Obsessive-Compulsive Disorder
Post-Traumatic Stress Disorder
Acute Stress Disorder
Generalized Anxiety Disorder
Anxiety Disorder Due to General Medical Condition
Substance-Induced Anxiety Disorder

Somatoform Disorders

Somatization Disorder
Undifferentiated Somatoform Disorder
Conversion Disorder
Pain Disorder: Associated With Psychological Factors,
    Associated With Both Psychological Factors and a
    General Medical Condition
Hypochondriasis
Body Dysmorphic Disorder

Factitious Disorders

Dissociative Disorders
Dissociative Amnesia
Dissociative Fugue
Dissociative Identity Disorder
Depersonalization Disorder

Sexual and Gender Identity Disorders

Sexual Dysfunctions: Sexual Desire Disorders, Sexual
    Arousal Disorders, Orgasmic Disorders, Sexual Pain
    Disorders, Sexual Dysfunction Due to a General
    Medical Condition
Paraphilias: Exhibitionism, Fetishism, Frotteurism,
    Pedophilia, Sexual Masochism, Sexual Sadism,
    Transvestic Fetishism, Voyeurism
Gender Identity Disorders: Gender Identity Disorder
    in Children, Gender Identity Disorder in Adolescents
    or Adults

Eating Disorders

Anorexia Nervosa
Bulimia Nervosa

Sleep Disorders

Primary Sleep Disorders: Dyssomnias, Parasomnias
Sleep Disorders Related to Another Mental Disorder
Other Sleep Disorders

Impulse-Control Disorders Not Elsewhere Classified

Intermittent Explosive Disorder
Kleptomania
Pyromania
Pathological Gambling
Trichotillomania

Adjustment Disorders

Other Conditions That May Be a Focus
of Clinical Attention

Psychological Factors Affecting Medical Condition:
    Mental Disorder, Psychological Symptoms,
    Personality Traits or Coping Style, Maladaptive
    Health Behaviors, Stress-Related Physiological
    Response

Medication-Induced Movement Disorders
Relational Problems: Related to a Mental Disorder or
    General Medical Condition, Parent-Child Relational
    Problem, Partner Relational Problem, Sibling
    Relational Problem
Problems Related to Abuse or Neglect: Physical Abuse
    of Child, Sexual Abuse of Child, Neglect of Child,
    Physical Abuse of Adult, Sexual Abuse of Adult
Additional Conditions That May Be a Focus of
    Clinical Attention: Noncompliance With Treatment,
    Malingering, Adult Antisocial Behavior, Child
    or Adolescent Antisocial Behavior, Borderline
    Intellectual Functioning, Age-Related Cognitive
    Decline, Bereavement, Academic Problem,
    Occupational Problem, Identity Problem, Religious
    or Spiritual Problem, Acculturation Problem, Phase
    of Life Problem

Axis II: Personality Disorders and Mental Retardation

Personality Disorders

Paranoid Personality Disorder
Schizoid Personality Disorder
Schizotypal Personality Disorder
Antisocial Personality Disorder
Borderline Personality Disorder
Histrionic Personality Disorder
Narcissistic Personality Disorder
Avoidant Personality Disorder
Dependent Personality Disorder
Obsessive-Compulsive Personality Disorder

Mental Retardation

Mild Mental Retardation
Moderate Mental Retardation
Severe Mental Retardation
Profound Mental Retardation

Axis III: General Medical Conditions

Axis IV: Psychosocial and Environmental Problems

Problems that may affect diagnosis, treatment, and
prognosis of mental disorders, including problems with
primary support group, problems related to the social
environment, educational problems, occupational
problems, housing problems, economic problems,
problems with access to health care services, and
problems related to interaction with the legal
system/crime.

Axis V: Global Assessment of Functioning

A scale (1 to 100) rating the individual's psychological,
social, and occupational functioning.

*Note: In addition to the specific disorders listed here, most
categories include an NOS (Not Otherwise Specified)
diagnosis.*

Abnormal Psychology

Abnormal
A DISCOVERY APPROACH
Psychology

Steven Schwartz

Mayfield Publishing Company
Mountain View, California
London • Toronto

For on-line resources, visit the *Abnormal Psychology* Web site at www.mayfieldpub.com/schwartz

Library of Congress Cataloging-in-Publication Data

Schwartz, Steven.
   Abnormal psychology: a discovery approach / Steven Schwartz.
     p. cm.
   Includes bibliographical references and index.
   ISBN 1-55934-266-8
     1. Psychology, Pathological. 2. Psychiatry. I. Title.

   RC454.S3598 2000
   616.89—dc21

                              99-046116

Manufactured in the United States of America
10   9   8   7   6   5   4   3   2

Mayfield Publishing Company
1280 Villa Street
Mountain View, California 94041

Sponsoring editor, Franklin Graham; developmental editor, Barbara Armentrout; production editor, Lynn Rabin Bauer; manuscript editor, Beverley J. DeWitt; art director and cover designer, Jeanne Schreiber; text designer, Ellen Pettengell; cover art, Ewa Gavrielov; art editor, Amy Folden; illustrators, Judith Ogus, Alice and Will Thiede, John and Judy Waller, and Su Wilson; photo researcher, Brian Pecko; manufacturing manager, Randy Hurst. The text was set in 9.75/13 Palatino by GTS Graphics and printed on 50# Somerset Matte by R. R. Donnelley and Sons. Case studies in this book may resemble actual clinical studies but, unless otherwise indicated, any resemblance to actual studies or to persons living or dead is purely coincidental.

Acknowledgments and copyrights continue at the back of the book on pages 683–684, which constitute an extension of the copyright page.

In loving memory of my father,
Robert Schwartz

Preface

Imagine yourself at the breakfast table. A headline in the morning newspaper catches your eye—*Olympic Hopeful Dead*. Danielle Wood, a university student and champion swimmer, was found dead on the floor of her college dormitory room. Illegal drugs were found near her body. Questions fly through your mind as you read this sad story: Was her death murder? An accident? Suicide? The article does not mention a suicide note, but do people who take their own lives always leave notes? You realize that you do not know. You continue reading. Danielle's friends say that she was depressed about not making the Olympic swimming team, and that she recently broke up with her boyfriend. This raises further questions. What is depression? Does it drive people to suicide? What role, if any, did drugs play in her death? (The complete newspaper article is on pp. 2–4.)

Olympic Hopeful Dead

by Evan Moran
Daily Staff Writer

Danielle Wood's death was discovered around 5:30 p.m. on Sunday when Jayne Handley found her body. Handley, a junior long-distance swimmer at the university, had just returned to campus after her summer vacation and was eager to see her friend Danielle.

"I went into the room because it was unlocked and I heard music. I saw Danielle on the floor. She was just lying there, face up, with a vacant stare in her eyes. I called for help," Handley recounted.

The police believe that Danielle Wood, a 20-year-old junior, took her own life by consuming a large quantity of amphetamines and anabolic steroids. This was the third student suicide to take place on the campus in the past 12 months.

Suicide is equivocal in Danielle's case, however, because she did not leave a note.

Also, she was found on the floor in the middle of her dormitory room, which could mean that she died while trying to get help. On the other hand, she was reported to have been despondent over her recent breakup with her boyfriend, Luke Garson.

Olympic Hopeful

"What makes this tragedy particularly hard to take," said Dr. Carmel Garza, dean of students, "is that Danielle was a young woman who had come so far against some great odds. She had a terrible childhood. She worked hard at her schoolwork and at her swimming. She just missed making the last Olympic team, but she had hoped to make the next one. Money was a problem for Danielle. She supported herself waiting tables in a restaurant near the university, but she sometimes needed

A casual newspaper reader may never discover the answer to these questions. But imagine that you are a psychologist. How would you ascertain the truth about Danielle's death? You might begin by seeking further information about her history, for example. Has she had psychological problems before? Perhaps she was seen by social workers or psychologists at some time in the past. Their assessments could help to reveal why she was despondent. Interviews with people who knew Danielle may also yield important data. As a psychologist, you may also consult the research literature to find out whether people who commit suicide always leave notes. Gradually, by sifting through the relevant research literature and linking it to the information you were able to gather, you may be able to understand the events that took place in Danielle's dorm room.

This book is designed to teach you—a student of abnormal psychology—how to amass and analyze evidence in just this way. In other words, the aim of this book is to teach you how to think like psychologists do. Instead of simply presenting theories, research, and brief case studies (as most textbooks do), this book is organized to help you uncover the facts of abnormal psychology for yourself. To do this, the book relies on problem-based "discovery" learning.

A DISCOVERY APPROACH

This book is subtitled "A Discovery Approach" because it turns the traditional method of teaching abnormal psychology on its head. Instead of beginning with five or six introductory chapters and gradually working up to syndromes and treatments (with the occasional clinical vignette thrown in for illustrative purposes), this book begins with the story of Danielle Wood. Using primary documents—social work and psychological assessments, interviews with significant people in Danielle's life, and hospital documents—Chapter 1 shows how this student's life and tragic death reflect the major issues confronting abnormal psychology: What is a psychological disorder? What do we mean by "abnormal"? What are the causes of psychological disorders? How are they treated and can they be prevented?

The facts of Danielle's life are not presented in a pre-digested, summary form—like the case studies typically found in textbooks—but as original documents (actual psychology and social work reports, newspaper articles, court records, transcripts of therapy sessions, and so on). The use of primary clinical documents to present case materials makes this book unique. (The complete documents appear on pp. 5–8.)

UNIVERSITY HOSPITAL

Social Work Report

Date: December 1, 2000

Social Worker: Li Cheong, MSW, psychiatric social worker

Referral: Dr. Kahn requested this report on Danielle Wood, a 19-year-old sophomore who appears to have made a suicide gesture last week.

Sources: Family Service records, Luke Garson, Mrs. Mavis Wood, Coach Murray Lawrence

Danielle Wood was brought to the University Hospital on Saturday, November 25, having ingested an unknown quantity of tranquilizers. She was treated with stomach lavage and placed under observation.

Danielle is one of three children born to Edward and Louise Keogh. When she was 7, the police were contacted by Danielle's teacher, who believed that the child was being abused. Danielle sometimes came to school bruised and told other children that her father

UNIVERSITY HOSPITAL

Psychological Assessment

Date: December 4, 2000

Client: Danielle Wood, Robertson Hall, DOB: 3/17/1981

Tests Administered

Minnesota Multiphasic Personality Inventory (MMPI-2) (12/2/2000)

Thematic Apperception Test (TAT) (12/3/2000)

Rorschach Inkblot Test (12/3/2000)

Beck Depression Inventory (BDI) (12/3/2000)

Los Angeles Suicide Prevention Center Lethality Scale (12/2/2000)

Wechsler Adult Intelligence Scale (WAIS-III) (12/3/2000)

Clinical interview

Psychologist: Dr. Stuart Berg

Referral: Dr. S. Kahn, University Hospital

Reason for Referral: The client was referred by Dr. Kahn for personality assessment. She apparently attempted suicide, but she immediately telephoned for help, leaving some doubt about her actual intention and the potential threat she posed to herself.

As more documents are presented, you are encouraged to generate increasingly deeper questions: Danielle died in mysterious circumstances—was her death suicide? How can you tell? What are the signs of suicide? What causes someone to take her own life? To answer these questions, you must discover for yourself how social, personal, and biological factors interact to cause suicide and other behaviors, both normal and abnormal. In other words, you will be launched on a voyage of discovery from the very beginning of the book.

Although you will cover many of the same topics that students using a traditional textbook do—such as research methods, experimental results, and treatment modalities—you will learn about these topics within a clinical context. Thus, your learning will be deeper and more meaningful than mere superficial memorization. You will see why researchers tackle some questions and not others, and you will learn how research findings affect clinical practice (and vice versa). In addition, the discovery approach will provide you with learning skills that you will find useful in other courses and throughout your career.

ABNORMAL PSYCHOLOGY IS ABOUT PEOPLE

Unlike the brief clinical vignettes found in traditional textbooks, which have predetermined features and outcomes, the primary source documents used in this book are often ambiguous and "messy," just like the real world (and real people). People are not always predictable, and even professionals are human beings. Sometimes psychologists, judges, and lawyers get testy; sometimes they make mistakes. These all-too-human qualities are reflected in this book's primary documents. Thus, you will not be learning an idealized textbook version of abnormal psychology; you will be learning about living, breathing people. And 30 years of teaching abnormal psychology have convinced me that exposure to clinical cases from the very first day of the course is more stimulating and motivating than traditional teaching methods.

AN INTEGRATED ONE-SEMESTER COURSE

Instead of a loosely related set of topics—history of psychopathology, assessment methods, diagnosis, research techniques, legal issues—spread across 15 or 20 chapters, this book consists of 13 integrated chapters plus an epilogue. Thus, you can complete the entire book in one semester.

Each chapter contains primary case documents specially chosen to raise crucial issues. By learning how these issues pertain to the particular case, you will come to see all aspects of abnormal psychology—from basic research to legal dilemmas—as part of an integrated whole. In other words, you will learn not only *what* scientists and clinicians do, but you will also learn *why*. To reinforce this integrative theme, this book does not contain separate chapters on history, multiculturalism, treatment, legal issues, and so on. Instead, the primary clinical documents are presented in a sequence that raises each of these topics when it is relevant to the circumstances of a case. In this way, new concepts are introduced when they are necessary to answer clinical questions—you receive new information when you need it. As the sole author of this book, I was able to ensure that all of the chapters speak with a single voice.

This book contains just three introductory chapters with the first devoted to the case of Danielle Wood. The sequence of chapters has been designed to maximize and maintain your interest. For example, to provide an early opportunity for you to relate your own experiences to the problems of others, the clinical chapters begin with common everyday problems. In later chapters, attention is given to eating disorders, suicide, and other problems that disproportionately affect the college population. To demonstrate that many clinical problems are simply exaggerations of everyday behaviors, clinical chapters include the entire "spectrum" of problems ranging from common, everyday complaints (fear of public speaking, for example) to related clinical disorders (such as phobias and anxiety disorders). The growing influence of public health and the increasingly loud demands for clinical efficiency and accountability are reflected in the special emphasis given to prevention and to new developments in service delivery, such as managed care.

COMBINING SCIENCE AND CLINICAL PRACTICE

Abnormal psychology is a science, and most of this book is devoted to discussions of research. At every juncture, however, these discussions are related to the primary clinical documents. In this way, you will learn how research grows out of clinical problems. Of course, our present knowledge of psychopathology does not come entirely from controlled research studies. Clinical observations, especially detailed case studies, have made equally important contributions. Over the years, initial clinical observations have been refined, tested, and extended by increasingly sophisticated research. This book emphasizes this collaborative process by showing how clinical observations contribute, along with scientific research and theory, to the goal of helping people in distress.

To help you organize and assimilate the information in this book, all chapters begin with an outline of the topics to be covered as well as a set of learning objectives. Each chapter ends with an integrative summary that not only describes the current state of the chapter's topic but also points out likely future developments. The Epilogue does the same thing for the field of abnormal psychology as a whole. To help consolidate your learning, every chapter contains a list of key terms and key names (individuals who have been especially influential in advancing the field). Key terms appear in bold type in the text and are defined in a comprehensive glossary at the end of the book.

The book contains two types of boxes—"Highlight" and "Critical Thinking About Clinical Decisions." Highlights illuminate specific studies or issues in an intellectually stimulating way. Some examples are "Surfing for Sex," "Aboriginal Deaths in Custody," and "Are We Born Fearing Snakes?" Critical Thinking About Clinical Decisions boxes challenge students to apply what they have discovered to important problems. Sample topics include: "Sex Crimes and Misdemeanors," "Do We Get Less Intelligent With Age?," and "Can Surveys Be Trusted?" Highlights and Critical Thinking boxes are not just tacked on to the text; they are explicitly referenced and integrated into the relevant discussions.

A CRITICAL VIEWPOINT

In this book, disorders are grouped according to the scheme described in the American Psychiatric Association's *Diagnostic and Statistical Manual of Mental Disorders (DSM-IV)*. This does not mean that everything contained in the *DSM-IV* is uncritically accepted. Abnormal psychology is a rapidly moving field in which there are still more questions than answers. Neither the current *DSM*, nor any *DSMs* in the foreseeable future, can, or will, claim to be definitive. Informed criticism—of the type found in this book—is the only way to ensure that each new revision is better than the last.

On the subject of criticism, it is worth noting that new information on abnormal psychology is constantly being accumulated and no single research study is likely to be the last word on any issue. So it is wise to be cautious when interpreting research findings and accepting theories. Not all views deserve equal weight on every topic; some theories have more research support than others. Textbooks that treat all research findings, and all theories, as equally valid provide a distorted picture of the field. In this book, theories and research findings are subjected to critical scrutiny. Most often, combinations of biological, behavioral, and social factors best explain abnormal behavior. Thus, this book views abnormal psychology as a *biopsychosocial* science. As you will see, however, there are also times when psychoanalytic, humanistic, and other approaches may also provide valuable insights. Ultimately, the test of any theory or research finding (or of any abnormal psychology textbook, for that matter) is its value in helping us to understand people and help them to overcome their problems.

OTHER FEATURES

What else is special about this book? The coverage is up-to-date. The reference list includes articles and books published as recently as the year 2000. The book is also comprehensive. Just about every *DSM-IV* disorder, and practically all relevant theories of abnormal psychology, are discussed, including many topics omitted by other textbooks (from managed care and health economics to the shootings at Columbine High School). The book's illustrations are not simply decorative; they have been carefully designed to elucidate the concepts covered in the text. Finally, the primary documents—and the discovery approach to learning—make this book different from all other abnormal psychology textbooks.

TEACHING AND LEARNING TOOLS

To help students and instructors make the most out of this textbook, a comprehensive package of teaching and study aids is available.

For Instructors and Students

- The Web site (www.mayfieldpub.com/schwartz) provides tools for both instructors and students. For students it includes a Web tutorial, interactive Study Guide, Internet activities, virtual cases, and hot links. For instructors it includes a syllabus builder, an Instructor's Resource Guide, electronic transparencies, PowerPoint® presentation slides, an image bank, upcoming events list, on-line teaching forum, and more. (All instructor items are password protected. The password is found on the copyright page of the Instructor's Resource Guide or is available from your sales representative.)

For Instructors

- The Instructor's Resource Guide contains, for each chapter, a list of learning objectives, a chapter summary, lecture organizers, discussion topics and in-class activities, Internet and video resources, and more.
- The Instructor's CD-ROM includes the complete Instructor's Resource Guide, PowerPoint® presentation slides, electronic transparencies, and art from the text.
- The printed Test Bank contains more than 100 test items for each chapter, including multiple-choice, short-answer, true-false, and essay questions, topic identifiers for each question, and references to the source pages in the text.
- The computerized Test Bank is both Mac and IBM compatible.
- Transparency Acetates include important figures and images from the text, more than half in color.
- A complete list of videos is available to qualified adopters.

For Students

- The student Study Guide contains, for each chapter, a chapter outline, chapter summary, learning objectives, practice examination questions, activities for interactive review, and Internet and popular media resources.
- *Abnormal Psychology: An Interactive Cases and Activities Handbook* is designed to complement and add to the material in the text. It includes case studies in abnormal psychology (in addition to those in the text) accompanied by interactive activities.
- *Classic Studies in Abnormal Psychology.* Also by Steven Schwartz, this supplementary text describes 20 cornerstone psychological experiments in detail and places each in historical context.

ACKNOWLEDGMENTS

Although my name appears as the author of this book, no project of this magnitude could ever be the work of a single person. Many people have helped me. My sincere thanks go to Frank Graham, Barbara Armentrout, Lynn

Rabin Bauer, Jeanne Schreiber, Amy Folden, Brian Pecko, and the rest of the team at Mayfield who encouraged, cajoled, and stimulated me to complete this project, even when the obstacles sometimes seemed insuperable. On a personal level, I must add that no one has ever had a more understanding, devoted, loyal, and sympathetic friend than I have had in Frank Graham. One of the benefits of working on this project has been the opportunity to know Frank. I am indebted to Greg Schwartz, who contributed to this book in many ways— as a computer consultant, editor, critic, compiler of a 3,000-name index, and 60 pages of references. Carolyn Schwartz, who has been my inspiration for more than 30 years, is also the best editor I know; she read much of the manuscript and helped translate my prose into grammatical English. Mark Diamond found many of the references and is responsible for several of the clinical cases. My secretaries, Allison Vandertang and Suzanne White, helped with countless tasks (including putting up with me when the work was going slowly), and I owe a particular debt to Claire Farrugia who went beyond the call of friendship and read the entire manuscript aloud so that I could proofread the galleys.

I am also indebted to the following colleagues and friends who served as advisors and reviewers:

Ronald W. Belter, University of West Florida
Robert F. Bornstein, Fordham University
JoAnne Brewster, James Madison University
James F. Calhoun, University of Georgia
Bernardo J. Carducci, Indiana University Southeast
Elaine Cassel, Marymount University, Lord Fairfax Community College
June Madsen Clausen, University of San Francisco
Philip E. Comer, West Virginia University
Peter Ebersole, California State University, Fullerton

Lani C. Fujitsubo, Southern Oregon University
Bernard S. Gorman, Nassau Community College, Hofstra University
Shepard B. Gorman, Nassau Community College
Alan G. Glaros, University of Missouri, Kansas City
Michael J. Lambert, Brigham Young University
Travis P. Langley, Henderson State University
Richard L. Leavy, Ohio Wesleyan University
Kina Leitner, New York University
Arnold LeUnes, Texas A & M University
Robin J. Lewis, Old Dominion University
David J. Lutz, Southwest Missouri State University
Lily McNair, University of Georgia, Athens
Scott M. Monroe, University of Oregon
Michael L. Raulin, State University of New York, Buffalo
Roger N. Reeb, University of Dayton
Lynn P. Rehm, University of Houston
Beth Menees Rienzi, California State University, Bakersfield
Patricia Schoenrade, William Jewell College
James A. Schmidt, Western Illinois University
Edwin S. Shneidman, University of California, Los Angeles
Pamela E. Stewart, Northern Virginia Community College
T. Gale Thompson, Bethany College
Robert M. Tipton, Virginia Commonwealth University
Josh G. Weinstein, Humboldt State University
Robert J. Wellman, Fitchburg State College
David M. Young, Indiana University–Purdue University, Fort Wayne

Brief Contents

Contents

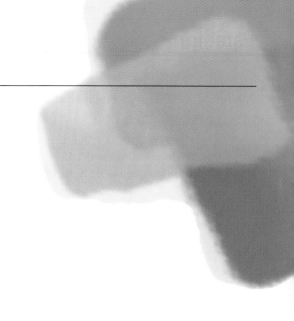

CHAPTER 2

Paradigms and Perspectives, Models and Methods 40

CHAPTER 3

Psychological Assessment, Classification, and Clinical Decision Making 94

CHAPTER 4

The Anxiety Spectrum
From Everyday Worry to Panic 134

CHAPTER 5

Effects of Stress on Health and Disease 188

CHAPTER 6

The Substance Disorder Spectrum 230

CHAPTER 7

Dissociative, Somatoform, and Factitious Disorders 274

CHAPTER 8
The Mood Disorder Spectrum
From the Blues to Depressive and Bipolar Disorders 316

CHAPTER 11
Intellectual and Cognitive Disorders 458

CHAPTER 12
Disorders of Childhood and Adolescence 504

CHAPTER 13

Sexual and Related Problems of Adult Life   552

EPILOGUE

Littleton, Colorado, and the Future of Abnormal Psychology 594

About the Author

Steven Schwartz is president of Murdoch University in Perth, Western Australia. After receiving his PhD in clinical psychology from Syracuse University in New York, he moved to Northern Illinois University, where, for 4 years, he taught abnormal psychology to undergraduates, as well as in the clinical psychology program, and consulted in child psychopathology at the Village of Progress Child Center. He then moved to the University of Texas Medical Branch in Galveston, where he performed clinical work and research in child psychopathology and trained clinical psychology interns.

Dr. Schwartz has been a visiting professor at Harvard and Stanford Universities and has also taught clinical psychology in the graduate program at the University of Western Australia and the University of Queensland, where he was also director of the psychology clinic. His other posts have included president of the academic board and professor and head of the Department of Psychology at the University of Queensland and executive dean of the Faculty of Medicine and Dentistry at the University of Western Australia. Dr. Schwartz is one of only a handful of non-medically trained professors ever to serve as the dean of a medical school.

Throughout his academic career, Dr. Schwartz has been awarded over $1 million in research grants and has received distinguished fellowships and prizes from such organizations as the National Institutes of Health, the Red Cross, the Brain Research Foundation, the World Health Organization, the North Atlantic Treaty Organization, the American Psychological Association, the Royal Society of London, the Australian Academy of Science, the Australian Academy of Social Science, and the Australian government. He has written over 100 journal articles in psychology, many of which are among the most highly cited papers in their field. He is also the author of nine books, including *Classic Studies in Abnormal Psychology,* published by Mayfield Publishing Company. In addition, Dr. Schwartz has written more than 250 articles for popular newspapers and magazines, successfully communicating science to the public.

Dr. Schwartz presented at the 1999 American Psychological Society meeting in Denver, Colorado, on case-based learning in abnormal psychology and is a frequent speaker both in the United States and abroad. When not traveling the world teaching and lecturing, he enjoys scuba diving, reading, and, of course, writing.

Abnormal Psychology

CHAPTER 1

CHAPTER OBJECTIVES

All of psychology is dedicated to one vitally important goal—understanding why people think and behave as they do. Abnormal psychology is just one part of this great quest for human understanding. Contrary to what you may sometimes see in movies or read in newspapers, people who have psychological disorders are not "crazy," nor are they fundamentally different from you and me. With few exceptions, their disorders are simply exaggerations of feelings and thoughts that everyone has from time to time. Far from being a stranger in our midst, the person with a psychological disorder is likely to be a neighbor, a member of the family, or even a friend. To illustrate how psychological disorders can devastate a person's life (and the lives of those who care about the affected person), this chapter introduces a university student named Danielle Wood. Through newspaper articles, diary entries, psychological reports, and other documents, you will learn about her background, her triumphs, and her tragic end. Danielle's story, which continues through the following chapters, will not only give you insight into the nature and causes of psychological disorders but will also show you how such disorders are diagnosed, treated, and sometimes prevented. This chapter provides an introduction to and overview of the topics, theories, and controversies that are discussed in more depth in the rest of this book.

The five main questions addressed in this chapter are

1. What is "abnormal" behavior?
2. How do different mental health professionals approach abnormal psychology?
3. What are the causes of psychological disorders? How can they be treated?
4. How do social attitudes affect diagnosis and treatment?
5. What makes abnormal psychology scientific?

The Death of Danielle Wood

CONTENTS

"Historic buildings, monuments, and traditions are important," university President Brad Reynolds said at his morning welcome to new students and parents, "but the university cannot stagnate; progress demands expansion." And expansion has clearly occurred. Graduates, transformed over the years into the parents of new students, are simultaneously shocked and impressed by the new glass-and-steel dormitories, the movie and theater complex, and the imposing new engineering building. Still, after a few hours strolling around the campus, most former students manage to convince themselves that nothing really important has changed since their undergraduate days. The sorority and fraternity houses look splendid in the hazy September light, and the campus's neatly trimmed lawns are covered in a blanket of orange leaves, just as they remember them. The notice boards are still filled with posters, flyers, and scribbled notes: a party for first-year students on Friday night, the dramatic society's tryouts for aspiring actors and support crew (no experience required), roommate wanted, used books for sale. Everywhere, groups of students chat and laugh. Parents stop for a rest at the new campus coffee shop, take in the setting, and are reassured. No harm will come to their children in a place like this.

As the daylight begins to fade, Dr. Carmel Garza, dean of students, gazes out of her office window at the parents and visitors saying their last goodbyes. Her eyes follow the cars down the main drive until she loses sight of them at the point where the road curves and leaves the campus. She is scheduled to speak to the new students in 15 minutes. The orientation speech and the dinner that follows are traditional, and Dr. Garza is looking forward to both. This is her fourth year as dean, and she is proud of the improvements in student life. Club membership is up, sports facilities for women are vastly improved, and so too are student health services. Dr. Garza is particularly pleased with the success of the support groups she has established for students from minority and disadvantaged backgrounds. She recalls what it was like for her when she first came to the university as a student 20 years ago. Lost and unhappy, she had contemplated dropping out. Only the support of her friends had kept her in school. She is planning to tell the new students about her own experiences and to let them know that help is available. But Dr. Garza never gets to make her speech. Just as she opens the door to leave, the telephone rings. The voice on the phone is controlled and professional: "This is Sergeant Timothy Harmon of the Metro Police. A student is dead. It looks like suicide. Please come to Robertson Hall as quickly as you can. The other students are very upset."

DOCUMENT 1.1

Newspaper Report of Danielle's Death

Olympic Hopeful Dead

by Evan Moran
Daily Staff Writer

Danielle Wood's death was discovered around 5:30 p.m. on Sunday when Jayne Handley found her body. Handley, a junior long-distance swimmer at the university, had just returned to campus after her summer vacation and was eager to see her friend Danielle.

"I went into the room because it was unlocked and I heard music. I saw Danielle on the floor. She was just lying there, face up, with a vacant stare in her eyes. I called for help," Handley recounted.

The police believe that Danielle Wood, a 20-year-old junior, took her own life by consuming a large quantity of amphetamines and anabolic steroids. This was the third student suicide to take place on the campus in the past 12 months.

Suicide is equivocal in Danielle's case, however, because she did not leave a note. Also, she was found on the floor in the middle of her dormitory room, which could mean that she died while trying to get help. On the other hand, she was reported to have been despondent over her recent breakup with her boyfriend, Luke Garson.

Olympic Hopeful

"What makes this tragedy particularly hard to take," said Dr. Carmel Garza, dean of students, "is that Danielle was a young woman who had come so far against some great odds. She had a terrible childhood. She worked hard at her schoolwork and at her swimming. She just missed making the last Olympic team, but she had hoped to make the next one. Money was a problem for Danielle. She supported herself waiting tables in a restaurant near the university, but she sometimes needed loans from the student financial aid fund that I administer."

Over the past summer, Danielle worked as a volunteer counselor in a program for abused teenagers. Ironically, according to Father John Annunzio, the program director, Danielle's goal was to give the teenagers a message of hope, help them learn to respect themselves, and teach them to never give up.

On the morning of the day that she was found dead, Danielle attended swimming training just as she did 6 days a week during the semester. Her coach, Murray Lawrence, did not notice anything wrong. "Danielle was always fairly matter-of-fact about her training. She didn't make the Olympic team the first time she tried, so she just kept on training. She would have continued training until she made the team. She liked to win races as much as anyone, but she never became hysterical when she won. She tended to keep her feelings under control."

Coach Lawrence said that Danielle's apparent suicide came as a shock and that he had no hint that she had been taking drugs. "Her times were a little slow last year, and she may have thought that steroids would build her strength. I guess she was very competitive in her own quiet way. I wish I could say more, but she was hard to get to know, and she tended to keep things bottled up inside. I can't believe that she would harm herself."

Background Full of Pain

Danielle did not often share details about her background, and no one in her small circle of friends knew much about her childhood. She sometimes referred to her adoptive mother, Mavis Wood, as her mother and, at other times, as her aunt. Although she spoke kindly of Mrs. Wood, Danielle seemed to lack adult parent figures, her friends said.

Danielle met Luke Garson in her first year of college. He was in her English class, and they both were considering majoring in human movement studies. Their relationship did not seem any rockier than most romances between first-year students, but Jayne Handley found Danielle deeply depressed by even minor spats. "I tried to comfort her when she and Luke had their fights, but she was difficult to console."

"Danielle and I had our problems, but we also had some great times. We even talked about marriage," said Garson. "She could be funny and kind as well as moody and jealous. I think she never got over the things that happened to her when she was a little girl."

History of Suicide

Early in her sophomore year, Danielle attempted suicide by taking a large quantity of tranquilizers. She was admitted to University Hospital for 5 days and later became an outpatient at the student counseling service. Her suicide attempt was reported to the police, and both her adoptive mother and her coach were informed.

Dr. Sally Kahn, a university health service psychiatrist, said that patient-

Danielle Wood (second from right) and her fellow swim team members practice for Olympic trials.

doctor confidentiality would ordinarily have required that Danielle's treatment be kept secret but that "Danielle regretted what she had done, and she wanted both her mother and her coach to know."

After a brief stay in the hospital, where she was treated with antidepressant medication and received psychological testing, Danielle asked to be discharged, according to her psychiatrist. Despite some qualms, Dr. Kahn agreed to see Danielle as an outpatient. After 5 months, her treatment was terminated because she was considered to be recovered.

Why did Danielle kill herself now?

"I wish I could tell you," said Dr. Kahn. "Then I might be able to prevent the same thing happening to others. Danielle would not let people get close to her, and she did feel rejected by her boyfriend. Combine this with the stress of swimming practice, constant worries about money, and the normal burden of university work, and it may all have been too much. You can never predict when accumulated stress will explode."

Dr. Stuart Berg, a university health service psychologist, is not completely convinced that Danielle committed suicide. "It is possible that Danielle's death was an accident. After all, there was no note, and she was found in the middle of the floor, not in bed. Maybe she did not deliberately set out to kill herself. In trying to improve her athletic performance, she may have simply overdone the drugs. Or she may have been making a suicide gesture, attempting to call attention to her problems. We will never know which one of these explanations is correct. Indeed, they may all be correct; behavior often has more than one explanation."

Around 100 people attended Danielle's funeral. University President Brad Reynolds talked about Danielle, about challenges that she had faced and barriers that she had overcome. Father Annunzio praised her volunteer work with abused teenagers. Mrs. Wood sat silently, but after the funeral, she told friends that she was considering suing the university for not taking proper measures to prevent Danielle from harming herself.

Perhaps the most telling comments at the service were those of Danielle herself. Reading from her high school yearbook, Father Annunzio quoted her farewell message as captain of the swimming team: "Set your standards high, higher than you think you can ever achieve, and then struggle as hard as you can to achieve them. Success is within each of us. We have only ourselves to blame if we fail."

Mrs. Wood sits alone at her kitchen table at 3:00 a.m. She has been unable to sleep more than a few hours at a time since learning about Danielle's death. The same thought keeps going around in her mind: "What could I have done?" She knew that Danielle had been troubled over the summer. Except for swimming, she had hardly left the house, and she had spent a lot of time sleeping, even taking afternoon naps. Mrs. Wood knew that Danielle had not been eating properly. She even knew that Danielle was taking pills. Danielle had told her that they were vitamins, and Mrs. Wood had believed her. "I should have given her more time," she thinks. "I should have taken her to the doctor. If only I had done something."

 UNIVERSITY HOSPITAL

Social Work Report

Date: December 1, 2000

Social Worker: Li Cheong, MSW, psychiatric social worker

Referral: Dr. Kahn requested this report on Danielle Wood, a 19-year-old sophomore who appears to have made a suicide gesture last week.

Sources: Family Service records, Luke Garson, Mrs. Mavis Wood, Coach Murray Lawrence

Danielle Wood was brought to the University Hospital on Saturday, November 25, having ingested an unknown quantity of tranquilizers. She was treated with stomach lavage and placed under observation.

Danielle is one of three children born to Edward and Louise Keogh. When she was 7, the police were contacted by Danielle's teacher, who believed that the child was being abused. Danielle sometimes came to school bruised and told other children that her father had slept in her bed. An investigation revealed systematic sexual and physical abuse by her father over a period of almost a year. Louise Keogh at first claimed to know nothing about her husband's behavior. She later admitted she knew but felt helpless to do anything.

Charges were brought against Edward Keogh, and all three children were removed from the family and placed in separate foster homes. Danielle was 8 years old at the time. Since then, Danielle has had little contact with her natural siblings.

Shortly before his trial was set to begin, Edward Keogh committed suicide by shooting himself. Mrs. Keogh became seriously depressed and had to be hospitalized for 17 weeks. On two occasions, she received electroshock treatment, and she has been treated with antidepressant medication ever since. Danielle has seen her natural mother only three times in the past 11 years.

Danielle was placed in the home of Mavis and John Wood. They had received special training from the Department of Family Services in how to deal with abused children, and they had sheltered others before Danielle.

The Woods felt a special attachment to Danielle from the very beginning. Reports state that they treated her as if she were their natural child, and by all indications Danielle thrived in their home. A social work report prepared for the family court when Danielle was 9 praised the care provided by Mr. and Mrs. Wood. At the time, Danielle appeared to be a shy and quiet girl who seemed well-adjusted to her circumstances. The family court judge must have agreed because she awarded the Woods custody. Danielle has used their name since she was 10 years old.

Danielle's new parents encouraged her to pursue her interest in swimming and even paid for her coaching. Danielle showed early talent as a swimmer.

John Wood died suddenly of a heart attack when Danielle was 16. His life insurance provided sufficient funds for Mavis and Danielle to live on, but not enough for professional coaching. However, Danielle was able to obtain employment as a waitress and used her earnings to pay for a swimming coach herself.

Danielle entered the university last year, intending to major in human movement studies and pursue her swimming career. She met Luke Garson at a party for first-year students and has been dating him exclusively ever since. Danielle trained hard for last year's Olympics. In fact, she reduced her course load so that she could devote more time to training. She made it all the way to the national tryouts, but she missed selection. According to Luke, she took this hard and was very "depressed." For a few days, she refused to leave her room, and she neither ate nor washed. Finally, at the urging of Carmel Garza, the dean of students, Danielle returned to class and to swimming.

About 2 weeks ago, Luke told Danielle that he planned to go home for Thanksgiving and that he would be away for 5 days. He did not invite Danielle to go with him. She did not want him to go, but he was determined. He told her that they were too dependent on one another and needed some time apart. Danielle seemed to accept this, but later, by her own admission, she took "10 or 12 Valiums" and called the campus emergency number for help.

Evaluation: Danielle is a needy person whose early history has made her sensitive to any sign of rejection. Her suicide gesture was a way of calling attention to herself and control-ling Luke. Danielle does not have many friends, nor does she belong to any church or uni-versity clubs. She is not close to her natural family. She requires a network of social support so that she does not again become excessively dependent on one person and therefore so vulnerable. Continued social work supervision after discharge is recommended.

Dean Garza sits gazing at the social work report, the events of the previous week repeating themselves in her mind: Danielle being carried off on a stretcher, the tearful questions from distressed students, her own interview with Sergeant Harmon, and the painful session with Mrs. Wood. Now she has to go over it all again. She has no choice. The memo from Brad Reynolds is quite clear: "As the President, I need to know exactly what happened and how such a tragedy can be prevented in the future." Dean Garza turns once again to the file. (*Note:* The tests mentioned in Document 1.3 are described in detail in Chapter 3.)

DOCUMENT 1.3

Psychological Assess-ment Prepared After Danielle's Previous Suicide Attempt

UNIVERSITY HOSPITAL

Psychological Assessment

Date: December 4, 2000

Client: Danielle Wood, Robertson Hall, DOB: 3/17/1981

Tests Administered

Minnesota Multiphasic Personality Inventory (MMPI-2) (12/2/2000)

Thematic Apperception Test (TAT) (12/3/2000)

Rorschach Inkblot Test (12/3/2000)

Beck Depression Inventory (BDI) (12/3/2000)

Los Angeles Suicide Prevention Center Lethality Scale (12/2/2000)

Wechsler Adult Intelligence Scale (WAIS-III) (12/3/2000)

Clinical interview

Psychologist: Dr. Stuart Berg

Referral: Dr. S. Kahn, University Hospital

Reason for Referral: The client was referred by Dr. Kahn for personality assessment. She apparently attempted suicide, but she immediately telephoned for help, leaving some doubt about her actual intention and the potential threat she posed to herself.

Behavioral Observations and History: The client was seen on two separate testing sessions. On each occasion, her appearance and behavior were the same. She wore a man's shirt, jeans, and deck shoes. Her hair was long and messy, and she wore no makeup. There were dark circles under her eyes.

The client avoided eye contact, looking down at the table or over the examiner's shoulder. She kept her hands clasped in her lap and never spoke spontaneously. She did respond to questions, but her answers were always brief and unelaborated. The client did not appear delusional or out of contact with reality; she was able to complete the tests and to provide a family history. It seemed as if everything she said or did required considerable effort.

The client told me that she had taken an overdose of "pills" because of a fight with her boyfriend. She felt that her boyfriend might be "getting tired of her" and she felt that she "could not live" if she were to lose him.

Family History: (See Social Work Report.)

Intellectual Assessment: The client's scores on the WAIS-III place her in the "above-average" range of intelligence. Although she understood the instructions, the test results were probably a low estimate of her abilities. On several occasions, she produced the correct response but so slowly that the time required to receive credit for the response had already expired. As a consequence, her lowest scores were on those subscales that require quick responses. This slowness was particularly apparent on the performance tasks. Slowness is often found among depressed people, and it is consistent with the client's general depressed appearance.

Personality Assessment: The validity scales of the MMPI-2 were all in the average range, indicating that the profile could be safely interpreted. The main feature of Danielle's MMPI-2 is the elevated depression score. The client reports feeling apathetic and indifferent to her usual activities. She believes that her life is no longer under her control. Her energy is gone, and so too is her ability to feel pleasure. The client's elevated hypochondriasis and hysteria scores reflect her tendency to complain of numerous physical symptoms and to respond to stress with illness.

Danielle's Rorschach responses contained considerable evidence of depression, and her BDI score was in the seriously depressed range. Her responses indicated considerable self-dislike and self-blame. She also indicated that she had thought of killing herself.

Based on the test results, behavioral observations, and clinical interview, it appears that the client has a distinctly unfavorable self-concept. Despite her athletic achievements and her success at the university, she feels that she has been a failure and that she has let people down. Her TAT responses reflect her preoccupation with success and her fear of failure. On several occasions, she indicated her guilt at the way she has hurt others and her fear of the future. She feels that she is more sensitive and that she feels rejection more intensely than most people.

The client's interpersonal relationships tend to create conflict. She wants to get close to others, but she fears rejection and loss. She is continually testing others to see if they really love her. Eventually this behavior produces the very result she wishes to avoid. That is, people ultimately fail a test, and the client's fears are confirmed.

Individuals with dependent personalities, and with this pattern of guilt, self-blame, and hopelessness, are at risk for suicide. Her score on the suicide lethality scale places her in the "moderately dangerous" category. Although her recent suicide attempt may be viewed as a way of gaining attention and perhaps of manipulating her boyfriend, such behavior may also be a reflection of underlying self-destructive tendencies.

It is possible that her early experiences have given her a sense of "learned helplessness." She could not control her father's behavior, and as a consequence, she may have learned to feel helpless in protecting herself against hurt.

The client should be monitored on an outpatient basis, and psychological and medical treatment should be initiated and maintained at least until the danger of suicide passes.

Diagnostic Considerations: The client meets all of the criteria in the 4th edition of the Diagnostic and Statistical Manual of the American Psychiatric Association (DSM-IV) for a diagnosis of major depression. In addition, she seems to have had a long-standing pattern of behavior that is characteristic of a personality disorder, especially the dependent type. She has recently experienced some mild stress (breaking up with her boyfriend), and her global psychological functioning is definitely impaired at present. Her activities prior to the current episode show that she is capable of a high level of psychological functioning.

Axis I (clinical disorders): Major depression

Axis II (personality disorders): Dependent personality

Axis III (general medical conditions): None

Axis IV (psychosocial and environmental problems): Breakup with boyfriend. Severity: 2, mild.

Axis V (global assessment of functioning): In past year: 80; current functioning: 50 (out of a maximum of 100).

Jayne and Luke sit opposite one another. Dr. Berg is on Luke's right, halfway between the two students. Jayne is talking: "I just wish . . . I just would have liked . . . If only she had waited. I could have talked to her. Maybe I could have kept her from doing it. I didn't even have a chance to say goodbye."

Dr. Berg listens intently, but he says nothing. His experience has taught him that these first post-traumatic counseling sessions must proceed slowly. He is correct.

After a brief silence, Jayne continues with some feeling: "I don't think I'll ever forgive you, Luke. It's all your fault. You could never make a commitment to her. You kept her on a string, but she was never sure about you. You were not there for her when she needed you."

Luke does not respond. He stares down at the floor, his hands tightly gripping the arms of the chair.

Dr. Berg can no longer remain silent: "Jayne, I can see how angry you are. It's only natural to look for a guilty person, a scapegoat, when something like this happens. If we can direct all of our pain and anger at another person, we can avoid facing reality. But the truth is that Danielle did this to herself, and our friendship and love were not enough to stop her."

Luke still says nothing. Inside, he knows that Jayne is partly right. He was ambivalent about his relationship with Danielle; maybe he didn't provide the commitment and devotion that she needed. He feels responsible for her death.

Jayne begins to cry. "Why did she do this?" she sobs.

"You can't believe how I feel," Luke says at last. "When it first happened, I tried to convince myself that it was an accident. Danielle took steroids and uppers to improve her performance. She just took too many. But I knew all along that was not true."

Although Luke's words seem to suggest strong emotions, they are said in a flat, expressionless voice. Not once, while he is talking, does he lift his eyes from the floor. Dr. Berg sees that Luke is depressed and perhaps in more psychological distress than Jayne. He tries to draw him out.

"I know this is hard," Dr. Berg says, "but you must face your feelings, and you must work through all of this so that you can get on with the rest of your life. We will probably never know for sure whether Danielle's death was deliberate or an accident. We will have to learn to live with not knowing."

The silence in the room seems to last a very long time. It becomes a kind of weight pressing down on Luke, forcing the words out of him. He speaks slowly and softly: "It wasn't an accident, and it was at least partly my fault. We didn't see each other during the summer because I spent most of the vacation backpacking through Europe. When I got back, around three weeks ago, I didn't immediately call Danielle. She knew that I was home, but she didn't call me either. I guess I wasn't sure whether I wanted to continue our relationship, and Danielle was testing me. Anyway, she eventually called me. She was friendly, and we talked mainly about my trip. We live about six hours apart, and because we were both coming back here in a week, we agreed to wait and see each other when we got back to college. The day before I left home, I received a package from Danielle. It contained a compact disc of her favorite music and a card that said, 'When you listen to this music, please think of me.' At the time I thought she was trying to keep our relationship going. Now I realize that she was saying goodbye."

Jayne sobs, and tears begin to flow down Luke's face as well. Dr. Berg passes around a box of tissues. For the first time that afternoon, he begins to relax. It might take a little while, but he knows that these two will make it.

President Reynolds always makes a good impression standing at a podium. Although he is largely bald and approaching 50, his 6-foot 3-inch height and well-cut suits give him an image of authority and power. New students admire him, and, just as important, so do their parents. President Reynolds likes greeting the new students and their parents on the first day of each academic year. He likes to tell them about the history of the university and about faculty and student achievements over the past year. On this day, a year after Danielle's death, he also wants to tell them about a new program that the university is initiating, a program inspired by Danielle. President Reynolds does not refer to her explicitly, but some members of the audience—Carmel Garza, Jayne Handley, Stuart Berg, Sally Kahn, Mavis Wood, Murray Lawrence, Father Annunzio, and Luke Garson—are thinking of her as Reynolds begins to speak:

> Suicide has been called the taboo topic, something we should not talk about in polite company. Suicides are hushed up, disguised, and reported as accidents. The truth is that we all feel guilty and ashamed when someone we know commits suicide. We feel

guilty because we think that we should have been able to prevent such behavior, and we feel ashamed because we did not succeed.

It is easy to avoid responsibility for helping suicidal people by saying that they are psychologically disturbed and should be looked after by mental health professionals. But this is not enough. Suicide is one of the leading causes of death among adolescents and young adults, and the number of university students who attempt suicide is rising at an alarming rate. We cannot simply rely on mental health professionals. We all must do something.

This year, along with the usual information on courses, clubs, and calendars, students will find a six-page pamphlet on suicide included in their registration packets. It contains the warning signs of an impending suicide. Look out for these signs among your friends. If they get seriously depressed, make remarks about not being around much longer, give away prized possessions, and talk about ending it all, get in there and help. Refuse, for your friends' sakes, to keep their plans secret. If they won't get help, then get help for them. The telephone numbers to call are in the pamphlet.

This year, we will also be holding special classes for dormitory resident advisers, who will be taught how to recognize the danger signs of suicide and how to obtain help. We are also beginning a peer education program in which resident advisers and other students trained in stress management will give talks to groups of students.

I realize that my remarks will probably make a few parents in the audience today uneasy. You may wonder whether all this talk about suicide is healthy. You may fear that it will put the idea in students' heads. I understand your anxiety, but it is time for suicide to come out of the closet. We must talk about it and confront it directly. We must end the conspiracy of silence that surrounds it. All of us must make education and prevention our responsibility.

HOW DID DANIELLE DIE?

Was Danielle's death a suicide, a plea for attention that went horribly wrong, or the unintended result of drug abuse? It is impossible to say. She left no note, but most suicides do not (Leenaars, 1988). She did send Luke her favorite music disc, along with a message that sounded very much like goodbye. On the other hand, Danielle's previous suicide attempt was halfhearted, and this could have been just another gesture that got out of hand. Perhaps she unintentionally overdosed on drugs and was struggling toward the door for help when she died. There is evidence both for and against all of these possibilities. We shall never know which one is correct. This is not unusual. Unlike the idealized case descriptions ordinarily found in textbooks, real life is rarely tidy. Ambiguity is the norm. We must learn to tolerate this ambiguity, to evaluate the various probabilities, and to make the best judgments that we can given the information available.

In some ways, Danielle's story is depressingly familiar to clinical psychologists. The backgrounds of young adults who attempt suicide are filled with stories of broken homes, social isolation, intense competition,

and drug abuse (Lewinsohn, Rhode, & Seeley, 1993; McIntosh, 1991). But, there are also ways in which Danielle was different from other young suicide victims. For example, she took the performance-enhancing drugs known as anabolic steroids. These drugs are known to produce serious physical and emotional disorders (Yesalis & Bahrke, 1995). More important, she was abused as a child and raised in a foster home after her father committed suicide. These are hardly common occurrences, even among those who take their own lives. The interplay between abstract laws of behavior and the characteristics of specific individuals, between global generalizations and local exceptions, is a recurrent theme in abnormal psychology.

Understanding Danielle—understanding anyone, including ourselves—is not easy. The questions that arise from Danielle's story (Was she suffering from a mental disorder? Could her death have been predicted? Could it have been prevented?) are really specific examples of the questions that have occupied students of abnormal psychology for centuries (What is abnormal behavior? How do we know it when we see it? What causes it? How do we treat and prevent it?). The answers to these questions are constantly changing. As so-

Hopelessness and depression are emotions we all experience occasionally. Why, for Danielle, did they end in death?

cial attitudes evolve, our definition of abnormal behavior, our theories about the causes of psychological disorders, and our ideas about how these disorders should be treated change accordingly. Nevertheless—despite the undeniable influence of social values on all aspects of behavior—the dominant theme of this book is that abnormal psychology is (or should be) a scientific enterprise. This chapter introduces the key concerns of abnormal psychology by showing how they apply to Danielle. Focusing on a single case makes these abstract issues concrete. However, Danielle's story has wider significance. As you will see, every case study is really a miniature study of abnormal psychology itself.

One word of caution. At some time in our lives, we have all felt hopeless and depressed. Because Danielle had similar feelings, it is only natural to identify with her and to worry about our own mental health. The best way to handle this is to examine Danielle's case—and the other cases in this book—in depth. You may be similar to the people described, but are you identical? You should also talk to other students. You will probably find that they have had thoughts and experiences similar to yours. Identifying with people in distress is not something to worry about. It is a reflection of your humanity and concern for others.

WHY DID DANIELLE DIE?

Although we may never know exactly *how* Danielle died, she is dead and we must try to understand *why* she died. Everyone who knew Danielle has a different answer. Coach Lawrence blames the intense swimming competition and Danielle's frustration at not winning a place on the Olympic team. Dr. Kahn, the psychiatrist, focuses on stress and drug abuse. The psychologist, Dr. Berg, although uncertain about whether Danielle really did intend to kill herself, believes that her poor self-concept and dependent personality could have driven her to such a desperate act. The social worker, Li Cheong, thinks that Danielle's limited social support network may have played a role. Mrs. Wood blames genetics because Danielle's biological father took his own life. Who is right? It is difficult to say. All of these people may be partly correct. People from different backgrounds, including professionals, tend to emphasize different causes, but behavior rarely has just one cause. (For more about the academic backgrounds and training of various types of mental health professionals, see Highlight 1.1, p. 12.) Genetics, life experiences, learned habits, and the social context influence everything we do. Modern clinical psychologists refer to behavior as **biopsychosocial** because biological, psychological, and social forces all interact to determine our every action (Freedman, 1995; McLaren, 1998). This section describes some of the possible causes of abnormal behavior, with special reference to Danielle.

Can Depression and Suicidal Behavior Be Inherited?

"Biology is destiny," claimed Sigmund Freud (1856–1939), founder of the school of psychology known as psychoanalysis. Although Freud meant that our personalities are strongly determined by whether we happen to be born male or female, his statement has much wider applicability. We are biological organisms, and it should not be surprising that our biochemistry, physiology, and anatomy affect the way we behave. Because we inherit most of our biological characteristics, it seems plausible that our personalities, and even our everyday behaviors, should have a genetic origin. Mrs. Wood certainly feels this way. She believes that Danielle inherited a suicidal personality from her father. Most people would agree. If eye color is inherited, why not aggression or shyness or a tendency toward self-destruction? Research evidence suggests that inheritance plays a role in

Who's Who in Mental Health

Several professions play a role in helping people in psychological distress. Dr. Berg, the **clinical psychologist,** holds a Doctor of Philosophy (PhD) degree. Some clinical psychologists hold Doctor of Psychology (PsyD) degrees. Both require four or more years of graduate study after the completion of a bachelor's degree. The difference between the two degrees is mainly a matter of emphasis. The PhD requires an extensive dissertation on a specific aspect of psychology, whereas the PsyD requires a less elaborate dissertation and intensive clinical training. In addition to their degrees, clinical psychologists complete an internship in which they are closely supervised in various aspects of clinical work. Nearly all states also require psychologists to be certified or licensed. This usually means passing a special examination.

In addition to psychological assessment and therapy, clinical psychologists are trained in the main areas of psychology—developmental, physiological, experimental—with particular attention given to research techniques. Doctoral programs in counseling and school psychology are similar to those in clinical psychology, but their emphasis is on everyday problems (career guidance, marriage counseling) rather than on mental disorders. It is becoming increasingly common for psychologists to do postdoctoral study to refine their skills in one or more specialties, such as the problems of children or sexual disorders. Because of their background in research, psychologists tend to be empiricists. They demand justification for the application of treatments, and they are likely to be skeptical and cautious about any claims that cannot be verified empirically. Although they recognize and accept the role of biology in behavior, most

psychologists would follow Dr. Berg in emphasizing the causal role of psychological factors, such as Danielle's low self-concept, in behavioral problems.

Dr. Kahn, the **psychiatrist,** is a medical doctor with an MD degree. She has completed internship and residency training, during which she received supervised experience in the treatment of mental disorders. Dr. Kahn is not only licensed by the state to practice medicine, she is also certified by a professional board of psychiatry, which requires an examination. Because she is a medical doctor, Dr. Kahn can perform physical examinations and administer medical therapies. Psychiatrists have traditionally been the only mental health professionals permitted to prescribe medications, although limited prescribing rights may be given to specially trained psychologists. Contrary to popular belief, psychiatrists are not required to study academic psychology in any depth. Also unlike psychologists, psychiatrists are not required to conduct research as part of their training. Because they are doctors, most psychiatrists conceptualize psychological problems as "illnesses" or "disorders," although they recognize that psychological factors play an important role.

Psychoanalysts are mental health professionals trained in the specific approach to treatment known as psychoanalysis. Although there are different schools of psychoanalysis, all are derived from the writings of the Austrian physician Sigmund Freud. Training requires several years of practical experience, and all trainees must, themselves, be psychoanalyzed. Most psychoanalysts are qualified psychiatrists, but psychologists and others can become psychoanalysts as well. Psychoanalysts view behavioral problems as the result

of unconscious conflicts arising from early childhood experiences. They would almost certainly blame Danielle's death on her horrible childhood.

Li Cheong holds a Master of Social Work (MSW) degree. Her training included courses in social policy and sociology, and considerable practical work in interviewing and counseling. **Social workers** function both inside and outside hospitals. Although they are involved in therapy, their main goal is to integrate people into their respective communities. Social workers emphasize interpersonal causes of problem behavior (such as Danielle's small network of friends).

Psychiatric nurses are concerned with the treatment of hospitalized patients. In most psychiatric hospitals, the nurse is the person who looks after most aspects of daily life. In addition to nursing training, psychiatric nurses study aspects of psychology and psychiatry, and they receive supervised experience working in psychiatric wards. Like psychiatrists, psychiatric nurses tend to view behavioral problems as analogous to medical illnesses.

In addition to the mental health professions mentioned so far, there are many others concerned with mental and emotional disorders. For example, members of the clergy are sometimes trained to do personal counseling, whereas occupational, music, art, and other therapists play a largely rehabilitative role, helping people to learn skills that are useful for adjusting to life after discharge from a hospital. Finally, there are many self-appointed "therapists" who are neither formally trained nor licensed. Because there is no professional organization to oversee them, the quality of their services cannot be guaranteed.

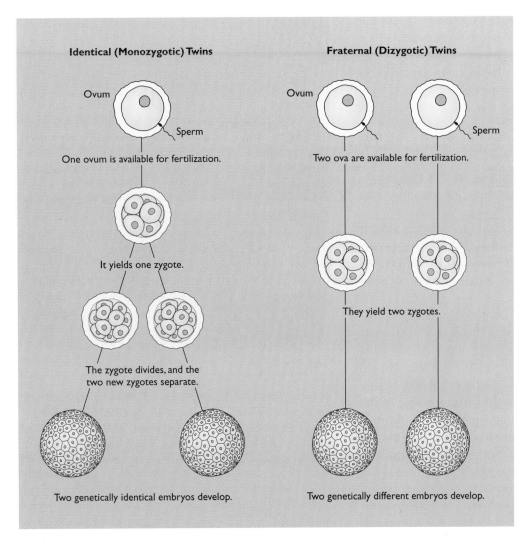

FIGURE 1.1 The Genetics of Identical and Fraternal Twins. *Identical (monozygotic) twins develop from a single ovum that splits into two embryos after fertilization. Both embryos have exactly the same genes. Fraternal (dizygotic) twins develop from two separate ova that are fertilized at the same time. They share about half their genes in common. From: Schickedanz et al. (1998, p. 75).*

learning disorders, reading disability, alcoholism, and many other disorders (Plomin & Rende, 1991). Even our social attitudes are claimed to be partly inherited (Plomin et al., 1997; Tesser, 1993).

When psychologists wish to establish whether genetics plays a role in behavior, the best evidence comes from people who are closely related. Studies comparing monozygotic (identical) twins, who come from the same zygote, or fertilized egg, and dizygotic (fraternal) twins, who come from two simultaneously fertilized eggs, are particularly important because monozygotic twins have identical genetic endowments (Figure 1.1). If behavior has a genetic origin, then the more closely related people

are, the more similarly they should behave. This is exactly what has been found. An identical twin whose brother or sister commits suicide is more likely also to commit suicide than a fraternal twin whose brother or sister commits suicide (Lester, 1986). This finding suggests that Mrs. Wood may be correct; suicide may have a genetic basis. However, genetics cannot be the whole story because the **concordance rate** (the proportion of identical twins who both commit suicide) is only 21%. If genetics alone causes suicide, then the concordance rate among identical twins should be close to 100% because they have identical genes. In reality, the concordance rate would never actually reach 100% even if genetics were solely responsible because some twins would die of natural causes before fulfilling their suicidal destiny. However, the low 21% figure means that factors other than genetics and natural deaths play a moderating role in determining who commits suicide.

One possible moderating factor is stress. Genetics may provide what is known in abnormal psychology as a diathesis (a vulnerability or predisposition to commit suicide), but suicide occurs only if the individual encounters some precipitating stress, such as the depression produced by rejection or loss, for example. This **diathesis-stress model** of psychological breakdown can explain the 21% concordance rate for suicide among identical twins on the assumption that both twins harbor a diathesis that makes them prone to suicide, but only the twin who encounters the required stress actually carries out the act.

Getting back to the question posed in the heading of this section, it is entirely possible that Danielle inherited a diathesis for depression and a set of personality traits from her father. Of course, it is equally possible that the diathesis was the result of her early childhood experiences. Danielle's diathesis made her vulnerable to the stress produced by not winning a place on the Olympic team and by losing her boyfriend. Together, the diathesis and stress could have driven her toward self-destruction. Unfortunately, it is rarely possible to say in advance that a person has a diathesis, nor can we say with any certainty what type of stress is likely to set it off. Thus, the diathesis-stress model has limited predictive value. It is usually invoked as an explanation *after* someone has behaved abnormally.

If Danielle did inherit a predisposition toward depression, it means that she must have differed physiologically or anatomically from people who do not inherit such a disposition. Let's look at the role played by physiology and anatomy in abnormal behavior.

Did Danielle's Death Have a Physiological Origin?

After her first suicide attempt, Danielle was treated with antidepressant medication. Drug therapy for psychological disorders has become so common, it is difficult to believe that it has been only 45 years since the first modern psychotropic medications (drugs that can alleviate the symptoms of psychological disorders) came into routine clinical use (Kline, 1954). Drugs were known to affect behavior before then (B. A. Maher & Maher, 1985), but mainly for the worse; they caused rather than cured psychological disorders. Over the years, specific drugs

In the early history of medicine, illness was believed to be caused by an imbalance of the four humors. Too much black bile ("melancholer") caused depression; too much phlegm caused apathy and sluggishness; too much blood made one passionate; and too much yellow bile ("choler") caused anger and bad temper.

have been linked to specific disorders (Grabowski & VandenBos, 1992). Danielle, for example, used amphetamines and anabolic steroids. Amphetamines are stimulants that, initially at least, make people more alert and energetic. Over time, however, the body quickly builds up a tolerance to them, so that increasing amounts are needed to achieve the desired stimulating effect. Habitual abusers frequently take dosages large enough to kill nonusers. At these high dosages, amphetamines can cause people to lose contact with reality and behave violently (Peet & Peters, 1995). The anabolic steroids that Danielle used to improve her sporting performance can also produce serious psychological disorders (Yesalis & Bahrke, 1995). The very existence of drugs that cause psychological disorders by affecting the body's physiology and other drugs that relieve these disorders by the same mechanism is compelling evidence that abnormal behavior can have a physiological origin (Holmes & Nadelson, 1999).

The idea that psychological disorders can have physical causes dates back at least to ancient Greece, when all of nature was divided into four basic elements: water, air, fire, and earth. These elements, in turn, were considered the building blocks of four body fluids known as the humors.

Phlegm was the bodily equivalent of water, blood equated to air, yellow bile was equal to fire, and black bile (also known as melancholer) was the equivalent of earth. In a healthy body, the Greeks believed, the humors are in a state of equilibrium. Ill health results from disharmony: too much of one humor, too little of another.

Greek physicians would have blamed Danielle's depression on an excess of black bile, or melancholer. They would have reasoned that "black" moods must be caused by a black substance such as melancholer. The more melancholer, the blacker the mood. Echoes of the classical theory can still be heard every time we describe a depressed person as "melancholy."

The Greeks were good at a great many things, but physiology was not one of them. (Aristotle, the great Greek philosopher, insisted that the function of the brain was to cool the blood.) Still, their explanation for depression has a decidedly modern ring. Today's theories continue to attribute depression and suicide to imbalances in brain chemistry (Hollandsworth, 1990). It is never wise to be too superior when judging the theories of the past, as Highlight 1.2 explains.

In addition to having a basis in aberrant physiology, abnormal behavior can also be caused by damaged anatomy. For example, the memory loss and intellectual deterioration found among older patients is associated with brain atrophy (Maurer, Riederer, & Beckmann, 1990), and tumors can cause mental retardation, irritability, and depression (Haug, Brain, & Aron, 1991). Blows to the head (especially those that leave blood clots) can cause a variety of behavioral disorders (Wood, 1990), and depressions such as Danielle's have also been linked to anatomical causes (Depue & Iacono, 1989).

It has been known for more than a century that infectious illnesses can cause abnormal behavior. Even before the discovery of the germ theory of disease, doctors knew that the sexually transmitted illness syphilis could lead to dementia and death. The modern scourge AIDS can also invade the brain, producing behavioral and cognitive disorders (Wormser, 1992). Other somatic causes of abnormal behavior include low birth weight (Friedman & Sigman, 1992), poisons, and environmental pollution (especially by lead) (Schroeder, 1987).

Given the numerous somatogenic causes of psychological disorders, it is not surprising that some medical practitioners assume that all psychological disorders have a somatic origin—"behind every twisted thought lies a twisted molecule" (B. Simon, 1978, p. 41). This extreme somatic view has never been dominant among

Although Anton Mesmer's "magnetic fluid" cure was ultimately judged to be fraudulent, it gave rise to the notion that sometimes symptoms of physical illness are psychological and can be cured by suggestion.

psychologists and social workers like Dr. Berg and Li Cheong, however. They prefer psychological (the Greek word *psyche* means "mind") and social explanations for abnormal behavior.

Was Danielle's Death Caused by Psychological Factors?

Modern readers have little difficulty accepting the idea that Danielle's death was the long-term result of her horrifying childhood, her reaction to not making the Olympic team, or her despair over the loss of her boyfriend (or all three). It seems self-evident to us that such experiences produce disordered behavior. Yet, this was not always the case. Like most of the other scientific ideas that we take for granted today, the theory that behavior disorders have psychological causes developed over time.

Mesmerism and the Birth of Modern Abnormal Psychology Although Galen (129–199 AD), a classical Greek physician, wrote extensively about the ways that our thoughts and emotions can make us ill, it took 1,800 years before the idea really caught on. The person responsible, although he never knew it, was Franz (also known as Friedrich) Anton Mesmer (1734–1815). According to Mesmer, illness results when "magnetic fluid" becomes blocked in parts of the body. To help clear these blockages, Mesmer filled a tub with iron filings and bottles of special "mesmerized" water. Patients suffering from a variety of conditions sat around the tub

Why We Should Never Judge the Past by the Present

Historical studies of the suffering (pathology) of the mind (psyche), or psychopathology, have always been more interesting to historians than to clinicians and scientists. There are at least three reasons for this. The first is the abstract nature of historical knowledge. No one would claim that a thorough understanding of the ancient Greek view of depression makes it any easier for a modern psychologist to help people like Danielle. A second reason for ignoring the history of psychopathology is that it is rather unpleasant. Mistreatment, punishment, cruelty, and superstition abound. The third reason is that historical studies are difficult. Original materials (manuscripts, notes, letters) are often unobtainable. Even when the required sources are available, interpreting them centuries later, from the perspective of a different culture, is a tricky process. History, like most other human pursuits, is subject to intellectual fads, and the views of historians have changed markedly across time.

Consider, for example, what historians of the future might think looking back at our modern society. Depending on the documents and artifacts that survive, they might conclude that our diets consisted solely of pizza and hamburgers and that most of us believed that Elvis Presley came back from the dead. Based on newspaper stories and films, they might think we believed that abnormal behavior is caused by devils who take possession of people's bodies and that ritual exorcism is a common form of psychological treatment, or psychotherapy.

This sounds unlikely and strange. How could historians of the future jump to such unwarranted conclusions? The truth is, it's easy; we do it all the time. Consider, for example, the discovery by archeologists of Stone Age skulls with carefully cut symmetrical holes. The cutting was done with a stone implement called a trephine; hence the procedure involved in doing the cutting is called trephining (or, sometimes, trepanning). Some of the skulls show evidence of healing, which means that people occasionally survived the operation. Because many of the skulls that had been trephined also show evidence of other head trauma (fractures, for example), it is possible that trephined individuals had been involved in battle. Trephining could have been a way of removing the splinters of bone and blood clots produced by blows to the head (W. B. Maher & Maher, 1985).

This is not a widely accepted theory, however. Most psychologists believe that trephining was not a treatment for battle wounds but a treatment for "mental disorders." To them, trephining was a way of releasing the evil spirits that the ancients believed were responsible for mental illness. The idea that trephining was a way to release madness-causing demons from the skull appears to have originated in a book called *Men Against Madness* (Selling, 1940), which provided no evidence for this assertion. Yet the "demonic" explanation still persists. Why? Because it fits a particular intellectual fashion, the tendency to view human history as a reasonably steady progression (with the occasional stumble) from ignorance, superstition, and cruelty to true knowledge and humane generosity. By assuming that our current theories and practices are always wise and that previous generations and ancient cultures were ignorant, we are succumbing to what historians call presentism—imposing the standards of one civilization on another.

Presentism colors most published histories of abnormal psychology. Perhaps admitting that members of ancient cultures may have been as intelligent and humane as we are threatens our belief in progress and our sense of intellectual superiority. Whatever the reason, the persistence of presentism is unfortunate; it not only devalues other times and cultures, it also denies us the opportunity to learn from them.

Consider, for example, Faron's (1968) well-known study of the Mapuche Indians of Chile. Faron relates the story of a young Mapuche named Secundinas Huenchulaf. Secundinas suffered from headaches that resisted all available

grasping flexible metal rods, which served as antennae. Magnetic fluid flowed from the tub through the antennae and into patients' bodies. Mesmer, dressed in a lavender cape, circulated around the room, every so often tapping a patient on the shoulder with a "magic wand." The patient would fall to the floor in a kind of seizure and, upon awakening, would be cured.

The French medical community, who thought Mesmer a fraud, convinced King Louis XVI to establish a Royal Commission to examine Mesmer's claims. The commission ran several tests. It substituted plain tap water for the mesmerized variety and found no change in the cure rate. Eliminating the tub of filings and its associated paraphernalia also made no difference to the number cured. The commission concluded that there was no such thing as magnetic fluid and that Mesmer's treatments were worthless. To explain why people seemed to have been cured, the royal commissioners argued that these people were never physically ill in the first place. Their illnesses were psychological—and that

treatments. Finally, his father took him to see a local medicine man, or shaman, who advised trephining to allow the evil spirits that were causing the headaches to escape. According to Faron, the shaman

> cut two "holes," one above each ear, in an operation which lasted for approximately three hours. The shaman used a stainless steel knife . . . boiled rags to mop up the blood, sea gull fat to smear over the wound and keep out the air, and an ordinary needle and strong white thread to sew the scalp in place. . . .
>
> During the few months I knew Secundinas, he had no headaches, was a very alert young man and, apparently, reasonably well adjusted. (p. 77)

Close inspection of the wounds led Faron to discover that the shaman never actually cut any holes in Secundinas's skull, but only in the skin of his scalp. The shaman was using the power of suggestion. He realized that Secundinas would feel better if he *believed* that the evil spirits were released. The actual operation was not necessary. How should we interpret Faron's story? Is it another illustration of the silly superstitions of primitive cultures, as presentism might suggest, or is it an example of the sophisticated use of suggestion to help an ill patient?

Presentism can seriously bias psychological research. For example, Michel Foucault, in his influential history of abnormal psychology, *Madness and Civilization* (1967), claimed that in the Middle Ages people with mental disorders were loaded onto boats and sent out to sea. These "ships of fools" were often denied permission to dock, so they sailed from one port to another or simply drifted on the ocean. According to Foucault, these ships were primitive concentration camps designed to separate people who behaved abnormally from the rest of society. Over the years, the ship of fools story has been repeated and elaborated many times (Weckowicz & Liebel-Weckowicz, 1990). Yet, there is no evidence that these ships ever existed.

An investigation by W. B. Maher and Maher (1982) traced the source of the ship of fools story to a book published in 1494 by a comic writer called Sebastian Brant. The book consists of a series of satirical poems about a fictional group of "fools" who were being sent from their native land to the Land of Fools. Each fool represented a human foible (pride, greed, and so on). Brant's book became famous and was widely translated. It also inspired a famous painting, "Ship of Fools," by Hieronymous Bosch. Although Brant's book was fiction (and not even about the mentally ill), Foucault found it sufficiently reliable to assert that there actually were ships of fools. It is surely no coincidence that Foucault's ship of fools story happened to support his view that the mentally ill have always been rejected and banished by society. Over the years, writers have repeated Foucault's claims, citing him as the authority. In this way, a historical inaccuracy has been perpetuated.

Presentism can distort psychological research. For example, as this 15th-century painting by Hieronymous Bosch exemplifies, the "ship of fools" was a popular allegorical device used in the early Renaissance to ridicule aspects of society. It was not a method for dealing with the mentally ill, as Michel Foucault has claimed.

is why they were eliminated by "suggestion." The commission's report was the first official acknowledgment that illness can be caused (and cured) by psychological factors alone.

Mesmer faded into obscurity, but his disciples, encouraged by the Royal Commission's report, discarded the tub, the robes, and the magic wand and concentrated on the power of suggestion. Patients were mesmerized (placed in a trance) and told that their symptoms would disappear when they awoke. Over the next century, "mesmerism" was replaced by **hypnosis**, and the idea that behavior disorders can be caused psychologically became increasingly accepted. Today, all psychologists would agree that Danielle's early experiences would have contributed to her personality, affected her behavior as a young adult, and influenced her death.

Possible Psychological Contributions to Danielle's Death

As we have seen, there were many possible psychological causes for Danielle's apparent suicide. This section highlights the six most often associated with depression and suicide.

Learned Helplessness   Danielle was abused by her father. She was helpless to stop the abuse, and those who could have stopped it, her mother, for one—did nothing to help her. This experience could have led Danielle to adopt an attitude of "learned helplessness." Abused children often come to believe that they are unable to control their lives (Barahal, Waterman, & Martin, 1981; Kelley, 1986). Learned helplessness leads them to react to life's inevitable blows with depression and, in some cases, suicide (Green, 1978; Overmier & LoLordo, 1998; Seligman, 1975).

Loss of Trust   Her father's abuse and her mother's complicity could have taught Danielle not to trust others (J. L. Jackson et al., 1990). This may be why she demanded frequent demonstrations of love and devotion. Ironically, her insecurity and lack of trust ultimately sabotaged her relationship with Luke, the relationship that she worried most about preserving.

Guilt and Self-Blame   The victims of sexual abuse often feel guilty, as if, in some way, they encouraged the abuser's illicit behavior (Jehu, 1992). Danielle's guilt feelings were reinforced by her father's suicide, for which she may have felt partly responsible. Guilt often results in low self-esteem. Danielle's poor opinion of herself may have made it easier for her to engage in self-destructive behaviors. As discussed earlier, suicide victims are often full of self-blame, and many come from troubled backgrounds (Overholser, Spirito, & Adams, 1999; Sorenson & Rutter, 1991).

Modeling   Her father's suicide may have served as a model for Danielle's later violence against herself. A history of family violence often leads to more violence, not only against others but also against oneself (Ammerman & Hersen, 1992). Peers may also serve as models. The suicides of other university students may have helped Danielle reach the decision to take her own life (Robbins, 1986).

Loss   Divorce, parental death, and adoption are all linked to emotional problems later in life (J. B. Kelly, 1998; Kurtz, 1995; S. Schwartz & Johnson, 1985). Danielle experienced all three. The death of Danielle's adoptive father could have further reinforced her sense of helplessness and perhaps even her depression (Paykel, 1982). Danielle's failure to make the Olympic team (an-other loss) and the apparent loss of her boyfriend may have been the last straws.

Social Isolation   Li Cheong's concern—that Danielle lacked a wide social support network—may have been well-founded. People with limited or unsatisfying social interactions are more prone to depression and more difficult to treat than those with a circle of supportive friends (Heikkinen, Aro, & Lonnqvist, 1993; Lewinsohn, Zeiss, & Duncan, 1989; Morano, Cisler, & Lemerond, 1993).

Any or all of these psychosocial causes could have contributed to Danielle's death. As already noted, however, no potential cause can be considered in isolation. An individual's personality results from the interaction of genetics, physiology, and experience. It is rare that any single factor is entirely responsible for a behavior. Indeed, even the interaction of psychological and biological factors may not provide a complete explanation. Social and cultural factors must also be considered.

Was Danielle's Death the Result of Social and Cultural Factors?

In 1518, just before the feast of Mary Magdalene, a woman who lived in Strassburg began to dance madly and speak in "tongues." She did this daily until she was sent to the chapel of St. Vitus in nearby Hohlenstein for help (Rosen, 1969). The woman continued her dancing, and within days she was joined by more than 400 people. After a month or so, the dancers began to disperse. This was not the first report of a "dancing mania" (period of excitement and unfocused physical activity). In 1374, a monk named Peter of Herental described a strange sect of traveling peasants, artisans, and servants who danced their way across Europe. They would enter a village, throw off their clothing, dance wildly through the streets, roll on the ground, bang their heads, foam at the mouth, and babble in strange tongues. Sometimes the villagers would join in. By the end of the 16th century, St. Vitus' Dance had become institutionalized. It occurred once each year on the festival of St. John. The dancing was believed to protect dancers from illness for the next year. The term **St. Vitus' dance** is still in use today to describe the odd muscle movements that accompany some forms of brain disorder, especially brain damage caused by high fevers (Swedo et al., 1993). It is possible that at least some of the 16th-century St. Vitus dancers also suffered from brain damage (F. E. James, 1991).

Speaking in tongues in some churches today may be similar to the "dancing manias" of Europe in the Middle Ages, like St. Vitus' dance and tarantism.

A related type of dance frenzy known as tarantism was seen in medieval Italy (Sigerist, 1943). Episodes occurred mainly in summer. Feeling a sudden pain, people would run into the street, hopping, jumping, and dancing. At the time, tarantism was blamed on the bite of the tarantula spider. Today, the phenomenon is usually attributed to the dangers and uncertainties of medieval life. The economic system that functioned so well under the Romans had been destroyed, along with confidence in the social order. Medieval Europeans were fearful, helpless, and superstitious. They sought relief in the pagan orgies that had been banned with the advent of Christianity. By attributing their behavior to a spider bite, villagers were able to justify acting in ways that would otherwise have been punished as sinful. A remnant of tarantism exists in the Italian folk dance called the tarantella.

Before we succumb to presentism and conclude that the dancing manias were proof of the ignorance and superstition of medieval Europeans, it is worth noting that speaking in tongues and rapturous "dancing" continued to be a feature of many 18th- and 19th-century religious movements. The "whirling dervishes," acolytes of the Turkish Islamic priests, and the Shakers of New England are two examples. Similar behaviors are even found today among charismatic and Pentecostal religious sects. Thus, we should have no reason to feel superior to our ancestors. The same forces that shaped

their behavior—economic hardship, cultural expectations, and social attitudes—continue to influence our behavior today.

Economics   The frequency of psychological disorders (as measured by mental hospital admissions) increases when unemployment increases (T. Jackson, 1999; Rabinowitz et al., 1995). Even in good economic times, mental hospital admissions are more common among the lower socioeconomic classes than among the middle or upper classes (Hollingshead & Redlich, 1958).

Cultural Expectations   Behavioral disorders can often be traced to cultural expectations. For example, in the past 30 years, society's idea of what constitutes an attractive female figure has changed drastically. Rather than having the fuller figures of the past, the women portrayed in modern magazines and movies tend to be very thin (Berel & Irving, 1998). This emphasis on thinness may be one reason why cases of anorexia nervosa (a form of intentional starvation) are increasing in Western countries (Garner & Garfinkel, 1980). (Anorexia nervosa is discussed in detail in Chapter 13.) For an example of how cultural change can affect the expression of disordered behavior, see Highlight 1.3.

Social Stereotypes   People who do not conform to social stereotypes can find themselves isolated and ostracized.

Running Amok

Human behavior does not operate in a vacuum. We are all influenced by the culture in which we live. Consider, for example, this description of the Malaysian phenomenon of running amok (sometimes spelled "amuck" in English). The following report is fairly typical:

> On the 8th July 1846, Sunan, a respectable Malay house-builder in Pinang, ran amok . . . , and before he was arrested killed an old Hindu woman, a Kling, a Chinese boy, a Kling girl about 3 years old in the arms of its father, and wounded two Hindus, three Klings, and two Chinese, of whom only two survived. On his trial it appeared that he was greatly afflicted by the recent loss of his wife and child, which preyed upon his mind and quite altered his appearance. A person with whom he had lived up to the 15th of June said further, "He used to bring his child to his work, since its death he has worked for me; he often said he could not work as he was affected by the loss of his child. I think he was out of his mind, he did not smoke or drink, I think he was mad." On the morning of the amok this person met him, and asked him to work on his boat. He replied that he could not, he was very much afflicted. He had his hands concealed under his cloth, he frequently exclaimed, Allah, Allah! He daily complained of the loss of his wife and child. On the trial Sunan declared he did not know what he was about, and persisted in this at the place of execution, adding "As the gentlemen say I have committed so many murders I suppose it must be so." The amok took place on the 8th, the trial on the 13th, and the execution on the 15th July—all within eight days. (Quoted in Spores, 1988, pp. 41–42)

According to Spores (1988), it was traditionally expected that Malaysian warriors, when faced with overwhelming opposition, would "run amok." They would crash into the enemy, lashing widely with their sharpened swords. Ultimately, the warrior would be killed, but his death (the warriors were all men) would be covered in glory. In the 19th century, civilians, faced with severe financial or social hardship, mimicked the warriors by also running amok. These frenzied rampages usually began with an attack on someone they knew, but as the episode continued, strangers were attacked indiscriminately. Ultimately, the amok runners were either captured or killed. Those captured denied any memory of the episode.

Running amok was a frequent occurrence during the 19th century. At the time, Malaysia, including what is now Singapore, was a feudal society in which people had few civil rights. There was no organized justice system, and those who could not pay their debts were forced into slavery. Amok was common probably because it was similar to behavior considered heroic in battle and almost certainly because it provided an escape valve for frustrations that may otherwise have boiled over into open revolution against the feudal social system.

The frequency of amok began to decrease as the British consolidated their hold over the country. The British brought tribal peace and economic order. They developed laws, courts, and various administrative structures that enabled business to be carried out rationally and fairly. The British also eliminated debt slavery, the feudal system, and the arbitrary confiscation of property. In their place, they established a judicial system. These massive social changes removed both the purpose and the cultural legitimacy of amok; by the middle of the 20th century it was extinct. Today, the most likely place for an indiscriminate killing spree to occur is not Malaysia but the United States. Because the United States is not a feudal society, we must look for different causes from those that operated in Malaysia. Some likely possibilities are the availability of guns, the glorification of violence in the media, and drug abuse. There is one way that 19th-century Malaysia and 20th-century America are alike, however. In both countries, behavior is shaped by social and cultural forces.

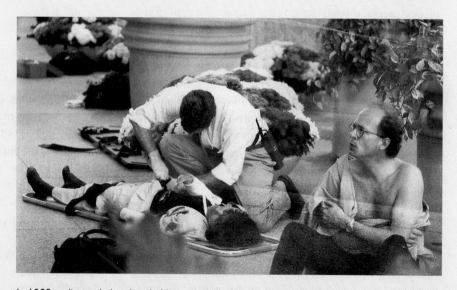

In 1993, a disgruntled and probably emotionally disturbed law client "ran amok" in a San Francisco office tower. Using an arsenal of high-powered guns, he killed eight people and wounded many more before killing himself.

Being cut off in this way can cause abnormal behavior. This is why behavior disorders, including depression, drug abuse, and suicide, are more prevalent among those who reject stereotypic sex roles (Carson, 1989) and those, like Native Americans, whose cultural values differ from the majority (Meketon, 1983; Muhlin, 1979).

The effect of cultural factors on behavior can be conceptualized within the diathesis-stress model described earlier. Specifically, poverty, prejudice, and social expectations produce stress. When combined with an appropriate diathesis, this stress can result in disordered behavior (see Al-Issa, 1982). Because both a diathesis and social stress are required to produce abnormal behavior, we would not expect everyone faced with prejudice or other social stresses to develop a behavior disorder, and, of course, not everyone does.

So, was Danielle's death related to social factors? It is difficult to say. She had financial problems, and she came from an unhappy background of which she was apparently ashamed. These factors could have made her already low self-esteem even lower, and there were two other suicides in her school in the past year that may have served as models. Combined with the other biological and psychological factors already described, these social influences could well have helped push Danielle over the edge to self-destruction.

The Cause of Danielle's Death: What Can We Conclude?

Causal attributions are difficult because, in most cases, our data are correlational. We know, for example, that suicide is more common among the relatives of people who commit suicide than it is in the general population. Because Danielle's father took his own life, it is tempting to conclude that his suicide in some way caused hers, but this conclusion may not be warranted. A correlation between two events does not necessarily mean that one causes the other. Danielle and her father may both have been driven to suicide by some third factor, an inherited disposition, for example. The problems of correlational research are discussed in Chapter 2. As will be shown, it is probably best to conceptualize the various causes of abnormal behavior as **risk factors.** In other words, Danielle's genetic background, childhood experiences, drug abuse, disappointment at not making the Olympic team, and fear of losing her boyfriend placed her at special risk for committing suicide. Whether any specific factor or combination of factors actually caused her to take her life, we are not yet able to say.

Despite the long list of causes discussed so far, the most common explanation for abnormal behavior has not yet been mentioned. If you ask people why Danielle attempted suicide, most will reply that she tried to harm herself because she suffered from a depressive mental illness. "Mental illness" explanations for behavior disorders are ubiquitous, yet it is not entirely clear what they mean. Let's take a closer look at this concept.

WAS DANIELLE MENTALLY ILL?

Danielle took drugs—anabolic steroids, amphetamines, and, in the past at least, tranquilizers. She may have tried to kill herself on one previous occasion, or she may have been seeking attention and help. Either way, she managed to get herself admitted to a hospital psychiatric ward. Mental health professionals considered her to be depressed enough to require treatment with medication and psychotherapy. Finally, Danielle died young, probably as a result of suicide. Does all this make her abnormal? Does it make her mentally ill? It depends on what we mean by "abnormality" and "mental illness." There is no single, universally applicable definition of abnormality, nor does everyone agree on exactly what behaviors constitute signs of mental illness. As you will see in this section, there are many different ways of judging whether behavior is abnormal; no single one is applicable in all circumstances. Abnormality, it turns out, is one of those ambiguous concepts that psychologists must learn to tolerate.

Danielle's Behavior Was Unusual

According to one relatively straightforward view, abnormal behavior differs from normal behavior mainly in degree. Thus, everyone gets depressed from time to time. It is when depression becomes severe enough to lead a person to contemplate suicide that it becomes "abnormal." Declaring unusual or extreme forms of behavior to be abnormal implies that whatever characterizes the majority of people is "normal." This is why we commonly refer to the average body temperature of 98.6° Fahrenheit (37° Celsius) as "normal" and to deviations from the average as "abnormal." Because it relies on averages and departures from the average, this way of defining what is normal and abnormal is called statistical. Terms such as *sexual deviant* are derived directly from this statistical view of abnormality—*deviants* are people who deviate from the norm. From a statistical viewpoint, Danielle's behavior was certainly abnormal. Most university students do not take amphetamines or anabolic steroids, nor do they try to harm themselves.

Applying the statistical definition usually requires dividing a continuous variable into discrete categories: normal and abnormal. Blood pressure is a good example. It varies along a continuum. Most people fall somewhere in the middle of the range; some are higher than average; others are lower. People with high blood pressure are considered to suffer from "hypertension." They require a special diet and, in some cases, medication. In other words, people with high blood pressure are considered to have a disease. Yet, the definition of hypertension is purely statistical. The number of people who are diagnosed as hypertensive depends on where we place the line that divides normal from abnormal. If a small deviation from average is considered abnormal, the number of people judged to be hypertensive will be large. If only very high blood pressure is considered abnormal, the number of hypertensive patients will be small. By deciding how high blood pressure must be before it is considered abnormal, we not only transform a continuum into discrete categories, but we also determine the number of people each category will contain. In other words, nature does not assign people to normal and abnormal categories; people do.

In abnormal psychology, as in medicine, people who deviate from the norm are often placed in discrete diagnostic categories. An alternative to this categorical approach is to describe people using a number of different psychological dimensions. Thus, instead of diagnosing Danielle as a dependent personality, Dr. Berg could have described her using a profile of measures—of intelligence, dependence, depression, and so on. The relative advantages and disadvantages of the categorical and dimensional approaches are discussed in Chapter 3. For now, it is enough to say that clinicians overwhelmingly favor categorical descriptions. In practice, dimensional descriptions are typically converted into categories to facilitate their practical application (Widiger & Trull, 1991).

The statistical approach to defining abnormality requires the balancing of costs and benefits. For example, Danielle's first suicide attempt put her in the hospital, where she was kept under close observation. It would be expensive (not to mention intrusive) to hospitalize and observe everyone who hints at suicide. Many of those confined would not be in any real danger. To make sure that limited hospital resources are allocated to those most likely to benefit, psychologists try to confine only those who are in serious danger. Instruments such as the Los Angeles Suicide Prevention Center Lethality Scale (Shneidman, Farberow, & Litman, 1970) administered by Dr. Berg to Danielle are used to help make such

Sports commentator and former NFL football coach John Madden must travel all over the country for games, but he has a fear of flying. For him, the solution is to travel in a customized bus.

judgments. Based on their scores, people are categorized as either "dangerous," and put under observation, or "not dangerous," and treated less intrusively. In this way, a continuum is divided into categories and resources are allocated to those who need them most. (For more on cost-benefit analysis, see Critical Thinking About Clinical Decisions 1.1.)

Despite its widespread acceptance, the statistical approach to abnormality has some flaws. First, because they are relative, statistical definitions of abnormality are tied to a particular time and place. In a population of pygmies, where most people are small, a person who would appear to be of average height to us would seem a grossly abnormal giant. Second, the statistical approach can lead to ridiculous conclusions if we try to apply it too widely. What happens, for example, when extremes are desirable? Is it really abnormal to be too beautiful, too happy, too intelligent, or too healthy? Clearly not. We need some additional criteria to separate desirable from undesirable traits. One frequently suggested possibility is to consider behavior to be abnormal when it produces distress.

Danielle's Behavior Produced Distress

Danielle experienced considerable personal anguish. She was upset about not making the Olympic team and miserable over Luke's apparent rejection of her. If behavior that produces distress is abnormal, then Danielle's behavior was certainly abnormal.

How Many Suicides Can We Afford to Prevent?

For practical purposes, clinical psychologists frequently find it necessary to divide a diagnostic continuum into discrete categories. For example, people may be classified as "suicidal" or "not suicidal" based on their scores on a measure of suicidal tendency. Special precautions may be taken for those classified as suicidal. Because special precautions are expensive, the number of people classified as suicidal is really a matter of costs and benefits.

Consider, for example, the accompanying graph, which contains the results of a hypothetical measure of "suicide lethality" administered to a random population. Lethality scores range along a continuum from "not suicidal" to "suicidal" (shown on the horizontal axis of the graph). If the lethality scale is valid, people who are actually suicidal should score higher than those who are not suicidal. That is, their scores should fall somewhere in the right-hand bell curve. In practice, a small number of nonsuicidal people (most of whom score in the left-hand bell curve) achieve a higher score than people who are actually contemplating suicide. Their scores suggest that they are suicidal when they are not. These are known as **false-positives**; their scores fall in the region where the two graphs overlap. Suppose we are psychologists working at a large clinic. To prevent people from harming themselves, we must recommend hospitalization and observation for those most at risk. Do we hospitalize everyone with scores to the right of Cutoff 1 or everyone with scores to the right of Cutoff 2?

If we use Cutoff 1, we will eliminate any false-positives. Everyone identified as suicidal will really be suicidal. On the other hand, many people who are suicidal will be missed and not hospitalized. If we use Cutoff 2, we will hospitalize every potential suicide, but we will also hospitalize many false-positives who are not suicidal. The two cutoffs have different patterns of costs and benefits. Cutoff 1 has lower costs but may miss some suicides. Cutoff 2 has higher costs (more people hospitalized needlessly) but prevents more suicides. Which cutoff is correct? There is no answer to this question. It depends on the resources available and our attitude toward hospitalization. Cutoff 2 requires more resources and results in the hospitalization of many nonsuicidal people. Cutoff 1 costs less but will miss some suicidal people. As you can see, making a diagnostic judgment is not just a matter of giving someone a test and noting the result. It also depends on our available resources, the number of false-positives that we are willing to tolerate, and our willingness to hospitalize people who may not need it.

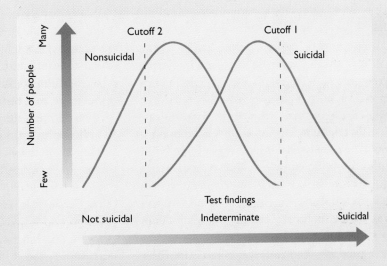

Measure of Suicide Lethality

The distress approach to defining abnormality overcomes some of the problems of the statistical definition. Consider fear of flying, for example. Traveling salespeople who fear flying but need to fly to earn their living may find their fear sufficiently troubling to warrant professional help. Other people who fear flying but who do not need to travel can just avoid airplanes; their fear causes them no personal distress. The personal distress criterion allows us to make a distinction between the salespeople and the others even though both groups would be considered abnormal using the statistical definition.

Allowing people to decide for themselves whether their behavior is abnormal relieves psychologists from having to make judgments about the behavior of others. But people are not always the best judges of their own behavior. Danielle may well have believed that her future was hopeless and that suicide was her only option. This does not mean that we should simply accept her judgment and allow her to kill herself. When it is believed to be in a person's or society's best interest, the government can act as *parens patriae* (the parent of the people) and make decisions on behalf of an individual. In practice, this means that people judged to present a danger to themselves or to others can be committed to treatment facilities against their will (Bongar, 1991; Sales, 1993). If her suicidal intent had been known and judged serious, this is exactly what would have happened to Danielle.

Involuntary treatment is a controversial matter, one that we will return to several times in this book. For now, it is enough to emphasize that people who are treated involuntarily need not be personally distressed for their behavior to be considered abnormal. This means that we must rely on something other than the personal distress criterion to make such judgments. One possibility is to evaluate behaviors by the functions they serve. Normal behavior allows individuals to adapt to their social and physical environment; it facilitates individual and social goals. Abnormal behavior is maladaptive; it results in unfavorable or harmful outcomes for the individual or society. This focus on behavioral outcomes falls squarely in the philosophical tradition known as utilitarianism.

Danielle's Behavior Was Not Functional

Judging behavior by what it achieves is a natural outgrowth of **utilitarianism,** a philosophy developed by the 18th-century English scholar Jeremy Bentham (1748–1832). Bentham's philosophy is usually described as "hedonistic" because he viewed whatever gave pleasure to both the individual and society as right and whatever gave pain as wrong. Bentham's rule for judging behavior was to value most those behaviors that provided "the greatest good for the greatest number" (Heilbronner, 1980).

Utilitarians consider behavior to be abnormal only when it is maladaptive, when it harms the individual or society. Thus, alcoholism, violence, and drug abuse are all maladaptive (and therefore abnormal) because they threaten our individual and collective survival. Behaviors that prevent individuals from fulfilling their potential (debilitating fears, for example), are also maladaptive. Danielle's drug abuse, her dependent personality, her depression, and her attempts to harm herself were all maladaptive, and therefore abnormal, using the utilitarian criterion.

Because utilitarians judge a behavior by the function it serves, the same behavior can be normal or abnormal depending on what people are trying to achieve and the circumstances in which they are trying to

Jeremy Bentham (1748–1832) founded the philosophy of utilitarianism, which considers behavior abnormal if it harms the individual or society.

achieve it. Violent aggression against another person is maladaptive and abnormal when it is unprovoked or when it threatens social cohesion. The same behavior is adaptive, and normal, for soldiers at war (Ellard, 1989).

Although it has some intuitive appeal as a political philosophy, utilitarianism has always had its critics. They claim that some activities are wrong and objectionable even when they benefit the majority of people. Slavery in the Old South, for example, produced significant economic advantages for the White majority, yet few would argue (even then) that slavery is a good way to organize society. Similar problems arise in applying the utilitarian criterion to the behavior of individuals. Should we consider sexual sadism (harming another for sexual gratification) or sexual relations between adult men and children to be adaptive, and therefore normal, just because the individuals concerned find willing partners? If your answer is no, then you must believe that some behaviors are abnormal even if they are not personally distressing and even if they bring pleasure to the individuals concerned. Your belief is part of a long tradition. Throughout history, society's views on what constitutes moral, ethical, and proper behavior have played a crucial part in defining abnormality.

Danielle's Behavior Violated Social Values

To a large extent, society defines what is considered to be abnormal behavior. Western societies consider sui-

Famed Japanese film director Juzo Itami committed suicide in 1997, when he learned a magazine was going to publish a story about his alleged affair with a 26-year-old employee. His suicide note said this was the only way he could assert his innocence. In Western societies, without the traditions of Bushido and hara-kiri, a public figure committing suicide in a similar situation would appear to be admitting guilt.

cide to be abnormal except in rare circumstances (among people suffering from terminal or debilitating illnesses, for example). Nevertheless, there were, and there still are, societies in which suicide is actually required under some circumstances. For example, the 17th-century Japanese code of Bushido considered failure to one's lord to be a fatal disgrace that could be expiated only by suicide. As recently as World War II, Japanese soldiers were expected to sacrifice their lives for their emperor. A Japanese soldier who chose not to commit hara-kiri would have been considered abnormal. Not only soldiers have been required to take their own lives, so have civilians. The Indian custom of suttee, for example, required that a widow be cremated with her husband. Wives were expected to throw themselves on their husbands' funeral pyre. Even today, in some parts of India, a wife who chooses to live after her husband dies is considered to be abnormal.

Most societies disapprove of behavior that is statistically rare, personally distressing, and maladaptive. But social disapproval is more than just a combination of the definitions already discussed. It is actually a fourth definition of abnormality, quite separate from the others. Behavior can be common, adaptive, and not distressing and still be considered abnormal if it is socially

disapproved. This is understandable. Social relations are based on a shared knowledge of how people will act in familiar situations. If everyone were to behave unpredictably, society as we know it would be impossible. Still, we do not want to go too far and force everyone into a dull conformity. A balance between allowing people to express their individuality and at the same time allowing society to function is required. This balance is often difficult to achieve. The majority may be tempted to force the minority to conform. In extreme cases, people are persecuted just for being different. This, in fact, is what has happened to homosexuals. Critical Thinking About Clinical Decisions 1.2 provides some background on this subject.

Society's definition of acceptable behavior is constantly changing. Behavior considered abnormal at one time or in one place may be considered perfectly normal at or in others. Yet the important role played by social and cultural norms is not always recognized. Before 1973, psychiatrists considered homosexuality to be an "illness." Then, as attitudes changed, the American Psychiatric Association voted this "illness" out of existence. What kind of illness can be eliminated by a vote? Can doctors vote diabetes or malaria out of existence?

Was Danielle's Behavior Caused by an Illness?

Danielle's behavior met all of the criteria for abnormality: It was deviant statistically, caused her personal distress, was maladaptive, and was socially disapproved. She even received a psychiatric diagnosis. But was she ill? One way to answer this question is to turn to the origin of modern scientific medicine in the early 19th century.

General Paresis and Mental Illness　As far back as the 16th century, doctors noted that patients who harbored **delusions,** bizarre or false ideas, were not all alike. Some believed that people were plotting against them, others believed that they were receiving messages from God, and still others had delusions of grandeur (an exaggerated sense of self-importance). Over the years, clinicians observed that people with delusions of grandeur often became forgetful and foolish as they grew older. Eventually, they became paralyzed and died. These seemingly disparate symptoms occurred together frequently enough to constitute a distinct **syndrome** known as general paralysis of the insane, or **general paresis.**

By the 1860s, autopsies had demonstrated considerable brain damage among patients who had died from general paresis. This was not surprising given that the patients were often paralyzed. At first, alcohol and tobacco were blamed because many sufferers drank and

Homosexuality and the Politics of Psychiatric Diagnosis

Homosexuality was a common feature of classical Greece (B. Simon, 1978). It was considered neither abnormal nor a threat to society. With the rise of Christianity, biblical injunctions against homosexuality were used as a reason to prohibit homosexual practices and punish offenders. As nations developed, secular governments continued the persecution of homosexuals. From the 16th century to as recently as 1861, the penalty for violating one of these laws in England was death (Bayer, 1981). Homosexuals were not permitted to immigrate to the United States, and those who were born in America were denied jobs. In the 19th century, medical scientists began to show an interest in homosexuality. The dominant view was that homosexuality was an inherited trait, perhaps influenced by certain environmental factors (poor upbringing, for example). Doctors disagreed about what should be done with homosexuals: Some recommended incarceration in asylums; others favored trying to convert them into heterosexuals. Everyone agreed, however, that homosexuality was abnormal. In 1952, when the American Psychiatric Association published its first official manual of psychiatric disorders, homosexuality was included.

Despite the American Psychiatric Association's claim to scientific objectivity, its judgment that homosexuality was a psychological disorder disregarded a considerable body of evidence to the contrary. For example, in 1948 Alfred Kinsey (1894–1956) and his colleagues published a landmark study on the sexual behavior of American males (Kinsey, Pomeroy, & Martin, 1948). This study reported a much higher incidence of homosexual behavior than had previously been believed—too high, argued Kinsey, to represent an illness. Kinsey believed that homosexuality was one of many learned sexual orientations. In the 1950s, Evelyn Hooker (1957, 1993), a psychologist, studied the psychological functioning of homosexuals by giving personality tests to homosexuals who were working in the wider community, as well as to heterosexuals of the same age, intelligence test scores, and education. She found that clinicians could not tell the two groups apart. Homosexuals were judged to be as well adjusted as the heterosexuals. She concluded that the reason psychiatrists considered homosexuality a disorder was that they met only troubled homosexuals in their practices. Well-adjusted homosexuals had no need to visit psychiatrists.

With the emergence of the gay rights movement as a political force in the 1960s, the American Psychiatric Association was forced to reconsider its classification of homosexuality as a disorder. In 1973, the members of the Association voted 58% to 42% to delete homosexuality from its manual of disorders. From that day forward, homosexuality was no longer a recognized mental disorder. What caused the American Psychiatric Association to alter its view? Was it new findings proving that homosexuality was not a mental disorder? The answer is probably no. The association was merely acknowledging an increasing social tolerance for alternative sexual preferences (see Kirk & Kutchins, 1992, for a detailed discussion of the political history of psychiatric diagnoses).

With the development of an organized gay rights movement in the late 1960s, homosexuals became more visible, and views in the United States about homosexuality began to change. In 1973, the American Psychiatric Association decided homosexuality no longer should be classified as a mental disorder. Here, gay rights activists participate in a 1993 civil rights march in Washington, D.C.

smoked, but so too did many people who never developed general paresis. In the 1880s, reports appeared linking general paresis with the sexually transmitted disease syphilis. More than half the general paresis patients reported having had syphilis at some time in their lives. These reports were suggestive but puzzling. If syphilis was responsible for the syndrome, all of the general paresis patients should have had the disease, not just half. Either the relationship between syphilis and general paresis was spurious or those who claimed never to have had syphilis were not telling the truth. They may have been embarrassed to admit it or genuinely unaware that they had ever had the disease.

Because self-reports are unreliable, demonstrating a relationship between syphilis and general paresis required some objective way of knowing whether a person with general paresis had ever had syphilis. The German neurologist Richard von Krafft-Ebing (1840–1902) came up with a foolproof method. He knew that the overt signs of syphilis (genital sores) disappeared after a few weeks, while the disease lingered in the body making people immune to future infection. Capitalizing on this immunity, Krafft-Ebing injected patients who claimed never to have had syphilis with material taken from syphilitic sores. Not one developed the symptoms of syphilis. This meant that they had all been previously infected. Thus, Krafft-Ebing established a clear link between syphilis and general paresis.

It is doubtful that Krafft-Ebing's experiment could be conducted today. He deliberately exposed people to an incurable and, at the time, fatal disease. Modern ethical codes forbid us from endangering people in this way. At the time, however, general paresis was a major health menace, and the risks to a small number of terminally ill people may have seemed a small price to pay given the potential benefits. Ironically, not long after Krafft-Ebing's experiment, a blood test for syphilis was developed that could identify those who had been infected without risking anyone's health.

Once the link between syphilis and general paresis was made, scientists devoted themselves to finding a cure. Arsenic compounds were sometimes successful but also poisonous and potentially lethal. Patients were deliberately infected with malaria because the high temperatures associated with that disease could kill the organism that causes syphilis; unfortunately, they sometimes also killed the patient. Ultimately, these primitive methods were replaced by antibiotics. The result was that, in less than a century, a common psychological disorder whose symptoms were delusions of grandeur, forgetfulness, and intellectual decline was found to be the

The Mad Hatter in Lewis Carroll's Alice in Wonderland *is based on real life. In Victorian England, hatters were notorious for irrational behavior, which was eventually traced to poisoning from the mercury used to treat the felt for hats.*

result of an underlying physical illness and curable. Doctors were encouraged by this success to look for the underlying physical causes of other behavioral problems. And they were successful. By the early 1900s, a physical basis had been established for other behavior disorders—the mental deterioration associated with alcoholism and with old age, for example. Even the irrational behavior of the notorious "mad hatters" of *Alice in Wonderland* fame was traced to brain damage caused by the mercury used to treat the felt from which hats were made.

Despite these notable successes, and notwithstanding many valiant attempts (including numerous autopsies of people with behavioral disorders), 19th-century researchers were unable to link the majority of behavioral disorders to any specific disease. As a consequence, clinicians began to refer to these as **functional disorders,** disorders that had no physical basis. These functional disorders were called "mental illnesses."

Differentiating Between Physical and Mental Disorders

If functional mental illnesses are not diseases, then what are they? The answer is that they are analogies. We act as if mental illnesses are physical illnesses, even though we know that, in many cases, they are not. Treating mental illnesses as analogous to physical illnesses allows us to achieve two purposes, one humanitarian and one scientific. The humanitarian purpose is to obtain help for people in distress. By calling people mentally ill, we place them in the same category as those who are physically ill. Instead of considering them sinners, eccentrics, or simply evil, we classify them as sick, thereby making it legitimate to use society's limited health resources to help them (Szasz, 1961).

The scientific purpose behind treating mental illnesses as analogous to physical diseases is to allow clinicians and researchers to apply to abnormal behavior the methods that have worked so well in medicine. Clinicians observe which symptoms and signs seem to go together to form syndromes. Researchers direct their efforts toward uncovering a syndrome's underlying cause. Once the cause is known, treatments can be devised to eliminate the underlying illness.

The analogy between medical and psychological disorders fits with clinical training methods. For most of the 20th century, clinicians were mainly psychiatrists trained not in psychology but in medicine. It was natural for them to apply their medical training to abnormal behavior. There is nothing inherently wrong with this. This book describes many important insights produced by the analogy between medical and psychological illness. But the analogy is not perfect; it has suffered from illusory correlations, cultural biases, and illness inflation.

Illusory Correlations   Unless there is some independent way to identify the underlying "illness" (equivalent to the blood test for syphilis), attributing abnormal behavior to mental illnesses can lead to circular reasoning. For example, Dr. Berg believes that Danielle took drugs and behaved in a self-destructive manner because she had a psychological disorder. How does he know that she had a psychological disorder? Well, she behaved self-destructively, didn't she? By invoking an illness analogy, Dr. Berg has not produced an explanation for Danielle's behavior, only the illusion of an explanation.

Cultural Biases   Most physical illnesses are universally recognized. People who have general paresis are ill no matter who they happen to be or where they happen to live. Whether they are Indian widows, Japanese warriors, or American college students is irrelevant. Cultural identity is relevant, however, when determining whether a suicide will be considered abnormal. Similarly, it is ludicrous to imagine a meeting of doctors voting to remove diabetes or malaria from their list of official diagnoses, as happened with homosexuality. To be

fair, there are some psychological disorders that are universally recognized (Al-Issa, 1982), but the majority are linked to certain cultures and times (Szasz, 1961).

Illness Inflation   Even within a single society, there is often no definitive way to decide who is mentally ill. Are terminally ill people who commit suicide mentally ill? Are people who become severely depressed over the death of a loved one mentally ill? Are hermits and beachcombers mentally ill? Are people who leave all of their money to their cats mentally ill? Where do we draw the line? Because there are no objective tests available to establish a diagnosis of mental illness, practically anyone who experiences a problem in life can be classified as mentally ill. This is why the number of mental illnesses is constantly inflating. Today, it includes people who are out of touch with reality, the depressed, some criminals, children who have trouble learning, people who do not like the way they look, unhappy couples seeking a divorce, people who do not like sex, people who like sex too much, mentally retarded people, addicts, alcoholics, those with stress-related physical illnesses, self-centered people, those whose personalities have been deemed inadequate, and numerous others. The idea that all of these people are sick in the same way that a person with general paresis is sick stretches the illness analogy far beyond its breaking point.

Let us now return to the question posed at the start of this section: Was Danielle's behavior caused by an illness? There turns out to be no simple answer. Danielle may have been depressed, and depression (as we will see in later chapters) certainly has some of the characteristics of an illness. It is also possible that she had an unfortunate accident or that she made a deliberate choice to end her life based on her bleak view of the future. We may find Danielle's death regrettable and tragic, but this does not mean that she was sick. Whether we decide to call her sick is a matter of benefits and costs. On the benefits side, calling Danielle sick could have allowed her to be hospitalized against her will and treated, and this may have saved her life. On the costs side, Danielle would have been deprived of her civil rights. Also, a mental illness label would have stuck with Danielle, coloring not only how others would treat her but also how Danielle would think about herself (Goffman, 1961; Rosenhan, 1973). Given that many mental diagnoses are ambiguous, subjective, and culture-bound, it seems wise to apply them with great caution, and only when the potential benefits of diagnosing someone as mentally ill outweigh the costs.

COULD DANIELLE'S DEATH HAVE BEEN PREDICTED?

Danielle was abused by her father, who later killed himself. She had made at least one previous suicide gesture, and she took drugs. Psychological tests showed Danielle to be depressed, dependent, and perhaps even a little guilty about the events of her childhood. Does this mean that she presented a serious suicide risk? How serious? Answering such questions—predicting behavior—is one of the main goals of scientific psychology. It is easy to see why. If Danielle's behavior had been predicted, steps could have been taken to prevent her death and save her family and friends considerable anguish. This section is concerned with how psychologists go about making such predictions.

Why Clinical Predictions Are Often Uncertain

At the time of her hospitalization, Danielle was referred to Dr. Berg for a **psychological assessment;** one purpose of the assessment was to gauge the likelihood that she might try to harm herself. Although the terms *assessment* and *testing* are often used synonymously, they are not identical. An assessment includes the entire process by which data are gathered, integrated, and interpreted. Psychological testing may be involved in that process, but tests are only one source of assessment information. Assessments also rely on observations, interviews, and histories. Dr. Berg, for example, began by talking to Danielle. He noted her sad demeanor, tearfulness, and feelings of hopelessness. He knew her history from Li Cheong's social work report, and he knew that she was in the hospital because of a suicide gesture. The psychological tests revealed Danielle's low self-concept, dependent personality, depression, and lack of hope. After considering all of the available information, Dr. Berg recommended that Danielle be placed on medication and monitored as an outpatient. He must not have considered her a serious enough suicide risk to require continued hospitalization.

Dr. Berg's task was not unusual; psychologists are often required to make predictions about how people will behave. Although the specifics vary from case to case, behavioral predictions are always uncertain. In this section, we review some of the reasons for this uncertainty. The first lies in the nature of the diagnostic process.

Diagnosis   A diagnosis serves four main purposes. First, it provides a convenient way to refer to a syn-

drome. Rather than describe people as having delusions of grandeur, deteriorating intelligence, and paralysis, we can simply say that they have general paresis. The second purpose of a diagnosis is to provide a focus for research. Once a syndrome has been identified and labeled, researchers from different parts of the world can study it with some expectation that they are all studying the same condition. Ultimately, someone may discover the cause of the syndrome (as in general paresis), and then the diagnosis can fulfill its third purpose—suggesting an appropriate treatment. Finally, after sufficient cases have been studied, diagnoses can serve their fourth purpose, providing information on which to base a **prognosis** (a prediction), such as the expectation of paralysis and death for untreated cases of general paresis.

Although some psychiatric diagnoses fulfill all four purposes, many do not. They may provide a convenient label for a correlated set of behaviors and a focus for research, but only a few are tied to specific treatments and even fewer can predict the future with any degree of precision. Had Danielle been diagnosed as having pneumonia, we would have known that she had a bacterial infection that would respond to antibiotic treatment. We would also have known that if she remained untreated, her breathing capacity would have gradually deteriorated until she died. But Danielle was not diagnosed as having pneumonia. Dr. Berg said that she was depressed and dependent. Although we can guess at how she got that way, Dr. Berg's diagnoses do not suggest a specific etiology or treatment, nor do they lead to a specific prognosis. Depressed and dependent people may try to kill themselves, but, then again, they may not. Psychiatric diagnoses are full of such uncertainties.

Self-Reports   Uncertainty can also arise from the imprecise nature of clinical data. Self-reports, for example, often constitute the main source of clinical information, yet they are notoriously unreliable. It is not that people consciously intend to deceive clinicians (although sometimes they do); it is just that most people are poor judges of their own behavior. Some exaggerate their problems; others minimize them. A clinician's questions may be misunderstood or misinterpreted. For example, one medical survey found that 35% of men could not answer the question "Are you circumcised?" correctly (Lilienfeld & Graham, 1958). Ethnic and cultural background, education, even attitudes toward psychological problems have all been found to affect the way people respond to a clinician's questions and, as a consequence, add to the uncertainty of clinical data (S. Schwartz & Griffin, 1986).

People have long believed that lunacy increases when the moon is full. But studies have shown that this common belief, depicted here in an 18th-century French engraving, is an illusory correlation.

Illusory Correlations Each year, thousands of psychological tests are performed at a cost of millions of dollars. The purpose of these tests is to help psychologists formulate a diagnosis, understand a person, make a prediction, or produce a treatment plan. In some cases, tests appear to be administered simply because they are available—to have them "on the record." Although there are no specific data on how psychological tests are used in clinical practice, a study of medical laboratory tests ordered by 111 California doctors (Wertman et al., 1980) found that 32% of tests produced absolutely no change in diagnosis, prognosis, therapy, or understanding of the patient's condition. There is little reason to believe that psychological tests are any different. For example, it is not clear what Dr. Berg got out of the intelligence test or the Thematic Apperception Test administered as part of his assessment of Danielle. (These specific tests and others are described in Chapter 3.)

Even when test data are potentially relevant, predictions based on test results may not be justified because some psychological tests have low **predictive validity,** that is, they are only weakly correlated with future behavior (Gregory, 1992). Unfortunately, tests with low predictive validity (like the Thematic Apperception Test) continue to be used. At least part of the explanation for their continued popularity is the existence of **illusory correlations,** which were first demonstrated by Chapman and Chapman (1969). These researchers exposed university students to a series of drawings accompanied by manufactured personality descriptions of the supposed artists. The same drawings were presented several times, each time with a different personality description. By the end of the presentations, every drawing had been matched with every personality description. In the next stage of the experiment, students were asked to recall which picture went with which personality description. Because every picture was paired with every description, the students should have been as likely to recall one pair as another. But this is not what happened. The students recalled specific pairs of drawings and personality descriptions more often than others. For example, they recalled that a drawing showing a person staring down at the floor had been matched with a personality description suggestive of depression. They did not recall that the same drawing had also been matched with other, nondepressed personality descriptions. It seems that students expected depressed people to draw pictures of people staring down at the floor. This expectation led them to recall the pairing that was consistent with their preconceived belief and to ignore or forget the others. By remembering only evidence consistent with their expectations, the students could have convinced themselves that drawings offer insights into personality even though the relationship between drawings and personality descriptions was completely random. The students would have formed an "illusory correlation."

There are many examples of selective attention to evidence in the clinical literature. For example, Dawes (1988) quotes a clinical psychologist who wrote: "I cannot think of a single psychological problem—from anxiety and depression, to fear of intimacy or of success, to alcohol or drug abuse, to spouse battery or child molestation—that is not traceable to the problem of poor self-esteem" (p. 12). Because people with low self-esteem frequently seek help, this psychologist concluded that psychological problems are *caused* by low self-esteem. But the psychologist has observed only people who seek his help for psychological problems. It is possible that an even larger number of people with low self-esteem never develop psychological problems. The psychologist has no way of knowing because these people never consult him. The correlation between self-esteem and mental illness may be illusory.

Illusory correlations can have tragic consequences. In a notorious British child abuse case that took place in 1988, sexually abused children were found to lack a certain reflex in the muscles of the rectum. Focusing only on positive cases, the doctors concluded that any child who lacked the reflex was the victim of sexual abuse (J. Evans, 1989). In reality, there was no basis for this conclusion. Many nonabused children also lack the reflex (Reardon et al., 1992). The doctors did not know this, however, because they studied only abused children. By focusing solely on cases that supported their preconceived expectation, they gave a clinical sign (the absence of the reflex) the illusion of validity. Based solely on this illusion, children who were later found never to have been abused were removed from their homes, causing considerable pain and anguish to their families. Predictions must always take into consideration both confirming and disconfirming evidence. For a discussion of this point, see Critical Thinking About Clinical Decisions 1.3.

Clinical Versus Statistical Prediction

Clinicians are taught to gather as much information as possible, providing, of course, that gathering the information produces no harm. In practice, however, large volumes of information often prove difficult to use. There seems to be an inherent limitation to the amount of information that a human being is capable of handling at any one time (H. A. Simon, 1957). Perhaps this is why Dr. Berg seems to have ignored some of Danielle's test results in his assessment.

A potentially serious by-product of information overload is overconfidence; the more information they have available, the more confident clinicians become in the accuracy of their predictions. The relationship between the amount of information available and confidence is the subject of a frequently cited study by Oskamp (1965). He presented clinical psychologists with increasing amounts of case material and, at various stages, tested the psychologists' understanding of the case. He found that they became more convinced that they understood the case as the amount of information available to them increased, even though tests showed them to be no better at predicting outcomes than they were with fewer items of information. Findings such as

these suggest that clinicians are not always good judges of their own accuracy.

Meehl (1954) called the type of reasoning used by Oskamp's psychologists "clinical" and distinguished it from an alternative approach to clinical prediction, which he called "statistical." Although neither approach was precisely defined, Meehl thought of clinical reasoning as largely intuitive and certainly nonquantitative, whereas the statistical approach was exactly that—reasoning based on a statistical formula. Note that statistical and clinical reasoning do not differ in the data they use, but in the way the data are combined and evaluated. Clinical reasoning requires intuitive judgments based on a patient's history, present behavior, and test results. The statistical approach requires that judgments be reached through the application of statistical formulas. Dr. Berg's evaluation of Danielle's suicide potential was made clinically. An alternative, statistical procedure would have used a formula to predict whether Danielle would try to harm herself. This formula would have consisted of a set of weights assigned to certain predictive signs (so much for writing a suicide note, so much for previous attempts). These weights, which had been determined by previous research, would have been combined using a statistical formula to yield a probability that Danielle would attempt suicide.

Meehl (1954) claimed that predictions made by following statistical rules are at least as accurate, and sometimes more accurate, than clinical judgments. This claim was hotly contested, and the debate raged on in the psychology literature for many years (see S. Schwartz & Griffin, 1986, for a review). The bulk of the relevant research (Dawes & Corrigan, 1974) shows that Meehl was indeed correct—statistical formulas are better than unaided clinical judgments in predicting behavior. Boredom, fatigue, distraction, and illness affect human judgments, but statistical formulas are immune to such things. Because formulas capture the knowledge of expert clinicians while eliminating their unreliability, they are usually superior. One outgrowth of statistical formulas is the use of computerized psychological test interpretation programs (Mezzich et al., 1994). These are discussed further in Chapter 3.

To return to the question posed at the outset of this section—Could Danielle's death have been predicted?—the answer must once again be equivocal. It is possible to predict behavior in general terms, but such predictions are never entirely precise. Further refinements of our predictive instruments are essential if we wish to prevent tragedies like Danielle's from happening to others. The ability to predict is essential but not sufficient.

Measuring the Practical Value of Psychological Tests

Even when tests have high predictive validity, their practical value can still be low. Let us return to the suicide lethality scale discussed in Critical Thinking About Clinical Decisions 1.1. Like all scales, this one has a different detection rate depending on the population being assessed. Suppose, for example, that the scale can identify 90% of the hospitalized depressed people who will attempt suicide. This means that the scale will be able to identify 9 out of every 10 potential suicides in the population of hospitalized depressed people. Like every test, the lethality scale is not perfect. It not only misses 1 in 10 potential suicides, it also produces false-positives (in this case, people who are mistakenly classified as suicidal even though they will never harm themselves). Let us say that our lethality scale has a false-positive rate of 10%. This means that 1 out of every 10 people that the scale predicts will commit suicide will never actually make a suicide attempt.

Is this a useful scale for clinical practice? Before we can say, one more item of information is required. We must know the number of hospitalized depressed people who attempt to kill themselves. At first glance, this may not seem important. If the lethality scale identifies Danielle as suicidal, isn't the probability that she will attempt suicide 90%? The answer is no. To see why, imagine that studies have found the **prevalence** (also known as the **base rate**) of suicide among hospitalized depressed patients to be 5%. In other words, 50 out of every 1,000 such patients attempt suicide (1,000 × 0.05). Because our lethality scale identifies 90% of the potential suicides, we would expect it to identify 45 of the 50 suicidal people (50 × 0.90). Five suicides will be missed. Because our lethality scale has a false-positive rate of 10%, 95 of the 950 people who are not suicidal (950 × 0.10) will be falsely classified as potential suicides. The percentage of

true-positives out of the total number of suicide predictions (the test's **predictive value**) is 32% (45/140). In other words, even if a suicide prediction scale with 90% accuracy predicts that a person will attempt suicide, the odds are still more than 2 to 1 *against* her trying to harm herself. (This example appears in the outcome table for 1,000 hospitalized depressed people.)

Now, what happens if, instead of hospitalized depressed patients, the lethality scale is administered to a population more likely to attempt suicide—patients like Danielle who have made a previous suicide attempt? The prevalence of suicide in this population is, say, 15%. The

outcome of administering our suicide prediction scale to this population is summarized in the outcome table for 1,000 people with a history of suicide. As may be seen, the test correctly identifies 135 and misses 15 suicidal patients. Of the remaining 850, 85 are false-positives, and the others are correctly classified as nonsuicidal. The percentage of true-positives (135) out of all positives (220) in this high-risk population—the test's predictive value—is 61%, much higher than in the population with a lower prevalence. Clearly, knowing the prevalence is essential if we want to make accurate predictions about a person's behavior.

Outcome of a Suicide Lethality Scale Administered to 1,000 Hospitalized Depressed People (prevalence = 5%)

Test prediction	Actual future behavior		
	Suicide	No suicide	Total
Suicide	45 (true-positives)	95 (false-positives)	140 (all positives)
No suicide	5 (false-negatives)	855 (true-negatives)	860 (all negatives)
Total	50	950	1,000

Note: Predictive value = 45/140 = 32%.

Outcome of a Suicide Lethality Scale Administered to 1,000 People with a History of Suicide (prevalence = 15%)

Test prediction	Actual future behavior		
	Suicide	No suicide	Total
Suicide	135 (true-positives)	85 (false-positives)	220 (all positives)
No suicide	15 (false-negatives)	765 (true-negatives)	780 (all negatives)
Total	150	850	1,000

Note: Predictive value = 135/220 = 61%.

Once we know who is likely to attempt suicide, we then need to know what to do to prevent it.

COULD DANIELLE'S DEATH HAVE BEEN PREVENTED?

Mrs. Wood wants to sue the university for negligence. She feels that the health service doctors and psychologists had a duty to care for Danielle and that measures should have been taken to prevent her from harming herself. The courts would certainly agree; psychologists whose patients commit suicide following treatment have been successfully sued (Bongar, 1991). These legal judgments imply that psychologists know how to keep people from engaging in self-destructive behaviors; otherwise they could hardly be held negligent. Yet psychologists have few ways to prevent people from harming themselves or, indeed, to prevent any type of behavior disorder from developing. Despite its importance, prevention is the most poorly researched aspect of abnormal psychology. Where they exist, prevention programs are discussed in connection with the specific disorders described in later chapters. As will be seen, these programs fall into three categories: primary, secondary, and tertiary.

Primary Prevention

Primary prevention is what most people mean by prevention. Its goal is to eliminate the cause of a problem and thereby prevent its occurrence. This is most easily achieved when two conditions are met: (a) the cause of the disorder is known, and (b) a method of prevention is available. One example of a successful primary prevention program is the mass immunization of children, which has eliminated such formerly common diseases as polio.

Although primary prevention is most likely to be successful when a condition's precise etiology is known, disorders can sometimes be prevented even when their cause is unclear. Cholera, for example, was almost totally eliminated by restricting the public's access to contaminated water supplies. At the time, health officials had no idea why the water caused the disease; they only knew the two were related. Quarantines have also proved effective, even when the exact nature of a disease's transmission was unknown. Other examples of successful primary prevention programs include education about diets, food inspections, improvements in food processing (pasteurization of milk, for example),

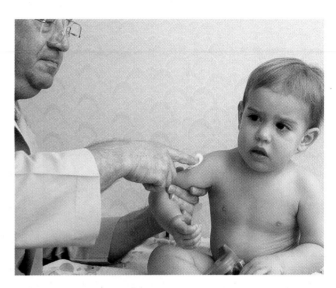

The polio vaccine, which has been virtually 100% successful in preventing polio, is a notable example of primary prevention, or the elimination of the cause of an illness or disease.

water-supply fluoridation, mandatory seat belt (and motorcycle helmet) laws, highway speed restrictions, and clean air acts.

The primary prevention of behavior disorders has been impeded by difficulties in defining abnormal behavior. If researchers cannot agree about what they mean by abnormal behavior, then how can they tell whether their prevention programs are successful? Despite this stumbling block, some generally accepted behavioral disorders have been controlled and even eradicated by primary prevention. The removal of lead from interior house paint and the changeover to unleaded gasoline, for example, have eliminated two sources of brain damage and mental retardation in children (Romieu et al., 1995; Schroeder, 1987). Because so few behavior disorders are amenable to such direct intervention, however, most attempts to prevent behavior disorders have relied on education. Providing information about safer-sex practices has reduced the spread of sexually transmitted diseases and their consequent behavioral symptoms. Anti-drug campaigns have reduced drug abuse and, as a consequence, its concomitant behavioral disorders. Because poverty and unemployment are connected with mental illness (Brenner, 1973), social welfare programs can also have important preventive effects. For efficiency, primary prevention efforts are often targeted at those most "at risk" to develop psychopathology. Some examples are stress-reduction training for soldiers in combat and counseling for families

Secondary prevention, such as early intervention by counselors after the death of a schoolmate, can help survivors cope with their feelings and prevent them from developing long-term problems.

about to divorce (S. Schwartz & Johnson, 1985). President Reynolds's attempt to educate students about suicide is also an example of primary prevention.

Despite these and other notable efforts, the primary prevention of behavior disorders remains a largely unrealized hope. Substantial progress is not likely to occur until we learn more about the causes of behavior disorders and about the interventions that will prevent them from developing. At present, we are woefully ignorant about both.

Secondary Prevention

Secondary prevention takes place at a later stage than primary prevention, after the abnormal process has begun but before the disorder is fully developed. Its goal is early identification and amelioration. An example of a successful secondary prevention program is the routine screening of newborns for the presence of phenylketonuria (PKU). PKU is a genetically caused disorder that makes people unable to metabolize certain amino acids (S. Schwartz & Johnson, 1985). Unless the diet of affected individuals is controlled, mental retardation and other problems are inevitable. Although genetic engineering may soon permit us to correct such genetic defects before birth, primary prevention of PKU is not presently possible. Secondary prevention is another

matter. Because PKU can be identified by a screening test shortly after birth, babies found to be affected can be placed on special diets. If this occurs early enough, the symptoms can be completely prevented. The costs of screening are much lower than the cost of caring for PKU-affected children (Dhondt et al., 1991).

Although there are few reliable screening tests for psychological problems, early identification is still possible, especially in times of crisis. The suicide prevention program described by university President Reynolds is an attempt to enlist the aid of students in identifying as early as possible those students who are likely to harm themselves. People identified in this way would be provided with special counseling, and, if necessary, special precautions could be taken. Because people who have recently experienced traumas are most likely to develop behavior disorders, postdisaster therapy is another form of secondary prevention. Dr. Berg's counseling and support for Luke and Jayne was an attempt to keep their grief and guilt from leading to long-term psychological problems.

Similar early interventions have been used with people exposed to natural disasters and other forms of psychological stress (L. G. Peterson & O'Shanick, 1986). When the ferry *Herald of Free Enterprise* sank in the North Sea in 1987, for example, counselors worked in round-the-clock shifts with both survivors and relatives (Dalgleish, Joseph, et al., 1996). These early interventions were designed to prevent long-term problems from developing.

Secondary prevention is based on the assumption that early intervention is better than treating a disorder after it develops. This seems reasonable when applied to physical illnesses. Mass screenings for PKU, tuberculosis, and certain forms of cancer and other illnesses can prevent considerable suffering and keep medical costs down (D. R. Cohen & Henderson, 1988). There are times, however, when secondary prevention may not be the most efficient way to spend our resources. Mass screening for the early identification of dental cavities using new high-technology imaging instruments, for example, would cost considerably more than routine dental checkups without significantly reducing the number of cavities (D. R. Cohen & Henderson, 1988). The money spent on such a program would be better used for other health purposes.

Sometimes, early identification may actually be counterproductive. For example, in the days when the only "treatment" choice available to the seriously mentally ill was incarceration in large mental hospitals, early identification meant only that they would spend more of their lives locked away. Even today, when considering an early detection program, psychologists should be sure that their treatments are sufficiently effective to outweigh the potential harm caused by labeling someone "disturbed." One of the primary ethical rules of clinical work is "First do no harm."

Tertiary Prevention

The goal of tertiary prevention is to limit the after-effects of psychopathology and to rehabilitate those with behavior disorders. Treatment can take place in hospitals and other institutions as well as in psychologists' offices. In all cases, the aim is to help the individual return to a better level of psychological functioning or, at the very least, to prevent a disorder from getting any worse. Danielle's counseling after her first suicide attempt was an example of tertiary prevention. Her treatment took place initially in the hospital and later as an outpatient. The goal was, first, to prevent any future recurrence of suicide and, second, to help Danielle return to her previous level of psychological functioning. Clearly, the success of tertiary prevention depends on the effectiveness of our treatments. Of the three types of prevention, tertiary prevention, especially treatment, has been the most intensely researched. The results of this research appear at appropriate places throughout this book.

Impediments to Tertiary Prevention

A problem limiting the success of tertiary prevention is making appropriate services available to those who need them. Teachers, social workers, doctors, the police, and the courts are often the first people to come into contact with disturbed people. Frequently, they are unaware of what treatments are required and available. If the distribution of services is ever to be improved, there needs to be much greater cooperation among these various professions. After all, there is little point in developing and testing treatments if people are never referred for them.

Even when appropriate interventions are available, they may not be administered for legal reasons. Danielle, for example, voluntarily left the hospital although Dr. Kahn believed that she should have remained on the psychiatric ward a little longer. Dr. Kahn did nothing to force Danielle to stay in the hospital because she did not feel that Danielle represented a danger to herself. Had she felt otherwise, Dr. Kahn could have kept Danielle in the hospital by legal means (commitment). The laws governing who can be committed, and how, vary from state to state. In most cases, minors can be committed for treatment by court order without a legal hearing. All that is required is a mental health professional to say that such treatment is warranted. In emergencies, adults can also be committed for short periods on the certification of one or two doctors. If it is necessary to keep an adult in the hospital longer than a few days, however, a full hearing is required. Those seeking the commitment (relatives, the police) will have to present "clear and convincing" evidence that the individual needs to remain in the hospital. The usual reasons are the person's inability to care for him- or herself or the danger he or she poses to self or society. Just keeping someone in a hospital does not mean that the person will be treated. Even committed patients have the right to refuse treatment in certain circumstances (Fulford, 1989).

Preventive efforts are sometimes inhibited by the confidentiality traditionally granted to the therapist-client relationship. For example, relatives may not be told of a family member's suicide attempt. Is this appropriate? This is not an easy question to answer. Most psychologists believe that effective treatment requires the trust that comes from knowing that one's private revelations will not be disclosed to others. The American Psychological Association's (1990) Code of Ethics states that "psychologists have a primary obligation to respect the confidentiality of information obtained from persons in the course of their work as psychologists" (p. 392).

Rules for Killing People

On Wednesday, January 20, 1993, Jack Miller killed himself by allowing his arm to drop. This simple act released a clip from around some plastic tubing, which in turn allowed carbon dioxide gas to flow from a canister to a mask that covered his face. Eighteen minutes later, he was dead. Jack Miller wanted to die because the pain he experienced from bone cancer had made his life a living hell. In deciding to kill himself, he felt that he was taking charge of his own life.

Public opinion polls show that most respondents accept that people should have the right to die with dignity. The courts have officially recognized the right of terminally ill or incurable patients (or their relatives, in some cases) to reject treatment and choose death instead. In some instances, it has been found legal for doctors to withhold food and water from patients, literally allowing them to starve to death. Yet *actively* assisting someone to commit suicide (rather than passively allowing people to die) is illegal in the majority of states and throughout Canada ("Canada Court Denies," 1993). Attempts to legalize physician-assisted suicide have so far been unsuccessful. Dr. Jack Kevorkian, the retired pathologist who constructed the apparatus Jack Miller used to kill himself (and who has helped dozens of other people die) has stood trial several times for murder. On each occasion, he

was acquitted. His defense was that he only made suicide possible; he never killed anyone. Kevorkian's run of acquittals was broken in 1999. He had videotaped himself administering a lethal injection to a patient and allowed the videotape to be played on national television. Using the tape as evidence, prosecutors convinced a jury to find him guilty of second-degree murder.

One reason often given for taking a hard line against assisted suicide is the fear of abuse. Patients may be encouraged to commit suicide by insurers or governments as a way of controlling spiraling medical costs. Even without such encouragement, patients who are worried about the high cost of care may choose suicide to avoid becoming burdens on their families. A second argument against helping patients kill themselves is that such decisions are often made when patients are feeling depressed about their illness or when they are in severe pain and not thinking clearly. It is possible that treatment for their pain or depression could lead them to change their minds about wanting to die. A final reason for opposing physician-assisted suicide is moral. Some people argue that a doctor's mission is to preserve life, not to end it. Allowing doctors to assist in suicide is to abandon the profession's most important ethical rule.

On the other side are people such

as Kevorkian and Timothy Quill (Quill, Cassel, & Meier, 1992), a doctor who has admitted helping a leukemia patient commit suicide rather than face a life of pain and suffering. Kevorkian views physician-assisted suicide as not only humane and ethical but also an opportunity for the dying person to save lives through organ donation (Kevorkian, 1988). Quill and his colleagues argue that physician-assisted suicide is not only permissible, but in some cases is more humane than keeping the terminally ill alive. They believe that terminally ill patients fear abandonment and loss of control as much as they fear pain and death. Human dignity, they suggest, includes being allowed to die when life is no longer worth living. Quill and his colleagues have proposed that physician-assisted suicide be permitted when patients are incurable, suffering severely, getting all the treatment available, repeatedly requesting death, thinking clearly (and are not just despondent), and when an independent doctor agrees. Quill would also require both doctors and the patient to sign some sort of agreement. Clearly, this would completely eliminate physician-assisted suicide from being made available to people like Danielle.

There is some evidence that Quill's views are becoming more acceptable to the community at large. Despite an investigation into his self-confessed "crime"

However, psychologists have a responsibility to society as well as to their clients. A client with AIDS who plans to have unprotected sex poses a threat to many people. Keeping such information confidential would pose a major threat to public health. Similarly, a child who is being abused may need a psychologist's protection even if this means revealing facts gained in confidence from the perpetrator of the abuse. In some cases, a homicidal or suicidal patient may have to be committed involuntarily, a process that involves breaching confidentiality by informing the courts of

the danger. Although the law varies across jurisdictions, and some psychologists continue to resist the notion of breaching confidentiality under any circumstances, the American Psychological Association's code of ethics recognizes that confidentiality can be breached in certain situations.

As medical technology advances and patients can be kept alive indefinitely, new ethical questions arise. Are there times when death is preferable to life? Should doctors help people commit suicide? These issues are complex and emotional; they present a serious chalof helping a patient commit suicide, a grand jury failed to indict him, and a committee of doctors declined to take any action against him. The fine line between what is considered appropriate medical behavior and what is not is especially stark in The Netherlands. In 1993, the Dutch Parliament extended legal protection to doctors who assist people in committing suicide, while leaving **euthanasia** (mercy killing) on the legal books as a crime punishable by up to 12 years' imprisonment (Steinfels, 1993). The distinction requires that the patient, not the doctor, perform the final act.

The general public remains unsure of its own position on physician-assisted suicide. For example, some California opinion polls have found citizens in favor of physician-assisted suicide. Yet, in 1992, a California ballot initiative to legalize the practice was defeated. In contrast, in 1997, Oregon passed the Death with Dignity Act, which permits patients to be given lethal prescriptions. Fifteen people used this method to end their lives in 1998 (Chin et al., 1999). The Oregon law requires that the lethal drugs be self-administered. Books are being published instructing people about how to take their own lives (Humphry, 1991), while philosophers and ethicists argue about the potential deleterious effects that sanctioning physician-assisted suicide will have on society and on future generations (Guillemin, 1992).

For some years, the debate about physician-assisted suicide has been conducted by lawyers, doctors, and ethicists (Steinberg & Youngner, 1998). Psychologists have not been widely involved. This is unfortunate because psychological research could potentially clarify many of the controversial issues. Among the issues that psychologists could and should address are the influence of depression (and other psychological disorders) on the request to die, the impact of physician-assisted suicide on the family, and the exact quality-of-life variables that cause patients to request death over life. By addressing these questions, psychologists could bring psychological science to bear on a pressing and important social issue.

In 1989, Dr. Jack Kevorkian, the most prominent advocate of physician-assisted suicide, designed a "death machine" from old household appliances, magnets, and switches. The patient can switch it on to release a lethal but painless combination of chemicals into an intravenous tube.

lenge to all those who work in the "caring" professions, as Highlight 1.4 emphasizes. For this reason, ethical codes must be kept under close scrutiny and revised when necessary as new developments and dilemmas arise.

Economics and Prevention

Psychological problems are among the top 10 reasons employees miss work. Each year $20 billion is spent on mental health services (Organization for Economic Co-operation and Development [OECD], 1992). Half this amount is financed directly by the government; the rest comes from private insurance or directly from consumers' pockets. Whenever a third party (the government or an insurance company) pays the larger part of a bill, the demand for services increases. **Health maintenance organizations (HMOs),** for example, operate by providing health care to individuals and families for a fixed yearly fee. To control their costs, HMOs try to limit services by providing them only to those subscribers who can really benefit.

Traditional insurance companies are also interested in controlling their costs. For this reason, most have instituted peer review. Panels of experts examine patient records and decide whether a clinician's treatment conforms to certain practice "guidelines." If it does not, insurance benefits could be denied. Because services are so costly, denying an insurance claim is tantamount to denying treatment.

These various attempts to control costs by determining who will receive treatment and the type of treatment they will receive are known collectively as **managed care.** They are part of a worldwide trend toward greater accountability in the helping professions. The movement began in medicine, where costs have escalated dramatically with only a marginal impact on health status (OECD, 1992). To ensure that resources are being spent where they will do the most good, governments and insurance companies are pressuring clinicians to show that their treatments are not only effective but also the least expensive way to achieve the desired result. Needless to say, many clinicians are not happy with this pressure. They are concerned about their professional autonomy. Psychologists argue that it is in their clients' best interest to allow clinicians to decide how people should be treated. The insurance companies and government agencies, who pay the bills, say that psychologists are just protecting their own incomes. The truth, as usual, lies somewhere between these two extremes. Clinical autonomy is important, but no psychologist can expect to be given a blank check.

Because it is usually cheaper to keep people from developing behavior disorders than to treat them after disorders develop, it seems inevitable that increasing emphasis will be given to primary and secondary prevention. This change in focus, from treatment to prevention, presents an important opportunity for psychologists because their research training makes them uniquely equipped to do the research necessary to develop practice guidelines and prevention programs. Rather than resist managed care, as some clinicians are inclined to do, psychologists should embrace it as a challenging opportunity. They should keep in mind that the moral and practical justification for spending society's resources on research in abnormal psychology is the goal of helping others.

CHAPTER 1 IN PERSPECTIVE

Real life is often ambiguous. We will never know for sure whether Danielle intended to kill herself. What we do know, however, is that her life went tragically wrong. The goals of abnormal psychology are to understand why such tragedies happen, to learn how to predict them before they happen, and to devise ways of preventing them. Accomplishing these goals requires research into how heredity, physiology, early experience, and cultural values shape behavior. But research alone will not ensure that help goes to all those who need it. The services that people receive also depend on their individual desires, social preferences, economics, and, to a certain extent, the fashions of the day.

Key Ideas

Defining Abnormal Behavior

Although most serious behavior disorders are universally recognized, many others are culture specific. This is why there is no single, universally accepted definition of abnormal behavior. Instead, we have some guidelines, which vary in their applicability depending on the case. According to these guidelines, abnormal behavior is unusual, maladaptive, and causes distress. It also typically violates social norms.

The Disease Analogy

Some behavior disorders are diseases (general paresis is the most famous example). Others are called mental illnesses for humanitarian reasons—people who are "ill" are entitled to help. In such cases, the term "illness" cannot always be taken literally. It is an analogy, designed to achieve a specific purpose. The analogy can also help scientists apply the scientific methods that have worked so well in medicine. In some cases, however, the illness analogy can obscure the social nature of much abnormal behavior.

Causes of Abnormal Behavior

Behavior disorders rarely have a single cause. They arise from the complex interaction of our genetic endowments, physiology, anatomy, developmental histories, and the social context in which we live. Genetics may make a greater contribution to certain disorders, whereas others are largely the result of early experience, but it is rare to find any disorder in which both genetics and environment do not play some part.

Diathesis-Stress Model
It is often noted that the same traumatic experience can produce a severe disturbance in one person and no disturbance at all in another. The diathesis-stress model explains this by assuming that the person who develops the disturbance was particularly vulnerable to the stress. It is possible, for example, that Danielle inherited a diathesis for depression from her father. (Of course, it is equally possible that the diathesis was the result of her early childhood experiences.) Unfortunately, we cannot usually tell in advance who has the diathesis or what type of stress will cause a behavior disorder to develop. So, the diathesis-stress model has limited predictive value.

The Importance of History
There are fads and fashions in both science and history. This makes studying the history of abnormal psychology a humbling experience. Each generation of researchers and clinicians, including our own, believes that its views are the last scientific word. Yet each generation's theories are invariably rejected, or at least modified, by the next. It is certain that the psychologists of the future will consider today's theories of abnormal behavior to be primitive and misguided. This does not mean that studying history is a waste of time. If we know where others have gone wrong, we can at least avoid repeating their mistakes.

Clinical Predictions
Psychologists are often called upon to predict behavior. Because they depend on self-report and tests with imperfect predictive validity, their predictions are often uncertain. Clinicians do not al-

ways realize how uncertain their predictions are. They fall victim to the illusion of validity, ignore disconfirming evidence, and become overconfident in their predictions.

Prevention
There are three types of prevention: primary, secondary, and tertiary. Thus far, psychologists have put most of their effort into tertiary prevention (treatment and rehabilitation). The rising costs of health care as well as legal and practical impediments to treatment are likely to make primary and secondary prevention increasingly important in the coming years.

Key Terms

base rate
biopsychosocial
clinical psychologist
concordance rate
delusion
diathesis-stress model
    of etiology
euthanasia
false-positives

functional disorder
general paresis
health maintenance
    organization (HMO)
hypnosis
illusory correlation
managed care
predictive validity
predictive value

presentism
prevalence
prognosis
psychiatric nurse
psychiatrist
psychoanalysts
psychological assessment
psychopathology
psychotherapy

risk factors
social worker
St. Vitus' dance
syndrome
true-positives
utilitarianism

Key Names

Jeremy Bentham
Michel Foucault

Sigmund Freud
Alfred Kinsey

Richard von Krafft-Ebing
Franz Anton Mesmer

CHAPTER 2

CHAPTER OBJECTIVES

It has been said that the Native American Eskimo people have many different words for snow. Because it is such an important part of their lives, they see nuances and textures in snow that are invisible to the inhabitants of warmer climates. Scientific theories have a similar ability to shape how we view the world. Behaviorists, for example, have many different ways to describe learning. In contrast, psychoanalysts have a small vocabulary for learning but have a rich set of concepts to describe unconscious and symbolic processes. This chapter describes the different ways in which psychologists understand and study human behavior. The social, economic, and ethical aspects of psychological research and treatment are also discussed. To give focus to the various issues, the chapter shows how different theoretical approaches (paradigms) explain what happened to Danielle Wood.

The five main questions addressed in this chapter are

1. What are the main paradigms of abnormal psychology?
2. How did these paradigms evolve?
3. What are the characteristic methods used by each paradigm to study and treat psychological disorders?
4. What are the similarities and differences among paradigms?
5. Is it possible to apply more than one paradigm to the same person?

Paradigms and Perspectives, Models and Methods

CONTENTS

As we saw in Chapter 1, Danielle's life began and ended unhappily. Is it possible to understand what happened to her? Can we prevent the same thing from happening to others? These are not easy questions to answer. Danielle had more than one problem: She was prone to depression and guilt, she mistrusted others (with some reason), she was dependent, she lacked self-esteem, and she took drugs. Because each of these problems was at least partly responsible for the others, the various aspects of Danielle's behavior cannot be studied in isolation. We must understand how they interact. This is not easy. Complex interactions are difficult to unravel because psychological evidence can almost always be interpreted in more than one way. To make the task of assembling and interpreting clinical and research data manageable, those who work in the field of abnormal psychology find it useful to adopt a theoretical framework—a coherent set of guiding principles—for construing behavior.

These theoretical frameworks go by many different names: paradigms, viewpoints, perspectives, models, and approaches. To some extent, the varying terminology stems from the desire to be different. One writer's "perspectives" are another's "models" and yet another's "approaches." At a deeper level, however, the variety of terms conveys an important message. Theoretical frameworks determine how we *approach* the task of understanding others, the *viewpoints* that we adopt, the data that we *perceive,* and the theoretical *models* that we develop.

We like to think that science proceeds by the gradual accumulation of new facts and findings. In practice, however, advances often come abruptly, in revolutionary leaps. Between revolutions, a particular theory dominates a field. Research techniques associated with the authoritative theory become standard, and most scientists conform to the dominant view. These periods of conformity last until the next revolution, when the dominant theory is replaced with a new, incompatible, one. In the physical sciences, pioneers such as Isaac Newton and Albert Einstein were responsible for such revolutionary changes. Thomas Kuhn (1962), a well-known philosopher of science, refers to the drastic changes in outlook that characterize the history of science as "paradigm shifts." A **paradigm** is the conceptual framework within which a scientist works. It determines the questions researchers try to answer, the methods they use, and the theoretical explanations they will accept.

At present, abnormal psychology does not have a completely dominant paradigm. Instead, it is characterized by several competing paradigms. One with a long history is the biological paradigm, which concentrates on the organic factors that can cause abnormal behavior. Almost the opposite position is taken by the sociocultural paradigm, which emphasizes the cultural and social factors underlying abnormal behavior. Between these two extremes lie a variety of other paradigms. Psychoanalysis emphasizes early experience and unconscious conflicts. Behaviorism and its offshoot, the cognitive paradigm, focus on the ways in which behaviors and cognitions are learned and unlearned. The humanistic paradigm concentrates on the guiding role of self-concepts and personal values in determining behavior.

Scientists working within the biological paradigm concentrate on genetics, disease, brain chemistry, and other biological etiologies. Not surprisingly, their approach to treating people like Danielle consists mainly of biological interventions (the administration of antidepressant drugs, for example). In contrast, clinicians working in the cognitive paradigm focus on the pathological thinking underlying Danielle's depression (the idea that losing a swimming competition means that one is worthless, for example). Psychoanalytic psychologists take a third approach, searching for the cause of Danielle's depression in unconscious conflicts (guilt about her father's death, for instance). Psychoanalytic treatment requires that these conflicts be made conscious and "resolved."

Although a shared paradigm facilitates communication by providing scientists and clinicians with a common language, rigid paradigms can also impede progress by restricting scientists' thinking. Sometimes, even a common language can produce barriers. For example, clinical psychologists who work in medically related paradigms may refer to the people they treat as *patients*, whereas less medically oriented psychologists prefer the term *clients*. As we shall see, this seemingly small difference may have major implications for the way psychologists approach their work. (This book uses the term *client* to refer to people treated by psychologists).

Because of their different points of view, proponents of one paradigm sometimes consider those who work in a different one to be misguided, naive, or even stupid. The inevitable result is minimal collaboration and poor communication across paradigm boundaries. This is unfortunate, because none of the currently available paradigms is sufficiently robust to deal with all types of psychopathology. (This is why no single paradigm is dominant.) By concentrating solely on one paradigm, scientists are certain to miss something important in an-

Metaparadigm: overarching theoretical framework (truism) which is that we are biological organisms. There are proximal (immediate) cause (body rxh) & distal (distant) factors (state of CNS ← other factors) of beh. outside

other. In this book, there are frequent references to all of the various paradigms, especially their relative ability to explain different types of abnormal behavior. This chapter introduces the major paradigms and places them in historical perspective. Its aim is to identify the main questions that different paradigms try to answer, and to describe the way they go about answering them. Where possible, attempts are made to forge bridges across paradigms.

ABNORMAL PSYCHOLOGY'S METAPARADIGM

Discussions of paradigms tend to emphasize their differences. This is understandable, but it is nevertheless misleading. Stressing the differences among paradigms makes the field of abnormal psychology seem incoherent, a jumble of different theories each competing for adherents. This chapter takes a different direction, emphasizing similarities. To make this task easier, this discussion of paradigms begins with a description of abnormal psychology's "metaparadigm," the overarching theoretical framework to which all current paradigms subscribe. This metaparadigm provides a superstructure into which the specific paradigms may be incorporated.

The metaparadigm is based on a truism—we are biological organisms. Every thought we have, every emotion we experience, everything we do is determined by our biology. We cannot lift a finger, shed a tear, feel sorrow, or laugh with joy without some corresponding activity taking place in our brains, spinal cords, glands, and muscles. In this concrete sense, all behavior, normal or abnormal, is biological. You might wonder, then, how there can be any paradigm other than the biological one. The answer hinges on the distinction between the proximal and distal causes of behavior. Although the proximal (immediate) cause of any behavior can always be found in the activities of the central and autonomic nervous systems (Figure 2.1) and its associated organs (muscles, glands, and so on), the state of the central and autonomic nervous systems, at any point in time, is the result of many distal (distant) factors including heredity, early experience, and a host of social and psychological influences.

All of the current paradigms of abnormal psychology take for granted that the immediate causes of our behavior are biological. Where they differ is in the emphasis they give to different distal causes and in the methods they use to validate their theories. The psychoanalytic paradigm, for example, assumes that certain early experiences can produce unconscious conflicts that affect behavior later in life. Freud himself admitted that these distal conflicts must leave some trace in the central nervous system (otherwise they could not affect behavior), but the psychoanalytic paradigm is not concerned with central nervous system activity. Rather, its focus is on the relationship between certain distal causes (unconscious conflicts, for example) and abnormal behavior. Likewise, strict behaviorists, whose concern is the relationship between distal antecedent stimulus conditions and subsequent behavior, do not deny that the immediate causes of behavior are biological. Their position is that central nervous system activity may be disregarded because a thorough knowledge of antecedent stimulus conditions is all that is necessary to predict a person's behavior.

Unlike the psychoanalysts and the behaviorists, scientists and clinicians working within the biological paradigm are not concerned with unconscious conflicts or antecedent stimulus conditions. Instead, they focus on the distal biological causes of abnormal behavior (genetics, disease, and brain injury). Nevertheless, it is worth emphasizing that these biological causes serve precisely the same explanatory role in the biological paradigm that unconscious conflicts serve in the psychoanalytic paradigm and that antecedent stimulus conditions serve in the behavioral paradigm: They are assumed to affect the central nervous system, which, in turn, controls behavior.

The relationship between the distal and proximal causes of behavior constitutes abnormal psychology's metaparadigm (Figure 2.2). This metaparadigm provides coherence to what might otherwise appear to be a chaotic field. Although it is true that communication and collaboration across paradigms is not as great as it should be, it should be obvious from Figure 2.2 that the various paradigms are not inherently in conflict. Abnormal behavior has multiple causes, and no paradigm can, by itself, explain everything. By emphasizing different distant causes of behavior, the paradigms may be viewed as complementary rather than competing. The following sections of this chapter look individually at the various paradigms and their logic, as well as their characteristic methods.

BIOLOGICAL PARADIGM

All scientists working in the field of abnormal psychology—whatever paradigm they favor—begin by observing behavior. These observations, usually in the form of

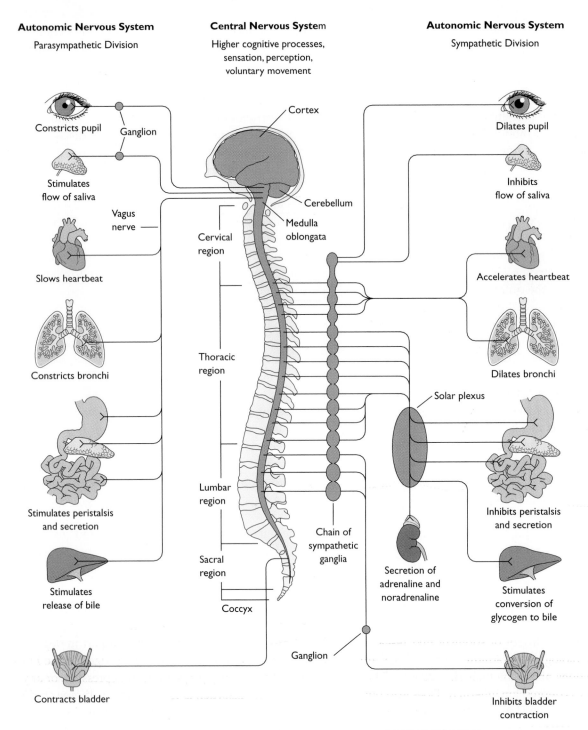

Autonomic Nervous System

Parasympathetic Division

Constricts pupil

Ganglion

Stimulates
flow of saliva

Vagus
nerve

Slows heartbeat

Constricts bronchi

Stimulates peristalsis
and secretion

Stimulates
release of bile

Contracts bladder

Central Nervous System

Higher cognitive processes,
sensation, perception,
voluntary movement

Cortex

Cerebellum

Medulla
oblongata

Cervical
region

Thoracic
region

Lumbar
region

Sacral
region

Coccyx

Chain of
sympathetic
ganglia

Ganglion

Autonomic Nervous System

Sympathetic Division

Dilates pupil

Inhibits
flow of saliva

Accelerates heartbeat

Dilates bronchi

Solar plexus

Inhibits peristalsis
and secretion

Secretion of
adrenaline and
noradrenaline

Stimulates
conversion of
glycogen to bile

Inhibits bladder
contraction

FIGURE 2.1 The Central and Autonomic Nervous Systems. *The central nervous system consists of the brain and spinal cord and controls higher cognitive processes (such as speech), sensation, perception, and voluntary movements. The sympathetic division of the autonomic nervous system consists mainly of nerves originating in the thoracic and lumbar regions of the spinal cord; the parasympathetic division arises directly from the brain or lower (sacral) spine. Strong emotions, such as fear, trigger the sympathetic division, which in turn produces a variety of physiological effects: pupil dilation, dry mouth, faster heart-beat, and so on. The parasympathetic division reduces arousal once the threat—and its related strong emotion—dissipates. Thus, the proximal causes of behavior are biological activity in the central and autonomic nervous systems, whereas heredity, experience, and a host of other psychosocial factors represent the distal causes of behavior.*

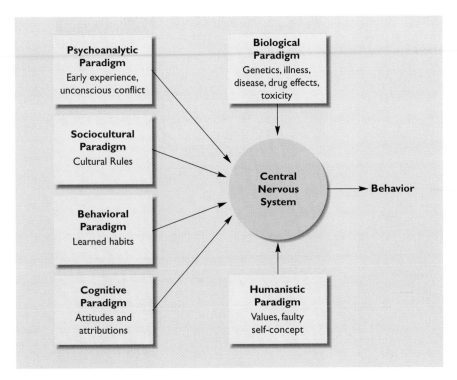

FIGURE 2.2 **Causes of Behavior According to the Six Paradigms.** *The proximal cause of all behavior is activity in the central nervous system and its effectors—a fact accepted by all the paradigms. Where they differ is in the emphasis they give to various distal causes.*

case studies such as Danielle's, play the same role in abnormal psychology that chemical reactions play in chemistry and the movement of the planets play in astronomy. They constitute the phenomena that psychologists attempt to understand. Case studies are invaluable sources of hypotheses about abnormal behavior, but they can provide only weak support for an explanatory theory. To gather evidence that is less subject to bias and more generalizable than that provided by case studies, researchers employ a variety of sophisticated research methods. In the biological paradigm these methods are applied to questions about the biological causes of behavior disorders: Is depression inherited? Does lead poisoning cause mental retardation? Do hormonal imbalances cause aggression? This section introduces the main questions asked by the biological paradigm, its characteristic methods, and its current status.

Biological Paradigm Question 1: Are Certain Types of Abnormal Behavior Inherited?

Danielle was prone to depression and probably took her own life; so too did her father. Does this mean that

Danielle's death was in some way caused by the genes she inherited from her father? Researchers have devised several techniques to try to answer this type of question.

Pedigree Studies   Depression and suicide sometimes run in families (Roy, Rylander, & Sarchiapone, 1997; Roy, Segal, & Sarchiapone, 1995). Scientists working within the biological paradigm are particularly interested in such family histories because they suggest, but do not prove, that heredity may play a part in depression and suicide. The first step in investigating the hypothesis that heredity plays a role in depression, or any other behavior disorder, is to perform a pedigree study in which the family trees of **probands** (individuals with the disorder under investigation) are searched for relatives with similar disorders. If heredity is involved, there should be more cases of depression among the proband's relatives than in the general population. Because close relatives are more alike genetically than distant relatives, we would also expect the incidence of depression and suicide to be higher in a proband's immediate family than among distant relatives. In other words, identical twins should be more alike than fraternal

Depression and suicide are unusually common in some families, suggesting that heredity plays a role. Ernest Hemingway's father, brother, and a sister committed suicide, as did his granddaughter Margaux. Hemingway and his father probably suffered from manic-depression; Margaux, once a model and movie actress, had suffered from depression and bulimia.

twins, who should be more alike than cousins, and so on.

Pedigree studies have found that depression and suicide follow the pattern expected for an inherited behavior disorder. Both are more common among the relatives of probands than in the general population, and both are more likely to be found among a proband's close relatives than among more distant ones. Although these findings are consistent with a genetic influence, they are not, by themselves, sufficient to prove that a tendency toward depression and suicide is genetic. Because relatives tend to grow up in comparable neighborhoods, eat the same foods, and share similar experiences, it is possible that these environmental factors—and not heredity—are responsible for their similar behaviors. Perhaps both heredity and environment are jointly responsible for depression and suicide. As noted in Chapter 1, only 21% of monozygotic twins who commit suicide have brothers or sisters who also take their

own lives (Lester, 1986). Because identical twins are genetically identical, environmental factors must be responsible for any differences within the pair. Such an interaction between heredity and environment is not unusual. Few behavior disorders are entirely the result of heredity or environment; most result from a combination of both. The appropriate research focus, therefore, is not on whether heredity *or* the environment has *any* influence on a behavior disorder, but on their *relative* influence.

Twin Studies   There are two ways to study the relative influences of heredity and environment. One is to examine people who have been adopted early in life and raised apart from their natural relatives. If such people resemble their natural parents and siblings more than the members of their adoptive families, then we can say that genetics is more important than the environment in

Comparing brain scans of identical twins can help researchers learn how a disorder affects brain structure. Here, scientists at the National Institute of Mental Health examine 3-D brain surface renderings of identical twins in a study of schizophrenia.

Heritability: determine the extent to which heredity contributes to a particular beh. disorder.

shaping the behavior in question. Danielle, for example, seems to have behaved more like her natural than her adoptive father. This suggests that genetics may have been a more important influence on her behavior than her later environment. This is a common finding. Children whose natural parents suffer from severe depression are often found to become depressed themselves, even when they are raised in adoptive families whose members are not prone to depression (Tsuang & Faraone, 1996; Wender et al., 1986).

The most powerful adoption studies involve monozygotic twins who, for one reason or another, were separated early in life and raised in different families. Because they have identical heredity, any differences found between twin pairs must be the result of the environments in which they were raised. By examining identical twins reared apart, it is theoretically possible to determine the extent to which heredity contributes to a particular behavior disorder. This is known as the disorder's **heritability.**

In practice, such studies are exceedingly difficult to conduct. One problem is that even separated twins may still grow up in similar environments. This is because social service agencies try to place children in homes similar to their natural ones and many children are adopted by relatives. We do not know, therefore, whether twins reared apart behave similarly because they are genetically identical or because they have been raised in similar environments. To separate the effects of heredity and environment, we need to find monozygotic twins who were raised in dissimilar environments from early in life, and such twins are exceedingly rare. To make research even more difficult, we do not know which aspects of the environment are important causes of depression and suicide. So, even when twins are raised in different environments (upper class versus lower class, rural versus urban, and so on), we cannot be sure that these differences are important. Figure 2.3 illustrates how adoption and twin studies can be combined to estimate heritability.

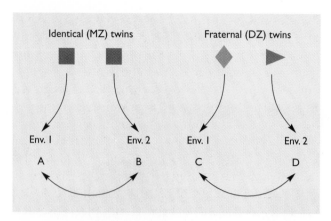

FIGURE 2.3 Separating the Influence of Genetics From That of Environment on Identical and Fraternal Twins. *Adoption studies compare monozygotic (MZ), or identical, twins and dizygotic (DZ), or fraternal, twins who were separated early in life and raised in dissimilar environments. Higher correlations among monozygotic twins than among dizygotic twins represent the influence of genetics.*

Prospective Studies Separating and measuring the relative effects of heredity and environment is made particularly difficult by the retrospective nature of most clinical research. Because we do not normally study probands until *after* they have come to a clinician's attention, we have no direct way of knowing what they were like before they became depressed (or suicidal or schizophrenic), nor do we know what events they experienced over the years. We must depend on the memories of clients, relatives, friends, and clinic records for all of our information. Unfortunately, these sources are subject to a variety of subtle and not-so-subtle biases. These include selective forgetting (all families have experiences they would just as soon forget), distortions, and outright fabrications designed to avoid blame and guilt. In addition, clinic data may be missing or selectively recorded by a therapist with a biased viewpoint. For all of these reasons, retrospective data on the behavior of natural and adoptive parents and on the childhood behavior of probands who are now adults are rarely trustworthy. The best way to avoid the difficulties presented by retrospective data is by conducting a prospective study—that is, by identifying potential high-risk patients before they develop a disorder and following them over time to see if any disorders develop. By studying a large enough population for a long enough time, subjecting them to periodic psychological assessments, and keeping track of their life experiences, it may be possible to identify the environmental causes of psychological disorders.

Because of the time and the expense required, prospective studies are relatively rare. Compromises are often necessary; these can make the results of prospective studies difficult to interpret. For example, one common difficulty is obtaining a sufficiently large sample of people to study. Only a small portion of the population will develop any particular disorder, so to ensure that a prospective study has a large enough sample, researchers target people who have a high risk of developing the disorder under investigation. They may, for example, study children whose parents have been diagnosed as depressed. This is a reasonable approach, but as we shall see in Chapter 3, psychiatric diagnoses are not always reliable. Inevitably, some children will be incorrectly included in the high-risk group. Others who are genuinely at high risk will be lost to the study because their families move from the area. These difficulties are not unique to studies of heredity; they affect research in all of the paradigms of abnormal psychology.

Behavior, we have seen, is determined by a variety of interacting causes. Separating out any individual cause can be extraordinarily difficult. This does not mean that research into the genetic bases of behavior disorders is futile. Although no single study is likely to be definitive, the cumulative results of many studies may permit us to draw reasonable conclusions, especially when the findings all seem to point in the same direction. This is certainly the case for heredity. Decades of research have confirmed the importance of genetics as a distal cause of behavior disorders (Plomin & Rende, 1991).

Future researchers will find their work made easier by advances in molecular genetics. Instead of attempting to measure the influence of heredity through pedigree and adoption studies, scientists will soon be able to use biochemical techniques to examine the molecular constituents of genes directly. Using such modern techniques, the Human Genome Project (Collins, 1995; T. F. Lee, 1991; Marshall & Pennisi, 1996) is attempting to describe the biochemical structure of all human genes. As this work progresses, it will become increasingly possible to identify differences in the genes of disordered and nondisordered people. Once this is possible, the next step will be the development of ways to repair "damaged" genes (Blum et al., 1997; R. C. Williams, 1991).

No matter how sophisticated biochemistry becomes, however, we are never likely to find a single gene that causes people to take their own lives. Behavior disorders such as depression and suicide are far too complex to be caused by a single gene. They are much more likely to be the end result of many genes interacting with one another and with the environment (as described by the diathesis-stress model). Thus, even when we know everything there is to know about the molecular action of genes, we will still need to understand how the environment plays its crucial role if we are to help people achieve their full potential. (See Highlight 2.1 for a historical perspective on the acceptance of heredity's role in human behavior.)

Assessing Genetic Hypotheses: A Matter of Accumulation   Assessing heritability—testing any genetic hypothesis—is a time-consuming and methodologically complex process. No single study is definitive. Instead, we gradually increase our belief that a disorder is inherited by accumulating data from a variety of different sources. When these data all point in the same direction, our belief in the genetic hypothesis is strengthened. For example, our belief in the hypothesis that suicide is partly genetically determined would be strengthened by finding that

- Suicide occurs more commonly in the families of suicidal people.
- Suicide occurs more frequently in close relatives than in distant relatives.
- Adopted children resemble their natural parents more than their adoptive parents.
- Children with suicidal parents or close relatives are "at risk" and therefore more likely to commit suicide than other children.
- There are molecular (DNA) differences between suicidal and nonsuicidal people.

At present, there are limited data for all except the last of these points, suggesting that there may well be a genetic component in suicide.

Biological Paradigm Question 2: Is Abnormal Behavior a Disease?

The biological paradigm is sometimes characterized as a "medical" (or "biomedical") model of abnormal behavior. There are two reasons for this. First, those who work in the biological paradigm tend to use medical terms, such as *symptom, syndrome, diagnosis, etiology, pathology,* and *treatment.* Second, it is often assumed that behavior disorders that have their roots in biology are, by definition, illnesses that should be managed by health care professionals. (See Document 2.1 for an illustration of a biological approach to understanding and treating Danielle.) The confusion of biological causes with illness is nothing new. An editorial in the *Journal of Mental Science,* published in 1858, declared: "Insanity is purely a

disease of the brain. The physician is now the responsible guardian of the lunatic and must ever remain so" (quoted in Bentall & Pilgrim, 1993, p. 71). A century later, Hunter and MacAlpine (1963) stated boldly that "the lesson of the history of psychiatry is that progress is inevitable and irrevocable from psychology to neurology, from mind to brain, never the other way round" (quoted in Bentall & Pilgrim, 1993, p. 71). The belief that behavior disorders are biological in origin and best left to doctors to treat continues to dominate modern medicine despite the failure of researchers to find biological causes for the majority of behavior disorders (Charlton, 1990).

DOCUMENT 2.1

Doctor's Notes in Danielle's Hospital Chart

The social work report and the psychological assessment, as well as the patient's symptoms, confirm my provisional hypothesis that the patient is suffering from a depressive illness. I am ordering blood work to assess hormone levels and will monitor these to ensure that the depression is not secondary to hormone deficiency. Although Danielle seems calmer today, I am continuing suicide precautions for another 3 days. I have started the patient on a course of antidepressant medication, which will be reviewed in 2 weeks. Diagnosis: major depressive episode.

Sally Kahn, MD
December 5, 2000   ■

Over the years, considerable energy has gone into arguing about the value of the medical model, with writers taking extreme positions on either side. Thomas Szasz (1961) called the notion of mental illness (which he equated with physical disease) a myth invented to legitimize the allocation of social resources to certain categories of people. He also objected to the metaphoric use of the term *mental illness,* described in Chapter 1, on the grounds that it misleads people into "medicalizing" what are really "problems in living." In contrast to Szasz, Nancy Andreasen (1984) advocated the opposite position. She claimed that most, if not all, behavior disorders are really neurological illnesses. Other writers have expressed opinions that fall between these two extremes. Who is correct? Thus far, neither side has provided sufficient evidence to make its case.

The use of medical terminology, for example, does not necessarily reflect an illness model of behavior disorders. Even behaviorally oriented clinicians who explicitly reject the illness model may still refer to *pathologies,*

Do Only the Strong Deserve to Survive?

Although most psychologists are now willing to accept that certain behavior disorders may be at least partly inherited (Blum et al., 1997; Snyderman & Rothman, 1988), this has not always been true. For much of the 20th century, psychologists resisted the notion that heredity plays a significant role in human behavior. Their resistance was a reaction to the woeful history of genetic hypotheses, particularly in the past century.

In the 19th century, Charles Darwin's theory of evolution by natural selection (those organisms that are best adapted to their environment are most likely to survive and pass on their abilities to their offspring) was transformed by the English philosopher Herbert Spencer into a doctrine known as social Darwinism. Spencer's thesis was that personality traits, moral behavior, and intellectual abilities are subject to the same evolutionary forces that shape physical characteristics. Some people are born morally superior; others inherit criminal tendencies. Some people inherit high intelligence; others are born (and remain) stupid. Because healthy, virtuous, intelligent people are more likely to survive and to attract the best mates, the weak will eventually perish. It was Spencer, not Darwin as often thought, who coined the phrase "survival of the fittest" to describe how nature ensures the continual improvement of the human race.

The social Darwinists believed that welfare programs and specialized treatment facilities for the chronically ill represent a misguided humanitarianism because they interfere with natural selection. Poverty and psychological disorders are moral defects that originate from an innate biological inferiority. By allowing the poor and the troubled to perish, humanity will eventually rid itself of the scourges of poverty and illness. The social Darwinists founded the Eugenics Society, which was dedicated to promoting "ideal" matings and, on occasion, to sterilizing people who were believed to be not so ideal. (**Eugenics** literally means "the production of fine children.")

Spencer's ideas were especially welcomed in the United States, where the ruling elite readily accepted the proposition that success is a sign of inherent superiority and failure, the result of a personal defect. By the 1930s, 20,000 "lunatics," "moral perverts," and "degenerates" (all considered at the time to be genetically inferior) were forcibly sterilized under various eugenics laws (Mazumdar, 1992). Restrictive immigration laws were also enacted to prevent members of "degenerate" races (mostly southern Europeans) from entering the country. When the Nazis gained power in Germany in the 1930s, their first eugenics laws were modeled on those enacted in the United States. The Nazis proceeded to take social Darwinism to a nightmarish extreme. In an attempt to wipe out mental illness, they initiated mass killings of patients in mental hospitals and children diagnosed as mentally retarded. The gas chambers that were later used to murder millions of Jews were first used on these unfortunate people. After the war, when the Nazi horrors were revealed to the world, eugenics was discredited as a "science."

One of the great ironies of eugenics is that it was based on a scientific and logical fallacy. By assuming that genet-

disorders, and *diagnoses.* More important, the mere discovery that a behavior or trait has a distal biological cause does not mean that it is an illness (Gorenstein, 1992). Consider homosexuality. Suppose researchers find that homosexuality is a biological rather than a social phenomenon (a possibility discussed in Chapter 13). Would this discovery mean that the American Psychiatric Association was wrong and that homosexuality is a disease after all (see Chapter 1)? The answer is clearly no. After all, if homosexuality has a neurophysiological cause, so too does heterosexuality. To be logically consistent, we would have to say that heterosexuality is an illness because it is "caused" biologically. Similarly, because hair color and eye color are biologically determined, redheads and people with green eyes would also have to be considered ill. You can see the absurdity; we cannot conclude that abnormal behavior is an illness just because it has a biological cause.

As noted in Chapter 1, what we decide to call an illness (or a disorder or a pathology) is determined by history, social values, and the relative costs and benefits of labeling people ill. This is true not only for behavior disorders, but for physical illnesses as well. In modern Germany, for example, low blood pressure is considered to be an illness that requires medical attention. Thousands of patients are under treatment with 1 of more than 85 different drugs. In England and Spain no such medical condition is recognized, and, consequently, no patients are being treated (Clare, 1989). This does not mean that there are no people with low blood pressure in England

ically transmitted traits are immutable, the eugenicists made the mistake of confusing a **genotype** (a person's genetic endowment) with a **phenotype** (the way in which a genetic endowment is expressed). Although it is true that genotypes are determined biologically, phenotypes are affected by both biological and environmental factors. For example, phenylketonuria (PKU), which was described in Chapter 1, is a genetic condition with a distinctive genotype. Nevertheless, PKU's symptoms can be prevented by restricting the diet of affected individuals. In this way, an environmental manipulation (such as diet) can change the phenotype of a genetic condition.

It may soon be possible to alter genotypes directly by manipulating individual genes (Blum et al., 1997). When this becomes a reality, there will be no limit to the extent to which phenotypes may be altered. Given the abuses of the past, we will have to keep a close watch on these new technologies to ensure that they are used for the benefit of humanity and not for its destruction (Knoppers & Chadwick, 1994).

In addition to exterminating people deemed "defective," the Nazis also had plans to create a "master race." One project was Lebensborn ("Life Spring"), which established group homes in which to raise children of Hitler's elite SS officers and "racially valuable" women. Here, some of those specially selected women are exercising at a "school for brides" in 1939.

and Spain. There are proportionally the same number as in Germany; they are just not considered sick. National differences reflect the relative wealth of countries (Germany is richer and can afford to treat more people) as well as cultural attitudes toward what constitutes an illness.

Calling the biological paradigm a medical model clarifies nothing. It simply confuses the distal biological causes of behavior with economic, social, and legal judgments about whom society considers sick. The result of this confusion has been considerable rhetorical heat but not much theoretical light. It is time to move beyond sterile debates about whether behavior disorders are illnesses and to focus instead on the causes, treatment, and prevention of abnormal behavior.

The Evolution of a Biological Hypothesis

Theories in the various paradigms have a characteristic natural history, from observations to hypotheses to theoretical explanations. The best way to see how a paradigm shapes theory and research is to examine how it transforms observations into theories. This section illustrates the biological approach by focusing on depression. Note that many of the research methods described in this section are also used by researchers working in other paradigms.

Naturalistic Observation   In the 1950s, clinicians began using the drug reserpine to treat high blood pressure. Reserpine is derived from rauwolfia (snakeroot), a plant

51

prized for centuries for its calming effect. Although reserpine was effective in lowering blood pressure, clinicians noted that it sometimes had an unpleasant side effect: It made people depressed. Further research revealed that reserpine lowers norepinephrine levels. By putting these two observations together, clinicians stumbled across one possible biological cause of depression—diminished levels of norepinephrine.

The origin of the norepinephrine hypothesis is not atypical; many theories can be traced back to a fortuitous clinical observation. Indeed, naturalistic observation—observing phenomena as they occur in nature—is the most prevalent scientific method. In some sciences (astronomy, for example), it is the only method. Clinical case studies are psychology's most commonly used type of naturalistic observation. Although they have given rise to important research programs, case studies have serious shortcomings as research tools. One problem is that the same person is both therapist and scientific observer. These roles are not always compatible. The therapist-observer may be biased, selectively reporting or distorting the case to support a particular theory. Case studies are also difficult to generalize. Because each case has its unique features, we are never quite sure whether the findings of a particular case study can be applied to other people. Clearly, more rigorous research is required before researchers can give much credence to a naturalistic observation.

Correlational Studies   The next step in the evolution of the norepinephrine hypothesis was to ensure that the initial clinical observations were not unique events. The easiest way to do this was to study more cases. In the 1960s, researchers assembled observations on a large number of hypertensive patients treated with reserpine. They found that many, although not all, reported depression. These observations were reassuring because they suggested that the first reported cases were not unique. There did, indeed, seem to be a **correlation** (a relationship) between two variables—treatment with reserpine and depression. Based on this relationship, it would have been tempting to conclude that reserpine causes depression. Unfortunately, such a conclusion would not have been warranted. A correlation between two variables does not mean that one causes the other. Other explanations are always possible (Patten & Love, 1994). For example, the hypertensive patients may have become depressed worrying about the long-term consequences of their high blood pressure. The reserpine may have had nothing to do with their depression.

Researchers were aware of this possibility, so their next step was to compare hypertensive patients who were treated with reserpine with those who were not. They found that patients who received the drug had a greater likelihood of becoming depressed. These observations placed the norepinephrine hypothesis on somewhat firmer ground. Although all hypertensive patients might have been expected to worry about their health, only those who received the drug became depressed. Still, even this finding did not prove that diminished norepinephrine causes depression. It is possible that patients who are offered medication—any medication—will consider themselves sicker than those who are not treated. If this is true, then drug-treated patients will worry more about their health and become depressed more often than untreated patients. To rule out this possibility, researchers had to move to the next stage in the natural history of biological research, a controlled experiment.

Controlled Studies   In a controlled experiment, researchers manipulate one variable and observe the changes produced in another. Experimenters call the variable they manipulate the **independent variable;** the one they observe is known as the **dependent variable.** To determine whether it is specifically reserpine's effect on norepinephrine, and not just any drug treatment, that causes depression in hypertensive patients requires a controlled experiment with at least two groups of people. One group, the **experimental group,** is treated with reserpine while the other, the **control group,** receives some other form of treatment, either another method of lowering blood pressure or, more usually, a **placebo** (in this case, an inert tablet designed to look like reserpine). In this experiment, the independent variable is treatment (reserpine or placebo) and the dependent variable is a measure of depression.

If such an experiment showed that people treated with reserpine (but not those who received the placebo) become depressed, we would have more reason to believe the norepinephrine hypothesis. But we could still not be entirely sure. Perhaps the members of the experimental group were more depressed than those in the control group even before the experiment began. To rule out this possibility, researchers try to ensure that there are no preexisting differences between the experimental and control groups. One way to achieve this is to choose subjects so that each member of the experimental group is matched with a member of the control group on every relevant variable (family history, age, and so on). Unfortunately, researchers do not always know which subject characteristics are relevant and which ones they can ignore. They attempt to get around this by randomly assigning people to groups. They hope that, by selecting people at random from the population being studied, they will wind up with two similar groups.

The effects of extraneous variables can be subtle. For example, a researcher who knows that a person is receiving reserpine might expect that person to become depressed. This expectation, in turn, might lead the researcher to show more concern for that subject than for someone not receiving the drug. The researcher might ask the person getting reserpine more questions about his or her moods, for example. These questions could cause the person receiving the drug to become concerned and perhaps even depressed. In other words, by treating people who receive the drug differently from those who receive the placebo, the researcher could unwittingly affect the results of the experiment.

Even when experimenters treat all experimental subjects similarly, it is still possible that those who know they are receiving a drug that could possibly cause depression will behave differently from those who know they are receiving a placebo. Those getting the drug may brood about the possibility of drug-induced depression, for example. Their brooding could affect the outcome of the experiment. To avoid these expectancy effects, patients and researchers should be kept "blind" (unaware of who is receiving the drug and who is getting the placebo). Such experiments are described as **double-blind** (Figure 2.4, p. 54). Those responsible for determining whether people in the experiment have become depressed should also be kept blind to avoid biased evaluations.

Ethical Challenges   Thus far, we have seen how research on the norepinephrine hypothesis evolved from clinical observations to controlled studies. At each evolutionary stage, confirmatory evidence placed the norepinephrine hypothesis on an increasingly firmer footing. Yet doubts remained. One problem is that all of the studies discussed so far were conducted with people who had high blood pressure. It is possible that reserpine causes depression only in hypertensive people, and not in anyone else. This would complicate the norepinephrine hypothesis considerably because it would suggest that neurotransmitter levels do not operate alone. Instead, it would seem that an interaction between high blood pressure and reserpine causes depression. The next step, therefore, is to administer reserpine to people

who do not have high blood pressure. At this stage in the natural history of research, we encounter a rather different type of problem from those discussed so far. Giving potentially harmful drugs to people who are not sick (and who will, therefore, derive no therapeutic benefits) may be unethical.

Scientists are primarily motivated by curiosity and a search for scientific knowledge. Nevertheless, they must consider the social context in which they live and work before planning their studies. Whether an experiment is concerned with animals or people, there are ethical obligations to which all scientists must adhere (American Psychological Assn, 1990; McNeill, 1993). Probably the most important ethical issue in abnormal psychology is the problem of voluntary, informed consent. A basic tenet of ethical research is that people must voluntarily consent to participate. To do this, research participants must be informed of all the potential risks and benefits of the study, and they must have the capacity to make a considered judgment. Voluntary consent means more than simply getting someone to agree to participate. Children asked by their teachers, prisoners asked by their wardens, and soldiers asked by their commanding officers may agree to participate in research because they are being asked by someone in authority. They may fear the consequences should they decline. In such cases, their participation is not truly voluntary. It is usually best if recruitment is conducted by the researcher rather than a person who has authority over potential participants.

Informed consent requires not only that potential volunteers be informed of the relative risks and benefits of participation but that they be informed in a way that they can understand. This requirement is especially difficult to fulfill when people are kept blind to whether they are being treated (Brownell & Stunkard, 1982). Informed consent is also problematic when research focuses on special populations such as children, those who are mentally retarded, and people who are severely disturbed. Members of these groups may lack the capacity to make decisions for themselves. Those given responsibility for the care of these people must consent on their behalf. This is an important responsibility, which must be exercised with great care.

Even when informed consent is obtained, it is still up to researchers to demonstrate that a study is worth doing. Usually, this requires a comparison of a study's risks and benefits. When the risks to those studied outweigh the expected benefits (to the participants and to society), the study should not be conducted. Finally, all

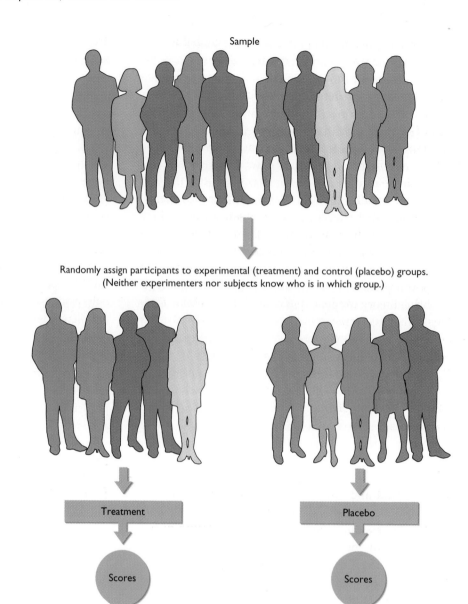

FIGURE 2.4 **A Controlled, Double-Blind Experiment**

research participants deserve anonymity; they should never be identified without their consent.

Accumulating Evidence Carefully controlled experiments provide the best test of a scientific hypothesis, but they are not always feasible. No one would suggest, for example, that randomly chosen children be subjected to child abuse (such as that experienced by Danielle) to see whether they become suicidal later in life. Because such experiments cannot be conducted for ethical reasons, scientists have looked for alternative ways of testing hypotheses. **Analogue experiments,** using animals as "analogues" (from the word *analogy*) for people, have sometimes yielded useful results (Ellison & Bresler,

1974). These experiments can never be definitive, however, because it is difficult to generalize from animals to people. (Who knows whether an animal's depression is similar to that of a human?) Moreover, research ethics also forbid subjecting animals to unnecessarily harmful procedures. Another type of analogue experiment, in which people with mild forms of depression are studied instead of patients, can produce important findings (Vredenburg, Flett, & Krames, 1993), but such experiments are of more value to researchers in some of the other paradigms than they are to biological researchers. People with nonclinical forms of depression are unlikely to subject themselves voluntarily to hormonal assays, drugs, and other biological manipulations.

Biological Paradigm

For many theoretical problems in psychopathology, the correlational approach to research is the only practical one. Rather than attempt to conduct the definitive experiment, researchers seek to support their theories by accumulating correlational evidence from a variety of different sources. For example, the discovery that antidepressant drugs known as monoamine oxidase (MAO) inhibitors *increase* the amount of norepinephrine in certain neurons supports the hypothesis that depression is the result of *decreased* levels of norepinephrine. The finding that tricyclic antidepressant drugs, which are chemically different from MAO inhibitors, also increase norepinephrine levels (Snyder, 1991) adds further support to the norepinephrine hypothesis. Despite the support provided by these studies, however, the norepinephrine theory cannot explain all of the available findings. Other neurotransmitters have also been implicated as possible causes of depression (Snyder, 1991). (These research findings are discussed in Chapter 8.) For now, it is enough to say that the issue is not settled, and evidence both pro and con continues to accumulate. This is also part of the natural history of a scientific hypothesis.

Biological Paradigm: Current Status

For practical and ethical reasons, much biological research into the causes of abnormal behavior is correlational. Depression, for example, has been found to correlate with low neurotransmitter levels, enlarged brain ventricles, and various other physiological and anatomic anomalies (Beats, Levy, & Forstl, 1991; Depue & Iacono, 1989; M. L. Scott et al., 1983). The precise mechanisms by which these biological anomalies produce the behaviors that we associate with depression (hopelessness, guilt, and so on) is rarely made clear. This is why biological theories, despite their grounding in observable physiology and anatomy, often seem surprisingly vague. This vagueness applies even to biological theories that are incontestably true. Consider, for example, the syndrome of general paresis, which was discussed in Chapter 1. As noted, one of its well-known behavioral manifestations is delusions of grandeur. Today, a century after the discovery that general paresis is caused by the syphilitic spirochete, we still cannot say why many infected people develop delusions of grandeur (or why some do not). We are also unable to say why some people who have never had syphilis develop similar delusions. Until we can answer such basic questions about how infections, lesions, hormones, and so on, actually produce specific behavior disorders, the biological paradigm will not fulfill its great promise; it will remain an assemblage of intriguing correlations (Gorenstein, 1992).

PSYCHOANALYTIC PARADIGM

In contrast to the biological paradigm, which derives its methods from the laboratory, the psychoanalytic paradigm uses techniques derived from the psychological clinic to answer questions about the unconscious causes of behavior: Is abnormal behavior determined by unconscious conflicts? Do long-forgotten childhood experiences influence adult behavior? Are dreams meaningful? The paradigm, which consists of both a theory of behavior and a treatment for behavioral disorders, is derived from the work of Sigmund Freud.

Sigmund Freud: Hysteria, Hypnosis, and the Unconscious

Sigmund Freud was born in 1856 and spent most of his life in Vienna. While still a medical student, Freud got caught up in biomedical research. Although he showed promise as a scientist, on graduation Freud chose to enter the more lucrative world of private medical practice. He nevertheless maintained his biomedical research interests, publishing papers on brain anatomy, neurology, and a well-known monograph on the effects of cocaine. In 1885, Freud was made a clinical lecturer in neurology at the University of Vienna. This was an ideal situation for him because he could do some teaching and research without giving up his private practice. It also made him eligible for a travel grant. Freud used the money to visit Paris, where he worked at the Salpêtrière under the great neurologist Jean Charcot (1825–1893). Charcot was one of the founders of the medical specialty of neurology. Not only was he the first person to describe important conditions—including amyotrophic lateral sclerosis (Lou Gehrig's disease)—he was also a pioneer in studying psychological disorders. On Freud's return to Vienna, he began to specialize in the ancient problem of hysteria. Like his contemporaries, he treated patients with a combination of rest, baths, massage, and electric currents. In 1889, he again journeyed to France, this time to study with Hippolyte Bernheim. On his return, Freud began to use Bernheim's hypnotic "suggestion" technique. He would hypnotize patients and suggest that their symptoms would be gone when they awoke. The outcomes were mixed; some patients benefited, but many did not.

Only 25 years after Sigmund Freud and Josef Breuer suggested in
Studies on Hysteria *that subconscious memories may cause physical*
symptoms, psychoanalysis had developed to the point that theoreti-
cians held regular international conferences, such as the one Freud at-
tended in The Hague in 1920.

Freud frequently discussed his cases with Josef Breuer (1842–1925), an older and distinguished Viennese doctor. It was in one of these discussions that Freud first heard about Anna O., a patient that Breuer had treated in the early 1880s. Anna O. had a variety of symptoms, including headaches, paralysis, and speech disturbances. At first, Breuer tried Bernheim's technique. He hypnotized the young woman and told her that when she awoke, her symptoms would be gone. Anna O. did not respond. In fact, her condition deteriorated. Breuer took a different tack. He had noticed that hypnosis prompted Anna O. to recall past events. He encouraged this. One day, while under hypnosis, she relived the trauma of her father's death (for which she wrongly felt responsible), and her symptoms disappeared. Breuer concluded that Bernheim was wrong. Hypnotic suggestion does not, by itself, cure hysteria. Patients must also relive traumatic memories and express the associated emotions. Breuer called this release of pent-up emotions **catharsis,** from the Greek word meaning "to purge or to purify."

Freud decided to use the cathartic method with his own patients. Over the years, he and Breuer compared notes and refined their treatment. Eventually, they pro-

duced a theory: Hysterical symptoms are the physical manifestations of pent-up emotions. In a book called *Studies on Hysteria* (1895/1956), Breuer and Freud elaborated on their idea. They claimed that the details of some childhood traumas are too disturbing to be admitted into consciousness. So, these memories are kept unconscious through a process they called **repression.** The repressed incident (along with its associated emotions) is not completely forgotten. Instead, it acts like a festering sore, producing hysterical symptoms for years after the traumatic event.

Sometimes the connection between a hysterical symptom and its precipitating event is clear. For example, Breuer and Freud (1895/1956) describe a man who developed pain in his hip joint after watching his brother undergo a painful joint operation. More commonly, however, the relationship between the precipitating cause and the hysterical symptom is "symbolic" rather than direct. One example was the patient who was so disgusted by some distant event in her life that she developed the hysterical symptom of vomiting. Whether symptoms are direct representations of traumatic events or symbolic derivatives of early traumas, Freud and Breuer believed that they could be eliminated provided the original trauma could be recalled. In an important break with previous practice, Breuer and Freud began to use hypnosis not as a cure in itself but as a means of uncovering unconscious memories. In the decades following the publication of *Studies on Hysteria,* Freud treated patients for 5 or 6 days each week. He analyzed their dreams, their slips of the tongue, and their free associations. Eventually, he used these data to construct an elaborate theory of personality and behavior. Freud called this theory psychoanalysis, and it became the foundation of the psychoanalytic paradigm.

Psychoanalytic Paradigm Question 1: What Is the Personality, and How Does It Influence Behavior?

According to Freud, mental functioning takes place at more than one level. In an arrangement that has been likened to an iceberg, only the smallest part of mental functioning, the exposed tip of the iceberg, is available to awareness. Another, somewhat larger part of the iceberg lies immediately below the surface. This is the **preconscious,** which contains material that is not in immediate awareness but is available when needed. Although it may require some mental effort, we can usually recall information, such as a telephone number, that resides in the preconscious. By far the largest part of the iceberg,

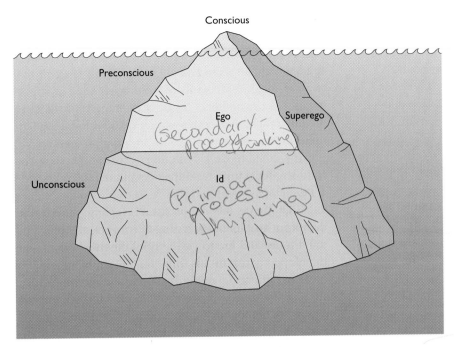

FIGURE 2.5 A Schematic Illustration of the Personality. *Freud compared personality to an iceberg. Only a very small part is conscious. A somewhat larger part is preconscious—available to conscious awareness with some mental effort. But by far the largest part of personality is unconscious, unavailable to the individual without massive psychoanalytic effort.* From: S. Schwartz and Johnson (1985, p. 13).

the **unconscious,** lies deep beneath the surface and out of awareness. The unconscious contains traces of past experiences, impulses, and desires. It also provides a home for the basic biological instincts, including the sex drive. Unconscious material may sometimes reach consciousness (in dreams, for example), but when this occurs the material is usually experienced as foreign.

Psychoanalytic theory divides the adult personality into three interacting parts: the **id,** the **ego,** and the **superego.** At first, only the id exists. It is ruled by the **pleasure principle,** which requires that biological needs, such as hunger, thirst, and sex, be immediately satisfied. When this is impossible, wish-fulfilling fantasies (known as **primary-process thinking**) provide a temporary solution. The solution is temporary because fantasies do not really satisfy biological needs. This is when the ego takes over. The ego mediates between the id and the external world. By permitting the individual to work toward a goal (**secondary-process thinking**), the ego allows the individual to satisfy important needs without violating the demands of civilized society. The superego is, in a sense, an optional personality characteristic. It is possible to exist without one, and individuals are thought to vary in the extent of its development.

The superego consists of an internalized moral code similar to a conscience. Inevitably, there are times when the id's demands for immediate gratification conflict with the superego's moral code. At such times, the ego's job is to strike a compromise among the id, the superego, and the real world. Figure 2.5 illustrates the interrelationships of the personality's parts.

Psychological Energy Freud viewed human beings as complex energy systems. Psychological energy comes from the instinctual desires of the id. Among the instincts that Freud considered most important were the life instincts, which have as their goal the survival of the individual (hunger, sex); the death instinct (which is manifest in war); and the death instinct's derivative, aggression. Freud called the psychological "energy" derived from life instincts **libido.** He conceived of it as a type of "fuel" for the ego, for the superego, and for psychological functioning in general. In keeping with the concept of psychic energy, psychoanalytic ideas are also referred to as psychodynamic.

Personality Development Intellectually, Freud owed a considerable debt to the 17th-century philosopher

Thomas Hobbes (1588–1679), whose political treatise, *Leviathan* (1651/1973), depicted human beings as governed by selfishness, lust, greed, and aggression. Hobbes believed that humans, if left unchecked, always try to satisfy their impulses by whatever means possible, including war, rape, and theft. Civilization depends on the restraint imposed on people by outside forces, such as the police. Freud's views were similar to Hobbes's. People, he believed, are hedonists who, left to their own devices, always seek to gratify their impulses. Freud's views differed from Hobbes's in one respect. Civilization does not depend solely on external forces such as the police; individuals can also internalize society's rules into the superego, he believed. By punishing transgressions with feelings of guilt and shame and by rewarding socially approved behaviors with increases in self-esteem, the superego acts as a kind of internal police force.

According to psychoanalysis, the superego develops through a process called **identification.** Children want to be like their parents. To accomplish this, they identify with (adopt) their parents' standards of proper behavior. Because children have two parents, they can make two identifications. The balance between these identifications determines not only a child's moral standards but also his or her sexual identity. If the identification process goes awry, the result is a damaged conscience and an uncertain sexual identity. These two basic ideas—(a) people are born savages and must be socialized to behave morally, and (b) sexual identity is not innate but develops out of early family experience—formed the cornerstone of Freud's theory of psychosexual stages of development.

The Psychosexual Stages   From the psychoanalytic point of view, early life experiences are the crucial determinants of adult personality. Every child must face an inevitable series of conflicts with the world. These conflicts occur in "stages," each requiring some kind of adjustment. The oral stage, which comes first, occurs at a time when the child achieves pleasure from sucking, eating, and later, biting. If, for some reason, a child is frustrated at this stage, **fixation** will result. Some libido will remain "fixated" at the oral stage, and the individual will crave the satisfaction of oral needs—by smoking, for example. If fixation occurs later in the oral stage, the individual may become someone who abuses others verbally (perhaps a "biting" speaker).

The next stage—the anal stage—represents the first challenge from civilization to the primary-process pleasure-seeking id. Toilet training requires that defecation, which is a biological reflex, be brought under social control. Overly harsh training may suffocate a child's spirit, producing a personality that slavishly conforms to all of society's demands. On the other hand, a failure to resolve the conflicts of the anal stage could lead to lifelong rebellion, a never-ending battle between the individual and society.

An even more threatening conflict between the child's natural urges and the demands of civilized society develops during the phallic stage. Now it is the genitals that are the site of pleasurable feelings, and it is at this point that the **Oedipal conflict** occurs. According to Freud, males are forced, through fears of castration, to repress their natural desire for their mothers and to identify with and pattern themselves after their fathers. Although a similar process, called the **Electra complex,** occurs for females, its resolution is not as clear. The outcome of all of this turmoil during the phallic stage of development has implications for later social and sexual behavior. If the conflicts are not successfully resolved, individuals may not be able to adopt mature adult sexual roles. The phallic stage also marks the birth of the superego. During the latency stage, children are supposedly indifferent to sex. Instead, their identification with their parents becomes stronger. The child adopts the mannerisms and values of his or her same-sex parent. In this way, the child becomes indoctrinated into his or her culture.

The final stage of development, the genital stage, marks the adult personality. It is when interpersonal skills, friendships, and social attachments develop. A fully developed, genital, personality requires a successful passage through the four preceding psychosexual stages. Table 2.1 summarizes Freud's developmental stages.

Anxiety and Defense Mechanisms   **Anxiety** is an affective state characterized by unpleasant feelings of dread and fear. Over the years, Freud proposed several etiologies for anxiety. Although they differed in their details, the etiologies shared one essential feature. They all attributed anxiety to repression, a psychological process by which unacceptable impulses and thoughts are kept out of consciousness. Repression is a way of protecting the ego, but it is rarely successful. Unconscious repressed material creates anxiety and a host of hysterical, and other, symptoms.

On the basis of his clinical observations, Freud concluded that repressed thoughts and impulses almost al-

TABLE 2.1	Freud's Psychosexual Stages of Development	
Stage	**Age (approximate)**	**Characteristics**
Oral	Birth to 18 months	Pleasure is derived from sucking, eating, and biting. Frustration results in fixation.
Anal	18 months to 3 years	Toilet training requires that a biological reflex be brought under social control. How conflicts are resolved affects tendency to conformity or rebellion.
Phallic	3 to 4 years	Pleasure is derived from genitals. Resolution of Oedipal conflict and Electra complex affects later social and sexual behavior.
Latency	6 to 12 years	Libidinal energies redirected to discovering new interests and skills.
Genital	12 years to maturity	Pleasure is derived from sexual relationships. Interpersonal skills, friendships, and social attachments develop.

ways concern sex. It is possible, however, that this conclusion was biased by his patient population. Freud's patients were all middle-class Viennese, mainly women, and mainly hysterics. They were hardly a representative sample of the world at large. It is possible that Freud would have reached different conclusions had he had a wider sample of patients.

Based on his patients' reports, Freud came to believe that traumatic sexual experiences such as rape and incest were the cause of most, if not all, psychological disorders. He later modified this view. Reasoning that traumatic sexual experiences could not possibly be as common as his patients' reports suggested, Freud concluded that the sexual incidents they described never actually happened; they were just fantasies. His change of view led him to modify his theory. Anxiety and many psychological disorders are not necessarily the result of repressed sexual *trauma*—they can also be caused by unacceptable sexual *fantasies*. Freud's unwillingness to believe that sexual trauma was as common as his patients claimed could have been a function of the times in which he lived. Sexual behavior, especially deviant sexual behavior, was a taboo subject in polite 19th-century society. Freud may have decided that his patients' descriptions of incest and rape were fantasies because of his desire to make his theories more acceptable to his contemporaries (Masson, 1992) or, as some psychoanalysts have claimed, to make them more acceptable to himself (Kupfersmid, 1992). One wonders what Freud would have made of Danielle's case. If Danielle's father had not admitted to his crime, Freud might have concluded that Danielle's report of sexual abuse was also only a fantasy.

When anxiety is troublesome, relief may be obtained by the use of **defense mechanisms,** which operate unconsciously and always involve some distortion of reality. Among the principal defense mechanisms are repression, which we have already encountered; sublimation, the channeling of libido into socially acceptable behaviors (creating erotic works of art, for example); projection, attributing one's problems to external sources rather than to oneself ("I do not hate her; she hates me"); rationalization, inventing sham reasons for behavior ("I am not prejudiced, but allowing homosexuals to serve in the army may affect teamwork"); reaction formation, adopting attitudes that are opposite to those that are producing anxiety (a person who fears being homosexual may become an avid anti-gay campaigner, for example); and denial, the outright rejection of reality (as in the patient who deliberately starves herself and claims that she is still too fat). Defense mechanisms can be ordered along a continuum of reality distortion (Figure 2.6). At one end is sublimation. It requires relatively little misrepresentation, and it can help people to improve their social functioning. At the other extreme is denial, which almost always results in a considerable perversion of reality. The other defense mechanisms fall somewhere between these two extremes. People who habitually rely on reality-distorting defense mechanisms are more likely to be considered maladjusted than those who rely on sublimation and rationalization.

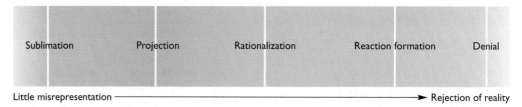

| Sublimation | Projection | Rationalization | Reaction formation | Denial |

Little misrepresentation ⟶ Rejection of reality

FIGURE 2.6 **The Spectrum of Defense Mechanisms**

Psychoanalytic Paradigm Question 2: How Should Psychological Disorders Be Treated?

Psychoanalysis is more than a theory of personality and behavior; it is also a treatment for psychological disorders. As we have seen, Freud began treating patients using Bernheim's hypnotic suggestion technique ("When you awake, your symptoms will disappear"). He later added Breuer's cathartic method, using hypnosis to help patients retrieve repressed memories. Freud soon found that neither technique was completely satisfactory. The effects of hypnotic suggestion were rarely permanent, and some people could not be hypnotized. To encourage the recollection of repressed memories among nonhypnotizable people, Freud developed another way of helping them "concentrate" their thoughts. He had his patients lie back on a couch with their eyes closed while he sat alongside them with his hand on their forehead, encouraging them to talk about themselves. One day, a patient who had been lying on the couch for some time remarked that she was not sure exactly what the doctor wanted to hear. To Freud, this remark came as a revelation. Patients need not be hypnotized to be suggestible; unhypnotized patients can also be influenced by the therapist. To ensure that his patients were not simply saying what they thought he wanted to hear, Freud developed the **free association** technique, which requires patients to relate whatever comes into their minds, no matter how irrelevant or nonsensical. Free association eventually displaced hypnosis as Freud's main therapeutic tool.

Freud's therapy was particularly concerned with dreams, which he believed represent a "pathway" to the unconscious. The manifest, or obvious, content of dreams masks a latent content to which the manifest content is symbolically connected. He believed that, by careful dream analysis, therapists could uncover unconscious conflicts that patients resist revealing through free association. Over time, Freud became increasingly occupied with the analysis of what he called the **transference** relationship—a tendency for patients to transfer their habitual modes of interpersonal behavior, love as well as hate, to the therapist. Through an analysis of the transference relationship, patients can come to understand and change the way they react to other people. Freud offered patients interpretations of the transference relationship that were designed to help them gain insight into their behavior. Armed with this insight, patients were able to release the psychic energy they were expending to keep unacceptable thoughts repressed. By working through the ramifications of repressed material as it came to the surface (noting how it influences behavior), patients were able to release their repressed feelings, and, as a result, their symptoms disappeared.

Modifications to Psychoanalysis by Neo- and Post-Freudians Freud was initially shunned by his German and Austrian medical colleagues, who found his "obses-

Freud's therapy has been called the "talking cure." To encourage patients to speak freely rather than saying what they thought he wanted to hear, Freud often had them lie on this couch in his office.

Carl Jung (1887–1961) broke with Freud over the centrality of sex drives and established "analytical" psychology, whose emphasis on self-actualization influenced the humanistic paradigm.

Erik Erikson (1902–1994) extended Freud's theory into an examination of the development of the personality over the life span.

sion" with sexual matters distasteful and perhaps even depraved. It is likely that psychoanalysis would have remained a marginal activity of interest to only a few people had it not been for World War I. Soldiers, in reaction to the horrific conditions in the trenches, developed a variety of "hysterical" symptoms (blindness, deafness, tremors) that rendered them unfit for duty (Stone, 1985). These symptoms were treated as disciplinary problems, and the soldiers were punished for their behavior. But the punishment did not work. The incidence of symptoms became so great that army discipline was threatened. British psychoanalysts offered the army their services, which were gratefully accepted. These clinicians gave the soldiers' symptoms a name. They were not cowards; they were suffering from a mental condition known as shell shock, a condition treatable by psychoanalysis. By redefining the soldiers' behavior and giving it a label, and by purporting to know how to treat it, psychoanalysts soon found themselves in demand in Great Britain and later in the United States. After the war, Freud's fame began to spread. He was awarded honorary degrees and his works were studied carefully. Despite his fame, his theories were never widely accepted in his own country. In 1938, Freud was driven out of Austria by the Nazis. He fled to England, where he died a year later, at the age of 83. Psychoanalysis did not stagnate with Freud's death, however. Neo- and post-

Freudians extended, and in some ways transformed, psychoanalysis in ways never anticipated by Freud.

Carl Gustav Jung (1887–1961), for example, was a Swiss psychiatrist who seemed set to become Freud's heir when the two broke up over matters of theory. Jung was less interested in sex drives than Freud. He preferred instead to concentrate on the spiritual and mystical forces that we supposedly inherit from our ancestors in the form of a genetic data bank he called the **collective unconscious.** Jung eventually went on to establish his own "analytical psychology," which emphasized the need for **self-actualization** (the development of all aspects of the personality to their highest potential). This idea was taken up again in the humanistic paradigm, which is discussed later in this chapter. Where Freud stressed the influence of the past, particularly early childhood experiences, on behavior, Jung stressed the ability of people to set and meet goals. In his career, Jung wrote extensively about many psychological topics, including personality traits and psychological assessment.

Other early collaborators were Alfred Adler (1870–1937), whose "individual psychology" stressed the human need to "strive for superiority" in some aspect of life, and Erik Erikson (1902–1994), who extended Freud's theory of psychosexual development beyond childhood to show how personality continues to develop throughout life. Erikson proposed an eight-stage

TABLE 2.2 Erikson's Stages of Development	
Stage	**Psychosocial crisis**
Birth to adolescence	
Infancy	Trust versus mistrust. Realization that needs will be met leads to trust in others and self.
Toddlerhood	Autonomy versus shame and doubt. Physical maturation gives sense of being able to do things for self.
Early childhood	Initiative versus guilt. Increasing abilities promote exploration and expand experience.
Middle childhood	Industry versus inferiority. Accomplishments and skills provide basis for self-esteem.
Adolescence to old age	
Adolescence	Identity versus identity diffusion. Biological and social changes of adolescence occasion a search for continuity of self.
Early adulthood	Intimacy versus isolation. Sense of self provides the basis for sexual and emotional intimacy with another adult.
Middle adulthood	Generativity versus stagnation. Concern for children and future generations reflects need to leave something of oneself.
Late adulthood	Integrity versus despair. Acceptance of one's life as having meaning gives one a sense of dignity.

Note: From Cobb (1998), p. 66.

model of development, with each stage presenting a new challenge or crisis (Table 2.2). The way in which each of these crises are resolved determines how a person deals with the next stage. A particularly important crisis, with profound consequences for later development, takes place at Erikson's fifth stage, which occurs between ages 12 and 20. This is known as the **identity crisis.** To resolve the identity crisis, adolescents and young adults must make important life choices—about careers, goals, and social commitments, and about the type of people they wish to become.

Jung, Adler, and Erikson all influenced the development of the humanistic paradigm (discussed later in this chapter). They differed from Freud in their more optimistic view of human beings. Erikson, especially, emphasized the resilience of the ego and its ability to overcome many adversities. He believed that we are not necessarily the prisoners of our early experiences. Given the right circumstances, we can overcome early traumas and grow into fulfilled human beings. Because they considered the ego to be the most important aspect of the personality, Erikson and other neo-Freudians (including Freud's daughter Anna) are referred to as ego psychologists.

Variations on Freud's general themes have ap-

peared (and in some cases, disappeared) over the years. In general, the trend has been away from his reliance on biological instincts as the main determinant of personality development and toward a greater role for social determinants. The role of the ego has continued to be strengthened as well. In its general orientation and basic philosophical position, however, psychoanalysis remains relatively unchanged. Unconscious motivation remains paramount (W. L. Kelly, 1991).

The Evolution of a Psychoanalytic Hypothesis In the previous section, we saw how a biological hypothesis about the cause of depression, which originated in case studies, was refined and verified by increasingly sophisticated experimental tests. Psychoanalytic hypotheses are also derived from case studies, but few have been tested empirically. Instead, Freud relied on his considerable knowledge of medicine, literature, and anthropology to find symbolic meanings in his patients' symptoms, thoughts, and dreams. If he could weave these symbolic meanings into a plausible explanation for the patient's behavior, Freud considered his hypotheses valid. Experimental verification of psychoanalytic hypotheses was neither necessary nor, according to Freud, possible. The psychoanalytic approach to developing and validating a hypothesis is illustrated by one of Freud's best-known case studies, a person known today as the Rat Man (Freud, 1909/1959c).

Freud's patient was a well-educated, aristocratic young military man who had suffered from various anxieties since childhood. In the years preceding his visit to Freud, the man's problems had become much worse. He feared that some harm would come to his father (even though he was long dead) and also to the woman he loved. The young man found it nearly impossible to keep these fears out of his mind. He considered killing himself by cutting his throat with a razor—an impulse that he had thus far managed to resist.

Freud gave his patient his standard free-association instructions:

> I made him pledge himself to submit to the one and only condition of the treatment—namely, to say everything that came into his head, even if it was *unpleasant* to him, or seemed *unimportant* or irrelevant or *senseless*. (p. 297, italics in original)

The young man described being on a recent military exercise when he heard the apocryphal story of a prisoner who was stripped naked, tied face down, and tortured by having a large pot of rats turned upside down over his buttocks. Imagining the rats eating their way through the prisoner's anus, the young man got the idea that this torture was happening to his dead father and to the woman he loved. Time and again, he would see a mental picture of his father and the woman being devoured by the rats. He tried to avoid these recurrent images by castigating himself ("Whatever are you thinking of?"), but this provided only temporary relief.

Ultimately, the man convinced himself that the fate of the woman, and his dead father, depended on his repaying a debt (that he did not actually owe) to a fellow soldier. He became obsessed with paying this nonexistent debt, compelled by his belief that this was the only way to ensure the safety of his father and of the woman he loved. When the other soldier refused to accept money that he was not owed, the young man sought Freud's help. His plan was to obtain a medical certificate stating that his health required the other soldier to accept payment. Freud refused to play along, insisting instead that his patient continue his free associations. Eventually, the young man described how he was supposed to marry a wealthy cousin and establish

> a business connection with the firm [which] would offer him a brilliant opening in his profession. The family plan stirred up in him a conflict as to whether he should re-

main faithful to the lady he loved in spite of her poverty, or whether he should follow in his father's footsteps and marry the lovely, rich, and well-connected girl who had been assigned to him. And he resolved his conflict, which was in fact one between his love and the persisting influence of his father's wishes, by falling ill; or, to put it more correctly, by falling ill he avoided the task of resolving it in real life. (p. 336)

The illness that the young man used to avoid making a choice took the form of obsessions (recurring thoughts) and compulsions (ritualistic behaviors). For example, as the patient and his "lady"

> were sitting together during a thunderstorm, he was obsessed, he could not tell why, with the necessity for *counting* up to forty or fifty between each flash of lightning and its accompanying thunderclap. On the day of [his lady's] departure he knocked his foot against a stone lying in the road, and was *obliged* to put it out of the way by the side of the road, because the idea struck him that her carriage would be driving along the same road in a few hours time and might come to grief against this stone. But a few minutes later it occurred to him that this was absurd, and he was *obliged* to go back and replace the stone in its original position in the middle of the road. (p. 327)

To explore the relationship between the young man's problems and his obsession with rats, Freud asked him to free-associate. According to Freud,

> rats came to have the meaning of *"money."* The patient gave an indication of this connection by reacting to the word *"Ratten"* [rats] with the association *"Raten"* [installments] . . . When . . . I told him the amount of my fee for an hour's treatment, he said to himself . . . "So many florins, so many rats." Little by little he translated into this language . . . his father's legacy . . . the . . . request to pay him [the fellow soldier] back . . . [all] served to strengthen the money significance of rats. . . . (p. 350)

To elucidate further the symbolic meaning of rats, Freud drew on his knowledge of literature, science, and philosophy. He used the Rat-Wife in Henrik Ibsen's play *Little Eyolf* (and *The Pied Piper of Hamelin*) to show that rats can represent children. He cited Goethe's *Faust* to show that rats can also represent oneself ("For in the bloated rat he sees a living likeness of himself"). At various points, he quoted Shakespeare, Socrates, the philosopher Schopenhauer, and anthropological studies of the Southern Slavs. Readers of the case study cannot help but be impressed by the range of Freud's references.

In the end, Freud attributed his patient's problems to an ambivalent relationship with his father, who once beat him for biting someone and who was also a heavy gambler. (The young man referred to his father as a *Spielratte*, or play-rat.) As a young man, Freud's patient often wished for his cruel father's death, and when his father actually died, the young man felt responsible. (For parallels with Danielle, see Document 2.2.) The man's obsessions and compulsions were manifestations of his unconscious hatred for his father. His impulse to commit suicide was both a way of punishing himself for hating his father and, at the same time, escaping from responsibility. After 12 months of analysis and interpretation, Freud reported that his patient's obsessions and compulsions disappeared. Unfortunately, the young man died soon after, in World War I.

DOCUMENT 2.2

Thematic Apperception Test (TAT) Story Produced by Danielle for Her Psychological Assessment

> This is a young girl and, I think, what looks like a ghost behind her. Let's see, the ghost is haunting her. She had something to do with the ghost's death. Maybe she even killed him, or maybe she didn't really kill him, but she wanted him to die. Now she is haunted by the ghost because she feels guilty about his death. I think the dead person is probably a relative.

Dr. Berg's interpretation: Danielle may have sometimes wished that her father would be punished, perhaps by death, for the way he treated her. When this wish came true, she may well have blamed herself, not only for his death, but for his sexual abuse as well. She turned her anger on herself, and her suicidal impulses may be motivated, at least in part, by a desire to punish herself for the death of her father. ∎

Were Freud's interpretations correct? This question is not easily answered. As we have already seen, Freud considered psychoanalytic hypotheses verifiable only within clinical sessions. His yardsticks for validity were plausibility and internal consistency. In other words, as long as his interpretations appeared plausible, and did not contradict one another, he considered his theories valid. In Freud's hands, psychoanalysis became a "closed" system, justified by its own rules and not open to external evaluation or experimental investigation. Its explanations of behavior were all *post hoc* (after the fact). Because it made no predictions, and therefore could not be disconfirmed, many psychologists rejected psychoanalysis as more a matter of faith than science.

Psychoanalytic Paradigm: Current Status

All scientists who work in the field of abnormal psychology, whichever paradigm they favor, are indebted to psychoanalysis for establishing the legitimacy of psychological theories about—and treatments for—behavior disorders. Those who suffer from psychological disorders also owe psychoanalysis a debt of gratitude. By providing an explanation and a treatment for psychological disorders, Freud gave sufferers hope and dignity. He also changed the way we think about both normal and abnormal behavior. Today, almost all psychologists accept the importance of childhood experiences, and few deny the existence of unconscious motivation. Moreover, most psychologists believe, along with Freud, that behavior disorders are not mysterious ailments that affect certain weak people but the unhappy outcome of the anxiety and conflicts that affect us all.

Of course, any theory that tries to explain all of human behavior has set itself an ambitious goal. It is probably not surprising, therefore, that psychoanalysis has not been entirely successful. There is much that the theory cannot explain. Does this mean that psychoanalysis should be dismissed from modern psychology? Not necessarily. Although it may not explain *everything*, psychoanalysis may still be valuable—provided that it explains *something*. It is on this second point that opinions differ.

Critics argue that psychoanalysis is too vague to be of any scientific value. This is not entirely fair. It is true that psychoanalytic concepts are abstract and unobservable, but this is not unusual; all theoretical concepts are abstract and unobservable. Even physics, the hardest of sciences, relies on unobservable concepts such as gravity to explain natural phenomena. As long as they can be reliably inferred from observable phenomena, there is nothing inherently unscientific about nonobservable concepts. A second criticism is that psychodynamic theorists rely largely on case studies to support their theories. This was certainly true of Freud, who based his theories on a small number of cases and who argued that psychoanalytic theory could only be "tested" in the clinic. We must, however, distinguish between Freud and psychoanalysis. Although Freud may not have thought it necessary to do so, psychoanalytic hypotheses can be subjected to experimental test. Freud's reluctance to conduct objective experiments is a reflection on him, not his theory.

This brings us to the crucial question. Does psychoanalysis lead to clear-cut, testable hypotheses? Here is where the theory often fails. Many of its explanations and hypotheses are untestable. As an example, consider this explanation of enuresis (bed-wetting) by a neo-Freudian:

> Infantile (nocturnal) enuresis is a sexual discharge. Urinary excretion originally served as an autoerotic activity which gave the child . . . satisfaction . . . the enuresis represents a substitute and equivalent of suppressed masturbation. . . . (Fenichel, 1946)

Can you think of any observations that could prove or disprove Fenichel's hypotheses (that urination is erotic; that enuresis is a substitute for masturbation)? No? Well, you are in good company. Most psychologists find themselves similarly unable to think of ways to test this and many other psychoanalytic hypotheses. Because most psychoanalytic hypotheses are not testable scientifically, psychologists do not consider the theory to be scientific. Partly in reaction to psychoanalysis, psychologists sought to develop a paradigm that was both psychological in content and testable scientifically. The result was the behavioral paradigm discussed next.

BEHAVIORAL PARADIGM

Behaviorism is not a specific theory; it is an umbrella term for a group of interrelated ideas. Nevertheless, as a general worldview, the behavioral paradigm represents the major alternative to psychoanalytic theory. Unlike psychoanalysis, the behavioral paradigm did not develop from clinical observations; it was born and raised in the psychological laboratory, and it was developed to answer rather different questions.

Behavioral Paradigm Question 1: What Are the Basic Elements of Behavior?

It is usually agreed that the first experimental psychology laboratory was established by the German philosopher and psychologist Wilhelm Wundt (1832–1920) at Leipzig University in the 1880s. Experimental psychology became popular almost immediately, and, by the turn of the century, laboratories had been established at universities around the world. The first experimental psychologists were mainly structuralists. Their interest was in the internal structure of what they called the mind or, as it is known today, consciousness. Subjective impressions were their raw data, and introspection (subjective reporting on the contents of one's own thought) was their preferred technique. A typical structuralist study required people to introspect about the sensations produced by different stimuli, colors, for example. Most reported that purple produced both blue

The German philosopher and psychologist Wilhelm Wundt (1832–1920), standing in the center behind the table, set up the first experimental psychology laboratory to test how the mind works.

and red sensations. Experimenters then asked people whether purple is more *bluish* than *reddish*. They could not agree. Some thought purple was more blue; others thought it was more red. Arguments about whether purple is more bluish than reddish raged in the psychological literature, but they were never resolved because experimenters had no way of deciding which subjects were correct. After a while, researchers gave up, and structuralism was replaced by functionalism.

The functionalists believed that psychology should forget about the elements of the mind and focus on what the mind does, that is, on perception and cognition. Although their emphasis on function heralded the modern era in experimental psychology (most modern psychologists are concerned with function), the functionalists did not have the opportunity to map out a complete research program of their own. Before they could get one under way, their dominant position was usurped by the school of psychology known as behaviorism.

The term *behaviorism* was coined by a functionalist with interests in animal behavior, John B. Watson (1878–1958). Watson's *Psychology as the Behaviorist Views It* was a manifesto for a new type of human psychology. He rejected all previous psychological theories as subjective, speculative, and "mentalistic." Psychology, Watson argued, should not be concerned with thoughts or sensations but with behavior—the observable activities of animals and human beings. His belief that psychology could safely ignore consciousness is not difficult to understand. He studied animal learning, a field in which consciousness was, at the time at least, a largely unnecessary construct. Interestingly, despite his back-

In his experiments with the salivary response of dogs, Ivan Pavlov (1849–1936) discovered the conditioned reflex.

ground in animal psychology, Watson denied that in-born instincts (or other genetic traits) are important determinants of behavior. All behavior, he believed, was learned through experience.

Psychology as the Behaviorist Views It was a philosophical work, and not entirely original. Many of its ideas were taken from 18th-century philosophy, and its basic learning theory came directly from pioneering work done in Russia on the conditioned reflex.

The Conditioned Reflex   Although many came before him, the person most associated with the modern concept of the conditioned reflex is the Russian scientist Ivan P. Pavlov (1849–1936). Pavlov was a physiologist whose work on the circulatory and digestive systems won him the Nobel Prize in 1904. The next year, while involved in a research program designed to test Sechenov's ideas about the ways in which reflexes develop, Pavlov conducted one of the most famous series of experiments in psychology.

During his work on the digestive system of dogs, Pavlov found that puppies are born with an innate salivation reflex that is set off by the sight of food. As a physiologist, he knew that nerve fibers convey information about food in the mouth to the brain, which, in turn, triggers the production of saliva. As Pavlov, and every other dog owner, had noticed, animals also salivate when they simply see food, even if it is not placed in their mouths. Food that is only seen, but not tasted, cannot stimulate the mouth's nerve fibers, so there must be some other explanation for why dogs salivate. Pavlov's theory made use of the *psychic reflex*. Through experience, animals learn to associate the sight of food with food in their mouths. Eventually, the sight of food produces the same salivary response as real food in the mouth.

Pavlov rejected introspection and decided to study animal behavior the same way he studied physiology, objectively. He began by surgically redirecting a dog's salivary gland from inside to outside the animal's mouth. This allowed him to measure with great accuracy the amount of saliva the dog secreted. Using an elaborate apparatus (Figure 2.7), he rang a bell and measured the amount of saliva produced (none in the beginning). He then began following the bell with food. As expected, the food triggered the production of saliva. After repeating this procedure several times, Pavlov rang the bell on its own. This time, the dog produced a little saliva. After a few more trials in which the bell and food were paired, Pavlov again presented the bell on its own. This time the salivary response was stronger. By alternating paired and unpaired trials, Pavlov showed how a bell, which formerly elicited no saliva at all, could come to elicit considerable saliva.

This simple demonstration (no control groups or elaborate statistics) revolutionized psychology. Pavlov had showed how new reflexes are formed by association with innate ones. He went on to explore the implications of his deceptively simple finding while at the same time elaborating a technology he called conditioning. Conditioning requires a neutral stimulus (the bell, in his case), which is known as the **conditioned stimulus,** or **CS.** At the outset, the CS produces no response other than curiosity. This contrasts with the **unconditioned stimulus,** or **UCS** (the food), which automatically produces the **unconditioned response,** or **UCR** (salivation). The UCS and UCR are *unconditioned* because no training is required to produce a connection between them. By pair-

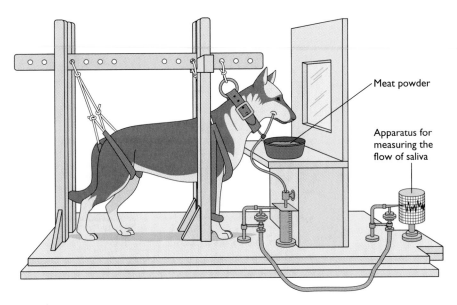

FIGURE 2.7 **Pavlov's Conditioning Apparatus**

ing the CS and the UCS, the CS eventually comes to elicit the **conditioned response,** or **CR.** The CR is similar but rarely identical to the UCR. For example, Pavlov's dog always produced more saliva in response to the food than to the bell, even after many pairings. (See Figure 2.8 for a schematic outline of Pavlov's famous experiment.)

Pavlov went on to show that conditioning works with practically any neutral stimulus or innate reflex, even an unpleasant one. For example, a mild electric shock applied to an animal's leg produces an innate reflex—withdrawal of the leg. A neutral CS (say, a bell), if paired with the shock a sufficient number of times, will eventually come to elicit the same response. Moreover, the animal's fear of being shocked (manifested by heavy breathing, barking, and sweating) also becomes associated with the CS, and it will show its fear every time it hears the bell. Pavlov's work, especially the idea that fear can be conditioned, made a great impression on John Watson, who was trying to convince his fellow psychologists that behaviorism was a viable paradigm for psychology. For Watson, conditioning not only offered a research program and a research method, it also offered a way to demonstrate behaviorism's superiority to psychoanalysis.

Behavioral Paradigm Question 2: Can Psychological Symptoms Be Learned?

In 1909, Freud published one of his most famous case studies, the *Analysis of a Phobia in a Five-Year-Old Boy,* better known as the case of Little Hans (Freud, 1909/1959a). When Hans was 8 years old, he developed an unreasonable fear, a phobia, of horses. He was afraid that one might bite him, and he refused to leave his house for fear of encountering a horse. Freud noted that Hans described his father in the same way he talked about horses, referring to both as "proud" and "very white" and on one occasion asking his father not to "trot" away. Another similarity: Hans's father had a black beard and wore glasses, and Hans particularly feared white horses with black mouths and blinkers. Finally, Hans was fond of crawling into his mother's bed when his father was away. Based on this information, Freud concluded that Hans's fear of horses was a symbolic representation of his real fear, his father. According to Freud, Hans was sexually attracted to his mother and jealous of his father, whom he viewed as a rival for his mother's affections (the Oedipal conflict). These hostile feelings were threatening to Hans; after all, his father was much bigger and stronger than he was. Thus, he protected himself by displacing his unwanted feelings onto horses. For Freud, most phobias are ultimately traceable to such underlying conflicts.

Watson was skeptical. He believed that Freud had ignored relevant data. Specifically, in a letter to Freud, Hans's father had mentioned that his son had once witnessed an accident in which large horses pulling a loaded wagon were thrown to the ground, where they flailed their legs and cried until they were rescued. Watson believed that this experience could have produced the boy's fear through Pavlovian conditioning. Along with his assistant, Rosalie Rayner, Watson set out to prove that behaviorism was superior to psychoanalysis by showing that conditioning alone can produce a phobia in a young child.

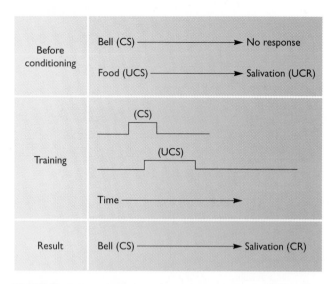

FIGURE 2.8 **A Schematic Outline of Pavlov's Experiment.** *Before training, the food alone elicits salivation. During learning, the bell and the food are paired. After training, the bell alone is sufficient to elicit salivation.*

John Watson, the founder of behaviorism, and Rosalie Rayner showed that a phobia can be induced by conditioning rather than by unconscious conflicts, as Freud theorized. They startled Little Albert, an 11-month-old, with a loud noise whenever they showed him a white rat; eventually, they claimed, he generalized his fear of the rat to all furry objects.

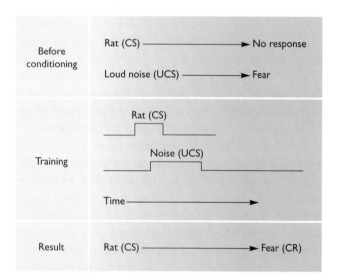

FIGURE 2.9 **A Schematic Outline of Watson and Rayner's Experiment.** *Before training, the noise alone elicits fear. During learning, the rat and the noise are paired. After training, the rat alone is sufficient to elicit fear.*

Watson and Rayner's experimental subject was an 11-month-old infant they deliberately called Little Albert so that he would be compared with Freud's patient Little Hans. Their technique is depicted in Figure 2.9. They startled Albert with a loud noise (the UCS) while he played with a small white laboratory rat (the CS). Before the experiment, Albert liked playing with the rat, but after several pairings of the rat and the noise, Albert no longer wanted anything to do with the animal.

Showing him the rat, even without any accompanying noise, was enough to make him afraid (the CR). His conditioned fear "generalized" beyond the rat to include other furry objects (such as a sealskin coat). Watson and Rayner (1920) concluded that phobias were not the result of unconscious conflict but of conditioning.

In reality, Watson and Rayner's results were more equivocal than they acknowledged. According to Watson and Rayner's own description, Albert showed no fear if he was permitted to suck his thumb when the rat was around, a strange sort of phobia. It is also not clear whether his "fear" really generalized to furry objects such as the sealskin coat. Watson and Rayner's descriptions were crude at best, and the only evidence they provided for the generalization of Albert's fear to the sealskin coat was that the baby "fretted" when they showed him the garment. (Whether Albert would have also fretted when shown a cloth coat was never tested.) Most troubling of all is the failure of other experimenters to replicate Watson and Rayner's results (B. Harris, 1979). Despite these weaknesses, Watson and Rayner's paper stirred psychologists' imaginations. Many came to believe that neurotic symptoms could be produced, and perhaps even cured, by conditioning.

Operant Conditioning   Whereas psychoanalysis viewed behavior as driven by internal emotions, drives, desires, and conflicts, Watson's human being was essentially an empty "black box." Watson believed that thoughts, feelings, and even neurophysiological processes could be safely ignored and that an independent science of be-

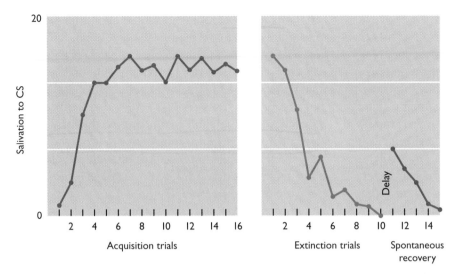

FIGURE 2.10 **Acquisition and Extinction of an Operant.** *The left-hand graph depicts the acquisition of a conditioned response. Drops of saliva produced to the CS (prior to the presentation of the UCS) are plotted on the vertical axis; the number of conditioning trials appears on the horizontal axis. The CR gradually increases until it tops out at about 12 drops of saliva. After 16 conditioning trials, the experimenter switches to extinction. The results appear in the right-hand graph. Note that the CR gradually decreases to zero but then recovers when testing begins again after a delay.* From: S. Schwartz (1986, p. 21).

havior could be developed solely around observable stimuli and responses. In his view, complicated behaviors, such as those performed by a rat navigating its way through a laboratory maze, are made up of a chain of simple stimulus-response (S-R) reflexes, with each response serving as the stimulus for the next one. The job of psychology, according to Watson, is to study these (S-R) units, to describe how they are formed, how they are organized into chains, and how they may be altered. The black-box approach to psychology reached its height in the work of B. F. Skinner (1904–1990), who sometimes seemed to argue not only that cognitive processes should be ignored but that they do not even exist. According to Skinner, thoughts, ideas, feelings, opinions, and even free will are simply convenient fictions; all behavior is controlled by the stimulus environment in which the organism lives.

Skinner identified two types of conditioning: the Pavlovian type, which he called respondent (also known as **classical conditioning**), and his main interest, **operant** (or instrumental) **conditioning.** Operant conditioning derived from the work of Edward L. Thorndike (1874–1949), whose interest was animal learning. Thorndike observed that animals seemed to learn tasks by "trial-and-error." To escape from a special laboratory box, for example, they might try pushing on a door, pulling a handle, jumping onto shelves, and so on. In the beginning, animals try a variety of ways to escape from the box. Behaviors that lead nowhere are abandoned, but those that move the animal closer to its goal are repeated. Thorndike called this tendency to repeat behavior that leads to favorable outcomes the "law of effect." Skinner refined and extended Thorndike's law of effect to create a technology of operant conditioning. Specifically, he showed how operants (emitted behaviors) that are followed by reinforcing (rewarding) consequences are likely to be repeated, whereas those that lead to unpleasant consequences are likely to be abandoned. By repeating reinforced behaviors that are instrumental in helping it to achieve its goal, the animal learns to escape from the box.

Skinner ingeniously exploited the power of operant conditioning. For example, he taught a pigeon to play ping-pong by first reinforcing the bird (giving it food) for picking up a paddle. Once the bird had learned this operant well, Skinner withheld reinforcement until the bird pointed the paddle toward the ball. This gradual shaping process, in which successive approximations to the desired response were rewarded, continued until the bird was able to hit the ball with the racket. By teaching a pigeon to respond differently to different stimuli, Skinner (1976) also showed how a pigeon could learn to guide a missile.

Once learned, an operant must continue to be reinforced (although not on every occasion), or it will gradually disappear, or extinguish (Figure 2.10). The same thing occurs in classical Pavlovian conditioning when a CS is repeatedly presented without the UCS (the CR gradually disappears). Extinction is not the same thing as forgetting. If subjects are removed from the experimental environment for a rest, they are likely to show the conditioned behavior again on their return. Pavlov called this phenomenon spontaneous recovery. Both he and Skinner concluded that conditioned behavior can be temporarily inhibited without being forgotten. Skinner applied this concept to punishment, which he differentiated from negative reinforcement. The latter refers to the removal of a noxious stimulus on the emission of an operant (stopping a loud noise contingent on a subject's performing the desired behavior, for example). Punishment, on the other hand, refers to following a behavior with a noxious stimulus (scolding a child for misbehaving, for instance). Whereas negative reinforcement leads to learning, Skinner argued that punishment results in only a temporary inhibition of behavior. As soon as the punishment is removed, the behavior returns. (More recent studies have challenged this view; Hilgard & Bower, 1975.)

In Skinner's hands, operant conditioning proved a powerful model for explaining some types of behavior disorders. He showed how partial reinforcement schedules (in which operants are reinforced only part of the time) can produce pathological gambling (the gambler does not expect to be reinforced each time). Similarly, compulsive behavior (checking the stove, lights, and locks several times before leaving the house) may be maintained over a lifetime by once in a while finding the stove on or a door unlocked. Skinner also showed how new stimuli can take on reinforcing qualities by being associated with **primary reinforcers** such as food. Despite Skinner's ingenuity, neither operant nor classical conditioning can account for all learned behavior. Consider typing, for example. We do not teach students to type by pairing key strokes with unconditioned stimuli, nor do we encourage students just to hit keys at random, waiting for reinforcement to tell them which key strokes they should repeat. No, we ask students to learn by observing and copying what the typing teacher does. Learning by observation is known as **modeling.**

Modeling   Modeling is a type of indirect conditioning (Bandura, 1986). To take a simple example: A child who observes a friend getting her way after throwing a temper tantrum might learn to behave similarly. In conditioning terminology, the observing child's tendency to throw a temper tantrum is vicariously reinforced by seeing what happened to her friend. (For another example of modeling, see Document 2.3.)

DOCUMENT 2.3

Newspaper Story
One Month After
Danielle's Death

Another University Student Attempts Suicide

by Evan Moran
Daily Staff Writer

Just one month after the tragic death of Danielle Wood, another university student has attempted to take her own life. Millicent Pommeroy was found unconscious in her dormitory room by her roommate, Margaret Sangster, at 11:30 p.m. last night. She was taken to University Hospital, where her condition is described as stable.

Sangster, still visibly shaken this morning, was able to give an account of her grim discovery. "I found Millie in her bed. The lights were on, the radio was playing, and there were open bottles of pills on her desk. I tried to wake her up, but she would not budge. I panicked. I called 911. Thankfully, the paramedics got here fast."

Millicent Pommeroy was not a close friend of Danielle Wood, but the two girls did know one another through class. Sangster reports that Pommeroy had mentioned Wood on several occasions.

"When Danielle Wood died, Millie read everything she could about her in the papers. Millie said she could understand why Danielle might want to take her own life. She seemed to take a special interest in Danielle."

Millicent had recently broken up with her boyfriend of many years, and she was feeling despondent. According to Sangster, Millicent also had problems "at home." She frequently argued with her family about her decision to drop out of her premed course and her lack of attention to her studies.

Dr. Carmel Garza, dean of students, said that the entire campus is in shock over this suicide attempt so soon after the death of Danielle Wood.

"Copycat suicides, in which one person's suicide attempt becomes a model for others, are one of the most tragic aftermaths of suicides. I hope that this will be the final such tragedy on our campus. I want to say to students, please, if you are feeling despondent, contact my office or the Counseling Service. We do not want any more tragedies on campus."

Although modeling can be construed in conditioning terms, it requires some extra assumptions. For example, the observer must *attend* to the model and *understand* the connection between the model's behavior and the contingent reinforcement. The observer must also store what has been learned in *memory* and *recall* the information in the appropriate circumstance. Finally, the observer must be capable of performing the required behavior. Just watching a tennis star win a tournament will not, by itself, make an observer a proficient tennis player. Modeling, in other words, is not a simple mechanical process. Instead, it views the learner as an active participant, and it invokes a number of nonobservable processes (attention, understanding, memory, and recall) that would probably have made Watson feel distinctly uncomfortable. The need to rely on nonobservable processes to explain modeling suggests that Watson and Skinner's strict behaviorism—which ignores all internal causes of behavior—may not be capable of dealing with all of the complexities of human behavior. Another example of why it is often necessary to postulate internal causes of behavior comes from the studies of mediated learning.

Mediated Learning How do we learn to avoid potentially threatening situations? Avoidance learning experiments conducted in the 1930s and 1940s (Miller, 1948, for example) set out to answer this question by studying rats who were given an electric shock. As might be expected, the electric shock produced pain, signs of fear, and efforts to get away from the shock. By pairing the shock (UCS) with the sound of a buzzer (CS), the experimenters conditioned rats to avoid the buzzer. After a few pairings, the sound of the buzzer elicited the same behavior as the shock itself.

This sounds like a typical example of classical conditioning, but there is another step. The experimenters found that the buzzer had become a negative reinforcer. Rats learned new "avoidance" responses (jumping over walls, opening doors) just to turn off the buzzer. To explain why the animals bothered to learn responses just to avoid a harmless buzzer, the experimenters assumed the existence of an internal state called fear. In other words, through classical conditioning, the buzzer had come to induce fear. This fear, in turn, motivated the rats to learn avoidance responses. Put another way, their learning was *mediated* by a desire to escape the internal state of fear produced by the buzzer—hence, the term **mediated learning.** Because this account of avoidance learning is based on both classical and instrumental conditioning, it is known as the **two-process theory** (Mowrer, 1939). Figure 2.11 schematically illustrates it.

Although some have questioned the details of the two-process theory (Makintosh, 1983), the avoidance conditioning paradigm has proved useful in explaining why phobias fail to extinguish even though they are rarely, if ever, reinforced. People who develop a fear of flying (because of some early experience or, more likely, through modeling) feel fear whenever they must travel

According to the theory of modeling, this boy is "fixing" his lawn mower just like his father does because he has attended to his father's model, understood the purpose of his father's behaviors, stored what he learned in his memory, and recalled the information in an appropriate circumstance.

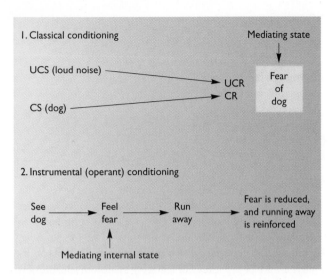

FIGURE 2.11 Two-Process Theory of the Acquisition of Phobias. *The fear response is first learned by classical conditioning and then maintained by instrumental (operant) conditioning (escape from the feared object is rewarded by a reduction in fear).*

a long distance by plane. This fear motivates them to drive or take a train instead of flying. The avoidance response (driving or taking the train) is negatively reinforced (by fear reduction). Because fear reduction is reinforcing, and because avoidance responses keep the phobic person from entering the feared situation, phobias are notoriously resistant to extinction.

By invoking the idea of mediating internal states, behavioral theorists were able to provide a clear alternative to psychoanalytic formulations. Instead of repressed conflicts, fear and anxiety were the result of conditioning. Over the years, behaviorists attempted to reconcile psychoanalysis and behaviorism, with the best-known attempt being Dollard and Miller's *Personality and Psychotherapy* (1950). Although this work has not been influential in either field (psychologists in both camps prefer to stress their differences rather than their similarities), behaviorism has moved a long way from the sole concentration on overt stimuli and responses advocated by Watson and Skinner. Internal processes, including thoughts and feelings, have been incorporated into behavioral research and treatment.

Behavioral Paradigm Question 3: Can Psychological Disorders Be Unlearned?

From the very beginning, Watson was concerned with the practical applications of behaviorism to psychological problems. While on the staff of the psychology department at Johns Hopkins University, he worked closely with the staff of the psychiatry clinic (most of

whom were Freudians), looking for ways to apply behavioral principles to clinical problems. One of the first to take up the challenge was a student, Mary Cover Jones, who in 1924 first produced and then treated a fear of white rats in a young boy named Peter. Jones's treatment consisted of pure classical conditioning. She presented the rat (CS) to Peter and at the same time gave the boy food (UCS). The pleasant sensations produced by the food were eventually associated with the presence of the rat, and the child was no longer frightened.

The idea that fears can be overcome by exposing people to feared situations, while at the same time eliciting an incompatible response (pleasure), was the basis for the treatment known as **systematic desensitization** developed by Joseph Wolpe (1969). In its original form, systematic desensitization requires the phobic person to imagine a series of gradually more frightening scenes (the **anxiety hierarchy**) while at the same time trying to relax as deeply as possible. For example, a person who fears heights might be asked to imagine increasingly frightening scenes involving heights (standing near a window, standing on the roof of a skyscraper, leaning over the edge, and so on). While imagining these scenes, the person attempts to relax all of his or her muscles. Two Pavlovian conditioning processes are supposedly at work here. First, extinction occurs because of the repeated presentation of feared situations (the CS) without any untoward consequences (that is, without a UCS). Second, the technique involves new conditioning. Relaxation replaces fear as the response to feared scenes.

The principle of extinction also found wide applicability in treatment. Knight Dunlap (1932), for example, had people deliberately repeat an unwanted behavior (a facial **tic,** for example) over and over until it extinguished. A modern technique known as flooding (G. Martin & Pear, 1992) deliberately exposes people to aversive stimuli (fear-provoking situations, for example) to facilitate extinction. Aversive conditioning is yet another way of applying classical conditioning principles to treatment. In an early application, people with drinking problems were given alcohol followed by injections that induced vomiting. The result was the classical conditioning of nausea to alcohol (see Kazdin, 1978). (For a rather different application of aversive conditioning, see Highlight 2.2.)

Operant conditioning principles have also been applied to the treatment of behavior disorders. Most often, this involves arranging an individual's environment so that unwanted behaviors (a child's temper tantrums, for instance) are not reinforced but allowed to extinguish while desirable behaviors (cooperative play) are shaped and reinforced. In some circumstances, operant condi-

Is Bed-Wetting a Symptom or an Illness?

One early application of aversive conditioning to problem behavior was Mowrer and Mowrer's (1938) demonstration that conditioning could eliminate bed-wetting. They had bed wetters sleep on a special sheet, which contained electrical contacts. The first drops of urine closed the circuit and set off a bell, which awakened the child. After a while, the children learned to get up on their own. This apparatus was commercialized and sold through a national retailer. It was so successful that it made money despite being sold with a money-back guarantee.

Because they saw enuresis as a symptom of an underlying sexual conflict, Freudian psychologists argued that treating bed-wetting with this apparatus was like bathing a feverish patient in ice water. The patient's fever will diminish, but whatever is causing the fever will remain unaffected. The patient is still sick, so we can expect other symptoms to develop until the underlying illness is cured. Because the cause of bed-wetting—the underlying sexual conflict—remained unaffected by Mowrer and Mowrer's treatment, Freudians believed that other symptoms were sure to develop. This prediction is known as the **symptom-substitution hypothesis.**

Clearly, the psychoanalytic and behavioral paradigms construe the same problem very differently. One sees the etiology of enuresis as an unconscious conflict; the other blames faulty learning. One recommends psychotherapy to resolve the underlying disturbance; the other views conditioning as the treatment of choice. Is there a way to choose between the two? The answer is yes. We can study children treated behaviorally and find out whether they develop new symptoms, as the Freudians predict. Mowrer and Mowrer did just that, and they failed to confirm the symptom-substitution hypothesis. On the contrary, they found that the elimination of bed-wetting produced unexpected positive effects. Brothers and sisters ceased their ridicule; mothers were no longer angry about having to change the sheets. Instead of fostering symptom substitution, elimination of bed-wetting resulted in an *improvement* in overall psychological adjustment. Thus, data collected from behaviorally treated children failed to support the symptom-substitution hypothesis. Such empirical tests of hypotheses are the essence of the behavioral paradigm.

tioning may be used to condition physiological responses through a process known as biofeedback. For example, using suitable equipment, it is possible to provide hypertensive patients with continuous feedback on their blood pressure. Some patients are able to use this feedback to lower their blood pressure (Basmajian, 1989).

The diversity and complexity of **behavior modification** (or **behavior therapy,** as it is sometimes called) are illustrated in discussions found throughout this book. It should be kept in mind that the success of various forms of behavioral treatment does not mean that behavioral explanations for the etiology of various pathological conditions are correct, any more than the success of a particular tranquilizer in treating anxiety means that anxiety is caused by the lack of tranquilizers. (Critical Thinking About Clinical Decisions 2.1 takes a closer look at the flaws in this reasoning.) The successful explanation, treatment, and prevention of behavior disorders requires direct knowledge of the variables responsible for problem behavior.

The Evolution of a Behavioral Hypothesis

Imagine this experiment. A dog is confined in a cage with an electrified floor. The animal receives painful shocks every time electricity flows through the floor, but it cannot escape because there is no way out. Later, that dog and some new ones are placed in another box to eat. This box also has an electrified floor, but this time there is an escape route. In the new environment, a buzzer rings before the electricity is turned on. Dogs who had never been shocked before quickly learn to make an avoidance response. As soon as they hear the buzzer, they stop eating and make their escape. The dog that had been shocked before behaves quite differently. Instead of learning to escape, the animal simply lies down on the grid and passively accepts its fate. According to psychologist Martin Seligman (1975), the previously shocked dog failed to learn to escape because its earlier experience had taught it to be helpless.

There are obvious similarities between the helpless dog and depressed people like Danielle. As had the dog, Danielle had experienced painful events that were beyond her control (abuse by her father, for example). She may have also had a tendency to give up trying in the face of adversity (when she first failed to make the Olympic swimming team, for instance). Seligman did not take the superficial similarities between the helpless dog and people as proof of the hypothesis that depression and suicide are the result of "learned helplessness."

Just Because You Are Dead Does Not Mean You Were Hanged

Because certain behavioral problems (fears, for example) may be induced by conditioning, it is tempting to conclude that all such problems are the result of conditioning. Unfortunately, such a conclusion is unwarranted. It is like arguing that because hanging results in death, all dead people must have been hanged.

Not all psychologists are aware of this logical trap. Consider, for example, the claim that the odd behavior of severely disturbed children results from the failure of their early environment to reinforce proper behavior (Seifert, 1990). What is the evidence for this claim? Well, reinforcement shapes behavior. The children behave strangely, so they must not have been reinforced properly. It should be obvious that this reasoning is circular.

The psychologists are saying that disturbed children act abnormally because they were not reinforced for acting properly, and they know this to be true because the children act strangely.

Because we cannot ethically rear children in impoverished environments, the best way to establish the validity of the reinforcement etiology (or any other explanation for abnormal behavior) is to study children longitudinally. Longitudinal studies examine a group of individuals over an extended period of time. Because they observe the same people at each stage, longitudinal studies provide information about the development of behavior that is not available any other way. By following children over the course of time, we can observe their rein-

forcement history and see which ones become disturbed. Longitudinal studies also permit researchers to test prevention programs. By comparing children exposed to the prevention program with those not exposed, we can determine whether the program reduces the likelihood that a child will become disturbed. Because it requires that subjects be studied over many years, longitudinal research is very expensive. A common cost-saving ploy is to perform the research retrospectively, to explore the pasts of disordered individuals to see what reinforcers they experienced in their youth. Because memories can be selective and biased, however, retrospective studies are poor substitutes for longitudinal research.

He sought corroborating evidence from independent sources.

Seligman found, for example, that shocked dogs have depleted levels of a class of neurotransmitter known as catecholamines. Because catecholamine levels in humans are *increased* by antidepressant drugs, and because antidepressant drugs seemed to reduce learned helplessness in previously shocked dogs, there seemed to be a connection between the physiological state of dogs who had learned to be helpless and the physiological state of depressed people. In laboratory experiments, Seligman found that exposing people to loud, uncontrollable noise led them to feel helpless. These helpless people performed as poorly on cognitive tests as did those who were clinically depressed. These analogue experiments provided further support for the hypothesis that learned helplessness may be responsible for at least some of the behaviors that we associate with depression.

Revisions Based on More Precise Observations Although the learned helplessness theory appeared plausible and was substantiated by corroborating evidence,

it could not account for several well-known characteristics of depression in humans. For example, depressed people tend to blame themselves for their condition. Is it not strange for people who feel helpless to blame themselves? Depressions also tend to dissipate gradually over time. Why should people who feel helpless get better? Why do some not get better? To account for these characteristics, the learned helplessness theory had to be revised. First, a distinction was made between universal and personal helplessness. The former applies to events beyond an individual's control, whereas the latter refers to events that are within a person's control. Both types of helplessness can cause depression, but only the second produces self-blame. Depressions that result from universal helplessness are temporary and dissipate quickly, whereas depressions based on self-blame tend to be more chronic. This modification to the theory helped it to account for more of what was known about depression, but it was still far from complete. It did not account for some of the other symptoms of depression (loss of appetite, sleeplessness) nor for the tendency of some peoples' moods to alternate between depression and elation. We will look at this and related matters more closely in Chapter 8. For now, the important point is that the learned helplessness hypothesis is typical of hypotheses within the behavioral paradigm. Most have to be modified many times to account for experimental results and clinical observations. This is a natural part of their evolution.

Comparison With Psychoanalysis Seligman looked for corroborating evidence from a variety of sources. He also devised experimental tests and interpreted the results in terms of his theory. Perhaps most important, his hypothesis was open to refutation by experimentation. If he had found that loud, uncontrollable noise did not lead to learned helplessness, this would have been strong evidence against his hypothesis. Contrast this with the psychoanalytic approach, which seeks to verify its hypotheses only within the confines of the psychoanalytic setting. Freud viewed suicide as self-punishment for real or imagined sins; he believed that the Rat Man wanted to kill himself because of the guilt he felt concerning his father's death. Freud's only evidence for the validity of this hypothesis was his interpretation of the symbolic connection among rats, the Rat Man's father, guilt, and death. He had no objective measures of guilt, nor did he attempt to find corroboration outside of the therapy. His hypothesis, unlike Seligman's, was essentially immune to refutation. To behaviorists (and to scientists in general), hypotheses that cannot be refuted are, by definition, not scientific. That is why behaviorists have taken every opportunity to put psychoanalytic assertions to empirical test (see Highlight 2.2 for more information).

Behavioral Paradigm: Current Status

From its beginnings barely a century ago, behaviorism has grown to become a major force in modern psychology. Few psychologists today deny the main tenets of behaviorism—the emphasis on objective measurement, the need to put theories to experimental test, the importance of experience, and the crucial role of the stimulus environment in determining behavior. Nevertheless, the explanations of human behavior provided by the behavioral paradigm are far from complete.

For example, behavioral therapists have assumed that all behavior is under the control of external stimuli. Provided with the right stimulus and reinforcer, people can learn just about any behavior. Yet, laboratory studies have repeatedly shown that there are specific constraints on the behaviors that organisms learn. For instance, it is much easier to condition a phobia to a spider

than to a flower (Ohman, 1979). Similarly, inducing nausea following the ingestion of food produces a stronger aversion response than following food with electric shock (Garcia & Rusiniak, 1980). These findings suggest that human beings may be biologically primed to learn certain behaviors. They are not as malleable as Watson considered them to be.

The black-box approach to predicting and controlling behavior leaves little role for events occurring within an organism. Skinner, perhaps the most radical behaviorist, insisted that cognitive phenomena (opinions, attitudes, and so on) were, at best, mere epiphenomena, unimportant by-products of the true causes of behavior. He claimed that cognitive phenomena such as attitudes and opinions are forms of "verbal behavior" controlled by external contingencies in the same way as any other behavior. To anyone other than a staunch Skinnerian, such a radical stance appears absurd. What would have happened, for example, if someone had held a gun to Skinner's head and made him say aloud "behaviorism is rubbish"? Would he have changed his opinion or just his verbal behavior? (This example comes from Chomsky, 1973.) If you agree that his opinion would have remained unchanged, then opinions must be something different from verbal behavior. Clearly, if opinions exist and they affect behavior, we would be foolish to omit them (and other cognitive phenomena) from our theories. In recent years, there have been several attempts to enlarge the behavioral paradigm to incorporate mental states (Dujovne, Barnard, & Rapoff, 1995; Zinbarg et al., 1992). Initially, psychologists retained the main features of the behavioral paradigm. Cognitions were considered mediators to be understood within the context of mediated learning. Gradually, cognitions have taken on an increasingly independent theoretical role. They have become more than simply responses to stimuli; they have become independent causes of behavior. The idea that cognition can cause behavior eventually became the central tenet of the cognitive paradigm.

COGNITIVE PARADIGM

Danielle blamed herself for not making the Olympic swimming team. She felt inadequate and became depressed, perhaps even suicidal. Another unsuccessful swimmer, with a background different from Danielle's, might have responded differently. She might have acknowledged the superior skill of the competitors or blamed the situation ("I am never my best on hot

B. F. Skinner (1904–1990), the most famous behaviorist, focused his research on animals and attempted to show that, with the appropriate reinforcers, any behavior can be learned. He also developed a teaching machine, the precursor of programmed instruction, to apply his behavioral theory to human learning.

days"). Both swimmers may have been equally disappointed about not making the team, but in Danielle's case this disappointment led to self-blame and self-destruction, whereas in the other case it did not. From a strictly behavioral view, the two girls were exposed to exactly the same stimulus event: failing to make the Olympic swimming team. So, why do they respond so differently? According to the cognitive paradigm, the two girls react differently because they place different interpretations on the same event. One considers herself a personal failure and worthless; the other is more philosophical. The cognitive paradigm views such individual interpretations as crucial in determining how people behave.

Cognitive Paradigm Question 1: Can Cognition Be Studied Scientifically?

As we have already seen, the first experimental psychologists were structuralists whose goal was to isolate the basic elements of thought using introspection. Although it took some years, it eventually became clear that stucturalism was a failure. Structuralism was replaced with functionalism. The functionalists changed the focus of

psychology from what thoughts *are* to what thoughts *do*, a more tractable problem for scientific study. The functionalists were soon overshadowed by the behaviorists, however, who went on to dominate psychology for the first half of the 20th century. The behaviorists eschewed all "mentalist" constructs, banishing structuralism, functionalism, and most of psychoanalysis from psychological science. The behaviorists argued that an objective science of behavior could, and should, be built solely on the analysis of stimulus-response relationships.

It was not until the 1950s that cognitive concepts once again began to find their way into psychology journals. This time, however, those interested in cognitive psychology avoided the mistakes of their structuralist and functionalist ancestors. The modern approach to cognition was similar to the method used by the classical geneticists. Before the identification of DNA and other advances in microbiology, geneticists approached their subject entirely from the outside. They crossbred plants and animals, observed their offspring, and tried to infer the biological mechanisms that could have produced the observed variations. The modern cognitive psychologists adopted a similar approach to study cognition. They began by observing how organisms behave in different situations. Thus, a person who looks at a cloudy, threatening sky and reaches for an umbrella is assumed to have formed an *expectation* of rain. This expectation cannot be seen, of course; it is a hypothetical mental entity inferred from observing someone's behavior in a specific situation. By inferring mental concepts from objective behavior, the modern cognitive psychologists turned what was formerly a mentalistic pseudoscience into an enterprise that was just as objective and scientific as behaviorism. In recent years, cognitive studies have dominated experimental psychology. However, only a small portion of cognitive psychology has been applied in the clinic. These clinical applications have centered on four types of cognitions: attributions, appraisals, beliefs, and expectancies.

Cognitive Paradigm Question 2: How Do We Construe Our World?

Attributions are inferences that we make about the causes of events, our own behavior, and the behavior of others (see Fiske, 1992, for a historical review). We make such attributions every day. Say, for example, that you are about to go out for the evening and your partner criticizes your appearance. You ask yourself whether you really do look bad or whether your partner is just being grouchy after a hard day. Perhaps your partner is really

TABLE 2.3 Types of Attributions

	Internal	
	Permanent	**Temporary**
Global	I'm not smart enough to handle college courses.	I had a cold and was feeling awful.
Specific	I've never been good at math.	I didn't know the answer to the first question, and I froze.

	External	
	Permanent	**Temporary**
Global	Essay tests are hard.	With three midterms on the same day, I couldn't cram for them all.
Specific	The teacher liked/ didn't like me.	The test was on the one thing I did/ didn't study.

angry about something else and has picked this way to show it. These are all attributions about your partner's behavior. In the psychology literature, attributions are categorized in three ways: internal or external, temporary or permanent, and specific or global (Table 2.3).

Internal attributions assign the causes of behavior to factors within ourselves, whereas external attributions assign causes to aspects of the environment. Danielle's self-blame is an example of an internal attribution, whereas the other, hypothetical, swimmer's claim that the heat affected her performance is an external attribution. Internal attributions may be permanent ("I failed because I am worthless") or temporary ("I failed because I was ill on that day"). External attributions can also be permanent ("Olympic swimming trials are always held in hot weather") or temporary ("I did poorly because of the heat that day"). Finally, attributions may be specific ("I am not a good swimmer") or global ("I can't do anything right").

People develop characteristic attributional styles. Some regularly attribute their behavior to internal causes, whereas others emphasize external ones (Dodge, 1993). Depressed and suicidal people like Danielle tend to make internal, permanent, global attributions for negative events ("I failed to make the team because I am an undeserving person"). They blame their setbacks on their personal inadequacies and assume they can do nothing to overcome them. The cognitive paradigm views such an attributional style as one cause of depression (Frazier, 1991). Thus, the goal of treatment in the cognitive paradigm is to change a person's attri-

butional style (Alford & Beck, 1997; A. T. Beck, 1991). Document 2.4 shows how Dr. Berg focused on Danielle's negative attributional style after her first suicide attempt. Although the idea that psychological disorders are the result of faulty cognitions seems plausible, it should be noted that the opposite may be equally likely—faulty cognitions may be caused by psychological disorders. Alternatively, both cognitions and disorders could result from the biological causes mentioned earlier.

DOCUMENT 2.4

Transcript From One of Danielle Wood's Cognitive Therapy Sessions

This exchange comes from a therapy session conducted by psychologist Dr. Stuart Berg with Danielle Wood after her first suicide attempt. Note the way Dr. Berg focuses on Danielle's negative attributional style.

DANIELLE: I'm not sure I understand what you mean when you say that I get depressed because of the way I think about things.

DR. BERG: Why do you think you get depressed?

DANIELLE: Well, I think I get depressed when everything goes wrong—for instance, when I practice for a swimming meet and then get sick, or get beaten because of a bad night's sleep. Then, I get depressed.

DR. BERG: How does losing a race make you depressed?

DANIELLE: Well, if I lose, I'll never get to the Olympics.

DR. BERG: So losing can cost you a lot. Still, if losing a race makes people seriously depressed, then wouldn't everyone who loses be depressed? Is that what happened? Was everyone but the winner depressed enough to try suicide?

DANIELLE: No, but maybe it wasn't as important to them.

DR. BERG: OK. Who decides what's important?

DANIELLE: I do.

DR. BERG: Right. And that's why I believe we must look at your way of viewing swimming meets, the way you make winning important, and the way in which losing may affect your chance to be in the Olympics.

DANIELLE: OK.

DR. BERG: The first thing you must see is that the way in which you look at the outcome of a swimming meet affects you; it is your thoughts that trouble you. You lose a race, and you feel depressed. You have trouble sleeping, lose your appetite, and may even wonder whether there's any point in continuing to try.

DANIELLE: I have been thinking about giving up swimming. I thought it would be better not to try than to keep losing.

DR. BERG: Because?

DANIELLE (*tearful*): I'll never make the Olympic team.

DR. BERG: And what does that mean to you?

DANIELLE: That I'm just not good enough.

DR. BERG: And?

DANIELLE: I will always be a failure. I will never be happy. My life will be one big zero.

DR. BERG: How do these thoughts make you feel?

DANIELLE: Miserable.

DR. BERG: So it's the meaning you give to losing a meet that makes you miserable. Your *belief* that you're doomed to failure and will never be happy is what is actually making you unhappy. You've convinced yourself that a failure to get on the Olympic team means that you will never be happy. Each loss simply reinforces this belief. Yet most people in the world never get near an Olympic team, and they still manage to be happy. ■

Appraisals   No one can escape **stress;** it is part of living. To get along in life, we must learn to cope with the many sources of stress (**stressors**) that we encounter every day. In the behavioral paradigm, stress is construed as a characteristic of the environment, a stimulus that gives rise to conditioned and unconditioned responses (collectively forming a stress reaction). Treatment, in the behavioral paradigm, involves helping people to substitute effective coping responses for poorer ones. In the cognitive paradigm, on the other hand, stress is not viewed as something external to the person. Stress is located internally. It arises from a person's appraisal of the environment. The same external environment may be appraised as stressful by one person and not stressful by another.

The best-known studies of stress appraisal have been conducted by Richard Lazarus (1993). Lazarus showed subjects a stressful film depicting, among other things, Australian aboriginal initiation rites in which males had their penises operated on. The film was accompanied by a soundtrack that either denied the threat in what was being shown ("The boys are not distressed by the initiation rite") or emphasized it ("The boys are suffering severe pain"). The soundtrack was designed to affect the way subjects appraised the film. The non-threatening soundtrack was expected to produce a benign appraisal (and, therefore, little stress), whereas the

threatening soundtrack was expected to lead to the opposite appraisal (and considerable stress). This is just what Lazarus found. Those who were told that the boys were feeling pain had faster heart rates, sweated more, and reported more psychological distress than did those who were told that the boys felt no pain. In other words, people's emotional reaction to the film was determined not by the film itself but by their appraisal of the film. This appraisal, in turn, determined how subjects coped with the perceived threat. Those who appraised the film as threatening tried to ignore it or leave the room. Note how Lazarus's experimental method allows him to avoid the criticism leveled at attributions (that disorders cause attributions rather than the other way around). In his experiments, it is clear that appraisals precede and determine stress.

Because the cognitive paradigm views appraisals as determining how people will react, helping people to reach more accurate evaluations of external events is one of its treatment goals. Thus, people who are anxious when speaking in front of audiences may interpret the departure of a member of the audience as indicating that their speech is going badly. Such an appraisal may increase their anxiety even further. This could be avoided, however, by teaching speakers to appraise the situation differently. Perhaps the person who left early had an urgent appointment. In this way, changing interpretations may reduce anxiety about public speaking.

Beliefs   According to psychologist Albert Ellis (1962; Ellis & Dryden, 1997), **beliefs** are long-term ways of thinking about oneself and the world. Unlike appraisals or attributions, beliefs are not specific to a particular social situation; they represent a person's characteristic mode of thinking. Ellis views psychological disorders as largely determined by irrational beliefs like these: It is a dire necessity for an adult human being to be loved or approved by virtually every significant other person in the community; one should be thoroughly competent, adequate, and achieving in all possible respects to consider oneself worthwhile; it is awful and catastrophic when things do not go as one prefers; human happiness is externally caused, and we have no ability to control our sorrows; because something strongly affected one's life at one time, it should always have a similar effect; there is invariably a right, precise solution to human problems, and it is catastrophic if this perfect solution is not found (Ellis, 1962).

Irrational beliefs color the way that people appraise and interpret everyday events. Those like Danielle, who need constant reassurance, continually seek signs of ap-

Albert Ellis, the founder of rational-emotive therapy, believes that psychological disorders are largely caused by irrational beliefs. His approach to therapy focuses on challenging these beliefs rather than on changing behavior.

proval. They are quick to see signs of rejection in others and to consider themselves worthless whenever they fail to live up to their own high expectations. They may mentally castigate themselves, saying to themselves "I am such a failure" (see Meichenbaum, 1977). Ellis's **rational-emotive therapy** is designed to expose and challenge these irrational beliefs. Using a combination of logical argument, modeling, and a variety of other techniques, Ellis attempts to get people to abandon what he calls the unreasonable "shoulds" and "musts" that keep them from leading fulfilling lives (Ellis & Dryden, 1997).

As you can see, Ellis's "beliefs" have much in common with "attributions." When faulty, both may be responsible for psychological disorders. Moreover, like attributions, Ellis's beliefs can just as easily be the *result* of psychological problems as the *cause*.

The Evolution of a Cognitive Hypothesis

Hypotheses, in the cognitive paradigm, are inferences about the type of cognitive mechanism that might account for a pattern of behavior. **Expectancies,** for example, are cognitions about what will happen in the future. They can exert powerful effects on our behavior and on the behavior of those we interact with. (Recall that a researcher's expectancies can even affect the outcome of experiments unless they are conducted double-blind.)

Albert Bandura (1986), whose work on modeling has already been mentioned, believes that expectancies develop from vicarious learning (modeling). Through our own experiences and by observing what happens to others, we learn what to expect in common social situations. For instance, the rude and slightly drunk football player who is rejected by the girl he would most like to date directly experiences the consequences of his behavior (rejection). At the same time, his friends learn what to expect should they behave similarly. Bandura identified two general types of expectancies, outcome and efficacy. An outcome expectancy is a person's belief that a behavior will lead to a particular outcome (asking someone out will lead to a date, for example). Efficacy expectancies are beliefs about one's personal ability to execute a behavior ("I won't have the nerve to ask someone for a date"). If people have low efficacy expectations, they may limit their lives and avoid situations where they expect to fail. (They may not ask for dates, for example.) Those with high efficacy expectations will try and keep on trying. Indeed, they may even try harder when faced with a tough challenge.

Demonstrate That the Variable Has Value in Predicting Behavior Bandura argues that psychological treatments should be focused on raising people's belief in themselves. As a demonstration, Bandura, Adams, and Beyer (1977) studied adults whose fear of snakes had led them to abandon outdoor recreational activities. Some dreamed of snakes, and a few even found their work disrupted. The researchers began by asking the snake phobics to perform a graded series of tasks: look at a caged snake, pet it, hold it, and so on. Few would comply. Some were too frightened even to enter a room containing a caged snake. Not surprisingly, the participants rated their self-efficacy as very low. During the next phase of the research, some participants were gradually enticed into performing at least some of the tasks (touching the snake, for example), while others just watched the therapist "model" the required behaviors. Over time, people in both conditions increased their self-efficacy ratings to varying degrees. The largest increases were made by those who actually performed some of the behavioral tasks. In the final phase of the research, the participants were asked again to perform the various snake-related tasks. Bandura and his colleagues found a strong relationship between self-efficacy ratings and subsequent behavior. Those participants who increased their ratings the most were able to perform the largest number of snake-related tasks. The researchers concluded that improvements in perceived self-efficacy were responsible for the changes in the participants' behavior.

Generalize and Seek Corroborating Evidence   An important part of establishing the value of a hypothesis is to show that it applies in other contexts (that it generalizes). One powerful demonstration of expectancies at work is Rosenthal and Jacobson's (1968) study of schools (which was actually performed before the study by Bandura and his colleagues). Rosenthal and Jacobson told teachers that certain children in their classes were exceptionally bright. Although the children were actually selected at random, they were later found to have excelled in their studies. Somehow, the teachers' expectations that the children would do well affected the way in which they treated the children, which in turn affected their school performance.

Cognitive Paradigm: Current Status

Although the cognitive paradigm developed as a reaction to the narrow views of Skinner and others, it does not represent a radical departure from behaviorism. You may have noted, for example, that the attributional view of depression (considering oneself a habitual failure) has much in common with the behavioral concept of learned helplessness. Both hypothesize that a person's past experience produces a characteristic reaction to life's setbacks—resignation, the feeling that nothing one does will make any difference. This similarity is not accidental. There are at least three crucial ways in which the behavioral and the cognitive paradigms are similar.

First, like behaviorists, those who work in the cognitive paradigm are reductionists (they break complex behaviors down into simpler constituents). Second, like behaviorists, cognitive psychologists stress the importance of objective measures of behavior and of testing theories empirically. Finally, if we construe the stimulus-response relationship (the very essence of the behavioral paradigm) as the relationship between antecedent conditions and behavior, then those working in the cognitive paradigm have exactly the same goals as the behaviorists. Both want to describe, predict, and control the antecedent conditions that determine human behavior.

It is just as well that cognitive psychologists think

like behaviorists because this means the two paradigms can work together. This compatibility is particularly valuable in the clinic, where psychologists usually want to change *both* cognitions and habits. They do this by exploiting the reciprocal relationship between behavior and cognition. Changing behavior can sometimes lead to changed cognitions. Bandura and his colleagues (1977) showed this when they found that the best way to change people's self-efficacy ratings was to get them to engage in specific behaviors (to enter the room containing the snake, for instance). To exploit the reciprocal relationship between behavior and cognitions, cognitive therapists often give clients "homework" assignments in which they are asked to engage in specific behaviors that the therapists hope will change their cognitions. Similarly, behavior therapists may try to change cognitions as a way of getting clients to change their behavior (A. A. Lazarus, 1989). Because behavior therapists routinely include cognitive techniques in their work with clients and cognitive therapists include behavioral approaches in their work, it is probably not accurate to consider behavior modification and cognitive therapy to be totally separate approaches.

The cognitive paradigm has broadened the scope of abnormal psychology, provided psychologists with a richer set of antecedent variables, and given them a wider appreciation for what is meant by behavior (not just overt motor movements but also thoughts). The cognitive paradigm emphasizes the characteristic of human beings that makes us most human, our ability to think. Still, despite its focus on our most human of traits, the cognitive paradigm steers clear of dealing with the larger questions about life—why we live the way we do, what we hope to gain from living, what the meaning of existence is. These are the province of the humanistic paradigm.

HUMANISTIC PARADIGM

In many respects, the humanistic paradigm is a response to behaviorism. In his novel, *Walden Two* (1948/1976), B. F. Skinner described his vision of utopia: a world in which operant conditioning principles were systematically applied to ensure that everyone behaved in socially acceptable, self-fulfilling ways. Years later, in a nonfiction book called *Beyond Freedom and Dignity* (1971), Skinner elaborated on this theme. His argument went something like this: Although we may think that we are the initiators of our own behavior, our free will is just an illusion. Everything that we do is determined by

Behaviorism

reinforcement contingencies. ("A person does not act on the world, the world acts upon him," p. 271.) As long as we are already being controlled by the reinforcement contingencies in our environment, we may as well explicitly use them to produce behaviors that society values. Skinner, you can see, was a strict determinist. Given a particular stimulus situation and a specific reinforcement history, an organism has no choice but to behave in predetermined ways. Ironically, given that they differed in most other ways, Freud's view on the matter of free will was little different from Skinner's. He, too, believed that our behavior is determined by our experiences. We may think that we are in control of our lives, but, in most cases, what we do and how we feel is unconsciously determined by events that took place years before.

To those who work in the humanistic paradigm, strict determinism is an anathema. They view human beings as independent agents who are free to make choices and to control their own destinies. Like the existential philosophers of the post–World War II era, the humanists argue that this freedom is an essential component of mental health (Frankl, 1973; R. May, Angel, & Ellenberger, 1958). People who are (or feel) powerless to control what happens to them will inevitably become psychologically disturbed. The humanists argue that we must resist the social forces that seek to stifle the individual if we are to maintain our freedom, or individuality, and our mental health.

The humanistic paradigm is sometimes referred to as existential-humanistic, but there are some differences between the two points of view (Yalom, 1980). The humanists are optimists. They believe that, given the right conditions, we are all able to lead fulfilling, anxiety-free lives. The existentialists are more pessimistic. For them, anxiety cannot be avoided. It arises from the inevitability of death (or, as they call it, nothingness). We fear death, yet we know it is unavoidable. Unless we find meaning in our lives, we will succumb to **existential anxiety**—the feeling that our lives are purposeless. Despite their differences, both schools are concerned with helping people find meaning in life. Their therapies aim to enhance human dignity by establishing the conditions that allow people to make free choices about their own behavior.

Humanistic Paradigm Question 1: What Is the Proper Subject of Psychology?

In the first American textbook of psychology, published in 1892, William James (1842–1910) devoted consider-

In the early part of the 20th century, William James's (1842–1910) emphasis on the self as psychology's main subject dominated the field.

able space to the self, the repository of conscious experiences that tell us who we are and makes each of us unique. For James, the self (or **self-concept**) was the sum total of our needs, plans, desires, values, perceptions, and memories. Despite its intuitive appeal, the concept of the self was dropped from mainstream psychology during the years of the behavioral ascendancy. In the 1950s, the humanists rediscovered the self and made it a central part of their paradigm. In focusing on the self as psychology's main subject matter, they emphasized the uniqueness of each individual. This was in direct contrast to the behaviorists, who focused on the similarities among people.

According to Carl Rogers (1902–1987), one of the pioneers of the humanistic paradigm, an individual's experiences, feelings, perceptions, and values come together to form the self-concept (Rogers, 1967). Values are acquired in two ways, from experience and from other people. Those that develop from experience contribute to our personal development; they make us who we are. In contrast, values imposed by others seem foreign and prove difficult to integrate into our self-concept. This is especially true when values are adopted just to conform to another's wishes. Say, for example, that we adopt the religious beliefs of our parents and relatives just to please them. To do this we may deny our own private doubts. The result is conflict. Our public self (the one that goes along with our parents) and our real self are not "integrated." Unless we can somehow bring the two together, we will lose sight of our own values and feelings, and we will suffer psychologically.

Humanistic Paradigm Question 2: What Is the Aim of Existence?

The humanists view human beings as naturally cooperative and constructive. They believe that we all strive to reach our maximum potential (to self-actualize) given the right conditions—an integrated self and healthy interpersonal relationships. Negative behaviors, such as cruelty and selfishness, and behavior disorders arise only when the natural drive toward self-actualization is thwarted by stress, unhealthy relationships, or other forces outside the person. Note the stark contrast between this view and Freud's idea that humans are naturally selfish, instinct-ridden, pleasure-seeking, id-dominated creatures who must be socialized by society.

What does it take to become self-actualized? According to the humanists, it takes a positive self-concept, a belief in oneself. How does one achieve this? From the unconditional love that we receive from others. Unconditional love allows us to take chances, to explore options without fear that others will stop loving us. If love is provided only conditionally, we will mold ourselves into the person that our parents and others want us to be in order to ensure their continued love. This could well have been what happened to Danielle. Her psychological problems may have arisen, at least in part, from trying to ensure the love of other people by being a star athlete.

What does a human being need to achieve self-actualization? According to Abraham Maslow (1908–1970), one of the most influential humanists, this simple question requires a complicated answer. Our needs are organized hierarchically (Goble, 1970). At the bottom are the most basic: food, air, water, and sex (Figure 2.12). Next come safety, love, esteem, and so on, until we reach the highest level, which is self-actualization. We begin by fulfilling needs at the lowest level because without air, food, and water, the other needs have little meaning. Once the basics are assured, we seek safety, and then we seek love, and so on. As we gratify our needs at one level, the needs at the next level up become more im-

portant. If, for any reason, our needs at a level are not satisfied, conflict ensues, and progress through the levels is blocked. If, at any time, a need at a lower level ceases to be gratified, we go back (regress) to that level until the need is once again satisfied and progress up the hierarchy can begin again. Those who manage to make it to the top of the needs hierarchy are free and autonomous individuals; they are able to make choices unfettered by unfulfilled needs at lower levels.

Humanistic Paradigm Question 3: How Can We Help People to Self-Actualize?

Humanistic therapists do not typically treat people who are severely disturbed, nor are they concerned with the elimination of specific problems such as phobias. Instead, their focus is on personal growth, on helping people achieve their maximum potential. In other words, the goal of humanistic therapy is not to modify behavior but to set the conditions for people to take responsibility and change themselves.

Carl Rogers's client-centered therapy is probably the best-known humanistic approach to treatment (Rogers, 1951). Rogers believed that therapeutic progress requires that (a) individuals be given **unconditional positive regard** (clients must be respected as people no matter how they behave) and (b) therapists empathize with those they treat (therapists must show that they see the world as the client does). Client-centered therapists achieve rapport with clients, and at the same time demonstrate their empathy, by reflecting back to the client his or her own feelings. This exchange between Danielle's psychologist and her friend Jayne (from Dr. Berg's session with Danielle's friends in Chapter 1) shows this approach clearly:

JAYNE: I don't think I'll ever forgive you, Luke. It's all your fault. You could never make a commitment to her [Danielle]. You kept her on a string, but she was never sure about you. You were not there for her when she needed you.

DR. BERG: Jayne, I can see how angry you are. It's only natural to look for a guilty person. . . .

As you can see, Dr. Berg is not simply repeating Jayne's words. He is trying to distill the meaning and emotion behind what she is saying and to communicate these back to her. As therapy continues, Dr. Berg hopes that Jayne will come to feel that he is concerned about her but not judgmental. In this way, he hopes to give her

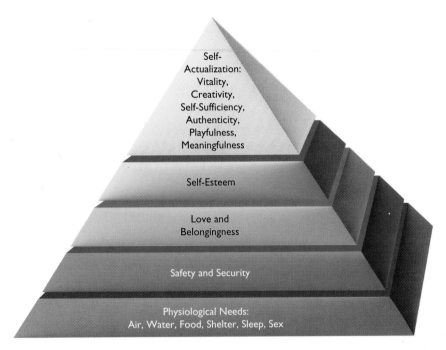

FIGURE 2.12 **Maslow's Hierarchy of Needs.** From: Maslow (1970).

the confidence to face her own guilt over Danielle's death—feelings that would otherwise remain suppressed.

Another humanistic treatment, gestalt therapy, was developed by Frederick (Fritz) Perls (1893–1970). It involves acting out past experiences and even dreams in an attempt to permit the client to reexperience early conflicts and resolve them (Perls, Hefferline, & Goodman, 1973). Logotherapy, developed by Viktor Frankl (1905–), is known for its use of a specific therapeutic technique, paradoxical intention (Frankl, 1978). This involves a deliberate exaggeration of symptoms. Compulsive eaters may be instructed to eat even more; compulsive hand washers, to wash even more often. The therapist does not actually expect these instructions to be carried out. The idea is to show people that they can control their symptoms rather than be controlled by them.

Humanistic Paradigm: Current Status

No example of the evolution of a humanistic hypothesis is included in this section because the humanistic paradigm does not have a specific research program, nor does it have characteristic research methods. In fact, the humanistic paradigm is hardly a scientific paradigm at all. It is more of a philosophical position. Still, the para-

digm's emphasis on the self, on personal responsibility, and on free will, as well as its optimistic view that people are not totally slaves to their earlier experiences, strikes a resonant chord with many people. It is also consistent with the way behavior is viewed in the legal context. Our entire system of law is predicated on the notion that people are responsible for their acts.

Because humanistic psychologists have tended to ignore research, the value of their theories and treatments has rarely been demonstrated empirically. Like Freud, the humanists rely on their observations of people in therapy both for their data and for the proof of their hypotheses. Rogers is the exception. He and his students have devoted considerable effort to assessing client-centered therapy and to studying psychotherapy in general (Rogers, 1954).

The humanistic approach was at its most popular in the 1960s, a time of social upheaval in which the values of society were subject to intense questioning. Since that time, its popularity has declined. The paradigm has been criticized (mainly by behaviorists) as vague, unscientific, and overly simplistic ("touchy-feely" is one of the less kind characterizations). Critics also point out that, despite the vastly different rhetoric, some humanistic ideas are not really very different from behavioral and cognitive ones. Compare, for example, humanists' idea that people develop psychological problems when they do not feel in control of their lives with the behavioral concept of learned helplessness and the cognitive concept of faulty internal attributions.

Finally, psychologists working in other paradigms sometimes express resentment that the label "humanistic" has been appropriated by a single paradigm. Because they try to help others, all psychologists consider themselves humanistic. Even aversive conditioning may be humanistic if it is used to relieve suffering. There is no point in arguing about which paradigm is more humanistic (such an argument will never be settled), but it is worth noting that one of the most human of traits is our need to live and work with other people. The sociocultural paradigm emphasizes the social nature of our behavior.

SOCIOCULTURAL PARADIGM

In 1927, the anthropologist Bronislaw Malinowski, who had previously conducted studies of Australian aboriginal families, published *Sex and Repression in Savage Society*. Malinowski studied the sexual behavior of the Trobriand Islanders (Melanesian islands of Papua New Guinea) seeking evidence for Freud's theory of psychosexual development, which, at the time, was widely accepted. Malinowski found no evidence for an Oedipal conflict among the islanders and concluded that Freud's theory was "culture-bound," that is, that it applied only in Western society. Malinowski was followed by Ruth Benedict (1934) and Margaret Mead (1949), both of whom argued that what is considered normal (or abnormal) behavior depends entirely on one's culture. You might think that judging "savages" by seeing how well they conform to Western theories of behavior is rather arrogant, and you would be correct. Nevertheless, these pioneering studies were a step forward from the 19th-century view that different cultures are simply primitive versions of ourselves. As the linguist Edward Sapir (1929) wrote, "The worlds in which different societies live are distinct worlds, not merely the same world with different words attached" (p. 209). The same is true for people who lived in different historical times.

Over the years, doubts have been expressed about the accuracy of some of the data reported in early anthropological studies (Cote, 1994; Freeman, 1983), and there are strong differences of opinion about the *extent* to which culture affects behavior. Nevertheless, few anthropologists, sociologists, or psychologists working to-

What is considered abnormal behavior varies from society to society. In parts of Mexico, for example, penitentes are a common sight in Easter week processions. This self-flagellation, representing the suffering of Christ, is considered an expression of utmost devotion.

day would deny that culture exerts strong effects on what is considered normal behavior. We human beings, after all, are social animals. We spend our lives in relationships with other people and with society in general. It would be strange indeed if our behavior were not influenced by the culture in which we live. We have already encountered examples of cultural relativity in Chapter 1. The behavior known as amok, for instance (described in Highlight 1.3), was prevalent in feudal Malaysia but died out with the cultural changes instituted by the British. We also saw that suicide has different meanings for Indian widows, Japanese warriors, and American university students. Finally, even the definition of a physical illness depends on the sociocultural context. Low blood pressure, you will recall, is a treatable illness in Germany but not in England.

Although it may seem reasonable to accept that sociocultural factors play a role in creating and maintaining disordered behavior, researchers in abnormal psychology have given the idea little more than lip service. They have downplayed social and cultural differences and emphasized psychological universals—laws that apply to all people. This emphasis is probably inevitable in the biological paradigm, which focuses on the distal biochemical causes of behavior. It is also understandable in the behavioral paradigm, in which researchers are searching for general laws of learning. It is less easy to understand how the cognitive and humanistic paradigms can also ignore culture, because culture has its strongest effects on just the types of behavior that these paradigms are interested in: language, concepts, values, beliefs, attributions, and so on.

Consider, for example, the finding that Puerto Rican and Mexican American populations living in the United States rate themselves as being in far poorer health than do doctors who have given them physical examinations (Shweder & Sullivan, 1993). In contrast, Euro-Americans' self-ratings tend to agree with their doctors' ratings. When they do differ, it is in the other direction—Euro-Americans think they are healthier than do their doctors. Why the difference? One possibility is that members of some Latino ethnic groups find it difficult to say that they feel in good health when another family member is suffering. That is, for some ethnic groups, health is a communal rather than a personal state. The practical significance of this ethnic-group difference for public health surveys (which often simply ask people to rate their overall health) should be obvious. The implications for abnormal psychology are equally important. Our enduring beliefs about ourselves (not just how healthy we are, but our attitudes and values) are influenced by our culture. A science of abnormal psychology built entirely around urban, White, Western, middle-class people is doomed to provide an impoverished, if not incorrect, picture of human behavior.

The Sociocultural Paradigm's Question: How Do Cultural Factors Contribute to Our Understanding of Abnormal Behavior?

Cultural psychology is an interdisciplinary field that includes anthropology, psychology, and linguistics as well as parts of other social and biological sciences such as economics and genetics (Shweder & Sullivan, 1993). It is related to what has traditionally been called cross-cultural psychology (Kagitçibasi & Berry, 1989), but cultural psychology puts greater emphasis on the differences among cultures, whereas cross-cultural psychology tends to focus on the universal psychological principles that apply across cultures.

Both cultural and cross-cultural psychologists are interested in differences in the way abnormal behavior is manifested in different cultures. Too often, however, this interest has led simply to the collection of oddities.

It is easy to be fascinated by the exotic conditions found in different societies. *Koro,* the fear among some Southeast Asian men that their penises will be absorbed into their abdomen; *windigo,* the fear, once found among Algonquin Indian warriors, of being turned into a cannibal; *latah,* imitating the words and movements of others, often accompanied by swearing, found among some Malaysian women; and *kitsunetsuki,* the fear found among rural Japanese of being turned into a fox, are all strange enough to make us curious (Simons & Hughes, 1985; Yap, 1951). But collecting and describing odd illnesses does not do much to advance our understanding. Anyway, odd illnesses are not found only in foreign cultures.

We have odd fears that other cultures do not have (of growing old and ugly, of failure). We even have a condition in our culture, Tourette's disorder, that is similar to *latah* (see Chapter 12). By themselves, these cultural differences are not psychologically significant. People in different cultures also speak different languages, but this does not mean that the cognitive mechanisms underlying the acquisition and use of language differ from one culture to another. Similarly, the existence of cultural differences in behavior tells us little about the way that behavior disorders are acquired, maintained, or treated in different cultures. To advance our knowledge of abnormal psychology, we need to know *how* and *why* different cultures foster different behaviors.

Cultural Stereotypes Intentional weight loss to the point of starvation was given the name anorexia nervosa by an English doctor in 1874. The majority of sufferers are teenage women, and most claim that they are losing weight to improve their appearance. It is alleged that this disorder (which is dealt with in some detail in Chapter 12) is becoming increasingly common in Western society while remaining rare or nonexistent in traditional cultures (Swartz, 1985). Cultural differences are attributed to the increasing preference for thin female figures in Western films, magazines, and advertisements over the past 25 years. You need only compare photographs of the late Marilyn Monroe with today's film stars to see how much our idea of the ideal female form has changed since the 1950s. The idea that a cultural stereotype could produce a life-threatening condition —a condition that is rare or nonexistent in other cultures—indicates the powerful effects that cultural values can exert on behavior. Nevertheless, not all teenage girls are anorexic, and some anorexics are boys.

The standards of attractiveness vary from culture to culture and from era to era. In 1900, the S-shaped corset suppos-edly followed and enhanced the natural lines of the figure. In contrast, in the 1990s, the ideal female figure had barely any curves at all.

As always in abnormal psychology, it is impossible to isolate one single cause for abnormal behavior. Cultural values act along with other forces (genetics and life experiences) to produce abnormal and normal behavior.

Cultural Interpretations   Depressions like Danielle's have inspired a large number of etiological theories. We have already mentioned several—biochemical aberrations, guilt turned inward toward oneself, learned helplessness, negative internal attributions, and discord between one's public self and one's true self. There is one etiological factor that we have not yet mentioned, and that is culture. Despite the universalism implied in the theories that we have discussed so far, depression seems to vary considerably across cultures. Surveying depression in different cultures, Kleinman and Good (1985) found that

> sadness, hopelessness, unhappiness, lack of pleasure with the things of the world and with social relationships has dramatically different meaning in different societies. For Buddhists, taking pleasure from the things of the world and social relationships is the basis of all suffering: a willful dysphoria [depression] is thus the first step on the road to salvation. For Shi'ite Muslims in Iran, grief is a religious experience, association with the recognition of the tragic consequences of living justly in an unjust world; the ability to experience dysphoria fully is thus a marker of depth of person and understanding. Some societies, such as the Kaluli of Papua New Guinea, value

full and dramatic expression of sadness and grieving. (p. 3)

This is consistent with the finding that the same type of stress that leads to depression in Westerners leads to physical complaints in China (Kleinman, 1986). Whether this means that cultures give different emotional interpretations to the same physical state (as in Lazarus's appraisal theory) or that members of different cultures have different physiological reactions to the same emotion remains to be determined (Shweder & Sullivan, 1993). What is certain is that such findings mean that we must qualify the theories of depression that we have discussed so far. Unless the cultural issue is addressed, they will be applicable only in Western cultures.

Acculturation Stress   The United States and other Western countries, such as Canada and Australia, are multicultural societies. More liberal immigration laws have radically altered the ethnic makeup of most large cities. New York City, for example, saw a 20% drop in its non-Hispanic White population in 20 years while at the same time welcoming a large number of people from the Caribbean, Africa, and Asia (Shweder & Sullivan, 1993). New York and other large cities now have tribal associations for Africans with ties back to Africa and temples with direct relationships to Asia. Although many consider cosmopolitan cities more interesting than cities

The process of acculturation—choosing which traditions to keep and which to change—can be stressful for immigrants and refugees. These Muslim women continue to dress in the traditional way—in chadors, long sleeves, and long skirts—while the young man with them has chosen more typical California beach garb.

made up of a single ethnic group, they are also more complicated socially. Ethnic groups tend to cluster into certain neighborhoods and in certain professions. The New York City fire department, for example, is an Irish enclave, whereas people of Puerto Rican descent make up the majority of garment industry workers (Shweder & Sullivan, 1993). Ethnic groups vary markedly in their tolerance for different behaviors. Smoking is more common among Asian immigrants than among White middle-class Americans. Italian Americans are more likely to seek medical care for minor conditions than are people of Irish descent (S. Schwartz & Griffin, 1986). With multiculturalism, it has become difficult, if not impossible, to identify a truly dominant culture whose values and behavior can serve as the baseline for what is "normal."

Recent ethnic immigrants must learn to adapt to their new culture, a process called **acculturation.** Acculturation almost always involves some degree of stress. The amount of stress—as reflected in social and behavioral disorders—depends on the ethnic group (refugees experience more stress than other immigrants), the nature of the larger society (multicultural societies produce less stress than homogeneous societies), and a host of other factors (Kagitçibasi & Berry, 1989). Psychological studies of acculturation have the potential to assist both migrants and the larger society in minimizing the disorders caused by acculturation stress.

Sex Role Stereotypes   Attitudes toward the sexes, and their respective social roles, vary across cultural and so-

cial groups. In traditional societies, for example, women increase in status with age, whereas just the opposite is true in the West (J. K. Brown & Kerns, 1985). Mid-life crises, in which people question the purpose of their lives and sometimes radically change direction, are characteristic of North America but may not exist in the Orient (Ward, 1987, cited in Kagitçibasi & Berry, 1989). We are used to thinking of women as emotional and retiring but of men as stoic and aggressive. In some developing countries these distinctions between the sexes do not exist (Kagitçibasi & Berry, 1989). Sex role stereotyping seems to affect women more than men. For example, when men and women in 14 countries were asked to describe their self-concepts (what they were like) and their ideal self-concepts (the kind of person that they would prefer to be), J. E. Williams and Best (1987) found that men were fairly happy being themselves, whereas women's ideal was more masculine than their real self-concept. Male-dominated cultures not only produce women who are unhappy with themselves, they can also produce prejudice against women, which, in the extreme, can lead to victimization. For an example, see Highlight 2.3.

The Evolution of a Sociocultural Hypothesis

One of the most commonly mentioned sociocultural causes of disordered behavior is unemployment. The negative psychological effects of unemployment were first described in the Great Depression of the 1930s (Bakke, 1934). Because there were no reliable measures of psychological disorders available to researchers in those days, their mental health evaluations were largely impressionistic. This is not an uncommon occurrence in the sociocultural paradigm, where most hypotheses are based, at least at first, on qualitative data. Although these data are sufficient to suggest fruitful hypotheses, qualitative research is not normally sufficient to demonstrate a relationship. To measure correlations, we need numbers. So, the next step was to use quantitative scales of psychological health to assess the effect of unemployment on mental health. Survey research of this type is a common research tool in the sociocultural paradigm. Such research has confirmed that job loss ordinarily leads to a deterioration in psychological health (Feather, 1990).

Descriptive Data Collection   Interestingly, the negative effects of unemployment on mental health are highly variable. They depend on the unemployed person's age,

Witches and Victimization

In 1484, Pope Innocent VIII issued a papal bull urging the courts of the Holy Inquisition to go on a witch hunt. To help the ecclesiastical judges identify those who were "abandoning themselves to devils" (quoted in Szasz, 1971, p. 7), two medieval priests, Jakob Sprenger and Heinrich Krämer, published a manual for witch hunters called the *Malleus Maleficarum* ("The Hammer of Witches"). According to the *Malleus*, women are the source of all evil because of their insatiable carnal lust (Sprenger & Krämer, 1486/1948). Their rapacious sexuality makes them easy prey for the devil. This pseudoscientific nonsense was then used as a justification for the persecution of women. Before the *Malleus*, witches came in both sexes. After the publication of the *Malleus*, it was mainly women who were persecuted for witchcraft. Torture was used to make them confess their sins. Those who still refused were usually banished; some were burned at a stake. Although the practice of witch-burning was never as widespread as some present-day accounts would suggest, witches were burned on and off for hundreds of years, and the practice did not completely die out in Europe until the 18th century.

According to the *Malleus*, witches possess the devil's mark, an area of the skin that is insensitive to pain. To search for the devil's mark, witch hunters stuck pins into the bodies of suspected witches. Because numbness is also associated with hysteria, some historians have claimed that the witches suffered from hysteria. They were persecuted, not because they were women, but because the superstitious, ignorant, and cruel people of the 15th century feared

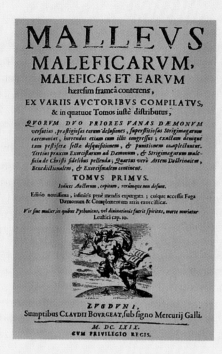

After the publication in the late 15th century of Malleus Maleficarum, *a manual for witch hunters, only women were accused of being witches. This manual used pseudoscientific stereotypes about women's sexuality to justify persecuting women who violated social norms.*

and loathed the devil-possessed mentally ill (Zilboorg & Henry, 1941).

Are these interpretations justified? Was demonology a commonly accepted explanation for hysteria? Were the mentally ill persecuted? Probably not. There is considerable evidence that medieval society viewed mental illness as something quite different from witchcraft. For example, mental hospitals were established during the Middle Ages throughout Europe and England. The grounds for admission were similar to those used today (dangerousness, an inability to look after oneself). Being possessed by

the devil was *not* one of the reasons for admitting people to these institutions. At medieval court proceedings held to determine whether a person was "sane" and able to function independently in the community, demonic possession was almost never raised as an issue, nor do records kept at the time refer to demonic possession or even sin as causative factors in abnormal behavior (W. B. Maher & Maher, 1985).

Demonology was never the dominant theory of abnormal behavior in the Middle Ages. Witches were persecuted because they questioned established authority or, more often, because they annoyed men. For some reason, the idea that witch trials were a way to keep women in line has never appealed to psychologists, who have grasped at other explanations, no matter how far-fetched. For example, Caporael (1976) has suggested that the Salem, Massachusetts, witch trials of 1692 were instigated by witnesses who were experiencing delusions and hallucinations brought on by ergot, a parasitic fungus that grows on grains and causes hallucinations. This theory, although clearly in the spirit of the modern biological paradigm (Caporael's paper was published in the prestigious journal *Science*), cannot explain one crucial fact. If the whole episode was the result of poisoned cereal or bread, why were three quarters of the accused witches women? Could part of the answer be that many of these women had violated social norms by inheriting property, having illegitimate children, or simply having sharp tongues? Could it have something to do with all of the judges being men?

According to the sociocultural paradigm, unemployment affects people differently, depending on how they meet their psychological needs after they lose their job.

gender, income, social support, interest in work, and the length of time that the person is out of work (Ezzy, 1993). Thus, the longer a person is out of work, the more likely he or she is to suffer psychological effects. Of course, this is only a correlational relationship. It is also possible that the causal direction is the other way round—people who have psychological problems take longer to find jobs. Because we cannot ethically perform experiments to find out (we cannot pick people at random, throw them out of work, and see if they develop psychological disorders), we must seek confirmation for our hypotheses in the overall pattern of observed relationships. For example, the finding that people who are committed to their jobs are more likely to develop disorders when they lose them than are those who hate their jobs suggests that it is losing the job that causes the disorder rather than the opposite.

Although these various relationships are clearly important, by themselves they are only descriptive. They tell us how different people react to unemployment, but not why. This descriptive phase is a natural first step in the evolution of a sociocultural hypothesis. It supplies the raw materials for the next stage, which involves providing a theoretical explanation for the observed relationships.

Sociocultural Explanations   Like most theories, sociocultural ones tend to evolve over time (see Ezzy, 1993, for a review of theories). One of the earliest theories of the effects of unemployment described the unemployed as passing through a series of stages. First they experience shock; then they attempt to find another job. When this fails, they become distressed, and finally they become resigned and apathetic. As you can see, this theory is little more than a description of the behavior of the unemployed; it does not try to explain why the behavior occurs. Nevertheless, it is often necessary to begin with such descriptive theories because they provide the necessary framework for the more complicated ones that follow.

One way of explaining the effects of unemployment on the individual is to examine what the unemployed person loses. Losing one's job not only means losing income, it also means losing contact with coworkers, losing

Can Surveys Be Trusted?

Sociologists have frequently implicated social class as a possible factor in disordered behavior. For example, in their pioneering study on the relationship between social class and psychological well-being, Hollingshead and Redlich (1958) showed that severe psychological disorders were nine times more likely to develop at the bottom of the social ladder than in the top social class. They also found that severe disorders were found more often in the poorest areas of cities than in the more affluent suburbs. This finding suggests that the stress produced by poverty, unemployment, and crowded urban housing may contribute to the production of severe psychiatric disorders.

One problem with Hollingshead and Redlich's conclusion is that it was based on admissions to public psychiatric hospitals. Because people in lower socioeconomic classes are more likely to wind up in such institutions than are middle-

and upper-class people (who have access to private facilities), the researchers' sample may have been biased toward overestimating the prevalence of disorders among the lower classes. In the same way, a study of private hospitals would have overestimated the prevalence of disorders among the middle and upper classes. The best way to avoid such biases is to study an unbiased sample, one in which every member of the population has an equal chance of appearing.

One approach to constructing an unbiased sample is to survey every household in a city. Another possibility is to select households at random from a variety of lower- and middle-class neighborhoods. Members of the selected households are then surveyed. As a check on their reports, all public- and private-hospital records can be examined to see whether the members of these households have been hospitalized.

Such large-scale epidemiological surveys tend to confirm Hollingshead and Redlich's finding: The poor are more likely to be hospitalized with severe psychiatric disorders than are members of the middle or upper class. Although this seems consistent with the idea that economic and social stress can produce severe disorders, it is also possible that the cause goes the other way: Disordered behavior may cause people to fall into poverty. Perhaps both disordered behavior and poverty are related to some genetic factor. Poverty and disordered behavior may interact so that each has an effect on the other. It's difficult to tease these relationships apart. Short of performing completely unethical experiments (separate identical twins and raise one in a high-social-class environment and the other in a low-social-class environment), we must make do with correlational data.

status, losing the chance to work toward organizational goals, and losing an externally imposed time structure to one's day. To the extent to which these things are necessary to mental health, unemployment will produce disordered behavior. This way of explaining the effects of unemployment looks for causes within the individual. The theory seems plausible, but it cannot explain why some unemployed people do not develop psychological problems. To do this, we need to look outside the individual to the social situation.

Suppose it is true that psychological health depends on our chance to use our skills, interact with other people, and so on. Work is not the only way to get these things. We can also get them from volunteer work and from family members. Thus, it is no surprise that some unemployed individuals remain psychologically well-adjusted. They may be fulfilling their psychological needs in other ways. Although an improvement over

the simple view that needs can be met only at work, even this more sophisticated idea is still inadequate. It treats people as passive, when, in practice, they are often able to shape their environment to meet their needs. What is required is a theory that combines environmental and psychological factors with what we know about human behavior. For example, unemployment removes people from an environment that fulfills many of their psychological needs. If these needs are not met in their new environment, and if they are unable to shape their environment to meet their needs, then they will develop psychological disorders.

This progression from simple to increasingly sophisticated interactions between the person and the environment is typical of sociocultural theories. Note, however, that these theories are largely after the fact and subject to several methodological biases. (Critical Thinking About Clinical Decisions 2.2 explores the question of bias in surveys more fully.) To be useful from a practical clinical view, theories must be able to make new, verifiable predictions. Moreover, they must be applicable at some level to individuals. It is not enough to know that there is a statistical association between unemployment and mental health in some parts of the population: Social groups do not come to the clinic; individuals do. Theories that do not make testable predictions (or at least provide falsifiable explanations) and that are not applicable to individuals are difficult to apply in the clinic. For instance, it is difficult to give an example of the sociocultural paradigm's view of Danielle because the paradigm does not focus on individuals.

Sociocultural Paradigm: Current Status

For the past 200 years or more, we in the Western democracies have been looking forward to the day when science, education, and consumer-based capitalism will replace traditional shamanism and poverty. We have encouraged assimilation among ethnic groups in our countries and fostered "progress" and "development" among those in foreign countries. Yet, ethnic consciousness is stronger than ever. All around the world, and right in our own cities, ethnic groups are asserting their own identities and values. It is time to admit that we will never homogenize people. We must take cultural variations seriously, understand their role in daily life, and examine how they influence behavior.

This does not mean that abnormal psychology is entirely culturally relative. We know that severe psychological disorders are universal; they occur in more or less the same form in most countries of the world (Al-Issa, 1982). This is not surprising. After all, we human beings all share a similar genetic endowment. We are all born with the capacity to learn, for example. This shared endowment makes it possible for us to treat people from another culture as human beings instead of as weird and incomprehensible aliens. But it does not make everyone the same. Our universal biological endowment is molded by the culture in which we live. To take a simple example, almost all people are born with the biological capacity to learn a language (Chomsky, 1980), but the specific language that a person learns depends on his or her culture. The goal of the sociocultural paradigm is to describe and understand how culture interacts with universal biological and psychological traits. In the words of Shweder and Sullivan (1993), psychology must develop a concept of "universality without the uniformity" (p. 517).

CHAPTER 2 IN PERSPECTIVE

Each paradigm construes behavior in its own way. From the point of view of the biological paradigm, depressions like Danielle's are the result of genetic factors and perhaps biochemical abnormalities. The psychoanalysts, on the other hand, would emphasize Danielle's early sexual trauma and her repressed guilt. The behaviorists would concentrate on learned modes of responding, especially learned helplessness, whereas the cognitive psychologists would concern themselves with negative attributions. The humanistic psychologists would be most interested in Danielle's self-concept and her ability to make choices; the sociocultural theorists would be mainly concerned with social forces (need for success, for example) that might drive someone to take her own life.

To a certain extent, these various positions are all useful ways of construing behavior. They may even all be correct. As indicated in the metaparadigm presented at the beginning of this chapter, psychological disorders frequently have more than one cause. Sometimes, the various paradigms seem to be saying essentially the same thing in different ways (consider, for example, the behavioral concept of learned helplessness, the cognitive notion of faulty attributions, and the humanistic idea that depression is caused by the perceived inability to achieve one's goals). Given that disorders have more than one cause and given the apparent overlap in explanations, some people have argued that the best approach is an eclectic one. That is, why not combine the various paradigms? Clinical psychologists frequently use techniques from more than one paradigm, so why shouldn't researchers do the same thing? Sometimes they do. But it must be kept in mind that there are important differences between the clinic and the laboratory. The clinician's goal is to help the patient. It makes sense for the clinician to take a pragmatic approach and try whatever works. The researcher's goal is different. The researcher wants to develop valid theories of behavior. This is done by testing hypotheses, not by simply accepting all theories as equally valid. From the scientific viewpoint, the existence of more than one paradigm is healthy because it makes for competition among researchers. By trying to provide better explanations than their competitors, scientists will help to improve our understanding of abnormal behavior.

Key Ideas

Paradigms

A scientific paradigm is the conceptual framework in which a scientist works. It contains a set of assumptions (some implicit) about which phenomena to study, which explanatory concepts are legitimate, and which scientific methods should be used to collect data. A shared paradigm allows scientists to communicate with one another, and, to a large extent, it defines a scientific discipline. Shared paradigms can also blind researchers to facts and interpretations from another paradigm.

Metaparadigm

Human beings are biological organisms. Everything a person does, thinks, and feels is ultimately the result of activity in his or her central nervous system and its associated organs. For this reason, the proximal cause of behavior is always biological. The state of the central nervous system at any moment in time is the result of a variety of distal causes, including those studied by the various paradigms of abnormal psychology. Each of the paradigms emphasizes a different set of causes, but they overlap to some degree, and they also interact.

Biological Paradigm

The biological paradigm emphasizes the distal genetic, biochemical, and anatomical causes of behavior. Treatment is viewed as biological as well (drugs, for example). Researchers in the biological paradigm may get their hypotheses from case studies, but they prefer to test them under controlled laboratory conditions. Despite the rigorous research approach on which they are based, biological theories of abnormal behavior often sound vague. Researchers may point out a relationship between a biological variable (infection with syphilis, say) and some behavior disorder (delusions of grandeur) but may fail to say how one causes the other.

Psychoanalytic Paradigm

The psychoanalytic paradigm emphasizes the etiological role of unconscious conflicts in behavior disorders. Although Freud's successors have given an increasingly important role to conscious forces, therapy in the psychoanalytic paradigm still requires the uncovering of repressed material. Psychoanalytic hypotheses arise from case studies, and they are confirmed by finding consistent evidence within the same or additional cases studies. Because many psychoanalytic hypotheses are not testable empirically, most research psychologists do not consider psychoanalysis to be scientific. Nevertheless, psychoanalytic ideas are pervasive in most areas of abnormal psychology.

Behavioral Paradigm

From its origins in studies of animal learning, the behavioral paradigm has developed to encompass just about all aspects of how our behavior varies with changes in the environment. The paradigm views behavior disorders as examples of faulty learning. Treatment involves new learning (or the extinction of old learning). Research in the behavioral paradigm takes place in the clinic as well as the laboratory. Controlled studies are common, as are studies of the way a single individual responds to environmental changes (such as changes to schedules of reinforcement). The behavioral paradigm stresses the objective measurement of behavior.

Cognitive Paradigm

The cognitive paradigm focuses on the role of beliefs, attitudes, appraisals, and attributions on behavior. It is dominated by the idea that at least some behavior disorders are the result of irrational, faulty, or just plain destructive beliefs. Treatment involves changing beliefs by a combination of logical argument and behavioral techniques such as conditioning. Research in the cognitive paradigm consists of both laboratory and clinical studies and, like the behavioral paradigm, usually involves objective measures of behavior. Cognitions are often inferred on the basis of objective measures.

Humanistic Paradigm

More of a philosophical position than a scientific program, the humanistic paradigm starts from the idea that all people can be well-adjusted if they are given the freedom to be themselves and develop to their full potential. This optimistic view is in direct contrast to the psychoanalytic idea that people are naturally uncivilized and that the constraints of society are required to keep them in line. Treatment, from the humanistic viewpoint, is designed to establish the conditions that allow people to make free choices. The humanistic paradigm has no characteristic research methods, nor does it have a specific research program.

Sociocultural Paradigm

The sociocultural paradigm emphasizes both psychological universals and cultural uniqueness. How we learn is determined by our heredity, whereas what we learn is determined by our culture. Disordered behavior is not entirely relative, however. Some disorders, especially the serious ones, occur in more or less the same form in all cultures. There is no separate treatment in this paradigm, although if there were, it would focus more on changing the environment than changing the person. Sociocultural research consists mainly of observational and epidemiological studies. Although sociocultural theories can rarely be tested experimentally, their predictions may still be assessed by looking for confirmations in a variety of settings using a variety of measures.

Key Terms

acculturation
analogue experiment
anxiety
anxiety hierarchy
attribution
behavior modification
    (behavior therapy)
behaviorism
belief
catharsis
classical conditioning
collective unconscious
conditioned response (CR)
conditioned stimulus (CS)
control group
correlation
defense mechanism

dependent variable
double-blind experiment
ego
Electra complex
eugenics
existential anxiety
expectancies
experimental group
fixation
free association
genotype
gestalt therapy
heritability
id
identification
identity crisis
independent variable

libido
mediated learning
modeling
Oedipal conflict
operant conditioning
paradigm
paradoxical intention
phenotype
pleasure principle
preconscious
primary-process thinking
primary reinforcers
proband
rational-emotive therapy
repression
secondary-process thinking
self-actualization

self-concept
stress
stressor
superego
symptom-substitution
    hypothesis
systematic desensitization
tic
transference
two-process theory of
    avoidance learning
unconditional positive regard
unconditioned response
    (UCR)
unconditioned stimulus
    (UCS)
unconscious

Key Names

Alfred Adler
Josef Breuer
Jean Charcot
Albert Ellis
Erik Erikson

Viktor Frankl
Carl Gustav Jung
Thomas Kuhn
Richard Lazarus
Abraham Maslow

Ivan Pavlov
Frederick (Fritz) Perls
Carl Rogers
Martin Seligman
B. F. Skinner

Edward L. Thorndike
John B. Watson
Joseph Wolpe
Wilhelm Wundt

CHAPTER 3

CHAPTER OBJECTIVES

Science is possible only when the objects of study can be defined and measured. Physicists must be able to define and measure what they mean by mass, motion, and acceleration. Chemists must be able to define and measure atomic weights. Similarly, psychologists who are interested in studying the disorders of behavior must be able to define these disorders (describe their characteristic signs and symptoms) and measure (assess) their severity in different people. Unlike physics and chemistry, abnormal psychology is not yet fully scientific. There is still considerable disagreement about the definition of the various disorders, and psychological measures are not as precise as those used in the physical sciences. Nevertheless, as you will see in this chapter, much progress has been made. We have the beginning of an objective classification system for psychological disorders, and our measurement instruments are becoming increasingly sophisticated.

The main questions addressed in this chapter are

1. What are the strengths and weaknesses of the current diagnostic system?
2. What are the main elements of a clinical diagnosis?
3. What are the common assessment instruments used by clinicians?
4. How do clinicians integrate statistical and clinical information to make judgments and decisions about clients?

Psychological Assessment, Classification, and Clinical Decision Making

CONTENTS

As described in Chapter 1, Danielle Wood attempted suicide in her sophomore year. She was admitted to University Hospital under the care of Dr. Sally Kahn, who referred her to a psychologist, Dr. Stuart Berg, for a psychological assessment. Dr. Kahn hoped that this assessment would tell her more about Danielle—her personality, her ability to cope with stress, her intellectual and emotional strengths, and her potential for further suicide attempts. Dr. Kahn planned to use this information to decide whether special suicide precautions were needed and to formulate a suitable treatment plan. Dr. Berg began his assessment by examining the case history assembled by the social worker, Li Cheong. He then interviewed Danielle, noting her demeanor and behavior as well as her answers to his questions. Dr. Berg also administered several psychological tests. Using the information gained from the case history, interview, and tests, Dr. Berg produced a psychological assessment for Dr. Kahn (see Document 1.3).

Interactions like those among Dr. Kahn, Dr. Berg, and Danielle are repeated every day in clinics around the world. Assessment is one of a psychologist's most important, and most common, tasks. Assessments are used mainly to make diagnoses and plan treatments, but they may also be used for other purposes. They can help to determine whether a person accused of a crime is competent to stand trial, whether a parent should be given custody of children in a divorce case, whether a person should be committed to (or released from) a hospital, whether a child requires special education, or whether an applicant will be given a job. A psychological assessment that compares a client's behavior before and after treatment can also indicate whether treatment was successful. In some cases, assessments may even reveal the etiology of psychological disorders. Such etiological information is essential if the prevention of behavior disorders is ever to become a reality.

The clinician's assessment toolbox includes interviews, behavioral observations, and tests. Which assessment techniques a clinical psychologist uses depends on the specific questions to be answered and on the paradigm in which the psychologist works. For example, psychoanalytic clinicians favor assessment techniques that are designed to uncover unconscious conflicts, whereas behavioral psychologists prefer to assess the environmental characteristics that elicit and maintain problem behaviors. This chapter describes several approaches to assessment and attempts to put each into a theoretical context. The chapter is divided into three main sections. The first is concerned with the science

and practice of psychological assessment. Because many assessments are undertaken to reach a diagnosis, the second section addresses diagnosis and classification. The third section is concerned with the ways (both good and bad) that clinicians use assessment data to make judgments and decisions.

PSYCHOLOGICAL ASSESSMENT

A psychological assessment consists of more than just administering and interpreting tests. It is a complex intellectual activity that includes formulating hypotheses about a person, deciding what data are necessary to confirm or disconfirm these hypotheses, gathering the required data, interpreting them, and, finally, drawing conclusions (Groth-Marnat, 1990). At each stage in the assessment process, the psychologist must be alert to factors that could compromise the integrity of the assessment. For example, interviews and tests may not always provide accurate information, adherence to a paradigm may blind a clinician to contradictory data, and clinical inferences may not always be justified. An important aspect of clinical expertise is knowing how much weight to give to different data sources and how much confidence to put in clinical inferences.

This section describes both assessment devices and the assessment process. Throughout the discussion, factors that might threaten the integrity of assessment data are highlighted. The discussion begins with the most ubiquitous of all assessment techniques, the interview.

Clinical Interviews

Whatever paradigm a clinical psychologist adopts, interviews almost always play an important role in the assessment process (Gorman, 1993; Wiens, 1983). The goals of an assessment interview are to gather information about a client's history, life situation, personal relationships, and outlook for the future; to assess the client's current functioning; and, often, to make a clinical diagnosis. Good interviewers gain information, not only from what people say, but also from their general appearance, tone of voice, body posture, facial expressions, and eye contact. Experienced interviewers know that a tearful tale about losing a lover told by a young woman with "dark circles under her eyes" (Document 3.1) means something quite different from a relaxed client's bland statement that she and her boyfriend "had an argument."

DOCUMENT 3.1

Behavioral Observations From Dr. Berg's Assessment of Danielle

The client was seen on two separate testing sessions. On each occasion, her appearance and behavior were the same. She wore a man's shirt, jeans, and deck shoes. Her hair was long and messy, and she wore no makeup. There were dark circles under her eyes.

The client avoided eye contact, looking down at the table or over the examiner's shoulder. She kept her hands clasped in her lap and never spoke spontaneously. She did respond to questions, but her answers were always brief and unelaborated. The client did not appear delusional or out of contact with reality; she was able to complete the tests and to provide a family history. It seemed as if everything she said or did required considerable effort.

The client told me that she had taken an overdose of "pills" because of a fight with her boyfriend. She felt that her boyfriend might be "getting tired of her," and she felt that she "could not live" if she were to lose him. ∎

Rapport is essential in a client-therapist relationship. In Good Will Hunting, Dr. Maguire (Robin Williams) is able to break through to Will Hunting (Matt Damon) in part because they both come from the same Irish American blue-collar neighborhood in Boston.

People find it easiest to speak frankly and freely with clinicians with whom they establish **rapport** (a warm and trusting relationship). By being attentive to the emotions that lie behind what a client says and by reflecting these emotions back to the person in a nonjudgmental way, clinicians try to make people feel comfortable about revealing themselves. Sometimes, clinicians must actively draw people out, encouraging them to speak (Document 3.2). Establishing rapport can take considerable time, so clinicians must learn to be patient. The process is too important to be rushed.

DOCUMENT 3.2

Excerpt From Dr. Berg's Clinical Interview With Danielle's Friends

LUKE (*haltingly, in a flat, expressionless voice without lifting his eyes from the floor*): You can't believe how I feel. When it first happened, I tried to convince myself that it was an accident. Danielle took steroids and uppers to improve her performance. She just took too many. But I knew all along that that wasn't true.

DR. BERG (*seeing that Luke is depressed—and perhaps in more psychological distress than Jayne—and trying to draw him out*): I know this is hard, Luke, but you must face your feelings, and you must work through all of this so that you can get on with the rest of your life. We will probably never know for sure whether Danielle's death was deliberate or an accident. We will have to learn to live with not knowing.

The silence in the room seems to last a very long time. It becomes a kind of weight pressing down on Luke, forcing the words out of him.

LUKE (*slowly and softly*): It wasn't an accident, and it was at least partly my fault. . . . ∎

The quality of the information gained from an interview is in part determined by the "match" between the interviewer and the interviewee. Female clients, for example, may be reluctant to talk frankly about sexual matters with male psychologists (and vice versa). Similarly, members of minority groups may have difficulty communicating their views to White, middle-class interviewers (Paurohit, Dowd, & Cottingham, 1982). Mismatches between clients and clinicians can lead to miscommunication. Cultural differences may be interpreted as signs of disordered behavior (Dauphinais & King, 1992). Or, bending over backward to be culturally sensitive, clinicians may make the opposite error: They may mistakenly attribute abnormal behavior to cultural differences (Betancourt & Lopez, 1993). Clearly, good interviewers are always vigilant for signs of cultural, sexual, or other biases.

Structured Versus Unstructured Interviews Clinical interviews fall along a continuum that ranges from loose, unstructured conversations at one end to formal, structured interactions at the other. Unstructured interviews are largely spontaneous. The therapist and the client change topics whenever a new direction is warranted. Although the unstructured format of such interviews gives psychologists the freedom to explore important matters as they arise, the conversations are not really random. Clinicians focus on the issues that their preferred paradigm deems relevant to understanding and helping troubled people. For example, a psychologist working in the psychoanalytic paradigm might concentrate on a client's interesting dream, whereas a humanistic psychologist might try to steer the conversation around to the person's self-concept.

Because unstructured interviews follow unpredictable paths, it is not surprising that independent clinicians, assessing the same person, may reach different conclusions. Adding more structure forces all interviewers to cover the same material in the same sequence, thereby increasing the probability that they will reach the same conclusion (McReynolds, 1989). Consider, for example, the **mental status examination**, a semistructured interview used mainly as a screening device to assess a person's current neurological and psychological status along several dimensions: memory, sensation, activity level, mood, and clarity of thought (Trzepacz & Baker, 1993). The mental status examination involves behavioral observations as well as questioning. Although more structured than the typical clinical interview, the mental status examination still gives clinicians the freedom to devise case-specific questions and to pursue interesting leads as they arise. Document 3.3 contains an excerpt from Dr. Kahn's mental status examination of Danielle at the time of her admission to the hospital. It illustrates Dr. Kahn's attempt to determine whether Danielle is "oriented" in time and place (that she knows where she is and why).

DOCUMENT 3.3

Excerpt From Danielle's Mental Status Examination

DR. KAHN: What is your name?

DANIELLE: Danielle Wood.

DR. KAHN: Can you tell me where you are right now?

DANIELLE: In the hospital.

DR. KAHN: What is today's date?

DANIELLE: December third.

DR. KAHN: Do you know why you are here?

DANIELLE: Because I tried to hurt myself. ∎

Although a mental status examination introduces structure to the clinician-client interaction, doctors do not always agree on its results (Molloy, Alemayehu, & Roberts, 1991). Clinical agreement can be increased, however, by making interviews even more prescriptive— that is, by limiting the clinician's freedom about what questions to ask and in what form to ask them. Interchanges of this type are called **structured interviews.** Document 3.4 illustrates Dr. Kahn's use of a structured clinical interview to determine whether Danielle is suffering from a major depressive episode. Notice how Dr. Kahn's interview questions are designed to obtain diagnostic-specific data. By forcing clinicians to go through the questions one by one and by not allowing them to deviate from the interview protocol, structured interviews increase the likelihood that different clinicians will reach the same conclusion.

DOCUMENT 3.4

Excerpt From Dr. Kahn's Structured Interview for Diagnosing Major Depression

Adapted from Spitzer et al. (1992, p. 625).

Dr. Kahn's questions	Reason for question
Can I ask you some questions about your mood?	Depression is marked by a depressed mood.
In the last month, has there been a period of time when you were feeling depressed or down most of the day, nearly every day? (What was that like?)	A depressed mood most of the day, nearly every day, as indicated either by subjective account or by observation by others, is a sign of depression.
What about being a bit less interested in most things or unable to enjoy the things you used to enjoy? (What was that like?)	A markedly diminished interest or pleasure in all, or almost all, activities most of the day, nearly every day (as indicated either by subjective account or by observation by others of apathy most of the time) is a sign of depression. ∎

Although some clinicians fear that overly structured interviews inhibit the development of rapport, the available evidence indicates that this is not so (McReynolds, 1989). However, structured interviews do have certain drawbacks. Suppose, for example, that Dr. Kahn wants to predict whether Danielle, who usually attends swimming practice on Monday mornings (when the weather is fine), will attend practice on a particular Monday. It would be easy to produce a structured interview to predict whether Danielle will attend practice on a given day. ("Is it Monday?" "Is the weather fine?") These questions will usually lead to the correct prediction. However, one Monday Danielle wakes up with an ear infection. This reduces the probability that she will attend practice to zero. If Dr. Kahn slavishly sticks to her structured interview, she will fail to make the correct prediction because the interview protocol does not contain a question about ear infections. In contrast, a flexible clinician, who follows up unusual occurrences, has no trouble reaching the correct judgment. (This example is adapted from Meehl, 1954.) Because people are all individuals who belong to different ethnic and cultural groups, no interview can be completely predetermined. "Ear infections," and other special circumstances, mean that clinical interviewers must always be ready to use their expert judgment about what questions to ask, what to follow up, and what to ignore (S. Schwartz, 1991).

Validity of Interviews   In psychometrics, the science of psychological measurement, tests are valid if they really measure what they are purported to measure. The validity of a clinical interview (its ability to provide trustworthy information about a person's psychological status) hinges largely on the skill and experience of the interviewer (Okun, 1982), but even skilled interviewers may be misled. Members of minority groups may react to interview questions in unexpected ways (Dauphinais & King, 1992). Clients being assessed as the result of a court order or because their parents, teachers, or spouses insisted on it may not wish to reveal their true feelings. Even "voluntary" clients may produce distorted information. For example, Danielle's depression affected her self-concept; she denigrated her achievements and portrayed herself in an unrealistic light. Severely disturbed clients may be unable to express themselves at all.

Some clients provide misleading information because they are genuinely unaware of their own behavior; others exaggerate their problems. Inaccuracies can sometimes arise in subtle ways. For example, medical researchers have found that patients vary greatly in their definitions of pain (Gorman, 1993). When a doctor palpates part of a patient's body and asks if it hurts, the patient's definition of pain determines whether the answer is yes or no. Patients with the same condition may answer differently if they have different subjective ideas about pain. Similarly, psychologists who inquire about

"anxiety" should expect considerable variability in the replies they receive.

In summary, clients' perceptions; their interpretations of psychologists' questions; their background, education, and attitudes toward psychological problems all affect their answers to interview questions. Of course, interviewers may be biased as well. They may emphasize information that is consistent with their preferred paradigm, discounting or even ignoring inconsistencies. For all these reasons, psychologists rarely rely solely on interviews for clinical information. Most prefer to supplement interviews with psychological tests.

Intelligence Assessment

The modern era in psychological testing began with the work of the British scientist Francis Galton (1822–1911), a committed social Darwinist who coined the word *eugenics* (see Chapter 2, Highlight 2.1). To help identify people with "superior intellects," Galton devised several measures of "intelligence," but these turned out to lack validity. For example, they failed to differentiate eminent intellectuals from ordinary citizens, nor could they predict university grades. Galton did set the stage, however, for a more valid test to be developed in France by Alfred Binet.

Binet's Test   Like Sigmund Freud, Alfred Binet (1857–1911) studied medicine under Jean Charcot at the Salpêtrière in Paris. Instead of following a medical career, however, Binet shifted to psychology, where he studied individual differences. Binet might have quietly pursued this research for the rest of his career had the government not asked him to take on a practical assignment. Specifically, Binet was commissioned to develop an assessment device that could be used to predict which schoolchildren would need special education. Binet compiled a "battery" of 30 tests covering communication, memory, and number skills, as well as the ability to understand and reason about common situations.

Binet and his colleagues published their test in 1905. In a later revision, they introduced the concept of **mental age,** which they contrasted with actual, chronological, age. A child of 10 with a mental age of 15 is above average in intelligence, whereas a child of 10 with a mental age of 5 is below average. A few years later, the German psychologist Louis Stern (1871–1938) showed how the relative performance of children at different ages could be compared by taking the ratio of their mental and chronological ages. In 1916, the Stanford University psychologist Louis Terman (1877–1956) published a

In the early 1900s, French psychologist Alfred Binet (1857–1911) and his colleagues introduced the concept of mental age.

In 1916, Louis Terman (1877–1956) published the Stanford-Binet test, a modified version of Binet's scale, and coined the term IQ (intelligence quotient).

modified version of Binet's scale (the Stanford-Binet) that became widely used in the United States. It was Terman who invented the term **intelligence quotient** as well as its abbreviation, IQ. The Stanford-Binet has been continually revised (Thorndike, Hagen, & Sattler, 1986), but its popularity has been eclipsed by the intelligence tests developed by David Wechsler. See Table 3.1 for examples of tasks that children of various ages should be able to perform, according to the Stanford-Binet.

Wechsler's Tests   David Wechsler (1896–1981) was a psychologist at New York's Bellevue Hospital when he published his first intelligence test in 1939. The Wechsler-Bellevue intelligence test was divided into two scales—verbal and performance—each consisting of several subtests (vocabulary, arithmetic, arranging blocks into designs, and so on). Each of the two scales yielded an IQ score (in addition to a Full Scale IQ score). Wechsler also introduced the modern method of calculating IQs, which is explained in Critical Thinking About Clinical Decisions 3.1. The Wechsler-Bellevue was so well received that Wechsler devoted the rest of his career to refining it. Over the years, he published many more tests designed for use with children as well as adults. Each followed a similar formula: five or six verbal subtests and approximately the same number of performance tests.

In 1939, David Wechsler (1896–1981) introduced a method of calculating IQs so that they remain stable with age. The Wechsler intelligence scales are now more commonly used than the Stanford-Binet scale.

TABLE 3.1   Representative Tasks From the Stanford–Binet

Age	Task
2½	Points to toy object that "goes on your feet" Names *chair, flag* Can repeat two digits
4	"In daytime it is light, after night it is . . . ?" "Why do we have houses?"
6	"What is the difference between a bird and a dog?" "An inch is short; a mile is . . . ?" "Give me _____ blocks" (up to 10)
9	"Tell me a number that rhymes with *tree*." "If I buy 4 cents worth of candy and give the storekeeper 10 cents, how much money will I get back?" Repeats four digits in reversed order
12	Defines *skill, muzzle* "The streams are dry _____ there has been little rain." ". . . 'In an old graveyard in Spain, they have discovered a small skull which they believe to be that of Christopher Columbus when he was about ten years old'. . . . What is foolish about that?" Repeats five digits in reversed order

Note: Adapted from Gleitman (1981, p. 590).

Wechsler's most widely used adult test is the one Dr. Berg administered to Danielle, the Wechsler Adult Intelligence Scale-III, (WAIS-III; Wechsler, 1997). The test is popular because it has several important characteristics. First, it has high **reliability** (the psychometric term for a test that yields consistent results). When the WAIS-III is administered twice to the same person in similar circumstances, it produces a similar score. This type of reliability is known as test-retest reliability. Reliability is essential, but to be useful, a test of intelligence must also have high validity—that is, it must actually measure "intelligence." There are several ways to judge the WAIS-III's validity. For example, it has "face" and "content" validity because it contains tasks that span many of the verbal and performance skills associated with intelligence. It also has "predictive" validity because scores on the WAIS-III are reasonable predictors of educational and career attainment (Kaufman, 1990).

Other Wechsler tests include the Wechsler Intelligence Scale for Children-III (WISC-III; Wechsler, 1991), which is suitable for children between the ages of 6 and 16, and the Wechsler Preschool and Primary Scale of Intelligence-Revised (WPPSI-R; Wechsler, 1989), which is aimed at younger children. Along with the WAIS-III, these are among the most widely used psychological tests in the United States (Lubin, Larsen, & Matarazzo, 1984; Piotrowski & Keller, 1989). Although they were designed to measure intellectual functioning (Sattler,

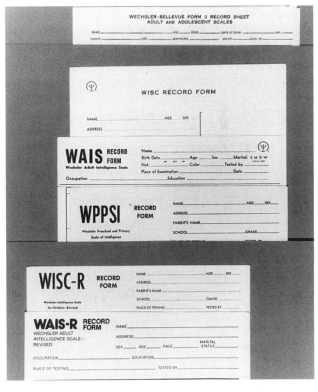

The Wechsler family of intelligence tests has evolved over the years but all share characteristic features such as verbal and performance subscales. Wechsler-Bellvue Intelligence Scales © 1947, WAIS © 1955, WAIS-R © 1981, WISC-R © 1974, WPPSI © 1963 and 1967, all © by The Psychological Corporation, a Harcourt Assessment Company. Reproduced by permission. All rights reserved.

Do We Get Less Intelligent With Age?

According to Binet, a child whose actual age is 6, but whose intelligence test performance is the same as the average 4-year-old's, has a "mental age" of 4. Similarly, a 12-year-old whose performance is equivalent to the average 10-year-old's, has a mental age of 10. Although both children are two "mental" years behind the performance of their peers, they are not equally backward. A 6-year-old who has a mental age of 4 has achieved only two thirds the level of the average 6-year-old (4 ÷ 6), whereas a 12-year-old who has a mental age of 10 has achieved five sixths the level of the average 12-year-old (10 ÷ 12).

To reduce the difficulty of comparing children of different ages, psychologist Louis Stern suggested that comparisons be based on the ratio of a child's mental and chronological ages. Thus, the 6-year-old with a mental age of 4 has a mental-to-chronological-age ratio of 0.67 (4 ÷ 6), whereas the 12-year-old with a mental age of 10 has a ratio of 0.83 (10 ÷ 12). Stern's ratio makes it clear that the two children are not equally behind others of their same age.

Louis Terman suggested multiplying Stern's ratio by 100 to remove the decimal point—so, 0.67 becomes 67 and 0.83 becomes 83. Terman called this number the intelligence quotient, or IQ. The average child at any age has an IQ of 100 (try the arithmetic to see why). IQ scores greater than 100 represent above-average performance, whereas scores lower than 100 indicate below-average performance. Although neat and tidy, there was a problem with Terman's IQ scores. That is, people seemed to become less in-

telligent as they aged. To see why, imagine a precocious 8-year-old who answers every question on the Binet scale correctly. At age 8, this child receives the top mental age score possible on the test, which is 16. The child's IQ is 200 [(16 ÷ 8) × 100 = 200]. If the same child still gets all the items correct at age 16, then the child's IQ shrinks to 100 [(16 ÷ 16) × 100 = 100]. Even worse, the same perfect performance at age 32 produces an IQ of 50 [(16 ÷ 32) × 100 = 50]. This is clearly absurd.

To get around this problem, Wechsler replaced the ratio IQ formula with a new one that compared a person's performance with that of others at the same age:

$$IQ = \frac{\text{Score on test}}{\text{Mean score for age group}} \times 100$$

Wechsler's formula rested on the assumption that IQ remains stable with age. This does not mean that Wechsler

expected people to answer the same number of questions correctly at age 60 as at age 20. What he expected was that a person's *relative* achievement—compared with that of others of the same age—would remain more or less constant. Thus, a person who achieves an average score for 20-year-olds when aged 20 should achieve an average score for 60-year-olds when aged 60. On Wechsler's tests, the mean IQ is always 100, and the standard deviation is 15 for every age group. A person who scores two standard deviations above the group mean has an IQ score of 130, whereas a person who scores two standard deviations below the mean has an IQ score of 70. By noting how many standard deviations above or below the mean a person falls, it's possible to assign an IQ score to any level of performance (as the graph of the bell curve illustrates). Because these IQ scores are based on how far a person deviates from the mean, they are known as **deviation IQs.**

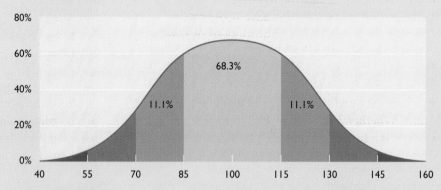

The distribution of IQ scores in the population follows a bell curve in which 100 is the most frequent score. More than two thirds of all people score between 85 and 115 on IQ tests.

1992), it is sometimes possible to make inferences about other aspects of a person's behavior from a WAIS-III protocol. (As an example, see Dr. Berg's remarks on Danielle's intelligence test results in Document 3.5.)

DOCUMENT 3.5

Excerpt From Dr. Berg's Interpretation of Danielle's Intelligence Test

The client's scores on the WAIS-III place her in the "above-average" range of intelligence. Although she understood the instructions, the test results were probably a low estimate of her abilities. On several occasions, she produced the correct response but so slowly that the time required to receive credit for the response had already expired. As a consequence, her lowest scores were on those subscales that require quick responses. This slowness was particularly apparent on the performance tasks. Slowness is often found among depressed people, and it is consistent with the client's general depressed appearance. ■

It is important to keep in mind that the IQ is a relative measure. It shows where a person stands in relation to a peer group (say, White, 20-year-old females). If we measured height using deviation scores, we would assign a "height quotient" of 100 to anyone whose height was average for the population. The average person in a population of pygmies would have the same height quotient (100) as the average person in a population of amazons, even though the average amazon might be twice as tall as the average pygmy. IQ scores are similar. They do not reflect any specific amount of knowledge. Indeed, there is evidence that intellectual achievement is increasing in the general population. People today must answer more questions correctly than their parents or grandparents had to, in order to achieve the same IQ score. Whether this means that humans are getting smarter is addressed in Highlight 3.1.

Personality Assessment

Intelligence (whatever it may be) is not the only important human characteristic. We also have our individual personalities. When we describe a friend who hates to spend a night at home as sociable, or when we describe a firefighter as heroic, we are implying that their behavior is caused by certain **personality traits.** As an explanation of behavior, traits have an intuitive appeal; they fit with our everyday observations of people. To psychologists interested in personality, however, traits are more than just handy descriptions; they are enduring aspects of the personality. In theory at least, measuring personality traits should allow us to predict how a person will act in various situations: For example, shy people should avoid social contact; heroes should act courageously. Alas, people are rarely so simple. Cowards may act courageously, and sociable people may occasionally prefer to be alone. Social situations determine behavior just as much as enduring personality traits do (Bandura, 1986; Mischel, 1968, 1973). This is one reason why the personality measures described in this section can never predict behavior with certainty.

Projective Personality Tests   Although they were developed in Europe, projective personality tests have always been more popular in the United States. Steeped in psychoanalysis, American psychologists developed the "projective hypothesis" in the early part of the 20th century (Frank, 1939). According to this hypothesis, people "project" their unconscious drives, feelings, wishes, and conflicts onto the "screen" provided by ambiguous stimuli. Tests using stimuli that elicit a wide range of different responses became known as projective tests or techniques.

Perhaps the best-known projective technique is the Rorschach inkblot test developed by the Swiss psychoanalyst Hermann Rorschach (1884–1922). Rorschach was not the first to study inkblots; Alfred Binet used inkblots in his work on intelligence testing. However, Binet focused on the various shapes and forms that people see in inkblots, whereas Rorschach set out to develop a measure of unconscious conflict. Rorschach did not believe he could learn about unconscious conflicts from the shapes people reported seeing in inkblots because, as a psychoanalyst, he accepted that overt reports are censored by the ego. Rorschach decided to concentrate instead on the perceptual and cognitive processes that underlie perception. He believed that psychologists could uncover repressed conflicts by noting which aspects of an inkblot elicit a person's reaction.

Although Rorschach claimed to find relationships between personality and inkblot characteristics, such as color and shading, these relationships were not straightforward. For example, nonpatients who reported seeing relatively common shapes (people, for example) often reported perceived movement ("people dancing"). In contrast, people with mood disorders also reported seeing people, but they did not perceive movement ("people standing still"). Rorschach concluded that personality assessment could not be based on a single perception (both groups saw people) but only on the simultaneous

Are People Getting Smarter?

IQ tests are deliberately designed to have a mean of 100. So, by definition, the average score cannot change over time. However, when researchers went back and looked at the raw data (the actual number of test questions that people answered correctly), they were surprised to find massive increases over the past century. That is, people can answer more questions today than they could 100 years ago. Judged by today's standards of performance, around half of all Americans in 1918 had IQ scores of around or below 75 (Flynn, 1984, 1987; Herrnstein & Murray, 1994). This increase in scores had been masked by the use of deviation IQ scores (which were explained in Critical Thinking About Clinical Decisions 3.1).

The largest improvements over time have been on performance subtests. This is surprising because these subtests (mazes, puzzles) seem the least likely to be affected by improved schooling. Clearly, something has had an important influence on people's abilities, but what? Some have suggested that diet is responsible, but in industrialized countries, diet has been more than adequate for decades. Better education is another possibility, although, as already noted, most of the improvement in IQ performance has been on the performance subtests, which tap skills that are not really part of the school curriculum. A third possibility is that television and computer games have made the visual-spatial skills measured by performance subtests more important than they were in the past.

At present, we do not have sufficient information to decide whether any of these explanations for the increase in intelligence test performance is correct. One thing seems certain, however. The change in performance scores has happened too quickly to be explained by genetics. The large improvements in IQ test performance clearly show that the environment has important effects on whatever is measured by intelligence tests.

Have IQs risen in recent decades because television and computer games have sharpened children's visual-spatial skills?

consideration of all of a person's perceptions, and the characteristics of the inkblot that elicited them. He admitted that this was difficult to do, but he believed the effort to be worthwhile because inkblot interpretation offered a way of bypassing the ego's defenses. Document 3.6 contains part of Dr. Berg's interpretation of Danielle's responses to Rorschach images. Figure 3.1 shows some sample responses to an inkblot image.

In the years following his death, interest in Rorschach's test grew. Reports began to circulate about the test's ability to reveal hidden personality conflicts. "Blind" personality descriptions made by clinicians with no knowledge of individuals other than their Rorschach protocols, were said to be uncannily accurate. Over the years, various systems have been devised to score and interpret the Rorschach test (Exner, 1990). However, some clinicians use inkblot responses not as a test but as a kind of unstructured interview, a way of getting people to talk (Frank, 1990). For example, if a client sees sexual activity in an inkblot, the clinician can use this as an entry into a discussion of the client's sexual history and attitudes toward sex.

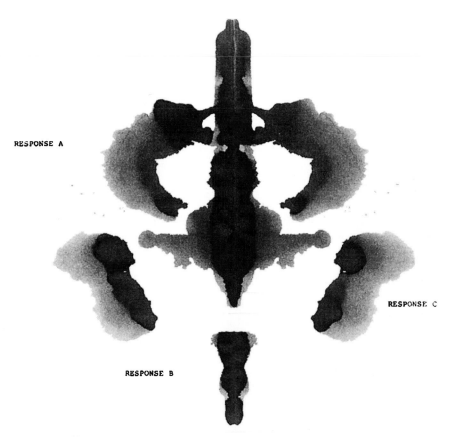

RESPONSE A

RESPONSE C

RESPONSE B

FIGURE 3.1 Sample Responses and Scoring of a Rorschach-Type Inkblot.
Response A: "Two kids jumping on either side of a large pogo stick." Where are they?
"Here are the kids; here is the pogo stick." What makes it look like that? "Their shape,
here, you can see their hands holding on to the stick, and they seem to be bouncing in the
air." Scoring: Location—large detail (everything except the three unconnected parts of the
inkblot); Determinants—form, human movement. Response B: "A ballerina." Scoring:
Location—large detail; Determinants—form, human movement. Response C: "Storm clouds in
a dark blue sky." Scoring: Location—large details; Determinants—form, shading, color. From:
S. Schwartz (1993, p. 27).

DOCUMENT 3.6

Dr. Berg's Interpretation of One of Danielle's Rorschach Responses

Danielle tended to respond primarily to the noncentral aspects of the stimulus cards. Specifically, her responses were determined by peripheral details rather than the overall appearance of the stimulus cards. This focus on minor details may indicate an unwillingness to confront her problems. She may prefer to dwell instead on unimportant details as a way of avoiding her main difficulties. Danielle was frequently affected by color, suggesting that she has strong emotions that may be affecting her judgment. She did not perceive any human movement, which may suggest depression. ■

The popularity of the Rorschach test in the United States inspired psychologists to use their ingenuity to develop new projective instruments. From the 1930s through the 1960s, the number of projective tests increased dramatically. One of the most popular was the Thematic Apperception Test, or TAT. The brainchild of Henry Murray, a surgeon who turned to psychology as a second career, the TAT requires subjects to make up stories about rather vague pictures mounted on cards (Murray, 1943). The cards are designed to elicit stories about what Murray saw as basic human "needs" (dominance, achievement, and so on) as well as common social and interpersonal problems. Although Murray intended that a minimum of 20 cards be administered,

A TAT image like this one elicited Danielle's response in Document 3.7.

most clinicians use only those cards they believe relevant to a specific case and ask clients to produce more than one story. Typically, a client is asked to say what is happening in the picture, what the people are thinking or feeling, and what the outcome will be. One of Danielle's TAT stories appears in Document 3.7.

DOCUMENT 3.7

Transcript of One of Danielle's TAT Stories

DR. BERG: Can you tell me who the people in this picture are, what is happening between them, what they are thinking or feeling, and what will happen in the future?

DANIELLE: This is a young man and an older person—no, not a person, a spirit, a ghost. The young man is very sensitive and worried, maybe guilty, about something . . . I don't know what. He doesn't know that the ghost is behind him. The young man is sad and worried about what someone thinks. The ghost is friendly. The ghost wants to send the man a message. I don't know what the message is. Maybe . . . it's not his fault. I think that the young man will get the message. I think it will get through.

Dr. Berg's interpretation: Danielle's story is consistent with the

picture, although she sees a young man where many people see a woman. This may be her way of distancing herself from the sad emotions and guilt that she believes the person in the picture is experiencing. The young man is being visited by a ghost, who brings a message of forgiveness ("it's not his fault"). This could be Danielle's dead father saying that his death was not Danielle's fault or that her failure to make the Olympic team was not her fault. The story's optimistic ending suggests that Danielle may see her future in brighter terms than she has in the past. ∎

Although many different TAT scoring systems have been developed over the years (Groth-Marnat, 1990), most clinicians use the test as a supplement to the interview—to uncover potential problems and make impressionistic judgments. One common technique is to search for consistent themes. Is aggression (or guilt or dependence) featured in several stories? In line with the projective hypothesis, Murray assumed that people "project" their own needs and feelings onto the "hero" of their story. So, clinicians also try to assess the adequacy of the hero. Is the hero assertive or passive? Successful or unsuccessful? Depressed or happy? Clinicians also try to judge how closely a person's story fits the picture. Is the story a reasonable one, given the picture? Are new elements introduced? Although creativity is an important trait, a story that is too distant from the picture might suggest that a person has lost contact with reality.

In addition to the standard TAT, there is a Children's Apperception Test, or CAT (Bellak, 1986), which uses pictures of household animals to stimulate children to make up stories. There are also versions of the TAT depicting Black or Hispanic people (Aiken, 1989). Although this sensitivity to developmental, racial, and ethnic differences is laudable, there is little evidence that any of these variations is more (or less) reliable or valid than the standard TAT (R. J. Cohen, Swerdlik, & Phillips, 1996; S. Schwartz & Johnson, 1985).

Projective Tests: Current Status   The migration of European psychoanalysts to America in the 1930s and 1940s strongly influenced the development of clinical psychology. By the end of World War II, American clinical psychologists were routinely using projective tests in their work. Following the war, academic psychology began a period of rapid growth. Because psychology training emphasized controlled experimentation and rigorous research, it was inevitable that psychologists would turn their attention to the validity of projective tests. On the whole, these validity studies produced disappointing results. In the typical validity study, researchers compared personality descriptions derived from projective tests with other indices of personality and noted how closely they agreed. For example, Rorschach claimed that creative people see human movement in inkblots ("ballerinas dancing," for instance). To test this assertion, psychologists administered the Rorschach to well-known artists and nonartists. They found no difference; artists did not report human movement more frequently than nonartists. The researchers concluded that seeing human movement in inkblots is not a valid sign of creativity. Such negative findings were typical. Rorschach claimed that people who see objects in the white areas of inkblots (rather than forms produced by the ink) are rebellious and have difficulty cooperating with authority figures. Yet, when psychologists compared the inkblot perceptions of convicted criminals with those of a group of law-abiding citizens, they found no difference. Hundreds of these "validity" studies have been reported; very few have substantiated predictions derived from projective tests (R. J. Cohen et al., 1996).

To be fair, Rorschach never claimed that individual signs are good indicators of personality. He believed that valid personality descriptions must rely on the totality of a person's perceptions. To examine this assertion, psychologists had eminent Rorschach experts produce personality descriptions and diagnoses using the total pattern of a person's responses. These were "blind" interpretations; the experts had no information about the people they were diagnosing other than their Rorschach responses. When experts' assessments were compared with those produced by clinicians who had firsthand knowledge of the individuals involved, there was little agreement. Personality descriptions based on the total of all responses were no more valid than those based on individual Rorschach signs; other projective tests fared no better (Hersen, Kazdin, & Bellack, 1983).

Some psychologists have criticized this research on procedural grounds (Acklin, McDowell, & Orndoff, 1992), and a firm core remains committed to the use of projective techniques (Acklin, 1995; Aronow & Moreland, 1995; Aronow, Reznikoff, & Moreland, 1994; Moreland, Reznikoff, & Aronow, 1995). Why do clinicians still cling to projective tests despite the flimsy evidence for their validity? Some find the negative research findings difficult to reconcile with their clinical impression that projective tests yield valid information (Karon, 1978). A second reason for the persistence of projective tests is that many clinicians do not use them as tests at all, but as extensions of interviews, as ways of generating, rather than confirming, hypotheses. For example, a person whose Rorschach protocol contains many sexual responses may have particular problems with sexual function or gender identity. Used in this way, projective tests can be a rich source of hypotheses about how a person views the world. But they are only hypotheses. They must be confirmed using valid measures of personality and behavior.

Self-Report Tests In response to the perceived shortcomings of projective tests, many psychologists turned to self-report inventories and questionnaires. Because their scoring usually involves counting rather than interpreting responses, self-report tests are often called objective tests. Perhaps the best known is the Minnesota Multiphasic Personality Inventory (MMPI), which was developed by two University of Minnesota researchers, psychologist Starke Hathaway and psychiatrist J. Charnley McKinley (Hathaway & McKinley, 1943). Their test is called multiphasic because it measures several personality dimensions simultaneously.

Hathaway and McKinley did not begin with a personality theory. Instead, they combed psychology textbooks, novels, folk stories, anecdotes, and clinical case studies for self-descriptive statements: "I sometimes keep on a thing until others lose their patience with me," "Bad words, often terrible words, come into my mind and I cannot get rid of them," "I often feel as if things are not real," "Someone has it in for me," "I like mechanics magazines." These descriptive statements were collected and presented to psychiatric patients, hospitalized medical patients, and adults who were not patients. They were asked to indicate which statements were self-descriptive. Statements that failed to discriminate between the psychiatric patients and others were eliminated. In other words, if everyone replied "true" to the statement "I sometimes keep on a thing until others lose patience with me," that statement was eliminated. Items that discriminated among the groups were retained, no matter how strange the item seemed. For example, if psychiatric patients responded "no" to the statement "I like mechanics magazines" and nonpatients responded "yes," the item was included in the test even if Hathaway and McKinley had no idea why the groups responded differently.

Because test items were not chosen according to a theory of abnormal psychology but purely on their ability to discriminate among groups, the MMPI approach to test construction is sometimes called dustbowl empiricism. Hathaway and McKinley ultimately assembled around 500 items keyed to one or more subscales. The subscales were mainly measures of traditional psychiatric diagnoses (depression, schizophrenia, paranoia). An additional scale, Social Introversion, was constructed by choosing items that discriminated between outgoing and shy university students. Over the years, other scales have been developed using the same empirical approach (Butcher et al., 1989a; Graham, 1987).

For decades, the MMPI has been the most widely used clinical self-report test (Lubin et al., 1984; Piotrowski & Keller, 1991). It is used in psychiatric institutions, psychology clinics, personnel offices, and military bases. It has also stimulated considerable research (A. F. Friedman, Webb, & Lewak, 1990). On the whole, validity studies have found reasonable evidence for the ability of the test to predict clinically relevant outcomes, such as how people will respond to treatment. Predictive validity is best when the overall pattern of subscale scores is considered (Webb, McNamara, & Rodgers, 1981).

An updated version of the MMPI, the MMPI-2, was published in 1989 (Butcher et al., 1989a; Butcher & Williams, 1992). To make the test suitable for use in the 1990s, many of the original items were rewritten to reflect contemporary language, and new items were added. The new test was administered to a representative sample of the general population. This process is known as **standardization** (R. J. Cohen et al., 1996). Standardization results in a set of "norms" that represent the distribution of scores in the standardization sample. By comparing a person with the standardization sample, we can tell if the person is average for the population, above or below average, and by how much. To be of practical value, the standardization sample must represent the population on which the test will be used. On this score, critics have claimed that the MMPI-2 standardization sample was better educated than the population at large and omitted some minorities. This may be why profiles generated by the two versions of the MMPI do not always agree (Adler, 1990).

The first step in interpreting an MMPI protocol is to inspect its "validity scales," which are intended to help clinicians determine whether an individual is responding to the test openly and honestly. High scores on the validity scales warn the examiner that the person's responses should not be accepted at face value. For example, the L, or Lie, scale contains such items as "I gossip a little at times." Because such behavior is so common, a "no" response to a Lie-scale item may reflect an attempt to portray oneself in a socially desirable light. The F, or Frequency, scale contains bizarre statements, such as "My soul sometimes leaves my body" and "There are persons trying to steal my thoughts and ideas." Because

even seriously disturbed patients rarely endorse these items, those people who do are either not reading the questions or trying to fake a psychiatric illness. The K, or Correction, scale attempts to measure defensiveness, a trait that may affect scores on the clinical scales. To reduce the effects of defensiveness, K-scale scores are sometimes used to "correct" the clinical scales. Specifically, a person with a high K-scale score and a moderately high score on one of the clinical scales is considered to be similar to a person with a low K-scale score and a high score on the clinical scale. The "Cannot Say" score is simply the number of items that a person fails to answer. A high number of omitted items suggests a reading problem, defensiveness, or uncooperativeness. It could also mean that a person is indecisive, often a sign of depression. Table 3.2 describes the MMPI-2 validity and clinical scales.

The MMPI-2 introduced several additional validity scales. The Back-Page Infrequency scale attempts to determine whether an examinee's attention has wandered during the testing session by including rarely endorsed items in the final pages of the test. The Response Inconsistency scale compares responses to the same statement phrased in different ways. For example, to be consistent, an examinee who answers yes to the statement "I never speak at parties" should answer no to the statement "I always speak at parties."

If a client's scores on the validity scales are within the expected range, the examiner then turns to the clinical scales (see Table 3.2). MMPI results are expressed as T-scores, which have a mean of 50 and a standard deviation of 10. Scores above 70 are considered particularly significant (Butcher et al., 1992; Graham, 1987; Webb et al., 1981). Danielle's MMPI profile appears in Document 3.8. Note that her validity scales (L, F, K) were all within normal limits and that her depression score was the only one above 70.

Although it is the most widely used, the MMPI is not the only empirically derived self-report test. There is, for example, a special version for adolescents, the MMPI-A (Butcher et al., 1989a). In addition, the California Psychological Inventory (McAllister, 1986) is similar to the MMPI in most respects, except that it is intended to measure the dimensions of the normal, rather than the abnormal, personality (Groth-Marnat, 1990). The Personality Inventory for Children, designed for use with children up to age 16, is actually aimed at parents (Wirt, Lachar, Klinedinst, & Seat, 1977). It has been found to predict which children will require special education and counseling (Dreger, 1982).

Other self-report measures of personality are con-

DOCUMENT 3.8

Danielle's MMPI Profile

Note: For an explanation of the scale labels, see Table 3.2.

MMPI-2™

S.R. Hathaway and J.C. McKinley
Minnesota Multiphasic
Personality Inventory - 2™

Profile for Basic Scales

Minnesota Multiphasic Personality Inventory - 2
Copyright © by THE REGENTS OF THE UNIVERSITY OF MINNESOTA
1942. 1943 (renewed 1970). 1989. This Profile Form 1989.
All rights reserved. Distributed exclusively by NATIONAL COMPUTER SYSTEMS, INC.
under license from The University of Minnesota.

"MMPI-2" and "Minnesota Multiphasic Personality Inventory - 2" are trademarks owned
by The University of Minnesota. Printed in the United States of America.

Name _Danielle Wood_

Address _Robertson Hall_

Occupation _Student_ Date Tested _12/2/2000_

Education _15_ Age _19_ Marital Status _0_

Referred by _Dr. Kahn_

MMPI-2 Code _____

Scorer's Initials _____

| T or Tc | L | F | K | Hs+.5K 1 | D 2 | Hy 3 | Pd+.4K 4 | MF 5 | Pa 6 | Pt+1K 7 | Sc+1K 8 | Ma+.2K 9 | Si 0 | T or Tc |

TABLE 3.2 MMPI Validity and Clinical Scales

Scale Label	Scale Name	Description
L	Lie	Validity items that test honesty of answers; a high score indicates an attempt to look good
F	Frequency	Validity items that test thoughtfulness of answers; claiming unusual behavior may reflect a desire to appear abnormal
K	Correction	Validity items that test whether the person is trying to protect self-image
HS	Hypochondriasis	Preoccupation with physical complaints and concerns
D	Depression	Low mood, hopeless, pessimistic, often irritable
Hy	Hysteria	Physical symptoms that help the person avoid responsibilities or stress
PD	Psychopathic Deviation	Antisocial and rebellious, disregards others' rights
Mf	Masculinity-Femininity	Male: aesthetic interests; Female: assertive and aggressive (females who score higher than 70 have masculine traits; males who score higher than 70 have feminine ones)
Pa	Paranoia	Suspicious, delusions of persecution or grandeur
Pt	Psychasthenia	Anxious, fearful, guilty, indecisive
Sc	Schizophrenia	Disturbances in thinking, delusions
Ma	Hypomania	Emotional excitement and low frustration tolerance
Si	Social Introversion	Shy and sensitive, conforming, and insecure

Note: From Butcher et al. (1989b).

tinually appearing (R. J. Cohen et al., 1996). Most are more specific than the MMPI. For example, Aaron Beck has developed a self-report measure to assess depressive attributional style (Beck, 1991). Beck's Depression Inventory was one of the tests that Dr. Berg administered to Danielle. It consists of 21 sets of four-choice items. For example, one set consists of the following four items:

0 I am not particularly discouraged about the future.
1 I feel discouraged about the future.
2 I feel I have nothing to look forward to.
3 I feel that the future is hopeless and that things cannot improve.

The client chooses the one statement in each set that best describes his or her current feelings. The number preceding each statement represents the points attributable to it. The client's score is the total of the points attributed to each endorsed statement. The higher the score, the more serious the depressive condition.

Computerized Personality Tests Practically anyone can administer and score an MMPI, but interpreting the results is difficult. Because of the large number of possible patterns (Dahlstrom, Welsh, & Dahlstrom, 1972), computers have been enlisted to administer, score, and interpret the MMPI (Butcher, 1987). Sophisticated computer programs present test questions, record responses, and scan large research databases to extract personality descriptions that correspond to an individual's pattern of scores. These descriptions are woven together into printed reports that are often indistinguishable from those produced by experienced clinicians.

Computerized test scoring and interpretation is inexpensive. Computers can also increase efficiency by asking only those questions required to reach a reliable conclusion. (Allowing computers to determine the sequence and number of questions is known as adaptive testing.) Computers can even be used to automate routine reporting, such as writing hospital discharge summaries (Mezzich et al., 1994).

Along with these advantages, computerized test interpretation also has disadvantages. It is easy to be misled into believing that just because an interpretation is produced by a computer, it must be valid. In reality, much of the data found in computer-generated test interpretations is not based on controlled research, or even statistical formulas, but on clinical lore. As described in the discussion of statistical versus clinical decision making in Chapter 1, clinical lore is almost always less valid than judgments based on statistical formulas (Dawes, Faust, & Meehl, 1989). To improve the validity of computerized interpretations, attempts have been made to distill clinical lore into a set of statistical formulas that may be applied automatically to specific profiles. These statistically based personality interpretations are likely to be more valid than those that simply mimic a clinician's judgment, but we cannot take this for granted. Formulas must be validated in the same way as any other assessment device (Matarazzo, 1986).

Computerized reports have legal implications as well. If a person is harmed by a report, it is unclear whether legal liability lies with the company that produced the software or the psychologist who used it (or with both). Because psychologists may ultimately be responsible for the consequences of computer-generated reports, they should take considerable care when using them. The American Psychological Association's (1986) *Guidelines for Computer-Based Tests and Interpretations* recognizes this responsibility by making it clear that psychologists who use computerized interpretations should know whether the computer-generated report is based on controlled research, a statistical formula, or on clinical opinion. In the last case, psychologists should ensure that they have sufficient information to weigh the credibility of these opinions before relying on the computer's interpretation. Irrespective of how a computer report is generated, clinicians should not just slavishly accept everything the computer report says. Professional ethics require psychologists to use computerized reports cautiously. Assessments must ultimately rely on psychologists' scientific knowledge and clinical experience.

Neuropsychological Assessment

Modern technology has made it possible to produce high-resolution images of both the structure and function of the brain. These imaging techniques, which are described in detail in Chapter 11, can provide clear pictures of the location and extent of brain damage. Yet, despite their sophistication, these images may still miss

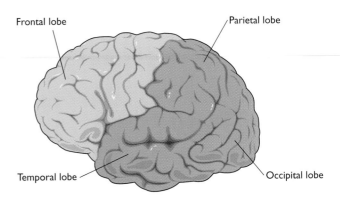

FIGURE 3.2 **Functional Anatomy of the Cerebrum**

subtle disturbances of brain function (Crawford, Parker, & McKinlay, 1992). To detect these subtle signs of disturbance, psychologists have developed **neuropsychological tests** (D. I. Margolin, 1992). These tests are used to help clinicians make diagnoses and to assess the effects of treatment and rehabilitation programs on people who have sustained head injuries, suffered strokes (blockage or bleeding from a brain blood vessel), developed degenerative diseases or cancer, or who engage in substance abuse (Tupper & Cicernone, 1991). By choosing tests appropriately, neuropsychologists are often able to pick up neurological deficits that are not identifiable any other way. In children, neuropsychological tests are also used to assess the effects of prematurity, illness, lead poisoning, and other developmental and environmental factors on neurological functioning.

Neuropsychological tests range from brief screening instruments that are used to determine whether more intensive testing is required to comprehensive test batteries that take most of a day to administer. In between are numerous specialized tests designed to provide information about specific aspects of brain functioning (Boulton, Baker, & Hiscock, 1990; Crawford et al., 1992). Choosing the appropriate instrument for a particular person requires an understanding of brain-behavior relationships. Because not all clinical psychologists have the required knowledge, neuropsychological testing has become a specialty within psychology.

Localization of Brain Damage   Neuropsychological tests exploit known brain-behavior relationships to help localize the site of brain damage. **Localization of brain damage** is largely a process of logical deduction. For example, because the occipital lobes (the back part of each of the brain's cerebral hemispheres; Figure 3.2) are the

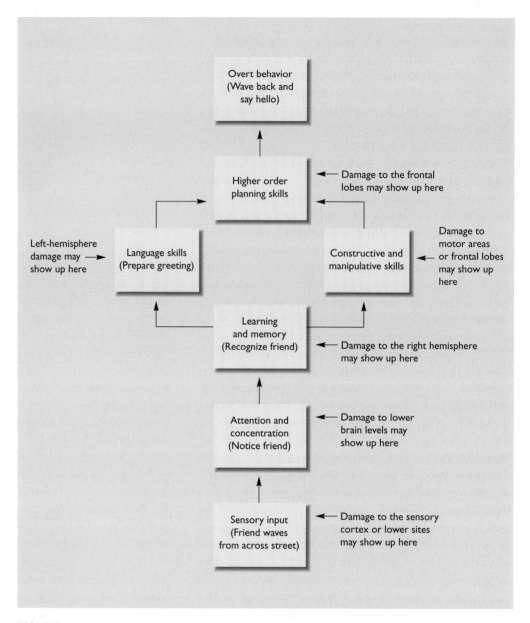

FIGURE 3.3 **Conceptual Model of Information Flow as a Function of Brain Organization.**
Adapted from: Bennett (1988).

primary visual areas of the brain, the neuropsychologist begins by inferring that a person with a visual-perception deficit probably has occipital lobe damage. Because the left and right occipital lobes process information from opposite sides of the environment, the neuropsychologist infers that a visual deficit that is evident only when stimuli are presented to the left is likely to reflect damage to the right occipital lobe. If the deficit involves recognizing familiar objects, the brain damage can be further localized in the forward part of the right occipital lobe because this is the area responsible for giving meaning to visual stimuli (D. I. Margolin, 1992).

Figure 3.3 contains an organizational structure for understanding the process of neuropsychological testing. It depicts, in rough outline, the information processing required for you to recognize a friend waving hello from across the street and to return the greeting. The process begins at the bottom with sensory input. In this case, your friend waves from across the street. This input must be attended to if processing is to proceed. If you do not notice your friend waving, information processing will not proceed. In the next stage, information stored in memory is retrieved and used to interpret the stimulus. This stored information includes your friend's name and appearance. Language skills are required to understand what your friend is saying and to produce a suitable reply. Higher order planning skills may also come into play (telling you that greetings should be returned), and motor skills are required for you to wave back. Brain damage at any stage in the information flow may produce behavioral defects. An inability to retrieve information from memory may manifest itself in an inability to remember your friend's name. A language deficit may make you unable to reply correctly. The goal of neuropsychological testing is to localize a deficit to one of these information-processing stages and then to associate these processing stages with specific brain sites. A deficit in sensory input, for example, implies damage to the sensory cortex (or the lower brain structures leading to the sensory cortex). A difficulty in language processing implies damage to one of the left hemisphere areas that control language in most people.

To assess the various stages of information processing, neuropsychologists administer tests. Based on the results, they try to localize behavioral deficits to specific brain sites or processes. To ensure that no potential deficits are missed, some neuropsychologists administer a fixed test battery to all clients. The Luria-Nebraska Neuropsychological Battery (Golden, 1989) and also the Halstead-Reitan Battery of neuropsychological tests (Reitan & Wolfson, 1985) are among the most popular neuropsychological test batteries. They tap most of the information-processing stages depicted in Figure 3.3. Despite the virtues of standard batteries, some neuropsychologists argue that they are a mistake. They believe that a flexible, probing attitude is necessary to uncover subtle brain-behavior relationships (Walsh, 1987). Such psychologists prefer to use specific tests such as the Wechsler Memory Scale-Revised (Wechsler, 1987), which measures learning and memory, and the Bender Visual-Motor Gestalt Test (Bender, 1938). According to Piotrowski and Keller (1991), the Bender Gestalt is the third most commonly administered psychological test. It consists of figures that the client must copy one at a time (Figure 3.4). Some drawing errors—drawing objects sideways or upside down, simplifying them, mixing features of one object into another, numerous erasures—are associated with brain damage (Lacks, 1984).

Neuropsychologists also use tests of higher order thinking skills that measure the ability to plan ahead (by negotiating a path through a maze, for instance), set goals, solve problems, and form logical categories. An example of the last is the Wisconsin Card Sorting Test (Berg, 1948), which consists of 64 cards each containing varying numbers of shapes (triangle, star, cross, or cir-

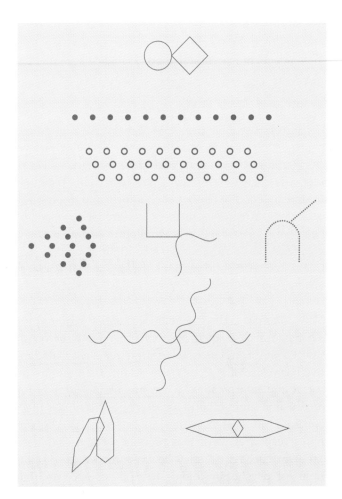

FIGURE 3.4 Bender Visual-Motor Gestalt Test Figure.
Clients must reproduce the designs from memory.

cle) in one of four colors. No two cards are identical in shape, color, and number. The client must sort these cards into four piles without knowing whether the piles should be based on color or shape. After each card is placed, the examiner indicates whether the testee is right or wrong. Through trial and error, the client ultimately learns how the examiner wants the cards sorted. At that point, the examiner shifts the rules. Instead of shape, the client now must sort the cards according to number (or vice versa). An inability to make the required reversal is a sign of damage to those parts of the brain associated with higher order thinking skills.

Children and Brain Damage Children present special challenges for neuropsychologists. The effect of brain damage in children depends not only on the location of the damage but also on the child's age when the damage was sustained and the time elapsed since the damage occurred (S. Schwartz & Johnson, 1985). This is why tests designed and validated on adults cannot be used with children unless they are modified to take developmental level into account (Koppitz, 1975).

Behavioral Assessment

Behavioral psychologists have developed a heterogeneous set of assessment techniques collectively known as **behavioral assessment.** As its name suggests, behavioral assessment is concerned with describing the environmental conditions that elicit and maintain problem behaviors. In contrast to more traditional approaches, behavioral assessment is not limited to a small number of assessment "sessions." It is a continuous process that tracks behavior throughout treatment (Bellack & Hersen, 1988).

SORC Analysis   The essential information required for a behavioral assessment is summarized by the acronym **SORC.** The "S" refers to the stimuli that elicit maladaptive behavior. Most often, these stimuli are found in the social and interpersonal environment. "O" stands for organismic (individual) characteristics that may affect behavior (physical disabilities, for instance). The "R" denotes responses, or actual problem behaviors. These problem "behaviors" may be overt motor acts, cognitions, or psychophysiological responses such as high blood pressure. In a behavioral assessment, particular attention is devoted to assessing the frequency, duration, and intensity of the problem behaviors. "C" refers to the consequences—both positive and negative—that follow a problem behavior. These consequences are assumed to determine the behavior's frequency and intensity. To obtain the necessary information for a SORC analysis, behavioral psychologists use a wide variety of procedures, including interviews, self-report measures, and direct observation (Ciminero, Calhoun, & Adams, 1986).

Behavioral Interviewing   The questions asked in a behavioral interview are often indistinguishable from those asked in any other type of interview. They cover physical health, history, current problems, family and peer relationships, and so on. The similarity to other interviews is superficial, however, because the goals of a behavioral interview are different from the goals of, say, a psychoanalytic interview. Instead of attempting to uncover unconscious conflict, the behavioral interviewer seeks answers to specific "what" questions (Ullmann & Krasner, 1975): *What* behaviors occurring in *what* situations, with *what* consequences are causing a problem? In the case of children, this information may often be gained by interviewing parents or teachers rather than the children themselves (Mash & Terdal, 1981).

Self-Report Measures   Although behavioral assessment often makes use of self-report scales, these are not employed to infer underlying personality traits or psychodynamic conflicts. Instead, behavioral psychologists use self-reports (or, in the case of children, parental reports) to learn more about the antecedents and consequences of problem behaviors. Hersen and Bellack (1988) describe around 300 behavioral tests, scales, inventories, and techniques. Self-report inventories may also be used to learn about a person's thoughts in different situations. A. T. Beck's (1991) measure of depressive attributional style is a good example. Instead of self-reports, psychologists often use behavior-problem checklists to identify problem behaviors in children (McMahon, 1984). Lists of problem behaviors ("cries a lot," "hits others," "has nightmares") are given to parents, caregivers, and teachers, who must then indicate those that are problems for the child and how frequently the problems occur.

Direct Observation of Behavior   Although interviews and self-report measures are important sources of information, they are subject to various biases. People may not always be willing (or able) to say exactly what is troubling them. In such cases, observations of actual behavior can provide clinicians with information they cannot obtain in any other way. These observations can be made naturalistically (observing children in their classrooms, for instance), or they can be made in the clinic. Clinic observations are easier to arrange and control than naturalistic ones, but it should be kept in mind that the clinic environment is artificial. People may act one way in the clinic and another way in their everyday environment. Another problem with direct observations is that observers can get tired and miss, or incorrectly observe, behaviors. To avoid this, behavioral observations are often confined to brief periods. Whether observations are made in the clinic or naturalistically, observers must be carefully trained and the **interrater reliability** of their observations—that is, the degree of agreement and consistency among observers—must be assessed as for any other assessment device.

   An example of behavioral assessment by direct observation is the behavioral avoidance test, which measures how long a person can tolerate exposure to an anxiety-producing situation (R. J. Cohen et al., 1996). A person who fears enclosed spaces, for example, may be asked to remain alone in a small room. The amount of time the person spends in the room is a behavioral mea-

To gather information about the behavior of young children, observation is an essential tool because children lack the language skills to give accurate self-reports and to take most psychological tests.

sure of the person's fear. (The shorter the time, the greater the fear.) The behavioral avoidance test not only measures the severity of a person's fear, it also provides a yardstick for judging treatment success. That is, we would expect the amount of time the person spends in the room to increase if treatment is successful.

Self-monitoring is an important part of practically all behavioral assessment (Kratochwill & Sheridan, 1990). It involves counting the number of times one engages in a behavior and noting one's feelings or cognitions at the time. If you are attempting to stop smoking, for example, your behavior therapist might ask you to record each cigarette you smoke, the prevailing social circumstances (alone, with strangers), and your feelings and thoughts at the time (tired, tense, happy, thinking about work). Self-monitoring makes people self-conscious. You may smoke less just because you are monitoring yourself and because you know that a psychologist will be examining your smoking record. Because the very act of self-monitoring may affect behavior, it is known as a **reactive measure.** Reactive measures can obscure treatment effects. A therapist may think behavioral treatment is responsible for reducing a client's smoking when it is the reactive self-report measure that is really responsible. One way to demonstrate treatment effects is to show that people who receive treatment have better outcomes than those who engage only in self-monitoring without receiving treatment.

Ongoing Behavioral Assessment Behaviorally oriented psychologists try, as far as possible, to build assessment directly into their treatments. In a sense, each client is considered a mini-experiment whose goal is to determine the value of a specific treatment for a particular

person (Yates, 1970). Such mini-experiments may use a "reversal," or ABAB, experimental design. **ABAB experiments** have four phases. In the first phase (A), the psychologist collects baseline data on the frequency and intensity of the problem behaviors. In the second phase (B), treatment is introduced, and any changes in behavior are noted. However, an improvement may be coincidental (it might have occurred even without treatment). To show that the treatment was responsible for the improvement, it is necessary to demonstrate that the treatment and the behavior are "functionally" related. This is accomplished by "reversing" the treatment. Thus, in the third stage, treatment is discontinued (A) while behavior continues to be monitored. If the problem behavior returns to its baseline frequency, therapy is reinstated (B). If the positive changes noted earlier occur once again, the psychologist can feel relatively confident that the treatment is responsible. Figure 3.5 illustrates the phases of a hypothetical ABAB experimental design.

There are instances when ABAB designs are not appropriate. For example, if a therapeutic intervention produced a marked weight gain in a person who had refused to eat, psychologists would not reverse this effect and return the patient to starvation just to be sure that it was their treatment that was responsible. Reversals may also be impossible when clients have been taught new skills. For example, we would not try to make clients who have successfully undergone assertiveness training submissive again just to be sure that the assertiveness training had worked. In such cases, it is sometimes possible to demonstrate a functional relationship between a treatment intervention and a behavior by measuring several independent behaviors in the baseline phase. If the behaviors are truly independent, an intervention applied to one should not affect the others. For example, a person who refuses to eat may not only be starving but may also be excessively active. The psychologist can take baseline measures of both caloric intake and activity level. A treatment program aimed at increasing caloric intake can then be instituted. If caloric intake and activity level are independent, this program should affect only eating, not activity level. A second intervention can then be targeted at reducing the person's activity level. If this intervention proves successful, the psychologist can reasonably conclude that the individual treatments were each responsible for specific behavioral effects. Because more than one behavior is measured in the baseline phase, this experimental design is known as a **multiple-baseline experiment.**

ABAB and multiple-baseline experiments are only two of many **single-subject experimental designs** (E. E. Jones, 1993). Although such experiments are generally

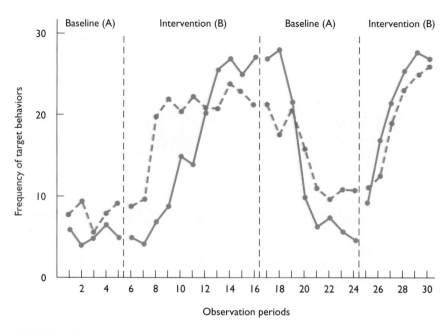

FIGURE 3.5 **Results of a Hypothetical Behavior Modification Study Following an ABAB Design.** Adapted from: Bordens & Abbott (1999, p. 288).

associated with the operant (Skinnerian) tradition of behavioral therapy, they are applicable to any therapy aimed at changing specific behaviors (Barlow & Hersen, 1984).

Psychophysiological Assessment

Various physiological instruments may be used to record and make inferences about behavior. A penile plethysmograph, for example, is a pressure-sensitive device used to record changes in penis size; it reflects a male's state of sexual arousal. By presenting suitably chosen photographs or films, it is possible to determine whether a male is aroused by deviant stimuli (young children, for example). Because it relies on a physiological response, the plethysmograph can record sexual arousal without requiring an overt verbal report (Abel, Rouleau, & Cunningham-Rathner, 1986).

Electromyographs record muscle tension. Like the plethysmograph, the electromyograph may also be used to determine a person's physiological response to stimuli without requiring an overt response. For example, an electromyograph can record muscle tension while a person who fears public speaking makes a speech. We would expect recorded muscle tension to decrease with successful treatment. Sometimes, just providing people with information about the state of their muscle tension can lead to tension reduction (Hatch, Fisher, & Rugh, 1987). Providing people with information about a phys-

iological process in the hope of changing their behavior is known as **biofeedback.**

The best-known physiological recording apparatus is the **polygraph,** a device that simultaneously measures respiration rate, heart rate, and several other forms of physiological activity. The polygraph is commonly known as a *lie detector,* a term made popular by William Moulton Marston in the early years of the 20th century. Marston, the creator of the *Wonder Woman* cartoon, claimed that people who tell lies experience emotions that are measurable using the polygraph (Lykken, 1981). Although the polygraph has been used in criminal investigations and to screen job applicants, there is little evidence for its validity as a general screening device to measure "honesty" (Gale, 1988; Steinbrook, 1992). This is why many states and foreign countries have placed restrictions on its use, especially in personnel selection. The unquestioned acceptance of the polygraph by some police forces and employers should serve as a warning. We cannot assume that assessment devices that rely on technical equipment are more "scientific" than paper-and-pencil tests. The reliability and validity of all tests—physiological or paper-and-pencil—must be demonstrated through careful research. Psychologists' professional ethics demand that they consider a measure's reliability and validity when drawing inferences from it that can have serious consequences for the individual being assessed.

Classifying a disorder requires more than anecdotal evidence. Because he has not been willing to submit to psychological assessments, Theodore Kaczynski (the Unabomber) has been variously "diagnosed" as obsessive-compulsive, delusional, antisocial, paranoid, or narcissistic. His vehement objections to an insanity plea have led some people to speculate that he has paranoid schizophrenia because one of its hallmarks is the refusal to be labeled mentally ill.

CLASSIFYING ABNORMAL BEHAVIOR

Classifying disorders into diagnostic categories and giving them labels permits shorthand communication. Instead of having to describe a person's behavior in detail, clinicians can say that the person is depressed and others will have an idea about what the person is like. In some cases, diagnoses can also convey important information about treatment. Classification is also an essential first step in uncovering the etiology of disorders. Doctors once spoke of "the fevers," lumping together those caused by malaria with fevers caused by pneumonia, infection, and the common cold. Not surprisingly, the specific causes of these different illnesses were not discovered until scientists began making distinctions among the conditions. The same applies to abnormal behavior. We cannot hope to find the causes of behavior disorders if we consider them all part of one undifferentiated category. Our understanding of psychopathology must begin with a generally accepted set of classifications.

Because classification had its impetus in the medical context, it is almost always referred to as diagnosis even though there are other nonmedical ways of classifying

people, which are also discussed in this chapter. To show how our current classification and diagnostic system came to develop the way it has, the discussion begins with a brief history of the classification and diagnosis of mental disorders.

The First *DSMs*

Before the 19th century, people whose behavior was considered abnormal were looked after by general practitioners, priests, social welfare agencies, friends, or relatives. After the American and French revolutions, however, democratic governments began to accept greater responsibility for their citizens, even those considered deranged. Newly built state hospitals began to admit "mentally disturbed" people (Scull, 1989). Clinicians who worked in these state hospitals began to specialize in psychological disorders. As one of their first tasks, these new specialists set out to describe their patients and to classify them into diagnostic categories. They began by making meticulous observations of patients. They noted symptom patterns (syndromes), which they grouped into categories based on similarities in appearance and natural history. Next, they attempted to explain how and why different conditions develop by inferring underlying disease states. Later, by trying out different interventions and noting their effects, they developed treatments.

By the late 1800s, accurate diagnosis—classifying patients into more or less homogeneous categories—became scientific medicine's major preoccupation. It was inevitable, therefore, that mental health professionals would adopt a similar approach and devote themselves to describing and classifying their patients. Foremost among these classification-oriented mental health specialists was Emil Kraepelin (1856–1926).

Kraepelin, a German psychiatrist who had studied psychology with the pioneer experimental psychologist, Wilhelm Wundt (1832–1920), wrote his first paper on classification while still a medical student (Pasamanick, 1959), and he remained interested in classification throughout his career. In his last published work, which appeared one year after his death, Kraepelin classified all the mental disorders known at the time into 13 categories. In addition to grouping together disorders with a presumed common etiology, he also created descriptive categories based on symptom similarity. Although the names have changed and the number of categories has grown, the mixed etiological and descriptive diagnostic system we use today is a direct descendant of the one devised by Kraepelin.

Emil Kraepelin (1856–1926) was a pioneer in the classification of psychological disorders and the attempt to discover similarities and differences among them.

In 1948, the United Nations' World Health Organization produced the *International Statistical Classification of Diseases, Injuries, and Causes of Death (ICD).* This comprehensive list of diseases included "mental" disorders. Although the *ICD* was intended to foster international cooperative research by creating a common **nosology** (naming scheme), its terminology for mental disorders was not adopted in the United States. Instead, the American Psychiatric Association produced its own *Diagnostic and Statistical Manual of Mental Disorders (DSM)* in 1952. The American Psychiatric Association preferred to have its own diagnostic scheme because the mental health profession in the United States was dominated by psychoanalysts. They rejected the *ICD*'s emphasis on physiological etiologies, stressing instead the role of traumatic experiences. Because psychoanalysts believe that almost all mental disturbances are reactions to real or imagined trauma, the *DSM* called all nonorganic disorders *reactions* (depressive reaction, schizophrenic reaction, and so on). It also contained a category called **neuroses** for people whose psychological problems were not sufficiently severe to require hospitalization. In 1968, the American Psychiatric Association produced a revised diagnostic scheme called the *DSM-II*

(American Psychiatric Assn, 1968). The *DSM-II* no longer labeled everything a reaction. Otherwise, it was not a major departure from its predecessor. Yet, as soon as it was published, it came under critical attack. For historical reasons, these criticisms are discussed here. However, as you will see later in this chapter, many criticisms of the early *DSM*s remain equally valid today.

Criticism 1: Diagnoses Are Social Constructions   Among the first, and most vocal, critics of the *DSM*s were the **anti-psychiatrists,** a group that included Thomas Szasz, whose views were introduced in Chapter 2. The anti-psychiatrists argued that if we take the environmental view seriously—if we accept that mental disorders are produced by bigotry, poverty, poor parenting, unemployment, and other environmental factors—then mental disorders are not medical diseases. They are social dilemmas that are not the responsibility of medicine or clinical psychology but fall instead within the realm of religion, politics, and ethics. The anti-psychiatrists alleged that, by assigning medical diagnoses to what are really social problems, the mental health establishment was simply trying to maintain its professional prestige and power (Szasz, 1971). The American Psychiatric Association's deletion of homosexuality from its diagnostic manual in 1973 (as described in Chapter 1) gave credibility to the anti-psychiatrists' claim that diagnoses were simply social constructions (M. Wilson, 1993).

Criticism 2: Diagnoses Lack Reliability   Whereas the anti-psychiatry movement criticized the philosophy underlying the *DSM-II*, psychologists criticized it on methodological grounds. They pointed out that diagnoses are useful only if they have high interrater reliability. Independent clinicians, using the same diagnostic criteria and evaluating the same person, should come up with the same diagnosis. (For information on assessing diagnostic reliability, see Critical Thinking About Clinical Decisions 3.2.) Clinicians should also be able to discriminate people with different diagnoses from one another. Unfortunately, empirical studies found that many diagnostic categories had low reliability and discriminative ability (see Kirk & Kutchins, 1992, for a review). One reason for the poor showing was that diagnoses were often stated in vague terms. For example, the *DSM-II* described people with "inadequate personality" as having "ineffectual responses to emotional, social, intellectual, and physical demands . . . inadaptability, ineptness, poor judgment, social instability, and lack of physical and emotional stamina" (American Psychi-

Clinical Agreement: Better Than Chance?

The obvious way to assess diagnostic reliability is to ask clinicians to assign people to diagnostic categories and note the number of times they agree. In practice, however, such studies are difficult to conduct. First, the clinicians being studied must be equally expert. Otherwise, low levels of agreement may reflect differences in diagnostic skill rather than diagnostic reliability. Second, all clinicians should receive the same amount of information about the people they are diagnosing. Finally, clinicians must make their judgments independently. Allowing them to consult one another will produce spuriously high levels of agreement.

Even when these methodological conditions are met, the results of reliability studies are often difficult to interpret. Take an extreme case. Two clinicians diagnose 100 people simply by flipping a coin. Heads, a person is assigned to category A; tails, to B. Because the coin will come up heads about half the time, each clinician will assign about 50 people to each category. Because their assignments are random, the clinicians will sometimes agree by chance. The probability that both clinicians will assign the same person to category A is .25 (.50 × .50). The same is true for category B. Adding the probabilities of agreement for both categories, we find that two clinicians who assign people to diagnostic categories by the flip of a coin will still agree

about 50% of the time (.25 + .25 = .50). Because the clinicians will agree half the time by chance alone, diagnostic reliability can be shown only if they agree more than half the time. How much more? This is not an easy question to answer; it depends on a disorder's prevalence.

The prevalence, or base rate, is the number of cases of a particular disorder found in a population (see Critical Thinking About Clinical Decisions 1.3). If the prevalence of suicidal tendencies in the general population is 10%, this means that in a random sample of 100 people, we would expect 10 to be suicidal. Now, suppose two clinicians have no idea how to spot potentially suicidal people. They could still achieve a high rate of agreement by choosing 10 people at random from the population of 100, classifying them as suicidal, and calling everyone else nonsuicidal. The result would be at least an 80% interrater reliability. To see why, let's give each person in the sample a number from 1 to 100. The table shows what happens when

one clinician arbitrarily assigns persons 1–10 to the suicidal category and the other clinician assigns persons 91–100 to the suicidal category. Although the two clinicians assign different people to the suicidal category, they both assign the same 80 persons (numbers 11–90) to the nonsuicidal category. Thus, they agree at least 80% of the time even though they chose their suicidal groups arbitrarily.

Because chance agreement inflates reliability, researchers usually express reliability using a statistic known as **kappa (κ),** which indicates the level of interrater agreement over and above the level expected by chance alone (J. Cohen, 1960, 1968).

Keep in mind that no diagnostic system is perfectly reliable. The level of reliability required for everyday clinical use varies with the treatments available. For example, diagnoses that lead to dangerous treatments or the deprivation of liberty need to be more reliable than those with more innocuous consequences.

Hypothetical Results From a Study in Which Clinicians Arbitrarily Classify 10 out of 100 People as Suicidal and the Rest as Nonsuicidal

Catetory	Clinician 1	Clinician 2
Suicidal	Persons 1–10	Persons 91–100
Nonsuicidal	**Persons 11–90**	Persons 1–10
Nonsuicidal	Persons 91–100	**Persons 11–90**

atric Assn, 1968, p. 44). Given this subjectivity, it is not surprising that clinicians could not agree about whether a person is "ineffectual," "inept," or "lacks stamina."

Criticism 3: Diagnoses Lack Validity In addition to questioning the reliability of diagnostic categories, psychologists also attacked their validity (their claim to represent a specific abnormal psychological state). One critic of diagnostic validity was David Rosenhan (1973),

who arranged for "pseudopatients" (psychologists, physicians, a painter, a housewife, and himself) to present themselves to psychiatric hospitals claiming to hear voices. Apart from feigning this symptom and using false names and professions, the pseudopatients answered all questions honestly and made no attempt to appear abnormal. Nevertheless, nearly all were diagnosed "schizophrenic." Once they were admitted to a hospital, the pseudopatients' task was to convince

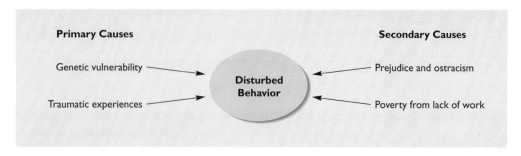

FIGURE 3.6 **Primary and Secondary Causes of Behavior Disorders**

the medical staff that they were "sane" so they could be discharged. They stopped talking about their hallucinations. When asked, they reported no symptoms and claimed to be feeling well. Nurses described the pseudopatients as "friendly," "cooperative," and "exhibiting no abnormal indications." Yet, pseudopatients spent from 7 to 52 days in the hospital, with an average stay of 19 days. During that time, not a single one was unmasked by hospital staff. Because hospital staff could not tell the fake clients from real ones, Rosenhan concluded that psychiatric diagnoses lack validity.

Critics of Rosenhan's study cried foul; clinicians, they claimed, were just being properly cautious. Suppose, they argued, that instead of claiming to hear voices, pseudopatients had consumed a pint of blood, stumbled into the hospital emergency room, and vomited the blood on the floor. Wouldn't doctors have been justified in thinking that they needed treatment for a serious disorder, even if, following the episode, they appeared fine?

This criticism was probably justified, but Rosenhan's attack on diagnostic validity did not rely solely on what happened to the pseudopatients. After the last pseudopatient had been discharged, Rosenhan informed the staff of one teaching hospital that sometime within a 3-month period one or more pseudopatients would attempt to gain admission. He asked the hospital staff to try to expose the phony patients. Forty-one of the 193 people admitted to the hospital during the 3-month period were alleged by staff, with high confidence, to be pseudopatients. This finding was embarrassing for the hospital because Rosenhan had lied; he never sent any pseudopatients. The people accused of being phonies were *real* patients. Again, clinicians could not tell real patients from fake ones. Rosenhan concluded that clinicians may show reasonable levels of agreement about who is schizophrenic but that their diagnoses are not valid. Normal people were diagnosed as schizophrenic, whereas seriously disturbed people were diagnosed as normal.

Criticism 4: Diagnostic Labels May Become Self-Fulfilling Prophecies

Even valid diagnostic systems may be pernicious if the act of giving a person a diagnosis itself causes harm. Recognizing the effects of labeling, sociologists distinguish primary from secondary causes of abnormal behavior (Scheff, 1966, 1975), as shown in Figure 3.6. Initially, psychopathology arises from causes within an individual or from an individual's experience. For example, a person may have contracted a disease such as general paresis, inherited a predisposition toward mental illness, or undergone a traumatic experience. Once the person begins to behave abnormally, however, a second force comes into play—society's reaction. Like the lepers of the past—and today's people with AIDS— people diagnosed as mentally ill may be socially disadvantaged and stigmatized. They may be ridiculed, shunned, feared, and isolated. Even old friends may avoid them, and they may find it difficult to obtain housing and jobs. To adapt, they withdraw from social contacts. In some cases, they become aggressive toward those who mistreat or ignore them. In this way, the diagnosis becomes a self-fulfilling prophecy. Eventually, diagnostic labels even begin to affect how people think about themselves. They may lose faith in their ability to control their own lives and become dependent on mental health professionals. In effect, the labels themselves become causes of abnormal behavior.

The effects of labeling were dramatic in Rosenhan's study. Doctors and nurses interpreted normal behavior as "pathological." Boredom was construed as nervousness, and anger at mistreatment was interpreted as pathological aggressiveness. Pseudopatients who kept diaries were described as engaging in "writing behavior." It seemed that once a person was diagnosed mentally ill, everything that person did, even writing, was viewed as pathological. Even after discharge, the pseudopatients (all of whom were behaving normally) could not escape their diagnostic label. Most were given the diagnosis of "schizophrenia, in remission." This suggests that, despite the pseudopatients' superficial normality, clinicians still considered them disturbed underneath.

Response to the Critics: *DSM-III* and *DSM-III-R*

As criticisms of the *DSM-II* grew louder, the mental health professions, especially psychiatry, began to suffer. Insurance companies claimed that diagnoses were so unreliable that no one knew which treatments were appropriate for which clients. They began to deny claims for reimbursement of the costs of psychiatric treatment. At the same time, the dominant theoretical view (that behavior disorders are mainly the result of traumatic experiences) meant that research funds were directed mainly to psychologists and other social scientists. Facing severe losses to their clinical income from insurance companies and unable to obtain research grants, psychiatrists decided to revamp their image by revising the *DSM-II*. The third revision of the *Diagnostic and Statistical Manual (DSM-III)* was published in 1980, and a further revised edition (the *DSM-III-R*) appeared in 1987. Over the years, the *DSM* was translated into 20 languages and became the standard nosology in many parts of the world.

Although pressure from clinicians resulted in the retention of some low-reliability, psychoanalytically derived diagnoses in the revised system (Kirk & Kutchins, 1992), the new *DSMs* did have significant advantages over the old ones. The most important was their attempt to introduce objective diagnostic criteria. Interrater reliabilities for *DSM-III* diagnoses ranged from around 50% to as high as 90%, with most falling in the 70–80% range (American Psychiatric Assn, 1980; Andreasen & Carpenter, 1993; Werry et al., 1983). These reliabilities were inflated somewhat because the clinicians who participated in *DSM-III* reliability studies did not always make their diagnoses independently (see Critical Thinking About Clinical Decisions 3.2 and Kirk & Kutchins, 1992). Nevertheless, *DSM-III* reliabilities compared favorably with diagnostic reliabilities achieved in many areas of medicine. After all, radiologists don't always agree when evaluating chest X rays, cardiologists disagree about the meaning of electrocardiograms, and pathologists do not always agree about whether a tissue sample is malignant (S. Schwartz & Griffin, 1986).

Despite the widespread adoption of the *DSM-III* and *DSM-III-R*, even their admirers admitted that they were not perfect (Spitzer, Williams, & Skodol, 1983).

Further revisions were inevitable. Indeed, planning for the fourth edition of the *DSM* began almost as soon as the *DSM-III-R* was published. The *DSM-IV* is the edition presently in use.

The *DSM-IV*

In 1988, the American Psychiatric Association appointed a task force to begin work on a fourth revision of the *Diagnostic and Statistical Manual of Mental Disorders (DSM-IV)*. The reason for beginning work so soon after the publication of the *DSM-III-R* was the World Health Organization's (1992) planned 10th revision of the *International Statistical Classification of Diseases (ICD-10)*. To ensure the comparability of research data collected in different countries (an essential condition for cooperative research), the United States government, along with other members of the United Nations, agreed to maintain consistency between its diagnostic systems and those contained in the *ICD-10*.

The *DSM-IV* was developed in three stages. In the first, work groups consisting of clinicians and researchers conducted systematic literature reviews to identify problems in the *DSM-III-R* diagnostic criteria. The second stage involved analyses of previously collected data, whereas the third stage consisted of field trials conducted to assess the reliability of the diagnoses. To encourage widespread debate, options for revising the *DSM-III-R* were published first in preliminary form (American Psychiatric Assn, 1991). The *DSM-IV*, which was published in 1994, represents an evolutionary rather than a revolutionary development of the *DSM-III-R*. Although it attempts to provide scientific justifications for its various diagnostic criteria, the quality of these justifications varies considerably across the disorders. Many of its diagnostic criteria are still based on little more than clinical opinion. Others represent compromises among clinicians, researchers, and special interest groups. It is worth keeping in mind that, like the *DSM-III-R*, the *DSM-IV* is not just a scientific document; it is also a political statement in which organized mental health professionals stake out what they consider to be their territory.

We have already seen one example of the political nature of psychiatric diagnoses—the removal of homosexuality from the *DSM*. Another example is "premenstrual dysphoric disorder" (PMDD; Rivera-Tovar, Pilkonis, & Frank, 1992). PMDD is a constellation of symptoms (irritability, sleep disorders) allegedly

Since the first edition in 1952, the DSM has been rewritten four times in an attempt to make diagnoses of mental disorders more objective, reliable, and valid. The DSM's classification system differs somewhat from that of the ICD, which is used in the rest of the world.

experienced by some women during a certain stage of the menstrual cycle. One of the work groups preparing the *DSM-IV* proposed that PMDD be included to encourage research and to provide treatment for those women who needed it. The response from critics was loud and immediate (see Chase, 1993). They claimed that PMDD was simply a form of the normal premenstrual syndrome that affects many women. Including it in the *DSM-IV,* they claimed, would define normal female behavior as deviant, stigmatizing women and promoting discrimination. Heated arguments appeared on both sides. Eventually, a political compromise was reached. The *DSM-IV* relegated PMDD to an appendix. Clinicians can use the term if they wish, and the subject will be debated again when the *DSM* is next revised.

Most *DSM-IV* diagnostic categories are less political than PMDD, but they have other types of problems. For example, the *DSM-IV* attempts to group together disorders with similar symptoms. Thus, depression caused by substance abuse is classified with mood disorders

rather than with substance-induced disorders. This does not mean that a single organizing principle underlies all *DSM-IV* categories. Some categories (schizophrenia and other psychotic disorders) contain disorders with similar symptoms; others group together disorders with similar causes or etiologies (such as brain damage); still others, such as the developmental disorders, are grouped based on the age at which symptoms first appear. This mixed type of nosology reflects our uneven knowledge about the etiology of mental disorders. Researchers simply do not know enough about the causes of mental disorders to group all of them according to their etiologies. This is not a problem peculiar to abnormal psychology. Doctors group ulcerative colitis, irritable bowel syndrome, and several other conditions together in a category known as inflammatory bowel diseases (Kirsner & Shorter, 1980). These conditions are grouped together because of the similarity in their symptoms, not because there is any evidence for their common etiology.

At this stage in our knowledge, a mixed diagnostic system like the *DSM-IV* is probably inevitable. The best we can hope for is that the diagnostic categories are sufficiently reliable that researchers can use them to investigate the causes of psychopathology and that clinicians can use them to help choose appropriate treatments.

DSM-IV TABLE 3.3 Main *DSM-IV* Diagnostic Categories and Chapter(s) in This Book in Which They Are Discussed

Diagnostic Category	Brief Description	Chapter
Disorders usually first diagnosed in infancy, childhood, or adolescence	These range from pervasive disorders that affect every aspect of life to minor ones, such as elimination disorders. The common bond is the age of first diagnosis.	12
Mental retardation and learning disorders	Disorders of intellectual functioning and communication.	12
Delirium, dementia, amnestic and other cognitive disorders	Mainly disorders of memory and cognitive function with presumed neurological causes (brain damage, brain disease).	11
Eating disorders	Undereating and overeating.	12
Mental disorders due to a general medical condition	Includes emotional and cognitive effects of physical illnesses.	5
Substance-related disorders	Alcohol and drug (prescription and illicit) problems.	6
Schizophrenia and other psychotic disorders	Disorders marked by a loss of contact with reality.	9
Mood disorders	Includes depression, extreme elation, and mood alteration.	8
Anxiety disorders	A mixed group of fear- and dread-related conditions.	4
Somatoform disorders	Mainly disorders with physical complaints.	7
Factitious disorders	Intentional faking of physical illness.	7
Dissociative disorders	Loss of memory and personal identity.	7
Sexual and gender-identity disorders	Problems with sexual functioning and gender identity.	13
Sleep disorders	Sleep difficulties with various causes.	12, 13
Impulse-control disorders not elsewhere classified	A mixed group of disorders including shoplifting, fire setting, gambling, and others.	10
Adjustment disorders	Reactions to life circumstances (death, divorce).	13
Personality disorders	Disorders of "character," such as antisocial, dependent, and histrionic personality disorders	4, 10
Other conditions that may be a focus of clinical attention	A wide variety of problems that may require clinical intervention (academic, occupational, intellectual).	Throughout

Specification of Diagnostic Criteria in the *DSM-IV*   The *DSM-IV* divides behavioral disorders into 18 major categories, each containing a set of disorders (Table 3.3). Each disorder, in turn, has its own set of diagnostic criteria. These have been formulated to make them as objective as possible. To illustrate how *DSM-IV* criteria differ from earlier ones, Table 3.4 compares the general *DSM-IV* criteria for schizophrenia with the *DSM-II* criteria for that disorder. As may be seen, the *DSM-II* description contains few details and gives little guidance to the clinician about such matters as the length of time

that symptoms must be in evidence before a person can be diagnosed schizophrenic. In contrast, the *DSM-IV* description is more complete and objective. It is worth noting that Rosenhan's pseudopatients—who were diagnosed as schizophrenic using the *DSM-II* criteria—would not be diagnosed as schizophrenic using the *DSM-IV* criteria (because the *DSM-IV* requires that hallucinations persist for at least 1 month and that signs of disturbance be apparent for at least 6 months).

Although the *DSM-IV* is an improvement over earlier *DSM*s, it is far from perfect. The criteria for schizo-

DSM-IV **TABLE 3.4** A Comparison of the *DSM-II* and *DSM-IV* Diagnostic Criteria for Schizophrenia

DSM-II

This large category includes a group of disorders manifested by characteristic disturbances of thinking, mood, and behavior. Disturbances in thinking are marked by alterations of concept formation, which may lead to misinterpretation of reality and sometimes to delusions and hallucinations, which frequently appear psychologically self-protective. Corollary mood changes include ambivalent, constricted, and inappropriate emotional responsiveness and loss of empathy with others. Behavior may be withdrawn, regressive, and bizarre.

DSM-IV

A. *Characteristic Symptoms:* Two (or more) of the following, each present for a significant portion of time during a 1-month period (or less if successfully treated):

   1. delusions

   2. hallucinations

   3. disorganized speech (e.g., incoherence)

   4. grossly disorganized behavior

   5. negative symptoms (no show of emotion, for example)

   Note—Only one symptom is required if delusions are bizarre or hallucinations consist of a voice keeping up a running commentary on the person's behavior or thought, or two or more voices conversing with each other.

B. *Social/Occupational Dysfunction:* For a significant portion of the time since the onset of the disturbance, one or more major areas of functioning, such as work, interpersonal relations, or self-care, is markedly below the level achieved prior to the onset.

C. *Duration:* Continuous signs of the disturbance persist for at least 6 months. This 6-month period must include at least 1 month of symptoms that meet the criterion set out under "A" (Characteristic Symptoms).

Note: Information from *DSM-II* is adapted from American Psychiatric Association (1968, p. 33) and information from *DSM-IV*, American Psychiatric Association (1994, p. 285).

phrenia still include vague phrases such as "for a significant proportion of the time." Moreover, because a diagnosis requires the presence of only two of five "characteristic symptoms" (or just one under certain conditions), it is possible for two people to receive the same diagnosis without sharing any symptoms.

Multiaxial Classification The *DSM* uses a multiaxial classification system. Each axis represents a different item of information. Axis I contains a person's primary clinical diagnoses (major depression, for example). Axis II is used to describe any existing personality disorders, such as antisocial personality (see Chapters 4 and 10). Separating primary diagnoses from personality disorders ensures that clinicians, who tend to focus most of their attention on a person's immediate clinical disorders, do not ignore long-term personality dispositions. Axis III is used to describe nonpsychiatric medical conditions that may play a role in a person's problem. Axis IV is used to indicate psychosocial or environmental problems that may affect the diagnosis, treatment, or prognosis of a mental disorder (death of a family member, for example). Axis V consists of a global assessment of a client's psychological functioning. Although the *DSM-IV* contains several measurement scales suitable for measuring global functioning, the assessment is usually made using the Global Assessment of Functioning scale, which describes social and occupational functioning (Table 3.5). The lowest ratings are given to people who are having trouble looking after themselves, and the highest ratings are given to those who are employed, are involved in social activities, and have no overt behavioral disorder. Ratings can be made for current as well as past functioning. Axis V ratings are used to plan a treatment program, measure its impact, and predict treatment outcome. Structured interviews are available to lead clinicians through the process of making *DSM-IV* diagnoses (Bech, 1993; see also Document 3.4).

Examples of how *DSM-IV* diagnoses are applied appear in Documents 3.9 and 3.10. Document 3.9 comes

TABLE 3.5 Global Assessment of Functioning Scale

Consider psychological, social, and occupational functioning on a hypothetical continuum of mental health–illness. Do not include impairment in functioning due to physical (or environmental) limitations.

Code (Note: Use intermediate codes when appropriate, e.g., 45, 68, 72.)

Code	
100 91	Superior functioning in a wide range of activities, life's problems never seem to get out of hand, is sought out by others because of his or her many positive qualities. No symptoms.
90 81	Absent or minimal symptoms (e.g., mild anxiety before an exam), good functioning in all areas, interested and involved in a wide range of activities, socially effective, generally satisfied with life, no more than everyday problems or concerns (e.g., an occasional argument with family members).
80 71	If symptoms are present they are transient and expectable reactions to psychosocial stressors (e.g., difficulty concentrating after family argument); no more than slight impairment in social, occupational, or school functioning (e.g., temporarily falling behind in schoolwork).
70 61	Some mild symptoms (e.g., depressed mood and mild insomnia) *or* some difficulty in social, occupational, or school functioning (e.g., occasional truancy, or theft within the household), but generally functioning pretty well, has some meaningful personal relationships.
60 51	Moderate symptoms (e.g., flat affect and circumstantial speech, occasional panic attacks) *or* moderate difficulty in social, occupational, or school functioning (e.g., few friends, conflicts with peers or co-workers).
50 41	Serious symptoms (e.g., suicidal ideation, severe obsessional rituals, frequent shoplifting *or* any serious impairment in social, occupational, or school functioning (e.g., no friends, unable to keep a job).
40 31	Some impairment in reality testing or communication (e.g., speech is at times illogical, obscure, or irrelevant) *or* major impairment in several areas, such as work or school, family relations, judgment, thinking, or mood (e.g., depressed man avoids friends, neglects family, and is unable to work; child frequently beats up younger children, is defiant at home, and is failing at school).
30 21	Behavior is considerably influenced by delusions or hallucinations *or* serious impairment in communication or judgment (e.g., sometimes incoherent, acts grossly inappropriately, suicidal preoccupation) *or* inability to function in almost all areas (e.g., stays in bed all day; no job, home, or friends).
20 11	Some danger of hurting self or others (e.g., suicide attempts without clear expectation of death; frequently violent; manic excitement) *or* occasionally fails to maintain personal hygiene (e.g., smears feces) *or* gross impairment in communication (e.g., largely incoherent or mute).
10 1	Persistent danger of severely hurting self or others (e.g., recurrent violence) *or* persistent inability to maintain personal hygiene *or* serious suicidal act without clear expectation of death.
0	Inadequate information

Note: From American Psychiatric Association (1994, p. 32).

from Dr. Berg's assessment of Danielle Wood conducted after her unsuccessful suicide attempt. Document 3.10 comes from Dr. Berg's assessment of William Cole, a university student who is also depressed and has the chronic disease diabetes mellitus. (We will learn more about William Cole in Chapter 5.) Note how multiaxial classification can provide useful benchmarks by which to judge the effects of a treatment. For example, Dr. Berg believes that treatment should restore Danielle to a higher level of functioning than it will William. (William's chronic medical problem makes it difficult for him to achieve a high level of functioning.)

DOCUMENT 3.9

Multiaxial Diagnosis of Danielle Wood

The client meets all of the *DSM-IV* criteria for a diagnosis of major depression. In addition, she seems to have had a long-standing pattern of behavior that is characteristic of a personality disorder, especially the dependent type. She has recently experienced some mild stress (breaking up with her boyfriend), and her global psychological functioning is definitely impaired at present. Her activities prior to the current episode show that she is capable of a high level of psychological functioning.

Axis	Classification	Danielle Wood's classification
Axis I	Clinical disorder	Major depressive disorder
Axis II	Personality disorder	Dependent personality
Axis III	General medical conditions	None
Axis IV	Psychosocial and environmental problems	Failure to achieve sports goals
Axis V	Global assessment of functioning	GAF at present: 50; highest level past year: 95 ■

DOCUMENT 3.10

Multiaxial Diagnosis of William Cole

The client is an insulin-dependent diabetic who is moderately depressed and has become socially isolated. He does not feel in control of his illness. His illness becomes worse under stress (final examinations, for example). At such times, he may also fail to comply with treatment (perhaps a disguised call for help). The client has low self-esteem. Recommend that he attend a diabetic support group. Exposure to others in similar circumstances may help him acquire better coping skills while at the same time increasing his sense of belonging and his self-esteem. Therapy will also be helpful. Therapy should include training in stress reduction, coping skills, and the skills necessary to increase social support. Antidepressants may also be helpful in the short term.

Axis	Classification	William Cole's classification
Axis I	Clinical disorder	Mood disorder due to diabetes with depressive features
Axis II	Personality disorder	Dependent personality
Axis III	General medical conditions	Diabetes mellitus
Axis IV	Psychosocial and environmental problems	Academic problems, illness
Axis V	Global assessment of functioning	GAF at present: 50; highest level past year: 70 ■

Diagnosis and Classification: Current Status

The *DSM-IV* is open to many of the same criticisms as its predecessors. Not all of its diagnostic categories are derived from research (many are based on little more than clinical opinion), it contains disorders with no known etiology, many of its diagnoses have no current treat-

Behavioral disorders sometimes elude precise classification. Australian pianist David Helfgott's unusual behaviors are evident in the biographical movie Shine, *yet his psychiatrist has not been able to diagnose him. His psychiatrist says that Helfgott is not autistic or schizophrenic or manic in the clinical sense and that the closest label for what ails him may be "schizoaffective disorder."*

ment implications, the reliability of some of its diagnostic categories is still too low, and its diagnostic labels still carry stigmatizing connotations. These deficiencies are taken by some critics as evidence for the futility of classifying behavior disorders into discrete diagnostic categories. Some critics argue that there is simply no clear distinction between normal and abnormal behavior. Everyone gets unhappy sometimes; the difference between unhappiness and depression is really a matter of degree rather than a difference in kind. Even if this is true, however, it does not necessarily follow that classification is futile. There are no discrete boundaries between colors either. Yet it is still possible, and valuable to artists, to distinguish gray from black and pink from red.

Taking a related tack, some critics attack the descriptive nature of many diagnostic categories. For example, the *DSM-IV* labels a shoplifter a "kleptomaniac." This label tells us little more about the person than we already knew—the person shoplifts. Because the label kleptomaniac tells us nothing about the etiology or treatment of shoplifting (it simply describes the behavior it is meant to explain), critics argue that diagnosis is a waste of time. Again, this conclusion does not neces-

Are People More Than Simple Labels?

The *DSM*s have all followed Kraepelin's **categorical** approach to **classification.** First, diagnostic categories are constructed by grouping together related symptoms to form syndromes. Then, people are assessed to see how closely their symptoms match those of a specific syndrome or disorder. A person who displays a sufficient number of the relevant symptoms is said to meet the "criteria" for that disorder. This approach to classification is familiar and easy to learn. Its major disadvantage is that it conveys little information about any specific individual. This is inevitable. Putting people into categories emphasizes their similarities; individual differences that make people unique are lost.

Instead of trying to place people in preexisting categories, researchers and clinicians could describe an individual on a series of personality dimensions—aggressiveness, mood, rigidity, honesty, energy. You may have a friend who is currently depressed. Your friend is also very honest, always tired, rarely aggressive, and often rigid and moralistic. The *DSM-IV* would describe your friend as suffering from a depressive episode. True as far as it goes, but it hardly gives much of a picture of what your friend is like. A **dimensional classification** approach would include all of your friend's characteristics, thereby providing a richer, more lifelike picture than is possible with a categorical diagnosis. But flexibility and richness come at a cost. Dimensional descriptions are more complex and harder to summarize than categorical diagnoses, and, more important, there is no consensus about the appropriate dimensions to use. One solution is to use statistical techniques such as **factor analysis** to determine which dimensions "go together." Patterns produced by dimensions that seem to covary could be given names, thereby producing an alternative to traditional diagnoses.

Although researchers have found some correspondence between statistically derived diagnostic categories and those contained in the various *DSM*s, many psychiatric categories have no statistical counterpart (S. Schwartz & Johnson, 1985). A study in which people were independently assigned to *DSM-III* and statistically determined categories (Gould, Bird, & Jaramillo, 1993) failed to find any one-to-one correspondence between the two types of diagnoses. This does not mean that one approach to diagnosis is necessarily better than the other. The purpose of diagnostic classification is to provide information that can be used to help troubled people. Diagnostic systems should be judged on how well they achieve this purpose. Thus far, there is little evidence for the superiority of either statistically derived or categorical diagnoses. In fact, their validity has been found to be about the same (Gould et al., 1993).

sarily follow. Grouping together people whose problems appear similar may lead to etiological discoveries (as in general paresis). Descriptive categories are also useful for investigating treatment effectiveness. No treatment will be effective for mental disorders in general; treatments need to be assessed as to their effectiveness for people with similar problems.

The stigmatizing and self-fulfilling effects of labeling remain a serious concern for all diagnostic systems. In the past, to avoid stigmatizing people, clinicians have replaced one label with another. "Lunatics" became "mentally ill," while "imbeciles" became "mentally retarded," "intellectually challenged," or even "exceptional." This ploy rarely works for long because the new label soon takes on the same stigmatizing connotations as the old one. A better approach is to promote more positive attitudes toward people with psychological disorders. Still, the stigmatizing potential of labels should never be ignored, and, where practical, diagnoses should be kept confidential. More important, before giving anyone a diagnostic label, professionals should ensure that the clinical benefits of labeling outweigh the stigmatizing effects. When dealing with human beings in distress, we should always keep in mind the important clinical rule stated in the Hippocratic corpus 2,000 years ago: First do no harm.

To be fair, the *DSM-IV* does recognize that people should not be reduced to single diagnostic labels. Its multiaxial system recognizes that social support and physical health also affect behavior. Of course, even a multiaxial diagnosis does not fully describe complex human beings. The details that make each of us unique are inevitably lost in any categorical diagnostic system, as Highlight 3.2 explains. Again, this does not mean that *DSM-IV* diagnoses are useless. Diagnoses are not meant to describe everything that makes an individual unique. (How much does the diagnosis of "pneumonia" tell us about a person?) The purpose of a diagnosis is to provide information that can be used to help troubled people. Diagnostic systems should be judged by how well they achieve this purpose. For example, one purpose of diagnosis is prediction, and long-term follow-ups have found that diagnoses do predict psychological problems later in life (Gillberg, Hellgren, & Gillberg, 1993; Vetter & Köller, 1993).

To summarize, it is true that reliability is a problem for some *DSM-IV* diagnostic categories, and we are still ignorant of the etiology and treatment of many behavior disorders. However, this is more a criticism of the slow progress in abnormal psychology than of the *DSM-IV*. The refinement of diagnostic labels is a continuous process that involves incorporating new discoveries as they are made. The work is difficult, and progress slow, but, by incorporating the latest research into its nosology, each new *DSM* has the potential to improve on the last.

CLINICAL JUDGMENT AND DECISION MAKING

Every day, psychologists make decisions that affect the lives and well-being of others. Although many of these decisions are routine, others are characterized by uncertainty. Clinical information is rarely perfectly reliable; the outcomes of treatment strategies are never perfectly predictable. Understanding how clinicians make decisions in the light of uncertainty has been the subject of intensive psychological research over the past 15 years (S. Schwartz, 1991, 1994; S. Schwartz & Griffin, 1986; Turk & Salovey, 1988). This work is based mainly on the notion of bounded rationality.

"Bounded Rationality" and Judgment Heuristics

It is generally agreed among clinicians that more information leads to better judgments than does less information. This is one reason why new psychological tests are constantly being developed. However, there are inherent limitations to the amount of information clinicians are capable of handling (H. A. Simon, 1957). Because the information-processing capacity of clinicians is limited, providing them with more information may not improve their judgment. In fact, by trying to process too much information clinicians may overload their cognitive capacity, thus reducing their diagnostic accuracy (Sisson, Schoomaker, & Ross, 1976). When complex cognitive tasks such as diagnosis make demands that are beyond their information-processing capacity, clinicians simplify the task. As a result, clinical judgments that appear illogical and irrational when examined in the context of the larger problem may be perfectly reasonable within the "bounds" of the simplified problem.

One way to simplify complex cognitive tasks is to rely on stereotyped cognitive strategies such as **judgment heuristics.** These strategies, or rules of thumb, are useful ways to reduce cognitive load. Under certain circumstances, however, they can lead decision makers astray. When this happens, judgment is *biased*. Over the past 20 years, psychologists have described several general judgment heuristics (Kahneman, Slovic, & Tversky, 1982; S. Schwartz, 1991, 1994). The two most frequently studied heuristics are availability and representativeness.

Availability Heuristic Clinicians are often called on to estimate probabilities. For example, they may be asked to estimate the probability that a person will attempt suicide. One way to do this is to use the *availability heuristic*, which states that easy-to-recall ("available") events are more likely to occur than are those that are difficult to recall. Using the availability heuristic, clinicians attempt to recall instances when similar clients attempted suicide. The easier it is to bring such events to mind, the higher they will rate the probability that the current client will attempt suicide. This availability heuristic usually "works" because events that are easy to recall (that are more "available") are often more frequent. Unfortunately, there are exceptions. For example, Christensen-Szalanski and colleagues (1983) asked clinicians to estimate the frequency of death from various diseases. They found that clinicians overestimated deaths from some diseases (heart disease, for example) and underestimated deaths from others (asthma). In general, diseases that received more coverage in journals were rated as more lethal than those that received little written attention. The authors concluded that journal coverage makes a disease more "available," which, in turn, increases its subjective frequency.

Representativeness Heuristic Clinical judgments based solely on how closely a specific client "represents" a stereotyped case can often be traced back to the *representativeness heuristic* (Kahneman et al., 1982). Consider, for example, the case of C. S. (adapted from Dawes, 1988):

> C. S. had trouble in the tenth grade when she failed two courses. A psychological assessment revealed superior intelligence but personality assessment showed her to be shy and introverted; she also had trouble making friends. As a consequence, she spent long hours in her room reading books. Because C. S. had no unusual ideas and did want to make friends, the psychologist predicted that her poor grades and isolation would be temporary. A few

years later, C. S. graduated and went on to college and graduate school where she studied literature.

Given this background, do you believe that C. S. went on to a career in business or that she is a librarian? If you think it more likely that she is a librarian, you are probably engaging in representative thinking. You believe that she is a librarian because she fits your stereotype of a librarian. Your prediction ignores the much greater base-rate probability that C. S. works in business. (There are many more businesspeople than librarians.) When all we know about a person is that she was shy in 10th grade, it seems rather naive to ignore the relevant base rates and predict that she is a librarian. The fact that we ignore base rates shows the strength of the representative heuristic.

Framing The way in which a problem is stated (or framed) can affect clinical judgments. For example, people have been shown to prefer a treatment with a 60% probability of success to a treatment with a 40% probability of failure, even though both treatments have an identical, 60%, probability of success (Kahneman et al., 1982). The only difference between the two treatments lies in the way the problem is framed.

Overconfidence As noted, human information-processing capacity is limited and easily overloaded. Nevertheless, the more information clinicians have available, the more confident they become in the accuracy of their judgments. Oskamp (1965) found that psychologists became more convinced that they understood a case as the amount of information available to them increased, as described in Chapter 1. This confidence was not reflected in their performance, however; they were no better at predicting outcomes with more information than they were with less.

Decision Aids and Decision Analysis

To help clinicians improve their decision making, psychologists have developed decision aids. One approach already discussed is to distill the combined wisdom of many clinicians into a statistical formula (see the discussion of clinical versus statistical decision making in Chapter 1). Another uses the power of computers to develop expert systems.

Expert systems are computer programs that solve problems and give advice by making inferences from a database. Unlike the equally "intelligent" computer systems that control manufacturing or laboratory equipment, expert systems operate interactively. In theory at least, expert systems can help the clinician to structure a problem, suggest potential hypotheses, point out logical weaknesses, and evaluate decisions. None of these functions can be performed by statistical decision aids (S. Schwartz, Griffin, & Fox, 1989).

A computer that "thinks" like an expert has significant appeal. Because it can explain the basis for its recommendations—by tracing through its reasoning process—an expert system can also serve in a teaching role. Consider the following exchange between a neuropsychologist and an expert system:

COMPUTER: Is the patient's illness progressive?

CLINICIAN: Why? *(Why do you want to know this?)*

COMPUTER: This will help to determine whether the patient's illness is psychogenic.

CLINICIAN: Explain.

COMPUTER: If:
1. The illness is not progressive and
2. remissions occurred and
3. onset was gradual
Then: It is probable that the illness is psychogenic.

In this example, the clinician asked the neuropsychological expert system the question Why? (that is, "Why are you asking me for this information?"). The system then explained the reasoning behind its question by tracing backward through its rules. Many computer scientists and most psychologists believe that an ability to provide convincing explanations for their advice will ultimately determine how acceptable computer consultants are to clinicians (S. Schwartz et al., 1989).

Decision analysis is a set of procedures for making decisions under conditions of uncertainty. It proceeds by breaking down complex decisions into smaller, more tractable, problems and then combining the answers to these into an overall measure of outcome attractiveness. When performing a decision analysis, clinicians must consider both the probability and the **utility** (subjective value) of all possible decision outcomes. The probability of each outcome is multiplied by its utility to obtain the "expected utility." The decision that leads to the highest expected utility (probability × utility) is usually considered best. An example of how the subjective expected utility (SEU) approach to decision making could have been applied to Danielle after her first suicide attempt appears in Figure 3.7.

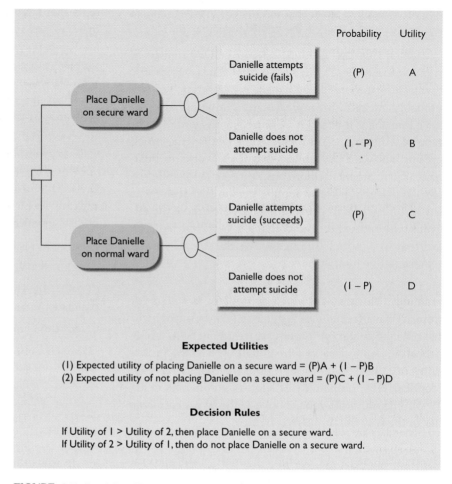

FIGURE 3.7 **Decision Tree Representation of a Clinical Judgment**

The simplified decision tree in Figure 3.7 represents the process of deciding whether Danielle, a potentially suicidal patient, should be placed in a secure ward. Decision trees should be read from left to right; a rectangle represents a specific choice, whereas an oval indicates that two or more outcomes can take place. In the decision analysis depicted in Figure 3.7, each choice can result in two possible outcomes: Danielle attempts suicide or she does not attempt suicide. The probability of the first outcome is P, and the probability of the second is $1-P$ (the probabilities of all outcomes associated with each branch must sum to 1). Each outcome has been assigned a utility, represented by the letters A, B, C, and D. Although no numbers have been assigned to these utilities, it is safe to assume that false-positives (incorrectly classifying Danielle suicidal) are less serious than false-negatives (misclassifying Danielle as not suicidal when she is), which can possibly result in death. Of course, the utilities for both are lower than for making an appropri-

ate judgment. Although it is impossible to know, it is interesting to speculate about whether Danielle's death could have been avoided if she had consulted a clinician who had then had the opportunity to perform a decision analysis.

SEU theory requires decision makers to maximize their expected utility. This does not mean that clinicians should always choose the most likely alternative. Depending on the utilities assigned to each outcome, even an unlikely outcome can wind up maximizing one's utilities. Examples of possible decision rules are given at the bottom of Figure 3.7.

Decision Aids: Current Status

Although statistical formulas, expert systems, and decision analysis have been shown to be valuable in different contexts, clinicians have been slow to adopt them. Except for automated psychological test interpretations, clinicians have preferred to emphasize clinical reasoning. Among the reasons advanced for this is the feeling that the research on clinical judgment has not been entirely fair. Most studies have been applicable to only some aspects of clinical practice (diagnosis, for example), and these aspects may not be the most important. Other objections are more practical. Clinicians are always pressed for time, and most decision aids require that data be systematically collected and scored. Similarly, because they require that data be collected across many people, decision rules are difficult to formulate.

Although these objections have merit, by far the most important is the feeling that a reliance on "num-

bers" or external aids diminishes the importance of the clinician and devalues the individual patient. Base rates, statistical formulas, and decision analysis appear far removed from living, breathing people. The statistical approach, by definition, refers to groups of patients, whereas clinicians are interested in one specific case. Decision aids will be accepted only if they are perceived to improve clinical practice. Researchers working in the field of clinical decision making are beginning to perform studies on the practical value of decision aids. As the results of these studies begin to appear, decision-making research may begin to make a greater impact on clinical practice.

CHAPTER 3 IN PERSPECTIVE

Danielle's suicide attempt brought her to Dr. Berg, who performed a psychological assessment. This assessment consisted of more than just administering and interpreting tests. Assessment is a complex intellectual activity that includes formulating hypotheses, deciding what data are necessary to confirm or disconfirm these hypotheses, gathering the required data, interpreting them, and drawing appropriate conclusions. Psychologists have devoted considerable energy to developing assessment instruments, yet some of the most popular ones lack evidence for their reliability and validity. Their continued use demonstrates the power of

clinical tradition in clinical practice.

The outcome of Dr. Berg's assessment of Danielle included a diagnosis. Diagnoses are not just labels; they attempt to summarize, in a convenient form, what is known about the etiology and course of various disorders. Not only are reliable and valid diagnoses useful for clinical practice, they serve an essential role in research. Separating different disorders is the first step in uncovering their etiology and developing useful treatments. Diagnostic schemes are constantly in evolution. Each revision attempts to incorporate new scientific findings, clinical experience, and changing social values. Because our cur-

rent diagnoses vary in their reliability and validity, and because they can have pernicious effects, clinicians must constantly weigh the costs and benefits of giving someone a diagnosis.

Although assessments involve tests, interviews, and behavioral observations, the final report always represents the clinician's best judgment. Psychologists have attempted to minimize the potential biases to clinical judgment by devising decision aids. These aids will probably not make an important impact on clinical practice, however, until sufficient evidence for their clinical value accumulates.

Key Ideas

Reliability and Validity
A reliable assessment device produces consistent results. At a minimum, assessment devices must have high interrater reliability. Where possible, they should also have high test-retest reliability. In clinical practice, test-retest reliability is difficult to achieve because people and circumstances change. Clinical assessment devices must also be valid. A face-valid device is one that seems, on the surface, to be measuring what it claims to. A content-valid assessment device covers the

important aspects of whatever it is measuring. Because they do not reflect the practical value of the information provided by an assessment device, face and content validity are less important than other types, such as predictive validity (the ability to predict an important outcome).

Interviews
Regardless of the paradigm a clinical psychologist adopts, interviews play an important role in assessment. They are used to gather information about a per-

son's current problem, history, life situation, personal relationships, and outlook for the future. Clinical interviews fall along a continuum that ranges from loose, unstructured conversations at one end to formal, structured interactions at the other. Unstructured interviews give clinicians maximum flexibility, but structured interviews produce more reliable data.

Intelligence Tests
Modern intelligence testing began with Binet, whose goal was practical—to

predict which children would do well in school. His mental-age measures were superseded by Wechsler's deviation IQ scores, which permit people to be compared across age groups and through the life span.

Projective Tests

Projective tests are based on the idea that people project their unconscious drives, feelings, wishes, and conflicts onto the "screen" provided by stimuli that elicit a wide range of responses. Projective tests include the Rorschach inkblot test, the Thematic Apperception Test (TAT), and many others. Despite meager evidence for their reliability and validity, projective tests are widely used.

Self-Report Tests

Because their scoring usually involves counting rather than interpreting responses, self-report tests are often called "objective" to differentiate them from the more subjective projective tests. The most widely used self-report test is the empirically derived Minnesota Multiphasic Personality Inventory (MMPI). Many self-report scales incorporate validity checks (such as the MMPI validity scales) and are easily adapted for computer scoring and interpretation.

Neuropsychological Assessment

Neuropsychological assessment is a specialization within psychology. Its goal is to use brain-behavior relationships to help localize the site of brain damage (and to understand brain function). Neuropsychological assessment involves an assortment of psychological tests, direct observation, and modern imaging techniques.

Behavioral Assessment

Behavioral psychologists have developed a heterogeneous set of assessment techniques collectively known as behavioral assessment. The aim of these techniques is to describe the environmental conditions that elicit and maintain problem behaviors. Behavioral assessment is not limited to a small number of assessment "sessions." Using self-report measures, psychophysiological devices, and direct behavioral observations, behavior therapists track behavior throughout treatment.

Purposes of Diagnostic Classification

Diagnoses enhance communication by allowing clinicians to summarize a constellation of symptoms. They also allow researchers to evaluate hypotheses on relatively homogeneous groups. Some diagnoses have etiological validity (the cause of a disorder is known), and some have therapeutic implications.

Criticisms of Diagnoses

Critics of psychiatric diagnoses have argued that psychological disorders are not like medical diseases; they are really social problems. They argue that giving such problems diagnoses is misleading, potentially stigmatizing, and gives too much power to mental health professionals. Even scientists who admit that diagnostic classifications can serve a useful purpose have criticized the poor reliability and validity of many categories. Ultimately, the argument about whether diagnoses are worthwhile boils down to one of costs and benefits. Most mental health professionals believe that the benefits outweigh the costs, although they acknowledge the need for care in applying diagnoses, and for continued research to improve them.

Clinical Judgment

There are inherent limitations to the amount of information clinicians are capable of handling. As a result, they simplify complex clinical tasks by using stereotyped cognitive strategies such as judgment heuristics. These heuristics can bias clinical judgment. To help clinicians improve their decision making, psychologists have developed decision aids. The most popular approach is to distill the combined wisdom of many clinicians into a statistical formula. For some problems, it is possible to use expert systems for advice. When probabilities and utilities are known, decision analysis also can aid clinical decision making.

Key Terms

ABAB experiment
anti-psychiatrists
behavioral assessment
biofeedback
categorical classification
deviation IQ
dimensional classification
DSM (Diagnostic and Statistical Manual of Mental Disorders)
factor analysis

ICD (International Statistical Classification of Diseases)
interrater reliability
intelligence quotient (IQ)
judgment heuristics
kappa
localization of brain damage
mental age
mental status examination
multiple-baseline experiment

multiaxial classification system
neuropsychological tests
neuroses
nosology
objective tests
personality traits
polygraph
projective personality tests
psychometrics
rapport

reactive measure
reliability
self-monitoring
single-subject experimental designs
SORC analysis
standardization
structured interview
utility
validity

Key Names

Alfred Binet	Emil Kraepelin	Hermann Rorschach	David Wechsler
Francis Galton	J. Charnley McKinley	Louis Stern	
Starke Hathaway	Henry Murray	Louis Terman	

CHAPTER 4

CHAPTER OBJECTIVES

Is there anyone alive who has not, at some time or another, felt anxious? The "butterflies" fluttering in your stomach before an examination, the "nervousness" you feel before an employment interview, the pounding of your heart as you hear footsteps on a dark night—these are all signs of anxiety. Anxiety is not necessarily bad. It can motivate you to study harder for examinations and prepare better for job interviews; it can also place you on guard against danger. In other words, anxiety can help you cope with the challenges of everyday life.

When anxiety gets out of control, however, this helpful emotion turns pernicious. Instead of helping you to cope, it interferes with your daily life. You may feel anxious much of the time, regardless of the circumstances. You may withdraw from activities you would normally find pleasurable. People to whom this happens are said to have an anxiety disorder, a diverse set of problems that tend to grow progressively worse if left untreated.

Tens of millions of people suffer from anxiety disorders. Fortunately, it is an area where much is known about both etiology and treatment. This chapter reviews the relevant clinical and laboratory research, focusing for illustrative purposes on the story of Carole Ballodi, a veteran of war.

The three main questions addressed in this chapter are

1. What are anxiety disorders?
2. How do they develop?
3. Can anxiety disorders be treated?

The Anxiety Spectrum
From Everyday Worry to Panic

CONTENTS

Students of abnormal psychology are faced with a bewildering collection of disorders. Some involve bizarre behaviors rarely encountered in ordinary life (hallucinations, for example). Others seem little more than exaggerations of everyday behavior. Get too sad, and you are "depressed." Drink too much, and you are a "substance abuser." There is no discrete line separating disordered from "normal" behaviors; they shade subtly into one another. At one time or another, all of us behave in ways that may be construed as abnormal. This is why abnormal psychology is an applied branch of general psychology, not a separate science. The theories and techniques developed to understand "normal" behavior are also applicable to psychological disorders. Building on the first three chapters, Chapter 4 shows how concepts derived from various branches of psychology can illuminate both common and pathological forms of fear and anxiety. By introducing several widely used treatment and prevention techniques, this chapter also builds a foundation for the discussions of clinical treatment that appear in later chapters. The chapter begins by introducing Dr. Carole Ballodi, whose history provides a context for many of the discussions that follow.

A CASUALTY OF WAR

"War is hell," said U.S. General George Patton. It exerts a terrible toll on everyone involved—both victims and survivors. After the Civil War, the Surgeon General of the Union Army found that many soldiers suffered from "nostalgia," a severe form of depression brought on, he believed, by their prolonged absence from home (P. G. Bourne, 1970). World War I veterans were said to suffer from "shell shock," brain concussions caused by the exploding shells. In World War II, soldiers were described as suffering "battle fatigue," a condition marked by intense fear and terror (Sutker, Allain, & Winstead, 1993). Vietnam veterans displayed similar symptoms, although these may not have been apparent until months, even years, after their discharge (Keane et al., 1992). Documents 4.1 and 4.2 suggest that Carole Ballodi, a medical doctor, may be yet another casualty of war.

Carole Ballodi's panic attacks were triggered by flashbacks of her Gulf War experiences ministering to injured and dying soldiers.

DOCUMENT 4.1

Defense Department
Report on Gulf War
Episode Involving
Captain Carole
Ballodi, MD

Department of Defense

Commendation Report

On the night of 24 February, three seriously injured infantry soldiers were transported by helicopter to Medivac Unit 4 CB, which was under the command of Captain Carole Ballodi. Captain Ballodi and her team of medics and nurses began to stabilize the wounded in preparation for surgery, when they found themselves under fire. They called for assistance, but before air strikes could be ordered, their Medivac unit was hit by a rocket. One of the wounded soldiers was struck in the head by shrapnel and killed instantly while Captain Ballodi was taking his pulse. A nurse was gravely injured. Although electrical supplies were cut off, and the shelling continued, Captain Ballodi and her team managed to tend to the wounded until the shelling stopped. She then assisted in an emergency surgery that required the amputation of one soldier's leg. Captain Ballodi's actions during that night saved the lives of the injured soldiers. She is worthy of the highest commendation.

DOCUMENT 4.2

Initial Interview
Between Dr. Carole
Ballodi and Psychia-
trist Dr. Sally Kahn

 UNIVERSITY HOSPITAL

Psychiatry Service

Consultation Transcript

Reason for referral: Carole Ballodi is an internal medicine specialist at University Hospital. She was brought to the emergency room complaining of chest pain. A physical examination proved negative. Because of her agitation, she was referred for a psychiatric consultation.

DR. KAHN: Tell me, what do you consider your main problem?

DR. BALLODI: I have these pains in my chest and feel like I can't catch my breath.

DR. KAHN: When does this occur?

DR. BALLODI: One time was in my car. I was just about to get on the bridge. I was at the toll booth when I heard a helicopter overhead. I panicked. I couldn't catch my breath. I broke out in a sweat, and I could feel my heart pounding. I felt like there was a tight band across my chest. I got dizzy, hot, and nauseous. And I was very frightened. I thought I was dying.

DR. KAHN: Can you recall what thoughts were going through your head when this happened?

DR. BALLODI: Actually, I can. I thought that the helicopter sounded like the ones that delivered the wounded to the Medivac unit in Kuwait. I think I just panicked.

DR. KAHN: You panicked?

DR. BALLODI: Yes. I was afraid that the helicopter would come down and crash into my car.

DR. KAHN: What would happen to you?

DR. BALLODI: I would be disabled for life and have to use a wheelchair.

DR. KAHN: So, you were thinking about these things and then began to feel the chest pain?

DR. BALLODI: I'm not sure—it all seemed to happen together. I was thinking about the helicopters and my car, and then I felt the pain in my chest and had trouble breathing.

DR. KAHN: What happened next?

DR. BALLODI: I pulled over to the side and just sat there. Traffic backed up behind me, but there was nothing I could do. It was like it was happening to someone else. Finally, someone called an ambulance.

DR. KAHN: What happened in the hospital?

DR. BALLODI: I felt better by the time I got to the hospital. They ran the usual tests but found nothing. They suggested that I see you.

DR. KAHN: Have you "panicked" at any other time?

DR. BALLODI: Yes. Mostly at night. I wake up at two or three in the morning. I'm covered in sweat and my heart is racing. I can hardly catch my breath. I think I'm going to die.

DR. KAHN: Is there anything specific that set all this off?

DR. BALLODI: I had a patient die in my office. It brought back the war. I never used to, but now I spend hours each night going over things that have happened in the past. I relive what happened in Kuwait. It's like a videotape that I play over and over again in my mind while I ask myself whether I could have done things differently.

DR. KAHN: What do you do when you wake up during the night?

DR. BALLODI: I usually check all the windows and door locks and then I go back to sleep.

DR. KAHN: What about your work?

DR. BALLODI: I can't concentrate on anything. I've taken practically all of my sick days.

DR. KAHN: What are you doing about your problems?

DR. BALLODI: Mostly I stay home, hoping that rest will help. I have a few drinks to help me sleep.

DR. KAHN: Has this worked?

DR. BALLODI: Well, the drinks knock me out, but I'm missing lots of work.

DR. KAHN: Do you go out with friends?

DR. BALLODI: No. I'm afraid to leave home. I'm afraid to get in my car. I might have another incident. I'm not interested in seeing anyone, and sex leaves me cold.

DR. KAHN: Do you ever see anyone you served with in the Gulf War?

DR. BALLODI: No. I was never really bothered by the war, but I don't want to talk to anyone. Who knows what they might think? I don't know what's happening to me. I think I'm going mad.

THE ANXIETY SPECTRUM

Carole Ballodi told Dr. Kahn that when she heard the helicopter overhead, she "panicked." We all know what she meant. Panic! You're very scared. Your heart beats so hard you think it will burst through your chest. You can barely catch your breath. Your mouth is totally dry, and you are dizzy and shaking. This can't be real. It's not happening, not to me. You feel like you are going to faint, maybe even die.

Panic is not, by itself, an abnormal behavior. It is simply the intense fear produced by an especially frightening situation: You lose control of your car on an icy road; you turn around in the shopping center and can't see your little brother anywhere; you hear footsteps following you down a dark street. It is perfectly normal to

DSM-IV   **TABLE 4.1**   *DSM-IV* Definition of a Panic Attack

A discrete period of intense fear or discomfort, in which four (or more) of the following symptoms developed abruptly and reached a peak within 10 minutes:

1. Palpitations, pounding heart, or accelerated heart rate	8. Feeling dizzy, unsteady, light-headed, or faint
2. Sweating	9. Derealization (feelings of unreality) or depersonalization (being detached from oneself)
3. Trembling or shaking	10. Fear of losing control or going crazy
4. Sensations of shortness of breath or smothering	11. Fear of dying
5. Feeling of choking	12. Paresthesias (numbness or tingling sensations)
6. Chest pain or discomfort	13. Chills or hot flushes
7. Nausea or abdominal distress	

Note: From American Psychiatric Association (1994, p. 395).

be frightened in such situations. However, Carole Ballodi "panicked" in her car when she heard the sound of a helicopter, and panicky feelings have wakened her from sleep. She reacted as if she were in danger even though no objective threat was present. The *DSM-IV* refers to such episodes as **panic attacks** and describes them as shown in Table 4.1.

Fear, Panic, and the Anxiety Disorders

Fear is a negative emotion that occurs in response to some immediate threat or danger. A panic attack consists of an abrupt and intense feeling of fear accompanied by somatic symptoms, usually in the absence of any objective danger. The physical symptoms of fear and panic—sweating, rapid pulse, shallow breathing, hot flushes, and nausea—are produced by the arousal of the sympathetic division of the autonomic nervous system. In a process known as the **alarm reaction** (Selye, 1976), the sympathetic nervous system and its associated glands increase the amount of sugar in the blood (to provide extra energy), speed up heart and respiration rates (to make more oxygen available for muscle exertion), reduce the blood supply to vessels near the skin (to reduce bleeding in case of injury), and increase the supply of proteins that cause blood clotting (to prevent excessive blood loss should injury occur). In this way, fear serves a positive purpose. It helps mobilize the body's defenses quickly in situations requiring fight or flight (running away) from an enemy. Figure 4.1 shows many of the physical responses triggered by the alarm (or emergency) reaction.

Panic attacks that are invariably triggered by specific stimuli (such as the sound of a helicopter) are called "situationally bound" or "cued" attacks. In contrast, unexpected "uncued" attacks can occur anytime and any-

where. Carole even seemed to have them when she was asleep, which is not a rare occurrence (Krystal et al., 1991). There is also a "predisposed" type of panic attack, which is somewhere between a cued and an uncued attack. Predisposed attacks usually occur in a particular situation, but they are not as inevitable as cued attacks. Although the various attacks sound different, in practice it is often difficult to tell them apart, and many people have all the types (Rapee et al., 1992).

Clearly, Carole Ballodi's episode on the bridge fits the *DSM-IV* definition quite well. Her fear came on suddenly and was accompanied by many of the physical symptoms in Table 4.1. However, a panic attack is not, by itself, a psychological disorder. Isolated panic attacks are common, especially among adolescents and college students (Asmundson & Norton, 1993; King et al., 1993). However, when panic attacks become frequent, when they occur in combination with other symptoms, or when they seriously affect a person's quality of life, they may be a sign that a psychological disorder—most likely an anxiety disorder—is present.

Anxiety is a negative emotional state marked by foreboding and somatic signs of tension, such as a racing heart, sweating, and often, difficulty breathing. (*Anxiety* comes from the Latin word *anxius*, which means constriction or strangulation.) Anxiety is similar to fear but with a less specific focus. Whereas fear is usually a response to some immediate threat, anxiety is characterized by apprehension about unpredictable dangers that lie in the future. Low levels of anxiety are adaptive; they help us avoid danger ("I don't think I like the look of that dark street") and plan for the future ("I better study for the final exam or I will fail"). Persistent high levels of anxiety, however, are always maladaptive; they restrict social life and destroy peace of mind.

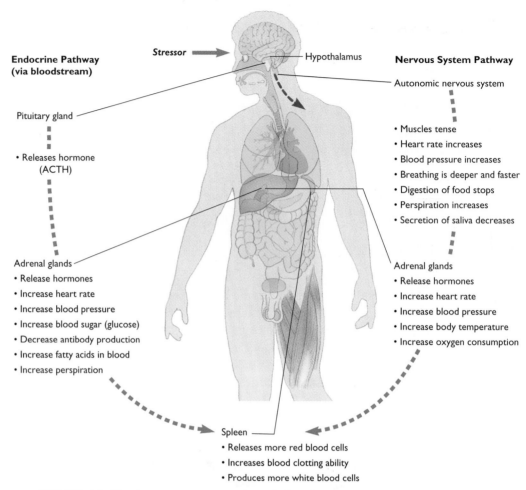

**Endocrine Pathway
(via bloodstream)**

Stressor

Hypothalamus

Nervous System Pathway

Autonomic nervous system

Pituitary gland

• Releases hormone
(ACTH)

• Muscles tense
• Heart rate increases
• Blood pressure increases
• Breathing is deeper and faster
• Digestion of food stops
• Perspiration increases
• Secretion of saliva decreases

Adrenal glands
• Release hormones
• Increase heart rate
• Increase blood pressure
• Increase blood sugar (glucose)
• Decrease antibody production
• Increase fatty acids in blood
• Increase perspiration

Adrenal glands
• Release hormones
• Increase heart rate
• Increase blood pressure
• Increase body temperature
• Increase oxygen consumption

Spleen
• Releases more red blood cells
• Increases blood clotting ability
• Produces more white blood cells

FIGURE 4.1 *The alarm reaction starts a chain of physical responses through both hormonal and nerve pathways (ACTH = adrenocorticotropic hormone).*

Some researchers have suggested that fear and anxiety are fundamentally different emotions, so different that they are controlled by different parts of the central nervous system (Gray, 1991). According to one theory, fear originates in the lower parts of the brain (the midbrain and hindbrain), whereas anxiety is associated with the **limbic system,** which connects the lower brain to the cerebral cortex (Figures 4.2 and 4.3). Attempts have also been made to link fear and anxiety with different neurotransmitters and brain chemicals (Barondes, 1993). Despite a considerable amount of research, however, these theories remain equivocal (Nutt & Lawson, 1992). Although the proximal cause of fear and anxiety certainly lies in the brain and its associated chemical reactions (see the metaparadigm in Chapter 2), both fear and anxiety remain mainly psychological constructs.

Freud viewed anxiety, especially repressed sexual anxiety, as the cause of many psychological disorders, especially those called the **neuroses.** Over the years, as Freud's influence waned, *neurosis* became merely a de-

scriptive term for any distressing mental or behavioral symptom that did not involve a serious break with reality. Eventually, even this limited use disappeared. The *DSM-IV* makes no mention of the neuroses. Instead, it contains a diverse group of specific disorders. The present chapter is primarily concerned with the most common of these, the **anxiety disorders** (R. C. Kessler et al., 1994). The *DSM-IV* contains ten disorders in which anxiety is the main defining feature (Table 4.2),* but anxiety plays a part in most, if not all, psychological disorders. It is also a feature of everyday life. We all have fears and worries, perhaps not serious enough to merit a diagnosis, but troubling just the same. One way to conceptualize the effects of anxiety is to think of a spectrum similar to the one produced by light passing through a

———

*The *DSM-IV* includes an 11th diagnostic category for "anxiety disorders not otherwise specified." Vague references to disorders "not otherwise specified" appear throughout the *DSM.* Because they have no specific symptoms, etiology, or treatment, these disorders are not discussed in this book.

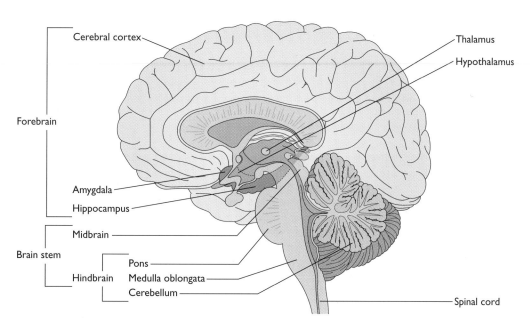

FIGURE 4.2 **Major Brain Structures**

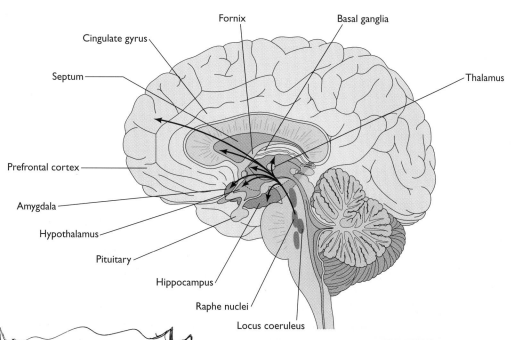

FIGURE 4.3 **The Limbic System.** *Except for the pituitary, all the highlighted areas in the forebrain are part of the limbic system and normally receive signals from neurons that secrete mood-altering neurotransmitters. Some neurotransmitter pathways are indicated by arrows.*

DSM-IV   **TABLE 4.2**   The *DSM-IV* Anxiety Disorders

1. **Specific phobia:** fear that is out of proportion to any objective threat
2. **Social phobia:** fear of situations in which one may be evaluated by others
3. **Obsessive-compulsive disorder:** intrusive recurrent thoughts (**obsessions**) or ritualistic actions (**compulsions**) or both
4. **Generalized anxiety disorder:** free-floating anxiety in many situations without any objective threat
5. **Panic disorder:** fear of having panic attacks or being in places where panic attacks can occur
6. **Agoraphobia:** fear of being alone away from help and protection; in extreme cases, a fear of leaving home
7. **Acute stress disorder:** a short-term reaction to an emotional trauma
8. **Post-traumatic stress disorder:** a long-term response to a traumatic incident, characterized by anxiety, emotional numbness, and the continual reliving of the traumatic event
9. **Substance-induced anxiety disorder:** usually drug-induced fearfulness
10. **Anxiety disorder produced by a general medical condition:** anxiety symptoms caused by an illness—for example, an overactive thyroid gland

prism (Figure 4.4). One end contains the fairly mild worries that affect daily life ("Will I pass the final exam?"), whereas the other end contains severe anxiety disorders that affect a person's entire life. Of course, there are many shades in between.

Comorbidity and the Anxiety Disorders

People often show signs of more than one disorder (T. A. Brown, Barlow, & Liebowitz, 1994). For example, Carole Ballodi was afraid to get in her car (perhaps she had a specific phobia), had panic attacks and feared having another (possibly a sign of a panic disorder), stayed home because of her fear of another panic attack (agoraphobia), avoided people because of what they might think about her (social phobia), seemed to be reliving her war experiences (post-traumatic stress disorder), and checked all the locks when she awoke at night (obsessive-compulsive disorder). This does not mean that Carole actually has all these disorders (she doesn't), but some overlap is not unusual. **Comorbidity** (in which several disorders seem to "go together") is probably inevitable because panic and its related symptoms and signs occur in practically all of the anxiety disorders. This is why they are often difficult to differentiate (Wittchen et al., 1995).

Anxiety disorders not only seem to go with one another, they are also frequently accompanied by depression (Zinbarg et al., 1992). This association is so common that L. A. Clark and Watson (1991) theorized that anxiety and depression may share a common feature. That is, they both involve emotional distress, but they vary in how this distress is expressed. In anxiety, emotional dis-

tress leads to physiological arousal, which produces sweating, rapid breathing, and so on, whereas in depression, emotional distress produces a negative mood. We will not fully understand anxiety disorders or depression until we can explain their high comorbidity (T. A. Brown & Barlow, 1992).

As we delve further into Carole Ballodi's history, you will see that anxiety disorders are largely exaggerations of our everyday fears and worries. Because some people seem to approach life with anxiety and fearfulness, this chapter also includes discussions of avoidant personality disorder and obsessive-compulsive personality disorder. These are not anxiety disorders (they are more like maladaptive personality traits), but they are characterized by many of the same behaviors.

FEARS AND PHOBIAS

On the basis of their discussion, Dr. Kahn felt certain that Carole Ballodi was suffering from an anxiety disorder, probably related to her war experiences. Before Dr. Kahn could be more certain, however, she had to consider the possibility that Carole's behavior was the result of a general medical condition. A variety of medical disorders can cause symptoms similar to Carole's (an overactive thyroid gland, heart disease, vitamin deficiencies, respiratory disease, brain tumors). Because alcohol, caffeine, and many prescription and illicit drugs can also cause anxiety symptoms, Dr. Kahn had to be sure that Carole's behavior was not substance-related (or related to withdrawal from a substance). Thus, Dr. Kahn began by ordering a medical history as well as physical

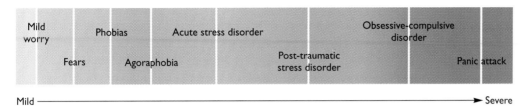

FIGURE 4.4 **The Anxiety Spectrum**

and laboratory examinations. These found no evidence of a relevant medical condition or substance-induced anxiety. Increasingly certain that Carole's problem was a reaction to her war experiences, Dr. Kahn prescribed a tranquilizer to help Carole sleep and asked psychologist Dr. Stuart Berg to assess Carole and to help formulate a treatment plan. An excerpt from Dr. Berg's report appears in Document 4.3. The tests administered by Dr. Berg were described in Chapter 3, except for the Mississippi Scale for Combat-Related Post-Traumatic Stress Disorder (Keane, Caddell, & Taylor, 1988). This test is specifically designed to measure the signs and symptoms of combat-related anxiety disorders. Additional excerpts from Dr. Berg's report appear later in this chapter.

 UNIVERSITY HOSPITAL

Psychological Assessment

Date: November 5, 2001

Client: Dr. Carole Ballodi, University Hospital, DOB: 3/7/1959

Tests Administered

Minnesota Multiphasic Personality Inventory (3/11/2001)

State-Trait Anxiety Inventory (3/11/2001)

Mississippi Scale for Combat-Related Post-Traumatic Stress Disorder (4/11/2001)

Anxiety Disorders Interview Schedule for DSM-IV (3/11/2001)

Thematic Apperception Test (4/11/2001)

Psychologist: Dr. Stuart Berg

Referral: Dr. S. Kahn, University Hospital

Reason for Referral: The client was referred by Dr. Kahn for personality assessment and treatment planning. She seems to have a history of panic attacks and an increasing reluctance to leave home or interact with others. The client is a medical practitioner and a Gulf War veteran who seems to be reliving her war experiences.

Behavioral Observations and History: The client was seen for two separate testing sessions. She was well dressed and alert but seemed tense. She fidgeted in her seat and rubbed her hands together continuously. She drank a great deal of water during the assessment sessions, explaining that her mouth was unusually dry. However, she responded to all questions and was able to provide a detailed history.

DOCUMENT 4.3

Excerpt From Dr. Berg's Psychological Assessment of Dr. Carole Ballodi (behavioral observations and early history)

> Dr. Ballodi was an only child born to older parents. Her father, an army officer, was 47 when she was born; her mother, a housewife, was 39. Dr. Ballodi's father died when she was 9; her mother died last year. Although she remembers missing her father for years after he died, Dr. Ballodi recalls her childhood as mainly happy. She was close to her mother, who was her "best friend" but perhaps a little overprotective. Dr. Ballodi says that she was a good student who received high marks. On the other hand, she had few friends because she was always rather shy.
>
> Dr. Ballodi's first memory of being fearful was her childhood fear of snakes. Although she cannot recall ever being injured by a snake, Dr. Ballodi feared visits to the family's summer cottage because of the snakes in the area. She recalls that her mother also feared snakes. From the time she was 8 years old, Dr. Ballodi refused to go walking alone in the woods around the summer cottage for fear of encountering a snake. She would only go walking if her father accompanied her. Even then, she set out with considerable trepidation and was always relieved to return to the cottage. The only other childhood fear Dr. Ballodi could recall was her fear of the dark. She insisted on going to sleep with a light on, and with her mother in the room reading her a story. This was a preference that her mother indulged.

From Everyday Fears to Phobias

Carole Ballodi's childhood fears were not unusual. At one time or another, everyone is afraid of something: snakes, storms, airplanes, or going to the dentist. Fear is an important evolutionary adaptation (Katerndahl, 1992). Fear of failure motivates us to work hard, fear of injury motivates us to avoid harmful situations, fear of enemies binds us to our families and tribes, and fear of punishment is one reason we try not to harm others. But fear can also be debilitating. It can torment us, destroy our sleep, and rob our lives of pleasure. In extreme cases, it can cause disease, even death.

According to the *DSM-IV*, fears are different from phobias. A phobia consists of a persistent and irrational fear coupled with a desire to avoid the feared object or situation. Phobic people display extreme fear when exposed to feared stimuli; they may even have a panic attack. When questioned about their behavior, they recognize that their reaction is excessive, yet they permit their fear to disrupt their everyday lives. "Rational" fears, on the other hand, are not phobias. If you hurry home after hearing a storm warning on your car radio, you are not displaying a phobia—no matter how frightened you may feel. On the other hand, if your fear of storms is so intense that you give up your job to move to a city with a different climate, uprooting your family and causing financial hardship, then you have a phobia.

In practice, it is sometimes difficult to separate everyday fears from specific phobias. Often, the difference is simply a matter of degree (Zinbarg et al., 1992). Fears become phobias when they disrupt daily life enough to justify clinical intervention. Of course, the same fear may be construed differently by people who live in different environments. For example, Carole Ballodi's intense fear of snakes presented a bigger impediment to her when she was a child spending summers in the country than when she was an adult living in a large city. It has been estimated that about 11% of the population meet the criteria for a specific phobic disorder at some time in their lives (Magee et al., 1996). Once a phobia gets started, it tends to last a lifetime unless it is specifically treated.

The *DSM-IV* distinguishes three categories of phobias: specific phobia, social phobia, and agoraphobia. People with specific phobias fear certain objects, organisms, and places. People with social phobia have an excessive concern about being evaluated by others. Agoraphobia is the fear of being alone and unprotected in a threatening place. This section of the chapter deals with specific and social phobias. Agoraphobia is discussed later in this chapter, along with panic disorder.

The five main *DSM-IV* diagnostic criteria for a specific phobia are summarized in Table 4.3. The *DSM-IV* also includes a sixth criterion, which requires that a person's fears or panic attacks not be better "accounted for"

Horror movies like Arachnophobia *use people's everyday fears to build suspense. Why does fear in this situation elicit interest rather than avoidance?*

DSM-IV   TABLE 4.3   Main *DSM-IV* Criteria for a Specific Phobia

A. Marked and persistent fear that is excessive or unreasonable, cued by the presence or anticipation of a specific object or situation (e.g., flying, heights, animals, receiving an injection, seeing blood).

B. Exposure to the phobic stimulus almost invariably provokes an immediate anxiety response, which may take the form of a situationally bound or situationally predisposed Panic Attack. Note: In children, the anxiety may be expressed by crying, tantrums, freezing, or clinging.

C. The person recognizes that the fear is excessive or unreasonable. (In children, this feature may be absent.)

D. The phobic situation(s) is avoided or else is endured with intense anxiety or distress.

E. The avoidance, anxious anticipation, or distress in the feared situation(s) interferes significantly with the person's nor-mal routine, occupational (or academic) functioning, or social activities or relationships, or there is marked distress about having the phobia.

F. In individuals under age 18 years, the duration is at least 6 months.

G. The anxiety, Panic Attacks, or phobic avoidance associated with the specific object or situation are not better accounted for by another mental disorder, such as Obsessive-Compulsive Disorder (e.g., fear of dirt in someone with an obsession about contamination), Post-traumatic Stress Disorder (e.g., avoidance of stimuli associated with a severe stressor), Separation Anxiety Disorder (e.g., avoidance of school), Social Phobia (e.g., avoidance of social situations because of fear of embarrassment), Panic Disorder With Agoraphobia, or Agoraphobia Without History of Panic Disorder.

Note: From American Psychiatric Association (1994, pp. 410–411).

by some other condition (panic disorder, for example). Most *DSM-IV* diagnoses include a similar criterion. Rather than repeat this criterion over and over again, it is taken for granted in this book that clients should be given the diagnosis that best accounts for their symptoms.

Over the years, writers have developed a huge vocabulary of phobia names. To name a new phobia, all you have to do is take the suffix *phobia* (which comes from *Phobos*, the Greek god who was said to have frightened his enemies to death) and add it to the Greek or Latin word for the feared object. This is how we get *claustrophobia* (fear of closed spaces), *cardiophobia* (fear of heart disease), *arachnophobia* (fear of spiders), and even *anglophobia* (fear of things English). Of course, simply giving a disorder a name (even a pretentious Greek one) does not mean that we know what causes it or how to treat it. Jargon is never a substitute for knowledge. The *DSM-IV* ignores phobia names, opting instead for a simple four-way classification: fears of the natural environment (insects, storms); fears of blood, injection, or injury; situational fears (cars, planes, heights, elevators, and tunnels); and a mixed category of "other" less common fears.

Determinants of Fears and Phobias

People can be afraid of almost anything; the *Encyclopedia of Phobias, Fears, and Anxieties* (Doctor & Kahn, 1989) has more than 2,000 entries. Some of the more common fears may be found in Table 4.4. Note that some objects and situations are more commonly feared than others. Hardly anyone is afraid of kittens, whereas millions of people fear spiders. Our fears are determined by the complex interaction of cultural norms (fears vary across cultures), heredity (we may be genetically programmed for certain fears), and our learning experiences.

Cultural and Social Determinants   To a large extent, our culture determines the objects and situations we fear (Tuan, 1980). The Aborigines of Central Australia, for example, have an intense fear of violating sacred tribal sites (Strehlow, 1985). Those who violate taboo areas are subject to "bone-pointing." A tribal elder takes the leg bone of a kangaroo, dips it into an anthill, covers the end with human hairs, and points it at the transgressor while chanting a curse. Aborigines fear bone-pointing so much, some of those subjected to the curse have reportedly died from fright (Basedow, 1925).

Even within a society, different minority groups have different fears. African Americans, for example, are

TABLE 4.4 Common Fears and Phobias		
Death	Flying	Snakes
Dentists	Heights	Storms
Enclosed places	Illness	Traveling alone
	Injury	

three times more likely to report specific phobias than White Americans (D. R. Brown, Eaton, & Sussman, 1990), and women report more phobias than men (Davey, 1994). The racial differences may reflect higher stress levels among African Americans (Neal & Turner, 1991). The usual explanation for the gender difference relies on social roles. The traditional male role, which emphasizes courage and bravery, may make men more reluctant to report their fears than women. To test this hypothesis, K. A. Pierce and Kirkpatrick (1992) asked men and women to respond to a fear survey in one of two conditions: (a) while wired to a mock "lie detector" or (b) without the lie detector. They found that males reported more fears when they thought they were wired to a lie detector, whereas females produced the same number of fears in both conditions. This result is consistent with the idea that men prefer to hide their fears. Unless they feel that their lies will be detected, males keep their fears to themselves. There is one complication, however. Even in the lie detector condition, males reported fewer fears than females. So, even when the reporting bias is minimized, males still seem to have fewer fears than females.

Hereditary Determinants   Most birds flee when they encounter an owl (Hinde, 1954). They also fly away when confronted with a stuffed owl or a cardboard cutout shaped like an owl. In fact, birds fear and avoid anything that vaguely resembles an owl. Chickens act the same way around hawks or anything that looks like a hawk. Are these fears learned? Or are birds and chickens born fearing owls and hawks? Experiments with chicks raised in captivity suggest the latter. These chicks showed signs of agitation and consternation when exposed to cardboard cutouts resembling hawks. Because they exhibited no fear of cutouts designed to resemble other birds and because they had never seen a live hawk, the chicks could not have acquired their fear through experience; it had to be innate (Barondes, 1993).

John Watson (1930) believed that humans are also born with innate fears. These include fear of unexpected loud noises, sudden loss of support, jerky movements,

Are We Born Fearing Snakes?

As a child, Carole Ballodi feared snakes, and a survey of almost 12,000 English children aged 4 to 14 found that she was not alone. The fear of snakes was found to be the most common of all animal fears (R. Morris & Morris, 1965). Contrary to Watson's conditioning theory, most of these children were similar to Carole; that is, they had never been harmed by a snake. Although this fact alone might suggest that the fear of snakes is innate and not learned, psychoanalysts have a different interpretation. They view the ubiquitous fear of snakes as symbolic. For them, snakes represent the penis. Thus, the fear of snakes is a symbolic representation of repressed sexual conflict.

One problem with the psychoanalytic theory is that chimpanzees also fear snakes (Tuan, 1980), and no one has tried to argue that guilt-ridden chimpanzees repress their sexual anxiety. A more likely hypothesis is that the fear of snakes, in both human beings and chimpanzees, is innate. This hypothesis received experimental support from Hebb (1946), who presented a painted wood replica of a snake to chimpanzees raised in captivity. By the age of 4 or so, these animals began showing signs of fearing the wooden snake. Their fear increased over the next few years, reaching a peak at age 7. Because they had never been harmed by (or even seen) a snake, Hebb concluded that the chimpanzees' fear was innate.

Human children show a similar pattern. Until the age of 2 or so, they are not frightened of snakes. By age 4, many begin to show signs of discomfort and, by age 6, most children show definite signs of fear when confronted with a snake. The similarity between the chimpanzees and human infants suggests that the human fear of snakes is also innate, but it is always tricky to generalize across species. Mineka (1979), for example, found that rhesus monkeys raised in captivity do not fear snakes. Because ethical considerations prohibit scientists from raising a child in captivity, we cannot conclude with certainty that the fear of snakes is innate in humans. However, the evidence suggests that this is at least a possibility.

and pain. (And they may include the fear of snakes, as Highlight 4.1 explores.) Watson argued that other fears, which make their appearance later in life, are acquired through classical conditioning. That is, a neutral stimulus repeatedly paired with one of the innate fear-producing stimuli eventually comes to elicit fear itself. Although some fears may be acquired in this way, Watson almost certainly overstated his case. Even fears that make their first appearance later in life can still be innate. Babies are unable to walk for months after birth, yet the ability to walk is innate. Walking evolves spontaneously as a child's neurological system matures.

Like walking, some fears require a certain amount of neurological maturation before they become apparent. A good example is the fear of strangers. This fear has clear survival value because it helps keep children away from potential predators. Babies less than 3 or 4 months old show no fear of strangers. They do not complain when they are picked up by someone they have never seen before. By the time they are 7 or 8 months old, however, practically all children complain loudly when approached by a stranger (Schaffer & Emerson, 1964). Around the same time, children show distress when parted from their caregivers (usually their parents). What has happened in that time? Have all strangers been repeatedly paired with loud noises or

In preschoolers, not wanting their mother to leave is a sign of cognitive development. When they were babies, they were unable to distinguish between their parents and other adults.

other innate fear-producing stimuli, as Watson alleges? For most children, the answer is no. The reason newborn infants do not show any fear of strangers is because they cannot distinguish between strange and familiar people. As their nervous systems mature and they become able to tell one person from another, their fear becomes manifest (Abe et al., 1993). Note that the fear of strangers is not a sign of psychopathology; it is a normal part of development. Only when the fear of being separated from one's caregivers persists into later childhood and affects social and academic functioning does it become the sign of a disorder (**separation anxiety disorder**).

Although it is possible that Carole Ballodi's fear of snakes was inherited from her mother, it is more likely that Carole learned her mother's fear through modeling. Yet, not every child models his or her parents' fears. There seem to be stable individual differences in fearfulness that make some people more vulnerable to develop fears than others. This vulnerability may well have a genetic component. We know, for example, that breeding can produce fearful or fearless animals (Gray, 1987), and we also know that people differ in their general level of anxiety from soon after birth (Kalin, 1993). Pedigree studies have found a tendency for fear to run in families (Kendler, Neale, et al., 1992; Last et al., 1991), and identical twins raised apart have been found equally likely to develop fears and to be afraid of similar things (Plomin & Rende, 1991). One possible mechanism for the genetic transmission of fear is the sensitivity of an individual's alarm reaction. That is, some people may inherit a lower threshold for fear than others—it takes less to set off their alarm reaction (Gabbay, 1992). When faced with stress, highly reactive people (a category which may include Carole Ballodi) are more likely to develop phobias than more temperate people.

Although there is evidence for a genetic vulnerability to develop fears, such vulnerabilities can also be acquired through experience (Figure 4.5). For example, the death of Carole's father and her mother's overprotectiveness could have produced Carole's fearfulness. Thus, vulnerability to develop fears may be genetic and psychological, and it is often difficult to separate the two.

Learning Experiences   Although Watson's list of innate fears was probably too small, few psychologists disagree with his assertion that most fears are learned, either through classical conditioning or operant conditioning, or, more often, some combination of both. In either case, behaviorists construe what is learned not as some subjective emotional state called fear but as

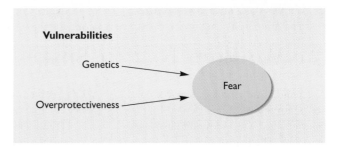

FIGURE 4.5 Sources of Fearfulness. *Vulnerability to fear can be both genetic and psychological.*

learned "avoidance." Thus, Carole Ballodi's childhood fear of snakes was characterized by her avoidance of the woods. Fear of flying is evidenced by the avoidance of airplanes. Rather than relying on introspective self-reports, defining fear in terms of avoidance allows behavioral psychologists to measure fear objectively. A person who will not even enter a room containing a non-poisonous snake is more fearful than someone who is willing to enter the room but will not touch the snake. Objective measures of fear are useful for assessing treatment outcome. The more successful the treatment, the closer the person should get to the feared object. Despite the considerable advantages of the avoidance approach to defining fear, there are times when it is not possible to define fear in this way. Some fears—death, drought, unemployment—do not involve any overt avoidance. Some people feel fearful without being able to specify any object or cause. Such "free-floating anxiety" cannot be measured in terms of avoidance because there is no specifically feared object or situation.

The two-process theory of fear, introduced in Chapter 2, postulates that a phobia is acquired initially through classical conditioning. Over time, the person comes to avoid situations related to the one in which the original conditioning took place. Once it is generalized, the avoidance response fails to extinguish because avoiding feared objects reduces anxiety, which, in turn, instrumentally reinforces future avoidance. Consider, for example, the recollections of a 20-year-old university student who had an intense fear of dentists:

I was not afraid of the dentist, at least not in the beginning. Then, when I was about nine, I fell down a flight of stairs. I couldn't move my leg, and it hurt very much. An ambulance took me to the hospital, where I had to wait in the emergency room. A child was screaming. I had to wait for a long time before X rays were taken of my leg. The only other X rays I had ever had before were at the dentist. I was taken on a stretcher to the operating room. The room was being used, so I had to wait outside the door. Even though I was feeling drowsy from the medicine they gave me, I could hear the sounds of a saw cutting off a plaster cast. The sounds of the saw, and the smell of disinfectant, reminded me of the dentist's drill and the smell of his office. I fell asleep, and when I awoke, my leg was in a plaster cast, and it hurt very much. Months later, when the cast was removed and the pain was gone, I was scheduled to visit the dentist. I convinced my mother to put off that appointment and the next. Now, even calling for an appointment makes me upset.

This student's fear of the dentist seems to have begun with the classically conditioned association of the saw and the disinfectant smell with the dentist's office. It then generalized to even calling for an appointment. Similar reports of traumatic experience are common among people with fears and phobias (Kirkby et al., 1995; Öst, 1991). But such retrospective reports must be interpreted cautiously. People may have inaccurate memories of past events, or they may exaggerate them to justify their current fears. If a traumatic experience with a feared object were the cause of phobias, we would expect fewer such experiences among people without phobias. Yet, Merckelbach and colleagues (1992) found that people who do not fear spiders report the same number of aversive experiences with spiders as those who do. Similarly, people who are not afraid of dogs report the same number of aversive experiences as those who are (Doogan & Thomas, 1992).

To deal with the finding that many phobias arise without any traumatic history (Menzies & Clarke, 1995; Merckelbach et al., 1992; Ollendick & King, 1991), behaviorists note that fears may be acquired indirectly by observing fear in others (Kleinknecht, 1994). Such observational learning was demonstrated by Mineka (1985), who found that rhesus monkeys raised in captivity were not afraid of snakes until they observed the fearful reactions of monkeys raised in the wild. Similarly, Carole Ballodi may have developed her fear of snakes by observing her mother's fear. Indeed, just being warned about snakes may be enough to create a phobia in highly susceptible people (Merckelbach et al., 1996).

Although observational learning may account for many fears acquired in the absence of aversive experiences, exposure alone may not be sufficient for fears to develop. For example, Mineka's monkeys did not develop fears of flowers or a toy rabbit, even when exposed to apparently fearful models (1985; see also M. Cook & Mineka, 1991). Perhaps observational learning

What causes fear of flying? Most people who are afraid to fly, such as the participants in this flying desensitization program, have never been in a plane crash.

produces phobias only for dangerous objects and situations that evolution has genetically "prepared" us to fear (Ohman & Soares, 1993). Of course, even this "preparedness" hypothesis has difficulty accounting for fears of harmless insects like cockroaches (Davey, 1994).

Most of the emphasis so far has been on classical conditioning, but fears may also be instilled by instrumental conditioning. Recall, for example, that Carole was apprehensive about sleeping in the dark. Her mother let her leave a light on and read her to sleep, an activity that she found pleasant. This may have reinforced Carole's fear of going to sleep alone in the dark. As Carole was indulged on many occasions, she may have developed the instrumentally conditioned habit of not going to sleep without a bedtime story and the light on. As suggested by the two-process theory, once instilled, fears may be maintained by instrumental conditioning

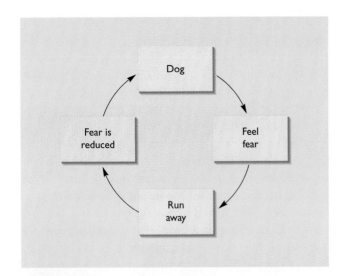

FIGURE 4.6 *Fears may be maintained by instrumental conditioning.*

(Figure 4.6). Carole feared walking in the country because the prospect of encountering a snake produced anxiety. Because anxiety is distressing, Carole was motivated to reduce it by avoiding country walks. This ploy was successful; her avoidance of walks was reinforced by anxiety reduction. In this way, anxiety reduction strengthened her avoidance of walks. Every time she avoided a walk, future avoidance became increasingly likely.

Although fears may be acquired through conditioning, Watson's claim that any stimulus is as likely as any other to become associated with fear was almost certainly exaggerated. Valentine (1930), for example, found it easier to condition his daughter to fear caterpillars than to fear a pair of binoculars. Once again, it seems as if human beings have a disposition to develop some fears (snakes, spiders, heights) and not others. Whether a person develops a specific fear or phobia depends on the person's developmental stage, traumatic conditioning experiences, exposure to fearful models, and genetic and cultural background (Davey, 1995).

Cognitive Determinants As discussed in Chapter 2, how we interpret (appraise) the prevailing social context helps to determine whether we feel fear. This was demonstrated in a classic experiment by Schacter and Singer (1962). They secretly gave some people the stimulant drug epinephrine, which produces autonomic arousal similar to that of an alarm reaction. Because the subjects in this experiment were unaware that they had received an arousal-producing drug, they interpreted their arousal as elation, anger, or fear, depending on the social situation prevailing when the drug was administered. That is, they attributed their arousal to emotions caused by the social context. In contrast, people who knew they had received the drug felt no emotion at all, even though they were in similar social situations. The difference was one of cognitive attribution. People who knew they had received the drug felt no emotion because they correctly attributed their arousal to the drug rather than to the social context.

Cognitive behavior therapists believe that some people habitually make fearful attributions. They overestimate the probability of risk and, at the same time, underestimate their personal ability to cope (Stopa & Clark, 1993). Bandura (1986) has suggested that, in some people, this perceived inability to cope is responsible for *both* anxiety and avoidance behavior. In other words, the real cause of fear is not the feared stimulus itself but feelings of inadequacy in dealing with the challenge it presents. Fearful thoughts may become self-fulfilling prophecies. For example, being afraid of failure on an examination may make people fail. Consider the thoughts running through the mind of this anxious student during a final exam in introductory psychology:

> This is the final exam. It counts sixty percent. If I fail this, I'll fail the course. I'll have to do it again next year, and I won't graduate. Everyone else will be gone, but I'll still be here, without any friends. Everyone will think I'm stupid. I should have studied more. I can't remember anything. This essay question is about conditioning. I'll never be able to write an entire page. I wish it were not so hot in here. It's stifling. I can't think. My shirt is getting wet under my arms. Everyone will see the stains. "In conditioning, the CS stands for the conditioned stimulus." They're already beginning to leave. How do they do it? I am too stupid for this. What will my parents say? They'll be so disappointed. I think I'll try the next question. "What is the projective hypothesis?" I don't know which essay to do. I'd better go back to the last question, or I'll never finish. I know it's related to projective tests. Only thirty minutes left. Everyone is leaving now. I'll be the only person in the room. "What is the CS-UCS interval?" Got to calm down; I'm really sweating now. I'd better try another question. "What are the origins of IQ tests?" No time. I'd better go back. There goes another one finished. I'm going to fail; I know it. What's the point? I'll go on to the last question. Why did I ever take this course? I can feel my heart beating. Boy, it's hot. Only fifteen minutes left. No use going on. There's not enough time. I'll never be any good at tests. I'll just leave now.

This student's fear of failing is an example of the fear of evaluation, a common fear among university students.

From Performance Anxiety to Social Phobia

Carole Ballodi was never treated for her childhood fear of snakes or the dark. Like most people, she just learned to live with her fears. Although she did well in school and entered college at age 17, Carole found the competition for grades daunting. She particularly dreaded oral presentations. She would do whatever she could to avoid them. If a paper was acceptable instead, she would choose that option, even if it meant more work. Eventually she sought treatment from her college counseling center. During his structured diagnostic interview, Dr. Berg asked Carole to tell him how she had felt when she had been required to make a class presentation. An excerpt from this interview appears in Document 4.4.

DOCUMENT 4.4

Excerpt From Interview Between Dr. Berg and Carole Ballodi (Carole's feelings about class presentations)

It would start months before the day of the presentation. I would try to prepare, but I couldn't concentrate. I'd keep thinking about what would happen if I failed. I'd tell myself that everyone in the class found the work easier than I did. This made me feel inadequate. Sometimes, I'd think there was no use in working because I was going to fail anyway. On the day, I would wake up in a sweat. As I entered the room, my mouth would get dry, my hands cold and damp, my heart would race, and I'd feel as if I couldn't catch my breath. I'd try to concentrate, but I couldn't. I'd keep thinking about failing and about how bad I would feel. People would present before me, and I would think that they were smarter than me. I tried to overcome my fear, to think positive thoughts. I borrowed a book on relaxation from the library. I was referred to a counseling-center psychologist, but the thought of talking to her terrified me. Still, I wanted to be a doctor, and I knew I had to get over my fear, so I went to the center and sought help. ■

Carole's concerns are exceedingly common (M. B. Stein, Walker, & Forde, 1996). The fear of examinations and speaking in front of other people ("stage fright") are both forms of **performance anxiety,** a common complaint among college students, especially younger ones (Yarbrough & Schaffer, 1990). But performance anxiety is not limited to students. Employment tests, driver's license tests, even medical examinations can produce feelings of apprehension and dread in many people

(Sloboda, 1990). Although moderate levels of anxiety may actually facilitate performance (G. Jones, 1995), high levels of anxiety always lower performance (Sarason, 1980). In extreme cases, anxiety may render people unable to perform at all. It can produce eating and sleeping disorders, and, in severe cases, it can make sufferers physically ill (Cairns et al., 1991).

Performance anxiety occurs in both Western and Eastern cultures (Sharma & Sud, 1990; Yue, 1994). In developing societies, however, where females have only recently begun to participate in higher education, performance anxiety is higher among female than among male students (Sharma & Sud, 1990). Cultural sensitivity is often necessary when interpreting performance anxiety. Among Native American cultures, for instance, it is considered improper, impolite, and even disloyal to stand out from one's peers (Dasen, Berry, & Sartorius, 1988; Kagitçibasi & Berry, 1989). A fear of rejection, rather than of performance evaluation, may cause members of such cultures to do poorly on examinations.

Performance anxiety is rarely the result of a traumatic experience (Hofmann, Ehlers, & Roth, 1995). It is more often related to shyness and lack of confidence (Schwarzer & Wicklund, 1991). People who have a low opinion of their own abilities become self-conscious when performing in front of others, especially when they think their performance is being evaluated (Alden, Teschuk, & Tee, 1992; Schwarzer & Wicklund, 1991). Preoccupation with fear of failure distracts them from concentrating on their performance (Clark & Beck, 1988). It is worth noting that the attributions made by performance-anxious students are similar to those made by depressed people (A. T. Beck, 1991), and many performance-anxious people report feeling depressed (A. T. Beck & Clark, 1991).

Because people with performance anxiety can usually interact successfully with others (provided they do not have to perform), few seek professional help. Like Carole, they consider talking to a psychologist just another type of "performance" they would rather avoid. For some people, however, the fear of being evaluated by others extends beyond performances to most aspects of social interaction. These people may curtail their social lives, even sacrifice their careers, to avoid threatening social situations. In the *DSM-IV* diagnostic scheme, such persons are likely to be suffering from social phobia (Heimberg et al., 1993).

Social Phobia   As already noted, performance anxiety is common, and many fears have a social dimension (Stravynski, 1995). But social phobias, which begin in

DSM-IV	**TABLE 4.5** Main *DSM-IV* Diagnostic Criteria for Social Phobia

A. A marked and persistent fear of one or more social or performance situations in which the person is exposed to unfamiliar people or to possible scrutiny by others. The individual fears that he or she will act in a way (or show anxiety symptoms) that will be humiliating or embarrassing. Note: In children, there must be evidence of the capacity for age-appropriate social relationships with familiar people and the anxiety must occur in peer settings, not just in interactions with adults.

B. Exposure to the feared social situation almost invariably provokes anxiety, which may take the form of a situationally bound or situationally predisposed Panic Attack. Note: In children, the anxiety may be expressed by crying, tantrums, freezing, or shrinking from social situations with unfamiliar people.

C. The person recognizes that the fear is excessive or unreasonable. Note: In children, this feature may be absent.

D. The feared social or performance situations are avoided or else are endured with intense anxiety or distress.

E. The avoidance, anxious anticipation, or distress in the feared social or performance situation(s) interferes significantly with the person's normal routine, occupational (academic) functioning, or social activities or relationships, or there is marked distress about having the phobia.

F. In individuals under age 18 years, the duration is at least 6 months.

G. The fear or avoidance is not due to the direct physiological effects of a substance (e.g., a drug of abuse, a medication) or a general medical condition and is not better accounted for by another mental disorder (e.g., Panic Disorder With or Without Agoraphobia, Separation Anxiety Disorder, Body Dysmorphic Disorder, a Pervasive Developmental Disorder, or Schizoid Personality Disorder).

H. If a general medical condition or another mental disorder is present, the fear in Criterion A is unrelated to it, e.g., the fear is not of Stuttering, trembling in Parkinson's disease, or exhibiting abnormal eating behavior in Anorexia Nervosa or Bulimia Nervosa.

Note: From American Psychiatric Association (1995, pp. 416–417).

adolescence, represent an exaggerated form of performance anxiety in which the fear of social evaluation can produce panic attacks and can severely restrict a person's life (Schneier et al., 1992). Around 13% of the general population meets the criteria for social phobia at some time in their lives (Magee et al., 1996), with most cases found among the young and relatively few in the elderly (Sheikh, 1992; Verberg et al., 1992). Like most anxiety disorders, social phobia affects more females than males (M. H. Rapaport, Paniccia, & Judd, 1995). Social phobias may sometimes be traced to a specific triggering event (say, an embarrassing inability to find a date for the senior prom), but most cases appear to develop without any specific trigger. Instead, social phobias usually develop slowly in people who either inherit a tendency toward shyness or become shy early in life (Fyer et al., 1993; Kagan & Snidman, 1991). The main *DSM-IV* diagnostic criteria for social phobia appear in Table 4.5.

Dr. Berg believed that Carole Ballodi exhibited some of the behaviors associated with social phobia. To explore this further, he used the *Anxiety Disorders Interview Schedule for* DSM-IV (*ADIS-IV*; Di Nardo, Brown, & Barlow, 1994), a structured interview designed to help clinicians gather information relevant to diagnosing anxiety disorders. An excerpt from Dr. Berg's interview appears in Document 4.5.

DOCUMENT 4.5

Excerpt From Interview Between Dr. Berg and Carole Ballodi (diagnosing a potential social phobia)

DR. BERG: In social situations where you might be observed or evaluated by others, do you feel nervous?

CAROLE: I don't really want people to know what happened to me.

DR. BERG: Are you overly concerned that you might say or do something that might embarrass or humiliate you in front of others, or that others will think badly of you?

CAROLE: I would be embarrassed if the people I work with knew how I have been behaving. They might think I was mad.

DR. BERG: What do you anticipate before going into social situations?

CAROLE: I get a bit worried; I will have to pretend that everything is OK.

DR. BERG: Do you avoid social situations because you are afraid that you will have a panic attack?

CAROLE: I would not want anyone to see me having one. ■

From Document 4.5, it seems that Carole avoids social situations and worries that her coworkers might find out about her recent problems. This sounds like social phobia, but she does not meet criterion C: She does not feel that her fear of social evaluation is unreasonable. She may be correct. Being considered mentally ill might well harm her medical career. Dr. Berg concluded that although Carole has some features of social phobia, her condition may be better described by some other disorder.

The *DSM-IV* distinguishes several subtypes of social phobia:

1. *Performance type:* The phobic stimulus involves public performance of activities that can be engaged in comfortably if the individual is doing them while alone (such as playing a musical instrument, giving a speech, or urinating).
2. *Limited interactional type:* The phobic stimulus is restricted to one or two socially interactive situations, such as going out on dates or speaking to authority figures.
3. *Generalized type:* The phobic trigger includes most social situations.

The independence of these subtypes is open to question. Clinic clients display the signs of more than one subtype, and usually other disorders as well (S. M. Turner et al., 1991). An added diagnostic complication is that the generalized subtype of social phobia seems indistinguishable from another *DSM-IV* condition, avoidant personality disorder (Heimberg et al., 1993).

Avoidant Personality Disorder People have different personalities. Some are aggressive; others are timid. Some are gregarious; others are shy. Taken to extremes, practically any personality trait can impair social functioning and create personal distress. Aggressive people may get into legal trouble; shy people may lead unsatisfying social lives. When personality traits are extreme enough to produce deleterious effects on a person's life, the affected person is said to have a personality disorder. These personality disorders usually become apparent in late childhood or early adolescence, and, once they appear, they change little over the years.

As you will recall from Chapter 3, the *DSM-IV* diagnostic scheme includes several axes. Axis I is used to describe clinical disorders such as social phobia, whereas personality disorders are coded on Axis II. This makes it possible for a person to be diagnosed as suffering from both a clinical disorder on Axis I and a personality disorder on Axis II. However, Axis I and Axis II disorders often overlap. In some cases, they are just slightly different versions of the same condition (Oldham et al., 1995). The *DSM-IV* contains 10 Axis II personality disorders. Many

are discussed in Chapter 10, but some are better discussed in other chapters along with similar Axis I disorders. Avoidant personality disorder is discussed here because of its close relationship to performance anxiety.

The hallmarks of **avoidant personality disorder** are extreme shyness and concern about social evaluation. Like people with generalized social phobia, those with avoidant personality disorder feel as if they are constantly being evaluated, even by strangers. Some males even report being unable to urinate in front of others in public rest rooms. Although people with avoidant personality disorder would prefer to be sociable, they avoid social contact because they fear embarrassment and criticism. Avoidant personality disorder, which seems to occur about equally in men and women, has a prevalence in the general population of about 0.5–1% (American Psychiatric Assn, 1994). The *DSM-IV* diagnostic criteria for avoidant personality disorder are summarized in Table 4.6. Keep in mind that extreme shyness and evaluative concern may be developmentally appropriate for young children, and may not be signs of a personality disorder.

Avoidant personality disorder is not exactly equivalent to generalized social phobia. For example, social phobias may sometimes result from specific traumatic experiences, whereas avoidant personality disorder usually develops gradually. But the differences between the conditions are minor. In practice, generalized social phobia and avoidant personality disorder are interchangeable diagnoses. Choosing between them depends on whether a clinician views the fear of social evaluation as a clinical disorder or a long-standing character trait.

Overcoming Fears and Phobias

While a college student, Carole Ballodi sought help for her performance anxiety. Depending on the orientation of the counseling-center psychologist, she could have received a variety of treatments. (All of the paradigms discussed in Chapter 2 have made contributions to the treatment of specific fears and phobias.) This section describes the most common approaches to treatment.

Measurement Comes First The first step in establishing a treatment program is assessment. Accurate measurement is essential not only for treatment planning but also for evaluating treatment outcome. Fears and phobias may be measured by self-report, behavioral observation, and physiologically.

DSM-IV TABLE 4.6 Main *DSM-IV* Diagnostic Criteria for Avoidant Personality Disorder

A pervasive pattern of social inhibition, feelings of inadequacy, and hypersensitivity to negative evaluation beginning in early adulthood and present in a variety of contexts, as characterized by four (or more) of the following:

(1) avoids occupational activities that involve significant interpersonal contact because of fears of criticism, disapproval, or rejection

(2) is unwilling to get involved with people unless certain of being liked

(3) shows restraint within intimate relationships because of the fear of being shamed or ridiculed

(4) is preoccupied with being criticized or rejected in social situations

(5) is inhibited in new interpersonal situations because of feelings of inadequacy

(6) views self as socially inept, personally unappealing, or inferior to others

(7) is unusually reluctant to take personal risks or to engage in any new activities because they may prove embarrassing

Note: From American Psychiatric Association (1994, pp. 664–665).

Self-Report One popular way to obtain quantitative information about fears is to use a **fear survey** schedule. Fear surveys require people to assign numeric values to fear-producing stimuli. For example, Carole Ballodi's college counseling-center therapist asked her to indicate the behavioral consequences of her fear of public speaking and also its intensity using a scale that ranged from 1 (*none at all*) to 5 (*very much*) (Figure 4.7). In addition to a fear survey schedule, the psychologist used specially designed self-report inventories to assess Carole's performance anxiety (Mandler & Sarason, 1952; McCroskey, 1983; Sarason, 1984, 1991; Spielberger, 1980). Of course, the drawbacks associated with self-report inventories that were discussed in Chapter 3 (such as the need to portray oneself in a socially desirable light) also apply to fears and phobias.

Physiological Measures Physiological measures of autonomic arousal can tell us how a person is reacting in threatening situations. Such measures are not contaminated by social desirability, but they are often impractical because they require sophisticated equipment, such as a polygraph, and trained operators. Moreover, physiological measures reflect only the examinee's *state* at a particular time; they are not useful for measuring a general *tendency* toward social anxiety (McCroskey, 1983).

Behavioral Observations Behavioral observations are more practical than physiological measures because they are less intrusive. "Wiring up" a person for physiological recording may, in itself, increase anxiety. Behavioral observations are also probably more valid than physiological recordings. Autonomic arousal is only in-

directly related to fear. As we have already seen, an alarm reaction may be appraised in different ways depending on the social context in which it occurs. Thus, we cannot conclude that an autonomically aroused person is experiencing fear. Behavioral assessments are most reliable when judges make specific observations under standard conditions. For example, the Behavioral Assessment of Speech Anxiety, or BASA (Mulac & Wiemann, 1983), requires subjects to make a brief speech, which is videotaped. Trained observers then watch the tape and rate the severity of a variety of behaviors that have been found to reflect stage fright.

Establish a Trusting Relationship No matter what treatment is used, an important factor in helping someone to overcome any problem is to establish a trusting relationship. Because fearful clients are often embarrassed about their behavior, a clinician who treats fears as silly may wind up making clients feel more embarrassed and even less inclined to go through with treatment. To avoid this, therapists must get clients to trust them. Building trust begins by explaining the planned treatment, including its risks and benefits. Informed clients, those who know what is about to happen and why, feel more in control and are more likely to benefit from treatment (Eccles et al., 1993).

Set Treatment Targets Many different treatments have been developed to deal with common fears, as well as with performance anxiety and social phobia (Juster, Heimberg, & Holt, 1996; Menninger, 1994; Schooling & Emmelkamp, 1993; Zarate & Agras, 1994). Although each has its specific aspects, they all share the same "active

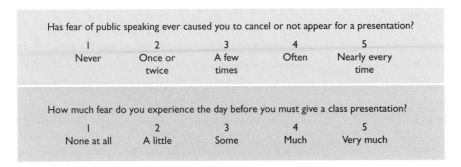

Has fear of public speaking ever caused you to cancel or not appear for a presentation?

1	2	3	4	5
Never	Once or twice	A few times	Often	Nearly every time

How much fear do you experience the day before you must give a class presentation?

1	2	3	4	5
None at all	A little	Some	Much	Very much

FIGURE 4.7 **Sample Items From a Public-Speaking Fear Survey**

ingredients": motivating people to change, ensuring that they prepare, and exposing them to the feared stimulus.

Motivation   Motivation is important because people with phobias may resign themselves to their fear. For example, people with social phobia may lose their desire to even enter social situations. For such people, the first step in any treatment program must be motivational. One way to start is by setting specific treatment goals. Because people are more committed to achieving goals they set for themselves, the anxious person should set his or her own objectives. These should be challenging but realistic. Unrealistic goals will only lead to failure and disappointment.

Preparation   Preparation is crucial to successfully overcoming performance anxiety and social phobia. Even the calmest person will perform poorly if he or she is unprepared. The problem is that preparing elicits thoughts of failure and humiliation, which make performance-anxious people feel even more frightened. One of the reasons that performance-anxious people are so often unprepared is that preparing makes them anxious. Not preparing helps alleviate anxiety in the short term but makes it worse in the long term. It virtually guarantees poor performance. Overcoming performance anxiety requires that the cycle of anxiety and avoidance be broken (Derry, 1988). Carole, for example, was put on a preparation schedule. She set herself tests to see whether she was achieving her goals. Success is intrinsically rewarding, but the psychologist also encouraged Carole to give herself rewards (a little gift, for example) for achieving her goals. Following a preparation schedule not only ensured that Carole was prepared for her presentation, it also increased her self-confidence.

Exposure   People with phobias habitually avoid the feared object or situation (Davey, Burgess, & Rashes,

1995). Successful treatment almost always requires overcoming this avoidance and getting the client to confront the fear. Carole's self-confidence was increased by gradually exposing her to the dreaded class presentation. She practiced speaking alone in the classroom, and when she was ready the counseling center had her join a group of students with performance anxiety (Albano et al., 1995). This group provided Carole with an audience of sympathetic listeners, who also provided social support. Social support has been found to reduce the "worry" aspect of performance anxiety (Bolger & Eckenrode, 1991; R. E. Smith, Smoll, & Barnett, 1995).

The active ingredients of motivation, preparation, and exposure are usually implemented using one or more of the main therapeutic approaches: psychodynamic, humanistic, behavior modification, and cognitive-

For people in this rural Georgia church, overcoming their fear of handling poisonous snakes is the ultimate test of their willingness to put their life in God's hands. What motivation, preparation, and exposure enables them to overcome their phobia?

behavior modification, or some combination of approaches.

Psychoanalytic and Humanistic Treatments Psychoanalysts view fears and phobias as surface manifestations of unconscious conflicts. Guilt produced by repressed sexual and aggressive impulses generates anxiety, which is displaced onto an object or situation with some symbolic connection to the impulse. Fear of the dentist, for example, may be a symbolic representation of conflicts originating during the oral stage of psychosexual development. Over the years, psychoanalytic theory has evolved and broadened to include other etiological factors, such as dependency, but the idea that phobias are symbolic representations of repressed impulses remains central to psychoanalytic theory (Arieti, 1979).

Not surprisingly, psychoanalytic treatment consists of uncovering the repressed memories assumed to underlie fear and avoidance. Dream interpretation, free association, and other psychoanalytic techniques are used to lift repression and make unconscious conflicts conscious. Psychoanalysts may also expose patients to their fear (Wolitzky, 1995). In such cases, exposure is not expected to extinguish the fear but to help retrieve repressed conflicts and desires. Because phobias are thought to protect people from repressed impulses that are too painful to confront, psychoanalysts believe that any attempt to eliminate a phobia without resolving the underlying unconscious conflict is doomed to fail. There is little empirical evidence for this belief. Behavioral treatment typically confronts phobias directly, often with excellent results.

The humanistic approach to treatment emphasizes the development of a therapeutic relationship. The humanistic therapist provides an accepting, empathic listener, who gives clients "unconditional positive regard" (usually evidenced by reflecting back to the client the emotions the client is expressing). This allows clients to trust the therapist and to follow the therapist's suggestions, which assists clients in overcoming their problems. Although clinicians should develop good relationships with clients, the humanistic approach is fairly vague and may not be much better than a placebo.

Behavioral Treatment Behavioral treatments focus on one or another form of exposure. Perhaps the best-known exposure technique is systematic desensitization, which was introduced in Chapter 2 (St. Onge, 1995). The technique has three parts. The first is relaxation training. Clients are taught to relax, usually by al-

ternating the tensing and relaxing of various muscle groups combined with controlled breathing. The idea is to make people aware of their muscle tension so they can learn to relax. Biofeedback focused on muscle tension may also assist some people to relax. One common procedure is to vary the pitch of a tone to reflect muscle tension—the higher the pitch, the greater the tension. People learn to reduce the pitch of the tone and thereby learn to reduce muscle tension. The second part of systematic desensitization is the construction of an anxiety hierarchy in which fear-related images are arranged according to the degree of anxiety they elicit. The third part of desensitization involves the graded presentation of hierarchy images while the person attempts to maintain a relaxed state. The rationale is that one cannot be both fearful and relaxed at the same time. Thus, a fearful person who can learn to relax while imagining anxiety-provoking scenes will eventually cease being afraid. Desensitization can be conducted with the hierarchy items presented in imagery, in filmed scenes, or in vivo (in real life). In vivo exposure to the elements of a fear hierarchy is especially helpful with children, who may have difficulty visualizing the images required by the traditional desensitization procedure (Menzies & Clarke, 1993). One variation is to present both relaxation instructions and the anxiety hierarchy by computer (F. R. Wilson, Omeltschenko, & Yager, 1991).

In another variation, the college counseling-center psychologist conducted Carole Ballodi's desensitization in a group. Everyone used the same anxiety hierarchy (Document 4.6). This approach gave members of the group an opportunity to "perform" in front of a sympathetic and nonthreatening audience (Albano & Barlow, 1996; Heimberg & Juster, 1994).

DOCUMENT 4.6

Group Anxiety Hierarchy for Fear of Public Speaking for Carole Ballodi's Group

Fear-Provoking Image

1. Seeing the calendar that shows one day left before my presentation.
2. Taking my seat in the classroom on the day of my presentation.
3. Waiting while other students make their presentations.
4. Hearing my name called to step forward to the front of the room.
5. Standing in the front of the classroom.
6. Beginning my presentation. ■

In some cases, systematic desensitization must be altered. For example, unlike most other phobics, people who are afraid of blood show a slowing rather than an acceleration of their heart rates when they are confronted with the feared stimulus. Sometimes their heart rate becomes so slow that they faint. Based on this observation, Öst and colleagues (1989) devised a desensitization procedure that requires people who fear blood to tense rather than relax their body muscles while imagining feared situations. The idea is to keep them from fainting (Hellstrom, Fellenius, & Öst, 1996).

In systematic desensitization, clients are gradually exposed to fearful stimuli and all efforts are made to keep anxiety in check. In contrast, **flooding** requires fearful individuals to become "flooded" with emotion through exposure to their most feared stimulus. Because their fear is not "reinforced" (nothing bad actually happens), exposure to frightening situations should eventually cause the fear to extinguish. **Implosive therapy** is a type of flooding in which exposure is done through imagery rather than in vivo (Hogan & Kirchner, 1968). Here is an example of a therapist using implosive therapy with a person who is afraid of snakes:

> Picture the snake out in front of you, now make yourself pick it up. Reach down, pick it up, put it in your lap. Feel it wriggling around in your lap. Leave your hand on it, put your hand out and feel it wriggling around. . . . Okay, feel him coiling around your hand again, touching you, slimy, now he is going up on your shoulder and he is looking you right in the eye. He is big . . . and he is ugly . . . and he is ready to strike and he is looking at you. . . . Look at those sharp fangs. . . . He strikes out at you . . . feel it biting your eye and it is going to pull your eye right out and down your cheek. It is kind of . . . eating it. (Hogan, 1968, pp. 423–431)

Although psychologists have reported success applying flooding and implosive therapy to fears, outcomes vary widely (King & Tonge, 1992). Some people show extinction within the treatment session, only to have their fear return, more or less at its former level of intensity, at the next session (S. M. Turner, Beidel, Long, et al., 1992).

In addition to systematic desensitization and flooding, behavior therapists have developed a set of other therapeutic techniques. For example, clients may be "shaped" to approach feared objects by reinforcing (usually with social reinforcement) small "steps" in the right direction. A person who fears public speaking, for instance, may be reinforced for attending class, sitting through other people's talks, standing in front of the room, and so on. By combining operant conditioning with systematic desensitization, therapists can reduce fear while gradually helping clients to confront phobic stimuli.

Modeling (vicarious conditioning) is also used to help clients overcome fears and phobias. For example, the members of Carole Ballodi's therapy group watched films of people giving presentations. Watching these films provided opportunities for positive observational learning. Sarason (1980) found that just listening to a formerly anxious person describe the strategies she had used to overcome performance anxiety helped other anxious people to improve their performance. Some people with fears may also be helped by skill training. For example, people with social phobia may benefit from training in how to initiate conversations and how to behave in social situations (S. M. Turner, Beidel, & Cooley-Quille, 1995).

Cognitive–Behavioral Treatment   The goal of cognitive-behavioral treatment is to help clients learn to reappraise feared situations so that they can replace maladaptive cognitions about danger and failure with positive cognitions (Davey et al., 1995; Dobson, 1988; O'Neil & Spielberger, 1979). Document 4.7 contains an excerpt from a therapy session the college counseling-center psychologist conducted with Carole Ballodi. Note how the psychologist engages in cognitive restructuring, helping Carole to replace her original explanation of why other students volunteered to present first (they are smarter) with another, less threatening one (they just wanted to get it over with).

DOCUMENT 4.7

Excerpt From Carole Ballodi's Cognitive–Behavioral Therapy Session

PSYCHOLOGIST: How did you feel when some students volunteered to make their oral presentations first?

CAROLE: I figured that they were not worried; they were probably smarter than me. I knew that I didn't belong in this school. I'll probably never get into medical school.

PSYCHOLOGIST: And what did you do while you waited for your turn to speak?

CAROLE: I panicked. I got hot, my breath came very fast. I felt queasy. I had to leave the room.

PSYCHOLOGIST: How did you feel?

CAROLE: Angry with myself and unhappy. I thought I would always mess up.

PSYCHOLOGIST: Perhaps your interpretation of the situation was wrong. Is it possible that there was some other reason why some students volunteered to make their presentations first?

CAROLE: Well . . . maybe they were nervous. Maybe they just wanted to get it over with.

PSYCHOLOGIST: And when you think that, how do you feel?

CAROLE: Better. Maybe I'm not the only one who finds presentations tough.

PSYCHOLOGIST: Perhaps your fear of messing up a presentation is actually making you mess up. You believe that you will embarrass yourself. This makes you unable to concentrate on the presentation, and then, because you can't concentrate, you wind up messing up. ■

One cognitive-behavioral technique that has been applied to performance anxiety is stress inoculation (Meichenbaum, 1985), a procedure that is meant to be an analogue to immunization. Stress inoculation begins with an educational phase in which people are taught about the role played by negative self-statements in performance anxiety. Sometimes readings are assigned, a technique known as bibliotherapy (Register et al., 1991). Next, clients are taught a set of more accurate self-statements that they can practice in stressful evaluative situations. These statements are not overly positive exaggerations ("I am going to get an A+") but reasonable expectations ("If I practice the slow-breathing technique that I've been taught, I'll be able to help myself stay calm. I've been studying regularly, so I should do well if I stay calm"). In the final stage, clients are taught coping skills designed to help them deal with, rather than avoid, evaluative situations. One such skill is thought-stopping, which involves saying "stop" whenever fear-producing thoughts come to mind. Eventually, the incidence of such thoughts decreases (Wolpe, 1981).

Cognitive restructuring, stress inoculation, and other cognitive techniques have been applied with success to a variety of fears and phobias (Harvey & Rapee, 1995). Yet the rationale for cognitive treatment is not entirely clear. The *DSM-IV* diagnostic criteria for phobias include the requirement that sufferers know their fears are unreasonable. But if phobics already know their fears are unreasonable, what faulty cognitions are left for cognitive therapy to change? Perhaps the secret behind cognitive therapy's success is that therapists do more than simply change cognitions. They also urge their clients to confront feared objects and situations. Perhaps it is exposure to feared stimuli, rather than cognitive restructuring, that reduces fear.

Both behavioral and cognitive therapies include exposure to the fear-inducing event, such as taking a test, but one emphasizes changing behavioral responses and the other emphasizes changing cognitions about the event.

If exposure is the active ingredient, then cognitive therapy may be just a special form of behavior therapy. But the opposite is also possible; behavior therapy may be a special form of cognitive therapy. Modern theories of conditioning recognize that organisms are not passive participants in learning experiments. They must somehow notice that the conditioned and unconditioned stimuli go together, store this association in memory, and recall it when next confronted with the unconditioned stimulus. All of these require cognition (Newman et al., 1994; Persons, 1995). Looked at in this light, classical and instrumental conditioning (and behavior therapy in general) may be just a technique for instilling certain cognitions about the self and the environment (Craske & Barlow, 1991). Whether behavior therapy is a form of cognitive therapy or vice versa, one thing seems clear: The distinction between behavioral and cognitive treatment is not as great as many writers claim.

Self-Exposure As already noted, exposure in some form is part of all successful treatments for fears and phobias (Emmelkamp, 1994; Ritchie, 1992). Even psychoanalysts, who believe that phobias are the result of repressed conflicts, still try to get people to confront their fears (McCullough, 1993). But exposing oneself to feared objects and situations does not necessarily require the presence of a therapist. Sometimes, self-exposure is all it takes to overcome phobias and other anxiety disorders (Marks, 1994). In some circumstances, self-exposure may even be preferable to therapist-accompanied exposure. Clients who leave treatment entirely to the therapist may attribute improvements to the therapist rather than to themselves. On the other hand, those who take charge of their own treatment—who treat themselves by self-exposure—may develop feelings of mastery and enhanced self-esteem. Such clients are more likely to cope successfully with anxiety in the future.

Initially, it may be difficult to persuade some clients to expose themselves to feared objects and situations. Many people need at least a little experience with therapist-accompanied exposures before they feel sufficiently confident to face anxiety-producing stimuli on their own. For this reason, therapists may have to mix imagery and therapist-accompanied in vivo exposure with "homework" assignments in which clients expose themselves to phobic stimuli. Self-help manuals are often useful to assist clients with these homework assignments (Marks, 1994).

Drug Treatment At some point, practically everyone with performance anxiety, social phobia, or any other anxiety disorder will be offered anxiolytic drugs (*lysis* is Greek for "dissolve"; anxiolytics "dissolve" anxiety). Barbiturates, the initial anxiolytics, were widely used in the first half of the 20th century, but they made people groggy and physically dependent. In the 1950s, the propanediols (such as Miltown) came into use, but they were soon replaced by the faster acting **benzodiazepines,** which remain the most popular anxiolytics today. All benzodiazepines are descendants of chlordiazepoxide (Librium), whose anxiolytic effects were discovered accidentally by researchers observing how various chemical compounds affect animal behavior (Gelenberg, Bassuk, & Schoonover, 1991). As we shall see several times in this book, similar chance observations led to the discovery of many modern medications.

Diazepam (Valium) is the most widely prescribed benzodiazepine. This fast-acting drug, which reaches its peak blood concentration in about 1 hour, was introduced in 1963 and quickly became the most widely sold

Generic name	Common U.S. trade name
alprazolam	Xanax
chlordiazepoxide	Librium
clorazepate	Tranxene
diazepam	Valium
flurazepam	Dalmane
oxazepam	Serax

TABLE 4.7 Common Benzodiazepines

prescription medicine in the world. In recent years, alprazolam (Xanax), a high-potency benzodiazepine, has become the drug most often chosen for people who need ongoing treatment (Lipman & Kendall, 1992). Because alprazolam comes in sustained-release form, only one tablet per day produces a therapeutic effect (Schweizer et al., 1993). Table 4.7 contains the chemical (generic) names and the U.S. trade (brand) names of the most commonly prescribed benzodiazepines.

The precise action of the benzodiazepines is not well understood. It is known that they have only minor effects on organs outside the nervous system (although they do produce skeletal muscle relaxation, which makes them useful in treating muscle spasms and convulsions). In the brain, benzodiazepines seem to augment the inhibitory effect of gamma-aminobutyric acid (GABA), a neurotransmitter that inhibits neurons from firing. Beyond this, however, the details become somewhat sketchy, and considerable research work remains to be done.

Although there have been reports that benzodiazepines can induce depression, these are largely anecdotal, and most clinicians consider these drugs to be relatively safe (Gelenberg et al., 1991). Even when large doses are taken by people attempting suicide, they are almost never fatal. This does not mean that benzodiazepines do not produce problems. They are known to cause drowsiness (so they may adversely affect performance), they interfere with normal sleep, and they can harm cognitive functioning (Hindmarch, 1990). They are also associated with injury due to falling, especially in the elderly (Ray et al., 1992).

Even standard doses of benzodiazepines may cause tolerance, in which people require larger and larger doses to achieve the same therapeutic effect (Rickels et al., 1990). Terminating benzodiazepines after a prolonged period of use produces withdrawal symptoms (insomnia, dizziness, headache, and loss of appetite) and may also produce "rebound" anxiety, in which the individual experiences anxiety as, or even more, severe than before treatment. Benzodiazepines and alcohol make a particularly dangerous combination because their combined effects are stronger than the effects of either alone (Harangozo, Magyar, & Faludy, 1991). This is why benzodiazepines should never be given to people suspected of alcohol abuse. They are also not appropriate during pregnancy. Mothers who take them may have babies who are born addicted and who must undergo withdrawal soon after birth. Psychological dependence on benzodiazepines can be just as serious a problem as physical dependence. Instead of learning effective ways of coping with panic-inducing situations, habitual benzodiazepine users may come to rely on the drug to get them through, and they may panic when the drug is withdrawn (Schweizer et al., 1990).

New drugs are constantly being developed. Each has its own pattern of advantages and disadvantages. For example, the non-benzodiazepine anxiolytic buspirone (BuSpar) has the benefit of not causing drowsiness. Still, it is used less often than the benzodiazepines because it is slow acting (it needs a few days or longer to build up its effects). Beta-blockers (drugs used to lower blood pressure) may reduce some forms of performance anxiety without causing sleepiness like the benzodiazepines. Beta-blockers work by dampening the responsiveness of the sympathetic nervous system. One dose, taken before a performance, reduces the racing heartbeat and fast breathing associated with performance anxiety. Unfortunately, beta-blockers may have serious side effects: They can provoke asthma attacks in susceptible people, and they can cause impotence and depression. Because of these side effects and because tolerance quickly develops, beta-blockers can only be used short term. Teaching people behavioral and cognitive skills that can be applied in many anxiety-provoking situations is more likely to lead to long-term benefits without causing unwanted side effects.

Self-Help   Everyone has fears. They may not be serious enough to meet the diagnostic criteria for a phobia, but if they interfere with the quality of your life, then you should do something about them. Fortunately, fears respond to psychological treatment. Behavior therapy and cognitive therapy have proved to be effective in helping people overcome their fears. There are also some steps that you can take yourself, as outlined in Highlight 4.2.

Carole Ballodi's Psychological Evaluation

Carole Ballodi had a panic attack at the bridge. This attack was apparently cued by the sound of a helicopter.

She has also had uncued panic attacks, usually at night. Her anxiety about future attacks has affected her occupational and social functioning. Dr. Kahn prescribed tranquilizers and asked Dr. Berg for a psychological assessment. Document 4.3 contained the behavioral observations and history section of his assessment report. From these, we learned about Carole's childhood fear of snakes and of being left to sleep in the dark. In the interview excerpt in Document 4.4, Carole described her college fear of class presentations. Document 4.8 brings us back to the present. In this excerpt from his psychological assessment, Dr. Berg summarizes his findings, describing Carole as anxious not only at the time of testing (state anxiety) but chronically (trait anxiety). She is unable to enjoy life and sees the world as full of threats that are beyond her control.*

DOCUMENT 4.8

Excerpt From Dr. Berg's Psychological Assessment of Carole Ballodi

Personality Assessment: The validity scales of the MMPI-2 were all in the average range, indicating that the profile could be safely interpreted. The main features of Dr. Ballodi's MMPI-2 are the elevated psychasthenia, depression, and social introversion scores. Dr. Ballodi is anxious, guilty, and depressed, and she avoids social contact. She views the world as a threatening place that harbors forces beyond her control. These forces could easily harm her. Dr. Ballodi is so anxious that she finds it difficult to feel any pleasure. The State-Trait Anxiety Inventory confirms that Dr. Ballodi is currently feeling considerable anxiety about most aspects of her life. In addition, her score on trait anxiety was high. This indicates a general tendency to react to major and minor challenges with intense fear and anxiety. Dr. Ballodi's Thematic Apperception Test responses indicate that she is ambivalent about social relationships. She wants to get close to other people but fears that they may find out about her emotional problems and reject her. Thus, she avoids social contact.

According to her answers to the Anxiety Disorders Interview Schedule for *DSM-IV*, Dr. Ballodi has always been anxious. As a child, she feared snakes. This is a common fear in young children, indeed so common that some scientists believe that humans may be biologically prepared to develop a fear of snakes. Dr. Ballodi's mother also feared snakes. Thus, it is possible that Dr. Ballodi's fear could have been modeled

---

*The techniques mentioned in this assessment are described in this chapter or in Chapter 3.

Self-Help for Fears

To help yourself cope with fears, follow these steps:

1. *Confront your problem.* It is normal to avoid facing problems, especially those that make us fearful. However, changing requires that we first admit that we need to change. Try to get past the rationalizations and take an objective look at yourself. Are you really incapable of doing college-level work, or are you terrified by tests? Are you really not interested in a law career, or do you fear speaking in front of others? Are you really too tired to go to the party, or do you fear meeting new people?

2. *Critique your ideas.* Get in the habit of questioning yourself whenever you feel anxious. Identify the source of this feeling, and subject your fearful ideas to criticism. Are other people really so interested in you that they observe your every move, just waiting for you to embarrass yourself? Does each test constitute an assessment of you as a human being? Ask yourself, "What is the absolute worst thing that can happen?" Imagine it happening. Is this really so catastrophic? Will you really be devastated?

3. *Rehearse and prepare.* Fear is decreased by preparation. Set targets for study, for performing in front of or for meeting others, and then reward yourself for achieving your targets. Try role playing. Copy the behaviors of people who have learned to cope with anxiety and practice them. The more you practice, the less you will be afraid.

4. *Learn to relax and develop coping skills.* Relaxation is inimical to fear. There are numerous self-help guides to relaxation. Study them and practice relaxing, especially before tests and performances. Use such coping skills as thought-stopping and positive self-statements ("I feel calm," "I know I will pass") to reduce fear.

5. *Keep trying and get assistance.* Fears are easier to avoid than to overcome. Success is not always swift. Don't expect to go from fear to fearlessness overnight. By all means seek assistance from psychologists.

---

after her mother's. As a child, Dr. Ballodi also feared going to sleep in the dark. These multiple fears add further support to the hypothesis that she has a disposition toward fearfulness and anxiety. This disposition could have been inherited or the result of the trauma caused by her father's death, her mother's overprotectiveness, or both. It is possible that her early experiences gave her a sense of "helplessness." Specifically, her father died when she was very young, and this may have been the beginning of her feeling that forces out of her control can cause her pain.

In college, Dr. Ballodi continued her history of fearfulness. She developed a fear of speaking in public, for which she received treatment. A combination of behavioral and cognitive treatment (as well as a supportive group of fellow sufferers) helped her overcome her performance anxiety without the use of anti-anxiety drugs.

The Mississippi Scale for Combat-Related Post-Traumatic Stress Disorder suggests that Dr. Ballodi's current problems may be related to her experiences in the Gulf War. . . . ■

Dr. Berg's next task is to formulate an appropriate diagnosis for Carole Ballodi from among the anxiety disorders discussed in the remainder of this chapter.

GENERALIZED ANXIETY DISORDER

People with generalized anxiety disorder are not fearful of specific objects or situations; they are apprehensive about everything. When a partner is late, they conclude that some tragedy has occurred. If their boss is preoccupied at work, they fear their job is in danger. Any chest pain means an impending heart attack. As soon as one cause for worry is eliminated, they find another. At night, they lie awake worrying about real or imagined problems. They have trouble falling asleep, and when they finally doze off, they are plagued by nightmares in which they are late, lost, or pursued by murderers. When there is nothing at all to worry about, people with generalized anxiety disorder worry anyway. Their anxiety arises without any provocation at all; it is simply "free-floating." Along with their many worries, people with generalized anxiety disorder are often restless and irritable. They describe themselves as being "on edge," and their muscles are often tense. The main *DSM-IV* diagnostic criteria for generalized anxiety disorder are summarized in Table 4.8.

Generalized anxiety disorder occurs in about 4% of the population, with females outnumbering males two

> **DSM-IV**   TABLE 4.8   Main *DSM-IV* Diagnostic Criteria for Generalized Anxiety Disorder
>
> A. Excessive anxiety and worry (apprehensive expectation), occurring more days than not for at least 6 months, about a number of events or activities (such as work or school performance).
> B. The person finds it difficult to control the worry.
> C. The anxiety and worry are associated with three (or more) of the following six symptoms (with at least some symptoms present for more days than not for the past 6 months). Note: Only one item is required in children.
>   (1) restlessness or feeling keyed up or on edge
>   (2) being easily fatigued
>   (3) difficulty concentrating or mind going blank
>   (4) irritability
>   (5) muscle tension
>   (6) sleep disturbance (difficulty falling or staying asleep, or restless unsatisfying sleep)
> D. The focus of the anxiety and worry is not confined to features of an Axis I disorder, e.g., the anxiety or worry is not about having a Panic Attack (as in Panic Disorder), being embarrassed in public (as in Social Phobia), being contaminated (as in Obsessive-Compulsive Disorder), being away from home or close relatives (as in Separation Anxiety Disorder), gaining weight (as in Anorexia Nervosa), having multiple physical complaints (as in Somatization Disorder), or having a serious illness (as in Hypochondriasis), and the anxiety and worry do not occur exclusively during Post-traumatic Stress Disorder.
> E. The anxiety, worry, or physical symptoms cause clinically significant distress or impairment in social, occupational, or other important areas of functioning.
>
> *Note:* From American Psychiatric Association (1994, pp. 435–436).

to one (Brawman-Mintzer & Lydiard, 1996; T. A. Brown, Barlow, & Liebowitz, 1994; Sherbourne et al., 1996). It seems especially common among the elderly (Flint, 1994). Although it is probably the most common anxiety disorder after phobias, generalized anxiety disorder is not frequently diagnosed in the psychology clinic. Many cases never get to the clinic because people "treat" themselves with alcohol. Even those cases that do get to the clinic often receive some other diagnosis because generalized anxiety disorder often occurs in conjunction with other disorders (Blazer et al., 1991; Kendler, Neale, et al., 1992). Carole Ballodi is an example. She meets many of the criteria in Table 4.8, but she would not be given a diagnosis of generalized anxiety disorder because she fails to meet criterion D, which rules out anyone who may have post-traumatic stress disorder or who fears having a panic attack.

Etiology of Generalized Anxiety Disorder

There is no single cause of generalized anxiety disorder. Psychoanalysts attribute generalized anxiety disorder to a conflict between the ego and the id. The ego attempts to prevent the id's sexual impulses from breaking through to the surface because it fears the punishment that might

ensue. But the ego's repressive strategy is only partly successful. Sexual impulses remain unconscious but not the associated fear of punishment. The result is that the person is always fearful and apprehensive but does not know why. From the psychoanalytic viewpoint, generalized anxiety disorder is a more serious condition than simple phobia. By displacing anxiety onto a specific object, phobias help to limit anxiety. All phobic people need to do is to avoid the feared object. People with generalized anxiety disorder have a more difficult time containing their anxiety because its source is within themselves. They carry it around wherever they go. Like most psychoanalytic hypotheses, this explanation for generalized anxiety disorder relies on clinical observations rather than controlled research for its support.

Some behaviorists view generalized anxiety disorder as a form of classically conditioned fear that differs from a simple phobia only in its greater generality (Wolpe, 1982). People with generalized anxiety disorder are always afraid because they are always encountering a feared stimulus. Wolpe (1982) gave the example of a person who had a guilt-producing sexual experience that took place in the dark and later developed a disorder in which anxiety was triggered by the dark, dusk, dark colors, and so on. Unfortunately, this formulation

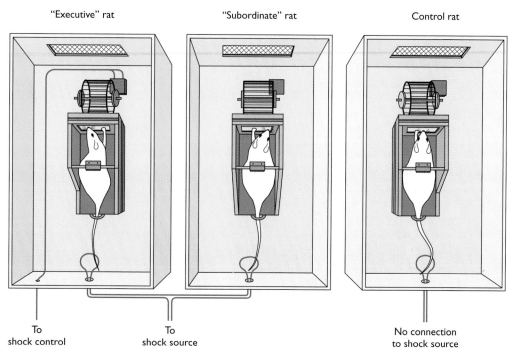

"Executive" rat   "Subordinate" rat   Control rat

To shock control   To shock source   No connection to shock source

FIGURE 4.8 **An Experiment Illustrating the Consequences of Controllability.** *The "executive" rat can control the electric shock to its tail by turning the wheel. The "subordinate" rat has no control over the shock. The control rat receives no shock at all. Neither the control nor the executive rat avoids the feeding place. The subordinate, on the other hand, becomes vigilant and anxious.* From: Seligman and Maser, 1977.

suffers from the same problem as conditioning theories of phobias—most cases of generalized anxiety disorder cannot be traced back to any particular traumatic experience (T. A. Brown et al., 1994).

To overcome the limitations of traditional conditioning theories, cognitive-behaviorists have shifted the focus from external stimuli (such as Wolpe's dark colors) to internal ones (Westling & Öst, 1995). Specifically, cognitive psychologists have proposed that people with generalized anxiety disorder fear loss of control and helplessness. Experimental support for this theory comes from several classical experiments conducted in the 1940s by Mowrer and Viek (1948). These researchers administered electric shocks to rats while the animals ate (Figure 4.8). Rats that were unable to control the shock came to fear and avoid the area in which they were shocked, even though this was also the place in which they were fed. These helpless animals never knew when danger might strike. They became vigilant and generally anxious. In contrast, rats who were taught how to terminate the shock—who were given a means of control—did not avoid the feeding place. It seemed that being in control helped them limit their anxiety (Mineka, 1992).

Helplessness and lack of control affect human beings in similar ways as animals. People with generalized anxiety are preoccupied with threats and constantly looking for signs of danger (Borkovec & Inz, 1990). This preoccupation with danger may be demonstrated in the psychology laboratory. In cognitive studies that require subjects to focus on a task, anxious subjects are more easily distracted by threatening distracters than are nonanxious subjects (M. W. Eysenck, 1992; Logan & Goetsch, 1993; MacLeod & Matthews, 1991).

Because most people have sexual and aggressive thoughts at one time or another and because everyone feels frightened or helpless sometimes, psychoanalysts, behaviorists, and cognitive psychologists all agree that generalized anxiety disorder develops only when there is a preexisting diathesis. Although there is evidence that the diathesis for generalized anxiety disorder may be inherited (Kendler, Neale, et al., 1992; Nigg & Goldsmith, 1994; Noyes et al., 1992; Roy et al., 1995; Swinson & Cox, 1993), there is also evidence that it is acquired. For example, neuropsychologists have reported that left cortical lesions produced by strokes may result in generalized anxiety (Castillo et al., 1993).We know that the social environment also contributes to the disorder

In As Good as It Gets, *Jack Nicholson plays a character with obsessive-compulsive disorder. One of his compulsions is avoiding the cracks in the sidewalk, causing him to weave in and out among the other pedestrians.*

because generalized anxiety disorder is more common in dangerous environments, such as war areas, inner-city ghettos, and other poor areas (Baum & Fleming, 1993; Blazer et al., 1991; Compton et al., 1991).

Treatment for Generalized Anxiety Disorder

The treatment of generalized anxiety disorder is determined largely by the theoretical orientation of the practitioner. Psychoanalysts use free association, dream interpretation, and other techniques to help people confront their repressed impulses and conflicts. Where practical, traditional behavioral clinicians use desensitization and other forms of exposure. Even when no specific triggering stimuli can be identified (or when there are too many), relaxation training may still help people reduce their level of anxiety (Zinbarg et al., 1992).

Cognitive interventions are usually aimed at the chronic worrying that is characteristic of generalized anxiety disorder (T. A. Brown, O'Leary, & Barlow, 1993). Clients are encouraged to confront their worries and to reappraise situations and events that they consider threatening (Butler et al., 1991; Craske, Rapee, & Barlow, 1992). Cognitive therapists may also try to combat helplessness with assertiveness training designed to increase clients' feelings of self-efficacy. Studies have found behavioral and cognitive treatments about equally effica-

cious in the treatment of generalized anxiety disorder, and both are better than no treatment at all (Barlow, Rapee, & Brown, 1992).

Anxiolytics are frequently prescribed for generalized anxiety disorder. Long-lasting drugs whose effects persist for hours or even days may be particularly useful because generalized anxiety disorder spans so many situations. Of course, medication, even when it temporarily relieves anxiety, does nothing to overcome helplessness or to teach new coping skills. As discussed earlier, people treated with drugs alone may relapse once the drug is removed.

In contrast to those with generalized anxiety disorder, in which the main features are worry and physical complaints, people with obsessive-compulsive disorder may not show any anxiety at all. As we shall see in the next section, however, anxiety does not have to be manifest to produce psychological distress.

OBSESSIVE-COMPULSIVE DISORDER

In Chapter 2, we encountered Freud's famous patient the Rat Man, who attempted to ward off unwanted thoughts by engaging in odd and repetitive behaviors. Today we would say that he was suffering from an obsessive-compulsive disorder. Obsessions are unwelcome, intrusive, and recurring thoughts or images that appear irrational and uncontrollable to the individual experiencing them. In psychoanalytic jargon, they are *ego dystonic* (involuntary) and *ego alien* (foreign). All of us have obsessive thoughts at times (Purdon & Clark, 1993)—about examinations, job interviews, something we should have said (or should not have said)—but obsessive people have them often. Carole Ballodi, for example, told Dr. Kahn she spends "hours each night going over things that have happened in the past. I relive what happened in Kuwait. It's like a videotape that I play over and over again in my mind while I ask myself whether I could have done things differently."

Compulsions are repetitive ritualistic behaviors (counting, cleaning, checking) that a person feels driven to perform to ward off some calamity. Carole Ballodi, for example, told Dr. Kahn that, when she awakened at night, she checked all the windows and door locks before going back to sleep. Compulsive people feel obligated to dress, clean house, or fold clothes in just the "right" way. Their rituals often involve repetitions: repeating certain phrases a set number of times, counting certain numbers, touching some religious icon, or going back several times to check that the doors are locked and the lights have been switched off. Often, compulsions are linked to obsessive thoughts. Thus, a person obsessed with infection and contamination may develop compulsive cleanliness rituals. A particularly extreme example comes from the late billionaire Howard Hughes (1905–1976). In his youth, Hughes was a well-known public figure, industrialist, aviation pioneer, and Hollywood producer. In his later years, however, he became a recluse obsessed with infection. Here are Hughes's instructions to his cook on how to open a can of fruit:

> The man in charge then turns the valve in the bathtub on, using his bare hands to do so. He also adjusts the water temperature so that it is not too hot nor too cold. He then takes one of the brushes, and, using one of the bars of soap, creates a good lather, and then scrubs the can from a point two inches below the top of the can. He should first soak and remove the label, and then brush the cylindrical part of the can over and over until all particles of dust, pieces of paper label, and, in general, all sources of contamination have been removed. Holding the can in the center at all times, he then processes the bottom of the can in the same manner, being very sure that all bristles of the brush have thoroughly cleaned all the small indentations on the perimeter of the bottom of the can. He then rinses the soap from the cylindrical sides and the bottom of the can. (Bartlett & Steele, 1979, p. 233)

Although obsessive-compulsive disorder is classified as an anxiety disorder, obsessive-compulsive people do not always appear overtly anxious. This is because their ritualistic behaviors keep their anxiety in check. However, if for some reason the person is prevented from performing a compulsive ritual, the typical result is intense—and very obvious—anxiety.

Diagnostic Issues

Obsessive-compulsive disorder affects between 2% and 3% of the population sometime in their lives, females more often than males (Douglass et al., 1995; Weissman et al., 1994). It generally makes its first appearance in late adolescence or early adulthood, often in conjunction with some significant life event, such as pregnancy or the start of a new job. The specific nature of obsessions and compulsions varies across cultures. In some cultures, obsessions and compulsions have religious themes, as in the examples from Egyptian investigations reported in Highlight 4.3. Sufferers become obsessed with sin and pray incessantly. In most modern countries, obsessions center around cleaning for women and checking ("Are all the appliances switched off?") for men (M. S. George et al., 1993; Noshirvani et al., 1991).

Despite the detailed diagnostic criteria contained in the *DSM-IV* (Table 4.9), the diagnosis of obsessive-compulsive disorder is often complicated because clients show considerable comorbidity (Chen & Dilsaver, 1995). Sometimes it is difficult to decide whether a person is depressed, phobic, obsessive-compulsive, suffering from a generalized anxiety disorder, or all four (Hunt & Andrews, 1995). The diagnosis is often based on the presumed etiology. Thus, even though Carole Ballodi showed some signs of obsessive worry and even though she compulsively checked window and door locks, Dr. Berg did not believe that she suffered from an obsessive-compulsive disorder because her behavior was probably the result of her traumatic war experiences.

Obsessive-compulsive disorder is an extreme exaggeration of everyday behavior. "Think before you act." "A place for everything and everything in its place." "Cleanliness is next to godliness." Everyday language is replete with exhortations to be thoughtful, orderly, and clean. This is usually good advice. Thoughtfulness, orderliness, and cleanliness are necessary ingredients in the success of most projects, but in obsessive-compulsive disorder, they become ends in themselves. People who are overly orderly and clean but who are not sufficiently affected to merit the diagnosis of obsessive-compulsive disorder may be given the Axis II

Cultural Influences on Obsessive-Compulsive Symptoms

Although obsessive-compulsive disorder was first described more than three centuries ago (Hunter & MacAlpine, 1963), the specific nature of obsessions and compulsions changes from time to time and place to place, reflecting changes in the dominant culture. In a compelling example of how culture influences obsessive-compulsive behavior, Okasha and his colleagues (1994) studied 90 Egyptian obsessive-compulsive clients who were being treated in a Cairo clinic.

Approximately 90% of the Cairo sample were Muslims, who are required to pray five times each day. The five daily prayer sessions each consist of certain phrases from the Koran, which must be read in certain specified sequences. Before each prayer, several parts of the body must be ritually washed in a specific order, three times each. Urinating and defecating before prayers negates the cleansing ritual, which must then be repeated from the beginning. For orthodox Muslim men, any contact with a female also requires a repetition of the cleansing ritual. Females are held to equally strict standards. They are not allowed to pray when menstruating, and after their period females must undergo a special ritual bath.

Reflecting the dominant religious culture, the compulsions displayed by the Egyptian clients studied by Okasha and his colleagues (1994) were concerned mainly with cleanliness and religion. For example, many felt compelled to repeat the washing rituals and prayers over and over again to make sure they were perfect. Perhaps because of the strict sexual prohibitions in Muslim cultures, many obsessions were concerned with sin, especially sexual thoughts and sexual attraction. The intimate connection between sin and obsessions is illustrated by the use of the Egyptian term *El Weswas* to mean both "devil" and "obsession."

Okasha and his colleagues (1994) found that sex and sin were also the main obsessions of the Christian members of their sample. However, the Christian group displayed far fewer compulsive rituals. This difference probably reflects the much greater emphasis on religious rituals among Muslims. Interestingly, the researchers reported that, despite the cultural differences between Muslims and Jews, Jewish obsessive-compulsives studied in Jerusalem were more similar to Egyptian Muslims than to Christians.

Okasha and coworkers' sample of obsessive-compulsives was dominated by males, whereas this is not the case in Western countries. It is possible that obsessive-compulsive disorder is more prevalent among men in Egypt than in the West, but the gender distribution could also be a cultural artifact. Egyptian women are reluctant to seek assistance outside of their families, and they tend to give precedence to the health needs of men. Females attend clinics only when their behavior becomes a burden to other members of their family. Men, perhaps because of their importance to the family's economic well-being, are encouraged to seek professional assistance. This may explain why the average age at first diagnosis for Egyptian females was much higher than for males. Another important difference between Egyptian and many Western obsessive-compulsives is that relatively few of the Egyptians were willing to admit that their behavior was illogical or silly. It seemed that the more bizarre their beliefs or their rituals, the *less* likely they were to admit their absurdity. Again, this difference may be attributable to their culture, which attaches a greater stigma to illogical thinking than to behavioral disorders.

The Egyptian findings illustrate how cultural values influence people with obsessive-compulsive disorders. Because cultural variables may also affect treatment outcome, clinicians must take them into account when devising treatment programs for members of different cultural groups (see also Chung & Singer, 1995).

---

diagnosis of **obsessive-compulsive personality disorder** (Rosen & Tallis, 1995; Skodol et al., 1995). The two disorders are not identical (D. W. Black et al., 1993). Obsessive-compulsive personality disorder is milder than obsessive-compulsive disorder. It does not involve intrusive thoughts or unwelcome rituals. It is a form of perfectionism in which inflexible individuals become preoccupied with details. (See Table 4.10 for the *DSM-IV* diagnostic criteria.) The disorder is characterized by orderliness and the desire to maintain tight control over oneself, one's routines, and the behavior of other people.

People with obsessive-compulsive personality disorder emphasize rules and insist on tight scheduling. They tend to concentrate on minor details and miss important issues. They like having their own way and tend to deny that other people may present reasonable alternatives. The disorder seems to be most common among males and has a prevalence in the general population of about 1%.

Both obsessive-compulsive disorder and obsessive-compulsive personality disorder are different from so-called compulsive gambling, smoking, or drinking. Gamblers, smokers, and drinkers are not necessarily

DSM-IV	**TABLE 4.9** Main *DSM-IV* Diagnostic Criteria for Obsessive-Compulsive Disorder

A. Either obsessions or compulsions:

Obsessions as defined by (1), (2), (3), and (4):

(1) recurrent and persistent thoughts, impulses, or images that are experienced, at some time during the disturbance, as intrusive and inappropriate and that cause marked anxiety or distress

(2) the thoughts, impulses, or images are not simply excessive worries about real-life problems

(3) the person attempts to ignore or suppress such thoughts, impulses or images, or to neutralize them with some other thought or action

(4) the person recognizes that the obsessional thoughts, impulses, or images are a product of his or her own mind (not imposed from without as in thought insertion)

Compulsions as defined by (1) and (2):

(1) repetitive behaviors (e.g., hand washing, ordering, checking) or mental acts (e.g., praying, counting, repeating words silently) that the person feels driven to perform in response to an obsession, or according to rules that must be applied rigidly

(2) the behaviors or mental acts are aimed at preventing or reducing distress or preventing some dreaded event or situation; however, these behaviors or mental acts either are not connected in a realistic way with what they are designed to neutralize or prevent or are clearly excessive

B. At some point during the course of the disorder, the person has recognized that the obsessions or compulsions are excessive or unreasonable. Note: This does not apply to children.

C. The obsessions or compulsions cause marked distress, are time consuming (take more than 1 hour a day), or significantly interfere with the person's normal routine, occupational (or academic) functioning, or usual social activities or relationships.

D. If another Axis I disorder is present, the content of the obsessions or compulsions is not restricted to it (e.g., preoccupation with food in the presence of an Eating Disorder; hair pulling in the presence of Trichotillomania; concern with appearance in the presence of Body Dysmorphic Disorder; preoccupation with drugs in the presence of a Substance Use Disorder; preoccupation with having a serious illness in the presence of Hypochondriasis; preoccupation with sexual urges or fantasies in the presence of a Paraphilia; or guilty ruminations in the presence of Major Depressive Disorder).

Note: From American Psychiatric Association (1994, pp. 422–423).

perfectionists, nor are they consumed by detail. They derive pleasure from their activities and do not perceive them as foreign. Obsessive-compulsive people are quite different. They get no pleasure from their behaviors, and most know that their obsessions and compulsions are odd and irrational.

Etiology of Obsessive-Compulsive Disorder

Like the other anxiety disorders, obsessive-compulsive disorder appears to run in families (Nigg & Goldsmith, 1994). Close relatives of people with obsessive-compulsive disorder tend to have either obsessive-compulsive personality disorder or obsessional behavior patterns (they may be slaves to routine, for example). Relatives also have a moderately high incidence of anxiety disorder (D. W. Black et al., 1992). Some family studies have

found obsessive-compulsive disorder to be related to neurological disorders and depression (Lenane et al., 1990; D. L. Murphy, Pigott, & Insel, 1990). One intriguing possibility is that obsessive-compulsive people have a diathesis for neurological disorders and depression, but special experiences produce obsessive-compulsive disorder instead. The nature of these "special experiences" varies depending on the paradigm.

Psychoanalytic Views According to psychoanalytic theory, the special experiences that produce obsessive-compulsive behavior take place early in life, when children learn to subjugate their id impulses to the demands of society. In toilet training, for example, children must learn to replace their instinctual impulses to defecate with socially approved toileting behaviors. The resolution of this conflict between a child's biological impulses

DSM-IV   TABLE 4.10   Main *DSM-IV* Diagnostic Criteria for
Obsessive-Compulsive Personality Disorder

A pervasive pattern of preoccupation with orderliness, perfectionism, and mental and interpersonal control, at the expense of flexibility, openness, and efficiency, beginning by early adulthood and present in a variety of contexts, as indicated by four (or more) of the following:

(1) is preoccupied with details, rules, lists, order, organization, or schedules to the extent that the major point of the activity is lost

(2) shows perfectionism that interferes with task completion (e.g., is unable to complete a project because his or her own overly strict standards are not met)

(3) is excessively devoted to work and productivity to the exclusion of leisure activities and friendships (not accounted for by obvious economic necessity)

(4) is overconscientious, scrupulous, and inflexible about matters of morality, ethics, or values (not accounted for by cultural or religious identification)

(5) is unable to discard worn-out or worthless objects even when they have no sentimental value

(6) is reluctant to delegate tasks or to work with others unless they submit to exactly his or her way of doing things

(7) adopts a miserly spending style toward both self and others; money is viewed as something to be hoarded for future catastrophes

(8) shows rigidity and stubbornness

Note: From American Psychiatric Association (1994, pp. 672–673).

and society's demands has important implications for later behavior. Children who are trained harshly may become obsessively orderly and conformist and remain this way throughout their lives. Freud supported this theory with case studies chosen to show that obsessive-compulsive symptoms have symbolic content. People who are guilty about sex, for example, may become compulsive hand washers. As is the case with other psychoanalytic explanations, there is little experimental evidence for the relationship between toilet training (or other early conflicts) and the later development of obsessive-compulsive disorder.

Behavioral and Cognitive-Behavioral Views   Once compulsive behaviors are established, it is not hard to see how they may be reinforced by their anxiety-reducing consequences. Hand washing reduces worry about germs and illness; compulsive checking reduces concern about potential burglary or fire. But how do compulsive rituals get started in the first place? One possibility is that compulsions are learned "superstitiously" (Skinner, 1948). Pure coincidences (rubbing a lucky rabbit's foot before winning a sporting event, for example) may lead people into ritualistic behavior patterns (rubbing a rabbit's foot before every contest). This explanation seems inadequate, however, because it fails to explain why we are not all obsessive-compulsives given

the frequency of such coincidences in everyone's lives. Another problem for the superstitious-learning explanation is that it fails to explain obsessions. Obsessive thoughts do not reduce anxiety—usually they increase it. Indeed, compulsions are widely viewed as ways of reducing the anxiety produced by obsessions. An intriguing alternative is that checking occurs in people whose visual memory lacks "vividness" (Constans et al., 1995). Thus, some people may repetitively check light switches and door locks because they cannot generate a clear memory image of themselves shutting off the lights or locking the doors.

In contrast to conditioning theorists, cognitive-behaviorists emphasize the importance of obsessive thoughts. From the cognitive-behavioral viewpoint, we all have distressing thoughts at one time or another, but people with a diathesis toward anxiety are unable to dismiss them from their minds (D. A. Clark & Purdon, 1995). They dwell on the unwanted thoughts, which makes them even more anxious. Compulsive rituals arise to distract people from obsessive thoughts and reduce the anxiety that accompanies them (Rachman & Hodgson, 1980).

Biological Views   Encephalitis, brain tumors, and closed-head injuries can all produce obsessive-compulsive behavior (Jenike, 1986). This suggests that the disorder is

Serotonin in Action

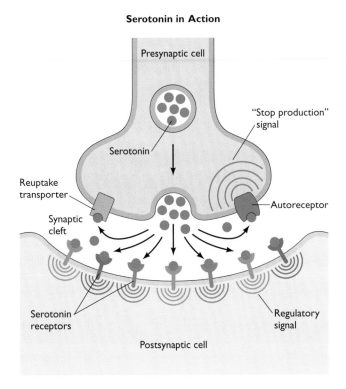

FIGURE 4.9 **Serotonin Receptors and Reuptake Transporters.** *Serotonin secreted by a synaptic cell binds to receptors on a postsynaptic cell and directs the postsynaptic cell to fire or stop firing. Serotonin levels in synapses are reduced by autoreceptors, which direct the cells to inhibit serotonin production, and reuptake transporters, which absorb the neurotransmitter. Antidepressants, such as Prozac and Paxil, increase synaptic serotonin by inhibiting its reuptake. Antidepressants can be similarly used to inhibit the reuptake of the neurotransmitter norepinephrine.*

at least partly physiological. The precise nature of the biological diathesis may lie in the metabolism of the neurotransmitter serotonin (Hollander et al., 1992). After a nerve impulse crosses a synapse, serotonin is reabsorbed into the nerve endings (Figure 4.9). Antidepressant drugs that block serotonin reuptake (fluoxetine, for example) also reduce the intensity and severity of obsessive-compulsive disorder (A. Wood, Tollefson, & Birkett, 1993). Most important, the stronger the dose, the better the therapeutic response (Lesch et al., 1991). Such dose-response relationships are usually taken as good evidence that the physiological effect of the drug, rather than the nonspecific placebo effect of treatment, is responsible for the improvement. These drug studies suggest that the diathesis for obsessive-compulsive disorder may be a defect in serotonin metabolism (Altemus et al., 1993). This hypothesis has been further strengthened by findings suggesting that obsessive-compulsive peo-

ple may have metabolic abnormalities in areas of the brain with high serotonin use, such as the caudate nucleus (Baxter et al., 1990; Paradis et al., 1992) and that treatment seems to normalize the functioning of these areas (J. M. Schwartz et al., 1996). These findings are promising, but serotonin metabolism is unlikely to be a complete explanation for obsessive-compulsive disorder. Defects in serotonin metabolism are also found in depression. We need a theory that explains why some people with the defect develop obsessive-compulsive disorder, whereas others develop depression.

Treatment for Obsessive-Compulsive Disorder

Obsessive-compulsive disorder is the most serious anxiety disorder. It involves chronic generalized anxiety, panic attacks, massive avoidance, and, often, serious depression. Freud considered obsessive-compulsive disorder to be among the most difficult disorders to treat. This was ironic, he thought, because people with obsessive-compulsive disorder knew they were "sick," hated their symptoms, and were highly motivated to change:

> This is a mad disease, surely. I don't think the wildest psychiatric phantasy could have invented anything like it, and if we did not see it every day with our own eyes we could hardly bring ourselves to believe in it. Now do not imagine that you can do anything for such a patient by advising him to distract himself, to pay no attention to these silly ideas, and to do something sensible instead of his nonsensical practices. This is what he would like for himself; for he is perfectly aware of his condition, he shares your opinion about his obsessional symptoms, he even volunteers it quite readily. Only he simply cannot help himself; the actions performed in an obsessional condition are supported by a kind of energy which probably has no counterpart in normal mental life. (Freud, 1917/1960, p. 270)

Freud's initial impressions have proven accurate over time; obsessive-compulsive disorder remains one of the most difficult anxiety disorders to treat. Nevertheless, each paradigm has tried to fashion a treatment approach. As you might expect, psychoanalytic treatment consists of making conscious the repressed conflicts presumed to be responsible for obsessive-compulsive behavior. Psychoanalysts do not attempt to inhibit the intrusive thoughts and ritualistic behaviors directly because they believe that these symptoms are keeping even more debilitating anxiety in check.

The behavioral approach to treatment usually consists of exposure and **response prevention** (Greist,

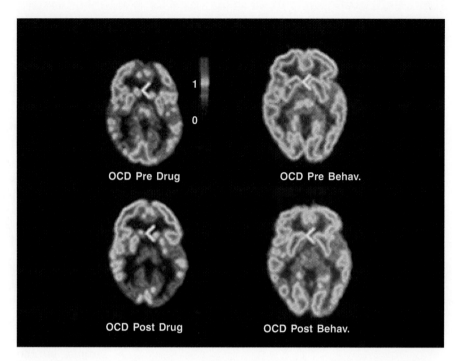

Drug treatment and behavior therapy can affect the brain physiology of people with obsessive-compulsive disorder, as shown in these PET scans before and after treatment. Although drugs can suppress symptoms, they still need to be combined with psychological treatment.

1994; Riggs & Foa, 1993). Clients who fear germs may be asked to enter a hospital, touch the walls, and even shake hands with patients while refraining from their normal ritualistic hand-washing response. Inhibiting hand-washing causes the person to experience the anxiety response that hand-washing is designed to avoid. Because nothing untoward actually happens, this anxiety is not reinforced. Thus, repeated exposures should cause the anxiety to extinguish. In a related manner, behavioral psychologists have treated obsessions using thought-stopping (requiring clients to say "stop" to themselves each time they begin to dwell on an obsessional thought). Perhaps the major problem faced by behavior therapists treating obsessive-compulsive disorder is getting clients to complete the treatment. Some people find behavioral treatment too threatening and drop out (Jenike, 1990). Cognitive restructuring may help some clients persist with therapy because it provides them with a set of motivating self-statements that they can use to help deal with anxiety-producing situations, including the anxiety associated with the therapy itself (Warren & Zgourides, 1991).

People with obsessive-compulsive disorder gain little relief from benzodiazepines or other antianxiety drugs, although, as already noted, some seem to respond to antidepressant medications such as fluoxe-

tine (Prozac; Baxter et al., 1992). Specific forms of compulsive behavior, such as trichotillomania (an irresistible impulse to pull one's hair) and onychophagia (compulsive nail-biting), have also responded well to antidepressant drugs. Those people who improve on drugs often show concomitant changes in brain activity as measured by PET scans (Baxter et al., 1992). Similar brain activity changes have been found among patients whose obsessive-compulsive symptoms improved after treatment with exposure and thought-stopping. Although this suggests that biological and psychological treatments affect brain physiology in similar ways (Abel, 1993), it should not be interpreted to mean that psychological treatment is superfluous. Drugs suppress symptoms; they do not teach people new behaviors. Clients treated solely with drugs may have to be treated indefinitely (C. T. Gordon et al., 1993). They also run the risk of serious side effects and relapse when the drug is terminated (Gersten, 1993; K. White & Cole, 1990).

In especially severe cases of obsessive-compulsive disorder, surgeons have destroyed a part of the brain structure known as the cingulum. Although this operation, called a cingulotomy, has been reported to reduce obsessive-compulsive behavior (Baer et al., 1995; Jenike et al., 1991), it may also produce personality change and

The symptoms of panic attacks, whether they are triggered by particular situations (such as subway tunnels) or are "uncued," are those of extreme and irrational fear, such as that depicted in George Tooker's painting The Subway.

interfere with cognitive functioning (Sachdev & Hay, 1995). Clearly, the destruction of brain tissue is a last resort—when all else has failed.

Although people with obsessive-compulsive disorder may show no overt signs of anxiety, this is not the case for those suffering from panic disorder. As we shall see in the next section, in panic disorder and agoraphobia the signs of anxiety are all too obvious.

PANIC DISORDER AND AGORAPHOBIA

As noted previously, panic attacks are common occurrences. They are associated with many psychological disorders (Battaglia et al., 1995; J. Johnson, Weissman, & Klerman, 1990) and also occur as part of everyday life. However, when panic attacks become recurrent and when people become so anxious about them that they change their lives to avoid them, then panic attacks can become a full-blown panic disorder. In the United States, panic disorder affects between 2% and 3% of adults (R. C. Kessler et al., 1994), and women are three times more likely to receive the diagnosis than men (Katerndahl & Realini, 1993). The disorder is rare in children (Moreau & Weissman, 1992). Panic disorder and related anxiety conditions appear to be universal, occurring in all cultures (Hollifield et al., 1990).

Panic disorder usually begins in early adulthood, and most people report clear memories of their first

panic attack. This initial attack, which may come on without warning, is often followed by further attacks. In such cases, the person comes to associate panic attacks with the situations in which they occur. Fearing further attacks, the client avoids these situations. Over time, panic attacks occur in other situations, which must also be avoided. As the number of situations that must be avoided increases, the person's movements become increasingly restricted. In this way, panic disorder often gives rise to agoraphobia.

The term *agoraphobia* was first used in 1872 by the German psychiatrist Carl Westphal (1833–1890) to describe a condition he observed in four male patients. Translated literally, agoraphobia means fear of the *agora*, the name of the marketplace in ancient Athens. Westphal chose the term because each of the four men had panic attacks when left alone in crowded open areas (Boyd & Crump, 1991). The lifetime prevalence for agoraphobia is around 7% (Magee et al., 1996). This makes it by far the most common fear seen in the psychology clinic (Marks, 1987). Although Westphal's initial observations were of four men, today agoraphobia is more common in women (Dick, Bland, & Newman, 1994; Horwath, Johnson, & Horning, 1993). It begins in early adulthood and is particularly common in older women (Lindesay, 1991). Although the gender difference is usually attributed to sex roles that make it more acceptable for women to be fearful than men, the incidence of agoraphobia in the two sexes has remained unchanged

DSM-IV   TABLE 4.11   Main *DSM-IV* Diagnostic Criteria for Panic Disorder With and Without Agoraphobia

A. Both (1) and (2):
   (1) recurrent unexpected panic attacks
   (2) at least one of the attacks has been followed by 1 month (or more) of one (or more) of the following: (a) persistent concern about having additional attacks; (b) worry about the implications of the attack or its consequences (e.g., losing control, having a heart attack, "going crazy"); (c) a significant change in behavior related to the attacks
B. Presence of agoraphobia in which the predominant complaint is anxiety about being in places or situations from which escape may be difficult or embarrassing, or in which help may not be available in the event of a panic attack or paniclike symptoms. (When this criterion is not met, the correct diagnosis is panic attack without agoraphobia.)
C. The panic attacks are not due to a general medical condition and cannot be better accounted for by another mental disorder.
 	
Note: Adapted from American Psychiatric Association (1994, pp. 402–403).

for decades. The entry of women into formerly "male" professions and other social changes have not had any effect on the incidence of agoraphobia (Bekker, 1996).

People with agoraphobia worry about having panic-like symptoms in places or situations from which escape might be difficult (or embarrassing) or in which help might be unavailable. The most frequently feared situations are shopping malls, cars, buses, trains, subways, wide streets, tunnels, restaurants, and theaters (Barlow & Craske, 1994). In a way, agoraphobia can be viewed as a primitive means of coping with panic attacks. That is, agoraphobic people avoid feared situations in the hope that doing so will help them avoid panic attacks. Some people with agoraphobia cannot avoid fearful situations; they may have to travel for work, for example. In such cases, they enter feared situations full of dread. Agoraphobic people, men particularly, may resort to alcohol or drugs just to get by. In extreme cases, they may escape by suicide (Henriksson et al., 1996), although this is rare (S. Friedman et al., 1992).

Diagnostic Issues

The *DSM-IV* provides diagnostic criteria for panic disorder with and without agoraphobia (Table 4.11). Criterion C is intended to rule out people who develop a fear of going out alone because of a realistic medical concern (a fear of going out alone after suffering a heart attack, for example). For the present discussion, the most important criterion is B because the idea that agoraphobia can exist without a history of panic attacks is controversial. Although it is true that people with agoraphobia often have a history of panic attacks (Faravelli et al., 1992),

agoraphobia and panic disorder do not always go together. In fact, epidemiological studies of the general population report that less than half of those who meet the criteria for agoraphobia report a history of panic attacks (Wittchen, Reed, & Kessler, 1998). In these people,

People with severe agoraphobia may be afraid to leave their homes and depend on others to bring them even basic necessities, a dependence that can strain marital and family relationships and lead to social isolation.

agoraphobia develops insidiously. They begin by fearing only a few situations (cars, tunnels). When placed in such situations, they feel fear. If the process goes no further, the *DSM-IV* would classify such people as suffering from situational phobias. However, if the fear continues to generalize, until practically all situations outside the home are potentially threatening, then the *DSM-IV* diagnostic scheme would classify the person as suffering from agoraphobia without a history of panic disorder.

The correlation between panic disorder and agoraphobia may result at least in part from biased sampling. Clinicians believe the conditions co-occur because only the most serious cases of agoraphobia seek clinical assistance, and most of these report panic attacks (Horwath, Lish, et al., 1993). In other words, agoraphobia and panic disorder may co-occur among clinic patients but not in the population at large. Until the relationship between the two disorders is better understood, it is probably wise to consider them separate but related disorders.

Carole Ballodi had a panic attack (perhaps several); she also feared leaving home. Yet, as will be seen later in this chapter, her main diagnosis was not panic disorder but post-traumatic stress disorder. This is because her panic attacks and fear were most likely the result of a traumatic experience. Panic disorder and agoraphobia are most often diagnosed in people who do not have clear-cut traumatic causes for their disorders.

Etiology of Panic Disorder With Agoraphobia

There are as many theories about panic disorder as there are schools of psychology. The psychodynamic formulation assumes that certain children are fearful by nature. These children experience an unconscious conflict. They wish to be independent, but they also fear being on their own. This conflict is exhibited symbolically by fears of being trapped, suffocated, and unable to escape (Shear et al., 1993).

Like most psychoanalytic theories, this explanation for panic disorder is difficult, if not impossible, to test by direct experimentation. However, there is indirect evidence that some people are predisposed to develop panic disorder. We know, for example, that panic disorder runs in families and that there is a greater concordance for such disorders among identical than fraternal twins (Weissman, 1993). There may even be specific genetic markers for panic disorders (Ayuso-Gutierrez et al., 1993).

Because of the genetic evidence, considerable research has been devoted to understanding the physio-logical causes of panic disorder (J. M. Gorman, Papp, & Klein, 1990). Some researchers have focused on emotional responsivity and regulation (J. D. Parker et al., 1993); others have explored the toxic effects of everyday substances such as nicotine and caffeine (Christensen, Bourgeois, & Cockroft, 1993). Still others have sought to link panic attacks with damage to particular brain sites (Papp, Coplan, & Gorman, 1992), neurochemical dysfunctions (George & Ballenger, 1992), even to a disordered balance mechanism that makes people feel as if they are fainting (Jacob et al., 1996). The bulk of the research, however, has focused on the way certain physiological processes may interact with cognitions to produce panic disorder. A good example is the relationship between carbon dioxide and panic attacks.

Carbon Dioxide–Induced Panic Attacks Although we are unaware of it, our breathing is controlled by a delicate and easily disrupted balance of chemicals. Without our conscious awareness, our respiratory system extracts oxygen from the atmosphere and excretes carbon dioxide, which plants then use to produce more oxygen. As long as the amount of carbon dioxide in our bloodstreams stays within certain limits, our breathing remains steady and effortless. If, for any reason, the amount of available carbon dioxide becomes too low, we begin to breathe rapidly. Rapid breathing can develop into **hyperventilation,** which is associated with respiratory and neurological symptoms. Often, hyperventilation can be stopped only by breathing into a paper bag. By rebreathing the same air over and over again, our carbon dioxide concentration is increased, and our breathing returns to normal.

Panic attacks sometimes begin with a feeling of suffocation followed by hyperventilation, which may at first be mistaken for pulmonary disease (Pollack et al., 1996). This has led researchers to hypothesize that panic attacks are triggered by abnormally low levels of carbon dioxide (Figure 4.10) or by an oversensitive internal monitoring mechanism that misjudges normal carbon dioxide levels as too low (Papp, Klein, & Gorman, 1993).

Experiments designed to assess the relationship between hyperventilation and panic attacks have found that inhaling carbon dioxide can produce panic attacks in people with a history of such attacks. Although this seems to support the hypothesis that carbon dioxide metabolism is responsible for panic attacks, other findings complicate the picture. For example, Rapee, Mattick, and Murrell (1986) showed that the effects of carbon dioxide depend on subjects' expectations. Subjects who were told that breathing carbon dioxide

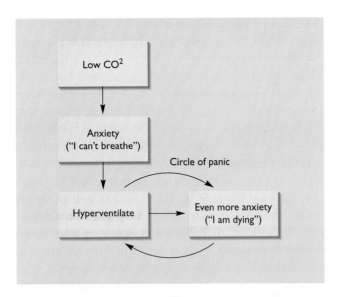

Low CO^2

↓

Anxiety
("I can't breathe")

↓

Circle of panic

Hyperventilate → Even more anxiety
("I am dying")

FIGURE 4.10 Carbon Dioxide's Link to Panic Attacks

would produce rapid breathing and increased heart rates were less likely to panic than those who were not told what symptoms to expect. This finding suggests that it may be the way in which the signs of hyperventilation are appraised that produces a panic attack rather than the hyperventilation itself (Papp, Klein, & Gorman, 1993). Perhaps this is why surreptitiously introducing carbon dioxide into room air does not produce panic attacks, even when it causes breathing rates to quadruple (J. M. Gorman et al., 1990).

The Mediating Effects of Cognition The relationship between carbon dioxide, cognitive appraisal, and panic was explored in more detail by Sanderson, Rapee, and Barlow (1989). They had subjects with a history of panic disorder breathe carbon dioxide through a specially designed apparatus. Subjects were told that they could reduce the concentration of carbon dioxide they were breathing by adjusting a dial each time a signal light switched on. For half the subjects, the light was on continuously (they were always in control), whereas the light never came on for the others. In reality, turning the dial had no effect on carbon dioxide level, so the experiment was concerned with perceived rather than real control. Eighty percent of the group who thought they had no control over the carbon dioxide level (because the light never came on) had a panic attack compared with only 20% of the group who believed that the carbon dioxide level was under their control. Because neither group really had control of the carbon dioxide level, this study showed that a cognitive appraisal (perceived control) plays an important role in the etiology of panic attacks.

People prone to panic attacks may have a general tendency to appraise benign physiological events as threatening. To test this hypothesis, Pauli and colleagues (1991) electronically monitored the heart rates of people for 24 hours as they engaged in their normal activities. These researchers found that people with a history of panic disorder responded with an accelerated heart rate every time there was a minor change in their heart rhythms. This suggests that these minor changes made them anxious. In related studies, researchers gave false biofeedback to panic-disordered subjects; the suggestion that their heart rate was increasing produced panic attacks in these susceptible subjects (Ehlers et al., 1988). Thus, it seems as if panic-prone individuals are highly sensitive to their internal physiology. Whenever they detect any change, no matter how slight, they become fearful.

Lactate-Induced Panic Attacks Three lines of evidence implicate sodium lactate, a by-product of normal metabolism, in panic attacks: (1) brain levels of sodium lactate increase during panic attacks (Dager et al., 1993), (2) giving sodium lactate to people with a previous history of panic attacks can induce a panic attack, and (3) drugs that are helpful in preventing panic attacks also block lactate-induced attacks. This suggests that excessive sodium lactate may be responsible for panic attacks. However, like carbon dioxide–induced attacks, lactate-induced attacks also have cognitive components. There is evidence that lactate-induced attacks can also be prevented by changing cognitive appraisals (Wittchen et al., 1998).

Mitral Valve Prolapse The mitral valve keeps blood from backing up in the heart. If it should prolapse (protrude) into the left atrium of the heart, it can produce symptoms very similar to those seen in panic attacks: difficulty with breathing, palpitations, and chest pain. **Mitral valve prolapse** is found in about 5% of the population, and it is particularly common in young women. Some studies of people with panic attacks have found a high comorbidity with mitral valve prolapse (Katerndahl, 1993); others have not (Wittchen et al., 1998). One reason for the conflicting findings is that diagnosing mitral valve prolapse from nonintrusive tests such as electrocardiograms is difficult, and experts often disagree. A second problem is that the experimenters who were interpreting the electrocardiograms usually knew which subjects suffered from panic disorder. Because interpretations were not "blind," experimenters may have been biased toward diagnosing prolapse in the panic-disorder group, even when the findings were equivocal (Wittchen et al., 1998; see also the section on biases in Critical Thinking About Clinical Decisions 4.1, which appears near the end of this chapter). At present, it seems best to be cautious and reserve judgment about whether panic disorders are related to mitral valve prolapse.

Fear of Fear   According to the *DSM-IV,* the diagnosis of panic disorder with agoraphobia is reserved for people who avoid public places because of their fear of having a panic attack. This is sometimes known as the "fear of fear" definition of agoraphobia (A. J. Goldstein & Chambless, 1978). To explain how such a fear of panicking might develop, the following list ties together the observations and experimental results discussed so far:

1. Many people have panic attacks, but only those who become excessively fearful of future attacks go on to develop panic disorder with agoraphobia.
2. People prone to panic disorder may inherit or develop a special sensitivity to their internal physiological state (Craske & Barlow, 1993; although see Antony et al., 1995, for an alternative view). This is why people with panic disorder are better than others at silently counting their own heartbeats (Ehlers & Breuer, 1992).
3. Because they notice any change in their physiology, people with panic disorder can easily become preoccupied with minor discomforts (Borden et al., 1993; Taylor, Koch, & McNally, 1992).
4. Should there be a minor change in respiration or heart rate, panic-prone people conclude that something serious is occurring and that they are not in control (Westling & Öst, 1995).
5. They begin to dwell on what might happen if their breathing or heart rate raced out of control. They would become incapacitated in public (Robinson & Birchwood, 1991). They might faint, hurt themselves, even die (Rapee, 1993).
6. These thoughts make them even more worried and vigilant.
7. A vicious cycle develops in which perceived sensations and catastrophic cognitions augment one another until they spiral into a full-blown panic attack.
8. To avoid being alone or unprotected during a panic attack, people restrict their movements. When this becomes excessive, they are diagnosed agoraphobic (Clum & Knowles, 1991).

Treatment for Panic Disorder

Both drugs and psychological treatments have been used by clinicians working with those with panic disorder.

Drug Treatment   Drugs are often prescribed for panic attacks; the idea is to prevent alarm reactions that trigger panic attacks. Early observations suggested that tricyclic antidepressant medications blocked panic attacks but had little effect on general anxiety, which responded to benzodiazepines (D. F. Klein, 1964). This observation was taken as support for the idea that the fear felt in a panic attack is physiologically different from the anxiety felt in generalized anxiety disorder. However, we now know that long-acting benzodiazepines, such as alprazolam, are helpful in people who have panic attacks with and without agoraphobia (Klosko et al., 1990). Thus, fear and anxiety may not be as different as once thought. Other drugs are also sometimes helpful. For example, antihistamines, normally associated with the treatment of allergies, can also reduce the intensity of panic attacks, as can antidepressants such as fluoxetine (Gelenberg et al., 1991; Poling, Gadow, & Cleary, 1991).

At present, no one knows why antihistamines and antidepressant drugs (which actually *increase* the neurochemicals associated with alarm reactions) should reduce panic. Because clinicians do not know how and why these drugs produce their therapeutic effects, they are often unable to predict when a drug will work or for whom. They can only give the drug a try and see what happens. Of course, clinicians do not need to know exactly how drugs work to use them, but until they have some idea of the underlying mechanism, drug treatment will remain a largely empirical exercise.

In contrast to drug treatment, most psychological treatments are theoretically based. They are aimed at one or more of the variables that contribute to the vicious "fear of fear" cycle: the preoccupation with internal bodily states, excessive physiological responsiveness to threat, faulty cognitive appraisals, or the quickly spiraling loss of control. A combination of drugs and psychological treatment can be effective in treating panic disorder (de Beurs et al., 1995).

Psychological Treatment   The aim of psychological treatment is to break the vicious cycle that maintains panic disorders with agoraphobia. Different treatments do this in different ways. For example, behavioral treatment uses relaxation to reduce the fear response, thereby reducing the alarm reaction. Behavioral treatment also uses exposure to help reduce the perceived threat of panic-inducing stimuli. Exposure may be gradual and combined with relaxation, as in systematic desensitization, or abrupt, as in flooding; it can be in imagery or in vivo. Agoraphobics, for example, may be taken to crowded public places (Craske et al., 1992; Mavissakalian, 1993). Therapists may deliberately expose clients to the somatic cues that trigger panic (see Barlow & Craske, 1994; Margraf et al., 1993). Specifically, clients may be asked to produce the sensations that trigger panic (by hyperventilating, for example). When signs of panic appear (dry mouth, increased heart rate), clients are shown how to use relaxation and cognitive restructuring to avoid a panic attack. Success in controlling panic in the psychology clinic gives clients the confidence they need to try out their coping skills outside the clinic. Two-year follow-ups have shown this type of treatment to be more successful than simple drug treatment (Craske, Brown, & Barlow, 1991).

Despite theoretical reasons for preferring one approach to another, the empirical evidence is that any type of exposure reduces the severity of both panic attacks and agoraphobia. In fact, simply telling patients treated in hospital emergency rooms for panic attacks to return to the scene of the attack reduces the probability of a second attack (Swinson et al., 1992).

Although exposure may help people approach fear-producing stimuli, it does not always prevent future panic attacks. Therefore, clients treated only with exposure are prone to relapse (Wade, Monroe, & Michelson, 1993). To prevent this, behavior therapists also train clients to react more calmly to the internal cues (heart and breathing rate changes, for example) that trigger panic. Clients may be trained in breathing techniques to help them control hyperventilation. Biofeedback may be used to reduce physiological responsiveness and to teach clients to control their heart and respiration rates.

Operant conditioning programs, in which clients are reinforced for exposing themselves to feared situations, frequently use family members to deliver reinforcement. This is especially important in agoraphobia because, in their attempt to be kind and understanding, family members may inadvertently reinforce avoidance behavior. Some therapists feared that family members might sabotage such programs because curing the agoraphobic might upset the family—they would no longer have the "sick" member to keep them together. Fortunately, researchers have reported just the opposite outcome (Craske et al., 1992). Helping people to overcome their agoraphobia actually improves their marital and family relationships. The social support of relatives and friends is an important ingredient in successful treatment (Fokias & Tyler, 1995; Violanti, 1996).

In addition to exposure and training in coping skills, clients who suffer from panic disorder may also benefit from cognitive restructuring (Barlow, 1988). The aim is to break the vicious cycle of noticing somatic cues, assuming they have dire implications, and then worrying oneself into a panic attack (Michelson & Marchione, 1991). Cognitive restructuring attempts to replace catastrophic appraisals of physiological events with more benign ones.

Studies have also shown the value of psychological treatment. For example, Clark and Salkovskis (1990) compared three groups of people: One received cognitive-behavior therapy, the second was treated with the antidepressant drug imipramine and applied relaxation training, and the third group was given no treatment (they were placed on a treatment waiting list). Subjects in the two treatment groups improved more than the waiting-list control subjects on a variety of measures: frequency and severity of panic attacks, the tendency to misinterpret bodily symptoms, scores on an anxiety inventory, and avoidance of feared situations. Subjects in the cognitive-behavior therapy group improved more than those in the drug and relaxation group (although fewer subjects in the cognitive-behavioral group completed the treatment program). In another therapy outcome study, Klosko and colleagues (1990) contrasted alprazolam with cognitive-behavior therapy, a placebo treatment, and being placed on a waiting list. Cognitive-behavior therapy was again found to be more effective than the other treatments, and relapse rates tended to be lower (Craske et al., 1991). Cognitive-behavior therapy has also proved useful in weaning patients from tranquilizers while minimizing relapse (Otto et al., 1993).

Building on the various treatment approaches, Bourne (1990) and Craske and Barlow (1993) have suggested the following general treatment program for panic disorder. The program treats the cognitive, physiological, and behavioral aspects of panic disorder rather than focusing on only one element:

1. *Cognitive restructuring.* Help clients to identify and change unrealistic appraisals. Provide them with cognitive explanations and strategies that they can use to reappraise their bodily sensations. ("You pay too close attention to your body. Every time your heart beat changes, you are not going to die.") Provide clients with coping statements. ("This is not pleasant, but I can handle it.")
2. *Relaxation training.* Teach clients to relax in the face of bodily changes.
3. *Breathing retraining.* Show clients how to avoid or short-circuit hyperventilation by controlling their breathing.
4. *Interoceptive (internal) exposure.* Expose clients to the internal cues that trigger panic (have them hyper-

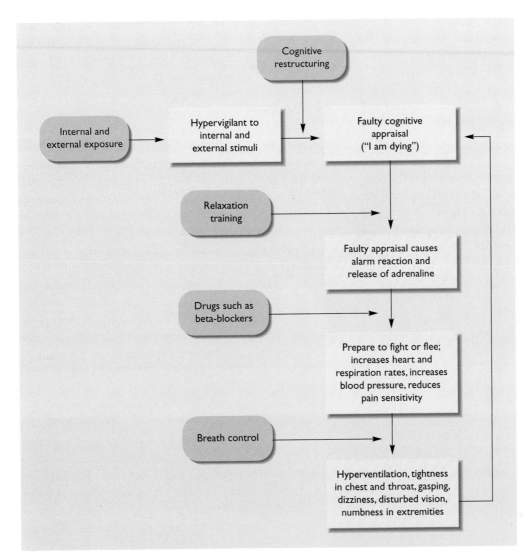

FIGURE 4.11 **Breaking the Panic Cycle.** *The panic cycle is broken at different places by different treatment techniques. Internal and external exposure is aimed at extinguishing the hypervigilant responses that begin the cycle. Cognitive restructuring is focused on the appraisal process, whereas relaxation training tries to cut off alarm reactions. Drugs aim to short-circuit the cycle by eliminating the motivation to fight or flee. Breath control tries to keep the alarm reaction from developing into a full-fledged panic attack. Note that this schematic has been simplified for illustrative purposes; treatment interventions can actually affect more than one aspect of the cycle. For example, relaxation training may also affect hypervigilance, and drugs may prevent an alarm reaction.*

ventilate, for example). Show them that these cues do not mean that dire consequences lie ahead.

5. *Situational exposure.* In vivo exposure to panic-producing stimuli can lead to extinction while also helping people cope with stress.

Of course, not all techniques can be applied to all patients. Sensitive clinicians tailor treatment to the needs and circumstances of the individual client. Figure 4.11 integrates theories of panic disorder with well-known therapeutic techniques and shows how each technique

attempts to disrupt the vicious cycle of cognitions, somatic vigilance, and panic. As we shall see in the next section, many of the same treatments apply when the trigger for panic attacks lies in traumatic stress.

POST-TRAUMATIC STRESS DISORDER

As noted early in this chapter, some Vietnam veterans showed no obvious signs of disturbance when they were discharged but developed psychological symptoms months, sometimes years, later (Keane et al., 1992).

Memories of a traumatic experience, such as during the Vietnam War, can trigger flashbacks months or years later. Some Vietnam veterans are so debilitated by flashbacks that they are unable to function in society and are living on the streets. Why are only some veterans affected so severely by post-traumatic stress disorder? What protects those who are able to live more successfully?

Essay

This also seems to have happened to Carole Ballodi, a Gulf War veteran (Sutker et al., 1994). She told Dr. Kahn that she was "never much bothered by the war" and that her ruminations about the war were recent. Like the Vietnam veterans, Carole had nightmares about the war, and during the day she was easily startled by unexpected noise (Pitman et al., 1990). Some veterans developed amnesia for traumatic war events, but most were like Carole; they could not stop remembering. Without warning, a sight or sound (such as a helicopter) could trigger a "flashback," a mental reliving of a war experience. Some veterans became depressed and emotionally numb (unable to feel joy or love). They developed physical symptoms (headaches, backaches, digestive upsets). Some sought relief in drugs; others acted out their inner turmoil in violent outbursts or suicide (Hobfoll et al., 1991; Keane et al., 1992). Nurses, soldiers who were never in combat, even civilians caught in the war developed similar symptoms (Z. Solomon et al., 1993).

Feeling rejected by society, Vietnam War veterans founded organizations to provide mutual support. Through political action, their plight became known. In 1980, the newly published *DSM-III* gave their disorder a name—post-traumatic stress disorder (PTSD). This was defined as an extreme anxiety response to traumatic, life-threatening events that were "outside the range of normal human experience." By giving veterans' problems a name, by making post-traumatic stress disorder a recognized mental condition, the *DSM-III* legitimized the veterans' claims for help. This is an example of how psychiatric nosology interacts with, and influences, society.

The main symptoms of post-traumatic stress disorder are anxiety, the avoidance of stimuli associated with the trauma, "flashbacks" in which the traumatic event is relived mentally, and a "numbing" of emotional responses (Table 4.12). Not surprisingly, post-traumatic stress disorder has been found to affect practically every aspect of everyday life (Warshaw et al., 1993).

It was recognized from the outset that, despite its origins, post-traumatic stress disorder is not limited to those who survived the Vietnam War. Carole Ballodi served in the Gulf War, which also produced its share of anxiety symptoms (Labbate & Snow, 1992). Severe trauma induces similar symptoms among the survivors of concentration camps (Kuch & Cox, 1992), floods and other natural disasters, train wrecks and car accidents, even new mothers who experienced difficult childbirths (Fones, 1996; Gelman & Katel, 1993; Palinkas et al., 1993; Taylor & Koch, 1995; Wilson & Raphael, 1993). Post-traumatic stress disorder also affects victims of violence, especially rape (Breslau et al.,

1991). Left untreated, these symptoms can last a lifetime (Potts, 1994).

Document 4.9 contains another excerpt from Dr. Berg's psychological assessment of Carole Ballodi. Dr. Berg used a self-report instrument, The Mississippi Scale for Combat-Related Post-Traumatic Stress Disorder (Sloan et al., 1995), to gauge the extent to which Carole's symptoms are related to her war experiences. Although she has symptoms of several anxiety disorders, he concludes that the most appropriate diagnosis is post-traumatic stress disorder.

DOCUMENT 4.9

Excerpt From Dr. Berg's Psychological Assessment of Carole Ballodi: Diagnosis

Dr. Ballodi followed in her father's footsteps and joined the army after finishing her medical training. She worked close to combat in the Gulf War and had at least one especially harrowing experience in which a patient died of wounds received while in her care. Dr. Ballodi did not display any serious psychological symptoms when she was discharged from the army but in recent weeks has developed a variety of symptoms. Dr. Ballodi is anxious in many situations and is clearly fearful of being evaluated by others. These are signs of generalized anxiety disorder and social phobia. She also has panic attacks, and she may have a checking compulsion. However, Dr. Ballodi best fits the criteria for post-traumatic stress disorder. She was exposed to horror and death, and she continuously relives the experience. She avoids situations that may remind her of the war, and she has lost interest in many aspects of her life. She has persistent signs of increased arousal, and the symptoms are causing her significant distress. She seems to have had a long-standing pattern of fearfulness but probably not sufficient to be considered an avoidant personality disorder. She has recently experienced stress (a patient died in her office), which reminded her of her war experience. Dr. Ballodi's global psychological functioning is definitely impaired at present, but her activities prior to the current episode show that she is capable of a high level of psychological functioning.

Axis I (clinical disorders): Post-traumatic stress disorder

Axis II (personality disorders): None (but may need to rule out possible avoidant personality disorder)

Axis III (general medical conditions): None

Axis IV (psychosocial or environmental problems): Death of patient

Axis V (global assessment of functioning): In past year: 90; current functioning: 40 (out of a maximum of 100) ■

DSM-IV TABLE 4.12 Main *DSM-IV* Diagnostic Criteria for Post-Traumatic Stress Disorder

A. The person has been exposed to a traumatic event in which both of the following were present:

(1) the person experienced, witnessed, or was confronted with an event or events that involved actual or threatened death or serious injury, or a threat to the physical integrity of self or others

(2) the person's response involved intense fear, helplessness, or horror. Note: In children, this may be expressed instead by disorganized or agitated behavior.

B. The traumatic event is persistently reexperienced in one (or more) of the following ways:

(1) recurrent and intrusive distressing recollections of the event including images, thoughts, or perceptions. Note: In young children, repetitive play may occur in which themes or aspects of the trauma are expressed.

(2) recurrent distressing dreams of the event. Note: In children, there may be frightening dreams without recognizable content.

(3) acting or feeling as if the traumatic event were recurring (includes a sense of reliving the experience, illusions, hallucinations, and dissociative flashback episodes, including those that occur on awakening or when intoxicated). Note: In young children, trauma-specific reenactment may occur.

(4) intense psychological distress at exposure to internal or external cues that symbolize or resemble an aspect of the traumatic event

(5) physiological reactivity on exposure to internal or external cues that symbolize or resemble an aspect of the traumatic event

C. Persistent avoidance of stimuli associated with the trauma and numbing of general responsiveness (not present before the trauma), as indicated by three (or more) of the following:

(1) efforts to avoid thoughts, feelings, or conversations associated with the trauma

(2) efforts to avoid activities, places, or people that arouse recollections of the trauma

(3) inability to recall an important aspect of the trauma

(4) markedly diminished interest or participation in significant activities

(5) feeling of detachment or estrangement from others

(6) restricted range of affect (e.g., unable to have loving feelings)

(7) sense of a foreshortened future (e.g., does not expect to have a career, marriage, children, or a normal life span)

D. Persistent symptoms of increased arousal (not present before the trauma), as indicated by two (or more) of the following:

(1) difficulty falling or staying asleep

(2) irritability or outbursts of anger

(3) difficulty concentrating

(4) hypervigilance

(5) exaggerated startle response

E. Duration of the disturbance (symptoms in Criteria B, C, and D) is more than 1 month.

F. The disturbance causes clinically significant distress or impairment in social, occupational, or other important areas of functioning.

Note: From American Psychiatric Association (1994, pp. 427–429).

The lifetime prevalence of post-traumatic stress disorder is around 7% (R. C. Kessler et al., 1995). The *DSM-IV* distinguishes between symptoms that last for 3 months or less and those that persist for more than 3 months. Acute stress disorders last less than 3 months; after 3 months, the disorder is chronic. This distinction recognizes that although traumatic experiences affect practically everyone, their effects are generally short-lasting. People who fail to return to their everyday lives after 3 months suffer from a more serious chronic disorder.

The *DSM-IV* recognizes that the symptoms of post-traumatic stress disorder may appear differently in children (Bremner et al., 1993). Children who have been abused, for example, often show behavioral changes (an outgoing child may become reclusive; a quiet child may start acting aggressive). Those who have been toilet trained may go back to soiling and bed-wetting.

Vulnerability to Post-Traumatic Stress Disorder

Although this is not the case for many psychological disorders, the etiology of post-traumatic stress disorder is defined in its diagnostic criteria—it is caused by an extraordinarily stressful, traumatic event. Given a severe enough trauma, even well-adjusted people may develop post-traumatic stress disorder (L. A. Clark, Watson, & Mineka, 1994). Yet most people manage to escape even the most terrifying events with no sign of an anxiety disorder, not even a phobia (Rachman, 1991). What protects such people? What makes others succumb? The usual answer to questions such as these is that some people are more vulnerable than others. They may have preexisting psychological disorders or a family history of psychological disorder (Breslau et al., 1991; Flach, 1990). Vulnerable people may inherit a disposition to develop post-traumatic stress disorder (Andreasen, 1995; True et al., 1993). Carole Ballodi, for example, seems to have a low threshold for fear conditioning (Shalev et al., 1992) or an oversensitive autonomic nervous system (Krystal et al., 1989) or both. There is evidence that people with post-traumatic stress disorder have higher levels of stress hormones than others (Yehuda et al., 1995), although this is equivocal (Boscarino, 1996). Certainly, people who develop post-traumatic stress disorder seem to have strong emotional reactions to life's problems (Z. Solomon, Mikulincev, & Flum, 1988).

Although it makes sense to look within individuals for the reasons why some develop post-traumatic stress disorder while others exposed to the same trauma escape unscathed, we should not discount the important role played by a person's social environment. Consider, for example, the finding that post-traumatic stress disorder is more common among African American and Hispanic Vietnam War veterans than among White veterans, especially White officers. Does this mean that, compared with White officers, African American and Hispanic enlisted men are less hardy, more autonomically responsive, and more prone to emotion-focused coping? Not necessarily. Forces outside the individual may also play an etiological role in post-traumatic stress disorder (Sutker et al., 1995). Minority-group soldiers were often given dishonorable discharges for offenses that may have been at least partly related to post-traumatic stress disorder (drug use, alcoholism). As a result of their dishonorable discharges, their career

Social support, such as that offered by storefront operations, is an important ingredient of successful therapy for people with post-traumatic stress disorder.

prospects were poor. White officers, on the other hand, were more likely to receive honorable discharges and to return home to intact families. Even when they had psychological problems, White officers—especially those who wished to pursue military careers—may have been reluctant to admit to them for fear of harming their careers. In contrast, veterans with poor social support and limited career prospects might have more to gain from admitting to a post-traumatic stress disorder (pensions and counseling, for example). The protective effects of a supportive environment may explain why the professional (mostly White) English and Argentinian soldiers who fought in the Falklands War rarely developed post-traumatic stress disorder (Summerfield & Hume, 1993).

Treatment for Post-Traumatic Stress Disorder

In the 1970s, as noted earlier, Vietnam War veterans established mutual support organizations that were instrumental in having post-traumatic stress disorder added to the *DSM-III*. Many of these organizations began as "rap groups," small self-help groups that met in storefronts and other convenient locations (Lifton, 1976). These rap groups provided an opportunity for veterans to share their troubles with sympathetic listeners. These groups were often the only forum in which they could express their guilt about the war and their anger at society for the callous treatment they had received.

With the publication of the *DSM-III,* mental health professionals began to devote increasing attention to post-traumatic stress disorder. Initially, they based their treatment programs on the established rap group model. Trauma victims were encouraged to discuss their troubles in groups made up of victims of similar traumas. It is generally accepted that the social support provided by these groups is an important ingredient of successful therapy (Boscarino, 1995; Hobfoll et al., 1991). However, group discussions alone may not always be sufficient. Other therapeutic interventions are also required. The most common behavioral intervention is exposure (Frueh, Turner, & Beidel, 1995). Victims are helped to confront their memories of the traumatic event so that their fear and anxiety can extinguish. Flooding, systematic desensitization, cognitive restructuring, and stress-management training are also used to help clients overcome their anxiety and to teach them how to cope with fear-provoking situations that may arise in the future (Foa et al., 1991). Sometimes assertiveness training is needed to teach people (rape victims, for example) how to deal with their anger (Keane et al., 1992). Antidepressant medication may also help reduce some of the symptoms of post-traumatic stress disorder (Davidson et al., 1990).

Cognitive processing therapy (Calhoun & Resick, 1993) is a therapy program developed specifically for the post-traumatic stress of victims of sexual assault. It combines aspects of exposure-based therapy with cognitive restructuring. The cognitions targeted for restructuring are those specific to rape: shame, feelings of responsibility, guilt. An important feature of this treatment program involves getting clients to write a detailed account of the sexual assault, which serves both as a form of exposure and as a way of getting clients to confront their feelings of anger.

Some therapists have reported successful treatment of post-traumatic stress disorder using a technique called eye movement desensitization, in which people are asked to visualize images of traumatic events. Once the image is clear, the clients are required to follow the movements of the clinician's finger (or a pencil) with their eyes while holding their heads immobile. They do this 10 or more times. For some unknown reason, tracking the therapist's finger with one's eyes is supposed to reduce the distress associated with post-traumatic stress disorder while, at the same time, eliminating nightmares and flashbacks (Marquis, 1991; S. A. Wilson, Becker, & Tinker, 1995). Most new treatments are heralded by enthusiastic reports extolling their virtues, and eye movement desensitization is no different. Trials that compare the treatment with plausible controls are the only way to determine if it is more effective than other treatments or than a simple placebo.

Early Intervention and Prevention

Because most psychological theories assume that the causes of psychological disorders are within individuals rather than in the social context in which they live, psychological treatment almost always focuses on the individual or small groups of people. Yet many victims of trauma never get to professional psychologists. For example, rape victims rarely seek psychological help in the period immediately following the attack (Koss, 1993). They do not see themselves as psychologically disturbed but as victims of a crime that they would rather forget. Unfortunately, the police, lawyers, and the press make sure that the attack is never far from mind. Some women may even find themselves being blamed for the attack. The stress builds up until it produces a stress disorder (Falsetti et al., 1995). It is at this point that victims seek assistance. Clearly, it would be preferable to intervene earlier, before post-traumatic stress disorder has a chance to develop, with education about what to expect and with cognitive restructuring and relaxation techniques (Foa, Hearst-Ikeda, & Perry, 1995). Special rape crisis centers, staffed with sensitive female clinicians, have been established for this purpose (Koss, 1993).

The prevention of post-traumatic stress disorder following a major disaster also requires early intervention. For soldiers, this means instituting treatment at the first sign of stress (FitzGerald et al., 1993). Such treatment may be conducted near, or even on, the battlefield. The goal, of course, is a quick return to combat, but such early treatment may also short-circuit the development of a full-blown stress disorder.

Early intervention is equally important in civilian disasters. Based on their experience providing mental health services for the survivors of an airplane crash, G. A. Jacobs, Quevillon, and Stricherz (1990) concluded that successful early intervention requires a carefully devised mental health disaster plan. Every community should have a coordinator who will have responsibility for deploying mental health personnel and resources.

Early intervention is especially important for rape victims, who may even find themselves being blamed for the attack and be reluctant to seek help until they have a stress disorder.

The coordinator should have access to an up-to-date register of suitably trained professionals (psychologists and others) who can be contacted quickly should the need arise. These staff should participate in a regular system of disaster drills. Suitable facilities for housing and treating survivors and their families should be identified, and, to prevent panic, communities should establish a formal procedure for providing information to victims and their families.

An example of such a community-based approach took place in the former Yugoslavia. During one of the longest sieges in history, the 400,000 residents of Sarajevo were attacked by rockets, grenades, and tanks. Many were killed; others had their homes destroyed. In November 1993, at the height of the fighting, the International Rescue Committee (a voluntary organization that provides resettlement services to refugees in the United States) and Bosnian mental health workers created the Corridor Mental Health Program (B. Smith & Surgan, 1996).

Corridor consisted of two major programs, counseling and public education. Because there were not sufficient mental health workers to serve the population, people from a variety of backgrounds—teachers, lawyers, managers—were enlisted and trained to be counselors. These counselors provided individual and group therapy to people living in frontline communities. They also provided visiting outreach programs for the elderly and disabled, as well as for those who were too agoraphobic to leave home. The education program used various media to disseminate mental health information. Corridor produced a magazine as well as radio and television spots. The goal was to dispel fear and despair. Acute and post-traumatic stress were explained and demystified. Media spots offered suggestions on how to cope and contained inspirational personal stories about people who were managing despite great adversity. Call-in shows featured advice from mental health professionals and interviews with people who were making it through trying circumstances. Because Corridor's counselors were undergoing the same traumas as everyone else, they were also provided with counseling to help them deal with the stress.

ASSESSING TREATMENT OUTCOME

New treatments, such as eye movement desensitization, are continually being developed by clinicians and researchers. Typically, these new treatments are first tested on clinic clients. Clinicians note how many improve and the extent of their improvement. Because clinic clients

Challenges in Assessing Treatment Outcome

CLIENT SELECTION

Deciding which clients to include in a treatment outcome study involves a tradeoff. Researchers may want to exclude clients with mild disorders because it may be easier to show improvement in clients whose symptoms are more severe. On the other hand, including a broad range of clients gives researchers a better idea of how effective the treatment will be in the real-world clinic population, which includes both severe and mild cases. Broad criteria will also make more subjects eligible for inclusion. This is often important because trials with small numbers of subjects may have insufficient statistical power to detect differences between groups.

BIASES

Because therapists may be biased (they may hope for a particular outcome), they should not know which subjects are receiving the treatment and which are controls. Such "blind" researchers are unable to subtly influence the results. Of course, clients may also have expectations, so they should be kept blind about whether they are in the treatment or the control group. In drug trials, it is relatively easy to keep both subjects and their doctors blind. Placebos can be designed to look just like the drugs being studied. In psychotherapy research, however, it is often difficult to disguise a treatment. At the very least, however, the clinicians who are evaluating the outcome measures, and judging which subjects improved and which did not, should be kept blind about which subjects are in the treatment group and which are controls.

OUTCOME CRITERIA

The dependent variable of a treatment trial is therapeutic outcome. In many studies, the choice of an outcome measure is straightforward. For example, an intervention aimed at suicide prevention should result in fewer self-inflicted deaths. For post-traumatic stress disorder, however, the appropriate outcome measure is not so clear. Researchers could measure the incidence of specific symptoms (nightmares per week, flashbacks per week) and expect that a successful treatment would reduce this incidence. Alternatively, researchers could use external indicators—time off work, number of hospitalizations, and the amount of medications taken—as indirect measures of mental health. A third possibility is to use psychological scales that measure depression, anxiety, and other symptoms, or quality-of-life measures can be used to assess global functioning. Because different outcome measures may produce different results, measures must be chosen carefully. Whichever outcome measure they use, researchers must be able to justify their choice.

PROSPECTIVE VERSUS HISTORICAL CONTROLS

Some studies compare treated clients to a "historical" control group of clients seen in the clinic some time before the trial began ("Mental Health," 1995). Although these historical controls are better than no controls at all, they are far from ideal because environmental events may affect the treatment and control groups differently. A change in the rules governing pensions for disabled soldiers, for example, could have dramatic effects on the treatment group but would not affect historical controls seen years before. It is better to select the treatment and control group from the same population and follow them prospectively for a specified time period.

STRATIFIED DESIGNS

By chance alone, randomization may fail to produce groups that are comparable on all the potentially important variables. To ensure comparability, researchers may assign clients to subpopulations (strata) before they are randomly assigned to the treatment or the control group. For example, if age is considered relevant to therapeutic response, the client population may first be divided (stratified) into age groups. The treatment and control groups may then be constructed by selecting clients randomly from each age group. Stratification is important when researchers know the crucial variables affecting outcome and when client samples are small.

CROSSOVER DESIGN

Sometimes it is possible to use clients as their own control by switching subjects between groups. Subjects in the experimental group "cross over" to the treatment group, and vice versa. This ensures that the two groups are completely comparable because each subject appears in each group. The drawback to this approach is that treatments can be affected by what came before. Trials using crossover designs must be analyzed carefully to ensure that such "order effects" do not confound the outcomes.

CLINICAL VERSUS STATISTICAL SIGNIFICANCE

Improvements on some measures may be statistically significant without necessarily being clinically significant (K. I. Howard et al., 1996). For example, given a large enough sample, a 1-point difference between the treatment and control groups on a depression scale may reach statistical significance. Technically, we would have to conclude that the treatment produced an effect, but this does not mean that the treatment will be clinically useful; its effects may be too small. The difference between a treatment's efficacy (as measured by a randomized control trial) and its practical clinical effectiveness is crucial to clinicians (Seligman, 1995). There is no practical value in a treatment that produces only trivial effects.

are not randomly selected (nor are they usually compared with an appropriate control group), clinical observations can never offer definitive proof of therapeutic effectiveness. Proof that a treatment is effective requires a controlled trial in which clients from a similar population are randomly assigned to either the treatment (say, eye movement desensitization) or some comparison group (Hollon, 1996; N. S. Jacobson & Christensen, 1996). If the treatment group improves more than the comparison group, we may assume that the treatment is responsible for the difference. Although randomized clinical trials may sound simple in theory, they are not easy to design. Small procedural changes can affect the way the trial results are interpreted. Critical Thinking About Clinical Decisions 4.1 examines just a few examples of the problems therapy researchers face.

CAROLE BALLODI: EPILOGUE

On the basis of his assessment and diagnosis, Dr. Berg recommended that Carole Ballodi be treated with a combination of techniques. While Carole was still on the tranquilizers prescribed by Dr. Kahn, Dr. Berg scheduled her for a series of relaxation training sessions. These were then combined with systematic exposure to her war memories. Exposure began with the sound of helicopters and worked up to the death of the soldier

while under her treatment. Gradually, Carole was able to think about and discuss her war memories with minimal anxiety. Carole was also exposed to memories of the patient who died in her office. Again, she was gradually able to think and talk about the incident with minimal anxiety.

In addition to relaxation and exposure, Dr. Berg helped Carole engage in cognitive restructuring, especially about the guilt she unreasonably felt over the soldier's death. To help her ease back into her life, cognitive therapy also focused on Carole's fear of social evaluation. She learned new cognitions ("My colleagues also have problems." "I will be a better doctor because I will understand what my patients are going through") as well as skills, such as controlled breathing, that she could use to calm herself when she felt the onset of panic.

When Carole felt sufficiently in control to leave home comfortably, she joined a group of people with panic and post-traumatic stress disorder. These group sessions provided her with ongoing social support and the opportunity to try out new social skills in a non-threatening environment. After two months, Carole was taking tranquilizers only occasionally to sleep. She was back at work and going out with friends. Although she still felt panic occasionally, she felt increasingly able to control it. Dr. Berg expected further improvement with continued group treatment.

CHAPTER 4 IN PERSPECTIVE

The *DSM-IV* contains a kaleidoscope of disorders. A few involve bizarre symptoms, such as hallucinations, but most are simply exaggerations of everyday behaviors. This is fortunate because it means the theories and techniques developed to understand and study typical behavior are also applicable to behavior disorders. This chapter focused on anxiety—an unpleasant feeling of dread and apprehension. Anxiety is valuable to our survival. It signals us that a potential threat is on the horizon,

and it mobilizes the necessary defenses. Anxiety can also cause psychological disorders. It can become attached to specific objects or situations, it can disrupt sleep and work, and it can cause people to withdraw from life. Anxiety disorders are relatively common in the population, although they may take different forms at different ages.

Although the various anxiety disorders have their specific symptoms, there is a considerable overlap, which suggests that anxiety disorders may have

related causes. These include not only learning but also a possible genetic disposition. Anxiolytic or antidepressant medications play an important role in the short-term management of anxiety disorders, but they can produce unpleasant side effects and cause physiological or psychological dependence. In the long term, the clients who fare best are those who learn new skills that allow them to cope with their anxiety.

Key Ideas

Fears and Phobias
Fears are determined by the complex interaction of heredity (inherited dispositions to be fearful in certain situations), developmental stage (different things

are feared at different ages), traumatic experiences (which cause fear by conditioning), cultural norms (fears vary across cultures), and instrumental learning (reinforced avoidance responses can

become fears). Although it is possible for people to fear just about anything, some fears are more common than others. We seem to inherit a genetic diathesis to fear objects and situations that threaten our existence. Fears are reasonable responses to objective threats, whereas phobias are unreasonable exaggerations of danger. Specific phobias are limited to a confined class of objects or situations, whereas social phobias apply to situations in which one may be evaluated by other people. Avoidant personality disorder is an Axis II diagnosis roughly equivalent to a chronic social phobia. Psychoanalysts believe that phobias represent a displacement of the anxiety produced by repressed conflicts. Behavioral psychologists implicate both classical and operant conditioning. However, because many phobias develop without any direct fear conditioning, modeling and other forms of vicarious learning are also likely to be involved. The crucial ingredient in the behavioral treatment of phobias is exposure. Even self-exposure can have positive therapeutic effects, especially when combined with cognitive restructuring for people who habitually catastrophize what are essentially trivial events.

Generalized Anxiety Disorder

Generalized anxiety disorder is marked by a multitude of physical complaints. Psychoanalysts attribute it to a fear of punishment for unconscious sexual and violent impulses. The traditional behavioral view is that it is a form of classically conditioned fear to a ubiquitous stimulus. However, because most cases of generalized anxiety disorder cannot be traced back to any particular conditioning experience, cognitive-behaviorists have concentrated instead on a tendency to be constantly on the lookout for signs of danger. Treatment is mainly determined by the theoretical orientation of the practitioner. Psychoanalysts try to get people to confront their repressed impulses and conflicts. Behavioral clinicians use relaxation and exposure (usually through desensitization). Cognitive interventions are aimed at helping people reappraise situations that they consider threatening, while at the same time increasing their sense of self-efficacy. Anxiolytics are often used alone or, preferably, in combination with psychological treatments.

Obsessive-Compulsive Disorder

Obsessions are unwelcome but uncontrollable thoughts and images; compulsions are repetitive ritualistic behaviors, such as counting, cleaning, and checking. Sufferers know that their obsessions and compulsions are irrational, yet they just seem unable to do anything about them. Psychoanalytic theory locates the etiology of obsessive-compulsive disorder in early childhood socialization experiences beginning with harsh toilet training. Behavioral psychologists believe that compulsive behaviors are reinforced by their anxiety-reducing consequences. What is not clear, from the behavioral formulation, is why compulsive behavior gets started in the first place. It is also not clear why obsessions persist despite their tendency to increase, rather than decrease, anxiety. Because antidepressant drugs that alter serotonin levels have a positive effect on obsessive-compulsive disorder, researchers working in the biological paradigm have suggested that obsessive-compulsive disorder may be the result of faulty serotonin metabolism. The goal of psychoanalytic treatment is to make conscious the repressed conflicts presumed to be responsible for obsessive-compulsive behavior. The most common behavioral approaches to treatment are exposure, response prevention, and thought-stopping. Cognitive-behavioral psychologists attempt to restructure the catastrophizing cognitions associated with obsessions and compulsions. Anxiolytics do not seem to help obsessive-compulsive people. Brain surgery has been used in intractable cases.

Panic Disorder

Characterized by sudden inexplicable feelings of dread, panic disorders occur in people who are constantly monitoring their own physiology. Any small physical event (a heart palpitation, for example) can make them anxious. This anxiety produces other physiological symptoms (rapid breathing, for instance), which make them even more anxious. They become trapped in a vicious cycle that can escalate into a full-blown panic attack complete with heart palpitations, hyperventilation, shaking, sweating, and feelings of suffocation. Researchers in the biological paradigm have attributed panic attacks to hyperventilation, sodium lactate metabolism, and mitral valve prolapse; psychoanalysts have implicated repressed conflicts. Pedigree studies suggest that some people may be genetically programmed to be fearful. Because cognitions can determine whether hyperventilation or sodium lactate causes a panic attack, the appraisal of physiological functioning may be more important than the physiology itself.

Agoraphobia

Panic attacks become associated with the situations in which they occur. Fearing further attacks, sufferers avoid these situations. Over time, the number of situations that must be avoided increases. Eventually, the person restricts movements outside the home because of fear of having a panic attack. When this happens, the person is said to be agoraphobic. Agoraphobia may also develop insidiously, without a history of panic attacks. In such cases, the fear of a few situations (cars, tunnels) gradually generalizes until practically any environment outside the home becomes a source of danger.

Acute and Post-Traumatic Stress Disorders

For most people, the effects of a trauma are short-lasting. They may experience a transitory acute stress disorder, but those who fail to return to their everyday lives after a few months may be suffering from post-traumatic stress disorder, a disorder that did not receive official recognition until the publication of the *DSM-III* in 1980. In the past, the diagnosis was associated with Vietnam veterans, but many types of trauma may induce the symptoms of post-traumatic stress disorder: avoidance, flashbacks, and a "numbing" of emotional responses. People vary in their vulnerability to post-traumatic stress disorder, suggesting that genetics or early experiences (or both) play a role.

However, the social environment is also important. Treatment usually involves group therapy combined with cognitive restructuring, relaxation, and exposure.

Sometimes, assertiveness training is required to teach people, such as rape victims, how to deal with their anger. Antidepressant medication may also help.

Secondary prevention in the form of crisis intervention can potentially prevent more serious disorders from developing.

Key Terms

acute stress disorder
agoraphobia
alarm (or emergency) reaction
anxiety
anxiety disorder
avoidant personality disorder
benzodiazepines
comorbidity

compulsions
efficacy (of a treatment)
fear survey
flooding
generalized anxiety disorder
hyperventilation
implosive therapy
limbic system

mitral valve prolapse
neuroses
obsessions
obsessive-compulsive disorder
obsessive-compulsive
   personality disorder
panic attack
panic disorder

performance anxiety
post-traumatic stress disorder
response prevention
separation anxiety disorder
social phobia
specific phobia
substance-induced anxiety
   disorder

CHAPTER 5

CHAPTER OBJECTIVES

Stress is a word that is used widely in both psychological writings and the popular press, so widely in fact that its meaning is not always clear. This chapter examines the concept of stress from a variety of viewpoints: historical, biological, social, and psychological. The value of a multidisciplinary biopsychosocial approach to stress is illustrated by an in-depth study of William Cole, a college student who suffers from a chronic illness. Although William's illness is physiological, the chapter shows that it is nonetheless profoundly affected by psychological factors including stress, emotions, and cognitions.

The four main questions addressed in this chapter are

1. What is stress and where does it come from?
2. How does stress affect psychological and physical health?
3. Why are some people more prone to suffer from the effects of stress than others?
4. How can people be helped to cope with stress?

Effects of Stress on Health and Disease

CONTENTS

W illiam Cole is a university student living with a chronic illness. Documents 5.1–5.3 describe his illness and its consequences. This chapter uses William Cole's story to illustrate the interplay between physical and psychological factors in health and disease.

DOCUMENT 5.1

William Cole's Hospital Record

UNIVERSITY HOSPITAL

Medical Record

CONFIDENTIAL

Name: William Cole

Sex: Male

DOB: 11/5/1982

Address: Mayne Hall, Room 17

Telephone: 555-3472

Next of Kin: Mrs. Iola Cole, 222 Southgate Avenue, Los Angeles, CA

Insurance Company: University Community Health Plan

Date of Admission: May 10, 2001

Date of Discharge: May 15, 2001

Discharge Diagnoses
1. hyperglycemia
2. insulin-dependent diabetes mellitus
3. depression
4. anxiety

Medications Administered: insulin (100 USP units per ml); fluoxetine (20 mg)

Tests Administered: glucose tolerance; full blood analysis

Emergency Room Note

5/10 at 10:00 a.m.: Patient is an 18-year-old African American male. He was brought to the hospital at 10:00 a.m. by ambulance after he collapsed during a final examination. At the time of his admission to the hospital, the patient was unconscious, and his respiration was shallow. He appeared dehydrated. There was a distinct "sweet" odor emanating from the patient's body. Ordered blood work, respiration, and intravenous fluid replacement. Consultant contacted.

Physician's Notes

5/10 at 11:00 a.m.: Saw patient for first time on ward 1 hour after admission. He was unconscious and had signs of acute ketoacidosis, probably caused by uncontrolled diabetes. Lab results confirmed the patient is diabetic. Treated with fluids and insulin.

5/10 at 4:30 p.m.: Patient has regained consciousness, and his blood glucose and ketone levels are returning to normal. Patient will remain on intravenous fluids, and a diabetic diet will be introduced gradually.

5/11 at 4:00 p.m.: Patient's color and general state have improved. He is eating and able to move around but seems withdrawn. Glucose tolerance test will be used to determine insulin demand. Nutritionist has been asked to help patient construct diet.

5/12 at 9:00 a.m.: Patient's blood levels have normalized, and a diet has been developed with the nutritionist. However, patient is still withdrawn and tearful. He says he has a severe headache. Psychological consultation with Dr. Stuart Berg ordered. He will see patient today.

5/13 at 10:00 a.m.: Dr. Berg considers patient to need assistance in coping skills. Will require outpatient psychological consultations. Antidepressant medication ordered.

5/14 at 4:00 p.m.: Patient still withdrawn and complaining of head pain but has asked to be discharged. Will leave tomorrow but will attend the diabetes clinic for monitoring and will continue to see Dr. Berg and other members of the clinical team as an outpatient.

DOCUMENT 5.2

Excerpt From an
Interview Between Dr.
Berg and William Cole

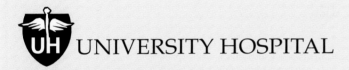 UNIVERSITY HOSPITAL

Interview With Patient

DR. BERG: How are you enjoying college?

WILLIAM: It's OK.

DR. BERG: What are you majoring in?

WILLIAM: I'm not sure yet.

DR. BERG: Well, it's still early. Many students don't choose a major in their first year. How are your grades so far?

WILLIAM: OK, I guess. I got one B and three Cs on my midterms.

DR. BERG: That's pretty good for a first semester.

WILLIAM: It's probably the best I can do.

DR. BERG: What makes you say that?

WILLIAM: I'm no brain. Not like some of the other students here.

DR. BERG: You must have done well in high school to get in here.

WILLIAM: Yeah, but I went to a pretty rough school. Most of the kids couldn't care less about going to college. The principal claimed I was the school leader. I really wanted to be a pilot, but diabetics can't be pilots.

DR. BERG: What made you different from the others?

WILLIAM: I had nothing better to do than study. I couldn't do sports, and I didn't hang out much with the other guys.

DR. BERG: Why couldn't you do sports or hang out?

WILLIAM: My mother was afraid I'd get hurt. I'm a diabetic.

DR. BERG: Having diabetes kept you from hanging out?

WILLIAM: Yeah. I get tired easily. I can't eat regular foods, and I can't go out drinking beer.

DR. BERG: Did you want to hang out?

WILLIAM: No . . . yes . . . sometimes.

DR. BERG: Is your diabetes under control?

WILLIAM: I guess not. Otherwise I wouldn't be here in the hospital.

DR. BERG: Is it usually under control?

WILLIAM: Yeah.

DR. BERG: What happened this time?

WILLIAM: I'm not sure. The last thing I remember was taking this final exam, and then I woke up in here with this damn headache. I get them all the time.

DR. BERG: Did anything special affect you recently?

WILLIAM: No. Just the usual.

DR. BERG: What have you been doing, say over the last week or two—before you went to the hospital?

WILLIAM: I've been studying.

DR. BERG: With anyone or alone?

WILLIAM: Alone.

DR. BERG: Have you been eating properly and taking your insulin?

WILLIAM: I guess.

DR. BERG: Aren't you sure?

WILLIAM: If you're going to get sick, you're going to get sick. There's not much you can do about it.

DR. BERG: Don't you think you are in control of your health?

WILLIAM: No. Not really.

DR. BERG: Let's get back to my earlier question. Did you take your insulin and stick to your diet before you got sick?

WILLIAM: I think so, but maybe I forgot once or twice.

DR. BERG: Why?

WILLIAM: Sometimes I get stressed out. You know. Hassles. Studying. My mom calling me up and worrying on the phone. I may have messed up.

DR. BERG: I can understand. Everyone has hassles. How about talking them over with your friends?

WILLIAM: I don't have any.

DR. BERG: Why not?

WILLIAM: I'm not sure. I guess I don't really fit in. I sometimes feel as if I'm treated more as a member of a race than as an individual.

DR. BERG: Do you feel lonely?

WILLIAM: Sometimes.

DOCUMENT 5.3

Psychology Consultation Note on William Cole

UNIVERSITY HOSPITAL

Psychology Service

CONFIDENTIAL

Consultation Note

Psychologist: Dr. Stewart Berg

Referral: Dr. M. Jankowitz

Reason for Referral: The client was brought to the Emergency Room in a diabetic coma. He responded well to medical treatment, but he seemed withdrawn and complains of chronic headaches. Dr. Jankowitz requested advice about the patient's state of mind and about the potential for his mental state to affect his illness.

Behavioral Observations: William Cole is an 18-year-old African American male. He is of average height but rather thin. He was neatly dressed and clean shaven. He entered my office slowly and hesitantly. Although he cooperated by answering questions, he volunteered little and seemed withdrawn. He avoided making eye contact, and his facial expression was tense. He frequently held his forehead in his hand.

History: William is a first-year student and the first member of his family to attend college. He is assisted by a student loan and has a job working in the library. His father works in an automobile factory, and his mother is a telephone company employee. They live in Los Angeles and see their son on holidays. He calls home every Sunday.

William reports being an athletic child with a close group of same-sex friends. He first learned that he had diabetes at age 13. His mother took him to the family doctor because he was always tired and thirsty and he urinated frequently. A blood test at the time confirmed the diagnosis. William's illness could not be controlled by diet. He required daily insulin injections. At first, William would not believe he was sick and resisted treatment. He continued to "hang out" with his friends and to play football and baseball. Eventually, however, he says he "accepted" his illness.

William reports that his mother became his nurse. She made sure that he followed a proper diet, checked his urine for sugar (several times each day), and administered his injections. She posted a chart of glucose test results on the bathroom door. William gradually lost contact with his friends. He says this was because his mother urged him to avoid sports or any other activity where he could get physically hurt.

A combination of diet and insulin kept William's condition stable for 5 years. The only exceptional incident occurred toward the end of his junior year in high school.

He was preparing for his examinations and was feeling left out because he did not have a date for the junior prom. He felt weak but kept going to school. He fainted in class and, although he quickly revived, was taken to the hospital, where he spent one day.

Since William entered college, he has had no serious diabetic episodes until the current one, although he has had trouble sleeping and has experienced loss of appetite. He claims not to have told any of the other students of his illness.

Brief Testing Results: The client's score on the Beck Depression Inventory was 16, placing him in the "moderately depressed" range. He has rather low expectations for the future ("I feel that I won't ever get over my troubles"). The client's responses to the Norbeck Social Support Questionnaire indicate a limited social support network, with no close friends. The client's Sickness Impact Profile confirms the restricted social life. He does not feel in control of his illness. The Social Readjustment Rating Scale score of 300 reflects sufficient stress to potentially affect his health.

Conclusions and Recommendations: William Cole is an insulin-dependent diabetic who is moderately depressed and has become socially isolated. He does not feel in control of his illness. His illness becomes worse under stress (final examinations, for example). At such times, he may also fail to comply with treatment (perhaps a disguised call for help). The client has low self-esteem. Recommend that he join a diabetic support group. Exposure to others in similar circumstances may help him acquire better coping skills while at the same time increasing his sense of belonging and his self-esteem. Psychotherapy would also be helpful. Therapy should include training in relaxation, stress reduction, coping skills, and social skills (to help him develop a social support network). Antidepressants may also be helpful in the short term.

Diagnostic Considerations

Axis I (clinical disorders): Major depressive episode due to a nonpsychiatric medical condition

Axis II (personality disorders): Secondary personality change due to a nonpsychiatric medical condition

Axis III (general medical conditions): Diabetes mellitus

Axis IV (psychosocial and environmental problems): Examinations, lack of social support, exacerbation of illness

Axis V (global assessment of functioning): Highest level of adaptive functioning in past year: 70; present functioning: 50

LIVING WITH CHRONIC ILLNESS: WILLIAM COLE'S STORY

William Cole, along with 10 million other Americans, suffers from diabetes mellitus (usually shortened to diabetes), a metabolic disease first described more than 2,000 years ago. Diabetes is caused by a deficiency of insulin, a hormone secreted by the pancreas. Because insulin is required to metabolize carbohydrates such as sugar, individuals with diabetes are unable to use carbohydrates effectively. The result is a state similar to star-vation. The brain is particularly affected because glucose (a carbohydrate) is the only nutrient that it can metabolize. In severe cases, diabetes leads to dehydration, an excess of acid in the body, and coma. Long-term sufferers may develop poor circulation, resulting in gangrene and other forms of tissue destruction. Prolonged diabetes can result in the loss of limbs and even blindness. Mild forms of diabetes may be controlled by a low-carbohydrate diet, but severe cases require insulin injections. Diabetic patients like William Cole, whose illness can be controlled only by insulin, are known as insulin-

For many people, such as William Cole, chronic illness can cause depression, which in turn can lead to social isolation, which can compound the depression.

dependent, or Type 1, diabetics. Type 1 diabetes is the third leading cause of death in the United States (Wertlieb, Jacobson, & Hauser, 1990).

PSYCHOSOMATIC VERSUS PHYSICAL ILLNESS: A DUBIOUS DISTINCTION

At first glance, diabetes may not seem particularly relevant to abnormal psychology; it is a physical disease. Traditionally, abnormal psychologists have limited their interest in physical diseases to the so-called **psychophysiological** or **psychosomatic disorders** (*psycho* = mind, *somatic* = body)—disorders in which psychological factors produce "real" physical diseases. These include, among others, peptic ulcer, asthma, hypertension, and headaches. Psychosomatic conditions were thought to differ from other physical illnesses because psychological factors played a significant role in their etiology.

Asthma, for example, was attributed to loss or separation, ulcers to stress-producing jobs, headaches to helplessness, and hypertension was supposedly the result of repressed anger. In recent years, it has become increasingly clear that this approach to physical illness is too simplistic. For example, we now know that many peptic ulcers are the result of a bacterial infection. However, the specific bacterium concerned, *Helicobacter pylori*, thrives in the acidic internal environment produced by a stressful job. In other words, a bacterial infection that thrives on stress results in a physical condition (peptic ulcer). This is a perfect example of the diathesis-stress model of psychopathology discussed in previous chapters.

Because of the interplay between physiological and psychological factors, distinguishing between pure physical illnesses and those with psychological components is now widely recognized as artificial and futile. Social and psychological factors affect *all* illnesses, from the common cold to cancer, from hernia to heart disease, from skin rashes to diabetes. In recognition of the interaction between psychology and physiology, a new field—**behavioral medicine**—has developed (Blanchard, 1994; Brannon & Feist, 1997; Epstein, 1992). Behavioral medicine researchers seek to learn how psychological factors (1) make people susceptible (or resistant) to illness, (2) alter the course of an illness, (3) determine compliance with medical treatment, and (4) affect health-related behavior. The last goal is increasingly important. As many of the scourges of the past (polio, for example) disappear, today's serious illnesses tend more and more to be the result of behavioral choices—smoking, using drugs, drinking alcohol to excess (Oyama & Andrasik, 1992). Understanding and preventing illness-causing behaviors such as smoking have the potential to do more to improve public health than building any number of new hospitals. The disciplines contributing to behavioral medicine are depicted in Figure 5.1.

Early versions of the *DSM* included a variety of "psychosomatic" disorders. These no longer appear in the *DSM-IV*, which refers instead to "psychological factors affecting a medical condition." This diagnosis is applied when psychological factors appear to cause, exacerbate, or delay recovery from a medical condition or when psychological factors interfere with treatment. The specific medical conditions affected are listed separately in Axis III. The *DSM-IV* also acknowledges that causality can go both ways—medical conditions can produce or exacerbate psychological problems. This "reverse" relationship is reflected in the diagnoses Dr. Berg gave to William Cole ("secondary mood disorder due to a nonpsychiatric medical condition" and "secondary personality change due to a nonpsychiatric medical condition").

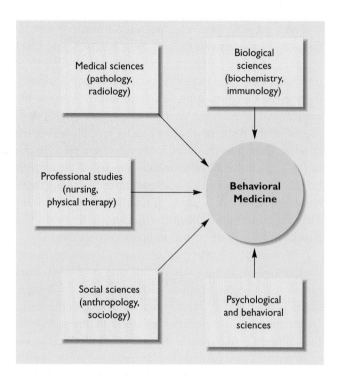

FIGURE 5.1 **Disciplines Contributing to Behavioral Medicine**

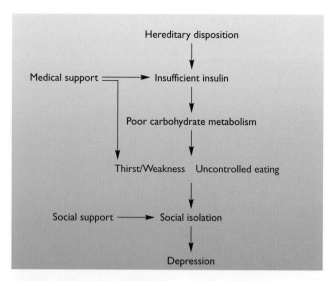

FIGURE 5.2 **The Interaction of Psychological and Physical Factors in Diabetes**

The *DSM-IV* includes several diagnoses that recognize the interaction between psychological variables and physical illness (for example, "sexual dysfunction due to a general medical condition"). However, these diagnoses hardly do justice to the complex interactions that take place between psychological factors and health. For example, insulin-dependent diabetics, like William Cole, may lead restricted lives. They cannot eat what (or when) they wish, they must continuously monitor the level of sugar in their blood, they are dependent on daily doses of insulin, and they live with the constant threat of serious complications. To make matters worse, diabetes (and anxiety) can cause sexual dysfunctions (A. M. Thomas & LoPiccolo, 1994). Not surprisingly, some people with diabetes become depressed and socially isolated. Preoccupied and unhappy, some stop monitoring their blood sugar or taking their insulin regularly. Poor monitoring and irregular insulin increase the probability of complications such as blindness. These complications further limit patients' lives, making them even more depressed and unhappy.

In extreme cases, some people with diabetes consider suicide a way out of their misery (Goldston et al., 1994). If they decide to kill themselves, they certainly have a convenient method available to them—they can stop taking their insulin, or they can take an overdose.

Psychological interventions, such as the provision of social support, are often aimed at helping clients to comply with their treatment regimen, thereby limiting complications. Thus, interventions designed to address psychological factors such as social isolation not only have direct psychological effects, they also help to reduce the severity of the physiological disease. Improved physical health, in turn, affects psychological well-being by reducing depression and social isolation. This is a typical pattern. Psychological and physiological variables continuously interact, one set of variables affecting and being affected by the other (Figure 5.2).

The aim of this chapter is to illustrate psychology's role in understanding and treating disease as well as in fostering health. Instead of focusing on the outdated idea of a special group of psychosomatic or psychophysiological illnesses, the chapter begins with a brief discussion of diabetes and its management. William Cole's case is used to highlight the psychological factors involved in the management of a chronic illness.

MANAGING A CHRONIC ILLNESS

The main task facing those with diabetes is the regulation of their blood sugar levels. In those who do not have diabetes, the body does this automatically. Like a thermostat that turns a furnace on and off to maintain a constant temperature, the body secretes or reduces insulin to maintain a relatively constant blood sugar level.

When the blood sugar level is high (after a meal, for instance), the pancreas secretes insulin, lowering the level. When the blood sugar level is low, insulin production is reduced, and blood sugar rises. Those with diabetes, such as William Cole, cannot rely on this automatic control system. They must consciously and deliberately regulate their blood sugar levels. Accomplishing this is a complicated and challenging task requiring considerable knowledge, special skills, and specific limitations in activity (Bradley, 1995; B. May, 1991).

The first step in managing blood sugar levels is to monitor them. This is done most accurately by blood testing. Step 1 is to prick a finger to obtain a drop of blood. The blood is then applied to a strip of paper impregnated with a special chemical. The chemical causes the paper to change color when the blood contacts it. Different blood sugar levels correspond to different colors. People with diabetes must repeat this test every day, sometimes twice each day. If monitoring shows that their blood sugar level is too high or too low, then they must take some action to lower or raise it. The correct action to take depends on a complex set of factors, including time of day, time since last meal, amount of insulin administered, and frequency of insulin administration.

To keep his blood sugar level stable, William Cole requires insulin injections twice a day, one before breakfast and one before his evening meal. Others need more frequent injections. Some receive their insulin from permanently fixed pumps that automatically deliver insulin directly into a blood vessel. Timely delivery of insulin is crucial to maintain blood sugar levels, but it is only half the equation. Insulin must be balanced by food intake. Too much insulin or too little food and the blood sugar level will be too low. Too little insulin or too much food and the blood sugar level will be too high. William's task is to maintain the delicate balance between food intake and insulin so that his blood sugar level remains in the healthy range.

Balancing insulin and food intake requires extensive knowledge about nutrition. To ensure that he consumes just the right amount of carbohydrates, William must know the nutritional value of everything he eats. Moreover, he must eat a certain amount of carbohydrates on a fixed schedule, whether he feels hungry or not. Eating too soon or too long after an injection will result in too high or too low a blood sugar level. William must plan his exercise just as carefully because exercise burns up sugar. His mother worried about his playing sports because she knew that a game of football or baseball would need to be balanced by an increase in carbohydrates or a decrease in insulin.

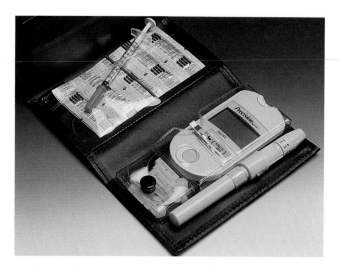

People with diabetes use a kit to monitor and help to regulate their blood sugar every day with diet and insulin injections. They are never able to forget that they have a chronic illness.

In summary, to stay healthy, William must have an extensive knowledge of nutrition and carbohydrate metabolism, considerable skill in blood monitoring and administering injections, and a willingness to organize his life to ensure that his blood sugar level remains in the normal range. Most of the time, he manages all of this quite well, but what happens when other aspects of his life begin to trouble him? How does his illness respond to life's inevitable disturbances? The remainder of this chapter is devoted to answering these questions. The chapter is organized according to the general stress and coping model depicted in Figure 5.3. In this model, the effect of stress (from whatever source) on health outcomes depends on the person's ability to cope with the stress. Coping, in turn, is moderated by social support, personality, cognitive variables, and health state. It is worth noting that poor health can itself be a source of stress, whereas good health may lower stress. The various aspects of the model (stress, coping, moderators, and health outcomes) are examined in the remainder of this chapter. The discussion begins with that ubiquitous term *stress*.

STRESS: ORIGINS, DEFINITIONS, AND THEORIES

William's hospitalizations coincided with school examinations and interpersonal challenges (the junior prom, for example). Today, most people accept that the psychological stress caused by exams and social anxiety can affect our health. Yet, like most ideas we take for

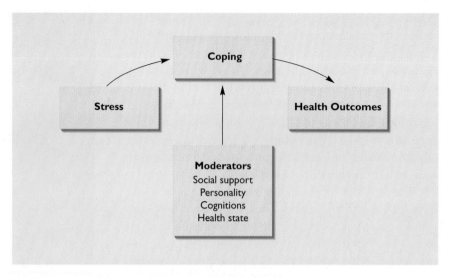

FIGURE 5.3 **Stress and Coping Model.** *The effect of stress on health depends on coping skills, which are influenced by various moderators.*

granted, the notion that our feelings affect our health has a long history. This section begins by placing our current views on **stress** and disease in a historical and theoretical context.

Origins

The Hippocratic corpus (see Chapter 1) contains frequent references to the effects of the emotions on health. For example, the ancient Greek teachers advised doctors to maintain a calm demeanor lest their patients become frightened. Showing fear, they believed, would exacerbate a patient's symptoms. Aristotle added anger as another emotion that, like fear, could cause illness. For centuries, doctors continued to believe in a causative link between strong negative emotions and illness, but this connection was broken in the Renaissance by the European philosopher René Descartes (1596–1650), who argued that the body and the *esprit* (French for "soul" or "mind") were separate entities that communicated through the pineal gland found at the base of the brain. This philosophical position has come to be known as Cartesian dualism.

According to Descartes, bodies are merely machines. They are part of the physical world, and they may be understood in mechanistic terms. To learn more about bodies, researchers make observations and conduct experiments. The mind, Descartes argued, is something else entirely. It has no physical presence, it cannot be observed, and its activities are not open to experimentation. Because the mind could not be studied empirically, medical scientists who were influenced by the Cartesian view focused on bodies. They devoted their efforts to uncovering disease-causing agents such as bacteria, ignoring psychological factors.

Psychoanalytic Views on the Physical Symptoms of Hysteria

Despite the objections of some philosophers, the notion that bodies are separate from minds and that physical illnesses are relatively unaffected by psychological factors dominated medicine from Descartes's time to the beginning of the 20th century. The classical view began to reemerge in the middle of the 19th century, when doctors first began to observe an illness called neurasthenia ("nerve weakness"; Abbey & Garfinkel, 1991). The symptoms of neurasthenia included fatigue, aches and pains, sore throat, and some low-grade fever. No physiological cause for neurasthenia was uncovered; it was blamed on hard work, striving for success, and changing sex roles. Although the diagnosis was common in the 1800s, it seemed to die out early in the 20th century (although today's diagnosis of "chronic fatigue syndrome" has some of the same symptoms; Abbey & Garfinkel, 1991). Neurasthenia is important, however, because its attribution to psychosocial causes provided the groundwork for Sigmund Freud's claim that the physical symptoms of hysteria were the bodily manifestations of emotional traumas experienced in early childhood (see Chapter 2).

According to Freud, childhood emotional traumas leave a residue of psychic energy that can be "converted" into physical symptoms. Indeed, Freudians of-

Ancient Greek teachers, such as Hippocrates (c. 460–370 BC), recognized the effect of the emotions on health. This connection was disavowed in the Renaissance by René Descartes (1596–1650), who argued that the mind and the body are separate entities.

ten referred to hysteria manifested by physical symptoms as **conversion hysteria.** Note that hysterical symptoms often mimic those associated with physical disorders (such as blindness, deafness, and paralysis), but Freud did not consider hysterical patients to be physically sick (although, as discussed in Chapter 2, prominent neurologists such as Charcot disagreed). Still, it was only a small logical leap from hysteria to the notion of psychosomatic illnesses. In both cases, physical symptoms (feigned or real) result, at least in part, from psychological causes.

Psychosomatic Medicine

The field that came to be known as psychosomatic medicine received a considerable boost in scientific respectability from the work of the Harvard physiologist Walter Cannon (1871–1945). According to Cannon, organisms faced with a threatening stimulus mobilize their physiological resources to combat or escape the threat ("fight or flight") (Cannon, 1939). Cannon called the physiological response to threat the **emergency reac-**

tion and showed that it is controlled by the sympathetic nervous system and by hormones secreted mainly by the adrenal gland. Also called the alarm reaction, the emergency reaction follows a regular course. First, in the seconds following the perception of a threat, respiration deepens to take in the extra oxygen the muscles need for intense physical effort. There is an increase in the rate and strength of the heartbeat, which allows more oxygen to circulate around the body. The spleen, a repository for red blood cells, contracts and releases these oxygen-carrying cells into the bloodstream. The liver releases energy-producing sugar, while blood flow to the brain is increased. The pupils of the eyes dilate to increase visual acuity, and the blood becomes more likely to coagulate (to stop wounds from bleeding).

Once the organism has safely escaped or defeated the cause of the threat, the emergency reaction dissipates. However, if the threat persists, the emergency reaction may begin to affect an organism's health. For example, Cannon studied cases of shell shock and battle fatigue among soldiers confined to the trenches for long periods during World War I. He found that these soldiers

With his discovery of the emergency reaction and his study of World War I soldiers suffering from shell shock and battle fatigue, Harvard physiologist Walter Cannon (1871–1945) showed a connection between the mind and the body.

Walter Cannon suggested that, like the emergency reaction suffered by World War I soldiers, voodoo deaths were the result of autonomic reactions produced by fear of curses prepared by voodoo practitioners.

developed a variety of ailments, including peptic ulcers, headaches, and coronary heart disease. Cannon concluded that the soldiers' resistance to illness broke down because battlefield conditions produced frequent and persistent emergency reactions. Cannon also attributed voodoo deaths (in which members of tribal cultures allegedly die of fright when a "curse" is placed on them) to the intense autonomic reactions produced by fear. Stories about people who die of fright or sadness or a broken heart are also sometimes cited as evidence that death can be caused by psychological factors (Sue, Sue, & Sue, 1994). However, most such reports are anecdotal and difficult to confirm.

Specificity Theory

Early theories in the field of psychosomatic medicine consisted mainly of elaborations on Cannon's basic theme. For example, the psychiatrist Helen Flanders Dunbar (1902–1959) noted that stress affects people in different ways. In one person, a prolonged emergency reaction leads to heart disease, in another the result may be a peptic ulcer, and a third may wind up with arthritis. Dunbar postulated that these individual differences may be traced back to different personality types. Faced with prolonged threat, "coronary personalities" develop heart disease, "ulcer personalities" develop peptic ulcer, and "arthritic personalities" develop arthritis. Dunbar devoted considerable effort to describing these personalities. For example, she described the diabetic personality as "one fraught with anxiety, depression, paranoia, dependency conflicts, and sexual problems" (quoted in Wertlieb et al., 1990, p. 69).

Because Dunbar believed that certain illnesses are related to specific personality types, her theory became known as the **specificity theory of psychosomatic illness.** Specificity theory was elaborated by the psychoanalyst Franz Alexander (1891–1964), who claimed that specific unconscious conflicts produce specific diseases. For example, Alexander believed that dependent, love-demanding people who cannot find gratification in their everyday relationships develop peptic ulcers. On the other hand, people who repress hostile impulses develop high blood pressure.

Research on the specificity theory involved comparing patients with healthy people or with patients who suffered from some other condition. Any differences among the groups were considered to be a cause of the disease. For example, because diabetics were found to be more dependent than nondiabetics, Alexander concluded that dependency is one of the causes of diabetes. Similar logic was used to uncover causes for many other illnesses. Note that specificity theory flourished mainly in areas of medical ignorance. When there were no known physical causes for an illness, it was tempting to invent psychological ones. Before the bacteria that causes tuberculosis was discovered, this lung disease was also attributed to psychological causes (S. Schwartz & Griffin, 1986).

The main problem with specificity theory research was that the people being studied were already sick. Researchers had no way of knowing what the patients were like before they became ill. It is entirely possible that having diabetes may cause people to become dependent on others for help. That is, instead of a dependent personality causing diabetes, the relationship could go the other way—diabetes may cause people to develop dependent personalities. Because people cannot be assigned randomly to a personality type (or a psychological conflict) and then observed over time to see what diseases they develop, it is difficult to prove that a personality type or psychological conflict actually causes a disease. (See Critical Thinking About Clinical Decisions 5.1 for more on this subject.)

Another problem with the specificity theory was its implicit assumption that different emotional conflicts have different physiological effects. However, emotions are largely nonspecific and have similar autonomic effects (Steptoe, 1991). Thus, it is not normally possible to match specific emotional states with specific diseases. Instead, it seems more likely that the autonomic arousal produced by emotional turmoil exacerbates any disease. Realizing this, theorists working in the field of psychosomatic medicine have largely abandoned the specificity theory for the nonspecific stress theory. Instead of referring to certain illnesses as "psychosomatic," nonspecific stress theory acknowledges that all illnesses have psychological components.

Nonspecific Stress Theory

The emergency reaction described by Cannon is the body's way of coping with immediate threats. However, the emergency reaction cannot persist indefinitely. Long-term or frequently recurring threats cause the body to gradually wear out. Deterioration takes place in a series of stages described by the medical physiologist Hans Selye (1907–1982) as the **general adaptation syndrome,** or **GAS** (Selye, 1950).

The GAS begins with a threat that produces an

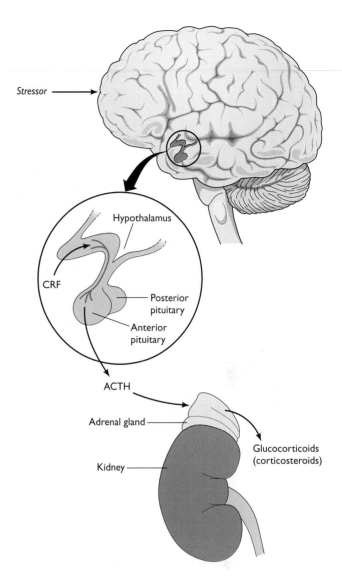

FIGURE 5.4 **Corticosteroid Release in Response to Stress.** *When the brain perceives a stressor, the hypothalamus releases CRF (corticotropin releasing factor) and other hormones. The CRF triggers the release of ACTH (adrenocorticotropic hormone, or corticotropin) in the anterior pituitary. The ACTH travels in the bloodstream to the adrenal glands, where it triggers the release of corticosteroids.* From: Sapolsky (1998, p. 33).

emergency reaction. Following the emergency reaction, the organism enters a "resistance" stage. If the emergency reaction can be described as the mobilization of the body's defenses, then the resistance stage is similar to all-out war. During the resistance stage, the organism uses its physiological resources to minimize tissue damage. Neurotransmitters carry mobilization commands to organs around the body. At the same time, the adrenal glands release corticosteroids ("stress hormones"), which further increase blood sugar for energy while reducing inflammation and pain (Figure 5.4). Body functions that are not directly related to avoiding harm

The Rise and Fall (and Rise) of the Type A Behavior Pattern

Because people cannot be assigned randomly to personality types, it is difficult to demonstrate a causative link between characteristic modes of behavior and particular diseases. Still, considerable effort has gone into trying to establish such links (H. S. Friedman & Booth-Kewley, 1987). Perhaps the most widely researched, and certainly the most frequently cited, behavior-disease relationship is the association between **Type A behavior** and coronary heart disease (CHD).

The main cause of CHD is the narrowing of the blood vessels supplying the heart, which starves the heart of blood. In the 1950s, California cardiologists, Meyer Friedman and Ray Rosenman, were studying cholesterol metabolism (Rosenman, 1986). It had long been suspected that the accumulation of fats like cholesterol in the blood was responsible for the narrowing of blood vessels. Even in the 1950s, people were being warned to limit the amount of fat in their diets. Yet, diet alone was unable to account for the observed fluctuations in blood cholesterol levels. Other factors, including psychological ones, seemed to be at work. For example, Friedman and Rosenman found that tax accountants had normal cholesterol levels early in the year, but, as the April 15 deadline for filing tax returns approached and they worked harder to meet the deadline, accountants' cholesterol levels became dangerously high. By June, with the pressure of the filing deadline behind

them, their cholesterol levels returned to normal. In a related study of couples, Friedman and Rosenman found that husbands were more susceptible to CHD than their wives, even when both partners consumed the same amount of fat. After ruling out the possible influence of sex hormones, the researchers turned to behavioral differences. Noting that husbands—at least in the 1950s—were more hard-driving and ambitious than their wives, Friedman and Rosenman hypothesized that, all other things being equal, people with

intense personalities are more likely to develop CHD than those who are more easygoing.

The idea that psychological factors are important in CHD was examined in more detail in the Western Collaborative Group Study (Rosenman et al., 1975). More than 3,000 healthy men between the ages of 35 and 59 were interviewed about their health, work habits, and diet ("Do you always feel anxious to get going and finish whatever you have to do?"). During this 15-minute interview, each man's rate of speech, posture, ag-

Researchers have not found a Type A personality prone to coronary heart disease (CHD), but they have found that hostile, angry people are more reactive to stress and to CHD than are more placid people.

(reproduction, digestion, growth) are gradually shut down. This only works for a time, however. If the threat persists, the body's defenses become progressively depleted. In the final stage, called exhaustion, illness becomes likely.

Any form of external pressure can trigger the GAS. People who have particularly demanding jobs may experience the first stages of a GAS every day. Because the

word **stress** is used to refer to both a cause (a "stressful" job, for example) and an effect ("I am feeling stressed"), Selye preferred to use the word **stressor** to refer to causes, reserving the word *stress* for the results produced by a stressor. In physics, stress is a force that distorts (strains) an object. A spring, for example, is strained by the application of a weight. Moderate stress causes the spring to compress. Severe stress, or stress

gressiveness, and signs of impatience (head nodding, knee jiggling, rapid eye blinking) were noted. Those who seemed impatient, competitive, and short-tempered were called Type A. The remaining subjects were called Type B. About half the sample fell into each category. The men were followed for the next 8 years. During that time, 257 of the original sample developed CHD. Of these, 178 had previously been classified Type A. Thus, Type A people were twice as likely to develop heart disease as Type Bs. Friedman and Rosenman concluded that Type A behavior contributes to CHD.

This conclusion immediately captured the public's imagination. Magazines published questionnaires designed to guide readers in classifying themselves as Type A or Type B ("Are you a competitive, always-on-the-go, ambitious, workaholic Type A person or a relaxed, easygoing, understanding, live-and-let-live Type B?"). Type A behavior, originally defined as a pattern of behaviors displayed in an interview, was reconceptualized as an enduring personality trait that could be measured by paper-and-pencil questionnaires (Jenkins, Zyzanski, & Rosenman, 1979). Family dynamics were studied to identify the child-rearing practices responsible for inculcating Type A behavior. In 1978, a panel of experts reviewed the literature and concluded that Type A behavior is an important risk factor for CHD, equal in its deleterious effect to smoking, high blood cholesterol, and inactivity (Brannon & Feist, 1992).

Within a few years after its publication, this conclusion was being challenged. Several long-term studies failed to find any relationship between Type A behavior and CHD; some found relationships between Type A and other illnesses but not CHD, and one study found that Type A people were more likely to survive an acute incident (a heart attack) than Type Bs (Haynes, Feinleib, & Eaker, 1983; Ragland & Brand, 1988a, 1988b). These contradictory findings could mean that Friedman and Rosenman were wrong: that Type A behavior is not a risk factor for CHD. Or they could mean that some measures of Type A behavior are more valid than others. A third possibility is that the contradictory results were due to sampling bias. In many studies, Type A people constituted the vast majority of subjects (Dembroski & MacDougall, 1983). Such studies load the dice in favor of finding a relationship between Type A behavior and CHD. To understand why, imagine a study in which all subjects are classified Type A. The outcome is preordained. Everyone who develops CHD will be Type A. The same bias is still present, although less extreme, when the majority of subjects are Type A.

These contradictory findings have led theorists to suggest that the Type A behavior pattern may be too complex to be a good predictor of CHD (J. J. Ray, 1991). Researchers dissected the Type A behavior pattern looking for specific behaviors that are related to CHD (Julkunen, Idanpaan-Heikkila, & Saarinen, 1993; Siegman & Smith, 1993). They found that it is not Type A behavior in general that predicts CHD but general tendencies such as hostility, cynicism, and anger. Hostile, angry people may be more "reactive" to stress than the placid Type Bs. When frustrated or angry, their blood pressure and heart rate increase faster and take longer to return to normal (Jorgensen et al., 1996; Lyness, 1993).

For obvious reasons, it is impossible to test the relationship between behavior and heart disease experimentally. Researchers cannot randomly assign people to hostile and nonhostile groups and then follow them up to see if they develop CHD. They can, however, do the next best thing; they can try to change people's behavior. Specifically, if hostility, cynicism, and anger predispose people to CHD, then changing these behaviors should reduce the risk. Some evidence has been found for this hypothesis. Reducing hostility, anger, and cynicism by stress management, relaxation, and cognitive therapy seems to reduce the likelihood of CHD (Brannon & Feist, 1992, V. A. Price, 1988; R. Williams, 1989). Thus, it does appear that some aspects of Type A behavior may be a risk factor for CHD, at least for some people (Thoreson & Powell, 1992).

applied for a prolonged period, causes the spring to break. In Selye's GAS model, stress in humans works the same way. We can cope with moderate levels of stress, but extreme stress causes us to break down and become ill (Jiang et al., 1996). Selye's view of the GAS is depicted in Figure 5.5.

Over the years, the boundaries of what constitutes a stressor have been gradually extended. Stressors have come to include not only physical threats, but also emotional experiences (divorce, for example), unpleasant internal states (fatigue), and also the subjective feeling of being under pressure. With such a broad definition, practically anything can be a stressor. Job loss, examinations, missing a train, sleeplessness, crowding, noise, loneliness, even going on vacation or winning the lottery can be sources of stress. Superficially, these stressors

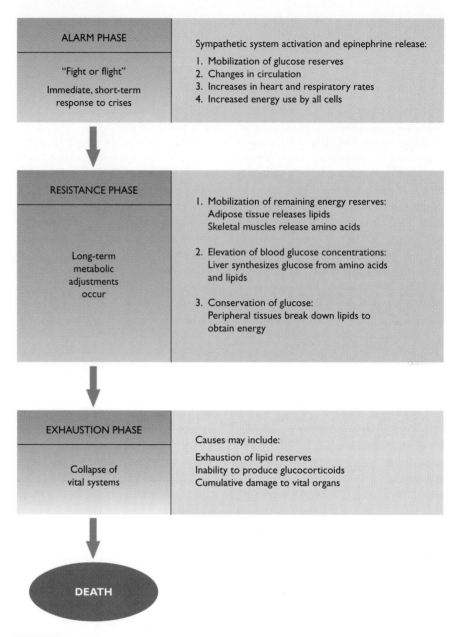

FIGURE 5.5 **Selye's General Adaptation Syndrome (GAS).** From: Martini (1989, p. 494).

seem to have little in common. Some are social; others are physical. Some are unpleasant; others (winning the lottery) are everyone's dream. Yet all stressors are related in one very important way—they have the potential to trigger a strong emotion leading to a GAS.

Selye's theory was the opposite of Dunbar's and Alexander's. He believed that the effects of stress are nonspecific. The same physiological response leads to widely different conditions. To explain why people develop different illnesses in response to stress, Selye postulated that genetic weaknesses, inadequate diet, infec-

tions, and other individual differences mediate the effect of stress. The specific mechanisms by which stress interacts with these mediating factors to produce illness are discussed next.

SOURCES OF STRESS

To summarize the argument so far, stress and physical illness go together. This is true not just for traditional psychosomatic conditions such as peptic ulcer but for

In Japan, where extremely long hours and little time off is common, karoshi (death from overwork) is an officially recognized cause of death for those who worked 24 hours straight or 16 hours a day for 7 days before they had a sudden heart attack or stroke or committed suicide.

metabolic conditions such as diabetes as well. Stressful cognitive tasks (school examinations), life events (the junior prom), even everyday annoyances can adversely affect blood sugar levels (see B. May, 1991, and Wertlieb et al., 1990, for reviews). Although the magnitude of the effect varies depending on the individual (Delameter et al., 1987), most clinicians agree that stress can exacerbate diabetes. This section describes some common sources of stress and uses diabetes to show how stress affects physical health.

Psychosocial Development

The transition from one developmental stage to another usually requires increasing autonomy and independence. For those who are unprepared (because of illness or for some other reason) **transitional stress** can be quite severe (Cairns et al., 1991; Shantz & Hartup, 1992). Take William Cole, for example. He first learned he had diabetes at age 13. This is not atypical; many cases of diabetes are first diagnosed in early adolescence. Adolescence is also a time when young people strive for independence and autonomy. It is a time when social relations are particularly important. An adolescent's self-esteem depends on peer acceptance, which in turn depends, to some degree, on conformity with local norms (Rathus & Nevid, 1992). The last thing William wanted was to be different from his friends. This is probably

why (as Dr. Berg notes in his report) William first denied that he was sick. He resisted treatment, continued to play sports, and tried to maintain the illusion that all was well so that he could remain "one of the guys."

William says that he eventually "accepted" his illness. He had little choice; he could not ignore his fatigue and thirst forever. However, William's acceptance of his illness came at a price. Learning that he had a chronic and incurable disease was a blow to his autonomy (he became dependent on his mother and his doctors for extra help and care), to his self-esteem (he was not able to participate in some activities), and to his feelings of efficacy (he did not feel in control of events; he felt powerless to prevent bad things from happening to him). His daily life and his future were suddenly restricted. Certain careers were no longer possible (William was unable to achieve his ambition to be an airline pilot, for example). Some activities became too dangerous. William withdrew from his friends and his external activities and became a loner. Even after entering the university, his low self-esteem made him hide his condition from other students.

Cultural Conflict

African Americans, Latinos, immigrants, and Native Americans all face some degree of pressure to assimilate into the White community. Yet members of these groups may be restricted by prejudice from full participation in economic and social life. Prejudice, itself, can lead to low self-esteem, which can be partly counteracted by the development of positive racial and ethnic identities. However, the stronger a person's racial and ethnic identity, the less likely the person is to assimilate into the White culture. This conflict—between assimilating or maintaining one's ethnic or racial identity—is the source of what L. P. Anderson (1991) called **acculturative stress** (see also Berry & Fons, 1994, and Pawliuk et al., 1996). William Cole felt the effects of such stress. He lived apart from his family and was one of only a few African American students at his college. College was a new world, and William may have found the acculturation stressful.

Catastrophes

When asked to imagine the psychological and social causes of stress, most people immediately think of large-scale cataclysmic events: floods, earthquakes, airplane accidents. A cataclysmic event is dreaded more than a common disease that affects one person at a time, even when the common disease kills more people. For example, fires and floods frighten people more than diabetes, even though diabetes kills far more people each year than fires and floods combined (S. Schwartz & Griffin, 1986). This excessive fear of horrific events seems to have deleterious effects on health. For example, in the months following the eruption of the Mount Saint Helens volcano in 1980, the number of emergency room visits increased by more than 30% compared with the number of visits before the eruption (P. R. Adams & Adams, 1984). Assuming that this is not a normal seasonal variation, it suggests that the eruption had a deleterious effect on the health of the local population. One possibility is that the eruption frightened people sufficiently to lower the functioning of their immune systems. This also seems to be what happened to people who lived near the Three Mile Island nuclear power plant at the time of the 1979 accident there (McKinnon et al., 1989).

One reason for the extreme stress produced by cataclysmic events is their unpredictability. Most of us go through life with optimistic attitudes. We act as if disasters only happen to others. When we are asked about the probability of having a car accident, going bankrupt, or dying young, most of us rate our luck as better than average (S. Schwartz & Griffin, 1986). We seem to share an illusion of invulnerability ("Bad things won't happen to me"). Catastrophes shatter this protective illusion; they show us how tenuous our good luck really is. This is

Catastrophes, such as Hurricane Andrew in Florida, shatter people's illusion of invulnerability and can lead to a deterioration in health in the months following the event.

why catastrophes frighten us more than more common killers such as diabetes. It is also why horrific experiences that threaten people's lives may produce symptoms long after the original event (see the discussion of post-traumatic stress disorder in Chapter 4).

Important Life Events

Major calamities can produce serious effects on health, but most stressors are more mundane—job loss, bereavement, divorce. These can lead to what the *DSM-IV* calls **adjustment disorders,** psychological disorders marked by anxiety, depression, withdrawal, and overall impairments in psychological functioning. These common life events also have the power to make people physically ill, or worse. A study of 96,000 Finnish widows and widowers, for example, found a doubled risk of death among survivors in the week immediately following their partner's death (Kaprio, Koskenvuy, & Rita, 1987). When bereavement is combined with other life changes, such as job loss, the risk of death is even greater.

One of the first researchers to study the relationship between life events and illness in a systematic way was the psychiatrist Adolf Meyer (1886–1950). An early adherent of Freud, Meyer broke with mainstream psychoanalysis when he left Europe for Baltimore's Johns Hopkins University in the early 1900s. To study the effects of stress, Meyer devised the "life-chart" technique. He would draw a time line (a graph of dates) with a person's illnesses on one side and significant life events on the other. Meyer claimed that illnesses often appeared just after significant life changes (especially job loss and separation).

Over the years, considerable evidence has been amassed to support Meyer's claim. For example, long-term unemployment has been found to be related to various illnesses, including heart disease, cirrhosis of the liver (probably from overuse of alcohol), hypertension, various psychiatric conditions, and suicide (M. H. Brenner, 1973; Pritchard, 1992). Unemployment not only reduces self-esteem and makes people dependent on others, it also produces poverty, which itself affects health (N. Adler et al., 1994; Carroll, Smith, & Bennett, 1994).

Separation, at any age, has also been related to illness. Divorced mothers, forced to work to make ends meet while coping with family pressures, are particularly vulnerable to illness (Waldrow, 1991). Studies of children separated from their parents, for example, have found prolonged separation to produce a range of disorders including depression (S. Schwartz & Johnson, 1985). Divorced men and women are more likely to visit doctors, drink excessively, and be admitted to mental hospitals than married people. The potentially fatal effects on the surviving partner of separation through death have already been mentioned.

Meyer's work influenced Thomas Holmes, a medical doctor who became interested in the relationship between life events and illness (Holmes & Rahe, 1967). Holmes routinely asked patients about their personal experiences before they had become ill. Like Meyer, he found a relationship between life changes and illness. By studying medical charts, Holmes produced a list of life events that seemed most often to precede illness. Some of these events were clearly unpleasant (divorce, separation), but others were positive (outstanding personal achievement). Holmes assumed that any life change, positive or negative, could produce stress if it required an adjustment in the way a person had previously lived.

Because marriage appeared to be a life event requiring adjustment for most people, it was assigned an arbitrary value of 500. Holmes then asked 400 adults to rate the remaining events relative to marriage (Does this event require more or less "readjustment" than marriage?). Raters assigned points to each event depending on the readjustment it required, ignoring whether the event was good or bad (Holmes & Rahe, 1967). Holmes called these ratings "life-change units." He and his coworkers transformed them into a scale that ranged from 0 to 100. The result was the Social Readjustment Rating Scale. This scale has since been revised and is called the Life Changes Scale (Miller & Rahe, 1997).

In addition to the assumed equivalence of positive and negative events, the Life Changes Scale also assumes that the effect of different stressors is cumulative. That is, the total amount of stress a person is experiencing is equal to the sum of the effects of the individual stressors. Thus, a person who begins college gets a score of 38 life-change units. A person who begins college *and* moves to a new residence gets a score of 63 or 85, depending on whether the person moves within the same city or to a different city. Holmes and his coworkers claimed that people with scores of 250–500 during the past year have a moderately increased chance of becoming physically ill or having a preexisting illness become worse. A score greater than 500 indicates a major crisis. People with this level of life-stress have a strong chance of becoming ill (Miller & Rahe, 1997). Table 5.1 depicts the Life Changes Scale completed by William Cole as part of his psychological evaluation.

The bold items in Table 5.1 are those that William Cole said were relevant to his life over the past year. William's score of 300 is known to be sufficient to exacerbate diabetes (Maes, Leventhal, & de Ridder, 1996). Following Holmes, scientists have repeatedly demonstrated a role for stressful life events in various physical and mental illnesses (Adams et al., 1994; Crandall, Preisler, & Aussprung, 1992; Monroe et al., 1996). Despite these findings, the relationship between life-stress and illness should be interpreted with caution. Most of the correlations are weak (Brannon & Feist, 1992). Moreover, as we have frequently seen, even strong correlations cannot be taken as evidence that life-stress causes illness. They could just as easily mean that illness causes life-stress. See Critical Thinking About Clinical Decisions 5.2 (pp. 210–211) for a discussion of some of the difficulties in interpreting life-stress research.

Everyday Hassles

William Cole's average day is full of hassles. Each morning, he must check to see that he has a sufficient supply of insulin and syringes. Twice each day, he has to measure out his insulin, prepare the skin around the injection site, and administer the injection. At other times during each day, he must test his blood sugar level. William has to keep a written record of his medication and adjust it according to the results of his blood tests and changes in his diet or activity level. Meals and snacks are another hassle. William must watch his diet carefully and eat only at specified times. Add doctor

TABLE 5.1 Life Changes Scale (bold items are those endorsed by William Cole)

Life Event	Points	Life Event	Points
Health		Change in arguments with spouse	50
An injury or illness that:		In-law problems	38
kept you in bed a week or more,		Change in marital status of your	
or **sent you to the hospital**	**74**	parents:	
was less serious than that	44	divorce	59
Major dental work	26	remarriage	50
Major change in eating habits	**27**	Separation from spouse:	
Major change in sleeping habits	**26**	due to work	53
Major change in your usual type or		due to marital problems	76
amount of recreation	28	Divorce	96
		Birth of grandchild	43
Work		Death of spouse	119
Change to a new type of work	51	Death of other family member:	
Change in your work hours or conditions	35	child	123
Change in your responsibilities at work:		brother or sister	102
more responsibilities	29	parent	100
fewer responsibilities	21		
promotion	31	*Personal and Social*	
demotion	42	Change in personal habits	26
transfer	32	**Beginning or ending school**	
Troubles at work:		**or college**	**38**
with your boss	29	Change of school or college	35
with coworkers	35	Change of political beliefs	24
with persons under your supervision	35	Change in religious beliefs	29
other work troubles	28	**Change in social activities**	**27**
Major business adjustment	60	Vacation trip	24
Retirement	52	New, close, personal relationship	37
Loss of job:		Engagement to marry	45
laid off from work	68	Girlfriend or boyfriend problems	39
fired from work	79	Sexual difficulties	44
Correspondence course to help you		"Falling out" of a close personal	
in your work	18	relationship	47
		An accident	48
Home and Family		Minor violation of the law	20
Major change in living conditions	42	Being held in jail	75
Change in residence:		Death of a close friend	70
move within the same town or city	25	Major decision about your immediate	
move to a different town, city,		future	51
or state	**47**	**Major personal achievement**	**36**
Change in family get-togethers	**25**		
Major change in health or behavior of		*Financial*	
family member	55	Major change in finances:	
Marriage	50	increased income	38
Pregnancy	67	decreased income	60
Miscarriage or abortion	65	investment or credit difficulties	56
Gain of a new family member:		Loss or damage of personal property	43
birth of a child	66	Moderate purchase	20
adoption of a child	65	Major purchase	37
a relative moving in with you	59	Foreclosure on a mortgage or loan	58
Spouse beginning or ending work	46		
Child leaving home:		William's total score:	300
to attend college	41		
due to marriage	41		
for other reasons	45		

Note: From Miller & Rahe (1997).

TABLE 5.2   Ten Most Frequently Endorsed Hassles and Uplifts

Hassles	Percent endorsing	Uplifts	Percent endorsing
Concerns about weight	52	Relating well with your spouse or lover	76
Health of a family member	48	Relating well with your friends	74
Rising prices of common goods	44	Completing a task	73
Home maintenance	43	Feeling healthy	73
Too many things to do	39	Getting enough sleep	70
Misplacing or losing things	38	Eating out	68
Yard work or outside home maintenance	38	Meeting your responsibilities	68
Property, investment, or taxes	38	Visiting, phoning, or writing someone	68
Crime	37	Spending time with family	67
Physical appearance	36	Home (inside) pleasing to you	66

Note: Adapted from Kanner et al. (1981).

visits and the occasional complication, and you can understand why William sometimes gets fed up.

To a lesser degree, daily annoyances plague all of us: time spent in rush-hour traffic or waiting at the bank, noisy neighbors, getting caught in the rain or snow, losing our keys. If we are lucky, we also have positive experiences: visiting with friends, performing well at school or at work, dining out. The Hassles Scale and the Uplifts Scale were designed to measure everyday irritations, or hassles, and positive events, or uplifts (Kanner et al., 1981). The Hassles Scale consists of 117 irritations and annoyances. Respondents indicate which of these occurred during the past month and then rate the severity of each one on a 3-point scale (the higher the score, the greater the stress). These ratings are important. Unlike the Life Changes Scale, which considers a life event to have the same impact on everyone who experiences it, the Hassles Scale explicitly acknowledges that people respond differently to the same event. The Uplifts Scale parallels the Hassles Scale but in the opposite direction. Respondents rate how good each uplift makes them feel. The test constructors believed that uplifts have the power to counteract hassles. Thus, a person's total stress is the difference between his or her scores on the Hassles and the Uplifts scales. Examples of the 10 most frequently occurring hassles and uplifts (as reported by a group of 100 middle-aged people) are contained in Table 5.2. Note that uplifts have higher scores than hassles. For this group, at least, everyday life is more positive than negative.

Daily hassles seem trivial when compared with some of the life events contained in the Life Changes Scale. Nevertheless, they can take their toll. For example, busy urban white-collar workers, who are exposed to many more daily annoyances than their rural counterparts, are considerably more likely to suffer from headaches, peptic ulcers, and hypertension. The inflammation that causes so much pain to arthritis sufferers is exacerbated by daily hassles (Thomason et al., 1992). Pregnant women whose lives are full of hassles are more likely to have premature and low-birth-weight babies than are women with more relaxed personal lives (Pritchard & Teo, 1994). Studies of those with diabetes have shown a correlation between the perceived severity of daily hassles and blood sugar levels (Wertlieb et al., 1990).

Across people and conditions, the Hassles Scale has been found to be a better predictor of psychological well-being than scales that measure major life events (Fernandez & Sheffield, 1995; Harran & Ziegler, 1991). The relationship between daily annoyances and health has also been demonstrated using other measures (Kohn & Macdonald, 1992). Interestingly, Uplifts Scale scores have not been found to add much predictive power (Gruen, Folkman, & Lazarus, 1988).

Chronic Illness

So far, stress has been viewed as a response to external life events and hassles. However, a chronic illness such as diabetes may, itself, be a significant source of stress (Maes et al., 1996; B. May, 1991). For example, in addition to the daily hassles William's diabetes engendered, his hospitalization during the examination period made it hard for him to study. In other words, William's illness added an extra stressor to the usual examination jitters. For those with diabetes, such as William, frequent absences from class or work and concern about future diabetes-related medical conditions are facts of life.

Interpreting Life-Stress Research

Although their results are intriguing, studies linking life-stress to health illustrate the dilemmas involved in conducting research in health psychology (Justice, 1994). Specifically, life-stress studies are subject to at least seven difficulties in interpretation:

1. Life-stress research is typically retrospective. Subjects are required to recall the events of the past 6 months, year, or in some cases, 2 years. This is not always easy for people to do (Raphael, Cloitre, & Dohrenwend, 1991). People who are sick and seeking an explanation for their illness may recall more stressful life events than healthy people, who have no particular reason to dwell in the past. Some people may have poor memories. In either case, relying on memory reduces the reliability of life-stress scales (Raphael et al., 1991). Because low-reliability measures, by definition, also have low validity (see Chapter 3), life-stress scales may not be valid measures of stress. The best way to eliminate the problem of selective recall is to conduct prospective studies in which people who experience life-stress are followed over time to see whether they become ill. Unfortunately, such prospective studies are rare.

2. The Life Changes Scale includes items that may, themselves, be signs of illness. For example, changes in eating or sleeping habits are as likely to be the *result* of illness as the *cause* of it.

3. The Life Changes Scale assumes that everyone agrees on the definition of the various events. However, people may disagree on what constitutes a "minor violation of the law" or "an injury or illness" (S. Schwartz, Richardson, & Glasziou, 1993; Wright, 1990).

4. Individuals may appraise life changes in very different ways. A person with specific retirement plans and the means to achieve them may look forward to leaving work. Another person, whose identity is intimately wrapped up in work, may dread the very prospect of retirement. The Life Changes Scale ignores these individual differences and assigns both people the same number of life-change

Many researchers doubt that positive and negative life events are equally likely to produce illness, and they question the Life Changes Scale. One group of researchers developed the Hassles Scale and the Uplifts Scale to reflect the difference.

William often feels frustrated because he cannot do everything he wishes. He wants to play sports, but he also wants to stay healthy and please his mother. Frustration and conflict are, themselves, significant sources of stress.

Chronic Pain and Headaches

Although pain is not itself an illness, it has the capacity to affect every aspect of our lives. The acute pain that accompanies a toothache or an illness or injury can keep us from thinking about anything else. Severe pain can affect immune system functioning (Page et al., 1993). Fortunately, healing usually ensures that acute pain will subside over time. In contrast, chronic pain persists indefinitely. People who suffer from the chronic joint pain of rheumatoid arthritis, repeated headaches, lower-back

pain, or the pain caused by the growth of tumors can look forward only to continued pain in the future. Often, this type of pain leads to depression (Banks & Kerns, 1996). About 65 million Americans are estimated to suffer from some form of chronic pain (S. Taylor, 1991). They are responsible for a large portion of the $100 billion that Americans spend on pain-relieving medications each year (S. Taylor, 1991).

Although chronic pain often has a physiological trigger, it may be exacerbated by stress. In severe cases, chronic pain may even be considered a psychological disorder. For example, the *DSM-IV* contains the diagnosis "pain disorder." The diagnostic criteria for this disorder include severe pain that is not feigned and that causes distress or an impairment in social, occupational, or other areas of functioning. Most important, the diag-

units, thereby lowering its predictive validity.

5. Social and ethnic groups may differ in their appraisals of life events (Dasen et al., 1988; Radley, 1993). Recall that in Maslow's hierarchy of needs (Chapter 2), social needs do not become important until basic needs are met. Thus, those of lower socio-economic status find financial misfortune (especially job loss) more stressful than do those of higher socio-economic status, who are more concerned about disruptions to personal relationships. Cultural differences also color how life events are perceived. The Japanese, for example, find minor violations of the law more stressful than do Westerners; older adults find sexual difficulties less stressful than younger people do (Masuda & Holmes, 1967). Researchers have tried to overcome cultural differences by validating life-change assessment measures on samples drawn from many sections of society (Dohrenwend et al., 1982). However, the validity of these scales may be short-lived. As cultures change and adapt, perceptions of stressors change as well (Dasen et al., 1988).

6. Life-stress researchers assume that both good and bad events produce illness. Yet there is little research to substantiate this assumption. For most people, winning a lottery is a much easier life change to deal with than withstanding a financial loss. A related problem is the weights assigned to different stressors (Birnbaum, 1992). Is "death of spouse" really more than twice as stressful as "marriage"? And is a "change in personal habits" really half as stressful as "marriage"? Does everyone weight events the same way? Most researchers believe that only unpleasant life changes (or at least those that are appraised as negative) cause stress and illness (Perkins, 1982). It might therefore be necessary to assign stressors to positive and negative categories so that their individual (and interactive) effects on health can be studied (Wheatley, 1990).

7. Life-stress studies are correlational. At best they may show that life-stress and illness are correlated, but they can never show that stress directly causes illness. It is always possible that some third factor is involved. For example, instead of affecting physical health directly, job loss and bereavement may cause people to turn to alcohol for solace. Excessive drinking may then cause illness. The various mechanisms (both direct and indirect) by which stress causes illness are discussed later in this chapter.

nosis requires that psychological factors (especially stress) play an important role in the onset, severity, exacerbation, or maintenance of the pain. The validity of the diagnosis of pain disorder is a controversial subject. Some authors have claimed that it is too inclusive and may lead to overdiagnosis (Fishbain, 1996). All agree, however, that pain is made worse by stress.

We also know that individuals may react very differently to the same level of pain: Some may continue work and social activities; others may drop out of life completely (M. P. Jensen et al., 1991). Those who cope well are optimistic, have good support networks, and feel in control of their lives (Gil et al., 1990; Lackner, Carosella, & Feuerstein, 1996). As will be shown later in this chapter, these characteristics also describe people who are resistant to stress.

William Cole complained of one of the most common forms of chronic pain, headaches. More than half the population—and perhaps as many as 80% of people—experience headaches each year (P. R. Martin, 1993). Over the years, complicated classification systems have been developed to characterize different types of headaches, but the two most common are tension and migraine. Tension headaches were traditionally thought to result from tense muscles in the neck and head, whereas migraine is thought to be caused by the contraction and dilation of blood vessels in the head. Migraines are more severe than tension headaches, often requiring a day or more to resolve. However, some research suggests that the differences between the two types of headaches are not so clear-cut; both types of headaches seem to be associated with the same physiological

Chronic pain, such as that caused by arthritis, is worsened by stress and can lead to depression. However, people who are optimistic, have a good support network, and feel in control of their lives are likely to react less negatively to chronic pain.

phenomena (P. R. Martin, Marie, & Nathan, 1992). It is possible that migraines and tension headaches have similar etiologies but that migraines represent a more severe form of headache.

Psychological variables moderate pain in two ways: through inhibition of pain impulses and by the production of chemicals called endogenous opioids. In its simplest form, psychological inhibition can be construed as shutting the "gate" that allows pain stimuli to be transmitted to the brain (Melzack & Wall, 1982). According to the gate control theory, pain stimuli are transmitted to the brain via the dorsal horns of the spinal column, which serve as a kind of gate. Pain stimuli open the gate, but inhibitory signals sent by the brain can close the gate and keep pain stimuli from reaching the brain. This seems to be what happens when soldiers are injured in battle; some do not feel any pain until after the battle is over (Melzack & Wall, 1982).

Endogenous opioids are chemicals produced by the body which, like opiates (heroin, for instance), can serve to reduce pain. There is some evidence that people who cope well with their pain produce higher levels of endogenous opioids than those who fail to cope (Bandura et al., 1987). It seems possible that, in addition to the endogenous opioids, males and females may also have specialized chemical pain-reduction systems (Mogil et al., 1993).

EFFECTS OF STRESS

To understand the complex web of interactions between external stressors and the stress produced by chronic illness, we need to take a closer look at the precise mecha-

nisms by which stress exerts its effects on physical and psychological health. Specifically, we shall examine two ways in which stress affects health: (a) the direct effects of stress on physiological functioning and (b) the indirect effects of stress on health-relevant behaviors.

Direct Physiological Effects of Stress

As we have seen in the discussion of the general adaptation syndrome, stress has direct effects on physiological functioning. It causes the release of certain hormones, increases the rate of blood clotting, raises respiration and blood pressure, and prepares the body for exertion. To mobilize the body's defenses, the GAS requires considerable energy. To obtain this energy, blood sugar levels are increased. Once the stressor is removed, blood sugar levels return to normal in those without diabetes. Among those with diabetes, however, blood sugar levels remain high (because there is insufficient insulin to reduce them). The resulting excess of blood sugar produces fatigue, irritability, and dehydration. In severe cases, diabetics may lose consciousness or even die. It is possible that the life-stress of starting college combined with the daily hassles William faced may have produced frequent emergency responses. These may have raised his blood sugar to the dangerous level that put him in the hospital.

The direct effects of stress on physiological functioning have also been implicated in cardiac arrests (heart attacks) and strokes (blood clots that destroy brain tissue). According to Sapolsky (1992, 1993) the corticosteroid hormones produced by the GAS have both beneficial and harmful effects. They reduce inflammation and inhibit pain, but they may also weaken neurons, especially in the hippocampus. In the short term, the body produces special proteins to protect neurons and other cells from hormone damage, but their effectiveness weakens with prolonged or repeated stress (Marcuccilli & Miller, 1994). Once the hippocampus has been weakened, it can no longer play its moderating role, and the stress response becomes difficult to "turn off."

Stress and the Immune System (Psychoneuroimmunology) Of all the ways in which stress directly affects physiological functioning, the most often cited, and certainly the most frequently investigated, is the effect of stress on the body's immune system. In recent years, **psychoneuroimmunology**—the study of the interactions among behavior, neurological and endocrine function, and the immune process—has become a lively field of multidisciplinary research (Cacioppo, 1994; Maier, Watkins, & Fleshner, 1994; Schmoll, Tewes, & Plotnikoff, 1992).

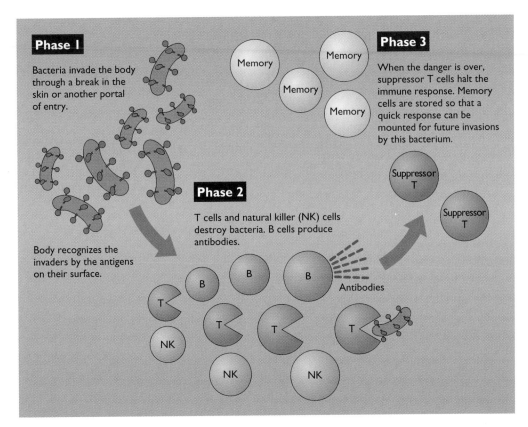

FIGURE 5.6 Immune Responses. *In antibody defenses, B cells multiply in response to specific antigens; some of the B cells become plasma cells, which secrete antibodies that destroy the antigens. In cellular defenses, killer T cells use lymphokine to attack the remains of specific antigens. Memory T and B cells recognize antigens from previous infections.*

The main organ of the body's immune system is the lymphatic system, a circulatory system that roughly parallels the one for distributing blood. The fluid that flows through the lymphatic ducts gets its name from the lymphocytes, or white blood cells, it contains. There are several types of lymphocytes; the best understood are the T cells, B cells, and natural killer (NK) cells. Lymphocytes are produced in the bone marrow, but they mature in various organs, including the spleen. Foreign invaders, such as bacteria, that make it past the body's first line of defense—the skin and mucous membranes—are attacked directly by T cells, which attempt to kill the invaders. Foreign substances known as **antigens** may also provoke the B cells to mount an indirect defense by secreting antibodies that bind with the invaders and mark them for later destruction. In addition to the body's mounting this primary immune response aimed at repelling invaders, some cells are held in reserve to be reactivated should the invader reappear. With repeated exposure, the supply of such "memory" lymphocytes can grow quite large and powerful. When their numbers are sufficient to prevent future infection,

the person is said to have acquired immunity to the invader. Vaccinations confer immunity by provoking the formation of memory lymphocytes under controlled conditions (Roitt, 1994). Figure 5.6 illustrates both antibody and cellular immune responses.

The term *psychoneuroimmunology* first appeared in the 1960s, but the field did not develop rapidly until Ader and Cohen (1975) showed that the immune system is subject to psychological control (see also S. Cohen, Tyrell, & Smith, 1993). Their procedure involved classical conditioning. The unconditioned stimulus (UCS) was a drug that suppressed the immune system (the unconditioned response). The conditioned stimulus (CS) was a saccharine and water solution. Laboratory rats were given the CS to drink, followed by an injection of the drug. After conditioning, the CS alone was enough to suppress the immune system—the immune system produced fewer lymphocytes than would normally be expected.

In the decades following this seminal study, more than 1,000 articles and books on psychoneuroimmunology have been published (see Ader & Cohen, 1993; S. Cohen & Williamson, 1991; Leonard & Song, 1996;

O'Leary, 1990; and Plotnikoff et al., 1991, for reviews). This vast literature repeatedly demonstrates that conditioning can affect the functioning of the immune system in both humans and animals and that life events, psychopathology, and daily hassles can reduce both the number and effectiveness of immune system cells (Coe et al., 1987; Schleifer et al., 1996). The mechanisms by which stress affects immunity are also becoming more clear (Ader & Cohen, 1993). We know, for example, that the corticosteroids and endorphins (natural pain reducers) produced during the GAS appear to decrease the effectiveness of natural killer cells (Van Ierssel et al., 1997).

Stress, Immune Response, and HIV Despite these important findings, not all of the crucial links in the chain connecting psychological stress, immune system activity, and illness have been forged. The logic underlying research in psychoneuroimmunology goes as follows: Stress impairs immune function, which, in turn, affects health. Ideally, therefore, research studies should include all three components: stress, measures of immune system functioning, and measures of health. In practice, however, most studies have concentrated on the effects of stress on immune functioning or the effects of stress on health (Figure 5.7). Studies showing that stress affects health by compromising the immune system are rare (Ader & Cohen, 1993). Moreover, those studies that are available provide an ambiguous picture of the relationship between stress and health. As an example, let us look at the work on HIV, the virus linked to AIDS.

Rabkin and her coworkers (1991) followed more than 100 men suffering from HIV. They found no relationship between life-stress, immune functioning, and illness in this group. A similar negative finding was reported by Perry and his colleagues (1992). In these studies, psychosocial factors seemed to have no clinically significant effect on the immune system (M. Stein, Miller, & Trestman, 1991). Taking another tack, some investigators have reported that exercise and stress management improve immune system functioning in HIV-positive men (Antoni et al., 1991). However, other investigators find the effects of stress management to be inconsistent (Van Rood et al., 1993). To confuse matters further, Kemeny and his colleagues (1994) found no relationship between stress produced by repeated bereavement (watching one's friends die of AIDS) and immune functioning among HIV-positive men. Clearly, considerable work remains to be done to explicate the precise links between stress, immune function, and illness.

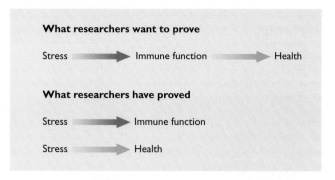

FIGURE 5.7 **Results of Research Into Links Between Stress and Health.** *Researchers still have not shown that stress produces the symptoms of illness even though it affects the immune system's functioning.*

Indirect Effects of Stress on Health

In addition to its direct physiological effects, stress can affect health indirectly by interfering with health-relevant behaviors. Consider William Cole, for example. To function well, William must adhere as closely as possible to a prescribed management regime. He must give himself the right amount of insulin at the correct time; he must eat the right foods (in the correct quantities) at the right time. He must monitor his blood sugar level by regularly testing his blood, and, if he finds something amiss, he must make the correct adjustments. Adhering to this regime requires memory skills (to remember the necessary actions), judgment skills (to figure out what to do if adjustments are required), and the motivation to take the necessary steps. To the extent that stress interferes with memory, judgment, or motivation, William's health will be affected.

Effects of Stress on Cognition Stress exerts profound effects on memory, judgment, and other aspects of cognition (Broadbent, Baddeley, & Reason, 1990; Burchfield, 1985; Christianson, 1992; Hockey, 1983). Studies of airline pilots, for example, have shown that as they become increasingly stressed, they become less alert. They have attentional lapses and become easily distracted. More important, highly stressed pilots are slow to make corrective adjustments, even when their instruments indicate such adjustments are necessary (Holding, 1983). In a similar manner, it is possible that stress was responsible for William's failure to take corrective action to adjust his blood sugar.

The effects of stress are insidious because they are not immediately apparent to the individual concerned.

Even when they were slow to respond to their instrument readings, pilots believed they were as efficient as they were when not under stress. In the same way, William may not have been aware that his judgment had been affected.

To make judgments about his condition and to choose the appropriate corrective actions, William must "process" information from a variety of sources. However, stress tends to affect information-processing capacity in complex ways (Christianson, 1992; Kozielecki, 1981). Stress does not always lead to poor decision making. As noted in Chapter 4, moderate amounts of anxiety (such as that produced by an upcoming performance, for example) may actually serve to focus attention on essential information. However, high levels of stress can shrink information-processing capacity to the point where important information is ignored. Studies of airline pilots have found them more likely to read their instruments incorrectly when flying in bad weather. Presumably, this is because coping with a storm produces stress (Broadbent, 1973). More dramatically, in the midst of a tense situation, the captain of the USS *Vincennes* ordered the shooting down of an Iranian passenger plane mistakenly identified as an attacking F-14 fighter. A subsequent inquiry showed that important information about the plane's flight path (it was ascending rather than descending, as would be expected of a fighter) was incorrectly processed (Bales, 1988).

Not only could stress have affected William's ability to process information, it may also have produced a tendency to cut corners and take chances. Stressed drivers, for example, have been found to engage in riskier maneuvers (dangerous passing, for instance) than relaxed drivers (Holding, 1983). Under stress, William might have been tempted to indulge in risky foods that he would have had no trouble resisting when he was not under stress.

Effects of Stress on Motivation   When under stress, those with diabetes may forget to check their blood or even to administer necessary injections. As we have seen, part of the reason is cognitive: Stress affects judgment. However, another part of the reason is motivational. Diabetics may eat the wrong foods or skip an injection when they are irritated, annoyed, lonely, or frustrated (B. May, 1991). In some cases, they may be punishing themselves; in others, they may be making a veiled cry for attention and help. It is possible that William's poor management of his diabetes may have been an unconscious call for help because of his loneliness and the difficulties he was having in adjusting to the college environment.

The Stress–Illness Cycle

As already noted, illness can be a source of stress. It can interfere with cognitive and emotional functioning and exacerbate the effect of external stressors. For example, poorly controlled blood sugar led to William's hospitalization. Being in the hospital kept him from completing his examinations. Missing exams meant he was behind his class. Worrying about making up his exams added to his burden of stress, which just made him sicker.

Illness can also produce stress through its effects on social functioning. Because of the effect on his blood sugar, William withdrew from active sports. Because he could not drink beer, he stopped going out with his friends. At college, he was a loner with a poor self-image. As a consequence, he lacked a social support network to help him deal with the stresses and strains of college life. Some illnesses produce stress because they are perceived as a sign of weakness. For example, people with liver disease resulting from the overuse of alcohol and people with AIDS resulting from intravenous drug use are often stigmatized and shunned because their illness is perceived as self-inflicted (Weiner, 1993).

Clinical psychologists working with people like William need to be sensitive to the many ways in which physical, social, and psychological factors interact. Recall that Dr. Berg administered the Sickness Impact Profile (Bergner et al., 1981) and the Norbeck Social Support Questionnaire (Norbeck, 1984) as part of his assessment of William because he knew that illness often leads to social withdrawal and that a lack of social support could amplify the stressful effects of William's illness.

Helping people like William requires that we somehow break the tendency for stress and illness to feed off one another (Figure 5.8). However, before we examine how this might be accomplished, we need first to examine why some people seem better able to withstand stress than others. Specifically, we need to understand differences in coping skills.

FACTORS THAT MODIFY THE EFFECTS OF STRESS

Coping means finding effective ways to adapt to the problems and difficulties presented by stress. For William, coping requires learning to implement the

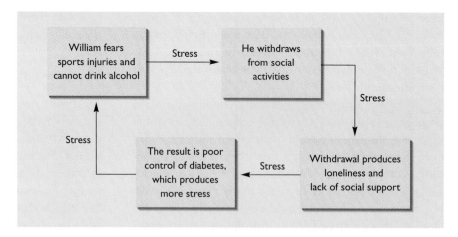

FIGURE 5.8 **The Reverberating Effects of Stress and Chronic Illness.** *The key to helping people with chronic illness and stress is to break the cycle.*

procedures necessary to control his blood sugar while, at the same time, adjusting to the social and psychological consequences of his chronic illness. In general, successful coping is marked by compliance with the treatment regime, by acceptance of the limitations and challenges of the illness, and by attempting to lead as "normal" a life as possible. Unsuccessful coping is evidenced by poor treatment compliance, shame, and social isolation. Clinical studies have found that successful coping is just as important a determinant of blood sugar control among those with diabetes as is life-stress (Spiess et al., 1994).

As a group, those with diabetes do not comply well with their prescribed treatment (B. May, 1991). Almost 80% administer insulin in an unhygienic manner, 75% test their blood sugar incorrectly, and more than half fail to adhere to their diets. Poor compliance is not surprising in chronic conditions, especially those in which the treatment regime is complicated. However, noncompliance also occurs when treatment is simple. For example, among women who have had breast cancer, fewer than half follow their doctors' recommendations for simple breast self-examinations (S. E. Taylor et al., 1984). Because compliance is essential to long-term health, considerable research has been devoted to clarifying why patients fail to comply with the recommended treatment. This research has identified several important factors (people comply better with clear instructions; warm doctor-patient relationships facilitate compliance), but the most important factor seems to be the way in which people appraise the stress produced by illness (S. M. Miller, Shoda, & Hurley, 1996). Some people deny being sick; others make a hobby out of it. Denial reduces compliance, whereas obsessive attention to one's health in-

creases compliance (but, as will be seen, at a price). In this section, we will see that treatment compliance depends on learning to cope with stress.

Appraisals

The effects of a stressor depend to a large extent on how the stressor is perceived. Thus, the first step in coping is to appraise the stress-producing situation (S. E. Taylor & Aspinwall, 1996). The appraisal of life events results in emotional, physiological, and behavioral responses that interact with one another in complex ways to determine how people cope with illness (Figure 5.9).

According to R. S. Lazarus (1993), whose theory was described in detail in Chapter 2, there are two types of appraisal: primary and secondary. In primary appraisal, the individual assesses the personal implications of an event. Events may be appraised as irrelevant, beneficial, or stress-inducing. Secondary appraisal is concerned with what, if anything, should be done. If an event is appraised as stress-inducing, the individual may then appraise the harm done (say, William decides to play a sport and dramatically lowers his sugar level) and decide how to prevent a future recurrence. If the harm has not yet been done (William has not yet played), appraisal may take the form of how to avoid or minimize harm (by eating something sweet, perhaps). Appraisals often include a comparison of costs and benefits (measuring blood sugar levels and eating sweets may take more time than simply playing and hoping for the best, but failure to assess his sugar levels may mean that he will have a bad reaction). Cognitive appraisals need not be so calculated or rational; they do not even have to be

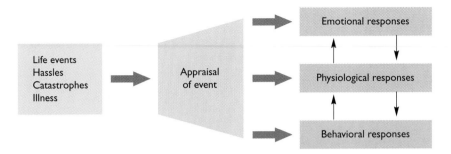

FIGURE 5.9 *The effects of life events depend on how they are appraised.*

conscious. However, at some level, our response to stress is always based on our personal *perception* of external events.

William at first tried to deny that he was really ill. (He was doomed to fail, of course, because his symptoms were too severe to ignore.) Denial is a primitive form of coping, but it can sometimes be useful. If an illness is untreatable, denying the facts may help the ill person make the most of what life remains. On the other hand, if a condition can be helped by a change in behavior, denial may make matters worse. Smokers who continue their habit after they are found to have heart disease endanger their health by denying the facts. A less extreme form of denial is to admit that one has an illness but to minimize its seriousness. Again, if treating life-threatening illnesses as minor annoyances allows a person to lead a fuller life than would otherwise be the case, a little denial is probably a good thing. However, if carried too far, denial can lead people to ignore the limitations imposed by illness—and possibly to take unwise health risks.

In contrast to those who minimize their illness, some people cope by becoming obsessed with their condition. They devote a lot of their energy to managing their disease. If their obsessiveness increases their quality of life, then it is a reasonable way of coping. On the other hand, if their extreme concern with their health causes other activities and relationships to suffer, then it is not a successful way of coping. Instead of controlling their illness, obsessive people may wind up achieving the opposite; they may find that their illness controls them. What is required is a happy medium between minimization and obsessive attention that provides a balance between controlling illness and not letting it take over one's life. Lazarus and his colleagues (Folkman & Lazarus, 1990; Lazarus, 1993) call denial and obsessiveness **emotion-focused coping.** The goal of emotion-focused coping is to manage feelings to make ourselves feel better (Pennebaker, 1993). **Problem-focused**

coping, on the other hand, involves making a plan of action and dealing directly with the stressor (Bhagat, Allie, & Ford, 1995). For example, when faced with a difficult final exam, emotion-based coping could take the form of avoiding thinking about the exam in order to reduce anxiety. In contrast, problem-focused coping would involve formulating a schedule for studying and a procedure for self-assessment.

It is important to know when to apply different types of coping. Relying on emotion-focused coping when problem-focused coping could result in a better outcome leads to sad results. However, problem-focused coping works only when a person has the ability to remedy the situation by taking some action. When events are not in a person's control, problem-focused coping may lead to frustration and more stress. When action is futile, it makes more sense to rely on emotion-focused coping.

Why do some people manage to cope successfully with their illness, whereas others never seem to be able to adjust? At least part of the answer lies in the coping resources available to the individual.

Social Support

Coping is not simply a matter for the person who is ill. It involves family members and friends as well. Some family members try to distance themselves from the ill relative (perhaps to avoid the pain of a loved one's suffering). Others derive enhanced self-esteem from helping the individual cope (Kovacs & Feinberg, 1982). Provided that it does not lead to overprotectiveness and dependency, the latter attitude is more helpful to someone attempting to come to grips with a chronic illness. Coping is a particular problem for children with diabetes, who may not have the cognitive or physical resources necessary to maintain the daily diabetic regime. For children, successful management often requires enlisting parents and siblings and making each responsible for some aspect of daily management (Wertlieb et al., 1990). Some families post schedules for blood sugar testing on the bathroom wall. Parents may wear wristwatch alarms to remind them to check their child's blood sugar or to administer insulin. Any activity that involves a change in routine—going to the movies, out to eat, or on a vacation—must be carefully planned by the entire family to ensure that the child eats regular meals, that blood sugar is monitored, and that medicines are administered when needed.

Given that all family members are affected by one member's chronic illness, it is not surprising that family conflict affects how well chronically ill people cope (Wertlieb et al., 1990). People with diabetes who live in harmonious families seem to have better control of their blood sugar than do those who live in distressed or unhappy families. It should be noted, however, that some studies have failed to find a strong relationship between family harmony and diabetic control (Gowers et al., 1995; Kovacs et al., 1989). One possible reason for the discrepant results is the reliance on self-report. Members of dysfunctional families may be reluctant to admit that disharmony exists. To get around self-censorship, Gustafsson (1987) observed families containing children with diabetes while the families were engaged in active decision making (planning a meal, furnishing a home). Conflicts during decision making were found to be related to poor control of blood sugar up to 5 years after the initial observations. This finding, which is not contaminated by self-report, suggests that family harmony and coping are related.

Although families are the most important source of social support for children, for adolescents and young adults, their peers are. Adolescents with diabetes who have close and supportive friends have better control of their illness than do those who are socially isolated (Wertlieb et al., 1990). To be effective, however, social support must be consonant with a person's stage of development. For example, daily questioning ("Have you had your insulin this morning?") improves treatment compliance in young children but actually makes it worse in adolescents, who resent this intrusion on their autonomy and independence (Wertlieb at al., 1990).

Social support contributes to health in several ways. First, by providing acceptance, social ties may help maintain self-esteem. Second, friends provide help in times of trouble and sympathetic ears for the expression of painful feelings. Third, members of self-help groups, such as the group for those with diabetes to which William was referred, are important sources of new information about the disease and its control (see Coyne &

Social support is essential for people with chronic illness. Such support can come from family, friends, or community agencies, such as this one for people with AIDS.

Downey, 1991, and Gerin et al., 1992, for detailed discussions of the health effects of social support). Of course, it is always possible that people who are sick withdraw from social contact. In such cases, illness has affected their social life rather than the other way around. Something along these lines certainly happened to William. Nevertheless, a disease-specific social support group may still help William comply with treatment and control his diabetes. We should not expect miracles, however. Social support does not act in a vacuum. As described in the next section, individual differences and external social events can moderate the effects of social support. There may even be times when social support is not beneficial, as explained in Highlight 5.1.

Individual Characteristics

Stress affects people in markedly different ways; an event that has a devastating effect on one person may hardly affect another. This section looks at some of the reasons for these individual differences: knowledge, hardiness, self-esteem, locus of control, and attributions.

Knowledge At first glance, coping with treatment may appear to be simply a matter of knowledge. Once the patient knows what needs to be done, and why, compliance should follow. However, studies that have assessed the knowledge that those with diabetes have of their disease have found little or no relationship between knowledge and treatment compliance (B. May, 1991).

When Social Support Increases Stress

To be of value, social support must work to facilitate positive goals. Friends who want to take you out for a pizza the night before an important exam may think they are being supportive, but the outcome of their behavior may be your failing the exam.

A compelling demonstration of the potential costs of social support may be found in a study by Baumeister and Steinhilber (1984). These researchers examined baseball World Series records from 1924 to 1982 and basketball semifinal and championship series for the years 1967 to 1982. They were particularly interested in the success of the home team. Teams playing at their home field or stadium have an audience of supporters to cheer them on. This is a form of "social support" that is usually interpreted as giving the home team an advantage over the visitors. Overall, the statistics confirmed this advantage. Both baseball and basketball teams are more successful in front of their fans. However, this advantage was evident only early in the season. End-of-season championships, such as the World Series, produced quite the opposite results. Home teams were more likely to lose. The pressure of playing in front of fans, of not wanting to lose at home, may cause a team to "choke." Teams actually performed better without the social support provided by their hometown crowds.

Knowing what to do (and why) does not guarantee healthy behavior. One reason that knowledge does not guarantee healthy behavior is that the illusion of invulnerability discussed earlier leads most of us to minimize the probability of bad outcomes. Medical students and students of clinical psychology are exceptions. They tend to err in the opposite direction, exaggerating their susceptibility to illness. They may even develop the signs and symptoms of the diseases they study. Overestimating one's susceptibility to illness is just as misleading and maladaptive as minimizing it. In both cases, knowledge does not guarantee appropriate behavior.

Hardiness   People who withstand stress when their coworkers, friends, and relatives break down may possess certain protective personality traits. Optimists, for example, tend to withstand stress better than pessimists. Around examination time, optimistic students report less fatigue and fewer colds, aches, and pains than their pessimistic peers. **Hardiness** is a particular form of optimism (Bernard et al., 1996; Kobasa, Hilker, & Maddi, 1979). Hardy people are committed to their work and believe that they have at least partial control over events. They view change as a challenge and an opportunity to grow. They downplay the importance of setbacks by putting them in the perspective of an entire life. When stress occurs, hardy people try to cope by addressing the specific problem in a positive way (P. G. Williams, Wiebe, & Smith, 1992). In a prospective study of business executives (Kobasa et al., 1979), hardiness was found to be negatively related to illness. There is also some evidence that hardiness and optimism are inherited dispositions (Schulman, Keith, & Seligman, 1993). These findings are certainly worth further investigation, but we should be careful not to overemphasize them. Most of all, we should avoid characterizing people who fall ill as lacking healthy personality traits, as is pointed out in Highlight 5.2.

Self–Esteem   Being different, not being able to do the same things as others, takes its toll on self-esteem. Low self-esteem, in turn, leads to a discrepancy between a person's real and ideal self. As noted in Chapter 2, psychologists working in the humanist paradigm attribute many psychological problems to a discrepancy between one's real and ideal selves. William Cole, for example, had a negative self-concept despite his accomplishments. He told Dr. Berg that he felt less able than the other students.

Because self-esteem is built up over the years, the age at which an illness begins and its duration affects a person's sense of self-esteem (Wertlieb et al., 1990). William's diabetes began when he was just entering his teenage years, a time when peer group interactions and acceptance are especially important. Therefore, he may have been particularly vulnerable to developing low self-esteem.

Not every ill person has low self-esteem. Studies of those with diabetes have found some to have higher self-esteem than their nondiabetic peers (Wertlieb et al., 1990). Some researchers have assumed that diabetics must have low self-esteem (if they are truthful), and any indication of high self-esteem simply reflects a denial of reality (C. Ryan & Morrow, 1986). Such claims are not

Personality, Stress, and Cancer

Cells that proliferate beyond control and have the capability to spread to other parts of the body are called malignant. *Cancer* is the generic term for any form of malignancy, not only noticeable tumors but also blood and lymphatic diseases, such as leukemia.

There is no doubt that certain behaviors can alter the risk of cancer. Smoking vastly increases the risk of lung cancer; sunbathing makes people more susceptible to skin cancer (A. G. Glass & Hoover, 1989). Some researchers have claimed that stressful life events can also produce or exacerbate cancer (Geyer, 1993), whereas stress management can extend the life of cancer patients (Fawzy et al., 1993; Spiegel et al., 1989). Numerous studies have been conducted to investigate the psychosocial influences on cancer (B. L. Anderson, Kiecolt-Glaser, & Glaser, 1994). There is only one problem; every positive finding seems to be matched by a negative one. Thus, Dean and Surtees (1989) reported a negative relationship between life-stress and the recurrence of breast cancer. That is, women with severe life-stress were *less* likely to have their breast cancer recur than were women with low levels of life-

What factors predispose some children to cancer? Clearly, genetics must play some role, but how do theories about personality and ability to deal with stress apply to children with cancer?

stress. Many such inconsistent results have been reported (J. R. Edwards et al., 1990; McGee, Williams, & Elwood, 1994).

To explain these inconsistent findings, researchers have invoked another factor—personality. Specifically, when faced with stress, some specific personality types are more likely to develop

only insulting to people with diabetes, they also ignore the possibility that success in overcoming the limitations of an illness can build self-esteem.

Locus of Control   Adults are usually considered responsible enough to comply with treatment. However, not all people accept this responsibility. In theory, at least, people who have an external **locus of control**—who believe that external forces are more likely to determine what happens to them than their own actions—should be less likely to adhere to a treatment regime than those who have an internal locus of control (Lefcourt, 1992). William seems to have an external locus of

control. This is illustrated by this interchange from his interview with Dr. Berg:

WILLIAM: If you're going to get sick, you're going to get sick. There's not much you can do about it.

DR. BERG: Don't you think you are in control of your health?

WILLIAM: No. Not really.

Studies of locus of control have produced a mixed picture (B. May, 1991; Wertlieb et al., 1990). Some report an external locus of control among chronically ill people; some do not. One possible reason for the discrepant results is the reciprocal effect of health status on locus of

cancer than others. This is hardly a new idea. The classical Greek physician Galen wrote extensively about the relationship between personality and illness. Using various personality measures, modern researchers have reported that depressed people and people who suppress their emotions have an increased risk of developing cancer. In a 30-year follow-up of 1,000 Johns Hopkins medical graduates who had taken personality tests while still in medical school, Shaffer and his colleagues (1987) found that people who repressed their emotions (as judged by the tests) were 16 times more likely to develop cancer than were those who expressed their emotions. In related research, helping people express their emotions through psychological treatment has been found to reduce recurrences of cancer and to lengthen overall survival time (H. J. Eysenck, 1991). This pattern of findings suggests that stress and personality interact to produce illness. However, once again, positive findings are matched by negative ones. Cassileth and his colleagues (1985) found no relationship between social ties, marital history, job satisfaction, hopelessness, or helplessness and either

the recurrence of cancer or the survival time of patients with cancer.

Some critics have objected to the very idea that psychological variables are related to cancer. If we are not careful, they fear, we may develop a form of "healthism" in which psychologists blame victims for their illness (Schmidt, Schwenk-mezger, & Dlugosch, 1990).

At present, matters seem to be at an impasse. Some researchers insist that stress, alone or in combination with personality, causes cancer. Others deny that any hard scientific evidence exists. Further progress depends on resolving several important issues:

- Different researchers focus on different aspects of life-stress and personality, and a bewildering variety of personality measures (of varying reliability and validity) are presently in use. This alone could account for the inconsistent results. The field needs standard definitions and a standard set of acceptable measures.
- Cancer is a diverse set of conditions. Some may be linked to stress and personality, and some may not be. By treating different forms of cancer as the

same thing, researchers may obscure the true underlying relationships.

- Cancer develops slowly, often over a period of years. It is difficult to demonstrate a precise causal relationship between episodes of stress and an illness that may not become apparent until many years later. This difficulty is exacerbated by the retrospective nature of most studies. However, even prospective studies, in which personality is measured while people are still healthy, have difficulty making causal links across long periods of time.
- The active link between smoking and cancer is tar. The link between sunbathing and cancer is ultraviolet radiation. What is the link between life-stress and cancer? Animal research suggests that immune system suppression is the cause (Vogel & Bower, 1991), but, thus far, there is no definitive human data evidence linking stress, immune suppression, and cancer.

control. Dr. Berg interviewed William shortly after an incident in which his blood sugar level had gotten out of control. It is not surprising that, at such a time, William did not feel in control. But beliefs can change. If William had been asked the same questions when his diabetes was in good control, he might have shown a more internal locus of control.

Despite uncertainties about the precise relationship between locus of control and illness, there is ample evidence that feeling in control helps reduce stress. Feelings of control come from three factors: familiarity, predictability, and controllability. Familiarity reduces stress by making us more aware of what to expect. This is why your first job interview is likely to elicit a greater alarm

reaction than your second or third. Predictability exerts an effect on stress independent from familiarity. In a demonstration of the effects of predictability, laboratory rats produced a more intense autonomic reaction to unpredictable electric shock than to shocks of exactly the same voltage occurring on a predictable schedule (Weiss, 1977). Indeed, animals who received unpredictable shocks developed peptic ulcers at a much greater rate than did rats who received predictable shocks. Providing the animals with a way of avoiding or shutting off the shock reduces the stress response even further. This last finding suggests that controllability also determines a stressor's effect (Tsuda et al., 1989). Similar effects have been found among older people placed in nursing homes without their consent (Rodin, 1986). They decline rapidly and die sooner than people who are allowed to choose for themselves where they will live and to determine their own daily activities.

Health Beliefs and Attributions Instead of focusing on a global belief such as internal-external locus of control, some researchers have studied the relationship between more specific beliefs and treatment compliance. For example, among those with diabetes, such as William, adherence to the treatment regime may be related to specific beliefs about themselves and their illness (B. May, 1991). Among these are beliefs about

- susceptibility ("I will not develop complications.")
- severity ("Diabetes is not really all that serious.")
- the benefits of compliance ("If I stick to the regime, I'll be all right.")
- the costs of compliance ("My injections keep me from going out at night.")

Brownlee-Duffeck and her colleagues (1987) used these beliefs to predict both blood sugar levels and adherence. After controlling for knowledge about diabetes and age differences, they found that health beliefs account for 27% of the variability in blood sugar levels and 59% of the variability in treatment adherence among adolescents. The corresponding figures for adults were 19% and 41%. It is not surprising that health beliefs were better predictors of adherence than of blood sugar levels. Even when adherence is perfect, blood sugar levels may vary depending on numerous physiological and emotional factors.

Looking at the specific beliefs, Brownlee-Duffeck and her colleagues found that adherence to the treatment regime among adolescents was related to their perception of the costs (restrictions in social life, for example). Among adults, on the other hand, adherence was related to the perceived benefits. It is likely that interventions designed to increase adherence could benefit from incorporating such individual differences (some people focus on costs; others, on benefits) into their treatment programs.

One unusual result of the study by Brownlee-Duffeck and her colleagues was their finding that, among adolescents, those who perceived their illness as severe (and their susceptibility to complications as high) had poorer adherence to treatment than did those who minimized their illness. This relationship was exactly the opposite of the one the researchers expected to find. One explanation is that people who do not adhere to treatment are just being realistic. They know that with

their severe illness they are more likely to develop complications, so why waste their effort? This explanation implies that health beliefs may both affect behavior and be affected by behavior (B. May, 1991).

A similar interaction occurs at the level of cognitive attributions. That is, the attributions that affect how people react to an illness are also affected by the illness. For example, William may have noted that his blood sugar goes down whenever he has an examination. As a consequence, he may have an extra-large meal before future exams. As B. May (1991) points out, however, this attribution may not be valid. Perhaps it was not test anxiety but getting up early to do some last-minute studying (and, consequently, altering the time of his morning injection) that lowered his blood sugar level. Unless William gets up early before every exam, eating more food might actually cause him more harm than good.

HELPING PEOPLE COPE

Practically every type of psychological treatment has been applied to helping people cope with stress, chronic pain, and the management of illnesses such as diabetes (Bradley, 1994; Rubin & Peyrot, 1992; Shillitoe & Christie, 1990). The main aim is to reduce stress, thereby reducing pain and preventing illness or exacerbations of illness. The general term **stress management** has come to be applied to the various approaches to reducing stress (Lehrer & Woolfolk, 1993). Some treatments take a direct approach, teaching relaxation and other stress-reduction skills. Others take an indirect approach. They attempt to change cognitions and behaviors, which may, in turn, lead to better health through better diabetic management. Every coping process and every coping resource are potential candidates for intervention. Thus, psychologists may try to build a person's self-esteem, provide social support, or even reorient a person who has an external locus of control into someone with a more internal one. Using William Cole as an example, this section describes some of the ways in which psychologists promote health and help people cope with stress. Although these approaches are discussed separately here, in practice, they are often combined into comprehensive treatment packages.

Stress Reduction Through Relaxation

William Cole's treatment actually began while he was still in the hospital. Dr. Jankowitz, the emergency room

Date	Time	Stress level (1–10)	Trigger	Symptoms	Thoughts
11/10	9:30 a.m.	9	Class presentation	Headache, sweaty, muscle tension	I am going to "go blank."
11/11	5:00 p.m.	5	Overslept	Headache, muscle tension	I'll be late for support group.
11/12	9:00 p.m.	9	Invited to movies by classmates	Muscle tension	I may not be able to talk, may get tired

physician, prescribed the antidepressant drug fluoxetine. Dr. Berg, the psychologist, believed that this was only a short-term treatment. He recommended that William have psychotherapy and join a diabetes support group. William accepted these recommendations.

Dr. Berg's first step was to encourage William to keep a "stress diary" (Barlow & Rapee, 1991). In this diary, William recorded the daily events that precipitated stress and the intensity of his reaction on a scale that went from 1 (*minimal stress*) to 10 (*severe stress*). He also noted his symptoms and his thoughts. This diary was used for a variety of purposes. It served as a baseline from which to judge the effectiveness of therapy (successful treatment should reduce the intensity of William's stress). It also provided important information on the skills William needed to learn and the changes he had to make to his life to cope with stress. Part of William's stress diary appears in Document 5.4.

Because muscle tension figured prominently in William's diary, Dr. Berg began treatment by teaching William to relax using E. Jacobson's (1938) progressive muscle relaxation technique (Figure 5.10). William was instructed to alternately tense and relax different groups of muscles. For example, focusing on the muscles of the lower arm, he would make a fist and then relax it. The goal was to make him aware of muscle tension and to give him practice in relaxing different muscle groups. When muscle tension is not a prominent symptom, therapists may use alternate relaxation techniques, such as transcendental meditation, in which the person focuses attention on quietly repeating a specific syllable (the mantra), or hypnosis. In each case, the underlying rationale is that relaxation is incompatible with stress. Individuals who learn to relax in stressful situations should have fewer and less intense alarm reactions. Fewer alarm reactions mean less strain on the heart, the nervous system, and the immune system.

In one dramatic demonstration of the power of relaxation, middle-aged heart attack survivors were randomly assigned to one of two conditions (M. Friedman & Ulmer, 1984). One group received advice from cardiologists about exercise, medications, and diet. The second group received the same advice plus continuing counseling on how to relax (eat slowly, smile at others and laugh at yourself, admit mistakes, and take time to enjoy life). The two groups were followed for 3 years. During that period, members of the relaxation group had only half the number of heart attacks as the first group. Friedman and Ulmer note that "no drug, food, or exercise program ever devised, not even a coronary bypass surgical program, could match the protection against recurrent heart attacks" of simply learning to relax (p. 141).

Relaxation training also helped William comply with his diabetes treatment regime. Evidence shows that relaxation training given to patients undergoing treatment for various diseases, including cancer, made them less fatigued and depressed and more likely to finish the treatment course (Decker, Cline-Elsen, & Gallagher, 1992; Vasterling et al., 1993). The benefits of relaxation training are not limited to people being treated for an illness. Employers have found that offering training in relaxation, and other aspects of stress management, at the workplace can improve employee performance (Quick, Murphy, & Hurrell, 1992). In highly stressful environments, whole communities

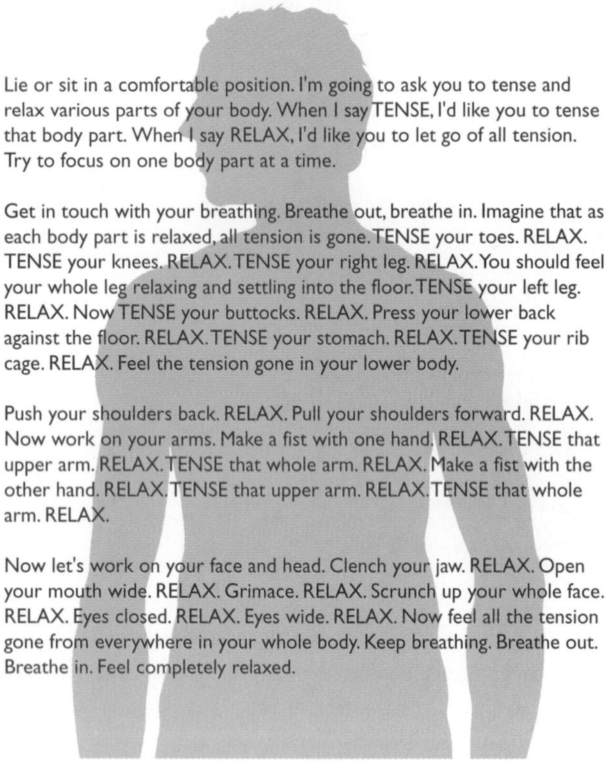

Lie or sit in a comfortable position. I'm going to ask you to tense and relax various parts of your body. When I say TENSE, I'd like you to tense that body part. When I say RELAX, I'd like you to let go of all tension. Try to focus on one body part at a time.

Get in touch with your breathing. Breathe out, breathe in. Imagine that as each body part is relaxed, all tension is gone. TENSE your toes. RELAX. TENSE your knees. RELAX. TENSE your right leg. RELAX. You should feel your whole leg relaxing and settling into the floor. TENSE your left leg. RELAX. Now TENSE your buttocks. RELAX. Press your lower back against the floor. RELAX. TENSE your stomach. RELAX. TENSE your rib cage. RELAX. Feel the tension gone in your lower body.

Push your shoulders back. RELAX. Pull your shoulders forward. RELAX. Now work on your arms. Make a fist with one hand. RELAX. TENSE that upper arm. RELAX. TENSE that whole arm. RELAX. Make a fist with the other hand. RELAX. TENSE that upper arm. RELAX. TENSE that whole arm. RELAX.

Now let's work on your face and head. Clench your jaw. RELAX. Open your mouth wide. RELAX. Grimace. RELAX. Scrunch up your whole face. RELAX. Eyes closed. RELAX. Eyes wide. RELAX. Now feel all the tension gone from everywhere in your whole body. Keep breathing. Breathe out. Breathe in. Feel completely relaxed.

FIGURE 5.10 Script for Jacobsonian Relaxation Session

have benefited from such training (Ingham & Bennett, 1990; Rutter, Quine, & Chesham, 1993).

Biofeedback

Because headaches came up often in William's stress diary, Dr. Berg augmented relaxation training with biofeedback designed to teach William to reduce the muscle tension in his head and neck. Biofeedback is often used as an adjunct to stress-management programs (Hovanitz & Wander, 1990; Shahidi & Salmon, 1992). For example, biofeedback has been used to try to reduce the muscle tension that seems to accompany some headaches, and to lower blood pressure. Initial claims for biofeedback—that it might be a cure for migraines, hypertension, peptic ulcers, and many other conditions— are now clearly seen to have been exaggerated (N. E. Miller, 1974). Biofeedback has beneficial effects in some conditions for some people, but, when used alone, the benefit of biofeedback for relieving stress and reducing symptoms is probably no greater than that provided by relaxation training. However, biofeedback is more effective when combined with relaxation, home practice, and other therapies (Blanchard, 1992; Gauthier, Côté, & French, 1994).

Recently, biofeedback has been used in more innovative and promising ways. Instead of attempting to affect physical health directly, some clinicians are employing biofeedback to teach people skills that they can use to help manage their illness. For example, Harver (1994) used biofeedback to help people with asthma recognize when their respiratory pathways were narrowing. Individuals who can anticipate that their breathing is about to become labored can take the appropriate medication, thereby avoiding an asthmatic episode. William Cole could gain a similar benefit were he able to associate some bodily sensations with high or low blood sugar levels, but no suitable feedback training program is presently available.

It has frequently been claimed that aerobic exercise (sustained exercise that increases cardiovascular fitness) reduces the anxiety and depression often associated with stress. Numerous studies show that those who exercise live longer and spend fewer days in the hospital than those who do not (Paffenbarger et al., 1986). Of course, it is always possible that people who are sick do not feel like exercising. As we have frequently seen, it is difficult to separate cause and effect when dealing with correlational data.

Behavioral and Cognitive–Behavioral Treatment

Behavioral and cognitive therapies are used to teach people to reduce stress; to inculcate new coping skills; and to modify the beliefs, cognitions, and emotions that affect their health. In William Cole's case, Dr. Berg concentrated on William's belief (expressed during his assessment) that he was not in control of his illness and on William's apparent performance and social anxieties (as reflected in his stress diary). Using a combination of the skill training discussed in Chapter 4 (having William practice giving talks, for example) and cognitive restructuring, Dr. Berg attempted to raise William's confidence and self-esteem while at the same time giving him a sense of being in control—of his illness and of his stress. An example from one of William's cognitive restructuring sessions appears in Document 5.5.

DOCUMENT 5.5

Excerpt From a Cognitive Restructuring Session Between Dr. Berg and William Cole

DR. BERG: Why do you think you are not in control of your illness?

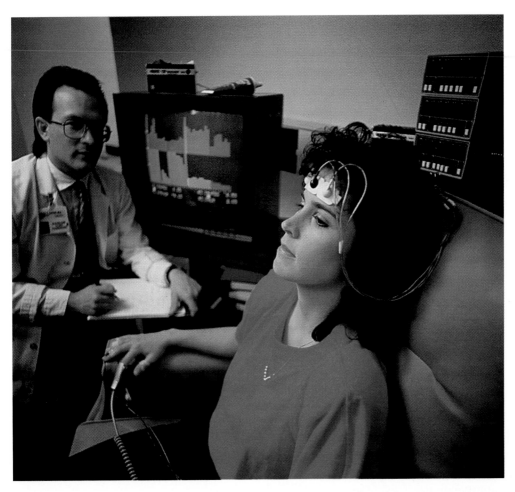

Biofeedback has been successfully used to help people manage asthma, and it shows promise with other illnesses as well.

WILLIAM: I wound up in the hospital, didn't I?

DR. BERG: How did it happen?

WILLIAM: I got stressed out by my exam.

DR. BERG: If you were less anxious about tests, would you have lost control?

WILLIAM: I don't know. Probably not.

DR. BERG: What if you could learn to cope better with tests, perhaps by learning better study skills and by putting tests in a more realistic perspective? Would you be better able to control your diabetes then?

WILLIAM: Yes, I guess I would.

DR. BERG: That's what we'll do then. We'll focus on how to take tests and on how not to let them make you anxious. We will do the same thing with social invitations. Your diary says that they make you anxious as well. Once you learn to manage stress, you may also find it easier to manage your diabetes, and then you will find yourself in better physical and mental health. ■

The entire technology of the behavioral paradigm, including modeling, behavioral contracting, and conditioning, may be used to help people develop new coping skills. For example, people with diabetes who fear needles are likely to miss injections. Helping them to overcome this fear through desensitization, for instance, would have obvious benefits in helping them comply with treatment. Reward-based programs, in which those with diabetes are reinforced for keeping to their diets or their blood sugar monitoring schedules, can have a similar effect.

The importance of social support provided by friends, family, or special support groups has already been noted. William Cole attended such a group for people with diabetes. Membership in this group gave William much-needed peer interactions, helped him overcome his feeling of being alone and isolated, and allowed him to practice desirable social skills (see Document 5.6). Sometimes, just talking about one's

DOCUMENT 5.6

**Letter From William
Cole to His Parents**

Dear Mom and Dad,

    I just wanted you to know that I have been feeling better since getting out of the hospital. I have been careful about my diet and insulin. The Dean has allowed me to take a makeup exam so I will not have to repeat any subjects or anything.

    You may not always find me in when you call anymore. I am going to meetings with a group of students with diabetes. I'm the only Black student in the group. I did not know any of the students before, but they seem OK.

    They also have me going to a psychologist. Not because I'm crazy, or anything. They think it will help me keep on top of stress. I don't know if it will do any good, but I'll give it a try.

    Please don't worry about me. I'll see you soon.

                Love,
                William

painful experiences can have health benefits (Francis & Pennebaker, 1992).

Given the evidence from human and animal studies suggesting that immune functioning is decreased by stress, psychological interventions have also targeted the immune system. Using a wide variety of therapeutic techniques, including relaxation, hypnosis, exercise, conditioning, and cognitive therapy, psychologists have been able to increase the level of immune functioning (Kiecolt-Glaser & Glaser, 1992; Zakowski, Hall, & Baum, 1992). Of course, the problem of clinical significance that affects the field in general also applies to treatment studies. Specifically, it has still not been demonstrated that increasing immune system function has a direct beneficial effect on health. (Keep in mind that, apart from AIDS, most infections increase immune function, yet this increased production of white blood cells is hardly an indicator of good health.)

Family Interventions

Stress and illness have profound effects not just on physical functioning but also on psychological and social identity (Kaplan, 1996; Morse & Johnson, 1991). Suffering affects a person's self-concept, and it subjects other family members to a burden that may require different family members to take on different caregiver roles. The spouse of someone receiving painful chemotherapy, for example, must cope not only with caring for the patient, but also with other family matters, and with fears for the

patient's future. Sometimes, family therapy is required to help families deal with the burden of one member's illness. Self-help groups for patients and their families (such as the one William Cole enrolled in) are often useful sources of social support.

Environmental and Community Interventions

Because stress-related disorders often result from threatening environments, community interventions can sometimes be as effective as individual treatment. For example, increased police patrols reduce the stress that comes from living in high-crime areas, antipoverty programs reduce the stress that comes from poverty, and employment programs help to reduce the stress created by job loss. Combinations of behavioral and cognitive interventions have also been used to modify a community's health-relevant behaviors. For example, people at high risk for illness may be taught strategies to minimize the risks while, at the same time, learning how to avoid dangerous behaviors (Bennett et al., 1991). A good example is the prevention of HIV infection. Many college students believe that AIDS is something that happens to other people; they do not feel at risk because most do not inject drugs and because they know their partners. The result is that college students may fail to practice safer sex, even though heterosexual transmission of HIV has become increasingly common. Behavioral and cognitive interventions need to be aimed at (a) teaching people the real risks, (b) teaching them about safer sex, (c) modify-

Self-Help in Coping With Stress

Even without psychological interventions, there are some things you can do to help yourself cope with stress.

1. *Appraise the situation.* Isolate the problem. Find out as much as you can about the stressor, its causes, and its correlates. Consider alternate actions.
2. *Examine your appraisal.* Is it realistic? Avoid catastrophizing. If you have failed an examination, is it really the end of the world? Perhaps you can try again. A study plan may help. Even if you cannot erase the failure,

you may find you are better at something else. Catastrophizing leads to stress. Realistic appraisals lead to calm but hopeful acceptance.
3. *Be aware of your defenses.* Are you denying reality? Are you rationalizing?
4. *Reduce stress and practice coping skills.* Learn to relax. Talk to friends. Exercise. Eat and sleep well. Join self-help groups where appropriate.
5. *Take the necessary actions, but do not be impulsive.* Consider possible actions, and list the pros and cons of each. Do

not be impulsive. Do not take an action just because of the need to do something. However, once you have decided what to do, then do it. Procrastination just produces more stress.
6. *Remain flexible.* Adaptive behavior means not being locked into any course of action. You must be willing to change direction when the situation warrants it.

---

ing health beliefs (so that they feel the illness can be controlled), and (d) assertiveness training so that they have the ability to insist on safer sex (Kelly et al., 1993; Lear, 1995; Ostrow, 1990; Woolf & Jackson, 1996).

A coordinated community approach to HIV prevention was applied in San Francisco (Coates, 1990). Interventions included educational materials presented on television, in print media, at schools, and at worksites. These materials not only warned of the dangers of unprotected sex, they also gave instruction on safer sex and how to use needles. This had the effect of giving people control over their health and the risks they might take. At the same time, these educational materials also tried to destigmatize those infected with the virus. In addition, convenient blood assessment centers were es-

tablished. This program led to a marked decrease in the incidence of unprotected sex (Coates, 1990). Similar community interventions have targeted heart disease and injury reduction (Peterson & Roberts, 1992).

No matter what psychological intervention is used, sociocultural factors must be taken into account (Radley, 1993). We cannot begin to help people cope with stress and illness until we first understand how they perceive stress and illness (Dasen et al., 1988). For example, members of some minority groups and women do not perceive themselves to be at risk of contracting AIDS (Mays & Cochran, 1988). Special efforts must be made to target these groups and their beliefs if prevention is to be successful.

CHAPTER 5 IN PERSPECTIVE

In the past, a small number of conditions were labeled psychosomatic or psychophysiological (ulcer, asthma, headaches, hypertension). Today, this distinction between illnesses with and without psychological components is considered artificial. Psychological fac-

tors play a role in *all* illnesses. The opposite is also true; all illnesses have psychological effects. The reciprocal effects of stress and illness are best understood using a "stress and coping" model. That is, the effects of various stressors on health are mediated by coping, which,

in turn, depends on an individual's coping resources. Psychological interventions may be aimed at reducing stress before it exerts its pernicious effects or at building up coping skills, which can help a person deal with stress when it occurs.

Key Ideas

Specificity Theory

Early theories in the field of psychosomatic medicine postulated a specific connection between certain personalities and certain diseases. This specificity theory claimed that specific unconscious conflicts produced specific diseases. For example, dependent, love-demanding people who could not find gratification in their everyday relationships were said to develop ulcers. However, it is also possible that the illness itself caused the person to become dependent on others for help. Because people cannot be assigned randomly to a personality type (or a psychological conflict) and then observed over time to see what diseases they develop, it is difficult to prove that a personality type or psychological conflict actually causes a disease.

Type A Behavior

The most frequently cited behavior-disease relationship is the association between Type A behaviors and coronary heart disease. Initial studies found Type A men twice as likely to develop heart disease as the calm, cool, and collected Type Bs. However, subsequent studies produced mixed results. It now appears that it is not Type A behavior in general that predicts coronary heart disease but habitual hostility, cynicism, and anger.

Stress

Selye's general adaptation syndrome, or GAS, was an elaboration of Cannon's emergency reaction. There are three stages: emergency (or alarm), resistance (during which the organism uses all of its physiological resources to minimize tissue damage), and, finally, the exhaustion stage (in which illness and injury become likely). Selye used the word *stressor* to refer to external threats to well-being that could trigger a GAS. Over the years, stress has come to mean not only physical threats, but also psychological threats (divorce, for example), internal states (fatigue, physical illness), and also the subjective feeling of being under pressure ("stressed out"). Strong or repeated stress causes

the body's defenses to crumble, making illness likely.

Sources of Stress

Stress can arise from developmental transitions, from catastrophes, from life events, and from everyday hassles. People who lead stressful lives may be more likely to develop various illnesses than those who lead more placid existences. However, the data need to be interpreted cautiously. They are mainly correlational and largely retrospective. Also, the effects of stressors may be mediated by individual differences.

Direct Effects of Stress on Health

Stress has been shown to weaken the nervous system, making it more prone to injury from incidents such as stroke. Stress also reduces the effectiveness of the immune system. Additional research is required, however, to clarify whether stress-induced reductions in immune function lead directly to illness.

Indirect Effects of Stress on Health

In addition to its direct physiological effects, stress affects health indirectly by interfering with health-relevant behaviors. Stress affects memory, judgment, and other aspects of cognition. Under stress, people may engage in unhealthy behaviors or fail to comply with recommended treatments.

Coping With Stress: Types of Appraisals

The first step in coping is to appraise the stress-producing situation. Primary appraisal involves an assessment of the implications of an event for the individual. Events may be appraised as irrelevant, beneficial, or stress-inducing. Secondary appraisals are concerned with what, if anything, should be done. Cognitive appraisals need not be rational or even conscious. However, response to stress is always based on our *appraisal* (conscious or unconscious) of the threat and our perception of how to deal with it.

Emotion-Focused Versus Problem-Focused Coping

Emotion-focused coping is aimed at managing feelings. In contrast, problem-focused coping attempts to challenge stressors directly by making a plan of action and dealing with the source of stress. Problem-focused coping works best when a person has the ability to remedy the situation by taking some action. However, when events are really not in a person's control, problem-focused coping may lead to frustration. Emotion-based coping may be more productive in these instances.

Coping Resources

Some people manage to cope successfully with their illness, whereas others never seem to be able to adjust. At least part of the answer lies in the coping resources available to the individual. Social support, for example, provides a source of help in times of trouble and gives people a way of expressing their painful feelings to one another. Other factors that affect coping include knowledge (about health practices), hardiness, high self-esteem, an internal locus of control, and health beliefs. We must keep in mind, however, that coping resources not only affect health, they are also affected by health. For example, social support helps people cope with illness, but illness may make people stay home and interact less with friends. Similarly, high self-esteem aids coping, but illness can reduce self-esteem. It is important to keep in mind the reciprocal nature of these interactions among health, stress, and coping.

Helping People Deal With Stress and Illness

The most widely applied intervention strategy for helping people cope with stress is relaxation. The underlying rationale is to teach people how to use relaxation to reduce the intensity and frequency of emergency reactions and GASs. Fewer GASs mean less strain on the heart, the nervous system, and the immune system. Exercise, biofeedback, behavior modification, self-help groups, and many other interventions have all been found useful in helping people cope with stress. However, as in other areas of clinical psychology, sociocultural factors must be taken into account when planning treatment. Because stress often affects families, they should also be considered when formulating treatment plans. In some cases, community interventions can help to reduce sources of stress and to educate people about healthy behavior (thereby reducing the overall risk of illness in the population).

Key Terms

acculturative stress
adjustment disorders
antigen
behavioral medicine
conversion hysteria
coping

emergency (alarm) reaction
emotion-focused coping
general adaptation syndrome
    (GAS)
hardiness
locus of control

problem-focused coping
psychoneuroimmunology
psychophysiological disorders
psychosomatic disorders
specificity theory of psycho-
    somatic illness

stress
stressor
stress management
transitional stress
Type A behavior

Key Names

Franz Alexander
Walter Cannon

René Descartes
Helen Flanders Dunbar

Adolf Meyer
Hans Selye

CHAPTER 6

CHAPTER OBJECTIVES

Chemicals that alter moods or behavior have been used for
thousands of years by people from just about every culture and
society. This chapter is concerned with why so many people use
these psychoactive substances, the problems such substances can
cause, how to help people who want to stop using substances,
and how to prevent people from taking them up in the first
place. The case of Davey Blackthunder, a Native American, is
used to illustrate many of the points made in the discussion.

The four main questions addressed in this chapter are

1. Why are psychoactive substances so popular?
2. What are the potential dangers of using psychoactive
   substances?
3. How are substance-related disorders treated?
4. Can substance-related disorders be prevented?

The Substance Disorder Spectrum

CONTENTS

Psychoactive substances—chemicals that alter our moods or behavior—touch every aspect of modern life; they affect the way we live, work, relax, and the way we die. In the United States, the total cost of substance abuse in 1992 (the most recent year for which estimates are available) was $98 billion. This money went toward preventing, treating, or remediating the pernicious effects of psychoactive substances (Swan, 1999). Reflecting the enormity of the problem, the *DSM-IV* contains more than 100 "substance-related" diagnoses, making this the largest single category of psychological disorders. Although each diagnosis is given a specific definition, the line between substance-related disorders and everyday behavior is often blurred. For example, just as shyness shades imperceptibly into social phobia (see Chapter 4), there is no precise boundary between social drinking and alcohol abuse. Like many psychological problems, substance-related disorders are often just exaggerations of common behaviors. How common? The 1992 U.S. National Household Survey on Drug Abuse conducted by the Substance Abuse and Mental Health Services Administration estimated that 12.8 million Americans use illicit drugs, 111 million use alcohol (52% of the population over 12 years of age), and 61 million smoke (SAMHSA, 1995).

Like the anxiety disorders described in Chapter 4, psychoactive substances form a spectrum. At one end are everyday substances, such as the caffeine found in coffee, soft drinks, and tea. At the other end of the spectrum are illicit and potentially dangerous substances, such as "crack" cocaine. A variety of other substances lie between these two extremes. The *DSM-IV* identifies 11 different substance categories, many with multiple entries, and a large "other" category to cover the multitude of less frequently used psychoactive substances (see Wyatt, 1996, for an example). Table 6.1 summarizes the main *DSM-IV* substance categories used by American college students (Johnston, O'Malley, & Bachman, 1995).

Listing such disparate substances in the same table may seem a little strange. After all, there is a difference between hankering for a cup of coffee for breakfast and injecting heroin. Coffee is familiar, practically everyone drinks it, and it rarely interferes with anyone's life. Heroin, on the other hand, can be devastating. Based on what we know about their effects, it is easy to believe that caffeine and heroin have little in common. Yet, from a psychological point of view, their similarities far outweigh their differences: People first try them for similar reasons, and the same psychological mechanisms maintain their continued use. Moreover, as we will see later

Caffeine is the psychoactive substance most used by U.S. college students.

in this chapter, similar treatments are applied to help people whose disorders stem from different substances. For all of these reasons, the chapter focuses on the most frequently used substances and emphasizes the commonalities that exist across the substance spectrum. The aim is to show how concepts derived from various branches of psychology and other sciences can help us to understand both everyday substance use and substance-related disorders. The case of Davey Blackthunder, which is introduced next, is used throughout the chapter to show how everyday substance use and rare forms of substance abuse are related.

AGONY OF A GASOLINE SNIFFER

When we think of substance abuse, we automatically think of pills, syringes, and alcoholic drinks. Yet there are substances that can produce mind-altering effects without being ingested or injected. These are the **inhalants**—breathable chemical vapors produced by many substances, including paint thinners, certain glues,

TABLE 6.1   The Substance Spectrum: Most Common Psychoactive Substances Used by American College Students

Substance	Common sources (street names)
Alcohol	Beer, wine, liquor (booze, grog)
Amphetamines	Amphetamine, methamphetamine, and related drugs (ice, glass, crank)
Caffeine	Coffee, tea, cola drinks, cocoa, chocolate
Cannabis	Marijuana, hashish (pot, hash, weed, Mary Jane)
Cocaine	(coke, blow, crack, free-base)
Hallucinogens	LSD (acid), mescaline, psilocybin, MDMA (ecstasy)
Inhalants	Gasoline, paint, cleaning fluid, aerosols, butane, amyl nitrate (poppers)
Nicotine	Cigarettes, cigars
Opioids	Codeine, morphine, heroin (horse)
Phencyclidine	PCP (angel dust)
Sedatives, hypnotics, anxiolytics	Benzodiazepines, barbiturates (downers, ludes)
Other	Anabolic steroids, betel nuts

Note: Substance list is adapted from Johnston et al. (1995).

DSM-IV   **TABLE 6.2**   *DSM-IV* Diagnostic Criteria for Substance Intoxication

A. The development of a reversible substance-specific syndrome due to recent ingestion of (or exposure to) a substance. Note: Different substances may produce similar or identical syndromes.
B. Clinically significant maladaptive behavioral or psychological changes that are due to the effect of the substance on the central nervous system (e.g., belligerence, mood lability, cognitive impairment, impaired judgment, impaired social or occupational functioning) and develop during or shortly after use of the substance.
C. The symptoms are not due to a general medical condition and are not better accounted for by another mental disorder.

Note: From American Psychiatric Association (1994, p. 184).

dry-cleaning fluid, aerosols, and, of course, gasoline (Dinwiddie, 1994; NIDA, 1996b). Just breathing these substances is enough to produce a severe form of **substance intoxication disorder**—a syndrome that may include one or more of the following: mood lability, belligerence, cognitive impairment, and impaired social or occupational functioning. Intoxication takes place during, or shortly after, exposure to the substance and fades away as the substance is broken down and excreted by the body. See Table 6.2 for the *DSM-IV* diagnostic criteria for substance intoxication.

Inhalant use is most prevalent among young people, who find these substances cheap and easily accessi-

ble (Espeland, 1997). Although fewer than 1% of college students report using inhalants (Johnston et al., 1995), 6–9% of U.S. high school seniors use inhalants in a given year (Johnston et al., 1996). The intoxicating effects of inhalants make users feel temporarily euphoric, but they can lead to hearing loss, brain damage, liver disease, and even death. Perhaps one of the most tragic aspects of inhalants is the havoc they cause to the youth of indigenous populations—Australian Aborigines, Aleuts, Eskimos, and other Native Americans (Mail & Johnson, 1993). The story of the young Native American Davey Blackthunder, as it is related in Documents 6.1–6.4, clearly illustrates this problem.

DOCUMENT 6.1

Excerpt From Davey
Blackthunder's (age
10) Hospital Discharge
Summary

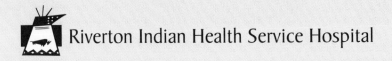

Riverton Indian Health Service Hospital

Discharge Summary

Patient's Name: Davey Blackthunder

Date: August 4, 1994

Age: 10

Attending Physician: Dr. H. Roundtree

This 10-year-old boy was brought to the Emergency Room by his mother. He was feverish and claimed to be seeing ghosts. Because he was agitated, I prescribed Valium. We observed the boy over the course of 24 hours, during which time his symptoms subsided. A blood test revealed that the level of lead in his blood was seven times the local average. The boy lives in a rural area where there are few cars and, therefore, little exposure to gasoline fumes. Clearly, the lead in his blood did not come from car exhaust. Most likely, the boy's high lead levels are the result of sniffing gasoline, which, in turn, produced his symptoms. A social work report was ordered. The social worker considered the boy a "child at risk" for substance abuse and recommended careful monitoring and treatment. After two days, the boy's symptoms subsided. On the fourth day, he was released to return home. He was enrolled in a special drug rehabilitation program and will receive social work visits.

DOCUMENT 6.2

Excerpt From Social
Work Conference on
Davey Blackthunder
(age 16)

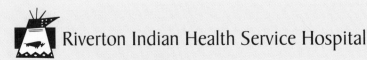

Riverton Indian Health Service Hospital

Social Work Conference

Patient's Name: Davey Blackthunder

Date: July 19, 2000

Age: 16

Social Worker: Lee Wright

Conference Participants: Horace Blackthunder (father) and James Blackthunder (uncle)

LEE WRIGHT: Thanks for coming. I realize that you may be a bit uncomfortable talking to me. May I offer you a cup of coffee? It will help you relax.

HORACE BLACKTHUNDER: Thanks. Make it black.

JAMES BLACKTHUNDER: Same. Mind if I smoke? Everyone in our family does. Davey is a chain smoker. He just lights one cigarette after another.

LEE WRIGHT: No. Go ahead and smoke, if it helps you relax. I wanted to talk to you about Davey. I am getting worried about him. I think he is sniffing gasoline regularly, and he seems to have lost a lot of weight.

HORACE BLACKTHUNDER: I think you are right.

LEE WRIGHT: Could we go over the background again?

HORACE BLACKTHUNDER: Davey is one of my three kids. He has two brothers. We all live together on the Riverton Reservation. My brother James is out of work, so he is also living with us until he gets back on his feet.

LEE WRIGHT: What about Davey's mother?

HORACE BLACKTHUNDER: She left us about three years ago.

LEE WRIGHT: Are you working?

HORACE BLACKTHUNDER: I have a part-time job as a laborer on a construction site.

LEE WRIGHT: How about Davey?

HORACE BLACKTHUNDER: He quit school and got a job, but he was fired for being high at work.

LEE WRIGHT: How long has Davey been sniffing gasoline?

JAMES BLACKTHUNDER: The kid has been at it since he was tiny. We had him in the hospital with lead poisoning when he was little, maybe nine or ten.

LEE WRIGHT: What happened at that time?

HORACE BLACKTHUNDER: Davey got all hot and said he was seeing ghosts. We got him in the hospital, and he came around.

LEE WRIGHT: Did you know he was sniffing gasoline?

HORACE BLACKTHUNDER: I knew, we all knew. We tried to stop him. We gave him hell, even beat him.

JAMES BLACKTHUNDER: Nothing we did made any difference.

LEE WRIGHT: What happened after he was discharged from the hospital, that first time?

HORACE BLACKTHUNDER: He went to a residential program. He talked with the doctor.

LEE WRIGHT: Did that help?

HORACE BLACKTHUNDER: For a time, it did. He seemed to stay clean; he even went to school regularly, but it didn't last. He only stopped sniffing when he lived in the program. Once the program was over and he came home, he got bored. There are no jobs around and there aren't likely to be any. He went back to his old gang and started imitating the others. He drank beer and smoked pot when he had the money. He even got into heroin when he could. Most of the time, all he could afford was gasoline.

LEE WRIGHT: Well, I think it is a good idea to try a program again—maybe away from the people he is imitating. We could enroll him in a program at Two-Tree Reservation.

JAMES BLACKTHUNDER: We find this very shameful; we like to handle things like this at home. But maybe we should give this a try.

Social Work Recommendation: Refer to Two-Tree Reservation Substance Abuse Program. Davey is at risk for serious consequences. He requires careful monitoring and treatment. There is a strong possibility that he will continue his gasoline sniffing and cause permanent damage to his health.

DOCUMENT 6.3

Emergency Room
Report on Davey
Blackthunder (age 17)

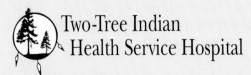

Two-Tree Indian Health Service Hospital

Accident and Emergency Department

Incident Report

Date: October 10, 2001
Time: 3:15 a.m.

A young male, around 17 years of age, was driven to the Accident and Emergency Department by an older man, who identified himself as Alan Arnold, a drug counselor. Two orderlies on a smoking break were outside and spotted the car on its arrival. They helped rush the patient into the treatment room. A bloodstained towel was wrapped around the young man's right arm. Removing the towel revealed several jagged, deep cuts to the forearm just below the elbow. Blood was gushing from a cut artery, and bone was visible. The patient had a faint pulse and shallow respiration. Four units of blood were transfused, and he was placed in intensive care.

DOCUMENT 6.4

Alan Arnold's Testimony at an Inquiry Into the Incident That Put Davey Blackthunder (age 17) Into the Hospital

In the Matter of Davey Blackthunder

COUNSEL FOR MEDICAL EXAMINER: Please state your name and occupation.

MR. ARNOLD: Alan Arnold. I am a counselor in the substance abuse treatment program at the Two-Tree Reservation.

COUNSEL FOR MEDICAL EXAMINER: This is a program for Native Americans?

MR. ARNOLD: Yes.

COUNSEL FOR MEDICAL EXAMINER: Is Davey Blackthunder enrolled in your program?

MR. ARNOLD: Yes.

COUNSEL FOR MEDICAL EXAMINER: How long have you known Davey Blackthunder?

MR. ARNOLD: I first met him two days before the incident that put him in the hospital. He was brought to the reservation by his father and uncle, who live in Riverton, a community about three hundred fifty miles west of Two-Tree. Their social worker thought that Davey would do better in a new environment.

COUNSEL FOR MEDICAL EXAMINER: What was your initial impression?

MR. ARNOLD: Well, I had a couple of beers with Davey's father and uncle—since they weren't clients—just to relax them so that I could get some background information. They told me that Davey had been sniffing gasoline on and off for years. Certainly, he seemed in pretty bad shape. He was skinny, weak, and seemed to have no energy. He told me and the other boys that he had seen God and that he would "see him again soon." I remember at his first meal with us, we served some red punch, and Davey kept sniffing at it, as if it were gasoline.

COUNSEL FOR MEDICAL EXAMINER: What happened on the night of the incident?

MR. ARNOLD: Davey spent the day by himself. He refused dinner and went off to his room. I visited him twice. Both times, he just stared out the window and puffed on a cigarette; he would not talk. Around two in the morning, I heard the sound of screaming and glass breaking. Davey had punched his hand through his window and his arm was spurting blood. I grabbed a towel and tried to put pressure on his artery, but he kept fighting me. Several other boys heard the commotion and came to help. We tried to tie a tourniquet around Davey's arm, but he kept pulling it off. We did finally manage to get him in the car and drive him to the hospital, but he lost a lot of blood.

COUNSEL FOR MEDICAL EXAMINER: Why did he punch through the window, do you think?

MR. ARNOLD: I don't know, but there was a can of gasoline in his room. The handle had a shoelace wrapped around it. I think he had probably tied the can to his face. I have seen this done before. The fumes may have made him lose control. Sniffing gasoline often leads to violence. ■

PSYCHOACTIVE SUBSTANCES ARE UBIQUITOUS

Davey Blackthunder almost died at 17, his life nearly lost to substance abuse. Residential rehabilitation programs kept Davey from sniffing gasoline while he lived away from home, but he reverted to gasoline sniffing whenever he returned to his environment. Driven by boredom, lack of work, and despair about the future, Davey chain-smoked, drank beer, smoked pot, and used heroin when he had the money. Otherwise, he and his friends lost themselves in a cheap and accessible gasoline-induced oblivion. The use of multiple substances is known as **polysubstance abuse**, a common pattern not only among Native Americans but also among many other substance users (Beauvais, 1996; Harrison, Fulkerson, & Beebe, 1997).

As you can see from Documents 6.1–6.4, the adults in Davey's life also used psychoactive substances: alcohol (beer), caffeine (coffee), and nicotine (cigarettes). Substances also played a part in the story of Danielle Wood (see Chapter 1), who tried to improve her athletic performance with anabolic steroids and died from an overdose of amphetamines (both substances are discussed later in this chapter).

At first glance, inhalants may seem different from these other substances. Many people drink beer, millions smoke, but few tie gasoline cans to their faces. Yet, if we look beneath the surface, Davey's behavior is not as outlandish as it first may seem. Sniffing gasoline allowed Davey to alter his psychological state (to get "high") while also providing him with peer group acceptance and, initially at least, a shared social activity. As you will see in this chapter, these are the main reasons for using *any* substance.

Because the *DSM-IV* contains more than 100 substance-induced disorders, it is not possible to review each one in this book. Instead, this chapter emphasizes the common features of psychoactive substance use by focusing on the four substances most frequently used by American college students: caffeine, nicotine, alcohol, and marijuana. Just about everyone who reads this book will have tried one or more of these substances; many people routinely use all four. This chapter looks at the history and chemistry of these substances and examines their physiological, psychological, and social effects. The aim of this discussion is to identify the reasons why people use these, and other, substances and why their use can sometimes lead to serious psychological disorders. Finally, we will look at treatments designed to help people overcome substance-related disorders and prevention programs intended to keep people from using

These Filipino street children, like other inhalant users, sniff glue in order to alter their psychological state and to share the activity with their peers.

psychoactive substances in the first place. The chapter shows how insights gained from an examination of the four most commonly used substances can be applied to rarer forms of substance use, such as the inhalants that almost killed Davey Blackthunder.

Caffeine

If you need any proof that practically everyone uses psychoactive substances at one time or another, just consider **caffeine.** It is practically everywhere. The only way you can avoid it is to shun coffee, tea, many popular soft drinks, cocoa, and chocolate. Even then, you may not succeed because caffeine is also found in headache, diet, and cold medications. Given its ubiquity (Figure 6.1), it should come as no surprise that 92–98% of adults in North America consume caffeine regularly (Heishman & Henningfield, 1992).

It is said that the first people to use caffeine were the Chinese, who began drinking tea 1,000 years ago, and Native South Americans, who ingested caffeine by chewing cocoa beans. When the technique of roasting coffee beans was developed in the 15th century, coffeehouses sprang up around the Muslim world. Although alcohol is forbidden in the Koran, coffee is not

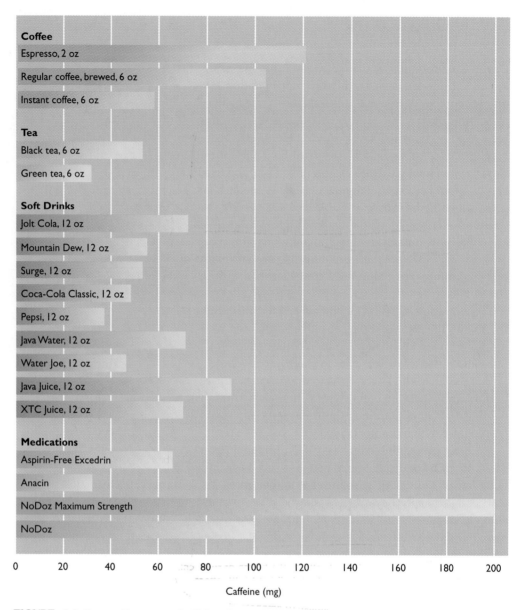

FIGURE 6.1 **Some Common Caffeine Sources.** From: "What Caffeine Can Do" (1997).

mentioned. Nevertheless, Muslim religious leaders attacked coffee as intoxicating and tried to have it banned. They were unsuccessful, and coffee eventually became so well liked in the Muslim world that it was known as the "wine of Islam." Tea, coffee, and cocoa became popular in Europe during the 17th century, when they were recommended for their health benefits. For more on the use of psychoactive substances as medicines, see Highlight 6.2, later in this chapter. By the 18th century, coffeehouses had spread throughout Europe, where they became centers for commerce, the exchange of news, and political and intellectual debates. People would spend many hours in coffeehouses, giving them ample opportu-

nity to ingest large quantities of caffeine. Today, coffee remains the world's most popular source of caffeine.

Action Caffeine belongs to a class of chemicals called stimulants, whose main psychoactive effect is to make us more alert. Nicotine (the subject of the next section) belongs to the same class of substances. Amphetamines and cocaine, less readily available stimulants, are described in Table 6.3.

Within 45 to 60 minutes after drinking a cup of coffee or munching a chocolate bar, caffeine is absorbed from the stomach and the intestines. Once in the bloodstream, it causes blood pressure, pulse rate, and stom-

TABLE 6.3	Examples of Stimulants (other than caffeine and nicotine)
Name	**Description**
Amphetamine	A synthetic (manufactured) compound that comes in legal prescription versions and illegal street versions, such as "speed." Amphetamine powder can be inhaled ("snorted") or injected. There is also a smokable form known as "ice" because of its clear crystal appearance. Inhaling or injecting amphetamines produces an intense, pleasurable feeling (a "rush"). Between 1% and 3% of college students report using some type of amphetamine in the past month (Johnston et al., 1995). Amphetamines enhance neurotransmitter concentration, especially norepinephrine and dopamine. This increased concentration produces alertness and arousal. Originally intended as an asthma medication, amphetamines still have several medical uses. For example, they may be prescribed for people with attention deficit disorder (discussed in Chapter 12); they may help people with rare forms of sleep disorder, such as narcolepsy (excessive sleepiness); and because they suppress appetite, they are sometimes used as diet aids. Initially, amphetamines make people feel alert, energized, strong, and happy. After long-term use, however, they produce many negative effects. Because they suppress appetite, they can cause malnutrition and dehydration. They may also cause severe anxiety and serious cognitive distortions, such as hallucinations (Wolkoff, 1997). As Danielle Wood's story showed, large doses of amphetamines can also be fatal.
Cocaine	Derived from the South American coca plant, cocaine, or coke, comes in several forms and was once an ingredient in Coca Cola (Musto, 1992). Cocaine produces stimulatory effects similar to those produced by amphetamines. Also like amphetamines, cocaine can be injected, snorted, or smoked in forms known as free-base and crack. Crack, which refers to the sound heard when the cocaine is smoked, is relatively cheap and, therefore, popular among younger people (B. D. Johnson et al., 1994). Smoking cocaine produces an intense and rapid high, which, for unknown reasons, is felt more intensely by men than by women (Lukas et al., 1996). Two percent of college students admit to using one or more forms of cocaine in the past month (Johnston, 1995). Cocaine acts to enhance the action of dopamine and other neurotransmitters, thereby increasing arousal while at the same time producing a variety of psychological effects including (after prolonged use) paranoia, anxiety, panic attacks, and even a psychotic disorder (Yudofsky, Silver, & Hales, 1993). Withdrawal does not seem to produce symptoms unless cocaine use extends over a considerable period (Gawin & Kleber, 1992). Cocaine used by pregnant women adversely affects the health of their children (Sprauve et al., 1997). Cocaine may also have indirect health effects. For example, people who inject cocaine (or any other drug) increase their exposure to HIV, hepatitis, and other diseases. Similar to amphetamines, cocaine can be fatal in large doses (Harlow & Swint, 1989).

ach acid production to increase. In the nervous system, caffeine acts as an antagonist to the neuroinhibitor adenosine (Ammon, 1991). Antagonists are chemicals that reduce the potency of other chemicals. By diminishing the inhibitory effect of adenosine, caffeine increases the activity of other neurotransmitters—specifically, glutamate, norepinephrine, serotonin, and possibly dopamine. These various effects combine to make people more aroused. Because caffeine also causes fat stores to be broken down, thereby releasing energy, it is sometimes used by athletes preparing for a competition (Dodd, Herb, & Powers, 1993). Using caffeine in sports can be dangerous because it is a powerful diuretic (it increases the excretion of liquid from the body). Because the physical exertion of sports causes intense sweating, adding the diuretic effect of caffeine can result in severe dehydration. The use of performance-enhancing drugs by athletes is one of the most worrying developments in modern sports, as Highlight 6.1 points out.

Health Effects   Although it is widely used and generally regarded as safe, caffeine may still have adverse

Threatening Mind and Body

The ambition to compete and win is as old as history. Equally ancient is the use of potions to ensure victory. Ancient Greek epic poems refer to various nostrums that were believed to increase strength, and the Vikings ate hallucinogenic mushrooms to prepare themselves for battle. The modern version of these ancient potions made its first appearance in the 1950s, when the spectacular size and performance of Russian weight lifters at the Olympics were found to result from **anabolic steroids.** Steroids are drugs derived from hormones. The term *anabolic* means growing or building, and refers to the drug's ability to increase size and strength. Specifically, anabolic steroids help the body to retain protein, thereby accelerating the growth of muscles, bones, and skin. Chemically, anabolic steroids are synthetic derivatives of the male hormone testosterone.

In response to the Russian victories, American firms began to manufacture their own anabolic steroids. Initially, these drugs were claimed to have medical value. They were supposed to improve appetite and promote healing after surgery. The U.S. Food and Drug Administration no longer accepts these claims and forbids the manufacture or use of anabolic steroids for any purpose. Of course, this does not stop people from making or using them. The United States is home to a multimillion-dollar black market in illegal steroids.

The first Americans to use anabolic steroids were athletes who competed in sports where strength provides a cru-

After testing positive for a diuretic, Zhang Yi of China was expelled from the 1998 World Championships and suspended from competitive swimming for 2 years.

cial advantage: football players, weight lifters, javelin throwers. During the 1970s, other athletes started using them as well. Highly competitive athletes such as Danielle Wood, the swimmer whose tragic death was discussed in Chapter 1, were enticed by the promise of improved performance (Elliot & Goldberg, 1996). By the 1990s, anabolic steroids were not only being used in most sports, but also by people simply trying to perfect their physiques (D. M. Scott, Wagner, & Barlow, 1996). In recognition of their dangers, anabolic steroids

have been banned by all national and international sporting bodies, and most have instituted drug testing regimes. Competitors caught using performance-enhancing drugs face severe sanctions.

Anabolic steroids may be taken as pills or by injection. Either way, they present numerous dangers to health. In men, anabolic steroids not only shrink the testicles and reduce the sperm count, they also produce impotence, baldness, and difficulty urinating. Because the drugs are derived from the male sex hormone, they foster masculine characteristics. Females who take them develop facial hair, deeper voices, and find that their breasts shrink. In both males and females, anabolic steroids produce acne, tremors, high blood pressure, and liver damage. In children and adolescents, they can also halt growth.

Anabolic steroids are notorious for their effect on mood. "Roid rages," in which anger erupts suddenly, may lead to violence. When anabolic steroids are withdrawn, users sink into a deep depression. Even if none of these events occurs, users who share needles to inject steroids increase their exposure to AIDS. Also, because the anabolic steroids currently available on the black market are all made in uncontrolled, illegal factories, they are often contaminated with poisonous materials. Thus, even if the steroids don't get you, the contaminants probably will. Considering the risks, anyone who uses illegal anabolic steroids is foolhardy indeed.

effects on health (Benowitz, 1990). For example, it increases the production of stomach acid, which may worsen digestive disorders and can cause acid reflux ("heartburn"). Insomnia, poor sleep, and anxiety are also the potential results of overuse of caffeine. From time to time, it has been suggested that caffeine may cause various illnesses, including cancer, high blood pressure, or

heart disease. It has proved difficult to establish links between caffeine and these diseases, however, because of the difficulty in ruling out other causes, such as smoking, lack of exercise, differences in genetic dispositions to disease, and the presence of other biologically active materials in caffeine-containing substances (coffee, tea, and chocolate contain more than just caffeine).

Psychological Effects   Because caffeine is a stimulant, many people consume drinks containing it to combat drowsiness, increase alertness, and boost energy. Paradoxically, many people also consume caffeine to relax. Indeed, it is common for some people, especially in the United Kingdom, to drink a cup of tea to help them to fall asleep. The use of caffeine as a relaxation aid was illustrated in Document 6.2, when the social worker, Lee Wright, offered coffee to Davey's father and uncle:

LEE WRIGHT: Thanks for coming. I realize that you may be a bit uncomfortable talking to me. May I offer you a cup of coffee? It will help you relax.

The relaxing effect of caffeine may have a physiological basis. We know, for example, that laboratory animals under stress consume more stimulants than unstressed animals (Goeders & Guerin, 1994; Miczek, Hubbard, & Cantuti-Castelvetri, 1995). It is possible that stimulants, at least at some dosage levels, may relieve anxiety in some people. On the other hand, it is also possible that the relaxing effect of caffeine is not the result of its chemical action but of expectancies and social reinforcements. If we expect caffeine to be relaxing, it probably will be. The roles played by physiology, expectancies, and social reinforcement in substance use and anxiety reduction are discussed in more detail later in this chapter.

Nicotine

Nicotine is the primary psychoactive ingredient in tobacco, a plant that has grown in the Americas for centuries. Tobacco was brought to Europe by Christopher Columbus and other explorers in the late 15th century (Brannon & Feist, 1992). The word *nicotine* is derived from the name of the 16th-century French writer Jean Nicot, who was one of the first Europeans to extol tobacco's medicinal qualities. Tobacco's popularity spread throughout the world in the 17th century, and it became an important source of revenue for the American colonies. Even back then, not everyone welcomed tobacco. The 17th-century Chinese emperor threatened to decapitate anyone caught selling the plant or its seeds. The emperor's threat, like all subsequent attempts to prohibit tobacco, was unsuccessful. By the 18th century, governments gave up trying to ban tobacco and started to tax it instead. Before long, they were making as much money from tobacco as were the people who grow and sell it (a situation that persists today).

From the outset, tobacco was used in many different ways. Native Americans smoked it in pipes, whereas Europeans preferred to sniff ground tobacco (snuff). Eighteenth-century Americans chewed tobacco leaves and smoked cigars. Cigarettes first appeared in the middle of the 19th century. They took a while to catch on because men considered them effeminate and the women of the day preferred snuff. By the 1920s, however, cigarette smoking had become, and remains, the dominant form of tobacco use (although cigars made something of a comeback in the 1990s).

In the 1960s, 32% of adult females and more than half of all adult males in the United States smoked (U.S. Department of Health and Human Services, 1990). With the publication of reports suggesting that smoking is a risk to health, the subsequent health labeling on cigarette packages, and the banning of smoking in most workplaces and public buildings, the incidence of smoking began to decrease (Husten, Chrismon, & Reddy, 1996). The decline has been more dramatic for males than for females (Remington et al., 1985; U.S. Department of Health and Human Services, 1990). Despite the downtrend in smoking, around one fourth of college students still report smoking and around 12% of high school seniors are heavy smokers, consuming half a pack of cigarettes or more per day (Dryfoos, 1990; Johnston et al., 1995). Smoking (like most forms of substance use) decreases as income and level of education increase (Gfroerer, Greenblatt, & Wright, 1997; J. P. Pierce et al., 1989). Davey Blackthunder, you may recall, was a chain smoker, as were his father and uncle.

While cigarette consumption has been decreasing in the United States, it has been going up in other parts of the world (American Medical Association Council on Scientific Affairs, 1990). Tobacco companies market their product aggressively in developing countries, where information about the dangers of smoking has not been widely disseminated.

Action   Nicotine, tobacco's psychoactive substance, is a powerful stimulant, so toxic that it has been used as a natural insecticide. A small amount instantly kills a variety of insects. In humans, nicotine is one of the fastest acting psychoactive substances. Within seconds of a smoker's puffing on a cigarette, nicotine reaches the smoker's brain (Bock & Marsh, 1990). It activates specific receptors in the midbrain that produce increased arousal. By stimulating the sympathetic nervous system, nicotine also produces a mild form of alarm reaction—increased heart rate, rapid breathing, and constricted blood vessels. The end result is similar to the one produced by caffeine—smoking makes people more alert and less drowsy.

The packs of Marlboro and Salem in this cigarette stand in central Beijing reflect the growing interest of U.S. tobacco companies in Asia. Although cigarette consumption has declined substantially in the United States, China now has the world's largest population of smokers.

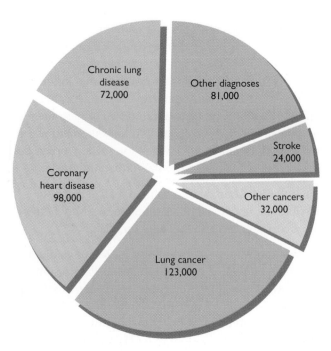

FIGURE 6.2 *Each year 430,000 U.S. deaths are attributable to cigarette smoking (average annual number of deaths, 1990–1994).* From: CDC (1997).

Health Effects   Although nicotine is toxic in large doses, it has not been definitely linked to any disease at the levels found in cigarettes. However, this is not true of the other compounds present in tobacco smoke, many of which are known to be dangerous to health. For example, carbon monoxide, the poisonous gas found in automobile exhaust emissions, is also present in cigarette smoke. It reduces the smoker's oxygen supply, thereby affecting the heart and other circulatory organs. Tar (the organic chemicals suspended in smoke droplets) contain several known carcinogens (substances that can cause cancer). Many other dangerous substances, such as formaldehyde (a well-known carcinogen) and nitric oxide (a poisonous gas), are also found in tobacco smoke.

The effects of smoking on health have been known for decades. In 1948, researchers began a prospective study of more than 5,000 people living in Framingham, Massachusetts. Their aim was to identify the factors that contribute to heart disease. The now-famous Framingham Heart Study revealed a number of risk factors (characteristics that seem to be associated with an increased risk of disease). Somewhat unexpectedly, at least at the time, high among those risk factors was smoking (Dawber, 1980). The Framingham study was

the first evidence that tobacco smoking was related to heart disease. It was followed by a study of 8,000 men of Japanese descent, which found smoking also to be a risk factor for stroke (brain damage caused by the blocking or bursting of blood vessels in the brain; Abbott et al., 1986). Smokers have three times as many strokes as people who have never smoked. A 34-year follow-up of the Framingham study shows a continuing association between smoking and a range of diseases years after smoking ceases (Freund et al., 1993).

In addition to heart disease and stroke, smoking is a risk factor in respiratory diseases such as bronchitis and emphysema (Burchfiel et al., 1995), in stomach ulcers, and in diseases of the mouth (Brannon & Feist, 1992). Labor studies have found that smokers are more likely to miss work because of illness than nonsmokers (U.S. Department of Health and Human Services, 1990). Exposure to the smoke of other people's cigarettes, pipes, and cigars (passive smoking) is also a health risk, especially for young children (J. M. Wu, 1990). Many people are killed each year by fires caused by smoking, especially those caused by falling asleep while smoking in bed (Fielding, 1985). Overall, one in every six deaths in the United States is in some way related to smoking (U.S. Department of Health and Human Services, 1990). Figure 6.2 summarizes the various causes of deaths attributable to smoking each year in the United States.

TABLE 6.4   The Health Benefits of Smoking Cessation

- After 1 year, excess risk of coronary heart disease drops by about 50%.
- After a few years, the risk of bladder cancer drops by about 50%.
- After 5 years, the risk for oral and esophageal cancer drops by about 50%.
- After 5–15 years, the risk of stroke is similar to that of people who have never smoked.
- After 10 years, the risk of lung cancer drops about 30–50%.
- After 15 years, the risk of coronary heart disease is similar to that of people who have never smoked.

Note: Adapted from *The Surgeon General's 1990 Report* (1990, pp. 2–10).

Although smoking is related to several types of cancer (Heineman et al., 1994; Muscat et al., 1997), the best-known link is the relationship between smoking and lung cancer. Interestingly, some studies find a strong connection between cigarette smoking and cancer, whereas others report a weaker association (Brannon & Feist, 1992). These differences do not mean that epidemiological research is invalid or sloppy. Discrepancies arise because cancer has many causes. In addition to smoking, pollution, diet, genetics, and a host of other factors have been linked to cancer. People who smoke the same number of cigarettes each day will nevertheless have different prospects of developing cancer depending on where they stand on the other factors.

Exploiting the complexities in the literature, cigarette manufacturers, and even some scientists, have argued that cigarette smoking is not, by itself, a major cause of illness. For example, the late British psychologist Hans Eysenck (1916–1997) argued that *both* the habit of smoking and vulnerability to disease are mediated by our genetically endowed personalities (Eysenck, 1991). Cancer, he claimed, occurs most often in people with genetically determined cancer-prone personalities (mainly people who find it difficult to cope with stress). These are also the people most likely to smoke. Eysenck's claims failed to convince many investigators. Their skepticism arose from studies of people who quit smoking. If Eysenck were correct—that personality, not smoking, causes illness—then giving up smoking should not improve health outcomes. After all, people who give up smoking still retain their disease-prone personalities. On the other hand, if smoking does cause illness and death, quitting should improve health. And this is just what has been found (Table 6.4). Although their personalities remain unchanged, people who give up smoking increase their life expectancy and reduce the likelihood that they will develop cancer (Tsevat, 1992).

Warnings were required on cigarette packages in 1965, and televised cigarette commercials were banned

in 1972. Yet tobacco companies continued to deny any link between smoking and illness. Lawsuits by smokers who contracted cancer were usually unsuccessful for two reasons: (a) it is difficult to prove that any particular person's illness was the result of smoking and not some other factor, and (b) people voluntarily chose to smoke even though cigarette packages contained health warnings. Tobacco companies began to come under intense pressure in 1992, when the United States Supreme Court ruled that manufacturers could be held liable for injuries to the health of smokers if it could be proved that they deliberately conspired to misrepresent the dangers of smoking. Lawsuits were filed by state governments claiming just such a conspiracy and seeking reimbursement for the public money spent caring for people made ill by tobacco. At first, the companies fought the suits, claiming no conspiracy existed. However, in 1997, the smallest American tobacco company, the Liggett Group Inc., acknowledged that cigarettes may cause cancer and agreed to turn over thousands of documents indicating that tobacco companies were aware of smoking's effects on health but conspired to keep these effects from the public. Rather than face years of lawsuits, the companies agreed to create a fund containing billions of dollars to compensate governments and victims and to pay for smoking-cessation programs. (The details of how this fund will be used may take years to decide.) The companies also agreed to further limitations on the advertising and distribution of tobacco. Notwithstanding the manufacturers' damaging admissions, millions of people continue to smoke.

Psychological Effects   Despite nicotine's arousing effects, most smokers, like most coffee drinkers, claim that they smoke to relax. Recall that the hospital orderlies who first saw Davey at the emergency room were on their smoking break (Document 6.3), and remember how James Blackthunder lit a cigarette before talking to social worker Lee Wright (Document 6.2). The process of taking a cigarette out of a pack, lighting it, and so on, may have helped James gain the poise and composure he needed to proceed with the interview. The claim that smoking is relaxing is supported by the observation that smoking increases under stressful circumstances (Pomerlau & Pomerlau, 1990). This paradox—nicotine and caffeine increase sympathetic arousal but are perceived to be calming—may have a physiological explanation. The body releases a class of chemicals (beta-endorphins) when it needs to control pain. These chemicals act in ways similar to opioid drugs (which are described in Table 6.5); they inhibit pain and produce feelings of pleasure. At high dosages, nicotine seems to stimulate the release of the body's natural opioids, thereby reducing anxiety (Pomerlau & Pomerlau, 1990). Caffeine may have a similar effect. Of course, the relaxing effects of cigarettes and coffee may be, at least in part, the result of expectancies and social reinforcement, a possibility discussed later in this chapter.

Although Eysenck's claims about disease-prone personalities lack support, personality may play a role in nicotine use. Despite the well-known health risks, millions of people continue to smoke. Eysenck (1991) suggested that this phenomenon may be partly explained as a behavioral expression of the personality trait of **extroversion**. According to Eysenck, extroverts are born with low levels of arousal. Low arousal is perceived as aversive, so extroverts continuously seek stimulation—and smoking is a source of stimulation. Not all extroverts smoke, of course. There are other ways to raise arousal; some may drink lots of coffee. However, once extroverts start smoking (because of peer pressure, rebelliousness, or for some other reason), they are likely to continue because smoking provides the stimulation they crave (Breslau, Kilbey, & Andreski, 1993).

Alcohol

Alcohol (more accurately, ethanol) is the second most commonly used psychoactive substance in the United States. It is found in wine, liquor, spirits, beer, cider, and many cold medications. Although the per capita sale of alcohol has been decreasing in most industrialized countries since the 1970s, more than 90% of Americans still consume alcohol from time to time, and more than 50% of the population over 12 years of age use alcohol regularly. Eighteen percent of 12- to 17-year-olds and 65% of college students report using alcohol in the past month, and more than 80% of college students have used alcohol in the past year (all alcohol use statistics are from Johnston et al., 1995, 1996). Unlike smoking, alcohol use is positively correlated with educational attainment. College graduates drink more than those who ended their educa-

tion after high school (although college students with low marks drink more than high-performing students; Presley & Meilman, 1992). International comparisons suggest considerable cross-cultural variability in alcohol consumption depending on availability and cultural prohibitions (Helzer & Canino, 1992; Yamamoto et al., 1993).

Around 10% of 18- to 25-year-olds are especially heavy drinkers who consume five or more drinks on a single occasion at least five times a month. Although Whites have the highest rate of overall alcohol use at 53%, all ethnic groups seem to have similar rates of heavy drinking. However, heavy drinking is more common among younger rather than older White men, whereas the pattern is reversed among African American men (Helzer & Canino, 1992). In all ethnic groups, males are much more likely than females to be heavy drinkers (Presley & Meilman, 1992). The higher rate of heavy drinking among males is the result of several factors. First, society is more likely to condemn women than men for heavy drinking (Gomberg, 1988). Second, women cannot physically tolerate the same amount of alcohol as men. Blood levels of alcohol build up more quickly in women than in men of the same size because women have less of the enzyme that helps break down alcohol in the stomach before it enters the bloodstream (Helzer, Bucholz, & Robins, 1992).

Alcohol is one of the oldest psychoactive substances. Relics suggest that people fermented cereals to produce alcoholic drinks as early as 9,000 years ago (J. Warner, 1992). By the time of the ancient civilizations, there was already a god of wine (Bacchus), and alcohol has played a significant role in religious ceremonies ever since. The New Testament records Christ as referring to wine as his blood, and wine is still consumed in many Christian communities as a symbolic representation of the blood of Christ. As already noted, the Islamic faith takes the opposite view and forbids the use of alcohol.

The technique of distillation, first used in Europe in the 13th century, made it possible to produce low-cost, but highly potent, alcoholic beverages (J. Warner, 1992). Drinking to the point of intoxication became common, but this was rarely considered a major social problem until the 18th century. The reason for the change of attitude was partly economic. The British Industrial Revolution was built around dependable labor. Because alcohol caused workers to become less reliable, the British Parliament imposed restrictions on its sale. These restrictions set off a series of riots and civil disturbances, and the restrictive laws were repealed in 1743.

Unlike in England, where the campaign against alcohol was motivated by economics, in the United States it was seen as a war against sin. In the 19th century,

In spite of the 18th Amendment prohibiting alcohol (1919–1933), many people ignored the law and made their own home brew.

On the balance of evidence, Davey Blackthunder's injury was probably the result of his use of inhalants. There are three general types of inhalants: solvents (such as paint thinners and gasoline), gases (aerosols, refrigerants, and the nitrous oxide canisters used to whip cream), and nitrites. Originally, nitrites came in small glass capsules, which were "popped" open and inhaled (hence, their street name "poppers").

Inhalant fumes produce an initial period of stimulation and a change in mood; they can also distort perception and cognition. Ultimately, however, the effect of gasoline fumes and most other inhalant substances is to depress bodily functions. Deep breathing of inhalant vapors also produces a loss of self-control and violent behavior like that evidenced by Davey. Long-term inhalant use can damage the liver, kidneys, blood, bone marrow, and nervous system. When used in concentrated form (as when Davey Blackthunder tied a gasoline can to his face), inhalants can replace oxygen in the lungs, causing death by asphyxiation. Clearly, given the dangerous nature of his substance use, Davey needs professional assistance. ■

members of the Women's Christian Temperance Movement occupied bars and led prayer meetings against drinking. In 1919, the movement succeeded in getting alcohol prohibited in the United States by constitutional amendment. Alcohol remained illegal for 13 years, but prohibition proved difficult to enforce. "Bootleggers" produced illegal alcohol for sale in bars called speakeasies. Crime families, flush with money earned from illegal alcohol, bribed politicians and police to protect their empires. Because it created as many social problems as legal alcohol, the prohibition amendment was repealed in 1933.

Action   Chemically, alcohol is a **depressant.** It lowers arousal and makes people drowsy (Yi, 1991). Some of the other depressants included in the *DSM-IV* are described in Table 6.5. Inhalants, such as the gasoline fumes sniffed by Davey Blackthunder, may also have depressant-like effects, as the medical incident report on Davey (displayed in Document 6.5) explains.

DOCUMENT 6.5

Excerpt From Medical Incident Report on
Davey Blackthunder

In the Matter of Davey Blackthunder

Conclusion: The role of inhalants
Davey Blackthunder's injuries were self-inflicted. The staff of the Two-Tree Reservation Drug Program and the Reservation Hospital acted properly and with due speed to provide the necessary assistance.

Alcohol exerts a variety of effects on the central nervous system, but one of its most important is to reduce inhibition, which is controlled by the GABA neurotransmitter system (see Chapter 2). The result is that drinkers lose some degree of self-control. The effects of alcohol on the sympathetic nervous system and on the body's organ systems are the opposite of those produced by stimulants such as caffeine and nicotine—alcohol dilates blood vessels, decreases blood pressure, lowers heart rate, and slows respiration. Although small amounts of alcohol are exhaled as vapor by the lungs—which can be measured by roadside breathalyzers—most of the ingested alcohol goes to the liver, where it is gradually broken down (metabolized) and excreted. The average person can metabolize about one "standard drink"—the equivalent of 1 glass of beer or wine or 1 ounce of 90-proof liquor—per hour. Neither black coffee nor splashing cold water on one's face makes any difference in the rate at which alcohol is metabolized; there is no quick way to sober up.

Health Effects   Moderate amounts of alcohol, especially wine, may reduce the likelihood of coronary heart disease (Kinsella et al., 1993). On the other hand, chronic use of alcohol can damage the heart and just about every other organ in the body (O. Ray & Ksir, 1993). Alcohol irritates the digestive system, causing inflammation and bleeding. Prolonged and intensive use of alcohol can turn the liver into nonfunctioning, fibrous tissue. This syndrome, which is known as cirrhosis, is the seventh most frequent cause of death in the United States (O. Ray & Ksir, 1993). Because it reduces the functioning of

TABLE 6.5   Depressants Other Than Alcohol

Name	Description
Sedatives, hypnotics (sleep-inducing drugs), and anxiolytics (anti-anxiety drugs)	Barbiturates (Seconal, Nembutal, and others) were first used in 19th-century Germany as sleeping aids. They became popular in the United States during the 1950s, but habitual users soon found that they were unable to sleep without them and that they had adverse effects on their health (Abadinsky, 1993). Methaqualone (Quaalude), a more modern drug, acts in a similar manner to barbiturates but is less dangerous. Benzodiazepines (e.g., Valium) are considered safer than either barbiturates or methaqualone. The main effect of all sedative and anxiolytic drugs is to depress bodily functions. Around 1% of college students report using tranquilizers or sleeping medications in the past 30 days (Johnston et al., 1995). At low doses, these drugs are calming and promote sleep, but they can affect memory and interfere with psychosocial functioning (Warneke, 1991). The abrupt cessation of any of these drugs after prolonged use can cause neurological symptoms, including seizures. Because alcohol, sedatives, and anxiolytics all affect the GABA system (McKim, 1991), mixing alcohol and these drugs produces a strong and potentially deadly effect (Fils-Aime, 1993).
Opioids	*Opioid* is the general term for substances derived from the opium poppy plant. Known as opiates or narcotics, these include opium, morphine, and heroin; synthetic variants, such as methadone; and naturally occurring brain substances, such as beta-endorphins (Jaffe, 1991). Opium was once prized for its ability to reduce pain, but it was so habit-forming that it was replaced with morphine. When morphine also turned out to be habit-forming, it was replaced with heroin, which was also habit-forming. Eventually, scientists understood that all opioids are habit-forming. Although they may produce a brief feeling of elation, opioids are depressants (Barinaga, 1992). Fewer than 1% of college students report using opioids in the preceding month (Johnston et al., 1995), but there are more than 1 million users in the general American population (A. Goldstein, 1994). Chronic users have a short life expectancy, not just because of overdoses, which can cause instant death, but also because of AIDS from shared needles, accidents caused by impaired judgment, suicide, and homicide (opioid users occupy a dangerous world; Hser, Anglin, & Powers, 1993). There is also evidence that opioids reduce the functioning of the immune system, thereby lowering resistance to disease. Although opioid use has been decreasing since the early 1990s (Johnston et al., 1995, 1996), the number of opioid-related visits to hospital emergency rooms has actually increased (SAMHSA, 1994). Part of the reason for the rise is the increasing strength of opiates, which produces more overdoses (A. J. Jenkins et al., 1994). Although special drugs such as Narcan can reverse an overdose (R. Martin, 1997), many users fail to get help in time.

the body's immune system, excessive alcohol use also speeds the course of infections such as AIDS (National Institute on Alcohol Abuse and Alcoholism, 1992). A very high blood alcohol level can be fatal, although most people become unconscious before drinking enough to kill themselves.

Because alcohol has no vitamins, minerals, or proteins, heavy drinkers, who often neglect food in favor of alcohol, may become malnourished and suffer from vitamin deficiencies. Poor diet can produce severe disorders. One well-known cluster of alcohol-related neurological symptoms is the Wernicke-Korsakoff syndrome. Named after two neurologists, this syndrome is the result of a vitamin B (thiamine) deficiency. Sufferers become confused and disoriented; they develop double vision, report "blackouts," and suffer a variety of memory losses. The Wernicke-Korsakoff syndrome is a type of dementia—a brain disease that affects cognitive functioning. Abstaining from alcohol and eating a balanced diet may produce some degree of recovery from demen-

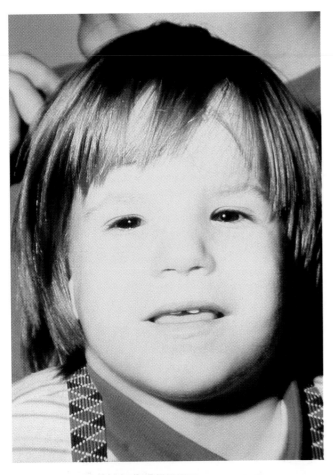

Signs of fetal alcohol syndrome include wide-set eyes, a fold of skin over the inner corner of the eye, a low nasal bridge and short nose, and an indistinct philtrum (the vertical groove between the nose and the upper lip).

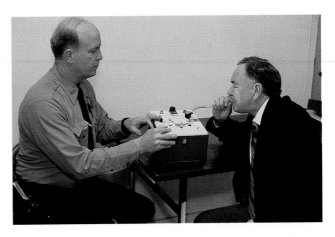

The police use breathalyzers to check the blood level of drivers they suspect of being intoxicated.

tias (G. B. Jensen & Pakkenberg, 1993), but in many people the damage is permanent. The dementias are discussed in detail in Chapter 11.

Heavy drinking during pregnancy can put a fetus at risk of developing fetal alcohol syndrome, which is marked by retardation, hyperactivity, facial deformities, heart defects, and organ malfunctions (Phelps & Grabowski, 1992; O. Ray & Ksir, 1993). Even when they consume the same amount of alcohol, African American women and female members of certain Native American tribes are more likely to have children with fetal alcohol syndrome than are members of other groups (Gordis, 1991). Their increased vulnerability appears to be the result of genetic differences in alcohol metabolism (Gordis, 1991). This finding serves as an important reminder that our response to alcohol is not just a function of how much we drink, but also of our genetic endowment (not to mention our nutritional status, our size, our diet, and many other factors).

Psychological Effects Moderate amounts of alcohol make most people feel talkative and relaxed. This is why Mr. Arnold offered Davey's father and uncle some beer (see Document 6.4):

MR. ARNOLD: Well, I had a couple of beers with Davey's father and uncle—since they weren't clients—just to relax them so that I could get some background information.

While drinkers may relax, even modest amounts of alcohol can affect cognition (Sayette, 1993). One general effect of alcohol on cognition is to limit the focus of attention. After a few drinks, we concentrate on only the immediate and the most obvious cues in our environment, ignoring complexities and long-term consequences. For example, you may feel like talking back to a professor or to your supervisor at work, but a sober consideration of the consequences will probably inhibit you from actually saying anything. Under the influence of alcohol, however, you may not consider the long-term consequences and just lash out. This narrowing of focus to the immediate is called alcoholic myopia (Steele & Josephs, 1990).

As the amount of alcohol in the bloodstream builds, vision becomes blurred, hearing grows less acute, and motor control begins to break down. It is these effects that make drinking and driving so dangerous. Indeed, alcohol is associated with around half of all automobile accidents (Painter, 1992).

The level of cognitive and motor impairment produced by alcohol depends on its concentration in the blood. Concentrations below 0.05% of blood by volume usually produce feelings of relaxation, with minimal cognitive or motor effects. Higher concentrations affect judgment and motor coordination. For most average-

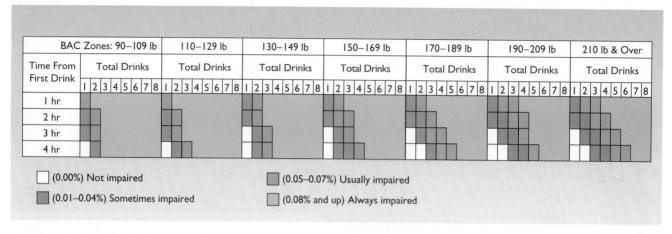

FIGURE 6.3 **Approximate Blood Alcohol Concentration (BAC) and Body Weight.** *The legal limit for BAC is .08% in some states and .10% in most others. For people under 21 years of age, some states have set a BAC limit of .02%.* From: Insel & Roth (2000, p. 254).

sized people, a blood volume concentration of 0.05 is reached after two standard drinks (two cans of beer, two shots of liquor, or two glasses of wine). However, smaller people may reach the 0.05 level after only one drink. The reason for the difference is blood volume. Because bigger people have more blood, they must ingest more alcohol to reach the same concentration. Figure 6.3 shows the relationship between blood alcohol concentration (BAC) and body weight.

Not only is judgment affected by alcohol but so are the attributional processes required to interpret and control emotions (Stritzke, Lang, & Patrick, 1996). For example, alcohol makes some people feel sexually aroused. Because their judgment is impaired, they may interpret innocent signs as indicating that another person feels the same way. Couple this with disinhibition, and it is not surprising that people influenced by alcohol may do things they would never do while sober. Alcohol's disinhibiting effect is what makes people believe that it is "stimulating" even though it is a depressant. Excessive disinhibition can sometimes lead to aggression (Bushman, 1993; Ito, Miller, & Pollock, 1996). Aggression, combined with impaired judgment, makes alcohol a factor in child abuse (B. A. Miller, Downs, & Testa, 1993), as well as in many suicides, murders, and rapes, especially "date rapes" (Modestin, Berger, & Ammann, 1996; Painter, 1992).

Cannabis

Despite being illegal, cannabis is the fourth most commonly used psychoactive substance among American college students. Fifteen percent admit to using it in the preceding month (Johnston et al., 1995). More than 65.2 million Americans (31.1%) have tried cannabis at least once, and almost 18 million (8.5%) have used it within the past year (Johnston et al., 1995). From 1979 to 1992, cannabis use among young people declined, but the trend reversed in 1993, and cannabis use increased through most of the 1990s.

Cannabis is actually a short name for *Cannabis sativa*, a type of hemp plant that produces several psychoactive substances. Marijuana (also known as pot, weed, and by many other names) is a mixture of the dried shredded flowers and leaves of the plant. Hashish is a sticky resin obtained from cannabis flowers; and hash oil is a liquid distilled from hashish. Cannabis users usually roll the substance into a cigarette known as a joint or smoke it in a pipe. One well-known type of water pipe is the bong. In the 1990s, users began slicing open cigars and replacing the tobacco with cannabis to produce what is known as a blunt. Some users mix cannabis into foods or use it to brew tea.

The psychoactive ingredient in marijuana is delta-9-tetrahydrocannabinol, usually called THC. Ordinary marijuana is about 3% THC, but some types can contain 20 times as much. At such high doses, THC can produce distorted sensations and perceptions (hallucinations). Technically, this makes cannabis a **hallucinogen**, but the *DSM-IV* classifies it in a separate category because perceptual distortions do not always accompany cannabis intoxication. Several hallucinogens are described in Table 6.6.

Cannabis is one of the oldest crops cultivated by human beings (see Grinspoon & Bakalar, 1993, for a history of marijuana). Ten-thousand-year-old clay pots unearthed in Taiwan were found to have strands of hemp

TABLE 6.6	Common Hallucinogenic Substances
Name	**Description**
MDMA	Widely known as ecstasy, MDMA has both hallucinogenic and amphetamine-like stimulating qualities. Although fewer than 1% of the college-age population admits to using the drug in the past 30 days (Johnston et al., 1995), MDMA use is concentrated in large cities, where it is used by groups of people at "rave" parties. MDMA destroys neurons, especially those containing dopamine. It not only produces hallucinations but also a loss of motor control (C. Fischer et al., 1995).
Natural (plant-derived) substances	Psilocybin (found in certain mushrooms), DMT (from the bark of the South American virola tree), mescaline (a cactus derivative), and other naturally occurring hallucinogens produce varying degrees of cognitive distortions depending on their concentration and on users' expectations. (People who expect to see changing colors or bright lights are more likely to experience these sensations than those without such expectations.)
LSD	**Lysergic acid diethylamide,** or **LSD,** is one of the most powerful hallucinogens and one of the most commonly used. Between 1% and 2% of college students say they have used LSD in the preceding month (Johnston et al., 1995). Derived from a fungus that grows on grain, LSD (commonly called acid) was first synthesized in 1938. It became popular in the 1960s when it was touted as an aid to self-insight. LSD comes in tablets, in capsules, or soaked into absorbent blotter paper, which can be chewed. The physical effects of LSD are similar to those of stimulants: increased heart rate and blood pressure, loss of appetite, sleeplessness, and dry mouth. LSD's psychological effects depend on the amount ingested, individual differences, expectations, and the social context. Typical reactions include rapid mood swings, distortions in time, and hallucinations. Sensations become confused, and some people claim to "hear" colors and "see" sounds (a phenomenon known as synesthesia). People who find such sensory experiences frightening label their experience a "bad trip." If trips are bad enough, they can trigger a mood or a psychotic disorder (American Psychiatric Assn, 1994). Although LSD symptoms usually disappear in 6–12 hours, a "hallucinogen persistent disorder" marked by flashbacks (repeats of some LSD experiences) may persist indefinitely, even among people who never again ingest LSD (American Psychiatric Assn, 1994).
PCP	Because its profile of psychological effects differs from those of LSD and MDMA, the *DSM-IV* puts phencyclidine (PCP) in a different category. Yet PCP is also a powerful hallucinogen. Widely known as angel dust, PCP was developed in the 1950s as a surgical anesthetic. However, many people given PCP had hallucinations, so the drug is now used only in operations on animals (Altura & Altura, 1981). Even low doses of PCP can precipitate a psychotic state in which sensation and judgment are so impaired that death may occur by accident or by suicide. Around 3% of high school seniors report using PCP in the past year (Johnston et al., 1996), often smoking it in a mixture with tobacco or marijuana.

fiber in their decorations. For centuries, and until fairly recently, hemp fiber was a major source of cloth (the first Levi jeans were made of hemp), rope, canvas, and paper. Hemp was also used in religious ceremonies and as medicine. In the 1800s, more than 100 scientific papers were published on the therapeutic effects of cannabis. Doctors recommended it for many specific diseases and also as a general analgesic and hypnotic. Despite its availability, history, and widespread medical use, cannabis gradually lost favor to aspirin, barbiturates, and injectable drugs that produce a quicker response. By the turn of the 20th century, cannabis was hardly used in medicine.

Changing social attitudes also worked against cannabis. In the early decades of the 20th century, lurid media reports portrayed drug users as criminals and dope fiends. In response, state legislatures moved to outlaw opioids and cocaine. Because alcohol was also prohibited, the authorities feared that people would turn to cannabis, so they banned it as well. The first states to ban cannabis were located in the Southwest. This was not a coincidence. Cannabis was widely used in those states because it was popular among the Mexican American population. In the 1930s, the federal government stepped in and made cannabis subject to such

Social attitudes toward psychoactive substances change from generation to generation. In the 1800s, cannabis was regarded as a medicine. But during Prohibition, it, like alcohol, was banned by many states. This 1936 film was meant as a cautionary tale, portraying evil marijuana dealers leading the children of Middle America astray.

heavy taxes that no one could afford to use it recreationally; the tax became the equivalent of a national ban. At the time, the cannabis tax produced little public controversy. The White majority had few qualms about prohibiting a drug used mainly by a rural ethnic minority. In fact, the cannabis ban remained uncontroversial until the 1960s, when cannabis became the substance of choice among the "hippie" culture. Activists then began to seek ways to have the substance legalized, a goal they have not yet attained.

Action   Within a few minutes of inhaling cannabis smoke, users experience dry mouth, rapid heartbeat, some loss of coordination, and slower reaction times.

Blood vessels in the eyes expand, and blood pressure rises. The membranes of certain nerve cells contain protein receptors that bind to THC. Once in place, THC stimulates chemical reactions that produce the euphoria that users experience when they smoke cannabis. Why should we have such THC receptors? It turns out that there is a naturally occurring chemical in the body, anandamide, that is similar to THC and that binds to the same receptors. Anandamide also produces feelings of elation (Fackelmann, 1993).

Health Effects   Many people use cannabis regularly with little obvious effect on their health. In fact, the most common physiological effects reported by cannabis users are feelings of thirst and hunger ("the munchies"). However, cannabis smoke contains many of the same ingredients as tobacco, so cannabis smoking can result in the same respiratory problems as cigarette smoking: cough, colds, and lung disease. In fact, because cannabis smokers try to keep the smoke in their lungs as long as possible, smoking a marijuana joint may actually have a greater effect on respiratory health than smoking a cigarette. Cannabis also increases blood pressure and heart rate, so it may have particularly negative effects on people with heart or circulatory diseases.

On the positive side, cannabis or THC may be a useful adjunct in the treatment of cancer, AIDS, and other conditions. Unfortunately, the U.S. Food and Drug Administration does not recognize cannabis as a treatment, so it is not legally available to patients, except in those states that have passed overriding legislation. For more on the therapeutic history of cannabis, see Highlight 6.2.

Psychological Effects   The psychological effects of cannabis are highly variable. They depend on the amount of THC ingested, the expectations of the individual, and the social context. Some people feel nothing at all when they smoke marijuana. Most report feeling lazy, relaxed, and mildly elated (a state usually summarized as feeling "stoned"). Because THC suppresses the neurons in the information-processing system of the hippocampus, a part of the brain that is crucial for learning and memory, cannabis may produce a memory disturbance. Distorted perceptions (sights, sounds, time, touch) have also been reported (Mathew et al., 1993). Occasionally, cannabis users suffer sudden feelings of anxiety and have paranoid thoughts (O. Ray & Ksir, 1993). In rare cases, cannabis may even induce a psychotic disorder (American Psychiatric Assn, 1994).

To sell their products, advertisers often focus on products' mood-altering effects. Highly caffeinated soft drinks are marketed to teenagers as the source of high-energy fun, while coffee is marketed to adults as the source of calm intimacy.

WHY ARE PSYCHOACTIVE SUBSTANCES SO POPULAR?

Why do we use psychoactive substances? According to ethologists, scientists who observe natural behavior in humans and animals, substance use is a "displacement" activity, something we do in place of another behavior. For example, psychoanalysts view smoking as a way of obtaining oral gratification, a displacement for the breast. Such simple explanations, however, hardly do justice to the complex web of factors controlling substance use.

Perhaps the most obvious reason for using a substance is to change our state of consciousness. Nicotine and caffeine increase arousal and make us more alert. If we need to get started in the morning or if we are having trouble concentrating on our work, a cup of coffee or a cigarette may help. Similarly, when we are tense, alcohol or cannabis may help us to relax. In other words, we use psychoactive substances to produce specific psychological effects. To sell their products, marketers and advertisers emphasize the effects of substances on consciousness, mood, and energy. Alcohol and cigarette advertisements routinely show people socializing and having a good time, while coffee is associated with calm intimacy. New,

high-caffeine drinks, such as Jolt and Red Bull, are aimed at younger consumers. Advertisements for these drinks promise increased power and energy. Cigarette manufacturers may deliberately increase the amount of nicotine in their product to provide a greater stimulating effect (Christen, 1996; D. A. Kessler et al., 1997).

Although they are important, the physiological effects of substances are only part of the story. Many people smoke and drink alcohol at the same time. Are they trying to become more alert or less alert? Probably neither. As you will see, substance use is the complex result of several interacting factors: exposure and availability, reinforcement, expectancies, social and cultural context, and biological variables.

Modeling and Availability

Before we can use a substance, we must first know that the substance exists and second, have access to it. In the case of caffeine, modeling is almost universal. From childhood, we are exposed to numerous models. Parents, friends, practically everyone uses caffeine in one form or another. Alcohol use is also widely modeled. Children can identify the smell of alcohol (beer, wine, or whiskey) by the age of six (Noll, Zucker, & Greenberg, 1990).

Substances, Medicine, and Morality

Modern medicine puts great effort and resources into finding treatments for identified diseases. In olden times, however, the approach was quite the opposite. Explorers would return from faraway places bearing exotic plants and ointments, which hucksters would then try to promote as cures for various ailments. For example, practically all psychoactive substances were first welcomed as medicines. Eighteenth-century doctors extolled tobacco as a wonder drug that could cure headaches, heal peptic ulcers, increase sex drive, and (believe it or not) sweeten the breath (Parrott, 1991). Amphetamines were introduced as a treatment for asthma, and the medicinal value of opioids was praised by no less an authority than Sigmund Freud. After a time, however, each of these substances became stigmatized and shunned. Consider the history of cannabis, for example.

Eighteenth-century doctors prescribed cannabis for coughs, venereal disease, headache, urinary incontinence, and to stimulate the appetite (Grinspoon & Bakalar, 1993). For the next 100 years, cannabis remained a respectable middle-class medicine recommended by the leading physicians of the day. It was prescribed for Britain's Queen Victoria and sold in American pharmacies. Yet when Congress passed the Controlled Substances Act in 1970, cannabis was placed on Schedule I. This is the most restrictive of the act's five schedules, reserved for substances with no medical value and unsafe to use even under a doctor's supervision.

There were many reasons for the change in attitude, but one was certainly morality. For many people, the use of psychotropic drugs was a sign of moral weakness, almost a sin. Professionals held a similar view. Early versions of the *DSM* did not classify substance-related problems as psychological disorders but as signs of deficient character. Temperance societies objected to cannabis for the same reasons they eschewed alcohol —it was immoral. Cannabis use was widely seen as the first step on the road to using more dangerous substances, such as cocaine and opium.

In the decades since the passage of the Controlled Substances Act, a battle has waged between the Food and Drug Administration (FDA), which has authority over drugs sold in the United States (and continues to believe that cannabis is unsafe and without medical value), and a combination of users, medical patients,

In the 1990s, buyers' clubs were created to dispense marijuana for medical use, especially to people with AIDS, cancer, and other diseases causing chronic pain and loss of appetite. The practice has been controversial, however, and is being debated at the state and federal levels.

Cigarette smoking is also easy to observe. Even with restrictions in advertising, there are few American children who are not exposed to cigarette smoking early in life. Children see people smoking on television, in movies, and in everyday life (after all, one third of Americans smoke). In recent years, well-known celebrities have also brought cigar smoking back into vogue. If they want to experiment with tobacco, young people have little difficulty. Attempts to restrict cigarette sales to minors are easily circumvented. In many countries, especially in Asia, there are few restrictions on advertising, and tobacco exposure is even more common than in the United States. Exposure to cannabis usually comes later than exposure to nicotine, caffeine, and alcohol. Because it is illegal in many countries, cannibis is not advertised and rarely modeled by parents. Most users are exposed by observing peers, usually in adolescence or early adulthood.

and scientists who believe that cannabis has sufficient health benefits to justify its use under a doctor's supervision.

One such health benefit is cannabis's ability to suppress the nausea caused by anticancer and anti-AIDS treatments. The FDA permits synthetic THC to be used for this purpose but not smoked cannabis. However, some patients are too nauseous to keep the THC tablets down and would prefer to smoke cannabis instead. A second potential medical application of cannabis stems from its ability to reduce excess pressure in the eyeball, which enables it to prevent damage to the optic nerves of people with glaucoma. Cannabis was used for this purpose until 1991, when permission was withdrawn by the FDA, which claimed that new drugs rendered cannabis unnecessary. Although some patients believe that cannabis is an effective addition to glaucoma treatment, they are denied access to the drug. A third medical use for cannabis is in reducing the pain suffered by people with multiple sclerosis (a disease in which the fatty covering of nerve cells is gradually destroyed). Although the FDA denies that cannabis is more effective for this purpose than other painkillers, many patients disagree. Finally, because THC stimulates the appetite, AIDS patients claim it helps them stave off the weight loss that often accompanies the disease. Cannabis smoke is a more efficient way to administer THC in AIDS patients than

tablets because AIDS damages the digestive system, making it more difficult for those with the disease to absorb THC through the intestines than to take it in through the lungs.

Because cannabis is illegal, anyone who uses it, even for health purposes, is liable for prosecution. This is what happened to Kenneth and Barbara Jenks. Kenneth contracted AIDS from a tainted blood transfusion and then passed the infection on to his wife (Grinspoon & Bakalar, 1993). Both were in their 20s and suffered from nausea, vomiting, and appetite loss. They learned about cannabis in 1989 and decided to give it a try. They regained weight and were healthier. Kenneth was even able to work full time. In 1990, acting on a tip, narcotics officers raided their home, held a gun to Barbara's head, and seized the two cannabis plants they grew to avoid the high costs of buying it on the street. The couple was found guilty of illegally cultivating marijuana, but their conviction was overturned on appeal. The Jenkses were allowed to use cannabis medically, as were a few other people. However, when the word got out, and many AIDS sufferers sought similar permission, the federal authorities refused. They argued that cannabis is no more effective than THC tablets and claimed that cannabis damages the immune system. This last point is especially important. AIDS already weakens the immune system; anything that weakens it further would make the

condition even worse. Because there were no carefully controlled studies of the effect of cannabis on the immune system, researchers at the time of the ban offered to conduct controlled clinical trials. Thus far, however, the federal government has withheld permission for them to perform such research, although, as previously noted, some states have passed overriding legislation permitting the medical use of cannabis.

Some psychoactive substances induce paranoia (unreasonable fear) in their users. It seems that cannabis has the same effect on some governments. There is no denying that cannabis has damaging effects on health and we should do all we can to prevent young people from taking it up. But we should also examine the possibility that it may be useful under medical supervision. We know that small amounts of alcohol protect against heart disease and that opiates help ease pain. It is possible that cannabis may also have value in medical care. Our challenge is to learn how to use psychoactive substances in ways that maximize their health-giving properties while avoiding the problems of unrestricted use.

Because we see so many people using caffeine, alcohol, and nicotine, often in happy surroundings such as coffee shops, parties, and restaurants, and because these substances are heavily promoted in the media and by peers, it is not surprising that most of us decide to give at least one of them a try. Modeling is also important for less common substances. For example, Davey Blackthunder was exposed to gasoline sniffing by members of his peer group, who seemed to be getting something

from the experience, and gasoline was easily accessible to him. Thus, for Davey at least, gasoline sniffing met the criteria of modeling and availability.

The more exposure we have to substance use and the more salient the models, the more likely we are to use a substance ourselves. Thus, children whose parents use alcohol to excess are more likely to try alcohol than are children whose parents abstain or drink moderately (Chassin et al., 1993). Also, adults who use substances

In recent years, celebrities such as Madonna and David Letterman have brought cigar smoking back into vogue.

are often less careful about monitoring their children and preventing their use of substances (Chassin et al., 1993).

Contrast the familiarity and availability of caffeine, nicotine, and alcohol with our knowledge of and access to amphetamines. Amphetamines are also stimulants, but they are not widely used. Few of us see our parents or friends using them, and they can be legally obtained only with a doctor's prescription. Because we are less likely to be exposed to them and because they are more difficult to get, we would expect fewer people to use amphetamines than caffeine—and we would be correct. Fewer than 3% of college students admit to using amphetamines in the preceding month (Johnston et al., 1995).

Reinforcement

Modeling and availability might determine which substances we are most likely to try, but other factors determine whether we will keep using those we do try. One of the most important is the positive reinforcement we get from changing our mental state (A. Goldstein, 1994). Caffeine makes us more alert; alcohol makes us relaxed and uninhibited. Davey's gasoline sniffing made him high. These changes in mental state are perceived as pleasurable because they stimulate the brain's "pleasure center," the part of the brain that gives rise to subjectively pleasant feelings (Korenman & Barchas, 1993; Olds, 1956). Although the exact location of the pleasure center is a matter of debate, it seems to be closely related to the dopamine system (Blum et al., 1996; A. Goldstein, 1994). One of the reasons that people continue to use substances is to experience the reinforcing feelings produced when substances stimulate the brain's pleasure center (Figure 6.4).

The reasons for using a substance may change over time. Consider smoking, for instance. Because young people are so heavily exposed to smoking models and because cigarettes are so easily accessible, it should come as no surprise that most smokers try their first cigarette as teenagers (Kandel & Logan, 1984). Most of the time, they find the experience unpleasant. The first few cigarettes may cause coughing, dizziness, nausea, even vomiting. It is amazing that anyone would wish to repeat the experience, especially since most adolescents know the health risks before they light up their first smoke (Quadrel, Fischhoff, & Davis, 1993). Yet, many go on to become smokers. One reason has already been mentioned—nicotine stimulates the brain's pleasure center. Another reason is peer group acceptance. Teenagers whose siblings or friends smoke are more likely to begin smoking than are those with no peers to emulate or impress (U.S. Department of Health and Human Services, 1990). Teenagers often associate cigarette smoking with glamour and independence; in some cases, smoking is a way of rebelling against adult strictures. Because smoking is followed by peer approval, as well as by desired changes in mental state, it is reinforced. Exactly the same group dynamics reinforce the use of alcohol, cannabis, and other substances.

Social reinforcement is an important determinant of substance use because substances are an integral part of social activity. Going out for a cup of coffee, a drink, or a smoke is something we often do with other people. The positive reinforcement produced by pleasant social interaction encourages substance use. In tense situations, substances are especially reinforcing because they take some of the friction out of social encounters. This is why social worker Lee Wright offered Horace and James Blackthunder coffee, and why counselor Alan Arnold offered them beer. Caffeine is a stimulant, whereas alcohol is a depressant, yet they both helped to smooth these difficult social interactions by shoring up the participants' poise and giving them something to do with their hands. The substances also allowed them to become involved in a shared activity as they eased into their interviews. The ability of substances to smooth social interactions makes them socially reinforcing.

In addition to positive reinforcement, negative reinforcement (escape from an aversive state) also plays an important role in substance use. Feeling tired or unable to concentrate is an unpleasant feeling. If a cigarette or a cup of coffee dissipates our fatigue and makes us more alert, we will be reinforced to try the same "cure" again the next time we feel tired or distracted. Similar negative reinforcement comes from substances that reduce feel-

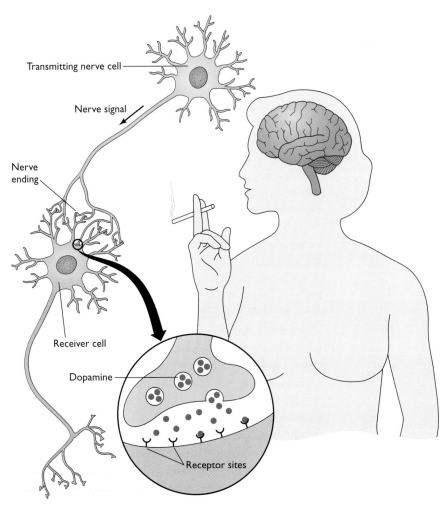

FIGURE 6.4 **The Chemical Process of Dependence on Nicotine.** *Nicotine stimulates neurons to release dopamine, which is associated with pleasure.*

ings of anxiety and depression (Chassin et al., 1993; King et al., 1993; Manley, 1992). A social form of negative reinforcement is the avoidance of ridicule ("Come on and try it. Are you chicken?"). Davey Blackthunder's friends might have ostracized him if he had refused to sniff gasoline (Lo et al., 1993).

Expectancies

As already noted, some people are in the habit of drinking a cup of caffeine-containing tea before going to bed. They say it aids slumber. But how can a substance that increases blood pressure, pulse rate, and arousal help people relax and fall asleep? We have discussed part of the answer; increases in arousal are reinforcing for low-arousal people, and stimulants affect the brain's pleasure center, releasing pleasurable endorphins. But there is another factor operating as well—cognitive expectan-

cies. If we believe that a cup of tea will help us to sleep or that a cigarette will help us relax, then they probably will have these effects even though both tea and cigarettes contain stimulants.

Experiments have repeatedly shown the power of expectancies to influence our psychological reaction to substances. For example, people who expect alcohol to relieve their inhibitions feel less restrained when given a drink purported to contain alcohol, even when the drink contains no alcohol at all (Cooper et al., 1992). These expectancies about the effects of substances are the result of direct experience with a substance as well as exposure to parents, peers, and the media (P. M. Miller, Smith, & Goldman, 1990). Positive expectancies about substances (smoking is sophisticated, alcohol makes us funnier, cannabis increases aesthetic appreciation) are one of the main reasons that people experiment with substances in the first place.

Social and Cultural Context

The reinforcement produced by peer group acceptance is an important determinant of substance use. Remember, Davey Blackthunder did not sniff gasoline when he was a resident in the rehabilitation program. It was only when he returned to his previous environment and joined up with his old gang that he returned to gasoline sniffing. This suggests that, in part at least, peer group social reinforcement encouraged Davey to sniff gasoline. Economic factors are also related to substance use (E. Smith, North, & Spitznagel, 1993). Remember that Davey sniffed gasoline only when he could not afford alcohol and drugs. Whole economies are similar. People in poorer countries may prefer one substance to another for economic reasons (de Almeida-Filho et al., 1991).

Substance use is a particularly serious problem for some ethnic groups. For example, Australian Aborigines and Native Americans like Davey Blackthunder have a higher incidence of substance-related problems than the population at large (Beauvais, 1996; Mail & Johnson, 1993). At least part of the reason for the high use of substances among Native American populations is historical. Europeans sometimes used substances, especially alcohol, as a way of subduing indigenous peoples. The continued high rates of substance use are the result of poor employment prospects, poverty, and despair about the future. To make matters more complicated, Western-style interventions designed to assist people with substance-related problems are not always appropriate to native cultures. For example, Native American norms emphasize the welfare of the group over the individual. In such cultures, it is difficult to single out a specific person as needing special treatment. Also, as we saw in Document 6.2, shame may be attached to needing psychological assistance. Families like Davey's prefer, as Davey's father put it, to "handle things like this at home." Understanding substance use, and helping people with substance-related problems, requires sensitivity to the ways in which cultural norms affect substance-related behavior (Caputo, 1993).

Biological Variables and Individual Differences

Some people may be genetically programmed to favor certain substances (Cadoret et al., 1987). If they are exposed to these substances, people with such predispositions are more likely than others to use them again. Evidence for such a predisposition among smokers comes from a study of male twins, which found moderate levels of concordance for smoking (Carmelli et al., 1992). Adoption studies have also provided evidence that substance use is at least partly genetic (A. Goldstein, 1994; Sigvardsson, Bohman, & Cloninger, 1996).

Genetics certainly play a role in alcohol use (C. C. H. Cook & Gurling, 1991; Kendler, Heath, et al., 1992). A possible mechanism for a predisposition to alcoholism is the DRD2 gene found on chromosome 11 (Blum & Noble, 1993). About 66% of excessive alcohol users (people whose alcohol use has caused them problems) carry this gene, whereas it is present in only 20% of the rest of the population. The existence of the DRD2 gene does not mean that some people are born "alcoholics." The same gene is also associated with other substances, including nicotine and opioids, and with compulsive binge eating and gambling (Blum et al., 1996). According to Blum and his colleagues (1996), the DRD2 gene could mark a "reward deficiency syndrome." Specifically, the brain pleasure centers of people who possess this gene may be less responsive than normal. Such people require intense stimulation to produce a pleasurable response (a reward). To gain this stimulation, they may use greater amounts of substances than other people. Compulsive eating and gambling as well as thrill-seeking behaviors, such as those characterizing extreme sports, are further examples of the ways in which reward-deficient people seek to provide greater stimulation to their brain pleasure centers.

Some people with the DRD2 gene may never develop substance-related problems because they have also inherited competing dispositions that counteract the effects of DRD2. For example, as many as half of all people of Asian descent lack one of the enzymes that helps break down alcohol in the liver. When they drink alcohol, they experience an "alcohol-flush syndrome" that includes a blushing red skin, dizziness, and nausea (Agarwal & Goedde, 1991). The alcohol-flush syndrome may be unpleasant enough to prevent affected people from drinking, even if they have inherited the DRD2 gene.

It is important to note that one third of problem drinkers do not have the DRD2 gene. This suggests that there may be two different types of people who develop problems with alcohol: (a) those with the DRD2 gene and a family history of excessive drinking, who develop alcohol-related problems early in life, and (b) those without the gene, whose drinking problems develop late in life and whose social and occupational functioning is only mildly affected (Yoshino & Kato, 1996; Schuckit & Smith, 1996). Drinking in the second group seems mainly affected by environmental factors (expo-

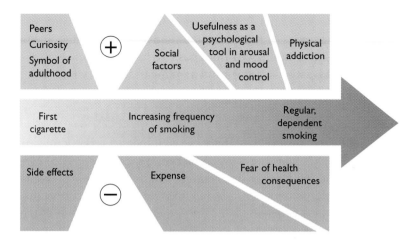

FIGURE 6.5 **Psychological, Behavioral, Social, Economic, and Biological Factors Affecting Different Stages in the Development of Smoking.** Data from: Stephney (1980, pp. 325–344).

sure, social reinforcement), whereas drinking in the first group may be more influenced by genetics.

Reasons for Substance Use: Summary

Although caffeine can trigger an anxiety disorder, and high doses can cause death, the *DSM-IV* does not consider caffeine to be as serious a potential problem as nicotine, alcohol, cannabis, inhalants, and, other substances. Most people use caffeine with little effect on their health or their everyday psychological functioning. Yet from a psychological point of view, caffeine is not very different from other psychoactive substances. Caffeine use depends first on being exposed to the substance, usually through direct modeling, and, second, on being able to obtain it. Whether we use caffeine depends on whether our peers are using it and whether we expect it to produce beneficial effects. Caffeine's physiological effect on us varies depending on our inherited dispositions, and our continued use of caffeine depends on its positive and negative reinforcing qualities.

In other words, exposure, modeling, and availability entice people to use caffeine, just as they enticed Davey Blackthunder to use inhalants and millions of college students to smoke cigarettes, drink alcohol, and use cannabis. Moreover, the same psychological, social, and biological variables that reinforce and maintain the use of caffeine also reinforce and maintain the use of other substances (Figure 6.5). The almost universal use of caffeine tells us that, given the right set of circumstances, almost everyone will use psychoactive substances.

POTENTIAL PROBLEMS OF SUSTAINED SUBSTANCE USE

The average American consumes 200 mg of caffeine per day, the equivalent of two strong cups of brewed coffee. Of course, many people consume much more. High caffeine consumption can induce caffeine intoxication, which is marked by restlessness, excitement, an inability to sleep, flushed face, muscle twitching, and in especially severe cases, rambling speech, heart rate abnormalities, and agitation (American Psychiatric Assn, 1994). Very large doses can even be fatal. Alcohol and cannabis also produce well-documented intoxication syndromes (American Psychiatric Assn, 1994). For some people, the whole point of using alcohol or cannabis is to become intoxicated. Intoxication was certainly the main reason why Davey Blackthunder and his friends sniffed gasoline.

You probably know people who routinely consume cup after cup of coffee without showing any signs of intoxication. Similarly, you may know people who show no signs of intoxication even after consuming significant amounts of alcohol or cannabis. You may wonder why these people seem immune to the intoxicating effects of these substances. The answer is **tolerance.** With repeated use, our bodies come to tolerate substances. Three cups of coffee may be enough to produce caffeine intoxication in a nonuser, whereas a much larger amount may have little or no effect on a habitual coffee drinker. Tolerance eventually develops to most (but not all) substances.

How much of a substance users consume, and how often, is partly determined by the amount of a substance in the user's body. For example, when long-term smokers are given reduced-nicotine cigarettes in place of their normal brand, they smoke more (and inhale more deeply) than they normally do (Herning et al., 1981; Maron & Fortmann, 1987). In other words, smokers adjust their habit to maintain a certain level of nicotine in their bodies. If nicotine levels fall below the desired level, they become irritable, restless, distractible, and hungry (Bock & Marsh, 1990). These symptoms are known as nicotine **withdrawal syndrome** (American Psychiatric Assn, 1994). The *DSM-IV* also contains diagnostic criteria for alcohol withdrawal syndrome, which is marked by tremor, sweating, nausea, and anxiety. In severe cases, people withdrawing from alcohol may experience disturbances in consciousness, including hallucinations (known as delirium tremens, or the DTs). Withdrawal symptoms may be so severe that people continue using a substance just to avoid them. In such cases, substance use is being maintained by a form of negative reinforcement.

In the *DSM-IV* diagnostic scheme, intoxication and withdrawal syndromes are called **substance-induced disorders.** These are disorders in which the problematic behaviors—intoxication, withdrawal, sleep disorder, anxiety disorder—are caused by using certain substances. Not all substances have recognized withdrawal syndromes. For example, the *DSM-IV* does not describe a withdrawal syndrome for caffeine or cannabis. This does not mean that withdrawal from these substances produces no symptoms; caffeine withdrawal is frequently associated with headaches, for example (Silverman et al., 1992). Caffeine and cannabis withdrawal syndromes are omitted from the *DSM-IV* because they are usually mild and unlikely to interfere with everyday functioning.

The positive effects produced by psychoactive substances are often followed by negative effects. Thus, highs are often followed by "crashes." According to the **opponent-process theory,** this shifting between positive and negative feelings is a natural aspect of self-regulation (R. L. Solomon, 1980). As tolerance develops, chronic substance users require increasing amounts of a substance to produce any effect. When the effects of the substance wear off, the person experiences withdrawal symptoms, including an intense craving for the substance. This craving can be set off by any cue, even the sight of a needle or a pipe, and it does not subside until the substance is once again ingested (Grant et al., 1996). Eventually, the substance ceases to produce any positive feeling of elation;

users continue to consume it, however, just to satisfy the craving. At this point, the motivation for taking a substance has moved from positive (to get high) to negative (to satisfy cravings and avoid withdrawal symptoms).

Substance Use Versus Substance Abuse

For most people, substances do not present a problem. They consume only moderate amounts, too little to interfere with their everyday functioning. This is an important point to keep in mind: Substance use, by itself, is not a psychological disorder. Substances present a psychological problem only when they produce adverse consequences. Consuming a glass of wine with dinner does not lead to adverse consequences for most people; thus it is not a sign of a psychological disorder (it may even be healthy for the heart). In contrast, drinking to the point of intoxication and missing classes the next day could be a sign of what the *DSM-IV* refers to as a **substance abuse disorder.**

The *DSM-IV* diagnostic criteria for substance abuse appear in Table 6.7. As you can see, the diagnosis requires a *recurring* pattern of substance-related difficulties. A single episode, such as a single instance of driving while intoxicated with alcohol, is not sufficient to make the diagnosis. According to the *DSM-IV*, all substance categories except caffeine and nicotine are liable to be abused. By the criteria contained in Table 6.7, Davey Blackthunder would be considered to be a person who abused inhalants.

Substance Dependence

Chronic substance abuse may lead to an even more serious substance use disorder, **substance dependence disorder.** Substance dependence means much the same thing as addiction, an older term that has been seriously overused in recent years. In addition to substances such as nicotine and opioids, writers have claimed that people can be addicted to chocolate, soap operas, work, even to sex. (See Chapter 13 for more on sex addiction.) When a term is used this broadly, it loses any specific meaning. To be more precise, the *DSM-IV* uses the term *dependence* rather than addiction. Table 6.8 contains the main *DSM-IV* diagnostic criteria for substance dependence.

According to the *DSM-IV*, all categories of substances except caffeine can produce dependence. Dependence develops at different rates for different substances, depending on how long the substance stays in

DSM-IV **TABLE 6.7** Main *DSM-IV* Diagnostic Criteria for Substance Abuse

A. A maladaptive pattern of substance use leading to clinically significant impairment or distress as manifested by one (or more) of the following, occurring within a 12-month period:

  (1) recurrent substance use resulting in a failure to fulfill major role obligations at work, school, or home (e.g., repeated absences or poor work performance related to substance use; substance-related absences, suspensions, or expulsions from school; neglect of children or household)

  (2) recurrent substance use in situations in which it is physically hazardous (e.g., driving an automobile or operating a machine when impaired by substance use)

  (3) recurrent substance-related legal problems (e.g., arrests for substance-related disorderly conduct)

  (4) continued substance abuse despite having persistent or recurrent social or interpersonal problems caused or exacerbated by the effects of the substance (e.g., arguments with spouse about consequences of intoxication, physical fights).

B. The symptoms have never met the criteria for substance dependence for this class of substance.

Note: From American Psychiatric Association (1994, pp. 182–183).

DSM-IV **TABLE 6.8** Main *DSM-IV* Diagnostic Criteria for Substance Dependence

A. A maladaptive pattern of substance use, leading to clinically significant impairment or distress, as manifested by three (or more) of the following, occurring at any time in the same 12-month period:

  (1) tolerance as defined by either of the following:
    (a) a need for markedly increased amounts of the substance to achieve intoxication or the desired effect
    (b) markedly diminished effect with continued use of the same amount of the substance

  (2) withdrawal, as manifested by either of the following:
    (a) the characteristic withdrawal syndrome for the substance
    (b) the same (or a closely related) substance is taken to relieve or avoid withdrawal symptoms

  (3) the substance is often taken in larger amounts or over a longer period than was intended

  (4) there is a persistent desire or unsuccessful efforts to cut down or control substance abuse

  (5) a great deal of time is spent in activities necessary to obtain the substance (e.g., visiting multiple doctors or driving long distances), use the substance (e.g., chain smoking), or recover from its effects

  (6) important social, occupational, or recreational activities are given up or reduced because of substance use

  (7) the substance use is continued despite knowledge of having a persistent or recurrent physical or psychological problem that is likely to have been caused or exacerbated by the substance (e.g., current cocaine use despite recognition of cocaine-induced depression, or continued drinking despite recognition that an ulcer was made worse by alcohol consumption).

Note: From American Psychiatric Association (1994, p. 181).

the body. Fast-acting substances result in quicker dependence than slow-acting substances (Hallfors & Saxe, 1993; J. T. Sullivan & Sellers, 1992).

Once substance dependence forms, people begin to organize their lives around satisfying their craving. Job, school, family, and friends give way to the need for the substance. The chronic use of substances may also change body chemistry because many substances actually replace the body's natural chemicals. For example, opioids reduce the production of natural endorphins, and benzodiazepines replace the body's natural production of GABA. When substances are discontinued, the body takes a while to restart its natural production. In the interim, the person experiences withdrawal symptoms. As we have already seen, these symptoms are often so unpleasant that people continue to use a substance long after the initial sources of positive reinforcement have disappeared and even in the face of strong social disapproval. In contrast to substance-induced disorders, such as intoxication, the *DSM-IV* classifies substance abuse and dependence as **substance use disorders.**

Note that the *DSM-IV* criteria for dependence include more than just the presence of tolerance and withdrawal. There are two reasons for including the additional criteria. First, not all substances produce physical signs of tolerance and withdrawal. LSD and cannabis, for example, are rarely associated with physiological withdrawal. Second, the opposite is also true: Tolerance and withdrawal can exist without the craving for a substance that marks dependence. For example, patients who are given strong painkillers after surgery may show signs of tolerance and withdrawal when their pain medication is discontinued without showing any of the craving usually associated with dependence.

By using a broad set of diagnostic criteria for substance dependence, the *DSM-IV* acknowledges that psychological dependence can occur without physiological dependence. LSD, as already noted, does not seem to produce tolerance or significant withdrawal symptoms. Yet people may still use it repeatedly, may steal to get money to buy it, may crave it when it is unavailable, and may find it difficult to stop using it. Such people are considered "psychologically dependent" on LSD even though they are not physiologically dependent. To distinguish between the two types of dependence, the *DSM-IV* allows the substance dependence diagnosis to be specified as "with" or "without physiological dependence." In reality, most substance abuse disorders are sustained by a combination of physiological and psychological dependence.

In general, the substances most likely to produce dependence (a) have social reinforcing qualities (peer acceptance, for example); (b) produce tolerance; (c) produce withdrawal symptoms; (d) lead to significant mood changes; and (e) affect pain, alertness, arousal, or stress (Rodin & Salovey, 1989). Even when substances possess all four characteristics (as in the case of alcohol), dependence is not guaranteed. Scientists once thought that people who abuse alcohol enter an inevitable downward spiral in which they become increasingly dependent (Jellinek, 1946), but we now know that alcohol abuse does not necessarily lead to dependence (Schuckit et al., 1993). Despite the widespread abuse of alcohol, fewer than 10% of drinkers meet the criteria for dependence in any 1-year period (R. C. Kessler et al., 1994). What is still not entirely clear is why some alcohol abusers become dependent, whereas others do not (Sobell & Sobell, 1993).

It is important to emphasize that dependence is much the same disorder whatever the substance involved. Although the college student who lights up a cigarette after class may seem to be a world apart from Davey Blackthunder sniffing gasoline with his friends, the same psychological mechanisms are at work in both cases. Habitual use of either substance can produce tolerance, and quitting either one results in withdrawal symptoms (American Psychiatric Assn, 1994). Quitting is difficult for both smokers and gasoline sniffers, even though both are aware of the harm they are doing to themselves (U.S. Department of Health and Human Services, 1988).

OVERCOMING SUBSTANCE DEPENDENCE

Substance use is often a difficult habit to break. Even people who are highly motivated to quit may not necessarily succeed. This section illustrates the problems people face in giving up substances and some of the proposed solutions. Because the use of nicotine and alcohol is so common, the main focus of this section is on these two substances, but the discussion also shows how lessons learned from helping people give up common substances may be applied to less frequently used substances, such as Davey Blackthunder's inhalants.

Stages in Overcoming Substance Dependence

As summarized in Figure 6.6, people with substance dependence are thought to go through a series of stages in the process of giving up a substance. This model was

FIGURE 6.6 **Stages in Giving Up a Substance**

originally put forward by Lichtenstein and Glasgow (1992) to describe the process of quitting smoking, but it is applicable to practically any substance (see also R. A. Martin, Velicer, & Fava, 1996; Prochaska, 1996). From not even thinking about giving up the substance (the precontemplation stage), people move through the contemplation stage, in which they are thinking about giving it up in the next 6 months, to the action stage (in which they actually quit). In the final, maintenance, stage, they consolidate their treatment gains and attempt to avoid relapse. Many people pass through these stages on their own, without the assistance of psychologists; however, an increasing number of people are seeking professional help. Most psychological treatment programs are aimed at the action stage; the majority also address maintenance issues. Public health programs are aimed either at preventing people from smoking in the first place (primary prevention) or at the precontemplation or contemplation stages, in which case they are designed to convince smokers to quit.

Detoxification

Once the action stage is reached, the first step in many treatment programs is **detoxification** (removal of the substance from the body). Smokers must stop smoking; alcohol-dependent people must stop drinking; heroin users must give up their drug. Substance abusers who have overdosed may be treated with special drugs (R. Martin, 1997).

To minimize withdrawal symptoms and maximize the probability that an individual will continue treatment, detoxification is usually a gradual process (Dackis & Gold, 1991). Sometimes, people undergoing detoxification may be prescribed anxiolytics and antidepressants to help with the stress of the withdrawal process (McCreery & Walker, 1993; Weddington, 1992). Care must be taken, however, to limit the use of these drugs to ensure that people do not give up one substance only to start using another. Although detoxification can take place anywhere, residential facilities (hospitals, drug treatment centers) often provide the safest environment for people undergoing withdrawal.

Beginning in the 1980s, inpatient facilities became increasingly popular not only for detoxification but also for the later stages of treatment. There are many well-known clinics specializing in helping people give up substances (e.g., the Betty Ford Clinic, Daytop Village, Phoenix House). However, inpatient treatment is more expensive than outpatient treatment, and there is little evidence that the extra expense necessarily produces better outcomes (Alterman et al., 1994).

Anti-smoking ads, such as this one, and education programs are aimed primarily at preventing people from smoking in the first place but also at people in the precontemplation or contemplation stages of quitting.

The Betty Ford Clinic is one of the most famous inpatient facilities where people go for detoxification programs, although there is little evidence that they are more effective than less expensive outpatient programs.

Antagonist and Aversive Drugs

Detoxification does not, by itself, constitute a treatment. Many substance-dependent people go through cycles of detoxification followed by abuse and dependence followed by detoxification again (Vaillant, 1992). To break this cycle, clinicians may prescribe an antagonist to block the action of the substance. For example, people dependent on opioids may be given naltrexone, a drug that blocks the action of opioids. Naltrexone has had only modest success in helping people overcome opioid dependence, although it may assist people who are dependent on alcohol (O'Malley et al., 1996; Schuckit, 1996).

Using an aversive approach, people who are dependent on alcohol may be prescribed a drug called Antabuse. If they take Antabuse and then consume alcohol, they will become quite ill—their hearts will race, they will vomit violently, and they may break out in soaking sweats. In theory at least, people who take Antabuse will stop drinking alcohol to avoid becoming ill. The equivalent of Antabuse for smokers is silver nitrate gum. Chewing it while smoking produces a foul taste in the mouth. Unfortunately, these aversive treatments rely on people's actually taking the Antabuse or chewing the silver nitrate gum. A person who wants to drink without becoming sick needs only to stop taking the Antabuse, a smoker needs only to stop chewing the gum—and that is just what many people do (Børup, Kaiser, & Jensen, 1992; E. J. Jensen et al., 1991).

Substance Replacement and Maintenance

In theory at least, substance replacement can help to minimize withdrawal symptoms. For example, nicotine-containing chewing gum and nicotine-releasing transdermal skin patches can replace the nicotine lost when people stop smoking (Bock & Marsh, 1990). Unfortunately, by itself, nicotine replacement does not appear to help people quit smoking (Gottlieb et al., 1987; Hill, Rigdon, & Johnson, 1993; U.S. Department of Health and Human Services, 1990). Some of those who do quit may become dependent on the gum or patch (Hughes et al., 1991). On the other hand, nicotine replacement may help people quit smoking when combined with psychological treatment (J. R. Hughes, 1993). Because nicotine gum is difficult to use correctly (and can produce digestive upsets), nicotine skin patches may be preferable.

Some forms of substance dependence may be so difficult to give up that users settle for replacing a dangerous substance with a less dangerous one that they can stay on indefinitely. This is known as maintenance treatment. The most common drug maintenance program involves substituting the synthetic opioid methadone for the more dangerous opioid heroin (E. A. Warner, Kosten, & O'Connor, 1997). An alternative to methadone is a drug called LAAM (levomethadyl acetate hydrochloride). LAAM's main advantage over methadone is that it is longer acting. Methadone needs to be taken once a day, requiring either a daily trip to a clinic or take-home dosages. LAAM need only be administered a few times a week. Although maintenance treatment may help some people wean themselves off heroin, it is almost certain that participants in such programs will become dependent on methadone or LAAM.

Self-Help Groups

Self-help groups have a long history in treating people with substance dependence. Alcoholics Anonymous (AA), for example, has been offering a self-help program around the world since 1935 (Nathan, 1993). Al-Anon is a related organization that provides support for the families of people dependent on alcohol. There are similar programs for people dependent on opioids and other substances (N. S. Miller, Gold, & Pottash, 1989). Self-help groups are extremely popular; there are more than 1 million AA members in North America alone (Chappel, 1993). Although there are differences from one AA group to another (H. A. Montgomery, Miller, & Tonigan, 1993), the AA program usually progresses through a series of 12 steps. Alcohol-dependent people must first acknowledge their dependency, must then put their trust in a spiritual being ("a power greater than ourselves"), and must make amends to people whom they have harmed (Chappel, 1993). Progression through the steps requires attendance at AA meetings, sometimes every day. These meetings give alcohol-dependent people the opportunity to talk to others who share their problems, and new members are encouraged to lean on long-term members for support. Because people are not randomly assigned to AA or a control group, it is not possible to conduct controlled clinical trials on the effectiveness of AA. The available evidence seems to suggest that many people drop out of AA after a short time, but those who manage to stick with the program do seem to benefit (Emrick et al., 1993; Pisani et al., 1993).

Multimodal Treatment

Practically all treatment programs for substance dependence combine several different methods, a strategy

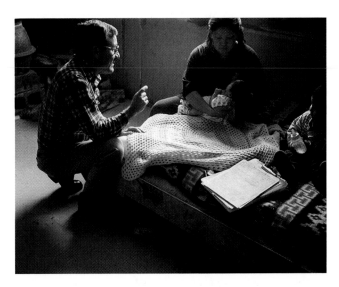

Health care workers, such as this visiting nurse, on Native American reservations must be sensitive to the cultural norms of their patients.

known as **multimodal treatment.** The general idea is to wean people away from a substance; help them manage their craving; and give them the skills necessary to cope with social stress, anxiety, and other potential causes of substance abuse. For example, a stop-smoking program might include insight-oriented therapy, cognitive therapy, training in coping skills, social support, relaxation, and **behavioral contracting,** in which people are fined or rewarded depending on whether they keep to the terms of a contract (Galanter, 1993; Higgins et al., 1993; W. R. Miller et al., 1992; Silverman et al., 1996).

As already mentioned, aversive conditioning using drugs such as Antabuse has also found a place in treating substance abuse. Aversive conditioning without drugs may also be tried. Typically, psychoactive substances are paired with noxious stimuli, either in vivo or in imagination (Callner, 1975; Cautela, 1996). One variation of aversive conditioning used with smokers is to have them puff rapidly on cigarettes until they feel so nauseated that the very thought of smoking becomes aversive. In theory, the rapid smoking technique is applicable to any smoker, although care should be taken in using it with people who have heart disease because their health may be adversely affected by rapid smoking. Note that, like drug-based aversion, aversive conditioning is dependent on a person's motivation to continue a treatment program even when the program involves unpleasant experiences.

Document 6.6 contains counselor Alan Arnold's treatment plan for Davey Blackthunder. Note the use of many different treatment modalities, each aimed at ad-

dressing another reason for Davey's dependence on gasoline sniffing and other substances. Also note the addition of a seminar on Native American culture. Substance abuse has been the tragedy of many indigenous communities around the world (Mail & Johnson, 1993). Overcoming substance-related disorders is not easy under any circumstances, but it is particularly difficult among native cultures, which must somehow integrate treatment and prevention programs into their social norms (Novins et al., 1996). As you can see, the Two-Tree Reservation Substance Abuse Program tries to provide participants with a sense of cultural identity. The idea is that people who have pride in their identity also have pride in themselves and are more likely to stick with treatment (D. G. Fisher, Lankford, & Galea, 1996). The treatment program also includes traditional healers (medicine men) who add a culturally relevant dimension to treatment.

DOCUMENT 6.6

Alan Arnold's Treatment Plan for Davey Blackthunder

Goal: Complete Abstinence From Inhalants

1. *Minimize withdrawal symptoms:* Detoxify Davey by complete withdrawal from inhalants. Valium will be used for a maximum of 7 days to help Davey deal with any withdrawal symptoms. He will be allowed cigarettes, but not alcohol, during the detoxification and withdrawal process.

2. *Social support:* Davey will be enrolled in a self-help support group consisting of members of the drug program, which meets daily for 1 hour. The group discusses all aspects of their struggle with substance abuse as well as ways to avoid relapse. Davey will also be assigned a "buddy" whom he can contact for support outside of group meetings.

3. *Culture:* Group seminars on the tribe's history and culture are mandatory for everyone enrolled in the Two-Tree program. These seminars emphasize the ancient history and cultural achievements of Native Americans. Native American philosophies of community and discipline are also discussed. Medicine men participate and employ folk medicine to help participants. The goal is to build self-esteem by giving participants pride in their culture.

4. *Cognitive-behavioral therapy:* Davey will be enrolled in a cognitive-behavioral therapy program, which has five specific interventions:

    A. *Cognitive self-statements:* Davey will be taught self-statements that stress the negative health consequences of substance dependence and the benefits of quitting.

    B. *Social skills:* Through role playing, Davey will be taught how to reject substances offered by friends.

Assessing Treatment Outcome

Designing a study of treatment effectiveness requires researchers to make several important choices (Burnam, 1996). First, they must decide whom to treat: a random sample, a representative sample, a group of volunteers? Most treatment outcome studies rely on self-selected volunteers. Because volunteers may be more motivated to succeed than the average substance user, studies relying solely on volunteers may produce outcomes that are better than those obtained when participants are chosen at random. By randomly assigning participants to treatments, researcher can ensure that their estimate of treatment effectiveness is close to the effectiveness that will be achieved in the real world of the clinic.

Once the treatment population is defined, researchers must decide how to deal with people who drop out of treatment before the end of the program. Should they be ignored? Should they be considered failures? Because some of the dropouts may well go back to substance abuse and dependence, ignoring them will result in an overestimation of the program's success. The conservative approach is to assume that all dropouts are abusing substances and count them as treatment failures even if this leads to an underestimate of a program's success.

Next, the researcher must decide on a definition of success. Is one day without the substance enough? Two days? A week? Is complete abstinence necessary, or can some substance use be tolerated? This last question has been the subject of considerable disagreement. The AA program is based on the notion that alcohol-dependent people must abstain completely from drinking. Indeed, one of the steps in the program requires participants to admit that they are unable to control their drinking. In contrast, some psychologists have claimed that "controlled drinking" is an achievable goal for at least some alcohol-dependent people (Sobell & Sobell, 1976). After years of controversy about whether controlled drinking is possible or whether abstinence is the only way to prevent alcohol abuse (Pendery, Maltzman, & West, 1982), the answer seems to be that it depends on the person and the place. Some alcohol-dependent people are able to learn to control their drinking (Finney & Moos, 1991; Rosenberg, 1993), whereas for others, complete abstinence is the only way to ensure that they do not slip back into old habits.

Having chosen an outcome criterion, researchers must give it an operational definition. Should the researcher rely on participants to be honest, or should biochemical assays be used to verify their reports? The choice of an operational definition is crucial because different operational definitions may produce different research results. For example, studies that rely on self-report usually claim higher success rates than studies using biochemical drug tests (Magura & Kang, 1996). This suggests that self-report is not a reliable method for determining if a person is using a substance. Biochemical tests are more objective, although there is some evidence that the threat of a biochemical assay is enough to prompt honest self-reporting (D. K. Wilson et al., 1993). Even biochemical tests have their drawbacks. For example, treatment programs that include nicotine replacement obviously cannot use

C. *Relaxation training:* Davey will be taught systematic relaxation to show him how to relax without the aid of substances.

D. *Behavioral contracting:* Davey will be offered a contract in which he will receive privileges for staying substance free and will sacrifice privileges if backsliding occurs.

E. *Aversive conditioning:* In a later phase of treatment, we will try to help Davey give up cigarettes by using rapid smoking (frequent deep inhaling) to create an aversive reaction to tobacco. ■

In addition to culture, clinicians must also be sensitive to gender issues when planning treatment programs (Hamilton, 1991; Room, 1996; M. D. Stein & Cyr, 1997). For example, many female (and some male) substance abusers are victims of sexual abuse (Harrison et al., 1997; Wilsnack et al., 1997). They may require special therapists. Women in treatment may also need help in making suitable arrangements for their dependent children (Copeland & Hall, 1992).

One of the reasons so many therapists favor the multimodal approach is the lack of evidence favoring one treatment approach over another (McLellan, 1992). As discussed in Critical Thinking About Clinical Decisions 6.1, valid treatment outcome data are difficult to collect. Although it is clearly necessary to determine the answer, it may be some time before we are able to say with any certainty which approach to substance dependence is best for which person.

the presence of nicotine in the body to indicate relapse. In such cases, biochemical tests may be able to find other evidence of smoking, such as the presence of carbon monoxide.

A final decision for researchers is how long to follow up smokers into the maintenance stage. Since relapse can occur at any time, the choice of a follow-up period is necessarily arbitrary. Most researchers consider 6 months to be a minimum.

To show how variable treatment outcomes can be, the table summarizes the results of hundreds of studies designed to assess the value of stop-smoking programs (J. L. Schwartz, 1987). Because they used different populations, defined outcome in many different ways, and treated dropouts differently, and because some of the studies lacked appropriate controls, the precise quitting rates they report are not comparable. The successful reports for acupuncture and hypnosis are especially suspect (Parrott, 1991). Still, there are some trends worth noting. Taking the medians as estimates of treatment effectiveness, only 30–40% of the participants in

a stop-smoking program will quit and remain abstinent for 12 months. Treatment programs for other substances produce similar results. Are these results good or bad? It depends. Since many substance users stop on their own, without even the assistance of psychologists or self-help groups, only the toughest cases might decide to participate in a treatment program. Thus, a 30–40% success rate may not be too bad.

Summary of Quit-Smoking Outcome Studies

| Type of program | Percentage of smokers who quit | | | |
| | After 6 months | | After 12 months | |
	Range	Median	Range	Median
Self-help	0–33%	17%	12–33%	18%
Nicotine gum	17–33	23	8–38	11
Nicotine gum plus behavior modification	23–50	35	12–49	29
Hypnosis	0–60	25	13–68	19.5
Physician advice	5–12	5	3–13	6
Acupuncture	5–34	18	8–32	30
Rapid smoking	7–62	25.5	6–40	21
Rapid smoking combined with other treatments	8–68	38	7–52	30.5
Multimodal program	18–52	32	6–76	40

Note: Adapted from J. L. Schwartz (1987).

Relapse Prevention

Most substance abuse treatment programs have high relapse rates. For example, practically all quit-smoking programs are successful at first, but after a time, 70–80% of participants begin smoking again. Some treatment programs attempt to improve on this by training people to deal with the potential causes of relapse before they occur. For example, quitting smoking commonly leads to weight gain, and some smokers return to smoking just to control their weight (Talcott et al., 1995). In such cases, relapse may be prevented by teaching these people how to control their diets before they begin to gain weight. Although this sounds like a logical strategy, outcome studies have not found relapse prevention programs, as they are presently conducted, particularly effective (Lichtenstein & Glasgow, 1992). The main factor influencing relapse seems to be treatment length. Longer, more intense treatments produce better results than brief treatments (Lichtenstein & Glasgow, 1992).

Treatment of Substance Dependence: State of the Art

Despite the best efforts of generations of psychologists, substance dependence remains difficult to treat. A 25-year follow-up of men treated for heroin dependence found that 75% were either dead, in jail, or still abusing heroin; only 25% were substance-free (Hser et al., 1993). Still, we know that it is possible for people to quit because many have overcome substance dependence, often on their own without any treatment (Lichtenstein & Glasgow, 1992; Finney & Moos, 1991). There are many different treatment programs currently in use for both dependence and abuse, and no single program seems to work for everyone. This is understandable. People differ in their genetic sensitivity to substances and their reasons for using them (Brannon & Feist, 1997; C. A. Cloninger, 1987; K. O'Connor & Stravynski, 1982). Specific treatments, targeted at the reasons an individual uses a substance, are likely to be more successful than global treatments applied to everyone.

Substance dependence is often associated with other psychological disorders (Higuchi et al., 1993; M. B. Kushner, Sher, & Beitman, 1990; McFall, Mackay, & Donovan, 1992). It is often difficult to determine whether substance abuse is the cause of another psychological disorder or its result, or both (T. P. Johnson et al., 1997). In most cases, however, it is necessary to treat any serious psychological disorders before people can moderate their use of substances. The problems of **mentally ill chemical abusers (MICAs)** are especially severe (Kutcher et al., 1992). MICAs, who are most often young males, are generally poor, homeless, sickly, and likely to get into legal difficulties. In the past, they may have been institutionalized, but today they are more likely to be found on the street, where substances are easy to obtain (Polcin, 1992). Although some attempts have been made to enroll MICAs in self-help groups (S. Caldwell & White, 1991), treating them remains a great challenge (Hansell, 1997).

PREVENTION OF SUBSTANCE-RELATED DISORDERS

Although they vary in their specifics, all clinical-based programs for substance dependence focus on the individual. The social forces maintaining substance abuse—peer pressure, lack of knowledge, advertising (in the cases of nicotine and alcohol), and legal restrictions—are rarely addressed. Clinical programs are also expensive; they involve multiple sessions, and only limited numbers of people can be treated at one time. They may be justified for those people whose substance dependence has proven recalcitrant to any other intervention, but their relatively modest success makes them a costly option. In contrast, prevention programs have the potential to save money because keeping disorders from developing is usually cheaper than treating disorders after they develop. Because certain types of substance abuse are more prevalent among some minority groups (Native Americans, for example), and among poorly educated people (Lichtenstein & Glasgow, 1992), prevention programs may benefit people who are unable to access or afford clinical treatment.

Legal Restrictions

Perhaps the most straightforward approach to the primary prevention of substance abuse and dependence is to use the legal system. (See Chapter 1 for a discussion of primary and secondary prevention.) For example, over the years, increasingly severe legal restrictions have been placed on cigarette and alcohol advertising. These restrictions have had only minimal effects, however, because manufacturers usually contrive to gain public exposure in other ways (by sponsoring sporting events, for example).

Because legal restrictions on exposure have had limited success, public health authorities have argued that restricting access might be a more effective means of preventing substance abuse (Jansen, 1996). There are many other ways to use the law to restrict access. We can, for example, forbid sales to minors, or we can require a doctor's prescription to purchase a substance. Regrettably, neither of these strategies has been particularly effective. Although cigarettes can be sold legally only to adults, minors have little difficulty obtaining them ("Accessibility," 1996; "Estimates," 1996; Jason et al., 1996). Unscrupulous doctors have sold prescriptions to children, and most prescription drugs can also be purchased on the street.

Another approach to restrict access is to ban substance use in certain settings. Smoking, which was once common in offices, restaurants, planes, and theaters, is now prohibited in most public areas. As the number of places where smoking is permitted decreases, smokers have fewer opportunities to pursue their habit. Thus, making smoking inconvenient reduces its prevalence.

Perhaps the ultimate in primary prevention through legal restriction is complete prohibition; substances are simply outlawed. Anyone caught using, selling, or even possessing an illegal substance is liable to criminal prosecution. The U.S. government, for example, periodically declares "war" on drugs and appoints a tough leader (a "czar") to pursue the campaign. This was the approach taken to alcohol in the United States in the 1920s, and, as we have already seen, it failed miserably. People still drank, but the purity of what they drank was suspect, and criminals thrived by providing illegal liquor to those with the money to buy it. Because prohibition has produced crime and been a failure every time it has been tried, countries such as Great Britain and the Netherlands have experimented with making psychoactive substances available through government-controlled distribution points. In this way, the authorities can ensure the purity and potency of the substances people use, eliminate the criminal black market that presently provides illegal substances, and obviate the need for substance-dependent people to steal in order to support their habit. Thus far, such legalization has not won much favor in the United States. For a more detailed discussion of the pros and cons of legalizing substances, see Highlight 6.3.

Global Educational Programs

Although people who use substances are usually aware of the health risks, they tend to believe that these risks apply more to other people than to themselves (Gibbons, McGovern, & Lando, 1991). This feeling of invulnerability, which applies to adults as well as adolescents (Quadrel et al., 1993), may explain why people continue to use dangerous substances even when they know that they are harmful (Gibbons et al., 1991). Educational programs have been targeted directly at these mistaken feelings of invulnerability. Health warnings, mass media campaigns, and school health programs (see Sussman, 1996, for example) are all designed to convey the message that substance dependence presents a danger to everyone. Since health warnings made their first appearance on cigarette packages, the incidence of smoking has decreased. It is tempting to conclude that it was the health warnings that were responsible. This conclusion may not be entirely justified, however. Smokers may be aware that packages contain warnings, but few spend much time reading them, and even fewer can remember what they say (P. M. Fischer et al., 1989). Similarly, although media campaigns and educational programs targeted at schools make people more knowledgeable about the dangers of smoking (E. L. Thompson, 1978), they do not seem to have a strong effect on the act of smoking itself. The main value of health warnings is in moving those who use substances from the precontemplative to the contemplative stage of the substance-quitting process, at which point other, more powerful interventions take over.

Specific Educational Programs

Global educational programs provide information about substances, but they do not address the factors that maintain substance use: peer pressure, mood changes, advertising, avoidance of withdrawal, and stress reduction. Specific educational interventions designed to teach those at risk how to resist these influences and temptations, and how to deal with stress and withdrawal, may have a greater chance of succeeding (Jansen, 1996). Using a method he calls "skillstreaming," A. P. Goldstein and his associates (1990) attempt to teach children and adolescents the skills necessary to refuse substances. Goldstein has identified 20 core refusal skills, including "knowing your feelings," "using self-control," "responding to teasing," and "dealing with being left out." The skillstreaming process, which takes place in groups, begins with the teacher modeling the skill. This is followed by role playing, in which adolescents attempt to employ the skill. All participants receive feedback on their performance. Good performances are reinforced and rewarded. When they have acquired their new skills, the participants practice them as homework. A sample curriculum for teaching the refusal skill "responding to teasing" appears in Table 6.9.

Schools can be effective venues for educating young people about substance abuse. Because school attendance is compulsory, schools offer opportunities to reach all population groups, including those at special risk for drug abuse (such as children with behavior problems or learning disabilities). School-based prevention programs do have an effect, especially when they include a parents' or caregivers' component that reinforces the messages sent to children and opens opportunities for family discussions about substance use (Dusenbury, Falco, & Lake, 1997). Although most school programs are aimed at primary and high school students, even college students benefit from a substance abuse curriculum (Coleman et al., 1997).

One of the most important reasons why adolescents experiment with substances is peer pressure. It is possible, therefore, that adolescents may be deterred from using substances if they can be helped to resist the blandishments of their peers—"just say no." This is the aim of R. I. Evans's "inoculation" program (Evans, Smith, & Raines, 1984). Based on the stress inoculation procedure described in Chapter 4, Evans's program aims to build self-esteem, inculcate the coping skills necessary to deal with peer pressure, and reward adolescents for abstinence. Evans shows teenagers films of adolescents encountering and resisting peer pressure and encourages participants to model the behavior they see in the films. Inoculation programs have been found to deter substance use, especially smoking, not only immediately but after 2 years (Evans et al., 1984). However, after 4–6 years, students who received inoculation are about as likely to use substances as students who received only normal health education (Brannon & Feist, 1992). The

Minimizing Harm

For many people, substance abuse is morally wrong; the Catholic Catechism of 1992 classifies it as a sin (Riding, 1992). However, immorality and illegality are not the same thing. Many morally questionable behaviors—adultery, for example—are not criminal offenses in the United States. Why, then, are some psychoactive substances illegal? There are three main reasons. First, substances such as heroin are illegal because they pose a serious danger to individuals or to society. They kill 1%–2% of users each year, those who share needles are in danger of contracting AIDS, and people may turn to crime to feed their habits (Langer & Tubman, 1997). A second reason for making some substances illegal is to keep people from becoming substance dependent and having their lives ruined. Even substances that do not cause dependence may be banned because they may entice people to use other substances that are more habit forming. For example, as they get more money, heavy users of inhalants, like Davey Black-thunder, may progress to injectable drugs such as heroin (Schutz, Chilcoat, & Anthony, 1994). A third reason for making substances illegal is the social cost of dependence. If society is forced to spend its scarce resources caring for the health effects produced by substance dependence, it will have fewer resources for other purposes, such as schools, transportation, and hospitals.

These are all good reasons for making substances such as heroin illegal, but they do not explain why alcohol and nicotine remain legal. Both are notorious for causing dependence, both fill hospitals with patients, and both are responsible for large numbers of deaths each year. The answer is that America did once try to make alcohol illegal, but failed. Fed up with spending money chasing bootleggers and the danger presented by impure alcohol, the public supported the repeal of prohibition in 1933.

In the United States, county workers burn confiscated marijuana plants (top). In The Netherlands, teenagers roll a legal joint in a café (bottom). Which approach to substance abuse causes the least harm: prohibition or legalization?

The prohibition of other psychoactive substances has been no more successful than was the prohibition of alcohol in the 1920s. For example, almost one third of Americans (including Bill Clinton) admit to using cannabis, an illegal substance, at one time in their lives. As in the prohibition era, impure street substances cause illnesses, and sometimes death. A fortune is expended chasing those who grow, manufacture, and supply substances as well as those who turn to crime to support their dependence. Another fortune is expended paying to keep those who get caught in prison. Some writers have argued that the consequences of making substances illegal

are perhaps worse than the effects of the substances themselves. Perhaps it is time to admit that some people are always going to use psychoactive substances and concentrate on minimizing the negative consequences. This emphasis on secondary prevention is known as the harm-minimization approach (Byrne, 1996). If illegal psychoactive substances were made legal, we could ensure that users get pure substances, clean needles, education, and appropriate health care. Society would not only save the money currently spent on police and prisons, it could tax all substances just as cigarettes and alcohol are currently taxed. The result could be an increase in government revenue for other purposes.

The logic in favor of legalizing psychoactive substances may appear sound, but there is another side to the argument (Campbell, 1996). Opponents of legalization fear, with good reason, that more people will use psychoactive substances if they are made legal. Down the line, this could mean more dependence and more substance-related illness. Road accidents and accidents at work could also increase if more people began using psychoactive substances. Governments who distribute psychoactive substances are also worried about their potential liability. By making available to the public substances known to be dangerous, the government may open itself to lawsuits from anyone who becomes ill. Clearly, there are positives and negatives attached to making psychoactive substances legal. Still, we know that prohibition has not worked. Perhaps it is time to experiment with the controlled distribution of substances (as the British and Dutch do) just to examine the effects and to measure whether the benefits outweigh the costs. It may be time to start treating substance abuse and dependence as a disease whose harm can be limited rather than as a sin for which people should be condemned.

TABLE 6.9 Example of Skillstreaming: Teaching Children to Respond to Teasing

Steps	Trainer's notes
1. Decide if you are being teased.	Are others making jokes or whispering?
2. Think about ways to deal with the teasing.	Gracefully accept it; make a joke of it; ignore it.
3. Choose the best way and do it.	When possible, avoid alternatives that foster aggression, malicious counterteasing, and withdrawal.

Suggested content for modeling displays

School or neighborhood: Main actor ignores classmate's comments when refusing an offered cigarette.

Home: Main actor tells sibling to stop teasing about refusal to smoke.

Peer group: Main actor deals with teasing about smoking by making a joke of it.

Note: From A. P. Goldstein et al. (1990, p. 42).

problem seems to be that social situations change with time. Coping skills that are effective in middle school may not work as well in high school. The most effective prevention programs are long term, extending over the school career with repeat interventions (called "boosters") to reinforce the original prevention goals. Once again, family-focused prevention efforts that include parents as well as children have a greater impact than strategies that focus on children only.

Minimum-Cost Interventions

Family Doctors   Most people visit a doctor at least once each year. Thus doctors (as well as their assistants and nurse counselors) are in an excellent position to help educate people about substances (K. M. Carroll & Schottenfeld, 1997). Medical advice is generally respected, and doctors can prescribe any necessary medications (tranquilizers, for instance, or nicotine-replacement skin patches). Physicians trained in client-centered counseling techniques are more likely to be effective than those who simply provide information, but even untutored doctors can have beneficial effects (Lichtenstein & Glasgow, 1992). Although any particular doctor may influence only a small number of patients, the large number of doctor-patient interactions could still result in a substantial effect across the entire population. See Critical Thinking About Clinical Decisions 6.2 for an analysis of the cost-effectiveness of this sort of intervention.

Worksite Programs   As their name suggests, worksite programs are delivered to workers, and sometimes their families, at their place of employment. With the cooperation of employers, workers are given time off to attend these programs and may even be rewarded for success. Worksite programs are not only more convenient for the participants, they can be designed to fit the organization and coordinated with its rules about using substances such as alcohol and nicotine. Like doctors, worksite programs may help only a small number of people at each site, but the overall effect of programs at many worksites is potentially huge (K. K. Fisher, Glasgow, & Terborg, 1990; also see Critical Thinking About Clinical Decisions 6.2). In an attempt at secondary prevention, some employers use chemical tests to screen employees for substance use. Such programs raise certain ethical problems (Forrest, 1997). If such screening is considered part of routine occupational health and safety (substance abuse can produce dangerous work situations), then normal medical ethics should apply. Employees should be given full information on the purpose of the screening tests and must voluntarily consent to screening. Employees who produce positive results should be given access to their blood or urine sample so that they can get an independent analysis. If screening is not conducted as part of occupational health, but as a prelude to dismissal and criminal prosecution, then employees should have the same rights as anyone involved in a criminal investigation (Schorling & Buchsbaum, 1997).

Cost-Effectiveness Analysis

New treatment programs almost always mean additional expense. With the increasing costs of health-related services and the advent of managed care, not all new treatment programs can be funded. Priorities must be set (Booth & Murphy, 1997). **Cost-effectiveness analysis** is the tool that health economists use to set these priorities. A cost-effectiveness analysis is designed to answer one simple question—which of several alternative health programs provides the greatest value for the money?

The table contains a hypothetical cost-effectiveness analysis. Three stop-smoking programs are compared: C is a clinic-based treatment program requiring multiple visits to a psychologist, B is a worksite program, and A consists solely of advice given by family doctors to their patients. The cost per person of each program is shown in the second column. Doctor counseling is the least expensive of the three programs. It requires only a few extra minutes added to the end of an office visit. Because worksite interventions involve professional time and the preparation of materials, they are more than three times as expensive as doctor advice. Clinic-based treatment is the most expensive intervention of all. It requires multiple visits at high professional fees. The third column summarizes the expected outcome of each program in terms of the extra years of life each should provide. Using the extra years of life produced by each program as a measure of outcome is appropriate because smoking-related illnesses are known to shorten life expectancy. In this analysis, every person who quits smoking is expected to gain an average of 10 extra years of life.

As you can see, doctors' advice has only a small effect. Perhaps 5 of every 100 people receiving only doctors' advice give up smoking. Each one of these people increases his or her life by 10 years. Thus, the average number of extra years of life gained per person receiving doctors' advice is 5 people × 10 years/100 = 0.5. Worksite programs have a better outcome; 10% of participants give up smoking, producing an average of 1 extra year of life per person treated (10 people × 10 years/100 = 1). Clinical treatment is the most effective of the three; 30% of those treated give up smoking, producing an average of 3 extra life years per person (30 people × 10 years/100 = 3).

The cost-effectiveness ratios shown in the table reflect the cost for every *extra* year of life gained by switching from the lowest cost program (doctors' advice) to one of the higher cost programs (either worksite or clinic treatment). The cost of every extra year of life gained by switching from the lowest to a higher cost program is known as the marginal or incremental cost. As you can see, switching from doctors' advice to clinical treatment saves more years of life than switching to a worksite program, but the cost for every extra year of life produced by switching to the clinical program is almost 20 times more than the cost for a year of life added by switching to a worksite program. If funds are limited, it is more cost-effective to switch from doctors' advice to worksite treatment (incremental cost is $20 per extra year of life year gained) rather than to clinical treatment (whose incremental cost per extra year of life gained is $398).

As the cost of health care continues to rise, cost-effectiveness analyses will take on increasing importance in allocating resources. In the future, it will not be sufficient to show that psychological treatments provided in private offices and clinics have beneficial effects. It will also be necessary to show that these treatments are cost-effective—that they produce outcomes at lower costs than the available alternatives.

Example of a Cost-Effectiveness Analysis: Cost per Extra Year of Life Gained by Switching From a Low-Cost Stop-Smoking Program to a Higher Cost Program

Program	Cost per person	Extra years of life per person treated
A. Doctors' advice	$5	0.5
B. Worksite program	$15	1
C. Clinic-based program	$1,000	3

Cost-effectiveness ratios

Marginal cost for each extra year of life produced by switching from A to C:	($1,000 − $5) ÷ (3.0 − 0.5) = $398
Marginal cost for each extra year of life produced by switching from A to B:	($15 − $5) ÷ (1.0 − 0.5) = $20

A century ago, if smokers could not stop by themselves, they had only some questionable remedies to turn to, such as Seroco Tobacco Specific.

Encouraging Self-Help   Another approach to secondary prevention is self-help. Most people who successfully overcome substance dependence do so without attending any treatment program. Of course, people who overcome substance dependence without specific treatment have been exposed to media campaigns, health warnings, legal restrictions, family and doctor advice, and many other nonspecific interventions. Although it is difficult to judge the influence of these nonspecific interventions on any individual, they may be responsible for moving people from the contemplative to the action stage in the process of giving up a psychoactive substance. To help people give up substances without professional intervention, public health authorities produce brochures, books, and instruction guides (Lichtenstein & Glasgow, 1992).

CHAPTER 6 IN PERSPECTIVE

Psychoactive substances have an ancient history. Most were originally hailed for their medicinal qualities, only to be later condemned as scourges. The truth usually lies somewhere between these two extremes. Today, psychoactive substances are ubiquitous; practically everyone has used at least one at some time in our lives. These substances form a spectrum, from common everyday substances such as caffeine to highly dangerous ones such as crack cocaine. The *DSM-IV* contains more than 100 substance-related disorders. Although the *DSM-IV* attempts to make each of these disorders distinct, they have many commonalities. People first try different substances for similar reasons, and the continued use of different substances is maintained by similar psychological mechanisms. In addition, treatment and prevention of different substance disorders often make use of similar interventions. Because psychoactive substances can cause health and social problems, there have been numerous attempts to restrict access to them by making them illegal. Regrettably, prohibition has almost never succeeded. Harm-minimization may be a more achievable (and more cost-effective) goal for treatment and prevention programs.

Key Ideas

Caffeine, Alcohol, Nicotine, and Cannabis: The Four Psychoactive Substances Most Commonly Used by College Students

Caffeine, nicotine, alcohol, and (even though it is illegal) cannabis are the four psychoactive substances most commonly used by American college students. Caffeine is found in many drinks, as well as in headache, diet, and cold medications. Nicotine is the psychoactive ingredient in tobacco. Alcohol is found in wine, beer, spirits, and many medications, whereas cannabis is a type of hemp plant whose leaves and other constituents may be ingested in a variety of ways. Caffeine and nicotine are stimulants. Along with less common substances such as amphetamines and cocaine, they combat drowsiness, increase alertness, and help produce energy. Alcohol is a depressant. Like sedatives, anxiolytics, opioids, and most inhalants, alcohol slows body processes and induces sleep. Cannabis has a variety of stimulant and depressant effects. It also has the potential to produce sensory and cognitive distortions (similar to those produced by hallucinogens such as LSD and MDMA).

Health Effects of Common Substances

Although caffeine and nicotine may be dangerous to health in large doses, they have not been linked to any specific illness at the levels typically consumed by college students. However, many of the other compounds present in tobacco smoke have been linked to serious health conditions. In controlled doses, alcohol and cannabis may have beneficial effects on health for some people. However, at higher doses, alcohol can cause serious health problems, and cannabis smoke may be as dangerous as cigarette smoke.

Psychological Effects of Common Substances

Although both caffeine and nicotine are stimulants, many people claim to find them relaxing. The relaxation produced by these substances, and by other stimulants, may be a reflection of their ability to enhance the body's natural opioids. Relaxation may also be the result of cognitive expectancies and social reinforcement. A third possibility is that some personality types (extroverts) are chronically underaroused, a state they find unpleasant. Because stimulants increase their arousal to "normal" levels, they find these substances produce pleasant feelings. Even modest amounts of alcohol and cannabis can adversely affect cognition. Cannabis commonly disrupts memory. These cognitive disruptions combined with disinhibition may lead people to do things they would never do without the influence of alcohol and cannabis.

Factors Influencing Substance Use

Given the well-publicized health risks, why does anyone begin to use substances such as nicotine, alcohol, opioids, and others? Part of the reason is social conformity. For example, smokers usually try their first cigarette as teenagers, a time when peer group acceptance is especially important. Certain personality traits—extroversion, for example—may also encourage people to use substances. The specific effects of a substance on an individual depend on the person's inherited disposition. Continued use of a substance depends on its positive and negative reinforcing qualities.

Potential Problems of Sustained Substance Use

Using substantial amounts of many substances can result in intoxication. Chronic use of substances may also produce tolerance, forcing users to continually increase the amount they consume to achieve the same effect. Abruptly giving up a habitually used substance can produce the unpleasant symptoms characteristic of withdrawal. Tolerance and withdrawal are known as substance-induced disorders. This differentiates them from substance use disorders, such as substance abuse and the even more serious disorder, substance dependence. Substance dependence is marked by a craving that profoundly shapes people's lives.

Overcoming Substance Dependence

Breaking a habit can be viewed as a multistage process. First, the person must decide to change. Next comes an active attempt to change. Finally, the new behavior must be maintained. Most psychological interventions are aimed at the active stage; many also target the maintenance stage. Practically all treatment programs aimed at substance abuse and dependence are multimodal (they combine several treatment methods). The general idea is to help people manage their craving and to give them the social and cognitive skills necessary to cope with social stress, anxiety, and other causes of substance dependence. Sometimes, replacing one substance with another, less dangerous one (nicotine patches, for example) can assist the treatment process. In addition to positive treatments, aversive conditioning has also been widely used to help people who are dependent on substances. Treatment studies are difficult to compare because they use different subject populations, apply different criteria of success, use different outcome measures, and follow up participants for different lengths of time.

Preventing Unhealthy Habits

Psychological interventions are expensive; they involve multiple sessions, and only limited numbers of people can be treated at one time. Their relatively modest success makes them a costly intervention for the general public. In contrast, public health interventions have the potential to reach many more people at much less cost. Although they may be valuable in getting people to think about quitting, outright prohibition and global educational programs have not proved successful in reducing substance dependence. Family doctor counseling, worksite programs, and self-help strategies have the potential to help many people give up substances. Although none of these approaches is likely to be as successful as psychologist-run clinical programs, they may still be justified on the grounds of cost-effectiveness.

Key Terms

alcohol (ethanol)
anabolic steroids
antagonist
behavioral contracting
caffeine
cannabis
cost-effectiveness analysis
depressant
detoxification

extroversion
fetal alcohol syndrome
hallucinogen
inhalants
lysergic acid diethylamide
  (LSD)
mentally ill chemical abusers
  (MICAs)

multimodal treatment
nicotine
opponent-process theory
polysubstance abuse
psychoactive substance
stimulant
substance abuse disorder
substance dependence disorder

substance intoxication disorder
substance-induced disorders
substance use disorders
THC
tolerance
withdrawal syndrome

Key Names

Hans Eysenck

CHAPTER 7

Dissociative, Somatoform, and Factitious Disorders

CONTENTS

In his book *Psychopathology of Everyday Life,* Sigmund Freud (1938) described an encounter with a young man on a train. After some desultory small talk, their conversation drifted to their mutual plight as European Jews. The young man decried the treatment his people were receiving from Hitler's Nazis. Quoting the *Aeneid,* he expressed the hope that future generations would revenge the wrongs of the present day. Freud immediately pointed out an error in the quotation; the young man had omitted the word *aliquis* (Latin for "someone"). Rather than let the matter drop, Freud's companion responded by saying: "I understand you claim that forgetting is not without its reasons; I should be very curious to find out how I came to forget this indefinite pronoun *'aliquis'*" (p. 18).

Freud accepted the challenge, instructing the young man to tell him "frankly and without any criticism everything that occurs to your mind after you focus your attention . . . on the forgotten word" (p. 19). In other words, he asked the man to "free-associate" to the word *aliquis.* Beginning with *liquid* and *fluid,* the young man moved on to three Catholic saints: St. Simon, who was murdered in childhood; St. Augustine, whom he had recently read about in an article titled "What St. Augustine Said Concerning Women"; and St. Januarius, whose congealed blood—preserved in a church in Naples—is said to liquefy on the same day each year.

At this point, the young man's free associations stopped. Freud asked him why he hesitated, and the young man replied: "Something occurred to me . . . but it is too intimate a matter to impart. . . . besides, I see no connection and no necessity for telling it" (p. 21). Freud urged him to say what was on his mind. Eventually, the young man revealed that his thoughts were of a woman "from whom I could easily get a message that would be very annoying to us both" (p. 21). Freud instantly asked whether the message was that the woman was pregnant. The surprised young man agreed and asked how Freud had guessed. Freud's response was that all of the man's associations were related to missed menstrual periods: the liquid, saints' names that were also the names of months (August and January), the child murder, and the miracle of the blood. To Freud, the cause of the original misquote was clear. The passage from the *Aeneid* expressed a wish for posterity, but the young man did not entirely welcome a new generation—at least not in the next 9 months. The young man's unwillingness to face up to his potential fatherhood led him to omit the word *aliquis* from the quote.

Freud used this example to support his theory that everyday memory lapses may be caused by the repression of troubling thoughts and feelings. (See Chapter 2

Freud used the case of Anna O. to put forward his theory, which is the foundation of psychoanalysis, that unconscious thoughts and emotions can produce psychological disorders.

for a more detailed discussion of Freud's theories.) Freud (1938) noted that repression may not always be effective; disturbing ideas and emotions may still make their way into consciousness, but usually in a disguised form. He gave several examples. A female patient, worried about her pregnancy, wrote a letter in which she substituted the word *stork* for *stock.* When Freud told a male patient, who was in serious financial difficulty, that he needed a new medicine, the patient replied, "Please do not give me big *bills* because I cannot swallow them." These word substitutions, which seem to be motivated by unconscious worries, came to be known as "Freudian slips."

By using examples from everyday life, Freud hoped to demonstrate that repression is not an abnormal process, but the ego's routine way of defending itself against unacceptable thoughts and impulses. One of the recurrent themes of this book is the continuity between normal and abnormal behavior—and Freud certainly agreed. He maintained that everyday memory lapses and slips of the tongue obey the same psychological principles, and are explainable by the same theories, as psychological disorders. The difference between them is one of degree. Repression, a normal psychological

DSM-IV	TABLE 7.1 Main *DSM-IV* Dissociative, Somatoform, and Factitious Disorders

Dissociative disorders

Dissociative amnesia: psychologically caused loss of memory

Dissociative fugue: flight from familiar surroundings accompanied by memory loss

Depersonalization disorder: the feeling of being detached from one's body

Dissociative identity disorder: multiple "personalities" in the same person

Somatoform disorders

Conversion disorder: physical symptoms, usually confined to a single organ or system, which usually mimic the symptoms of a neurological condition (paralysis, blindness)

Somatization disorder: multiple, vague physical complaints (dizziness, palpitations)

Pain disorder: preoccupation with pain

Hypochondriasis: morbid preoccupation with imagined illness

Body dysmorphic disorder: obsessive concern with presumed defects in appearance (size of breasts, hair loss)

Factitious disorder

Feigning symptoms to get attention

---

process, causes a mental disorder when it becomes so pervasive that it interferes with either occupational or social functioning.

Over the years, many of Freud's views have been challenged by other theorists, but the idea that unconscious thoughts and emotions can produce psychological disorders still seems to prevail when it comes to the *DSM-IV* categories discussed in this chapter—dissociative disorders and somatoform disorders. **Dissociative disorders** derive their name from their main symptom— the "dis-association" of the personality. Our personalities are the totality of our inner experiences and our behaviors. Normally, the various parts of our personalities are glued together by our memories. These allow us to recognize friends and loved ones and to predict the response we can expect from others if we behave in certain ways. Our memories also help to provide us with an identity: a set of preferences, abilities, needs, values, and goals. In the dissociative disorders, our memories and sometimes our identities become detached ("dissociated") from one another. We may forget the past or, in some cases, even who we are.

Somatoform disorders are marked by physical symptoms that mimic those produced by disease (*somatoform* means "similar to the body"). They differ from the stress-related organic disorders discussed in Chapter 5 in that people with somatoform disorders have no obvious physical illness. The absence of a physical illness also differentiates the dissociative disorders from brain disorders that produce similar symptoms (these brain disorders are discussed in Chapter 11).

Although there are no obvious physical reasons for their symptoms, you should not conclude that people suffering from somatoform and dissociative disorders are deliberately faking. People with dissociative disorders have real memory losses, and people with somatoform disorders really do believe that they are physically ill, are about to fall ill, or are physically deformed. People who *intentionally* pretend to be sick are classified as either **malingerers** (who pretend to be sick to avoid commitments or to gain some advantage) or as suffering from a **factitious disorder** (in which people feign illness for no personal gain other than attention).

Following Freud's early work, the dissociative and somatoform disorders were originally classified together as *neuroses* (see Chapter 3 for the history of the term *neurosis*). The current *DSM-IV* categorizes them separately because of their rather different clinical appearance. They are grouped together in this chapter because of the apparent role played by unconscious processes in both types of disorder. Factitious disorders are also included because their superficial similarity to somatoform disorders presents clinicians with an important diagnostic challenge. Table 7.1 summarizes the disorders discussed in this chapter. The chapter begins with the case of Helen Fairchild, a woman whose lost past appears to have returned to haunt her.

UNWELCOME MEMORIES

Just before her 27th birthday, Helen Fairchild consulted Dr. Dorothy McLean for help in dealing with a variety of symptoms. Documents 7.1–7.5 tell the beginning of Helen's story. The rest is revealed in documents presented throughout the chapter.

DOCUMENT 7.1

Dr. Dorothy McLean's Assessment and Preliminary Treatment Plan for Helen Fairchild

Dorothy McLean, Ph.D.
Psychologist

Brief Intake Assessment and Preliminary Treatment Plan

Date: September 3, 1999

Client: Helen Fairchild, 34 Genesta Circle

DOB: 9/17/1972

Tests Administered

Structured Clinical Interview for DSM-IV

Dissociative Disorders-Revised (SCID-D)

Beck Depression Inventory

State-Trait Anxiety Inventory

MMPI-2

Reason for Referral: Helen Fairchild was self-referred. She says that she is distracted, has no sexual desire, sometimes feels that life is not real, and has no memory for parts of her past.

Behavioral Observations and Brief History: Helen Fairchild, a 27-year-old White female, reports feeling distressed for the past few months. Her husband of 7 years left her 3 months ago and moved in with his secretary. Helen says that she never had much interest in sex and found little enjoyment in intimacy. Since her husband left, Helen has developed recurrent stomachaches, dizziness, hot flushes, and headaches. She sought medical advice, but no physical cause was identified. Her family doctor prescribed painkillers for her headaches. She denies any illness or substance use.

Helen has found it difficult to concentrate and has been having trouble at work. She has not been completing tasks, has been missing appointments, and sometimes has missed whole days of work. On several occasions, she found herself driving in the country when she was supposed to be at work. On these occasions, she was unable to recall how she had gotten to the country or what she had done during the preceding hours. She finds this loss of memory distressing, especially since she also has few memories of her childhood. Sometimes she feels that life is not "real" and that she is simply "playing a role." She says that she feels as if she is standing outside herself, watching herself go through the motions of everyday life.

Helen was carefully dressed and groomed. Although she seemed quiet, she was not weepy, nor did she seem particularly anxious. Although she was responsive to questions, she would lapse into silence and from time to time had to be prompted to respond.

Assessment: Helen's score on the Beck Depression Inventory was in the "mildly depressed" range with some answers indicating low self-esteem. The SCID-D indicated several important signs of a dissociative disorder (amnesia, feelings of depersonalization, and derealization). The validity scales of the MMPI-2 were in the average range, but Helen had an elevated hysteria score. In general, she seemed to be a mildly depressed woman with a variety of physical complaints coupled with feelings of unreality and memory loss.

Diagnostic Considerations: Helen seems to be mildly depressed, but she also has distinct signs of dissociative disorders, such as depersonalization and amnesia. It is premature to make any specific diagnosis, but the following are possibilities:

Axis I: Dissociative amnesia (and perhaps fugue)
    Depersonalization disorder
    Somatoform disorder
    Depressive disorder

Axis II: No diagnosis

Axis III: No medical reason has been uncovered for memory loss, headache, and stomachache; could be signs of a somatoform disorder

Axis IV: Husband left home to live with another woman

Axis V: GAF = 45 (at time of assessment)

Preliminary Treatment Plan: Although Helen's problems may be a reaction to her husband's infidelity and abandonment, there are some troubling and puzzling aspects to this case. Helen has no interest in sex, and she has unexplained gaps in her childhood memories. She also seems to have "blank" periods when she cannot recall where she was or what she was doing. Putting these together, it may be possible that Helen has repressed sex-related childhood memories that have led her to fear sex. One possibility may be childhood sex abuse. This would be consistent with her stomachache, which could be a "body memory" of what happened to her. Her dissociative symptoms may arise from the same source. Therapy will be targeted at uncovering evidence for such early abuse. Free association and hypnosis may help her to recover these memories. If such evidence is uncovered, Helen will be enrolled in a support group for trauma survivors. She will also need to confront her abuser.

DOCUMENT 7.2

Excerpt From Transcript of Treatment Session Conducted by Dr. Dorothy McLean With Helen Fairchild

Dorothy McLean, Ph.D.
Psychologist

Transcript of Treatment Session: Helen Fairchild

Client: Helen Fairchild

Therapist: Dr. Dorothy McLean

DR. MCLEAN: The hypnotic induction is now complete. Are you relaxed?

HELEN: Yes.

DR. MCLEAN: Last time we met, you had trouble recalling your childhood. Do you think there is something that you might not want to remember?

HELEN: I don't know. I guess it's possible that I do not want to remember some things.

DR. MCLEAN: Perhaps the events you do not want to remember were so painful that you just cannot bear thinking about them.

HELEN: Maybe.

DR. MCLEAN: In my experience, people who have problems like yours sometimes turn out to have been molested as children. Do you think that is what you are afraid to remember?

HELEN: I don't know.

DR. MCLEAN: You know, sometimes our bodies recall things even when our brains do not. Your stomachache, for example. It may be your body's way of remembering what happened to you as a child. Maybe you were molested and your stomach was injured. Your hot flushes may have a similar origin.

HELEN: I guess that makes sense. My stomach may have been hurt.

DR. MCLEAN: Early sex abuse would also explain your lack of desire and interest in sex.

HELEN: I suppose it is possible that something terrible happened. The only really horrible thing that I can recall from my childhood was the death of my friend Jacqueline when I was only seven.

DR. MCLEAN: Tell me what you remember.

DOCUMENT 7.3

Newspaper Article Reporting Accusations of Murder

Woman Accuses Father of Decades-Old Murder

by Jack Gregory

Helen Fairchild, a 27-year-old office worker, has accused her father, Stanley Fairchild, age 57, of murdering her school friend 20 years ago.

On the basis of Ms. Fairchild's charge, police have reopened the murder case of Jacqueline Buchanan, which has remained unsolved for 20 years. Jacqueline, who had just celebrated her seventh birthday, went missing after visiting the Fairchild home. Her naked body was later found in some bushes on the north bank of the Torrens River. She had been raped and strangled.

Because he was the last adult to see Jacqueline, police investigators questioned Stanley Fairchild at the time. He claimed that the girl was perfectly all right when she left his home. The police theorized that someone had accosted Jacqueline as she walked home from the Fairchild house, but no suspects were ever found.

A few months ago, after Helen Fairchild's husband left her to live with his secretary, Fairchild became distressed and sought the assistance of a psychotherapist, Dr. Dorothy McLean. During her treatment, Fairchild recalled incidents of Jacqueline's rape and murder, which had taken place 20 years earlier. Not only did she recall details of the slaying, Fairchild also recalled that her father had sexually abused her on many occasions.

According to Dr. McLean, the young Helen was so traumatized by what she saw that she put all the details out of her mind. In treatment, however, these terrible memories came flooding back. Dr. McLean says that these "repressed memories" were causing Helen's psychological problems. Curing her required that the memories be brought to the surface.

Stanley Fairchild denies the charges. The police are investigating.

SUPERIOR COURT

TRANSCRIPT OF TRIAL

In the Matter of Stanley Fairchild

Cross-Examination of Helen Fairchild by Counsel for the Defense,
Michael Moriarity

COUNSEL FOR THE DEFENSE: You have testified on direct examination that your
father drove you and Jacqueline to the river. He left you in the backseat of the
family car while he raped and strangled Jacqueline on the riverbank.

COUNSEL FOR THE DEFENSE: Yet you never told this story to anyone at all for the
next 20 years.

HELEN FAIRCHILD: No. I did not.

COUNSEL FOR THE DEFENSE: Why not?

HELEN FAIRCHILD: I could not remember it. I must have been so traumatized that
I repressed my memories.

COUNSEL FOR THE DEFENSE: These are interesting words: "traumatized,"
"repressed." Where did you learn them?

HELEN FAIRCHILD: I don't know what you mean.

COUNSEL FOR THE DEFENSE: Well, they sound like the sort of words that might be
used by a psychologist. Did you learn them from Dr. McLean?

HELEN FAIRCHILD: I may have.

COUNSEL FOR THE DEFENSE: Was she the first to suggest that you may have been
"traumatized"?

HELEN FAIRCHILD: Yes. I think so.

COUNSEL FOR THE DEFENSE: Did the memories of the murder appear to you all
at once?

HELEN FAIRCHILD: No. I had many hypnosis sessions in which I gradually recalled
details of what happened that day.

COUNSEL FOR THE DEFENSE: Were these memories spontaneous?

HELEN FAIRCHILD: I don't know what you mean.

COUNSEL FOR THE DEFENSE: Did they just come to you, or did Dr. McLean lead you
to them?

HELEN FAIRCHILD: They are my memories.

COUNSEL FOR THE DEFENSE: Yes, but did Dr. McLean point you toward them? Did
she suggest that you had been sexually abused, for example?

HELEN FAIRCHILD: She may have, a few times.

DOCUMENT 7.5

Transcript of Dr.
Dorothy McLean's
Testimony at the Trial
of Stanley Fairchild

SUPERIOR COURT

TRANSCRIPT OF TRIAL

In the Matter of Stanley Fairchild

Cross-Examination of Helen Fairchild by Counsel for the Defense,
Michael Moriarity

COUNSEL FOR THE DEFENSE: What was your first impression of Helen Fairchild?

DR. MCLEAN: She came to see me shortly after her husband left her. She reported problems at work: an inability to concentrate, missed days, and forgetfulness. She said that she was simply going through the motions of life—going to work, looking after her kids. She said that nothing seemed real. It was like she was outside her body watching herself. She also said that her stomach and head hurt and that she had hot flushes, although doctors could find nothing wrong. She also said that she had no sexual desire.

COUNSEL FOR THE DEFENSE: What did you make of these symptoms?

DR. MCLEAN: She sounded as if she was showing signs of depersonalization, somatoform disorder, and dissociative amnesia.

COUNSEL FOR THE DEFENSE: Did she have other problems with her memory?

DR. MCLEAN: Yes. She said she was unable to recall events from her childhood.

COUNSEL FOR THE DEFENSE: When did you first suggest to Helen that she had been sexually abused by her father? When did you first plant this idea in her mind?

DR. MCLEAN: I did not plant the idea. Helen remembered it. Even her body seemed to remember, although the memory was disguised as hot flushes and a stomachache.

COUNSEL FOR THE DEFENSE: But Helen had never made any such accusation prior to seeing you in therapy. The pediatrician who looked after her as a child never noticed any sign of abuse, nor did her mother, her neighbors, her grandparents, or her teachers. Perhaps her stomachache was simply that, a stomachache.

DR. MCLEAN: I don't think so. I believe that the details of her abuse and the rape and murder of Jacqueline were so traumatic that Helen not only repressed them but also hid them from others.

COUNSEL FOR THE DEFENSE: If she repressed these details so well that she completely forgot them, and never mentioned them to anyone, and no one ever noticed anything, how did she come to mention them to you?

DR. MCLEAN: I may have asked her whether any such event occurred in her childhood.

COUNSEL FOR THE DEFENSE: How do you know that what she told you was the truth?

DR. MCLEAN: People do not lie about such things. Besides, Helen's memories were like films, full of detail. She believed them strongly. She was able to recall them because I made her feel safe and gave her the strength to face her past. I also helped her by placing her under hypnosis.

COUNSEL FOR THE DEFENSE: Are you sure that her memory was spontaneous?

DR. MCLEAN: Of course.

COUNSEL FOR THE DEFENSE: You never suggested to her that she may have been sexually abused and then repressed any memory of the abuse?

DR. MCLEAN: I may have, on a few occasions. Many of Helen's problems were those associated with childhood abuse. Her memory gaps, her forgetfulness at work, her stomach pain, headaches, her lack of desire for sex, all of these things come from her repressed sexual trauma. I may have pointed her in the right direction, but the story came from her. I only facilitated her getting in touch with her past.

Trevor Rees-Jones (center), the sole survivor of the car crash that killed Princess Diana, was repeatedly summoned for questioning. Finally, 6 months after the accident, he began to experience what his psychiatrist called "windows of memory." His inability to remember the accident was likely due to trauma-induced amnesia.

DISSOCIATIVE DISORDERS

After 20 years of silence, Helen Fairchild accused her father of sexual abuse and of raping and murdering her childhood friend Jacqueline Buchanan. Helen's accusations arose out of treatment for several psychological problems, including memory loss, poor occupational functioning, lack of sexual desire, headaches, hot flushes, and unexplained abdominal pain. Dr. McLean, Helen's psychologist, believed that all of these problems were the result of Helen's repressed memories of sexual abuse and murder. She also believed that Helen recovered these memories under treatment. On the other hand, Stanley Fairchild's defense lawyer argued that the memories were created by Dr. McLean. Who was correct? Were Helen's memories planted by her psychologist, or were they real? Can long-forgotten traumatic events produce psychological symptoms many years later? Do bodies have memories separate from minds? These questions, and related ones, are addressed in this chapter. To answer them, we must examine the dissociative, somatoform, and factitious disorders in some detail. We begin with two dissociative disorders, amnesia and fugue.

Amnesia and Fugue

Anyone living in the final years of the 19th century would be forgiven for thinking that human memory is extremely fragile. The popular and professional literature of the day was replete with reports of people who had suddenly lost all or part of their memories or who

Hollywood sometimes uses a fictionalized version of retrograde amnesia as a plot device to create suspense (as in Alfred Hitchcock's Spellbound) or to change a personality (as in Mike Nichols's Regarding Henry). In this film, Harrison Ford plays a ruthless lawyer who loses his memory after being shot in the head and becomes a kinder, more ethical person.

In contrast to Hollywood's version of amnesia, the outcome is often bittersweet. Here, Irene Tomiczek wipes away a tear after she has been reunited with her daughter Cheryl, an amnesia victim known only as "Jane Doe" for a year until she was reunited with her family at South Florida State Hospital.

had dramatically changed their personalities—or both. As the century drew to a close, such cases began to disappear from the literature. Perhaps the syndrome vanished. More likely, it just went out of style. There are fads in abnormal psychology as in anything else. With the rise of cognitive psychology in the 1970s, memory again became a central concern of psychologists. Clinicians and scientists were once more on the lookout for memory defects, and they seemed to find them in ever-increasing numbers (Lussier et al., 1997).

As Freud demonstrated, finding memory slips is easy. We all forget things: shopping lists, telephone numbers, birthdays, anniversaries. However, when memory gaps are too great for ordinary forgetfulness, when a person cannot recall important life events or even who she or he is—and when memory loss is associated with psychological trauma—then **dissociative amnesia** (psychogenic memory loss) may be suspected (Spiegel, 1997).

There are two main types of amnesia. An inability to form new memories is known as *anterograde* (forward) amnesia. Sufferers can remember events that occurred before a traumatic experience, but new events are forgotten shortly after they occur. For example, a person may remember everything that occurred before an automobile accident but not after the accident. Each day, the person awakes believing that the accident took place the day before. *Retrograde* (backward) amnesia is exactly the opposite; events that took place before a traumatic event are forgotten. A person may not recall anything that

happened before an automobile accident while remembering events that occurred after the accident. Almost all cases of dissociative amnesia are of the retrograde type.

Helen Fairchild displayed retrograde amnesia in a *localized* form. She could not recall events that took place during certain intervals—what she did when she missed work, what happened during parts of her childhood—but otherwise her memory was intact. In more severe cases, memory loss is *generalized.* Sufferers fail to recognize relatives and friends and cannot recall any details about their past before the traumatic event. Yet they still retain all their talents and abilities (they can still read, for example, or play the piano). Generalized retrograde amnesia occurs more frequently in Hollywood movies than in real life, but it is not entirely unknown in the clinic. Table 7.2 contains the main diagnostic criteria for dissociative amnesia.

Was Helen Fairchild suffering from dissociative amnesia? As you saw in Document 7.1, Dr. McLean thought this was a possibility. Helen had memory lapses that were too extensive to be characterized as ordinary forgetfulness, and she was having trouble coping at work and at home. Helen was not a substance user, and she had experienced the trauma of having a childhood friend murdered. Thus Helen does seem to meet most of the *DSM-IV* criteria for dissociative amnesia.

When a person not only develops retrograde amnesia but also leaves home and adopts a new identity, the appropriate diagnosis is **dissociative fugue** (see Table 7.3 for the main *DSM-IV* diagnostic criteria). In extreme

DSM-IV **TABLE 7.2** Main *DSM-IV* Diagnostic Criteria
for Dissociative Amnesia

A. One or more episodes of inability to recall important personal information, usually
of a traumatic or stressful nature, that is too extensive to be explained by ordinary
forgetfulness.

B. The disturbance does not occur during the course of another disorder, nor is it a direct result of substance abuse, brain injury, or a general medical condition.

C. The symptoms cause clinically significant distress or impairment in social, occupational, or
other important areas of functioning.

Note: Adapted from American Psychiatric Association (1994, p. 481).

DSM-IV **TABLE 7.3** Main *DSM-IV* Diagnostic Criteria
for Dissociative Fugue

A. The predominant disturbance is sudden, unexpected travel away from home or one's
customary place of work, with an inability to recall one's past.

B. Confusion about personal identity or assumption of a new identity (partial or complete).

C. The disturbance is not exclusively part of another dissociative disorder, substance abuse, or
a general medical condition.

D. The symptoms cause clinically significant distress or impairment in social, occupational, or
other important areas of functioning.

Note: Adapted from American Psychiatric Association (1994, p. 484).

cases, people may move to another town, assume a new name, start a new job, and even change their personalities. However, most fugues are not so dramatic. People do not begin entirely new lives; they simply wander away from home for brief periods (Loewenstein, 1991). The majority are soon found or return home on their own, claiming not to know why they left, where they had been, or what transpired in their absence.

Helen Fairchild displayed many of the features of dissociative fugue: She missed work and found herself inexplicably in the country, she had no memory for certain aspects of her past, and her occupational functioning was impaired. On the other hand, she knew who she was and did not assume another identity (few people do; American Psychiatric Assn, 1994).

It seems as if Helen met most of the diagnostic criteria for both dissociative amnesia and fugue, but there is another possibility. Helen's symptoms could have been the result of an undetected brain injury. Several types of brain damage can produce disorientation, flight, and memory loss. This is why it is vital to distinguish between organic brain conditions and the dissociative disorders. Unfortunately, this is not always easy. As you will see in Chapter 11, all of the symptoms associated

with dissociative amnesia and fugue may also be produced by organic brain syndromes (Maisto, Galizio, & Connors, 1991; Squire & Butters, 1992). To make matters even more complicated, brain injury and psychological trauma may go together. For example, a mugging or rape can easily result in *both* brain injury and psychological trauma.

Special assessment scales and interview schedules, such as the Structured Clinical Interview for Dissociative Disorders (SCID-D) used by Dr. McLean, may help clinicians to differentiate the various dissociative disorders from organic disorders, as well as from one another (Steinberg & Hall, 1997; Vanderlinden et al., 1993). There are also several clinical signs that may help to distinguish organic from dissociative amnesia and fugues: (a) organic amnesias usually result from degenerative diseases that develop gradually, whereas dissociative amnesias come on suddenly; (b) organic amnesias are typically anterograde, whereas dissociative amnesias are almost always retrograde; (c) dissociative amnesia is associated with severe psychological stress; and (d) people with organic amnesias do not usually take on new identities.

Based on these four signs, it seems likely that Helen's dissociative symptoms were most probably psychogenic. They came on suddenly after her husband left her, and her amnesia was retrograde. Keep in mind, however, that these indicators are not perfect. Sophisticated psychological and medical tests may be required to determine the cause of a memory loss, and sometimes even they produce equivocal results.

Etiology and Treatment of Amnesia and Fugue Because dissociative amnesia and fugue are rare, we know little about their family patterns and course (C. A. Ross, 1991). They seem to occur most often after a severe psychological trauma, such as the death of a loved one, combat, or following natural disasters such as an earthquake (Bremner et al., 1993; Cardena & Spiegel, 1993; Kihlstrom, Tataryn, & Hoyt, 1993; Loewenstein, 1991). All psychologists, irrespective of their theoretical bent, view these and other forms of traumatic stress as the essential cause of dissociative amnesia and fugue. Because of the close association between traumatic stress and dissociative symptoms, it is not surprising that amnesia and fugue frequently accompany the post-traumatic stress disorder discussed in Chapter 4 (Eriksson & Lundin, 1996).

A possible behavioral explanation for amnesia is derived from the notion of **state-dependent learning** (Bower, 1981). In a state-dependent learning experiment, participants learn different materials (two lists of words, for example) in two distinct mental states (say, one while sober and one while inebriated). Later, the participants are asked to remember words from each list while sober and again while inebriated. Typically, people in the sober state recall best the words they learned when sober and those in the inebriated state recall best the words they learned while inebriated. In an extreme example, after a night spent drinking, it may be necessary for a sober person to get drunk again to recall the location of his or her car keys. If state-dependent learning is at work, then events that occurred when someone was under great stress may well be forgotten once the stress disappears, thereby creating amnesia. It would follow that the only way to recall these lost events is to once again subject the person to great stress. Clearly, this is an impossible hypothesis to test in any ethical experiment or treatment.

The aim of psychoanalytic treatment is to help patients with amnesia and fugue to uncover the repressed material that caused them to lose their memories or wander off. In the same way that Freud asked the young man on the train to say whatever came to his mind, patients in psychoanalysis may be asked to free-associate beginning with the last remembered events prior to the onset of amnesia or fugue. If this is not successful, they may be asked to tell their complete life stories in the hope that some retrieved memory might trigger the recall of relevant material (Combs & Ludwig, 1982). In some cases, therapists may emulate Dr. McLean and use hypnosis to uncover memories that are otherwise unavailable to consciousness.

Because they do not know that anything is wrong, people in fugue states rarely refer themselves for treatment. Any treatment that does take place usually occurs after they recover their memories. For this reason, therapy for fugue is aimed at preventing future episodes. Cognitive and behavioral interventions, such as stress management and stress inoculation (see Chapter 4), may be particularly valuable because they provide people with more adaptive ways to cope with stress and conflict than escaping their lives or forgetting who they are.

Depersonalization Disorder

In addition to her memory gaps, Helen felt alienated from her own life. As Dr. McLean noted in her psychological assessment

> Sometimes she [Helen] feels that life is not "real" and that she is simply "playing a role." She says that she feels as if she is standing outside herself, watching herself go through the motions of everyday life.

Dr. McLean followed up these feelings with Helen during one of her treatment sessions. A transcript of part of that session appears in Document 7.6.

DOCUMENT 7.6

Excerpt From Transcript of One of Helen Fairchild's Treatment Sessions With Dr. Dorothy McLean

HELEN FAIRCHILD: I think I'm going crazy.

DR. MCLEAN: Why do you think that?

HELEN FAIRCHILD: It's hard to explain. It's like I'm dreaming even when I'm awake.

DR. MCLEAN: Dreaming?

HELEN FAIRCHILD: Yeah. I can see myself as if I were another person. I'm outside myself, and I can see my face, my hair. I feel like a robot, not really in control of myself.

DR. MCLEAN: You see yourself from the outside?

HELEN FAIRCHILD: Yes. And my hands and feet look enormous. Way bigger than they really are. I don't see how I can get my shoes on. I know this all sounds weird; I just can't seem to get past it.

DR. MCLEAN: Get past what?

DSM-IV   TABLE 7.4   Main *DSM-IV* Diagnostic Criteria
for Depersonalization Disorder

A. Persistent or recurrent experiences of feeling detached from, and as if one is an outside observer of, one's mental processes or body (e.g., feeling like one is in a dream).
B. During depersonalization, reality testing remains intact.
C. The depersonalization causes clinically significant distress or impairment in social, occupational, or other important areas of functioning.
D. The depersonalization is not exclusively part of another disorder, a general medical condition, or substance abuse.

Note: Adapted from American Psychiatric Association (1994, p. 490).

HELEN FAIRCHILD: This feeling that I'm not really me. I feel like an actor playing a role, going through the motions of living but living someone else's life. ■

Helen appears to meet most of the *DSM-IV* diagnostic criteria for a **depersonalization disorder** (summarized in Table 7.4). As you can see, in a depersonalization disorder, the sense of "self" becomes dissociated from the rest of the personality. Like Helen, people with depersonalization disorders may believe that their hands and feet are too large or too small, or they may have the impression that they are outside their bodies viewing themselves from a distance. Sometimes they feel mechanical, as though they were robots. **Derealization,** the feeling that the world is not real or of living in a dream, often accompanies depersonalization.

Similar complaints may be found in people suffering from other psychological disorders. For example, people with schizophrenia may also complain that they are not "real," but they fail to meet criterion B. In contrast to people with a depersonalization disorder, who realize that the world is still there and that they are not really robots, people with schizophrenia lose touch with reality. Some come to believe that they really are robots.

People who fall into trances during socially sanctioned religious or cultural rituals do not have a depersonalization disorder. However, a person who falls into a trance claiming to be "possessed," and whose behavior differs markedly from that of other members of his or her culture, may well be suffering from a dissociative disorder. At present, the most appropriate diagnosis for such a person would be depersonalization disorder, but a new diagnosis known as "dissociative trance disorder" is currently being considered for possible inclusion in the next edition of the *DSM* (American Psychiatric Assn, 1994).

Criterion D in Table 7.4 presents a major diagnostic challenge. Substance abuse can produce feelings of de-

personalization (Mathew et al., 1993) and so can several organic illnesses (Sacks, 1998). Sacks, for example, describes cases in which the nerve fibers responsible for proprioception (sensory feedback from one's own muscles, tendons, and organs) were destroyed. Like those with depersonalization disorder, people with faulty proprioception feel detached from their bodies. They may claim that their feet or hands are too large or small or that their limbs belong to someone else. One of Sacks's patients woke during the night to find a cold, hairy leg in bed with him. He couldn't stand the idea of sharing his bed with such a monstrosity, so he pushed it over the side. To his surprise, he also wound up on the floor. No amount of argument could convince this patient that the disembodied leg was actually part of his body and that by throwing it over the side, he had actually thrown himself out of bed.

Although the incidence of depersonalization disorder is unknown, feelings of unreality and derealization are common complaints (Putnam, 1991). The disorder usually begins in the teenage years and is associated with psychological trauma (Hollander et al., 1997). It follows an unpredictable course, which waxes and wanes in response to life-stress.

As we have seen, Helen Fairchild showed signs of each of the three dissociative disorders discussed thus far: amnesia, fugue, and depersonalization. But we have not yet examined the best-known dissociation disorder—in which several "personalities" share a single body. Dissociative identity disorder combines elements of the other dissociative disorders and takes them to the extreme.

Dissociative Identity Disorder

From Janus, the ancient Roman god with two faces, through the witch trials of colonial America, to Robert

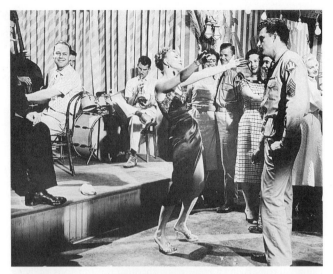

The 1957 film The Three Faces of Eve *introduced the general public to multiple personality disorder (later renamed dissociative identity disorder in the DSM-IV). The personality Eve White is a shy housewife, puzzled by the unfamiliar shoes in her closet. The personality Eve Black is a fun-loving flirt—and someone who wears such shoes. The personality Jane, who appears during therapy, is a relatively well-adjusted compromise of the two.*

Louis Stevenson's classic novel *The Strange Case of Doctor Jekyll and Mr. Hyde* (1896), and into the present, the public has always found the idea of two people sharing the same body to be morbidly fascinating. The modern era in the study of "multiple personality" began in 1908, when the pioneering clinical psychologist and founder of the *Journal of Abnormal Psychology*, Morton Prince, published *The Dissociation of a Personality*. Prince's book was a biographical study of "Sally Beauchamp," who consulted him because of headaches and blackouts. Under hypnosis, Sally revealed three personalities—The Saint, the Devil, and the Woman—each with its individual feelings, tastes, and memories.

Although other cases were reported in the literature, it was not until 1957, when Thigpen and Cleckley published *The Three Faces of Eve*, that the idea of multiple personality really captured the public's imagination. Like Sally Beauchamp, Eve White sought treatment for headaches and blackouts. In therapy, she changed from a quiet woman to Eve Black, a sexy extrovert. Later, she became Jane, a stable woman. The popularity of *The Three Faces of Eve*, and the subsequent award-winning film, spawned a literary genre. Chris Sizemore, the real-life "Eve," wrote her own book, *A Mind of My Own* (1989), in which she described a few more personalities not included in Thigpen and Cleckley's original. Indeed, personality inflation became characteristic of the genre.

Each new case seemed to have more personalities than the last (Merskey, 1995). Schreiber (1975) described Sybil's 16 personalities, and Keyes (1981) catalogued Billy Milligan's 24. As the number of personalities multiplied, some psychologists became skeptical about their reality. As will be seen in this section, practically every aspect of multiple personality (or **dissociative identity disorder,** as the *DSM-IV* prefers to call it) is the subject of intense controversy (Piper, 1994; Weissberg, 1993).

Diagnosis of Dissociative Identity Disorder The main *DSM-IV* criteria for the diagnosis of dissociative identity disorder are summarized in Table 7.5. Although a memory disturbance similar to Helen Fairchild's is one of the criteria, Helen did not display the disorder's main distinguishing sign—at least two separate identities that come forward in turn to take charge of an individual's behavior. In dissociative identity disorder, each of these

DSM-IV   TABLE 7.5   Main *DSM-IV* Diagnostic Criteria
for Dissociative Identity Disorder

A. The presence of two or more distinct identities or personality states (each with its own relatively enduring pattern of perceiving, relating to, and thinking about the environment and self).

B. At least two of these identities or personality states recurrently take control of the person's behavior.

C. Inability to recall important personal information that is too extensive to be explained by ordinary forgetfulness.

D. The disturbance is not due to the direct physiological effects of a substance (e.g., blackouts or chaotic behavior during alcohol intoxication) or a general medical condition (e.g., complex partial seizures). Note: In children, the symptoms are not due to imaginary playmates or fantasy play.

Note: From American Psychiatric Association (1994, p. 487).

identities has its own characteristic personality, habits, and memories. When a particular identity is in control, the person acts accordingly—quiet when a shy personality is dominant, outgoing and brash when an extroverted personality is in control. One personality may be aware of the other's existence, but, more often, a personality is unaware of what is happening when another personality is in control.

Clinicians have claimed that alternative personalities, or *alters,* can differ physiologically: in handedness, visual acuity, blood pressure, autonomic arousal, and even in the illnesses they suffer (Coons, Bowman, & Milstein, 1988; Putnam, Zahn, & Post, 1990; Sue et al., 1994). If such claims were true, they would give considerable force to the idea that different personalities can inhabit the same body. In reality, the evidence for physiological differences among alters is equivocal at best (S. D. Miller & Triggiano, 1992). Indeed, the whole idea that more than one personality can inhabit a single body is probably misleading. It is more objective to say that people with dissociative identity disorder act *as if* their bodies were inhabited by several personalities. Also, note that a diagnosis of dissociative identity disorder requires the multiple personalities to persist over time. A temporary

incident, or one brought on by substance abuse, does not qualify.

In addition to the formal *DSM-IV* criteria, clinicians also look for telltale signs that may signal the possibility of a dissociative identity disorder (Kluft, 1987; Putnam, 1989). For example, people who report finding letters in their own handwriting that they cannot remember writing and who complain of headaches and blackouts (as did Sally Beauchamp and Eve) may be harboring more than one personality. People who refer to themselves by different names or call themselves "we" are also suspect. Keep in mind, however, that the habit of using different names for different personalities is sometimes the result of a therapist's suggestion (Merskey, 1992).

The symptoms of dissociative identity disorder overlap those produced by other disorders including schizophrenia (C. A. Ross et al., 1990). Diagnostic instruments have been developed to aid diagnosis, but their validity is difficult to establish (D. G. Fischer & Elnitsky, 1990). Still, there are certain cases in which dissociative identity disorder appears to be the most appropriate diagnosis. For example, most clinicians would suspect that the newspaper report contained in Document 7.7 describes an example of dissociative identity disorder.

DOCUMENT 7.7

Newspaper Report Suggesting a Possible Case of Dissociative Identity Disorder

Professor's Secret Life

by Evan Moran

It seems even history professors can have secret lives.

Responding to a complaint from neighbors, Metro Police officers Rob Martin and Selena Quadrio made a routine visit to 34

Mountain Drive. Their plan was simply to ask the residents to lower the volume of their stereo, which could be heard a block away.

When their knocks went unanswered, the two officers let themselves in through the unlocked door. They found the two-room apartment in a shambles. Broken furniture, wine bottles, old clothing, and rotting food littered the floors. The red velvet draperies had holes in them, and the red carpets were extensively stained. The stereo volume was up high, and the CD player was programmed to keep repeating the same disc.

The bedroom, which featured a mirrored ceiling and a round bed, reeked with the smell of rotting food. Used condoms were on the floor. A woman dressed only in stockings and a garter belt lay face down and unconscious on the bed. The officers turned the woman over and checked to see if she was breathing. At this point she awoke and started struggling with Officer Quadrio. The woman scratched and kicked Officer Quadrio but was eventually subdued.

The woman, who said her name was Meg Warne, was taken to University Hospital. Police later identified her as Dr. Kaye Golding, of the university's History Department. Dr. Golding has no previous police record. Within an hour of her admission to the hospital, Dr. Golding admitted to her true identity. When police informed her of her behavior and her claim to be Meg Warne, Dr. Golding denied any knowledge of the incident or of any person called Meg Warne. She denied ever being in an apartment on Mountain Drive.

Dr. Golding told police that she had been suffering from severe headaches and from blackouts, periods for which she has no memory.

University officials refused to comment on what Dr. Golding was doing at the apartment.

Is Dissociative Identity Disorder Becoming More Common? Dissociative identity disorder is usually diagnosed first in adolescence or early adulthood, although it may sometimes begin in childhood. It is not only more common in women than in men, but it also seems to run in families (C. A. Ross, Norton, & Wozney, 1989). The incidence of dissociative identity disorder has been rising for the past 50 years. A review conducted in the 1940s found that only 76 cases had ever been reported in the literature (W. S. Taylor & Martin, 1944). By 1970, the number of published cases had grown to 100. The number reached 200 in the mid-1970s, 300 by 1980, and by the 1990s, cases in the thousands appeared (Kluft, 1991; Putnam, 1989; C. A. Ross, 1991).

The increasing incidence of dissociative identity disorder is largely an American phenomenon (Darves-Bornoz, Degiovanni, & Gaillard, 1995). It is rare in other countries (Merskey, 1992). For example, based on a survey of Swiss psychiatrists, Modestin (1992) estimated that dissociative identity disorder occurs in only 0.05–0.1% of Swiss psychiatric outpatients. Interestingly, Modestin found that three psychiatrists reported more than half the cases. This could mean that these clinicians were "biased" toward making this diagnosis or that they were recognized experts to whom other clinicians referred suspect cases of dissociative identity disorder. Unfortunately, because the diagnoses were not confirmed by a second clinician, it is not possible to determine which of these two explanations for the variability among clinicians is correct.

To avoid the problem of clinician bias, C. A. Ross and his colleagues (1991) used a standard screening instrument and a structured diagnostic interview to determine the prevalence of multiple personalities among American psychiatric inpatients. Their estimate was 3.3%, 30 to 60 times the Swiss estimate. Because inpatients have more severe conditions than outpatients, we might expect the prevalence of dissociative identity disorder to be somewhat higher in Ross and colleagues' study than among Modestin's Swiss outpatients, but not 30 to 60 times as high.

The reason for the high, and apparently increasing, incidence of dissociative identity disorder in the United States is not entirely clear. C. A. Ross (1989) has suggested a sociocultural explanation. Freud originally attributed dissociative disorders to childhood sexual abuse. He saw them as ways to repress childhood traumas. Freud's belief that his patients were sexually abused as children was an anathema to his contemporaries, who put him under considerable social pressure. Eventually, Freud repudiated his original theory and replaced it with the idea that children "fantasize" about sexual activity. Ross suggests that Freud may have been correct the first time; sexual abuse is common and it does produce mental disorders, especially dissociative identity disorder. The low incidence of dissociative identity disorder may have been deliberate. Freud and other therapists avoided making the diagnosis of dissociative identity disorder because they did not want to face up to the sexual abuse of children.

Ross's theory has several virtues. First, there does seem to be a connection between dissociative identity disorder and childhood sexual abuse. (This is why Dr. McLean first suggested that Helen Fairchild may have been abused.) Second, Ross's theory can explain why more women seem to suffer from dissociative identity disorder than men—girls are more often the target of sexual abuse (Ross & Norton, 1989; see also Chapter 13). Nevertheless, there are other possible explanations for the apparent increase in prevalence. High on the list are the constantly changing diagnostic criteria (Kihlstrom et al., 1993). For example, although the *DSM-IV* makes a clear distinction between dissociative identity disorder and schizophrenia, this has not always been the case. Blackouts, memory lapses, and feeling under the control of another person are all common among people with schizophrenia (C. A. Ross et al., 1991). It is possible that some people who meet today's *DSM-IV* diagnostic criteria for dissociative identity disorder would have been diagnosed schizophrenic in the past (Rosenbaum, 1980). As the schizophrenia diagnosis became more precise, people who formerly fell into that category were given the diagnosis of dissociative identity disorder instead, thereby increasing its incidence.

There are fads and fashions, even in diagnosis, and it is possible that some clinicians have simply replaced other diagnoses with dissociative identity disorder because the latter is more fashionable (Bliss, Larson, & Nakashima, 1983). There does seem to be a modern tendency to look for multiple personalities. Putnam (1992), for example, argues that Anna O. was not suffering from "hysteria" as Breuer and Freud believed (see Chapter 2), but was really a case of dissociative identity disorder. It pays to be suspicious about this rush to find multiple personalities. Books and movies such as *The Three Faces of Eve* provide an easily accessible script for anyone who wants to assume the role of a person with a dissociative identity disorder. As already noted, clinicians may unwittingly reinforce such role playing by encouraging people to give names to their various personalities and then by addressing each one by name (Merskey, 1992; Piper, 1994; Weissberg, 1993). The use of hypnosis gives the diagnostic enterprise a legitimacy that it may not deserve (Spanos, 1994; Spanos, Weekes, & Bertrand, 1985).

A final reason why dissociative identity disorder

may be increasing in the United States is the willingness of the American legal system to accept multiple personality as a defense (Owens, 1997). For example, men accused of violent crimes such as rape have claimed to be suffering from dissociative identity disorder and blamed one of their alters for committing the crime (see Highlight 7.1). Dissociative identity disorder has also been used by victims as grounds for criminal charges. For example, a woman allegedly suffering from dissociative identity disorder claimed that one of her alters consented to sex while a nonconsenting alter was raped (Keyes, 1981; Sue et al., 1994). Countries whose legal systems reject such defenses and accusations seem to have far fewer cases of dissociative identity disorder than the United States.

Etiology and Treatment of Dissociative Identity Disorder

Although they differ in detail, all schools of psychology attribute dissociative identity disorder to traumatic experiences. As already noted, these often involve physical and sexual abuse (Boon & Draijer, 1993; Coons et al., 1988; Kluft, 1984, 1985; C. A. Ross, 1989; C. A. Ross et al., 1990). According to psychoanalytic theory, these anxiety-producing memories are successfully repressed, and a new personality is created to take "responsibility" for all of the "forgotten" feelings and memories (J. P. Shapiro, 1991).

Not everyone who is abused as a child develops a dissociative identity disorder, however, so other factors must also be involved (Sanders & Giolas, 1991). Bliss (1986) has suggested that one such extra factor is a susceptibility to "self-hypnosis" (the ability to put oneself into a hypnotic state). We know that hypnosis can be used to induce forgetting in suggestible people, and we also know that people with dissociative identity disorder are highly suggestible and easily hypnotizable. Putting the two together, it is possible that people prone to dissociative identity disorder hypnotize themselves into forgetting painful memories (Frischholz et al., 1992; Kihlstrom, Glisky, & Angiulo, 1994). An alternate personality is created to protect the abused child from direct involvement with sexual abuse. Future psychological problems are dealt with by creating additional personalities. Although it may sound plausible, it is not clear how this theory can be tested except in highly artificial lab experiments (Spanos, 1986).

Psychodynamic therapy is devoted to helping people lift their repression and "work through" conflicts associated with early trauma. In the past, this has meant picking one of the personalities and focusing on that personality's memories. For example, Thigpen and

Is Dissociative Identity Disorder Real?

Is dissociative identity disorder a sham, simply an excuse to avoid responsibility for one's actions? For some psychologists, the answer is yes (Coons & Bradley, 1985; Merskey, 1992; Piper, 1994). Their skepticism is fueled by people like Kenneth Bianchi, the notorious Hillside Strangler who plagued California in the late 1970s. Bianchi claimed to be a victim of dissociative identity disorder and, therefore, not responsible for his crimes. Before his trial, Bianchi was "hypnotized" by psychologist John Watkins. While under a trance, eyes closed, head nodding, Watkins deliberately asked a second personality to come forward:

WATKINS: I've talked a bit to Ken but I think that perhaps there might be another part of Ken that I haven't talked to. And I would like to communicate with that other part. And I would like that other part to come to talk with me. . . . And when you're here, lift the left hand off the chair to signal to me that you are here. Would you please come . . . and lift Ken's hand to indicate to me that you are here. . . .

Bianchi's hand lifted and then he and the interviewer had the following conversation:

WATKINS: Are you the same as Ken or are you different in any way?

BIANCHI: I'm not him.

WATKINS: You're not him. Who are you? Do you have a name?

BIANCHI: I'm not Ken.

WATKINS: You're not him? Okay. Who are you? Tell me about yourself. Do you have a name I can call you by?

Kenneth Bianchi, accused of killing several women in Southern California, claimed that one of his alters was responsible for the crimes. Did he have dissociative personality disorder, or did his psychologist, instead, give him cues to act as if he did?

BIANCHI: Steve. You can call me Steve. (J. R. Schwarz, 1981, pp. 139–140)

Steve later said that he, not Ken, had committed the murders. Rorschach tests administered to Steve and Ken allegedly showed them to be different personalities. Yet the well-known psychiatrist Martin Orne testified that Bianchi was faking (Orne, Dinges, & Orne, 1984). According to Orne, Watkins provided Bianchi with cues about how he was expected to behave. By asking to talk to other personalities and by encouraging Bianchi to behave in a bizarre fashion, Watkins let Bianchi know how a "multiple personality" should act (see also Coons, 1991). This criticism is not new.

Many years before, Morton Prince was alleged to have encouraged Sally Beauchamp to develop her various personalities by hypnotic suggestion (Mc-Curdy, 1941).

Do cues in the hypnotic situation help people to fake a dissociative identity disorder? One way to answer this question is to compare Bianchi's behavior with the behavior of people specifically asked to pretend to suffer from dissociative identity disorder. Such a possibility was explored in a laboratory experiment by Spanos and his colleagues (1985), who asked university students to pretend to be an accused murderer who was being examined by a psychiatrist. They hypnotized some of the students and then interviewed them using Kenneth Bianchi's interviews as a script. Spanos and his colleagues found that the students adopted new names and feigned amnesia. In other words, they acted just like Bianchi. Clearly, it is possible for anyone to pretend to have more than one personality. Bianchi's jury may have guessed this because they found him guilty.

Although it is wise to be skeptical about the claims of people who stand to gain substantially from faking a dissociative identity disorder, it is not warranted to consider all cases to be hoaxes. Certainly, most professionals believe in the existence of multiple personalities (Dunn et al., 1994). It is worth remembering, however, that judgments about whose disorder is real and whose is a simulation are difficult to make.

Cleckley (1957) began treating Eve by working with Jane, her most "competent" personality. Ultimately, a fourth personality called Evelyn emerged who represented an integration of the other three personalities. However, as Chris Sizemore (the real Eve) revealed in her own book (1989), her treatment was not as successful as Thigpen and Cleckley suggested. Over the years, she developed many more personalities.

To avoid the continued spawning of personalities, modern treatments attempt to fuse a person's various personalities into a single one (International Society for the Study of Dissociation [ISSD], 1997; Putnam, 1989; Putnam & Loewenstein, 1993; C. A. Ross, 1989). Therapists may videotape interviews with each personality and show these to the other personalities. Diaries, letters, and other information may also be shared. The hope is that the various personalities will fuse into one when they share the same memories. The new fused personality can then be taught to cope with anxiety in ways other than by forming new personalities.

Drugs may also be used to treat people with dissociative identity disorder. For example, because there is a high degree of comorbidity between dissociative identity disorder and other psychological problems, particularly depression and anxiety, antidepressants and anti-anxiety medications are often prescribed. Other drugs, such as Amytal Sodium and Pentothal Sodium (so-called truth serums), have been used to help people regain supposedly lost memories (Kluft, 1988). Using drugs to get people to reveal matters that they would otherwise keep to themselves is as old as recorded history. The Latin proverb *in vino veritas* (wine brings truth) is but one example. Like alcohol, Amytal and Pentothal Sodium release inhibitions, allowing people to reveal memories that would otherwise remain repressed. Unfortunately, such memories may be state-dependent and forgotten once the drug wears off. Also, we cannot assume that drug-induced memories are always accurate.

Behaviorists view dissociative identity disorder as an extreme form of normal behavior. Each of us displays different behaviors and moods in different situations. These various roles and moods are elicited by environmental stimuli, but, in dissociative identity disorder, certain stimuli produce exceptionally dramatic changes in behavior and mood. For example, a person may behave in a hostile fashion whenever a police officer is present, even if the officer presents no threat. Such a person may appear perfectly happy and at ease yet suddenly become belligerent and hostile when the police officer appears. The dramatic change makes it appear as if the person has more than one personality. Although plausible, this explanation seems oversimplified. For example, it does not explain why one personality is often unaware of the existence of an alter.

Although the behavioral explanation for dissociative identity disorder seems inadequate, behavioral treatment may still be useful. For instance, teaching people with dissociative identity disorder coping skills to help them deal with stress could reduce their need for alters. Behavioral therapists also use positive reinforcement to encourage clients to display their most healthy personality (Kohlenberg, 1973).

To date, there are no controlled outcome studies of treatments for dissociative identity disorder. Our knowledge comes mainly from clinical case reports (Coons, 1986; Kluft, 1985). These suggest a highly variable outcome. In some cases, the condition may last for years and be highly resistant to treatment (Putnam & Loewenstein, 1993), whereas in other cases considerable progress can be made (Ellason & Ross, 1997). Treatment is less likely to be successful the longer a dissociative identity disorder exists, so early diagnosis and intervention are recommended to prevent a more resistant condition from developing.

Did Helen Fairchild Have a Dissociative Disorder?

Helen Fairchild sought psychological assistance from Dr. McLean after her husband left her. Under treatment, she recovered memories of childhood sexual abuse at the hands of her father, whom she also accused of the rape and murder of her childhood friend Jacqueline Buchanan. The validity of Helen's memories, which were unsubstantiated by any other evidence, were challenged by her father's lawyer.

Clinically, Helen displayed at least some signs of dissociative amnesia, fugue, and depersonalization, but she did not show the main feature of a dissociative identity disorder, the existence of multiple "personalities." One aspect of her clinical presentation that has not yet been discussed was her headaches, hot flushes, and stomach pain. Because Helen's physical complaints seemed to have no organic cause, Dr. McLean believed that they may have signaled a somatoform disorder.

SOMATOFORM DISORDERS

The *DSM-IV* describes five somatoform disorders: conversion disorder, somatization disorder, pain disorder, hypochondriasis, and body dysmorphic disorder. As you will see, there are important differences among these disorders, but there is also a general unifying theme—all of the somatoform disorders are construed as physical manifestations of psychological (usually unconscious) problems (van der Feltz-Cornelis & van Dyck, 1997).

Conversion Disorder

William Harvey (1578–1657), physician to King James I and mapper of the human circulatory system, was a keen clinician. Among his many case reports were several cases of pseudocyesis (false pregnancy):

> I am acquainted with a young woman, the daughter of a physician with whom I am very intimate, who experienced in her own person all the usual symptoms of pregnancy; after the fourteenth week, being healthy and sprightly, she felt the movements of the child within the uterus, calculated the time at which she expected her delivery, and when she thought, from further indications that this was at hand, prepared the bed, cradle, and all other matters ready for the event. But all was in vain. Lucina . . . deity of childbirth . . . refused to answer her prayers; the motions of the fetus ceased; and by degrees, . . . as the abdomen increased so it diminished; however, she remained barren ever after. (Harvey, 1847, pp. 189–190)

From classical times through Harvey's day and well into the 20th century, cases such as this were diagnosed as "hysteria" (see Chapter 2). Freud and Breuer's famous patient, Anna O., had among her many symptoms a false pregnancy. Hysteria was once considered to be a physical, usually a neurological, disease. However, after Breuer and Freud published their studies on hysteria, professional opinion began to change. Today, it is generally agreed that hysteria is a psychological condition. According to Freud's theory, repressed sexual conflicts are "converted" into physical symptoms, which represent these conflicts in a disguised form. Hysterical paralysis of the hand, for example, may be a symbolic representation of guilt over masturbation. Although the term *hysteria* is no longer used and Freud's influence is much reduced, echoes of the past may still be heard in the *DSM-IV*'s name for hysteria—**conversion disorder** (L. Miller, 1997).

Although a number of false pregnancies have been reported, conversion disorders normally consist of pseudoneurological symptoms that affect sensory or motor functioning (Boffeli & Guze, 1992). Sufferers complain of paralysis, blindness, deafness, seizures, odd tingling sensations, and anesthesias (loss of feeling). Note

that sexual symptoms are excluded because they fall into a separate diagnostic category.

Sometimes, conversion symptoms may be bizarre. Individuals may complain of being unable to hear when lying down but report that they hear perfectly when sitting upright. They may claim to be unable to speak loudly, only softly. A common complaint is *globus hystericus*, the feeling of having a lump stuck in one's throat (Harris, Deary, & Wilson, 1996). More commonly, however, conversion symptoms mimic those of real illnesses. They can be differentiated from physical illness because laboratory tests and examinations are negative and because there is no long-term physical deterioration or improvement as might be expected with a genuine medical condition. However, in some cases, the similarity between conversion symptoms and medical illness is so great that only ingenious examinations can distinguish them (see Highlight 7.2). Clinical lore holds that people with conversion symptoms show what the 19th-century French clinicians called *la belle indifférence* (a lack of concern) about their supposed illness. In practice, this response is rare. Most people with conversion disorder are troubled by their symptoms.

When making the diagnosis of conversion disorder, it is important to consider a person's social and cultural environment (Alexander, Joseph, & Das, 1997). In some evangelistic church services, people may fall into a trance or have "seizures." Because they are culturally accepted parts of such religious ceremonies, these symptoms are not signs of a conversion disorder.

The main *DSM-IV* diagnostic criteria for conversion disorder appear in Table 7.6. As you can see, Helen Fairchild's stomachaches (and possibly her hot flushes and headaches) met most of the diagnostic criteria for a conversion disorder.

Medical disorders such as multiple sclerosis, myasthenia gravis (progressive muscular weakness), and others may produce strange symptoms that are easily confused with conversion disorders. The extent of this confusion was illustrated by Slater and Glithero (1965), who followed up people who had been diagnosed as suffering from conversion symptoms 9 years earlier. Sixty percent had either died or been diagnosed as suffering from a physical disease. More recent studies have confirmed that people diagnosed as having a conversion disorder often turn out to have a physical disease, although not as often as reported by Slater and Glithero (Kent, Tomasson, & Coryell, 1995; Mace & Trimble, 1996).

Clearly, it is important to be cautious when concluding that a person's symptoms result from a conversion

Separating Conversion From Somatic Symptoms

The noted 17th-century clinician Thomas Sydenham (1624–1689) observed that hysterical symptoms can mimic any disease. According to Sydenham, the only way to tell whether symptoms are real or the result of a conversion disorder is to investigate the events preceding their appearance. If a symptom is preceded by a "disturbance of mind," the diagnosis is conversion disorder. Today, more than 300 years after Sydenham's death, high-tech laboratory tests and expensive diagnostic equipment are available to help clinicians determine whether symptoms are somatic (Morota et al., 1994). Yet the physical status of many symptoms remains equivocal. Increasingly, medical tests are being supplemented with diagnostic methods derived from psychological research.

For example, Bryant and McConkey (1989) examined a 33-year-old man whose symptoms began after being hit in the right eye with a rifle butt during military training. The young man first reported partial sight and then no sight at all in his injured eye. When medical examinations and tests uncovered no physical reason for his blindness, Bryant and McConkey devised a psychological test of his visual ability. They designed an apparatus (see the illustration) that included a screen containing three triangles. One of the three was always in a different spatial orientation from the others (pointing up when the others pointed down and vice versa). The apparatus also produced a tone. Below each triangle was a switch that could turn off the tone. The man's task was to learn to pick out the triangle that differed in orientation and use the switch under that triangle to turn off the tone. On some (but not all) trials, the correct triangle was illuminated. With his good

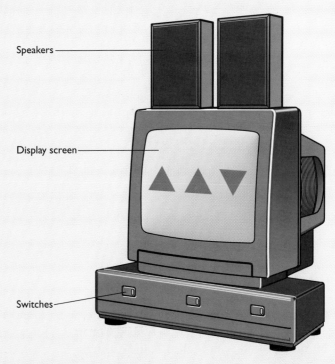

Apparatus Used by Bryant and McConkey (1989) to Assess a Visual Conversion Disorder

eye covered, the man performed the task many times. Even though he supposedly could not see, the man's performance improved when the triangle was illuminated. When the experimenters encouraged the man to improve his accuracy, his performance improved even further. All the while, he claimed to be unable to see the screen.

By distinguishing between the young man's verbal reports and his actual performance, Bryant and McConkey showed that his problem was not somatic but psychological. Does this mean that the young man was consciously faking? Not necessarily. As used by today's cognitive psychologists, the term *unconscious* is different from Freud's uncon-

scious (Kihlstrom, Barnhardt, & Tataryn, 1992). Freud's unconscious was a repository for psychic energy and conflicts. The modern view relates the term to the location of cognitive processing: Perceptual and cognitive processes that take place out of awareness are considered to be "unconscious." Thus the young man may have thought that he was blind because his visual processing was taking place outside of awareness. A similar explanation may be applied to the observation that people with "hysterical" blindness usually manage to get around without bumping into the furniture—they are unaware of their own visual perceptions (Hilgard, 1994).

DSM-IV TABLE 7.6 Main *DSM-IV* Diagnostic Criteria for Conversion Disorder

A. One or more symptoms or deficits affecting voluntary motor or sensory function that suggest a neurological or other general medical condition.

B. Psychological factors are judged to be associated with the symptom or deficit because the initiation or exacerbation of the symptom or deficit is preceded by conflicts or other stressors.

C. The symptom or deficit is not intentionally produced or feigned (as in factitious disorder or malingering).

D. The symptom or deficit cannot, after appropriate investigation, be fully explained by a general medical condition, or by the direct effects of a substance, or as a culturally sanctioned behavior or experience.

E. The symptom or deficit causes clinically significant distress or impairment in social, occupational, or other important areas of functioning or warrants medical evaluation.

F. The symptom or deficit is not limited to pain or sexual dysfunction, does not occur exclusively during the course of a somatization disorder, and is not better accounted for by another disorder.

Note: From American Psychiatric Association (1994, p. 457).

disorder. There have been tragic cases of supposed conversion disorders that later turned out to be medical conditions (Bokey, 1993; J. B. Jones & Barklage, 1990). For example, Fishbain and Goldberg (1991) described a man who was hit on the head with a glass bottle during a fight. He did not lose consciousness, and a neurological examination and an X ray were both normal. However, when the police attempted to take him to jail, the man claimed that he was unable to move his left arm and leg. After several demands, he was able to move his arm and leg. But, when he tried to accompany the police to the patrol car, he claimed to be unable to walk. Because he could move his limbs when he tried and a medical examination was negative, the man was believed either to have a conversion disorder or to be faking in order to avoid jail. However, further testing with a CT scan revealed a blood clot on the right side of his brain. This blood clot interfered with automatic movements such as walking but not with conscious, deliberate movement. Figure 7.1 exemplifies another way of distinguishing conversion disorder from problems of a physical origin.

Prevalence, Family Patterns, and Course Although Breuer, Freud, and their contemporaries treated many people with conversion disorders, modern clinicians rarely see a case. Psychoanalytic psychologists consider the apparent decrease in the prevalence of conversion disorders evidence for Freud's view that such disorders are the result of repressed sexual conflicts. They argue that Freud's turn-of-the-century Vienna was sexually inhibited and that today's more open attitude toward sex has eliminated the main cause of conversion disorders.

Because the few sexual taboos that do remain today apply more to women than to men (as they also did in Freud's time), then we should expect to find a higher prevalence of conversion disorders among women than men. This is indeed the case (Tomasson, Kent, & Coryell, 1991; Viederman, 1986), although men may also develop pseudoneurological symptoms in stressful situations (Streuning & Gray, 1990).

An alternative, sociological, explanation for the sex differences focuses on the specific symptoms reported by the different sexes. Consider, for example, G. C. Watson and Buranen's (1979) report that men are more likely to have false "heart attacks" than women. These false heart attacks are rarely considered signs of a conversion disorder even when the man involved meets all the *DSM-IV* diagnostic criteria. Women, on the other hand, are more likely to seek medical help for dizziness, weakness, and nausea—symptoms which, in the absence of an obvious medical condition, are usually considered signs of a conversion disorder. Thus, it is possible that the sex differences in the prevalence of conversion disorder are at least partly explainable by different complaints. The symptoms reported by females are more "suspect" than those reported by males, even when the complaints of both sexes are medically unsubstantiated. Perhaps what needs to be studied is not why conversion disorders are more common among females but why false heart attacks are *not* seen as signs of a conversion disorder in men.

In addition to sex differences, there are marked regional and national differences in the prevalence of conversion disorders. In the United States, most cases occur

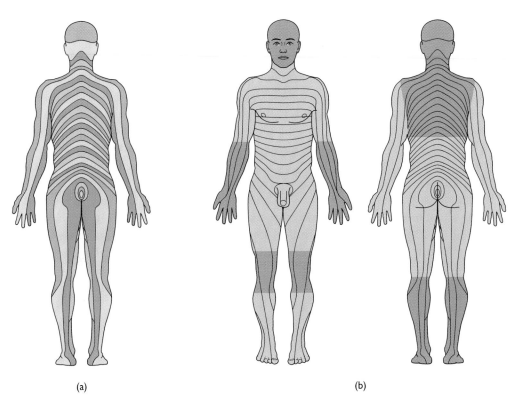

(a)   (b)

FIGURE 7.1 Patterns of Neural Innervation (a) and Typical Areas of Anesthesias in Patients Suffering From a Conversion Disorder (b). *Conversion disorders can sometimes be detected because the physical symptoms make no anatomical sense. If numbness has a psychogenic rather than a neurological origin, areas of pain insensitivity may not correspond to the actual structure of the nervous system. Part b adapted from plate 150,* Atlas of Human Anatomy.

in people from rural areas, especially among those with little education, low income, and fundamentalist religious backgrounds (Binzer, Andersen, & Kullgren, 1997; Folks, Ford, & Regan, 1984). Although its prevalence has declined in Western countries, conversion disorder still remains common in developing societies (Pu et al., 1986) and among newcomers to the United States (Drinnan & Marmor, 1991). Before we conclude that people from rural areas and developing countries are less sophisticated than we are, we should note that cross-national comparisons are difficult (Alexander et al., 1997; Gureje et al., 1997). Most of the world relies on the *ICD* (WHO, 1993) rather than the *DSM* diagnostic criteria. The *ICD* has no category exactly equivalent to the *DSM-IV*'s conversion disorder. Clearly, this makes it difficult to compare diagnoses in different countries. The only justifiable way to show that prevalence varies across countries is to design a cross-national comparison study in which diagnoses in both countries rely on the same criteria; this has not yet been done.

Etiology and Treatment Conversion disorder has had more explanations than practically any other psychological complaint: wandering wombs, planetary magnetic forces, neurological lesions, unconscious conflicts. Every fad in the history of psychology makes its appearance in the study of hysteria. Moreover, these fads never completely fade away. Thus, even though twin and adoption studies have failed to find significant evidence for a genetic factor in conversion disorder (Torgersen, 1986), many scientists believe that a genetic basis must exist.

As recently as the 1980s, some writers were still arguing that conversion symptoms always have a medical explanation (Ford & Folks, 1985). Certainly, many people with conversion disorder also have a concomitant somatic disorder (Binzer et al., 1997). However, the vast majority of psychologists have opted for either the psychoanalytic or a cognitive-behavioral view.

Psychoanalysts view conversion disorders as manifestations of repressed, usually sexual, conflicts in the symbolic form of somatic symptoms (Edelmann, 1992). Symptoms provide a **primary gain** to the person with a conversion disorder—they keep unacceptable conflicts at bay. For example, people with conflicts about expressing anger may develop hysterical muteness. Symptoms also provide a **secondary gain** in the form of sympathy and attention. It is important to keep these two types of gain separate (Kirmayer, Robbins, & Paris, 1994).

Psychoanalytic treatment is aimed mainly at the primary gain. It involves uncovering conflicts, showing how they contribute to the apparent illness, and helping people to express their psychological needs in less debilitating ways. In addition, the emotional catharsis that comes from releasing repressed sexual energy, combined with new insights into one's behavior, is supposed to help people give up their symptoms. As usual, the evidence for these claims comes mainly from clinical observations and small trials (Ochitil, 1982).

Psychoanalytic treatment for secondary gain is subsidiary. It is aimed at removing the attention and sympathy that reinforce the "sick" role. In contrast, behavioral and cognitive clinicians focus almost entirely on secondary gain (Blanchard, 1994; Mullins, Olson, & Chaney, 1992). They believe that a conversion disorder is most likely to develop when (a) an individual is under stress, (b) the person knows enough about an illness to mimic its symptoms, and (c) there is some reinforcement (secondary gain) for being "sick." The person need not consciously pretend to be sick. Symptom formation can take place outside of awareness.

In theory, systematic desensitization should reduce situational anxiety, thereby alleviating the source of somatic complaints. For example, children who become nauseous at school could be taken through a series of graded exposures to school similar to the desensitization of a phobia (Lesage & Lamoontagne, 1985). In practice, desensitization alone is rarely sufficient to overcome a conversion disorder. People with conversion disorders are reluctant to admit that their problems might be psychological. They rarely undergo systematic desensitization because they avoid referrals to mental health professionals. Instead, they prefer to make the rounds of medical practitioners. Even if such people could be returned to active life (by receiving a "prize" for returning to school or a "bonus" for returning to work), they would still have to admit that their illness was at least partly psychological. For many people, remaining ill is preferable to making such an admission. Bogus medical treatments (in which people are prescribed placebo pills) may help such people by giving them a face-saving way of attributing their improvement to medical rather than psychological treatment (Solyom & Solyom, 1990).

People who have successfully avoided responsibility because of "illness" have had their symptoms strongly reinforced. Overcoming their habitual "avoidance through sickness" might require family therapy targeted not just at the "patient" but also at those people in the person's social environment who are reinforc-

ing and maintaining the conversion symptoms (Brazier & Venning, 1997). At the very least, the family and friends of people with a conversion disorder need to be taught not to reinforce the symptomatic behavior. Assertiveness training as well as training in specific social skills may also assist people with conversion symptoms to abandon the view that they are weak and sick. None of this is possible, of course, until the therapist overcomes the main obstacle—getting people with conversion disorder into treatment in the first place.

Treatment follow-up studies have produced a mixed picture (Krull & Schifferdecker, 1990; Mace & Trimble, 1996). In general, children and adolescents respond better to treatment than do adults (Gooch, Wolcott, & Speed, 1997). The longer conversion symptoms are present, the poorer the treatment prognosis.

Although the departure of Helen Fairchild's husband provided an obvious source of psychological stress and although she did develop troubling physical symptoms that could not be medically explained, we are not quite ready to diagnose her as having a conversion disorder. We must first consider whether another somatoform disorder, somatization disorder, better describes her pattern of symptoms and signs.

Somatization Disorder

From classical times through Breuer and Freud's famous studies, hysteria received more attention than practically any other psychological disorder. The 19th century was the age of classification in science, and hysteria was no exception. Hysterics were divided into two main types, those with multiple complaints and those whose complaints centered around a specific organ or system. The latter would today receive the diagnosis of conversion disorder. The former, people with multiple complaints, were the specific interest of a French doctor, Pierre Briquet (1796–1881), who published a textbook on the symptoms and treatment of hysteria in 1859. Based on his observations of more than 400 patients (almost all women), Briquet systematized what had previously been a haphazard catalogue of symptoms: chest pains, paralyses, changes in consciousness, and so on. His work became so well known that hysteria marked by multiple complaints was called **Briquet's syndrome.** Although this term is still occasionally encountered, it has been largely replaced by the *DSM-IV* diagnosis, **somatization disorder.**

The *DSM-IV* diagnostic criteria for somatization disorder are summarized in Table 7.7. Note that the di-

> **DSM-IV**   TABLE 7.7   Main *DSM-IV* Diagnostic Criteria
> for Somatization Disorder
>
> A. A history of many physical complaints beginning before age 30 that result in treatment being sought or significant impairment in social, occupational, or other areas of functioning.
> B. Each of the following criteria must have been met, with individual symptoms occurring at any time during the course of the disturbance:
> (1) four pain symptoms: pain related to at least four different sites or functions
> (2) two gastrointestinal symptoms other than pain (nausea, bloating, vomiting)
> (3) one sexual symptom other than pain (erectile dysfunction, indifference)
> (4) one pseudoneurological symptom (tingling, paralysis, loss of balance, double vision).
> C. Either (1) or (2):
> (1) After appropriate investigations, the symptoms in Criterion B cannot be fully explained by a medical condition or substance abuse.
> (2) If there is a related medical condition, the complaints exceed what might be expected from history and lab findings.
> D. The symptoms are not intentionally produced.
>
> *Note:* Adapted from American Psychiatric Association (1994, pp. 449–450).

agnosis depends on having at least eight physical complaints spanning several bodily systems. There is another *DSM-IV* diagnostic category, **undifferentiated somatoform disorder,** for people with only one or two unexplained symptoms. Helen Fairchild's complaints were more typical of an undifferentiated somatoform disorder—headache, hot flushes, stomachache, loss of interest in sex. In both somatization disorder and undifferentiated somatoform disorder, the symptoms significantly affect everyday life, they are not explainable physiologically, and they are not consciously feigned.

People with a somatization disorder describe their symptoms with much associated drama ("I almost died when . . ."). Yet they are frequently inaccurate when reporting their medical histories. Jumping from doctor to doctor, telling each a different story, people with somatization disorder leave a trail of inconsistencies. Clinicians must cut through this confusion and piece together an accurate history by talking to relatives, reading doctors' reports, and reviewing hospital records. Although laboratory tests are almost always negative and physical examinations are normal, doctors may still prescribe medication to relieve symptoms. For example, Helen was given a painkiller for her headache. It is also common for somatization patients to be prescribed tranquilizers and antidepressants. Because they see many doctors and undergo numerous hospitalizations and surgical procedures, people with somatization are prone to **iatrogenic disorders** (illnesses caused by treatment). They may, for example, develop infections

from surgery or have adverse reactions to drugs.

Given the potential negative consequences of ignoring a physical illness, it is wise for clinicians to consider all somatic symptoms as potentially the result of some medical condition until they can be proven otherwise. Vague, even bizarre, symptoms can still have a physical cause. For example, in multiple sclerosis, which has already been mentioned, hard patches called plaques replace the usual neural coverings in the brain or spinal cord. These plaques cause dizziness, paralysis of different parts of the body, and various peculiar sensory phenomena that come and go as the plaques disappear and pop up somewhere else. Crohn's disease (an autoimmune disorder in which the body produces antibodies against itself) produces diarrhea, pain, arthritis, skin rashes, mood changes, and a host of other symptoms. Before making the diagnosis of somatization disorder, careful investigations are required to rule out these and other physical illnesses.

There are a few suspicious signs that may alert clinicians to the possibility of a somatization disorder. Complaints that span biological systems—gastrointestinal, neurological, respiratory—are suspect because there are relatively few medical conditions that affect multiple organ systems (although note that Crohn's disease affects the gastrointestinal, dermatological, and skeletal systems). Complaints that last for decades without any deterioration or improvement are also suspicious because most illnesses either get better or worse. Of course, it is possible to have a somatization disorder as well as a physical illness at the same time. So clinicians should

Mind Versus Body: The Case of Chronic Fatigue Syndrome

Woody Allen once wrote: "If there is a mind-body split, which would you prefer?" Clearly, you want both, because one is useless without the other. The complete interdependence of mind and body is one of the main themes of this book. In Chapter 5, we saw how psychological factors, especially stress, can affect physical illnesses. That chapter criticized the old-fashioned idea that some illnesses are psychosomatic (ulcers, high blood pressure), whereas others are not. Using the case of a person with diabetes, the chapter showed how psychological, social, and physical factors are involved in all diseases, even those that have a clear physiological component. A similar point needs to be made about the somatoform disorders. By definition, somatoform disorders involve physical complaints in the absence of medical disease. Yet a rigid distinction between mind and body is as out of place in somatoform disorders as it was in our discussion of physical illnesses in Chapter 5 (van der Feltz-Cornelis & van Dyck, 1997).

Consider, for example, the disorder known as chronic fatigue syndrome (Fukuda et al., 1994). The syndrome's main symptom is persistent or relapsing fatigue that is not the result of exertion; that is not alleviated by rest; and that negatively affects occupational, educational, or social functioning. The diagnosis requires four or more of the following symptoms: impaired memory or concentration, sore throat, tender lymph nodes, muscle pain, joint pain, headaches, a sleep disturbance, and postexertion malaise. The diagnosis requires that the person not have any other illness or substance abuse problem that could explain the fatigue. There are no laboratory tests that can confirm chronic fatigue syndrome; it is diagnosed only when other possible causes of the fatigue are excluded.

Perhaps it has already occurred to you that this syndrome bears considerable resemblance to a somatoform disorder—multiple symptoms across several body systems that affect occupational and social functioning with no obvious cause. A person with the symptoms of chronic fatigue syndrome who is seen in a psychiatric clinic is likely to be diagnosed as suffering from a somatoform disorder. The same person seen in a medical clinic would likely be diag-

nosed with a physical disorder, namely, chronic fatigue syndrome (S. K. Johnson, DeLuca, & Natelson, 1996). Psychologists search for the cause of a person's symptoms in the events of his or her personal life; medical researchers seek a physical explanation (a virus, for example).

Who is correct? Both are. As argued in Chapter 5, the distinction between mental and physical illness is artificial and leads to misleading conclusions. All conditions involve both psychological and physical factors. Thus, a person with chronic fatigue syndrome may well have experienced some psychological trauma that has contributed to his or her pattern of symptoms. Similarly, people with somatization disorder may have a physical condition that has contributed to their psychological distress by leaving them weak and easily fatigued (even if that condition remains unidentified). As psychologists, it is vital that we keep in mind that we are dealing not with a disembodied mind that affects a body but with a whole person. The symptoms that people display in the clinic always reflect the interaction of minds and bodies.

---

always be alert to signs of an underlying medical condition, even among people who meet all the criteria for a somatization disorder. (For a discussion of this point as exemplified by chronic fatigue syndrome, see Critical Thinking About Clinical Decisions 7.1.)

Prevalence, Family Patterns, and Course It is difficult to estimate the lifetime prevalence of somatization disorder because each version of the *DSM* has used different diagnostic criteria. The best estimate is somewhere between 0.2% and 2.0% of women and less than 0.2% of men (Faravelli et al., 1997). However, these figures may be too low because people with a somatization disorder may be diagnosed as suffering from an anxiety, mood,

dissociative, or personality disorder, all of which show a high comorbidity with somatization disorder (F. W. Brown, Golding, & Smith, 1990; Golding, Smith, & Kashner, 1991; M. P. Rogers et al., 1996). Estimates of the prevalence of somatization disorder in men may be especially low because, in some cultures, it is not considered "masculine" to complain about being sick. At least one third of the men referred to psychologists because of multiple somatic complaints probably meet the diagnostic criteria for a somatic disorder (Golding et al., 1991) even though they do not necessarily receive this diagnosis.

Because those with somatization disorder receive medical workups and undergo unnecessary procedures, even a small number of cases of the disorder can greatly inflate hospital costs (Purcell, 1991). It has been estimated that about 3% of all hospitalizations in Denmark are for people with somatization disorder (Fink, 1992). Danish adults with somatization disorder averaged 22 hospital admissions each over a 20-year period.

The prevalence of somatization disorder varies greatly across cultural groups (Gureje et al., 1997). It is more common among Chinese Americans than among Caucasian Americans (Hsu & Folstein, 1997), and it seems to be especially common in India (Chandrassekaran, Goswami, & Sivakumar, 1994). The way in which symptoms are reported also varies considerably from one culture to another (Janca et al., 1995). For instance, reports of "feeling like worms are crawling under the skin" are common in Africa but hardly ever encountered in the United States or Europe (American Psychiatric Assn, 1994). Other culture-specific syndromes (*koro, windigo, latah,* amok) were discussed in Chapter 2. Across cultures, somatic symptoms are correlated with emotional distress; the greater the distress, the more symptoms reported by both males and females (Piccinelli & Simon, 1997).

In females, somatization disorder typically begins in late adolescence (C. R. Cloninger et al., 1986), usually with menstrual complaints. Males usually begin with interpersonal problems, delinquency, and truancy, followed by somatization disorder later in life. In both sexes, once the somatization pattern sets in, individuals do not remain symptom-free for very long. As a consequence, they find it difficult to maintain jobs or stable relationships. Fortunately, with the increasing presence of psychologists in hospitals and clinics, somatization disorder is less likely to result in unnecessary operations and procedures than in the past.

Etiology and Treatment   Somatization disorder runs in families (Guze, 1993). Close relatives of females diagnosed as having somatization disorder tend to have a similar disorder themselves (C. R. Cloninger et al., 1986; Guze et al., 1986; Ziegler & Schlemmer, 1994). Male relatives report fewer medical complaints than female relatives. Instead, they tend to abuse alcohol and drugs, and many have histories of criminal activity (C. R. Cloninger et al., 1984). Researchers have hypothesized that males express negative emotions by abusing substances and engaging in criminal behavior, whereas females develop multiple medical symptoms (Lilienfeld, 1992). Children who have an adoptive parent with somatization disorder have a greater risk of developing the same disorder, even though they are not biologically related (American

Psychiatric Assn, 1994). This suggests that family patterns are most likely the result of environmental factors like modeling rather than genetics.

Because people with somatization disorder reject any suggestion that their problems are psychological, few consent to participate in psychological treatment. Most are seen by medical practitioners (Escobar, 1996). Not surprisingly, there are few data on the efficacy of psychological treatment. Treatment programs rely on combinations of case reports and theoretical speculation for their justification. As they do conversion disorders, psychoanalysts view somatization disorder as the manifestation of psychological conflicts, usually sexual, in the symbolic form of somatic symptoms (Edelmann, 1992). There is certainly evidence that people diagnosed as having a somatization disorder report being sexually abused as children (Kinzl, Traweger, & Biebl, 1995; Pribor et al., 1993; Salmon & Calderbank, 1996). As for conversion disorder, psychoanalytic treatment is aimed mainly at the primary gain. It involves uncovering conflicts, showing how they contribute to the apparent illness, and helping people to express their psychological needs in less debilitating ways. As in conversion disorder, behaviorists focus mainly on the secondary gain produced by somatic symptoms. They argue that it is not uncommon for an anxious person to develop physical symptoms such as nausea, vomiting, and sexual performance problems. However, if these symptoms help the person gain attention and escape an uncomfortable situation, they will be reinforced and become habitual. Treatment usually involves **response prevention** (keeping the client from consulting a medical practitioner for an imagined illness, for example). The ultimate goal of behavioral treatment is to remove the reinforcement or secondary gain, thereby allowing the symptoms to extinguish.

An alternative to psychoanalytic or behavioral treatment is the cognitive approach, in which somatoform symptoms are seen as a way of avoiding responsibility. Attributing one's problems to sickness is often preferable to admitting to some personal fault (T. Smith, Snyder, & Perkins, 1983). Cognitive therapists try to get people to accept responsibility for their behavior (to change their attributions) while at the same time teaching them the skills they need to cope with anxiety and frustration in more adaptive ways. Cognitive therapists must be cautious, however, because confronting people with the apparent psychological nature of their problems may drive them away from treatment (Solyom & Solyom, 1990).

DSM-IV   **TABLE 7.8**   Main *DSM-IV* Diagnostic Criteria for Pain Disorder

A. Pain in one or more anatomical sites of sufficient severity to warrant clinical attention.

B. The pain causes clinically significant distress or impairment in social, occupational, or other important areas of functioning.

C. Psychological factors are judged to have an important role in the onset, severity, exacerbation, or maintenance of the pain.

D. The symptom is not intentionally feigned.

E. The pain is not better accounted for by a mood, anxiety, or psychotic disorder. It is also not related to sexual intercourse.

Note: Adapted from American Psychiatric Association (1994, p. 461).

Although you might imagine that the *DSM-IV* categories of conversion disorder and somatization disorder cover practically all possible physical complaints, there is yet another somatoform disorder, called **pain disorder,** that the *DSM-IV* reserves for people whose main physical complaint is pain.

Pain Disorder

Pain is normally caused by injury and illness. It is a sign that some aspect of biological functioning has been disrupted. In recent years, much has been learned about chronic pain, and special clinics have been established to help people manage their pain (Wall, Melzack, & Bonica, 1994). Because a person's response to pain is a complicated function of tissue damage, social background, personality, coping skills, and social supports, successful treatment often requires a combination of physiological and psychological interventions.

Despite the close relationship between neurophysiological and psychological factors in causing pain, the majority of people who attend pain clinics have obvious medical conditions. Their pain is the result of illness or injury. What then is a pain disorder? According to the *DSM-IV*, it is pain that seems related to psychological factors and that severely disrupts occupational, family, or social life (see Table 7.8 for diagnostic criteria). Pain associated primarily with a medical condition is not considered to be a pain disorder, although such pain could still be noted on Axis III in the *DSM-IV* diagnostic scheme. Pain disorder is diagnosed only when psychological factors are either dominant or very important and when pain is not related to sexual intercourse. As you can see, Helen Fairchild seems to have met most of the diagnostic criteria for pain disorder.

There is some justification for including pain disorder in the *DSM-IV*. Chronic pain may lead to unemployment, disability, divorce, and drug abuse. It is also a significant cause of depression. Most important, it can often be helped by psychological treatment. However, the value of having a pain disorder diagnosis separate from the other somatoform disorders is not clear. Most people with pain disorder have other medical and psychological disorders as well (Ekselius et al., 1997). Creating a new diagnosis called pain disorder is only justified if it improves theoretical understanding or clinical treatment. At present, there is no evidence that the *DSM-IV* diagnosis does either (Fry, Crisp, & Beard, 1997).

The somatoform disorders discussed thus far—conversion, somatization, and pain disorder—all involve complaints about physical symptoms. The two remaining somatization disorders, hypochondriasis and body dysmorphic disorder, are different. Sufferers do not necessarily have physical symptoms. Their main problem is obsessive worry about their normal health and appearance. That is, they perceive illness and deformity where neither exists.

Hypochondriasis

Jerome K. Jerome's *Three Men in a Boat* (1889) is one of the comic classics of English literature. Among its many memorable scenes is the following satire of a person who is constantly concerned with his health:

> I remember going to the British Museum [library] one day to read up the treatment for some slight ailment of which I had a touch—hay fever, I fancy it was. I got down the book, and read all I came to read: and then in an unthinking moment, I idly turned the leaves, and began to indolently study diseases, generally. I forget which was the first. . . . I plunged into some fearful, devastating scourge, . . . before I had glanced down the list of . . . "symptoms,"

it was borne in upon me that I had fairly got it.

I sat frozen with horror: and in the listlessness of despair, I again turned over the pages. I came to typhoid fever—read the symptoms—discovered that I had typhoid fever, must have had it for months without knowing it—wondered what else I had got; turned up St. Vitus's Dance—found, as I expected that I had that too—began to get interested in my case, and determined to sift it to the bottom, and so started alphabetically—read up ague, and learnt that I was sickening from it, and that the acute stage would commence in about another fortnight. Bright's disease, I was relieved to find, I had only in a modified form and, so far as that was concerned, I might live for years. Cholera I had, with severe complications; and diphtheria I seemed to have been born with. I plodded conscientiously through the twenty-six letters, and the only malady I could conclude I had not got was housemaid's knee. . . .

Zymosis I had evidently been suffering with from boyhood. There were no diseases after zymosis, so I concluded that there was nothing else the matter with me. . . .

Then I wondered how long I had to live. I tried to examine myself. I felt my pulse. I could not at first feel any pulse at all. . . . I tried to feel my heart. I could not feel my heart. It had stopped beating. . . . I patted myself all over my front from . . . my waist up to my head, and I went a bit round each side, and little way up the back. But I could not feel or hear anything. I tried to look at my tongue. I stuck it out as far as ever it would go, and I shut one eye, and tried to examine it with the other. I could only see the tip, and the only thing I could gain from that was to feel more certain than before that I had scarlet fever. . . . (pp. 7–9)

A famous literary hypochondriac is Argan, Moliére's protagonist in Le malade imaginaire (The imaginary invalid), *written in 1672. Here Argan, as depicted by Honoré Daumier, dreams about a number of death scenes: being bled to death, preparing a will, appearing as a corpse, and being measured for a coffin.*

Nothing much has changed in the century since Jerome wrote his book. Every pharmacy is full of useless treatments for imaginary ailments such as zymosis. As an aside, notice how many of the "diseases" mentioned by Jerome no longer exist. As in abnormal psychology, classification of medical conditions is an ever-changing process. Medical diseases come and go and change their names just as often as psychological ones do.

Hypochondriacal behavior is as old as medicine itself. Ancient healers, such as Galen, attributed morbid health concerns to disorders of the *hypochondrium* (abdomen)—hence, the name **hypochondriasis.** For centuries, hypochondriasis was considered to be the male form of hysteria. (Only females could have true hysteria because only females could have a wandering uterus.) As we have already seen, the *DSM-IV* has redefined hysteria as a conversion disorder, a condition that affects both sexes. Hypochondria refers to obsessive health concerns in both men and women. People with hypochondriasis are preoccupied with the fear of disease. They are neither delusional nor malingering; they simply worry constantly about being ill. They take ordinary physical sensations—an occasional cough, a stomachache—as signs of serious illness. As may be seen from Table 7.9, the *DSM-IV* diagnostic criteria for hypochondriasis explicitly require that a person continues to believe that he or she is ill despite a negative medical evaluation and physician reassurance to the contrary. Indeed, a persistent belief that one is ill, and disappointment when a doctor fails to confirm this self-diagnosis, are the hallmarks of hypochondriasis (Kellner, Hernandez, & Pathak, 1992).

Because the concerns of those with this disorder may involve several different body systems, it is not always easy to differentiate hypochondriasis from somatization disorder. The two may occur together (Barsky,

DSM-IV **TABLE 7.9** Main *DSM-IV* Diagnostic Criteria for Hypochondriasis

A. Preoccupation with fears of having, or the idea that one has, a serious disease based on the person's misinterpretation of bodily symptoms.
B. The preoccupation persists despite appropriate medical evaluation and reassurance.
C. The belief in Criterion A is not of delusional intensity and is not restricted to a circumscribed concern about appearance.
D. The preoccupation causes clinically significant distress or impairment in social, occupational, or other important areas of functioning.
E. The duration of the disturbance is at least 6 months.

Note: From American Psychiatric Association (1994, p. 465).

Wyshak, & Klerman, 1992), and both tend to affect many family members (Noyes et al., 1997). Nevertheless, there are some differences between hypochondriasis and the other somatoform disorders. Unlike Helen Fairchild, who complained of physical symptoms such as stomach pains and headache, hypochondriacal people misinterpret *normal* bodily symptoms (Clark & Salkovskis, 1990). They fear particular diseases rather than just symptoms, and, most important, hypochondriacs usually fail to profit from adopting a "sick" role. They do not avoid work or family responsibilities. Instead, their preoccupation with illness is a kind of hobby (Haenen et al., 1996). As Jerome K. Jerome showed, hypochondriacal behavior may appear humorous, but an obsessive preoccupation with one's health exacts a severe toll on family and social life. Sufferers spend much of their spare time and money on self-help books, doctor visits, and patent medicines. The homes of people with hypochondriasis are filled with medical literature, and their bathroom cabinets overflow with the prescriptions of many different doctors.

When making the diagnosis, clinicians must once again keep in mind that no medical examination is foolproof and no laboratory test is 100% accurate. As already mentioned in the discussions of conversion and somatization disorders, there are difficult-to-diagnose medical conditions that can affect multiple body systems. It is also possible to be sick and hypochondriacal at the same time. Clinicians must remain open to the possibility that what appear to be hypochondriacal complaints may have a physical cause.

Estimates of the prevalence of hypochondriasis range from 3% to 13% (Kellner, 1985), with equal numbers of men and women. Prevalence is not closely related to education, social class, or ethnicity. Although medical conditions occur most frequently in the elderly,

hypochondriasis is not strongly correlated with age (Barsky et al., 1991). At any age, hypochondriasis is a chronic condition that waxes and wanes but never completely disappears (Barsky et al., 1993). Note that periods of less than 6 months during which an individual is preoccupied with illness are not sufficient for the diagnosis.

Etiology and Treatment In common with those with the other somatoform disorders, people with hypochondriasis resist any suggestion that their problems are psychological. Because they refuse to consult mental health professionals, they are rarely seen in psychology clinics. Thus, our knowledge of etiology and treatment outcome is based on the small number of atypical hypochondriacal people who agree to participate in psychological research and to attend psychological clinics. Despite these limited data, the various schools of psychology each have an explanation for hypochondriacal behavior. These tend to follow paradigmatic lines. Psychoanalytically inclined psychologists focus on repressed conflicts, whereas family-oriented clinicians emphasize the role of family dynamics. Not surprisingly, behavioral psychologists construe hypochondriasis as a reinforced set of learned behaviors. In their view, hypochondriasis may be precipitated by illness or a hypersensitivity to body sensations and pain (Barsky et al., 1993). Once the disorder begins, the concern of friends, family members, and colleagues reinforces and maintains the individual's preoccupation with personal health. An alternative behavioral explanation for hypochondriasis construes the condition as a phobia—a fear of becoming ill. It follows, then, that exposure to the feared stimuli (visiting hospitals, for example) combined with response prevention may be useful ways to treat hypochondriasis (Visser & Bouman, 1992; Warwick & Marks, 1988).

Cognitive psychologists attribute hypochondriacal

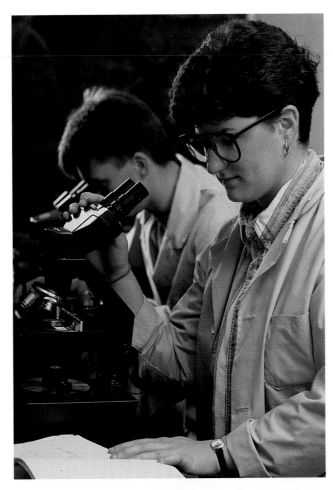

Among medical students, unusually high anxiety about health is common, a syndrome called medical students' disease, or nosophobia. Perhaps because they are studying illnesses, they are prone to attributing serious causes to benign symptoms.

behavior to an attributional bias. Like Jerome's character, who fears he has zymosis, people with hypochondriasis have a tendency to attribute serious illness to benign symptoms—a phenomenon known as "somatosensory amplification." To demonstrate this bias, Hitchcock and Mathews (1992) asked college students to offer likely explanations for a sore elbow. Most students offered mundane explanations, such as a sports injury. Hypochondriacal students, on the other hand, tended to attribute the complaint to a serious underlying disease, such as cancer, for example. This finding supports the idea that people with hypochondriasis attribute everyday symptoms to serious illness. This does not necessarily mean that this attribution bias causes hypochondriasis. The students studied by Hitchcock and Mathews were hypochondriacal before the experiment. It is possible that their attribution bias was the *result* rather than the cause of their disorder. The only way to establish that an

attribution bias *causes* hypochondriasis is to identify people with this attribution bias before they become hypochondriacal and then to study them longitudinally to see if they develop the disorder.

Despite the uncertainty surrounding the causal nature of attributional biases, the goal of cognitive therapy is to modify them, usually through cognitive restructuring ("Just because I have an ache or a pain does not mean that I'm seriously ill"). In cognitive-behavioral treatment, cognitive restructuring is combined with behavioral interventions, such as response prevention (Salkovskis & Warwick, 1988). The evidence suggests that a combination of cognitive and behavioral treatment can reduce the frequency of hypochondriacal behavior (Warwick et al., 1996).

Body Dysmorphic Disorder

In contrast to people with hypochondriasis, who are preoccupied with their health, people with **body dysmorphic disorder** are obsessed with supposed defects in their appearance. Hair loss, skin blemishes, scars, the shape of their nose, the size of their breasts, practically anything can become the focus of concern. Although these defects are either imaginary or highly exaggerated, people with body dysmorphic disorder become self-conscious; they may give up social commitments and stay away from work just to avoid anyone seeing them (W. A. Myers, 1992; Phillips et al., 1993). In severe cases, social isolation becomes so extreme that people perceive suicide as their only way out (Phillips et al., 1993). Table 7.10 summarizes the main *DSM-IV* diagnostic criteria for body dysmorphic disorder.

Some people with body dysmorphic disorder check mirrors frequently; they may even purchase special magnifying lenses to study themselves more closely. Other sufferers avoid mirrors and photographs entirely, not wishing to see their alleged defects. Some people with body dysmorphic disorder try to camouflage their problem by wearing wigs, growing beards, or even stuffing socks into undergarments to enhance a "small" penis. Others undergo surgical procedures—enhancements, reductions, sometimes both. Such procedures rarely provide a permanent solution.

Body dysmorphic disorder usually begins in adolescence, a time when young people are particularly conscious about their appearance. In a survey of college students, Fitts and her colleagues (1989) found that 70% indicated at least some dissatisfaction with the way they look, with a higher figure for women than for men. Few adolescents go on to develop the full disorder, but once

DSM-IV	TABLE 7.10	Main *DSM-IV* Diagnostic Criteria for Body Dysmorphic Disorder

A. Preoccupation with an imagined defect in appearance. If a slight physical anomaly is present, the person's concern is markedly excessive.

B. The preoccupation causes clinically significant distress or impairment in social, occupational, or other important areas of functioning.

Note: From American Psychiatric Association (1994, p. 468).

body dysmorphic disorder begins, it is likely to continue indefinitely. The disorder is more common among single or divorced adults than among married ones, and females outnumber males three to one (Veale, Boocock, et al., 1996). This sex difference probably reflects the great value that our culture places on a female's appearance.

Body dysmorphic disorder has much in common with obsessive-compulsive disorder (see Chapter 4). Obsessive thoughts about presumed physical defects interfere with an individual's social and occupational functioning (McKay et al., 1997). Body dysmorphic disorder may also be construed as a type of social phobia (dysmorphobia) in which people avoid social occasions because they fear being rejected because of the way they look (Phillips, 1991).

As with obsessive-compulsive disorder and phobias, treatment is often difficult because people with body dysmorphic disorder tend to avoid confronting the source of their anxiety (Snaith, 1992). Nevertheless, positive outcomes have been reported for behavioral treatment (McKay et al., 1997) and for cognitive-behavior therapy (Veale, Gournay, et al., 1996). Some people respond well to antidepressants (Cotterill, 1996; Phillips, 1996).

After numerous plastic surgeries, Michael Jackson has dramatically changed his appearance since he was a child star with the Jackson Five. Although females are more likely than males to have body dysmorphic disorder, appearance is more important to performing celebrities than to people in other walks of life.

Munchausen syndrome takes its name from the fictional Baron Munchausen, who traveled from town to town (sometimes on a cannonball) with fanciful tales of battle wounds.

Did Helen Fairchild Have a Somatoform Disorder?

Dr. Dorothy McLean hypothesized that Helen Fairchild was suffering from both dissociative and somatoform disorders. We have seen that Helen did indeed meet many of the diagnostic criteria for dissociative amnesia, fugue, and depersonalization. She also displayed signs of an undifferentiated somatization disorder, a pain disorder, and at least some signs of a conversion disorder. Thus, Dr. McLean seemed to be correct. However, there is one further possibility that must still be excluded. That is, Helen could have been faking. The *DSM-IV* diagnostic category for people who feign symptoms is called factitious disorders.

FACTITIOUS DISORDERS

In 1784, Rudolf Erich Raspe published *Baron Munchausen's Narrative of His Marvelous Travels and Campaigns in Russia*. Raspe described the life of Baron Karl Friedrich Hieronymous von Munchausen, allegedly a retired Russian army officer, who traveled from town to town spinning wild and unsubstantiated stories of his heroism, including detailed descriptions of his extensive battle wounds. In honor of Raspe's hero, **Munchausen syndrome** became the name applied to people who wandered from hospital to hospital pretending to be ill (Zuger, 1993). The *DSM-IV* calls Munchausen syndrome a factitious disorder—a condition in which people pretend to be sick. Document 7.8 contains a typical example of Munchausen syndrome.

DOCUMENT 7.8

Hospital Discharge Summary for Patient With Munchausen Syndrome

Ellen Grant was admitted to the hospital from the emergency room. She had presented with an abscessed leg wound. On admission, her leg was severely swollen and discolored, with clear indication of a bacterial infection. She could not walk on her leg because of the pain, and she had a fever of 104°F (40°C). She explained that she had accidentally dropped her knife while preparing her husband's dinner. The knife had landed in her calf and, although she had cleaned the wound, it had somehow become infected.

Mrs. Grant was admitted to the ward and put on intravenous antibiotics. At the same time, the wound was cultured and the culture sent to the pathology laboratory for analysis. The wound responded well to treatment.

Pathology indicated that the bacteria causing the infection were intestinal in origin. When asked about how such bacteria might have found their way to her calf, Mrs. Grant described the similarities between intestinal bacteria and other forms, a subject on which she was quite knowledgeable. She suggested that the lab may have been in error.

Mrs. Grant indignantly denied purposely rubbing feces into the wound to cause infection, although this remains the most likely explanation. ■

As indicated earlier, people with factitious disorders should not be confused with malingerers. Malingerers also fake their symptoms, but they always have a clear reason for doing so. They may wish to avoid jury duty or a final examination, or they may be attempting to provide evidence for a lawsuit. Malingering may even be a way of keeping fed and warm for the winter (see Document 7.9). Malingering is not always unhealthy—hostages who pretend to be sick to escape from their captors have good reason to malinger. Factitious disorders, on the other hand, are more difficult to

> **DSM-IV**   TABLE 7.11   Main *DSM-IV* Diagnostic Criteria
> for Factitious Disorder
>
> A. Intentional production or feigning of physical or psychological signs or symptoms.
> B. The motivation for the behavior is to assume the sick role.
> C. External incentives for the behavior (such as economic gain, avoiding legal responsibility, or improving physical well-being, as in malingering) are absent.
>
> *Note:* From American Psychiatric Association (1994, p. 474).

explain. Sufferers pretend to be sick without any obvious reward or incentive (other than attention).

DOCUMENT 7.9

Interview Between Eric Fienes and Hospital Psychologist, Louis De Souza

Eric Fienes, aged 60, has come to the admissions office of a large public hospital in Florida, where he is being interviewed by the staff psychologist, Dr. Louis De Souza.

DR. DE SOUZA: Tell me your problem.

ERIC: I hear voices.

DR. DE SOUZA: What do they say?

ERIC: "You are a miserable louse. We hate you."

DR. DE SOUZA: We?

ERIC: No, not we, "I."

DR. DE SOUZA: I thought you said, "We hate you."

ERIC: Yes.

DR. DE SOUZA: Have you been to this hospital before?

ERIC: No.

DR. DE SOUZA: Our records show that you were here last year at this time, as well as the year before.

ERIC: Oh.

DR. DE SOUZA: Both years, you came in November and left in April.

ERIC: Yes, I did.

DR. DE SOUZA: Where were you the rest of the year?

ERIC: Boston.

DR. DE SOUZA: Is this your way of spending your winter in Florida at the taxpayer's expense?

ERIC: No, I really hear voices.

DR. DE SOUZA: Do you have any place to live? Did you come here with money?

ERIC: No. I think I should be in the hospital. I hear voices. ■

The main *DSM-IV* diagnostic criteria for factitious disorder appear in Table 7.11. As you can see, the primary criterion is pretending to be ill or intentionally manufacturing symptoms (as Ellen Grant did in Document 7.8) or both. There is no obvious reason for the behavior; sufferers just wish to appear physically sick or psychologically disturbed (Nicholson & Roberts, 1994). Diagnosis can be particularly complicated when parents use their children as "proxies" for their own factitious disorders (McQuiston, 1993). In such cases, it is often difficult to tell whether the child is really ill or whether the parents are falsifying their child's symptoms (Mehl, Coble, & Johnson, 1990). A diagnosis of factitious disorder by proxy is being considered for inclusion in the next *DSM* (American Psychiatric Assn, 1994).

There are two main factitious disorder subtypes. In one, the symptoms are primarily psychological, whereas in the other they are mainly physical. In both subtypes, individuals may use drugs and other substances to enhance their symptoms. People with factitious disorder often present their illness in dramatic terms: "I barely made it here alive. One more day and I probably would have died." Because their speech is filled with medical terms and they are knowledgeable about clinical routines, their presentation is usually sufficiently realistic to get them admitted to a hospital. Indeed, the medical histories of people with factitious disorder often contain multiple hospitalizations, numerous tests, and even surgical procedures (Gunatilake, De-Silva, & Ranasinghe, 1997). In one notorious case, a woman with factitious disorder had both her breasts removed because of suspected cancer (McDaniel et al., 1992). Scar tissue from unnecessary operations may later cause serious conditions. It is ironic that medically treating individuals with a factitious disorder can actually make them physically sick with an iatrogenic illness.

Once their illness is proven false, people with factitious disorder quickly develop "complications" or new symptoms. When they are finally forced to leave the hospital, they simply turn up at another. Some spend their lives traveling from city to city seeking hospitals where they are not already known. Even though the local doctors may suspect that a patient is faking, they may admit the patient to the hospital anyway. They are just being cautious. After all, even fakes can get sick. Deciding whether a symptom is real or phony requires considerable skill. The diagnosis should be made only when all medical explanations for a symptom are eliminated or when there is clear evidence that a symptom has been manufactured.

Although factitious disorder is relatively rare in both sexes, the available evidence suggests that it occurs more often among males than among females (S. Taylor & Hyler, 1993). The disorder seems to begin in early adulthood and is typically difficult to treat. Although the subject of much speculation (Plassmann, 1994), there are no generally accepted etiological theories or treatment programs for factitious disorder. Many professionals are reluctant to expend their energies on people who are faking their symptoms, so the factitious disorders have received little clinical attention. However, some treatment success has been reported using a combination of behavioral, cognitive, and insight-based approaches (P. E. Parker, 1993; K. Schwarz et al., 1993). Solyom and Solyom (1990), for example, reported the successful treatment of factitious paralysis with a combination of behavioral and cognitive treatment. Specifically, they eliminated reinforcement for symptomatic behavior (the person's physical complaints were ignored), and they provided the person with a placebo medical treatment. As they do with the somatoform disorders, placebos allow people with factitious disorders to save face by attributing their recovery to medical treatment rather than having to admit that they were never really physically ill.

There is no suggestion in any of the documents either that Helen Fairchild was suffering from a factitious disorder or that she was malingering. Her symptoms were those belonging to dissociative and somatoform disorders. For Dr. McLean, the common element that tied together each of Helen's complaints was her memory of childhood abuse and the murder of her friend. These memories not only "explained" Helen's dissociative and somatoform symptoms, they also formed the basis for the charges brought against Stanley Fairchild. Yet the defense attorney suggested that Helen's memories were not real but had instead been planted in her mind by Dr. McLean. Was he correct? Were Helen's memories false?

RECOVERED MEMORIES

Helen's charges against her father were based on memories she supposedly recovered in treatment. Except for the murder of her friend, her case is far from unique. Beginning in the 1970s, numerous charges of early childhood abuse have been made by adults who allegedly recovered repressed memories in therapy (Yeager & Lewis, 1997). Many American states deliberately modified their statutes of criminal limitations expressly to permit charges based on recovered memories to be tried decades after the alleged events (Horn, 1993). In court, adults have described being beaten and raped as children, being forced into sex acts, and even being made to participate in black magic rituals involving animal and human sacrifice. Some of these charges have led to convictions.

Recovered-memory cases have produced a storm of controversy. Some writers have argued that such memories are accurate recollections of repressed traumatic events acceptable as evidence in court. Others have claimed just the opposite—recovered memories are inaccurate and not reliable unless corroborated by other evidence. This section evaluates the evidence both for and against the validity of recovered memories. It also looks at the ethical responsibilities imposed on psychologists who are treating patients they suspect may have been subjected to childhood abuse.

Recovered Memories May Be Accurate

According to the ancient philosopher Plato, our memories are like warehouses full of wax impressions, each containing sounds, sights, and smells. When we want to retrieve a particular memory, we go to the proper part of the warehouse and just lift the block of wax off the shelf. Continuing with the wax analogy, indistinct memories are similar to partly melted wax impressions (or blurry old photographs). First, the details fade, then the main parts, and finally, the memory is forgotten. Although it has the virtue of simplicity, Plato's concept of memory is hopelessly oversimplified. The problem is that forgetting is often temporary. We may be unable to remember a name, a face, or a song title. Yet hours, days, or even weeks later, the missing information pops back into our minds. Clearly, the information could not have faded away like an old photograph. If we can recall it, then the information must still reside somewhere in memory.

Because we have all had the experience of recalling previously forgotten information, it is easy to believe that long-forgotten personal memories may come

At least half a dozen people who had been sexually abused as children by Father James Porter (shown here at his sentencing) had repressed the memory; of the sixty-some who remembered, many had conduct or addictive disorders.

flooding back in psychotherapy. It is also easy to believe that traumatic events can be pushed out of consciousness. Indeed, the *DSM-IV* diagnostic category of dissociative amnesia owes its existence to the notion that traumatic memories can be repressed (Leavitt, 1997). There are also physiological mechanisms that could explain how such repression occurs (Bremner et al., 1995, 1996). If traumatic memories can be repressed, as the *DSM-IV* claims, and if forgotten information may be recalled at a later date, then it follows that repressed memories of childhood abuse could surface in the course of psychotherapy.

This was certainly Sigmund Freud's experience. In treatment, many of his patients recounted episodes of early childhood sexual abuse. As noted earlier, Freud originally believed that these were accurate recollections of real experiences. Later, he changed his mind. His patients were not reporting actual events, Freud argued, only fantasy expressions of their wishes and desires. Modern writers have charged Freud with deliberately covering up his patients' claims of sexual abuse. They argue that Freud invented the fantasy interpretation in order not to offend the conservative professional elite upon whom his career was dependent (Masson, 1992).

The large number of confirmed cases of child sexual abuse leaves little doubt that such abuse is not unusual. There is also proof that such traumatic events

may be forgotten by the victims (Scheflin & Brown, 1996). Cases of child sexual abuse have been independently verified even when the victims had no memory of their occurrence (Martinez-Taboas, 1996). Recovered memories of abuse have also been independently verified (Scheflin & Brown, 1996).

In summary, sexual abuse of children does occur. It may then be forgotten and remembered at a much later time. Keep in mind, however, that most victims of abuse do not forget what happened to them, and many recovered memories are later shown to be inaccurate (Loftus, 1993). These inaccurate memories are not always deliberate fabrications; they are examples of memory elaboration or construction, a process that is described next.

Recovered Memories May Be Inaccurate

Beginning in the 1930s, the British psychologist Sir Frederick Bartlett (1886–1969) studied memory by asking people to recall brief stories (Bartlett, 1950). He found that people distorted these stories in systematic ways. For example, when asked to recall a story about Native Americans, British students changed the word "canoes" to "boats" and "paddling" to "rowing." Clearly, these British students were not simply reading back a copy of the story from some wax tablet stored in their memories; they were *reconstructing* the story in the light of their own experience (which did not include canoes or paddling, but did include boats and rowing).

Because memories are *constructed,* how people are questioned can exert an important influence on what they remember. In a frequently cited study, Loftus (1979) showed students a film of an automobile accident. Immediately after viewing the film, the students were asked questions about what they had just seen. One group of students was asked, "About how fast were the cars going when they *crashed* into one another?" Another group was asked, "How fast were the cars going when they *hit* one another?" A week later, subjects returned to answer questions about the film. On this second occasion, all subjects were asked, "Did you see any broken glass?" Although there was no broken glass in the film, subjects who had been asked the *crashed* question a week earlier remembered seeing broken glass twice as often as those asked the *hit* question. Apparently, *crashes* are more likely to produce broken glass than *hits.* Loftus's experiment showed that memory may be reconstructed differently depending on questions asked after the original event. In a related study, Garry, Loftus, and Brown (1994) were able to convince people that they had once been lost in a shopping mall even though no such event had ever occurred.

Studies such as these made Stanley Fairchild's lawyer skeptical about the accuracy of Helen's memory of childhood sexual abuse. Some psychologists are equally skeptical about the validity of recovered memories (Garry, Loftus, & Brown, 1994; Loftus, 1993; Loftus & Rosenwald, 1995; Shapiro et al., 1993). They believe that therapists can influence the kind of memories their clients construct. This is especially true when therapists actively lead their clients to recall memories of abuse. For example, in *The Courage to Heal,* Bass and Davis (1988) write: "If you are unable to remember any specific instances [of being raped] but still have a feeling that something abusive happened to you, it probably did" (p. 21). Wakefield and Underwager (1992) found that Bass and Davis's book has been involved in more than 100 cases in which repressed memories of abuse were recalled years later. Partly in response to this book, parents accused of child abuse by their adult children have formed a support group called the False Memory Syndrome Foundation.

Given the constructive nature of memory, it is possible that Dr. McLean induced Helen to create false memories of abuse and of witnessing a murder. By using hypnosis to give the process a false appearance of scientific legitimacy (Sheehan, Grigg, & McCann, 1984), Dr. McLean may have led Helen to accept the idea that she was abused.

Dr. McLean's interpretation of Helen's stomach pain as a "body memory" may have also contributed to Helen's belief that she was once abused. Clearly, the stomach has no memory, but many psychologists, including practically all psychoanalysts, believe that physical symptoms may be symbolic reflections of repressed conflicts. In their eyes, a stomach pain could well represent a repressed sexual trauma. Of course, as Stanley Fairchild's defense lawyer said, a stomachache could also be just a stomachache. Without an objective test, it is not possible to tell which symptoms are symbolic representations of underlying conflicts and which are not. Unfortunately, this has not stopped therapists with a strong belief in recovered memories from interpreting even the most innocuous physical symptoms (dry mouth, for instance) as signs of abuse (Lindsay & Read, 1994).

Dr. McLean's continued repetition of the story of the murder and rape could also have distorted Helen's memory. We know that it is relatively easy to forget the original source of a repeated story (Tulving, 1993). De-

spite Dr. McLean's claims, it is possible to believe strongly that one's memory is accurate even when it is later proved to be wrong (Brewin, Andrews, & Gotlib, 1993; Frankel, 1994; Neisser & Harsch, 1992).

A troubled person like Helen, who is looking for an explanation for her problems, might be tempted to blame early abuse for her current difficulties. Certainly, most people who recover memories of sexual abuse in treatment are facing emotional and psychological distress at the time their memories are recovered. Often there is a precipitating event similar to Helen's desertion by her husband.

Dr. McLean suspected that Helen was a victim of sexual abuse from the first day they met. In her initial assessment, she noted that "therapy will be targeted at uncovering evidence for such early abuse." In other words, from the outset, Dr. McLean set out to uncover evidence that Helen was the victim of sexual abuse. To gain this evidence, she suggested that many people with Helen's problems were abused as children, and she directly asked Helen many times whether she had any such memories. She hypnotized Helen to help her recover these lost memories. By leading her in a particular direction, it is possible that Dr. McLean influenced Helen unduly.

Given the vulnerability of people in treatment and the potential damage to individuals and families from false accusations, and given the evidence for both sides of the recovered-memory debate, how should psychologists act when faced with a client they believe may have been abused as a child?

Ethical Responsibilities

Practically all of the professional groups that deal with people in psychological treatment have issued statements and guidelines about how psychologists should act in cases where memories may be recovered (Australian Psychological Society, 1994; Working Group on Investigation of Memories of Child Abuse, 1996). All of these statements recognize that memories of early childhood abuse may sometimes be forgotten, only to be remembered much later in life. That is, they all admit that it is possible to recover memories of early childhood abuse. However, they also recognize that individuals may sometimes construct memories of early abuse that seem real to them but that never happened (Yapko, 1994).

Professionals, especially research-trained psychologists, should be aware of the evidence for the constructive nature of memory. Psychologists should know that memory is subject to distortion by leading questions

In a much-publicized case about recovered memory, Eileen Franklin (center) accused her father of child abuse and killing her best friend when she was 8 years old. The jury convicted him of murder based solely on her testimony. After 6 1/2 years, his conviction was overturned, in part because the trial judge had obstructed the defense argument that Franklin's "memories" were created from news reports of the murder.

and suggestions. They should also know that memories recovered under hypnosis or by using drugs are no more or less accurate than any other memories.

Because of the constructive nature of memory, the guidelines recommend that ethical psychologists should never suggest to clients that they were abused. They should adopt a neutral stance, gathering evidence for and against alleged acts of abuse in an unbiased way. Even a client's spontaneous claims of abuse should be subjected to careful investigation. Neither the strength of a person's belief in a memory, nor its spontaneity, nor the number of details recalled is a valid indicator of whether a memory is accurate. In the absence of external corroboration, there is no scientific way for a therapist to know which memories are valid and which are false. Thus, psychologists should never testify that a memory is true without corroborating evidence.

By not following these guidelines, Dr. McLean left herself open to a civil lawsuit. For example, in 1994, a father whose daughter accused him of child abuse sued his daughter's therapist for malpractice. He claimed

that the therapist had violated professional ethics by using suggestion and leading questions to create a distorted memory in his daughter's mind. The father won. Similarly, people who have made accusations of abuse against their fathers and later retract them have blamed their therapists for convincing them to make unfounded charges. Some of these retractors have brought civil lawsuits against their therapists. In July 1995, a woman in Minneapolis won $2.5 million from a psychiatrist whom she accused of planting memories in her mind. Clearly, by violating her profession's code of ethics, Dr. McLean put herself in a vulnerable legal position.

Dr. McLean may have acted unethically, but this does not mean that Helen's memories were inaccurate. Was Helen abused? Was her father a rapist and a killer? Without corroborating evidence, we will never know for sure. We can only judge by the information available. Read Document 7.10, which contains part of the jury summation by Stanley Fairchild's lawyer. Imagine that you were a member of the jury. How do you think you would vote?

DOCUMENT 7.10

Excerpt From the
Summation for
the Defense

SUPERIOR COURT

TRANSCRIPT OF TRIAL

In the Matter of Stanley Fairchild

Summation by Counsel for the Defense, Michael Moriarity

Ladies and gentlemen of the jury, you have heard testimony about the constructive nature of memory. You have heard how Dr. McLean, Helen's psychologist, continuously probed her for evidence of abuse and murder. Dr. McLean violated professional ethics by telling Helen that people with her psychological problems were often molested as children. Dr. McLean asked Helen repeatedly about whether she had any such memories. When Dr. McLean heard of her childhood friend's murder, she suggested that this terrible tragedy was tied to the alleged abuse. In this way, Dr. McLean created Helen's memories. She took a vulnerable woman, a woman who had been abandoned by her husband, a woman who was suffering psychologically, and she planted in her mind an explanation for the shambles of her life. It wasn't Helen's fault: It was all because she was abused as a child. She rewarded Helen for producing detailed memories of abuse by showing special interest in them and encouraging her to recall more details.

Remember, ladies and gentlemen, that despite Helen's claims of physical and sexual abuse by her father, she had never before mentioned it to anyone. Not a soul has ever seen any evidence. Her neighbors suspected nothing. Her mother and sister say nothing ever happened. Her teachers never noticed a thing, nor did her family doctor. There is no corroborating evidence that Stanley Fairchild committed any crime at all. Fairness requires that you acquit him and let him return to his family.

CHAPTER 7 IN PERSPECTIVE

Although they are among the most written about psychological disorders, we know surprisingly little about the etiology and treatment of the dissociative, somatoform, and factitious disorders. One reason for this is a reluctance on the part of clinicians and researchers to become involved with people who may be malingering. Another is the lack of sophisticated theories. Although they use different terminology, the major paradigms take a remarkably similar view and recommend comparable treatments. Clearly, there is much left to learn about these puzzling disorders.

Key Ideas

Dissociative Amnesia and Fugue
Dissociative amnesia involves memory loss. When a person not only develops amnesia but also moves away from home and perhaps even adopts a new identity, the diagnosis is dissociative fugue. Because the symptoms associated with dissociative amnesia and fugue may also be found in organic brain syndromes or may be induced by substance abuse, clients must be carefully evaluated. Most instances of dissociative amnesia and fugue are brief (hours or days), with travel limited to one city. Generalized memory loss and intercity travel occur infrequently; taking on an entirely new identity is rarer still. Recovery is typically rapid, and recurrences are unlikely. All psychologists, irrespective of their preferred paradigm, construe memory loss and

fugue as ways of escaping traumatic stress. In some cases, amnesia and fugue may represent state-dependent learning. Because they do not know that anything is wrong, people in fugue states rarely refer themselves for treatment. Treatment usually takes place after the person recovers and is aimed at preventing future episodes.

Depersonalization Disorder

People with depersonalization disorder feel as if their body parts have changed in size, or they may have the impression that they are outside their bodies, viewing themselves from a distance. Sometimes they feel mechanical, as though they are robots. They realize that these perceptions are not accurate, but they find their misperceptions compelling. Although the incidence of depersonalization disorder is unknown, it is a common complaint among both psychiatric patients and the general population. The onset of the disorder is usually sudden and associated with stress. The treatment literature is sparse and inconclusive. Although the psychological literature seems to take for granted that the symptoms of depersonalization are psychogenic in origin, physical conditions and substance abuse can produce similar symptoms.

Dissociative Identity Disorder

In dissociative identity disorder, formerly known as multiple personality disorder, two or more separate identities recurrently come forward to take charge of a person's behavior. Each identity has its own characteristic personality, habits, and memories. Dissociative identity disorder is more common in women than in men, and it also seems to run in families. Although they differ in the details, all schools of psychology attribute dissociative identity disorder to traumatic experiences, particularly childhood physical and sexual abuse. Because many, perhaps most, abused children do not develop a dissociative identity disorder, abuse alone is not a sufficient cause. Other factors must also be involved. These may include the ability to put oneself into a hypnotic state. Some cases of dissociative identity disorder are clearly frauds. In other cases, clinicians may inadvertently encourage behavior consistent with dissociative identity disorder by the questions they ask and the cues they provide. Treatment attempts to fuse disparate personalities into a single person. Behavioral therapists usually include coping skills in their treatment programs. They may also use reinforcement to encourage clients to display their most healthy personality. To date, there are no controlled outcome studies of treatments for dissociative identity disorder. Clinical case reports suggest that the longer a dissociative identity disorder persists, the more difficult it is to treat. Thus, early diagnosis and treatment may prevent a more resistant condition from developing.

Conversion Disorder

Conversion disorder—pseudomedical complaints in otherwise healthy people—gets its name from Freud's theory that the energy associated with unconscious conflicts is "converted" into physical symptoms. These symptoms may sometimes be bizarre, but usually they mimic real illnesses. Caution is required because some people diagnosed as having a conversion disorder have later turned out to have serious medical conditions. Education, social attitudes, and cultural norms affect both the way conversion symptoms are presented and their frequency. Psychoanalysts assume that conversion symptoms are the result of repressed conflicts. Behaviorists try to eliminate any reinforcement that might be maintaining the symptoms. Treatment may require family therapy targeted not just at the "sick" person but at those people in the person's social environment who are reinforcing the conversion symptoms. Assertiveness and social skills training may help the person with conversion symptoms overcome the view that he or she is dependent and weak. Often, it is difficult to get clients into treatment because they are reluctant to admit that their problems might be psychological. Placebo medical treatments may give them a face-saving way of undergoing treatment. Follow-up studies have found that children and adolescents respond better to treatment than adults do. The longer that conversion symptoms are present, the poorer the prognosis.

Somatization Disorder

Somatization disorder is characterized by multiple physical complaints spanning several bodily systems, with no medical explanation and without conscious faking. The prevalence of somatization disorder is difficult to measure because culture affects how (and how frequently) symptoms are expressed. There is a tendency for somatization disorder to run in families, although this may reflect environment as much as genetics. In females, somatization disorder typically begins in late adolescence, whereas males are diagnosed later following a history of interpersonal problems. In both sexes, once the somatization pattern sets in, individuals do not remain symptom-free for very long. Few somatization clients consent to participate in psychological treatment, so there are few data on treatment efficacy. Those treatments that exist follow paradigmatic lines. For example, psychoanalysts try to uncover unconscious conflicts, show how they contribute to the apparent illness, and help people to express their psychological needs in less destructive ways. Behaviorists see somatization as instrumental behavior aimed at gaining reinforcement. For them, symptoms are a way of gaining attention and escaping uncomfortable situations. Response prevention may allow the behavior to extinguish. Cognitive psychologists construe somatoform symptoms as ways of avoiding responsibility. Cognitive therapy consists of learning to cope with anxiety and failure in more adaptive ways.

Pain Disorder

An individual's response to pain is a complicated function of tissue damage, social background, personality, coping skills, and social supports. Pain that seems related to psychological factors and that severely disrupts occupational, family, or social life constitutes a pain disorder. Pain associated primarily with a medical condition or with sexual intercourse is noted on Axis III. The value of having a diagnosis of "pain" disorder separate from the other somatoform or factitious disorders has not been thoroughly tested.

Hypochondriasis

Hypochondriasis, preoccupation with disease, is common and occurs in all social and educational classes. Unlike other somatoform disorders, hypochondriasis does not seem to produce secondary gain. Because it is possible to be sick and a hypochondriac at the same time, clinicians must always remain alert to the possibility that what appear to be hypochondriacal complaints may have a physical cause. Once established, hypochondriasis waxes and wanes but never completely disappears. As in the other somatoform disorders, hypochondriacs resist the suggestion that their problems are psychological and refuse to attend psychology clinics. Etiological theories reflect the various paradigms. Psychoanalysts focus on repressed conflicts, family therapists emphasize the role of family dynamics, and behavioral psychologists construe hypochondriasis as either a reinforced set of learned behaviors or a phobia—a fear of becoming ill. Cognitive psychologists attribute hypochondriacal behavior to a tendency to attribute benign symptoms to illness.

Body Dysmorphic Disorder

Body dysmorphic disorder is characterized by an obsessive preoccupation with a supposed "defect" in appearance. Although the defect is either imaginary or highly exaggerated, sufferers may become so self-conscious that they avoid social commitments, stay away from work, or even commit suicide. Body dysmorphic disorder usually begins in adolescence and has much in common with obsessive-compulsive disorder, with a specific focus on presumed physical defects. Treatment is difficult because people focus on their presumed physical defect and resist any suggestion that any psychological problem may be involved.

Factitious Disorder

People with factitious disorder pretend to be sick. Unlike malingerers, who have a clear reason for pretending to be ill, people with factitious disorder pretend to be sick without obvious reward. Parents may even falsify the symptoms of their children. Although the *DSM-IV* suggests that factitious disorder is more common among males than females, there are no reliable estimates of prevalence, nor are there any widely accepted etiological theories or treatment programs.

Key Terms

body dysmorphic disorder	dissociative fugue	malingerer	somatoform disorders
Briquet's syndrome	dissociative identity disorder	Munchausen syndrome	state-dependent learning
conversion disorder	(multiple personality	pain disorder	undifferentiated somatoform
depersonalization disorder	disorder)	primary gain	disorder
derealization	factitious disorder	response prevention	
dissociative amnesia	hypochondriasis	secondary gain	
dissociative disorders	iatrogenic disorder	somatization disorder	

Key Names

Sir Frederick Bartlett	Pierre Briquet	William Harvey	Thomas Sydenham

CHAPTER 8

CHAPTER OBJECTIVES

Emotions are an important part of what makes us human: They warn us when danger is near, and they allow us to gain pleasure and enjoyment out of life. When emotions get out of hand, however, the result can be tragic. This chapter revisits the story of Danielle Wood, whose death was described in Chapter 1. By examining what happened to Danielle, and to Bernard Louis (a man whose euphoria did not mean he was happy), this chapter shows how exaggerated emotional states lead to psychological disorders and how these disorders may be treated and prevented.

The five main questions addressed in this chapter are

1. What are mood disorders?
2. What causes mood disorders?
3. How are mood disorders treated?
4. What is the relationship between mood disorders and suicide?
5. Can mood disorders and suicide be prevented?

The Mood Disorder Spectrum

From the Blues to Depressive and Bipolar Disorders

CONTENTS

efore reading this chapter, you should refamiliarize yourself with the tragic story of Danielle Wood, the student whose death was described in Chapter 1. Danielle's death, which devastated her friends and family, was made worse by the uncertainty surrounding it. Like most people who take their own lives, Danielle did not leave a note explaining her actions. It was months later, when her adoptive mother finally found the strength to sort through Danielle's belongings, that her diary was discovered buried among various class notes. As you can see from the excerpts in Document 8.1, there seems little doubt that Danielle's death was suicide.

DOCUMENT 8.1

Excerpts From
Danielle Wood's Diary

Monday, August 12, 2001
I don't blame Luke for dumping me. It's really my fault for being so jealous. This is how it's always been with me and probably how it always will be. Now I'll have to go back to college and face him and everyone else.

Tuesday, August 13, 2001
Noisy neighbors. Barking dogs. Meddling mothers. Know-it-all doctors. No one cares. No one understands. Tonight I was so angry, I slammed my door so hard that it fell off its hinges.

Wednesday, August 14, 2001
I don't want to go back to school. How can I face Luke, and Jayne, and everyone?

Friday, September 9, 2001
Luke is the only person I have ever loved and the one I really wanted to love me back. But I know now that I do not deserve him. He's far too good. Still, I do not see how I can go on without his love and affection. Life will be empty without him.

Saturday, September 10, 2001
I finally got here, but now that I'm at school, I just can't seem to do anything. I just lie here. Not sleeping really, not eating, not doing anything. I'm so tired, but I just can't sleep. I keep thinking that I should do something—wash my hair, iron my clothes. But I just can't be bothered. What's the use? There is no point. There is really no way out of this. I should just get it all over with.

As you will learn in this chapter, Danielle's diary entries reflect the classic signs of depression: sadness, hopelessness, self-blame, anger, insomnia, and loss of appetite. Depression is one of several **mood disorders,** abnormal conditions characterized by persistent extremes of mood. Depression represents one pole of the mood spectrum (Figure 8.1). The other pole, which is known as **mania,** is marked by extreme elation. People who are in the grip of mania have lots of energy, form grandiose plans (to make a fortune or cure cancer), display a cavalier attitude toward money, and usually have a strong sex drive. At first glance, this may not seem to be much of a problem. Who would not like to feel great, have lots of energy, and not worry about money? But looks can be deceiving. If Danielle's mood was too low, then the mood of people with mania is too high. Left unchecked, mania can cause just as many difficulties as depression. It may seem surprising (because they appear so different), but the two poles of the mood spectrum are closely related. Some individuals oscillate between depression and mania; a few even manage to be manic and depressed at the same time (McElroy et al., 1992).

Happily, most of us spend the bulk of our time somewhere in the middle of the mood spectrum, neither very high nor very low. But moods are volatile. A telephone conversation, a walk in the park, or a dinner with

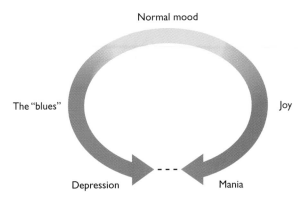

FIGURE 8.1 The Mood Spectrum. *Most of the time, we find ourselves in the middle, not too high or too low. Notice that the two extremes, mania and depression, are closer to one another than they are to the normal mood state. In fact, some people actually cycle between depression and mania, and a few manage to be both depressed and manic at the same time.*

As Star Trek fans know, Mr. Spock differs from humans because he, as a Vulcan, does not experience emotion. Sometimes his cold rationality is an advantage, but at other times his lack of emotion cuts him off from intuition and social connection.

friends can lift our mood. On the other hand, a bad day at work, failing an exam, losing a tennis match, indeed any of life's disappointments can bring on the "blues." Sometimes, even success can bring us down. You might be surprised at the number of people who feel deflated after passing an exam or winning a sports contest (J. R. Miller, 1994). When our mood rises, we feel happy, energized, confident, and optimistic. When we get the blues, we feel sad, tired, and pessimistic. We snap at our friends and family, and we become preoccupied ("How could I have missed that serve?" "I should have studied harder." "Now that I have my degree, what's next?"). Self-esteem takes a dive ("I'm not much good." "Perhaps I'll never succeed at anything"). We may decide to drown our sorrows in a drink, or maybe just to go to bed.

The main difference between the blues, an emotion we all experience, and a mood disorder is one of degree (Flett, Vredenburg, & Krames, 1997). The blues pass quickly. In a day or two, we pick ourselves up and start again. However, when a negative mood persists, affecting social and occupational functioning, clinicians begin to suspect the presence of a mood disorder.

This chapter is concerned with the diagnosis, etiology, treatment, and prevention of mood disorders. It also includes a discussion of suicide, which is sometimes (but not always) caused by a mood disorder. The points made in this chapter are illustrated by reference to the stories of Danielle Wood and Bernard Louis, a man whose manic episodes severely affected his life. Before turning to the specific mood disorders, the chapter first puts them into context by examining what psychologists mean when

they talk about normal and abnormal emotions. As you will see, mood disorders (like anxiety, somatoform, and most of the other disorders discussed in this book) are mainly exaggerations of everyday emotions.

EMOTIONS: NORMAL AND PATHOLOGICAL

Admirers of the original (and often-repeated) *Star Trek* television series and films will recall the Starship *Enterprise*'s Vulcan officer, Mr. Spock. Spock differed from earthlings in two ways: He had odd, pointy ears and he was never emotional. Unlike Captain Kirk, Spock was never tempted by the seductive outer-space sirens who regularly tried to lure the space mariners to destruction. Even when the murderous Romulans seemed certain to destroy the *Enterprise,* Spock never panicked. As he

The use of ritual ceremonies, such as shivas and funeral masses, to help people express grief over the death of a loved one, is common to all cultures.

coldly evaluated the ship's predicament, the other crew members would accuse Spock of being "inhuman." To them, the essential characteristic of a human being is the ability to feel emotions—and most psychologists agree.

The importance of emotions in our lives is apparent in our language. There are more than 400 English words to describe feelings (joy, passion, ecstasy, sorrow, anger, fear, lust, love, grief, and so on), each with a slightly different meaning. Emotions are so much a part of life, we never stop to ask ourselves why they exist in the first place. What is the biological function of negative emotions, such as fear and sorrow? Why did they evolve? Would we not be better off being unemotional like the Vulcan Spock?

As is the case with many questions surrounding evolution, the first place to look for answers to these questions is in the works of the founder of the theory of evolution through natural selection, Charles Darwin (1809–1882). In his book *The Expression of Emotions in Man and Animals* (1872), Darwin hypothesized that emotions evolved because they have survival value. Take fear, for instance. Fear helps us to survive because when we are afraid of something, we flee and avoid possible harm. Sorrow also has survival value. Parent-child bonds are cemented by the feelings of sadness parents and their children experience when they are separated. To avoid sadness, parents stay close to their children, thereby increasing their offspring's chances of survival. Of course, it is possible to have too much of a good thing. Unrelenting fear or sorrow can be so debilitating that, instead of increasing, they can *decrease* a person's chances of survival. Danielle's story is an example of the havoc that can be caused when sorrow turns into an in-

tense negative **mood** (a period dominated by a specific emotion).

To summarize, emotions are a vital part of what makes us human, and they serve important evolutionary purposes. Even negative emotions, such as fear and sorrow, have survival value, provided they stay within limits. However, when emotions are too extreme or a mood state lasts too long, the result may be a mood disorder. There is no sharp demarcation between the everyday blues and depression nor between joy and mania; moods shade into one another. Where clinicians draw the line between normal moods and a mood disorder depends to a great extent on cultural norms. In our society, moods that cause social and occupational functioning to suffer are usually, but not always, considered disordered. Under some conditions, even intense and prolonged periods of sadness can be perfectly normal. An example is the emotion felt during grieving.

Grieving

The loss of a loved one or a friend usually sets off a grieving process. Whether the loss is through death, divorce, or separation, the first reaction is usually emotional numbness and disbelief punctuated with acute bouts of distress. All the world's societies have developed ways to help people come to terms with loss. Funerals, for example, have evolved over the centuries to help people cope with their sorrow and disbelief. The ritualized nature of funerals, which include special prayers and ceremonies, provides roles for friends and relatives (as pallbearers, readers of prayers, or guests), allowing them to show their support for the grieving

DSM-IV   TABLE 8.1   Main *DSM-IV* Mood Disorders

Unipolar (depressive) disorders

Major depressive disorder: At least 2 *weeks* of depressed mood or loss of interest in everyday activities plus additional symptoms such as insomnia.

Dysthymic disorder: At least 2 *years* of depressed mood for more days than not accompanied by signs of depression less severe than those of major depression.

Bipolar disorders

Bipolar I disorder: A mixture of depression and mania.

Bipolar II disorder: A mixture of depression and milder forms of mania.

Cyclothymic disorder: Alternating moods.

person. Social support is an important determinant of how quickly, and how well, people cope with the grieving process (Kissane, McKenzie, & Bloch, 1997).

Within a week or so after a loss, disbelief is replaced with a period of pining for the lost person. The survivors dwell on their loss, have trouble sleeping, neglect other aspects of life, and display anger at their fate ("Why me?"). This stage may last months or years, but most people eventually acknowledge the permanency of their loss ("I am now a widow"). In the final stage of grieving, people gradually regain their interest in life, and their sadness abates. The whole process may take a year or more and may involve significant periods of psychological distress. Still, the process is perfectly normal. In fact, not grieving over the death of a loved one would be viewed by most psychologists as abnormal. Because grieving is normal, treatment is not indicated unless people become dangerous to themselves or are unable to function (S. Jacobs, 1993). In such cases, clinicians would probably consider the individual concerned to be suffering from one of the *DSM-IV* mood disorders described next.

DSM-IV Mood Disorders

According to the *DSM-IV*, there are two general types of mood disorder: **unipolar** and **bipolar.** The "poles" referred to by these diagnostic labels are the extremes of the mood spectrum—depression and mania. Unipolar mood disorders are characterized by depression, whereas bipolar disorders combine depression with manic periods. Both unipolar and bipolar disorders are divided into subtypes. The unipolar subtypes include a relatively mild condition known as **dysthymic disorder** and a more serious one called **major depressive disorder.** Bipolar disorders are divided into **bipolar I,** which

mixes depression and mania, **bipolar II** (depression and mild manic episodes), and **cyclothymic disorder** (cycling between elevated and depressed moods). The *DSM-IV* diagnostic scheme for mood disorders is summarized in Table 8.1.

This chapter begins with an examination of the two depressive disorders—major depressive disorder and dysthymic disorder. As you will see, they differ mainly in degree; dysthymic disorder is a milder version of a major depressive disorder.

DEPRESSIVE (UNIPOLAR) DISORDERS

Depression is as old as recorded history. King Saul's fits of despondency are graphically described in the Old Testament. The Hippocratic corpus also contains numerous references to depression, or as it was known then, melancholia. **Melancholia** is derived from the Greek word *melancholè*, which means "black bile," one of the four bodily humors. Ancient healers believed that depression, a "black" mood, resulted from an excess of black bile. The idea that depression is caused by a chemical imbalance in the body remains popular today.

Over the centuries, hundreds of books have been published on depression. Perhaps the most famous is Robert Burton's (1577–1640) classic, *The Anatomy of Melancholy,* published in 1621. This encyclopedic review of depression (it cited more than 1,000 authors) was revised five times during Burton's lifetime. Today, after 80 editions, *The Anatomy of Melancholy* holds the record for the most frequently reprinted book in the history of abnormal psychology. Burton, who suffered from bouts of depression, defined melancholy broadly to include not only what today would be considered the unipolar mood disorders but also several of the anxiety disorders.

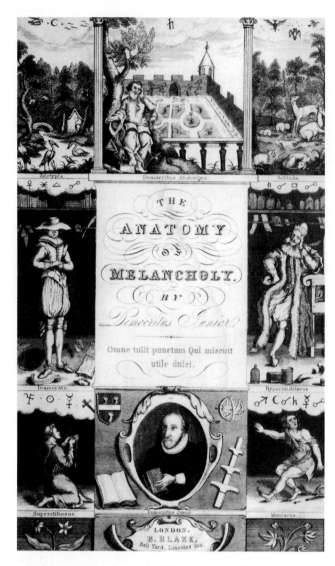

Robert Burton's The Anatomy of Melancholy (1621) is perhaps the most famous book ever written about depression. The varieties of melancholy it describes are now diagnosed as both mood and anxiety disorders.

Mood and anxiety disorders are kept separate in the *DSM-IV* (as they have been in this book), but Burton was correct; they are closely related. As you will see later in this chapter, anxiety and mood disorders often co-occur (Swendsen, 1997).

Burton's book describes symptoms and syndromes and reviews various causes of depression, including early childhood experiences, genetics, and other modern-sounding theories. About one-fourth of Burton's book is given over to "love-melancholy," a condition that was also discussed at great length by the legendary Arabian doctor Avicenna (980–1037). Both Burton and Avicenna describe how an unhappy love affair can produce depression and feelings of worthlessness, which can lead

to suicide. Their descriptions of lovesickness are reminiscent of Danielle's feelings about possibly losing Luke (see Document 8.1).

Signs of Depression

The signs of depression are common. We all experience periods of sadness and self-doubt, although these are not usually severe enough to qualify for a psychological diagnosis (McClure, Rogeness, & Thompson, 1997; Rosal et al., 1997). Typically, these feelings begin with a reaction to some stressful life circumstance (losing one's job, for example). If these feelings dissipate within 6 months, the *DSM-IV* labels them an **adjustment disorder with depressive features**—a transient reaction to a stressful circumstance. A **major depressive episode** may appear superficially similar to an adjustment disorder, but it is more extreme. It is not a passing reaction to life's vicissitudes, but a serious mental disorder (Mintz et al., 1992).

Major Depressive Episode

Signs The hallmark of a major depressive episode is a sad mood. Depressed people feel down and apathetic. They may go through the motions of daily existence—get up, go to class, go to the library—but there is no enjoyment in it. Life seems dull and gray, and formerly pleasurable activities no longer bring any enjoyment. (This inability to feel pleasure is known as **anhedonia**.) Starting a new activity seems impossibly difficult. Sufferers describe themselves as constantly tired and just barely dragging themselves through life. Depressed people may talk and think slowly; some may be unable to get out of bed in the morning. This psychomotor slowness was apparent when Dr. Berg talked to Danielle Wood after her first suicide attempt (Document 8.2). Although slowness is more typical, some depressed people become agitated. Instead of lying around in bed, they are unable to sit still. They pace the floor, shaking their heads and restlessly wringing their hands.

DOCUMENT 8.2

Dr. Berg's Observations of Danielle Wood at the Time of Her Psychological Assessment

Her hair was long and messy, and she wore no makeup. There were dark circles under her eyes.

Among those who have struggled with severe depression are journalist Mike Wallace and comedian Joan Rivers.

The client avoided eye contact, looking down at the table or over the examiner's shoulder. She kept her hands clasped in her lap and never spoke spontaneously. She did respond to questions, but her answers were always brief and unelaborated. . . . It seemed as if everything she said or did required considerable effort. ■

A major depressive episode may affect the way people sleep; they may wake in the night or early morning and be unable to return to sleep. (On the other hand, some depressed people sleep all the time.) Changes in appetite (usually eating less but sometimes eating more), loss of interest in sex, and a wide variety of aches and pains are also associated with a major depressive episode. Some writers believe that the presence of these so-called vegetative symptoms (appetite change, sleep disturbance, loss of sex drive, fatigue) is what distinguishes a major depressive episode from less severe forms of depression (Buchwald & Ruddick-Davis, 1993).

Although a down mood and vegetative symptoms are the most obvious signs of a major depressive episode, cognition and memory are often affected as well (Brand, Verspui, & Oving, 1997; Burt, Zembar, & Niederehe, 1995; Mathews & MacLeod, 1994). Depressed people have difficulty concentrating on cog-

nitive tasks (Hartlage et al., 1993; Mialet, Pope, & Yurgelun, 1996). They tend to see the downside of everything, dwelling on their failures and ignoring their successes. Because of their pessimism, they lose motivation. Why struggle and work hard when things are bound not to work out? As Danielle wrote in her diary, "What's the use? There is no point." This lack of hope for the future may have contributed to her death ("There is really no way out of this").

Depressed people judge themselves to be less liked and less capable than other people rate them (Gotlib & Hammen, 1992). This discrepancy between how depressed people view themselves and how others regard them may be the result of faulty cognitive attributions (see Chapter 2 for a detailed discussion of attributions). Depressed people like Danielle Wood tend to make negative self-attributions ("I failed to make the swimming team. Therefore, I'm worthless and will never accomplish anything in life"). These evaluations persist even though they are not shared by others. Danielle, for example, saw herself as a failure despite considerable evidence to the contrary (Document 8.3). In some people, these negative cognitions can lead to "anger attacks"—sudden intense spells of anger associated with a surge of autonomic arousal including such symptoms as a rapid

DSM-IV **TABLE 8.2** Main *DSM-IV* Diagnostic Criteria for a Major Depressive Episode

A. Five (or more) of the following symptoms have been present during the same 2-week period and represent a change from previous functioning; at least one of the symptoms is either (1) depressed mood or (2) loss of interest or pleasure. (Symptoms due to a general medical condition or delusions and hallucinations which seem unrelated to mood are omitted.)

(1) Depressed mood most of the day, nearly every day as indicated either by subjective report (feels sad) or observations made by others. (In children and adolescents this may appear as irritability.)

(2) Markedly diminished interest or pleasure in all, or almost all, activities most of the day, nearly every day.

(3) Significant weight loss when not dieting or weight gain (for example, a 50% change in body weight in a single month), or a decrease in appetite nearly every day. (In children this may appear as a failure to make expected weight gains.)

(4) Insomnia or hypersomnia (greater than average sleep) every day.

(5) Psychomotor agitation or retardation nearly every day (observable by others).

(6) Fatigue or loss of energy every day.

(7) Feelings of worthlessness or excessive or inappropriate guilt (which may be delusional) not merely self-reproach about being sick.

(8) Diminished ability to think or concentrate or indecisiveness.

(9) Recurrent thoughts of death (not just fear of dying), recurrent suicidal ideation, or suicide attempt.

B. The symptoms cause significant distress or impairment in functioning and are not the result of substance abuse or a general medical condition.

Note: From American Psychiatric Association (1994, p. 327).

heart rate, sweating, flushing, and a feeling of being out of control (Fava et al., 1993).

DOCUMENT 8.3

Excerpt From Dr. Berg's Psychological Assessment of Danielle Wood

. . . the client has a distinctly unfavorable self-concept. Despite her athletic achievements and her success at the university, she feels that she has been a failure and that she has let people down. Her TAT responses reflect her preoccupation with success and her fear of failure. On several occasions, she indicated her guilt at the way she has hurt others and her fear of the future. ■

The *DSM-IV* diagnostic criteria for a major depressive episode are summarized in Table 8.2. Notice how heterogeneous an episode can be. One depressed person may feel sad, eat too much, and sleep a lot, whereas another may eat very little and hardly sleep at all. In children, a depressive episode may look different again. Children are more likely to be irritable than sad, for example, and they may show different symptoms at different developmental stages. Depressed babies tend to be listless and apathetic, toddlers have numerous physical complaints, whereas the depressive episodes of adolescents resemble those of adults (S. Schwartz & Johnson, 1985).

Pessimism, guilt, and self-blame are not attractive traits. People who exhibit them are often unpopular. This is why depressed people lose friends and why the divorce rate is high in marriages with a depressed partner (Gotlib & Hammen, 1992). It is difficult for people to change because depression has a tendency to feed on itself. The vicious cycle begins with depressed people becoming irritable and short-tempered. They snap at their partners and their children. Regretting their behavior, depressed people feel guilty about mistreating their loved ones. These guilt feelings make them even more depressed (Hammen, 1991b).

Comorbid Conditions Depression and physical illness often go together; hormonal disorders, brain damage, and a wide variety of other illnesses have been associated with depression (W. A. Gordon & Hibbard, 1997; Peyrot & Rubin, 1997; Zheng et al., 1997). In some cases, it is the physical illness that actually causes the depression. After all, being ill is a fairly depressing experience. Causality can also go in the opposite direction—depres-

Mood disorders are often accompanied by drug abuse. The career of Brian Wilson of the Beach Boys was derailed for many years as he battled depression and drug abuse. He became reclusive and for a while put himself in the hands of a controversial therapist who took 24-hour control of his life.

sion can cause physical illness. For example, researchers have observed that depression reduces immune system functioning, and medical patients often report that their physical health improves when their depression lifts (D. L. Evans et al., 1992; Von Korff et al., 1992).

In addition to comorbid physical conditions, there is considerable psychological comorbidity as well. Depressed children frequently display other problems, especially unruly misbehavior (Brady & Kendall, 1992; Lewinsohn, Rohde, & Seeley, 1993). In adults, depression

is often accompanied by substance abuse. Danielle Wood, you will recall, used both performance-enhancing drugs and tranquilizers. The use of tranquilizers is especially common because most depressed people are anxious as well (Coryell, Endicott, & Keller, 1992; Flint, 1997; Rohde, Lewinsohn, & Seeley, 1990; Zinbarg et al., 1994). Indeed, generalized anxiety disorder (see Chapter 4) and major depressive episodes often co-occur, and they are not always easy to tell apart. They share many important features including irritability, distractibility, poor memory, guilt, and worry (Goldberg, 1995). Because of the high comorbidity between generalized anxiety disorder and depression, the diagnosis of "mixed anxiety-depression" is included in the *International Classification of Diseases* (WHO, 1992) and is being considered for inclusion in the next *DSM* (American Psychiatric Assn, 1994).

Psychological Assessment   Clinical diagnosis is often supplemented by psychological assessment designed to measure the extent and severity of a person's depressive symptoms (Knight et al., 1997). Perhaps the most widely used assessment device for depression in the United States is the Beck Depression Inventory (A. T. Beck & Steer, 1993). Each question on the inventory describes a specific symptom of depression, which must be rated using a severity score that ranges from 0 to 3. The person being assessed simply circles the answer that corresponds to his or her mood at the time of testing. The questions are divided into 21 general topics (sadness, pessimism, and so on). The higher the score, the more serious the symptoms. Document 8.4 contains part of the Beck Depression Inventory completed by Danielle when she was assessed by Dr. Berg following her first, unsuccessful, suicide attempt.

DOCUMENT 8.4

Excerpt From Danielle Wood's Responses (circled) to Items From the Beck Depression Inventory

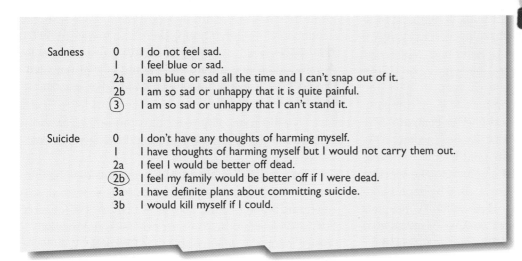

Sadness	0	I do not feel sad.
	I	I feel blue or sad.
	2a	I am blue or sad all the time and I can't snap out of it.
	2b	I am so sad or unhappy that it is quite painful.
	(3)	I am so sad or unhappy that I can't stand it.
Suicide	0	I don't have any thoughts of harming myself.
	I	I have thoughts of harming myself but I would not carry them out.
	2a	I feel I would be better off dead.
	(2b)	I feel my family would be better off if I were dead.
	3a	I have definite plans about committing suicide.
	3b	I would kill myself if I could.

Major Depressive Disorder

A major depressive disorder consists of one or more major depressive episodes. If the episodes persist for 2 or more years, the disorder is considered "chronic." In the past, it was common to divide major depressive episodes into two categories: endogenous and exogenous. *Endogenous depressions* were thought to be biologically caused, whereas *exogenous depressions* were extreme reactions to external events, such as excessive grieving over a death in the family. Although this distinction may seem logical, in practice, it has not proven useful. Both endogenous and exogenous depressions have the same signs and symptoms, have similar courses, and respond similarly to treatment. For these reasons, the endogenous-exogenous distinction was dropped from the *DSM-IV*.

Depressive disorders can be very debilitating. Wells and his colleagues (1989) examined 11,000 people who were being treated for either a medical or a psychological problem. They compared people who were depressed with those suffering from heart disease, digestive disorders, endocrine diseases such as diabetes, and other physical conditions. All of the participants were asked to complete a questionnaire about their physical and social functioning, the number of days they spent in bed, and their subjective perceptions of their own health. The researchers found that depressed people were more likely to spend time in bed, had more difficulty pursuing their normal activities, and perceived themselves to be worse off than people with chronic medical problems like diabetes, arthritis, and asthma.

Clearly, depression takes an enormous toll not only on the individual, but also on society—particularly the economy. Each year, the United States spends between $12.4 billion and $19.2 billion treating depression. In addition, depression induced absence from work (or reduced productivity at work) results in a huge loss to national productivity, and a substantial cost to business. Estimates suggest that in the United States alone, lost productivity caused by depression wipes $24 billion off national economic output each year. In 1998, the director of health care planning for one large company reported that depression was costing his company $7.1 million a year, roughly 1.3% of its net income. This amount included medical costs paid by the company, lost productivity of depressed employees who worked below their capacity, absenteeism caused by depression, and the effects of depressed workers on their colleagues (depression results in a greater number of errors that other employees must correct, thereby reducing their productivity).

Dysthymic Disorder

Dysthymic disorder is a chronic, relatively mild, depressive disorder that lasts at least 2 years but may last for decades (Rush, 1993). In children or adolescents, the diagnosis requires that the symptoms last at least 1 year. The person may experience occasional symptom-free days, but symptoms never disappear completely for more than 2 months at a time. In addition to a depressed mood (or irritability in children and adolescents), the *DSM-IV* diagnostic criteria for dysthymic disorder require the presence of at least two specific depressive symptoms (Table 8.3). People who have a dysthymic disorder combined with occasional major depressive episodes are said to suffer from a condition called **double depression.**

In clinical practice, depressive disorders do not always fit neatly into a diagnostic category (D. N. Klein et al., 1996). Some people complain of short depressive episodes that include only a few depressive symptoms. Others report that they get seriously depressed for a few days every month or two. People whose symptoms do not fit the standard criteria for dysthymic or major depressive disorder are called "atypical" depressive disorders in the *DSM-IV* even though they probably constitute the majority of depressed people (First, Donovan, & Frances, 1996).

Prevalence and Course of Depressive Disorders

Clinical depression is the "common cold" of psychological disorders (Gotlib, 1992). Between 8% and 20% of the population will experience a major depressive episode sometime in their lives (R. C. Kessler et al., 1994). Each year, at least 100 million people in the world develop some form of depression, and the number of cases seems to be rising in most countries, putting considerable pressure on health expenditures (Cross-National Collaborative Study Group, 1992; Unutzer et al., 1997). The widespread use of psychoactive substances, mass international migrations, the breakdown of the traditional family, crime, unemployment, and poverty all make some contribution to the rising incidence of depressive disorders. Figure 8.2 illustrates this increase in mood disorders as it is seen among the relatives of bipolar patients.

Depression has historically been considered a condition affecting adults. Before the 1970s, it was considered rare among young people (S. Schwartz & Johnson, 1985). Over the past 20 years, however, the number of cases among young people like Danielle Wood has steadily increased. Today, depression has become pri-

DSM-IV   TABLE 8.3   Main DSM-IV Diagnostic Criteria
for Dysthymic Disorder

A. Depressed mood for most of the day, for more days than not, as indicated either by subjective account or observation by others, for at least 2 years. Note: In children and adolescents, mood can be irritable and duration must be at least 1 year.

B. Presence, while depressed, of two (or more) of the following:

(1) poor appetite or overeating

(2) insomnia or hypersomnia

(3) low energy or fatigue

(4) low self-esteem

(5) poor concentration or difficulty making decisions

(6) feelings of hopelessness

C. During the 2-year period (1 year for children or adolescents) of the disturbance, the person has never been without the symptoms in Criteria A and B for more than 2 months at a time.

D. The symptoms cause clinically significant distress or impairment in social, occupational, or other important areas of functioning.

Note: Adapted from American Psychiatric Association (1994, p. 349).

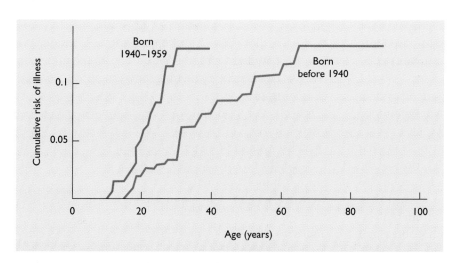

FIGURE 8.2 **Risk of Mood Disorders in People Born Before 1940 and People Born 1940–1959.** *This graph compares two groups of relatives of bipolar patients. At every age, those born between 1940 and 1950 have a much higher risk of developing bipolar illness or a related psychosis.* From: Gershon & Rieder (1992, p. 131).

marily a disorder of young people (Lewinsohn, Hops, et al., 1993; Lewinsohn, Rohde, Seeley, & Fischer, 1993). A person's first major depressive episode is now more likely to occur before age 19 than after, although, as already mentioned, it may present differently in children from the way it presents in adults (Burke et al., 1990; Weissman et al., 1991). As discussed later in this chapter, one of the outcomes of the increasing incidence of depression among young people is an increasing rate of youth suicide (Lewinsohn, Rohde, & Seeley, 1993). De-

pression is likely to become an even more serious mental health problem in the future than it is today because depressions that begin early in life are likely to become chronic (Harrington et al., 1990; Rohde et al., 1990; Winokur et al., 1993). Even dysthymia, if it starts early enough in life, can be a danger sign for future major depressive episodes (Wells et al., 1992).

Although major depressive episodes can develop over only a few days, most begin gradually, usually with a prolonged period of anxiety or mild depression.

Although they can last for years, most episodes improve within 9 months to 1 year (Tollefson, 1993).

Sex, Ethnic, and Cultural Differences

Except possibly in Japan (Sartorius et al., 1983), women are more than twice as likely as men to be diagnosed as depressed (Ernst & Angst, 1992; Strickland, 1992). Women's depressive episodes also are more severe, last longer, and are more apt to recur than those of men (Winokur et al., 1993). This sex difference, which is not present in childhood, becomes apparent by adolescence (Allgood-Merten, Lewinsohn, & Hops, 1990). Why women should be more prone to depression than men has been the subject of substantial debate. Indeed, any suggestion that women are different from men—in any way—is guaranteed to produce at least some dispute (see Eagly, 1995, and the comments on her article, for example). Some writers try to explain away sex differences in depression by claiming that they are simply artifacts. Women, they say, are more likely to seek assistance for psychological problems than men, so they turn up more often in the statistics. Depressed men presumably cope in other ways.

If females seek psychological help more often than males, we would expect to find more females than men in all of the *DSM-IV* diagnostic groups. Because we do not, alternative explanations have been offered that specifically target depression. For example, critics of the *DSM-IV* allege that the diagnostic criteria for mood disorders are subtly biased to include more women than men. Still another explanation for the sex difference is that men mask their depression with alcohol abuse and criminal behavior (Modestin, Hug, & Ammann, 1997). Instead of being diagnosed as depressed, they are diagnosed as substance abusers or as suffering from an antisocial personality disorder (antisocial personality disorders are discussed in Chapter 10).

Although these explanations are all plausible, it is difficult to obtain any definitive data to support them. At the same time, there are other data that shed a different light on the sex difference. Gotlib (1992), for example, found that women who are raising children and who are not employed outside the home have a higher than average risk of developing depression. These women tend to lose social contacts and feel isolated. They may spend the day brooding about their predicament, and yet feel helpless to change their circumstances (Nolen-Hoeksema, 1991). As will be discussed later in this chapter, feelings of powerlessness are frequently associated with depression. Interestingly, in communities where all women work (the Amish people of Pennsylvania, for example), depression is equally common in both sexes (Egeland & Hostetter, 1983).

In addition to sex differences, researchers as far back as Kraepelin have been interested in sociocultural differences (Leff, 1992). They have found that the prevalence of depression varies across ethnic groups. For example, Native Americans and people of Southeast Asian background are reputed to have higher rates of depression than the rest of the population (Chung & Okazaki, 1991; Kinzie et al., 1992; Okazaki, 1997; Vega & Rumbaut, 1991). The signs and symptoms of depression are also said to differ among ethnic and cultural groups. Vegetative symptoms are supposedly more common among members of Asian, Latin, and Mediterranean cultures, whereas a loss of interest in formerly pleasurable activities and feelings of worthlessness are more common among northern Europeans (American Psychiatric Assn, 1994; Kleinman, 1991).

Although these ethnic and national differences undoubtedly exist, it is important to emphasize that they are dwarfed by cross-cultural similarities. Consider the results of studies using the World Health Organization (WHO) Depression Screening Instrument (a checklist consisting of a series of true-false questions, such as "Did you ever wish you were dead?" or "Have you lost interest in sex?"). To validate the instrument, the WHO checklist was administered to people in Switzerland, Canada, Iran, and Japan (Sartorius et al., 1983). Although minor national differences were noted, these were overwhelmed by the enormous cross-national similarities. Sadness, anhedonia, anxiety, lack of energy, inability to concentrate, and ideas of worthlessness characterized depression in every country surveyed.

Although the symptoms and signs of depression are similar across cultures, they are not unique to unipolar depressive disorders; they occur in the bipolar disorders as well. As we shall see in the next section, however, there are important differences between bipolar disorders (which mix depression with mania) and unipolar depressive disorders.

BIPOLAR DISORDERS

Although it is possible to experience manic episodes without any periods of depression, clinicians dating back to ancient Greece have noted that this is exceedingly rare. In the vast majority of people, manic episodes are either preceded or followed by depression (although there may be intervening periods of relative calm). By the 19th century, it was taken for granted that depression and mania go together. This is why Kraepelin coined the term *manic-depressive* to describe people with wide mood swings (see Chapter 3). The *DSM-IV* term *bipolar* conveys a similar picture: episodes of elevated mood (one pole) alternating with periods of depression (the other pole). Somewhat confusingly, the term *bipolar* is also applied to people who display only manic episodes. The *DSM-IV* assumes that their depression is there but has not yet become manifest. Document 8.5 introduces Bernard Louis, a man whom we first encounter in the midst of mania.

Manic, Hypomanic, and Mixed Episodes

The hallmark of a **manic episode** is an overly elevated mood. Manic people feel high and excited, although, like Bernard Louis, they are also easily irritated. In addition to an expansive mood, manic episodes are marked by grandiosity. In the grip of mania, people believe that they have unusual abilities and that they can accomplish anything. Bernard Louis's idea of building a country club in his backyard may sound absurd, but manic episodes often involve such wild schemes. Convinced of their great wealth, manic people have been known to hand out money to strangers they meet on the street or

DOCUMENT 8.5

Note Dictated by Psychiatrist, Dr. Kahn, When Admitting Bernard Louis to the Hospital

UNIVERSITY HOSPITAL

Intake Note

CONFIDENTIAL

Admitting Physician: Dr. Sally Kahn

Bernard Louis was brought involuntarily to the admitting ward by county police who were acting on a court order that had him committed for 24 hours of psychiatric observation.

Mr. Louis is a large man, well over 6 feet tall. He weighs more than 200 pounds. When he appeared at the hospital, his face was very red, and his hair and clothing were disheveled. Otherwise, he seemed normal. According to his wife, who accompanied him to the hospital, Mr. Louis had been working alone, 18 hours a day, building a "golf course" in their suburban backyard. His plan was to turn their half-acre lot into a private country club with a clubhouse. He hoped to sell memberships at $5,000 a year. The clubhouse would offer catering facilities as well as a bar and pro shop. He planned to build sand and water traps and to invest in a fleet of motorized golf carts. When his wife suggested that he might be getting a little carried away, Mr. Louis lost his temper, shouted in rage, and threatened to leave her for another woman. He claimed to have four girlfriends whom he regularly "satisfied" ten times a night. Two days earlier, when his wife had left the house, Mr. Louis had taken all her jewelry to a pawnshop. He had used the money to invite strangers off the street to an all-night party that finally had to be stopped by the police. Mr. Louis had not slept at all for three days before his wife obtained the court order that brought him to the hospital.

Mr. Louis was difficult to interview because he talked nonstop. He complained that he was being persecuted and that his wife was just jealous of the many women who were after him because of his sexual prowess. There was nothing wrong with him. In fact, he claimed to have ". . . never felt better in my life." When asked if he was happy, Mr. Louis responded, "Am I happy? Why, if I felt any happier, you could sell tickets. I'm so happy, it should be illegal."

DSM-IV **TABLE 8.4** Main *DSM-IV* Diagnostic Criteria for a Manic Episode

A. A distinct period of abnormally and persistently elevated, expansive or irritable mood, lasting at least 1 week (or any duration if hospitalization is necessary).

B. During the period of mood disturbance, three or more of the following symptoms have persisted (four if the mood is only irritable) and have been present to a significant degree:

(1) inflated self-esteem or grandiosity

(2) decreased need for sleep

(3) more talkative than usual or a perceived pressure to keep talking

(4) flight of ideas or subjective experience that thoughts are racing

(5) distractibility (attention is easily drawn to unimportant or irrelevant stimuli)

(6) increase in goal-directed activity (either socially, at work or school or sexually), or psychomotor agitation

(7) excessive involvement in pleasurable activities that have a high potential for painful consequences (buying sprees, sexual indiscretions, foolish business ventures)

C. The mood disturbance is sufficiently severe to cause marked impairment in occupational functioning or in usual activities or relationships with others or to necessitate hospitalization to prevent harm to self or others, or there are psychotic features. The symptoms are not the result of substance abuse, a medical conditions or drug treatment.

Note: From American Psychiatric Association (1994, p. 332).

to make enormous wagers at racecourses or casinos.

In the midst of a manic episode, people find it impossible to focus on a single task. Their minds race from one idea to another, a phenomenon known as "flight of ideas." They begin various grand projects but do not see them through to completion. Not only are their thoughts rapid and unfocused, but their physical activities are also energized and chaotic. They have little need for sleep, and their sex drive is heightened. Manic individuals speak quickly and rarely fall silent. Their speech is so rapid, and they switch topics so often, that they may become incoherent. Document 8.6 contains a brief excerpt from the intake interview between Dr. Kahn and Bernard Louis. Note that Mr. Louis is not only grandiose and incoherent, but also easily irritated.

DOCUMENT 8.6

Excerpt From Intake Interview Between Dr. Kahn and Bernard Louis

BERNARD LOUIS: I don't know what I'm doing here. Here, here ye, the court is now in session. Bring on the witnesses, bailiff. I am an innocent man. The old bag just wants me out of the way so she can keep the country club for herself and get rich. Oh, I wish I was a rich man, all day long I'd diddle diddle dum. Funny, I —

DR. KAHN (*interrupting*): What is so funny?

BERNARD LOUIS: Funny? Funny? You think I'm funny? Well, people laughed at Einstein, you know, and also at Carnegie. Who are you to laugh at me? You are an incompetent doctor. You just keep laughing. I'll show you. You'll be sorry that you laughed. Laughing on the outside but crying on the inside, just like in the opera. ■

The main *DSM-IV* criteria for a manic episode are summarized in Table 8.4. Although the emotional tone of depression and manic episodes are "poles" apart, notice that some of their respective diagnostic criteria (distractibility, insomnia) overlap. Some people display manic symptoms while having a depressed mood. They are said to have a **mixed episode.** Clinical lore holds that the presence of "mood-incongruent symptoms" (crying while elated, laughing when depressed) indicates a more severe disorder than one in which the symptoms are mood-congruent, but there is little research evidence to support this hypothesis (Fennig et al., 1996).

In addition to a manic episode, the *DSM-IV* diagnostic system also allows for a milder form of disturbance known as a **hypomanic episode,** which is marked by an elated mood, little need for sleep, and intense periods of activity. This may not seem like much of a disorder, and sometimes it isn't. Still, everything, including good moods, can be taken to extremes. Liveliness is great, but not if it turns into frenzy. Enthusiasm is wonderful, but if it gets out of hand, it can become fanaticism. This is the hidden face of hypomania. Superficially, affected individuals are elated and industrious, but peek below the surface and you will see a tendency to skip from one activity to another, an inability to carry out plans to their completion, and a low tolerance for frustration. Because they feel energetic and healthy, hypomanic (and manic) people do not seek professional assistance, nor do they recognize that anything is wrong with them. Like Bernard Louis, they may have to be treated as involuntary patients.

Specific Bipolar Disorders

The three main bipolar disorders are

1. *Bipolar I disorder* consists of one or more manic or mixed episodes. In most cases, individuals will also have had one or more major depressive episodes. This is the type of disorder experienced by Bernard Louis.
2. *Bipolar II disorder* is characterized by recurrent major depressive episodes and at least one hypomanic episode.
3. *Cyclothymic disorder* involves periods during which hypomanic symptoms are present alternating with periods of mild depression over the course of 2 years (or 1 year in children and adolescents). These periods may be mixed with periods of normal moods.

The *DSM-IV* makes provision for several additional mood disorders. "Mood disorder due to a general medical condition" consists of a depressed or irritable mood that is clearly related to an illness. For someone to receive this diagnosis, his or her mood disturbance must be sufficiently serious to affect normal social or occupational functioning or to cause distress. "Substance-induced mood disorder" is, as its name suggests, a mood disorder related to the use of drugs or alcohol (or the discontinuation of these substances). Even prescription drugs may cause depression in some people (Patten & Love, 1997). There is also a high comorbidity between bipolar disorders and substance abuse (Regier et al., 1990). Because substances such as cocaine can cause manic behavior, and because many people use alcohol and drugs to control their moods, it is often impossible to tell whether changes in mood are the result of substance abuse or are responsible for it.

Another type of mood disorder, **premenstrual dysphoric disorder,** is being considered for inclusion in the next *DSM*. The proposed diagnosis refers to a depressed mood that seems to recur at the same time during each menstrual cycle and that may, therefore, be related to sex-linked hormonal changes (Parry, 1997). There is resistance to the inclusion of this diagnosis in the next *DSM* because of the minimal research evidence for its existence and its worrysome potential to perpetuate the stereotype that women's emotions are less controllable than are those of men.

In practice, the distinction between bipolar and other mood disorders is not so simple. Some authors claim that bipolar disorder is simply a more severe form of major depressive disorder, whereas others believe that the two conditions are distinct (Faraone, Kremen, & Tsuang, 1990). Although there is evidence for both points of view, there is a compelling reason to believe that the two types of disorders are different: The disorders respond to different treatments. Given this important distinction, and the incomplete state of our present knowledge, it is probably best to keep the two disorders separate (Coryell & Winokur, 1992).

Bipolar disorders present important diagnostic challenges because manic-like behaviors may result from several physical and mental conditions. Certain brain tumors may cause manic behaviors, and psychoses can produce a flight from one idea to another. The best way to differentiate bipolar disorder from these other conditions is to focus on mood. Few conditions other than bipolar disorder result in an exaggerated elated mood.

Prevalence and Course of Bipolar Disorders

Bipolar disorders are rarer than unipolar disorders. Only around 1 person in 100 will develop a bipolar disorder in his or her lifetime (R. C. Kessler et al., 1994). Although it is not the case with unipolar disorders, men and women are equally likely to be diagnosed with a bipolar disorder, although more women than men fall into the bipolar II category, in which depressive symptoms dominate (Goodwin & Jamison, 1990).

There do not appear to be marked ethnic differences in the prevalence or presentation of bipolar disorders (Karno et al., 1987), but there is a tendency for bipolar disorders to be diagnosed more often among members of higher rather than lower socioeconomic groups (Goodwin & Jamison, 1990). On its own, this fact is not easily interpreted. It could simply mean that wealthier and better educated people have greater access to mental health services, or it may have some deeper theoretical significance. Many famous people have allegedly suffered from bipolar disorders (Herman Melville, Ernest Hemingway, Winston Churchill, Vincent van Gogh, Vivien Leigh, Pyotr Tchaikovsky, and many oth-

Kay Redfield Jamison, a professor of psychiatry who has had bipolar disorder for more than 30 years, has written a popular book called The Unquiet Mind, *which puts forth the hypothesis that bipolar disorder has links to creativity.*

ers). Although not all of these people came from the higher social classes (certainly Melville did not), writers have speculated that there is some relationship between mood swings and great achievement. Perhaps the rush of ideas produced by a manic episode or the intense emotion and morbid preoccupation with death that are so common in a major depressive episode foster creativity (Schildkraut, Hirshfeld, & Murphy, 1994; Whybrow, 1994). Such speculations should be treated cautiously, however. The problems associated with retrospective diagnoses have been pointed out in previous chapters. We also know that most artists do not suffer from mood disorders and that the vast majority of people who suffer from mood disorders are not particularly creative. (Bernard Louis sold insurance.) It is always important to be wary of illusory correlations, no matter how compelling they may appear. (For more on illusory correlations, see Chapter 3.)

About 15% of people initially diagnosed with some form of depression go on to experience manic or hypomanic episodes (NIMH/NIH Conference Statement, 1985). The cyclical pattern varies among individuals. Some people have brief manic episodes alternating with long periods of depression, whereas others have brief depressive and manic episodes. Still others have periods of relative calm between manic and depressive episodes. Although some people with bipolar disorder have only a few manic episodes over the course of their lives, others, known as rapid cyclers, can have four or more episodes of mania and depression in a single year.

Although the first signs of bipolar disorder usually appear in early adulthood (Burke et al., 1990), bipolar disorders may also occur in young people (Gershon et al., 1987). The onset of a bipolar disorder is typically sudden. Full-blown manic episodes develop within a few days and usually end as abruptly as they began (Winokur et al., 1993). Follow-up studies have found the prognosis for bipolar disorder to be poor. Even among those who are treated, relapse is common, and social and occupational functioning becomes progressively worse over the years (Coryell et al., 1993; Deister & Marneros, 1993; Keller, Baker, & Russell, 1993).

DIAGNOSTIC SPECIFIERS

In addition to the symptoms and signs already described, mood disorders (both unipolar and bipolar) may have other associated features. For example, people may have odd motor disturbances (ranging from complete immobility to bizarre postures and movements). When such features are present, the *DSM-IV* diagnosis is expanded to include the **diagnostic specifier** "with **catatonic features.**" If the mood disorder includes severe delusions (a belief that one was sent by God to save the world, for instance), it is described as "with **psychotic features.**" Other specifiers include the ancient word **melancholic,** which is used today to describe mood disorders in which the main feature is a loss of interest in previously enjoyable activities (Rush & Weissenburger, 1994). There is some suggestion that melancholic mood disorders may be more resistant to treatment than those marked by sadness or elation (Duggan, Lee, & Murray, 1991). Seasonal disorders (such as **seasonal affective disorder,** or **SAD**), affect up to 5% of the population and recur at specific times of the year (Lewy, 1993). Typically, people feel depressed in winter, improve in spring, and then become depressed again as autumn turns to winter.

Postpartum depressions are those that occur in the 4 weeks following childbirth (Walther, 1997), although signs of depression may have also been present during pregnancy (Kitamura et al., 1996). Most of these episodes are mild and brief, but intense episodes do oc-

DSM-IV	TABLE 8.5	Main *DSM-IV* Specifiers Applicable to Mood Disorders
Specifier	**Description**	
Catatonic features	Clinical presentation characterized by psychomotor disturbance.	
Psychotic features	Clinical presentation marked by loss of contact with reality.	
Melancholic	Loss of interest in previously pleasurable activities.	
Seasonal	Mood disorder associated with a particular season.	
Postpartum	Onset within 4 weeks of childbirth.	

cur, and these may presage the development of a major depressive disorder (Fossey, Papiernik, & Bydlowski, 1997). In severe cases, the depression is probably not caused solely by the birth of a child but is likely to be the end result of many preexisting factors including low self-esteem (Fontaine & Jones, 1997; Whiffen, 1992).

The various specifiers are not only useful in classification, they can also help in prognosis. We know, for example, that seasonal mood disorders tend to improve as winter ends. We also know that the specifiers tend to be stable over time—a second episode is likely to warrant the same specifier as the first (Coryell et al., 1994). Table 8.5 summarizes the main *DSM-IV* diagnostic specifiers.

ETIOLOGY OF MOOD DISORDERS

Because mood disorders have vegetative symptoms and because they may be triggered by disease and by certain drugs, biologically oriented researchers have concluded that they must have a physiological etiology. At the same time, noting that mood disorders have numerous psychological symptoms and often follow stressful events, psychologically oriented researchers have focused on possible social and psychological causes. Although it is useful for researchers to concentrate their efforts, the distinction between physical and psychological causes is oversimplified and artificial. According to the metaparadigm presented in Chapter 2, the proximal cause of depression—indeed, the proximal cause of all behavior, normal or abnormal—is biological activity taking place in the central nervous system. Understanding mood disorders means knowing how genetic, physiological, social, and psychological factors act on the central nervous system to produce their troubling symptoms. This section examines various causes of mood disorders. As you will see, unipolar depressive disorders receive the most attention; the literature on the etiology of bipolar disorders is fairly thin.

Genetics

Kraepelin noted a "hereditary taint" in cases of mood disorders, an impression that has persisted ever since. Although the diagnostic criteria for mood disorders have been repeatedly revised, the research data accumulated over the past 100 years strongly suggest that these disorders run in families. There are many examples. One famous one is the artist Vincent van Gogh and his family, who seem to have had more than their share of mood disorders. During what appear to have been manic

Vincent van Gogh was prone to bleak depressions (once even cutting off his ear) interspersed with periods of prolific creativity. He may have suffered from a mood disorder, as did most of his close relatives.

TABLE 8.6   Average Risk for Mood Disorders in First-Degree Relatives of People With Mood Disorders

	Percentage of relatives with	
Patient's disorder	**Major depressive disorder**	**Bipolar disorder**
Major depression	9.1	0.6
Bipolar disorder	11.4	7.8
No disorder (general population)	8	<1

Note: From R. Katz and McGuffin (1993) and various epidemiological studies.

episodes, Vincent produced numerous paintings, sometimes several in a single day. On the other hand, when he was depressed, van Gogh produced nothing. In a period of severe distress, he cut off part of his ear before finally taking his own life. Vincent's brother Cornelius also committed suicide, and their sister, Wilhelmina, spent decades in psychiatric hospitals. Another brother, Theo, supported Vincent for most his life but was said to suffer from major depressive episodes. The writer Ernest Hemingway and his granddaughter Margot are a more recent tragic example of multigenerational suicide.

For reasons discussed earlier, it is not possible to conclude from historical data alone that a mood disorder was responsible for van Gogh's marvelous paintings or Hemingway's novels. Nevertheless, mood disorders did seem to run in their families. Clusters of mood disorders have been found in systematic family studies. The first step in these studies is to diagnose probands (index cases) using carefully specified criteria and structured interviews. This is followed by a search for relatives, who are then evaluated in the same manner. Although the exact figures vary depending on the specific criteria used to define depressive and bipolar disorders, most studies have found (as Table 8.6 illustrates) that first-degree relatives (parents, siblings, children) of people with mood disorders are more likely to have mood disorders themselves than are people without affected relatives (Hammen, 1991a; Sadovnick et al., 1994). Child probands are especially likely to have many similarly affected relatives (Neuman et al., 1997). Bipolar disorders also seem to run in families, including the family of Bernard Louis (Document 8.7).

Referral: Dr. Kahn requested this report on Bernard Louis, a 49-year-old insurance salesperson who was involuntarily admitted to the hospital last week.

According to his wife, Bernard Louis is one of two children. His parents are deceased, and his sister, Phoebe (52), lives in California. According to Mrs. Louis, Bernard's mother was frequently depressed. Although she was never hospitalized, she was treated with antidepressant medications over many years. Bernard has told his wife that his mother had little to do with the children when they were young. His most common memory was of his mother lying in her bed, alone, for much of the time. Mrs. Louis also reported that Phoebe Louis has had a lifelong tendency to become depressed and is currently being seen by a psychologist.

Mrs. Louis stated, and a check of hospital records confirmed, that Bernard was admitted to University Hospital 3 years ago after he had gone 3 days without sleep. On the day of his admission, Mr. Louis had withdrawn all of his savings from the bank and was talking about investing in a diamond mine which would make him "a billionaire." Mr. Louis responded well to treatment and was discharged after 12 days. He was not seen again in the hospital until the current admission. However, his wife reports that he has consulted both psychologists and psychiatrists in the interim. These consultations were for depression. Mr. Louis was treated with a combination of medications and psychological treatment. Mrs. Louis noted that both of her husband's hospital admissions were preceded by business setbacks. Before his previous admission, he had lost a great deal of money when a business he had invested in had gone bankrupt. More recently, he had found that an employee had embezzled a large sum of money from his insurance firm. ■

DOCUMENT 8.7

Excerpt From a Social Work Report on Bernard Louis

Social Worker: Li Cheong, MSW

Of course, these findings do not necessarily mean that mood disorders are genetic; shared environments can also be responsible. Depressed parents, for example, may provide family environments that foster depression in their children (Burge & Hammen, 1991). Still, not all children of depressed parents become depressed themselves (Conrad & Hammen, 1993). There must be some special diathesis that makes some children especially vulnerable. The most likely candidate is some form of genetic predisposition.

The existence of a genetic diathesis for mood disorders is supported by studies that compared identical and fraternal twins. Twins tend to live in closely similar environments, but they differ in their genetic similarity. Identical twins share all their genes, whereas fraternal twins, like siblings in general, have only about half their genes in common. Twin studies have found that the probability of an identical twin developing a mood disorder given that his or her twin has a mood disorder is approximately 79%. For fraternal twins, the corresponding concordance figure is around 24% (R. Katz & McGuffin, 1993; Kendler et al., 1994; McGuffin, Katz, & Rutherford, 1991). This difference suggests that genes contribute to the development of mood disorders. Nevertheless, because 21% of identical twins are discordant (they do not develop a mood disorder despite having an identical twin brother or sister with such a disorder), nongenetic factors must also play an etiological role (Baron, 1991).

Searches for the gene or genes responsible for mood disorders began with a search for specific genetic markers, genetic material present in relatives with mood disorders. Finding such material requires two important ingredients: technology capable of identifying parts of chromosomes and a sufficiently large number of affected family members who can be studied over several generations. The required technology is now widely available. Suitable populations are another matter. Modern society is transient and mobile; tracking down relatives is often difficult. Researchers have been forced to focus on communities that are geographically or socially isolated, particularly ones in which members intermarry or in which all members descend from a small number of ancestors. One such study concentrated on several large Orthodox Jewish families in Jerusalem who had a high prevalence of mood disorders. The researchers claimed to find evidence for a "bipolar disorder gene" located on the X chromosome (Baron et al., 1987). Unfortunately, subsequent studies have not replicated this finding.

A similar study was conducted among the Amish people of Pennsylvania. The Amish are a close-knit group whose members seldom leave or marry outside their community. It is also helpful that the Amish eschew drugs and alcohol. This means that their mood disorders cannot be attributed to substances. Studies of Amish families with a high prevalence of mood disorders claimed to find a genetic marker (Egeland et al.,

1987). Sadly, like those of the Jerusalem studies, these results have proved difficult to reproduce (Berrettini et al., 1990; Kelsoe et al., 1989).

Given the accumulated data, it seems reasonable to conclude that genetics plays a role in rendering people susceptible to mood disorders (Monroe & Simons, 1991). Nevertheless, we should keep in mind the distinction between genotype and phenotype (see Chapter 2). A genetic diathesis (genotype) does not guarantee that a person will develop a mood disorder; even identical twins may still be discordant. Environmental and psychological factors interact to determine whether (and in what form) a mood disorder develops. For example, Bernard Louis may have inherited a tendency to develop bipolar disorder, but his manic episodes seem to have been triggered by financial disasters (see Document 8.7).

What Is Inherited?

If genetics plays a role in the development of mood disorders, then it follows that sufferers must inherit something that renders them especially susceptible to mood disorders. Three possibilities have received the bulk of research attention: disturbances in the regulation of the chemical neurotransmitters that mediate communication among neurons, hormonal imbalances, and disturbances in biological rhythms.

Faulty Neurotransmitter Regulation   As we have seen, in ancient times, mood disorders were attributed to an imbalance in the chemicals (humors) of the body. As described in Chapter 2, this ancient theory was put on a more scientific footing in the 1950s, when it was observed that about 15% of patients treated with reserpine to reduce their high blood pressure were found to develop major depressive episodes. Because reserpine was thought to reduce the level of a neurotransmitter known as norepinephrine, researchers hypothesized that depression might be the result of diminished levels of norepinephrine. Around the same time that these observations were being made, clinicians using the drug iproniazid to treat tuberculosis noted that their patients not only improved physically, but they also seemed to be in a much better mood. Nathan Kline (1916–1982), a pioneer in the area of psychopharmacology, conducted clinical trials comparing the behavioral effects of iproniazid with those of a placebo. His findings supported the clinical observations; iproniazid was indeed effective against depression. By the late 1950s, the drug was being widely used to treat depression even though no one had any idea how it worked.

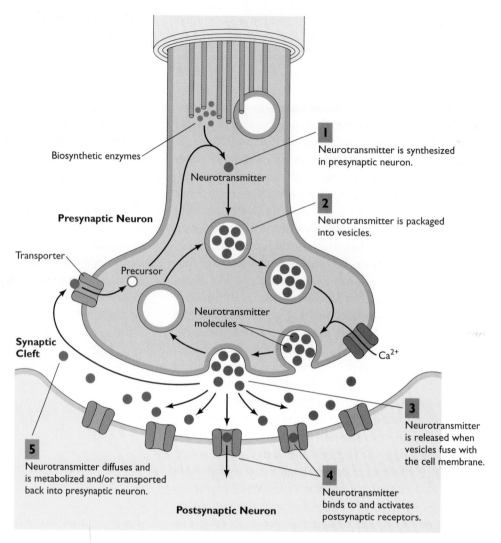

Biosynthetic enzymes

Presynaptic Neuron

Neurotransmitter

Transporter

Precursor

Synaptic Cleft

Neurotransmitter molecules

Ca²⁺

1 Neurotransmitter is synthesized in presynaptic neuron.

2 Neurotransmitter is packaged into vesicles.

3 Neurotransmitter is released when vesicles fuse with the cell membrane.

5 Neurotransmitter diffuses and is metabolized and/or transported back into presynaptic neuron.

4 Neurotransmitter binds to and activates postsynaptic receptors.

Postsynaptic Neuron

FIGURE 8.3 The Neurotransmitter Cycle. *Disruption of any stage of this process can lead to over- or underproduction of a neurotransmitter or interfere with its reuptake. A variety of drugs have been created to regulate the cycle of specific neurotransmitters.*

Ultimately, scientists discovered that iproniazid, like reserpine, affects neurotransmitter levels. Specifically, iproniazid inhibits the activity of an enzyme known as **monoamine oxidase (MAO)**, a chemical that plays a crucial role in neurotransmitter regulation. Under normal conditions, neurotransmitters are released from the axons of one or more neurons into the synaptic cleft (the space between neurons), where they stimulate the dendrites of adjacent neurons (Figure 8.3). After they have done their job, neurotransmitters are reabsorbed so that they do not accumulate in the synaptic cleft, overstimulating adjacent neurons. This is where MAO comes in. It facilitates the chemical breakdown and reuptake of neurotransmitters such as norepinephrine,

dopamine, and serotonin after they have done their job. Because iproniazid inhibits the activity of MAO, it slows the reuptake process. The result is a higher concentration of norepinephrine in the synaptic space and greater neural stimulation.

Because iproniazid, like reserpine, increases neurotransmitter levels while at the same time helping to lift depression, researchers became further convinced that depression results from diminished levels of neurotransmitters or, more precisely, their too rapid reuptake (Gold, Goodwin, & Chrousos, 1988). Not surprisingly, pharmaceutical companies rushed to market other **MAO inhibitors.** Unfortunately, these drugs had a serious drawback; they interact with certain foods to cause such potentially life-threatening conditions as stroke. This is why MAO inhibitors have been largely abandoned in favor of much less lethal antidepressant drugs.

Although the chemical action of modern antidepressant drugs is well understood, a number of questions about their effect on mood disorders remain unanswered (S. A. Montgomery & Corn, 1994). For example, if antidepressants elevate mood by slowing down the reuptake of neurotransmitters (a physiological effect that takes only hours to produce), why does it usually take weeks before any clinical improvement is noticed? Moreover, after clients have been on medication for 2 weeks, their neurotransmitters often return to premedication levels. In other words, the clinical improvement does not appear until neurotransmitter levels return to normal. This suggests that the therapeutic effects of antidepressants do not result from an increase in neurotransmitter levels, but from some other, more long-term process. One possibility is that, by increasing neurotransmitter levels, antidepressants overstimulate neuronal neurotransmitter receptors. Neurons adapt to this overstimulation by reducing the number of receptors, a process that takes several weeks. Perhaps it is the reduction in receptors, rather than the increase in neurotransmitter levels, that helps lift depression.

Although the level of neurotransmitters (or the number of receptors) may be related to depression, this hypothesis does not explain why some people cycle between depression and manic episodes. In the early days of MAO inhibitors, researchers hypothesized that manic states were the mirror of depressed ones—that is, that mania is the result of an *oversupply* of certain neurotransmitters (Schildkraut, 1965). Unfortunately, this simple formulation has never been substantiated. At present, the best guess is that shifts in the *relative* amounts of *different* neurotransmitters produce both depression and mania (Goodwin & Jamison, 1990). For example, neurotransmitters may be linked. An abnormally low level of one substance, such as serotonin, may be compensated for by a higher than normal level of another neurotransmitter. At present, this theory needs considerable elaboration before it will yield testable research hypotheses. Even then, it would not offer a specific explanation for mood disorders. Faulty neurotransmitter regulation is also associated with anxiety disorders and with the psychoses (see Chapters 4 and 9). For now, we can only conclude that neurotransmitter regulation probably does play some role in mood disorders, although the precise nature of this role remains to be determined.

Faulty Hormone Regulation   Because menopausal depression, postpartum depression, and maybe premenstrual dysphoric disorder all occur when there are changes in hormone production, investigators have sought to connect hormones with mood disorders (Leibenluft, Fiero, & Rubinow, 1994; Wisner & Stowe, 1997). This connection is given further support by the observation that hormone dysfunction, such as a reduction or an increase in the hormones produced by the thyroid gland, can cause mood disorders (Haggerty & Prange, 1995).

Perhaps the hormone that has been studied in greatest depth is cortisol, a substance produced by the adrenal cortex as part of the alarm reaction (see Chapter 5). Cortisol has attracted particular interest because people with abnormally high levels of cortisol (usually caused by taking large doses of hormones such as cortisone as a treatment for arthritis) often become depressed. One way to measure cortisol levels is to have people ingest a synthetic form of the hormone known as dexamethasone. If this is done late in the day, cortisol levels will normally be suppressed throughout the following day. However, when this **dexamethasone suppression test (DST)** is applied to people suffering from depression, they show either no or only minor cortisol suppression the next day (Holsboer, 1992). Researchers have interpreted this finding to mean that depression may be related to some abnormality in the system that regulates cortisol levels. This does not mean that depression is caused by high cortisol levels. It is entirely possible that the relationship goes the other way. That is, high cortisol levels may be a consequence rather than a cause of depression. Indeed, once the depression lifts, cortisol levels usually return to normal.

Although the dexamethasone suppression test was heralded as a potential biological indicator of depression, it has not proven particularly useful in practice. Because many conditions in addition to depression can affect cortisol regulation, the test is not precise enough to serve as a marker for depression (see Critical Thinking About Clinical Decisions 8.1). Moreover, the idea that hormone imbalances cause depression is an overgeneralization. Most women do not become clinically depressed at menopause or after giving birth, and most mood disorders occur in people who have normal hormone levels. Clearly, hormone imbalances alone cannot explain why some people develop mood disorders.

Biological Rhythms   Circadian rhythms reflect the inner workings of the body's biological clock. They regulate

When Negative Results Count More Than Positive Ones

Many clinicians believe that clinical tests are most useful when they yield a positive result. For example, a positive dexamethasone suppression test (DST) is usually taken as a sign of depression (McKnight, Nelson-Gray, & Barnhill, 1992). Yet there are occasions when a negative test result provides more information than a positive one. To see why, we must have a closer look at the clinical value of test results, using the DST as an example.

The probability of a true-positive test result (the probability that the DST will yield a positive result when a person is really depressed) is known as **test sensitivity.** The average sensitivity of the DST is .44. The probability of a true-negative test result (the probability that the DST will yield a negative result when a person is not depressed) is known as **test specificity.** The specificity of the DST is .93 for normal controls and around .77 for other psychiatric patients. Although these figures appear to be pretty good in isolation, they produce a different picture when they are considered together.

The table summarizes the expected results of administering the DST to a sample of 1,000 people, of whom 8% or 80 people, are depressed (this is about the national prevalence rate). Because the DST's sensitivity is 44%, we would expect the test to give a positive result for 44% of the 80 depressed people in the group. That is, the test will correctly identify 35. The remaining 45 depressed people will not be recognized because they test negative. For the 920 people who are not depressed, we would expect the DST to give a true-negative result for 93%, or 856. The remaining 64 will give a positive result. Taking these figures together, the predictive value of a positive result (the ratio of true-positives to all positives), is 35/99, or 35% (to refresh your memory on the predictive value of tests, see Critical Thinking About Clinical Decisions 1.3). What does this result mean for the DST? First, the probability that a person who tests positive is actually depressed is less than 50-50. In other words, a positive DST is no more revealing than tossing a coin. In contrast, the predictive value of a negative result, the ratio of true-negatives to all negatives, is 856/901, or 95%. In summary, a positive DST tells us next to nothing, whereas a negative DST tells us there is a high probability that the person is not depressed. The DST is an example of a test in which a negative result provides more information than a positive one.

Hypothetical Outcome of the DST Administered to 1,000 People Selected at Random		
	Actual status	
Test result	**Depressed**	**Not depressed**
Positive	35	64
Negative	45	856

Note: From Arana, Baldessarini, & Ornsteen (1985).

when we wake and when we sleep, when our bodies store fat, and many other aspects of daily life. Because mood disorders almost always involve a sleep disturbance, researchers have speculated that mood disorders may be at least partly the result of a disruption in the body's normal rhythm of sleep and wakefulness (Kupfer, Monk, & Barchas, 1988). (Figure 8.4 shows normal adult sleep stages.) This hypothesis is supported by the results of sleep studies that have found depressed people to have different sleep patterns from nondepressed people. One curious finding is that depressed people seem to enter **rapid eye movement (REM) sleep** (during which most dreams allegedly occur) earlier in the night than nondepressed people (Goodwin & Guze, 1984). This pattern is particularly obvious in melan-

cholic depression (Monroe, Thase, & Simons, 1992), and it remains apparent in electroencephalographic sleep recordings even when the overt signs of depression are gone (Benca et al., 1992). These findings, combined with the observation that partial sleep deprivation may temporarily help depressed people feel better (Riemann et al., 1996; Wu & Bunney, 1990), suggest that an aberration in the circadian rhythms controlling sleep may play a causative role in mood disorders. It is worth noting, however, that these findings and their interpretation are controversial (van-Bemmel, 1997).

In addition to circadian rhythms, the behavior of most organisms is also subject to seasonal rhythms. Birds and fish migrate with the seasons, arctic animals hibernate, caterpillars turn into butterflies, and amphibians

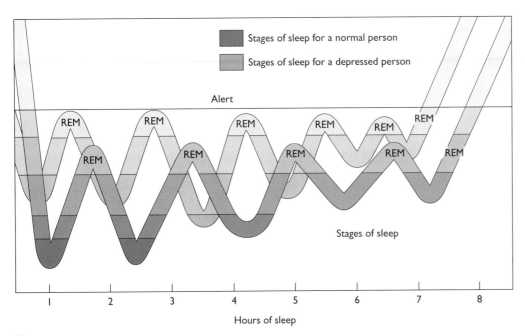

FIGURE 8.4 The Stages of Sleep in a Normal Adult. *Stage 1 (the lightest stage of non-REM sleep) occurs just after we fall asleep and just before we wake up. The other non-REM stages alternate with REM sleep in approximately 90-minute cycles throughout the night. Stages 3 and 4 occur only in the early stages.*

move between the sea and land. The trigger for many of these behaviors is a change in the amount of ambient light. Except at the equator, winter days are short and summer days are long. Many animals are sensitive to the change in the number of daylight hours that accompanies changes in season. The behavior of light-sensitive animals changes depending on the hours of daylight. Noting that people with seasonal affective disorder seem to become depressed at the same time each year, and generalizing from animal behavior, Wehr (1989) reasoned that seasonal mood changes may be activated by changes in the length of the day. (Figure 8.5 shows that SAD is more prevalent at latitudes farther from the equator.) Because sufferers of seasonal depression often improve in the longer days of spring, Wehr hypothesized that artificially increasing the length of short winter days might dispel the depression. Wehr tested this hypothesis by exposing a sample of depressed people to artificial sunlight. Patients awoke early, around 5 a.m., while it was still dark. They spent the next few hours reading, knitting, or listening to the radio while sitting in front of a bank of fluorescent lamps. Despite its simplicity, the experiment was a success. Within a few days to a week, subjects began to report feeling the way they usually did in the spring. Since this initial experiment, thousands of people have

been treated with "light therapy" (Dalgleish, Rosen, & Marks, 1996). The precise mechanism by which exposure to light lifts depression is not known. We do know that the production of melatonin (a hormone produced by the

From October to March, the Cafe Engel in Helsinki, Finland, offers its breakfast patrons the use of a lightbox with daylight-intensity light. The use of such lightboxes has been found to help people with seasonal affective disorder, especially those who live in latitudes where there is little daylight during winter months.

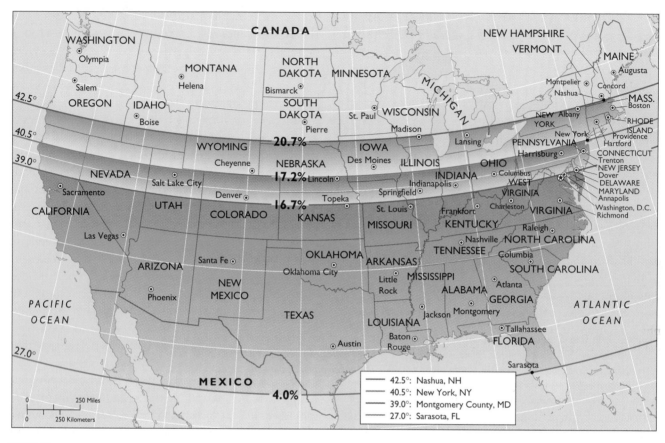

FIGURE 8.5 Prevalence of Seasonal Affective Disorder by Latitude. *SAD occurs less often at latitudes with longer hours of sunlight, and more often farther north.* Data from: L. N. Rosen et al. (1990).

brain's pineal gland) is decreased by light. So, seasonal depression may somehow be linked to excess melatonin (Schlager, 1994).

Biological Diathesis: Current Status There are compelling reasons for believing that biology plays an important etiological role in depression. The response of seasonal affective disorder to light therapy, the effectiveness of antidepressant drugs, the evidence for heredity, and the relationship between mood and hormonal imbalances are all compatible with a biological disorder (Honig & Praag, 1997). Yet despite considerable research over the past 50 years, it is still not possible to identify a specific biological diathesis for mood disorder. Most of the evidence is correlational and open to more than one interpretation. For example, although drugs that increase certain neurotransmitter or hormonal levels exert a powerful affect on mood, this does not prove that hormonal or neurotransmitter imbalances cause depression. Aspirin reduces fever, but no one believes that fevers are caused by a lack of aspirin. Similarly, the re-

search on biological rhythms, although intriguing, requires a more precise understanding of why seasonal mood disorders affect only certain people and what it is about the early onset of REM sleep that might cause some people to become depressed.

Psychosocial Factors

Although there is clear evidence that genetics plays a role in mood disorders, and we have several plausible candidates for the biological diathesis, it is important to keep in mind that the concordance rate, even among identical twins, is less than 100%. Thus, the environment must also play a role in determining who develops a mood disorder. We know, for example, that severe stress, especially divorce or the death of a loved one, is often associated with the development of a mood disorder (Hammen, 1991b; Post, 1992). We also know that chronic stress (lasting 12 months or more) presents a greater risk than short-lived stress (Brown & Harris, 1989). In this section, we look at how psychoanalytic, behavioral, cognitive, and social psychologists explain how stress interacts with preexisting vulnerabilities to produce mood disorders.

Psychoanalytic Views   According to Freud (1917/1959b) and his followers, depression is a form of grief produced in reaction to a loss, especially the loss of an important personal relationship through death, divorce, or separation. In a departure from normal grieving, people who become clinically depressed tend to blame themselves for their loss. Why do they do this? According to psychoanalysis, this pattern of self-blame is established early in life, usually because of the loss of parental affection. Rejecting parents, or early separation from one's parents through death, divorce, or desertion, can cause a child to become fixated at the oral stage of psychosexual development. Because children at this early developmental stage depend on their caretakers to satisfy their physical and psychological needs, fixation produces a passive and emotionally dependent adult. They blame themselves for their loss of parental affection; these children grow up feeling unwanted and worthless. They are angry about their loss, but they turn their anger inward, thereby setting the stage for a lifetime habit of self-blame, and a consequent vulnerability to depression.

In short, psychoanalysts view the diathesis for mood disorder as originating in the lack of a loving parent-child relationship. In more recent writings, psychoanalytic theorists have broadened this formulation. Psychoanalysts now believe that mood disorders can be traced back not just to the loss of parental affection, but to the loss, early in life, of any person who was of special importance to the child (Blatt & Zuroff, 1992). This traumatic childhood loss continues to exert its pernicious effects later in life (Maughn & McCarthy, 1997).

Behavioral Views   Like psychoanalysts, behavioral psychologists originally emphasized the loss of important relationships in the etiology of depression. Their basic premise is that the behavior of other people is an important source of reinforcement for our own behavior. For example, we share our innermost feelings and needs with a loved one because this brings reinforcement in the form of companionship, affection, and a sympathetic ear. Similarly, we are encouraged to tell humorous stories when our friends reinforce us with their laughter, and we work hard for sporting teams when our teammates respond with approval. When we lose a friend or loved one, we also lose the reinforcement they provided. As a consequence, we may go out less, tell fewer jokes, and lose interest in social activities; in other words, we

may become depressed (Lewinsohn, 1974). Once people become depressed, they set in motion a vicious cycle. Depressed people are bad company, so they are avoided. This furthers their isolation and makes them even more depressed. Even worse, if other people show sympathy for depressed friends and relatives, then the depressive behaviors may be reinforced and the depression may become chronic.

To account for depressions that do not involve the loss of a loved one, behavioral theories have been broadened to include more than just the loss of interpersonal reinforcement. Behavioral psychologists now believe that any life event that disrupts habitual behaviors can potentially lead to the loss of reinforcers and, therefore, to depression (Lewinsohn et al., 1980). Some behaviorists have also attempted to account for manic episodes in similar terms (Staats & Heiby, 1985). People who are excessively praised for some accomplishment feel energized and euphoric. This feeling is pleasant and reinforcing, so it elicits further activity, which creates further euphoria until the person spirals out of control.

The main problem with these behavioral formulations is their lack of specificity. We know that many people experience the loss of a loved one without becoming clinically depressed. Similarly, very few people respond to praise and success by becoming manic. To account for these well-known facts, behavioral theories assume that individual differences make some people more likely to develop mood disorders than others (Staats & Heiby, 1985). Because psychoanalytic theory makes the same assumption and also attributes depression to loss, there is little difference between the predictions made by the two theoretical views.

Cognitive Views   The cognitive approach to mood disorders was introduced in Chapter 2. Briefly, cognitive psychologists such as A. T. Beck (1991) view mood disorders as mainly the result of distorted attributions (Dodge, 1993). They believe that depressed people are biased toward negative attributions. These negative attributions constitute what Beck calls the **cognitive triad** of depression: negative feelings about the self, the world, and the future. People with depressive mood disorders also have characteristic ways of interpreting and responding to life events. These interpretations contain four logical errors:

1. *Arbitrary inference.* Depressed people interpret neutral events as negative reflections on themselves, often without any evidence. For example, every time Luke failed to call, Danielle interpreted this as a sign

that Luke was "getting tired" of her. A nondepressed person might interpret Luke's failure to call as a sign that he was studying or simply forgot.

2. *Selected abstraction.* Depressed people magnify minor events out of all proportion. If his date fails to laugh at a joke, a depressed man may conclude that the night was a total failure even when, in all other respects, his date seems to have enjoyed herself. The tendency of depressed people to dwell on negative events is also apparent in the laboratory studies of the memory for lists of emotionally laden words. Depressed people tend to recall more negative words than do nondepressed people (Mineka & Sutton, 1992; Burt et al., 1995).

3. *Overgeneralization.* Depressed people interpret any setback as clear evidence for their unworthiness (Robins, 1990). This was Danielle's reaction to not making the Olympic team. However, even trivial events can elicit similar responses. For example, if their bus breaks down, and they are late for work, depressed people blame themselves ("I should have taken an earlier bus").

4. *Magnification and minimization.* Depressed people magnify negative events and minimize positive ones. Danielle, for example, ignored the swimming achievements that almost got her a place on the Olympic team and focused instead on her failure to go as far as she would have liked.

According to cognitive psychologists, all four of these logical errors stem from low self-esteem. People who feel worthless distort events to justify their low opinion of themselves. These distorted appraisals then make them depressed. Once depression sets in, they tend to make more negative self-appraisals, assuring further "failures" and making them feel more worthless and even more depressed. Once this process takes hold, depression becomes self-perpetuating.

Like psychoanalysts and behaviorists, cognitive psychologists make room for individual differences in their theory. For example, A. T. Beck (1983) distinguishes between sociotropic and autonomous personalities. People who are *sociotropic* (who value social interaction and intimacy) get their sense of self-esteem from relationships. These individuals would be most likely to develop a mood disorder in response to the loss of a loved one (Hammen, Ellicott, & Gitlin, 1992; Segal et al., 1992). They react to their loss by seeking social support and assistance. *Autonomous* people get their sense of self-worth from specific achievements. They are most likely to become depressed if they fail to achieve a desired goal. They

react to such setbacks by blaming themselves (Robins & Luten, 1991). Like many people, Danielle seemed to be a little of both, sociotropic and autonomous. Both the loss of the swimming contest and her deteriorating relationship with Luke made her depressed. Although Beck's distinction between sociotropic and autonomous people has not proved especially useful in treatment or research (Haslam & Beck, 1994; Jolly et al., 1996), his goal was an important one. It is essential to identify the reason the same events produce mood disorders in some people but not in others.

The main tenet of the cognitive view is indisputable; the research evidence showing that depressed people are self-critical is overwhelming (Gotlib & Hammen, 1992; J. White et al., 1992). However, the evidence for other forms of distorted cognition is equivocal (Dykman et al., 1991; Haaga, Dyck, & Ernst, 1991). For example, when depressed people are asked to predict the likelihood that they will succeed at some laboratory task, cognitive psychologists might expect them to be pessimistic and underestimate their chances. In reality, depressed people are often accurate judges of their own behavior. In other words, they are able to perceive events accurately; they just exaggerate their importance and the consequences of failure.

Of course, the mere existence of a tendency toward self-blame does not necessarily mean that self-blame causes mood disorders (Haaga et al., 1991). It could be the other way around. Mood disorders could make people feel worthless. In order to show that cognitive attributions actually cause depression, we need some plausible mechanism by which cognitions and mood disorders can be related. One possibility is the concept of learned helplessness.

Learned Helplessness   In contrast to Beck's cognitive theory, which was derived from clinical observations, Martin Seligman's theory of **learned helplessness** was originally derived from animal research (Seligman, 1975). In the typical experiment, dogs were confined in a box with an electrified floor. They received electric shocks, which they could not avoid because there was no escape route. Later, the same dogs were tested in an apparatus known as a shuttle box. This box consisted of two compartments separated by a small partition. One side of the box had an electrified floor; the other did not. Once again electric shocks were delivered through the floor, but this time they were preceded by a buzzer or a light signal. The animals who were attracted to the electrified compartment by food or drink could avoid the pain of a shock by jumping over the wall whenever they

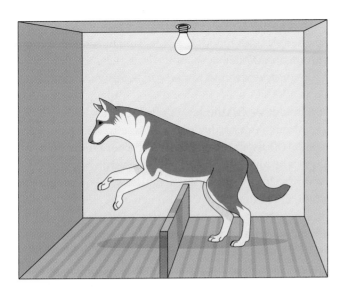

FIGURE 8.6 *In Martin Seligman's (1975) research into learned helplessness, dogs that had been confined in a box with an electrified floor and were unable to avoid being shocked were subsequently unable to learn to jump to safety over the partition in a half-electrified shuttle box at the signal of a buzzer or a light.*

heard or saw the signal (Figure 8.6). Animals who had never been exposed to the inescapable shock eventually learned to jump out of the electrified side of the box whenever the signal was presented. This allowed them to eat or drink in the electrified box without ever feeling any shock. The animals who had previously been exposed to the unavoidable shock never learned to make the required escape response. Instead, they just lay down on the grid, cowered, whined, and accepted their fate. According to Seligman, these animals had learned that painful outcomes were beyond their control. Instead of learning to avoid shock, they simply learned to act helpless.

Seligman noted parallels between the animal research and human depression. For example, many depressed people have experienced tragedy and loss over which they have had no control. In response, they may give up trying to cope and react to life's problems with passivity and helplessness. The similarity between Seligman's animals and depressed people was further supported by studies showing lowered neurotransmitter levels in dogs who had previously experienced unavoidable shock. Because antidepressant drugs seemed to help previously shocked dogs overcome their helplessness and learn to make the required avoidance response, it seems reasonable to conclude that learned helplessness in dogs and human depression are related phenomena. This conclusion was further strengthened

by laboratory experiments in which human subjects who were exposed to uncontrollable noise later had trouble solving cognitive problems when compared with people who were not previously exposed to uncontrollable noise (Hiroto & Seligman, 1975). Although most of the human research was conducted with college students rather than depressed patients, Seligman concluded that clinical depression is the result of learned helplessness. People become depressed because their life experiences (loss, rejection) have taught them that they have no control over events (Nolen-Hoeksema, Girgus, & Seligman, 1992).

Over the years, Seligman has gathered additional evidence for his learned helplessness theory (Peterson, Maier, & Seligman, 1993). His coordinated research program is an excellent example of how laboratory research and scientific theory can interact to produce helpful clinical insights. However, there were a few loose ends. We have already noted that depressed people blame themselves for their failures. But why should they blame themselves if they are helpless and not in control of their lives? Just as puzzling is why depression dissipates with time. Is learned helplessness only a temporary phenomenon? To answer these questions, the learned helplessness theory was modified to include cognitions and attributions similar to Beck's.

According to the revised learned helplessness theory, we attribute our failures and losses to either internal or external causes. Danielle, for example, attributed her failure to win a place on the Olympic team to internal failings ("I'm not any good"). Swimmers who were not depressed might blame circumstances ("I was ill on the day of the trials"). External attributions lead to temporary feelings of helplessness and depression but not to self-blame. Internal attributions, on the other hand, produce more chronic forms of depression in which low self-esteem and self-blame play an important role. Of course, there are degrees of severity even among internal attributions. Global internal attributions ("I'll never succeed at anything") are more pernicious than specific internal attributions ("I'll never succeed at Olympic swimming") because they are invoked on many more occasions. People who tend to attribute all of their failures to global personality traits ("I'm a total screw-up") are the most vulnerable and are said to have "depressive personality styles." An important prediction of the revised helplessness theory is that serious depressions require not only a triggering event (such as the failure to make the Olympic team) but also a depressive attributional style that assigns such failure to personal, usually global, failings (Alloy, Lipman, & Abramson, 1992).

More recently, learned helplessness theory has been further augmented with the introduction of the concept of **hopelessness** (Metalsky et al., 1993), a construct that combines helplessness with negative expectancies (Alloy et al., 1990). Hopelessness accounts for the frequent comorbidity of depression and anxiety. Specifically, helplessness develops out of negative life experiences and creates anxiety. If helplessness becomes chronic, attributions become more global—the person begins to believe that negative consequences are inevitable. Hopelessness then takes over, and depression becomes chronic (Waikar & Craske, 1997).

It is easy to see how Danielle Wood could have developed a tendency toward helplessness. As described in Chapter 1, when Danielle was a child, she was abused by her father, who committed suicide when his behavior was discovered. Early child abuse is often a precursor of adult psychopathology (Figueroa et al., 1997). Danielle's mother not only failed to protect Danielle from her father but neglected to look after her daughter following her husband's death. So, Danielle not only experienced loss as a child, but also helplessness. By the time of her death, Danielle may well have reached the point of hopelessness. She expected loss and pain and believed that she was unable to do much about them.

There is evidence that hopeful people are less likely to become depressed than are those who have given up hope (Nunn, 1996). Yet, despite the addition of the hopelessness construct, the learned helplessness theory has been criticized on several grounds. Investigators have questioned its specificity—anxious people also show signs of learned helplessness—and its causal significance—does depression precede hopelessness or vice versa? (Dohr, Rush, & Bernstein, 1989; Ford & Neale, 1985). Thus, although it has generated considerable research, learned helplessness does not provide a definitive etiological explanation for mood disorders.

Interpersonal and Social Support As we have seen, loss and stressful life events, especially the deaths of loved ones, are often associated with mood disorders. The effects of stress and loss can be minimized by supportive friends and family (McLeod, Kessler, & Landis, 1992). This is why mood disorders are less likely among people who have strong social support networks (Holahan & Moos, 1991; C. A. Patten et al., 1997). For example, HIV-positive homosexual men, who are at risk for developing AIDS, are less likely to develop depression if they have strong networks of social support (Hays, Turner, & Coates, 1992). Although social support seems to help guard against depression, it is also possible that poor so-cial support is a result rather than a cause of mood disorder. People with mood disorders are not congenial companions, and they frequently lack the social skills to maintain friendships (Joiner, Alfano, & Metalsky, 1992).

Psychological Diathesis: Current Status There is at least some support for each of the psychological theories. As the psychoanalysts predict, poor family relationships are common in the childhoods of many people suffering from mood disorders (Brown & Harris, 1993; Gotlib & Hammen, 1992; Hammen et al., 1990). There is little doubt that the loss of the affection of those to whom we are attached produces feelings of inadequacy and low self-esteem. It is also clear that helplessness, hopelessness, and depression often go together. Yet, despite these often-confirmed findings, psychological theories of mood disorders are still incomplete. First, they concentrate on depression while ignoring the manic end of bipolar disorders. Second, even within depression, psychological theories leave many questions unanswered. Do faulty attributions and learned helplessness cause the sleep and appetite disturbances that often accompany mood disorders? If yes, how? If not, what causes them? How does fixation at the oral stage of development explain the cyclic nature of many bipolar mood disorders? Why don't people stay miserable all the time? Death and disappointment touch all our lives. Why doesn't everyone become depressed? The answers to these questions require a theory that tries to link psychological and biological variables.

One possible link comes from studies showing that 20% of young monkeys separated from their mothers show depressive symptoms, including agitation and despair, when later subjected to social stress (Mineka & Zinbarg, 1991; Suomi, 1991). These same monkeys also have low levels of norepinephrine and increased cortisol. Most important, these monkeys remain highly reactive to stress throughout their lives. They avoid novel situations, and they show signs of withdrawal and despair whenever they are subjected to stress. Interestingly, the monkeys' fathers show similar reactions to stress. The stress reaction of both young and old monkeys is reduced by the administration of antidepressant medication. These results suggest that some monkeys inherit a biological diathesis toward mood disorders, but these disorders only develop when they lose maternal affection early in life. It is possible that early life stress "sensitizes" their nervous systems to become highly responsive to stress.

A similar early sensitization of the nervous system may occur in human beings who inherit a diathesis to-

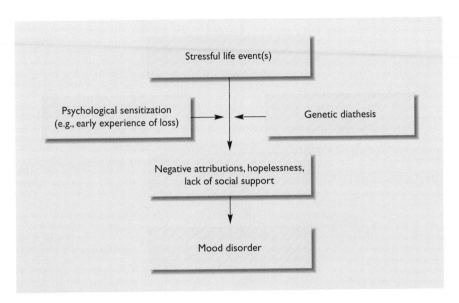

FIGURE 8.7 **Schematic Summary of Causes of Mood Disorders**

ward mood disorders and also experience rejection or loss early in life (Gotlib & Hammen, 1992). Such individuals may be especially vulnerable to mood swings when faced with stressors such as unemployment or the loss of a loved one. In an attempt to account for their moods, human sufferers construct a peculiar set of beliefs—they consider themselves to be loathsome and their futures to be hopeless. In this way, their cognitions become consistent with their mood. Note, however, that this logic can be turned around. Perhaps cognitions (worthlessness or grandiosity) come first and then cause mood changes. At present, it is not possible to be specific about the causal direction. Figure 8.7 summarizes the possible causative relationships in schematic form.

TREATMENT OF MOOD DISORDERS

In classical times, the treatment of depression was directed at the supposed excess of black bile. Bloodletting, the administration of drugs that caused vomiting and diarrhea, diets, massages, baths, and exercise were all prescribed. Even when doctors no longer believed in the four humors, diets, massages, and exercise continued to be prescribed, and they are still in use today (P. L. Cooper et al., 1997). This section describes biological treatments for both depressive and bipolar disorders, followed by a discussion of psychological and social interventions. Although it is convenient to discuss biological and social treatments separately, in practice, many people receive a combination of both.

Biological Treatments

Biological treatments cover a wide range, including electroconvulsive therapy, light treatment, sleep deprivation, and many other interventions. However, by far the most common biological treatment is the administration of mood-altering drugs.

Drug Treatment As already discussed, the treatment of depression with drugs began in the 1950s with clinical observations of the antidepressant effects of the MAO inhibitor iproniazid. Although MAO inhibitors are still available, their side effects are too serious to make them the drug of first choice. They are prescribed only for people who have failed to respond to other treatments. MAO inhibitors were first replaced by imipramine, which was originally synthesized to treat schizophrenia. It did not do much to help the symptoms of schizophrenia, but it did seem to lift people's depression. Thus, by accident rather than by design, imipramine became the first in a series of **tricyclic antidepressants.** Although these drugs work differently from MAO inhibitors, they also increase neurotransmitter levels. Specifically, they block the proteins that transport neurotransmitter residues back to synaptic terminals. This keeps the neurotransmitters from being reabsorbed, thereby increasing their level (Snyder, 1991).

Although most of the early research focused on norepinephrine, more recent drugs have targeted another neurotransmitter, serotonin. Fluoxetine (Prozac), for example, is an antidepressant drug that blocks the

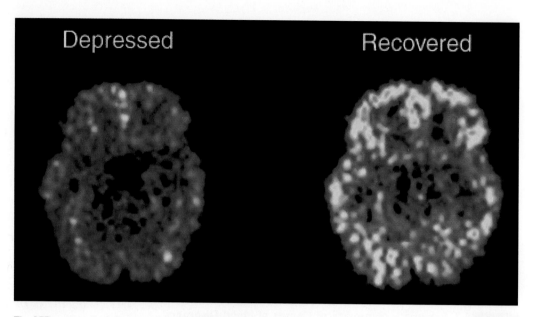

The PET scan on the left shows a depressed patient's brain; the scan on the right shows greatly increased activity in the prefrontal cortex after treatment.

reuptake of serotonin (thereby increasing serotonin levels) while leaving other neurotransmitters unaffected. Fluoxetine and related drugs are known as **selective serotonin reuptake inhibitors (SSRIs).** Despite some unwarranted claims that fluoxetine increases the probability of suicide (Mandalos & Szarek, 1990), the drug has become popular because it is not only effective against depression but also has relatively mild side effects (Strickland, 1992). These reduced side effects are especially important. It takes 2 weeks or more before any of the antidepressant drugs exert their therapeutic effect. During these 2 weeks, patients develop the side effects of the drugs but receive no benefits. Some give up the drugs in disgust. Because fluoxetine has few side effects, people are more likely to stick with it long enough to obtain the benefits. Reduced side effects also save money because drug side effects often require treatment (Hughes, Morris, & McGuire, 1997).

Most double-blind controlled studies have verified the effectiveness of modern antidepressants with adults (Anstey & Brodaty, 1995; D. N. Klein et al., 1988), although a few studies have reported little difference between antidepressants and placebos (Greenberg et al., 1992, 1994). These discrepant results may be attributable to the dependent variables used in different studies. For example, clinician ratings of drug effects are more positive than client ratings. There also appear to be marked individual differences in the response to antidepressants (Peselow et al., 1992). Autonomous people, for example,

respond better than sociotropic ones, and children may not respond at all (W. D. Ryan, 1992).

Because most depressions eventually lift whether they are treated or not, the main goal of drug treatment is to hasten recovery and prevent recurrence (Prien & Potter, 1993). The latter goal may require that patients be given "maintenance" doses of antidepressant medication for prolonged periods lasting months or even years (E. Frank et al., 1990; Kupfer et al., 1992; Stokes, 1993). After prolonged use, these medications can cause troubling withdrawal symptoms unless discontinuation is gradual (Lejoyeus & Ades, 1997; Rosenbaum & Zajecka, 1997). Remember, however, that antidepressants do not "cure" depression and that recurrences may still occur, even among those treated with maintenance doses (Greenberg et al., 1992).

As was the case with antidepressants, drug treatment for bipolar disorder was also discovered by accident. In the 1940s, John Cade (1912–1980), an Australian psychiatrist, studied people who had manic states, trying to find some biochemical cause for their behavior. One of his experiments involved injecting guinea pigs with urine samples taken from manic patients and noting whether the animals' behavior changed. Nothing happened. Cade could not find any particular ingredient that caused mania. Instead, he found that lithium urate (a salt found in everyone's urine) caused the guinea pigs to become lethargic. Since **lithium carbonate,** a naturally occurring salt, had the same effect, he concluded that it was the lithium that was calming down the animals. Lithium had been used by doctors for at least 100 years before Cade's experiments for a variety of disorders, without much evidence that it did any harm (or good, for that matter). Still, Cade played it safe and gave it to himself first. Noting no ill effects, he tried lithium out on one of his patients, with spectacular results. The patient, who Cade described as "dirty, destructive, mischievous, and interfering" and who had "enjoyed preeminent nuisance value in a back ward for years" became perfectly well. Lithium's dramatic effects are illustrated in Document 8.8, which contains nurses' observations from Bernard Louis's hospital chart.

DOCUMENT 8.8

Nurses' Notes From Bernard Louis's Hospital Chart

23 March 8:00 a.m.: Mr. Louis is in a state of manic excitement. He alternates between amiability and irritability, sometimes within a moment. He is talking incessantly and is restless, pacing the floor, unable to sit still. He commenced treatment with lithium carbonate.

25 March 10:00 p.m.: Although he is still talking rapidly, Mr. Louis has become far less irritable. He has even volunteered to assist with feeding and nursing other patients. This morning, he watched a television show for about 15 minutes, although he kept interrupting by talking out loud.

27 March 11:00 a.m.: It is clear that Mr. Louis is improving, in appearance and in behavior. He is much less distractible, he can carry on a conversation instead of a monologue, and he is getting along with all of the patients and staff.

29 March 2:00 p.m.: Mr. Louis is no longer manic. Although his mood remains good, he is behaving with decorum and seems almost serene. He has lost his pressure to keep talking, his irritability, and his need to keep moving. He seems ready for day visits home. ■

Perhaps Cade's most extraordinary discovery was that lithium was not only effective against mania, it also seemed to prevent the depressive episodes of bipolar disorder. Thus, although antidepressants helped relieve depression and strong tranquilizers calmed mania, lithium helped both conditions. Moreover, unlike imipramine or fluoxetine, lithium does not affect neurotransmitters. Instead, it seems to reduce the excitability of the nervous system.

Although Cade initially reported that bipolar disorder patients will not have a recurrent manic episode if they take lithium indefinitely, more recent studies esti-

mate the recurrence rate among treated patients to be around 40–50% (Harrow et al., 1990; R. E. Smith & Winokur, 1991). One difficulty in judging lithium's effectiveness is ensuring that people take their medication as prescribed. Some people stop taking lithium because they like the feeling of well-being and energy that accompanies a manic state (F. K. Goodwin & Jamison, 1990). Others forego lithium because of its side effects: diarrhea, stomach upset, weakness, and frequent urination. In high dosages, lithium can even be fatal. Ensuring patient compliance is especially important because discontinuing lithium actually *increases* the probability of a manic episode. In other words, discontinuing lithium may be worse than never taking it in the first place (Suppes et al., 1991).

Cade's discovery was very important, but lithium is not the final treatment for bipolar disorder. Other pharmaceuticals have been tried. These include anticonvulsant medications normally used to treat epileptic seizures (Small et al., 1991). The rationale for using anticonvulsives in people with bipolar disorder is that these medicines reduce the excitability of neurons, therefore making people less prone to wide mood swings (Gitlin, 1990; Post, 1992). Thus far, no alternative treatment has been found more effective than lithium.

Electroconvulsive Therapy Electroconvulsive therapy was first introduced in the 1930s. Like many drug treatments, it also had its origins in an accident. A Viennese doctor named Manfred Sakel noted that a patient who had accidentally been put in a coma by an overdose of insulin became less anxious and depressed. Sakel began to experiment with "insulin shock" treatment and reported that it had therapeutic effects on a variety of mental disorders. Because it was difficult to determine the exact amount of insulin required to produce a seizure without inflicting serious harm or even killing the patient, clinicians experimented with "safer" methods to induce seizures.

One of the first clinicians to use electric shock for this purpose was the Italian psychiatrist Ugo Cerletti (1877–1963). In 1938, Cerletti applied electrodes (flat metal disks) to the head of a man found confused and hallucinating on a railway station platform. He applied a current through these electrodes that rendered the man unconscious. After 11 such treatments, the man was well enough to return home. Cerletti later reported success in treating depression, and many other conditions, with his **electroconvulsive therapy** (now called **ECT**). Cerletti theorized that ECT produces special brain chemicals called aeroagomines, which act like drugs to cure mental

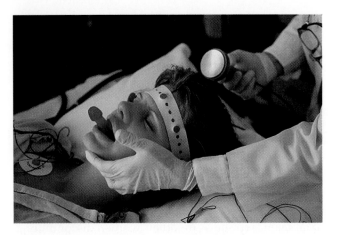

Today, precautions are taken to ensure that patients are not harmed by the seizures that accompany electroconvulsive therapy.

disorders. Toward the end of his career, Cerletti began giving ECT to animals and extracting what he believed to be an antipsychotic serum from their brains. He advocated injecting this serum into patients because he believed this to be safer than ECT, which, in Cerletti's time, was administered without anesthesia or muscle relaxants. Patients who made violent movements during seizures often wound up with fractures. Some patients sustained permanent brain damage. Because of these dangers and because no one believed Cerletti's ideas about aeroagomines anyway, ECT fell out of use in the 1950s. However, by the 1970s, ECT began to make a comeback. Today, ECT is used for depressed people who do not respond to drugs or psychological therapy.

In contrast to previous practice, today's ECT patients are given a general anesthetic so they are not conscious during the procedure. They also receive drugs that inhibit body movements. Electrodes are then placed on the head, usually on the right side only. Because the left side of the brain normally contains the speech centers, applying shock only to the right minimizes any disruption in communicative ability (Abrams, Swartz, & Vedak, 1991). Once the electrodes are in place, a current is passed through the head for about half a second. The patient's response is a convulsion (seizure) that lasts for around a minute, followed by a coma that lasts from a few minutes to half an hour.

ECT can bring a rapid clearing of a depression without the need to wait the weeks that are required with drugs or psychotherapy (R. D. Weiner & Coffey, 1988). Indeed, a single treatment may have strong effects, and five or six may bring the patient to a normal mood state (Klerman, 1988). Suicidal thoughts usually disappear at

the same time, so ECT can be lifesaving. However, ECT may have side effects. One of these is memory loss, especially for events just before the seizure. Modern practice is to minimize the number of treatments so that memory loss is not extensive and new learning is unaffected. More serious side effects are rare (Goldman, 1988), but they can occur. For this reason, ECT is generally reserved for people who do not respond to other forms of interventions. Adolescents and children are rarely treated with ECT, although results with younger age groups seem similar to those achieved with adults (Rey & Walter, 1997; Walter & Rey, 1997).

Theorists have suggested that ECT works by increasing neurotransmitter levels in the brain. Although this hypothesis is consistent with the drug research reviewed earlier, there is no direct evidence that ECT works this way. Without such evidence, the hypothesis is essentially identical to Cerletti's theory that ECT produces aeroagomines. The truth is that after almost 60 years of its use, we still have no theory to explain the therapeutic effects of ECT. The lack of a theory about how ECT works, coupled with reports of serious side effects, even death, have made ECT controversial. In the United States, this controversy has led to legal challenges. Spurred on by books and movies, such as *One Flew Over the Cuckoo's Nest,* that portray ECT as barbarous and by groups such as the Scientologists, who take a dim view of psychiatry in general, and ECT in particular, there have been many attempts to restrict the use of ECT or to ban it completely. Much of this effort has been directed against the use of ECT on people who are unable to give permission (such as elderly patients who are no longer capable of managing their own affairs). In such cases, guardians normally act on behalf of the person. However, courts have been inconsistent in determining whether guardians have the right to authorize ECT (*Austwick v. Legal Advocacy Service,* Ill. App. Ct., 9/7/95; *Guardianship of Ruth E.J. v. Ruth E.J.,* Wis. Ct. App., 9/6/95). Given the depth of feeling among its opponents, ECT seems destined to remain mired in legal and professional controversy for some time to come.

Light Treatment and Sleep Deprivation   For hundreds of years, clinicians have prescribed a trip to a sunny climate as the best cure for the winter blues. Light treatment provides similar benefits, but without the travel. People with seasonal affective disorder are exposed to a few hours of bright light every morning (Dalgleish et al., 1996). The light is designed to mimic the spectrum of sunlight. Efficacy data are not yet available, although there are positive clinical reports (Beauchemin & Hays, 1997). It is possible that people who improve with such treatment may indeed have had an excess of melatonin production. In any event, side effects are rare, although exposure to light may cause eyestrain and headache (Levitt et al., 1993).

Sleep deprivation, in which depressed patients are awakened whenever they enter REM sleep, has been reported to produce an improvement in about one half of treated depressed patients (Wu & Bunney, 1990). However, these positive effects are temporary. Most people relapse after a night's sleep. Some clinicians have claimed that combining sleep deprivation with light treatment produces a better effect than does sleep deprivation alone (Levitt et al., 1996).

Psychological Treatments

Medications, light, and ECT are aimed at alleviating the symptoms of depression. They do not teach people prone to depression how to cope with the loss of a loved one, unemployment, or any of the other triggers of depression. Psychological treatment, on the other hand, is designed to help people learn more effective ways of behaving. (Psychological treatments may be the *only* treatment for people who cannot take drugs or undergo ECT—pregnant women, for example.) Most psychological treatments have focused on depression rather than bipolar disorder (other than those that try to devise ways of making sure that people with bipolar disorder take their lithium).

Psychoanalytic and Interpersonal Treatment   Psychoanalytic treatment is designed to help patients achieve insight into the repressed conflicts that are presumed to be responsible for their mood disorder. Most often, these conflicts involve the loss of a loved one, accompanied by guilt and self-blame. Once the therapist has helped the person to recognize the conflict, the therapist encourages the person to release the inwardly directed hostility and, through this catharsis, eliminate their inner-directed anger.

Modern forms of therapy, such as **interpersonal therapy (IPT)** (Klerman, 1988), take a different approach. For example, IPT aims to help clients examine the ways in which their present social behavior keeps them from forming satisfactory interpersonal relationships (Burns, Sayers, & Moras, 1994). Instead of focusing on the past, IPT is concerned with the present, especially problems in adjusting to grief; fights with friends,

coworkers, and relatives; role transitions (new job, divorce); and social deficits (such as a difficulty in acquiring new relationships). In addition to gaining insight, clients are taught assertiveness and communication skills as well as other ways of improving their ability to form supportive relationships. IPT and some related forms of family therapy may also be effective in treating the bipolar disorders (Emanuels & Emmelkamp, 1997).

Cognitive-Behavioral Treatment   As its name suggests, cognitive-behavioral treatment combines cognitive and behavioral interventions. The cognitive component involves teaching clients to identify self-critical and negative thoughts, to note the connection between such thoughts and depression, and to challenge negative thoughts to see if they are supportable. If they are not, the client is taught to replace them with more realistic evaluations of present and future circumstances. An example, taken from Danielle's interview with Dr. Berg, appears in Document 8.9. Notice how Dr. Berg identifies and challenges Danielle's negative cognitions and how he attempts to replace them with more realistic, and more positive, ones. He does this by getting Danielle to examine her thoughts for errors (to "test her hypotheses") and to look at her failures in new ways (to make new attributions). Finally, Dr. Berg urges Danielle to focus on her successes and areas in which she agrees that she has succeeded.

DOCUMENT 8.9

Excerpt From Interview Between Dr. Berg and Danielle Wood Following Danielle's First Suicide Attempt

DR. BERG: Why do you say you're a failure?

DANIELLE: I lost the swim meet. Everyone was counting on me.

DR. BERG: But why does this mean that you are a failure?

DANIELLE: I'm not going to the Olympics, am I? I never get anything I want.

DR. BERG: Why do you think that you will never succeed at anything?

DANIELLE: I just won't.

DR. BERG: But why do you think so? What is the evidence that you will never succeed at anything? How many swimming competitions have you won?

DANIELLE: Lots.

DR. BERG: How many have you lost?

DANIELLE: Hardly any, but this was an important one.

DR. BERG: I appreciate that, but the truth of the matter is that you are really more of a winner than a loser, aren't you?

DANIELLE: Well, I have won, but not when it counted.

DR. BERG: Were there special circumstances surrounding the swimming meet? Were you ill or tired? Could you have trained harder?

DANIELLE: I was tired. I think I may have overtrained.

DR. BERG: Perhaps you will do better next time.

DANIELLE: I don't think there will be a next time.

DR. BERG: Why? Is this really your last chance for success? Does losing a swimming match really mean that you will never succeed at anything? How about your university studies? You have succeeded there.

DANIELLE: Well, yes, I guess so. ■

Outside of clinical sessions, some clients find that reading, videos, and self-help materials can help them understand and control their depression (P. Robinson et al., 1997; N. M. Smith et al., 1997). Clients are also urged to probe their negative thoughts when they are outside of therapy in the same way that Dr. Berg probed Danielle's. The idea is to get the client to be more reflective and to learn to substitute logical and positive interpretations for the illogical and negative ones that they habitually produce. In some versions of cognitive-behavioral therapy, clients are also taught problem-solving techniques (Nezu, Nezu, & Perri, 1989). Their purpose is to teach clients how to handle life's inevitable vicissitudes, rather than to react with passivity and depression. Children may especially benefit from a cognitive approach, especially if it teaches them to solve problems before they develop into major disorders (Munoz, 1993; Rudolph, Hammen, & Burge, 1997). In addition to changing thoughts and teaching problem-solving skills, cognitive-behavioral therapists encourage clients to engage in pleasant activities. Social skills training may be helpful in getting clients to interact more with other people and thereby gain additional sources of reinforcement (Hersen et al., 1984). Although most of the literature has concentrated on depression, there is some evidence that cognitive-behavioral therapy may also be useful in treating bipolar disorder (Chor, Mercier, & Halper, 1988).

Drugs Versus Psychological Treatment

One of the first studies to compare psychological with drug treatments for mood disorder was conducted by Rush and his colleagues (1977). They found that cognitive-behavioral therapy was superior to imipramine in the treatment of depression. This study stimulated a series of similar comparative trials, all of which showed cognitive-behavioral therapy to be at least as efficacious as imipramine (see Hollon et al., 1992, for example). Perhaps the most sophisticated of these comparisons was the National Institute of Mental Health Collaborative Research Project (Elkin et al., 1985), which added a placebo group to the comparisons (subjects in this placebo condition received an inert pill and were seen by a clinician, but no formal psychological treatment was administered).

Despite increasing methodological sophistication, there are significant methodological problems with just about all comparative studies (Lipman & Kendall, 1992). For example, few studies have monitored compliance with the drug regimen. Therefore, we cannot be sure that subjects in the drug condition were taking the drugs as prescribed. Remember, many people fail to take antidepressants because of their side effects. Also, because so many different factors can affect therapy outcome, a single study is rarely definitive. It is often necessary to combine the results of many different studies to get the full picture (see Critical Thinking About Clinical Decisions 8.2).

Several studies found that cognitive-behavioral treatment and interpersonal treatment reduce the probability of a relapse (Hollon et al., 1992; Hollon, Shelton, & Davis, 1993; Lewinsohn et al., 1990). Combining psychological treatments with antidepressant medication seems to produce a greater prevention effect than use of either treatment alone (M. D. Evans et al., 1992; Gotlib & Hammen, 1992). One reason for this is that people in psychotherapy are more likely to take their drugs regularly (Paykel, 1995). However, the research results are somewhat equivocal. Some studies report no extra benefit from combining drugs with psychological treatment (Hollon, Shelton, & Loosen, 1991). It is possible, of course, that some people may benefit more from drugs, whereas others benefit more from psychological treatment. Even among psychological treatments, some people may benefit more from cognitive therapy, whereas others may require intensive training in social and communication skills (Haaga & Davison, 1989). Careful clinicians always try to tailor their interventions to a client's individual needs. For example, Dr. Kahn used Danielle Wood's interest in exercise to devise a treatment plan to help Danielle after her suicide attempt. (Document 8.10).

Meta-Analysis: Getting the Total Picture

Treatment outcome studies are among the most difficult to conduct of all psychological experiments. Choosing an appropriate dependent measure, selecting treatment and control groups, standardizing treatments, and ensuring that experimenters and subjects are unaware of their status (keeping them "blind") are just a few of the problems facing treatment outcome researchers. Because so many different factors can affect treatment outcome, it is rare for a single study to yield definitive results. Instead, to judge the effectiveness of a treatment, we must somehow synthesize the results of many different studies. **Meta-analysis** is a set of techniques designed to find, appraise, and combine data across disparate studies.

A meta-analysis begins with a search for all relevant studies. This is generally done by using computerized databases such as PsycINFO and Medline. For example, a researcher may search these databases for all studies dealing with the effect of psychological treatment on depression. But this is only the beginning. Because researchers tend to publish only their positive findings, restricting a meta-analysis to published studies results in a biased (overly positive) picture of treatment effectiveness. It is important, therefore, for researchers to also obtain the results of unpublished studies and conference reports, which are more likely than published articles to contain negative results. Foreign language studies may also yield important data. Not all research in abnormal psychology is published in English.

After gathering the relevant studies, the researchers must then assess their relative value. This means examining their research methodology. For example, in treatment outcome studies, participants must be randomly assigned to treatment and control groups, and they must be comparable at the outset. Otherwise, one treatment may appear better than another purely because it is being applied to less seriously disturbed participants.

It is also important that whoever judges whether a treatment is successful is unaware of which participants are controls and which are in the treatment group. Experimenters who both administer a treatment and also judge the treatment's success may be biased toward positive outcomes. Where possible, participants should also be blind to whether they are in the treatment or the control group. In practice, this is difficult to ensure because people can often guess whether they are receiving an active medication. Sometimes, they notice the side effects; at other times, the effects of the drugs on mood are so profound they cannot be missed (Bystritsky & Waikar, 1994; Greenberg et al., 1994).

Even if the criteria mentioned so far are all met, studies may still yield ambiguous results depending on the dependent variable used to measure outcome. We know, for example, that therapists' ratings of outcome often differ from participants' ratings (Greenberg et al., 1992). To get around this problem, psychotherapy studies use multiple outcome measures (therapist and client ratings, checklists, and so on). This leaves the researcher with a problem. What if a treatment produces an improvement on one measure but not another? Which is the more valid? Answering this question is just as difficult as deciding what to measure in the first place.

Another important criterion for judging outcome studies is whether people who withdrew from the study were included in the analysis. Including all participants in the data analysis is known as an "intention to treat" analysis because the experimenters originally intended to treat everyone in the study. Studies that ignore dropouts will almost always produce misleading results.

The importance of analyzing all data is illustrated in the table, which summarizes a study by Hollon and his colleagues (1992). Their study compared antidepressant medication, cognitive treatment, and a combination of both. The first row of the table gives the results only for participants who completed the study; the second row of the table includes all participants. Notice the change in the apparent outcome. When all participants are included, all of the treatments appear less effective, and the difference between the worst and best treatments is substantially reduced.

It is important to keep in mind that even the best-designed outcome study may not predict how successful a treatment will be in routine clinical use. This is why researchers distinguish between treatment efficacy and treatment effectiveness. **Efficacy** is measured under ideal conditions—in double-blind, controlled studies in which subjects are carefully chosen, treatments are administered in a standardized fashion by experienced therapists, and compliance is monitored. **Effectiveness,** on the other hand, is measured in the "real world," where clients cannot be selected to fit certain profiles and where compliance cannot be guaranteed. For these reasons, a treatment's effectiveness is always lower than its efficacy.

Treatment Outcomes: Completers Only Versus "Intention to Treat"

Type of analysis	Percentage improved		
	Drug treatment	Cognitive treatment	Combined treatment
Completers only	56	62	69
Intention to treat	40	44	48

Note: From a study by Hollon et al. (1992).

DOCUMENT 8.10

Dr. Kahn's Treatment
Plan for Danielle
Wood

UNIVERSITY HOSPITAL

Treatment Plan

Doctor: Dr. S. Kahn

Patient: Danielle Wood

Goal: Improve depression and teach Danielle the coping skills necessary to help prevent relapse

1. Antidepressant regime: Prozac dosage will be adjusted based on Danielle's response over the next 4 weeks. Danielle will also be given Valium to be used as needed for anxiety.
2. Exercise: Danielle's self-esteem is largely tied up with her swimming. In recent weeks, she has neglected training. Getting back into an exercise routine will not only help build her self-esteem, it will also have the effect of keeping her active, an important part of combating depression.
3. Social support: Danielle will be enrolled in a self-help support group led by Dr. Stuart Berg. The group meets weekly to share their experiences of coping with depression. This will also allow Danielle to hear from others. It is important that she does not simply dwell on herself.
4. Cognitive-behavioral therapy: Danielle will receive cognitive-behavioral therapy from Dr. Berg. He will focus on the following:
   A. Replacing negative self-attributions with positive ones. The focus will be on Danielle's attributions of failure in sports and relationships. A more positive future focus will be developed. At the same time, her guilt needs to be addressed and reduced.
   B. Relaxation training to help Danielle deal with the anxiety of competition.
   C. Danielle will be asked to sign a "contract" indicating that she will not attempt to harm herself while in treatment and will always contact me or Dr. Berg whenever suicidal thoughts enter her mind.

Undertreatment

Epidemiological studies provide overwhelming evidence that mood disorders, especially unipolar depressive disorders, are seriously undertreated (Hirschfield et al., 1997). Some people do not seek help because they fail to recognize the signs of depression, others fear the stigma of "mental illness," and still others cannot afford treatment costs. Medical professionals also contribute to undertreatment. Many medical practitioners are poorly informed about mood disorders and the benefits of treatment (Shao et al., 1997). The damage to the individuals concerned, and to society as a whole, is significant. Individual suffering, reduced work productivity,

marital discord, and many other problems can be traced to untreated mood disorders. The worst outcome of an untreated mood disorder is a despair that becomes so extreme that the person takes his or her own life. However, as discussed next, mood disorders are not the only cause of suicide.

SUICIDE

Suicide is not a mental disorder; it does not appear in the *DSM-IV*, nor does it have a specific treatment. In some times and places, suicide has even been socially

Suicide Myths and Reality

Over the centuries, a folklore has developed around suicide. Some of the more prevalent myths, and the corresponding realities, are summarized here.

Suicide Myth	Suicide Reality
Those who talk about suicide never do it.	The vast majority of suicides give some warning.
Suicide is related to social class.	People of all social and educational classes commit suicide. Highly educated people, such as doctors, have among the highest suicide rates (North & Ryall, 1997).
Everyone who commits suicide is depressed.	Many people who commit suicide are not depressed. Indeed, suicides are most likely to occur just when it appears that a person has recovered from depression.
Suicide is influenced by weather ("the suicide season").	Suicides can occur at any time of year.
Suicidal people always want to die.	Most suicides are not sure they want to die. Many gamble with their lives, hoping that others will save them.
Only insane people contemplate suicide.	Suicidal thoughts are common in the normal population. Among the terminally ill, suicide may be a rational act.
Once people try suicide, they remain forever suspect.	Most people attempt suicide only once.
Those who unsuccessfully attempt suicide were never serious.	Some people are poorly informed about the lethality of different acts.

acceptable. The 17th-century Japanese feudal code of Bushido considered failure to one's lord a disgrace that could only be expiated by taking one's life. An echo of this ancient code was heard in the cries of Japanese kamikaze pilots who flew suicide missions in World War II for the honor of their emperor. Indian widows who immolated themselves on their husbands' funeral pyres were also behaving in socially acceptable ways. In contrast, Christian, Jewish, and Muslim societies have traditionally abhorred suicide. At one time, Christians who took their own lives were buried at crossroads with a stake through their hearts. Even today, when our social views are more tolerant, suicide is still considered a social disgrace.

Suicide is the end result of the complex interaction of social, psychological, and biological forces, and **suicidology** (the study of suicide) has become a scientific field in its own right (Leenaars, 1993). Still, many people who take their own lives do suffer from a mental disorder (Caldwell & Gottesman, 1992). Because suicide is frequently associated with depression, it has been included in this chapter.

Suicide: What Is It, and How Is It Studied?

Because of the shame and dishonor associated with taking one's own life, suicide has traditionally been a taboo topic, not discussed in polite company. As a consequence, a folklore has developed about why and how people commit suicide—a folklore whose beliefs are often incorrect (Highlight 8.1). Over the past 30 years, our knowledge about suicide has increased dramatically. Death and dying are now discussed openly, and a careful research literature has accumulated. This literature has shown that the motive for committing suicide varies from person to person (Maris, 1992). Some suicides are attempts to extract retribution or obtain martyrdom, others are a way to end a life of intolerable pain, and still others are the result of risk taking or "playing with death." Despite these varying motivations, there are certain commonalities among people who display suicidal behavior (Shneidman, 1992): They are seeking a solution to a problem, they wish to end consciousness, they have either psychological or physical pain (or both), they have frustrated psychological needs, they feel hopeless, they cannot see alternatives, and they are "escapers" rather than problem solvers. Although we think of suicide as the sole act of a person in despair, increasingly suicides involve more than one person (Jamison, 1997). Physician-assisted suicide was discussed in Chapter 1. Husbands have also been known to help terminate the lives of their chronically ill wives—although wives rarely help to kill their husbands (M. Rosenbaum, 1990).

It can be difficult to judge whether a death was caused by suicide. Some automobile-related deaths are intentional suicides, whereas others are the result of thrill seeking ("playing chicken"), where death was not the intention. Telling these deaths apart is not easy. Sometimes, a **psychological autopsy** consisting of interviews with a victim's friends and relatives may reveal the truth, but such after-the-fact reconstructions are notoriously difficult to conduct (D. C. Clark & Horton-Deutsch, 1992). Families may try to cover up the facts, and official records are rarely accurate. Determining the cause of death is easier if the deceased leaves a note, but suicide notes are not always informative (S. T. Black & Lester, 1995; Leenaars, 1996), and only 15% of suicide victims actually leave a note (Leenaars, 1992; O'Donnell, Farmer, & Catalan, 1993). Without a note, the psychological autopsy must rely on circumstantial evidence: Did the person put considerable care into planning the act? Did the person give away favorite possessions? Was the method of death guaranteed to be lethal (guns rather than pills, for example)? Sometimes, as in Danielle's case, it is impossible to decide whether a death was intentional. Even with the evidence of her diary, it is still possible that Danielle did not really intend to kill herself. She may have merely been trying to punish Luke or to call attention to her unhappiness.

Prevalence and Incidence

Suicide is universal and has occurred throughout history. It is among the top 10 causes of death in the industrialized world and a common cause of death among young people (Ryland & Kruesi, 1992). Although suicide occurs everywhere, cross-cultural comparisons are difficult because cultures treat suicide in different ways.

The suicide of a celebrity, such as Michael Hutchence of INXS, sometimes triggers other suicides.

Catholic, Muslim, and Jewish cultures tend to underreport cases because they consider suicide sinful. In other countries, ritual suicides, such as suttee (in which Indian widows toss themselves onto their husbands' funeral pyre), may go unreported because they are no longer officially sanctioned. In all countries, social attitudes have an important effect on suicide rates. Japan, which still unofficially accepts suicide as a way to make up for dishonor, has a higher suicide rate than China, where suicide is stigmatized (Group for the Advancement of Psychiatry, 1989).

Suicide Rates The reported suicide rate in the United States is 30,000 per year (one death every half hour or so); the actual number is probably higher. Many suicides go unreported because of the ambiguity surrounding the death or because they are covered up by families trying to avoid social stigma (Bongar, 1991). Although suicide rates do not vary much from year to year, they may be affected by short-term external factors. For example, when a celebrity commits suicide, clusters of similar suicides almost always occur (M. Gould et al., 1990). This macabre form of imitation may play a particularly strong role in many adolescent suicides (Berman & Jobes, 1991; Hazell, 1993). Highlight 8.2 looks at some possible causes of adolescent suicide clusters.

Adolescent Suicide Clusters

On the first Monday in February, 16-year-old Michele Money died after taking an overdose of pills. The next day, 15-year-old Mark Walpus died of a self-inflicted gunshot wound. On Friday, Tom Wacha, an 18-year-old senior, shot himself. Within 5 days, three students at Bryan High School in Omaha had committed suicide while two other students had made failed suicide attempts. Similar clusters have been reported before. For example, within 2 months, nine young members of the Shoshone tribe of Wyoming hanged themselves. In a 24-month period, 14 teenagers took their own lives in Cobb County, Georgia; most used guns or hanged themselves.

What causes these suicide clusters? There are many hypotheses, but few hard facts. The Bryan High School suicide victims knew one another, but not well. Two were from broken homes and one had recently argued with a family member about an automobile accident. But these are hardly rare events. Why did they lead to premature death? Why all in one week? There are no easy answers to these questions; many factors are at work. But one important element is the unintended effects of "glamorizing" suicide.

Schools often respond to suicide deaths with memorial services. The victims are given substantial attention, and their deaths become occasions for public grief. The publicity may stimulate other vulnerable and despondent youths to try suicide themselves. On the other hand, keeping suicides quiet does not necessarily prevent future deaths. Suicide prevention programs depend on open public discussion. Clearly, there is a balancing act required between educating the public about suicide and making sure that the publicity does not stimulate more suicides (H. Jackson, Hess, & van-Dalen, 1995). What is required is a suicide education program that avoids glamorizing victims and thereby encouraging vulnerable people to imitate their tragic behavior. Although there is little chance of getting the media to keep suicides quiet (especially famous suicides), it would be helpful if both the media and educational programs portrayed these deaths as pathetic and preventable events. In all cases, the methods used by victims to take their own lives should not be described in any detail, and all media stories and educational materials should include crisis-line telephone numbers for troubled people to call.

Age, Sex, and Ethnic Differences Although suicide is a relatively more common cause of death among young people than among older ones (because young people are less likely to die from disease), suicide is not uncommon among older persons (Figure 8.8). It is particularly prevalent among White males over the age of 65 (McIntosh, 1992; Wallace & O'Hara, 1992). Divorced, widowed, and other single people have higher suicide rates than married people (Figure 8.9). Contrary to what you might expect, only a small number of suicides involve a terminal illness (Clark & Fawcett, 1992). In all instances, more men than women take their own lives (Figure 8.8). One explanation for this sex difference is that women tend to have supportive social relationships. They may reject suicide as an option because their friends and children need and depend on them. We certainly know that the more children a woman has, the less likely she is to commit suicide (Hoyer & Lund, 1993). Men, on the other hand, tend to become socially isolated. This is especially true for elderly men. Retirement leaves them with little to do, no one to live for, and considerable time to dwell on death. Some find it difficult to live alone and to depend on their own resources (Zauszniewski, 1997). The sex difference in suicide rates may also reflect greater alcohol abuse among men. Alcohol, which reduces inhibitions and worsens a depressed mood, is a frequent ingredient in suicide (Rivara et al., 1997).

Although these various explanations for sex differences are all plausible, it is also possible that the differences may be artifactual—the result of different suicide methods. Females who try to kill themselves do not succeed as often as men because females tend to use less lethal means, such as pills, whereas men use guns (Group for the Advancement of Psychiatry, 1989). With the ever-increasing availability of guns, we might expect an increase in successful female suicides. There are alarming signs pointing in that direction (J. R. Rogers, 1990).

In the United States, suicide rates are highest for Native Americans and Whites, and many of these deaths are alcohol related (Clarke, Frankish, & Green, 1997; National Center for Health Statistics, 1992). Suicide rates are lowest for African Americans and people of Asian descent, including Japanese Americans (National Center for Health Statistics, 1992). The Japanese

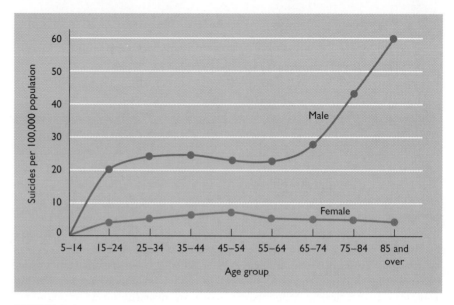

FIGURE 8.8 **Suicide Rate by Age and Gender.** Data from: Pamuk et al. (1998, Table 48).

American figures are interesting because the Japanese have a high suicide rate in their own country. This difference between expatriate and native Japanese illustrates the importance of culture in determining suicidal behavior. Japanese immigrants behave more like other Americans and less like native Japanese.

Despite cultural differences in the rate of suicide, the circumstances of people who take their own lives is remarkably similar across cultures. Suicides are most common among people whose families have been affected by death or divorce, who have unhappy love affairs, who suffer serious illness, or who experience severe economic setbacks.

Although suicide figures have been fairly stable for many years, there are some disturbing trends. For example, the suicide rate among young male African Americans has tripled in the past 30 years (Berman & Jobes, 1991). This increase has been attributed to powerlessness and alienation among an oppressed minority. Yet African American women have not shown a similar increase in suicide over the same period, and more African Americans than ever occupy managerial and professional positions. It seems almost as if suicide is one price African American men are paying for assimilation into middle-class American society.

Another disturbing trend is the dramatic increase in suicidal behavior among young homosexual males, who often lack adequate social support (Bagley & Tremblay, 1997), and successful suicides among young people in general. The suicide rate among adolescents has quadrupled in the past 50 years (Garland & Zigler, 1993;

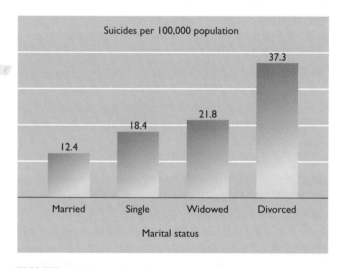

FIGURE 8.9 **Suicide Rate by Marital Status.** Data from: McIntosh (1991, p. 64).

National Center for Health Statistics, 1992; C. Peterson et al., 1993). Rates are rising most rapidly among White males between the ages of 15 and 20, although the incidence in other groups has increased as well (Berman & Jobes, 1991). Perhaps even more frightening are studies showing that large numbers of young people contemplate suicide at some time. A national survey of students in grades 9–12 found that 27% had thought about suicide in the preceding year and 8% had made a suicide attempt (Centers for Disease Control, 1991; see also Freiberg, 1991). Although many suicidal adolescents are clinically depressed (Pfeffer et al., 1993), a substantial number suffer from other disorders, and many have a

TABLE 8.7	Suicide Attempters Versus Suicide Completers	
Characteristic	**Attempters**	**Completers**
Sex	Female	Male
Age	Under 35	Over 60
Means	Low lethality (pills)	High lethality (firearms)
Diagnosis	None or rare	Depression; substance abuse
Setting	Public, easy to discover	Private and isolated

tendency toward impulsiveness (Lewinsohn, Rohde, & Seeley, 1993).

College students are particularly at risk (Hawton et al., 1995; Hays, Cheever, & Patel, 1996). They commit suicide at a rate twice as high as that of the noncollege population. In fact, suicide is second only to accidents as a cause of death among college students (Summerville et al., 1992). The highest risk is among male graduate students. The worst time is at the beginning of a semester, and the most common place is in a campus residence (as in Danielle's case). Because most suicides occur early in the semester, they are not generally a response to examination anxiety. Besides, most college-student suicides have average or even above-average grades. Despite their high grades, it is possible that suicidal students hold themselves to much higher standards than those to which most other students hold themselves and punish themselves when they fail to meet those standards (as in Danielle's despair over not making the Olympic team). Foreign students who come from cultures that put a high value on success may be especially at risk for suicide if their performance fails to meet the high expectations held for them (Sue & Sue, 1990). Like suicidal adolescents, suicidal college students also frequently suffer from a psychological disorder (Pfeffer et al., 1993).

Suicide is rare among children under 14, but it still occurs. When it does, parents often report that they were unaware that their children, especially their young children, were unhappy (Walker, Moreau, & Weissman, 1990). In some of these sad cases, children successfully hid their feelings from their parents. This is not surprising because troubled children may express their problems in disguised ways. In a particularly poignant example, Sokol and Pfeffer (1992) describe a suicidal 5-year-old engaging in fantasy play. The child described a mother and a father dog who fought over their puppy. Finally, the puppy kills itself, and, at the funeral, the mother and father dogs kiss and make up.

We know relatively little about suicide attempters because most do not seek help (Meehan et al., 1992).

From what little we do know, it appears that the typical suicide attempter is a teenage girl who ingests pills. This contrasts with the typical successful suicide—a male adult who shoots himself. Among teenagers it is estimated that there are 200 attempts for every successful suicide (Summerville et al., 1992). The equivalent ratio among adults is 4 attempts per successful suicide (McIntosh, 1992). This difference may mean that adults are more determined to die or that, because many adult suicides live alone, they are less likely to be rescued. Despite the differences between successful suicides and attempters, it is wrong to think of suicide attempters as a completely separate group from successful suicides (Lewinsohn, Rohde, & Seeley, 1993). By definition, attempters do not wind up killing themselves, but some attempters keep trying until they do (D. C. Clark & Fawcett, 1992; Maris et al., 1992; Meehan et al., 1992). The known differences between suicide attempters and completers are summarized in Table 8.7.

Causes

Because suicidal people are usually examined only after they have made a suicide attempt, the only way to study their behavior is retrospectively using a psychological autopsy. The usual sources of information are friends, crisis-line calls, interviews with relatives, diaries, and a suicide note left behind by the victim. Because most of this information is gathered after the fact, we can never be sure that it is not biased. Nevertheless, these data form the basis for most of the etiological theories discussed in this section.

Psychological Disorders and Suicide   A psychological disorder, usually a bipolar disorder or a major depression, appears in the history of many cases of suicide (D. C. Clark & Fawcett, 1992; Garland & Zigler, 1993; Shneidman, 1992). Interestingly, people rarely attempt suicide while in the depths of depression. The year following a major depressive episode is the most dangerous period (Klerman, 1982), perhaps because the person

Anomic Suicide: Australian Aboriginal Deaths in Custody

In the 1980s, 99 Australian Aboriginal people died, mainly of hanging, while in the custody of prison, police, or juvenile detention institutions. Ninety percent were males. Their median age was 29. A Royal Commission of investigation was established in response to public concern that these deaths were too frequent to discount the possibility of foul play. It is an appalling commentary on the life of Aboriginal people that so many believed it possible that these people were murdered by government officials.

To understand the circumstances of these deaths in custody, commissioners tried to piece together the lives of the individuals using official files and the testimony of friends and relatives. Slowly a picture emerged. Many victims were raised in foster or adopted homes and denied contact with their natural families. Some were given up for adoption voluntarily, but, in many cases, they were forcibly removed from their parents to be brought up in White society. Schooling was patchy. Many of the victims were de-

Disintegration of native cultures, such as that of the Aborigines in Australia or Native Americans in North America, often leads to despair and high rates of substance abuse and suicide. This group of Aborigines in a church-sponsored shelter are trying to overcome their addiction to wood alcohol.

scribed in school records as truant, intractable, and unteachable. Practically all of the victims had a history of legal troubles beginning in their teenage years. Their health ranged from poor to very

bad, and their medical records were full of dismissive entries ("drunk again"). Of the 99 victims, 83 were unemployed, and the others held only marginal jobs. Alcohol played a role in most of the deaths. For example, of the 22 deaths by hanging in police cells, 19 had dangerously high levels of blood alcohol.

The Royal Commission eventually concluded that all of the deaths were either suicides or the result of natural causes. The reason for these suicides was what Durkheim called anomie—the disintegration of native culture, bringing with it alienation, poverty, and substance abuse. The reason death occurred frequently in custody was because Aboriginal people spend considerable time in custody. This tragic story is not specific to Australia. Indigenous people in other countries (such as Native Americans) have similar histories and problems. Their plight will change only when we work out ways to find them a place, as a distinct people, within our society.

---

is still unhappy but now has the energy required to carry out self-destructive intentions.

Alcohol Abuse   Although it would be tempting to conclude that psychological disorders cause suicide, it should be kept in mind that most people with mood disorders do not kill themselves. Other factors must be present as well. Alcohol consumption has already been mentioned (Rivara et al., 1997). The presence of a psychological disorder, such as depression, combined with the poor judgment and reduced inhibition produced by alcohol create a lethal combination (D. C. Clark & Fawcett, 1992; G. E. Murphy et al., 1992; J. R. Rogers, 1992).

Sociocultural Factors   Émile Durkheim (1897–1951), a French sociologist, pioneered the sociocultural ap-

proach to suicide early in the 20th century. Durkheim classified suicides into three main categories. "Egoistic" suicide is the result of a failure to maintain social ties. Divorce, death, and social isolation all contribute to egoistic suicide. "Altruistic" suicide occurs when a person gives up his or her life for the greater community (as in the Japanese kamikaze pilots of World War II). Durkheim's third category, "anomic" suicide, refers to suicides that result from rapid social change, such as the destruction of native cultures by colonization and the accompanying social disintegration, substance abuse, and despair. Highlight 8.3 provides a tragic example of this type of suicide.

Although Durkheim believed that he was creating an explanatory theory of suicide, his categories are mainly descriptive, and his explanations are little more than correlations. Correlations alone cannot disentangle cause from effect because it is always possible for them to be reversed. For example, some people may lose their jobs because a mood disorder causes their work to suffer. If such people commit suicide, we cannot say that unemployment was the cause; it could just as well have been the mood disorder. In any event, Durkheim's theory makes no attempt to explain why most people—even downtrodden people who lose their jobs, their fortunes, and their spouses—do not kill themselves. To understand why social forces affect some people differently from others, we need to look not just at society but also within the individual.

Psychological Factors   Freud and his followers attributed suicide to the same dynamic that causes major depressive disorders. Specifically, Freudians construe suicide as a form of murderous anger at another person turned inward against oneself. A child whose mother dies may become angry about this loss, but the child is unable to vent this anger because its target, the dead mother, is unavailable. Instead, the child turns this anger inward. There is some evidence for the psychoanalytic view. For example, the incidence of parental death is higher in the childhood of suicides than among the general population (Paykel & Cooper, 1982). On the other hand, most people who lose their parents do not become suicidal later in life. Moreover, because the death of a parent may cause a severe family disruption (children may require foster care, for example), children may not get the opportunity to learn adequate social and coping skills. Faced with stress later in life, such individuals may find themselves unable to cope and prone to suicide.

Despite the confirmation of early loss in the childhood of many suicides, the overall evidence for the psychoanalytic view of suicide is far from compelling. Although hate and revenge are sometimes the motives for suicide, they are not the only reasons that people take their own lives (Shneidman, 1992). Shame, guilt, and hopelessness are considerably more common motives. Hopelessness is particularly important (A. T. Beck, Steer, et al., 1985; Weishaar & Beck, 1992). In a 10-year study of people admitted to the hospital with suicidal thoughts, A. T. Beck and colleagues (1985) found that those who went on to commit suicide differed mainly in their feelings of hopelessness. Hopelessness has also been found to be an important accompaniment of adolescent suicide (Marttunen et al., 1991). Young people depend heavily on their families for their sense of security and a positive attitude toward the future. Rejection, abandonment, and physical abuse destroy this security and are common factors in the backgrounds of suicidal young people (Berman & Jobes, 1991; Buist & Barnett, 1995; de Wilde et al., 1992; Maughn & McCarthy, 1997; McCauley, Kern, & Kolodner, 1997).

In addition to hopelessness, suicide is associated with impulsiveness, especially in adolescents (Spoont, 1992). Many adolescent suicides are not planned; they are spontaneous acts triggered by depression, alcohol, poor coping skills, and impulse (Brent et al., 1988). For urban adolescent males, impulsive behaviors are made more lethal because of the ready availability of guns. A survey of grade 11 boys in a large American city found that 47% claimed to have easy access to handguns (Callahan & Rivara, 1992). Irrespective of sex, motive, and means, youthful suicide attempters are alike in one way—they lack problem-solving skills. They fail to see alternatives to problems and to implement sound decision-making strategies (Sadowski & Kelley, 1994).

Genetics and Physiology   Danielle's natural father committed suicide. This is not unusual. Suicide, like depression, tends to run in families (Wender et al., 1986). The concordance rate for suicide among monozygotic twins is 20 times higher than it is among dizygotic twins (Roy et al., 1991). Because most suicidal twins are also depressed (or suffering from some other mental disorder), it may be their mental disorder, rather than the tendency toward suicide, that is inherited. In any event, there does seem to be a genetic factor involved, although it is worth noting that, even among monozygotic twins, the concordance rate for suicide is not 100%.

If inheritance plays a role in suicide, its influence may be expressed through its effects on neurotransmitters. Lower levels of serotonin (and dopamine) have been found among suicidal depressed patients than among nonsuicidal depressed people (Mann et al., 1992; Roy, Karoum, & Pollack, 1992). Low serotonin levels are also found in people who engage in violent behavior. This latter finding is consistent with the psychoanalytic theory that suicide is a form of violence directed against oneself (Edman et al., 1986). At present, however, the evidence is correlational. We have no proof that abnormal levels of serotonin and dopamine cause suicide. It is always possible that depression is responsible for *both* suicide and low levels of neurotransmitters.

Cause of Suicide: Current Status   One of the reasons that it is so difficult to understand suicide is the large

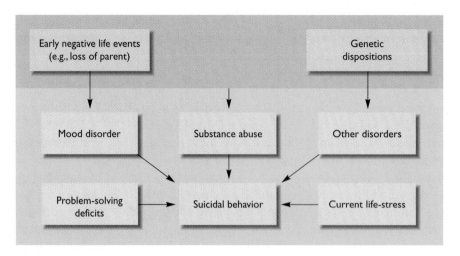

FIGURE 8.10 **Schematic Summary of Etiological Factors in Suicide**

number of contributing variables. Early negative life events, genetic predispositions, and psychological disorders all play a role, yet none of these variables, by itself, predicts who will commit suicide. Variables such as a deficit in social problem solving, substance abuse, and life-stress mediate the effects of genetics and early life events. Our current understanding of how all of these factors interact to cause suicide is summarized in schematic form in Figure 8.10. Early experiences and inherited vulnerabilities result in a tendency to develop psychological disorders (mood disorders, substance abuse, and other disorders). These disorders can lead to suicidal behavior provided that there is sufficient life-stress and the person has poor problem-solving skills.

Assessing Suicidal Intentions

As mentioned in Chapter 1, it is not easy to predict who will commit suicide; many suicides seem to happen without prior warning (Apter et al., 1993; Maris et al., 1992). After Danielle's hospitalization for attempted suicide, Dr. Berg was unable to predict that she would try again less than a year later. Based on the literature reviewed so far, plus clinical observations, suicidologists have identified a set of risk factors that seem to be correlated with suicide (Table 8.8). A problem for these risk factors is that they are based on data gathered from whole populations. When they are applied to specific individuals, they are only modest predictors of suicide (Pokorny, 1993). An examination of the backgrounds of 2,000 patients hospitalized for depression over a 10-year period failed to find any single set of predictors that would have identified the majority of those who went on to attempt suicide (R. B. Goldstein et al., 1991). De-

spite these difficulties, it is important not to disregard sudden mood changes or suicidal communications because *some* people who go on to commit suicide do give early warning signs. You should particularly become worried when someone you know becomes preoccupied with death, says goodbye, or gives away prized possessions (D. C. Clark & Fawcett, 1992).

To help counselors and psychotherapists determine who is at greatest risk of suicide, Edwin S. Shneidman, a renowned expert on suicide, has developed the Psychological Pain Assessment Scale (PPAS). Based on a traditional form of assessment tool called the projective test (which includes such instruments as the Rorschach inkblots and the Thematic Apperception Test), the PPAS uses pictures illustrating psychological pain to investigate suicide. Psychological pain, according to Shneidman, is the introspective experience of negative emotions such as anger, despair, fear, grief, shame, guilt, hopelessness, loneliness, and loss (Shneidman, 1993, 1998). These negative emotions, which Shneidman calls psychache, are directly related to suicidal acts. Like other projective tests, the PPAS consists of TAT-like pictures; the subject is asked to rate the psychological pain of the principal characters depicted in each picture. From the standpoint of the clinician, the goal of the PPAS is to assess the client's mental anguish, present and past, especially as it might relate to suicide. The obvious central implication of this approach for therapy is to reduce the client's heightened sense of upset and distress in order to thwart the heightened likelihood of suicide and address the particular psychological needs that are distressing the individual. The basic formula is elevated psychache plus constricted perceptions of life's options plus thoughts of being dead over being alive

TABLE 8.8	Risk Factors and Suicide	
Factor	**Low risk**	**High risk**
Sex	Female	Male
Marital status	Married	Single/divorced/living alone
Age	Middle years	Adolescence/old age
Psychiatric status	Normal/ character disorders/ situational disturbances	Depression/alcoholism/ conduct disorder/ schizophrenia
Setting	Rural	Urban/prisons
Religious activity	Regular churchgoer	Non-churchgoer
Nationality	Italian/Dutch/Spanish	Scandinavian/Japanese/ German-speaking countries

Note: Adapted from E. K. Stevenson et al. (1972).

equal suicide. The PPAS may prove helpful in identifying an individual's degree of risk for committing suicide, which might permit clinicians to better predict, and thus try to prevent, future suicide attempts.

Treatment and Prevention

Because there is no turning back a suicide, the professional ethics of psychologists require that they try to prevent people from harming themselves, even if this means breaking client-therapist confidentiality. Psychologists who do not take reasonable care to assess suicide potential and to take precautions against suicide can be successfully sued for negligence (Fremouw, Perczel, & Ellis, 1990). However, these ethical precepts are not universally accepted. Some writers argue that professionals are not always obligated to prevent suicide. Szasz (1986), for example, believes that people are free moral agents who should be allowed to end their own lives. Derek Humphry has written *Final Exit* (1991), a manual designed to help people end their lives, and we have already discussed Dr. Jack Kevorkian's suicide machine (see Chapter 1).

Because medical science can now keep some people alive indefinitely, there is considerable debate about the ethics of doing so. Perhaps people should be able to die with dignity when they no longer wish to live. Psychologist Bruno Bettelheim and writer Arthur Koestler committed suicide when they thought that old age and disability would force them to have lives of low quality (Fremon, 1991). Living wills, which require doctors to comply with the wishes of dying patients who no longer desire medical treatment, are recognized (but not always honored) in all states. The Netherlands even permits euthanasia (mercy killing) in certain cases. Thus far, U.S. legislatures have resisted this step. Who decides, politicians ask, when quality of life is not sufficient? Should vain actresses be allowed to take their own lives because they do not want to grow old? Szasz would argue yes, whereas most people would argue no. Certainly, most psychologists feel legally and professionally bound to save lives. To do this, they apply one or more of the interventions described next.

Crisis Intervention Crisis intervention is aimed at overcoming immediate problems. This is often done through the telephone crisis lines and walk-in prevention centers that were first established in most cities in the 1960s. The counselors who answer these phones and who work in these centers have been taught to maintain contact with the person in crisis, develop a relationship, clarify the source of stress, and recommend an action plan—usually a place the person can go for help. It is difficult to assess the effectiveness of crisis intervention centers because there is no ethical way to form a control group of suicidal people who do not receive advice. Although there is some evidence for a reduction in the suicide rate after hotlines are established (H. L. Miller et al., 1984), the overall evidence that they prevent suicide is weak (Dew et al., 1987).

Psychological Interventions The first issue to be faced in the treatment of suicide is the potential for another attempt. If the likelihood seems high (and that is often difficult to judge), then the safest place for the person is in the hospital (Comstock, 1992)—even if this means involuntary commitment. Once the immediate danger subsides, treatment is usually aimed at overcoming any

Preventing Suicide: What You Can Do

Suicidal people believe that their problems are enormous and insoluble. You may be able to save a life if you know how to respond to such hopelessness.

1. First, regard all threats as serious. If someone says "I'll die if I can't get a date for the prom," don't be flippant in your response. The problem is serious to the person, even if it seems trivial to you. The correct response is that suicide is not a solution and that other solutions may be available. Helping the person find a date may, in some cases, save a life.

2. Keep a close watch on friends you may consider depressed or suicidal. Gestures such as offering you gifts to "remember" them by are often signs of suicidal plans. When possible, try to eliminate the means (guns, drugs) until the crisis has passed.

3. Do not keep secrets. If a friend confides in you that he or she is planning suicide, refuse to keep this confidence. Encourage the person to seek help from a parent or some other responsible adult. Go with the person to show that you care what happens.

4. Give suicidal people a reason to live. Suicidal urges are transitory. If you can help the person get over the immediate crisis, there is a good chance that you can prevent a death. Ask your friend to help you with a project or to participate in some favorite activity.

immediate life-stress and at teaching clients how to go about solving problems before they become hopeless (Berchick & Wright, 1992). Obviously, if a mental disorder such as depression is present, it will have to be treated. Family therapy may also be useful in helping to improve communication and joint problem solving. Although these interventions seem to make practical sense, studies in which people were randomly assigned to intensive therapy or routine clinical contact have not yet been able to show that psychological treatment markedly reduces suicidal behaviors (Hawton, 1989).

Primary and Secondary Prevention Primary prevention programs are aimed at eliminating the risk factors that lead people to attempt suicide. These programs have recently been expanded in response to the alarming increase in suicide among young people. As we saw at Danielle's school, some universities distribute information on suicide to all new students. Included in these information packets are discussions of suicide, examples of warning signs, and pleas to watch over and recommend help for troubled friends. Crisis-line contact numbers are always included as well. Although such educational programs are well-intentioned, they are controversial. Some psychologists fear that educational materials that attempt to take the stigma out of suicide (so that students will not be ashamed to seek help) may subtly encourage suicidal behavior by implying that it is a normal response to stress. These critics of school-based programs argue that adolescent suicides are more likely to be discouraged if suicide is associated in their minds with a mental disorder. (No one wants to be thought of as "crazy.") The critics also note that there is little evidence that such school-based programs prevent suicide (Garland & Zigler, 1993; Spirito, Overholser, & Hart, 1991). Suicide clusters, such as those described in Highlight 8.2, have taken place in schools with elaborate suicide education programs. Perhaps school programs aimed at the entire school population miss the students who need such programs the most.

In contrast to primary prevention programs, which seek to eliminate the factors that lead to depression and suicide, secondary prevention programs are targeted at minimizing the risks for those already troubled enough to take their own lives—teenage boys who are depressed or who have made a previous suicide attempt, for example. Buddy programs, in which students are taught to look out for one another, may also permit professionals to intervene before it is too late. For suggestions about what you can do to help troubled friends, see Highlight 8.4.

Reducing Access to Means When the United Kingdom replaced domestic cooking gas with natural gas (which has a lower carbon dioxide content and is less lethal), the overall suicide rate decreased. It seemed that suicidal people who would have formerly died after turning on the gas in a closed room now lived long enough to be rescued. In other words, it is possible to reduce suicides by making the environment safer. A similar reduction in suicide rates has been achieved by preventing access to

What kinds of measures are most effective in preventing suicide? Because San Francisco's Golden Gate Bridge is such a popular location for suicide attempts, a suicide hotline has been installed for people who may be having second thoughts about taking their lives.

certain highly public places. For symbolic reasons, many suicides have jumped from the Golden Gate Bridge in San Francisco. Erection of a safety barrier that prevents pedestrian access to the edge of the bridge has resulted in a reduction in impulsive suicides. In the United States, most successful suicides use guns. Sixty-five percent of teenage suicides involve shootings. Given the success of changes in gas type in the United

Kingdom and of restricting access to certain popular suicide spots, some researchers have argued that restricting access to guns would also reduce suicide (Powell, Sheehan, & Christoffel, 1996).

It is difficult to prove or disprove such a claim. We clearly cannot randomly distribute guns to experimental and control groups and then sit back and see what happens. The best we can do is to rely on natural experiments.

TABLE 8.9   Elements Common to Suicide Postvention Programs

1. Information
- Following a suicide, obtain accurate information regarding the circumstances of the death.
- Acknowledge the death publicly without sensationalism.
- Provide accurate information to the media. Emphasize the tragic nature of the death and the positive steps taken by the company, institution, or community to cope.

2. Risk assessment
- Identify those at high risk for imitation, including friends of the deceased, especially those with a history of depression or suicide.
- Follow up high-risk people with the cooperation of relatives.

3. Promotion of healthy recovery
- Organize information sessions on the normal response to grief.

4. Prevention
- Offer information to staff and relatives on how to recognize people at risk.
- Provide an opportunity for people to learn problem-solving skills as an alternative to suicide.

Note: Adapted from Hazell (1993).

For example, J. H. Sloan and his colleagues (1990) compared suicide rates in Seattle, Washington, and Vancouver, British Columbia. These cities are similar in size, ethnic mix, and socioeconomic status, but they have vastly different gun laws. Vancouver strictly regulates ownership and availability. The researchers found that guns were much more likely to be used by suicides in Seattle than in Vancouver but that the overall rate of suicide in both cities was similar. This suggests that, if guns are unavailable, people find other ways to kill themselves. Similar findings were reported by Rich and his colleagues (1990), who compared suicide rates in the Canadian province of Ontario before and after 1978 (the year the local government outlawed handguns). These researchers also found no differences in suicide rates. Suicide by gunshot decreased, only to be replaced by an increase in the number of people leaping off high buildings.

The evidence is not all negative, however. Sloan and his colleagues (1990) found some evidence that, among young men, impulsive suicides were more common in Seattle than in Vancouver. This might mean that impulsive suicides are aided by the easy availability of handguns. In another study, Marzuk and his colleagues (1992) found suicide rates to be higher in Manhattan than in the other boroughs of New York. Part of the reason was the large number of people who leapt from Manhattan's skyscrapers. This finding does suggest that

the availability of means could increase the number of suicides, although the effect is hardly overwhelming.

Postvention   Suicide has a shattering impact on the survivors (C. Lukas & Seiden, 1990; E. B. Ross, 1997). Family and friends must cope not only with the death of a loved one but also with the circumstances of the death. **Postvention** (Shneidman, Farberow, & Litman, 1970) is aimed at helping relatives and friends cope with grief. Friends and relatives of a suicide victim often feel guilty and anxious because they believe that they should have done something to prevent the death. Sometimes they may become suicidal themselves (Ness & Pfeffer, 1990). Group therapy can sometimes help provide a supportive environment, but postvention involves more than just group therapy. Postvention also includes rumor control and identifying those people at high risk of imitation. A number of postvention programs have been developed, mainly for schools, but there are no compelling data yet available for their success. Elements common to postvention programs appear in Table 8.9.

Could Danielle Wood's Death Have Been Prevented?

In many ways, Danielle Wood was a suicide waiting to happen; her history combines many suicide risk factors. She had a family background of suicide, and she was sexually abused as a child by her own father. These experiences were breeding grounds for learned helplessness. Her helplessness was reinforced by severe early childhood losses, first of her father and then of her mother (when she was given up for adoption). She abused substances and was prone to depression. Danielle was also in the high-risk age group, and she was single. She had made a suicide attempt in the past and had recently experienced a potential breakdown in her relationship with Luke.

Despite these risk factors, Danielle's death was not inevitable. Perhaps if her college had instituted a suicide prevention program earlier, her friends would have recognized the danger signs and watched Danielle more closely. If substances had been more difficult to obtain, she might not have been able to find the means to end her life. The most tragic aspect of Danielle's death is the feeling that it might have been prevented if only she had followed through with the treatment she was offered after her first suicide attempt. She might have then learned the coping and problem-solving skills we must all develop to deal with life's inevitable problems.

CHAPTER 8 IN PERSPECTIVE

Mood disorders are among the most common and thoroughly studied of all psychological problems. Some facts are now widely accepted. We know, for example, that mood disorders tend to occur most often among people who have experienced a severe loss early in life. We also know that mood disorders run in families. Pharmaceuticals, ECT, and psychological treatments (alone or in combination) seem to help shorten depressive and manic episodes and prevent relapses. Cognitive and interpersonal therapies are also useful, especially for cases of depression. Despite these acknowledged advances in our understanding and treatment of mood disorders, our understanding of these disorders is far from complete; bipolar disorder, especially, has been neglected. Although it may seem plausible that people who have learned to feel helpless or hopeless and who have negative self-concepts should become depressed, it is not clear why they should cycle through periods of excitement and elation. Biological theories that focus largely on neurotransmitter levels also have trouble explaining the presence of alternating manic and depressive episodes. Thus, even though this is the longest chapter in this book, there is still much to learn about the etiology and treatment of mood disorders.

Key Ideas

Symptoms and Signs of Major Depressive Episodes and Disorders
Depression is marked by a sad mood, loss of interest in formerly pleasurable activities, sleep disturbances, changes in appetite, loss of interest in sex, irritability, inability to concentrate, and a wide variety of aches and pains. In adults, depression, physical illness, and substance abuse often go together. In children, the most frequently reported comorbid conditions are disorders of conduct. Dysthymic disorder is a moderate depression that lasts 2 years or more (1 year in children and adolescents).

Prevalence and Course of Depressive Disorders
Depression is common, and the number of cases seems to be rising, especially among young people. Women are more than twice as likely to be depressed as men. Although the prevalence of depression varies across ethnic groups, its symptoms are remarkably similar across cultures.

Symptoms and Signs of Bipolar and Mixed Disorders
Manic episodes are marked by an expansive mood, grandiosity, diminished sleep, heightened sex drive, and rapid-fire speech. In the grip of mania, people believe that they have unusual abilities and can accomplish anything. In reality, they have trouble concentrating on a single task. Hypomanic episodes are similar to manic episodes but milder. Bipolar disorders can consist only of manic episodes, but this is rare. Typically, manic or hypomanic episodes alternate with depressions. When the depressions are mild and mood is highly variable, the diagnosis is cyclothymia.

Prevalence and Course of Bipolar Disorders
Bipolar disorders are less common than unipolar disorders and affect men and women of different ethnic groups equally. The frequency and intensity of mood changes vary across individuals. The first signs of bipolar disorder usually appear in early adulthood, but the incidence of bipolar disorders seems to be rising among young people. Typically, onset is sudden. Follow-up studies have found the prognosis to be poor.

Etiology of Mood Disorders
The response of some mood disorders

to light therapy, the effectiveness of antidepressant drugs, the evidence for heredity, and the relationship between mood and hormonal imbalances are all compatible with a biological etiology. Yet, despite considerable research over the past 50 years, it is still not possible to identify a specific biological diathesis for mood disorder. The same is true for psychological causes. Psychoanalysts focus on the loss of affection and "fixation" in early childhood. Behavioral theories emphasize learned helplessness and loss of reinforcement. Cognitive theories focus on faulty attributions. Both biological and psychological theories largely ignore bipolar disorders. This leaves important questions unanswered. For example, how does fixation at the oral stage of development explain the cyclic nature of many mood disorders? Why don't depressed people stay miserable all of the time? The answers to these questions will probably require a theory that combines psychological and biological causes.

Treatment of Mood Disorders

Biological treatments for mood disorders cover a wide range and include ECT, light treatment, sleep deprivation, and the administration of mood-altering drugs. All of these treatments are symptomatic. Psychological treatment, on the other hand, attempts to teach people more effective ways of coping with problems. Comparing treatments is not easy because outcome studies are difficult to conduct and even the best-designed outcome study may not predict how successful a treatment will be in routine clinical use.

Suicide Prevalence

Suicide is the tragic result of the complex interaction of social, psychological, and biological forces. People who take their own lives are seeking a solution to a problem, wish to end consciousness, have intolerable psychological or physical pain, have frustrated psychological needs, feel hopeless, cannot see alternatives, and are "escapers" rather than problem solvers. Suicide is among the top 10 causes of death in the industrialized world and a common cause of death among young people. Divorced, widowed, and other single people have higher suicide rates than do married people. In all instances, more men than women take their own lives. In the United States, suicide rates are highest for Native Americans and Whites; many of these deaths are alcohol related. College students are also at high risk.

Causes of Suicide

One of the reasons that it is so difficult to understand suicide is the large number of possible causes. Early life events, genetic predispositions, and psychological disorders all play some role, yet none of these factors by itself is a good predictor of who will commit suicide. They are mediated by such variables as problem-solving skills, alcohol abuse, and life-stress. Because its etiology is complex, it is not easy to predict who will commit suicide.

Treatment of Suicide

The most immediate suicide treatment is crisis intervention, which is aimed at overcoming current problems and reducing the probability of a suicide attempt. If the probability seems high, then the safest place for the person is in the hospital. Once the immediate danger subsides, cognitive-behavioral treatment can be used to teach clients how to go about solving problems before they become hopeless. If a mental disorder such as depression is present, it must be treated. Family therapy may also be useful in helping to improve family communication and joint problem solving. Although these interventions seem to make practical sense, studies in which people were randomly assigned to intensive therapy or routine clinical contact have not yet been able to show that psychological treatment markedly reduces suicide.

Prevention and Postvention of Suicide

School-based primary prevention programs are designed to teach students the warning signs of suicide, give them information about crisis-line numbers, and encourage them to watch over and recommend help for troubled friends. Secondary prevention programs are similar, but they target high-risk people. Reducing access to lethal weapons and to popular suicide spots are also ways to reduce suicide rates. Postvention is aimed at helping relatives and friends cope with the grief of a suicide.

Key Terms

adjustment disorder with depressive features
anhedonia
bipolar mood disorder
bipolar I disorder
bipolar II disorder
catatonic features
circadian rhythms

cognitive triad
cyclothymic disorder
dexamethasone suppression test (DST)
diagnostic specifier
double depression
dysthymic disorder
effectiveness (of treatment)

efficacy (of treatment)
electroconvulsive therapy (ECT)
hopelessness
hypomanic episode
interpersonal therapy (IPT)
learned helplessness

lithium carbonate
major depressive disorder
major depressive episode
mania
manic episode
melancholia
meta-analysis
mixed episode

monoamine oxidase (MAO)
   inhibitor
mood
mood disorders
postpartum depression
postvention

premenstrual dysphoric
   disorder
psychological autopsy
psychotic features
rapid eye movement (REM)
   sleep

seasonal affective disorder
   (SAD)
selective serotonin reuptake
   inhibitor (SSRI)
suicidology
test sensitivity

test specificity
tricyclic antidepressant
unipolar mood disorder

Key Names

Robert Burton
John Cade

Ugo Cerletti
Charles Darwin

Émile Durkheim
Nathan Kline

Martin Seligman

CHAPTER 9

CHAPTER OBJECTIVES

Schizophrenia is a short-hand term used to describe a diverse group of disorders with severe psychological symptoms. Although new treatments allow many sufferers to lead higher quality lives than was formerly thought possible, most people with schizophrenia experience years, sometimes decades, of debilitating symptoms. Although there is compelling evidence that schizophrenia runs in families, there is equally strong evidence in favor of an environmental diathesis. Practically all researchers agree that schizophrenia is the result of the complex interaction of genetic, environmental, and social factors.

The four main questions addressed in this chapter are

1. How is schizophrenia diagnosed?
2. What causes schizophrenia?
3. How is schizophrenia treated?
4. What are the legal problems faced by people with schizophrenia and their relatives?

The Schizophrenias and Other Psychotic Disorders

CONTENTS

Schizophrenia is the most catastrophic of all psychological disorders. It typically strikes young adults, who may suffer for decades as schizophrenia wrecks their social relationships, impairs their thinking, impairs their health, and robs them of the ability to enjoy life. Schizophrenia also represents a massive drain on society's resources (Ho, Andreasen, & Flaum, 1997). Few schizophrenic patients can work, many require public assistance, and most require expensive treatment (Kirkby et al., 1997). Faced with unrewarding lives, people with schizophrenia may commit suicide. Their tragic deaths add yet another burden to the guilt and pain already borne by their families. This chapter focuses mainly on the diagnosis, etiology, and treatment of schizophrenia. However, because people with schizophrenia must somehow find a place in our society, the social, cultural, and legal aspects of their disorder are also reviewed.

Unlike those of anxiety or mood disorders, or of most of the other disorders discussed in this book, the signs and symptoms of schizophrenia are not simply exaggerations of everyday behavior. Some are rarely, if ever, encountered in daily life. Still, it is important to remember that, no matter how bizarre their behavior, people with schizophrenia are human beings with the same feelings, fears, desires, and hopes as everyone else. To help us keep in mind the human side of the tragedy that is schizophrenia, this chapter refers frequently to the story of Jennifer Plowman, which begins to unfold in Documents 9.1 and 9.2.

DOCUMENT 9.1

Transcript of a Commitment Hearing for Jennifer Plowman

COUNTY COURT

COURT TRANSCRIPT

Marion County

Presiding: Hon. Richard Harding

JUDGE: You are requesting that your daughter, Jennifer, be involuntarily committed to University Hospital? Are you represented by legal counsel?

ANNE PLOWMAN: No, Your Honor. I can't afford a lawyer.

JUDGE: I can see that you receive public assistance.

ANNE PLOWMAN: I do not want my daughter to wait for public assistance. Jenny refuses to go to the hospital on her own, and she desperately needs help.

JUDGE: Why do you say this?

ANNE PLOWMAN: Jenny has not left the house for days. She has not washed or changed her clothes. She just sits in her room. Sometimes I hear her talking to herself. Other times I can hear her laughing and swearing. Jenny says that she cannot come out of her room because people can read her thoughts. Your Honor, she desperately needs help.

JUDGE: Has she threatened you or anyone else?

ANNE PLOWMAN: No.

JUDGE: Has she harmed herself?

ANNE PLOWMAN: She won't wash or change her clothes.

JUDGE: But has she tried to hurt herself, cut herself, or something similar?

ANNE PLOWMAN: No. She says that there is nothing wrong with her.

JUDGE: I do not want to deprive Jenny of her liberty unless there is some good reason. Jenny is a 21-year-old adult. If she is not dangerous to herself or anyone else, then she should choose for herself whether she needs treatment.

ANNE PLOWMAN: Please, Your Honor. I'm so worried. Isn't there something you can do to help?

JUDGE: Perhaps we can talk her into going voluntarily into University Hospital. If not, I will commit her, but only for 72 hours so that she may be examined by Mental Health Services. Once I receive their report, I will decide how to proceed.

DOCUMENT 9.2

Description of Jennifer Plowman at the Time of Her Hospital Admission (from hospital records)

UNIVERSITY HOSPITAL

Intake Note

CONFIDENTIAL

Admitting Physician: Dr. Sally Kahn

Jennifer Plowman was committed involuntarily by Judge Harding for a 3-day evaluation. She arrived at the hospital by ambulance accompanied by her mother, Anne Plowman, and two male orderlies. Jennifer would not come to the hospital on her own, and the orderlies were required to transport her.

Although she is only 21, Jennifer appeared much older. Her clothing was dirty and covered with food stains, and her hair was greasy and matted. She seems not to have washed for some time. Jennifer had a blank facial expression and showed no obvious emotion.

Jennifer could not name the president of the United States. She did not know the date nor where she was. Although she could not (or would not) answer most questions on the mental status examination, she was not silent. She kept up a background chatter in which she jumped from one topic to another and often laughed unexpectedly. (Jennifer's words have been transcribed and recorded separately.)

Mrs. Plowman reported that her daughter had been acting strangely at home. For the past 6 months or more, she has been reluctant to leave the house. She would go out only if her mother pressured her. For the past month, she has refused to leave the house at all. At the same time, she began to claim that "people" could "read her mind." In recent weeks, Jennifer's behavior had become increasingly strange. She gave up washing and would laugh unexpectedly. Her mother would overhear Jennifer talking when alone in her room. On one occasion, she heard her daughter say, "Stop laughing. I am not funny." Jennifer was alone in her room at the time.

When Jennifer spoke, her speech was quiet, and her sentences were brief. Sometimes, her speech was difficult to follow because Jennifer would jump from one topic to another. Although she had periods of lucidity, these were short-lived.

Mrs. Plowman reported that Jennifer was adopted as a baby. Her natural mother had not played a role in her life. Mrs. Plowman believes that Jennifer's natural mother (who is now deceased) was "mentally ill." Jennifer has always been quiet. She lost her job as a file clerk and has been unemployed for 7 months.

When asked whether her husband was available for an interview, Mrs. Plowman simply replied, "No." Further questioning revealed that Edward Plowman, her husband, had died 10 months earlier.

Jennifer was admitted to the secure ward and arrangements were made for social work and psychological consultations.

THE GENESIS OF SCHIZOPHRENIA

We all can identify with people who are depressed or anxious. Most of us have "been there" ourselves, at least to some degree. There is nothing baffling or impenetrable about depression, or anxiety, or even mania. Schizophrenia is different. People with this enigmatic disorder behave in ways that most of us find incomprehensible. Like Jennifer Plowman, they may believe that other people can read their thoughts or that friends and neighbors are engaged in elaborate plots against them. In different historical periods, people who have displayed these behaviors have been called mad, crazy, insane, and lunatics. All of these pejorative terms refer to a group of disorders known as the psychoses. These disorders are characterized by gross distortions of reality. Sufferers are unable to tell what is "real" and what is not. Several psychotic disorders are described in the *DSM-IV*, but by far the most common is schizophrenia.

Although there are references to schizophrenic-like symptoms dating back to ancient times, descriptions of the modern schizophrenic syndrome seem to have originated in the 18th century (Torrey, 1980). Before then, mental disorders were not well differentiated—syndromes that we would consider to be quite separate were grouped together and considered to be different forms of a single disorder. Philippe Pinel (1745–1826), a French physician and surgeon, was one of the first to advocate separating and classifying disorders according to their main features. He believed that this would ultimately permit different disorders to be traced back to their unique physiological causes. One of Pinel's initial classifications contained people who displayed the signs that we currently associate with schizophrenia (Pinel, 1801/1962). Decades later, another French doctor, Benedict Morel (1809–1873), used the term *démence précoce* (premature mental deterioration) to describe a similar disorder.

Morel's contemporary Emil Kraepelin (whose work on psychiatric nomenclature was introduced in Chapter 3) devised a classification that included two psychotic conditions. Although they shared some of their presenting symptoms, Kraepelin's two types of psychoses differed in their respective courses and outcomes. In the first type, serious mental symptoms began early in life and followed a deteriorating course. In Kraepelin's second type of psychosis, symptoms followed a cyclical course in which periods of remission alternated with psychotic episodes. Kraepelin named the cyclic psychosis "manic-depressive disorder." (As discussed in Chapter 8, the *DSM-IV* name for this condition is bipolar disorder.) Kraepelin called the continuously deteriorating psychosis **dementia praecox**, which is simply a Latin translation of Morel's *démence précoce*. Kraepelin

Philippe Pinel (1745–1826) was one of the first physicians to differentiate and classify mental disorders. Among the ones he identified was what would later be known as schizophrenia.

believed that the deterioration he observed in dementia praecox was the result of a progressive organic brain syndrome that began early in life.

In contrast to Kraepelin, Swiss psychiatrist Eugen Bleuler (1857–1939) rejected the idea that the course of a disorder, alone, could ever distinguish one psychosis from another. Bleuler preferred to classify psychological disorders on the basis of their characteristic signs and symptoms, rather than on their course and outcome (Bleuler, 1911/1952). The *DSM-IV* adopted Bleuler's approach.

According to Bleuler, the symptoms of dementia praecox sometimes make their first appearance in adults rather than young people, and the course and outcome of the disorder are both more variable than Kraepelin acknowledged. Instead of following a deteriorating course, some people manage to recover, whereas others deteriorate only to a certain level and then stay there. Bleuler proposed that the name *dementia praecox* be replaced with *schizophrenia*, a term derived from the Greek words for split (*schizo*) and mind (*phrene*). It is important not to confuse Bleuler's concept of schizophrenia with the multiple, or "split," personalities described in Chapter 7.

Eugen Bleuler (1857–1939) coined the term schizophrenia *and advocated diagnosing mental disorders according to symptoms rather than course and outcome, which are more variable.*

Bleuler's "split" was not among personalities but among cognitions within a single personality. In schizophrenia, thoughts become split (disconnected) from one another. People race from one idea to the next, often with no obvious connection. Bleuler believed that a "loosening of associative threads" among cognitions was the common link among a set of heterogeneous disorders that he loosely grouped together and called the "schizophrenias":

> In this malady the associations lose their continuity. Of the thousands of associative threads which guide our thinking, this disease seems to interrupt, quite haphazardly, sometimes such single threads, sometimes a whole group, and sometimes even large segments of them. In this way, thinking becomes more illogical and bizarre. Furthermore, the associations tend to proceed along new lines. . . . Two ideas, fortuitously encountered, are combined into one thought. . . . Clang-associations [associations based on sounds such as rhymes] receive unusual significance. . . . Two or more ideas are condensed into a single one. . . . Thoughts . . . are not related and directed by any unifying concept of purpose or goal. It looks as though ideas of a certain category . . . were thrown into one pot, mixed, and subsequently picked out at random, and linked with each other by mere grammatical form or other auxiliary images. (Bleuler, 1911/1952, p. 14)

Document 9.3 contains a transcript of what Dr. Kahn called Jennifer Plowman's "background chatter," recorded during Jennifer's intake interview. The excerpt illustrates what Bleuler meant by a breakdown in associations. Note how Jennifer jumps from one idea to the next and how the word "year" produces the clang associations "leer," "jeer," and "tear," which then conjures up an old song lyric.

DOCUMENT 9.3

Transcript of Jennifer Plowman's "Background Chatter" at Her Intake Interview

Men need sex. I have had sex 10,000 times. That window is in the room because you want patients to know the color of the world. I know the president. He lives in town. I didn't like his movie. He just wants to win the Academy Award. His movie is my life. I made a movie once. It had lots of stars. The cameraman was my friend. The sound technician was excellent. Where are the mikes and cameras hidden? Is this logomouth here to get me nervous? My father died last year, leer, jeer, tears on my pillow, pain in my heart over you, what can I do? There is nothing wrong with me, you know. I don't know why I am here. I'm fine. ∎

Bleuler divided schizophrenic symptoms into two main categories: fundamental and accessory. According to Bleuler, the fundamental symptoms of schizophrenia are distorted thinking, a retreat into a personal fantasy world (he called this "autism," but it has little to do with the childhood autistic disorder described in Chapter 12 of this book), loss of initiative, impaired attention, and ambivalence. Note that none of these symptoms is unique to schizophrenia. Every one of us is ambivalent, indecisive, and distracted from time to time. In schizophrenia, however, these behaviors are greatly exaggerated. Bleuler's accessory symptoms included **hallucinations** (sensory experiences in the absence of external stimuli), **delusions** (unsubstantiated beliefs), odd motor movements, and bizarre behavior. Bleuler always referred to "the schizophrenias" rather than simply to schizophrenia. He insisted on the plural because he believed that several different but related disorders were responsible for psychotic behavior. He even called his book on the subject *Dementia Praecox or the Group of Schizophrenias* (1911/1952). Although this chapter uses the more common singular term *schizophrenia,* Bleuler was undoubtedly correct; schizophrenia is far from a homogenous diagnostic category.

Following Bleuler, the German psychiatrist Kurt Schneider (1959) divided schizophrenic symptoms into a first and second rank. Hearing one's own voice being spoken aloud, hearing voices commenting on one's own behavior, and the feeling that one's actions are controlled by other people were all first-rank symptoms. Schneider believed that these first-rank symptoms were specific to schizophrenia. Second-rank symptoms included other types of hallucinations and delusions, as well as mood changes. Although Schneider argued that schizophrenia can be diagnosed on the basis of first-rank symptoms alone, it has now become clear that these symptoms are not specific to schizophrenia; some are also found in bipolar disorder (see Chapter 8) and some organic disorders (O'Grady, 1990).

Kraepelin's definition of dementia praecox was relatively narrow (it was limited to conditions that begin in the teenage years and gradually deteriorate). Bleuler widened the definition to include people whose symptoms first appeared in adulthood and who did not necessarily deteriorate. From Bleuler's time until the 1970s, the definition of schizophrenia continued to broaden, and increasing numbers of people came to be considered schizophrenic. The trend to broader definitions was especially true in the United States, where clinicians invented categories such as "pseudoneurotic" and "pseudopsychopathic" schizophrenia to apply to people who did not have the symptoms of schizophrenia but whom clinicians suspected were really schizophrenic underneath. In Chapter 3, we encountered a study by Rosenhan (1973) in which people pretended to have "heard a voice" in order to gain admission to a mental hospital. This study provided a dramatic example of how broad the American concept of schizophrenia had become. The pseudopatients in Rosenhan's study were all successful at gaining admission to mental hospitals—all but one was diagnosed schizophrenic—solely on the basis of "hearing a voice" once. None had any other sign of mental disorder. Thus, it is not surprising that an international research project, conducted in the 1970s, found that American mental health workers were twice as likely as their European counterparts to diagnose a patient as schizophrenic (J. E. Cooper et al., 1972).

Clearly, it is impossible to make valid international comparisons if each country has its own definition of what constitutes schizophrenia. To bring American practice in line with that of Europe, the diagnostic criteria for schizophrenia were tightened considerably in the *DSM-III.* The *DSM-IV* refined the criteria even further. The result is that modern American diagnostic practice is now similar to that of other countries. Indeed, the diagnosis of schizophrenia is now associated with similar symptoms in most countries of the world (Warner & de Girolamo, 1995; Mason et al., 1997).

SYMPTOMS AND SIGNS

As already noted, the *DSM-IV* diagnostic criteria for schizophrenia are relatively narrow. Yet, despite this narrowing, there is no single symptom or set of symptoms that describes all schizophrenic people. The schizophrenic syndrome is heterogeneous in presenting symptoms, course, response to treatment, and outcome. These differences among people may mean that Bleuler was correct: Schizophrenia is not a single disorder. Alternatively, there may be a single underlying cause for schizophrenia, but environmental factors (and each individual's attempts to cope with schizophrenic symptoms) may change the way the disorder is manifested in different people (Gottesman, 1991).

In addition to schizophrenia, the *DSM-IV* describes seven other psychotic disorders, each of which shares some characteristics in common with schizophrenia (Table 9.1). **Schizophreniform disorder** appears similar to schizophrenia, but it has not yet become chronic. Be-

DSM-IV	TABLE 9.1 Main *DSM-IV* Psychotic Disorders

Schizophrenia: A psychotic disturbance lasting more than 6 months that includes one or more of the following: delusions, hallucinations, disorganized speech, or odd movements. There are five sub-types: catatonic, paranoid, disorganized, residual, and undifferentiated.

Schizophreniform disorder: A disorder with symptoms similar to schizophrenia but with a shorter duration.

Schizoaffective disorder: A combination of a mood disorder and symptoms similar to schizophrenia.

Delusional disorder: At least 1 month of delusions that are not bizarre in character and with none of the other symptoms of schizophrenia.

Brief psychotic disorder: Psychotic symptoms that last for less than 1 month.

Shared psychotic disorder: A psychotic disorder (usually a shared delusion) that seems to spread from one individual to another.

Psychotic disorder due to a general medical condition: Psychotic symptoms that develop directly from a medical condition.

Substance-induced psychotic disorder: Psychotic symptoms that are the result of substance abuse or exposure to a toxin.

cause the only difference between schizophreniform disorder and schizophrenia is the duration of symptoms, schizophreniform disorder should be considered a provisional diagnosis that may be altered to schizophrenia if the symptoms persist. **Schizoaffective disorder** is a combination of schizophrenic symptoms and mood disorder. However, the diagnosis requires that delusions and hallucinations must be present for at least 2 weeks in the absence of any mood symptoms. Like schizophrenia, schizoaffective disorder can become chronic, but the outcome is usually better than for schizophrenia (Craig, Bromet, Jandorf, et al., 1997; Tsuang & Coryell, 1993). People with **delusional disorder** are preoccupied with delusions for at least 1 month, but they do not meet the other criteria for schizophreniform disorder or schizophrenia. Nevertheless, a delusional disorder can still be debilitating. Sufferers may become asocial, and their delusions can persist indefinitely (Breier, 1993). **Brief psychotic disorder** is the name used to describe people who have psychotic symptoms that last for a short time but who then return to their previous level of functioning. **Shared psychotic disorder** (formerly known as *folie à deux*) refers to individuals who share similar delusions. The *DSM-IV* also contains diagnostic categories for substance-induced psychoses and for those resulting from brain damage or other medical conditions.

Although the *DSM-IV* contains diagnostic criteria for each of the psychoses, researchers have tended to neglect the other psychoses in favor of schizophrenia. For this reason, this chapter focuses on schizophrenia, al-though the other psychoses are mentioned when appropriate. Table 9.2 (p. 376) presents the main *DSM-IV* diagnostic criteria for schizophrenia.

Positive Versus Negative Symptoms

Schizophrenic symptoms are divided into two main categories: positive and negative. Positive symptoms reflect an excess or distortion of normal cognitive and emotional functions; negative symptoms reflect a reduction or loss of normal functions (Andreasen & Carpenter, 1993). The most common positive symptoms are delusions, hallucinations, and bizarre motor movements. The negative symptoms are similar to Bleuler's fundamental symptoms: loss of initiative, lack of emotional expression, and impoverished speech.

Although the distinction between positive and negative symptoms may have some practical value in predicting who will respond to treatment, it is a rather crude dichotomy (Cromwell & Snyder, 1993; Velligan, Mahurin, Diamond, et al., 1997). For example, positive symptoms do not seem to be closely related to one another. Some people with schizophrenia have only one positive symptom; others have many. Negative symptoms, on the other hand, are not specific to schizophrenia (they are also found in mood disorders). It is likely that the distinction between positive and negative symptoms will be modified in the future as our knowledge of schizophrenia increases (Peralta, Cuesta, & de Leon, 1995).

DSM-IV	TABLE 9.2 Main *DSM-IV* Diagnostic Criteria for Schizophrenia

A. *Characteristic symptoms:* Two (or more) of the following, each present for a significant portion of time during a 1-month period (or less if successfully treated):
   (1) delusions
   (2) hallucinations
   (3) disorganized speech (e.g., frequent derailment or incoherence)
   (4) grossly disorganized or catatonic behavior
   (5) negative symptoms . . . [flat affect, limited speech, lethargy]

B. *Social/occupational dysfunction:* For a significant portion of the time since the onset of the disturbance, one or more major areas of functioning such as work, interpersonal relations, or self-care are markedly below the level achieved prior to the onset (or when the onset is in childhood or adolescence, failure to achieve expected level of interpersonal, academic, or occupational achievement).

C. *Duration:* Continuous signs of the disturbance persist for at least 6 months. This 6-month period must include at least 1 month of symptoms (or less if successfully treated) that meet Criterion A (i.e., active-phase symptoms) and may include periods of prodromal or residual symptoms . . . [during which] the signs of the disturbance may be manifested by only negative symptoms or two or more symptoms listed in Criterion A present in an attenuated form (e.g., odd beliefs, unusual perceptual experiences).

D. *Schizoaffective and Mood Disorder exclusion:* Schizoaffective disorder and mood disorder with psychotic features have been ruled out because either (1) no major depressive, manic, or mixed episodes have occurred concurrently with the active-phase symptoms; or (2) if mood episodes have occurred during active-phase symptoms, their total duration has been brief relative to the duration of the active and residual periods.

E. *Substance/general medical condition exclusion:* The disturbance is not due to the direct physiological effect of a substance (e.g., a drug of abuse, a medication) or a general medical condition.

F. *Relationship to a Pervasive Developmental Disorder:* If there is a history of autistic disorder [see Chapter 12] or another pervasive developmental disorder, the additional diagnosis of Schizophrenia is made only if prominent delusions or hallucinations are also present for at least a month (or less if successfully treated).

Note: From American Psychiatric Association (1994, pp. 285–286).

Delusions

Delusions are unsubstantiated ideas and opinions. To be considered a potential symptom of schizophrenia, a delusion must be contrary to a person's background and must not be held by members of the person's cultural or ethnic group. For example, members of a cult who believe that the world will come to an end on a certain date are probably not showing signs of schizophrenia. On the other hand, educated middle-class Americans who believe that mice are scientifically advanced aliens who were sent to colonize the earth and destroy humanity most probably are.

According to her mother, Jennifer Plowman believed that "people" could "read her mind." This belief was explored by Dr. Stuart Berg, the psychologist who evaluated Jennifer on her second day in the hospital. Part of their discussion appears in Document 9.4. Note that Jennifer's speech is still disorganized but that it is possible for Dr. Berg to get some idea of Jennifer's delusion—outside her house, people can read her thoughts. Often, people with schizophrenia are less communicative than Jennifer. They produce little speech, and the speech they do produce is slow and devoid of content, a combination known as "alogia." Clinically, it sometimes appears that delusions are constructed by people to justify their hallucinations. Just try to imagine yourself in Jennifer's situation. You hear voices talking and laughing about you. You conclude that people are reading your mind. Why? Well, there must be some reason. Perhaps you possess special secrets. Clearly, you are worried, so you decide to stay home, where the thick walls of your house will keep people from reading your thoughts. There is indirect evidence that rationalizations such as these are developed to serve a protective psychological purpose. For example, schizophrenic people with active delusions seem less depressed and more content than those who have recovered and abandoned their delusions (Roberts, 1991). The implication is that delusions may help to protect schizophrenic people from having to admit to themselves that their odd sensory experiences and strange behaviors are the result of a mental disorder rather than external forces.

DOCUMENT 9.4

Transcript From an Interview Between Dr. Berg and Jennifer Plowman

DR. BERG: Jenny, your mother says that you refused to leave your house. How come?

JENNIFER: Come, lum, rum is a drink that sailors like.

DR. BERG: But, why did you refuse to go outside?

JENNIFER: I am fine. Why do I need to be here? The walls protected me at home.

DR. BERG: From what?

JENNIFER: Selegonite cannot get out of lead. There is lead in the bed and the walls and halls. Outside, they can get through.

DR. BERG: Who can get through?

JENNIFER: They can hear my thoughts. Without the lead, they leak out, and they can hear them. I can hear them laughing. They find out what I am thinking, and they laugh at their success.

DR. BERG: You believe that lead in the walls of your house keeps people from reading your mind. While you are outside of the house, without the lead to protect you, people will read your thoughts and laugh when they manage to get what they want.

JENNIFER: Yes. Like Superman. I know the secret because I am a rocket scientist. I have flown to space. I can develop new rockets that run on special minerals. I am too smart for this place. I should be at home. ■

Although Jennifer's delusions are relatively vague and incoherent, this is not always the case (B. A. Maher & Spitzer, 1993). Schizophrenic delusions can be systematic and elaborate. Some sound like plots for way-out science fiction or spy movies. For example, people with Capgras's syndrome believe that their friends or relatives (or even they, themselves) have been replaced by identical doubles (Ellis & de Pauw, 1994). They accuse their parents, siblings, and friends of being aliens, imposters, or humanlike robots. More typically, delusions concern persecution and conspiracies. A frequently recurring theme is that thoughts are being inserted into one's head. This idea is so common among schizophrenic people that Schneider made it one of his first-

rank symptoms. Incorrect but plausible delusions (my assistant is plotting to get my job) may also be found among schizophrenic people, but bizarre delusions have greater diagnostic value. The problem with plausible delusions is that they may not be delusions at all. After all, even delusional people can have enemies!

Despite their absurdity, bizarre schizophrenic delusions are not usually susceptible to rational argument. Most people with schizophrenia find it difficult to believe that others consider their ideas ridiculous; they cling to their beliefs even in the face of compelling negative evidence. For example, people with nihilistic delusions believe that they are dead. Even pricking them with a pin and drawing blood does not change their opinion. They simply conclude that dead people can bleed. Grandiose delusions (such as Jennifer's claim to be a rocket scientist) are also relatively common.

Delusions vary in the extent to which they disrupt everyday functioning. Some schizophrenic people are totally preoccupied with their odd beliefs, whereas others are only minimally impaired. In fact, you may never even know that some people have delusions because they are perfectly rational and can get along well except when someone brings up the subject of their delusion.

Hallucinations

We all have sensory illusions. At night alone in the house, you may think you hear a burglar when there is no one around. Walking across campus, you think you hear your name being called, and yet there is no one there (Heilbrun, 1993). These experiences do not mean that you are schizophrenic. It is only your imagination "playing tricks." In contrast, schizophrenic people consider such sensory illusions quite real.

Hallucinations are perceptions that occur without any external stimulus. Such perceptions occur in a variety of conditions, but bizarre delusions are most often associated with schizophrenia. Auditory hallucinations, such as hearing voices, are the most common type. Jennifer Plowman seemed to be having auditory hallucinations. Recall that her mother overheard Jennifer saying, "Stop laughing. I am not funny," even though Jennifer was alone in her room at the time. Visual, olfactory (particularly rotten odors), and tactile (touch) hallucinations—such as the feeling that bugs are crawling under one's skin—are also associated with schizophrenia in the United States (different cultures tend to produce different hallucinations; Azhar, Varma, & Hakim, 1993). To the person with active schizophrenia, these voices, odors, and sounds are not imaginary, they are really "out there." Even people with

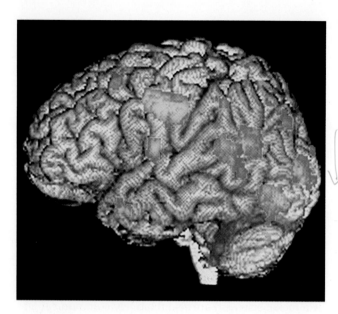

Imaging techniques, such as this PET scan (orange) superimposed on the white MRI image of a brain, show unusual brain activity during hallucinations. This patient saw heads that spoke to him; the visual (at right) and the auditory (upper center) areas of the brain are active, confirming that he "saw" and "heard" the hallucination.

doctoral degrees and considerable knowledge of psychopathology are reluctant to admit that their hallucinations could be illusory (Payne, 1992).

New imaging techniques have begun to give researchers insight into what is going on in the brains of people when they hallucinate. For example, it is now possible to use cerebral blood flow monitoring to examine brain activity during hallucinations. The technique involves injecting a special chemical into the bloodstream and monitoring the density of the chemical in different parts of the brain. The greater the density, the greater the blood flow in that area. Because active brain areas have an increased blood flow, monitoring the density of the chemical allows researchers to pinpoint active brain areas. One study using this technique found that the part of the brain most active during schizophrenic auditory hallucinations is the area responsible for speech production, not the brain area responsible for speech comprehension (McGuire, Shah, & Murray, 1993). This finding suggests that when schizophrenic people hallucinate, they are not "hearing" voices in their brain but are reporting their own thoughts (Hoffman & Rapaport, 1994).

Disorganized Speech

As you can see from the interview excerpts in Documents 9.3 and 9.4, Jennifer Plowman's speech was distinctly odd. She made up words, such as "logomouth"

and "selegonite" (these are known as *neologisms*), and she jumped from one topic to the next. At her intake interview, she went from sex to the president to movies to the Academy Awards. This phenomenon is known as *thought derailment,* as in a train going off its tracks. Jennifer also linked words together according to their sound, as in "come, lum, rum." These sound-based sequences are known as *clang associations.* Like Jennifer, people with schizophrenia often give irrelevant responses to questions, a phenomenon known as *tangentiality.* When the disorganization becomes extreme, the result is a mass of disconnected words ("word salad"). In contrast to Jennifer, many people with schizophrenia speak very little; others are excessively literal or concrete. For example, when asked by the admitting clinician, "How did you come to be here in the hospital?" one patient with schizophrenia answered, "I came by car."

The incoherent speech produced by Jennifer, and other people with schizophrenia, is often taken as a sign of an underlying "thought disorder" (Marengo & Harrow, 1993). Note, however, that the reasoning is circular. Schizophrenic speech is odd because people with schizophrenia have a thought disorder. How do we know that people with schizophrenia have a thought disorder? Well, they have odd speech, don't they? In any event, disorganized speech is not found in all people with schizophrenia, nor is it unique to schizophrenia. It may also be present during the manic phase of bipolar disorder (see, for example, Dr. Kahn's interview with Bernard Louis in Document 8.6).

Despite the considerable interest in schizophrenic speech over the years (S. Schwartz, 1982), most people with schizophrenia speak no differently from anyone else. It is the content of their speech (their delusions, for example) that is unusual, not their speech itself.

Disorganized or Catatonic Behavior

Left alone, some people with schizophrenia may not move a muscle for hours. At such times, they seem indifferent to events going on around them. This condition is known as catatonic stupor. Catatonic stupor may be accompanied by "waxy flexibility," in which people place or allow their limbs to be placed in uncomfortable positions (sitting with their hands on their heads, for example). They seem able to maintain these uncomfortable positions for long periods without apparent distress. In contrast to catatonic stupor, schizophrenia can also produce aimless, repetitive activity, such as pacing the floor or rocking back and forth in a chair (catatonic excitement). These repetitive movements may be accompanied by odd mannerisms, such as facial grimaces.

Catatonic symptoms have become less common in countries where antipsychotic medications are widely available, but they are still common in developing countries, such as Argentina.

The range of schizophrenic behavior is fairly wide: Patients may imitate other people's movements, act like robots, or refuse to cooperate with even simple requests ("negativism"). Like Jennifer, many people with schizophrenia neglect their personal hygiene, and some behave in socially unacceptable ways (shouting obscenities, for instance).

Catatonic symptoms seem to be far less common today than they were a century ago. In part, this is a beneficial result of the widespread availability of antipsychotic medications. It may also reflect a change in diagnostic sophistication. Many of the symptoms of encephalitis lethargica (sleeping sickness) are similar to those of catatonia. It is possible that at least some encephalitis patients were misdiagnosed as catatonic (Boyle, 1991).

Flat or Inappropriate Affect

Dr. Kahn described Jennifer as having a blank facial expression that was devoid of emotion. According to Bleuler, this is one of the principal signs of schizophrenia. He called it "flat" or "blunted" affect. Flat affect is also reflected in a monotonous speaking voice with few inflections. People with schizophrenia lose pleasure in previously enjoyable activities (anhedonia, a symptom also found in depression). In addition to being flat, schizophrenic affect at times may also be inappropriate—giggling at funerals, crying at parties.

There is evidence that affective symptoms first appear well before the development of schizophrenia. For example, home movies of children who develop schizophrenia later in life show that they displayed fewer positive emotions than their siblings years before the appearance of their schizophrenia (Walker, Grimes, Davis, & Smith, 1993).

Although people with schizophrenia superficially appear to have a flat affect, they may still have feelings that they keep inside. When shown emotion-producing films, people with schizophrenia (who appear unaffected on the surface) report having the same subjective emotions as people who are overtly emotional (Berenbaum & Oltmanns, 1992). This suggests that people with schizophrenia may feel emotions inside but not show their feelings overtly.

Social Withdrawal and Lethargy

Bleuler highlighted the schizophrenic tendency to withdraw from everyday social interaction and to retreat into a personal fantasy world ("autism"). Like Jennifer, most schizophrenic people spend their time alone, withdrawn from normal social activities. This may be one way they minimize sensory stimulation and protect themselves from further loss of control (Walker, Davis, & Baum, 1993). Indecisiveness, ambivalence, and apathy are among the most important negative symptoms of schizophrenia. Put together, they rob people of the energy they need to keep up with the activities of everyday life.

Additional Symptoms and Signs

In addition to the characteristic symptoms listed in criterion A, the *DSM-IV* includes several other important diagnostic criteria (see Table 9.2). First, the symptoms must affect the person's work or social life, or, in the case of a child, the symptoms must delay normal development. Second, the symptoms must persist for at least 6 months with an "active" phase—when symptoms are present—of at least 1 month. A "prodromal" phase before the active phase and a "residual" phase after the active phase also count toward the 6 months. In the prodromal and residual phases, only negative or mild versions of positive symptoms are present. The main effect of the 6-month diagnostic criterion is to restrict schizophrenia to chronic cases, as in Kraepelin's original formulation. The phases and course of schizophrenia will be described in more detail later in this chapter.

Because psychotic symptoms can be caused by various organic conditions (several are covered in Chapter 11), substance abuse, and prescription drugs, the diagnosis of schizophrenia can be made only after these other alternatives are excluded. Sometimes, a conclusion about the correct diagnosis is difficult to reach because people with schizophrenia may also use stimulants,

DSM-IV TABLE 9.3   *DSM-IV* Subtypes of Schizophrenia

Subtype	Dominant symptoms
Catatonic type	Odd motor activity, as reflected by one or more of the following: immobility, waxy flexibility, excessive motor activity, negativism, stereotyped movements, imitation of others, or odd movements.
Paranoid type	Delusions or auditory hallucinations without disorganized speech, catatonic behavior, or flat or inappropriate affect.
Disorganized type	Incoherent speech accompanied by bizarre and sometimes childish behavior plus flat or inappropriate affect.
Residual	Negative symptoms, or mild versions of the positive symptoms.
Undifferentiated	This category is reserved for those who meet the requirement of Criterion A (Table 9.2) but who do not fit any of the other subtypes.

hallucinogenic drugs, and alcohol (Turner & Tsuang, 1990). The *DSM-IV* also requires that mood disorders be ruled out before a person can be diagnosed as schizophrenic. When mood disorders and schizophrenic symptoms are both present in the active and residual phases, then the correct diagnosis is schizoaffective disorder, not schizophrenia. Finally, the *DSM-IV* criteria require that schizophrenia be kept separate from pervasive developmental disorders such as autism (see Chapter 12).

DIAGNOSTIC ISSUES

Among the issues involved in diagnosing schizophrenia are identification of the subtypes and some critics' objections to the diagnosis itself.

Subtypes

Kraepelin proposed three **subtypes** of schizophrenia, all of which are still recognized today: **catatonic**, **paranoid**, and **disorganized** (formerly known as "hebephrenic"). Although they have overlapping symptoms, the three subtypes are distinguished by their main presenting feature. In catatonic schizophrenia, either stupor or excitement predominate. Paranoid schizophrenia is marked by persecutory delusions, delusions of grandeur, or both. Jennifer's claim that she can develop rockets that run on special minerals is an example of a delusion of grandeur. On the whole, Jennifer's delusional system is rather vague and incoherent. In paranoid schizophrenia, delusions are usually more systematic and take the form of fantastic and elaborate conspiracies. Curiously, paranoid people are able to function well in areas not touched by their delusion. This is not true of those with disorganized schizophrenia, which is marked by incoherent speech,

formless delusions, and inappropriate affect. People who fall into this subtype have difficulty functioning in most settings. In addition to these subtypes, the *DSM-IV* has added a new one. The **residual** subtype consists of the negative or mildly positive symptoms seen in some patients after they have passed through the active phase of a schizophrenic episode. The various *DSM-IV* subtypes are summarized in Table 9.3.

Although clinicians and researchers claim to find them a useful shorthand for describing what patients are like, the various subtypes have limited value for anything else. They do not tell us who will respond to treatment, nor do we know whether the different subtypes have different causes. We do not even know whether a single subtype has more than one cause. It is possible that the subtypes are only different stages or different levels of severity of the same disorder. Interclinician reliability is lower for subtypes than for the overall schizophrenic diagnosis, and some people seem to move from one subtype to another over the course of their illness (McGlashan & Fenton, 1991).

Document 9.5 contains the preliminary diagnosis given to Jennifer at the time of her admission by Dr. Kahn. Note that Dr. Kahn has assigned Jennifer to the disorganized subtype because of her incoherent speech and flat affect. The description of Jennifer's behavior before her current episode suggests that she probably also has a schizoid personality disorder, which kept her socially isolated (schizoid personality disorder is discussed in Chapter 10). Jennifer does not suffer from a general medical condition, but she has experienced important psychosocial problems (her father's death and her loss of employment). Her general level of functioning at the time of her admission was fairly low; she was suffering from delusions, hallucinations, and impaired communicative ability.

DOCUMENT 9.5

Jennifer Plowman's Multiaxial Diagnosis (from her hospital chart)

Axis I (clinical disorder): Schizophrenia, disorganized type

Axis II (personality disorder): Possible schizoid personality disorder

Axis III (general medical conditions): None

Axis IV (psychosocial or environmental problems): Death of father, unemployment

Axis V (global assessment of functioning): GAF = 30 on admission. ■

Objections to the Diagnosis of Schizophrenia

The purpose of a diagnosis is not just to label someone. To be useful, a diagnosis should help us to understand the cause of a disorder, improve its treatment, or help prevent it. Over the years, many writers have claimed that the schizophrenia diagnosis accomplishes none of these goals and should be dropped as a diagnostic category (Goffman, 1961; Sarbin & Mancuso, 1980; Scheff, 1975; Szasz, 1961, 1971). These critics make four main points. First, there is no "gold standard" by which the accuracy of the schizophrenic diagnosis may be judged. Unlike for AIDS, for example, there is no laboratory test for schizophrenia. How can clinicians ever know that their diagnosis is correct if there is no independent method of verification?

The second common objection to the diagnosis of schizophrenia is its heterogeneity. As may be seen in Table 9.2, the *DSM-IV* criterion A for schizophrenia requires that two or more symptoms out of a list of five be present "for a significant portion of time during a 1-month period (or less if successfully treated)." Because only two symptoms are required and no symptom is considered more important than any other, the diagnosis of schizophrenia can be applied to very different people. One person may have delusions and disorganized speech, whereas another might have hallucinations and catatonic behavior. These two people have no symptoms in common, yet both are diagnosed schizophrenic. Because the population of schizophrenic people is so heterogeneous, it is difficult to see how they can all be suffering from the same condition. The third objection to the diagnosis of schizophrenia is the finding that clinicians do not always agree when making the diagnosis. As already mentioned, in the past, American clinicians used the diagnosis much more broadly than their European counterparts. The fourth objection is philosophical. Some writers believe that schizophrenia is not a mental disorder but a moral judgment made by the middle-class majority about the odd behavior of an eccentric minority (Sarbin & Mancuso, 1980).

These criticisms have varying levels of legitimacy. It is true that there is no objective test for schizophrenia, and the condition (as Bleuler noted) is heterogeneous. It is also true that this heterogeneity does sometimes make it difficult for clinicians to agree on a diagnosis. Yet clinicians do manage to agree 70%–80% of the time about who is suffering from schizophrenia; this is about the same level of interclinician reliability as many standard medical diagnoses (S. Schwartz, 1982). For example, experienced radiologists disagree about 30% of the time when evaluating chest X rays for tuberculosis, and pathologists frequently disagree about whether a tissue sample is malignant. Yet no one has argued that these diagnostic disagreements mean that tuberculosis and cancer are not legitimate diagnostic categories. We simply need better diagnostic tools. Indeed, one of the reasons the *DSM* is continuously being revised is to improve its diagnostic reliability.

The idea that schizophrenia is a moral judgment was taken seriously during the anti-psychiatry movement of the 1970s and early 1980s, but it went out of style in the face of the substantial evidence showing that schizophrenia is found in every culture, is at least partly inherited, and is often associated with various forms of brain damage. This evidence, which is reviewed later in this chapter, is difficult to reconcile with the idea that schizophrenia is simply middle-class name-calling. It is just as well that this peculiar idea has faded away because it was exceedingly cruel. Claiming that schizophrenia is simply a social judgment trivializes the enormous human suffering of people who have hallucinations, delusions, and other debilitating symptoms.

There is no doubt that schizophrenia is a heterogeneous diagnostic category. As research accumulates, the diagnosis will doubtless become more specific. It is typical in medical history to proceed from general categories ("the fevers," for example) to more specific conditions. Perhaps in the future we will have a new taxonomic system based on physiological and behavioral markers that will produce truly homogenous subgroupings of psychoses. Yet it would be incorrect to conclude that the present diagnostic criteria are worthless. As you will see in this chapter, researchers and clinicians have learned a great deal about the conditions we call schizophrenia. Their discoveries have led to treatments that have relieved suffering and increased our knowledge of human behavior. Each new increment to our knowledge brings us one step closer to unraveling schizophrenia's mysteries.

John Forbes Nash, a mathematician who won the Nobel Prize in economics in 1994, began suffering from paranoid schizophrenia in 1959. After 30 years of experiencing the various phases of the disease, he had a lasting remission, which is quite rare. His story is chronicled by Sylvia Nasar in A Beautiful Mind *(1998).*

COURSE OF SCHIZOPHRENIA

Like everything about schizophrenia, its course is highly variable. Schizophrenia usually makes its first appearance in adolescence, but it can appear later. Schizophrenia normally persists for years but may sometimes slip away more quickly. According to Breier and his colleagues (1991), the typical course of schizophrenia has three parts: a prodromal phase before symptoms appear; a deteriorating phase that lasts between 5 and 10 years, in which there are periods of active symptoms alternating with periods of better functioning; and, finally, a lengthy period of stable symptoms lasting into old age.

Prodromal Phase

The **prodromal phase** precedes the disorder and is marked by a deterioration from some higher level of functioning. Friends and relatives almost always notice personality changes—flattened affect, social withdrawal, and other negative symptoms—well before any positive symptoms appear. Even early in life, chil-

dren who later develop schizophrenia are different from their brothers and sisters. Judges asked to view home movies of children aged 1 to 5 playing with their siblings are able to pick out the children who later grew up to be schizophrenic (E. F. Walker & Lewine, 1990; E. F. Walker et al., 1993). The future patients were less emotionally responsive and had poorer motor coordination than their brothers and sisters (Bergman, Wolfson, & Walker, 1997).

In many cases, people in the early stages of schizophrenia are aware that their cognitive abilities are disintegrating. Consider a conversation related by Mrs. Plowman to Dr. Kahn (Document 9.6). The conversation took place between Mrs. Plowman and her daughter 7 months before Jennifer was hospitalized. Note how Jennifer attempted to rationalize her odd experiences.

DOCUMENT 9.6

Conversation Between Mrs. Plowman and Jennifer 7 Months Before Her Hospitalization

Mrs. Plowman related the following conversation to me just after her daughter's intake interview. I include it here because it seems to provide a good insight into Jennifer's behavior during the prodromal stage of her illness.

—S. Kahn

MRS. PLOWMAN: Jenny, why were you so upset last night? You just went right to bed without even talking to me.

JENNIFER: I had an upsetting experience. I was driving home, and I suddenly realized that I was lost. I didn't have a clue where I was. I tried to concentrate and figure out how I got there, but I seemed to keep drifting off. I kept thinking about other things.

MRS. PLOWMAN: But you were only driving home from the store.

JENNIFER: That's what was so scary. I couldn't figure out how I got lost. Every time I tried to figure it out, so many thoughts went through my head, I just couldn't concentrate on driving. I even started to think about navigating by the stars. The Milky Way constellation would point my way home. I started looking for the Milky Way. I saw a bright light and I followed it.

MRS. PLOWMAN: Well, you managed to get home safely, that's the important thing.

JENNIFER: I guess that I'm just stressed out. Dad's dying and my not working. I think I must be feeling all that stress. ■

To keep from disintegrating further, people in the early stages of schizophrenia may try to consciously control their thoughts and actions. Some time after Jennifer was hospitalized, Mrs. Plowman found the daily schedule reproduced in Document 9.7. It was prepared by Jennifer not too long before her hospitalization. Jennifer seems to have realized that she was losing control. Out of desperation, she decided to regiment every minute of her life in a last-ditch effort to maintain some semblance of order.

Active Phase

Once **active phase** symptoms appear, everyday life for people with schizophrenia becomes a harrowing profusion of ideas and images. In contrast to those in the prodromal phase, patients in the active phase do not seem to be aware that they are behaving strangely. Like Jennifer, they deny that their peculiar ideas are delusional or that their sensory experiences may only be hallucina-

tions. Because they are shunned by others, and partly for self-protection, most schizophrenic people withdraw into their own lonely and isolated worlds. The active phase can persist for weeks, months, or even years.

Residual Phase

In most cases, active symptoms eventually respond to treatment. However, a minority of patients never get beyond the active phase. Their course is said to be "continuous." (Table 9.4 summarizes the *DSM-IV* course specifiers.) Even those patients whose active symptoms diminish are unlikely to return to their premorbid level of functioning. Usually, negative symptoms and mild levels of positive symptoms persist in the residual phase. When negative symptoms alternate with active phase positive symptoms, the course of the disorder is said to be "episodic." In "single episodes," the active

DOCUMENT 9.7

Schedule Drawn Up by Jennifer 6 Weeks Before Her Hospitalization

Time	Activity
7:00–8:00	Shower, dry hair, make the bed, get dressed
8:00–8:15	Read passage from the Bible
8:15–8:30	Practice handwriting
8:30–8:45	Aerobics
8:45–9:00	Breakfast (one banana, cereal with milk, coffee)
9:00–10:00	Study word processing
10:00–11:00	Read newspaper
11:00–12:00	Wash clothes, clean windows
12:00–1:00	Aerobics and shower
1:00–1:30	Study word processing
1:30–1:45	Lunch (salad and three glasses of water)
1:45–2:45	Listen to music
2:45–3:15	Walk to library
3:15–4:30	Read at library
4:30–5:00	Walk home from library
5:00–6:00	Prepare dinner
6:00–6:20	Shower
6:20–6:35	Dinner (vegetables, bread, three glasses of water)
6:35–8:05	Study word processing
8:05–9:00	Go for walk
9:00–9:30	Read magazine
9:30–10:00	Choose clothes for tomorrow
10:00–10:20	Shower
10:20–10:40	Read passage from the Bible
10:40–11:00	Undress and change to night clothes
11:00–11:15	Meditate
11:15–11:30	Prepare schedule for tomorrow

DSM-IV	**TABLE 9.4**	*DSM-IV* Schizophrenia Course Specifiers

Episodic: Course characterized by active phases alternating with symptom-free phases or phases in which only negative, or mild positive, symptoms are present.

Continuous: Symptoms are almost always present.

Single episode: Used when a single psychotic episode is followed by either a symptom-free period or a period in which only negative symptoms remain.

phase is followed by a period in which there are either no symptoms or only negative ones.

Although Kraepelin thought that deterioration was inevitable, we now know that Bleuler was correct—some patients do recover (Harding, Zubin, & Strauss, 1992; Watt & Saiz, 1991), and even severely affected patients may improve (Breier et al., 1991; Hegarty et al., 1994). The best predictors of outcome are the level of premorbid functioning and the severity of symptoms in the active phase (Carpenter & Strauss, 1991; Menezes, Rodrigues, & Mann, 1997; Watt & Saiz, 1991). Given two people with good premorbid functioning, the one whose symptoms are predominantly negative is likely to have a poorer outcome than one with mainly positive symptoms (Breier et al., 1991). Overall, outcomes are better in developing countries than in the developed world, perhaps because of the greater tolerance of psychotic behavior in developing areas (L. Davidson & McGlashan, 1997; Jablensky et al., 1992).

Although the prognosis for those with schizophrenia is less pessimistic than Kraepelin thought, it is still not very good. About half of all people with schizophrenia relapse within 2 years of their first episode. The relapse rate is worst for those whose first episode occurred at a young age, probably because they never had the opportunity to develop adequate coping skills (Eaton et al., 1992). Life expectancy is also lower among schizophrenics. This is partly the result of a high rate of suicide (Heila et al., 1997; Roy & Draper, 1995) and deaths arising from exposure among the schizophrenic homeless. On the other hand, people who do manage to survive into middle and old age have a good chance of a reasonable quality of life free of active symptoms (Harding et al., 1992).

Process Versus Reactive Schizophrenia

It was once common to distinguish between "process" and "reactive" types of schizophrenia. Reactive schizophrenia is associated with good premorbid functioning, the sudden onset of active-phase symptoms in response to some traumatic event (such as a death in the family,

like that of Jennifer's father), and no obvious signs of neurological dysfunction. Paranoid schizophrenia is especially likely to be reactive. In contrast, process schizophrenia is characterized by poor premorbid functioning, a slow onset of active-phase symptoms, and signs of neurological damage. Reactive schizophrenia was supposed to be a "psychological" response to traumatic events (such as vicious military battles), whereas process schizophrenia was thought to be an insidious neurological disease. The main evidence in support of the process-reactive distinction is the better prognosis for people with reactive schizophrenia. As already noted, people with good premorbid functioning usually have better outcomes than process schizophrenics whose adjustment was poor even before they developed schizophrenia. Unfortunately, the process-reactive division has not held up over time. Although it is generally true that a good premorbid adjustment, acute onset, and the absence of neurological abnormalities are associated with a better prognosis, this is not always the case (Straube, 1993). Even people with good premorbid adjustment may develop chronic schizophrenia. The general view today is that schizophrenia cannot be divided into psychological and neurological forms. All cases of schizophrenia are the result of the complex interaction of physiological, psychological, and, as discussed next, cultural factors.

Course and Culture

Kraepelin, the principal designer of our modern diagnostic nosology, was also a pioneer of cross-cultural psychiatry (Jilek, 1995). He made several overseas study visits to Asia, the United States, Mexico, and Cuba. During these visits, Kraepelin noted cultural differences in the symptoms and course of dementia praecox. Since that time, other investigators have pursued similar investigations. One common finding, already mentioned, is that schizophrenia appears to have a more positive outcome in developing countries than in industrialized ones (L. Davidson & McGlashan, 1997; Weisman, 1997). Some researchers believe that this finding may be arti-

Life expectancy is low among homeless schizophrenics, who have a high rate of death due to exposure.

factual. The cultures of developing countries may be more accepting of divergent behavior than those of developed countries. For this reason, observers in developing countries may rate the outcome of schizophrenia as more favorable even if it is identical to the outcome in developed countries (Edgerton & Cohen, 1994). Alternatively, something in the social environment of developing countries may produce a more positive outcome (Weisman, 1997). Unfortunately, the social factors that lead to a better outcome for schizophrenia in developing countries have not yet been identified (Kulhara, 1994).

INCIDENCE, AGE OF ONSET, AND PREVALENCE

Schizophrenia is one of the most ubiquitous of the major psychological disorders. Although its presentation may vary from time to time and from country to coun-

try, the basic disorder remains recognizable in all times, in industrial and nonindustrial societies, and in every segment of the population—rich and poor, young and old, male and female. To find out how many people suffer from schizophrenia, and their demographic distribution, researchers must cope with many methodological difficulties.

Incidence

The incidence of a disorder is technically defined as the number of new cases that appear during a given period of time (usually 1 year). To determine the incidence of schizophrenia, researchers must begin with some method for finding cases. One possibility is a community survey in which every member of a community, or a selected sample of people from the community, is interviewed. Unfortunately, schizophrenia is too rare for such an approach. The number of people who would have to be surveyed to find a large enough schizophrenic sample is too great to be practical. For this reason, most incidence estimates are obtained by counting the number of new cases seen at treatment facilities (usually mental hospitals, but also doctors' offices and counseling centers) over the period of a year. This approach assumes that all cases are seen at these treatment services and that the clinicians who work in them are perfectly accurate diagnosticians. Neither assumption is likely to be true. In developing countries and in the poorer parts of industrialized countries, many people with schizophrenia lack access to treatment services. For those who do get to treatment, there is no guarantee that they will be diagnosed accurately. Even though the *DSM-IV* and the World Health Organization's *ICD-10* contain more explicit diagnostic criteria than earlier versions, there is still some variability in practice among clinicians and across countries.

Despite these methodological concerns, using the standard *DSM* and *ICD* criteria for schizophrenia, incidence rates are remarkably similar around the world. A review of 50 epidemiological studies (R. Warner & de Girolamo, 1995) conducted in both developing and developed countries, with many different age groups and clinicians, found the incidence of schizophrenia to be between .21 and .24 new cases per 1,000 people per year. (This figure must be age corrected as described in Critical Thinking About Clinical Decisions 9.1.) At these incidence rates, 1 out of every 4,000–5,000 people in the United States will be newly diagnosed as schizophrenic each year; this translates to about 50,000–60,000 new cases each year. From time to time, areas with a much

Standardizing Across Cultures: The Concept of Age Adjustment

Because cultural differences may reveal important clues about schizophrenia's etiology, researchers frequently wish to compare the incidence and prevalence of schizophrenia in different countries. If researchers find that there are more people with schizophrenia in India than in the United States, for instance, they can then look at other differences between the two countries—diet, health care, child-rearing practices, and so on. These differences may tell us why schizophrenia occurs more often in one culture than another. However, before researchers devote a lot of energy to searching for the cause of cultural differences, they must be absolutely certain that the differences they are investigating are real and not just the result of a statistical artifact.

Consider the United States and India. For illustrative purposes, let us say that epidemiological studies estimate that there are 500,000 people with schizophrenia in the United States and 1,500,000 in India. There are many more people diagnosed as schizophrenic in India, but this may be a statistical artifact. We would expect many more cases of

schizophrenia in India because India has a much greater population. To compare two countries of different sizes, we must change the raw number of cases into prevalence "rates," which are expressed as a fraction in which the numerator is the number of cases of schizophrenia and the denominator is a standard number of persons. Thus, we may find that there are 2.8 cases of schizophrenia per 1,000 people in India and 2.00 cases per 1,000 people in the United States.

Rates are an improvement over raw number of cases, but the comparison may still be flawed if the 1,000 people represented in the denominators of the two countries have different compositions. Life expectancy, for example, is lower in India. This means that there are more elderly people in a sample of 1,000 people from the United States than in a sample of 1,000 people from India, where people die at a younger age. If schizophrenia is associated with age, we will observe different rates of occurrence in the two countries, not because of any cultural differences, but simply because the longer people live, the more opportunity they have to develop schizophre-

nia. Clearly, what researchers need is a single value that summarizes the prevalence rate for each country while correcting for any differences in the age distribution of their populations. To get this single number the population estimates must be **age adjusted** or **age standardized.**

The direct method of age adjustment involves choosing a standard population and applying the occurrence rates observed in the countries being studied to the standard population. The choice of a standard population is arbitrary. Often, it is the population of a particular country at a particular time, such as the United States in 1990. Sometimes it is the world population. By applying the observed rates to the standard population, it is possible to compare the prevalence rates of different countries while correcting for any differences in the age distributions of their populations. Such comparisons have generally found the prevalence rate to be markedly similar in India, the United States, and most other countries (Thara, Padmavati, & Nagaswami, 1993).

---

higher incidence have been reported. On each occasion, further investigation has been able to attribute an apparent high incidence to local diagnostic practices: for example, the use of a broad and inclusive definition of schizophrenia (see Häfner & Gattaz, 1991, for example).

Recent reports suggest that the incidence of schizophrenia may be declining (Waddington & Youssef, 1994). However, this reduction may simply be an artifact produced by changes in diagnostic and treatment practices. For example, fewer people are being diagnosed schizophrenic today because many of the people who would have formerly received this diagnosis are now being diagnosed with schizoaffective disorder. In addition, early incidence estimates were based on the diagnosis of people admitted to mental hospitals. Today, hospitalization is less common. Many people with

schizophrenia live among the homeless and never come into contact with a mental health facility.

Although the incidence of schizophrenia may not have really declined, there has been a conspicuous change in its clinical appearance. As noted earlier, the catatonic subtype has become relatively rare in developed countries, although catatonic symptoms may still be found in developing countries (R. Warner & de Girolamo, 1995).

Age of Onset

The typical age of onset for schizophrenia is 14–25 for men and 24–35 for women, with negative symptoms making their appearance around 4 years before the first hospital admission (Lewine, 1991). By the age of 60, the cumulative incidence for men and women is equal, and almost no new cases of schizophrenia are identified after age 60 (Gottesman, 1991). Thus, although men show signs of schizophrenia earlier in life, women eventually catch up. The finding of an earlier onset for men, which was first noted by Kraepelin, has been replicated many times (R. Howard et al., 1993; Reicher et al., 1991). The earlier onset for males does not seem to be related to diagnostic procedures, nationality, occupational status, or help-seeking differences between the sexes (R. Warner & de Girolamo, 1995). Instead, the striking cross-cultural similarity of the sex difference in age of onset points toward a biological explanation (Basso et al., 1997). It has been suggested, for example, that the female hormone estrogen may reduce vulnerability to schizophrenia (Häfner et al., 1991).

Schizophrenia is more serious among men than among women. Men usually develop symptoms earlier and have longer and more frequent hospital stays (M. J. Goldstein, 1988; Iacono & Beiser, 1992; Mueser et al., 1990). Because schizophrenia usually begins later in females, they have a longer period of good premorbid adjustment. This may give them the chance to learn adaptive coping skills, which, in turn, gives them a better prognosis. This hypothesis is supported by outcome studies showing that when the age of onset is controlled, men and women have very similar outcomes (R. Warner & de Girolamo, 1995; see also Cernovsky, Landmark, & O'Reilly, 1997, and Jablensky & Cole, 1997).

Prevalence

The prevalence of schizophrenia—the total number of cases in the population—is determined by its incidence and its duration (prevalence = incidence × duration). Because schizophrenia is a chronic condition, people who are diagnosed schizophrenic tend to stay that way for years. The result is that cases tend to accumulate over time, producing a prevalence rate that is much greater than the incidence rate.

Researchers interested in schizophrenia have estimated three main types of prevalence rates. "Point prevalence" is the number of cases at any one time, "period prevalence" is the number of cases observed in a given period (usually 1 year), and "lifetime prevalence" is the number people in the population who have suffered from the condition at some time in their lives. The prevalence of schizophrenia varies depending on which estimate is used and which population is studied. For example, point-prevalence estimates for schizophrenia vary from 0.9 per 1,000 in the Pacific island nation of Tonga to 17.4 per 1,000 in Ireland (R. Warner & de Girolamo, 1995). Lifetime prevalence varies from around 0.6% to 2% (Keith, Regier, & Rae, 1991), with an average of about 1% (Karno et al., 1987; Regier et al., 1993; Sartorius et al., 1986). It has been estimated that around 4.5 million people in the United States are in the active phase of schizophrenia at any point in time (Carson & Sanislow, 1993). These people make up half of all hospitalized psychiatric patients.

Prevalence in developing countries is lower than in the developed world. Given that incidence rates are similar, the difference in prevalence between developed and developing countries does not reflect a true difference in the rate of occurrence of schizophrenia but rather the difficulty in finding cases and the shorter life expectancy in the developing world. (Because duration is multiplied by incidence to estimate prevalence, a shorter life span produces a lower prevalence.)

As is the case for incidence, there have also been occasional reports of geographic areas with extraordinarily high prevalence (R. Warner & de Girolamo, 1995). As noted, this may reflect local diagnostic practice. However, some of these reports may be the result of migration. Healthy people tend to leave economically depressed areas or areas of famine, whereas schizophrenic people, who lack the necessary resources to migrate, remain at home, driving up the apparent prevalence rate (Folnegovic & Folnegovic-Smalc, 1992). A similar phenomenon might account for the high prevalence rates of schizophrenia in the poor Aboriginal communities located on the outskirts of Australian cities (I. H. Jones & Horne, 1973). Schizophrenic people may stay in these communities while healthier people migrate to areas with greater employment opportunities. This is known as the "social drift" hypothesis, and it is discussed in more detail later in this chapter. An alternative hypothesis is that schizophrenia is more common in fringe communities because the intrusion of Western lifestyles disrupts traditional ways of life (Jablensky & Sartorius, 1975). At present, there is insufficient evidence available to choose between these two different explanations for increased prevalence in certain communities. It is also possible that both are true.

ETIOLOGY OF SCHIZOPHRENIA: GENETICS

One possible reason why the prevalence of schizophrenia is so similar from one country to the next is that it is an inherited condition. In the early decades of the 20th century, Franz Kallman (1938) examined the family members of more than 1,000 people with schizophrenia, all of whom were patients in a Berlin psychiatric hospital. He found that the more severe a person's disorder, the more likely it was that a member of the person's family would also show signs of mental disorder. Decades later, a Danish study reported a 30-year follow-up of 207 high-risk children, whose mothers were schizophrenic, and 104 low-risk children, who had no signs of mental illness in their families (Mednick & Schulsinger, 1968). Thirty-one members of the high-risk group developed schizophrenia compared with only two members of the low-risk group (one of whom should have been in the high-risk group because his mother was diagnosed schizophrenic after the study began). As may be seen in Document 9.8, schizophrenia ran in Jennifer Plowman's family as well. Over the years, there have been numerous investigations into the genetics of schizophrenia. The vast majority have confirmed the connection between genetics and schizophrenia.

DOCUMENT 9.8

Abridged Version of Jennifer Plowman's
Social Work Consultation Report

Date: December 20, 2000

Social Worker: Li Cheong, MSW

Referral: Dr. Kahn requested this report on Jennifer Plowman, a 21-year-old woman who has been committed by the court for assessment.

Sources: Hospital records, family service records, Mrs. Anne Plowman, Dr. Stuart Berg.

Jennifer Plowman is the adopted child of Anne and Martin Plowman. Jenny was born in Los Angeles, but she moved here with her adoptive parents when she was 7 months old.

Anne Plowman was 28 years old at the time of the adoption; her husband was 29. They had been married for 6 years. Both Martin and Anne were university graduates. Anne worked as an elementary school teacher until the couple adopted Jenny. She left work to raise her daughter. Martin started a retail electrical goods store when he was 30. The business thrived and expanded until he had stores at four locations. As their income improved, the family moved into a large house and traveled extensively on vacations.

Anne described Jenny as a "quiet" and "sensitive" child who preferred watching television to just about all other activities. She had a few close friends and seemed to do well in her schoolwork. Although her parents told Jenny that she was adopted, she never showed much interest in her natural par-

ents until she was 13, when she saw a television show about an adopted child who had sought out her natural parents. Jenny decided to do the same. Anne and Martin were against this, and there was considerable family friction over the issue. In the end, Martin reluctantly agreed to hire a lawyer to find Jenny's natural parents.

After a 2-month investigation, the lawyer reported that Jenny's mother was no longer alive. After giving birth at age 16 to Jennifer, she had spent the next 10 years in and out of Los Angeles mental hospitals and clinics. According to hospital records, Jenny's natural mother was diagnosed schizophrenic, undifferentiated type. She took an overdose of medication mixed with alcohol, thereby ending her life at age 26. Because Jenny's natural mother was unable to identify him, the identity of her natural father was never discovered.

After learning this tragic news, Jenny lost any further interest in her natural family and never mentioned the matter again. She graduated from high school and entered the university, where she continued to perform well in her studies. She was still "quiet" but otherwise seemed quite normal to her parents.

A few years ago, Martin borrowed quite heavily to expand his business further. When the economy went into recession, Martin could not meet his loan commitments. He was forced to sell his business and the family house, which he had mortgaged to raise further funds. Eventually, Martin was forced to declare bankruptcy. He found work as a salesperson with a local company, and Anne returned to teaching. They were getting by financially when Martin (aged 48 at the time) had a heart attack. Martin was never the same. He seemed to lack energy and drive. He became depressed and hardly worked. About a year after his first heart attack, he had a second one, which was fatal.

Martin had dropped his life insurance because he could not meet the yearly premium. Thus, his death put Jenny and Anne under great financial pressure. Jenny found a job as a file clerk but lost her job when she became forgetful and sloppy in her work. Anne's salary became their sole income. It was at this point that Jenny began acting strangely.... ■

Family Studies

Family studies begin by identifying a patient, who is called the **proband.** The next step is to examine the proband's relatives to see whether any suffer from schizophrenia or another psychotic disorder. As early as 1916, researchers used this **consanguinity method** to examine the genetic transmission of schizophrenia. The dependent variable in such studies is the **lifetime morbid risk,** the likelihood that a relative will suffer an episode of schizophrenia sometime between birth and

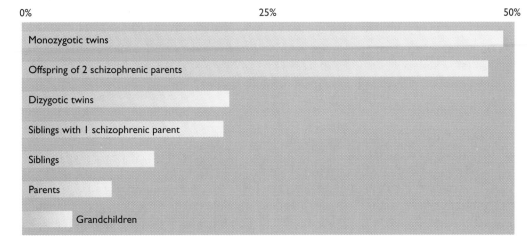

FIGURE 9.1 **Risk of Developing Schizophrenia for Relatives of People With Schizophrenia.** Adapted from: Gottesman & Shields (1972).

death. Because an older relative has fewer remaining years of life in which to develop schizophrenia than a younger one, lifetime morbid risk is usually adjusted to take into account relatives' ages. If heredity is important in schizophrenia, we would expect the lifetime morbid risk to be higher among the relatives of people with schizophrenia than in the general population. We would also expect lifetime morbid risk to be greater among relatives with a close genetic relationship to the proband than among more distant relatives.

Gottesman (1991), using data from about 40 studies conducted between 1920 and 1987, calculated the average lifetime morbid risk of developing schizophrenia for people with different degrees of relationship to a schizophrenic proband. These studies were not all of equal value. They suffered in varying degrees from biased sampling, variable diagnostic criteria, uncertainties about which twins were identical and which ones were dizygotic, and a host of other methodological problems. Still, the overall results, which are summarized in Figure 9.1, were remarkably consistent with a genetic hypothesis. Morbid risk increases with the number of genes that a relative shares with the proband. The greatest risk is among identical twins, who share all their genes; followed by first-degree relatives of schizophrenic people, who share 50% of their genes with the proband; nieces and nephews, who share 25% of their genes; and finally the general population, who have only a 1% risk of developing schizophrenia.

Twin Studies

The data summarized by Gottesman (1991) strongly suggest that genetic factors play a role in schizophrenia and

related disorders. This finding is further reinforced by the results of the already mentioned Danish high-risk study, which found that schizophrenic-like personality traits were three times as common in their high-risk group (people with schizophrenic parents) than in their low-risk group (Parnas et al., 1993). More recent studies have found evidence for the inheritance of schizophrenic symptoms, such as hallucinations and delusions, as well (Gambini et al., 1997). Despite these findings, genetics alone are not sufficient to explain the observed family patterns. Eighty-nine percent of schizophrenic probands did *not* have a parent with schizophrenia. Sixty-three percent had no relative, of any degree, with schizophrenia (Gottesman, 1991). This is not what we would expect to find if schizophrenia were simply an inherited condition. Clearly, other factors, such as the environment in which children are raised, also play a role.

Twin studies are one way to try to separate the effects of heredity from those produced by the environment. Specifically, if environmental factors determine who develops schizophrenia, we would expect monozygotic twins who are reared together to show a similar rate of concordance for schizophrenia to dizygotic twins reared together (even though monozygotic twins have the same genes, whereas dizygotic twins share only 50% of their genes). On the other hand, if genetics is paramount, we should expect to find a higher concordance rate among monozygotic twins (who share both their genes and their environments).

Like family studies, twin studies have produced mixed results. The reasons are similar: biased sampling, variable diagnostic criteria, uncertainties about which twins were identical, and even the way in which concordance was calculated. (Critical Thinking About Clinical

Measuring Concordance

Measuring concordance for schizophrenia among relatives requires several steps. The first is to identify a schizophrenic proband and then determine whether the proband's relatives also have schizophrenia. The answer to this question varies depending on the evidence required. A strict criterion, for example, might require a relative to have been hospitalized and diagnosed schizophrenic before he or she would be considered concordant. In contrast, a liberal criterion might only require the relative to have been diagnosed "psychotic." Strict criteria will produce lower levels of concordance than liberal ones. The first table illustrates this with data published by Gottesman and Shields (1972). The table summarizes the concordance rate for monozygotic and dizygotic twins using three different definitions of concordance. As you can see, the concordance rate increases markedly as the criteria become more liberal.

Even when two different researchers use the same criterion for determining concordance, they can still come up with different results because concordance may be calculated in more than one way. To see how the two methods differ, apply them to a hypothetical study in which 100 pairs of twins (200 people) were examined. In 50 pairs, both twins have been diagnosed schizophrenic, and in the remaining 50 pairs, only one twin has been diagnosed schizophrenic. These results are summarized in the second table.

METHOD 1: COUNT PAIRS

One way to measure concordance is to count the number of pairs in which both members have been diagnosed schizophrenic and express the result as a proportion of the total number of twin pairs in the study. For example, in the hypothetical study of 100 pairs in which 50 pairs had two schizophrenic members and 50 pairs had only one member who is schizophrenic, Method 1 produces a concordance of 50% (50/100).

METHOD 2: COUNT CASES

This method begins by identifying each case of schizophrenia in the study population and then counting the number of cases who have a schizophrenic brother or sister. Using this method, concordance is expressed as the proportion of cases in which both twins have been diagnosed schizophrenic over the total number of cases of schizophrenia in the study. In the hypothetical study, there were 50 pairs in which both members were diagnosed schizophrenic and 150 total cases of schizophrenia. Thus, Method 2 produces a concordance of 66% (100/150).

Note that, if concordance were perfect, both methods would produce the same result (100%). At lower rates of concordance, however, the two methods produce different results, making cross-study comparisons difficult (McGue, 1992; Torrey, 1992).

Concordance for Schizophrenia in Identical and Fraternal Twins Using Different Criteria	Concordance (%)	
Criteria for concordance	Monozygotic	Dizygotic
Hospitalized and diagnosed schizophrenic	42	9
Hospitalized but not necessarily diagnosed schizophrenic	54	18
All of those included by first two criteria plus others who were never hospitalized but were suspected	79	45

Note: From Gottesman & Shields (1972).

Outcome of a Hypothetical Twin Study	
Pairs in which both twins have been diagnosed schizophrenic	50
Pairs in which only one twin has been diagnosed schizophrenic	50
Total number of cases of schizophrenia (50 × 2 + 50 × 1)	150
Total number of pairs	100
Total number of individuals	200

Decisions 9.2 explains how concordance is determined.) Still, the majority of studies have found that monozygotic twins have much higher concordance rates for schizophrenia than do dizygotic twins (Gottesman, 1991; Onstad et al., 1991). This suggests that genetics is a more important determinant of schizophrenia than en-

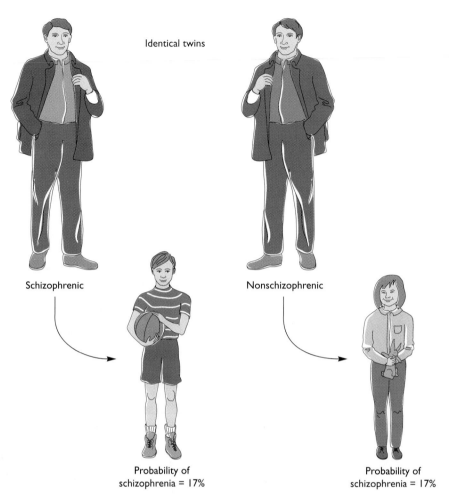

Identical twins

Schizophrenic

Nonschizophrenic

Probability of
schizophrenia = 17%

Probability of
schizophrenia = 17%

FIGURE 9.2 **Probability of the Offspring of Identical Twins Developing Schizophrenia.** From: Gottesman & Bertelsen (1989).

vironment. However, it is always possible that schizophrenia may be present in some form from birth (congenital) without being genetic. For example, the antipsychotic medications given to schizophrenic mothers during pregnancy may produce an abnormal intrauterine environment, which may affect the brain development of their children. It is possible that such children may be predisposed to develop schizophrenia in response to stress. Alternatively, a virus during pregnancy could affect neurological development and make children susceptible to schizophrenia (Stober, Franzek, & Beckmann, 1997). Both of these congenital causes would produce a higher concordance among twins than among other siblings because twins are exposed to the same intrauterine environment (Davis & Phelps, 1995).

To separate congenital from genetic causes of schizophrenia, Gottesman and Bertelsen (1989) studied the children of monozygotic schizophrenic twins who were dis-

cordant for schizophrenia (pairs in which only one twin had the condition). They found that the probability of finding schizophrenia in the next generation is 17%. Importantly, it did not matter whether it was a parent who had schizophrenia or a parent's identical sibling (an aunt or uncle). In both cases, the probability of a child's developing schizophrenia was the same, 17% (Figure 9.2). This is a striking finding. Children of nonschizophrenic parents whose aunts or uncles had schizophrenia have the same probability of developing schizophrenia as their cousins, whose parents actually had schizophrenia. This study suggests that genetics rather than events during pregnancy are responsible. The identical twin aunts and uncles who were not schizophrenic seem to be "carriers" who pass on the condition to their children.

If schizophrenia were entirely a function of heredity, we would expect to find a concordance of 100% among identical twins because they share all of their genes. Yet,

All four of the Genain quadruplets developed schizophrenia in their early 20s, providing evidence of a genetic etiology. However, the disorder took a different course for each of them. Myra eventually married and had two children. Hester, at the other end of the spectrum, spent a considerable time in the hospital and, at one point, was described as a hopeless case.

despite the widespread evidence for the inheritance of schizophrenia, no study has produced a concordance rate of 100% among monozygotic twins. It seems obvious that factors other than genetics must be involved. Perhaps being raised by a mentally ill parent or alongside a schizophrenic sibling determines who among those with "schizophrenic genes" will develop the disorder and what form it will take (Battaglia et al., 1995; Kendler & Walsh, 1995). This hypothesis is consistent with the results of a case study of the Genain quadruplets (a fictitious name). All four developed schizophrenia between the ages of 22 and 24. This seems compelling evidence for the genetic transmission of schizophrenia. Yet there were differences among the girls. Even though they shared 100% of their genes, each sister had a different course, symptoms, and outcome (D. Rosenthal, 1963). For example, two of the four sisters were floridly psychotic, showing severe symptoms, whereas the other two were much better adjusted. One of the four sisters eventually married and had children, two had fluctuating good periods and bad periods during which they had to be hospitalized, while the fourth sister spent her life in the hospital. These differences suggest that differences in the sisters' respective environments influenced the way these genetically identical sisters expressed their genetic disposition toward schizophrenia.

Adoption Studies

In the typical adoption study, researchers begin by identifying schizophrenic probands who were adopted soon after birth. The next step is to investigate the psychological history of the proband's natural and adoptive families to determine whether any family members have ever been diagnosed schizophrenic. Using this approach, Heston (1966) found that the risk of schizophrenia among the offspring of schizophrenic mothers who were adopted early in life was 16.6%. This figure is not much different from the average morbid risk for children raised by their own schizophrenic mothers (Gottesman, 1991). In other words, being raised by a schizophrenic mother does not increase the risk of developing schizophrenia. Over the years, other adoption studies have confirmed that the children of schizophrenic mothers tend to resemble their natural mothers more than their adoptive ones, even when they are adopted as infants (Kendler & Diehl, 1993).

One possible confounding variable in this research is the effect of adoption itself. Perhaps being adopted predisposes a person to develop schizophrenia. Wender and his colleagues (1974) investigated this possibility by comparing adopted children of both normal and "schizophrenic" parents (which in their study included parents with schizophrenia, schizophreniform, schizoaffective, and related disorders). The children in this study were adopted by either normal or "schizophrenic" families. The results are summarized in Table 9.5. As you can see, adopted children whose parents suffered from schizophrenia or a related disorder were almost twice as likely as adopted children from biologically normal families to develop some type of schizophrenic disorder. In contrast, children adopted from biologically normal families had the same probability of developing schizophrenia whether they were raised in normal or schizophrenic families. The implication is that being raised by a parent with schizophrenia does not increase the probability of developing the disorder. Further support for this idea comes from the finding that identical twins who are raised apart have the same concordance rates for schizophrenia as do those who are raised together by their natural parents (Gottesman, 1991).

In contrast to the studies reported so far, Tienari and fellow researchers (1987, 1991) have claimed that family variables do play an important role in determining whether a child will become schizophrenic. These researchers compared the children of schizophrenic mothers who were raised by adoptive parents with a group of matched control children. Like other researchers, they

TABLE 9.5	Schizophrenia and Related Disorders in Adopted Twins	

Parents		Adopted twins with schizophrenia and related disorders (%)
Biological	**Adoptive**	
Normal	Normal	10.7
Normal	Schizophrenia	10.7
Schizophrenia	Normal	18.8

Note: Data from Wender et al. (1974).

found that schizophrenia appeared more often among the children whose natural mothers were schizophrenic. However, they also found that adoptive families with schizophrenic children were more disturbed than other families. Few children became schizophrenic in nondisturbed families, even when their biological mothers were schizophrenic (see also Marcus et al., 1987). The researchers interpreted their findings as evidence that schizophrenia results from the interaction between family environment and genetics. Although this sounds plausible, keep in mind that, instead of family disturbance causing schizophrenia, the presence of schizophrenic members may have caused the families to become dysfunctional.

Markers

Underlying genotypes are often reflected in phenotypic traits known as markers. These markers are present not only in people with schizophrenia but also in their relatives. Prospective studies, in which people with the supposed markers are followed longitudinally to see if they develop schizophrenia, can help researchers to pinpoint the specific genetic causes of schizophrenia. Two potential cognitive markers for schizophrenia are attentional dysfunction and eye-tracking abnormalities.

Attentional Dysfunction   Kraepelin (1919) viewed distractibility as one of the most common features of dementia praecox:

It is quite common for them [schizophrenic patients] to lose both inclination and ability on their own initiative to keep their attention fixed for any length of time. . . . There is occasionally noticed a kind of irresistible attraction of the attention to casual external impressions. (pp. 6–7)

Distractibility in people with schizophrenia is often measured by performance on the Continuous Perfor-

mance Test (CPT), which requires people to identify a specific target letter or letter sequence from a rapidly presented population of letters. To perform well, people must focus their attention on specific visual patterns, something that distractible schizophrenic patients find particularly difficult to do (Nuechterlein, 1991). Of course, people with schizophrenia tend to do poorly on most cognitive tasks, so this finding alone is not of special significance. What makes the CPT so interesting is that relatives of schizophrenic patients, who are not schizophrenic themselves, also have difficulty with the CPT (Grove et al., 1991). The closer the relative, the more CPT performance is affected. For example, the children of schizophrenic patients tend to perform similarly to their parents (Erlenmeyer-Kimling & Cornblatt, 1992). These same children are likely to develop schizoid personality traits, and perhaps schizophrenia, later in life (Cornblatt et al., 1992). Electrophysiological studies of sensation and perception have confirmed that people with schizophrenia and their relatives seem to have special difficulty on tests such as the CPT, which require people to screen out irrelevant distracting stimuli (R. Freedman et al., 1991; Nuechterlein, Buchsbaum, & Dawson, 1994).

Further support for attentional deficit as a marker for schizophrenia comes from electrophysiological research, which focuses on the brain's electrical response to external stimuli. These studies have found abnormalities in the latency and size of the brain's response to stimuli in schizophrenic patients and their relatives (Shajahan et al., 1997; Van-Sweden, Van-Erp, & Mesotten, 1997).

Other measures of attentional performance also point toward attentional deficit as a marker for schizophrenia (Kern, Green, & Goldstein, 1995). These measures include the number of digits that can be recalled after a brief presentation and the comorbidity between schizophrenia and attention deficit disorder (Bellak, 1994; Granholm et al., 1997; Rund, Oie, & Sundet, 1996; see Chapter 12).

DOCUMENT 9.9

Comparison of
Jennifer Plowman's
Eye-Tracking Record
With the Record of
a Nonschizophrenic
Person

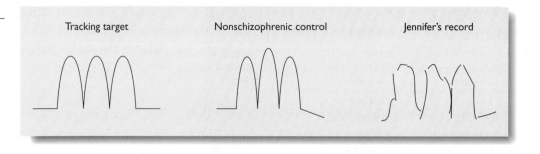

Tracking target   Nonschizophrenic control   Jennifer's record

Because attentional deficits not only run in families but also appear before any schizophrenic-like symptoms, they may reflect a genetic vulnerability to schizophrenia. For example, an inability to focus attention may impair a person's ability to process information, which, in turn, affects the individual's ability to engage in two-way communication (Velligan, Mahurin, Eckert, et al., 1997). However, because most of the family members who show attentional deficits will never show any schizophrenic symptoms, sensory deficits alone are clearly not sufficient to cause schizophrenia; other factors must also be involved.

Eye Movement (Tracking) Dysfunction   In his clinical descriptions, Kraepelin noted that people with dementia praecox had difficulty tracking a moving stimulus, such as a pendulum. Instead of smooth eye movements from side to side, Kraepelin's patients had frequent, jerky eye movements. (Document 9.9 illustrates Jennifer Plowman's eye-tracking record.) Kraepelin's observations have been repeated many times over the decades. On each occasion, schizophrenic patients were found to have eye-tracking abnormalities, whereas only a small number of nonschizophrenic people displayed any eye-tracking problem (Levy et al., 1993). These abnormalities in eye movement are also apparent in people at risk to develop schizophrenia (H. Schreiber et al., 1997). Specifically, about 50% of the first-degree relatives of people with schizophrenia have similar abnormalities (Iacono & Clementz, 1993; Katsanis et al., 1997; McDowell & Clementz, 1997). The same people also tend to do poorly on the CPT (Grove et al., 1991).

Researchers have hypothesized that eye-tracking problems and attentional impairments as indexed by the CPT or evoked potentials are markers for a specific "frontal-lobe" subtype of schizophrenia (Grove et al., 1992; Iacono & Grove, 1991). Because attention and cognition are at least partly dependent on the frontal lobes of the cerebral cortex, the finding of an attentional deficit is consistent with the results of anatomical, blood flow, and imaging studies that also seem to indicate the presence of some defect in the frontal lobes of at least some people with schizophrenia and their relatives (Deakin et al., 1997; Katsanis & Iacono, 1991; Knable & Weinberger, 1997; MacAvoy & Bruce, 1995).

How Many Genes Are Involved in Schizophrenia?

On average, children get half their genes from their mother and half from their father. This means that, if schizophrenia is the result of a single dominant gene, we should expect to find that 50% of children with one schizophrenic parent develop schizophrenia. The actual figure is only 17%, however. There are several possible ways to account for this discrepancy. One possibility is that schizophrenia is indeed the result of a single dominant gene but the gene has **variable expressivity** or **incomplete penetrance** (Carson & Sanislow, 1993; Kendler & Diehl, 1993). An example of a gene with complete penetrance is the gene that determines eye color. The underlying genotype is always reflected in the phenotype. When genes have variable expressivity, phenotypes vary in degree. Schizophrenia may be similar. An individual may carry the genotype but display varying degrees of psychopathology ranging from no symptoms at all through schizoid behavior to full-blown schizophrenia (C. M. Woolf, 1997).

If schizophrenia is the result of a single dominant gene (perhaps with incomplete penetrance), then it might be possible to identify its specific chromosomal location using linkage techniques such as those used to study mood disorders (see Chapter 8). Unfortunately, the current state of our knowledge of schizophrenic chromosomes is no better than that for mood disorders. Initial positive findings that have pointed toward potential "schizophrenic" genes have inevitably been followed by failures to replicate (Kendler & Diehl, 1993).

Although researchers are still trying to find the genetic site for schizophrenia, a definitive finding has not yet been made (Cao et al., 1997; Kirov & Murray, 1997; Schwab et al., 1997; Straub et al., 1997). Perhaps future research using more sensitive biochemical techniques will be more successful (Karayiorgou & Gogos, 1997). There is always the chance, however, that researchers are seeking something that does not exist. There may not be a schizophrenic gene. Instead, schizophrenia may be **polygenic,** the unlucky result of inheriting a number of interacting genes (Gottesman, 1991).

There are several reasons to believe that schizophrenia is polygenic. Polygenic inheritance would explain why only 17% of the offspring of a schizophrenic parent develop the condition themselves. (The probability of inheriting more than one gene is lower than the probability of inheriting only one.) Polygenic inheritance may also account for schizophrenia's varied course and symptoms, which seem too diverse to be caused by a single dominant gene. Finally, if schizophrenia is polygenic, then it is not surprising that linkage studies have produced inconsistent results. When several genes are responsible for a condition, we would not expect any single genetic marker to be present in all cases.

Whether schizophrenia is caused by one gene or many, there is little doubt that nongenetic factors play an important role. Remember, the concordance rate in monozygotic twins is only about 50%, even though these twins have identical genes. It seems reasonable to assume that some people inherit a vulnerability to schizophrenic breakdown. This vulnerability could take the form of a neurological defect, or it may be a personality trait, such as a tendency toward social isolation. In either case, an inherited vulnerability is not sufficient on its own to produce schizophrenia. Nongenetic factors must also be present. The best explanation is one derived from the diathesis-stress model. That is, the symptoms of schizophrenia are the result of an interaction between genetic and nongenetic factors.

ETIOLOGY OF SCHIZOPHRENIA: NONGENETIC RISK FACTORS

The precise causes of schizophrenia are still unknown. However, by comparing people with schizophrenia with those who do not have the disorder, it is possible to identify **risk factors** that are associated with a greater vulnerability to schizophrenia. The search for risk factors is an important research strategy in all areas of

health. We know, for example, that smoking is a risk factor for lung cancer and that a high level of blood cholesterol is a risk factor for coronary heart disease. Once such risk factors have been identified, they can serve as the basis for etiological theories and for potential interventions. For example, based on observed correlations between smoking and disease, scientists have hypothesized that something contained in cigarette smoke causes lung cancer. Research is then directed at identifying this cancer-causing substance, while treatment focuses on smoking cessation. Identifying risk factors is also important for epidemiological research. Schizophrenia is relatively uncommon, which means that many people have to be studied to find a sufficiently large sample. Using reliable risk factors, researchers can focus their efforts on people who are at high risk to develop schizophrenia, saving both time and money. This section reviews research on some of the common risk factors for schizophrenia and discusses the theories that have evolved to account for them.

Viral Infection

The idea that schizophrenia is the result of a brain infection comes partly from its rapid increase during the 19th century. Schizophrenic-like conditions were considered rare in the 18th century, but their incidence increased dramatically in the late 1800s (R. Warner & de Girolamo, 1995). In the United Kingdom alone, mental hospital admissions tripled between 1869 and 1900. This caused an editorial writer for the London *Times* of 1877 to quip that "if lunacy continues to increase as at present, the insane will be in the majority, and, freeing themselves, will put the sane in asylums" (quoted in Scull, 1979). At the time, many clinicians viewed the apparent growth in the number of cases as the result of improved mental health care. For the first time, they claimed, society was recognizing the needs of people with mental problems. However, if the increase in hospital admissions was entirely due to better services, there should have been at least some tapering off as the backlog of unrecognized cases was gradually reduced. This did not happen. Instead, the number of new cases continued to grow for decades. It is possible that some biological event (the birth of a new virus, for example) occurred sometime in the 1800s, producing the modern condition we know as schizophrenia (Hare, 1988).

The notion that schizophrenia may be the result of a virus that affects brain development in the fetus is consistent with the findings of research on fingerprints.

Among identical twins who are discordant for schizophrenia, about one third have different fingerprints. This suggests that some process has interfered with the normal biological development of the schizophrenic twin (Bracha et al., 1992). The virus hypothesis is also consistent with recent evidence that the antipsychotic medication clozapine is an effective antiviral agent (Jones-Brando et al., 1997). Perhaps antipsychotic agents such as clozapine work by inhibiting or destroying a schizophrenia-causing virus.

Despite these findings, the association between viral illnesses during pregnancy and later schizophrenia in offspring is not entirely positive. Although some researchers have found a relationship between maternal exposure to viral epidemics during pregnancy and later development of schizophrenia in offspring (W. Adams et al., 1993; Barr, Mednick, & Munk-Jorgensen, 1990; Kunugi et al., 1995; Mednick et al., 1988), others have failed to confirm such a relationship (Kendell & Kemp, 1989; also see R. Warner & de Girolamo, 1995, for a review).

One possible reason for the discrepant results is uncertainty about whether a specific woman contracted influenza during pregnancy. Just because an epidemic occurred in an area does not mean that every pregnant woman who lived in the affected area contracted the illness. One of the few studies that used doctors' records to substantiate that specific pregnant women had contracted influenza failed to find any increase in the prevalence of schizophrenia among the offspring of affected mothers, even after a period of 30 years (Crow & Done, 1992). Unfortunately, this negative finding does not completely settle the matter because it is possible that it is an infection other than influenza (or the drugs used by expectant mothers to combat illness) that produces a delayed effect on the fetus.

Looking at the viral issue in a different way, dozens of articles have been published on the season of birth of people with schizophrenia. Most report an excess of births in late winter or early spring, which means that their mothers were pregnant during the winter virus season (Modestin, Ammann, & Wurmle, 1995). Of course, there are other explanations for the seasonal finding. One possibility is that the finding is simply a methodological artifact (Eaton, 1991). Specifically, more people with schizophrenia are born in January than in later months because people born in January of any year are older than people born in February through December of that year. Because they have lived longer, people born in January have had more time to develop schizophrenia than those born in later months. One way to test the "artifactual" hypothesis is to examine season of birth in the Southern Hemisphere, where January and February are summer months and winter occurs in July and August. If more schizophrenics are born in July and August in the Southern Hemisphere, then the artifactual explanation is not likely to be correct. Unfortunately, the results of studies conducted in Australia and South America are equivocal; some find an excess of schizophrenic births in the winter months of July and August; others do not (M. S. Lewis, 1992).

In addition to the artifactual hypothesis, explanations of the supposed excess of schizophrenic births in winter and early spring have targeted seasonal variations in premature births, changes in endocrine output over the year, seasonal changes in diet, and, of course, variations in temperature (R. Warner & de Girolamo, 1995). However, the most common view is that the excess of schizophrenic winter births is the result of viruses such as influenza, which are more common in later winter and early spring. Specifically, viral exposure at a critical period of prenatal development causes subtle brain damage, which, in turn, produces a vulnerability to schizophrenia (Akbarian et al., 1993).

Cannon, Mednick, and Parnas (1990) have tied together genetic research with findings on season of birth. They hypothesize that viruses can trigger schizophrenia, but only in those people who have a genetic vulnerability. Birth injuries, complications of pregnancy, and low birth weight—which are all more common in the history of people with schizophrenia than in the population at large—may play the same triggering role. Thus, it may not be viruses alone that cause schizophrenia, but a variety of biological triggers interacting with a genetic vulnerability.

Life-Stress

Jennifer Plowman's illness was preceded by a year of considerable strain. Her father died, and she lost her job. This is not unusual. Studies that have followed people with schizophrenia over time have often found that active-phase episodes are preceded by significant life-stress (Norman & Malla, 1993).

Studies of the inmates of local jails in the United States have found that the prevalence of psychosis among inmates (around 6–8%) is higher than the prevalence among those newly admitted to jail (2–5%; Lamb & Grant, 1982). Because many inmates do not show signs of psychosis until after they are incarcerated, it seems that the stress of jail may be severe enough to produce a psychosis in vulnerable people (Teplin, 1990). Of course, it is also possible that nonpsychotic people were discharged, while psychotic inmates were kept behind bars. Such a selective discharge policy would artificially increase the prevalence without necessarily implying that the stress of prison is actually a cause of schizophrenia. Uncertainty about cause and effect also applies to studies that show schizophrenia to be more common among the homeless than in the general population (Fischer & Breakey, 1991). It is possible that the stress of being homeless contributes to the development of schizophrenia. Alternatively, people with schizophrenia may be unable to look after themselves and therefore become homeless.

One particular form of social stress that has been given special prominence is the stigma of being labeled schizophrenic. Goffman (1961) and Scheff (1966) have argued that once people are labeled schizophrenic, they are forced into a "sick" social role. They are denied employment, considered incapable of looking after themselves, and subjected to treatment (sometimes against their wishes). Eventually, such people come to believe that they are sick and act accordingly. These views were widely aired in the 1960s, and they do have some substance. All of us, including people with schizophrenia, are influenced by the reactions of others. However, genetic research has made it clear that there is much more to schizophrenia than mere labeling. Although it is important not to discount the social stigma associated with being labeled schizophrenic, few researchers today believe that hallucinations, delusions, and other schizophrenic behaviors are simply the result of having been called schizophrenic.

In summary, research on social stress has not produced great insight into the etiology of schizophrenia. Although social stress contributes to the development of the disorder, it is neither a sufficient nor a necessary cause of schizophrenia (Ventura et al., 1989). Many of us experience severe social stress without developing schizophrenic symptoms, and schizophrenia has been known to occur without any history of social stress.

Demographic and Socioeconomic Status

Schizophrenia has been associated with several intriguing demographic and socioeconomic findings. For example, schizophrenia is more common among people raised in large cities than among people brought up in rural areas or small towns (G. Lewis et al., 1992). New immigrants have higher than average prevalence rates and so do divorced and single people (Eaton, 1985). The explanation for these findings is not clear. Perhaps viruses are more common in big cities, or maybe big-city

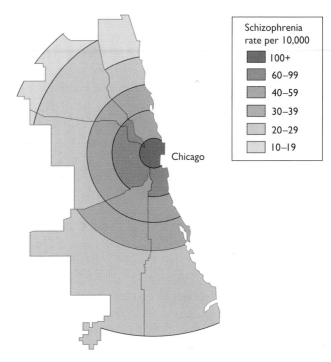

FIGURE 9.3 Prevalence of Schizophrenia in Chicago Neighborhoods in 1934. *The darkest area is downtown, where most of the residents were street people. Circling downtown were slums. They were bordered mainly by neighborhoods of skilled workers. Outside them were middle-class neighborhoods, and in the lightest area on the map were middle- to upper-class neighborhoods. Note how the rate of schizophrenia decreases as socioeconomic status increases.* Adapted from: Faris & Dunham (1939).

life is more stressful. Immigrants may have a special difficulty learning to adjust to their new culture. It is easier to explain why schizophrenia is more common among single than among married people—people with schizophrenia simply do not make good marriage prospects.

Social class is a particularly important variable in schizophrenia research. It is a standard finding that schizophrenia is more common among those in the lower social and economic groups (Faris & Dunham, 1939; Hollingshead & Redlich, 1958; R. Warner & de Girolamo, 1995). Figure 9.3 illustrates the relationship between socioeconomic status and the prevalence of schizophrenia.

Traditionally, two theories have been put forward to account for the relationship between social class and schizophrenia. The previously mentioned social drift theory blames the debilitating effects of mental illness. People with schizophrenia are impaired in their ability to compete economically, so they "drift" down the socioeconomic ladder. They wind up living in poorer neighborhoods, and they are not able to obtain the job that could help them move. In other words, the social drift theory argues that membership in the lower social classes is simply an offshoot of being schizophrenic. Social drift theory is supported by evidence that schizophrenic people often fail to achieve the occupational and socioeconomic status of their parents and family members (P. B. Jones et al., 1993). However, social drift theory is not able to explain why the relationship between social class and schizophrenia is often reversed in developing countries, where the prevalence of schizophrenia is greater in the higher social groups (R. Warner & de Girolamo, 1995).

Social stress theory proposes a direct causative role for social class. According to social stress theory, poor people are exposed to more economic and social problems than are those who are better off. These problems produce extra stress, which, in turn, helps breed schizophrenia. Social stress theory attributes the reversed relationship between social class and schizophrenia in developing countries to stresses caused by industrialization. Specifically, in developing countries, the better educated are under greater social stress with industrialization because they must learn to become part of a new and unfamiliar economic system, whereas the poor are left to their traditional subsistence living. This extra stress may be responsible for a higher prevalence of schizophrenia among the upper socioeconomic groups.

A third, more recent, theory highlights the relationship between the poor obstetric care available to members of the lower social classes and schizophrenia. For example, immigrants to the UK, who have a lower than average standard of obstetric care, also have a higher prevalence of schizophrenia (Eagles, 1991). Because obstetric care is poorer among the lower socioeconomic groups, their children experience a higher than average number of birth complications. These birth complications can cause brain damage, which may provoke psychiatric disorders, especially early-onset forms of schizophrenia (Eagles et al., 1990; Verdoux et al., 1997). This neurodevelopmental theory attributes the higher rates of schizophrenia among the upper social classes of developing countries to differences in access to medical care. In developing countries, the children of the wealthy get better medical care and are therefore more likely to survive a complicated birth than are the children of the poor. If birth complications lead to brain damage that ultimately results in schizophrenia, we would expect to find more cases among the upper classes because brain-injured children born to poor families in developing countries are not likely to survive. Of course, this theory depends on there being some relationship between brain

injury and schizophrenia. The evidence for such a relationship is reviewed later in this section.

Communication and Expressed Emotion

Freud concentrated most of his efforts on anxiety disorders and other neuroses while neglecting the psychoses. Apart from the claim that psychotic behavior represented regression to a primitive stage of development, Freud had little to say on the subject of schizophrenia. Nevertheless, many of his followers harbored the belief that family interactions were somehow responsible for psychoses. The so-called schizophrenogenic mother, for example, was thought to produce schizophrenia by her cold, domineering, and aloof attitude toward her children (Fromm-Reichmann, 1948; Hartwell, 1996). Parents of schizophrenic children were accused of sending confused messages to their offspring. For example, mothers might scold their children for speaking without permission and then accuse them of not wanting to share their thoughts with their parents. Such messages allegedly place children in a psychological "double-bind" from which they cannot escape except by schizophrenic breakdown (Bateson, 1959; Wynne & Singer, 1963). The evidence for this theory was always tenuous. Few researchers even bothered to study parent-child interactions. They based their conclusions about poor parental communication styles on how parents responded to TAT and Rorschach stimuli. Even those who do study real-life family interactions (for example, Tompson et al., 1997) run the risk of misinterpreting what came first, the faulty interaction or the schizophrenia. After all, it is always possible that the causal direction is the other way around—psychologically disturbed children affect the communication style of their parents. These blame-the-family theories added an additional burden of guilt to parents who already must cope with the heartbreak of having a disturbed child.

Although these early communication-based hypotheses were overstated, we do know that family relationships can influence the *course* of schizophrenia (Kuipers, 1992). Patients discharged to their own homes are more likely to return to the hospital or have an exacerbation of their symptoms if members of their family are hostile, critical, and overbearing. Such disturbed families are said to be high on a psychological dimension known as **expressed emotion** (Kavanagh, 1992). Document 9.10 is an excerpt from an interaction between Jennifer and her mother during one of Jennifer's visits home with Dr. Kahn. It illustrates what is meant by a high level of expressed emotion.

DOCUMENT 9.10

Expressed Emotion: Excerpt From a Conversation Between Jennifer and Her Mother

MRS. PLOWMAN: I have given my life to you, Jenny. Sacrificed everything. And this is what I get. You sit there in these long silences, saying nothing, making me worry.

JENNIFER: I have nothing to say.

MRS. PLOWMAN: This is what I deserve, right. For looking after you, for worrying about you. You should get your mind off your troubles. Read a book, or something.

JENNIFER: Please just leave me alone.

MRS. PLOWMAN: I just want to help you get better. ■

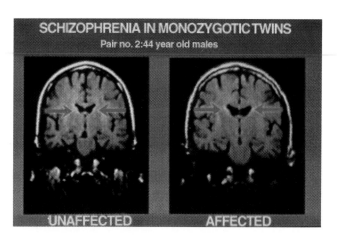

These MRIs of identical twins show enlarged lateral ventricles in the twin with schizophrenia.

High levels of expressed emotion in relatives is closely related to relapse among those with schizophrenia (Monking et al., 1997). Cross-cultural research suggests that high expressed emotion is less common in developing countries, where family members seem more tolerant of eccentric behavior than in developed countries. This may be one reason why the outcome of schizophrenia is more positive in developing countries (Craig et al., 1997; Jablensky et al., 1992; Lefley, 1992; Weisman, 1997). Note that the effect of expressed emotion is not specific to schizophrenia. Mood disorders are also made worse by families with high levels of expressed emotion (Hooley & Teasdale, 1989). Perhaps expressed emotion is just another form of stress (Miklowitz et al., 1991).

Because people with schizophrenia can relapse even when they live in calm environments with low levels of expressed emotion, expressed emotion is not a necessary cause of schizophrenic symptoms. We also know from the genetic studies that it is not a sufficient cause either. As we have stated many times in this chapter, both genetic and environmental factors are at work in schizophrenia (Tienari, 1991).

Brain Structure and Function

If viruses and birth injuries play a causative role in schizophrenia, they probably exert their effects by causing some form of brain damage (Waltrip et al., 1995). Brain imaging studies have attempted to identify these injuries. The most commonly reported abnormality is enlarged lateral ventricles (the cavities on each side of the brain that are filled with cerebrospinal fluid; Raz & Raz, 1990). The ventricles of people with schizophrenia have been found to be enlarged even before treatment, so the defect is not the result of receiving antipsychotic medication (Andreasen et al., 1990).

Some researchers have claimed that people with enlarged ventricles represent a subtype of schizophrenia that is characterized by a predominance of negative symptoms (McGlashan & Fenton, 1991). Other researchers believe that there are several different types of enlarged ventricles in schizophrenia (Nair et al., 1997). Although intriguing, these hypotheses have not proved to be of great theoretical value. The problem is that we do not have any good theory of why people with enlarged ventricles should develop the negative (or any other) symptoms of schizophrenia (Torrey et al., 1994). Enlarged ventricles tell us only that these people's brains have failed to develop normally.

Enlarged ventricles are not the only observed abnormality in people with schizophrenia. Researchers have also reported that people with schizophrenia have a smaller hippocampus and amygdala than nonschizophrenics. The hippocampus and the amygdala are part of the brain's limbic system, a part of the brain that is thought to be concerned with cognition and emotion (Gur & Pearlson, 1993). Researchers have also reported abnormalities on the left (language) side of the brain in some people with schizophrenia (Shenton et al., 1992). Curiously, other researchers have localized the schizophrenic defect in the right hemisphere (Cutting, 1994), and some say it can be in either one (Crow, 1997). To add to the confusion, another group of researchers claims that the problem is not localized to any part of the brain but is present in the whole brain (Sharif, Gewirtz, & Iqbal, 1993).

Researchers using regional blood flow have found decreased metabolic activity in the frontal lobes when schizophrenic subjects perform abstract problem-solving tasks (Gur & Pearlson, 1993). This effect is known as **hypofrontality** because it appears to be related to

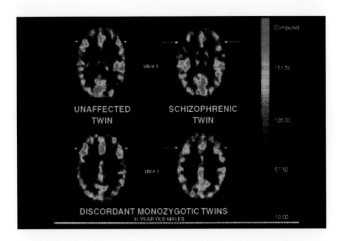

These PET scans of blood flow in identical twins when asked to perform a reasoning task show less activity in the frontal lobes of the twin with schizophrenia.

diminished activity in the frontal lobes (the area of the brain associated with emotional expression, planning, and some types of information processing). The negative symptoms of schizophrenia are correlated with poor performance on neuropsychological tests of frontal-lobe function, such as the digit span (I. Berman et al., 1997). Among identical twins who are discordant for schizophrenia, the schizophrenic twin may show hypofrontality, whereas the nonschizophrenic twin does not (K. F. Berman et al., 1992). This suggests that hypofrontality is not inherited but is the result of some brain injury. Unfortunately, results indicating hypofrontality, like many other findings in schizophrenia, are not always easy to replicate (Ebmeier et al., 1995).

In addition to enlarged ventricles, a smaller hippocampus and amygdala, damage to the left (or right) hemisphere, and hypofrontality, researchers have identified a host of other possible abnormalities in brain structure and function, some of which are progressive and change over the course of a person's illness (David & Cutting, 1994; DeLisi et al., 1997; Heinrichs, 1993). None of these defects is specific to schizophrenia (Raz & Raz, 1990), and not all cases of schizophrenia are associated with a brain abnormality (Palmer et al., 1997). About all we can say with confidence is that schizophrenia is sometimes associated with an abnormality in brain structure. The course and presentation of schizophrenia is so varied that it is unlikely scientists will ever find a single brain lesion that "causes" schizophrenia.

Brain Chemistry

Although the idea that body chemistry affects behavior goes back at least to Galen, modern attempts to link schizophrenia to brain chemistry date to the 1950s, when the hallucinogen lysergic acid diethylamide (LSD) first came into use. Because hallucinations are also present in schizophrenia, researchers hypothesized that investigations of the chemical structure of LSD might help us to understand the cause of schizophrenic symptoms. Investigations soon showed that LSD's chemical structure is similar to the structure of the neurotransmitter serotonin. Psilocybin, the active hallucinogenic ingredient in certain psychedelic mushrooms, has a similar structure. This coincidence of findings led to the hypothesis that at least some schizophrenic symptoms result from alterations to the function of serotonin.

Although LSD and psilocybin produce transient hallucinations, other drugs, such as phencyclidine (PCP, or angel dust), set off not only hallucinations but also delusions and paranoia. Unlike LSD, which affects serotonin, PCP affects the activity of the neurotransmitter glutamate.

Amphetamines and cocaine (especially in the potent forms called ice or crack) can set off schizophrenic symptoms in nonschizophrenics and exacerbate them in people who already have schizophrenia. However, unlike LSD or PCP, amphetamines seem mainly to affect the catecholamine neurotransmitter dopamine.

Reasoning by analogy, researchers have implicated serotonin, glutamate, and dopamine in schizophrenia. However, most have focused on dopamine. Their research can be summarized by three important findings:

1. If taken over a long period, antipsychotic medications known as **phenothiazines** may produce symptoms similar to those found in the movement disorder known as Parkinson's disease (tremors, jerky movements). We know that Parkinson's disease results from the destruction of dopamine-producing neurons. It is possible, therefore, that antipsychotic medications work because they somehow reduce dopamine activity in the brain.
2. The drug L-dopa, which is used to treat people with Parkinson's disease, works by increasing dopamine activity. Because L-dopa can produce some of the positive symptoms of schizophrenia, this is further evidence that some schizophrenic symptoms are related to increased dopamine activity.
3. Finally, because some types of antipsychotic medications ameliorate the positive symptoms of schizophrenia (and seem to work by reducing dopamine activity in the brain), it seems reasonable to conclude that excess dopamine activity is somehow responsible for the positive symptoms.

Put simply, drugs known to increase dopamine activity seem to provoke schizophrenic symptoms, whereas drugs that reduce dopamine activity tend to ameliorate them. Given this pattern of findings, it is easy to see why researchers have hypothesized that schizophrenic symptoms are the result of "excessive" dopamine activity. However, this hypothesis ignores the symptom-producing properties of LSD and PCP, neither of which primarily affects dopamine. The hypothesis is also based mainly on indirect evidence. We cannot open the brains of living people to measure the level of brain dopamine directly, so dopamine is measured indirectly by examining the blood or spinal fluid for the by-products produced by the breakdown of dopamine in the brain. It is like trying to judge how much alcohol people drink by counting the number of beer bottles in their garbage. Just as we can never be sure that the bottles reflect the amount the individual actually drank (someone else may have tossed them in the garbage), we can also not be sure that the presence of metabolic by-products of dopamine in the blood or spinal fluid reflects an excess of dopamine in the brain. It is always possible that these by-products got into these fluids for some other reason (because of a strange diet, for example). Future researchers will benefit from modern approaches that hold the promise of measuring brain dopamine directly (Potter & Manji, 1993).

The evidence presently available does not demonstrate conclusively that people with schizophrenia have a higher level of dopamine activity than nonschizophrenics do. Instead, it seems that people with schizophrenia have more dendritic dopamine receptors than do nonschizophrenics. These excess receptors make them more responsive to dopamine, even though their overall levels of dopamine are no different from those of nonschizophrenics. Before we conclude that extra dopamine receptors are somehow responsible for schizophrenic symptoms, there is one complication. Some antipsychotic drugs themselves can increase the number of dopamine receptors. Because most people with schizophrenia receive drug treatment, it is possible that the excess number of dopamine receptors observed by researchers is caused by drug treatment and, therefore, could not be responsible for the initial development of schizophrenic symptoms.

To find out whether an oversupply of dopamine receptors is responsible for the development of schizophrenic symptoms and not just the result of treatment with antipsychotic medication, we must study people with schizophrenia who have not been treated with drugs. If untreated people also have an excess of dopamine receptors, we can conclude that the drugs are not responsible. Unfortunately, untreated patients are exceedingly rare. Moreover, as shown in Figure 9.4,

there is more than one type of dopamine receptor (called D_1, D_2, and so on). Dopamine uptake at different types of receptors produces different effects on behavior. Clearly, the hypothesis that an oversupply of dopamine receptors is responsible for the positive symptoms of schizophrenia needs to be refined before the dopamine hypothesis can be substantiated. At the very least, the specific receptors responsible for schizophrenic symptoms need to be specified (Sharif et al., 1993).

Even if we could provide definitive evidence for an oversupply of dopamine receptors among untreated people with schizophrenia, the relationship between schizophrenia and dopamine would still be ambiguous. For example, among those patients who do respond to medication, it usually takes a few days or even a week or two before any improvement is noticed (Carson & Sanislow, 1993). Yet traditional antipsychotic medications have an immediate effect on dopamine activity. The lag before symptoms improve and the finding that some people do not improve at all suggest that schizophrenic symptoms reflect more than just dopamine activity. We have already noted that LSD and PCP can create schizophrenic-like behavior by their effects on other neurotransmitters, and some of the newer antipsychotic medications also target neurotransmitters other than dopamine (Lieberman et al., 1998; Meltzer, 1992, 1993). Perhaps it is the balance among different neurotransmitters that is important in schizophrenia rather than the absolute level of any particular neurotransmitter (Breier, 1995; Carlsson et al., 1997).

Risk Factors and Etiology: A Final Look

Uncovering risk factors and trying to understand how they contribute to the symptoms of a disorder is a common research strategy, not only in abnormal psychology but in many areas of medicine as well. Risk-factor studies have revealed the connection between cigarette smoking and lung cancer as well as the link between exposure to the sun and skin cancer. However, the risk-factor research strategy has certain drawbacks. The most obvious one is its reliance on correlations. Risk factors are associated with certain disorders, but this does not mean they cause them. The risk factor and the disorder could both be related to some third factor. For example, enlarged ventricles and schizophrenic symptoms may both be the result of birth trauma. To go beyond mere correlation, researchers must link risk factors to schizophrenic symptoms (Andreasen, 1997). For example, it is not enough to claim that neurotransmitter activity is involved in schizophrenia; researchers must also explain how neurotransmitter disturbances make people hear

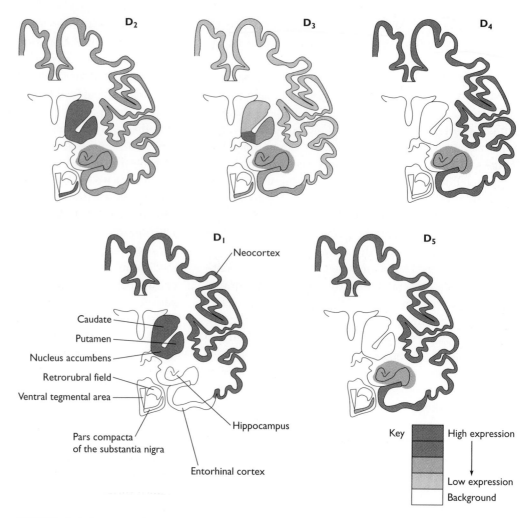

FIGURE 9.4 **Areas of Dopamine Receptor Activity.** *Five dopamine receptors have been identified to date. As shown, each one is more common in some parts of the brain than others. The D_2 receptor is particularly implicated in schizophrenia.* From: Meador-Woodruff (1998).

voices or believe that they are gods. Similarly, before we can say that viruses are implicated in schizophrenia, we need to explain how viruses contribute to the thought, emotional, and movement symptoms of schizophrenia.

At present, there are few, if any, etiological theories that make the required leap from risk factors to schizophrenic symptoms. Instead, researchers have devoted their efforts to finding new risk factors. Each new risk factor discovered is heralded as the "cause" of schizophrenia—heredity, viruses, birth trauma, social stress, brain damage, neurochemical imbalances, even a lack of breast feeding (McCreadie, 1997). Yet it is unlikely that a heterogeneous disorder such as schizophrenia will prove to have one single cause. It seems more likely that multiple interacting factors will be found responsible (Garver, 1997). Until more sophisticated theories are available, the best we can say is that there are numerous

risk factors, and no single one is sufficient on its own to cause schizophrenia.

TREATMENT

Over the centuries, people who would today be diagnosed schizophrenic have been subjected to a variety of treatments. Each new treatment is introduced with enthusiasm and accompanied by reports of its remarkable effectiveness. Inevitably, the initial excitement dies away when follow-up studies show that the treatment is not as effective as originally claimed. So let us establish one main point at the outset: There is no cure for schizophrenia—no pill, no operation, and no psychotherapy. Nevertheless, the quality of life of people with schizophrenia can be improved by medical, psychological, and social interventions (Falloon, Brooker, & Graham-Hole, 1992).

In the early 18th century, special hospitals were established for the mentally ill. For entertainment, English aristocrats would visit Bedlam and watch the inmates, as depicted in this 1733 painting by William Hogarth.

Hospitalization and Milieu Treatment

For at least 100 years, mental hospitals were considered to be the best place to treat psychotic people. Not only could drug and psychological treatment be delivered in the hospital, but the hospital environment (or milieu) was also thought to have beneficial effects of its own. Patients were sheltered from the everyday world, while doctors, nurses, and other staff created a joint culture in which patients interacted socially and gained a sense of independence by participating in ward government. **Milieu treatment** was considered to be an important factor in patient outcome. Even today, most people with schizophrenia spend at least some time in a hospital milieu program, although long-term hospitalization has fallen out of favor. The reasons for this change of opinion, and the current situation, are discussed in this section.

From Community to Asylum and Back Again For most of recorded history, psychotic people were either cared for at home by their families or permitted to roam the countryside, finding subsistence where they could. As Europe moved into the 18th century, doctors began to advocate a more "scientific" approach to the treatment of mentally ill people. The seriously disturbed began to be treated by "experts" in special hospitals. The first such hospital in the United States was established in Williamsburg, Virginia, in 1773. Others soon followed. These hospitals varied in quality. Some were humane and progres-

sive; others were dirty, violent, and degrading. One example of the latter was London's notorious St. Mary of Bethlehem hospital, widely known as Bedlam (a word that has become synonymous with mayhem).

Although the conditions in 18th-century Bedlam were deplorable, they must be viewed in the context of the times. Violent patients were kept in restraints because hospital authorities had few resources, and restraints were the cheapest way of keeping violent patients from harming themselves or one another. Bedlam was not just a warehouse, however. As the following quotation from a treatment manual written in 1765 shows, the daily life of the institution was designed as far as possible to provide a therapeutic milieu:

> [Matron's duty is to make sure that] such of the [women] patients as are low spirited or inclined to be mopish should be made to get up, and be sent out of their cells so that they may not creep back again to their beds: also to employ such as were capable at needlework when they were not otherwise busy rather than let them walk idle up and down the house. . . . (quoted in Alleridge, 1985, p. 29)

In areas without suitable hospitals, mentally disturbed people were placed in the care of boardinghouse proprietors, who looked after them for a fixed weekly fee. Like that of the hospitals, the quality of these private facilities varied widely. Lodgings catering to the rich were luxurious; those whose clientele was poor were often little more than hovels. Again, it is important to view this information in its historical context. The 1700s were hard times for the poor, whether mentally ill or not. Many lived squalid lives in conditions scarcely more comfortable than those provided for the mentally ill. Still, even at the time, there were protests and complaints about the treatment of the mentally ill. Unfortunately, when these complaints grew too loud, patients were simply set loose with nowhere to go. In a haunting premonition of the present situation in our large cities, psychotic people became vagrants. The British Parliament was so troubled by these homeless psychotics that it passed a vagrancy act that permitted judges to detain those who were "furiously mad." This law is the origin of our modern civil commitment laws (such as the one that sent Jennifer to the hospital), which are the subject of Highlight 9.1.

The most important figure in late-18th-century English treatment was the Quaker philanthropist William Tuke (1732–1822), who dedicated his York Retreat to the "moral-religious treatment of the mentally ill." Tuke's **moral treatment** involved kindness, comfort, calm, and heavy doses of the Protestant ethic. Plenty of manual

Civil Commitment

Jennifer Plowman did not want to go to a mental hospital. She was forced to go anyway because her mother and a judge thought it would be in her best interests. The process by which Jennifer was hospitalized is known as civil (as opposed to criminal) commitment. Most jurisdictions have emergency procedures similar to those used in Jennifer's case. Parents, friends, relatives, doctors, or the police who seek to have a person committed present their case to a judge, who may order an assessment of the person's current level of mental functioning. Commitment for longer periods requires an official hearing. The usual grounds for a longer commitment are an inability to care for oneself, being dangerous to oneself, or being dangerous to others. In theory, at least, the person in question has the right to legal representation, to examine witnesses, and to get an independent psychological assessment. In some jurisdictions, the person may even have the right to a hearing before a jury. In practice, however, most people are represented by court-appointed counsel who have little time to prepare, hearings are rushed, and judges must often make decisions based on minimal information (LaFrance, 1995). As a safeguard, all commitment orders must be reviewed periodically to ensure that involuntary hospitalization is still required (Weiner & Wettstein, 1993).

Civil commitment laws date back to the 18th century, when large public psychiatric hospitals were first opened (La Fond & Durham, 1992). If they would not go voluntarily, people were sent to these hospitals involuntarily. The justification then (and now) for depriving some people of their liberty is that the government has a duty to protect its citizens from harm (*parens patriae*, the state is the ultimate parent). When people cannot look after themselves or the public safety is endangered, the government can hospitalize people for their own good or the good of society (Turkheimer & Parry, 1992).

Civil commitment is a power that can be easily abused. In the 19th century, and even in the 20th, women who defied their husbands and people who opposed the government of the day were incarcerated as mental patients (Weiner & Wettstein, 1993). As recently as the 1980s, adolescents were involuntarily committed to psychiatric facilities by their parents even though they were not suffering from any mental disorder. Teenagers were essentially locked up because their parents did not approve of their behavior. Even today, children have fewer rights in the mental health system than adults do.

Civil commitment laws try to balance the rights of the individual against the rights of society. The "correct" balance is not fixed; it varies with changes in society. In the antiauthoritarian 1960s, the balance swung in the direction of individual rights. As a consequence, civil commitment became difficult. In the 1990s, the fear of violence is much in people's minds, and the commitment of potentially violent people has became easier (La Fond & Durham, 1992). The present concern with violence is probably overstated. Although serious mental disorders and violence are related, violence is still the exception among the mentally ill (Monahan, 1992). Anyway, it is difficult to predict which people will be violent or try to take their own lives (Lidz, Mulvey, & Gardner, 1993). By being overzealous and committing anyone who we think may be violent or may harm him or herself, we may be committing people who will never harm anyone. The general rule is that each individual should be treated in the least restrictive environment possible. Those who can safely be kept out of hospitals should be treated as outpatients.

Whether committed voluntarily or involuntarily, all patients take certain rights with them to the hospital. These include the right to treatment and to be housed in humane conditions. Hospitalized patients also have the right to know the consequences of a treatment and must consent to its use ("informed consent"; Hermann, 1990). As you can see, these rights may sometimes conflict. The right of patients to receive treatment may conflict with their right to refuse treatment. In practice, patient rights can be overridden if a patient is considered incompetent or dangerous.

As does the United States, most countries have some way of committing people for treatment. However, in less legalistic societies than the United States, the commitment process may not involve lawyers and courts. In Italy, for example, involuntary hospitalization can be ordered by a mayor (Whitney, Ruiz, & Langenbach, 1994). In Great Britain, the Mental Health Tribunal decides who should be committed. This tribunal is separate from the normal legal system and is run by clinicians, not lawyers. The tribunal bases its commitment decisions on the psychiatric needs of the person as well as on the person's potential danger to society. Systems run by clinicians are more likely to be biased toward committing people who might benefit from treatment than the American system, which is clearly biased toward protecting an individual's legal right to liberty.

In the late 18th century, reformers such as Philippe Pinel (here ordering the removal of the shackles from the inmates at Bicetre) recognized that the mentally ill needed opportunities for work and recreation if they were to have a chance of getting better.

work, organized recreation (such as concerts and poetry readings), and the inculcation of healthy habits were seen as paramount, along with removal from the normal environment. According to the reports of the time, moral treatment cured somewhere between 50% and 90% of patients. These figures were viewed with considerable suspicion even then. Nevertheless, moral treatment's apparent success made hospital reform a worldwide phenomenon. In Italy, Vincenzo Chiarugi (1759–1820) removed patients' restraints and provided all patients with opportunities for work and recreation. In France, Philippe Pinel and his colleagues introduced similar methods.

The first half of the 19th century witnessed an explosion in the number of mental hospitals throughout the world. In the United States, Dorothea Dix (1802–1887) spearheaded a national movement whose aim was to establish a modern mental hospital in every state. These hospitals were called asylums because they were intended to give disturbed people respite from the world and treatment in a therapeutic milieu. The asylums were so popular, they became severely overcrowded and remained so for more than a century. In 1830, there were approximately 200 or so mentally disturbed people hospitalized in the United States. By the 1950s, the number was 500,000. The numbers of hospitalized people did not begin to fall off until the 1960s, when antipsychotic medications made it possible for people with schizophrenia

to live outside the hospital. People who had spent most of their lives in mental hospitals were discharged in a process known as deinstitutionalization.

Deinstitutionalization   In the 1960s, there were two general ideas driving **deinstitutionalization** (Scull, 1989). The first was the belief that mental patients are better cared for in their home communities, where they are known and where they can participate in everyday life. The second idea grew out of 1960s radical politics. Mental hospitals were portrayed as tools by which the state robbed citizens of their freedom. Books and movies such as *One Flew Over the Cuckoo's Nest* portrayed mental hospitals as no different from jails. Hospitals were alleged to create more problems than they solved. What was formerly supposed to be a therapeutic milieu came to be seen as a repressive regime that enforced rigid conformity to rules and made patients apathetic, passive, withdrawn, and helpless. Deinstitutionalization became a romantic crusade to give "oppressed" patients back their rights and their freedom. Arguing that care should be provided in the least restrictive environment possible, the courts began to require that patients who could survive outside the hospital be discharged.

Community mental health centers and halfway houses were to be an essential part of deinstitutionaliza-

Principles of Community Care

Community care for people with schizophrenia has developed a bad name, mainly because of inadequate funding. But inadequate funding is not the entire story. People with schizophrenia experience multiple disadvantages. They are disadvantaged by poverty, disability, inadequate housing, few employment opportunities, and social stigma (Sartorius, 1997). They need much more than just mental health counseling (Hall & Brockington, 1991). They have the same ordinary needs that we all have—for shelter, food, clothing, and fulfillment—but they also have special needs for medication, training, and support. Therefore, a complete community service must provide more than just mental health and rehabilitation services. It must also include financial and legal assistance; housing (from apartments to group homes); and opportunities for social development, work, and leisure activities. To ensure that people are receiving the services they need, someone needs to help coordinate the disparate sources of help. E. Murphy (1991) has outlined the following principles of community care:

1. People with mental disorders and their families should be involved in planning and managing community services. Self-help groups should be encouraged.
2. Services should promote autonomy rather than dependence by offering people choices (in living arrangements, work, and social activities).
3. To the extent possible, people with mental disorders should be provided with a normal home environment, including contact with the general community.
4. People should be protected from discrimination and abuse.
5. Services should be organized on a small, local scale.

---

tion. In the United States, the Community Mental Health Center Act of 1963 authorized the federal government to construct and staff mental health centers throughout the country (Rochefort, 1993). These centers would provide the therapy, training, education, and supportive living environment required to keep patients functioning outside the hospital, as described in Highlight 9.2. Although some community mental health centers were established, few lived up to their stated aims. Instead of providing services to psychotic people, most concentrated on providing treatment for those with milder disorders, people who would have never been hospitalized in any event. When the federal government stopped funding community mental health centers directly and started providing money in "block grants" to the states, the level of support for community mental health centers dropped dramatically. Local politicians were very sensitive to the so-called NIMBY ("not in my backyard") syndrome. The public was sympathetic to the need for halfway houses, hostels, and other group living environments for mentally disordered people, so long as these facilities were not located in their neighborhood. To avoid annoying voters, state legislators arranged to spend their mental health block grants in other ways.

Despite the lack of community mental health services and homes on whose existence it was supposedly dependent, deinstitutionalization proceeded at a rapid pace. Between 1955 and 1985, the number of mental hospital patients in the United States decreased by more than 400,000. The vast majority were discharged without any plan for providing them with education, treatment, support, or even a place to live. Those lucky enough to be offered help were usually provided with services that were inferior to those available to them in the hospital. It is hard to avoid the conclusion that many state governments saw deinstitutionalization as a way to save money. It is ironic, therefore, that as people were discharged from the hospitals, the cost of caring for those left behind actually increased. Large institutions became less efficient to run when the number of patients fell because their overhead costs remained largely unchanged. They still had to employ doctors, nurses, cooks, and so on.

Although some of the patients discharged from hospitals survived in the community—mainly people who had family support and access to community mental health services—deinstitutionalization left many others unable to function. Without family support and with inadequate or nonexistent community mental health services, they simply joined the armies of homeless people haunting most big cities (Fischer & Breakey, 1991). Many entered into cycles of repeated hospitalizations and discharges. Others wound up in jail, even though they committed no crime other than the "crime" of being mentally ill (Torrey et al., 1992).

It is ironic that the deinstitutionalization movement, which saw as one of its missions the restoration of free-

In the 1960s, the deinstitutionalization movement led to the establishment of community mental health centers and residential halfway houses, which provide therapy and a supportive environment. In spite of the effectiveness of these community-based programs, government funds for them have decreased dramatically in subsequent decades.

dom to hospitalized mental patients, produced a situation in which people were simply allowed to wallow on the streets or in jails. As one psychiatrist put it, "Freedom to be insane is an illusory freedom, a cruel hoax perpetrated on those who cannot think clearly by those who will not think clearly" (Torrey, 1988, p. 34). Every so often, someone tries to do something to help the situation. News stories appear revealing the plight of the homeless mentally ill. If the stories are high profile, they create furious activity—blue-ribbon government committees are formed, reports are written, and then the issue gradually fades away. Meanwhile, little gets done. What has become clear is that people who cannot look after themselves, who may be violent, or who do not have access to the services they require to live in the community need protection. The best place for them is probably in a hospital, at least during the active phase of their disorders. The present situation is grossly inequitable. The wealthy find their way into private hospitals (J. W. Thompson et al., 1995), whereas those who cannot afford private hospital insurance are often consigned to the streets.

Somatic Treatments

Kraepelin believed that dementia praecox was a brain disease that would eventually yield to some form of somatic treatment. Despite his dedication to psychoanalysis, Sigmund Freud also believed that our provisional ideas in psychology will presumably one day be based on an organic substrate. Over the decades, many so-

matic treatments have been tried. Putting people into comas, first using insulin injections and later with electric shocks, was advocated in the 1930s and 1940s, even though there was limited evidence that such treatment had any effect on schizophrenia. (As noted in Chapter 8, electroshock therapy is now used mainly for severe depressive and bipolar disorders.) Psychosurgery, especially the disconnection of the frontal lobes from the rest of the brain, was also popular for a time, although again there was never much evidence for its effectiveness.

Perhaps the most important development in the somatic treatment of schizophrenia took place in the 1940s with the development of antihistamines. These drugs were found not only to relieve the symptoms of allergies such as hay fever but also to be useful in preparing people for surgical procedures. Antihistamines made people sleepy and less anxious. Attempts to maximize the tranquilizing effects of antihistamines in the 1950s resulted in the discovery of **chlorpromazine** (brand name, Thorazine) followed by other phenothiazines (sometimes referred to as major tranquilizers). The phenothiazines were the first **neuroleptic drugs** (*neuroleptic* is derived from an ancient Greek term meaning "take hold of nerves"). They act by blocking certain dopamine receptors. The phenothiazines were soon followed by the butyrophenones (Haloperidol) and the thioxanthenes (Navane).

Double-blind placebo control trials have shown neuroleptic drugs to be effective in reducing the positive symptoms of schizophrenia, but they have a smaller effect on the negative symptoms (Schooler, 1993). Neuroleptics seem to be equally effective for people from different racial backgrounds (Levinson & Simpson, 1992), although people of Asian origin may require lower doses than other people (Lin et al., 1989). Today, there are 20 or more neuroleptics on the market; practically every major pharmaceutical company has its own brand. Some people respond to one neuroleptic; some to another (Gitlin, 1990). This is a bit mysterious because the neuroleptic drugs in each category are very similar to one another (Kane & Marder, 1993). Unfortunately, some people with schizophrenia do not respond to any neuroleptic (around 25%), and many others respond only partially (Lewander, 1992).

Even among those who do respond, neuroleptics present a risk from drug side effects. The most troubling are the motor side effects that arise in the extrapyramidal neural pathways that connect the spinal cord to the brain. These include a shuffling walk, expressionless face, shakiness, and various odd movements. These side effects may be controlled by lowering

Neuroleptic medications can help the symptoms of schizophrenia, but they can also produce unpleasant side effects. Renowned jazz trumpeter Tom Harrell (recently voted the world's best trumpet player by Down Beat *magazine readers) has suffered from schizophrenia since his early 20s. Once, when his medication was causing serious tremors, he stopped taking it; the tremors stopped and he became less withdrawn and more confident but also began behaving erratically.*

the dosage or by the administration of additional drugs (Kane & Marder, 1993).

To reduce the probability of a relapse, schizophrenic patients are often kept on neuroleptic medication for long periods (Hogarty, 1993). Because patients may choose to discontinue their neuroleptic medication when they are feeling better, neuroleptics may also be administered by periodic injections rather than as tablets or pills. It is important to note, however, that long-term neuroleptic treatment, whether by injection or tablet, is associated with a movement disorder known as **tardive dyskinesia** (Morgenstern & Glazer, 1993). The symptoms include facial grimaces, jerky movements, lip chewing, and a host of other tics and odd movements. Tardive dyskinesia is often irreversible, particularly in females (Jeste & Caligiuri, 1993). In effect, people may be forced to choose between tardive dyskinesia and schizophrenic symptoms. Many choose not to take the neuroleptics (Hoge et al., 1991).

Ensuring that patients comply with drug treatment is an important aspect of therapy. No drug will be effective if patients fail to take it. For this reason, finding drugs that have fewer side effects is important. Several such drugs are now available. They are known as atypi-

cal neuroleptics. These drugs have a lower probability of producing extrapyramidal symptoms than the original neuroleptics while also having equal or better therapeutic effects (Borison, 1995; Fleischhacker & Hummer, 1997; Keltner, 1995; Moore et al., 1997; Petty, 1998; Rein & Turjanski, 1997). The most widely used atypical neuroleptic currently available in the United States is clozapine, whose antiviral properties have already been mentioned. This drug seems to reduce symptoms in patients who do not respond to traditional neuroleptics (Farmer & Blewitt, 1993; Rosenheck et al., 1997; Schooler, 1993; Young et al., 1997). Clozapine would probably be the most frequently used neuroleptic if it were not for one serious problem. It produces a potentially lethal blood condition known as agranulocytosis in about 1% of patients (Lindenmayer, 1993). In agranulocytosis, there is a dramatic lowering in the number of white blood cells and a consequent loss of immune function. People become prone to infections, which they cannot fight off. For this reason, frequent white blood cell counts are required so that treatment may be discontinued before an infection takes hold. Although the atypical antipsychotics are more expensive than traditional ones, they make up for their costs because people who comply

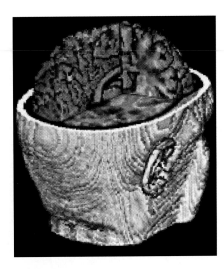

This combined 3-D PET and MRI scan shows the effect of clozapine on the brain. Activity is reduced in the area that includes the basal ganglia (the red structure just above the ear), which is rich in D2 dopamine receptors.

with treatment are less likely to require expensive hospitalization (Fichtner, Hanrahan, & Luchins, 1998).

Psychological Treatment

Few, if any, psychologists believe that schizophrenia can be cured by psychotherapy. Instead, the aim of psychological interventions is to delay relapse and to improve the quality of life for people with schizophrenia and for those who care for them. One approach is to try to reduce the level of expressed emotion in the families of people with schizophrenia.

Reducing Expressed Emotion   Research into expressed emotion has shown that relapse is at least in part determined by how people with schizophrenia are received by their immediate families when they are discharged from the hospital (G. Sullivan, Young, & Morgenstern, 1997). It seems logical, therefore, to try to reduce the relapse rate by helping the families and friends of schizophrenic patients lower their level of expressed emotion (Halford & Hayes, 1991). Treatment programs usually begin by educating families and other caregivers about schizophrenia and what types of behavior they should expect. They are also taught about antipsychotic medications and their side effects. Family assistance is enlisted in helping patients to stay on their medication because noncompliance is an important determinant of relapse (Haywood et al., 1995; Kane, 1997; Nageotte et al., 1997).

Families and caregivers are also trained in problem-solving and communication skills. The latter are particularly important because they help caregivers express themselves in ways that do not involve negative interactions and high expressed emotion. Support and counseling for the family are also needed because family members can be stigmatized and traumatized by a patient's condition (Lively, Friedrich, & Buckwalter, 1995). Local support groups in which family members and caregivers share their problems have now been supplemented by international support groups that communicate over the Internet. Anne Plowman's posting to an Internet support group appears in Document 9.11. Treatment programs aimed at reducing expressed emotion, combined with adherence to drug treatment, seem to produce a reduction in short-term relapse rates, although long-term relapses (2 or more years after treatment) still occur (Droogan & Bannigan, 1997; Hogarty, 1993; Kavanagh, 1992; Miklowitz & Goldstein, 1993).

DOCUMENT 9.11

Anne Plowman's Posting to an Internet Support Group for the Relatives of Schizophrenic People

From: Anne Plowman <anne@mail.com>
Newsgroups: alt.support.schizophrenia
Subject: Request for advice, ideas...
Date: Wed, 12 Nov 2001 21:36:40

My daughter, Jenny, is schizophrenic—she was diagnosed 1 year ago and has been hospitalized once. I am a widow. My husband died just before Jennifer's breakdown. Jenny has been taking medicine since she came out of the hospital, and her symptoms seem under control. She has stopped saying that people are reading her thoughts. She says that the medicine makes her feel dopey, but so far at least, she is still taking it. Although she seems to be better, she is not like her former self. She is listless and apathetic, and she is making no effort to get on with her life. I have tried hard to accept her as she is, although I believe that she could be doing better. She seems to lack self-discipline. She doesn't eat properly or exercise. I try not to show her how I feel because I know this will only make things worse.

I live in fear that Jenny will have another episode, and I wish there were more that I could do. When Jenny was little, we were so close. She used to tell me everything. Now, I don't feel as if I even know her anymore. I feel guilty because I am unable to do more, and sometimes I feel ashamed of her. Anyway, it helps me to express these feelings. When I write to this group, I feel as if I'm writing to people who understand. Please write to me if you have had similar experiences or if you have an idea about what could be done. I'd love to hear from you.
Thanks,
Anne

Token Economies For those who require long-term hospitalizations, token economies may be useful ways to inculcate and maintain desirable behavior on the wards. Token economies are really elaborate reinforcement programs in which each occurrence of a desired behavior (making one's bed, for example) is rewarded with a token, which can be exchanged for such privileges as time watching television. Patients who disrupt others or who act inappropriately are not rewarded and may even be fined. In a classic study, Paul and Lentz (1977) found that token economies help people with schizophrenia to learn more appropriate forms of behavior and to behave more appropriately while in the hospital, although there may be some falling back when people are discharged and token reinforcements are no longer available.

Social Skills and Cognitive Training Schizophrenic people who spend long periods in hospitals (or out of the hospital but removed from social interaction) may lack social skills (Benton & Schroeder, 1990). They need to learn the specific skills required to hold a conversation, go through a job interview, express their feelings, and maintain relationships (Bellack & Mueser, 1993; Liberman & Green, 1992). One way to teach these skills is to subdivide complex social skills into smaller units and then use role playing, modeling, and various programmed learning techniques to help people acquire these skills and use them in everyday life. Such skills

may also help give patients more confidence and reduce the effects of negative symptoms (D. J. Dobson et al., 1995). Psychologists should not have unrealistic expectations, however, because relapses will still occur (Bellack & Mueser, 1993).

Kingdon and Turkington (1991) reported a cognitive-behavior therapy program that began with an educational program in which patients were given non-stigmatizing (disease-related) explanations for their symptoms. Specifically, patients were told that stress produces symptoms such as delusions, hallucinations, and misinterpretations of events. Patients were taught to analyze their symptoms. For example, if they were "hearing voices," they were asked to consider whether the voices might have originated inside their head. They were also asked to note whether their symptoms were associated with stress. These interventions were aimed at giving people with schizophrenia the ability to examine their thoughts and perceptual experiences and to test them against reality (see also H. D. Brenner et al., 1992; McNally & Goldberg, 1997). Even when it is successful, such treatment will not cure schizophrenia, but it may make people more reflective. Treatment of this sort was given to Jennifer Plowman. The result is illustrated in Document 9.12, which is an excerpt from a follow-up interview with Jennifer 8 weeks after her initial hospitalization. Compare Jennifer's speech with her speech during her intake interviews (see Documents 9.3 and 9.4).

UNIVERSITY HOSPITAL

Case Note

Clinician: Dr. Stuart Berg

Clinician's Note: Part of this interview has been transcribed to provide a comparison with Jennifer's speech at intake.

DR. BERG: How have you been?

JENNIFER: Well, Dr. Berg, not perfect, but OK.

DR. BERG: What have you been doing?

JENNIFER: Taking it easy mostly, easing back into things. I may start looking for a job soon.

DR. BERG: Doing what?

JENNIFER: I'm not sure. I'm 21, but I don't really know what I want to do or what I'm good at. I don't think I ever really knew myself.

DR. BERG: What about your ideas—you know, that people could read your thoughts? That you possessed certain secrets?

JENNIFER: I have learned to cope. To be truthful, they are still there—not all the time, but sometimes. The difference is that now I know what they really are.

DR. BERG: How do you cope?

JENNIFER: I keep an eye on my own behavior so that I can stop peculiar ideas before they become too strong. Sometimes, when I think I've heard a voice, I ignore it and tell myself to act sane. If that doesn't work, I distract myself. I take a long walk, or listen to music, or just pick up a book. This gives me some control over myself.

DR. BERG: Are you taking your medication?

JENNIFER: I take the medicine because I'm afraid not to. But I hate the way it makes me feel, sleepy and dull.

DR. BERG: What will the future be like, do you think?

JENNIFER: I know that I am not cured and that I may always be ill. I wish I could just get going with life, but I can't seem to get started.

CHAPTER 9 IN PERSPECTIVE

Schizophrenia remains an enigma. Although it is safe to conclude that a vulnerability to psychosis is inherited, more than a century of research has so far failed to yield either a cause or a cure for this most debilitating of psychological disorders. We seem to have come about as far as we can with the present correlational research strategy of linking risk factors, such as social class or enlarged lateral ventricles, to the later development of schizophrenia. Further progress will almost certainly require a breakdown of schizophrenia into finer categories, as well as testable theories that specify the precise mechanisms by which risk factors produce various schizophrenic symptoms. For example, we need theories that indicate how enlarged ventricles produce paranoid ideas and how social class is linked to auditory hallucinations. Until such theories are available for testing, researchers will simply continue to add to the already long list of risk factors without being able to explain how any of them leads a person to believe that aliens have turned the population into robots or to sit for hours without moving a muscle. Similarly, until we know more about the etiology of schizophrenia, our treatments will remain aimed at ameliorating the symptoms of schizophrenia rather than at eliminating its cause.

Key Ideas

Schizophrenia and the Psychoses

Schizophrenia is the most common of the psychoses (disorders characterized by gross distortions of reality). Although references to schizophrenic-like symptoms date back to antiquity, the modern disorder seems to have been first described in the 18th century, although the precise definition of schizophrenia has varied over the decades.

Diagnosis

The *DSM-IV* diagnostic criteria for schizophrenia require that two of five symptoms be present (positive symptoms include delusions, hallucinations, disorganized speech, and grossly disorganized or catatonic behavior, whereas negative symptoms include limited speech and flat affect). The diagnosis also requires evidence of a decline from a previous level of functioning and the presence of disturbed behavior over a period of at least 6 months. The *DSM-IV* contains three main schizophrenic subtypes based on which symptom is dominant: catatonic, paranoid, or disorganized.

Course

The course of schizophrenia is divided into three stages: prodromal, active, and residual. The syndrome's first appearance is usually in adolescence or early adulthood, with alternating active and residual phases over many years. Although the prognosis is guarded, some patients seem to be recover sufficiently to function outside of institutions.

Number of Cases

The prevalence of schizophrenia in the population is about 1% (and about 1 new case per 5,000 people is added each year). Schizophrenic patients constitute approximately half of all hospitalized psychiatric patients. Men develop symptoms earlier and have longer and more frequent hospital stays than women do.

Heredity

The evidence from family, twin, and adoption studies suggests that there is a genetic factor that determines vulnerability to schizophrenia. However, the inherited trait appears to have variable expression (relatives may not be schizophrenic but may have related disorders). Unfortunately, linkage studies have not yet pinpointed a specific schizophrenic gene or genes, but behavioral markers have been identified (attentional disturbances, eye-tracking dysfunction). Because even identical twins have a concordance of less than 50%, it seems clear that heredity is not a sufficient explanation for schizophrenia. Heredity must interact with other causal factors.

Risk Factors and Etiology

Among the many risk factors that have been related to schizophrenia are season of birth, social class, life-stress, and expressed emotion in families. Etiology has been attributed to brain damage and neurochemical abnormalities (in dopamine, for example). At present there are few, if any, theories that tie risk factors directly to the schizophrenic symptoms that they are supposed to cause.

Treatment

Milieu treatment in hospitals, once the therapeutic mainstay, is now mostly limited to brief stays during the active phase of the disorder. Deinstitutionalization has resulted in an emptying out of hospitals, but alternative treatment resources have not always been provided in the community. People with schizophrenia are usually maintained on drugs, although medications (both old and new) may have serious side effects. Psychological and social treatments can also help to improve the role functioning and quality of life of people with schizophrenia and their families. Family therapy may be particularly valuable in helping families learn to cope with their own plight—facing life with a schizophrenic member.

Key Terms

active phase of psychosis
age adjustment (age standardization)
brief psychotic disorder
catatonic subtype

chlorpromazine
consanguinity method
deinstitutionalization
delusions
delusional disorder

dementia praecox
disorganized subtype
expressed emotion
hallucinations
hypofrontality

incomplete penetrance
lifetime morbid risk
milieu treatment
moral treatment
neuroleptic drugs

paranoid subtype
phenothiazines
polygenic inheritance
proband

prodromal phase of psychosis
psychoses
residual phase or subtype
risk factors

schizoaffective disorder
schizophrenia
schizophreniform disorder
shared psychotic disorder

social stress theory
tardive dyskinesia
variable expressivity

Key Names

Eugen Bleuler
Vincenzo Chiarugi

Dorothea Dix
Benedict Morel

Philippe Pinel
William Tuke

CHAPTER 10

CHAPTER OBJECTIVES

The notion that our personalities—our characteristic traits and habits—can be "disordered" is one of the oldest ideas in abnormal psychology, and also one of the most controversial. Some psychologists view the inclusion of personality disorders in the *DSM-IV* as an inappropriate attempt to "medicalize" what are really social problems; others believe that personality disorders constitute an important mental health issue. One point on which everyone agrees is that some personality traits (especially when they are extreme) can cause distress to individuals, families, coworkers, and to society as a whole. This chapter reviews the history and research on personality disorders. The first part of the chapter focuses on Eric Cooper, whose behavior is typical of the most carefully studied personality disorder: antisocial personality disorder. This chapter also touches on the impulse-control disorders, which, although they form a separate *DSM-IV* diagnostic category, are frequently associated with personality disorders. Case materials taken from the lives of individuals other than Eric Cooper are used to illuminate aspects of the various personality and impulse-control disorders.

The main questions addressed in this chapter are

1. What is personality?
2. How can a personality be disordered?
3. What is an impulse-control disorder?
4. Do we know what causes personality and impulse-control disorders?
5. Can people with personality and impulse-control disorders be helped?

Personality and Impulse-Control Disorders

CONTENTS

When we describe people who prefer spending a quiet night at home to attending a party as "introverted," or when we call ace fighter pilots "brave," we are implying that their behavior is *caused* by their personality traits. (Why do fighter pilots take to the sky? Because they are brave.) Such trait-based explanations of behavior have an intuitive appeal: They fit our beliefs about human nature. Some people are naturally shy; others, gregarious. Some are timid; others are brave. According to the *DSM-IV*, the sum of an individual's traits constitutes his or her **personality,** a set of "enduring patterns of perceiving, relating to, and thinking about the environment and oneself, which are exhibited in a wide range of important social and personal contexts" (American Psychiatric Assn, 1994, p. 630).

In theory, knowing someone's personality should allow us to predict how that person will behave. Shy people should avoid social contact. Brave people should act courageously. In reality, people are rarely so predictable. Under the right conditions, cowards may act bravely, and even sociable people occasionally prefer to be alone. Still, experience tells us that there is at least some consistency to people's behavior, and that maladaptive personality traits can cause distress. In Chapter 4, for example, we saw how some extremely shy people restrict their social lives to avoid anxiety. Because their behavior is maladaptive and causes them anguish, the *DSM-IV* considers such people to have a **personality disorder** (specifically, avoidant personality disorder).

Although both the *DSM-IV* and the *ICD-10* include a diagnostic category for personality disorders, the idea that a personality can be disordered is steeped in controversy (Elliott, 1991; Holmes, 1991; I. McKay, 1991; Sutker, 1994). For example, do career criminals really suffer from a personality disorder, or have they simply made a choice about how they wish to lead their lives? Experts disagree. They also disagree about which personality traits are debilitating enough to constitute a disorder. (The personality disorders in the *DSM-IV* differ from those in the *ICD-10*.) To make matters worse, no one knows what causes personality disorders, and they have no generally accepted treatments. Perhaps the fundamental problem with personality disorders is that they have so little in common. The *DSM-IV* personality disorders include excessive shyness, self-absorption, and schizophrenic-like behaviors. There seems little logical, empirical, or theoretical justification for grouping such disparate "disorders" into a single category.

Similar remarks apply to the **impulse-control disorders.** These range from fire setting, to stealing, fighting, gambling, and even to pulling one's own hair. Like the personality disorders, the impulse-control disorders

Can criminal behavior be attributed to personality disorder? Did Timothy McVeigh blow up the Murrah Federal Building in Oklahoma City because he has an antisocial personality disorder or because he believes he was making a political statement?

seem to have little in common. Moreover, they are not very specific. A failure to control impulses is characteristic of many psychological disorders. Still, because impulse-control disorders are often associated with personality disorders, it is convenient to discuss them together in this chapter.

To help illustrate the nature of personality and impulse-control disorders, this chapter makes frequent reference to the story of Eric Cooper, a man whose recent day in court is described in Document 10.1. A convicted thief and possible murderer, Cooper can nevertheless turn on considerable charm. He always shows remorse at what he has done and promises to make amends. Even his victims forgive him. Unfortunately, although Cooper appears contrite, he never genuinely reforms. He lies, cheats, steals, passes bad checks, and uses violence to further his aims. The journalist who wrote about Eric's trial in the article in Document 10.1 considered Eric's behavior to be a sign of a "character flaw." The *DSM-IV* uses a different term—**antisocial personality disorder.** Because antisocial personality disorder is the most thoroughly researched of the personality disorders, this chapter devotes much of its space to it, using it as a model for how personality disorders are conceptualized. Other personality disorders and the impulse-control disorders are discussed more briefly.

DOCUMENT 10.1

Newspaper Clipping
Describing Eric Cooper's
Day in Court

Violent Thief Asks (and Gets) Forgiveness

by Evan Moran
Daily Staff Writer

If you didn't know better, you would find Eric Cooper likeable. He can be warm. He expresses concern about the welfare of others. He is witty, well read, and he loves to talk over coffee.

On first meeting him, everyone likes Cooper. But he is human, and, like all of us, he does have a character flaw. He prefers to live a life of crime. He is a bankrupt who has been evicted from his last three homes for failing to pay rent. He has served numerous jail terms—for robbery, for nonpayment of child support, for forgery, assault, and possession of drugs. And now he is on trial for attempted murder.

Last year, Cooper refurbished an old music club on the East Side. Plasterers, plumbers, electricians, and decorators created a pleasant nightspot for those who love jazz. Unfortunately, business was slow. Cooper paid the contractors with checks, but these all bounced. His suppliers were also paid with bad checks, and so was his landlord.

Cooper kept this up for several months, issuing checks with no money to cover them. Finally, his creditors became impatient and threatened to call the police. First, Cooper tried to recoup the money through illegal gambling (one of his favorite pas-

times). This only got him deeper in debt. Then, after a long period of intense drinking, Cooper decided to rob the First National Bank branch in Westville. Unfortunately, the robbery went wrong. Eric wound up holding hostages at gunpoint. A plainclothes security guard, Shane Crockett, eventually overpowered Eric, but not before Eric's gun discharged, wounding the guard in the arm.

Yesterday, on the first day of his trial, as Cooper was being escorted into the court, he said to Crockett, who was waiting on a bench outside the courtroom, "I am so sorry about what happened to you. I don't care what happens to me, just as long as I know that you will be OK."

"I'm OK," replied Crockett.

"That's really great," said Eric. "I have been worried about you."

Similar exchanges took place with the other hostages. Eric apologized to each in turn. One hostage seemed so embarrassed that he just hung his head and looked away.

The trial was cut and dried. Eric admitted his crime, blaming his financial problems, alcohol abuse, and "bad judgment."

In determining sentence, Judge Warren allowed victim impact statements from the contractors who were left holding bad checks. Despite the losses they had suffered, most asked the judge for leniency. They forgave Eric and did not want to see him suffer. Many of the hostages testified that he treated them well. Even Shane Crockett, the man Eric shot, felt that the court should take Eric's "difficult circumstances" into account. The court psychologist's report indicated that Eric was suffering from a "personality disorder."

The judge, who knew that Eric had a long criminal history, was unimpressed. In sentencing Eric to 9 years in prison, the judge noted that Eric had a gift for making people like and forgive him.

In passing sentence, the judge said, "Clearly, you have a personality disorder, but you know the difference between right and wrong, so you are legally responsible for your actions in the eyes of the court. If people had been less willing to forgive you, your life might have gone differently. Perhaps you would have learned to accept the consequences of your behavior. I only hope that it is not too late."

DIAGNOSING PERSONALITY AND IMPULSE-CONTROL DISORDERS

In contrast with clinical disorders such as schizophrenia, personality disorders are supposed to arise from enduring character traits. We have already observed that people have different personalities. Taken to extremes, practically any personality trait can impair social functioning and create problems. Shy people may lead restricted social lives; those who are extremely aggressive may get into trouble with the law. When personality traits produce harmful effects on a person's life, the affected person is said to have a personality disorder. Table 10.1 lists the general *DSM-IV* criteria for a personality disorder.

Some personality disorders—antisocial personality disorder, for example—do not normally cause the individual who has them personal distress. Instead, the anguish is felt by other people, especially the person's victims. In such cases, diagnosis depends not on the self-perceptions of the individual concerned but on the effects of the person's behavior on others. This is not unusual in abnormal psychology. Recall that manic episodes (described in Chapter 8) are also not personally distressing; they mainly trouble other people. External perceptions are also important in the diagnosis of several impulse-control disorders. For example, **pyromania** (fire setting) and **kleptomania** (stealing without apparent gain) may not produce personal discomfort; they are diagnosed by their effects on other people. This is recognized in the definition of an impulse-control disorder—"the failure to resist an impulse, drive, or temptation to perform an act that is harmful to the person *or to others* (American Psychiatric Assn, 1994, p. 609, emphasis added).

All personality disorders, and most impulse-control disorders, begin to become apparent in late childhood or early adolescence, although some do not make their first appearance until adulthood (American Psychiatric Assn, 1994). Once these disorders appear, they change little over the years, and they affect behavior in numerous situations.

Categories Versus Dimensions

Because any personality trait, taken to extremes, can produce difficulties in living, some psychologists prefer to conceptualize personality disorders as the unlucky result of falling at the extreme of some personality trait—too shy, too hostile, too self-centered, and so on (R. D. Hare, Hart, & Harpur, 1991; Livesey et al., 1994). Because each of us can be described by noting where we fall on one or more personality traits, or "dimensions," some psychologists have advocated a **dimensional approach** to diagnosing personality disorders. Instead of employing the "exclusional" diagnostic categories of the *DSM-IV*—a person either meets the diagnostic criteria for a personality disorder or does not meet them—the dimensional approach to diagnosis describes people using a standard set of personality dimensions. Take Eric Cooper, for example. As you will see later in this chapter, the *DSM-IV* classifies him as meeting the criteria for a diagnosis of antisocial personality disorder. In contrast, a dimensional scheme might describe him as low

DSM-IV TABLE 10.1 General *DSM-IV* Diagnostic Criteria for a Personality Disorder

A. An enduring pattern of inner experience and behavior that deviates markedly from the expectations of an individual's culture. This pattern is manifested in two or more of the following areas:

(1) cognition (ways of perceiving and interpreting self, other people, and events)

(2) affectivity (the range, intensity, lability, and appropriateness of emotional response)

(3) interpersonal functioning

(4) impulse-control

B. The enduring pattern is inflexible and pervasive across a broad range of personal and social situations.

C. The enduring pattern leads to clinically significant distress or impairment in social, occupational, or other important areas of functioning.

D. The pattern is stable and of long duration and its onset can be traced back at least to adolescence or early childhood.

E. The enduring pattern is not better accounted for as a manifestation or consequence of another disorder.

F. The enduring pattern is not due to the direct physiological effects of a substance (a drug of abuse, a medication) or a general medical condition (e.g., head trauma).

Note: From American Psychiatric Association (1994, p. 633).

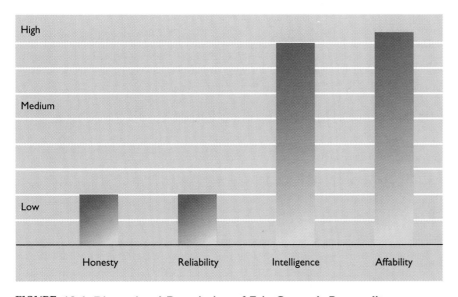

FIGURE 10.1 **Dimensional Description of Eric Cooper's Personality**

on the dimensions of "reliability" and "honesty" but relatively high on "intelligence" and "affability" (Figure 10.1).

The advantage of the dimensional approach is that it avoids pigeonholing people into narrow categorical boxes, thereby allowing them to be described in richer and more complex ways. Over the years, several attempts have been made to develop dimensional systems for describing personality (Cloninger, Bayon, & Przybeck, 1997; L. Goldberg, 1993). These have not had wide acceptance because psychologists have not been able to agree on which personality dimensions to use for this purpose (Widiger, 1991). Because there are a limitless number of potential personality dimensions and a lack of consensus on which ones to use, combining the dimensional and category approaches might offer the best solution (Pilkonis & Klein, 1997). Dimensions could be used to provide specific information about a person, and *DSM-IV* categories could be used for diagnostic purposes. At present, dimensional approaches are in limited use. Clinical diagnosis is dominated by the traditional categorical approach of the *DSM-IV*.

Implications of the Multiaxial Diagnostic System

In the multiaxial diagnostic system used by the *DSM-IV*, Axis I is used to describe the clinical disorders (including the impulse-control disorders), whereas personality disorders are coded on Axis II. (Refer to Chapter 3 for more detail on the multiaxial diagnostic system.) By using two axes, the *DSM-IV* encourages clinicians to at least think about personality disorders. If the personality disorders were coded on the same axis, it is likely that they would be overshadowed by the clinical disorders, which are usually more acute. By forcing clinicians to code personality disorders separately from clinical disorders, the *DSM-IV* multiaxial diagnostic system provides a more complex description of a person's problems than would be possible in a single-axis system. In practice, it is relatively common for a person to be diagnosed as suffering from a clinical disorder on Axis I while simultaneously suffering from a personality disorder on Axis II. For example, substance abuse (see Chapter 6) is often found in conjunction with antisocial personality disorder (Cloninger et al., 1997; Dinwiddie & Reich, 1993). As you can see from the court-ordered psychological assessment of Eric Cooper contained in Document 10.2, Cooper's diagnosis included both an Axis I substance abuse disorder and an Axis II diagnosis of antisocial personality disorder. (*Note:* The Psychopathy Checklist–Revised, listed under "Instruments" in Document 10.2, is a checklist of antisocial behaviors and symptoms [R. D. Hare et al., 1991].)

DOCUMENT 10.2

Excerpt From the Assessment of Eric Cooper by the Court Psychologist

MUNICIPAL COURT

Psychological Assessment

Date: December 4, 1999

Client: Eric Cooper

Instruments

Minnesota Multiphasic Personality Inventory (MMPI-2)

Thematic Apperception Test (TAT)

Wechsler Adult Intelligence Scale (WAIS-III)

Psychopathy Checklist–Revised (PCL-R)

Clinical interview

Psychologist: Dr. Aaron Lusted

Referral: Judge Warren

Reason for Referral: Judge Warren requested this presentencing report on Eric Cooper, a 30-year-old man who has been previously convicted of several crimes, including robbery and assault.

Behavioral Observations: Although the client was cooperative and friendly, he rarely made direct eye contact. Also, despite his general good mood, he would swear out loud and pound the table whenever he missed any questions on the intelligence test. There were no signs of delirium or alcohol intoxication, and the client was able to complete all tests with little prompting. The client reported that he had tried to rob a bank, while drunk, in order to pay his bills. He expressed concern that a guard was hurt during the attempted robbery and said he was pleased that no permanent damage was done. He asked whether there was a cure for his problem but when asked what his problem was, he said, "Bad luck, mostly."

Social History: [See Document 10.3, Social Work Report.]

Intellectual Assessment: The client's scores on the WAIS-III intelligence test place him in the above-average range of intelligence. His scores on the verbal scales were higher, in general, than his scores on the performance scale. This is not surprising in someone with the client's educational achievement.

Personality Assessment: The validity scales of the MMPI-2 were all in the average range, indicating that the test profile could be safely interpreted. The main feature of the profile was an elevated score on the psychopathic deviate scale. The client's responses revealed a self-centered person, whose own feelings always take precedence over those of other people, and a person who lacks empathy for the feelings and rights of others. He also has a strong tendency to act impulsively. . . . The client's TAT responses reflected a preoccupation with violence—there were numerous references to death, blood, and corpses—but no mention about how the characters in the story might respond or be affected by the violence. It was as if the client could not imagine what might be going through the heads of his own characters. . . . The client's responses to the Psychopathy Checklist (which assesses manipulative behavior and impulsivity), were those found among people who have been labeled "psychopaths"—people who lack empathy and are likely to use violence to achieve their goals.

Based on the test results, behavioral observations, and my clinical interview, it appears that the client is a person who has little empathy for or understanding of other people. He thinks mainly of himself, his needs, and his feelings. He is prepared to use violence to further his ends. Because he lacks empathy, the client is almost certain to have trouble in personal relationships. In addition, his self-centered attitude as well as his impulsiveness and willingness to use violence are likely to bring him into continued conflict with the law.

Diagnostic Considerations: The client meets the *DSM-IV* criteria for antisocial personality disorder; he also meets many of the criteria for a borderline personality disorder. In addition, he seems to have a pattern of substance abuse. He recently experienced stress from business problems, but his global functioning is only mildly impaired, and he is capable of a high level of psychological functioning.

Axis I (clinical disorders): Alcohol abuse

Axis II (personality disorders): Antisocial personality disorder
(possible borderline personality disorder as provisional secondary diagnosis)

Axis III (general medical conditions): None

Axis IV (psychosocial or environmental problems): Economic problems

Axis V (global assessment of functioning): GAF = 60

One commonly observed comorbidity is the strong link between mood disorders, social phobia, and avoidant personality disorder (Alpert et al., 1997; see also Fava et al., 1996). There are three possible explanations for this high level of observed comorbidity. First, it is possible that people with avoidant personalities (and social phobias) spend too much time alone and that this makes them prone to depression. A second possibility is that depression, social phobia, and avoidant personality disorder are separate conditions that happen to share a common etiology. That is, whatever causes depression also causes dependent personality and social phobia. A

third possible explanation for the observed comorbidity is that depression, social phobia, and avoidant personality disorder are really the same condition but with different names. As we saw in Chapter 4, there is little difference between long-term social phobia and an avoidant personality disorder. Perhaps depression, social phobia, and avoidant personality disorder are simply different aspects of the same condition.

Note that these three types of explanation (personality disorders cause Axis I disorders; both personality and Axis I disorders have a common cause; personality disorders are versions of Axis I disorders) apply not only to depression, social phobia, and avoidant personality but to any comorbidity between Axis I and Axis II disorders (Gerstley et al., 1990). At our present level of knowledge, it is not possible to say which of the three explanations is correct; different explanations may apply to different comorbidities. The important point is that coding personality disorders on a separate axis does not mean that their etiology is necessarily different from that of Axis I disorders. The two axes are better viewed as a diagnostic convenience with three main benefits. First, the use of a separate axis for personality disorders reminds clinicians to consider how long-term characterological traits affect the acute symptoms of an Axis I disorder. Second, Axis II information may sometimes be useful in choosing treatment programs, particularly when the presence of a concurrent personality disorder interferes with the treatment of an Axis I disorder. Finally, Axis II information may help in formulating a prognosis for an Axis I disorder. For example, the presence of a personality disorder may make the recurrence of an Axis I disorder more likely.

Types of Personality Disorders

The precise number of personality disorders and the names of these disorders have varied from one *DSM* to the next. The *DSM-IV* has settled on the 10 personality disorders listed in Table 10.2. It is important to keep in mind that these 10 disorders represent only a sample of the total number of potential personality disorders. For

Bess Myerson was Miss America in 1945, then a spokesperson for General Electric, and the cultural affairs commissioner for New York City. In 1988, she pled guilty to shoplifting $44 worth of nail polish, earrings, batteries, and sandals from a discount department store. Was she suffering from kleptomania?

DSM-IV TABLE 10.2 *DSM-IV* Personality Disorders

Diagnostic term	Primary personality characteristics
Paranoid personality	Distrust and suspicion of others, poor social relations
Schizoid personality	Restricted range of emotions and unstable relationships
Schizotypal personality	Eccentric behavior, including cognitive distortions
Antisocial personality	Disregard of the rights of other people
Borderline personality	Unstable relationships, poor self-image, impulsivity
Histrionic personality	Excessive emotional display and the pursuit of attention
Narcissistic personality	Grandiose feelings of superiority
Avoidant personality	Socially sensitive, inhibited, feelings of inadequacy
Dependent personality	Submissive and needing the care of others
Obsessive-compulsive personality	Preoccupation with order and control

example, there is no "Type A personality disorder" on the list, even though having a Type A personality may have serious health consequences (see Chapter 5). The personality disorders included in the *DSM-IV* owe their presence more to history and custom than to any scientific rationale about which constellations of personality traits constitute psychological disorders.

Types of Impulse-Control Disorders

As already noted, the impulse-control disorders constitute just as heterogeneous a category as the personality disorders (Hucker, 1997a). On the surface, at least, behaviors such as setting fires, stealing, pulling one's hair, and gambling do not seem to have a great deal in common. In an attempt to tie these seemingly disparate conditions together, and to separate them from the impulsive behavior that accompanies many other psychological disorders, the *DSM-IV* claims that the behavior of people with impulse-control disorders is different from the impulsiveness found in other conditions. For example, people in manic states often act impulsively (they may give away their money to a stranger, for example), but their impulsive behavior is not goal directed. In contrast, people with impulse-control disorders are said to feel a buildup of tension that can be relieved only by acting out their impulse—setting a fire, for instance. The implication is that tension accumulates until the individual can no longer resist lighting a fire. Once the fire is lit, the tension dissipates.

Despite this supposed difference, in the real world of the clinic it is often difficult to notice much difference between the type of impulsivity observed in the impulse-control disorders and the impulsivity found in other disorders. In fact, there seems to be much similarity between

the behavior of people with impulse-control disorders and people with other diagnoses, especially bipolar disorder and many of the personality disorders (McElroy et al., 1996). To justify a separate category for impulse-control disorders, the *DSM-IV* recommends that an impulse-control disorder (such as pyromania) not be diagnosed when a personality disorder (such as antisocial personality disorder) is more appropriate. In practice, there is little difference between the impulse-control disorders and some of the personality disorders, and clinicians find it hard to choose between them. The *DSM-IV* impulse-control disorders are described in Table 10.3.

Diagnostic Reliability

Interrater reliability is reasonably high for the individual diagnostic criteria of the various personality disorders (Merson et al., 1994). Nevertheless, clinicians still have difficulty deciding which personality disorder diagnosis is appropriate for which individual. The problem is that the same diagnostic criteria are applied to supposedly different disorders. Clinicians have no trouble agreeing that a person has poor social relations (one of the diagnostic criteria), but they do not agree about whether a person with poor social relations should be classified as borderline, schizoid, or avoidant personality disorder (each of which is marked by the same criterion—poor social relations). Similarly, hostility (another of the diagnostic criteria) is easy to recognize, but of little discriminatory value because it is a feature of more than half the personality disorders.

Given the overlapping diagnostic criteria, it is not surprising that there is a high comorbidity among personality disorders (Widiger & Corbitt, 1997; Widiger & Rogers, 1989). For example, like Eric Cooper, many

DSM-IV TABLE 10.3 *DSM-IV* Impulse-Control Disorders

Diagnostic term	Primary characteristics
Intermittent explosive disorder	Aggressive outbursts in which a person assaults others or destroys property. The outbursts are either unprovoked or out of proportion to the triggering event. The disorder is found more often among men than women.
Kleptomania	The stealing of worthless objects. Because the thief—for some reason, usually female—has nothing to gain (and the stealing is not motivated by anger or revenge), this behavior is believed to be intrinsically rewarding. That is, the act of stealing relieves tension.
Pyromania	The setting of fires purely to relieve tension and feel pleasure. Pyromania contrasts with arson, which is motivated by revenge or gain (or a delusion). Said to be more common in men, pyromania is rarely diagnosed.
Pathological gambling	Continued gambling despite personal loss and family harm. The most common of the impulse-control disorders, pathological gambling affects between 1% and 3% of the population. Sufferers do not know when to quit. Losses only spur them to gamble more, to win back what they have lost. Some have been helped by groups such as Gamblers' Anonymous, which is modeled after Alcoholics Anonymous. Whether pathological gambling is really a disorder or simply irresponsible behavior is the subject of considerable controversy.
Trichotillomania	The pulling out of one's own scalp, facial, or body hair. More common among women than men, this disorder is a type of compulsion, but it is not identical to obsessive-compulsive disorder because it usually does not involve obsessions.

people diagnosed with antisocial personality disorder are also given the diagnosis of borderline personality disorder (Paris, 1997; Zanarini & Gunderson, 1997). Although it is possible that these two personality disorders have similar causes, and therefore should be found together, it is also possible that their symptoms are so similar that they constitute the same disorder. Choosing between them may be so difficult that clinicians may find it easier to simply give people both diagnoses.

Impulse-control disorders are easier to distinguish from one another than are the personality disorders. After all, gambling is clearly different from stealing, and both are different from setting fires. The more difficult clinical judgment is when to apply an impulse-control disorder diagnosis and when a personality disorder diagnosis is more appropriate. Gambling, stealing, and fighting often go along with personality disorders. In such situations, the *DSM-IV* requires that the personality disorder take precedence. Perhaps this is why, with the exception of pathological gambling, pure impulse-

Baseball star Pete Rose was suspended from the game for gambling. Did he risk his career because of pathological gambling, or was he simply irresponsible?

control disorders are rarely diagnosed (American Psychiatric Assn, 1994).

Diagnostic Validity

The predictive value of the personality and impulse-control disorders is somewhat uncertain. Knowing that someone has a personality disorder tells us little about how different personalities develop, nor does it tell us much about how a person will behave in specific situations. Because they are more specific, impulse-control disorders may be better predictors of behavior (people with pyromania should start fires). However, despite the name, even people with impulse-control disorders sometimes control their impulses. People with pyromania have firefree periods, and people with kleptomania do not steal every day. Behavior is strongly determined by the social context. Under the right circumstances (when their boss is around, for example), gamblers may decide to moderate their betting. Similarly, people without an impulse-control disorder may be carried away by the excitement of a day at the races and bet all their money. Predicting how a person will behave in any situation requires that we understand not only the person's personality but also the social situation in which the behavior takes place (Mischel, 1997).

Diagnostic Biases

Clinicians must be on the alert for potential biases when making any diagnosis, but personality and impulse-control disorders are particularly susceptible to bias. For example, dependence, submissiveness, and allowing one's life to be directed by a spouse are all signs of a dependent personality disorder. However, they are also traits encouraged in females by many societies. If females adopt the dependent social role expected by their social group, are we really justified in calling their behavior a personality disorder? We might also ask ourselves why people who work 7 days a week, ignore their children, repress their emotions, and expect their families to relocate across the country as they climb the career ladder are not diagnosed as suffering from an *independent* personality disorder (M. Kaplan, 1983). Could it be because most such individuals are men and their behavior is socially sanctioned? And gender biases are not the only ones that clinicians must avoid. Unless clinicians are careful, their evaluation of other people may also be biased by social class, ethnicity, age, and education. As shown in the next section, each of these vari-

As Europe became industrialized in the late 1700s, cities became increasingly crowded with unemployed people, and the crime rate soared. However, the prevailing belief was that criminals were born, not created by social conditions. This Gustave Doré engraving depicts a street scene in the Whitechapel area of London.

ables can bias clinical judgments about who is suffering from a personality disorder.

EVOLUTION OF A PERSONALITY DISORDER: FROM PSYCHOPATH TO ANTISOCIAL PERSONALITY

The modern concept of antisocial personality disorder may be traced, at least in part, to the rise in crime in Europe during the 18th and 19th centuries. In the late 1700s, Europe's newly industrialized cities were crowded with unemployed people, whose very existence, in those days before unemployment insurance, depended on theft. Not surprisingly, crime became an important political and social issue. Instead of blaming the rising crime rate on a lack of social welfare programs, the governments of the day blamed genetics; they believed that criminals were born, not made. Most professionals agreed. One of the leading doctors of the time, Philippe Pinel, attributed criminal behavior to a *manie sans délire*, an inherited illness that causes people to act in an antisocial fashion even when they appear to be normal. British psychiatrists used the term **moral insanity** to describe the same condition (Prichard, 1835). People suffering from moral insanity were supposedly unable to tell right from wrong despite having normal intelligence and being "normal" in every other way. By the end of the 19th century, professional interest in so-called moral insanity grew strong enough to support the development of a new scientific field called **criminology**—the study of the causes, prevention, and treatment of criminal behavior.

Psychopaths and Sociopaths

The early criminologists were committed to the idea that criminality is genetic. One of the best known, the Italian doctor Cesare Lombroso (1835–1909), believed that inherited moral insanity could be recognized by defects in people's physical appearance: small skulls, asymmetrical faces, narrow foreheads, protruding ears, or prominent cheekbones. Lombroso called these supposed defects *stigmata* and argued that they signified a breakdown in evolutionary development. He believed that criminals were "throwbacks" to an earlier evolutionary stage, closer to apes than human beings. Claiming that different types of criminals had different patterns of physical stigmata, Lombroso became the champion of **physiognomy,** a pseudoscience based on the false idea that one's character is literally written all over one's face.

The idea that criminal behavior is inherited was an anathema to social reformers who hoped to create a more caring society. What is the point of trying to improve the lot of disadvantaged people if their destiny is genetically predetermined? In the 19th century, however, social reformers were in the minority. Most professionals followed the great classifier Emil Kraepelin, who agreed with Lombroso that criminal behavior was largely genetic in origin. In case descriptions reminiscent of Pinel's *manie sans délire,* Kraepelin described people who lied, cheated, committed crimes, and harmed others. He grouped such people into a diagnostic category he called *constitutional psychopathic inferiority.* The very name shows how close Kraepelin's thinking was to Lombroso's. "Psychopaths" were people who behaved in an antisocial manner. The cause of their behavior was genetic ("constitutional") and probably the result of some failure in evolutionary development ("inferiority"). Although he admitted that individuals considered

to be psychopaths in one culture—terrorists, for example—might be hailed as freedom fighters in another culture, Kraepelin still believed that social causes were secondary to genetics in the etiology of antisocial behavior.

Over the years, constitutional psychopathic inferiority was shortened (by dropping "constitutional" and "inferiority") to **psychopath.** But the idea that some people are born "inferior" persisted. In the 1930s and 40s, the Nazis justified the murder of millions of people by claiming that they were "purifying" the population —getting rid of people with bad genes. When the full horror of the Nazi extermination program became known after World War II, there was a backlash against genetic explanations for antisocial behavior. Instead of genes, psychologists attributed criminal behavior to such social factors as discrimination, deprivation, and poor role models. To mark this break with the past, the first *DSM,* published in 1952, abandoned the term *psychopath* entirely. Instead, it referred to a **sociopathic personality.** This change in nomenclature signified the dominance of social theories of antisocial behavior; criminals are made, not born.

Moral Insanity Revived

The term *sociopath* never entirely replaced psychopath. Indeed, psychopath was still a widely used diagnostic term when Hervey Cleckley published *The Mask of Sanity* in 1976. Cleckley, who was already famous for his coauthored book on multiple personality, *The Three Faces of Eve* (see Chapter 7), cemented his reputation as a popular writer with this frequently reprinted work. Using case studies, Cleckley resurrected the 19th-century idea of moral insanity, calling such people psychopaths. Cleckley's psychopaths were antisocial people who appeared "normal," even to professionals, but whose normality was really only a superficial "mask of sanity." Beneath the surface, Cleckley argued, psychopaths are deeply disturbed.

Because of their mask of sanity, psychopaths initially make a good impression. Like Eric Cooper, they can be friendly, intelligent, and show no overt signs of mental disorder. Yet they lead highly aberrant lives. They have dismal social relationships and disordered work histories, and they are often unreliable. On an impulse, they may give up a successful career to follow some momentary whim. Their projects, both legal and illegal, often turn out badly because, despite their intelligence, they fail to plan ahead. When confronted with evidence of their misbehavior, psychopaths first try to blame others. When this fails, they may admit their

Italian doctor Cesare Lombroso (1835–1909) believed that moral insanity was inherited and could be recognized by defects in people's appearance. In the frontispiece to his book Criminal Man *(1887), Lombroso grouped portraits of various kinds of criminals, purportedly to show similarities in appearance. In section A are shoplifters; in B, C, D, and F are swindlers; in E are German murderers; in G are gentlemen who fraudulently declared themselves bankrupt; in H are purse snatchers; and in I are burglars.*

misdeeds and feign regret, but their remorse and concern for their victims is not genuine, and their misbehavior is often repeated. Punishment does not deter them. In fact, psychopathic people engage in antisocial behavior even when they are almost certain to be caught and punished. It is as if they cannot see the future. When they are apprehended, psychopaths remain self-centered. Some have even been known to ask employers for references after being fired for stealing.

Eric Cooper has many of the characteristics of Cleckley's psychopaths. He can be friendly and intelligent (even his victims forgave him), but his behavior displays a flagrant disregard for the rights of others. Although he knows the difference between right and wrong and always claims to be remorseful, Eric does not hesitate to deceive others when it suits him. He rarely plans ahead, so he is repeatedly in trouble, but he never seems to learn from his experience. For examples from Eric's life, see Document 10.3, and for an example from recent history, see Highlight 10.1.

DOCUMENT 10.3

Court-Ordered Social Work Report on Eric Cooper

Date: December 1, 1999

Social Worker: Greg Sheridan, MSW

Referral: Judge Warren requested this presentencing report on Eric Cooper, a 30-year-old man who had been convicted of robbery and aggravated assault.

Sources: Court records, arrest reports, school records, interviews with Eric Cooper and Lenore Cooper (Eric's mother).

Eric Cooper is the only child born to Lenore and Edward Cooper. (Edward died in a hang-gliding accident when Eric was 5; Eric was raised by Lenore, a single mother.) Lenore Cooper reports that Eric always had a "bit of the devil" in him. When he was only 7, Eric stole money that his school was collecting to buy Christmas presents for needy children. His crime was detected when the piggy bank in which the money had been stored was found in his locker. At first, Eric denied any knowledge of how the bank had found its way into his locker, but when asked to explain the money in his pocket, he admitted his crime. Eric seemed contrite and remorseful, but the pattern of stealing (and getting caught) continued. During his elementary and junior high school years, Mrs. Cooper found her son in possession of toys, pens, wallets, a knife, an air rifle, and a radio. When asked to explain how he obtained these things, Eric would usually say he found them. In most cases, Mrs.

Cooper would later discover that they were stolen. Eric would always apologize and promise not to steal again, but he never kept these promises.

In junior high school, Eric was suspected of setting several fires in his school. These fires caused considerable damage to school property. On several occasions, Eric was seen in the vicinity of these fires, but there was never any proof connecting him to them.

In high school, Eric developed the habit of not coming home from school. The first few times, his mother panicked. She asked the police to search for him. Although it sometimes took as long as 2 days, Eric would always return unharmed. He usually refused to say where he had been, but from what his mother could find out, he had spent much of his time gambling. Eric played dice games, poker, bet on horses, and visited illegal casinos. Eric's interest in gambling continues to this day. Much of the money he has made (or stolen) has been lost in gambling.

In his last year of high school, Eric began an intimate relationship with a teacher. He was 17 and she was 24 (and married) when the affair began. The couple would meet after school at the teacher's apartment. The relationship was detected when the teacher became pregnant and named Eric as the father. Eric said he wanted to marry the teacher and raise the child, but when the teacher initiated divorce proceedings, Eric changed his mind. He claimed that he was seduced by the older woman.

Despite his extraordinary extracurricular life, Eric performed well enough at school to be admitted to college. Although his college marks were generally good, his academic career was punctuated by unpleasant incidents. For example, he was accused of cheating by another student but cleared when his accuser withdrew her claim. He had a string of girlfriends, but he did not stick with any one for very long. His style was to simply stop calling—no goodbyes and no explanation. While in college, Eric began to use alcohol and drugs, and he continues to use both today.

After graduation, Eric married his last college girlfriend. It was a violent relationship. Eric would "explode" and beat her, and he left her when she became pregnant. He never contacts her or his son, and rarely pays his required child support.

Over the years, Eric has managed to get a few jobs, but he has never kept one for very long. Often, there was no obvious reason for him to leave his employer; he just failed to turn up at work one day. He has also been constantly in debt and has a long history of paying bills with bad checks. Because he did not conceal his identity, his creditors had no trouble finding him, and he was convicted of fraud. He has also served time for robbery, drug dealing, burglary, possession of stolen goods, and selling pornography.

Eric began several businesses, including a stint running a

Was the President a Psychopath?

Charming, intelligent, engaging—all of these adjectives applied to President Bill Clinton. Yet, like the psychopaths described by Cleckley, he seemed to be unable to resist engaging in high-risk, and ultimately self-defeating, behavior. In retrospect, it seems obvious that he should have realized his sexual indiscretions would be discovered; so many people knew about them. It also seems obvious that he should have known his denials would be exposed as untrue; the others involved would act to protect themselves. Still, he persisted in denying any impropriety and blaming others for plotting against him. When confronted with clear evidence of his sexual transgressions, he grudgingly admitted minor wrongdoing. When the weight of evidence began to close in around him, he changed tack. He admitted his actions, asked for forgiveness, and displayed contrition. Like Eric Cooper, he even promised not to transgress again. Were his feelings of remorse genuine? We will never know for sure, but his pattern of behavior certainly showed many of the characteristics of a psychopath.

---

legal brothel in Nevada. His enterprises have always failed because he lost interest in them. His latest failure is the jazz club, whose unpaid bills precipitated the bank robbery that brought him once again into court.

Evaluation: Eric Cooper has led a life marked by irresponsibility. Stealing, lying, and a lack of concern for others have characterized his behavior since he was a child. Although his charm and intelligence allow him to give the appearance of remorse, there is little sign that he has reformed. Therapy may help, but it seems likely that Eric is destined to repeat his irresponsible behavior in the future. ■

Cleckley's Etiological Hypothesis: An Inability to Feel Emotions

For Cleckley, the failure to learn from experience was a central clue to the cause of psychopathic behavior. To explain why psychopathic people failed to profit from experience, Cleckley hypothesized that they are unable to experience normal emotions. They pretend to feel regret, affection, and fear, but they are really like actors, who simulate emotions they are not really experiencing. Because they do not feel anxiety about future punishment, psychopaths continue to commit antisocial acts for which they have been punished in the past.

Cleckley's hypothesis fit well with the behavioral psychology that dominated much of the 20th century. Translated into behavioral terminology, psychopaths were postulated to have a deficit in **avoidance learning.** Cleckley's hypothesis had been tested years earlier in an ingenious experiment by David Lykken (1928–), who compared people who fit Cleckley's description of a psychopath to nonpsychopaths in an incidental avoidance learning experiment (Lykken, 1957). The experimental apparatus consisted of red and green lights and three levers (Figure 10.2, p. 430). Subjects were required to learn to press the levers in sequence (for example, lever 3, followed by lever 1, followed by lever 2). Correct sequences illuminated a green light; incorrect sequences illuminated a red one. Through trial and error, the participants were expected to learn which lever-pressing sequences were correct. In one experimental condition, an incorrect sequence elicited an electric shock. Participants were told that these shocks were meant to help motivate their learning. The nonpsychopathic subjects learned the correct sequences more quickly when shock was used, whereas shock made no difference to the learning of the psychopathic subjects. As a result, the psychopathic subjects were shocked more times than the nonpsychopaths.

Lykken's result supported Cleckley's idea that the threat of punishment does not make psychopathic people anxious. Without anxiety to motivate them, psychopathic people take longer than nonpsychopathic people to learn to avoid shocks. Further support for this hypothesis comes from studies showing that psychopathic people show fewer biological signs of anxiety in the face of potential punishment than do nonpsychopathic people (Patrick, Cuthbert, & Lang, 1994).

DSM-IV Abandons Psychopathy

The experimental data collected over the decades are remarkably consistent with Cleckley's clinical observations (R. D. Hare, 1996; Lewis, 1991; Patrick et al., 1994). People who meet his definition of psychopath act on

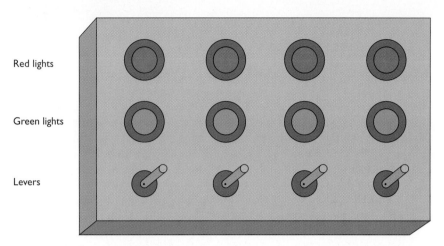

Red lights

Green lights

Levers

FIGURE 10.2 **Lykken's Experimental Apparatus for the Incidental Testing of Avoidance Learning.** *Subjects were told that they must learn to press levers in a certain sequence. Incorrect responses sometimes produced a painful electric shock. Even though subjects were not instructed to avoid shock, the nonpsychopathic subjects learned to do so, but the psychopathic subjects did not.* From: D. T. Lykken (1957).

their immediate instincts and seem not to fear punishment. Not surprisingly, like Eric Cooper, they are continuously in trouble. Despite these intriguing, and largely consistent, research findings, the *DSM-IV* abandoned both the term *psychopath* and the term *sociopath*, replacing them with *antisocial personality disorder*. The *DSM-IV* deliberately replaced Cleckley's psychopath—a clearly deviant person—with a diagnostic category that is so general it can accommodate practically anyone who behaves in an antisocial manner. Moreover, the new diagnostic criteria omit the hallmark of Cleckley's concept of psychopathy—an inability to feel emotions.

Why the change? The main reason is the *DSM-IV*'s attempt to make its diagnostic criteria as objective as possible (see Chapter 3). The *DSM-IV* criteria for antisocial personality, which appear in Table 10.4, focus on observable behaviors (such as impulsivity) and omit those that refer to presumed etiologies (such as a failure to feel emotions). Although the objective criteria strived for in the *DSM-IV* are an improvement over the subjective diagnostic criteria sometimes used in the past, it is curious that such a consistent body of psychological research has had so little effect on modern diagnostic practice. This seems to be an instance in which trying to be objective may have led professionals to abandon a potentially useful etiological theory.

As indicated in Table 10.4, the hallmark of the *DSM-IV*'s antisocial personality disorder is a flagrant

disregard for the rights of other people. Like Eric Cooper, people with antisocial personality disorder are often irresponsible, impulsive, and untrustworthy. Eric's repertoire also included behavior characteristic of at least three of the impulse-control disorders—pyromania (he lit fires when young), pathological gambling, and intermittent explosive disorder. This is not unusual; a lack of impulse control seems to be an intrinsic part of antisocial personality disorder. Eric was not diagnosed with pyromania or intermittent explosive disorder because the *DSM-IV* diagnostic criteria specifically exclude these diagnoses when a person is also diagnosed as having an antisocial personality disorder. He might well have been diagnosed with pathological gambling, however, had the psychologist known more about this aspect of Eric's behavior.

Because only three of seven criteria need be met for the diagnosis of antisocial personality disorder, the *DSM-IV* criteria can encompass confidence tricksters, thieves, charlatans, corrupt politicians, even devious used car salespeople. Because the category is so broad, it tells us remarkably little about a person's behavior. People with an antisocial personality disorder can have markedly different demeanors. Some, like Eric Cooper, can be charming; others may be surly and aggressive. In other words, despite its status as a disorder of "personality," the antisocial personality label tells us little about a person's temperament; it is really just a shorthand way

DSM-IV **TABLE 10.4** Main *DSM-IV* Diagnostic Criteria
for Antisocial Personality Disorder

A. There is a pervasive pattern of disregard for and violation of the rights of others occurring since age 15 years, as indicated by three (or more) of the following:

(1) failure to conform to social norms and respect lawful behaviors as indicated by repeatedly performing acts that are grounds for arrest

(2) deceitfulness, as indicated by repeated lying, use of aliases, or conning others for personal profit and pleasure

(3) impulsivity or failure to plan ahead

(4) irritability and aggressiveness, as indicated by repeated physical fights or assaults

(5) reckless disregard for the safety of self or others

(6) consistent irresponsibility, as indicated by repeated failure to sustain consistent work behavior or honor financial obligations

(7) lack of remorse as indicated by being indifferent to or rationalizing having hurt, mistreated, or stolen from another

B. The individual is at least age 18 years.

C. There is evidence of a conduct disorder with onset before age 15 years.

Note: From American Psychiatric Association (1994, pp. 649–650).

---

of saying that a person engages in a habitual pattern of irresponsible behavior. Often, this behavior brings the person in contact with the law (R. D. Hare et al., 1991). Nevertheless, it is important to note that an antisocial personality is not the equivalent of criminality. Not all criminals have a psychological disorder, and not all people who have antisocial personality disorder are criminals (Hart & Hare, 1997; see also Highlight 10.1).

In contrast to earlier editions of the *DSM*, the *DSM-IV* requires a long-term pattern of impulsivity, aggression, and deception for a diagnosis of antisocial personality disorder. There must be evidence of a conduct disorder in childhood (see Document 10.4 for an example in Eric Cooper's past and Chapter 12 for more on conduct disorder) and an adult pattern of antisocial behavior that is evident by age 15. By insisting on such a lifelong pattern, the *DSM-IV* seems to have moved back in the direction of Kraepelin's "constitutional psychopath," who is either born antisocial or who develops such tendencies early in life. In practice, the initial onset of antisocial behavior is difficult to document (Stoff, Breiling, & Maser, 1997). Objective information about a person's childhood is rarely available, retrospective reports by others are often unreliable, and people suspected of being antisocial cannot be trusted to give an accurate history of their own lives. Despite these uncertainties, the idea that people who are "psychopathic" are different from birth, or at least early childhood, is sometimes used to argue that they cannot help their ac-

tions—that they are simply suffering from an illness (see Critical Thinking About Clinical Decisions 10.1).

DOCUMENT 10.4

Elementary School Permanent–Record Note on Eric Cooper

Date: May 21, 1981

Teacher: Mrs. Bonnie Redman

Eric Cooper, a student in Class 6A, accompanied his class on a museum field trip. While the class was at the museum, Eric and another student, Brian Toohey, left the building. They could not be found when the class got ready to return to school. A search of the area proved futile, and the police were called. The class returned to the school without the boys, who were later found by the police outside a bar featuring topless waitresses and striptease. According to Toohey, Eric had taken $30 from my handbag while we were on the bus and then asked Toohey to go with him to a liquor store. Eric tried to use the money he had taken from my purse to buy alcohol and cigarettes. When the clerk refused to sell the boys anything, Eric and Toohey went to the bar. They were trying to gain admission when the police found them. Toohey was crying and very upset, while Eric seemed calm but contrite. He said he knew what he had done was wrong and that he would never do anything like it again. "Believe me," he said, "I have learned my lesson." ■

Criminal Responsibility: Bad or Mad?

On the night of June 23, 1993, John Bobbitt returned to his Virginia home after an evening of drinking. According to his wife, Lorena, he was drunk, and he forced her to have sex with him. John claimed that their sex was consensual. In any event, when John fell asleep, Lorena went to the kitchen and returned to the bedroom with a knife. She pulled down the sheets and cut off her husband's penis. She then left the house, drove a short distance, and threw the organ into a field. Soon afterward, she called police and told them where to find it. Surgeons managed to reattach the penis in an operation that lasted nearly 10 hours. In a barrage of publicity, Lorena stood trial for "malicious wounding." If found guilty, she faced a fine of up to $100,000 and a mandatory prison term of 5–20 years. However, following 7 days of testimony, the jury (seven women and five men) found Lorena Bobbitt "not guilty by reason of temporary insanity." They concluded that her act was the result of an impulse she could not resist. As required by Virginia law, the judge committed Lorena Bobbitt to a state mental hospital for a 45-day evaluation to determine whether she was a threat to herself or others. The doctors found that she was not, and she was released.

Lorena Bobbitt cut off her husband's penis while he was sleeping. She was found not guilty of malicious wounding by reason of insanity.

At the core of Lorena Bobbitt's winning defense was the testimony of a defense psychiatrist who said that she suffered from depression, post-traumatic stress disorder, and panic disorder, all caused by her husband's abuse. On the night in question, the psychiatrist testified, Lorena Bobbitt couldn't control an "irresistible impulse" to emasculate her

husband. The prosecution countered with experts who argued that Lorena Bobbitt never lost control of her impulses, but the jury obviously put more credence in the testimony of the defense expert.

Lorena Bobbitt's "insanity" defense has a long legal history. The rationale behind the defense requires that people who engage in criminal behavior be divided into two categories: those who are "bad" and those who are "mad." Both groups may engage in the same behavior (say, malicious assault), but the consequences differ. Bad people go to jail, whereas mad people may avoid prison altogether. The reason for treating the groups differently is that our legal system punishes only people who are responsible for their crimes and capable of defending themselves in court. Those who are not responsible for their actions at the time of a crime are committed for treatment. This is known as **criminal commitment** and contrasts with civil commitment for treatment or assessment (civil commitment is discussed in Chapter 9). People who, for one reason or another, are unable to defend themselves in court may also be committed, but they will be made to stand trial later if they recover sufficiently to participate in their defense.

Prevalence and Course of Antisocial Personality Disorder

Between 2.5% and 3.5% of the population, mainly men, meet the *DSM-IV* criteria for antisocial personality disorder (American Psychiatric Assn, 1994; Cloninger et al., 1997; Robins et al., 1984; Salama, 1988). Although the preponderance of men may reflect a difference between the sexes, it may also be the result of stereotypical sex roles (Giordano & Cernkovich, 1997). In our society, men are expected to be aggressive and to take more risks

than women. Men may be socially reinforced for behaving in ways consistent with at least some of the diagnostic criteria for antisocial personality disorder.

By the *DSM-IV*'s definition, antisocial personality disorder usually has its origins in adolescence, but it may begin even earlier (Clarizio, 1997; Loeber, 1991; Swanson, Bland, & Newman, 1994). In fact, poor impulse control and aggressiveness as a child are important predictors of antisocial personality disorder later in life (Foley, Carlton, & Howell, 1996; Hinshaw & Zupan, 1997; Manuzza et al., 1993). A typical sequence is for an impulsive pre-

Because **insanity** is a legal rather than a scientific term, its meaning is not determined by mental health professionals but by legislatures and courts. Thus, it is not surprising to find that the definition of insanity has varied with society's attitude toward crime and criminals. The modern usage of the term *insanity* has its origins in 19th-century England. Daniel M'Naghten, while attempting to assassinate the Prime Minister, murdered the Prime Minister's secretary instead. The jury found M'Naghten "not guilty by reason of insanity." The ensuing public outcry led the Law Lords (who interpret British law in the same way that the Supreme Court interprets American law) to establish a strict insanity defense. This became known as the **M'Naghten Rule.** Under this rule, a person is insane, and not responsible for criminal behavior, if the person is suffering from a mental disorder and *also* unable to tell right from wrong. This was the rule applied by the judge who sentenced Eric Cooper to jail (see Document 10.1). The judge recognized that Eric had a personality disorder, but this alone did not meet the legal definition of insanity. To be found not guilty because of insanity, Eric would have needed to be unaware that robbing banks, taking hostages, and shooting people is wrong. Because he did know that these acts are wrong, he was sentenced to jail.

Although many American states had adopted the M'Naghten Rule, others, such as Lorena Bobbitt's home state of Virginia, preferred an alternative—the **irresistible impulse rule.** Under this rule, a person who is unable to resist an impulse, as in a fit of passion, is considered temporarily insane and therefore not guilty of criminal behavior. Lorena Bobbitt's act of violence against her husband allegedly took place during such a fit of passion. A less well known rule, called the *Durham Rule,* was used by the Supreme Court in the 1950s. It stated that any person whose act is the product of a mental disease or mental defect is not criminally responsible for his or her actions. This is a much broader definition than either the M'Naghten or the irresistible impulse rule. Indeed, had the judge applied this rule to Eric, then he would have been acquitted. The Durham Rule is rarely applied today.

Today, the most commonly used definition of insanity is a 1984 revision of the M'Naghten Rule that limits the insanity defense to those people who, at the time of their crimes, were unable to appreciate the wrongfulness of their actions. Some states, such as Virginia, retain the irresistible impulse rule, and a few states have abolished the insanity defense altogether. These regional differences have produced deep concerns among both legal and mental health professionals about the validity of the insanity defense (Backlar, 1998). Why should the question of whether a person is insane depend on where he or she happens to live? Further doubts have been raised by disagreement among experts as to who is and is not legally insane. Expert witnesses often disagree (as in the Bobbitt trial), and there seems to be no valid way to determine which expert is correct (Hollweg, 1998). Finally, there is the question of equity and fairness. If treatment is going to be made available, why limit it only to those called legally insane? Why not make treatment available to everyone with a mental disorder? These many concerns and unanswered questions almost certainly guarantee that politicians, legal scholars, and mental health practitioners will be preoccupied by the insanity defense for some time to come (Reznek, 1998).

pubescent boy to be labeled as a "conduct problem" in school. In adolescence, the same boy is labeled "delinquent," and in early adulthood, he is diagnosed as antisocial (Lahey & Loeber, 1997). Girls usually show fewer problems before adolescence but then follow a pattern similar to that of boys (Zoccolillo, Tremblay, & Vitaro, 1996). About 40% of males and 24% of females who have conduct disorder as children wind up being diagnosed with antisocial personality disorder in later life (Robins, 1966). For both sexes, the longer a conduct problem persists, the less likely it is to be "outgrown."

The highest prevalence of antisocial personality disorder is among men aged 25–44 years. In middle and old age, the incidence of antisocial personality disorder declines. For example, the number of convicted criminals who are diagnosed as having an antisocial personality disorder drops off markedly with age (Harpur & Hare, 1994). It is not clear whether this means the disorder diminishes with age or whether people with antisocial personality disorder fail to live past middle age. We do know that many die young from suicide, homicide, accidents, and substance abuse (Plutchik & Van Praag, 1997).

Causes of Antisocial Personality Disorder

As already mentioned, 19th-century criminologists were convinced that antisocial behavior was inherited. By the middle of the 20th century, the pendulum of opinion had swung the other way—nurture had the upper hand. As the 21st century dawns, the pendulum has once again shifted back toward genetics. There is a difference, however, between today's views on the etiology of antisocial behavior and those of the past. Although modern scientists admit that genetics plays a role in antisocial behavior, few believe in the crude determinism of Lombroso and the Nazis. No one believes that there is a gene that makes a person a criminal. The modern view is that genetics and environment both contribute to every type of behavior, including antisocial behavior. In this section, we examine some of the ways in which heredity, biology, and experience interact to produce antisocial behavior.

Genetics   Considerable evidence points to a genetic element in antisocial behavior, particularly when the antisocial behavior includes aggression (Bohman, 1996; Carey & Goldman, 1997; Crusio, 1996; Dinwiddie, 1996; T. G. O'Connor et al., 1998; Rutter, 1996; Stallings et al., 1997). This evidence includes a higher concordance for antisocial traits among identical siblings than among nonidentical siblings (Jenaway & Swinton, 1993) and the finding that adopted children grow up to resemble their antisocial biological parents more than their nonantisocial adopted parents. In addition, pedigree studies have identified families with high rates of violent behavior among the male members. Highlight 10.2 profiles one such father-son pair.

Attempts to pinpoint the precise manner in which antisocial behavior is inherited have thus far proved unsuccessful. All of the simple explanations that have been offered to date (antisocial behavior is the result of an extra male chromosome, for instance) have proved to be blind alleys (Harmon et al., 1998). All researchers agree that the mechanism by which antisocial behavior is inherited is likely to be complicated. One popular theory is that an inherited tendency toward antisocial behavior is mediated by faults in the neurotransmitter system (Berman, Kavoussi, & Coccaro, 1997). Specifically, researchers have implicated low levels of serotonin as possibly contributing to violent antisocial behavior. A complication for this hypothesis is that some of the variables that affect serotonin levels may, by themselves, cause antisocial behavior. For example, disadvantaged people, whose diets are poor, may have low serotonin

levels. Their poverty also puts them at high risk of engaging in antisocial behavior. Is it their low serotonin that causes their antisocial behavior, or is it their poverty? (Perhaps it is both.) In addition to neurotransmitters, hormones have been linked to antisocial behavior—especially the male sex hormone, testosterone. The simple hypothesis is that excess testosterone causes aggression and violence. Although there is some correlational evidence for this hypothesis, the strength of the relationship between high levels of testosterone and violence remains equivocal (Brain & Susman, 1997).

There is a pressing need to clarify the ways in which genes affect antisocial behavior. Whether the necessary research is ever carried out depends on politics. In the United States in 1995, the federal government withdrew its financial support for a scientific conference on violence and genetics when some scientists and community groups protested (Nelkin, 1995). Opponents view genetic research as racially motivated, an attempt to redefine social problems in biological terms. They fear that genetic research will be used to stigmatize some minority groups as "born criminals." Stigmatizing minorities is a danger, of course, but such an outcome can be avoided by proper public education about the meaning of genetic findings. Banning research on the genetics of antisocial personality disorder for political reasons makes it impossible for researchers to get a complete picture about how genetics and environment interact to produce antisocial behavior.

Birth Trauma   Examining the medical histories of antisocial individuals led Brennan and Mednick (1997) to suggest that prenatal and postnatal accidents (such as anoxia caused by an umbilical cord wrapped around a baby's neck during childbirth) or early illnesses can produce brain damage, which, in turn, leads to poor impulse control and antisocial behavior. Poor nutrition can have a similar effect (Gottschalk, 1991). Because antisocial people are often poor in verbal skills, researchers have further hypothesized that the brain damage is most likely to be found in the left (language) hemisphere (Henry & Moffitt, 1997; Kavoussi, Armstead, & Coccaro, 1997). Although the logic sounds plausible, the evidence for brain damage in the left or right hemisphere of antisocial people is weak. Studies using modern imaging techniques to examine the brains of delinquent teenagers and antisocial adults have produced equivocal results. Moreover, most people who incur brain damage from birth trauma do not become antisocial (Henry & Moffitt, 1997; D. J. Stein et al., 1993).

Born to Be Wild

Willie Bosket Jr. describes himself as a "homicidal monster." His jailers in the New York State prison system agree. They built a special basement cell just for him, a dungeon in which Willie is kept in solitary confinement. The cell is lined with thick clear plastic, and video cameras monitor his every movement. Whenever anyone has to enter his cell, Bosket is chained backward to the inside of his cell door. When the door is swung open, he appears, suspended like a laboratory specimen.

How did Bosket get into this situation? It began when he was a child. Because of his constant stealing and fighting, Bosket was sent for psychological tests. These were never completed because he threatened to set fire to the office and kill the clinician. Bosket was 9 years old. Although impulse-control disorders were evident in his behavior (intermittent explosive disorder, pyromania, and kleptomania), the dominating diagnosis was antisocial personality disorder. Bosket did his best to live up to this label. When he was 15, he shot two New York City subway passengers to death. Over the years, he also knifed an

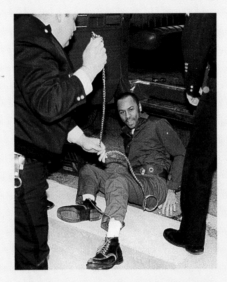

Willie Bosket Jr. followed his father's footsteps into a life of violent crime. Was his violence due to genetics or to environment? (Here, the guard is pulling Bosket with a chain after he tried to kick the guard as he was being taken from a van.)

elderly blind man, stabbed a prison guard, smashed another guard's skull with a lead pipe, choked a secretary, battered a teacher with a nail-studded club, sodomized many inmates, beat up a psychiatrist, and created general mayhem (throwing food and feces at guards).

Despite his wild behavior, Bosket is intelligent, and he can be charming. His cell is full of books, and he likes to converse about what he has read. His father was uncannily similar. Like his son, Bosket Senior had only a third-grade education. Like his son, he was sent to reform school at age 9. In fact, both father and son were sent to the same reform school. Both committed double murders, both were highly intelligent, and both liked to read. Bosket Senior was the first convict in New York history to be inducted into the Phi Beta Kappa honor society. He even worked for a while as a college teacher. He met his end when a botched escape attempt led to a shootout with the police. He killed his girlfriend and then himself. Bosket Junior believes that he inherited his violent tendencies from his father. Although environment may also play a role (the two men came from similar backgrounds), it is hard not to agree.

Sensation Seeking A hypothesis with a long history in psychology suggests that antisocial personality disorder is the result of low emotional arousal (Raine, 1997). The idea is that low arousal is an aversive state that people naturally try to escape. They do this by seeking the stimulation and excitement that comes from dangerous, often antisocial, behavior (Gabel et al., 1994). Recall from the social work report (Document 10.3) that Eric Cooper's father died in a hang-gliding accident. It is possible that he was a sensation seeker and that Eric inherited a similar tendency. Of course, stimulation seeking need not always lead to antisocial behavior. Successful businesspeople, mountain climbers, and even scientists may also crave stimulation, but their behavior is not antisocial. Clearly, sensation seeking alone is not a sufficient explanation for why some people develop antisocial personality disorder. We must also explain why such people seek stimulation in socially disapproved ways. One likely place to look is in early childhood family experiences.

Family Dynamics Psychodynamic theorists attribute antisocial and most other personality disorders to an absence of trust in other people (Gabbard, 1990). This loss of trust, which results from a lack of love during infancy, leads to emotional detachment. Children grow up unable to empathize with others; as a result, they become self-absorbed. The evidence for this view is the frequent finding of dysfunctional backgrounds, especially child abuse, in the histories of people with antisocial

Dead-Time Stories

"What a hot babe," teased Lollypop. "Should we get her?" asked Candyman.

These are the opening lines of a story written by an 11-year-old boy in which the "Bad Boyz" of Crime Alley circle and then close in on a horrified woman as she approaches her car. A Batman-style figure saves the day, but the story remains shocking. It is 1 of 30 sent by a schoolteacher to a newspaper (Hope, 1998). The children, 17 boys and 13 girls, wrote the stories as part of a school assignment in which they were asked to write about a chance meeting. Nearly all the boys' stories and half the girls' contain bloodshed and havoc. For example, an 11-year-old girl wrote "On the 18th of March, Elizabeth Jane Houston was murdered by an unknown man. He escaped justice. Elizabeth was killed by several knife wounds all over her body." A 10-year-old girl wrote "He got his gun

Does frequent exposure to violent behavior, such as that in many computer games, desensitize children to violence?

and pointed it at my face. Then he quickly got me in a headlock, the barrel of the gun firmly against my temple. . . . 'If anyone tries to stop me now, the girl is dead.'" Other stories included hijackings, murder, kidnappings, races to

the death, enslavement, violent arrests, chases by gunmen, armed robbery, and killings by aliens.

The teacher who sent the stories believes that they reflect the violence seen by the children on TV and in films, in computer games, and on the Internet. She worries that constant exposure to violence has left the children desensitized. They are so used to playing computer games that encourage firing on people pleading for help that they may have lost their natural inhibition to harm. Of course, there is a big difference between writing about violence and engaging in a violent act. Most children who see violence in the media do not become violent themselves. There are clearly other factors involved in determining who becomes violent, and under what circumstances.

---

personality disorder (Luntz & Widom, 1994). Again, however, there are many people who grow up with abuse who do not develop antisocial personality disorder, so family dynamics, on their own, are not a sufficient etiological explanation.

Modeling and Media Many lifelong habits are first developed in childhood, including antisocial ones. For this reason, a childhood spent with criminal models is an ideal training ground for children to learn antisocial behavior (Eron, 1997; Shaw & Winslow, 1997). More often, however, exposure to antisocial behavior is not direct, but through the media. Children get to see crimes, including violent ones, on television and in the movies, and they can even "perpetrate" a pretend form of violence by playing computer games. Some researchers and clinicians have claimed that exposure to violent movies, computer games, and rap songs is an important cause of violent antisocial behavior (Willis & Strasburger, 1998). Noting the influence of the media on behavior, politicians and even some psychologists have argued that

media violence should be censored to protect society from crime (McLeod, Eveland, & Nathanson, 1997).

It is difficult to avoid media violence, and there is evidence that exposure to violence and mayhem is coming to the notice of even young children, as Highlight 10.3 illustrates. We also know that violent crime among children and adolescents is increasing (Loeber & Hay, 1997). It seems sensible then to link the two together. Perhaps children who watch chainsaw massacres are more violent than those who prefer romantic comedies. Certainly, there is evidence that the number of hours spent watching media violence is a predictor of aggression, both in children and later in life (Huesmann, Moise, & Podolski, 1997). But it is only one of many predictors, and not a very strong one at that. The correlation between aggression among males and the time spent watching violent television programs in the United States is .25. In Australia it is .13, and in Finland .22 (Huesmann et al., 1997). These correlations are too small to explain or predict violence on their own (Barrett, 1997). Moreover, it is always difficult to infer causation from a correlation. Just as chil-

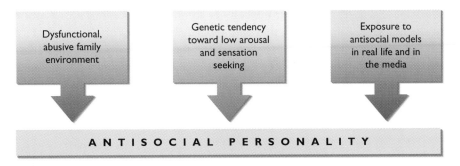

FIGURE 10.3 **Risk Factors for Antisocial Personality Disorder**

dren who like to play football watch more football on television than those who don't, perhaps aggressive kids are more likely to watch violent videos and play violent computer games. To make things even more complicated, there are strong counterexamples to the relationship between media violence and actual violence. Japan, for instance, is famous for its violent pornographic comics and gory cartoons, yet it suffers much less than other countries from violence.

The evidence boils down to this: Violence in the media is not a sufficient explanation for childhood violence. The easy availability of weapons (half of all juvenile murder victims are killed with a gun), temperament, poverty, and peer influences are probably as important or even more important determinants of violent behavior among children than is media violence (Adler & Denmark, 1995). Censorship of media violence may reduce violence among some susceptible children (at the risk of violating everyone else's right to free speech), but it is unlikely to eliminate what is really a complicated social problem with multiple causes.

Causes of Antisocial Personality Disorder: Summary
Like much human behavior, antisocial behavior has its origins in early childhood. Parents who provide an abusive and discordant environment are more likely to produce antisocial children than are parents who provide a stable and happy household. On the other hand, it is possible that the personality traits that lead parents to provide a poor home life—to drink too much, fight, and abuse their children—are at least partly inherited (and passed on to their offspring). Thus, early social background is not easily disentangled from genetics. Perhaps the best way to conceptualize our current knowledge of the causes of antisocial personality disorder is in terms of risk factors (Figure 10.3). A poor upbringing combined with exposure to antisocial models (in real life and in the media) and a possible genetic tendency toward low arousal and com-

pensatory sensation seeking are the main risk factors in the development of antisocial personality disorder.

Treatment of Antisocial Personality Disorder

Few adults with antisocial behavior seek treatment, and even fewer are motivated to change. The most common "treatment" for people with antisocial personality disorder is incarceration in a correctional facility. But incarceration is notoriously unsuccessful at rehabilitating most individuals, and repeat offenses are common. Psychological treatment does not usually thrive in involuntary settings such as prisons, yet there have been controlled studies showing the effectiveness of behavior therapy and behavioral staff training programs in reducing antisocial behavior, especially violence, by persons in institutions (Hamling, Harris, & Rice, 1997; Holbrook, 1997). Clinicians have also had some success in reducing violence using antipsychotic and antidepressant medications (Citrome & Volavka, 1997; Gitlin, 1993).

Given the difficulties encountered in treating antisocial personality disorder after it is established, some psychologists have emphasized prevention instead (Reid & Eddy, 1997). Prevention programs are usually aimed at children and adolescents from high-risk backgrounds (abused children, children in single-parent families, and children from marginal neighborhoods). These programs include one or more of the following elements: parent training; school-based counseling; removal of children from criminal environments; and rewards for positive behavior, such as studying or volunteer work (Henggeler et al., 1998). Recently, psychologists have been trying to tailor prevention programs to a child's social and ethnic background. Thus, programs aimed at Hispanic youths are delivered by Hispanic people familiar with the language and culture of the children and their families (Coatsworth et al., 1997).

Critical Thinking About Clinical Decisions 10.2 looks at the predictive task facing American clinicians, who have a legal obligation to assess the potential of their clients for violence. It is also essential to recognize the importance of social context in the commission of violent acts. As Document 10.5 illustrates, Eric Cooper did not enter the bank to commit violence, but the situation evolved that way—partly because of Eric's potential for violent behavior. Document 10.6 shows an actuarial assessment of Cooper's potential for violence, prepared in response to a parole board request after his incarceration for the bank robbery.

DOCUMENT 10.5

Police Report on
Eric Cooper's Bank
Robbery

Summary of Witness Statements

Reporting Officer: Salvadore Rogato

Date: November 16, 1999

Eight people were in the First National Bank, Westville Branch on Wednesday, November 15, when Eric Cooper entered the building. Three were customers speaking with the manager about a loan; one was a plainclothes security guard, Shane Crockett; and the remainder were bank staff. Eric Cooper went to a teller, Maria Lopez, and passed her a note on which he had printed, "This is a robbery. I have a gun. I do not want to hurt anyone, but I will use it if I have to. Put $10,000 in small bills in an envelope and pass it to me. Do not say anything to anyone." Ms. Lopez pressed a silent alarm, which was relayed to the Westville police station and was also picked up by Crockett on his earphone. As Ms. Lopez filled an envelope with cash, Crockett slowly strode over to place himself behind Cooper. He then reached out and tried to grab Cooper's wrist to put it in handcuffs. Cooper pulled out a small-caliber revolver. Crockett grabbed Cooper's hand, and a struggle ensued. During the struggle, Cooper discharged the gun, wounding Crockett in the arm. Despite his injury, Crockett was able to wrestle the gun away from Cooper. He held the gun on Cooper until the police arrived about 3 minutes later.

DOCUMENT 10.6

Actuarial Assessment
of Eric Cooper's
Potential for Violence

Parole Board Violence Report

Applicant: Eric Cooper

Date: October 23, 2001

Eric Cooper, a man with a history of aggression and violence, has applied for parole. The Parole Board has asked for this violence assessment. The following assessment is based on an actuarial formula using the base rates for violence among male offenders with a history of violent crimes and the 12 items of individual information summarized in the following table.

Eric Cooper's Status (in parentheses) on the Predictors Used to Assess Violence*

Psychopathy checklist (high)

Separation from one parent under age 16 (yes)

Victim injured in last offense (yes)

Presence of schizophrenia (no)

Never married (no)

Elementary school maladjustment (yes)

Female victim violence in past (yes)

Failure on prior conditional release (yes)

Property offense history (yes)

Age at last offense (30)

Alcohol abuse history (yes)

Antisocial personality disorder (yes)

Violence Report: On the basis of the actuarial formula, Eric Cooper has a probability of 80% or higher of committing a violent act in the first 6 months after release. Parole should be preceded by a period of home detention, and should be carefully supervised through all subsequent stages.

Psychologist:

Louis B. Jones, PhD

*Adapted from Harris et al. (1993).

Homicide is the second most frequent cause of death in the United States among young people between the ages of 15 and 24. What measures are effective in preventing this violence?

DIAGNOSIS, ETIOLOGY, AND TREATMENT OF THE *DSM-IV* PERSONALITY DISORDERS

This section contains descriptions, diagnostic criteria, and examples of the nine *DSM-IV* personality disorders not yet discussed plus two disorders recommended for further study. Following the *DSM-IV*, this discussion divides the personality disorders into three clusters. Cluster A includes the paranoid, schizoid, and schizotypal personality disorders. Individuals who fall into cluster A appear odd or eccentric. Cluster B includes the antisocial, borderline, histrionic, and narcissistic personality disorders. Individuals in Cluster B are dramatic, emotional, and erratic. Cluster C includes the avoidant, dependent, and obsessive-compulsive personality disorders. Individuals in Cluster C are anxious and fearful. Although this section is organized using the cluster system, keep in mind that these three categories presently have limited diagnostic value. It is not uncommon for the same person to be simultaneously diagnosed with personality disorders from more than one cluster (Phillips & Gunderson, 1996).

Cluster A: Paranoid, Schizoid, and Schizotypal Personality Disorders

Cluster A personality disorders are marked by eccentricity, not to the point of losing touch with reality, but sufficient for the individual to be perceived by others as odd.

Turbulent Weather Ahead

The United States is the most violent nation in the industrialized world (Potter & Mercy, 1997). After accidents, homicide is the most frequent cause of death among young people between the ages of 15 and 24. More than 2 million people are beaten, knifed, or assaulted each year, 23,000 fatally. These figures are as much as 10 times higher than those found in other developed countries, and they are low estimates. Much violence is underreported. Victims of rape or spousal abuse may feel that the attack was their fault or fear the loss of their reputation. They prefer to keep their victimization secret, thereby minimizing reported violence.

Reducing violent crime is the number one priority of police forces across the United States, and they have had some success (Shuster, 1998). Still, there is a long way to go. It would help considerably if we were able to predict who is likely to be violent, so that such people could be provided with the treatment they require and their potential victims could be warned to take precautions. Assessing their clients' potential for violence is a legal obligation of all American clinical psychologists. This obligation comes from three directions. First, as we saw in Chapter 9, the laws controlling civil commitment require clinicians to provide evidence that the person being committed is a danger to him- or herself or to others. A second obligation of clinicians, imposed by all states, is to inform the authorities whenever they suspect that children, those with disabilities, or older people are in danger of abuse by their caretakers. Finally, clinicians have an obligation to protect any third party from acts committed by their violent clients. In each of these cases (civil commitment, potential abuse, and possible violent acts directed at third parties) clinicians can carry out their obligations only by first making some assessment of a person's potential for violence.

Given that clinicians are required to make such assessments, it is fair to ask whether they are actually capable of meeting their obligations. Reviewing studies conducted in the 1970s, Monahan (1981) concluded that they were not. Clinicians were rarely accurate in predicting who would commit a violent act. This depressing news left the courts in a quandary. Although the clinicians were frequently called upon to assess a person's potential for violence (in custody and commitment decisions, in issuing restraining orders, in sentencing), it seemed that judges could not rely on the advice of clinicians to help them make such judgments.

Fortunately, psychologists did not despair; research into the correlates of violence continued. In a follow-up review, Monahan (1992) altered his previous pessimistic conclusion—psychologists, he believed, were getting better at predicting violent behavior (see also G. T. Harris, Rice, & Quinsey, 1997). There are many reasons for the apparent improvement. One is increasing exposure to violent people. Although the presence of a mental disorder is not by itself a strong predictor of future violence (Hamling et al., 1997), the number of violent people who are being seen by clinicians has been increasing. Almost 40% of mental hospital patients are violent in the weeks prior to admission (Steadman et al., 1994). Increasing exposure to violent people gives clinicians the opportunity to learn more about the conditions that foster violence. A second reason for the improved ability to predict violence is the increasing availability of base-rate information (Lidz, Mulvey, & Gardner, 1993). In the past, clinicians based their violence assessments solely on the characteristics of the individual. Unfortunately, information about an individual is not sufficient. Pre-

---

The disorders included in Cluster A all share at least a superficial similarity with the Axis I disorder of schizophrenia. Indeed, Cluster A personality disorders have sometimes been construed as milder versions or precursors of schizophrenia. As you can see from Table 10.5 (p. 443), there is considerable overlap among the Cluster A personality disorders, making it difficult for clinicians to differentiate them from one another (Livesley & West, 1986).

Paranoid Personality Disorder   The concept of paranoia has it roots in 19th-century psychoanalysis, which views this symptom as a form of "projection" (Bone & Oldham, 1994). Specifically, people with a **paranoid personality disorder** lack trust in others and constantly fear that their friends may be disloyal or unfaithful. As a consequence, people with paranoid personality disorder avoid revealing their thoughts and feelings. Often, they are perceived by others as hypersensitive. Those with this disorder may interpret even innocuous events (omission of their name from a roster, for example) as a sign that others are plotting against them. Document 10.7 contains an example of just such a situation. Any offers of assistance are taken as criticisms that the person is unable to cope on his or her own. Because they react to these perceived insults with anger, people with a paranoid personality disorder are perceived by others as hostile.

dicting violent behavior also requires knowledge of the base rates (the probability of violence in certain populations). As we saw in Chapter 3, changes in the base rate can have large effects on the accuracy of a prediction. In recent years, the accuracy of violence predictions has benefited from the availability of better base-rate information, which, when added to specific information about an individual, produces a more accurate prediction (Quinsey et al., 1998).

The ability of psychologists to predict violence has also benefited from closer community supervision of former hospitalized patients. Closer community supervision has made it possible to follow up people and learn when clinicians' predictions of violence were accurate and when they were not. Researchers receiving this feedback have been able to use it to improve predictive criteria (Monahan & Steadman, 1996). Another reason for increased predictive accuracy is the availability of professional training programs to teach clinicians how to make better predictions of violence (Quinsey et al., 1998).

The technology available to clinicians to assist them in assessing violence potential is steadily improving (Borum, 1996). Standardized assessment instruments (checklists, rating scales, standardized interview schedules) have helped to reduce observer errors and increase the reliability of clinical predictions (G. T. Harris et al., 1993; Loza & Dhaliwal, 1997). In addition, multivariate statistical techniques are being employed to devise statistical formulas that can be used to predict violence. As discussed in Chapter 3, statistical formulas are usually better predictors than unaided clinical judgment. To make such formulas easier for clinicians to use, psychologists have translated them into simple decision trees. For example, Gardner and his colleagues (1996) distilled a large number of statistical relationships into three simple yes-no questions: Has the person performed more than three prior violent acts? Is the person less than 18? Is the person a heavy drug user? "Yes" answers to all three questions indicate a high probability of violence. By noting the answers to these questions, it is possible to identify most violent people, who can then be pinpointed more accurately using more elaborate tests and interviews.

Although statistical prediction of violence represents an important breakthrough, it is important that those who use such predictions (especially the courts) understand their probabilistic nature. Violence, like most human behavior, is still largely governed by the social context. Because the situation is so important, we can never reach perfect accuracy in predicting violence. To ensure that users do not over- or underestimate the probability that a person will commit a violent act, Monahan and Steadman (1996) suggest that psychologists emulate weather forecasters. In forecasting the weather, meteorologists use both probabilities (a 70% chance of rain) and categories (hurricane watch, hurricane warning). Moreover, they always specify a duration for which the prediction is valid (the next 24 hours) and often suggest appropriate actions (in a hurricane watch, for example, people are urged to check their food and water supplies and to make sure they have batteries around). Monahan and Steadman suggest that psychologists adopt the communication style of meteorologists. Because many people misinterpret probabilities (particularly for rare events), they suggest that psychologists assign people to violence risk categories (low, moderate, high, and very high), each with relevant recommended actions and a duration for which the prediction is valid.

DOCUMENT 10.7

Police Officer Gary Johns's Report on and Interview With Gavin Marney

Record of Interview

Gavin Marney is a 36-year-old construction worker who got into a heated argument with a coworker whom he accused of stealing work from him. They traded blows. I interviewed Marney after being called to investigate the incident. I began by asking Marney why he had gotten into a fight with his coworker, Syd Maloney.

GAVIN MARNEY: He erased my name from the work roster.

OFFICER JOHNS: How do you know?

GAVIN MARNEY: My name is not on the roster.

OFFICER JOHNS: But how do you know Maloney was responsible?

GAVIN MARNEY: He has always hated me. He can't stand anyone smart, I know it. He always talks to others and laughs about me behind my back.

OFFICER JOHNS: But many people didn't make it onto the roster this week. The project is almost finished, and there is not much work left.

GAVIN MARNEY: Now you are siding with him. You're probably involved as well. I should have known. You're all alike. I just wish I could work for myself, away from all of you people.

OFFICER JOHNS: Would you like me to help negotiate with the supervisor for more work for you?

GAVIN MARNEY: I'm not incompetent; I can negotiate without your help.

At one time, paranoid personality disorder was viewed as a milder form of paranoid schizophrenia, but there are important differences between the two conditions. In contrast to people with paranoid schizophrenia (see Chapter 9), those with a paranoid personality disorder do not have delusions, hallucinations, or other forms of thought disorder (Bernstein, Useda, & Siever, 1995).

Charisma coupled with a paranoid personality disorder can have deathly consequences, as it did for David Koresh and his followers in Waco, Texas.

Instead, they are characterized mainly by their suspicion of other people. (Table 10.6 provides the main *DSM-IV* diagnostic criteria for paranoid personality disorder.) Today, most clinicians believe that paranoid personality disorder is at best only a distant member of the schizophrenic spectrum of disorders (Fulton & Winokur, 1993). Indeed, people with paranoid personality disorder are more likely to have depressed relatives than they are relatives with schizophrenia (W. Maier et al., 1994).

Sometimes, several people with paranoid personality disorder band together into groups with others who share their paranoid beliefs. Extremist groups who barricade themselves into armed enclaves to fight the "hostile government" may fit into this category (J. S. Masters & Masters, 1997). Of course, seemingly "paranoid" people may have real enemies, so this diagnosis should not be lightly applied to political or economic refugees or to people whose backgrounds may have actually included conspiracies and prejudice.

Paranoid personality disorder first becomes apparent in childhood and seems to occur more often in males than females (American Psychiatric Assn, 1994). It affects between 0.5% and 2.5% of the general population (American Psychiatric Assn, 1994). Because both brain damage and substance abuse may produce paranoid symptoms, care should be taken when making the diagnosis to exclude both of these possibilities (Morgenstern et al., 1997; Salmon et al., 1996). Few people with para-

TABLE 10.5   Comparison of Cluster A Personality Disorders and Schizophrenia on Selected Characteristics

Disorder	Characteristics			
	Negative symptoms (e.g., blunt affect)	Paranoid ideas	Family members with schizophrenia	Positive symptoms (e.g., thought disorder)
Schizophrenia	Yes	Yes	Yes	Yes
Cluster A personality disorders				
Paranoid personality disorder		Yes		
Schizoid personality disorder	Yes	Yes		
Schizotypal personality disorder	Yes	Yes	Yes	

DSM-IV   TABLE 10.6   Main *DSM-IV* Diagnostic Criteria for Paranoid Personality Disorder

A. A pervasive distrust and suspiciousness of others such that their motives are interpreted as malevolent, beginning by early adulthood and present in a variety of contexts, as indicated by four (or more) of the following:

(1) suspects, without sufficient basis, that others are exploiting, harming, or deceiving him or her

(2) is preoccupied with unjustified doubts about the loyalty or trustworthiness of friends or associates

(3) is reluctant to confide in others because of unwarranted fear that the information will be used maliciously against him or her

(4) reads hidden demeaning or threatening meanings into benign remarks or events

(5) persistently bears grudges, i.e., is unforgiving of insults, injuries, or slights

(6) perceives attacks on his or her character or reputation that are not apparent to others and is quick to react angrily or to counterattack

(7) has recurrent suspicions, without justification, regarding fidelity of spouse or sexual partner

B. Does not occur exclusively during the course of Schizophrenia, a Mood Disorder With Psychotic Features, or another Psychotic Disorder. . . .

Note: From American Psychiatric Association (1994, pp. 637–638).

noid personality disorder seek psychological treatment; they are too suspicious of the therapist. Those who do find their way into treatment may receive psychodynamic psychotherapy (Oldham & Bone, 1994), cognitive-behavioral therapy (M. H. Stone, 1993), and drugs (Joseph, 1997). Unfortunately, none of these approaches to treatment have met with much success.

Schizoid Personality Disorder   Schizoid personality disorder consists mainly of negative rather than positive symptoms. That is, the defining feature of schizoid personality disorder is not a delusion, obsession, or thought disorder—it is the *lack* of social relationships (Phillips & Gunderson, 1996). People with schizoid personality disorder prefer solitary pursuits and spend much of their time alone. (Document 10.8 exemplifies the isolation of one woman with schizoid personality disorder.) They have flat affect (a limited range of emotions), and they are indifferent toward the opinions of others. Because of their social isolation, people with schizoid personality disorder are socially inept and appear self-absorbed, cold, and aloof (Kalus, Bernstein, & Siever, 1995).

DOCUMENT 10.8

Veronica's Sunday

Veronica is a 32-year-old woman who works during the week as a security guard at a bank. This excerpt from a letter written by Veronica's sister, with whom she lives, to their mother, is a description of a typical Sunday in the life of this woman with a schizoid personality disorder.

Dear Mom,

I hope you are well, and over your cold. I am doing OK, but I'm worried about Veronica. She seems to be getting even more withdrawn. Let me tell you about Sunday. Veronica got up at 8:30 and switched on the television. She watched for an hour while still in bed. She then had some juice and coffee while watching a news show on television. At around 10:30, she fed Kat (the cat). She sat and watched the cat eat for a while and then spent 45 minutes washing and ironing her clothes. She organized her drawers and then had a shower and got dressed. By this time, it was noon. Her next activity was to sit on a chair directly in front of a window and read the newspaper that we get delivered. After about an hour of this, Veronica once again turned on the television. She watched a talk show, and then she went outside for a walk. When she returned home, she ate a tiny dinner and watched television until late, when she fell asleep. She did not utter a word to me, or anyone else, all day. . . .

The primary *DSM-IV* diagnostic criteria for schizoid personality disorder appear in Table 10.7. Note their similarity to the negative symptoms of schizophrenia (see Chapter 9). To keep the two disorders separate, the *DSM-IV* rules out schizoid personality disorder in people with schizophrenia (or any other psychotic disorder). It is also important that diagnosticians consider a person's social situation. For example, the diagnosis of schizoid personality disorder is inappropriate for people who have recently migrated from one culture to another. Although immigrants may show the signs of a schizoid personality disorder (immigrants often take a while to settle into their new surroundings), it would be unwise to make a diagnosis until they have had the opportunity to adjust to their new environment. Finally, the diagnosis should be reserved for people in distress, not for people who prefer and adjust well to living as "loners."

Although the term *simple schizophrenia* was once used to describe people with schizoid personality disorder, it, like paranoid personality disorder, is probably only a distant (at best) member of the spectrum of schizophrenia-related disorders (Fulton & Winokur, 1993; W. Maier et al., 1994). Schizoid personality disorder is no more common among the relatives of schizophrenic people than it is among the relatives of nonschizophrenic people. Like paranoid personality disorder, it is more likely to be found among the relatives of depressed than schizophrenic people. Indeed, it is not uncommon for depression and schizoid personality disorder to be found together, especially in adolescents and young adults (Belsher, Wilkes, & Rush, 1995).

Each of the various paradigms has its own view of the etiology of schizoid personality disorder. Psychodynamic (and most behavioral) theorists blame rejecting and abusive parents for causing their offspring to shun other people (Mahler, 1979). The trouble with this hypothesis is that precisely the same etiology is applied to paranoid personality disorder. What psychodynamic theorists do not explain is why some rejected children withdraw and develop a schizoid personality disorder, whereas others react with anger and become paranoid. Based on the restricted range of affect often displayed by people with schizoid personality disorder, cognitive theorists have hypothesized that their symptoms are the result of some deficit in processing emotional information (Kalus et al., 1995; Phillips & Gunderson, 1996). Psychophysiological theories include inherited dispositions and even a prenatal nutritional deficiency (Hoek et al., 1996). At present, there are insufficient data to allow us to choose among these various etiological theories.

People with schizoid personality disorder rarely seek treatment; they are too disengaged from others to care and too threatened by close relationships to get involved in psychotherapy (Kalus et al., 1995; Phillips & Gunderson, 1996). Those who do find their way into treatment usually suffer from some associated condition, such as substance abuse or depression. For those who are treated, psychoanalytic therapy focuses on working through the trauma produced by early rejection, whereas cognitive-behavioral therapy attempts to teach people the social skills they need to interact with others. There have been case reports of successful psy-

DSM-IV TABLE 10.7 Main *DSM-IV* Diagnostic Criteria
for Schizoid Personality Disorder

A. A pervasive pattern of detachment from social relationships and a restricted range of expression of emotions in interpersonal settings, beginning by early adulthood and present in a variety of contexts, as indicated by four (or more) of the following:

   (1) neither desires or enjoys close relationships, including being part of a family
   (2) almost always chooses solitary activities
   (3) has little, if any, interest in having sexual experiences with another person
   (4) takes pleasure in few, if any, activities
   (5) lacks close friends or confidants other than first-degree relatives
   (6) appears indifferent to the praise or criticism of others
   (7) shows emotional coldness, detachment, or flattened affectivity

B. Does not occur exclusively during the course of Schizophrenia, a Mood Disorder With Psychotic Features, another Psychotic Disorder, or a Pervasive Developmental Disorder. . . .

Note: From American Psychiatric Association (1994, p. 641).

chological treatment of schizoid personality disorder in young people (Herlihy, 1993), but, for most people, psychotherapy has produced only limited success (Belsher et al., 1995), and medications have not proved much better (Joseph, 1997).

Schizotypal Personality Disorder Like people with schizoid personality disorder, those with **schizotypal personality disorder** are loners who are unable or uninterested in forming relationships with other people. They prefer solitary activities to those involving others and, like people with schizoid personality disorder, they are often perceived as cold and unemotional. There are also similarities between schizotypal personality disorder and paranoid personality disorder. Both disorders are marked by suspicion of the motives of others and by

In Fatal Attraction, *Glenn Close portrayed a woman with a severe borderline personality disorder. Because of her obsession with the character played by Michael Douglas, she attempted both suicide and murder of his wife.*

ideas of reference, the belief that unrelated comments and events pertain to those with the disorder.

Clearly, the schizotypal personality disorder shares symptoms with both the schizoid and the paranoid personality disorders, but it differs in an important respect: Schizotypal personality disorder is related to schizophrenia (Battaglia & Torgersen, 1996). People with schizotypal personality disorder have peculiar thoughts, rambling speech, odd appearance, and eccentric behaviors. Put simply, schizotypal personality disorder seems to be a mild form of schizophrenia that occurs in approximately 3% of the population (American Psychiatry Assn, 1994). It is similar to the schizophreniform disorder described in Chapter 9. The main *DSM-IV* diagnostic criteria for schizotypal personality disorder appear in Table 10.8. Document 10.9 illustrates the appearance and behavior of someone with schizotypal personality disorder.

Because of the similarity between schizotypal disorder and the schizophrenia spectrum of disorders, researchers have tried to apply the diathesis-stress etiological model of schizophrenia to schizotypal per-

DOCUMENT 10.9

Conversation With a Clairvoyant

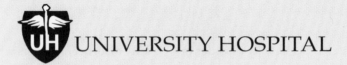

UNIVERSITY HOSPITAL

Emergency Room Consultation Note

Psychologist: Dr. Stuart Berg

Patient: Edgar Loosely

Date: 4/7/2001

Time: 22:00

Notes

This disheveled White male was brought in by the police, who were called after he was seen peeping into the bathroom of a house on University Avenue. Because the man seemed disoriented and disturbed, the police asked for a psychological consultation. I found the man, Edgar Loosely, dressed in ragged clothes. He was able to talk to me and to understand my questions. He denied hallucinations or delusions, and he was able to answer most questions on the Mental Status Examination. Nevertheless, he was decidedly odd, as may be seen in the following conversation:

DR. BERG: Why were you looking in the bathroom window of someone's home?

EDGAR LOOSELY: I was endeavoring to ascertain the veracity of my visions. You see, I have been given the divine gift of knowing the future. I am clairvoyant. I had a beatific vision revealing what would happen to the inhabitants of that abode, and I was confirming the validity of my vision.

DR. BERG: You were checking your clairvoyant predictions? Don't you know that you frightened the people in that home? What were your predictions?

EDGAR LOOSELY: I foresaw that they would partake of pizza and imbibe Coke tonight. I did not think that I would alarm them. I simply wanted to confirm the veracity of my vision.

DR. BERG: You wanted to see what they were eating and drinking?

EDGAR LOOSELY: Indeed.

DSM-IV TABLE 10.8 Main *DSM-IV* Diagnostic Criteria
for Schizotypal Personality Disorder

A. A pervasive pattern of social and interpersonal deficits marked by acute discomfort with, and reduced capacity for, close relationships as well as by cognitive or perceptual distortions and eccentricities of behavior, beginning by early adulthood and present in a variety of contexts, as indicated by five (or more) of the following:

(1) ideas of reference (excluding delusions of reference)

(2) odd beliefs or magical thinking that influences behavior and is inconsistent with subcultural norms (e.g., superstitiousness, belief in clairvoyance, telepathy, or "sixth sense"; in children and adolescents, bizarre fantasies or preoccupations)

(3) unusual perceptual experiences, including bodily illusions

(4) odd thinking and speech (e.g., vague, circumstantial, metaphorical, overelaborate, or stereotyped)

(5) suspiciousness or paranoid ideation

(6) inappropriate or constricted affect

(7) behavior or appearance that is odd, eccentric, or peculiar

(8) lack of close friends or confidants other than first-degree relatives

(9) excessive social anxiety that does not diminish with familiarity and tends to be associated with paranoid fears rather than negative judgments about self

B. Does not occur exclusively during the course of Schizophrenia, a Mood Disorder With Psychotic Features, another Psychotic Disorder, or a Pervasive Developmental Disorder.

Note: From American Psychiatric Association (1994, p. 645).

sonality disorder. Certainly, the diathesis appears to be similar. Schizotypal personality disorder is most commonly found in families with schizophrenic relatives (Battaglia et al., 1995; Kendler & Walsh, 1995), and people with schizotypal personality disorder exhibit attentional and eye-tracking deficits similar to those seen in people with schizophrenia (Keefe et al., 1997; Raine et al., 1997; Roitman et al., 1997; Voglmaier et al., 1997). The similarities between the two disorders do not end there.

Both have also been linked to higher than average levels of dopamine as well as to enlarged brain ventricles (Amin et al., 1997; Buchsbaum et al., 1997; Siever, 1995). As it is with schizophrenia, psychotherapy is of limited value in schizotypal personality disorder (Ewing, Falk, & Otto, 1996). The most successful treatment approaches mirror those used in schizophrenia—skills training (McKay & Neziroglu, 1996) and antipsychotic medication (Joseph, 1997).

Cluster B: Antisocial, Borderline, Histrionic, and Narcissistic Personality Disorders

People with Cluster B personality disorders tend to be self-absorbed. They find it difficult to empathize with others because they spend so much time and energy on themselves. In addition, they exaggerate the importance

of everything that happens to them, usually in a theatrical and overdramatic way. Because of their excessive self-concern and melodramatics, people with Cluster B personality disorders find it difficult to establish and maintain interpersonal relationships. Antisocial personality disorder has already been discussed, so this section focuses on the remaining three Cluster B disorders: borderline, histrionic, and narcissistic personality disorders.

Borderline Personality Disorder Although borderline personality disorder has been around for some time, until recently, it has lacked a precise definition. Clinicians and researchers who work from different paradigms have used the term *borderline* in several different ways: (a) to refer to people whose behavior fell at some hypothetical border between "neurotic" mood disorders and psychotic ones, (b) as a general term for the symptoms caused by mild brain damage, and (c) to describe people whose poor social relations are marked by manipulative suicide attempts (Gunderson, Zanarini, & Kisiel, 1995; Tyrer, 1994).

In an attempt to give systematic meaning to the term *borderline,* the *DSM-IV* has chosen to emphasize instability and impulsivity: See Table 10.9 for the main *DSM-IV* diagnostic criteria. According to the *DSM-IV,* people with **borderline personality disorder** are insecure

DSM-IV TABLE 10.9 Main *DSM-IV* Diagnostic Criteria
for Borderline Personality Disorder

A pervasive pattern of instability of interpersonal relationships, self-image, and affects, and marked impulsivity beginning by early adulthood and present in a variety of contexts, as indicated by five (or more) of the following:

(1) frantic efforts to avoid real or imagined abandonment. *Note:* Do not include suicidal or self-mutilating behavior covered in Criterion 5.

(2) a pattern of unstable and intense interpersonal relationships characterized by alternating between extremes of idealization and devaluation

(3) identity disturbance: markedly and persistently unstable self-image or sense of self

(4) impulsivity in at least two areas that are potentially self-damaging (e.g., spending, sex, substance abuse, reckless driving, binge eating). *Note:* Do not include suicidal or self-mutilating behavior covered in Criterion 5.

(5) recurrent suicidal behavior, gestures, or threats, or self-mutilating behavior

(6) affective instability due to a marked reactivity of mood (e.g., intense episodic dysphoria, irritability, or anxiety usually lasting a few hours and only rarely more than a few days)

(7) chronic feelings of emptiness

(8) inappropriate, intense anger or difficulty controlling anger (e.g., frequent displays of temper, constant anger, recurrent physical fights)

(9) transient, stress-related paranoid ideation or severe dissociative symptoms

Note: From American Psychiatric Association (1994, p. 654).

because they have a morbid fear of abandonment. They want to form close relationships, and, initially at least, they succeed. But their need for attention and reassurance eventually becomes too overwhelming, and their relationships break down. This is a recurring cycle—other people begin as perfect friends and evolve into enemies; there is no in-between. This tendency to categorize people as entirely good or entirely bad is known in psychoanalytic circles as *splitting*.

When relationships deteriorate, people with borderline personality disorder may threaten to harm themselves just to keep the connection going. If this does not work (and it rarely does), they may actually carry out their threats by mutilating or even killing themselves

(Barber et al., 1998). Document 10.10 reports the death of a young woman who may well have taken her own life because a relationship failed. In addition to self-harm, people with borderline personality disorder may engage in various forms of imprudent behavior—reckless driving, unsafe sex, gambling, and substance abuse (Rounsaville et al., 1998). It takes little provocation to make people with a borderline personality disorder hostile and aggressive (L. Carroll et al., 1998). Indeed, their moods tend to swing widely depending on the state of their interpersonal relationships. When these are going well, they may be elated, friendly, and good company. When their relationships are going badly, they become depressed, sullen, and aggressive.

DOCUMENT 10.10

Tragic Death of
a Borderline
Personality

Cult Member Commits Suicide by Immolation

by Evan Moran
Daily Staff Writer

Katherine Hurley, a 21-year-old fine arts student, died today. She doused herself in gasoline and set herself on fire in front of the Divine Light Center in Springbank.

Why did a young and talented woman like Katherine die? We may never know the whole story. Still, we can try to make sense of this tragic death.

Katherine was in the second year of her fine arts degree when she joined the Divine Light Center. The Center is the creation of cult leader Adam Aguirre, who claims to be a reincarnated Indian seer. Twenty-five people live in the Center and all donate their income to a general fund controlled by Aguirre. When she joined the Center, Katherine told her former roommate, Sybil Charles, that at last she had found a charismatic figure with whom she could identify. She idolized Aguirre, whom she believed was in direct touch with God.

Center members described Katherine as the most devoted of them all. Charles believed that Katherine also had a sexual relationship with Aguirre.

Although Katherine was initially happy at the Center, she soon became angry at what she described as Aguirre's "insensitivity." She devoted her life to Aguirre, and she wanted him to do the same for her. If he was not available when she wanted him, Katherine became intensely angry. On one occasion, she deliberately cut her wrists when he failed to keep an appointment, a Center member recounted.

In recent weeks, Katherine had become convinced that Aguirre was planning to abandon the Center and leave town. Katherine panicked at the thought of being left alone. Although Aguirre denied any such plan, Katherine was not appeased. Yesterday, after a loud argument with Aguirre, she sat down on the pavement outside the Center and ended her life in flames.

Borderline personality disorder occurs in about 2% of the general population (American Psychiatric Assn, 1994), mainly in females. As we have seen, sex differences in the incidence of a disorder can have many explanations. In the case of borderline personality disorder, social factors, especially sex role expectations, seem to play an important part (Becker, 1997). There is considerable overlap between the symptoms of antisocial personality and the symptoms of borderline personality disorder. (As noted in Document 10.2, Eric Cooper was given borderline personality disorder as a provisional secondary diagnosis.) There are some differences as well. Although people with both diagnoses are impulsive, reckless, unable to form stable relationships, and often hostile, borderline personality is also associated with a morbid fear of abandonment. It is possible that the underlying causes of the two disorders are similar but that women are socialized to be more frightened by being alone and to turn their aggression inward in the form of suicidal gestures rather than outward toward others (Paris, 1997). Through the process of socialization, similar etiological factors wind up producing somewhat different disorders. Of course, social roles change from one society to another, so it is important to keep in mind that practically all of the research and clinical reports concerning borderline personality disorder come from developed countries such as the United States. Traditional societies, such as those found in developing countries, have different sex roles. For example, in some societies women are almost guaranteed supportive relationships through a network of mutual family and community obligations. Perhaps this is the reason such societies have a low incidence of borderline personality disorder (Paris, 1996).

Susan Smith (center, in blue and white dress) murdered her two sons by driving her car into a lake and leaving them inside. Her motive appeared to be her fear of abandonment by her boyfriend, who she thought did not like her sons. She may possibly suffer from a borderline personality disorder.

Borderline personality disorder has been attributed to parental loss or abuse in childhood (Zanarini, 1997) or to post-traumatic stress later in life (Zlotnick, 1997). In both cases, psychological trauma is thought to produce a fear of further loss and a subsequent fear of abandonment (Sable, 1997). Although this seems a plausible theory, it is hardly specific to borderline personality disorder. Parental loss and abuse are found in the backgrounds of many psychological disorders. A similar lack of specificity may be found in the various biological explanations offered for borderline personality disorder—genetics, low levels of serotonin (Weston & Siever, 1993), thyroid dysfunction (Klonoff & Landrine, 1997), and brain damage (Van-Reekum, 1993) all occur in other disorders as well.

There have been many attempts to develop treatments for borderline personality disorder, but none has proved especially successful. Psychoanalytic psychotherapy concentrates on analyzing the transference relationship that develops between patient and therapist. The goal of treatment is to use the transference relationship as a model to show people the way in which they undermine their interpersonal relationships (Gabbard et al., 1994; Horwitz et al., 1996). A strong patient-therapist transference may also help people with borderline personality disorder to learn to trust others. As you can imagine, however, building a transference relationship and analyzing a client's interpersonal functioning is difficult with people whose relationships are characteristically turbulent. Following their usual pattern, borderline personality disorder patients begin by idealizing the therapist as a potential savior and later, through splitting, turn this completely around so that the therapist becomes a money-seeking charlatan. In such cases, analyzing the transference relationship takes some time, with many regressions along the way (Rosenbluth & Yalom, 1997; Wheelis & Gunderson, 1998). However, given the potential lifelong duration of borderline personality disorder, even prolonged treatment may be cost-effective if it helps people to stay at work and avoid hospitalization (Lazar & Gabbard, 1997; Stevenson & Meares, 1992).

Although cognitive-behavioral therapy may assist people with borderline personality disorder to lead more effective lives (Waldo & Harman, 1998), people with this disorder may find it difficult to complete a course of therapy. They may drop out of treatment at the first sign (real or imagined) that the therapist is neglecting them. To help such clients follow through with treatment, clinicians may first try to increase a client's emotional stability. For example, emotional awareness training, in which people with borderline personality disorder are given practice in recognizing their emotions (as well as those being experienced by others) and then taught ways to control their emotions, may help clients to cope with the stress of cognitive and behavioral interventions (Farrell & Shaw, 1994). Therapists, too, must make certain adjustments. For example, they must learn to deal with the manipulative behavior of clients who are hypersensitive to criticism and are always imagining that they are being rejected.

Assuming that people with borderline personality disorder can be kept in treatment, cognitive-behavioral therapists may employ a multimodal treatment strategy known as **dialectical behavior therapy.** This approach combines group and individual therapy, supportive counseling, and behavioral contracting (usually an agreement not to harm oneself) with skill training aimed at improving and maintaining relationships (Kern et al., 1997; Koerner & Linehan, 1997; Newman, 1998; Waldo & Harman, 1998). Support may also be given to friends and family members who need to learn what to expect and how to deal with a person who has a borderline personality disorder (Gunderson, Berkowitz, & Ruiz-Sancho, 1997).

In addition to psychological treatment, the entire spectrum of psychoactive drugs has been used with borderline personality disorder, usually in conjunction with some form of psychological therapy (Bendetti et al., 1998; Bornstein, 1997b; Goldblatt, Silverman, & Schatzberg, 1998; Hirschfeld, 1997; Salzman et al., 1995; Waldinger & Frank, 1989). The most effective drugs are the antidepressants (especially the SSRIs), which seem to reduce the impulsivity, depression, and rage that destroy relationships.

Histrionic Personality Disorder   Histrionic personality disorder is a direct descendant of the 19th-century concept of hysteria (see Chapter 2). In fact, at one point in history, histrionic personality disorder was known as "hysterical personality disorder." People with histrionic personality disorder do not have conversion symptoms (although they may have hypochondriacal concerns; Demopulos et al., 1996). They are mainly motivated by the need to be the center of attention (Widiger, 1998). To gain the notice they crave, people with this disorder may act seductively, dress in eccentric clothes, or act in a loud and boisterous fashion, as Sharlene does in Document 10.11. People with a histrionic personality disorder actively seek compliments and are easily upset by criticism. A stereotype of histrionic behavior is the envious actor who storms off the set when another member of the cast begins to attract notice. Because of their melodramatic displays, histrionic people are viewed as shallow and phoney.

DSM-IV   TABLE 10.10   Main *DSM-IV* Diagnostic Criteria for Histrionic Personality Disorder

A pervasive pattern of excessive emotionality and attention seeking, beginning by early adulthood and present in a variety of contexts, as indicated by five (or more) of the following:

(1) is uncomfortable in situations in which he or she is not the center of attention

(2) interaction with others is often characterized by inappropriate sexually seductive or provocative behavior

(3) displays rapidly shifting and shallow expression of emotions

(4) consistently uses physical appearance to draw attention to self

(5) has a style of speech that is excessively impressionistic and lacking in detail

(6) shows self-dramatization, theatricality, and exaggerated expression of emotion

(7) is suggestible, i.e., easily influenced by others or circumstances

(8) considers relationships to be more intimate than they actually are

Note: From American Psychiatric Association (1994, pp. 657–658).

DOCUMENT 10.11

Sharlene's Job Interview

Thirty-year-old Sharlene has been granted an interview for a job as a receptionist. She arrives dressed provocatively. Her top is cut low, and her short skirt is tight. She wears black stockings, very high heels, and strong perfume. She arrives late but does not make an excuse. Instead, she puts her hand on the arm of the male interviewer and begins to talk in a loud voice. Several times she crosses her legs in a provocative fashion.

"I know that I am absolutely the best person in the world for this job. I know how to make people feel comfortable when they come to the office. Hell, I know how to make people feel comfortable anywhere. [*Winks at the interviewer*] I prefer to work for a man; women can be so catty. Give me a man any day. [*Winks again*] I have learned how to get along with people because I have been through so much. I have really suffered—discrimination, long commutes, rudeness, you name it. [*Looks sad*] But I am too strong to be beaten. And now here I am. God, I am happy to be here. [*Laughs*] I can tell that we are going to make a great team." ■

Histrionic personality disorder appears to have a prevalence of 2–3% in the general population (American Psychiatric Assn, 1994) and is mainly diagnosed in women (Belitsky et al., 1996). This sex difference may be the result of sex role stereotypes—females are expected to be seductive and to overdramatize (Hamburger, Lilienfeld, & Hogben, 1996). Certainly, clinicians are more likely to assign this diagnosis to females than to males, even when the males show exactly the same pattern of behavior (Ford & Widiger, 1989). The main *DSM-IV* diagnostic criteria for histrionic personality disorder appear in Table 10.10.

Although people with histrionic personality disorder may seek treatment, they make difficult clients. They tend to use the therapeutic environment as another opportunity to play center stage and present exaggerated versions of their problems (Horowitz, 1997). Group treatment is generally not possible for people with histrionic personality disorder because of their need to monopolize the therapist's attention. Nor are histrionic people good candidates for insight-oriented therapy; they find it impossible to accept any but their own interpretations of their behavior. Perhaps the best therapeutic approach is to concentrate on helping people with this disorder to separate important problems from trivial ones, and to teach them how to pay attention to others. There are no specific drug treatments for histrionic personality disorder, although drugs may be used to treat any concurrent Axis I disorders (Joseph, 1997).

Narcissistic Personality Disorder   According to Greek mythology, Narcissus was a boy of legendary beauty who fell in love with his own reflection in the waters of a pond. He stared at his reflection until he wasted away to a flower. From this story, Freud derived the word *narcissistic*, meaning a person who is consumed with self-love. Freud's use of the term has evolved into the *DSM-IV*'s diagnosis of **narcissistic personality disorder.** People with this disorder are characterized by their strong sense of superiority. (Table 10.11 displays the main *DSM-IV* diagnostic criteria for narcissistic personality disorder.) They consider themselves to be important and demand special treatment. People with this disorder are often rude because they view rules and common courtesy as meant for others (Gunderson, Ronningstam, & Smith, 1995). Like people with histrionic personality disorder, narcissistic people crave attention.

DOCUMENT 10.12

Letter From a
Doctoral Student
to His Supervisor

Dear Professor Gray,

I am writing to express my disappointment with your supervision and my dismay at your failure to provide me with the research assistant that I requested. Clearly, I belong at a more prestigious, and forward-looking, university.

You know very well that my thesis research contains groundbreaking work that will revolutionize the way we look at English history. It is the kind of work that comes along once in a lifetime, and it is certain to be heralded as a great success when it is published.

I understand that you might be jealous of my work, but I cannot understand how you could fail to notice its importance. You say that doctoral students are not entitled to research assistants and must do their own library work. What you do not acknowledge is that I am not just any doctoral student and my work is not a typical dissertation. I am not one of the boring mass who are rushing through their research. I am going slowly because of the gravity of my findings. I wish that you could see how your envy might affect our field. I am going to find a supervisor who appreciates genius and is not afraid to break a few petty rules when this is necessary.

Sincerely,

Etienne Black

They dream of achieving powerful positions that will gain them the power and attention they seek. Sometimes, they succeed; many world leaders meet at least some of the *DSM-IV* criteria for a narcissistic personality disorder (Post, 1997). More often, however, narcissistic people exaggerate their own successes and envy the achievements of others, as the doctoral candidate who wrote the letter in Document 10.12 does. Beneath the surface, narcissistic people are so plagued by self-doubt that, even when they have reached a goal, they remain unsatisfied because success never brings them the level of adulation they desire.

In psychodynamic terms, narcissism starts in childhood. We are all narcissistic as children because the world seems to revolve around us. When we are hungry, someone feeds us; when we are cold, someone always caters to our needs. One of the most important tasks facing children during the process of socialization is learning that there are other people in the world, with their own feelings and needs. Learning to empathize with others is a skill that develops through childhood and the teenage years, so we must be wary of applying the *DSM-IV* criteria to young people (Kernberg, Hajal, & Normandin, 1998). However, by early adulthood, a narcissistic personality disorder should become clear. Once such a disorder develops, it tends to be ongoing (Ron-

ningstam, 1998). Narcissistic personality disorder affects about 1% of the general population (American Psychiatric Assn, 1994), mainly males.

Both psychodynamic and cognitive-behavioral approaches to the treatment of narcissistic personality disorder focus attention on helping people to become more realistic in their goals and to find satisfaction and fulfillment in the normal events of daily life (Rodin & Izenberg, 1997). Training in recognizing and empathizing with the emotions of others is an important adjunct goal of treatment. As in many other personality disorders, drugs may be used for some symptoms or for concurrent Axis I disorders (Joseph, 1997).

Cluster C: Avoidant, Obsessive-Compulsive, and Dependent Personality Disorders

The disorders in Cluster C share many characteristics with the anxiety disorders, including fearfulness and worry and a tendency toward depression (Alpert et al., 1997). In contrast to the anxiety disorders, however, Cluster C personality disorders tend to have an earlier onset, no clear cause, and a stable lifelong course. Two of the Cluster C disorders—avoidant and obsessive-compulsive personality disorders—were described along with the various anxiety disorders in Chapter 4. This

DSM-IV	**TABLE 10.11** Main *DSM-IV* Diagnostic Criteria for Narcissistic Personality Disorder

A pervasive pattern of grandiosity (in fantasy or behavior), need for admiration, and lack of empathy, beginning by early adulthood and present in a variety of contexts, as indicated by five (or more) of the following:

(1) has a grandiose sense of self-importance (e.g., exaggerates achievements and talents, expects to be recognized as superior without commensurate achievements)

(2) is preoccupied with fantasies of unlimited success, power, brilliance, beauty, or ideal love

(3) believes that he or she is "special" and unique and can only be understood by, or should associate with, other special or high-status people (or institutions)

(4) requires excessive admiration

(5) has a sense of entitlement, i.e., unreasonable expectations of especially favorable treatment or automatic compliance with his or her expectations

(6) is interpersonally exploitative, i.e., takes advantage of others to achieve his or her own ends

(7) lacks empathy: is unwilling to recognize or identify with the feelings and needs of others

(8) is often envious of others or believes that others are envious of him or her

(9) shows arrogant, haughty behaviors or attitudes

Note: From American Psychiatric Association (1994, p. 661).

section gives them only brief coverage, focusing instead on dependent personality disorder.

Avoidant Personality Disorder   As noted in Chapter 4, people with **avoidant personality disorder** are shy and socially uncomfortable. Unlike people with schizoid personality disorder, people with an avoidant personality disorder would prefer to be sociable, but they avoid social contact because they fear embarrassment and criticism. In practice, it is difficult to separate avoidant personality disorder from social phobia (Dahl, 1996), which is also discussed in Chapter 4. When social anxiety is long-standing, the diagnoses are probably interchange-able. Because shyness and social reticence are developmentally appropriate for young children (and because some cultural groups encourage social timidity for one or both sexes), a client's age and culture should be taken into account when making this diagnosis (Ono et al., 1996). Avoidant personality disorder occurs in around 1% of the population, and it affects men and women in equal numbers (American Psychiatric Assn, 1994). It is often found in conjunction with the Axis I diagnosis of depression (Alpert et al., 1997). Cognitive-behavioral treatments aimed at reducing social anxiety can also help people with avoidant personality disorder to lead fuller lives (Hofmann et al., 1995; Stravynski et al., 1994).

Obsessive–Compulsive Personality Disorder   As noted in Chapter 4, obsessive-compulsive behaviors fall along a continuum from relatively mild to severe (Stein & Hollander, 1997). **Obsessive-compulsive personality disorder** belongs at the mild end of the continuum. People who have this disorder do not display true delusions or even severe compulsions. Instead, they are characterized by a perfectionistic attitude toward daily life (Pfohl & Blum, 1995). People with this disorder try to maintain a rigid control over their routines and, when possible, the behavior of other people. They accomplish the latter by insisting on a tight adherence to rules and schedules. They feel that their approach to all matters is the only correct one, and they tend to deny that other people might have reasonable alternative views. Not surprisingly, they are viewed by others as moralistic, rigid, and stubborn. The disorder seems to be more common among males and has a prevalence in the community of

Adolf Hitler, whose goal was to conquer the world and establish a super-race, is an example of a world leader believed to have had a narcissistic personality disorder.

DSM-IV TABLE 10.12 Main *DSM-IV* Diagnostic Criteria for Dependent Personality Disorder

A pervasive and excessive need to be taken care of that leads to submissive and clinging behavior and fears of separation, beginning by early adulthood and present in a variety of contexts, as indicated by five (or more) of the following:

(1) has difficulty making everyday decisions without an excessive amount of advice and reassurance from others

(2) needs others to assume responsibility for most major areas of his or her life

(3) has difficulty expressing disagreement with others because of fear of loss of support or approval. *Note:* Do not include realistic fears of retribution.

(4) has difficulty initiating projects or doing things on his or her own (because of a lack of self-confidence in judgment or abilities rather than a lack of motivation or energy)

(5) goes to excessive lengths to obtain nurturance and support from others, to the point of volunteering to do things that are unpleasant

(6) feels uncomfortable or helpless when alone because of exaggerated fears of being unable to care for himself or herself

(7) urgently seeks another relationship as a source of care and support when a close relationship ends

(8) is unrealistically preoccupied with fears of being left to take care of himself or herself

Note: From American Psychiatric Association (1994, pp. 668–669).

about 1% (American Psychiatric Assn, 1994). In women, the impulse-control disorder of trichotillomania (hair pulling) is often found in conjunction with obsessive-compulsive personality disorder (Christenson, Ristvedt, & Mackenzie, 1993; Schlosser et al., 1994). Trichotillomania is a type of compulsion; its comorbidity with obsessive-compulsive personality disorder further demonstrates the relationship between personality and impulse-control disorders.

Dependent Personality Disorder   People with a **dependent personality disorder** have a strong need to be taken care of by someone else, preferably someone important (Bornstein, 1993). To fulfill this need, they tend to be submissive to the demands of their chosen caretaker, acting, at times, as if they were helpless to look after themselves. For example, instead of making decisions for themselves, they seek continual assistance, advice, and approval from other people (Meissner et al., 1996). As you can see from the *DSM-IV* diagnostic criteria summarized in Table 10.12, there is considerable overlap between dependent personality disorder and some of the other personality disorders (Hirschfeld, Shea, & Weise, 1995). Like people with histrionic personality disorder, those with dependent personality disorder have a strong need for approval. However, dependent people are timid, whereas histrionic people actively seek attention. Like people with borderline personality disorders, dependent people worry about being abandoned. Instead of reacting with rage, however, dependent people become sub-

missive. Finally, both avoidant and dependent personality disorders are characterized by feelings of inadequacy, but avoidant people tend to withdraw, whereas dependent people seek to develop relationships with people who can care for them.

Dependent personality disorder is one of the more common personality disorders (American Psychiatric Assn, 1994). Although the *DSM-IV* asserts that the disorder affects both sexes with only a small bias toward females, in the clinical setting females receive this diagnosis more often than males do (Bornstein, 1997a). This sex difference probably reflects the cultural stereotype of the dependent woman. Because young children are expected to be dependent and because some cultural groups foster dependent behavior among females (traditional Middle Eastern families, for example), caution should be taken in applying this diagnosis to children or to members of some cultural groups.

Although the precise causes of dependent personality disorder are not known, it is thought to begin with a fearful temperament (a genetic disposition) that evokes overprotectiveness from parents (Reich, 1996). Illness in childhood, abandonment, and traumatic loss can produce a similar overprotectiveness. Children may resent this attitude but may learn to submit rather than challenge their parents.

Few people seek treatment for dependent personality disorder. However, some may find their way into therapy for an associated Axis I anxiety or mood disorder (Skodol, Gallaher, & Oldham, 1996). In psychody-

In some cultures, such as traditional Middle Eastern ones, women are expected to be subservient and dependent. Such cultural norms need to be taken into account when considering a diagnosis of dependent personality disorder.

namic treatment, the therapist uses the transference relationship first to form a bond with the client, and then to teach the person how to separate. The idea is that, through the transference experience, the person will learn more effective modes of relating to others. Cognitive therapists try to help their dependent clients to recognize the faulty cognitions that produce their lack of self-confidence. Behavioral therapists use assertiveness training to enhance self-esteem by providing dependent clients with a nonsubmissive mode of relating to others. Relaxation training may also be helpful in reducing anxiety. Although people with this disorder usually go along with their therapist's treatment suggestions (they are submissive people), they are still difficult to treat because of their need for constant reassurance. Long-term treatment is probably not a good idea with dependent people because it may make them overly dependent on their therapist. On the other hand, support and self-help groups could be useful places for clients to practice new skills learned in therapy (provided, of course, that clients participate in the group and do not simply let others do all the talking). Drugs may be prescribed for the anxiety often experienced by people with dependent personality disorder (Joseph, 1997), but care should be taken because clients may use drug overdoses as a way of manipulating other people.

Personality Disorders Under Study

In addition to the three clusters of disorders already discussed, the *DSM-IV*'s appendix contains two personality disorders considered worthy of further study for possible inclusion in future editions of the *DSM:* depressive personality disorder and passive-aggressive (or negativistic) personality disorder.

The essential feature of **depressive personality disorder** is a tendency toward negative cognitions and depressed behaviors that begins in early childhood and occurs in many social contexts (Hirschfeld, 1994; Phillips et al., 1995). People with the proposed disorder are frequently gloomy, cheerless, and unhappy. They are rarely carefree and seem rarely to simply enjoy themselves and relax. Not only are they perceived by others as humorless, but they also seem to believe they have no right to be happy. People with the proposed diagnosis spend much time brooding, have low self-esteem, and are pessimistic about the future. There is substantial overlap between the depressive personality disorder and the dysthymic disorder discussed in Chapter 8. In fact, the only real difference is that the diagnostic criteria for depressive personality disorder give more weight to cognitions than do the criteria for dysthymia (Hartlage, Arduino, & Alloy, 1998). Before depressive personality disorder is included in the *DSM,* it will be important to demonstrate that it is somehow different from dysthymic disorder in prognosis, for example, or response to various treatments (Hirschfeld, 1995; Klein & Shih, 1998; Sherman, 1995).

The second personality disorder recommended by the *DSM-IV* for further study is **passive-aggressive (or negativistic) personality disorder.** This proposed disorder is characterized by negativistic attitudes and passive resistance to the demands of school and work. The affected individual habitually resents, opposes, and resists legitimate demands to function at the level expected of others. Through procrastination, "forgetfulness," stubbornness, and inefficiency, passive-aggressive people get workmates to shoulder the extra load they shirk (Trimpey & Davidson, 1994). Despite their habit of imposing on others, passive-aggressive people still feel unappreciated and complain about how others treat them. As a result, they are perceived as sullen, irritable, argumentative, cynical, and contrary. Whether passive-aggressive traits represent a psychiatric disorder is a matter of some controversy (Millon & Radovanov, 1995); perhaps such people are simply lazy. Because of the stigmatizing effects of labeling (see Chapter 3), "medicalizing" behavior by calling it a disorder is justified only when it leads to some positive outcome: prevention, research, or improved functioning. Further research is required before we can tell whether either of these diagnoses—depressive or passive-aggressive personality disorder—provides sufficient benefits to overcome the pernicious effects of labeling.

CHAPTER 10 IN PERSPECTIVE

Trait-based explanations of behavior appeal to our intuitive beliefs about human nature: People do seem to have different personalities. There is nothing wrong with being different, of course, but when personality traits cause distress, the person involved may be diagnosed as suffering from a personality disorder. Although such disorders have been recognized for some time, they remain controversial. Not only has their reliability and validity been questioned, but also their very existence. Some writers believe that personality disorders are not psychological disorders at all but simply a way of medicalizing human behavior, turning normal variations in temperament into diseases. Other critics believe that the criteria for at least some of the personality disorders contain unfair stereotypes about women and members of minority groups. The impulse-control disorders also seem to medicalize certain behaviors (stealing, fire setting, assault) that might otherwise be punished. The personality and impulse-control disorders are so heterogeneous that new disorders (such as passive-aggressive personality disorder) can be added without really seeming out of place. Unless psychologists develop a unifying rationale for these disorders, we may find that just about every personality type or impulsive behavior comes to be classified as a disorder.

Key Ideas

Categories Versus Dimensions

Personality disorders constitute distinct diagnostic categories; a person either meets the criteria for a personality disorder or does not meet them. Alternatively, people may be described by where they fall on a variety of personality dimensions. The dimensional approach provides richer descriptions and avoids pigeonholing people into narrow categories. Unfortunately, there are many possible personality dimensions, and no one knows which ones are appropriate for describing people.

The Multiaxial Diagnostic System and Comorbidity

Unlike the clinical disorders, which are coded on Axis I, personality disorders are coded on Axis II. It is common for a person to be diagnosed as suffering from a clinical disorder on Axis I while simultaneously suffering from a personality disorder coded on Axis II. What is unclear is whether one of these disorders causes the other, whether they share a common etiology, or whether Axis I and Axis II disorders are just two versions of the same condition.

Types of Personality and Impulse-Control Disorders

The 10 *DSM-IV* personality disorders represent a small sample of the potential personality disorders. The impulse-control disorders (including stealing, fire setting, aggressive outbursts, pulling one's hair, and gambling) are also just a subset of all possible impulse-control disorders. Why some possible disorders are included and others omitted is unclear but seems largely the result of tradition. Personality and impulse-control disorders are overlapping categories. For this reason, the *DSM-IV* recommends that an impulse-control disorder not be diagnosed when a personality disorder is more appropriate.

Diagnostic Issues

Clinicians often disagree about personality disorder diagnoses. The problem is overlapping criteria. For example, borderline, schizoid, and avoidant personality disorders are all marked by poor social relations. To make diagnosis easier, clinicians simply give people more than one personality-disorder diagnosis. Knowing that someone has a personality disorder tells us little about how different personalities develop, nor does it tell us much about how a person will behave in specific situations. In some cases, personality-disorder diagnostic criteria reflect cultural and gender stereotypes. Impulse-control disorders are easier to distinguish from one another than are the personality disorders, but they rarely occur on their own. Most often they are associated with some other disorder. Because they are more specific, impulse-control disorders may be better predictors of behavior (people with pyromania should start fires), although situational characteristics determine whether a person actually follows through on an impulse.

Antisocial Personality Disorder

At least since the 19th century, psychologists have recognized people whose selfish and amoral behavior placed them beyond the ethical bounds of society. These people were "morally insane" psychopaths or, in *DSM-IV* terms, they had an antisocial personality disorder. The hallmark of this disorder is a flagrant disregard for the rights of other people. The disorder is found mainly in males, it affects between 2.5% and 3.5% of the population, and its incidence decreases with age. Like much human behavior, antisocial personality disorder begins in childhood, especially among children from abusive or discordant families. Early childhood experiences are not easily disentangled from genetics, which may also play a role in the etiology of personality disorders. Exposure to antisocial models, both in real life and in the media, combined with a tendency toward low arousal and compensatory sensation seeking provide an especially risky environment for the development of antisocial personality disorder. Few people with antisocial personality disorder are motivated to seek treatment. Those who do find their way into treatment receive the full range of psychological and drug interventions.

Violence and Criminal Responsibility

Violent crime, committed by both adults and children, is common in the United States. It is possible that violence in the media is partly to blame, but poverty and the easy availability of weapons are also important causative factors. Whether violent criminals face punishment depends on whether they are responsible for their crimes and capable of defending themselves in court. Those who are not responsible for their actions at the time of a crime because they were "insane" are committed for treatment. *Insanity* is a legal term whose meaning is determined by legislatures and courts. Not surprisingly, its definition has varied with society's attitude toward crime and criminals. Because expert witnesses often disagree about who is insane, many professionals doubt the validity of insanity defenses, and some states have eliminated them.

Cluster A: Paranoid, Schizoid, and Schizotypal Personality Disorders

Cluster A personality disorders are marked by eccentricity, not to the point of losing touch with reality, but sufficient for the individual to be perceived by others as odd. The Cluster A disorders include paranoid personality disorder (marked by suspicion and distrust);

schizoid personality disorder (characterized by a lack of social relationships); and schizotypal personality disorder (which is more closely related to schizophrenia). Psychological treatments for Cluster A disorders mirror those used in schizophrenia—social skill training and antipsychotic medication.

Cluster B: Antisocial, Borderline, Histrionic, and Narcissistic Personality Disorders

People with Cluster B personality disorders are self-absorbed. They find it difficult to empathize with others, and they exaggerate the importance of everything that happens to them in a theatrical and overdramatic way. Because of their excessive self-concern and melodramatics, they find it difficult to establish and maintain interpersonal relationships. In addition to antisocial personality disorder, Cluster B disorders include borderline (marked by instability, impulsivity, and a fear of abandonment); histrionic (characterized by emotionality and attention seeking); and narcissistic (in which people develop a grandiose sense of self-importance). These disorders are difficult to treat but may sometimes respond to therapy, particularly a mixture of psychodynamic and cognitive-behavioral treatment. Drugs are also used, but mainly to treat associated conditions or specific symptoms.

Cluster C: Avoidant, Obsessive-Compulsive, and Dependent Personality Disorders

The disorders in Cluster C share many characteristics with the anxiety disorders. They are marked by fearfulness and worry, and they tend to co-occur with depression. In contrast to the anxiety disorders, however, Cluster C personality disorders tend to have an earlier onset, no clear cause, and a stable lifelong course. The disorders include avoidant (a long-term social phobia); obsessive-compulsive (in which people display perfectionistic attitudes); and dependent personality disorder (marked by submissiveness and the need to be cared for by a strong person).

Personality Disorders Under Study

In addition to identifying the three clusters of disorders already discussed, the *DSM-IV* contains an appendix detailing two personality disorders that are considered worthy of further study: depressive personality disorder (long-term dysthymia) and passive-aggressive (negativistic) personality disorder (characterized by a sullen, passive shirking of responsibilities). Whether these disorders provide sufficient extra information about prognosis or treatment remains to be demonstrated by further research.

Key Terms

antisocial personality disorder

avoidance learning

avoidant personality disorder

borderline personality
    disorder

criminal commitment

criminology

dependent personality disorder

depressive personality
    disorder

dialectical behavior therapy

dimensional approach
    to diagnosis

histrionic personality disorder

impulse-control disorder

insanity

intermittent explosive disorder

irresistible impulse rule

kleptomania

M'Naghten Rule

moral insanity

narcissistic personality
    disorder

obsessive-compulsive
    personality disorder

paranoid personality disorder

passive-aggressive (or
    negativistic) personality
    disorder

pathological gambling

personality

personality disorder

physiognomy

pyromania

psychopath

schizoid personality disorder

schizotypal personality
    disorder

sociopathic personality

trichotillomania

Key Names

Cesare Lombroso

David Lykken

CHAPTER 11

CHAPTER OBJECTIVES

Imagine being unable to read. Opportunities open to others—
to study and to work—are closed to you. How would you feel?
Inadequate? Stupid? Rejected? For many mentally retarded and
learning disabled people, these are not hypothetical questions.
Their lives are dominated by their intellectual disabilities. The
situation is even worse for people with cognitive disorders
because they face the additional terror of watching their intellectual skills slip away. This chapter summarizes what is known,
and what can be done, about the intellectual and cognitive
disorders.

The four main questions addressed in this chapter are

1. What is mental retardation and how does it differ from
   learning disabilities and cognitive disorders?
2. How can we help people live up to their intellectual
   potential?
3. Can we prevent intellectual and cognitive disorders from
   affecting people in the future?
4. What are the legal implications of intellectual and cognitive
   disorders?

Intellectual and Cognitive Disorders

CONTENTS

*M*oron, *fool, idiot, cretin, imbecile*—these are only a few of the pejorative terms that have been used through the ages to refer to people with **mental retardation,** those whose intellectual abilities fail to develop at the same pace as their peers. Until the second half of the 20th century, it was widely believed that most such individuals were unteachable. Even advocates of humane treatment limited their efforts to improving the conditions in which people with mental retardation lived rather than to improving their cognitive abilities. Doctors, teachers, and most other well-intentioned professionals believed that large custodial institutions, cocoons in which people with mental retardation could be removed and protected from the world, were the best places for them to reside. As we enter the new millennium, these views have changed dramatically. We are witnessing a revolution in both professional and lay attitudes toward mental retardation. Custodial institutions have been replaced by community-based and school programs. More important, pessimistic attitudes about how much people with mental retardation can be taught have been replaced with a new optimism. If there is one area of human frailty in which psychology has improved the quality of people's lives, it is in the intellectual and cognitive disorders.

The significant advances in the treatment and prevention of mental retardation that have grown out of psychological research are described in this chapter. At the same time, this chapter also discusses learning, motor skills, and communication disorders as well as the cognitive disorders. **Learning, motor skills,** and **communication disorders** are diagnosed when an individual's performance in these areas falls below the level expected for the person's age, schooling, and intelligence. Like mental retardation, these disorders are first noticed in childhood. In contrast, the **cognitive disorders** occur mainly among older people. They arise from temporary or permanent brain damage and attack the memories, personality traits, and cognitive skills that give each of us a unique identity. Sufferers are caught in the present moment, unable to relate to the past or to plan for the future. Grouping mental retardation, learning, motor skills, communication, and cognitive disorders in a single chapter does not mean they have a common cause. On the contrary, they have many important differences. The easiest way to illustrate these differences is to compare and contrast the various cognitive and intellectual disorders in the same chapter.

The chapter begins with a discussion of mental retardation, and then contrasts it with the learning, motor skills, and communication disorders. The focus next moves to the cognitive disorders, following the chronology of intellectual disorders from birth to old age. To provide a unifying focus, the discussions make frequent reference to the story of Helen Lee. First meeting her as a baby, we follow her progress through childhood and adolescence, and finally learn what happens to her as an adult.

MENTAL RETARDATION

There are hundreds of conditions that can retard intellectual development (Simonoff, Bolton, & Rutter, 1998). Some of these are inherited, others are acquired, and a few are the result of noninherited genetic "accidents." Helen Lee falls into the last group.

Helen Lee: A Child With Mental Retardation

Each of us inherits about 100,000 genes arranged on 23 pairs of chromosomes. Approximately 40,000 of these genes carry instructions for producing the human brain. With so many genes involved, there is considerable opportunity for something to go wrong. Recognizing this, pregnant women in high-risk categories (those older than 35, for example) are advised by their doctors to undergo screening for disorders that may affect the cognitive functioning of their unborn child. This is exactly what happened to Debbie Lee, a 36-year-old accountant, pregnant with her second child. At one of her prenatal checkups, her obstetrician gave her a brochure to take home and discuss with her husband, Michael. The brochure is reproduced in Document 11.1.

DOCUMENT 11.1

Brochure on Genetic Screening Given to Debbie Lee by Her Obstetrician

Prenatal Testing: Advice for Women Over 35

It is normal for pregnant women to worry about the health of their fetuses (unborn babies) and the possibility of birth defects. This is especially true of women older than 35 because certain birth defects are more common in the pregnancies of older women. The tests described in this brochure can detect some of these birth defects.

Decision 1

First, you must decide if you want a screening test. A *screening* test estimates the probability that your fetus has one of several birth defects. If the chances are high, it does not mean that your baby will have a defect. A second, *diagnostic,* test will have to be performed to determine whether the screening test is correct. Before deciding to undergo a screening test, it is vital that you talk to your doctor or a genetic counselor. They will be able to explain the meaning of test outcomes and your available choices.

How does the screening test work?

A sample of your blood is tested for substances made by your placenta or your fetus. Abnormal amounts of these substances may indicate a chromosomal defect. If the screening result is negative, it does not mean that your baby is guaranteed not to have a birth defect. It means that the risk is low and that further tests are unnecessary. (Avoiding further testing is good because there is a small possibility that the diagnostic test itself could cause a miscarriage.)

Decision 2

If the screening test is positive, it means that you have a higher than average risk for certain birth defects. You must then decide whether to undergo a diagnostic test. You should consult with a genetic counselor or your doctor before making this decision.

How does the diagnostic test work?

Amniocentesis. Between 12 and 14 weeks of pregnancy, a needle is inserted into your abdomen to remove a small amount of the fluid that surrounds your fetus. The chromosomes of fetal cells found in the fluid are examined for defects. Chromosomes are packages of genetic information found in every cell of the body. There is a small risk of miscarriage (about 1% of women tested). The results are available in about 2 weeks.

One of the birth defects that may be found by amniocentesis is Down syndrome, a common cause of mental retardation and heart defects in the babies of mothers over 35.

Decision 3

If the diagnostic test shows that your fetus has a birth defect, you will need to decide whether to terminate your pregnancy. Again, counseling is essential. A counselor can explain the type of birth defect that has been found and any available treatments. The counselor will discuss options for continuing or ending the pregnancy. You can then make an informed decision.

What should she do, Debbie wondered? According to the brochure, her age put her in the high-risk group. Positive screening and diagnostic tests would tell her whether her unborn child had Down syndrome. Her options at that point would include terminating the pregnancy or going forward with the knowledge that her child was likely to have both intellectual and physical disabilities. Debbie and Michael both held strong religious views against abortion; they would not consider terminating the pregnancy. Yet, they believed there was still sense in undergoing the tests. If their child had Down syndrome, they could prepare themselves by learning about the disorder and how to care for a child with it. If they were to decide that they would be unable to care for a disabled child, they could use that advance knowledge to make plans for their child's adoption.

Based on this logic, Debbie decided to undergo the screening test. The result was positive. Debbie and Michael next met with a genetic counselor. This counselor was nondirective; she saw her job as educational (Harper, 1993). She gave Michael and Debbie a realistic view of the genetic risks and the burdens they would face as caregivers and left it to them to decide (Folstein & Folstein, 1998). Debbie underwent amniocentesis. This test was also positive: Her baby had Down syndrome. After many days of discussion, Debbie and Michael decided to raise the baby themselves. They believed that even a child with this disability could have a fulfilling life. Debbie's pregnancy passed without complication, and she gave birth to a baby girl. The medical record made at the time appears in Document 11.2. The Apgar score referred to in Document 11.2 is a measure of infant health status named in honor of Dr. Virginia Apgar, one of the first pediatricians to specialize in newborn care. The score, which ranges from 0 (worst) to 10, is used to screen babies at risk for complications. Table 11.1 shows the five categories whose ratings (0–2) are added to get the final Apgar score.

DOCUMENT 11.2

Medical Record of
Helen Lee's Birth

UNIVERSITY HOSPITAL

Maternity Service

Obstetrician-Gynecologist: Sara Henderson, M.D.

Date: January 4, 1962

Mother's Name: Debbie Lee

Debbie Lee is a healthy 36-year-old woman with one previous child. Her husband, Michael Lee, is 33. Debbie had an uneventful pregnancy and carried her baby to term. Amniocentesis indicated Down syndrome.

Labor began at 11 p.m. on January 3 with mild contractions. Mrs. Lee arrived at the hospital at 11:30 p.m. and her amniotic fluid began to leak at midnight. Full dilation took 3 hours. Her female baby was delivered at 3 a.m. on January 4. The baby's skin had a blue tinge, and she was slow to initiate breathing. The baby's pulse was weak, and her muscles were limp. The baby was placed on a respirator for 6 hours. The baby's color remained poor, and she had abnormal heart sounds. A cardiology consultation was ordered. Visual appearance confirms the results of amniocentesis; the baby has the physical features of Down syndrome.

Birth weight: 6 lb, 1 oz

Apgar score after 1 minute = 3

Apgar score after 5 minutes = 5

TABLE 11.1   The Apgar Scoring System

	Rating		
Vital sign	**0**	**1**	**2**
Heart rate	Absent	Slow (below 100)	Over 100
Respiratory effort	Absent	Slow, irregular	Good, crying
Muscle tone	Flaccid	Some flexion of extremities	Active motion
Reflex responsivity	No response	Grimace	Vigorous cry
Color	Blue, pale	Body pink, extremities blue	Completely pink

Note: From Apgar (1953).

During Debbie's pregnancy, she and Michael set out to learn what they needed to know to raise a child with **Down syndrome.** They discovered that the syndrome was named for John Langdon Down (1828–1896), superintendent of a British asylum for children with mental retardation (Roizen, 1997). In 1866, Down described a subset of children who were different from other children with mental retardation. Down thought that these children looked like people from Mongolia, a group whom he believed to be intellectually inferior to the English. For this reason, he called the children *Mongoloids* and their condition *Mongolism*. When it came under fire in the 1960s as having racist connotations, the term was dropped from scientific use. It was replaced with "Down's syndrome," which evolved in the United States into the ungrammatical "Down syndrome." (It is still "Down's" in Great Britain.)

Down was correct about one thing: Children with this syndrome look physically different from birth (see Document 11.2). They have small heads and ears. Their heads have flat backs, their tongues are fissured, and their eyes have a fold of skin similar to that found among Asian people (hence, Down's Mongolism). Their hands are spadelike, with short fingers. Like Helen's, their muscles lack tone, and they have significant health problems, including a high incidence of heart defects. Mainly because of their heart problems, people with Down syndrome have traditionally died young. Today, with proper medical care, they live into middle and even old age (Jancar & Jancar, 1996).

From their reading, Debbie and Michael learned that mental retardation first becomes apparent in Down syndrome children during the first year or two of life. (Helen's intellectual assessment at just over 4 years of age, shown in Document 11.3, bears out that finding.) The Lees knew that their daughter's mental retardation was likely to cause her trouble in school, but they were not sure how much. To find out more about mental retardation and what can be done about it, Debbie and Michael joined a support group for parents of children with mental retardation, searched the Internet for information, and read books designed specifically for the parents of children with Down syndrome (see Selikowitz, 1997, for an example).

DOCUMENT 11.3

Helen's Early Intellectual Assessment

University School District Psychological Services

Intellectual Assessment

Child's Name: Helen Lee

Age: 4 years, 3 months

Mother's Name: Debbie Lee

Developmental Psychologist: John McAffery, PhD

Date: April 4, 1966

Tests Administered

Bayley Scales of Infant Development (BSID-II)

Vineland Scale of Adaptive Behavior, Interview Edition, Survey Form

Referral Request: Helen was referred by her pediatrician, Dr. Arlene Cohen, for assessment of her cognitive development, and for recommendations regarding remediation of any developmental delay.

History: Helen is a Down syndrome child who has been in special child care, including a stimulation program. Helen had cardiac surgery at age 1 to repair a congenital heart defect. She has been slow to reach important developmental milestones. She was 6 months behind in standing on her own and even now has an uncertain gait. She has speech, but it is limited to only a few words, and her pronunciation is indistinct.

Family Background: Debbie Lee was born in Canada but moved to the U.S. at the time of her marriage to Michael (who is 3 years younger). She has one other child (Carl, aged 11). She does not know of any mental illness or retardation in her family or in Michael's.

Behavioral Observations: Helen is small for her age. She seemed calm and peaceful but said little. The assessment was done by observation and maternal report.

Results and Analysis: Helen's scores on the Bayley scales are below those expected for a 51-month-old child. Her performance is more typical of a much younger child. For example, Helen is an uncertain walker. In her play with wooden blocks, she was able to stack them two or three high, but no more, and she was able to name only one picture, the dog ("doggie"). Helen's scores on the Vineland Scale of Adaptive Behavior show a similar profile of developmental delay. She is not toilet trained and needs help in feeding.

Recommendations: Continuation of the stimulation program, with an emphasis on self-help, expressive language, and motor skills. Review in 12 months.

Definition and Diagnosis

In their research, Debbie and Michael were surprised to learn that, prior to 1950, there were only two books on mental retardation written by psychologists (Burt, 1935; Sarason, 1949). Before that, mental retardation was viewed as a medical problem, with lawyers called in when involuntary commitment was considered necessary. Instead of using intelligence tests, doctors decided whether a person was mentally retarded on the basis of a clinical examination (Trent, 1995). As you might imagine, this subjective approach to assessment was open to bias. For example, working-class children were more likely to be diagnosed retarded than middle-class children (Trent, 1995). One of the arguments for the introduction of standardized intelligence tests was to bring objective rigor to the diagnostic process (J. Brown, 1992).

Role of Intelligence Tests Because intelligence tests were considered unbiased and because they predict academic success (at least for large groups), by the 1960s most states made intelligence testing a mandatory part of diagnosing mental retardation (Zenderland, 1998). The *DSM-IV* continued this tradition by requiring an intelligence test score of "approximately 70 or below" for a diagnosis of mental retardation. (Table 11.2 contains the main *DSM-IV* diagnostic criteria for mental retardation.) For those who cannot be tested by conventional methods, clinical judgment is still required, although instruments such as the Bayley Scales of Infant Development II (Bayley, 1993; see also Document 11.3) may help clinicians to be more objective. Mental retardation is coded on Axis II of the *DSM-IV*'s multiaxial diagnostic system. This allows any concurrent clinical disorders to be separately diagnosed on Axis I.

The *DSM-IV* equates degrees of mental retardation (mild, moderate, severe, profound) to progressively lower IQ scores. But this is not the only way to conceptualize mental retardation. Instead of using IQ scores, the American Association on Mental Retardation (AAMR) equates degrees of mental retardation to the level of support a retarded person requires (AAMR, 1992). For example, a person with only mild retardation may require only intermittent support, whereas those who are more severely retarded require pervasive support. Table 11.3 summarizes the *DSM-IV* subtype categories and IQ score ranges, the AAMR required levels of support, and the average expected outcome for different degrees of mental retardation.

The number of people in each *DSM-IV* subtype category decreases as we go down the IQ scale until we get to the profound range, where the number of cases exceeds those expected on a purely statistical basis. This excess of cases at lower IQ levels is the result of special environmental factors (injury or disease, for example) that produce mental retardation in individuals who

DSM-IV   TABLE 11.2   Main *DSM-IV* Diagnostic Criteria
for Mental Retardation

A. Significantly subaverage intellectual functioning; an IQ of approximately 70 or below on an individually administered IQ test (for infants, a clinical judgment of significantly subaverage intellectual functioning).

B. Concurrent deficits or impairments in present adaptive functioning (i.e., the person's effectiveness in meeting the standards expected for his or her age by his or her cultural group) in at least two of the following areas: communication, self-care, home living, social/interpersonal skills, use of community resources, self-direction, functional academic skills, work, leisure, health, and safety.

C. The onset is before age 18 years.

Note: From American Psychiatric Association (1994, p. 46).

DSM-IV   TABLE 11.3   *DSM-IV* Levels of Mental Retardation and Scores
on Intelligence Tests

DSM-IV subtype	IQ score range	Percentage of mentally retarded population	Required level of support	Average expected outcome
Mild	50–55 to approximately 70	85	Intermittent	Independent living and unskilled work
Moderate	35–40 to 50–55	10	Limited	Group home and some sheltered work
Severe	20–25 to 35–40	3–4	Extensive	Institutionalized but some self-help
Profound	Below 20 or 25	1–2	Pervasive	Total institutional supervision

would otherwise have been distributed throughout the IQ range (Zigler, 1967). This is shown in Figure 11.1.

It is ironic that intelligence tests were introduced as a way of making intellectual assessments more objective because we know today that they are not neutral measures and that they share some of the same bias problems as interviews. For example, unless special testing arrangements are made, people with hearing (or other) disabilities may be inappropriately classified as mentally retarded. More important are racial and ethnic biases. Although intelligence tests are standardized using samples representative of the entire population, we know that African American and Latino children typically score lower on intelligence tests than do other groups (Puente & Salazar, 1998). Because intelligence test scores are used to determine who is mentally retarded, African American and Latino children are over-

diagnosed relative to their numbers in the population. Calling members of these groups mentally retarded not only stigmatizes them, it also makes retardation at least partly a racial and ethnic phenomenon. (In reality, their low scores probably reflect the social and economic deprivation of many in these groups.) Everyone agrees that the assessment of intelligence should not be influenced by cultural diversity, although exactly how to conduct "culture-free" intelligence testing is a question that remains unanswered (C. R. Reynolds, 1995).

Role of Social Skills   In their readings, Debbie and Michael were struck by the controversies that have surrounded intelligence testing (Gould, 1996). They were particularly troubled by the relative nature of an IQ score. Recall the example used in Chapter 3. If we measured height the way we measure intelligence, a value of

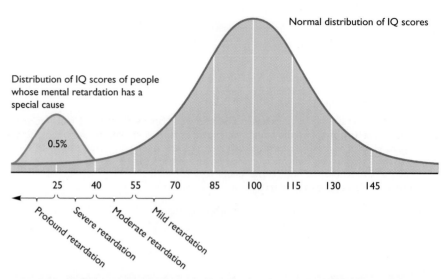

FIGURE 11.1 Normal Distribution of IQ Scores and Distribution of IQ Scores of People Whose Mental Retardation Has a Special Cause (such as disease or injury). Adapted from: Zigler (1967).

100 would be assigned to a population's average height regardless of whether the population consisted of giants or pygmies. A score of 100 would tell us that a person is average for his or her population but not how tall the person is. Similarly, IQ scores do not tell us much about intelligence. Knowing a person's IQ score (or "mental age") tells us little about how the person actually behaves. If we want to know whether a person is able to function in his or her environment, then we need to know more than just the person's intelligence test score. We also need to know how well the person adapts to his or her environment.

The assessment of social adaptation first became part of the diagnostic process in 1913, when the British Mental Deficiency Act required that "social adequacy"

be considered when diagnosing mental retardation. The idea was soon adopted in the United States, mainly because of the efforts of E. A. Doll (1889–1968), who was, for many years, director of the Vineland, New Jersey, Training School. Doll (1965) developed the Vineland Social Maturity Scale to help clinicians assess social adequacy. Since his pioneering work, many similar instruments have been developed (Zetlin & Morrison, 1998). Some tests have been computerized. For example, when Helen was 5, she underwent tesing with the California Adaptive Behavior Scale. The computer-generated report appears in Document 11.4. (Adapted from California Adaptive Behavior Scale. Copyright © 1995 Planet Press Enterprises. www.planetpress.org.)

 DOCUMENT 11.4

Assessment of Helen Lee's Adaptive Behavior at Around Age 5

University School District Psychological Services

Intellectual Assessment

Child's Name: Helen Lee

Age: 5 years, 1 month

Mother's Name: Debbie Lee

Developmental Psychologist: Dr. Elaine Bauman

Date: February 4, 1967

(Information for this evaluation was provided by Debbie Lee)

Tests Administered

California Adaptive Behavior Scale

Computer-Generated Assessment

The client's level of adaptive behavior was measured using the California Adaptive Behavior Scale, yielding an adaptive age equivalence of 2.63 years. Based on a chronological age of 5.08 years, adaptive age appears to be well below normal limits. With regard to specific areas, the highest level of functioning and the corresponding age equivalencies are given below:

Toileting: Cares for self at toilet (3.8 yrs)

Dressing: Dresses neatly without reminder (7.0 yrs)

Fastening: Maintained by caretaker

Eating: Drinks from cup/glass unaided (1.4 yrs)

Bathing: Soaps washcloth (2.5 yrs)

Grooming: Maintained by caretaker

Toothbrushing: Makes brushing strokes (3.0 yrs)

Personal Interaction: Responds to verbal greetings (2.5 yrs)

Group Participation: Knows to wait turn (3.0 yrs)

Receptive Language: Follows directions with 2 prepositions (3.0 yrs)

Expressive Language: Gestures to make needs known (1.25 yrs)

Leisure Time: Initiates own play activities (2.1 yrs)

Gross Motor: Stands by self (0.8 yr)

Perceptual Motor: Turns pages one by one (2.0 yrs)

Prevocation: Sorts by color (3.5 yrs)

Vocational: None. See Prevocational domain.

School Domain: The client's level of school readiness was measured using the California Adaptive Behavior Scale, yielding a school age equivalence of 2.20 years. Based on this score, participation in a nursery school level program is recommended. With regard to specific areas, the highest level of functioning and the corresponding age equivalencies are given below:

Reading: Identifies action in pictures (2.6 yrs)

Writing: Minimal

Number Skill: Minimal

Attention Span: Knows to wait turn (3.0 yrs)

Reliability Evaluation: Reliability for this evaluation is 95% based on a comparison of pairs of items embedded within the various domains. Inconsistencies were found between the following pairs of items:

No: Unwraps candy (1.8 yrs)

Yes: Unwraps candy/packages (1.8 yrs)

Note: These items should have been scored in a similar fashion (i.e., both yes or both no).

Validity Evaluation: Certain specific skills require prerequisite skills in order to be performed. The validity scale compares responses in one domain with prerequisite levels in another domain, to determine whether the responses are consistent (e.g., a client who enjoys social walks must first be able to walk; a client who indicates a need to use the toilet must be able to gesture to make his needs known). On this basis, validity for this examination was 97% based on a comparison of 30 pairs of items. Inconsistencies were found for the following items:

Yes: Enjoys social walks (1.0 yr)

No: Walks (1.0 yr)

Note: Any reported behavior (the first of the pair of items) must indicate that the prerequisite behavior (the second of the pair of items) is in the client's repertoire.

Recognizing the importance of social functioning, the *DSM-IV* diagnostic criteria for mental retardation require both a low IQ score and low adaptive functioning (see Table 11.2). Low intelligence, by itself, is not a disorder. Whether someone is "mentally retarded" depends on how that person adapts to his or her environment. If Helen Lee learns to overcome the obstacles that impede her development, if she learns to communicate, care for herself, and do some work, then she is not mentally retarded even though she has Down syndrome and scores low on intelligence assessments.

The *DSM-IV* requires that adaptive behavior be evaluated relative to a child's age and cultural group. This is because people at different developmental stages and from different cultural groups are expected to perform dissimilar tasks. For example, young children are not expected to live independently, whereas adults should be able to manage their own affairs. Because of these different age-related expectations, it is possible for an individual who has difficulty keeping up at school to adjust well as an adult when adaptive functioning is judged by different criteria.

How Many People Are Mentally Retarded? Using the relevant *DSM-IV* diagnostic criterion (an IQ score of "approximately 70 or below"), 2.5–3% of the population is potentially mentally retarded. This translates to between 7 and 8 million people in the United States. However, this IQ score cutoff is arbitrary. We could require a higher IQ cutoff and get a different result, as Critical Thinking About Clinical Decisions 11.1 points out. In practice, there are far fewer diagnosed cases of mental retardation than there are people whose IQ scores fall below 70 (Fryers, 1993; Gillberg, 1997; Katusic et al., 1996; Roeleveld, Zielhuis, & Gabreels, 1997). Put another way, the *administrative prevalence* (identified cases) is smaller than expected given the distribution of IQ scores (C. C. Murphy et al., 1995). Some people with low IQ scores slip through the administrative net; others develop a high enough level of adaptive skills to avoid being classified as mentally retarded.

The prevalence of mental retardation is associated with age; it increases through the school years and decreases in adulthood. Changes in prevalence with age can be explained by age-related changes in social and intellectual demands. When they start school, children who might previously have functioned well at home are faced with new challenges—cognitive, behavioral, and social. If they fail to adapt, they may be identified by school authorities as mentally retarded. Because intellectual and adaptive demands increase with each school year, the chances of a child's being identified as mentally retarded also increase. When the child leaves school, a new set of demands come into play. Individuals who had difficulty keeping up with their peers at school might find that they are capable of doing a job, taking care of themselves, and making new friends. Such people may no longer be considered mentally retarded. This is a crucial point worth emphasizing. When an individual's adaptive skills "fit" with the demands of the environment, then the person may still be able to function no matter what his or her IQ score happens to be. This is fortunate because it means that interventions aimed at improving adaptive skills can reduce the prevalence of mental retardation.

How Many People Do We Want to Be Mentally Retarded?

As discussed in Chapter 3, the distribution of IQ scores in the population conforms to a bell-shaped curve with a mean of 100 and a standard deviation of 15. What is often left unsaid is that intelligence tests are deliberately constructed to yield precisely this distribution. In other words, the bell-shaped curve is not an empirical discovery; it is determined in advance when the test is constructed. By specifying the distribution beforehand, the designers of intelligence tests ensure that approximately two thirds of the population will have an IQ of between 85 and 115 (one standard deviation above and below the mean). The *DSM-IV* defines mental retardation, in part, as an IQ score below 70 (two standard deviations below the mean). Thus, it limits the diagnosis to between 2% and 3% of the population. If, on the other hand, we were to use a higher IQ cutoff—say 75, the IQ cutoff preferred by the American Association for Mental Retardation (AAMR, 1992)—almost 10% of the population might potentially be mentally retarded. This is shown by the graph in this box. Put simply, the higher the IQ cutoff score, the more people who may be classified as mentally retarded.

Classifying more people as mentally

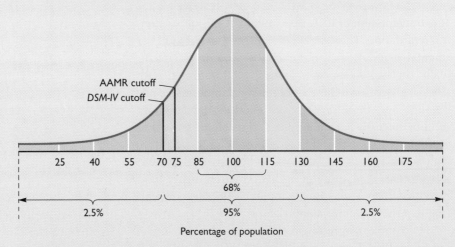

DSM-IV and AAMR Cutoffs for Mental Retardation. The DSM-IV *cutoff, at an IQ of 70, means that mental retardation affects 2–3% of the population. Using the American Association for Mental Retardation cutoff of 75, it affects 10% of the population.*

retarded may sometimes be justified. The diagnosis might make them eligible for special education and thus give them a brighter future. On the other hand, by using a higher score, society incurs the costs of providing special education to more students. Thus, setting the IQ cutoff score for mental retardation is a policy decision, not a scientific judgment. If society is willing to spend more money on education, then a higher cutoff may be justified. If we want to economize,

then a lower cutoff will save money and also limit the number potentially stigmatized by being labeled retarded. In summary, where we place the IQ cutoff for diagnosing mental retardation depends not on science but on our generosity as a society and our evaluation of the negative effects of labeling.

Causes

Michael and Debbie knew that mental retardation could be caused by genetic accidents such as the one that results in Down syndrome. What they were surprised to learn is that there are hundreds of other causes. Mental retardation can be caused by practically any condition that affects the development or working of the brain. Broadly, the causes of mental retardation can be categorized as genetic (including inherited conditions, genetic accidents, and mutations caused by exposure to X rays or other toxins), pregnancy complications (caused by alcohol, drug poisoning, or illness), birth trauma (caused by lack of oxygen or stressful delivery), childhood diseases or accidents, and social factors (poverty, poor nu-

trition, child abuse, or a deprived intellectual environment). Although it is not possible to describe all of the causes of mental retardation in this chapter, the main etiological factors and their significance are summarized in this section.

Inherited Diseases and Genetic Accidents   There are many genetically transmitted defects that can produce mental retardation. One relatively well known type of defect is an inherited inability to metabolize certain foods. More than 50 such disorders have been described, and new ones are being recognized all the time. Despite the large number of conditions, they are individually rare and, even in total, account for only a small number of cases of mental retardation. The best known of these inherited metabolic defects is **phenylketonuria,** or **PKU.** Affected children have difficulty metabolizing the amino acid phenylalanine. As a result, phenylalanine accumulates in their bodies, eventually leading to severe mental retardation. Notice that the gene responsible for the transmission of PKU does not, by itself, cause mental retardation. The gene is only part of the problem. For mental retardation to occur, the environment (specifically, diet) plays a crucial role. If a child affected with PKU is placed on a diet free of phenylalanine at an early enough age, then his or her intellectual development will be normal. Fortunately, it is possible to screen infants for PKU just after birth. Those who test positive can be placed on special diets. To help parents prevent future mental retardation in their children, many food products (Diet Coke, for example) carry labels indicating that they contain phenylalanine.

Of course, controlling a child's diet places financial and social burdens on families with PKU-affected children. Finding and purchasing special foods for the child takes time and requires that the person doing the shopping understand the labels on the products. Parents with poor education and low literacy may experience difficulty. This is another way in which a child's environment (parental education) interacts with a genotype (PKU) to determine phenotypic intelligence.

There are many other metabolic disorders that can result in mental retardation. *Tay-Sachs, Niemann-Pick,* and *Hurler's* diseases are the ones reported most often in the literature. They are each examples of lipidoses, diseases characterized by the degeneration of neural tissue. Tay-Sachs, which occurs most often among Jews of Eastern European descent, is marked by progressive neural atrophy (Goodman, 1994). Affected children begin to deteriorate in their first year of life, and they tend to die young. Some of these conditions can be detected by amniocentesis.

The metabolic disorders discussed so far are mainly recessive traits. For them to show up in children, both parents must be carriers. However, some types of mental retardation result from genetically dominant traits. These can affect children even when only one parent carries the gene. A few disorders appear to have more than one genetic etiology. For example, *tuberous sclerosis,* a disease that produces benign tumors in the brain and other organs, can result from a mutation or by inheritance from an affected parent.

The most common genetic cause of mental retardation, Down syndrome, is the result of a genetic abnormality known as *trisomy* (triplication) of the 21st chromosome. This triplication takes place during the reproductive process when sperm and egg cells split into

The majority of Down syndrome cases are caused by trisomy (triplication) of the 21st chromosome.

two. Normally each has half the number of chromosomes of the parent cell. Occasionally, however, one chromosome pair does not divide. Instead of 23 chromosomes each, one cell has 24 chromosomes and the other has 22. This accident is called *nondisjunction.* If a sperm or egg with an abnormal number of chromosomes merges with a normal cell, the resulting fertilized egg will have 3 chromosomes where there should only be 2. The majority of Down syndrome cases are caused this way. Affected individuals have three 21st chromosomes. Hence the scientific name for Down syndrome is **trisomy 21.** A small number of Down syndrome cases have causes other than nondisjunction (and slightly different genotypes), but the clinical result is similar (Hernandez & Fisher, 1996).

Although the cause of nondisjunction is not known, it is more common among older mothers. For women younger than 29, the risk is 1 in 3,000; for those over 34, the probability increases to 1 in 1,000. The probability climbs to 32 in 1,000 for mothers over 45. Interestingly, as screening becomes more common, fewer Down syndrome children are being born to older mothers (probably because many such pregnancies are terminated). The result is that Down syndrome is becoming relatively more common among the children of younger mothers (who do not undergo screening).

Having three 21st chromosomes leads to certain traits being overexpressed (more pronounced than normal). It is this overexpression that produces the signs and symptoms of Down syndrome. Because the amount of overexpression varies from person to person, there is a wide range of mental retardation and developmental delay noted among children with Down syndrome. The nonintellectual symptoms of Down syndrome also vary in severity. Some babies are born with heart defects, and

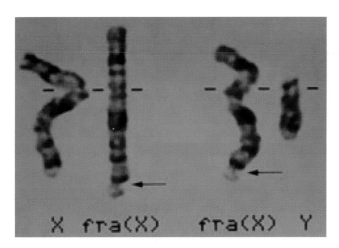

The indentation at the end of the X chromosome is what gives fragile X syndrome its name.

In people with Williams syndrome, the genes on chromosome 7 for elastin and for an enzyme called LIM kinease are missing.

others are not; some children have associated illnesses, such as epilepsy, and others do not (Korenberg et al., 1994). Researchers are currently trying to map all of the genes on the 21st chromosome with the goal of understanding which genes are overexpressed and how their expression may be altered (Patterson, 1995).

Another common genetic cause of mental retardation is the **fragile X syndrome** (Hagerman, 1996; Simonoff, Bolton, & Rutter, 1996). This syndrome takes its name from the unusual appearance of the X chromosome in affected individuals. Part of the chromosome is replicated many times. Affected individuals may have more than 1,000 copies of a particular genetic string. This confuses the protein production process, leaving affected individuals with low levels of the fragile X protein. The end result is mild to severe mental retardation.

Fragile X syndrome affects approximately 1 of every 2,000 males and 1 of every 4,000 females. Although there are some subtle physical signs, including large ears and a long face, the disease may be difficult to detect from physical appearance alone. DNA analysis is usually necessary. Although a treatment is not presently available, it may soon be possible to counteract fragile X syndrome with gene therapy. Specifically, a virus that infects specific cell types may be used to deliver the fragile X gene to depleted cells.

In addition to Down syndrome and fragile X syndrome, there are many other chromosomal abnormalities associated with mental retardation. The *Prader-Willi syndrome* (named after the clinicians who first described it) is caused by a genetic defect in chromosome 15 (Simonoff et al., 1996). This condition occurs in about 1 in every 15,000 births. The symptoms include short stature, obe-

sity, and mental retardation. *Angelman syndrome* (also named after the clinician who first described it) is another chromosome 15 disorder. It is characterized by jerky movements and seizures as well as by mental retardation (Simonoff et al., 1996). *Klinefelter's syndrome* is associated with one or more extra female chromosomes in males. Affected boys are tall and thin, their testes are small, and they do not mature sexually. Mild mental retardation may occur in some affected boys. *Turner's syndrome* occurs in females who have only one rather than two X chromosomes. These girls have only rudimentary ovaries and may also be mildly mentally retarded. *Cri du chat* syndrome is the result of one partially missing chromosome (part of the number 5 pair). Affected children are mentally retarded and have a weak meowing cry.

One of the most unusual genetic disorders is *Williams syndrome* (Pober & Dykens, 1996). Sufferers exhibit a curious combination of good cognitive abilities in some areas and retardation in others. For example, people with Williams syndrome may be articulate, fond of music, and avid readers yet unable to tie their shoes or do simple arithmetic. Williams syndrome appears rare (there are fewer than 25,000 known cases in the United States). It is sometimes called elfin-face syndrome because sufferers have pixielike narrow faces with broad foreheads, wide-spaced eyes, and sharp chins. They also have pixielike personalities—outgoing and gregarious. Although they speak fluently, people with this syndrome

People with Williams syndrome have a characteristic appearance, including narrow faces with broad foreheads, wide-spaced eyes, and sharp chins.

do not always understand what they are saying (Volterra et al., 1996). They also seem to have difficulty integrating their perceptions. For example, when asked to draw a picture of a complex object (such as a bicycle), one sufferer drew a chain, wheels, handlebars, and a seat, all unconnected with one another. Williams syndrome is the outcome of an inherited defect that results in missing genetic material on chromosome 7, including the gene that makes the protein elastin (which provides strength and elasticity to the walls of blood vessels). It is the missing elastin gene that accounts for the physical features of Williams syndrome. Because many individuals with Williams syndrome are not diagnosed until adulthood, they may have children of their own before anyone is aware of their disorder, thereby passing their genetic defect on to another generation. Figure 11.2 lists a number of the disorders caused by chromosomal abnormalities.

Pregnancy Complications, Birth Trauma, and Childhood Problems   Mental retardation can result from teratogenic (development-affecting) agents, infections, and maternal-fetal incompatibility. Examples of each of these are described in this section. In addition, diet during pregnancy can also affect unborn children. In developed countries, maternal diet is rarely poor enough to cause mental retardation. In the developing world, however, dietary deficiencies, such as a lack of iodine, can affect the mental development of fetuses (Brown & Pollitt, 1996).

Teratogenic Agents   Drugs used during pregnancy and, to a lesser extent, X rays may produce fetal malformations. Events such as the atomic bombing of Japan and the thalidomide disaster of the 1960s—in which a medication given to pregnant women led to the birth of hundreds of deformed children—illustrate the teratogenic power of such agents on the developing child. No one knows the number of children with mental retardation whose condition is the result of **teratogenic agents.** Nevertheless, drugs (legal and illicit), X rays, or other potentially harmful substances should be avoided by pregnant women unless they are absolutely necessary. Alcohol should also be avoided or at least severely cut back. In addition to physical deformities, the fetal alcohol syndrome described in Chapter 6 can result in mental retardation.

Prenatal Infection   Prenatal infections are a small factor in the causation of mental retardation (Camp et al., 1998). Nevertheless, illnesses such as rubella (German measles), if contracted in the early stages of pregnancy, can exert profound effects on the developing child. Syphilis, gonorrhea, and other sexually transmitted diseases can also affect unborn children. Public health interventions, including the use of condoms and vaccination programs, could eliminate such tragedies altogether. Unfortunately, many people are ignoring such programs, and some of these illnesses are now appearing in new drug-resistant strains.

Rh Factor   The Rh factor (or rhesus factor, after the monkeys in which it was first discovered) is an inherited protein found in the blood. Most of us have this protein, but about 15% of the population does not. When a mother is negative and a father is positive for the protein, some or all of the children will be positive. In such cases, the mother may produce antibodies against the protein in the fetus's blood. This may result in the child being mentally retarded. First pregnancies are usually not a problem, and complications can also be avoided in future pregnancies provided that mothers receive adequate prenatal care (Carlson, Eisenstat, & Ziporyn, 1996).

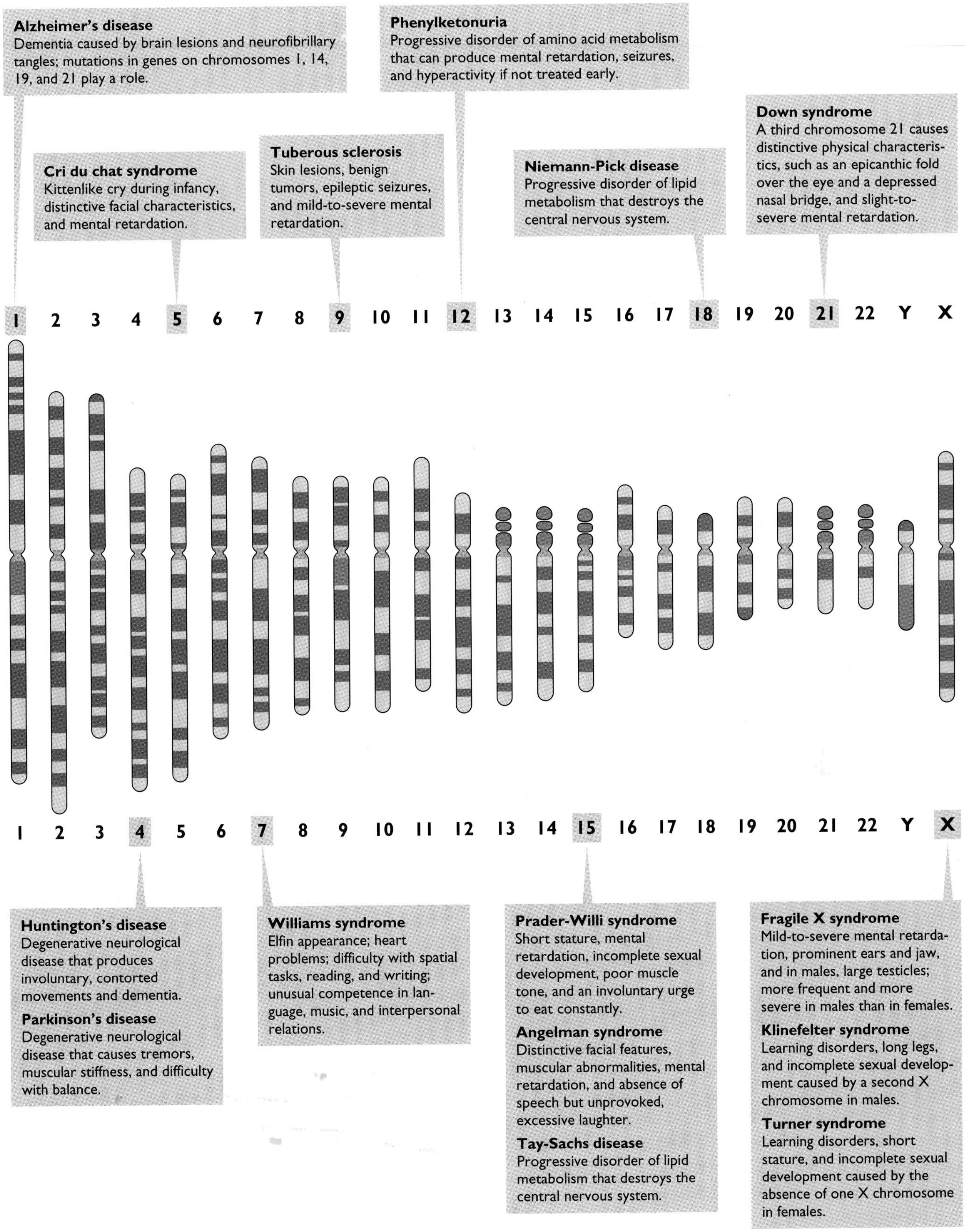
Alzheimer's disease
Dementia caused by brain lesions and neurofibrillary tangles; mutations in genes on chromosomes 1, 14, 19, and 21 play a role.
Phenylketonuria
Progressive disorder of amino acid metabolism that can produce mental retardation, seizures, and hyperactivity if not treated early.
Cri du chat syndrome
Kittenlike cry during infancy, distinctive facial characteristics, and mental retardation.
Tuberous sclerosis
Skin lesions, benign tumors, epileptic seizures, and mild-to-severe mental retardation.
Niemann-Pick disease
Progressive disorder of lipid metabolism that destroys the central nervous system.
Down syndrome
A third chromosome 21 causes distinctive physical characteristics, such as an epicanthic fold over the eye and a depressed nasal bridge, and slight-to-severe mental retardation.
1 2 3 4 5 6 7 8 9 10 11 12 13 14 15 16 17 18 19 20 21 22 Y X
1 2 3 4 5 6 7 8 9 10 11 12 13 14 15 16 17 18 19 20 21 22 Y X
Huntington's disease
Degenerative neurological disease that produces involuntary, contorted movements and dementia.
Parkinson's disease
Degenerative neurological disease that causes tremors, muscular stiffness, and difficulty with balance.
Williams syndrome
Elfin appearance; heart problems; difficulty with spatial tasks, reading, and writing; unusual competence in language, music, and interpersonal relations.
Prader-Willi syndrome
Short stature, mental retardation, incomplete sexual development, poor muscle tone, and an involuntary urge to eat constantly.
Angelman syndrome
Distinctive facial features, muscular abnormalities, mental retardation, and absence of speech but unprovoked, excessive laughter.
Tay-Sachs disease
Progressive disorder of lipid metabolism that destroys the central nervous system.
Fragile X syndrome
Mild-to-severe mental retardation, prominent ears and jaw, and in males, large testicles; more frequent and more severe in males than in females.
Klinefelter syndrome
Learning disorders, long legs, and incomplete sexual development caused by a second X chromosome in males.
Turner syndrome
Learning disorders, short stature, and incomplete sexual development caused by the absence of one X chromosome in females.

FIGURE 11.2 **Types of Mental Retardation and Neurological Disorders Caused by Chromosomal Abnormalities**

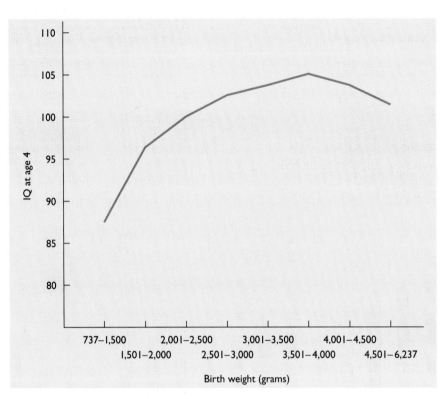

FIGURE 11.3 **Relationship Between Birth Weight and IQ at 4 Years.**
From: Broman et al. (1975).

Prematurity Premature birth—because of maternal illness, poor health, or other factors—results in children with low birth weights. Not long ago, very low birth weight infants did not survive. Today, modern medicine has made it possible to keep even tiny infants alive. Although it is difficult to identify precisely why low birth weight should produce slow cognitive development, it is clear that tiny infants are more likely to be mentally retarded than are normal sized infants (Zeanah, 1993). Interestingly, the relationship between birth weight and IQ is not linear, as shown in Figure 11.3 (Broman et al., 1975). IQ does increase with birth weight, but only up to 8.8 pounds (4 kilograms). For babies heavier than that, the relationship between birth weight and IQ is negative. This is because high birth weight is associated with maternal diabetes, a disease that can exert a profound effect on a child's intellectual functioning.

Postnatal Risks and Childhood Problems Despite improvements in obstetrics, some children are still injured during the birth process. The long-term effects of pressure, anoxia, and other birth traumas may include, among other things, mental retardation. Diseases such as meningitis and encephalitis, chemical insults such as lead poisoning, extremely poor nutrition—in fact, just about any disease, poison, or trauma—can result in mental retardation. Of course, these causes do not act in isolation; they almost always interact with social variables. A good example is lead poisoning. Ingesting lead can lead to mental retardation. The most common source of lead is a type of paint found solely in old buildings. Young children who live in such buildings eat lead-based paint as it flakes off the walls. Because economically disadvantaged people often live in older buildings, they are the ones affected. Thus, lead poisoning has both a physical cause (ingesting lead-based paint) and a social one (being too poor to live in modern housing). Addressing the social cause by improving housing can prevent future lead poisoning from paint (Lohiya et al., 1996).

Cultural-Familial Factors Although the causes of mental retardation discussed so far can exert devastating effects on individuals and their families, they account for a minority of mental retardation cases (although they are responsible for most of the serious and profound ones). Most mild cases of mental retardation are considered to be cultural-familial in origin. As its name indicates, **cultural-familial retardation** results from a combination of environmental (cultural) and genetic (familial) factors. The most important of the cultural factors is poverty and its correlates—low socioeconomic class, poor parental education, unstimulating environment. Mild mental retardation is most often found in uneducated families in the lower social classes (Islam, Durkin, & Zaman, 1993; MacMillan & Reschly, 1998).

The argument for familial factors begins with the assumption that intelligence is a polygenic trait (the result of many genes interacting). If we accept this assumption, and most researchers do, then the random assortment of genes that occurs during mating should produce a few extreme cases (both low and high IQs), just as it does for height or for weight. In other words, some cases of mental retardation are simply the result of genetic bad luck.

There is considerable evidence that appears to support the notion that genetic factors play a role in intelligence (Bouchard, 1996; Steen, 1996). For example, studies of adopted children have found that their IQ scores correlate better with the educational levels and IQs of their biological mothers than with those of their foster mothers. This is true even when they have no contact with their biological mothers and are raised by foster parents from infancy. Although these findings suggest that intelligence has a genetic component, they are not unequivocal. Foster parents are carefully chosen by adoption agencies. Most have average or above-average intelligence. This lack of variability among foster parents will produce lower correlations between them and their adopted children than between natural parents (whose intelligence test scores vary more widely) and their biological children.

Because of this ambiguity, researchers put more weight on studies showing that twins raised apart from birth still have high concordance for intelligence (Bouchard & Propping, 1993). Again, however, the results are not entirely clear-cut. Separated twins are often raised by relatives who provide similar environments. It could be these environmental similarities, not genetics, that produce the high concordance. What is required is evidence that identical twins reared apart from birth in vastly different environments are still highly concordant for intelligence. Unfortunately, such cases are rare. The largest study of such twins, and the study showing the highest concordance for twins raised apart, was reported over a period of years by the British psychologist Cyril Burt (1883–1971). Unfortunately, Burt's data are suspect, and no one is sure how much credence to give them (Mackintosh, 1995; Tucker, 1997).

Even if Burt's data were beyond reproach, it would be wrong to conclude that environmental variables are unimportant. Once again, it is crucial to distinguish between phenotype and genotype. Our maximum potential height depends on our genetic endowment. How tall we *actually* grow depends on our health and diet. Intelligence is similar. Our maximum performance on intelligence tests may depend on our genes, but our environmental experiences strongly influence our actual scores. This crucial point is sometimes lost in discussions about the genetics of intelligence, as Highlight 11.1 makes clear. Given the interaction between heredity and environment and the ambiguities in the data, it is not possible to state how much of intelligence is the result of nature and how much is from nurture (N. Brody & Crowley, 1995).

It is worth noting that almost all of the evidence collected on the inheritance of intelligence has focused on intelligence test scores. Adaptive behavior has been largely ignored. Yet as we have seen, the *DSM-IV* identifies an individual's ability (or inability) to adapt to his or her circumstances as an essential criterion in defining mental retardation. We cannot simply assume that adaptive behavior is inherited in the same way as intelligence. The neglect of adaptive behavior is a major omission in the research on the heritability of intelligence.

LEARNING, MOTOR SKILLS, AND COMMUNICATION DISORDERS

As we saw in Documents 11.3 and 11.4, the outlook for Helen Lee was guarded. As she grew older, this pessimism was confirmed. In Grade 2, Helen's IQ was estimated to be 54. She had difficulty learning to read, write, and do mathematics. She also had difficulty communicating her needs, and her clumsiness made her poor at childhood games. Despite special classes and instruction, Helen's performance remained far behind that of other children of her age. Given their daughter's obvious problems, Debbie and Michael were surprised to learn that Helen did *not* have a learning, motor skills, or communication disorder, at least not as defined by the *DSM-IV*.

Origins

Since World War II, the increasing importance of a skilled workforce has resulted in a growing concern about students who fail to learn in school. This concern, coupled with 20th-century advances in medicine, psychology, and education, produced a new field of specialization—*learning disabilities*. These included difficulties in learning to read, to write, and to do mathematics, as well as various language and coordination problems.

Biology Is Not Quite Destiny

Adoption studies have been a major source of support for the heritability of intelligence. In such studies, children raised from birth by foster parents undergo intelligence testing, as do their biological and foster mothers. Data from a hypothetical adoption study are summarized in the table.

As you can see in the table, the correlation between the intelligence test scores of natural mothers and their biological children was calculated to be .90, whereas the correlation between adoptive mothers and their children was only .10. Because the correlation between biological mothers and their children was stronger than that between adoptive mothers and their children, these results seem to provide clear evidence in favor of the heritability of intelligence. Does this mean that the children resembled their biological mothers more than they did their adoptive ones? Hardly. The

mean intelligence test score of the children was 101, exactly the mean score of the foster mothers, and much higher than the mean score of the biological mothers (89). How can this be?

The answer lies in the way correlations are calculated. Correlations are rank-order statistics. Provided the biological mother with the highest intelligence test score has the child with the highest score, and the biological mother with the second highest score has the child with the second highest score, and so on, the correlation between biological mothers and

children will be high, even if every single child in the study has a higher IQ score than his or her natural mother (a frequent finding in adoption studies). Why should adopted children have higher IQs than their biological mothers? Probably because their foster families provide stimulating intellectual environments that allow them to reach their intellectual potential. Even studies that reveal strong evidence for the heritability of intelligence do not negate the importance of environment. When it comes to intelligence, biology is not destiny.

Hypothetical Adoption-Study Data

	Biological mother	Adoptive mother	Child
Parent-child IQ score correlations	.90	.10	Not applicable
Mean IQ score	89	101	101

Over time, the term *learning disabilities* gave way to a new term, *academic skills disorders*, which the *DSM-IV* renamed *learning disorders* (at the same time separating academic skills disorders from coordination and communication disorders). Apart from confusing the public, these name changes and subdivisions have accomplished little. They reflect nomenclature fads rather than scientific progress. In this chapter, *learning disabilities* is used as an umbrella term to include learning, motor skills, and communication disorders.

A good birth date for the field of learning disabilities is 1861, the year the French neurologist Paul Broca (1824–1880) first observed that language disorders are correlated with damage to the left cerebral hemisphere (Broca, 1861). Broca was one of the first people to report a connection between brain anatomy and a cognitive function. Shortly after Broca's discovery, Carl Wernicke (1848–1905) described several other brain sites involved in language functioning (Wernicke, 1874). Stim-

ulated by Broca's and Wernicke's work, researchers began to look for the brain defects responsible for other cognitive disabilities, and they were at least partly successful. For example, clinicians described several *alexias* (specific reading disabilities caused by brain damage). Figure 11.4 shows the areas of the brain associated with language and reading disorders.

By the early part of the 20th century, it was taken for granted that some form of brain damage was responsible for all learning disabilities, even when there was no evidence for brain damage other than the disability itself. For example, Hinshelwood (1917) argued that reading disorders were the result of a brain defect that makes it impossible for affected people to associate meaning with words. How did he reach this conclusion? Well, some people have trouble learning to read, so there must be something wrong with their brains. When autopsies of dyslexic (reading-disabled) people revealed no visible brain damage, clinicians did not abandon

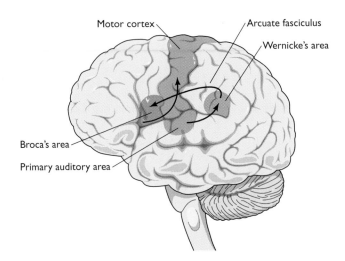

FIGURE 11.4 Areas of the Brain Associated With Language and Reading Disorders. *When a spoken word is heard, the auditory area of the cortex receives sensations, but the word is not understood until it is processed by Wernicke's area. A representation of the word is then transmitted through the arcuate fasciculus to Broca's area, where it is translated into a motor program. This program is supplied to the motor area of the cortex, which directs the speech apparatus to pronounce the word.*

their theory. Instead, they assumed that the damage was still present, but that it just was not visible on autopsy (Critchly & Critchly, 1978). Over the years, the brain damage underlying most learning disabilities remained elusive. As a consequence, learning disabilities progressively lost their connection with neurology. Educators and psychologists entered the field, shifting the emphasis from organic to behavioral and cognitive etiologies. However, as we shall see in Chapter 12, there is still some confusion about the role of brain damage in learning disabilities, particularly among children with attention-deficit disorder.

Diagnosis

According to the *DSM-IV,* learning, motor skills, and communication disorders are diagnosed when a person's performance in these areas is substantially below the level expected for the person's age, schooling, and intelligence. The *DSM-IV* defines the phrase "substantially below" as a discrepancy of more than two standard deviations between the person's performance on individually administered standardized tests of academic achievement and the person's IQ. This means that Helen, whose poor academic performance was consistent with her low IQ score, did not have a learning dis-

order, whereas people with high IQs who do poorly at school may have such disorders. (Highlight 11.2 looks at the potential for learning disorders in gifted children.) The *DSM-IV* diagnostic criteria for learning, motor skills, and communication disorders (which are summarized in Table 11.4) exclude people with vision, hearing, or other sensory deficits unless their disabilities are in excess of those associated with these deficits.

The logic of the *DSM-IV* diagnostic criteria rests on the assumption that it is possible to measure intellectual potential ("expected performance level") using IQ and other psychometric tests and that most children receive adequate instruction in reading, writing, and mathematics in the normal school curriculum. Both of these assumptions have been challenged, and some critics view the inclusion of learning disabilities in the *DSM-IV* as an attempt to overextend the range of mental disorders to include what are really educational problems (Naglieri & Reardon, 1993; see also Chapter 3).

Causes

Most learning disabilities, with the possible exception of mathematics disorder, affect boys more often than girls (Gross, Manor, & Shalev, 1996; Nass, 1993). In addition to brain damage and dysfunction, learning disabilities have many potential causes—early deprivation (emotional, cultural, or even sensory), genetics, emotional problems, inadequate schooling, or even growing up in a poor family (Ginsberg, 1997). A lack of motivation to learn, which is often a function of parental beliefs and cultural expectations, also influences whether children will display learning problems (Okagaki & Frensch, 1998). Once a child enters school, factors such as teacher expectations, poor teaching, and teaching methods can exert a strong influence.

Even among children raised in suboptimal environments, only a minority develop learning disabilities, suggesting that some children have a special psychological vulnerability that causes them to develop learning disabilities (Handwerk & Marshall, 1998). This vulnerability may extend to other mental disorders, explaining the high correlation between learning disabilities, depression, and adolescent suicide (Huntington & Bender, 1993; McBride & Siegel, 1997). Keep in mind, however, that these data are correlational, not causal. It is possible to turn the explanation around and hypothesize that having a learning disability is so frustrating and humiliating that it causes emotional problems and drives some people to suicide.

Smart People May Have Troubles, Too

It may seem a surprise to find "gifted" people discussed in a chapter devoted to intellectual and cognitive disorders. After all, gifted people are, by definition, superior in intellectual skills. Yet the 1975 Federal Education for All Handicapped Children Act specifically mentions gifted and talented children as groups needing special attention. These children were included in the Act because they often have special problems (Rimm, 1986). For example, Baumgarten (1930) studied children who could perform amazing feats at very young ages. One was a great chess master who could play 20 opponents simultaneously when he was only 8 years old. According to Baumgarten, such children often developed emotional problems because of their special abilities. This claim has been made many times since (Heehs, 1997).

One of the problems faced by those conducting research in this area is identifying who is actually gifted. The precocity of Baumgarten's children was an important cue to their special talents, but not all gifted people are precocious. Einstein supposedly did not speak until he was 4, nor read until he was 7, and Thomas Edison was considered mentally retarded by both his parents and his teachers (Holden, 1980). It seems as if some gifted individuals are easier to identify early in life than others. At present, the whole notion of "giftedness" is controversial (Benbow & Lubinski, 1996; Sternberg & Davidson, 1986). One problem is that the term is much too general. Few people are gifted in all areas; most shine in only a few. Sometimes a person can be gifted in one area and have a learning disorder in another (Brody & Mills, 1997).

The only large-scale attempt to study the development of gifted children remains Terman's famous longitudinal study, which began in the 1920s and continues to the present day (Vialle, 1994). Terman identified 1,528 California schoolchildren with IQ scores above 135. These children were interviewed, tested, and periodically reassessed over the years. Many became professionals, and most made more money than the national average. Despite the claims of Baumgarten and others, they were also *better* adjusted (according to their own reports) than the average population. Of course, there were a few "supergeniuses" in Terman's group, but no Einsteins, Tolstoys, or Beethovens. Perhaps it is only truly exceptional people who are at risk for mental disorders (see Nasar, 1998, for example). Despite years of study, there is still much we need to learn about how to nurture our most intellectually talented people (Friedman & Rogers, 1998).

TREATING MENTAL RETARDATION AND LEARNING DISABILITIES

At one time, it was common for people with mental retardation to be committed to large residential institutions (variously called hospitals or training schools). By today's standards, these institutions were dehumanizing, even horrifying. Some female residents were forcibly sterilized. In the middle of the 20th century, along with a general trend toward deinstitutionalization, mentally retarded people were transferred back to their homes and schools, and to community-based facilities for adults. The driving force was **normalization,** the idea that people with mental retardation should be helped to live as normal a life as possible—to work, make friends, even have families.

It was this same idea that led Debbie and Michael Lee to consult a plastic surgeon about Helen. They had heard that plastic surgeons could reconstruct the faces of people with Down syndrome. By making Down syndrome people look more "normal," surgery could increase their self-esteem and social "acceptability" (Katz, Kravetz, & Marks, 1997). Michael and Debbie considered the option of plastic surgery but decided not to proceed. Helen was already accepted by her peers, including her brother, and she seemed happy with herself. They feared that plastic surgery could have an effect opposite to the intended one—making her self-conscious about her appearance. They decided, instead, to find the best placement for Helen (the program that would allow her to develop to her maximum potential).

For some profoundly mentally retarded people, the best placement remains a residential institution. They cannot look after themselves and require too much care to be looked after by their families. For such people, institutions play a vital custodial role. Most institutions have also introduced behavior modification programs. Behavioral techniques such a "time out" (social isolation) are used to extinguish negative behaviors, such as aggression, whereas positive reinforcement is used to

DSM-IV   TABLE 11.4   *DSM-IV* Diagnostic Criteria for Learning, Motor Skills, and Communication Disorders

For each of the following disorders, the *DSM-IV* requires that the disturbance significantly interfere with academic or occupational achievement or some area of social life. Moreover, if mental retardation or a sensory defect is present (deafness, for example), then the disturbance must be greater than that usually associated with the condition.

DSM-IV disorder	Main clinical signs
Reading disorder	Below expected reading achievement.
Mathematics disorder	Below expected mathematics achievement.
Disorder of written expression	Below expected written communication skills.
Motor skills disorder	Below expected motor coordination skills; marked by delays in walking and other motor skills, clumsiness, and poor handwriting that is not due to a medical condition.
Expressive language disorder	Expressive language performance that is marked by poor vocabulary and poor verbal skills. Performance is substantially lower than expected based on nonverbal intellectual testing.
Mixed receptive-expressive language disorder	Difficulties in both expressing and understanding language.
Phonological disorder	Failure to use speech sounds appropriate for age and dialect (substitutions, pronunciation errors).
Stuttering	Fluency disturbances inappropriate to age. Marked by repetitions, prolongations, and blocking of speech.

teach new skills, such as toilet training. These behavior modification programs, combined with tranquilizing medications for agitated residents, have made these institutions far better places for the care of those with mental retardation than they were in the past. Still, they remain havens for those with no place else to go. Today, mentally retarded people who have learned at least some self-help skills are more likely to live at home or in community-based facilities than in institutions. Although home- and community-based programs vary in quality (Emerson & Hatton, 1996), most provide a better opportunity for individual development than could ever be provided in a large residential institution.

Most mentally retarded children live at home and attend a public school where they are educated in a normal classroom, in a special class, or a combination of both. Children with learning disabilities usually receive the same type of schooling as children who are mentally retarded do, although their respective educational goals may differ. For children with learning disabilities, the educational goal is for them to overcome their disorder (to learn to read, do mathematics, and so on). Similar educational goals may apply to mildly retarded children, whereas programs aimed at moderately retarded children focus mainly on self-help skills.

Collectively, the strategies used to help retarded and learning disabled children reach their goals are grouped together and referred to as **special education.** It is difficult to describe what special education is because it includes a heterogeneous group of techniques ranging from behavior modification to cognitive interventions and may also include medications (Delong,

Word-processing programs can provide scaffolds to help children with mental retardation or learning disabilities improve their written expression.

1995; Meltzer, 1993; Reid, Hresko, & Swanson, 1996; K. C. Williams, 1996). Special education seems to cycle through fads such as gentle teaching (Mudford, 1995), facilitated communication (Spitz, 1997), and sensory integration (Arendt et al., 1988). Each begins with great claims for its effectiveness, followed by disillusion when the new "breakthrough" turns out not to be a panacea.

One general approach that does seem to help children learn is called **scaffolding,** providing students with an assistive platform—or "scaffold"—on which to learn (Reid, 1998). Scaffolding strategies include teaching in novel ways so that students who would not learn well using the normal methods can perform at a higher level. For example, Helen Lee was taught some rudi-

mentary sign language to help her communicate with her parents and teachers. (Document 11.5 shows Helen's individualized education plan.) Research has shown that sign language provides a scaffold for students to learn other forms of communication (Powell & Clibbens, 1994). New "assistive technologies" are increasingly being used to provide a scaffold for learning. For example, the spell checkers and grammar checkers of computerized word-processing programs provide a scaffold for students who need help with their written expression. Similarly, speech synthesizers provide a scaffold for students with reading disorders, and talking calculators can assist students with mathematics disorder (Raskind & Higgins, 1998).

DOCUMENT 11.5

Helen Lee's Individual Education Plan

Individual Education Plan

(Initial)
Revised

Student's name: Helen Lee   **Date of birth:** January 4, 1962   **Sex:** (F) M

Grade: 2 plus special class

Race (circle): African American, Hispanic, (White,) Asian, Native American

---

Case manager: Mrs. Irene Reitman

Date of service initiation: September 4, 1969

Next diagnostic evaluation review: January 4, 1970

Parent or guardian: Debbie and Michael Lee   **Emergency contact:** Jenny Davis

Address: 12 Harpoon Hill, East Medina   **Address:** 13 Davies Crescent, Westwood

Telephone No.: 555-4546   **Telephone No.:** 555-9563

Disability or diagnosis: Down syndrome   Regular physical education? (Y) A

Special education services: Resource room   Extracurricular activities? (Y) A

Hours per week in regular education: 5   Y=Yes   A=Arrange

IEP Committee:

Parent: Debbie Lee

Nurse: Allison Hartley

Special Ed teacher: John Pyke

Instructional designer: Pam Davidson

Plan

Helen is a 7-year, 8-month-old girl with Down syndrome. She is physically independent, toilet trained, and able to feed herself. Her communication is rudimentary (mainly gestures), and she is not yet able to count. Her receptive language appears good, and she is social with her peers. She enjoys school, attends well, and plays with puzzles and toys.

<u>Academic Goals, Objectives, and Strategies</u>

Goal A. To increase communication skills

Objectives:
1. Helen will learn 10 new words per month.
2. Helen will learn to write the alphabet.
3. Helen will learn to write her name.

Strategies: Sign language training, in which Helen will be taught to sign certain key words, combined with simultaneous speech training (focusing on improving pronunciation). This will be followed by practice in letter-sound relationships.

Goal B. To increase numeracy skills

Objectives:
1. Helen will learn to count to 20.

Strategies: Use of counting blocks and counting games as practice.

One issue that has polarized professionals, parents, and politicians is whether children with mental retardation or learning disabilities should be taught in separate classes or whether they should be **mainstreamed**, placed in normal classes. Critical Thinking About Clinical Decisions 11.2 looks at the decision-making process Helen Lee's parents went through before reaching a compromise on the issue of mainstreaming. Students and parents are often ambivalent about whether they prefer segregation into special classes or integration into normal classes (Klingner et al., 1998). In special classes, students receive more individual attention, and they are not constantly comparing themselves (unfavorably) to quicker learners. On the other hand, the children in normal classes provide good role models for retarded and learning disabled children to imitate. Having mentally retarded and learning disabled children in their class also provides an opportunity for "normal" children to learn to accept "differences" among people and also to serve as mentors. This is important because there is still considerable community ignorance and prejudice about mental retardation. (Highlight 11.3 relates one example of the tragic results of such ignorance.) Given the pros and cons, the best option for most mentally retarded and learning disabled students is a flexible one, in which they receive segregated instruction where necessary and are integrated into normal classrooms where possible.

Primary and Secondary Prevention

Based on an examination of the case histories of 2,000 full-time residents of institutions for mentally retarded people, Stevenson and his colleagues (1996) estimated that, if all primary prevention strategies were used, the prevalence of severe and profound mental retardation could be reduced by 20%. These strategies include genetic screening and counseling, immunization, and the elimination of potential teratogenic agents, such as lead-based paint (Lennox & Kerr, 1997). There is also evidence that the severity of mental retardation, and of some learning disabilities, can be reduced through secondary prevention aimed at early intervention with children at risk. A good example is PKU. When appropriate dietary control is exercised, individuals with PKU can develop normally. For some at-risk children, early exposure to stimulation programs (such as Head Start) may improve school performance and social adaptation (Raver & Zigler, 1997; Zigler, 1995). Because mild mental retardation seems to occur most often in the lowest socioeconomic groups, efforts to understand and change the

Educating Helen

Although she was the correct age for Grade 2, Helen Lee still could not write or read. Yet her school advised her parents that she would attend a regular class. Debbie and Michael Lee were not sure that this was a good idea. Would Helen be able to learn in a regular class? Perhaps she would do better in a special class, where the teachers were trained to deal with mentally retarded children and where she would receive individual instruction. Decades ago, the question would not have arisen. Children with mental retardation and learning disorders were routinely segregated into special classes. In the 1970s, however, Congress, spurred on by court cases, passed laws that gave students with learning disabilities and mental retardation the right to study in the "least restrictive environment" according to their needs (Hayden, 1997). This has sometimes been interpreted to mean that, to the extent possible, children should be "mainstreamed" into normal classes.

Debbie and Michael went to see the school principal and guidance officer to voice their concerns. "There is no way that Helen could ever keep up with the mathematics and written expression lessons of a normal Grade 2 class, argued Debbie. The principal and the guidance officer agreed, but they stressed that Helen would still benefit from "inclusion."

"Education has a broader purpose than simply learning to read, write, and do arithmetic," said the principal. "It also serves social needs. By being in a normal class, Helen will learn to model the behavior of the other children, and they will learn to accept people like her who are different. Mainstreaming is best for *all* children. It teaches them important lessons."

Debbie and Michael understood the argument, and they wanted people to accept their daughter. But they were still concerned. Helen was a placid child who would probably not cause problems in the classroom, but would she actually learn? And would normal classroom teachers, who have not been trained in special education, be able to cope with her special needs? The guidance counselor responded by explaining that the school employed consultant teachers and teaching assistants just for this purpose.

Michael was still worried. In his reading, he had come across many educational fads. Was it possible that mainstreaming was just another one? In addition, the young couple who lived next door to the Lees had recently moved their children into a private school because they believed that their education was being slowed down by the retarded children in their classes. The principal acknowledged that this happens but suggested that such cases are rare. Most parents do not remove their children. Michael was unconvinced. Perhaps most parents simply cannot afford private schools.

Michael and Debbie eventually came to a compromise with the principal and guidance counselor. They devised an Individual Education Plan for Helen (see Document 11.5). She will spend part of her school day in a normal class but only for physical education, art, and music. She will spend the rest of the day participating in special programs tailored to her needs and abilities. These programs, which will be conducted by specially trained teachers, will focus on communication and basic self-help skills. As Helen improves her academic skills, she will gradually spend more time in normal classes and less time in special ones. In this way, Helen will get the best of both worlds—exposure to normal role models and a chance to get the individual instruction she needs to reach her potential.

dynamics of poverty may reduce the incidence of mental retardation (McDermott & Altekruse, 1994). On the other hand, if people with mental retardation "drift" down the social-class ladder (that is, poverty is the result rather than the cause of mental retardation), then reducing poverty may not affect the prevalence of mental retardation.

Tertiary Prevention

As mentally retarded and learning disabled people get older, the main challenge is to prevent deterioration and to maintain their independent quality of life at as high a level as possible (Rogers, Hawkins, & Eklund, 1998). This goal requires tertiary prevention strategies and a different focus from school programs. Postschool living requires practical skills, such as those needed to go grocery shopping (Morse, Schuster, & Sandknop, 1996). With training in such skills, most mildly retarded adults are able to live independently or in group homes, where they share the responsibilities of daily living with other disabled people (Turner, 1996).

Of course, there is more to life than self-care and grocery shopping. A fulfilling life also requires something meaningful to do. Employment in specially de-

Justice for All?

The police radio blares out the bare facts. An old lady has been raped and beaten to death. Police immediately arrest a relative, Richard Lapointe, a "mentally retarded" man who seems too interested in the details of the crime. Lapointe is taken to the police station and persuaded to waive his rights to silence and to legal representation. After being questioned all night, he signs a confession. Lapointe later disowns the confession, but the jury votes to convict him anyway.

This may sound like an unusual case, but it is all too usual (Pelka, 1997). There are many people with mental retardation currently serving time in prison for capital offenses. Some are almost certainly innocent; others had little understanding of the moral nature of their acts. In both cases, the criminal justice system seems to have treated mentally retarded people differently from nonretarded ones.

Let us return to the case of Richard Lapointe, who was convicted of the rape and murder of his wife's grandmother (see Pelka, 1997, for details). The only evidence against Lapointe was a confession written by the police and signed by Lapointe after a night of questioning. Lapointe waived his rights to self-incrimination and declined to have a lawyer, but it is not clear that he understood either of these rights. Although Lapointe has an IQ score of 92 (above the cutoff for mental retardation), he had a very low level of social adaptation. He also had poor eyesight and partial deafness. Lapointe lived with a tube surgically implanted into his skull to remove excess brain fluid. As a consequence, he was relatively weak. Yet he was convicted of a crime in which the victim was tied around the neck and wrists with strips of torn clothing, sexually assaulted, stabbed, and then burned when the killer set fire to her apartment.

To obtain Lapointe's confession, the police interrogators lied to him. They introduced themselves as "detectives" Friday and Gannon and claimed to be part of a special "task force" investigating the murder. Detective Friday told Lapointe that his fingerprints were found on the murder weapon. They showed him fake evidence that they claimed proved him to be the killer. The detectives told him that, if he did not confess, he would lose his children. There is no law against police lying to suspects, but someone of higher intelligence would not have been so easily deceived. Most of us would be suspicious when faced with detectives whose names come straight from *Drag-net*, but Lapointe did not get the joke. Lapointe agreed to sign a confession in return for being allowed to use the bathroom. He later withdrew that confession but, over the course of the night, was convinced to sign another. Lapointe trusted the police and wanted to please them. Instead, they deceived him into confessing to a crime that he probably did not commit.

To end such potential abuses, civil rights advocates recommend that police interrogations be videotaped. These tapes will provide juries with access to the process by which a confession is obtained, not just the police-authored end product. When tissue samples are available from crime scenes, DNA testing will also help courts to avoid convicting innocent people. Most important of all is the need to teach lawyers and judges about mental retardation. Even educated people equate mental retardation with Down syndrome. Juries find it hard to believe that people who look "normal" and whose IQs are close to average may still be mentally retarded. Lapointe was convicted, at least in part, because the jury did not believe that he was really mentally retarded.

---

signed workplaces (sheltered workshops) was once the only work option available to mentally retarded adults. Although they were better than nothing, jobs in sheltered employment rarely led to jobs in the wider economy (S. Katz, 1994). With the advent of federal laws making it illegal to discriminate against disabled people (including those who are mentally disabled), many people with mental retardation were able to find employment in private enterprise and the civil service (L. Harris and Associates, 1994). To make these jobs available, it is sometimes necessary to remove impediments from the workplace. For example, mentally retarded and learning disabled workers often require special nondistracting physical environments and tailored hours of work. In some cases, they need assistive technology, such as speech synthesizers, to help in reading. Making these adjustments and providing this technology has opened the world of work to many people who were formerly excluded. As opposed to sheltered work, **supported employment** initiatives increase the self-esteem of retarded people and raise their levels of job satisfaction and productivity (Wehman, Revell, & Kregel, 1991). The success of supported employment programs is evidence that, with the provision of an adequate foundation,

Supported employment in regular workplaces, such as bagging groceries at a supermarket, is preferable to sheltered workshops because it increases the self-esteem and productivity of people with mental retardation and learning disabilities.

mentally retarded people can lead fulfilling lives (Pueschel & Sustrova, 1997; Szymanski & Stark, 1996).

Helen Lee: An Adult With Mental Retardation

Helen Lee was one of the luckier people with Down syndrome. Although she had a slow start, her devoted parents and her cooperative school provided her with an environment that allowed her to learn to her full potential. By the time she left school, she was not only able to communicate verbally but she could also do simple math problems and read at a third-grade level. These skills, and her pleasant personality, helped her to find assisted employment in a home for older people. Helen's job was to help prepare meals for the residents and clean up afterward. She lived with her parents until she was 29 and then moved into a group home with three other disabled women. She lived in a town about 25 miles from her family home.

Michael and Debbie were pleased with Helen's accomplishments and grateful that she had achieved a good quality of life. Imagine their concern, therefore, when they received an unexpected report from Helen's supervisor at work. This report (which appears in Document 11.6) suggested that Helen's functioning was deteriorating. Michael and Debbie arranged to have their daughter examined by a neuropsychologist and a neurologist. The result confirmed their worst fears. Despite her young age, Helen seemed to be developing the degenerative brain disorder known as **dementia of the Alzheimer's type (DAT),** a disorder that is particularly common (and occurs heartbreakingly early) among peo-

ple with Down syndrome (Lendon, Ashall, & Goate, 1997; Schupf et al., 1998; Visser et al., 1997). Michael and Debbie realized that their life with Helen was going to take a new turn. They would now have to confront not only mental retardation, but also the cognitive disorder known as dementia.

DOCUMENT 11.6

Letter From Helen's Supervisor to Her Parents

Dear Mr. and Mrs. Lee,

I am writing to you out of concern for your daughter, Helen. As you know, I have supervised Helen for many years and have come to think of her as like my own child. That is why I am so worried. She seems not to be the same person she once was.

Just the other day, I asked Helen to pick up some empty trays from the lounge. She said she would and walked over to the lounge. But when she got there, she could not recall what she was supposed to do. I found her just sitting on a chair staring at the wall. This has happened a few times in recent weeks. Once, Helen went out to collect the mail and just kept on walking down the street. When we shouted for her to return, she seemed not to know who we were.

She is not only forgetful but also moody, not like her normal self. I am afraid that something is wrong and hope that you will not think me forward, but I think she needs to see a doctor.

Yours truly,

Bev Lingard ■

DEMENTIA AND THE OTHER COGNITIVE DISORDERS

By robbing people of their memories, cognitive disorders disconnect sufferers from their own lives and from the lives of their loved ones. Sufferers are caught in the present moment, unable to relate to the past or to plan for the future. The *DSM-IV* contains three main cognitive disorders: **delirium, dementia,** and **amnestic disorders** (Table 11.5). Each is characterized by a cognitive or memory deficit that represents a significant change from the person's previous level of functioning. Cognitive disorders, which are always the result of neurological dysfunction, are traceable to one of three possible causes: a general medical condition, a substance (drug or toxin), or a combination of both. By far the most common cognitive disorder is the one affecting Helen, namely dementia.

DSM-IV	TABLE 11.5	Main *DSM-IV* Cognitive Disorders

Dementia: Multiple cognitive deficits including forgetfulness, disorientation, concrete thinking, and perseveration (repetitive speech or movements).

Delirium: Cloudy consciousness accompanied by disorientation, memory deficits, perceptual disturbances such as hallucinations, and language deficits.

Amnestic disorders: Loss of past memories or an inability to learn new information.

For most of history, dementia (the technical name for what most people call senility) was considered to be rare, probably because people did not live long enough to develop it. As recently as the 1800s, the average life expectancy was about 45 years. Today, most residents of the developed world can expect to live well into their 70s and even into their 80s or 90s. As the number of older people increases, so does the prevalence of dementia. Far from being rare, dementia has become a major health problem.

The modern concept of dementia can be traced back to Phillipe Pinel, who first described a condition he called *demènce* in the 18th century. Sufferers experienced a gradual deterioration in cognitive functioning, similar to the one Kraepelin ascribed to dementia praecox (see Chapter 9), although Pinel's *demènce* began in adulthood rather than childhood. Pinel's student, Jean Esquirol (1772–1840), carried on his teacher's work, describing dementia as a brain disorder characterized by impaired reasoning, loss of memory, and difficulties in focusing attention (Esquirol, 1832). Esquirol differentiated three forms of dementia: acute, chronic, and senile. Acute dementia, the result of fever or hemorrhage, was curable. Once the fever was cooled or the bleeding staunched, the dementia disappeared. Today, this type of dementia would be called delirium (a condition discussed later in this chapter). Esquirol believed that chronic dementia was the result of either drunkenness or masturbation and was seldom cured. Senile dementia began in old age (*senium* is the Latin word for frail old age). It is the most similar of the forms to the modern *DSM-IV* concept. In Esquirol's own words, "Senile dementia . . . commences with feebleness of memory, particularly recent memory; attention . . . becomes impossible; the will is uncertain, the movements are slow" (quoted in Mahendra, 1988, p. 9).

Dementia can occur at any age. Helen, and other people with Down syndrome, may develop symptoms in their 30s and 40s, but the condition is most common among older people. As you can see from Document 11.7, the diagnosis of dementia is usually based on observable signs and symptoms as well as psychological and neu-

ropsychological tests. Increasingly, modern brain imaging techniques are also used as diagnostic aids. These techniques are the subject of Highlight 11.4 (pp. 488–489).

DOCUMENT 11.7

Psychological Assessment of Helen Lee

Date: November 5, 1997

Client: Helen Lee; DOB: January 4, 1962

Tests Administered
Mini Mental Status Examination (11/4/97)
Wechsler Memory Scale–Revised (11/4/97)
Wechsler Adult Intelligence Scale-III (11/4/97)
Halstead-Reitan Neuropsychological Battery (11/4/97)

Psychologist: Dr. Stuart Berg

Reason for Referral: The client, Helen Lee, was referred for psychological assessment. Helen, who has Down syndrome, has been increasingly forgetful and seems to have lost some cognitive skills. For example, she could previously count to at least 20, whereas now she has trouble counting at all. She has had to leave work and now even seems to be losing self-help skills that she formerly had. When left unsupervised, she often wanders off.

Behavioral Observations: Helen's blouse half hung out of her skirt, her hair was disheveled, and she was unsteady on her feet. During the testing session, her hand had a slight tremor, and she struggled to find the right words to express herself. In response to a general enquiry ("How are you feeling?") Helen said that she was "sad." Her parents, who accompanied her, denied ever having heard her say she was sad before. During assessment, Helen referred to me several times as "father."

History: [Please see case file.]

Assessment: Helen was not able to answer correctly any of the questions on the Mini Mental Status Examination. When questioned about the date, she was off by 2 years. She was unable to recall the names of three objects after 5 minutes, and she failed to recognize the president's name. It also proved impossible to administer the intelligence test and most of the memory scale because Helen was unable to concentrate long enough to respond. She could not learn new associations, nor could she perform the digit-symbol subtest. She had trouble even copying symbols. Helen had difficulty naming common objects and, at one point, referred to a radio as an oven. She could write only a few letters and could not perform any planning task. When given a clock face and asked to fill in the numbers, she omitted most, and those she included she put in the wrong place.

Diagnostic Considerations: The client seems to meet the *DSM-IV* diagnostic criteria for dementia. There are no signs of hallucinations or delusions nor of the confusion that is characteristic of delirium. Her cognitive ability seems to have gradually deteriorated from previous levels, to the extent that her social adaptation is now impaired. She has clumsy movements, misrecognizes common objects, and is unable to learn new material. She also seems to be depressed, a common finding in people with dementia. Because of its association with Down syndrome, Helen's dementia is most likely to be of the Alzheimer's type.

Diagnosis

Axis I: Dementia, probably of the Alzheimer's type (with early onset and depressed mood)

Axis II: Mental retardation (Down syndrome)

Axis III: (general medical conditions): Heart disease

Axis IV (psychosocial stress): Problems in accessing medical services

Axis V: Highest level of adaptive functioning in past year: 40; current functioning: 30 ■

DIAGNOSING DEMENTIA

The *DSM-IV* process for diagnosing dementia is depicted schematically in Figure 11.5. It consists of four steps (see also Weiner, 1996). First, the clinician must confirm that the person suffers from multiple cognitive deficits. The *DSM-IV* requires that these include a memory impairment and one or more of the following symptoms: **aphasia** (a language disorder usually associated with damage to the left cerebral hemisphere), **agnosia** (a failure to recognize familiar objects despite normal vision, touch, and hearing), **apraxia** (an inability to carry out desired motor actions despite normal muscle control—for example, an inability to dress oneself), or a disturbance in executive functioning (planning, organizing, or sequencing). Sometimes these symptoms can appear quite strange. One patient with visual agnosia attempted to put his wife on his head because he mistook her for his hat (Sacks, 1998).

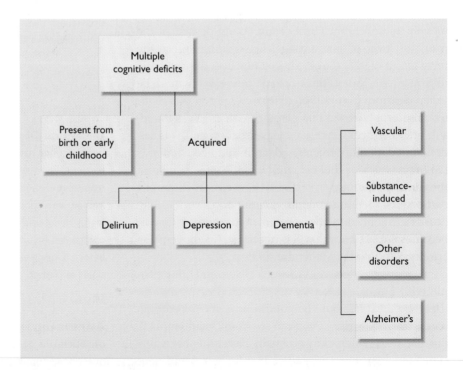

FIGURE 11.5 **Decision Tree for Diagnosing Cognitive Dementia**

DSM-IV   TABLE 11.6   Main *DSM-IV* Diagnostic Criteria for Delirium

A. Disturbance of consciousness (i.e., reduced clarity of awareness of the environment) with reduced ability to focus, sustain, or shift attention.

B. A change in cognition (such as memory deficit, disorientation, language disturbance) or the development of a perceptual disturbance that is not better accounted for by a preexisting, established, or evolving dementia.

C. The disturbance develops over a short period of time (usually hours to days) and tends to fluctuate during the course of the day.

D. There is evidence from the history, physical examination, or laboratory findings that the disturbance is caused by the direct physiological consequences of a general medical condition.

Note: From American Psychiatric Association (1994, p. 129).

Assessing cognitive deficits can be difficult in older people because they often tire easily. In most cases, their performance on cognitive tests is slower than that of younger people (Birren & Fisher, 1995). They will be penalized on "timed" tests but perform well on untimed ones (Poon & Siegler, 1991). Thus, depending on which tests are used, older people can appear cognitively impaired or normal (Butters, Delis, & Lucas, 1995). No matter which tests are used, it is crucial that clinicians be culturally sensitive. For example, in Western countries, people who do not know their birth date are almost certainly cognitively impaired. In cultures where birthdays are not celebrated, however, not knowing one's birthday may be perfectly normal. According to the *DSM-IV*, cognitive deficits are signs of dementia only when they impair social and occupational functioning. This criterion introduces another cultural element into the diagnostic process. Cultures that honor older people (the Chinese, for example), may tolerate cognitive impairments that our own society would consider debilitating.

The second step in diagnosing dementia requires the clinician to determine, on the basis of a client's family and medical history, whether the observed cognitive deficits are lifelong or acquired. By definition, dementia is acquired. People who have always been cognitively impaired, such as those with mental retardation, are excluded (unless, like Helen, they show signs of deterioration). Determining whether cognitive functioning has deteriorated is not always easy because self-reports are often unreliable (D. W. O'Connor et al., 1990). Some older people complain about their poor memories even though testing reveals few, if any, memory deficits (Benedict & Nacoste, 1990). Others never complain about their poor memories even though they have serious memory deficits. Determining whether cognitive skills have deteriorated requires an accurate informant who has known the client for some time.

Once the clinician has determined that a person has acquired multiple cognitive deficits, the third step in the diagnostic process is to rule out conditions that are superficially similar to dementia. The two most likely alternatives are delirium and depression.

Ruling Out Delirium and Depression

Delirium is a cognitive disorder marked by a "clouding" of consciousness most often found among older people (Lindesay, Macdonald, & Starke, 1990). It develops rapidly (within a few hours or days) and is present in 10–15% of emergency room patients (I. R. Katz, 1993). While delirious, patients seem to be unaware of where they are or what is going on around them. They have difficulty focusing, sustaining, or shifting attention; their memories may be poor; they may lose track of the day or even the month; their language may be rambling and incoherent; and they may have hallucinations and delusions. People who become delirious during the night have been known to pull off their bedclothes, claiming that their sheets are crawling with bugs. Hospitalized delirious patients have pulled catheters out of their arms and disconnected respirators that they need in order to breathe. In addition to showing cognitive symptoms, delirious people are often anxious, fearful, and irritable (Lipowski, 1990; Tune & Ross, 1994). The main *DSM-IV* diagnostic criteria for delirium are summarized in Table 11.6. In addition, there are several etiology-specific subtypes: delirium due to a general medical condition, substance intoxication delirium, substance withdrawal delirium, and delirium due to multiple etiologies.

Delirium has numerous causes: brain tumors, blows to the head, systemic diseases such as AIDS (Wise & Brandt, 1992), and intoxication with prescription (or illicit) drugs (Hobson, 1994; Hooten & Pearlson, 1996).

Seeing Inside the Brain

Until relatively recently, the only way to examine an individual's nervous system was to wait for the person to die and do an autopsy. Today, thanks to brain imaging technology, scientists can examine the structure and function of the living brain with minimal disturbance to the individual being studied (Bigler, 1997). One of the most widely used imaging techniques is **computerized tomography,** better known as **CT,** scanning (Lee, Rao, & Zimmerman, 1992). To perform a CT scan, multiple X-ray beams are revolved around the head. Transmitted radiation is computer analyzed to produce a cross-sectional image of the brain. Although CT scans do not produce clear pictures of brain tissue, they can show the outlines of certain structures, such as the brain's ventricles.

An imaging technique that is having an enormous impact on research is **magnetic resonance imaging,** or **MRI** (Lee et al., 1992; Sunaert et al., 1998). In MRI, powerful magnetic fields are used to attract the protons found in the nuclei of the body's hydrogen atoms. The protons are forced to change their alignment, giving off radio transmissions that are translated into images of the brain. The clarity of these pictures depends on the strength of the magnetic fields. Strong magnets can produce images that are almost as clear as photographs of brains taken at autopsy.

MRI provides a picture of brain *structure.* To answer questions about brain

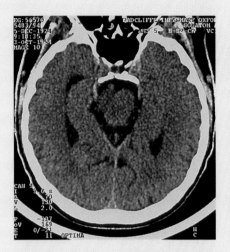

CT (computerized tomography) uses X rays to show brain structure in "slices." At the top of this axial (horizontal) scan of the healthy brain of a 70-year-old person is the front of the brain. The central dark areas are the ventricles, the inner cavities of the brain. The circular area at the upper center is the brainstem.

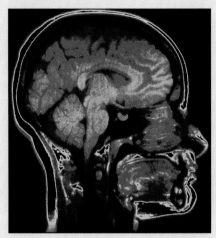

MRI (magnetic resonance imaging) is another way to show brain structure. This computer-enhanced MRI scan shows a normal brain with the pituitary singled out in green.

function (for example, which parts of the brain process different types of cognitive stimuli?) requires some way of imaging brain *fuction.* Functional MRI (fMRI) has developed for this purpose. It is a way of helping us see which parts of the brain are activated when we process information. The technique capitalizes on the increased blood flow produced by brain metabolism. Blood flows to activated parts of the brain. This produces magnetic signals that can be read by MRI. The result is a map of brain activity.

Positron emission tomography, or **PET,** scans can also reveal brain function (Frost & Wagner, 1990). The process begins with the administration of a radioactive form of the sugar glucose. Active brain cells metabolize the glucose, releasing radiation that is detected by the PET scanner. The result is an image of the metabolic activity in different parts of the brain. When people are required to perform certain cognitive tasks and the resulting radiation pattern is recorded, PET scans allow researchers to identify

---

Giving up a drug or substance (substance withdrawal) can also trigger an episode, especially among habitual drug users. **Delirium tremens,** for example, occurs when alcohol is withdrawn from habitual drinkers. In addition to these immediate causes, there are several psychological and social factors that can facilitate the development of delirium. These include severe stress, sleep deprivation, sensory deprivation (as in solitary confinement), and forced immobilization (as in patients being treated for serious burns; Lipowski, 1990). The appropriate treatment for delirium depends on the cause. If delirium is caused by a general medical condition, treatment focuses on curing the condition. If delirium is the result of substance abuse or withdrawal, then it is treated by either gradually withdrawing the substance or substituting another, less harmful one. Delir-

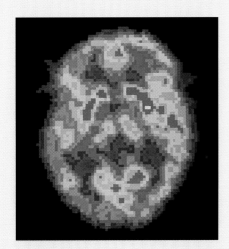

PET (positron emission tomography) scans use a radioactive tracer injected into the blood to show metabolic activity in the brain, such as that during normal sleep.

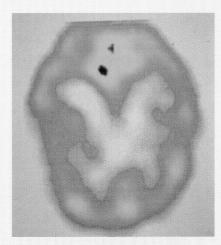

SPECT (single photon emission computed tomography) scans use a radioactive tracer and a rotating gamma camera to show brain activity. This axial section through the brain of a healthy 72-year-old person was taken above the level of the basal ganglia. The front of the brain is at the top. Blood flow appears as yellow and peach areas, highlighting brain activity. The white region in the center has low activity and corresponds to the ventricles.

lated. This is known as an event-related potential, or ERP. By recording ERPs from various sites on the head simultaneously, researchers can construct a topographic map that represents the electrical activity in various parts of the brain (Brunia, Mulder, & Verbaten, 1991). Comparisons of the topographic maps produced by people with different cognitive disorders can identify differences in information processing. Topographic maps may also be constructed using a technique called **single photon emission computerized tomography (SPECT)**. Like fMRI, SPECT scans monitor blood flow while people perform cognitive tasks (K. A. Johnson et al., 1998; Read et al., 1995). Because the active parts of the brain use more blood, changes in blood flow indicate which parts of the brain are active. By recording blood flow from different areas of the brain, researchers can produce a topographic map of brain activity during cognition. This technique provides similar information to fMRI.

the parts of the brain that are associated with different forms of mental activity (Tagamets & Horwitz, 1998). It is like "seeing" people think.

PET scans have serious drawbacks. Because they use radioactive materials and require considerable staff time, they are expensive; safety regulations limit individuals to one scan a year; and no woman of childbearing age may be

tested. For these reasons, researchers have turned to electroencephalographic (EEG) methods as a safer and cheaper alternative (Barcelo & Gale, 1997). EEGs are recordings of brain electrical activity made from the scalp (or directly from within the brain). By recording EEGs after the presentation of a stimulus (a flash of light, say, or a tone), the brain's electrical response to the stimulus can be iso-

ium normally disappears once its cause is identified and eliminated (Lipowski, 1990).

Although the two disorders share some symptoms, delirium can usually be differentiated from dementia by its rapid onset, short duration, alternating lucid intervals, the presence of hallucinations and delusions, and its minimal long-term effect on personality (Table 11.7). Keep in mind, however, that none of these differences is

absolute. For example, although they are more common in delirium, hallucinations and delusions are also found in 20% of dementia cases (Bolger, Carpenter, & Strauss, 1994). Moreover, it is possible to be delirious and also suffer from dementia, so a definitive diagnosis may not be possible until the delirium has cleared.

Ruling out depression as a cause of cognitive impairment is more difficult than ruling out delirium. Not

TABLE 11.7	Distinguishing Delirium From Dementia	
Characteristic	**Delirium**	**Dementia**
Onset	Rapid	Gradual
Duration	Short	Long
Degree of cognitive impairment	Varies, with some lucid intervals	Severe most of the time
Personality	Intact	Disorganized
Hallucinations	Active	Vague or none
Delusions	Prominent, especially of persecution	Vague or none
Affect	Anxious and fearful	Apathetic and unemotional

only are the symptoms of depression and dementia similar, but both conditions tend to co-occur among older people and those with Down syndrome (Sung et al., 1997). Some depressed people behave quite like people with dementia. They withdraw from their normal activities, lose interest in everyday life, and have difficulty concentrating or sleeping. In addition, their speech is confused and slow. The diagnosis of **pseudodementia** has been applied to people who show all the signs of dementia but are really suffering from depression.

Despite their similarities, there are important differences between dementia and depression. Depressive episodes have at least a vague beginning and an end, whereas dementia develops too gradually to pinpoint a date. Depressed people are aware of and complain about their cognitive functioning, and most respond to antidepressant medication. Neither of these is true of people with dementia (at least not in its later stages). There may also be subtle differences in the clinical presentation of depression and dementia. For instance, the symptoms of depression are usually worse in the morning, whereas dementia symptoms become more obvious late in the day when the person is tired (Heston & White, 1991). Using these various signs, it is possible for clinicians to separate pseudodementia from dementia. Keep in mind, however, that it is common to be like Helen—both depressed and suffering from dementia (Huppert, Brayne, & O'Connor, 1994).

Identifying the Subtype

Once a clinician has established that a client has acquired cognitive deficiencies that cannot be entirely accounted for by delirium or depression, the next step is to assign the dementia to one of the dementia subtypes: vascular, substance-induced, dementia due to general medical conditions, or dementia of the Alzheimer's type.

Vascular Dementia **Vascular dementia** (previously known as multi-infarct dementia) accounts for approximately 20% of dementia cases (Henderson, 1994). The lifetime risk of vascular dementia is 4.7% for men and 3.8% for women (Hagnell et al., 1992). The cause of vascular dementia is an interruption in blood supply to part of the brain, a condition known as a **stroke.** Typically, a stroke is caused by a blood clot in one of the brain's blood vessels. This "infarct" cuts off the supply of blood to the surrounding neural tissue. In some cases, the brain's blood supply is gradually reduced by arteriosclerosis, a generic name for any condition that causes blood vessels to become narrowed. In a few cases, blood vessels may burst. Whatever the cause, the result is the same. Neural tissue dies because of a lack of oxygen and nutrients. Unless there are numerous infarcts, widespread arteriosclerosis, or damage to large blood vessels, vascular dementia usually affects only a small part of the brain. The affected part may be visualized using modern imaging techniques (which were described in Highlight 11.4). When such tests are unavailable or their results equivocal, it may still be possible to localize brain damage using clinical signs and neuropsychological tests (McPherson, 1996; Reynolds, 1994). For example, vascular brain damage is usually localized to one side of the brain, so symptoms such as perceptual and movement disorders are often limited to one side of the body. Vascular dementia is associated with hypertension, diabetes, and smoking (Skoog, 1994).

Substance–Induced Persisting Dementia When there is evidence that the symptoms of dementia are related to drugs or poisons, the correct *DSM-IV* diagnosis is **substance-induced persisting dementia.** The word *persisting* is included to show that the dementia continues even after the substance is withdrawn. The list of substances that can cause dementia is endless—drugs (both

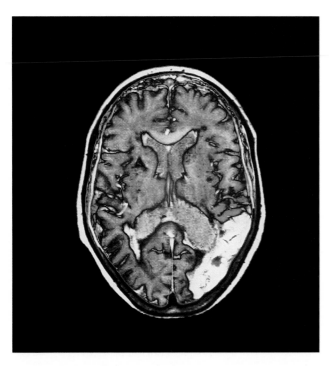

An MRI can show the location of vascular brain damage caused by a stroke. Here the hemorrhaged area of the stroke is the white area located in an occipital lobe of the cerebrum.

while, these symptoms are accompanied by a stooped posture, slow body movements, and a characteristic speech pattern in which the person speaks only in a soft monotone. Although dementia is not a necessary accompaniment of Parkinson's disease, approximately one third of people with Parkinson's develop a **subcortical dementia** (Biggins et al., 1992; Cummings, 1990). The symptoms of subcortical dementia consist mainly of psychomotor slowness and a memory defect (Whitehouse, Friedland, & Strauss, 1992). In common with most other types of dementia, depression frequently accompanies Parkinson's disease (Nagatsu et al., 1991).

Parkinson's disease is rarely diagnosed before age 50, but there are some famous exceptions, such as the actor Michael J. Fox, who began experiencing symptoms in his 30s. The lifetime risk is less than 0.1% and slightly more men than women are affected (Rao, Huber, & Bornstein, 1992). Parkinson's disease is more common in northern states than in the South, although the significance of this geographic difference is unknown (Malaspina, Quit Kin, & Kaufmann, 1994). Although some cases of Parkinson's are preceded by infections or blows to the head (as in the boxer, Muhammed Ali),

legal and illicit), alcohol, inhalants, lead, mercury, carbon monoxide, insecticides, and solvents. All act by destroying brain tissue or disrupting brain metabolism. Perhaps the most common cause of substance-induced dementia is alcohol abuse. An excessive intake of alcohol leads people to neglect their diets, which, in turn, produces cognitive disorders. Because alcohol is mainly associated with memory disorders (D. M. Smith & Atkinson, 1997), it is discussed in more detail later in this chapter in the section on amnestic disorders.

Dementia Due to Medical Conditions   Dementia is the potential result of a large variety of medical conditions. The *DSM-IV* singles out the following, most common, ones for special attention.

Parkinson's Disease   Parkinson's disease was mentioned in Chapter 9 in connection with the dopamine theory of schizophrenia. In **Parkinson's disease,** some of the brain's dopamine-producing cells spontaneously die (Nagatsu, Narabayashi, & Yoshida, 1991). The result is an undersupply of dopamine, which disrupts activity in parts of the brain that rely on dopamine. One such area is the basal ganglia, which play an important role in controlling motor behavior. As a result, people with Parkinson's disease develop tremors, rigid muscles, and difficulty initiating or stopping movements. After a

Usually, Parkinson's disease develops after people are 50. Michael J. Fox, who experienced his first symptoms when he was 30, is an exception. He has had brain surgery to reduce the stiffness and tremors on his left side.

Folksinger Woody Guthrie ("This Land Is Your Land") died in 1967 from Huntington's chorea. His children, including folksinger Arlo Guthrie, had a 50% chance of developing the disease but have fortunately escaped the disorder.

most cases are of unknown origin. Parkinson's disease may be treated with L-dopa (levodopa), a drug that enhances the production of dopamine. Although L-dopa may provide temporary relief from some troubling symptoms of Parkinson's disease, it can also produce symptoms similar to those of schizophrenia. If Parkinson's patients develop psychoses, they cannot be treated with most antipsychotic medications because these drugs worsen their motor symptoms (Musser & Akil, 1996). Researchers are guardedly optimistic that Parkinson's disease may soon be cured by transplanting normal dopamine-producing neural tissue into patients' brains (Koller & Paulson, 1995).

Pick's Disease   **Pick's disease** is named after Arnold Pick (1851–1924), an early investigator of aphasia (Pasquier & Petit, 1997). It is caused by the atrophy of the frontal and temporal lobes of the brain (Kertesz, 1996). In addition to the cognitive impairments usually associated with dementia, patients with Pick's disease also display the characteristic signs of frontal lobe damage, especially **disinhibition** (an inability to inhibit impulses; Mapou & Spector, 1995). Disinhibited people are sexually aggressive, socially tactless, and impulsive

(Mendez et al., 1993). The cause of Pick's disease, which first appears in people aged 40 or over, is unknown.

Huntington's Disease   First described by George Huntington (1850–1916), Huntington's disease is a form of **chorea** (a Greek word meaning "dance" but which refers today to brain syndromes that include irregular, jerky movements). Huntington's results from the progressive degeneration of the basal ganglia, a part of the brain involved in controlling movements and other functions (Harper, 1991). The first signs are a mild memory impairment, an inability to concentrate, and depression. Next come personality changes; sufferers become irritable and erratic. As the disease progresses, cognitive impairments become more noticeable (Savage, 1997). Sufferers may have paranoid delusions, especially the belief that they are being persecuted. Some act out on these beliefs by resorting to violence. Initially, Huntington's disease may be mistaken for schizophrenia, but as the condition progresses, the syndrome becomes unmistakable (there is no chorea in schizophrenia). Death occurs 10 to 20 years after the first symptoms appear.

The lifetime risk of Huntington's disease is less than 0.007%. Symptoms almost always appear by the age of

40. The condition seems to affect mainly people of European extraction; there are no reported cases among native Australian Aborigines or the Eskimos of North America, although the shorter life expectancies in these populations may mean that people are dying before the disease becomes manifest (Morris & Harper, 1991). Huntington's disease is caused by a single dominant gene (Gusella et al., 1993). Although the disease may be passed on by a child's mother or father, early-onset Huntington's disease is associated with inheritance from the father. This is one of very few cases in which the parental origin of a gene seems to affect the gene's expression (Rose, 1995). There is no cure for Huntington's, but carriers can be tested and may decide to forgo having children.

HIV Disease   The human immunodeficiency virus (HIV) —the AIDS virus—can enter the brain and cause dementia, even before there are any other signs of infection (Oldstone & Vitkovic, 1995; van Gorp & Buckingham, 1998). The resulting destruction of brain tissue produces a subcortical dementia manifested initially by mental slowness and deficits in memory as measured by recall but not in recognition memory (Butters et al., 1995; Portegies & Rosenberg, 1998). HIV patients also have motor dysfunctions, including a tremor and dizziness, as well as personality changes. People affected by AIDS become apathetic, depressed, and withdrawn. Because AIDS affects the immune system, it leaves the body vulnerable to numerous secondary infections that can also affect the brain and hasten the dementia process.

Creutzfeldt-Jakob Disease   In the early part of the 20th century, two clinicians, Creutzfeldt and Jakob, independently reported cases of dementia associated with symptoms similar to those of tardive dyskinesia (see Chapter 9). They described people who walked with a stiff gait, had trouble maintaining their balance, and had difficulty controlling their voluntary movements. These people also had a diminished ability to plan ahead and organize their behavior, two signs of frontal lobe damage. As **Creutzfeldt-Jakob disease** progresses, these movement symptoms are followed by memory defects, hallucinations, and delusions. Patients usually die within 2 years of diagnosis. Autopsies find nerve cells that look like "sponges," making the disease one of the spongiform encephalopathies, a category that includes "mad cow" disease (Allen, 1993).

Creutzfeldt-Jakob disease has been estimated to affect only one in a million people (A. J. Edwards, 1994). Because it is so uncommon, the disease would have been

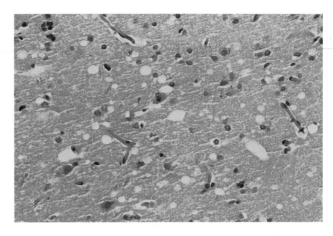

Nerve cells affected by Creutzfeldt-Jakob disease look spongy.

a mere curiosity if it had not been for Gajdusek's (1997) studies of kuru. Kuru is a spongiform disease found among the Fore tribe of Papua New Guinea. Its symptoms include dementia. Gajdusek won the Nobel Prize for showing that kuru is a very slow-growing virus that is transmitted through ritual cannibalism. The disease is transmitted when members of the Fore tribe eat the dead bodies of other tribe members, but symptoms do not appear for many years. In developed countries, Creutzfeldt-Jakob disease is not spread through cannibalism, but it may be transmitted by eating affected animals (Chesebro, 1991). Most cases of Creutzfeldt-Jakob disease are sporadic (they do not run in families), but cases that begin early in life (approximately 15%) may have a family history of brain disease. It is possible that these early-onset cases inherit a genetic diathesis that makes them especially susceptible to the virus.

Head Injuries, Tumors, and Other Brain Diseases   If they are severe enough, head injuries, tumors, and brain diseases can produce the symptoms of dementia. The behavioral effects of head injuries are determined by the location and extent of brain damage. For example, as already mentioned, frontal lobe damage usually results in disinhibition, a memory deficit, and a loss of the type of abstract reasoning needed to perform such tasks as mathematics (Butters et al., 1995; Stuss, Gau, & Hetherington, 1992). The precise cognitive and behavioral effects of brain injury depend on the victim's premorbid personality, coping skills, and the extent of his or her social supports. Brain injury can also cause the seizures associated with epilepsy (McLin, 1992).

Depending on their size and location, brain tumors and endocrine disorders may also produce cognitive impairments and personality changes resembling those

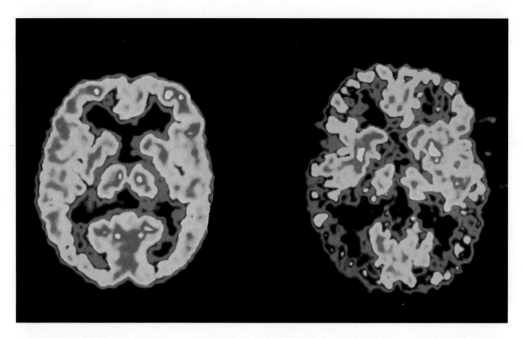

A comparison of PET scans of the brain of a healthy patient (left) and one with Alzheimer's disease (right) show high brain activity (red and yellow) in the healthy patient and a reduction in function and blood flow (blue and black) in the person with Alzheimer's.

found in dementia (Price, Goetz, & Lovell, 1992). Infectious diseases, such as syphilis (see the discussion of general paresis in Chapter 1), encephalitis (inflammation of the brain), and meningitis (inflammation of the membrane that surrounds the brain and spinal cord) may also produce some of the symptoms of dementia. Fortunately, all of these conditions are treatable or preventable. Brain tumors are treated with surgery, drugs, or radiation; endocrine disorders can be ameliorated by drug and diet; and infectious diseases can be prevented by immunization and safer-sex programs.

Dementia of the Alzheimer's Type   Dementia is considered to be an illness of old age. But, at a scientific meeting held in 1906, Alois Alzheimer (1864–1915) reported a case of "senile" dementia in a woman who was only 51. The woman had trouble recognizing common objects, frequent memory lapses, and difficulty speaking. Her personality also changed. In contrast to her former serene demeanor, she became impulsive and capricious. She also developed hallucinations and severe delusions of persecution. Most poignant of all was her own description of her disease: "I have lost myself." After the woman's death at age 55, Alzheimer performed an autopsy and found three abnormalities in her brain. First, she had many **neurofibrillary tangles** in her hippocampus and cerebral cortex. Neurofibrils are narrow fibers found within neurons. Scientists believe that these fibers provide structural support for neurons and also as-

sist in transporting neurotransmitters and other chemicals within nerve cells. In normal neurons, the neurofibrils are organized in symmetrical columns, but in Alzheimer's patient they were tangled and disorganized. The second abnormality that Alzheimer uncovered during the autopsy was the presence of numerous senile plaques. Modern protein sequencing has shown that these plaques contain a protein fragment known as beta-amyloid surrounded by the debris of destroyed neurons. The third abnormality that Alzheimer found was arteriosclerosis.

None of Alzheimer's observations were new. Neurofibrillary tangles, senile plaques, and arteriosclerosis had all been reported before (see Berrios, 1994). The main point of his 1906 paper was that dementia could occur in relatively young people. It was Emil Kraepelin who first referred to "Alzheimer's Disease," suggesting that so-called presenile dementia might be different from the dementia of old age. Although Alzheimer never accepted this idea, many others did—so many, in fact, that Alzheimer's disease became one of the most active research areas in medical science. Each year, more than 1,500 articles are published on Alzheimer-type dementia. Ironically, this huge body of research, which was stimulated by Kraepelin, has not substantiated his distinction between presenile and old-age dementia (Huppert et al., 1994). Except for the age at which they begin, the conditions are essentially identical. The only difference is that mental deterioration tends to progress

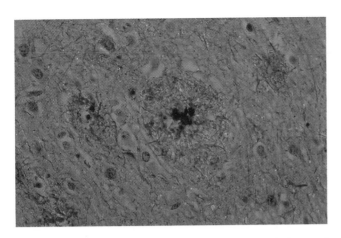

Neuritic plaques and neurofibrillary tangles are evident in the brains of people with Alzheimer's disease.

more quickly among people who show the first signs in their 40s and 50s. Today, it is common to refer to both presenile and senile dementia as Alzheimer's disease or dementia of the Alzheimer's type (DAT).

The bulk of modern dementia research is motivated by a desire to find the "cause" of Alzheimer's disease (Ishii, Allsop, & Selkoe, 1991). Researchers rarely question the assumption that DAT is a single disease. Yet DAT has few, if any, specific signs or symptoms (Geldmacher & Whitehouse, 1997). Neurofibrillary tangles and senile plaques are common in "healthy" older people who have no symptoms of dementia. It is possible that they are natural consequences of aging. This could mean that DAT is not a specific disease but simply an acceleration of the normal aging process (Huppert et al., 1994).

Over the decades since Alzheimer's case report, numerous anomalies have been found in the brains of older people with dementia (Filley, 1995). Unfortunately, none of these anomalies is specific to DAT. For this reason, DAT has become a clinical diagnosis that does not depend on any specific laboratory test or pathology. It is diagnosed only when other potential causes of dementia have been excluded. For example, if the symptoms of dementia come on suddenly and are accompanied by signs of focal brain damage (blindness or numbness, for example) in a person with a history of circulatory disease and if MRI or other laboratory evidence confirms a vascular accident, then the dementia is diagnosed as vascular. Similarly, dementia in a patient with a brain tumor or in a person who is infected with HIV will be diagnosed as dementia due to brain tumor or dementia due to HIV disease, respectively. DAT is diagnosed only when a person with an acquired cognitive impairment does not meet the diagnostic criteria for any other type of dementia—it is a diagnosis made by exclusion. Nevertheless, the diagnosis of DAT seems to have a high interrater reliability (McGuffin et al., 1994; Pearlson et al., 1992).

The *DSM-IV* diagnostic scheme allows clinicians to note whether DAT is accompanied by depression, delusion, or delirium. If none of these is present, DAT is said to be "uncomplicated." The *DSM-IV* also divides DAT into early onset (before the age of 65) and late onset (after age 65). Why 65? The reason is historic. In 1884, Otto Von Bismarck, then chancellor of Germany, decreed that citizens became entitled to social security pensions when they reached 65. This was copied by countries around the world until 65 came to symbolize old age. Keep in mind, however, that people live much longer today than in Bismarck's time. The *DSM-IV*'s use of 65 to denote old age seems rather young. In any event, the age cutoff is completely arbitrary and has no medical significance.

Prevalence, Incidence, and Course of Dementia

Alzheimer's is the most common form of dementia (Teri & Wagner, 1992) accounting for half of all cases. Four million Americans are currently affected (A. J. Edwards, 1994), and the number is increasing as the population ages. The *prevalence* of dementia rises with age from about 1% at age 65 to more than 10% of people in their late 80s (George et al., 1991; McGuffin et al., 1994; Skoog, Nilsson, & Palmer, 1993). The *incidence* of dementia also rises with age, from 2–3 cases per 100 people among those aged 75 to more than 5 cases per 100 in people over 80 (Brayne, 1993; Paykel et al., 1994). By the year 2040, more than 9 million people in the United States are expected to suffer from dementia (Max, 1993). Their care will cost billions of dollars.

At present, there are more women with dementia than men, but this may simply reflect the longer life expectancy of females. (The longer a woman lives, the greater the chance that she will develop dementia.) Dementia has a high prevalence and incidence among lower socioeconomic groups (Padgett, 1995), probably the result of poor health care, inadequate diet, and in some cases, substance abuse. Chronic conditions such as high blood pressure and vascular disease are poorly managed among those in lower socioeconomic groups. With better medical care and public health awareness, social class differences would probably disappear.

Cross-cultural estimates of prevalence and incidence are not always reliable because, as already mentioned, cultures have different attitudes toward and expectations of elderly people (Henderson, 1994). Cultural practices may distort estimates of dementia's prevalence and incidence. For example, surveys usually count only cases that live in a particular community. People who live in special institutions outside the community are missed. Thus, surveys may overestimate the prevalence of dementia in communities whose members prefer to keep elderly people at home and underestimate the prevalence in communities who institutionalize their elderly members.

Dementia caused by operable tumors, drugs, and treatable infections may be reversed, but such cases represent the minority. Most people with dementia, especially those with DAT, progressively deteriorate until they die (Cummings, 1992). In late-onset DAT, the average period between diagnosis and death is about 8 years (Trèves, 1991). In early-onset cases (about one fourth of the total), the period between diagnosis and death is much shorter, only 4.5 years (Heston & White, 1991). Both early- and late-onset cases usually begin with a mild memory disturbance that is often dismissed as mere forgetfulness. As time passes, the memory disturbance becomes more obvious (Butters et al., 1995). Not only does the person forget facts and events, but new learning becomes increasingly difficult. Initially, old memories are preserved, but eventually those, too, are lost. Personality changes, sometimes dramatic, come next. People with dementia become childish, irritable, and depressed. This is followed by increasing confusion, disorientation, aphasia, agnosia, and apraxia. In the late stages of dementia, people may lose control over body functions. Death usually follows soon after.

Risk Factors for, and Etiology of, Dementia

The list of potential etiologies for dementia is exceedingly long. It includes not only the specific causes of dementia that have already been discussed (tumors, blows to the head, the Creutzfeldt-Jakob virus) but also a disparate collection of risk factors that have been linked to DAT. For example, reports of high levels of aluminum in the brains of Alzheimer's patients gave rise to the theory that aluminum toxicity is the cause of DAT (Leigh & Swash, 1995). The evidence for this hypothesis is equivocal at best. Although it is true that kidney dialysis patients, who become intoxicated with aluminum, show signs of dementia, their symptoms are different from those of DAT. Furthermore, people who live in regions with high levels of aluminum in the water do not always have a greater incidence of DAT, and many people with DAT do not have excessive amounts of aluminum in their brains. The aluminum hypothesis is still supported by some scientists; however, it is clearly not a definitive explanation for DAT (Copestake, 1993). Autoimmune

disorders, deficient levels of neurotransmitters, viruses —the list of potential causes of DAT goes on and on. Few have managed to withstand close scrutiny.

So-called protective factors that supposedly prevent the development of DAT are equally suspect. For example, some writers have suggested that cigarette smoking has a protective effect because smokers, it seems, have lower rates of DAT than nonsmokers (Brenner et al., 1993). However, the relationship between smoking and DAT may be artifactual—smokers may just not live long enough to develop DAT. Education has also been identified as a potential protective factor. Educated people are alleged to have a lower risk of DAT because they keep up an active intellectual life (Stern et al., 1994). Before we prescribe more years of schooling as a way to prevent DAT, note that the correlation between education and protection from DAT may also be artifactual. Educated people tend to be wealthier, have access to better health care, eat better diets, live in better houses, smoke less, and take better care of themselves than do those who are less well educated. Any of these factors could be responsible for the lower incidence of DAT among the better educated.

Research and theory in the area of risk and protective factors seem to follow a distinctive pattern. Someone notices a correlation between some biological or environmental variable and DAT. Before long, the variable is being heralded as either the cause of DAT or an important factor in preventing DAT from occurring. Inevitably, further research throws doubt on the original observations. Before long, only a few diehards are left clinging to the original hypothesis; everyone else has moved on to the next one. The result is a landscape littered with discarded risk factors, etiological theories, and protective factors. Each has a few adherents, but none satisfactorily accounts for the prevalence, incidence, or course of DAT. This does not mean that researchers should cease looking. Observed correlations can lead to important discoveries. For example, the relationship between DAT and Down syndrome has been known for some time. Researchers following up this correlation have found a gene that predisposes people to develop Alzheimer's on chromosome 21, the same chromosome that is overexpressed in Down syndrome (Lendon et al., 1997).

A question that has preoccupied investigators is whether DAT can be inherited. This question remains largely unanswered because of the difficulties involved in researching a condition that usually does not become apparent until old age. Ordinarily, researchers would identify a person with DAT and then study that person's relatives to see whether they also have the disease. How-

DSM-IV TABLE 11.8 Main *DSM-IV* Diagnostic Criteria for Amnestic Disorders

A. The development of a memory impairment as manifested by impairment in the ability to learn new information or the inability to recall previously learned information.

B. The memory disturbance causes significant impairment in social or occupational functioning and represents a significant decline from a previous level of functioning.

C. The memory disturbance does not occur exclusively during the course of a delirium or dementia.

Note: From American Psychiatric Association (1994, p. 160).

ever, what happens if a relative gets run over by a bus while still in his 20s? Because he died with all his faculties intact, researchers may conclude that DAT does not run in families. It is possible, however, that the relative would have developed DAT if he had lived long enough. To determine whether DAT runs in families, researchers must follow relatives for many years in longitudinal studies. When they do, they find that 50% of the relatives of a person with DAT will develop DAT provided, of course, they live long enough (Pedersen & Gatz, 1991).

Cross-sectional twin studies are more practical than longitudinal ones. Unfortunately, they have produced ambiguous results. Some twin studies report little difference between monozygotic and dizygotic twin pairs in either the incidence or prevalence of DAT (McGuffin et al., 1994). These findings suggest that DAT is not inherited. Other studies have reported monozygotic concordance rates that are twice those of dizygotic twins. These results are consistent with a genetic involvement (Rose, 1995). These equivocal findings may be explained if there is more than one variety of DAT: a sporadic type and a type that runs in families. The familial type seems to be characterized by an earlier age of onset and rapid deterioration (Corder et al., 1993). Several researchers have suggested that the gene responsible for the familial type of DAT is apoE4, the one that controls the production of beta-amyloid, the major component of senile plaques (Farlow, 1992; Kowall et al., 1991; Quon et al., 1991).

Another possible interpretation of the genetic data is that it is not DAT that is inherited but the tendency to live a long life. The increased incidence of DAT in some families may not be evidence of an inherited disease but may simply be a consequence of living longer. The best way to differentiate these two possibilities is to compare the relatives of DAT patients with control subjects of the same age whose family members do not have DAT. If there is a specific genetic factor predisposing people to develop DAT, the relatives of DAT patients should have a higher probability of developing DAT than control subjects of the same age who do not have relatives with DAT.

AMNESTIC DISORDERS

Although one of the important signs of dementia is a memory disorder, there are people with memory disorders who do not have dementia. These people fall into a category that the *DSM-IV* calls amnestic disorders. People with amnestic disorders are able to perform simple memory tasks. They can usually attend to their immediate situation, retrieve old memories, and repeat a list of four or five digits. However, their cognitive impairment becomes obvious when they are required to hold on to an experience or to learn something new. For example, when asked to memorize the names of one or two objects, people with amnestic disorders forget them in a few minutes. This is why they feel as if they are continually meeting "new" people and being put into "new" situations.

Traumatic brain injury, stroke, exposure to highly toxic substances, and brain disease tend to produce amnestic disorders quickly, whereas drugs, chronic substance abuse (especially of alcohol, sedative medications, and tranquilizers), and nutritional deficiencies produce memory disorders that develop gradually. Diseases such as transient ischemic attacks (brief periods of reduced blood circulation) produce temporary amnestic disorders, whereas permanent brain injury, especially to the middle temporal lobes, usually produces an irreversible memory impairment. The *DSM-IV* refers to amnestic disorders that last for less than 1 month as transient; those that last longer are called chronic. The *DSM-IV* also distinguishes between amnestic disorders due to general medical conditions (vascular disease, head trauma, infection) and substance-induced persisting amnestic disorders, which persist after the effects of intoxication or withdrawal. The same diagnostic criteria apply to both types of amnestic disorders (Table 11.8). The only difference between the two is the presumed etiology.

An amnestic disorder, especially one caused by head trauma or substance intoxication, may begin with an episode of delirium. Because memory disorders are also common in dementia, care must be taken to rule out delirium and dementia before making the diagnosis of amnestic disorder. Amnestic disorders must also be distinguished from the dissociative amnesias discussed in Chapter 7. This distinction is not difficult to make. Unlike dissociative disorders, amnestic disorders always result from a general medical condition or a substance. Another hallmark of amnestic disorders is an inability to learn new material, whereas dissociative disorders are normally characterized by the forgetting of traumatic events.

One of the best-known amnestic disorders is Korsakoff's syndrome, which is the result of prolonged alcohol abuse. First described by Sergei Korsakoff in the 19th century, the syndrome results from two causes: (a) the poisoning of nerve cells by alcohol and (b) a vitamin B_1 (thiamine) deficiency caused by the poor diets of many heavy drinkers (G. Edwards & Peters, 1994; Oscar-Berman & Evert, 1997). The disorder is often accompanied by other signs of alcohol poisoning, such as inflammation of the nerves in the fingers and toes. Korsakoff's syndrome usually begins with an acute episode of delirium. When the delirium clears, the person is left with a severe memory deficit that affects mainly new memories. Typically, people with Korsakoff's syndrome can relate accurately the events of their childhood but are unable to say what happened an hour before. Despite their apparent inability to form new memories, people with Korsakoff's syndrome are not totally incapable of learning. They may be unable to verbalizable facts and events, yet they may still be able to learn unconsciously. For example, people with Korsakoff's can learn their way around nursing homes and hospitals, even though they claim not to recognize their surroundings. Similarly, they may learn to recognize the voices of nurses and doctors, even though they are unable to recall ever meeting them previously (Parkin, 1993). It seems as if explicit (verbalizable) learning is impaired, whereas implicit (unconscious) learning can still take place (Healy & Bourne, 1995). This learning can sometimes be enhanced by drugs, particularly SSRIs (P. R. Martin et al., 1995), but for most people with Korsakoff's, the memory impairment is irreversible.

TREATMENT AND PREVENTION OF COGNITIVE DISORDERS

Some types of dementia (and even some amnestic disorders) are reversible with treatment (Yodofsky & Hales, 1995). However, no single treatment works for all cases (Scheltens & van Gool, 1997; Spiegel & Irwin, 1996).

Treatment must be tailored to the specific case. Substance-induced dementia may be successfully treated by removing the offending substance. Thyroxin (a hormone produced by the thyroid gland) will usually reverse dementia (or at least prevent further deterioration) in people whose cognitive deficits are caused by **hypothyroidism** (low levels of thyroxin). The symptoms of Parkinson's disease may be controlled, at least temporarily, by L-dopa and, perhaps more permanently, by transplants of dopamine-producing brain tissue. Surgery can sometimes reverse dementia caused by brain tumors, and cognitive decline may also be delayed by ensuring that older people have regular exercise and good nutrition.

The symptoms of dementia and amnestic disorders may also be minimized by treating associated conditions. For example, antidepressant medications and cognitive-behavior modification may help to relieve the cognitive impairments caused by the depression that often accompanies dementia (Jozsvai, Richards, & Leach, 1996). In a similar manner, hallucinations and delusions can be treated with antipsychotic medications, and the cognitive disturbances caused by circulatory disease may be relieved by vasodilator drugs that increase blood flow. Vascular dementia can also be reduced by eliminating aggravating factors, such as smoking (Norris & Hachinski, 1991).

Unfortunately, the majority of people with dementia fall into the DAT category. For them, medical treatments are primitive, at best. For example, the first drug approved to treat DAT was tacrine hydrochloride, (brand name, Cognex). Tacrine hydrochloride prevents the breakdown of acetylcholine, a neurotransmitter known to be deficient in some people with DAT. The result is a modest improvement in cognitive functioning (Hasan & Mooney, 1994). Sadly, even these small gains disappear if the person stops taking the drug (Winker, 1994). Moreover, tacrine hydrochloride can have unpleasant side effects and, in some patients, can cause serious liver damage. Donepezil hydrochloride (brand name, Aricept) is now in more common use. It also inhibits the breakdown of acetylcholine but is less likely to cause liver damage. Neither of these drugs is a definitive treatment, but new treatments are under development, inspiring hope for the future (Becker, Giacobini, & Barton, 1997; Matsuoka & Satoh, 1998).

Because there is no specific medical cure for DAT or other forms of undifferentiated dementia, treatment usually involves more than just drugs. It also includes a variety of environmental and psychological interventions. The aims of treatment are to preserve the person's sense of independence and self-esteem, to keep up social contacts, and to provide as much enjoyment and meaning as is possible in clients' lives and in the lives of those who care for them (Howard & Rockwood, 1995; Whitehouse et al., 1992). If they cannot live at home, people with dementia and amnestic disorders will almost always be sent to nursing homes (Gatz & Smyer, 1992). Although they vary in standards, nursing homes are not ideal places for people with dementia. They focus mainly on the custodial aspects of care and often lack the personnel qualified to deal with dementia's psychological features. As a consequence, people who live in nursing homes often lose their sense of autonomy and self-worth. Without significant intellectual challenge and independence, their cognitive decline accelerates.

If possible, it is preferable to keep people with dementia and amnestic disorders at home. Often this requires certain modifications to both the home environment and daily routines (Corcoran & Gitlin, 1992). These modifications are designed to foster the person's sense of independence and control. For example, hand rails permit a person with apraxia to get around the house and to use the bathroom without assistance. Special chairs and beds that make it easy to sit, lie down, and rise, and remote controls that permit the television to be operated from a distance also promote independence. Printed labels or pictures on cupboard doors can help people with memory disorders to locate common household items. Colored arrows drawn on floors help people with dementia navigate around their homes without getting lost, and memory aids such as strategically placed reminders can help people to function more or less independently even while suffering from cognitive impairments (Bourgeois, 1992; Caplan & Lipman, 1995). Community services, such as meal preparation and visiting nurses, are also helpful in allowing people who would otherwise need institutional care to live at home.

Because dementia often involves significant disinhibition, sufferers have to be taught to regulate their own behavior. Specifically, they are trained to self-consciously scrutinize their behaviors and to silently remind themselves about how they should behave (Kohlenberg & Tsai, 1991). The idea is to replace unconscious inhibitory mechanisms with conscious ones.

Looking after a person with dementia can have a negative effect on the quality of a caregiver's life, as the letter from Helen Lee's mother to her own mother in Document 11.8 illustrates. Not surprisingly, family members burdened with the care of a relative with dementia may become depressed (Teri & Wagner, 1992). They may feel angry about their fate and guilty about

Notes and labels (such as "Alice's closet") can help people with dementia remember what they have to do and where things go.

their anger. Professionals need to recognize and address these problems. In addition to helping to maintain the independence and self-esteem of people with dementia, they should also include support services for their caregivers (Corrigan, 1995).

DOCUMENT 11.8

Letter From Debbie Lee to Her Mother

Dear Mom,

I'm coping better now. I think I have finally gotten my mind around the idea that Helen is never going to get better. A few years ago, I would not accept it. Michael has still not accepted it. He sometimes thinks that Helen is being difficult and that she could be more alert and responsive if she tried. I explain that it is the dementia, that she can't help it, and that she still loves him.

Of course, it's been hard, especially in the beginning. Helen may be retarded, but she knew she was being forgetful.

She used to say, "I don't know what is happening to me." I'd try to reassure her: "You're only tired, dear. I forget things, too." But I knew the truth. I knew she would eventually not know me. I knew she would become a stranger. And it broke my heart.

I know it was my choice, but sometimes I get angry that I have been stuck with her. I attend a group in which caregivers share ideas and give each other emotional support. I have also learned to think of the good times we had together. Still, sometimes I worry about who will take care of her when Michael and I are gone. When that happens, I put some old music on. Sometimes, I think I see her smile. I think, maybe some part of her is still there after all.

Love,

Debbie ■

It is much better to prevent cognitive disorders than to treat them. Sadly, our current state of knowledge does not permit us to do much. Treating high blood pressure reduces the probability of a stroke, and low-fat diets and certain drugs can prevent arteriosclerosis—two important causes of vascular dementia. Early diagnosis of diabetes mellitus and hypothyroid conditions will reduce the chances that these conditions will lead to cognitive disorders. Programs designed to combat alcohol and drug abuse and immunizations against the causes of encephalitis and meningitis are also important ways of preventing cognitive disorders from developing.

LEGAL IMPLICATIONS OF INTELLECTUAL AND COGNITIVE DISORDERS

As discussed in Chapter 10, our criminal justice system is predicated on personal responsibility. People with dementia or mental retardation may be unable to understand the implications of their behavior. Thus, they are considered to be legally "incompetent" and not responsible for their actions, even criminal ones (Grubb, 1994). Older people with cognitive disorders rarely engage in criminal behavior. They have neither the energy nor the physical capacity. However, in younger people with early-onset dementias (especially Huntington's disease and Pick's disease), disinhibition, depression, and a loss of judgment may combine to produce antisocial behavior. In such cases, perpetrators will not be found guilty of criminal behavior because, in the eyes of the law, their diminished mental capacity renders them unable to be held personally responsible for their actions.

A common legal consequence of intellectual and cognitive disorders is the loss of personal autonomy. People whose intellectual or cognitive impairments prevent them from making rational decisions may be declared legally incompetent and prevented from entering into contracts, disposing of property, or drawing up wills. Instead, a court-appointed executor or guardian is given the responsibility of administering the affected person's affairs (Payton, 1992). Guardians not only have the power to make financial decisions but also to determine where the person resides (at home or in an institution) and how the person's property will be distributed when he or she dies.

People who are declared legally incompetent may be unable to give informed consent for treatment. There are no hard-and-fast rules for determining whether a person is competent to give informed consent. In general, clinicians try to determine whether a person has the capacity to comprehend information about treatment options, to apply the information to him- or herself, to select from among the options, and to communicate a preference (Markson et al., 1994). A person does not have to agree with the doctor to be considered competent. It is only necessary to show that the person's thinking processes are rational in the light of his or her cultural and social situation (Cutter & Shelp, 1991). If a person is declared incompetent to give informed consent, the legal guardian will be given the responsibility for approving treatments.

As dementia progresses, the afflicted person becomes increasingly unable to participate in everyday life. As a consequence, the guardian takes on more responsibility, including the approval of treatment. Guardians are understandably reluctant to refuse any treatment that might potentially benefit the individual. As a consequence, people with cognitive disorders may be kept alive by modern medical technology well past the time when they can participate in, or enjoy, life's activities. Because many people dread living such a life, they have preempted the authority of guardians by preparing **living wills** while still legally competent. These wills, which are accepted in most jurisdictions, contain advance directives stipulating when medical treatment should be discontinued. Based on her experience with Helen, Debbie Lee decided to prepare the living will contained in Document 11.9 (adapted from Maklin, 1987, pp. 70–72).

To my family, my physician, my lawyer, and all others whom it may concern:

If the time comes when I can no longer take part in decisions for my own future, let this statement stand as an expression of my wishes and directions while I am still of sound mind.

If at such a time the situation should arise in which there is no reasonable expectation of my recovery from extreme mental or physical disability, I direct that I be allowed to die and not be kept alive by medications, artificial means, or "heroic measures." I do, however, ask that medications be mercifully administered to me to alleviate suffering even though this may shorten my remaining life.

This statement is made after careful consideration and is in accordance with my strong convictions and beliefs. I want the wishes and directions here expressed carried out to the extent permitted by law. Insofar as they are not legally enforceable, I hope that those to whom this will is addressed will regard themselves as morally bound by these provisions.

In the event that I should become comatose, or should enter a permanent vegetative state, or should become so impaired mentally or physically that I am incapable of meaningful communication with other persons, and if my doctors believe that recovery from this state is not likely to take place, I direct them to treat me as if I were actually dying, with all the requests and restrictions listed above. It is my strong belief that such states are, for me, the equivalent of death itself. I do not wish my body sustained by artificial feeding, antibiotics, blood transfusions, or cardiopulmonary resuscitation, nor do I wish to undergo any diagnostic studies likely to cause physical distress.

If any of my tissues or organs are thought to be of value to others as transplants or for tissue banking, I freely give my permission for such donation.

Should I become incompetent temporarily or permanently, I designate my husband, Michael, to serve as my representative and guardian for the purpose of making all medical decisions. I ask him to do so in the spirit of my requests and directions stated above. This power to make treatment decisions on my behalf shall remain effective indefinitely unless I recover competence to make such decisions.

Debbie Lee   Witness:

January 25, 2001

CHAPTER 11 IN PERSPECTIVE

People with mental retardation, long the subject of social concern, are finally getting a fair measure of professional attention. Confusion about the definition of mental retardation still exists, but the problems inherent in relying on intelligence test scores as the sole diagnostic criterion are now widely recognized. A definition based on both intelligence test performance and social competence is now the norm. The prevalence of mental retardation is difficult to determine with any precision because of varying definitions and diagnostic procedures. Although an overall estimate of 3% is widely accepted, the prevalence of mental retardation is a function of the demands made by society on the individual at different ages. The prevalence of learning disabilities, defined as lower than expected academic, language, or motor skills performance (when "expectations" are set by intelligence tests) also varies with social demands. In contrast to the past, most people with mental retardation and learning disabilities live, work, and study in the community. The philosophy of normalization combined with antidiscrimination legislation, special education, and supported employment programs have made it possible for people with intellectual disabilities to lead productive and fulfilling lives. Research advances have made the prevention of many intellectual disorders a realistic goal.

In contrast to mental retardation and learning disabilities, which are first diagnosed in childhood, the cognitive disorders affect mainly older people. These disorders, which all involve a deficit in cognition or memory, can have one of three causes: a general medical condition, a substance (drug or toxin), or a combination of both. Although the cognitive disorders all involve some form of neurological dysfunction, psychological factors play an important role in the expression of these disorders. Unfortunately, the treatment and prevention options for cognitive disorders remain limited.

Key Ideas

Defining and Diagnosing Mental Retardation

The *DSM-IV* diagnostic criteria for mental retardation require both a low IQ score and low adaptive functioning. Low intelligence test performance, by itself, is not a disorder. Whether someone is mentally retarded depends on how that person adapts to his or her environment. Adaptive behavior is evaluated relative to a person's age and cultural group because people at different developmental stages, and from different cultural groups, are expected to perform dissimilar tasks. It is possible for an individual who has difficulty keeping up at school to adjust well as an adult when adaptive functioning is judged by different criteria.

Causes of Mental Retardation

Mental retardation can be caused by practically any condition that affects the development or working of the brain. These causes can be genetic (including inherited conditions, genetic accidents, and mutations caused by exposure to X rays or other toxins), the result of pregnancy complications (caused by alcohol, drug poisoning, or illness), birth trauma (caused by anoxia or stressful delivery), childhood diseases or accidents, and socioeconomic factors (poverty, poor nutrition, or a deprived intellectual environment). Most mild cases are ascribed to cultural-familial retardation, a combination of unlucky inheritance and poor social environment.

Learning, Motor Skills, and Communication Disorders

Learning, motor skills, and language disorders, which are more common in boys than girls, are diagnosed when a person's performance in these areas is substantially below the level expected for the person's age, schooling, and intelligence (as measured by IQ). This definition depends on two questionable assumptions: that IQ reflects intellectual potential and that most children receive adequate instruction in the normal school curriculum. Like those of mental retardation, the causes of learning disabilities include genetics, medi-cal conditions, and social factors.

Treating and Preventing Learning Disabilities and Mental Retardation

Most people with intellectual disabilities live either at home or in the community. Only the most seriously affected need to live in institutions. The goal of treatment programs is normalization. Through special education and employment programs, people with intellectual disorders are given the opportunity to live as normal a life as possible. Primary prevention (such as immunization), secondary prevention (such as special diets for people with PKU), and tertiary prevention programs (sheltered or supported employment, for example) can reduce the burden of intellectual disorders on the community.

Dementia: Diagnostic Issues

The prevalence of dementia, in which cognitive functioning falls from previous levels, is increasing as the population ages. Dementia can be caused by a drug, an accident, or a medical condition. It can have specific symptoms (as in Huntington's disease) or diffuse ones. People with dementia always have a memory impairment. They may also have a language disorder, motor disabilities, disturbances in planning, and various agnosias (failures to recognize or identify objects despite intact sensory function). Depression, which shares many symptoms with dementia, usually has a more rapid onset and a more fluctuating course.

Dementia Types

Vascular dementia is caused by a sudden loss of blood supply to parts of the brain, resulting in the destruction of surrounding tissue. Vascular dementia affects men more often than women, probably because of their higher level of cardiovascular disease. Substance-induced persisting dementia is caused by a substance and continues even after the substance is withdrawn. Dementia may also be caused by a large variety of medical conditions. The *DSM-IV* singles out Parkinson's disease (a movement disorder caused by the destruction of dopamine-producing neurons), Pick's disease (caused by the atrophy of the frontal and temporal lobes of the brain), Huntington's disease (an inherited movement disorder), viruses such as HIV and the one that causes Creutzfeldt-Jakob disease, and trauma to the brain.

Dementia of the Alzheimer's Type (DAT)

DAT is the most common form of dementia, accounting for more than half of all cases. Although it is associated with neurofibrillary tangles and senile plaques, DAT is diagnosed when other potential causes of dementia are ruled out. DAT begins with a mild memory disturbance, which gradually becomes more obvious. Personality changes come next, followed by confusion, disorientation, aphasia, agnosia, and apraxia. In the late stages, the person may lose control over bodily functions. Early-onset cases progress more rapidly than late-onset cases. A disparate collection of risk factors have been linked at one time or another to DAT, but none can account for all cases or facets of the disorder. What can be said is that the

seem to run in families, and DAT is closely related to Down syndrome.

Delirium

Delirium is a rapidly progressing disorder of consciousness. Sufferers are forgetful, confused, incoherent, and unaware of where they are or what is going on around them. Many are also anxious, fearful, and irritable. Any illness, injury, or substance that affects the brain has the potential to cause delirium. Appropriate treatment depends on the cause. If delirium is due to a general medical condition, treatment focuses on curing the condition. If delirium is caused by a substance, it is treated by gradually withdrawing the substance. Normally, delirium will disappear once the cause is identified and eliminated.

Amnestic Disorders

People with amnestic disorders have difficulty learning new information and, in some cases, may be unable to recall previously learned information or events. Distant events are often remembered better than recent ones, and recall is usually affected more than recognition. Traumatic brain injury, stroke, or exposure to toxic substances can all produce an acute amnestic disorder. Drugs, chronic substance abuse, and nutritional deficiencies usually produce a more gradually developing disorder. Although people with amnestic disorders have difficulty with explicit verbal learning, they may still learn implicitly. Thus, they may benefit from psychological interventions.

Treatment and Prevention

Some types of dementia are reversible with treatment. For example, substance-induced dementia may be successfully treated by removing the offending substance, and administering thyroxin will usually reverse dementia in people with hypothyroidism. Unfortunately, most people with dementia have DAT, a condition for which drug treatments are crude at best. Social-psychological treatment aimed at maintaining independence and self-esteem may be helpful.

Looking after a person with dementia can have a negative effect on the quality of the caregiver's life, so it is important that the needs of caregivers not be ignored. Antihypertensive treatment, careful control of diabetes mellitus, immunizations against certain viruses, and moderate use of alcohol can help to prevent or delay the onset of dementia.

Legal Implications

People with severe mental retardation and dementia are legally incompetent and unable to make wills or administer their personal affairs. A court-appointed executor (or guardian) will be given responsibility for them. Because people with mental retardation or dementia are incompetent to give informed consent, the guardian is also the person responsible for agreeing that a treatment be administered. Most jurisdictions will also accept advance directives about treatment given by people while they were still competent.

Key Terms

agnosia
amnestic disorders
aphasia
apraxia
chorea
cognitive (impairment) disorders
communication disorders
computerized tomography (CT)
Creutzfeldt-Jakob disease
cultural-familial retardation
delirium tremens
dementia
dementia of the Alzheimer's type (DAT)
disinhibition
Down syndrome
fragile X syndrome
Huntington's disease
hypothyroidism
learning disorders
magnetic resonance imaging (MRI)
mainstreaming
mental retardation
motor skills disorder
neurofibrillary tangles
normalization
Parkinson's disease
phenylketonuria (PKU)
Pick's disease
positron emission tomography (PET)
pseudodementia
scaffolding
single photon emission computerized tomography (SPECT)
special education
stroke
subcortical dementia
substance-induced persisting dementia
supported employment
teratogenic agents
trisomy 21
vascular dementia

Key Names

Alois Alzheimer
Paul Broca
Cyril Burt
E. A. Doll
John Langdon Down
Jean Esquirol
George Huntington
Arnold Pick
Carl Wernicke

CHAPTER 12

It is natural to think of childhood as a carefree and innocent period in which youngsters feel loved and wanted. Unfortunately, for many children, childhood is full, not of affection and happiness, but of heartache and pain. Depression, anxiety, and all the other psychological problems that plague adults can affect children as well. In addition, there are psychological disorders that are particularly associated with childhood and adolescence because this is when they are normally first diagnosed. Although they are heterogeneous in both symptoms and etiology, these child and adolescent disorders are discussed together in this chapter because understanding them requires that we also understand how children and adolescents develop.

The main questions addressed in this chapter are

1. How does developmental psychology contribute to our understanding of psychological disorders among children and adolescents?
2. Why is it psychologically and biologically necessary for children to form close attachments to other people?
3. What happens when the attachment process goes awry?
4. What are the main psychological disorders first observed in childhood and adolescence?
5. What are the effects of a childhood disorder on other family members?
6. How can childhood and adolescent disorders be treated and prevented?

Disorders of Childhood and Adolescence

CONTENTS

Children are constantly changing. As they pass through childhood, they grow progressively taller, stronger, more mobile, and more verbal. In an attempt to impose order on this progression, psychologists typically describe development as a series of stages. We encountered Freud's psychosexual stages of development in Chapter 2. The Swiss psychologist Jean Piaget (1896–1980) and the neo-Freudian Erik Erikson (1902–1944) are famous for their stage theories of cognitive and personality development (Piaget, Gruber, & Voneche, 1995; Erikson, 1967), and there are many others (see Vygotsky, 1986, for example). These theories give the impression that development is an orderly process: The child advances through a series of stages and becomes an autonomous adult. Unfortunately, as Freud made clear, a safe passage through the developmental stages is not guaranteed. Because of disease, or genetics, or traumatic experiences (or a combination of all three), some children find the road to adulthood full of obstacles. Unless they are helped, such children are at risk for psychological disorders.

Diagnosing psychological disorders in childhood is not easy because behavior that is appropriate to one developmental stage may not be appropriate to another. We have already seen, in Chapter 11, how the intellectual capacity of a child is judged by school performance, whereas adults are assessed according to their ability to live autonomously. Another example of the importance of considering developmental stage when assessing behavior is bed-wetting. Wetting the bed is normal in a 1-year-old but not in a 10-year-old. The same principle applies to most childhood behaviors. To understand whether a child's behavior is "abnormal," we need to know what behaviors are "normal" for children at different stages of development. Studying abnormal behavior in its developmental context is the goal of the specialty area of clinical psychology known as **developmental psychopathology.**

The *DSM-IV* contains a large number of disorders that are first noticed in infancy, childhood, or adolescence. Some of these (mental retardation; learning, communication, and motor skills disorders) are reviewed in Chapter 11; others are covered in earlier chapters. The disorders discussed in this chapter are summarized in Table 12.1. These disorders (which are not all categorized as childhood disorders in the *DSM-IV*) are discussed together here because they may all be understood within a developmental context.

THE UNIVERSITY HOSPITAL PARENT SUPPORT GROUP

To give substance and coherence to the disparate disorders discussed in this chapter, we begin by introducing the members of the University Hospital Parent Support Group. This group was organized by psychologist Stuart Berg. Its members are parents of children under treatment for psychological disorders. Document 12.1 contains a transcript of the group's first meeting.

DOCUMENT 12.1

Transcript of the
First Meeting of the
University Hospital
Parent Support Group

UNIVERSITY HOSPITAL

Parent Support Group Transcript

DR. BERG: My name is Stuart Berg. I am a clinical psychologist working here at University Hospital. I want to welcome each of you to this first Support Group meeting. I know some of you, and I will look forward to meeting and working with all of you in the weeks to come. The goal of this support group is to help you to help your children and yourselves. You are all here because you have a child in treatment and because you indicated an interest in mutual support. Although these meetings will be unstructured, they do have a goal—to help you cope with a child who has a psychological disorder. Some of the issues we discuss will be practical: how to access government assistance programs, how to find a baby-sitter, how to get your child to the dentist. Because some parents whose children develop psychological disorders feel guilty and ashamed, as if they were the cause of their child's problems, we will also try to educate ourselves about what causes psychological disorders in children and what we can do about them. Because this is our first meeting, I thought it might be a good idea to go around and have each of you introduce yourself to the others. Let's begin on my left.

JOHN CHENEY: My name is John Cheney. I am a doctor, a radiologist, in this hospital. My son, Eddie, has autism. He is 8. I have no other children. I just couldn't handle any more.

INGRID CHENEY: I am Ingrid Cheney, John's wife. I do not work. My life is looking after Eddie.

PASQUALE ARMANTI: My name is Pasquale Armanti. I am a builder here in town. In fact, my company built this hospital. My wife, Francesca, couldn't have children. We adopted Paolo when he was a baby. My life hasn't been the same since. He has been in trouble since he could walk and nothing—

FRANCESCA ARMANTI (*interrupting her husband*): You are always picking on him. You never wanted Paolo. You always rejected him. Even when he was little, you spanked him—

PASQUALE ARMANTI (*interrupting his wife*): Lighten up! Listen to yourself. Who are you kidding? Paolo is out of control. He needs discipline.

DR. BERG: Perhaps we should get back to this later. Let's move on.

KAREN BEASLEY: I'm Karen. Karen Beasley. I'm 19 years old. I'm here on my own because my boyfriend Eric left us a few months ago. It's just me and Michelle now. Michelle is 4, and she won't talk. She won't hug me or let me hug her. She just stays in her room. Sometimes she watches TV; other times she just cries. Sometimes she hurts herself by banging her head against the wall. But even when she is hurting herself, she won't let me comfort her. I don't have a job. I never finished high school. Lately I've become fat. I'm dieting, but it doesn't help. I've been running, and even that doesn't work. That's me—a fat girl with no money, no boyfriend, and a kid who won't talk.

CELIA BEROFSKY (*to Karen*): How did you get into this mess? A baby at 15, abandoned at 19. And what makes you think you are fat? You're nothing but skin and bones.

KAREN BEASLEY: I am? But I feel fat.

DR. BERG (*addressing Celia*): Perhaps you can introduce yourself?

CELIA BEROFSKY: I am Celia Berofsky, and this is my husband, Michael.

MICHAEL BEROFSKY: Hi.

CELIA BEROFSKY: My son Gordon won't go to school. When we force him to go, he won't talk to anyone. I know this is just a phase that he will grow out of. Michael thinks so too. Our psychologist suggested that we come to this group, but I don't think we will be members long.

DR. BERG: Thanks, everyone, that was good. Perhaps one of you could start off the discussion by telling us about your experiences and the problems you are encountering. Everyone should feel free to ask questions. Now, who wants to start?

PASQUALE ARMANTI: I'll start. I am used to talking about Paolo. According to the psychologists at school and Dr. Gale, our private psychologist, Paolo has attention-deficit hyperactivity disorder. But this is not his only diagnosis. For a long time, they told me he had an oppositional defiant disorder, and he also supposedly has a conduct disorder. Once they suspected Tourette's disorder. I wonder if anyone knows what is wrong with Paolo. Maybe he's just a difficult kid.

TABLE 12.1 Disorders Discussed in This Chapter That Are Usually First Noticed in Childhood or Adolescence

Elimination disorders (enuresis and encopresis)

Disruptive behavior and attention-deficit disorders (oppositional defiant disorder, conduct disorder, attention-deficit/hyperactivity disorder)

Tic disorders (Tourette's, motor, and vocal tic disorders)

Pervasive developmental disorders (autistic, Asperger's, Rett's, and childhood disintegrative disorder)

Feeding and eating disorders (anorexia and bulimia nervosa, pica, ruminative disorder)

Sleep disorders (nightmares, sleep terrors, sleepwalking)

UNDERSTANDING DEVELOPMENTAL PSYCHOPATHOLOGY

Pasquale Armanti is a frustrated man. His adopted son, Paolo, had a problem, but exactly what was wrong was unclear. Paolo's diagnosis was constantly changing. To make matters worse, Pasquale and his wife, Francesca, were in conflict about the nature of their son's problems and what to do about them. Frustration and marital conflict are common among the families of children with psychological disorders. It is stressful for any family when one member has a psychological disorder; it is especially stressful when the affected person is a child.

Given their serious consequences, it is curious that, for most of recorded history, children's psychological problems were largely ignored (S. Schwartz & Johnson, 1985). Until the 18th century, there was not even a concept of "childhood" as a stage of development. Paintings, sculptures, and biographies portrayed children as little adults differing from grown-ups only in size and strength (Aries, 1962). There were no special children's games or literature, and even young children were expected to work full days. A major cultural shift occurred after the revolutions in America and France. Because citizens needed to be educated to participate in democratic processes, they established state-supported schools and kindergartens. For the first time in history, large populations of schoolchildren became available for study by educators and psychologists. By the early 20th century, governments around the world were supporting research into child development, sponsoring conferences, and publishing research results. In the middle of the century, child guidance clinics were established to assess and treat children's psychological problems. To help prevent psychological disorders from developing in the first place, researchers studied normal child development. Their goal was to identify, as early in life as possible, the risk factors for psychological disorders. Much of their work focused on childhood temperament.

Temperament and Behavior

Francesca was so happy when Paolo became available for adoption that she did not try to find out much about his biological parents. She knew that Paolo's mother was a teenager who refused to identify her baby's father. Much later, Francesca discovered that Paolo's biological father spent years in prison for a serious assault. The Armantis were in their 30s when they adopted Paolo. They had no other children, and little experience with children, so they were unaware of what to expect from a baby. Looking back now, however, it seems to them that Paolo may have been "difficult" from the first weeks of life (Document 12.2).

DOCUMENT 12.2

Transcript From Meeting of the University Hospital Parent Support Group: Francesca and Pasquale Discuss Paolo

DR. BERG: Francesca, tell us what Paolo was like as a baby.

FRANCESCA ARMANTI: He was a beautiful child—

PASQUALE ARMANTI (*Interjecting*): But noisy.

FRANCESCA ARMANTI: Yes, he was high-strung. He cried a lot. For his first six months, he rarely slept more than two hours at a time. I remember that it was hard to console him. I had to rock him for hours and even then he would start crying again as soon as I put him back in his crib. By the time he was a year old, he was a little calmer, but he was still strong willed. He would eat only when he felt like it; otherwise, he would spit food out. Potty training Paolo was like a war. ∎

Every child has a characteristic temperament; some are easier, and some are more difficult.

Paolo, like all children, displayed a characteristic temperament (Chess & Alexander, 1995; Strelau, 1998). *Easy children* have regular patterns of elimination, eating, and sleeping. They adapt readily to new environments, and, even when they are distressed, their emotional reactions are usually mild. *Slow-to-warm-up children* take longer to adapt to new situations than easy children, but they eventually adjust. Like easy children, their emotional reactions are mild. *Difficult children* like Paolo are another matter. They have irregular patterns of eating, sleeping, and elimination. They are slow to adapt to new situations and they have intense, usually negative, emotional reactions (such as tantrums).

Because these differences in temperament are obvious from the first day of life, before the environment can exert any effect, it is likely that they are biologically based. This belief is confirmed by twin studies that show a higher concordance for temperament among identical than among fraternal twins (Chess & Alexander, 1995). Difficult children are at risk to develop psychological disorders later in childhood and as adults (Chess & Alexander, 1995). They are particularly prone

to develop "acting out" or **externalizing disorders,** which involve behaviors that annoy or threaten others (Achenbach & McConaughy, 1996). Of course, not all difficult children develop psychological disorders, nor do all easy and slow-to-warm-up children avoid them. Some members of the latter groups will develop **internalizing disorders,** such as depression and anxiety, in which symptoms are directed inward. Whether children develop a psychological disorder depends on the fit between their temperaments and their environments (Chess & Alexander, 1999). A difficult child may develop significant problems if raised by parents who are rigid, demanding, and intolerant of individuality. Such problems might be avoided if the same child were raised by parents who are more flexible and tolerant.

Developmental Milestones

Francesca described toilet training Paolo as "like a war." Because she had no experience with other children, she had no way of knowing whether such "wars" were normal. This is not an unusual circumstance. Psychologists are often consulted by parents who wish to know whether their child's toilet training (or lack of it) is normal or abnormal. How do clinicians decide? Usually, toileting behavior is assessed in the context of the child's developmental stage. As they get older, children are expected to achieve certain developmental milestones (Table 12.2 provides examples). Unless there is an explanation (mental retardation, for example), children who fail to reach developmental milestones at the usual age are considered "abnormal." This is why wetting the bed is "normal" for a 1-year-old but "abnormal" for a child of 6. Indeed, the *DSM-IV* might consider the older child to be suffering from an elimination disorder.

Elimination Disorders

According to psychoanalytic theory (which has many adherents among clinicians who work with children), toilet training represents a conflict between the narcissistic id, whose goal is to immediately satisfy biological drives such as elimination, and society's demand that people use the toilet. Successful toilet training requires children to learn to delay their instinctual gratification until they can find a toilet. Other psychological paradigms place different constructions on elimination. Behaviorists, for example, focus mainly on improper toilet training techniques (Mellon & Stern, 1998). Despite their different emphases, all paradigms agree that **elimination disorders** are most likely to occur when training is

TABLE 12.2   Some Developmental Milestones

Age	Milestones
12 months	Begins to babble; recognizes names; walks with support
18 months	Produces first true words, with many mispronunciations; climbs stairs
24 months	Has 300-word vocabulary; runs; turns pages in a book
3 years	Develops self-reliance and flexible control of impulses (e.g., toilet training)
6–12 years	Understands fairness; forms same-sex friendships; adjusts to school
13+ years	Separates from family and develops a unique identity

Note: Adapted from Gard, Gilman, & Gorman (1993) and Stray-Gundersen (1995).

DSM-IV   TABLE 12.3   Main *DSM-IV* Diagnostic Criteria for Enuresis and Encopresis

Enuresis	Encopresis
A. Repeated voiding of urine into bed or clothes (whether involuntary or intentional).	A. Repeated passage of feces into inappropriate places (e.g., clothing or floor) whether involuntary or intentional.
B. The behavior is clinically significant as manifested by either a frequency of twice a week for at least 3 consecutive months or the presence of clinically significant distress or impairment in social, academic (occupational), or other important areas of functioning.	B. At least one such event a month for at least 3 months.
C. Chronological age is at least 5 years (or equivalent developmental level).	C. Chronological age is at least 4 years (or equivalent developmental level).
D. The behavior is not due exclusively to the direct physiological effect of a substance (e.g., a diuretic) or a general medical condition (e.g., diabetes, spina bifida, a seizure disorder).	D. The behavior is not due exclusively to the direct physiological effects of a substance (e.g., laxatives) or a general medical condition except through a mechanism involving constipation.

Note: From American Psychiatric Association (1994, pp. 107, 109–110).

harsh or inconsistent, especially when a child is resistant. "Difficult children," especially those with conduct disorders like Paolo Armanti, have a particularly hard time with toilet training (Foreman & Thambirajah, 1996). As you can see from the *DSM-IV* diagnostic criteria summarized in Table 12.3, children who fail to achieve toilet training by the usual age (or developmental level, if they are mentally retarded) are diagnosed as having **enuresis** (poor control of urination) or **encopresis** (poor control of defecation) or, in rare cases, both. Elimination disorders occur more often in boys than in girls and seem to run in families (American Psychiatric Assn, 1994). Although this implicates biology in their etiology, elimination disorders are also linked to child abuse (Cerezo & Pons-Salvador, 1998; Feehan, 1995). Behavioral therapy is usually successful for enuresis (see Chapter 2) and may help encopresis. It is frequently supplemented with cognitive therapy and antidepressants (Friman & Jones, 1998; Ondersma & Walker, 1998).

Paolo Armanti, a difficult baby, grew into a troublesome toddler. Everything was a struggle—feeding, sleeping, toileting. He was eventually toilet-trained and taught to feed himself, but his problems did not end there. In nursery school, kindergarten, and throughout his school years, Paolo was the undisciplined child whose behavior frequently disrupted his class. As we will see in the next section, Paolo's behavior earned him several *DSM-IV* diagnoses.

DISRUPTIVE BEHAVIOR AND ATTENTION-DEFICIT DISORDERS

Many children have mild temper tantrums and even arguments, but these rarely present a serious interpersonal problem. However, there are children who commit violent aggression such as hitting, biting, and kicking. Learning the difference between aggression—which harms others—and assertiveness—which is necessary for effective functioning in society—is an important part of growing up. As you can see in Document 12.3, Paolo Armanti had considerable difficulty learning to make this distinction.

DOCUMENT 12.3

School Report on
Paolo Armanti

Midvale Comprehensive School

Yearly Report

Student: Paolo Armanti

Grade: Two

Paolo's academic performance is below average. Although he has learned to count and to do simple addition and subtraction, he has not grasped the concept of fractions, and he is poor at other operations (division or multiplication). His reading is below grade level, particularly his comprehension. His schoolwork is marked by carelessness. He makes frequent errors and is easily distracted by things going on around him. Whenever he can, Paolo tries to get out of work. Intelligence testing conducted in preschool, and repeated this year, found Paolo's IQ to be above-average. It seems that his academic performance is not the result of poor intellectual capacity but, more likely, the result of a psychological disturbance.

Paolo's behavior is causing everyone at school considerable concern. He is constantly "on the go," and he almost never sits still. On the rare occasions that he does remain in his seat, he fidgets endlessly. At meals, games, or even when using the washbasin, Paolo never waits his turn; he always pushes ahead of the other children.

Paolo's behavior, over the course of the entire year, has been consistently negative. He often refuses to follow instructions. When his teacher insists, Paolo frequently loses his temper. He also picks fights with other children. He takes their food and their possessions, and seems to be constantly angry. On one occasion, Paolo took another child's baseball bat. When the child tried to take it back, Paolo hit him in the knee with the bat. The child required four stitches. On another occasion, he grabbed a girl's new pen out of her hand. When she demanded its return, he threw in on the floor and crushed it under his heel. When confronted with these behaviors, Paolo always denies wrongdoing, blaming the other children for "not sharing." Because of his behavior, Paolo has no friends in his class, or in the rest of the school. The school psychologist feels that Paolo may have an oppositional defiant disorder. Because children with this disorder may develop more serious long-term psychological disorders, the psychologist recommends that Paolo's parents seek professional assistance.

DSM-IV   TABLE 12.4   Main *DSM-IV* Diagnostic Criteria for Oppositional Defiant Disorder

A. A pattern of negativistic, hostile, and defiant behavior lasting at least 6 months, during which four (or more) of the following are present:

(1) often loses temper

(2) often argues with adults

(3) often actively defies or refuses to comply with adults' requests or rules

(4) often deliberately annoys people

(5) often blames others for his or her mistakes or misbehavior

(6) is often touchy or easily annoyed by others

(7) is often angry and resentful

(8) is often spiteful or vindictive

Note: Consider a criterion met only if the behavior occurs more frequently than is typically observed in individuals of comparable age and developmental level.

B. The disturbance in behavior causes clinically significant impairment in social, academic, or occupational functioning.

C. The behaviors do not occur exclusively during the course of a psychotic or mood disorder.

D. Criteria are not met for conduct disorder, and, if the individual is age 18 years or older, criteria are not met for antisocial personality disorder.

Note: From American Psychiatric Association (1994, pp. 93–94).

Oppositional Defiant Disorder

Paolo's parents were not surprised by the school report. They had observed similar behavior at home. Until they read the report, however, they had not realized that Paolo had a psychological disorder. They believed that children are "rebellious" at some stages in their lives and that Paolo would "grow out of it." They were driven to action by the school's belief that Paolo's behavior was affecting his social relations and causing him to do poorly at school. The Armantis consulted a psychologist, Dr. Connie Gale. She agreed that Paolo's behavior met the *DSM-IV* criteria for an **oppositional defiant disorder** (Table 12.4). She also agreed that children with this pattern of behavior are at risk for more severe problems as they grow older (Lahey & Loeber, 1997; R. Rogers et al., 1997). She told the Armantis that the diagnostic criteria for oppositional defiant disorder overlap with two other *DSM-IV* categories—conduct disorder and attention-deficit/hyperactivity disorder—one or both of which may also apply to Paolo. She undertook to conduct a more thorough assessment.

After discussing Paolo's history and his behavior with his parents, Dr. Gale conferred with his school. With the Armantis' permission, she observed Paolo at home and in class; she also examined his intelligence test results. She reviewed Paolo's behavior with his teacher, who also completed the Achenbach Child Behavior Checklist (Achenbach, 1991) as well as the Conners Teacher Rating Scale designed to screen children for attentional disorders (Goyette, Conners, & Ulrich, 1978). Paolo's Child Behavior Checklist profile appears in Document 12.4. As you can see, he scores in the 98th percentile (among the most extreme 2% of all children) on attention problems and on delinquent and aggressive behavior. His teacher's ratings on the Conners scale appear in Document 12.5. A score of 15 or above is regarded as indicative of an attentional disorder (Goyette et al., 1978). As you can see, Paolo received a score of 20.

To complete her evaluation, Dr. Gale arranged for Paolo to have vision, hearing, and medical examinations to rule out visual or hearing deficits that could be causing his problems. Finally, she interviewed Paolo. Considering all the information available to her, Dr. Gale reached a different conclusion from that of the school psychologist. Because of Paolo's above-average IQ score (see Document 12.3), Dr. Gale believed Paolo met the *DSM-IV* criteria for several learning disorders (see Chapter 11). He also met the criteria for conduct disorder and attention-deficit/hyperactivity disorder. Her next task was to explain these diagnoses to the Armantis and to plan a treatment program.

Paolo's Profile on
the Achenbach Child
Behavior Checklist

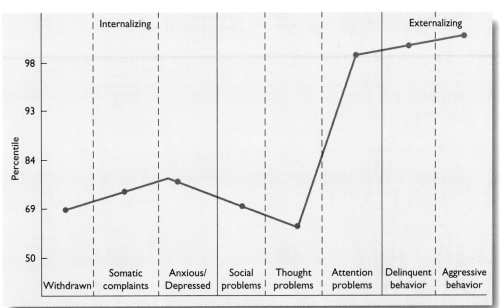

DOCUMENT 12.5

Conners Teacher Rating
Scale for Attention-
Deficit/Hyperactivity
Completed by Paolo's
Teacher

Classroom Behavior	Degree of Activity			
	(0) Not at all	(1) Just a little	(2) Pretty much	(3) Very much
Constantly fidgeting				✔
Demands must be met immediately—easily frustrated			✔	
Restless or overactive			✔	
Excitable, impulsive			✔	
Inattentive, easily distracted			✔	
Fails to finish things—short attention span			✔	
Cries often and easily	✔			
Disturbs other children				✔
Mood changes quickly and drastically		✔		
Temper outbursts; explosive and unpredictable behavior				✔

Conduct Disorder

The main *DSM-IV* diagnostic criteria for **conduct disorder** appear in Table 12.5. As you can see, many of these criteria also apply to antisocial personality disorder (see Chapter 10). This is not surprising, given that one of the diagnostic criteria for antisocial personality disorder is evidence of a conduct disorder before age 15. The main

difference between the two disorders is age. In theory, an adult may be given the diagnosis of conduct disorder, but in practice, antisocial personality disorder is used for individuals over age 18, whereas conduct disorder is applied to people under 18. The *DSM-IV* distinguishes two conduct disorder subtypes: childhood-onset (before age 10, as in Paolo's case) and adolescent-onset (for those who are older than age 10 when the characteristic

DSM-IV TABLE 12.5 Main *DSM-IV* Diagnostic Criteria for Conduct Disorder

A. A repetitive and persistent pattern of behavior in which the basic rights of others or major age-appropriate societal norms or rules are violated, as manifested by the presence of three (or more) of the following criteria in the past 12 months, with at least one criterion present in the past 6 months:

Aggression to people and animals

(1) often bullies, threatens, or intimidates others

(2) often initiates physical fights

(3) has used a weapon that can cause serious physical harm to others (e.g., a bat, brick, broken bottle, knife, gun)

(4) has been physically cruel to people

(5) has been physically cruel to animals

(6) has stolen while confronting a victim (e.g., mugging, purse snatching, extortion, armed robbery)

(7) has forced someone into sexual activity

Destruction of property

(8) has deliberately engaged in fire setting with the intention of causing serious damage

(9) has deliberately destroyed others' property (other than by fire setting)

Deceitfulness or theft

(10) has broken into someone else's house, building, or car

(11) often lies to obtain goods or favors or to avoid obligations (i.e., "cons" others)

(12) has stolen items of nontrivial value without confronting a victim (e.g., shoplifting, but without breaking and entering; forgery)

Serious violations of rules

(13) often stays out at night despite parental prohibitions, beginning before age 13 years

(14) has run away from home overnight at least twice while living in parental or parental surrogate home (or once without returning for a lengthy period)

(15) is often truant from school, beginning before age 13 years

B. The disturbance in behavior causes clinically significant impairment in social, academic, or occupational functioning.

C. If the individual is age 18 years or older, criteria are not met for antisocial personality disorder.

Note: From American Psychiatric Association (1994, pp. 90–91).

behaviors first appear). Three severity specifiers may also be applied—mild (behavior causes little harm), moderate (stealing, but little violence), and severe (when the person displays many criterion behaviors and causes considerable harm to others). Based on the number of criterion behaviors Paolo evidenced and his young age, Dr. Gale diagnosed Paolo as moderate conduct disorder, childhood-onset type.

Conduct disorders are distressingly common, affecting about 8% of boys and 3% of girls between the ages of 4 and 16 (Offord, Boyle, & Racine, 1991). Higher estimates may include children who live in threatening, high-crime neighborhoods and engage in aggressive antisocial behavior as part of gangs. For most such children, antisocial behavior may not be a sign of a psychological disorder but simply a way of life. Similarly,

immigrants from war-torn countries may have learned to use aggressive behavior to survive. Neither delinquents nor immigrants from war zones should be diagnosed with a conduct disorder because their behavior does not violate their "age-appropriate societal norms" (American Psychiatric Assn, 1994).

Each of the psychological paradigms has an etiological theory for conduct disorder. Beginning with the observation that conduct disorder runs in families, some theorists have suggested that it has a genetic basis. (Remember that Paolo's biological father spent time in jail for assault.) Adoption and twin studies have confirmed a genetic link (Carlson & Lahey, 1988; Lahey et al., 1988). Precisely what is inherited that causes conduct disorder remains unclear. Early reports that conduct disorder is related to an extra Y chromosome in males have been

Young people in gangs who come from high-crime neighborhoods should not be immediately diagnosed with a conduct disorder. They may be behaving according to age-appropriate societal norms.

largely discounted (Palermo et al., 1992). A more likely genetic mechanism may be the inheritance of a sensation seeking temperament (Geen, 1997). The idea is that conduct-disordered people, like Cleckley's psychopaths (see Chapter 10), are chronically underaroused. To make up for this, they are always seeking excitement. When their environment lacks socially acceptable opportunities for excitement, they turn to antisocial behaviors (Sarasalo, Bergman, & Toth, 1996).

Although genetics may predispose children to conduct disorders, it is not the whole story. The concordance rate for conduct disorders among identical twins is less than 1 (perfect), so environment must also play a role. One place to look for the environment's influence is in faulty family relationships. For example, psychodynamic psychologists believe that parental neglect or abuse can lead children, through displacement, to seek revenge on society (Bowers, 1990). This hypothesis is difficult to confirm experimentally; we cannot ask parents to abuse children deliberately for the sake of an experiment. However, there is evidence that the parents of children with conduct disorder tend to be rejecting and use severe physical punishment (D. R. Moore & Arthur, 1983; Straus & Donnelly, 1994). Both of these tendencies are revealed in the exchange between Pasquale and Francesca Armanti in Document 12.1. Remember, however, that parental aggressiveness could just as easily be the *result* of having a child with a conduct disorder as the cause of the child's disorder.

In addition to family dynamics, some theorists attribute conduct disorders to social factors, such as exposure to aggressive and criminal models, whereas others emphasize how extra parental and teacher attention can reinforce antisocial behavior (Dadds, 1997). Of course, parental neglect, exposure to antisocial models, and the reinforcement of antisocial behavior are not mutually exclusive. Many children experience all three (Dadds, 1997; Moore & Arthur, 1983). Whatever the cause or causes of conduct disorders, the outlook is poor for those whose disorder is first diagnosed in childhood (Dadds, 1997; Moffitt, 1993; Vitelli, 1997). Many such children go on to be diagnosed with antisocial personality disorder (Prinz & Connell, 1997). Many have high rates of marital instability, poor work histories, and a tendency to substance abuse (Myers, Stewart, & Brown, 1998). The relationship between age of onset and prognosis is similar for both sexes, although females are less likely than males to develop antisocial personality disorder as adults (Zoccolillo, 1993).

Children with conduct disorders may have learning disorders at the same time (Waldie & Spreen, 1993). It is possible that these learning disorders may be one of the causes of conduct disorders. Specifically, children who continuously fail at school feel humiliated because other children ridicule them. To win respect and ease the pain of repeated failure, such children may act out. While trying to control this disorderly behavior, teachers may actually reinforce it by giving disruptive children extra attention. Eventually, antisocial behavior becomes a well-rewarded habit. Although this hypothesis is plausible, keep in mind that it is based on a correlation between conduct and learning disorders. It is equally possible that the causal mechanism goes the other way around. Conduct disorders may cause learning disorders, perhaps by interfering with study time. It is also possible that conduct and learning disorders both result from the same cause. For example, both may result from distractibility—the main symptom of attention-deficit/hyperactivity disorder.

Attention-Deficit/Hyperactivity Disorder

As part of her evaluation, Dr. Gale observed Paolo at school. While Paolo's teacher talked to the class, Dr. Gale saw Paolo looking out the window at workers building a new wing on the building. When the workers stopped for lunch, Paolo became restless. He tapped the desktop with his pencil. When he noticed the teacher staring at him, he stopped tapping and started kicking the back of the seat in front of him. The girl sitting in that seat raised her hand to complain, and the teacher interrupted to ask Paolo to stop. He stopped, but only temporarily, and then started kicking again. As we have already seen, Paolo's failure to follow the rules that govern civil interaction have earned him the possible diagnosis of oppositional defiant disorder or conduct disorder. To these possibilities, Dr. Gale added **attention-deficit/hyperactivity disorder.**

Although Dr. Gale's diagnosis was new to Paolo's parents, it has a long and controversial history (Barkley, 1990). The notion originated with the work of Alfred Strauss and his colleagues (see Strauss & Kephart, 1955). Their goal was to identify childhood behaviors that could be used to diagnose brain damage in ambiguous cases (when there were no clear-cut signs of neurological impairment). Because children with brain damage were often very active, they argued that *hyperactivity* (a term they did not define) is a sign that a child is brain damaged. To get around the problem that hyperactive children did not show any hard signs of brain damage, the concept of *minimal brain damage* (or *dysfunction*) was introduced (Strother, 1973). Minimally brain damaged children were said to be hyperactive, impulsive, distractible, and emotionally labile. They had short attention spans, perceptual-motor deficits, poor coordination, and learning disorders. It seemed that the only problem that "minimally brain damaged" people lacked was brain damage! Recognizing this, the *DSM-II* introduced the neutral term *hyperkinetic reaction of childhood* to describe impulsive and distractible children who had no clear signs of brain damage.

Articles referring to hyperactive, hyperkinetic, and minimally brain damaged children began to appear with increasing regularity in the 1970s and 1980s. The *DSM-III* (American Psychiatric Assn, 1980) tried to bring order to this confused set of names with a new diagnosis, *attention-deficit disorder.* This disorder could occur in two forms: with hyperactivity or without hyperactivity. In other words, the *DSM-III* made inattention rather than hyperactivity the focus of the disorder. In 1987, however, the revised manual (*DSM-III-R*) reverted back to a single *attention-deficit/hyperactivity disorder* (typically abbreviated as ADHD). Subtypes were reintroduced in the *DSM-IV,* which recognizes three: predominantly hyperactive-impulsive, predominantly inattentive, and a combined type. The main *DSM-IV* diagnostic criteria for ADHD are summarized in Table 12.6.

Despite the many attempts to refine them, the *DSM-IV* diagnostic criteria still have problems. For example, criterion 1 and criterion 2 both require a child's developmental level to be considered when making the diagnosis, but the normative data necessary for this are unavailable. Clinicians do not know how much fidgeting is "excessive" for children at different stages of development. Moreover, children behave differently depending on the context. Some children have attentional problems at school, whereas at home they sit and watch television for hours. Because norms are unavailable for many attentional behaviors and because behavior depends on context, parents, teachers, and clinicians often fail to agree about which children suffer from ADHD (Lahey et al., 1998). Diagnostic unreliability may also explain the large regional differences in the prevalence of ADHD (Cooper & Ideus, 1995). In some school districts, many children are diagnosed with ADHD, whereas in other districts, the diagnosis is rare. Either some districts are underdiagnosing ADHD or some are overdiagnosing it. Sloppy diagnostic practices make it impossible to say which explanation is correct.

To improve diagnostic reliability and validity, the criteria contained in Table 12.6 should be applied only after a thorough assessment (Cantwell, 1996). As we saw, Dr. Gale not only talked to Paolo's parents, but also observed him at home and at school and talked to his teacher. Dr. Gale had Paolo medically assessed and interviewed him. Her goal was to establish the circumstances in which the criterion behavior occurs, to interpret this information in the light of Paolo's developmental, medical, and family history, and to rule out other explanations for his behavior. Unfortunately, few children receive such a careful assessment. Most are seen by family doctors or pediatricians for an hour or less before they are diagnosed ("The Age of Ritalin," 1998).

Like Paolo, most children with ADHD are boys; the sex ratio is about 5–9 boys for every girl (Gaub & Carlson, 1997). This may reflect a genuine sex difference or a social bias. That is, girls may not be diagnosed with ADHD because they rarely cause the discipline problems that lead to teacher intervention. When they are compared solely on measures of attention (rather than misbehavior or hyperactivity), there is little difference between boys and girls with ADHD (Breen, 1989).

ADHD is being diagnosed with increasing frequency (L. S. Goldman et al., 1998). This could be the result of greater awareness of the condition among teachers and parents, or it could simply reflect the way the welfare system works. Because ADHD counts as a disability, it qualifies children for special treatment under the Americans With Disabilities Act. Parents may actually want their children to be diagnosed with ADHD if this means they will receive special services. As well as in children, ADHD is increasingly being diagnosed in teenagers and adults (Faraone, Biederman, & Mick, 1997; Wender, 1995, 1997). Many adult cases are former ADHD children who have grown up and continue to show signs of an attentional disorder.

DSM-IV TABLE 12.6 Main *DSM-IV* Diagnostic Criteria for Attention-Deficit/Hyperactivity Disorder

A. Either (1) or (2):

  (1) six (or more) of the following symptoms of **inattention** have persisted for at least 6 months to a degree that is maladaptive and inconsistent with developmental level:

  Inattention

    (a) often fails to give close attention to details or makes careless mistakes in schoolwork, work, or other activities

    (b) often has difficulty sustaining attention in tasks or play activities

    (c) often does not seem to listen when spoken to directly

    (d) often does not follow through on instructions and fails to finish schoolwork, chores, or duties in the workplace (not due to oppositional behavior or failure to understand instructions)

    (e) often has difficulty organizing tasks and activities

    (f) often avoids, dislikes, or is reluctant to engage in tasks that require sustained mental effort (such as schoolwork or homework)

    (g) often loses things necessary for tasks or activities (e.g., toys, school assignments, pencils, books, or tools)

    (h) is often easily distracted by extraneous stimuli

    (i) is often forgetful in daily activities

  (2) six (or more) of the following symptoms of **hyperactivity-impulsivity** have persisted for at least 6 months to a degree that is maladaptive and inconsistent with developmental level:

  Hyperactivity

    (a) often fidgets with hands or feet or squirms in seat

    (b) often leaves seat in classroom or in other situations in which remaining seated is expected

    (c) often runs about or climbs excessively in situations in which it is inappropriate (in adolescents or adults, may be limited to subjective feelings of restlessness)

    (d) often has difficulty playing or engaging in leisure activities quietly

    (e) is often "on the go" or often acts as if "driven by a motor"

    (f) often talks excessively

  Impulsivity

    (g) often blurts out answers before questions have been completed

    (h) often has difficulty awaiting turn

    (i) often interrupts or intrudes on others (e.g., butts into conversations or games)

B. Some hyperactive-impulsive or inattentive symptoms that caused impairment were present before age 7 years.

C. Some impairment from the symptoms is present in two or more settings (e.g., at school [or work] and at home).

D. There must be clear evidence of clinically significant impairment in social, academic, or occupational functioning.

E. The symptoms do not occur exclusively during the course of a pervasive developmental disorder, schizophrenia, or other psychotic disorder and are not better accounted for by another mental disorder.

Note: From American Psychiatric Association (1994, pp. 83–85).

However, increasing numbers of ADHD diagnoses are being made in adults who were not diagnosed as children. Because the *DSM-IV* (criterion B) requires that some sign of attentional disorder be evident before age 7, the reliability of diagnoses first made in adulthood is questionable. (It is almost impossible to get reliable information about what an adult was like as a child of 7.) Whether the extension of ADHD to adults is a healthy trend depends on your point of view. It may mean that formerly undiagnosed people are getting the attention they deserve, or it may mean that people are escaping responsibility for their actions by blaming their behavior on a psychological disorder.

Despite numerous hypotheses, no one fully understands the etiology of ADHD. Lead poisoning, brain damage, birth defects, food additives, and too much sugar in the diet have all been blamed at one time or another, but none of these supposed causes has found strong empirical support (Barabasz & Barabasz, 1996; Barkley, 1996). At present, there is no generally accepted biochemical or neurological cause of ADHD. However, there is evidence that the problem runs in families. Among monozygotic twins, when one twin is diagnosed with ADHD, the other is more likely to receive the same diagnosis than among dizygotic twins (Eaves et al., 1993; Sherman, McGue, & Iacono, 1997). Although these data suggest that inheritance contributes to ADHD, even for identical twins the concordance rate is less than 1. In other words, genetics produces a disposition to ADHD, but environmental factors also play a role. Sadly, little research has been conducted to identify these environmental factors (even though their identification could lead to prevention programs). Most of the research effort has gone into treatment, specifically the use of stimulant drugs to control the symptoms of ADHD.

At one time or another, tranquilizers, antidepressants, and even antihistamines have been prescribed for ADHD, but today most cases are treated with stimulant drugs (Greenhill, 1998). The most commonly used drugs are methylphenidate (Ritalin), pemoline (Cylert), dextroamphetamine (Dexedrine), and a mixture of several amphetamines (Adderall), but methylphenidate has by far the largest market share. Stimulants can have dramatic effects. After only a few tablets, children who are constantly on the go calm down and focus their attention. Because stimulants produce a dramatic calming effect in children with ADHD, some writers have argued that a "paradoxical" calming response to stimulant drugs is diagnostic all by itself. In other words, if stimulant drugs lead to less hyperactivity and distractibility, then the child probably has ADHD. In reality, the response of people with ADHD is not paradoxical; it is not even unusual. Stimulants improve everyone's ability to concentrate (Rapoport et al., 1978). This is the reason for the worldwide popularity of caffeine and nicotine (see Chapter 6).

How do stimulants work? Pliszka, McCracken, and Maas (1996) proposed that ADHD is the result of a catecholamine neurotransmitter imbalance in the parts of the brain that control attention. Stimulant drugs act by increasing the amount of time that catecholamine molecules remain active in synapses. Because the cate-

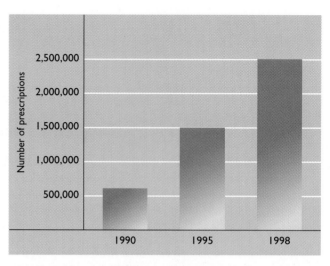

FIGURE 12.1 **Prescriptions of Methylphenidate (Ritalin) to Treat ADHD in Children Ages 5–18, 1990–1998.**
From: Safer, Zito, & Fine (1996); IMS America, quoted in Hurt (1998).

cholamine attentional circuits are complex, many different attentional problems can occur. This may explain why some people respond to one type of amphetamine but not another. The success of these drugs is a legend in the pharmaceutical industry. Prescriptions for methylphenidate increased 500% between 1990 and 1998, and the number keeps rising (Figure 12.1). There is ironic humor in the idea of American children being prescribed amphetamines so that they can concentrate during drug awareness programs designed to warn them of the dangers of amphetamines. It is worth noting that despite its effects on attention and behavior, methylphenidate does not improve long-term academic success (Gillberg et al., 1997); it simply makes children more manageable (Livingston, 1997).

A drawback to the use of stimulants is the likelihood of unpleasant side effects (Garber, Spizman, & Garber, 1997). These include sleeplessness, irritability, loss of appetite, and growth retardation. Pemoline can also cause liver damage. Taking drugs may also affect a child's self-concept. Children may learn to "externalize" responsibility for their behavior ("I can't control myself, so I must take medicines"). Externalizing responsibility could make children less responsive to learning self-control (Block, 1997; Garber et al., 1997). Skepticism about stimulant treatment has almost as long a history as stimulant treatment itself. In a provocative article titled "Pills or Skills for Hyperactive Children," O'Leary (1980) argued that ADHD children should learn new habits rather than simply rely on drugs. He offered a variety of behavior modification techniques. Since then, several cognitive-behavioral approaches to ADHD have also been developed (Braswell & Bloomquist, 1991; Ervin, Bankert, & DuPaul, 1996). Passions often run high in the debate over "pills or skills" (Garber et al., 1997), and some writers eschew medicine altogether (Block, 1997). In practice, the appropriate treatment for ADHD is not an either-or choice. Many ADHD children receive a combination of stimulants, cognitive therapy, and behavioral therapy, as well as various forms of special education (S. Goldstein & Goldstein, 1998).

Paolo Armanti is one of many children with multiple problems: learning disorders, conduct disorders, and ADHD. The outlook for him is guarded. Such children often develop antisocial personality disorder when they grow up (Lahey & Loeber, 1997; R. Rogers et al., 1997). To try to head off such an outcome, methylphenidate was prescribed for Paolo. At the same time, he was enrolled in a cognitive-behavior modification program conducted by his school psychologist. The goal of this program was to teach him to monitor his own behavior, to notice when his attention was wandering, and to engage in "self-talk" to keep his attention focused ("I am supposed to be looking at the teacher, not out the window"). Arrangements were made to allow Paolo to spend part of each week working on assignments in a quiet classroom without windows or other distractions. At the same time, to help his parents deal with Paolo, they were enrolled in a parent training program designed for the parents of children with ADHD (Fisher & Beckley, 1998). They not only learned how to administer methylphenidate, but also how to reinforce positive behaviors and extinguish negative ones. Parent training programs have been shown to help children as well as to reduce stress in parents (Anastopoulos et al., 1993). Francesca described the outcome of this treatment to the Parent Support Group as "mixed" (Document 12.6). Paolo's behavior changed more at school than at home, illustrating once again the contextual nature of ADHD. In addition, Paolo developed worrisome motor symptoms. Fearing that he might have a tic disorder, Paolo's family doctor referred him for further psychological, psychiatric, and neurological evaluation.

DOCUMENT 12.6

Transcript of Meeting of the University Hospital Parent Support Group: Francesca's Description of Paolo's Motor Disorder

FRANCESCA ARMANTI: Ritalin seemed to make more of a difference in Paolo at school than at home. I really didn't notice a lot other than that Paolo didn't seem to need much sleep. His teacher said he was not acting up as much at school. He still seemed to be having trouble learning, even with the extra attention he was getting. Pasquale wouldn't go to more than a few parent training sessions. He said it was a waste of time. We really got worried, though, when Paolo started making these strange jerking movements with his head and shoulders. After a month of this, we took him to the doctor, who thought we should consult Dr. Gale and a neurologist. He thought Paolo was either having a reaction to Ritalin or that he might have a disorder that produces these weird movements. ■

TOURETTE'S AND OTHER TIC DISORDERS

From the age of 7, the Marquise de Dampierre began acting strangely. She would snort, bark, and swear while at the same time making alarming facial grimaces and spasmodic hand movements. According to Dr. Jean Itard (1775–1838), who first described her case in 1825, the behavior of the Marquise was embarrassing to her aristocratic family (cited in Shapiro et al., 1978). Despite many attempts to help her, the Marquise was still swearing and snorting when she met Freud's teacher, Jean Charcot, 55 years later. Charcot passed his observations and Itard's case notes to his pupil Georges Gilles de la Tourette (1857–1904), who published them, along with several other case histories, in 1885. When Tourette was later incapacitated by a would-be assassin's bullet, Charcot decided to name the Marquise's condition after him.

Tourette's disorder is characterized by strange utterances (swearing, barking) and multiple motor tics (sudden repetitive but irregular movements). This apparently rare disorder appeared only in case studies until the 1970s, when a research literature began to develop. Although this literature burgeoned into a flood of books and articles (Shapiro et al., 1998), much about Tourette's disorder remains as mysterious as when it was first described in the 19th century. The *DSM-IV* diagnostic criteria for Tourette's disorder appear in Table 12.7. The *DSM-IV* also includes other tic disorders (chronic motor or vocal tic disorders, transient tic disorder) that have some, but not all, of the symptoms of Tourette's disorder. Unlike those for many psychiatric diagnoses, the criteria for Tourette's disorder have hardly changed from Tourette's original description. The criteria include vocal and motor tics that are generally chronic (although tic-free periods can occur). The disorder seems to occur in a similar form across all cultures (Staley, Wand, & Shady, 1997).

Like most childhood disorders, Tourette's disorder occurs more often in boys than in girls (Shapiro et al., 1998). It begins with facial tics, usually blinking or sniffing. In serious cases, it progresses to neck and shoulder

DSM-IV	TABLE 12.7 Main *DSM-IV* Diagnostic Criteria for Tourette's Disorder

A. Both multiple motor and one or more vocal tics have been present at some time during the illness, although not necessarily concurrently. (A tic is a sudden, rapid, recurrent, nonrhythmic, stereotyped motor movement or vocalization.)

B. The tics occur many times a day (usually in bouts) nearly every day or intermittently throughout a period of more than 1 year, and during this period there was never a tic-free period of more than 3 consecutive months.

C. The disturbance causes marked distress or significant impairment in social, occupational, or other important areas of functioning.

D. The onset is before age 18 years.

E. The disturbance is not due to the direct physiological effects of a substance (e.g., stimulants) or a general medical condition (e.g., Huntington's disease).

Note: From American Psychiatric Association (1994, p. 103).

jerking, head banging, arm flinging, and other peculiar movements. Sometimes, the tics are self-destructive (head banging, for instance). Odd verbalizations are always part of the disorder. People with Tourette's may sniff, bark, or, in a minority of cases, shout obscenities (a symptom known as *coprolalia*). As already noted, tics come and go, and old ones are replaced by new ones (Shapiro et al., 1998).

Tourette's disorder is characterized by motor tics and odd verbalizations. Here, Dr. Orrin Palmer (one of the people with Tourette's featured in Lowell Handler's Twitch and Shout: A Touretter's Tale, 1998) surprises a patient with his tic.

Tourette's disorder is different from the involuntary movement disorders (choreas) described in Chapter 11. People with Tourette's disorder can consciously inhibit their tics for brief periods, although this requires considerable effort. Because they can inhibit their symptoms at least part of the time and because their tics disappear during sleep, people with Tourette's were long considered to have a psychological disorder (Shapiro et al., 1978). Symptoms such as coprolalia were explained as either displaced aggression or the expression of poorly "defended" id impulses. Psychotherapy designed to uncover the unconscious conflicts causing Tourette's disorder did not meet with much success (Shapiro et al., 1998), and attention shifted to the neurochemistry of the illness (Murray, 1997). The discovery that small doses of haloperidol, a dopamine-suppressing drug used to treat schizophrenia, suppresses Tourette's symptoms in many people has led to the hypothesis that those with Tourette's may have an excess of dopamine (Murray, 1997). Further evidence for this hypothesis comes from the finding that drugs that increase dopamine levels, such as L-dopa, which is used in Parkinson's disease (see Chapter 11), tend to increase the severity of tics. Although promising, this hypothesis requires more research to identify the dopamine-dependent brain sites responsible for the symptoms of Tourette's disorder.

An important finding is that Tourette's disorder seems to be a genetically transmitted dominant trait (Barr & Sandor, 1998). This is why people with Tourette's disorder often have relatives who also have tic disorders (Hebebrand et al., 1997). They also have a high frequency of relatives with obsessive-compulsive disorder and ADHD, and many people with Tourette's disorder

Intense physical activity eases the symptoms of Tourette's disorder for some people. Both professional baseball player Jim Eisenreich and professional basketball player Mahmoud Abdul-Rauf, who suffer from Tourette's, found sports to be the activity in which they enjoyed spending time.

have these disorders themselves (D. W. Black, 1998; R. D. Freeman, 1997). Several writers have remarked on the substantial similarities between people with Tourette's disorder and people who stutter (Abwender et al., 1998; Pauls, Leckman, & Cohen, 1993). Both have facial tics and odd grimaces, particularly when they are in emotionally arousing situations, and both may be helped by haloperidol (Rosenberger, Wheeldeen, & Kalotkin, 1976). Coprolalia, surely the most peculiar symptom of Tourette's disorder, has also been noted among aphasic and schizophrenic patients (Lenneberg, 1967). There is presently no explanation for coprolalia, although it has been noted that stress makes it, and the other symptoms of Tourette's disorder, worse. In other words, Tourette's disorder, like practically all other psychological disorders, has both a genetic-physiological and a psychological component.

The *DSM-IV* estimates that Tourette's disorder occurs in 4 or 5 people out of every 10,000, but attempts to discover the precise prevalence have been hampered by the apparent rarity of the disease (Tanner & Goldman, 1997). There is some evidence, however, that the syndrome may be underdiagnosed (Mason et al., 1998). Every time a television show or magazine article discusses Tourette's, many people with Tourette's symptoms consult their doctors. Some of these people say that they have suffered from the symptoms all of their lives without knowing that their condition had a name.

Although other drugs are used, haloperidol remains the most common treatment for Tourette's syndrome. Unfortunately, people often discontinue treatment because of haloperidol's side effects, which, ironically, include a movement disorder similar to Parkinson's. The development of safer drugs for Tourette's disorder has been hampered by the small number of potential patients. Even with government assistance, drug companies are unlikely to recoup the hundreds of millions of dollars required to bring a new drug to market. One hope for the future is that the new antipsychotic drugs being used for schizophrenia will also help those with Tourette's disorder (Chappell, Scahill, & Leckman, 1997). For those who need treatment in addition to drugs (or who reject drugs because of their side effects), behavior therapy and cognitive-behavior therapy have been used to help people relax and to deal with the interpersonal and social problems caused by having a tic disorder (Peterson & Cohen, 1998).

Did Paolo have Tourette's disorder? As you can see from Document 12.7, he probably did not. Instead, his symptoms appeared to have been caused by methylphenidate. He was switched to antidepressants, which have beneficial effects in some people with ADHD (Popper, 1997). Paolo's case shows how the overlapping symptoms of many disorders can make diagnosis difficult. As you will see in the next sections, this was also true for Michelle and Karen Beasley.

DOCUMENT 12.7

Transcript From Meeting of the University Hospital Parent Support Group: Francesca, Celia, and Karen Discuss Their Children and Themselves

FRANCESCA ARMANTI: The doctors say Paolo may not have Tourette's disorder. He doesn't make sounds or shout. Anyway, you need to have symptoms for a year before you can make the diagnosis, and we didn't want to wait a year before doing something. The doctors decided to try a "drug holiday." During the summer vacation, Paolo was gradually tapered off Ritalin to see whether this made any difference. The experiment was a success. Paolo's tics stopped when his Ritalin was removed. The neurologist decided to put Paolo on the drugs they use for depression. He said these drugs also help kids like Paolo.

KAREN BEASLEY: I wish the doctors would give me some of that Ritalin. I could use something to kill my appetite. I want to eat, but I know I should lose weight. At least I exercise.

CELIA BEROFSKY: I told you before, you're already too skinny. You should be worrying about your daughter. That's the reason you're here, isn't it? Your daughter won't talk to you, and my son won't talk to his teachers. They make a good pair.

KAREN BEASLEY: I guess so. You know, I thought she would be better when Eric left. He used to beat her up. Once, he even broke her arm. But, you know, I need to look good. Eric said I was too fat. Maybe that's why he left. I diet and exercise like crazy, but I need to do more. I get so hungry I can't help eating. Like, I might eat a whole quart of ice cream or five— chocolate bars—sweets mainly. Then, I feel so bad, I just stick my fingers down my throat and throw it all back up. ∎

ATTACHMENT AND SEPARATION ANXIETY DISORDERS

Gordon Berofsky refused to go to school. When forced to attend, he would not talk. Michelle Beasley, who was physically abused by her father, wouldn't talk to her mother, nor would she let her mother comfort her when she cried. The functioning of both children was impaired enough to require treatment. This section discusses Michelle and Gordon in the context of three *DSM-IV* disorders: reactive attachment disorder of infancy or early childhood, separation anxiety disorder, and selective mutism.

Reactive Attachment Disorder

From relative obscurity, **reactive attachment disorder** exploded into public consciousness when it was used as a defense in the trial of a mother accused of killing her adopted son (Roebuck, 1997). Renee and David Polreis adopted David Jr. from a Russian orphanage. Early one morning in 1996, paramedics responded to a call from Renee. They found 30-month-old David lying on the floor unconscious, his body covered with bruises and blisters. Only his mother was at home with him, and she was phoning her lawyer. Despite medical efforts, David died later that morning. Police found two bloody wooden spoons, one wrapped in a blood-stained diaper, in the family garbage. They charged Renee with second-degree murder. Her defense, which received wide publicity, was that David Jr. had reactive attachment disorder, which caused him to beat himself to death in a fit of rage. The jury was not convinced; Renee was sentenced to 22 years in prison.

Although reactive attachment disorder was once considered a rare condition found only among neglected or abused children such as Michelle Beasley, the Polreis trial brought to light many alleged cases of the disorder. Children with this disorder, who refuse to be touched or held, appear unable to form strong emotional bonds (**attachments**), especially with their mothers. As we will see in the next section, such attachments are essential to normal development (J. P. Allen et al., 1998; Moss et al., 1998).

Attachment Formation Children go through a series of stages in the development of attachments (Schaffer & Emerson, 1964). They begin life comfortable with anyone who cuddles or cares for them. Between 6 and 12 months, they develop a strong attachment to their primary caregiver, usually their mother, but sometimes their father (Popenoe, 1996). Initially, the caregiver satisfies an infant's physical needs (for food, drink, warmth, and contact) while the infant satisfies the caregiver's need for love (by eye contact, cooing, and smiling). As children get older, their attachment takes on additional dimensions. In addition to meeting the child's physical needs, caregivers also meet a child's needs for intellectual stimulation and autonomy. They also serve as role models that children can imitate during the socialization process (Popenoe, 1996). Once attachments form, children become distressed when their caregivers leave them and relieved when they return. As the attachment bonds strengthen even further, children begin to fear strangers; the very presence of a strange face provokes distress and causes them to cling closer to their primary caregiver. Both attachments and the fear of strangers evolved because they have survival value. The safety of human infants (who are totally dependent on others) is best ensured by keeping their caregivers as close as possible and keeping predators away.

The separation of children from their caregivers is a common theme in myths and legends. Fairy tales about abandoned children separated from their mothers at a tender age appear in practically every culture. In these stories, children are left to grow up alone, or, like Romulus and Remus, they are raised by animals. Tarzan is an example of the latter theme. Normally, these children are presented as happy, frolicking with the animals of the forest or jungle. But some legends are gloomy. For example, Emperor Frederick II of Prussia, in an attempt to identify mankind's "natural" language, was supposed to have removed babies from their parents and raised them in total silence. With no language to imitate, he thought they would grow up speaking humanity's "pure" language. According to the tale, the experiment failed. Without the love of their parents, these babies died.

The idea that babies suffer, and even die, when deprived of love is not only a recurring theme in mythology, it is also featured in behavioral research as well. To study the development of attachments, psychologist Harry Harlow separated infant monkeys from their mothers, and from all other monkeys, for long periods (Harlow & Suomi, 1976). He found such separations left the monkeys profoundly disturbed. They huddled in corners, rocking back and forth for hours. They were unable to mate with other monkeys when they got older. Their problems were particularly severe if they were separated from their mothers for 6 months or more during their first year of life. An infant monkey's first year seems to be a **critical period,** a period of development when attachments must form if they are to form at all. Being introduced to their mothers after 12 months is too late.

No psychologist would repeat Harlow's experiment with human children; even his animal experiments would be ethically suspect today. In the first half of the 20th century, however, several "natural experiments" were conducted with human subjects. One type consisted of observing children raised in orphanages. Even taking into account the unfortunate conditions in many orphanages—rudimentary hygiene and minimal intellectual stimulation—children raised in them seemed to show a higher than expected number of psychological disorders. Psychoanalytically oriented researchers concluded that orphans separated from their mothers during their first year of life develop severe depression, leading to lifelong psychological disorders or, in severe cases, even death (Spitz, 1945, 1946). Observations of British children separated from their families to protect them from German bombing during World War II led to similar, if slightly less apocalyptic, conclusions (Bowlby, 1951). Over the years, these claims have been challenged and softened. Some children are resilient enough to sur-

Psychologist Harry Harlow found that separating infant monkeys from their mother for long periods left them profoundly distraught.

vive the most horrible beginnings without developing psychological disorders (Cowen, Work, & Wyman, 1997; Paris, 1998). Nevertheless, few psychologists doubt that a failure to form strong early attachments, for whatever reason, is bad for the mental health of both child and parent (Boris & Zeanah, 1998; Moss et al., 1998).

Diagnosis   The main *DSM-IV* diagnostic criteria for reactive attachment disorder of infancy or early childhood are summarized in Table 12.8. As you can see, the main feature of the disorder is a disturbance in attachments beginning before age 5. An unusual aspect of the disorder is that, contrary to the *DSM-IV* philosophy of using objective criteria, the diagnostic criteria for reactive attachment disorder include a presumed etiology (pathological care). The *DSM-IV* identifies two subtypes: an *inhibited* subtype consisting of children who fail to develop strong attachments (criterion A1) and a *disinhibited* subtype consisting of children who form numerous superficial attachments but no strong primary attachment (criterion A2). Michelle Beasley, whose difficulties are presumably the result of her father's abusive treatment, fits the inhibited subtype.

The *DSM-IV* considers reactive attachment disorder rare, but, as already noted, increasing numbers of cases are being diagnosed (Boris & Zeanah, 1998). It is not clear whether these new cases were always there but were missed before the disorder gained notoriety or whether the incidence of the disorder is increasing. The *DSM-IV* criteria are partly to blame. Because it is sometimes difficult to obtain accurate histories of childrearing, some clinicians ignore the etiological criteria (C and D); others do not. This not only leads to poor

DSM-IV TABLE 12.8   Main *DSM-IV* Criteria for Reactive Attachment Disorder of Infancy or Early Childhood

A. Markedly disturbed and developmentally inappropriate social relatedness in most contexts, beginning before age 5 years, as evidenced by either (1) or (2):

  (1) persistent failure to initiate or respond in a developmentally appropriate fashion to most social interactions, as manifest by excessively inhibited, hypervigilant, or highly ambivalent and contradictory responses (e.g., the child may respond to caregivers with a mixture of approach, avoidance, and resistance to comforting, or may exhibit frozen watchfulness)

  (2) diffuse attachments as manifest by indiscriminate sociability with marked inability to exhibit appropriate selective attachments (e.g., excessive familiarity with relative strangers or lack of selectivity in choice of attachment figures)

B. The disturbance in Criterion A is not accounted for solely by mental delay (as in mental retardation) and does not meet criteria for a pervasive developmental disorder.

C. Pathogenic care as evidenced by at least one of the following:

  (1) persistent disregard of the child's basic emotional needs for comfort, stimulation, and affection

  (2) persistent disregard of the child's basic physical needs

  (3) repeated changes of primary caregiver that prevent formation of stable attachments (e.g., frequent changes in foster care)

D. There is a presumption that the care in Criterion C is responsible for the disturbed behavior in Criterion A (e.g., the disturbances in Criterion A began following the pathogenic care in Criterion C).

Note: From American Psychiatric Association (1994, p. 118).

---

interclinician reliability, but also to overdiagnosis because more children meet criteria A and B than meet C and D (Boris et al., 1998; Richters & Volkmar, 1994). Another possible explanation for the increasing incidence is that children who would previously have received some other diagnosis (conduct disorder, for example) are now diagnosed with reactive attachment disorder (Minnis, Ramsay, & Campbell, 1996).

Etiology   As already mentioned, the *DSM-IV* diagnostic criteria for reactive attachment disorder (and the use of the term *reactive*) presume that the disorder is a *reaction* to pathological care: physical or emotional neglect, abuse, or frequent changes in caregiver. Pathological care can have profound effects on vulnerable people (Wang, 1997). Child abuse is particularly destructive (Popper & Steingard, 1996). Unfortunately, it is impossible to say whether all children who display poor attachments have experienced pathological care because accurate histories are sometimes difficult to obtain. In many cases, the presumption that pathological care is responsible for a reactive attachment disorder is just that, a presumption. Even when accurate information is available, it may still be difficult to pinpoint the exact cause of a child's disorder. Children adopted from orphanages

may have been abused by their parents, neglected by institutional staff, and handed over from one caregiver to the next. To cloud the etiological picture even further, some orphans are born to mothers who use drugs and alcohol. These children may have prenatal dietary deficiencies or fetal alcohol syndrome. Disentangling the various etiological factors is often impossible.

A problem with the *DSM-IV* diagnosis of reactive attachment disorder is that it locates the *disorder* in the child and the *cause* in parents who provide pathological care. Yet attachments are a two-way street. Parents may find it hard to form strong attachments to temperamentally difficult children. Some parents, especially those with depression, may have problems forming attachments even to easy children (Beardslee, Versage, & Gladstone, 1998; Condon & Corkindale, 1997). Some writers have postulated the existence of a maternal "bonding" disorder that prevents the formation of healthy parent-child attachments (Kumar, 1997). It is worthwhile keeping in mind that reactive attachment disorder is always the result of a two-way interaction.

Harlow's observation of a critical period for the formation of attachments seems to be supported by studies of children adopted from European orphanages. These studies have found that the older children are when

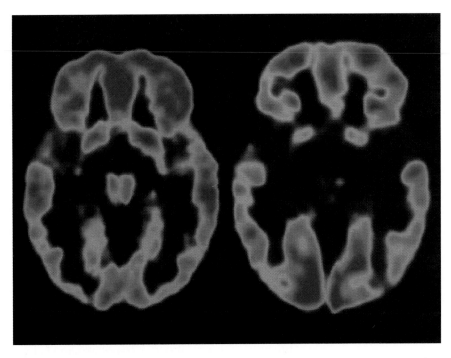

In these PET scans, the blue and black tones of a Romanian orphan (right) show that areas of the brain connected with emotion, such as the temporal lobe, are almost inactive in comparison with the scan of a child who is not an orphan (left).

they are adopted, the more likely they are to develop an attachment disorder (Chisholm, et al., 1995; Morison, Ames, & Chisholm, 1995). The critical age for attachment formation appears to be between 8 and 12 months. After this, children may have difficulties forming attachments, even with the best of parents.

Treatment   Michelle Beasley not only refuses to talk to Karen, she also cries inconsolably and bangs her head against the wall (see Document 12.1). Yet she will not let her mother console her. A variety of treatments have been tried and discarded for children like Michelle (Levy & Orlans, 1998). Karen, desperate for some way to connect with Michelle, decided to try a treatment she read about in a magazine. This treatment—*holding therapy*—requires parents to initiate physical contact with their child, by force if necessary (see Levy & Orlans, 1998). The idea is that contact is required to "break through" to children who "freeze" out their parents. Karen would sit on Michelle's bed and try to cradle her daughter in her arms. When Michelle struggled to escape, Karen would hold her tighter. On one such occasion, Karen accidentally crushed Michelle's face tightly into her chest. By the time Karen realized what she was doing, Michelle was beginning to turn blue from lack of

oxygen. Although she let go in time, Karen was afraid to try this treatment again.

While the advocates of holding therapy say that its safe application requires professional training, at $7,000 per course, many psychologists are skeptical about its rationale and efficacy. Like eye-movement therapy for post-traumatic stress disorder (described in Chapter 4), holding therapy is touted as a simple and quick cure for what is actually a complicated problem. Overcoming attachment disorder is a demanding process that almost always requires multiple treatment modalities (Hoyle, 1995; Levy & Orlans, 1998). At the very least, through role playing, modeling, and other methods, children must learn a set of social interaction skills. Because attachments are two-way processes, other family members will need counseling or therapy to identify impediments to attachment formation and to teach them how to reinforce appropriate behavior in the child. Adoptive families also need help accepting a child with psychological problems. In most cases, primary caregivers will require individual therapy to deal with feelings of guilt, inadequacy, and sometimes a secondary depression. Abusive parents require treatment for anger control. In addition, practically all parents benefit from the support provided by groups such as the University Hospital

Parent Support Group. It was through this group that Karen found respite care for Michelle and learned about treatment options from the Berofskys, whose son Gordon's problems appear to arise, at least in part, from too strong an attachment to his mother.

Separation Anxiety Disorder and Selective Mutism

At home, playing computer games, 10-year-old Gordon Berofsky seems to be a normal boy, but he has significant problems. He will not attend school, and when he does, he will not talk to his school-bus driver, the other children, or his teachers. Gordon has been seen by two psychologists and a psychiatrist and has received several diagnoses, as his mother relates in Document 12.8.

DOCUMENT 12.8

Transcript From Meeting of the University Hospital Parent Support Group: Celia and Michael Describe Gordon's Problems

MICHAEL BEROFSKY: Gordon is a sensitive boy who likes to be near his mom. He has always hated being left with a baby sitter. He would cry and cry. When he started third grade, he began having trouble getting out of bed in the morning. He would follow Celia as she made the beds and prepared meals. He would even stand outside the bathroom until she came out. Sometimes he would come to our bed in the middle of the night to see whether his mother was still breathing. He says he has nightmares about his mother dying in her sleep. I tried to get Celia not to baby the kid, but she just overprotected him to the point that he is now unable to stand on his own two feet.

CELIA BEROFSKY: Oh sure, blame it all on me. Like you were not there. You know how pathetic he was. He could barely let go of my hand when I took him to school. He is still the same. He is devastated every time he has to leave me. Besides, he is sickly. He has all these illnesses—headaches, tummy aches. The doctors seem to be unable to find out what is wrong. When I force him to go to school, he won't talk to anyone. He studies at home with me, and his work is excellent.

FRANCESCA ARMANTI: What treatment has Gordon received?

CELIA BEROFSKY: He has been to psychologists and psychiatrists. They say he has separation anxiety and that his not talking at school is selective mutism. He has had play therapy, behavior therapy, and a course of antidepressants. They all help a little, but sometimes I think this is just the way he is. ■

Diagnosis and Etiology The *DSM-IV* diagnostic criteria for **separation anxiety disorder,** which describe Gordon's behavior well, are summarized in Table 12.9. Note the importance of taking developmental level into account. It is normal for young children to be more uneasy about separation than older children. However, if young children exhibit more than the normal degree of separation anxiety, the *DSM-IV* categorizes them as having an early-onset separation anxiety disorder. Early-onset cases have a poor prognosis; many go on to develop adult anxiety disorders (Klein, 1995; Manicavasagar, Silove, & Hadzi-Pavlovic, 1998).

At one time, refusal to go to school was considered a relatively common type of phobia (Iwamoto & Yoshida, 1997; S. Schwartz & Johnson, 1985). It seems to occur equally often in boys and girls and is most likely to occur at transition points—entry to elementary school or at the beginning of junior or senior high school. Children who refuse to go to school need not have difficulty with schoolwork. Some may fear evaluation (recall the discussion of test anxiety in Chapter 4); others fear mixing with new children and may suffer from a social phobia or avoidant personality disorder. Some school refusers may fear bullying or ridicule. However, for children like Gordon, the term *school phobia* is misleading. It is not the fear of school that motivates Gordon to stay home; it is the fear of separation from his mother. Gordon's physical symptoms are an excuse to avoid school. Children like Gordon are different from truants, who skip school without their parents' knowledge to do something they like better, such as go to the beach or a ball game (Lee & Miltenberger, 1996). Gordon skips school to stay home, and his parents know all about it.

There are many possible causes for separation anxiety. In some cases, a child may have actually experienced separation from his or her parents through death or, more often, divorce. (Highlight 12.1 looks at the effects of the separation caused by divorce on children.) In other cases, separation anxiety may arise, as Michael Berofsky seems to believe, from overprotectiveness. Parents who worry excessively about harm coming to their child once the child is outside of their immediate purview communicate their anxiety to their child, who learns to fear separation. In some cases, the parents of children with separation anxiety disorder may have anxiety disorders themselves (Unnewehr et al., 1998; Eaves et al., 1997).

Staying home is reinforcing because it not only reduces anxiety but also offers secondary rewards, such as maternal attention. School refusal and separation anxi-

DSM-IV   TABLE 12.9   Main *DSM-IV* Diagnostic Criteria
for Separation Anxiety Disorder

A. Developmentally inappropriate and excessive anxiety concerning separation from home or from those to whom the individual is attached, as evidenced by three (or more) of the following:

(1) recurrent excessive distress when separation from home or major attachment figures occurs or is anticipated

(2) persistent and excessive worry about losing, or about possible harm befalling, major attachment figures

(3) persistent and excessive worry that an untoward event will lead to separation from a major attachment figure (e.g., getting lost or being kidnapped)

(4) persistent reluctance or refusal to go to school or elsewhere because of fear of separation

(5) persistently and excessively fearful or reluctant to be alone or without major attachment figures at home or without significant adults in other settings

(6) persistent reluctance or refusal to go to sleep without being near a major attachment figure or to sleep away from home

(7) repeated nightmares involving the theme of separation

(8) repeated complaints of physical symptoms (such as headaches, stomachaches, nausea, or vomiting) when separation from major attachment figures occurs or is anticipated

B. The duration of the disturbance is at least 4 weeks.

C. The onset is before age 18 years.

D. The disturbance causes clinically significant distress or impairment in social, academic (occupational), or other important areas of functioning.

E. The disturbance does not occur exclusively during the course of a pervasive developmental disorder, schizophrenia, or other psychotic disorder and, in adolescents and adults, is not better accounted for by panic disorder with agoraphobia.

Note: From American Psychiatric Association (1994, p. 113).

ety disorder make a dangerous combination. Children who show both signs develop sleep disorders and, in some cases, lifelong anxiety disorders (see Flakierska-Praquin, Lindstroem, & Gillberg, 1997). Critical Thinking About Clinical Decisions 12.1 provides more information on sleep disorders.

In addition to separation anxiety, Gordon's silence at school earned him the additional diagnosis of **selective mutism**, a disorder characterized by a lack of speech in some situations but not in others (Cline & Baldwin, 1994; see H. H. Wright et al., 1994, for a review and bibliography). Like Gordon, the typical child with selective (sometimes called elective) mutism speaks at home but refuses to speak at school. Unlike separation anxiety, selective mutism is relatively rare, affecting less than 1% of the clinic population, with slightly more girls than boys (Tancer, 1992). There is evidence, however, that the disorder is underdiagnosed. Because such children rarely cause problems at school, their behavior is tolerated by teachers (Kopp & Gillberg, 1997;

As she related in her autobiographical book I Know Why the Caged Bird Sings, *writer and poet Maya Angelou stopped speaking for 5 years after she was raped at age 8 by her mother's boyfriend.*

Suffer the Little Children

For many children of divorce, separation anxiety is an unavoidable part of life. Between half and two thirds of American marriages end in divorce; many of these breakups involve children. Divorce is rarely orderly, even when there are no children. Emotional turmoil, shock, and grief reverberate through the family, affecting parents, grandparents, other relatives, and friends. When divorce involves children, it can cause chaos in nearly every aspect of their lives.

Part of the problem is financial. Apart from movie stars and a few successful businesspeople, most working couples are made poorer by divorce. Even when they receive child support payments, custodial parents may struggle for economic survival. Not only do they have less money to meet their needs, hard-working parents also have less time to spend with their children. Children who may have been getting a considerable amount of attention before the divorce may find themselves increasingly left with child-care providers, sitters, or grandparents.

Studies have documented that separation from a parent and guilt over the breakup produce psychological disturbances in many children from divorced families (Lamb, Sternberg, & Thompson, 1997). What is not clear is whether these children would have fared better if their parents had stayed married. Some writers believe that divorce is preferable to living with parental conflict (Kelly, 1998); others argue that living in homes with parental conflict, although hardly a good thing, produces less psychopathology than family disintegration (Tapper, 1996). Both views are probably accurate. Some children are severely affected by divorce; more resilient children seem able to adapt (Emery & Coiro, 1997). The magnitude of psychological disturbance caused by divorce depends on the personality of the child, the psychological health of the parents, the extent of any conflict between the partners, and the financial circumstances of the custodial parent (Grych & Fincham, 1997; Lamb et al., 1997). Fortunately, individual and group therapy, as well as peer support groups, can help some children who are having difficulty adjust to their parents' divorce (Bogolub, 1995).

Kumpulainen et al., 1998). The main *DSM-IV* diagnostic criteria for selective mutism are contained in Table 12.10. Notice that the diagnosis does not apply to children who, for one reason or another, are uncomfortable with the local language (new immigrants, for example) or to children whose mutism lasts for less than 1 month.

Professional opinion is mixed about whether selective mutism is really a disorder in its own right or a type of social phobia (B. Black & Uhde, 1992). Although there is considerable overlap between the two (children are mute in situations that make them uncomfortable), social phobia is not the only reason for selective mutism. Traumatic experiences (sexual abuse, for example), instructions not to reveal sensitive family information, attention seeking, a need to defy authority (albeit in a passive-aggressive way), and even genetics can also result in selective mutism (Hayden, 1980; Simons, Goode, & Fombonne, 1997; Steinhausen & Adamek, 1997). Selective mutism is a more heterogeneous category than social phobia (Tancer, 1992), but the two disorders often go together (Dummit et al., 1997).

Treatment   Children like Gordon are difficult to treat because they typically refuse to talk to therapists. Psychodynamically oriented play therapy, family therapy, behavioral therapy, and drugs have all been tried. Gordon had all four! His first psychologist, a Freudian, spent months trying to engage Gordon in play therapy (see Cook, 1997). Gordon would play with her, but he would not talk. The best she could do was to get Gordon to use hand signals when he wanted a drink or needed to go to the bathroom. The therapist became frustrated—and so did Celia and Michael, who terminated the therapy. Thinking that there might be something about the school that was frightening their son, they enrolled Gordon in another school. He still refused to attend and was mute when forced. Gordon next saw a psychiatrist, who prescribed an antidepressant (fluoxetine). Antidepressants and, to a lesser extent, antianxiety drugs are sometimes prescribed for children with separation anxiety, reactive attachment disorder, or selective mutism (Pine & Grun, 1998). This is because depressed children may act different from depressed adults. In addition to being sad and tired, depressed children may also be defiant, combative, and anxious. Unfortunately, except for eliminating his nightmares, antidepressants made little difference to Gordon's other behaviors.

Gordon's second psychologist had a cognitive-behavioral orientation toward separation anxiety (see

To Sleep, Perchance to Dream

Gordon Berofsky had nightmares in which his mother was harmed. These dreams were so frightening and realistic that he would go to his parents' bedroom, his heart racing wildly, expecting to find that his mother had died (see Document 12.8). Nightmares occur sporadically in some adults and in practically all children, particularly those between 3 and 6 years of age (Leung & Robson, 1993). They usually occur in the middle of the night or in the early morning. In most children, nightmares involve a threat to the dreamer or, as in Gordon's case, to loved ones. Occasional nightmares are not serious. Most children are easily reassured. When nightmares are so frequent that they cause clinical distress or impair a person's functioning, however, the *DSM-IV* considers them signs of **nightmare disorder.**

After awakening from a nightmare, the dreamer soon realizes that he or she has been dreaming and is able to provide a coherent account of the dream (Buysse, Morin, & Reynolds, 1995). There is another type of disorder, however, in which children remain incoherent and terrified for a prolonged period after awakening. The *DSM-IV* calls this **sleep terror disorder.** In contrast to nightmares, "sleep terrors" occur early in the evening, during the first hour or two of sleep (Buysee et al., 1995). Awakened by a loud scream, parents rush to their child's bedroom to find the child disoriented and terrified—heart racing, breathing shallow, covered in sweat. Some children may run around the room in a frenzy. They may not recognize their parents and are not easily comforted. An episode may last 15–30 minutes, followed by a peaceful sleep and no memory of the incident (or any dream) the next morning. Sleep terrors may be accompanied by **sleepwalking disorder,** which also occurs early in sleep. Sleepwalkers move around their room (or even further afield) but do not recognize or respond to others. Like those with sleep terrors, sleepwalkers have no memory of the episode the next day.

Nightmares, sleep terrors, and sleepwalking are all examples of **parasomnias**—abnormal behavioral or physiological events that occur during sleep. They are different from **dyssomnias,** which are disturbances in the amount, quality, or timing of sleep. (See Chapter 13 for more on sleep disorders.)

Beginning with Freud, psychodynamic writers have considered dreams to be a window to the unconscious (Gaines, 1995). The meaning of Gordon's dreams seems transparent; he is worried about harm coming to his mother, or, in a wish-fulfillment sense, he may resent her overprotectiveness and desire harm to come to her. In Freudian theory, Gordon may harbor both of these contradictory feelings simultaneously. When he sleeps, these normally repressed feelings slip past his ego's defenses. Night terrors and sleepwalking are more difficult to understand from a psychodynamic perspective. Perhaps they are partially repressed dreams. Alternatively, they may be the result of an immature nervous system, which is why they are usually, but not always, outgrown. Physical conditions, including seizure disorders and respiratory disorders that limit oxygen intake during sleep, can cause night terrors and sleepwalking. Medications, such as the antidepressants given to Gordon, may also be responsible. Separating the various possibilities requires careful clinical judgment. Gordon's clinicians assumed that his nightmares were the result of separation anxiety (as was his selective mutism). They may have been correct, but they should not have jumped to conclusions. Responsible clinicians would have conducted the necessary investigations to rule out the possibility that drugs or an undetected medical disorder was responsible for his nightmares.

Levin et al., 1996). She employed cognitive restructuring (what is the worst thing that could happen if you talked?) and instituted a behavioral program designed to build Gordon's self-confidence. The latter program began with desensitization sessions in which Gordon's parents brought him to school after hours. With no children or teachers around, and with his parents present, Gordon was able to progress through a fear hierarchy that began with driving to school and went on to entering the grounds, the school building, and finally his classroom. He eventually reached the point where he was able to speak to the therapist in his classroom, provided that his mother was also present.

The next step was to gradually add other people to the group, but Gordon refused to speak if another person was present. Changing tack, the therapist had Gordon's parents videotape him answering questions posed by his mother. She then taped Gordon's teacher asking the same questions. By editing the two tapes, she produced a tape in which Gordon appeared to respond to the teacher's questions (see Blum et al., 1998). She repeatedly played this tape to Gordon and rewarded him with praise and toys during scenes showing him "answering" the teacher's questions. After many sessions, this **self-modeling** procedure induced Gordon to say a few words to the therapist. She then added more people

DSM-IV **TABLE 12.10** Main *DSM-IV* Diagnostic Criteria for Selective Mutism

A. Consistent failure to speak in specific social situations (in which there is an expectation for speaking, e.g., at school) despite speaking in other situations.

B. The disturbance interferes with educational or occupational achievement or with social communication.

C. The duration of the disturbance is at least 1 month (not limited to the first month of school).

D. The failure to speak is not due to a lack of knowledge of, or comfort with, the spoken language required in the social situation.

E. The disturbance is not better accounted for by a communication disorder (e.g., stuttering) and does not occur exclusively during the course of a pervasive developmental disorder, schizophrenia, or other psychotic disorder.

Note: From American Psychiatric Association (1994, p. 115).

to the tape. Gordon was now able to hear himself "answering" questions posed by various adults and children. At the same time, Celia and Michael were trained in contingency management. They implemented a program that assigned Gordon points for separation (staying with a sitter, for example). These points could be traded for "prizes," such as candy and toys. By the time of the first meeting of the University Hospital Parent Support Group, Gordon was still not attending school, but he was making progress. The therapist's plan was to begin inviting people to the room while Gordon viewed the tape, to try to generalize his talking to a more social situation.

Although Gordon was slowly improving, Karen Beasley had made only a small start in helping Michelle. Still, her story struck a responsive chord with John and Ingrid Cheney, whose son, Eddie, also had difficulty forming attachments. As you can see from Ingrid's description in Document 12.9, Eddie's attachment problems were different from Michelle's. They were the result of what the *DSM-IV* calls a pervasive developmental disorder.

DOCUMENT 12.9

Transcript From Meeting of the University Hospital Parent Support Group: Ingrid Describes Her Son

INGRID CHENEY: You know, Karen, listening to you talk about Michelle reminds me just how much of a relationship problem we have with Eddie. I mean, Eddie has never related to me at all. When he was an infant and then a toddler, I would go to him with my arms out, but he never reached out to signal that he wanted to be picked up. I don't think he really did. Even when I cuddled him, he never put his arms around my neck.

He just hung there limp, like a doll. He also never looks at me. He looks past me or through me but never at me—no eye contact at all. I sometimes think that he is attached to me; he certainly gets upset when we separate. But he doesn't relate to me as a person, just as an object. I'm just something he's used to having around, not someone he loves. ∎

PERVASIVE DEVELOPMENTAL DISORDERS

Pervasive developmental disorders are the most serious psychopathological conditions occurring in childhood. They are marked by poor interpersonal relationships, distorted thinking, defective perception, and inappropriate affect. At one time, these disorders were referred to as childhood schizophrenia, but it is now clear that they are different from schizophrenia. They are not associated with hallucinations or delusions, and the children do not develop schizophrenia when they grow up. The pervasive developmental disorders constitute a separate category of psychological disorder.

Our modern concept of pervasive developmental disorders dates to 1943, when psychiatrist Leo Kanner (1894–1981) published an article titled "Autistic Disturbances of Affective Contact" (Kanner, 1943). He described 11 children who displayed the syndrome later called infantile autism. Although Kanner was not the first to describe such children, his article ignited intense interest among clinicians and researchers. More than 300 books and thousands of articles have been published on autism, and the list grows each year. One result of this flood of research has been the differentiation of four pervasive developmental disorders. The first, **autistic disorder,** which seems to be present from birth

DSM-IV TABLE 12.11 Main *DSM-IV* Diagnostic Criteria for Autistic Disorder

A. A total of six (or more) items from (1), (2), and (3), with at least two from (1) and one each from (2) and (3):

(1) qualitative impairment in social interaction, as manifested by at least two of the following:

(a) marked impairment in the use of multiple nonverbal behaviors such as eye-to-eye gaze, facial expression, body postures, and gestures to regulate social interaction

(b) failure to develop peer relationships appropriate to developmental level

(c) a lack of spontaneous seeking to share enjoyment, interests, or achievements with other people (e.g., by a lack of showing, bringing, or pointing out objects of interest)

(d) lack of social or emotional reciprocity

(2) qualitative impairments in communication as manifested by at least one of the following:

(a) delay in, or total lack of, the development of spoken language (not accompanied by an attempt to compensate through alternative modes of communication such as gesture or mime)

(b) in individuals with adequate speech, marked impairment in the ability to initiate or sustain a conversation with others

(c) stereotyped and repetitive use of language or idiosyncratic language

(d) lack of varied, spontaneous make-believe play or social imitative play appropriate to developmental level

(3) restricted repetitive and stereotyped patterns of behavior, interests, and activities, as manifested by at least one of the following:

(a) encompassing preoccupation with one or more stereotyped and restricted patterns of interest that is abnormal either in intensity or focus

(b) apparently inflexible adherence to specific, nonfunctional routines or rituals

(c) stereotyped and repetitive motor mannerisms (e.g., hand or finger flapping or twisting, or complex whole-body movements)

(d) persistent preoccupation with parts of objects

B. Delays or abnormal functioning in at least one of the following areas, with onset prior to age 3 years: (1) social interaction, (2) language as used in social communication, or (3) symbolic or imaginative play.

C. The disturbance is not better accounted for by Rett's disorder or childhood disintegrative disorder.

Note: From American Psychiatric Association (1994, pp. 70–71).

or at least by age 3, is marked by poor social interactions, impaired communication, and odd motor behaviors. **Asperger's disorder,** named after Hans Asperger (1906–1980), the Austrian psychiatrist who first described it in 1944, is similar to autistic disorder but without the serious language and communication problems (Wing, 1998). **Childhood disintegrative disorder** affects children whose apparently normal development begins to deteriorate between the ages of 2 and 10. Finally, **Rett's disorder,** named after Andreas Rett (1924–1997), who described it in 1966, also involves the loss of previously acquired manual skills, but occurs earlier than childhood disintegrative disorder and is marked by an unnaturally small head.

Diagnosis

John and Ingrid Cheney were both 27 years old when Eddie was born. As we saw in Document 12.1, John is a radiologist. Ingrid was an associate professor of biochemistry, but she gave up her career to look after Eddie and now gives the occasional lecture on a part-time basis. Neither John nor Ingrid knows of any mental illness in their families, although Ingrid's brother had a developmental language disorder as a child. As you can see from Document 12.10, Eddie's problems became apparent early in life, and his behavior reflects almost all of the diagnostic criteria for autistic disorder, which are summarized in Table 12.11.

DOCUMENT 12.10

Transcript From Meeting of the University Hospital Parent Support Group: The Cheneys Talk About Eddie

INGRID CHENEY: My pregnancy and delivery were great. I felt well, and there were no problems. Eddie was a beautiful baby; people would look at him in his carriage and remark on how good-looking he was. He smiled a lot, but like I said, he never seemed to anticipate being picked up. When I would hold him, he would just hang there limp. Otherwise, he was perfectly normal.

JOHN CHENEY: Not quite perfectly. Remember when we thought he was deaf because he never seemed to turn to you when you called his name?

INGRID CHENEY: Of course, I remember. He was hardly aware of sounds.

JOHN CHENEY: Anyway, by the time Eddie was two, we knew something was seriously wrong. He would never look in anyone's eyes. Even when you held his head, he turned his eyes away. He said nothing intelligible, and he didn't seem to understand much either. Eddie's favorite pastime was tapping this one special pencil on any surface he could find. Tap, tap, tap, until you thought you would go mad. If you tried to take away his pencil, *he* would go mad.

INGRID CHENEY: It was around then that he started these strange movements—flapping his arms like a bird, rocking, whirling in circles, twisting his fingers in front of his face, grimacing. Other kids were going to nursery school and playing. Eddie was spreading feces all over my sofa.

JOHN CHENEY: And he was so rigid. Everything had to be just as he wanted it. You couldn't move any furniture without Eddie going into a fit. He would scream, flap his arms, and hit himself in the head. Even his routine had to be exactly the same every day. First supper, then television, then a bath, then bed. Any change, and he would have a tantrum. Living with him was exasperating.

INGRID CHENEY: And sometimes dangerous. I can't tell you how many times he has kicked me and bit me. I have had to hide all the knives, scissors, and anything else that he might hurt himself with. Not that he is all that sensitive to pain. He has had the most horrible wounds without showing any sign that they hurt.

DR. BERG: What is he like now that he is nine?

JOHN CHENEY: He talks, but his speech consists mainly of imitations of what he has heard someone else say, or something he heard on television. He likes music and can repeat whole songs after hearing them only once. He has learned to use some sign language—you know, the kind deaf people use. We have learned it, too. At least we can communicate a little that way.

DR. BERG: Does he go to school?

INGRID CHENEY: Yes, he is mainstreamed into a normal class for part of each day. He has special education the rest of the time, but he never plays directly with the other kids. And he is a handful at home. We rarely go out because we cannot leave him, and no one will baby-sit him. Vacations are only a dream.

DR. BERG: How has this affected you?

INGRID CHENEY: John works long hours and gets away from Eddie. For me, he is a constant companion. It has destroyed my life. I won't have any more kids because I can barely cope with Eddie. John and I fight about our lives, and we have discussed divorce. It's just too grim living like this. I feel like an old woman. ■

To distinguish autism from other pervasive developmental disorders, the *DSM-IV* defines it as beginning before age 3. Symptoms that appear later are not signs of autism. As mentioned earlier, retrospective parental reports about when symptoms first began are rarely reliable. However, autistic behaviors are so unusual that most parents notice something is "wrong" well before the child reaches age 3. The first sign is the child's lack of responsiveness. Eddie was typical. He did not form a normal parental attachment. He never anticipated being picked up by his mother, and when he was hugged, he did not hug back. Kanner's descriptions emphasized this aspect of autism. In fact, the term *autism* comes from the Greek word for *self*. Kanner believed that autistic children are alone within themselves, unable to relate to others. Eddie's failure to respond to his name or to other sounds gave his parents the impression that he was deaf. When they realized that he could hear, they interpreted his "deafness" as indifference. This impression was reinforced by his avoidance of eye contact—he looked through people rather than at them—and his insensitivity to pain.

As indicated in Table 12.11, a communication disturbance is always associated with autistic disorder. About 50% of people with autistic disorder never develop intelligible speech. The remainder learn to produce words, but they have difficulty using them to communicate (S. Schwartz, 1981). Instead, their speech is like Eddie's, mere parroting of what they have heard others say (a symptom called *echolalia*). Some autistic children may be able to learn to communicate using gestures or sign language (Seal & Bonvillian, 1997).

Although the *DSM-IV* emphasizes the communication disorder, most people with pervasive developmental disorders also have a cognitive deficit (Hooper &

The first sign of autism is a child's lack of responsiveness to a parent: his or her inability to respond to being picked up or hugged or to hearing his or her name.

Sally has a basket.   Anne has a box.

Sally has a marble. She puts the marble into her basket.

Sally goes out for a walk.

Anne takes the marble out of the basket and puts it into the box.

Now Sally comes back. She wants to play with her marble.
Where will Sally look for her marble?

FIGURE 12.2 **A Theory of Mind Experiment.** *Autistic people seem to lack a "theory of mind." They cannot appreciate the difference between what they know and the doll's knowledge, and so predict, in this experiment, that Sally will look for the marble in the box.* Adapted from: Frith (1989).

Bundy, 1998), although the exact nature of the cognitive deficit is unclear. Some psychologists describe it as a failure of executive functioning (Pennington et al., 1997; Russell, 1998). Executive functions include the allocation of attention, planning, and problem solving. There is no doubt that people with autism have problems in these, and other, cognitive tasks. However, until we have precise operational definitions of the executive functions, all we can say is that people with autism do poorly on many different cognitive tasks.

An intriguing approach to cognition among people with autism focuses on their "theory of mind" (Baron-Cohen, 1995). Interpersonal functioning requires the ability to assign mental states to oneself and others. To know whether to laugh with or console another person, we must be able to infer whether that person is happy or sad. Such inferences require an understanding that other people have mental states that contain feelings, wishes, and desires. Such an understanding is apparent in normal 2-year-olds but is missing in people with autistic disorder (Baron-Cohen, 1995; Lee & Hobson, 1998). Ingenious experiments have shown that people with autistic and Asperger's disorders are unable to see the world from another person's point of view, as Figure 12.2 exemplifies. Although people with mental retardation may have similar difficulties (Yirmiya et al., 1998), people with autistic disorder do poorly on "mind-reading" tasks, even when they have good language skills and high IQs. Simple experiments can produce dramatic results. For example, Baron-Cohen and his colleagues (1997) asked people with autistic and Asperger's disorders to infer the mental state of a person (happy, sad, angry) just from looking at photographs of

the person's eyes. Both groups were significantly impaired on this task. Yet the same individuals had no difficulty recognizing whether the eyes belonged to males or females. In other words, their difficulty is not perception but inferring mental states.

Kanner believed that the avoidance of change was an important sign of autism. Like Eddie, Kanner's autistic children insisted on keeping objects in their accustomed place and in maintaining routines. Any change might result in a *catastrophic reaction* (an intense temper tantrum). Eddie showed such reactions whenever his routine was rescheduled. His preoccupation with tapping a pencil and his stereotyped body movements (such as rocking, whirling, and hand waving) are also common in autism and most of the other pervasive developmental disorders.

Although special abilities in a limited area are not included among the *DSM-IV* diagnostic criteria, some children with pervasive developmental disorders may have special ability in music, drawing, arithmetic, or memory. Superior performance in some limited area has earned some people with a pervasive developmental disorder the label of *idiot savant* (literally, "retarded scholar"). Such people are featured in movies about people with autism. They are shown breaking top-secret military codes or beating casinos for huge sums of money. Unfortunately, these are only movies, and such genius is exceedingly rare. Most people with pervasive developmental disorders have no special intellectual or artistic abilities. In those few cases where special abilities are apparent, they usually occur in Asperger's disorder, and not in the other pervasive developmental disorders.

The diagnostic criteria for Asperger's disorder are essentially the same as those for autistic disorder, with one exception. Asperger's disorder does not involve a severe language problem. Because the two disorders are so similar, there is some doubt about whether Asperger's is a different disorder or simply a less severe form of autism (Schopler, Mesibov, & Kunce, 1998; Szatmari, 1998; Volkmar, Klin, & Pauls, 1998). Some psychologists prefer to think of an autistic "spectrum" of disorders ranging from mild Asperger's to severe autism (Myhr, 1998; Prior et al., 1998). Childhood disintegrative disorder and Rett's disorder fit into the spectrum less comfortably because they both have the additional characteristic of beginning with a period of normal functioning. Specifically, childhood disintegrative disorder requires at least 2 years of normal development followed by the loss of once-learned social, motor, and communication skills before age 10. (Table 12.12 presents the main diagnostic criteria for childhood disintegrative disorder.) Rett's disorder may occur earlier than childhood disintegrative disorder (after only 5 months of normal development) and involves a slowing down of head growth, poor coordination, and the loss of communication skills. (Table 12.13 displays the main diagnostic cri-

teria for Rett's disorder.) Both childhood disintegrative disorder and Rett's disorder are extremely rare, are associated with severe mental retardation, and tend to last for life. An unusual feature of Rett's disorder is the predominance of females; the other pervasive developmental disorders affect mainly males (Volkmar, 1996).

Epidemiology and Course

Kanner considered autism to be a rare disorder, and epidemiological studies have confirmed that it occurs in 4 or 5 of every 10,000 children aged under 15 years regardless of culture or social class (Sponheim & Skjeldal, 1998; Volkmar, 1998). Rett's disorder and disintegrative disorder of childhood are even rarer (American Psychiatric Assn, 1994). The specific prevalence of Asperger's disorder is difficult to estimate because its diagnostic criteria are so similar to those of autism that clinicians have trouble telling the two disorders apart. However, Asperger's disorder is probably no more prevalent than autism (Attwood & Wing, 1997).

The prognosis for children with pervasive developmental disorders is poor (Howlin, 1997). Most are destined to lives of little hope, often in institutions. There are some exceptions, however. People with mild autistic disorder or Asperger's disorder do better than those with other pervasive developmental disorders (Attwood & Wing, 1997; Larsen & Mouridsen, 1997). Some high-functioning children graduate from college, obtain jobs, and even publish books. Highlight 12.2 tells the story of one such woman. Sadly, even these successful people retain their "autistic aloneness." Few marry and have families; most remain outsiders for life (Morgan, 1996).

Etiology

Although everything from smothering mothers to perceptual defects to viruses has been implicated by one theorist or another, we still have no generally agreed on etiological theory for any of the pervasive developmental disorders of childhood (Volkmar, 1998). There are some notable trends, however. For a long time, theories that implicated parental behavior were dominant. Kanner partly blamed autistic disorder on "refrigerator" parents who behave in a cold, detached manner to their children. The famous child psychoanalyst Bruno Bettelheim (1903–1990) described autistic disorder as a defense against a destructive maternal environment (Bettelheim, 1967). Blame-the-parent theories were not limited to psychodynamic theorists; some behaviorists

**DSM-IV   TABLE 12.12   Main *DSM-IV* Diagnostic Criteria
for Childhood Disintegrative Disorder**

A. Apparently normal development for at least the first 2 years after birth as manifested by the presence of age-appropriate verbal and nonverbal communication, social relationships, play, and adaptive behavior.

B. Clinically significant loss of previously acquired skills (before age 10 years) in at least two of the following areas:

(1) expressive or receptive language

(2) social skills or adaptive behavior

(3) bowel or bladder control

(4) play

(5) motor skills

C. Abnormalities of functioning in at least two of the following areas:

(1) qualitative impairment in social interaction (e.g., impairment in nonverbal behaviors, failure to develop peer relationships, lack of social or emotional reciprocity)

(2) qualitative impairments in communication (e.g., delay or lack of spoken language, inability to initiate or sustain a conversation, stereotyped and repetitive use of language, lack of varied make-believe play)

(3) restricted, repetitive, and stereotyped patterns of behavior, interests, and activities, including motor stereotypes and mannerisms

D. The disturbance is not better accounted for by another specific pervasive developmental disorder or by schizophrenia.

Note: From American Psychiatric Association (1994, pp. 74–75).

DSM-IV   TABLE 12.13   Main *DSM-IV* Diagnostic Criteria for Rett's Disorder

A. All of the following:

(1) apparently normal prenatal and perinatal development

(2) apparently normal psychomotor development through the first 5 months after birth

(3) normal head circumference at birth

B. Onset of all of the following after the period of normal development:

(1) deceleration of head growth between ages 5 and 48 months

(2) loss of previously acquired purposeful hand skills between ages 5 and 30 months with the subsequent development of stereotyped hand movements (e.g., hand-wringing or hand washing)

(3) loss of social engagement early in the course (although often social interaction develops later)

(4) appearance of poorly coordinated gait or trunk movements

(5) severely impaired expressive and receptive language development with severe psychomotor retardation

Note: From American Psychiatric Association (1994, pp. 72–73).

---

held similar views. For example, Ferster (1961), a follower of B. F. Skinner, claimed that the home environment of children with pervasive developmental disorders failed to reinforce proper social behavior.

As evidence for their theories, both psychodynamic and behavioral researchers pointed to the failure of children with pervasive developmental disorders to form normal parental attachments. They assumed that the fault lay with the parents; somehow the parents failed to foster normal attachments. A test of this assumption was conducted by Kubicek (1980), who analyzed a filmed interaction between a mother and her 16-week-old child. This interaction took place 2 years before the child was diagnosed with autistic disorder. As a control, Kubicek

Thinking Like an Animal

Professor Temple Grandin is an animal behaviorist whose work has taken her around the world. She has designed more animal-handling facilities than any person alive, and she serves as a consultant to business and government. In addition to her doctoral dissertation, Grandin has published several books and more than 100 scientific papers. Her success is especially remarkable considering that she has a pervasive developmental disorder.

When Grandin was a child, she was much like Eddie Cheney. She stiffened when held, would not make eye contact, and did not respond to sounds. Like Eddie's parents, Grandin's mother thought her daughter might be deaf, but she turned out to have autism (or Asperger's disorder; it is difficult to tell in retrospect). Fortunately, Grandin was lucky. With the help of her mother and dedicated teachers, she learned to communicate. When she grew up, she decided to help others appreciate what it is like to have autism. In her talks and books (Grandin & Sacks, 1996; Grandin & Scariano, 1996), Grandin probes autism from the inside. She describes how a school bell sounded like a dentist's drill in her ear and how hugs were literally painful.

At first, Grandin's public talks were stilted and difficult to follow. She lacked the empathy required to understand her listener's point of view. Gradually, she learned how to connect with an audience, but Grandin is still noticeably "different." Social courtesies leave her puzzled, and social relations remain a mystery. She is single and celibate. To get along in social situations, she simply imitates what other people do.

Grandin believes that she has been successful as an animal behaviorist because she reacts to the world as an animal would. She is frightened by unpredictable noises and by any change in routine or in appearances. She just "knows" that cattle will be spooked by a shiny chain dangling from the side of a fence and that sheep prefer curved loading ramps to straight ones. Grandin knows that animals feel safe when they are supported around their sides and bellies because this is how she herself feels. When she was 18 years old, and experiencing what she describes as panic attacks, she lowered herself into a tight animal "squeeze" chute on a relative's farm and found the environment calming—so calming, in fact, that she designed a version of the device for her bedroom. A giant padded vise driven by an industrial compressor, this contraption enfolds her body in a snug cocoon.

Grandin gives the parents of children with autism hope. They flock to her speeches and buy her books, hoping to learn how to transform their children into university professors. Almost all of them will be disappointed. Tragically few people with autism develop independent lives, let alone successful careers.

Temple Grandin, who did not speak until she was 3 years old and is now an animal science professor at Colorado State University, is a high-functioning autistic who used her unusual perceptive skills (thinking in pictures) to develop a design to alleviate panic in livestock that are about to be slaughtered.

filmed a similar interaction between the same mother and the child's fraternal twin brother. Kubicek's analysis showed that the behavior of the boy who was later diagnosed autistic differed in several important ways from his brother's behavior. The first child did not respond to changes in his mother's facial expression, and he failed to respond to his mother's gestures or to her attempts to play. In other words, he seemed indifferent to his mother, whereas his brother responded to her attempts at intimacy. This suggests that it was the child, not the mother, who was hindering the formation of an attachment. Because there is no evidence that the parents of children with pervasive developmental disorders differ from other parents in personality or child-rearing practices (Koegel et al., 1983) and because such children often have normal siblings, blame-the-parent theories have largely disappeared. There is no reason for parents, whose lives have already been burdened by having a child with a pervasive developmental disorder, to also feel guilty for having caused their child's problems.

Parental behavior may not cause pervasive developmental disorders, but something must. The sex ratio (many more boys than girls for all the pervasive developmental disorders except Rett's disorder, which seems to affect only girls), the remarkable similarity of one child to another, and physical signs (such as the slowing down in head growth in Rett's disorder) all suggest that biology is a good place to look for etiological explanations. As you might expect, considerable effort has gone into determining whether there is a genetic basis for the pervasive developmental disorders. Because these disorders are relatively rare and families tend to be small (parents find it too hard to deal with additional children), it is difficult to recruit sufficiently large research samples to draw definitive conclusions. Nevertheless, it seems that pervasive developmental disorders do have a genetic component (Folstein et al., 1998; Gillberg, 1998; Mahoney et al., 1998). Cognitive and language disorders also appear with greater than average frequency among the relatives of people with a pervasive developmental disorder (Baron-Cohen & Hammer, 1997). It is likely that no single gene causes either a language disorder or a pervasive developmental disorder; it takes many genes acting together. At one time or another, practically every chromosome has been implicated in the genesis of pervasive developmental disorders (Assumpcao, 1998; Carratala et al., 1998), yet we still do not know which genes are actually responsible.

There have been reports of monozygotic twins in which only one had a pervasive developmental disorder (Kates et al., 1998). Given their identical inheritance, some other factor or factors must interact with genetics to produce a pervasive developmental disorder. One possibility is that pervasive developmental disorders, especially autistic disorder, are the result of an unlucky conjunction—a genetic predisposition to develop cognitive and language disorders combined with exposure to an environmental trigger. Possible candidates for this trigger include toxins, viruses, and a variety of illnesses (Barton & Volkmar, 1998; Bolte, 1998; Kemper & Bauman, 1998; Raja, Azzoni, & Giammarco, 1998; Rapin & Katzman, 1998). As yet, definitive triggers have not been identified; most have proved to be dead ends. To take a recent example, contrary to widespread publicity, autistic disorder is not the result of measles vaccinations (Duclos & Ward, 1998).

In an attempt to shed light on the pathology underlying pervasive developmental disorders, researchers have enlisted every conceivable blood test, hormonal assay, neuropsychological test, and imaging technique (Dawson et al., 1998; Hashimoto et al., 1998; Lincoln et al., 1998; Piven & O'Leary, 1997). Although these researchers have produced intriguing findings—smaller brains in people with Rett's disorder (Bauman, Kemper, & Arin, 1995) and an association between Asperger's disorder and Tourette's disorder (Marriage et al., 1993)—there is still no agreement on the neurological defects that cause the symptoms and signs of pervasive developmental disorders. All we can conclude at present is that people with autism and Asperger's disorder probably have a congenital vulnerability that combines with a trigger (a virus, a toxin, a birth trauma), resulting in an inability to form normal human attachments and, in people with autism, a language disability as well. In childhood disintegrative disorder and Rett's disorder, the trigger occurs later in childhood than in autism or Asperger's disorder, and mental retardation is almost always severe. There are no clear-cut biochemical, genetic, or neurological markers unique to any of the pervasive developmental disorders, but research using imaging and molecular genetic techniques may identify such markers in the near future.

Treatment

Children with pervasive developmental disorders of childhood have been subjected to just about every known psychological and medical treatment (Howlin, 1998; Shaw et al., 1998; Volkmar, 1998). For decades, psychoanalytically oriented psychotherapists labored to bring insight to children with pervasive developmental disorders. In 1975, the National Institute of Mental Health

(NIMH) published a treatment review that concluded: "Psychotherapy with autistic children of the kind designed to provide insight has not proved effective and in the light of our knowledge about autism is unlikely to do so" (p. 207). Most psychologists accept this verdict, although dynamic views of the pervasive disorders are not extinct (Ribas, 1998). To fill the void left by psychodynamic treatment, clinicians have used group therapy, family therapy, behavior therapy, psychoactive drugs, vitamins, sensory deprivation, sensory stimulation, music therapy, occupational therapy, walking balance beams, and spinning the children in circles (S. Schwartz & Johnson, 1985). None of these treatments can cure a pervasive developmental disorder, although effective early interventions may help to improve the quality of life of sufferers and their families (Gresham & MacMillan, 1998).

A continuing problem for clinicians, and for the families of people with pervasive developmental disorders, is the false hope given by well-meaning amateurs and outright charlatans. Consider, for example, the Cheneys' experience with an approach called facilitated communication, which they describe in Document 12.11.

DOCUMENT 12.11

Transcript From Meeting of the University Hospital Parent Support Group: The Cheneys Discuss One Treatment Approach

INGRID CHENEY: We were so desperate to break through to Eddie, we were willing to try anything. On the advice of another couple whose child had autism, we bought a computer and employed a facilitator to help Eddie communicate with us. The facilitator would gently hold Eddie's hand over the keyboard, and Eddie would type out what he wanted to say. This other couple told us that their boy, who could not even speak, used this method to communicate his feelings and needs to them. He even told them that he loved them. At first, Eddie did well. With the facilitator guiding him, he told us how frightened he was of his illness and how much he liked cocoa, and all sorts of things. I was so happy. I remember that first day spending three hours with Eddie and the facilitator exploring so many topics. I couldn't wait for her to return. Eddie had so much to communicate.

JOHN CHENEY: It was a fraud. You know, like that famous horse that supposedly could think and do mathematics but was really getting signals from its master. The facilitator was guiding Eddie toward certain keys. They were her messages we were getting, not Eddie's.

INGRID CHENEY: John's right; I was fooled. I wanted so much to talk to Eddie, I tried the method on my own, without the facilitator. Eddie never typed out anything with me. At first, I thought I just didn't understand the technique; then I thought, Eddie won't talk to me. Finally, I realized that I had built my hopes on air—there is no secret way to communicate with Eddie. ∎

The Cheneys' experience is not unusual. Facilitators with a day or two of "training" have convinced many parents that their technique helps people with pervasive developmental disorders to communicate thoughts and feelings they otherwise would not express. (In the precomputer age, the process was conducted by guiding the person's hand toward printed letters; in even earlier days, a ouija board could have served a similar purpose.) Facilitated communication is based on the notion that there is a person trapped inside the person with a pervasive developmental disorder. These trapped people have lots to say, and it takes a facilitator to allow them to say it.

Despite a total lack of empirical support, facilitated communication was rapidly applied, not only to individuals with communication disorders, but also to help people recover supposedly lost memories of child abuse (see Chapter 7). Research has confirmed John Cheney's view. It is not the person being facilitated whose thoughts are being communicated but the facilitator's (Edelson et al., 1998; Huebner & Emery, 1998). Still, the technique has its defenders. It seems that the problems of people with pervasive developmental disorders are so great and the desire to help them is so intense that parents, and even some professionals, allow their hopes to overwhelm the evidence (Twachtman-Cullen, 1998). Considerable time and money have been devoted to debunking quack cures for the pervasive developmental disorders. These resources would have been better spent on more productive scientific research.

Although there have been false trails, people with pervasive developmental disorders, and their families, can be helped to lead higher-quality lives. People with pervasive developmental disorders may be taught useful communication and survival skills, and those who care for them may benefit from learning useful coping skills. In either case, the most effective training techniques use combinations of behavior modification, behaviorally based special education, and speech therapy (Kunce & Mesibov, 1998; Larkin & Gurry, 1998). Using these techniques, children can be toilet trained (Wheeler, 1998), taught to play games (McClannahan & Krautz, 1999), and helped to acquire academic skills (Simpson & Myles, 1998). This should not imply that behavioral treatment can work miracles (Gresham &

Sign language is often effective in building the communication skills of children with pervasive developmental disorders who cannot speak.

MacMillan, 1998). Sometimes, the techniques fail. For example, some behavioral clinicians and researchers believed that they could teach spoken language to children with pervasive developmental disorders by "reinforcing" them with sweets for uttering a specific word when shown a particular stimulus. For example, the child may be shown an apple and given a candy for saying the word *apple*. After many conditioning trials, it is possible to teach even severely disabled children to say the right word to a stimulus. But this is not the same as teaching them to conduct a normal spoken conversation. They emit certain sounds in response to specific stimuli, but they do not know the meaning of what they are saying.

A more effective approach for building communication skills in children who cannot speak (or who only echo sounds) is to teach them the sign language used by deaf people (Seal & Bonvillian, 1997). As we saw in Document 12.10, John and Ingrid Cheney use sign language to communicate with Eddie. Of course, the degree to which children can be taught sign language is limited by their abilities. For example, severely disabled people with Rett's disorder have difficulty learning even simple conditioned responses (Smith, Klevstrand, & Lovaas, 1995).

If, as the research suggests, the problems faced by people with pervasive developmental disorders in forming attachments, engaging in social relations, and conducting normal conversations is partly because they lack a "theory of mind," perhaps they would benefit from being explicitly taught how to empathize with the feelings and thoughts of others. Research suggests that this "cognitive" treatment approach holds promise (Hadwin et al., 1997; Howlin & Barron-Cohen, 1998).

In addition to behavioral treatments, at one time or another just about every drug, vitamin, and herb has been administered to children with pervasive developmental disorders (Frischauf, 1997). Each of these treatments seems to pass through a cycle. At first, the drugs or vitamins or herbs are administered in a uncontrolled fashion by doctors who are willing to try anything to help their patients. Their reports are almost always glowing; a cure has been found! Parents are delighted, articles appear in the press, and stories run on television. Years later, when controlled trials are conducted and the drugs, herbs, or vitamins are compared with placebos under double-blind conditions, they are found to be ineffective or to produce minimal improvements only. There are no drugs, vitamins, or herbal treatments that cure pervasive developmental disorders, although some of these items may alleviate some symptoms (such as sleeplessness).

Behavioral treatments, sometimes combined with drugs, have made it possible for some children with pervasive developmental disorders to learn much-needed skills and have led to significant improvements in their social behavior. However, progress comes at great cost to their families. As we saw in Document 12.10, having a child with a pervasive developmental disorder affects every aspect of life and often leads to marriage breakdown (Catalano, 1998). The parents and siblings of people with pervasive developmental disorder need support, counseling, and respites during which the person with the disorder is looked after in a residential program, such as a summer camp.

Eventually, children with pervasive developmental disorders grow up, and a new set of problems arises. Adults with pervasive developmental disorders are faced with the same challenges as everyone else. They must learn to function sexually, care for themselves, make friends, engage in employment, and live autonomous lives. The lucky ones will live in group homes and work in autonomous or assisted employment (Unger et al., 1998; see Chapter 11). Sadly, most people with pervasive developmental disorders will not be able to meet the challenges of adulthood. They will never be autonomous or able to work in any type of employment. When their families are no longer able to look after them, they will reside not in group homes but in large institutions. John and Ingrid worry about what will happen to Eddie when he grows up. Making appropriate plans for adulthood is one of the greatest challenges facing the families of children with pervasive developmental disorders (Howlin, 1997).

Given the severity of most of the pervasive developmental disorders and their devastating effect on families, prevention would save much suffering. Unfortunately, until the genetic disposition and environmental triggers are clearly identified, the only preventive strategy available is for parents to receive genetic counseling on their risk of having a child with a pervasive developmental disorder (Simonoff, 1998). They can then make a decision about whether they wish to have children. Making a decision not to have children is difficult, and it is even harder when parents also have psychological disorders. For example, Karen Beasley could have trouble reaching a rational decision about whether to have another child. She is already having trouble dealing with Michelle, and she also seems to be gradually starving herself (see Document 12.7). Eating disorders like Karen's are explored in more detail in the next section.

Although people with anorexia nervosa look emaciated, they have a distorted image of their body and may even believe they are overweight.

FEEDING AND EATING DISORDERS

According to the *DSM-IV*, Karen's behavior is representative of one of the eating disorders: anorexia nervosa, bulimia nervosa, or a vague "not otherwise specified" category for those whose eating disorders do not quite meet the diagnostic criteria for either one. In addition, the *DSM-IV* appendix proposes a binge-eating disorder for potential inclusion in future *DSM* editions. All of these disorders, which are usually first observed in adolescence or early adulthood, as well as disorders first noted in infancy or early childhood—pica, rumination disorder, and feeding disorder of infancy or early childhood—are reviewed in this section.

Diagnosis

In 1874, Queen Victoria's doctor, Sir William Gull, published a paper on "appetite loss" (Gull, 1874). Already famous for helping to release psychiatric patients from the physical restraints commonly used at the time, Gull became even more famous for his case studies of young people who seemed to be deliberately starving themselves to death. Gull was not the first person to describe such people, but he was the most thorough (see Vandereycken & Van Deth, 1994, for a history of eating disorders). He noted that most of his starving patients were females who also displayed other symptoms, such as *amenorrhea* (cessation of menstruation), constipation, a slow pulse rate, and a passion for exercise. Although they would occasionally eat huge amounts at a single sitting (*binge-eat*), they would immediately vomit the food back up. To help these patients, Gull recruited the full armory of 19th-century medicines—preparations made from the bark of trees, tincture of mercury, iron tablets, quinine—but to no avail. Gull concluded that the disorder must be psychological and that the physical symptoms, such as slow pulse and amenorrhea, were the result of self-starvation. Gull named this condition **anorexia nervosa,** which is Latin for psychologically based loss of appetite. Although anorexia nervosa is a misnomer—initially, sufferers do not lose their appetites—Gull's name is still used today to refer to people who intentionally starve themselves.

According to the *DSM-IV*, anorexia nervosa usually begins in adolescence or early adulthood (Karen is 19) and affects mainly females (Walsh & Kahn, 1997). The disorder involves extreme weight loss, at least 15% below the expected weight for a person's age, sex, and height. Although they look emaciated, people with anorexia nervosa deny being ill. Like Karen, many are convinced they are overweight and need to diet. The self-esteem of people with anorexia nervosa is dependent on their body weight. Some take dieting to such extremes that they must be hospitalized and force-fed to prevent them from starving to death. The main *DSM-IV* diagnostic criteria for anorexia nervosa are contained in Table 12.14. In addition, the *DSM-IV* recognizes two subtypes: a *restricting type* consisting of people who lose weight by refraining from eating and a *binge-eating/purging type* marked by episodes of overeating followed by attempts to purge food from the body (by vomiting, for example). From Karen's description of her own behavior, she seems to fit the binge-eating/purging subtype. Although the *DSM-IV* considers the two to be separate subtypes, 30% of restrictors eventually become binge-eating/purgers (Strober, Freeman, & Morrell, 1997).

Binge eating is also the hallmark of another *DSM-IV* eating disorder, **bulimia nervosa,** or simply bu-

DSM-IV TABLE 12.14 Main *DSM-IV* Diagnostic Criteria for Anorexia Nervosa

A. Refusal to maintain body weight at or above a minimally normal weight for age and height (e.g., weight loss leading to maintenance of body weight less than 85% of that expected; or failure to make expected weight gain during period of growth, leading to body weight less than 85% of that expected).

B. Intense fear of gaining weight or becoming fat, even though underweight.

C. Disturbance in the way in which one's body weight or shape is experienced, undue influence of body weight or shape on self-evaluation, or denial of the seriousness of the current low body weight.

D. In postmenarcheal females, amenorrhea, i.e., the absence of at least three consecutive menstrual cycles. (A woman is considered to have amenorrhea if her periods occur only following hormone, e.g., estrogen, administration.)

Note: From American Psychiatric Association (1994, pp. 544–545).

DSM-IV TABLE 12.15 Main *DSM-IV* Diagnostic Criteria for Bulimia Nervosa

A. Recurrent episodes of binge eating. An episode of binge eating is characterized by both of the following:
   (1) eating, in a discrete period of time (e.g., within any 2-hour period), an amount of food that is definitely larger than most people would eat during a similar period of time and under similar circumstances
   (2) a sense of lack of control over eating during the episode (e.g., a feeling that one cannot stop eating or control what or how much one is eating)

B. Recurrent inappropriate compensatory behavior in order to prevent weight gain, such as self-induced vomiting; misuse of laxatives, diuretics, enemas, or other medications; fasting; or excessive exercise.

C. The binge eating and inappropriate compensatory behaviors both occur, on average, at least twice a week for 3 months.

D. Self-evaluation is unduly influenced by body shape and weight.

E. The disturbance does not occur exclusively during episodes of anorexia nervosa.

Note: From American Psychiatric Association (1994, pp. 549–550).

limia. (Table 12.15 contains the *DSM-IV* diagnostic criteria.) When they are anxious or depressed, people with bulimia gorge themselves (usually on so-called junk foods). During these episodes, they feel powerless to stop eating. Afterward, feeling guilty, they purge their bodies of food by some combination of vomiting, laxatives, diuretics, or enemas (the *DSM-IV* calls this the *purging subtype* of bulimia). Alternatively, they may try to lose weight by fasting or intense exercising (the *non-purging subtype*). Like anorexia nervosa, bulimia typically begins in adolescence and is found more often in women than in men (Walsh & Devlin, 1998). Although their behavior is similar to that of people with the binge-eating/purging subtype of anorexia nervosa, people with bulimia do not usually lose significant amounts of weight. Because they binge and purge in secret and

maintain a normal or higher body weight, people with bulimia can hide their problem for years. Sometimes, the first sign that anything is wrong is when the person attempts suicide—a not uncommon occurrence among people with bulimia or with the binge-eating/purging subtype of anorexia (Favaro & Santonastaso, 1997).

In addition to anorexia nervosa and bulimia, the *DSM-IV* appendix contains diagnostic criteria for **binge-eating disorder.** Although not yet an "official" psychological disorder, it is being evaluated for inclusion in future editions of the *DSM.* Like bulimia, the proposed binge-eating disorder is characterized by uncontrolled eating. However, sufferers neither purge their bodies of excess food nor do they fast or exercise excessively. They just eat until they are uncomfortably full. Not surprisingly, such people are obese. According to the *DSM-IV,*

Princess Diana admitted to being bulimic after frequent speculation in the press about her health. The pressure of being constantly in the spotlight and of having a less-than-happy marriage may have contributed to the development of her disease.

binge-eating disorder may affect 2% of the population, including a greater percentage of men than the other eating disorders (although they are still the minority).

There is considerable overlap among anorexia nervosa, bulimia, and binge-eating disorder. To help differentiate them, Table 12.16 summarizes the main similarities and differences. As noted previously, individuals who do not meet the precise diagnostic criteria for any of these eating disorders may be given the diagnosis of "eating disorder not otherwise specified."

A strange eating disorder, most often found among young children or pregnant women, is called **pica** (Phelps, 1998; Wren & Tarbell, 1998). The name comes from the Latin word for magpie, a bird known to eat practically anything. This is precisely the problem in pica. People with this disorder have been known to eat dirt, laundry starch, chalk, buttons, paper, cigarette butts, matches, sand, soap, toothpaste, and many other supposedly inedible substances. The main *DSM-IV* diagnostic criteria for pica appear in Table 12.17. Note that it is important to consider cultural practices when making this diagnosis. Members of cultures that sanction the consumption of odd substances, such as clay, are not suffering from a psychological disorder. The prevalence and cause of pica are unknown. Psychological theories tend to be vague ("fixation at the oral stage of develop-

ment"). Physiological explanations are not much better. Most are based on the idea that diet deficiencies (too little iron or zinc, for example) cause a craving for anything containing these missing minerals. Unfortunately for this theory, most of the items craved by people with pica do not actually supply the missing minerals.

The *DSM-IV* includes two other feeding disorders usually found in infants or young children: rumination disorder and feeding disorder of infancy or early childhood (Wren & Tarbell, 1998). **Rumination disorder** is marked by regurgitation of food, whereas **feeding disorder of infancy or early childhood** is manifested by inadequate eating. Both disorders are diagnosed only when there is no clear medical condition causing the symptoms. Little is known about the prevalence or etiology of either one (Wren & Tarbell, 1998).

Prevalence and Course

Each year, 18 of every 100,000 females and 2 of every 100,000 males is newly diagnosed with anorexia nervosa (Pawluck & Gorey, 1998). The incidence among adolescent females, and the sex ratio of 9 females to 1 male, has not changed for decades. In contrast, the incidence among women in their 20s and 30s has tripled since the 1950s (Pawluck & Gorey, 1998). This could mean that

TABLE 12.16 Similarities and Differences Among Eating Disorders

Symptom	Anorexia nervosa	Bulimia nervosa	Binge-eating disorder
Weighs less than 85% of expected weight	✓		
Considers self fat even though severely underweight	✓		
Has missed at least three menstrual periods	✓		
Obsessed with food and odd eating rituals	✓	✓	
Binges	✓*	✓	✓
Exercises excessively	✓	✓	
Gains weight			✓
Expresses dissatisfaction with appearance	✓	✓	✓
Considers bingeing beyond control	✓	✓	✓
Vomits or uses drugs to purge calories	✓	✓	
Disappears into bathroom for long periods (to purge)	✓	✓	

*Binge-eating/purging subtype

DSM-IV **TABLE 12.17** Main *DSM-IV* Diagnostic Criteria for Pica

A. Persistent eating of nonnutritive substances for a period of at least 1 month.

B. The eating of nonnutritive substances is inappropriate to the developmental level.

C. The eating behavior is not part of a culturally sanctioned practice.

D. If the eating behavior occurs exclusively during the course of another mental disorder (e.g., mental retardation), it is sufficiently severe to warrant independent clinical attention.

Note: From American Psychiatric Association (1994, p. 96).

more women in this age bracket are developing anorexia nervosa or that greater public awareness of its dangers has brought more clients to the attention of clinicians (or both). Nationally, the prevalence of anorexia nervosa in females is about 1 percent (Hoffman, 1994). Bulimia, which affects 2–3% of young women (Hoffman, 1994), also seems to be on the rise (Cotrufo, Barretta, & Monteleone, 1997). Adolescents and young adults are most vulnerable. One survey of navy personnel found a prevalence of 7% for males and 12% for females (McNulty, 1997a, 1997b).

The prognosis for eating disorders is poor. Left untreated, all eating disorders produce medical complications. Because they are overweight, people with the proposed binge-eating disorder are prone to high blood pressure and diabetes, as well as to gallbladder and heart disease. Rumination and other feeding disorders can result in "failure to thrive" (growth retardation and susceptibility to illness). Pica may cause injury or poisoning. Purging, even among people who do not lose weight, can result in heart failure due to the loss of electrolytes. If purging is violent, it can cause the stomach to rupture. On the less serious side, the acid in vomit causes tooth decay, inflammation of the esophagus, and can burn fingers pushed down the throat to induce vomiting.

As it progresses, anorexia nervosa depletes the body of nutrition. To protect itself, the body tries to conserve energy. Breathing, pulse, and blood pressure rates all drop, and hormone function slows. The nails and hair become brittle; the skin dries out and turns yellow. As insulating fat disappears, lanugo (the hair babies are born with) appears to keep the body warm. As starvation progresses, people lose calcium from their bones, making them brittle and prone to breakage; anemia is also common. Uncontrolled starvation eventually causes the death of 10% of people with anorexia nervosa (Hoffman, 1994; Nielsen et al., 1998). Adolescents with anorexia nervosa who are also severely depressed have the poorest prognosis (Saccomani et al., 1998). The prognosis for most people with an eating disorder is a lifetime struggle against binge eating, weight loss, depression, anxiety, and substance abuse (Pike, 1998; Sullivan et al., 1998). Remissions provide some respite, but eating disorders usually recur (Strober et al., 1997).

Etiology

Karen told the Parent Support Group that she had begun dieting when Eric left her, claiming that she was "too fat." Around the same time, her menstrual periods stopped. What she neglected to tell the others was that she was obsessed with eating and food rituals. Every morning, Karen would weigh precise portions of her food for the day on a kitchen scale. She would measure her liquid intake into jars. She stored each day's food and drink in special containers marked *breakfast, lunch, snack,* and *dinner.* At prescribed times, she would consume her daily ration of food and drink alone; she refused to eat in front of others. Karen would prepare separate meals for her 4-year-old daughter, Michelle.

Karen also failed to mention that she performed her exercise routine—400 sit-ups, 100 push-ups, and jogging in place for 1 hour—three times each day. Karen's behavior, common among people with anorexia and bulimia nervosa (Thornton & Russell, 1997), is reminiscent of the behavior of people with obsessive-compulsive disorder (see Chapter 4). Depression, anxiety, personality, and substance abuse disorders are also found among people with eating disorders. In addition, most people with anorexia nervosa also meet the diagnostic criteria for body dysmorphic disorder described in Chapter 7 (Rosen & Ramirez, 1998).

Since Gull's time, clinicians have assumed that eating disorders have psychological origins. Precisely what their psychological cause might be, however, varies from paradigm to paradigm; each has its characteristic spin. Freudian writers hypothesize that eating disorders (like other psychological symptoms) are symbolic representations of unconscious conflicts. One of the more imaginative Freudians has argued that females stop eating because of their unconscious fear of "oral impregnation" (Dally, 1969). It is not immediately obvious how such a hypothesis could be tested. Other psychodynamically oriented writers have focused on poor mother-child interactions (see Bruch, 1978, for example). The basic idea is that rejecting mothers induce feelings of self-hate in their daughters. The daughters hate their bodies, which they believe are too fat, and they diet to lose weight. Sometimes, hunger drives them to eat, but then they purge to get thinner. Although this view has

many adherents, the evidence that people with eating disorders have rejecting mothers and hate their bodies is mixed. Most people with eating disorders are unhappy with their figures (Cash & Deagle, 1997), but the majority have loving parents. Distorted body images (judging themselves and others to be heavier than they actually are) are found in many people with anorexia nervosa (Smeets et al., 1998), but some simply claim to prefer an ultra-thin look (Probst et al., 1998).

Behavioral psychologists, who take an operant conditioning view, presume that food avoidance or overindulgence is somehow "reinforced." For example, adolescents may gain attention and control over their parents by refusing to eat or by binge eating. While plausible, this is more an explanation for the maintenance of an eating disorder than for its origin. If control is the aim, why not throw temper tantrums or refuse to talk? Why do something self-destructive like giving up food? Anyway, the need-to-control theory conflicts with clinical experience. Adolescents with eating disorders are not usually rebellious. In fact, they are obedient children, conscientious students, and many are excellent athletes. Most people with anorexia describe themselves as perfectionists; the control they seek is over themselves, not others (Hornabacher, 1998).

The cognitive-behavioral view of eating disorders, particularly anorexia nervosa, sees them beginning with conditioned food aversions. For various reasons, some people learn to pair eating with mental images of obesity. Over time, such people become revolted by food. Continued food avoidance is maintained by the sense of self-control that the person develops as a result of being able to restrict food intake. Faulty attributions (such as "I need to diet because I am too fat") and other rationalizations ("You can't be too thin") are invented to justify continued food avoidance (Cooper, 1997).

Psychologists who prefer a family-systems approach claim that families with eating-disordered members are *enmeshed*—their respective roles are so blurred and family members so overprotective and involved in one another's lives that individuality and autonomy are lost (Minuchin, Rosman, & Baker, 1978). By absorbing themselves in their child's eating disorder, parents avoid dealing with their own relationship problems. Thus, the eating disorder serves to hold the family together. Although there is no doubt that eating disorders profoundly affect family functioning (Ross & Handy, 1997), family-systems theory, like "reinforcement" theories, explains how eating disorders are maintained *after* they are established. The family-systems approach does not explain why a child develops an eating disorder in the first place. (Why not depression, substance abuse, or some other problem the parents could focus on?)

Social-psychological explanations for eating disorders, especially anorexia nervosa, have focused on cultural standards of beauty. Noting that eating-disordered females outnumber males 9 to 1, sociologically oriented theorists have attributed eating disorders to a desire for the "ideal" female figure. Beginning in the 1970s, the ideal feminine body has become increasingly thin (Anderson & DiDomenico, 1992; Wiseman et al., 1992). As we enter the 21st century, the majority of Miss America contestants are 15% below the recommended weight for their height. In other words, most contestants meet the weight criteria for anorexia nervosa. The average woman (who is 5 feet 4 inches tall and weighs 142 pounds) who tries to look like the average fashion model (who is 5 feet 9 inches tall and weighs 110 pounds) has no choice but to diet or purge. Not surprisingly, Koszewski, Newell, and Higgins (1990) found that 6% of female undergraduates use laxatives or force themselves to vomit after eating. Once they begin down this path, some women find they cannot stop—they have developed an eating disorder. Presumably, slim figures are less important for males, which is why they have a lower incidence of eating disorders.

There is evidence for the social-psychological theory. For example, anorexia and bulimia occur most often among women who are especially concerned with their physique, such as models, dancers, and athletes (Neumaerker et al., 1998; Skowron & Friedlander, 1994; Sykora et al., 1993). Still, the sociological explanation is incomplete. It does not explain why females developed eating disorders in Gull's day (or in the 1950s and 1960s), when the ideal feminine form was considerably heavier than now. It also fails to explain why cultures that do not idealize thin female figures have essentially the same prevalence of eating disorders as the United States (Hoek et al., 1998). The social-psychological theory also fails to explain why African American women have a lower incidence of eating disorders than White women even though they live in the same culture (and there are plenty of thin Black models and actors).

One possibility is that ideals of feminine beauty, and other social-psychological factors, affect only vulnerable people. That is, heredity or some physiological malfunction, or both, predisposes certain people to develop eating disorders. The existence of such a predisposition is supported by studies of twins that have found a higher concordance for eating disorders (particularly anorexia

nervosa) among identical than fraternal twins (Garfinkel & Garner, 1982). Because the concordance rate among identical twins is less than 1, however, genes do not cause an eating disorder by themselves. Social and psychological factors are also involved. An example of the interaction between genes and environment is provided by Gorwood, Ades, and Parmentier (1998), who describe a young woman whose identical twin sister had a severe case of anorexia nervosa. Determined to avoid a similar fate, the unaffected sister adopted a deliberate weight maintenance program (a diet plan). By following this program, she never succumbed to the illness that devastated her twin sister.

In addition to a genetic vulnerability and a conducive environment, it takes a triggering event to precipitate an eating disorder. Just about any stressful life event can serve as a trigger—death or serious illness in the family, abandonment, personal illness, unemployment, failure at work or school, sexual conflicts, just about anything (Schmidt et al., 1997). For Karen, it was the departure of her boyfriend, who claimed that she was too fat.

Researchers looking for the physiological basis of eating disorders have focused on the neurotransmitters serotonin and norepinephrine, the same neurotransmitters implicated in both depression and obsessive-compulsive disorder (both of which often accompany eating disorders). Antidepressants, which work by increasing levels of serotonin and norepinephrine, help some people with eating disorders. This suggests that low levels of these transmitters play an etiological role in eating disorders. In addition to being associated with low serotonin levels, eating disorders and depression are also both associated with high levels of cortisol, a hormone released in response to stress. The excess cortisol seems to be the result of a malfunction in the hypothalamus (the part of the brain that controls eating and drinking). Thus, it appears that a malfunction in the part of the brain that controls appetite may be responsible for eating disorders, depression, and obsessive-compulsive disorder.

Treatment

There are few proven treatments available for rumination, feeding disorders, or pica, and not much research on the subject either (Weakley, Petti, & Karwisch, 1997). Most of the research effort has been directed toward anorexia nervosa and bulimia. Although people with bulimia may hide their problem, anorexia nervosa soon becomes painfully obvious. Yet people with both disorders deny that anything is wrong. Consider, for example, the

Starved Out

As the weeks passed, it became apparent to everyone in the Parent Support Group that Karen Beasley's condition was getting worse. She lost increasing amounts of weight until she became emaciated. Eventually, Dr. Berg persuaded her to leave Michelle with her mother and arranged for her to be admitted to University Hospital's special inpatient program for eating disorders.

Hospital care is a necessity for people whose weight loss puts them in danger of death. Yet managed care organizations and health insurers provide only meager benefits for the inpatient treatment of eating disorders (and Karen had no insurance anyway). Karen was lucky; her parents were willing to mortgage their house to pay the costs of her treatment. Many others who need treatment are simply unable to afford it. It is ironic that the psychological disorder with the highest mortality rate (about 10% of those with anorexia nervosa will die of their disorder) is the one that insurance companies refuse to cover.

In the 1980s, it was common for people with anorexia nervosa to spend weeks or even months in the hospital. They were not discharged until they reached the average weight for their age and height. With the advent of managed care and restrictions on health insurance benefits for psychological disorders, hospital stays are down to only a few days or a week. Karen was lucky to even find an inpatient program for eating disorders. Without enough insured patients to keep them going, most inpatient programs have closed. The National Alliance for the Mentally Ill, a lobbying group, has been campaigning for legislation to force insurance companies to treat mental illness as seriously as physical illness. But they have not had much luck getting insurers to cover eating disorders.

Stymied by legislative roadblocks, people with eating disorders are taking their fight to the courts. With the assistance of the National Association for Anorexia Nervosa and Associated Disorders, class action lawsuits have convinced some judges that eating disorders are physical illnesses and, therefore, qualify for the more liberal benefits paid for medical conditions. This came too late for Karen's parents, who are now $65,000 in debt, and steeped in guilt. They lie in bed at night wondering what they did to cause Karen's problems. Their lives have been destroyed by Karen's disorder—and by a cruel health system that denies care to those who need it most.

---

exchange between Karen Beasley and Celia Berofsky in Document 12.7. Denials like Karen's are the reason that people with eating disorders often fail to receive psychological treatment (Walsh & Devlin, 1998). By the time action is taken, many sufferers, especially those with anorexia nervosa, need to be hospitalized.

While patients are in the hospital, treatment consists of rest, a high-calorie diet (administered by tube feeding if necessary), and medications. In addition, patients may be enrolled in operant conditioning programs in which they are rewarded with social privileges for eating (Touyz & Beumont, 1997). Exposure to high-calorie food coupled with response prevention and systematic desensitization may help those who have developed a phobic aversion to eating (Boutelle, 1998). A variety of other treatments may also be employed (Wilson & Fairburn, 1998). For example, group therapy may provide people with eating disorders with much-needed guidance and mutual support. Cognitive-behavior therapy aimed at helping people with eating disorders change the distorted thinking that leads them to believe they look better skinny may also be helpful (Garner, Vitousek, & Pike, 1997).

Although hospitals are often the safest environment for people with serious eating disorders, hospital care is expensive. Health insurance companies and managed care organizations prefer people to be treated in cheaper outpatient programs (Bremer & Herzog, 1997; Hill & Maloney, 1997). As a consequence, many hospital-based programs have closed, as is explained in Highlight 12.3. Those programs that still exist maintain a fine line between caring for people with eating disorders and inducing a dependency that may retard their autonomous development as well as stigmatize them as psychiatric patients (Robin, Gilroy, & Dennis, 1998). For some adolescents, summer camps have proved a good compromise. In these camps, young people can be monitored, find support, adopt new eating habits, and learn to interact socially without the negative self-image that comes from psychiatric hospitalization (Tonkin, 1997).

Because of the demands of their sports, gymnasts and other athletes are particularly prone to eating disorders. Christy Heinrich, who was on the U.S. national gymnastic team in 1989, died from the effects of anorexia nervosa.

Drugs, such as appetite suppressants for binge eaters and lithium or antidepressants for people with anorexia and bulimia, have been used for some years, but their success has been modest at best (C. Freeman, 1998). Despite positive clinical reports, placebo-controlled, double-blind trials have shown that antidepressants help only a few people with anorexia nervosa when outcome is measured by weight gain or by improvement in psychological functioning (Attia et al., 1998). Findings such as these emphasize the importance of dietary and psychological treatment. Drugs play only a supplementary role (Garfinkel & Walsh, 1997).

Whether it takes place in or out of the hospital, treatment of eating disorders requires a team approach (Andersen, Bowers, & Evans, 1997). The first goal of

any treatment is to help the person gain enough weight to overcome any immediate health threats. The long-term goal is to help the person maintain a healthy weight. Both goals require the help of a medical practitioner, nutritionist, psychologist, and teachers (if still in school). Because family cooperation is essential in monitoring a person with an eating disorder, family therapy may help families to help the client (Eisler et al., 1997; Williamson et al., 1998).

Prevention

Because adolescent females are at highest risk of developing eating disorders, many colleges have initiated primary prevention programs. These programs, which are similar to those designed to prevent substance abuse, provide students with information about nutrition and health (Huon et al., 1998). This information may be presented in traditional ways—brochures, lectures, workshops, or films—and also in more innovative ways—such as by providing information about eating and nutrition in dining halls and by organizing group discussions (Daniel, 1988; Hotelling, 1988). Studies have found that students exposed to health and nutrition information in dining halls are less concerned about weight than are those who are not exposed (Koszewski et al., 1990; Weiss & Orysh, 1994).

Secondary prevention for high-risk groups has focused mainly on athletes. Coaches and instructors have been trained to monitor athletes and to identify the early signs of an eating disorder—body dissatisfaction, distorted body image, low self-esteem, overeating and purging. Some schools make self-assessment questionnaires available to students so that they can evaluate their own eating behavior and seek help if required (Probst et al., 1995). An example appears in Document 12.12.

At the tertiary level of prevention, one cost-effective intervention strategy is to train and supervise peer counselors (other students) to provide information and support to college students with eating disorders (Lenihan & Kirk, 1990). Studies of such programs have reported significant decreases in bingeing and purging as well as fewer obsessive-compulsive food rituals among students who met with peer counselors.

DOCUMENT 12.12

Self–Assessment Questionnaire Used to Identify Students at Risk for Eating Disorders

UNIVERSITY HOSPITAL

University Health Service
Eating Questionnaire

Eating problems can be serious. This questionnaire can help you to decide if you need more information or help. Check off each statement that applies to you:

Do I . . .

- ❑ Think about my weight constantly?
- ❑ Feel frustrated with dieting?
- ❑ Eat when I am lonely, angry, stressed, bored?
- ❑ Feel guilt about overeating?
- ❑ Eat when I am not hungry?
- ❑ Attempt to control my weight by fasting, dieting, vomiting, taking laxatives?
- ❑ Feel anxious if I miss exercise one day?
- ❑ Feel unworthy because I do not like my body?
- ❑ Wear loose clothes to hide my weight?
- ❑ Avoid looking in mirrors?
- ❑ Believe that I would become fat if I did not take active steps to control my weight?

If you answer yes to five or more of these questions, or know someone who would, you should contact the Eating Program Director at 555-6684 today.

CHAPTER 12 IN PERSPECTIVE

Child and adolescent development is generally conceived as a series of stages, but the process of development may not be orderly. Genetics, disease, and emotional trauma (acting separately or together) can result in one of the disorders covered in earlier chapters—depression, anxiety, and so on—or one of the childhood disorders discussed in this chapter, or both. Developmental psycho-pathology has become a specialty area of abnormal psychology. Although there is much that is still unknown, progress has been rapid. When the entire human genome (all of the genes that make up a human being) has been mapped, we will, for the first time in history, understand the diathesis for many childhood disorders. But genetics is not the whole story. Even when the genome is completely mapped, we will still need to identify and control the environmental triggers that produce psychological disorders in children if we are to prevent disorders from developing. In the meantime, we must perfect our treatments for the serious disorders of childhood and adolescence; many of those presently used are inadequate.

Key Ideas

Temperament

Because differences in temperament are noticeable from the first day of life, before the environment can exert any effect, they are most likely biologically based. "Difficult" children who have irregular sleeping, eating, and elimination patterns are at risk of developing externalizing psychological disorders (such as conduct disorder) as they grow older. (Internalizing disorders, such as depression, occur about as often among "easy" as among difficult children.) Whether children develop a psychological disorder depends on the fit between their temperaments and their environments.

Developmental Milestones

Developmental milestones are achievements that usually take place in a specific order at specific ages. For example, most children say their first word at 18 months. Failure to meet a developmental milestone may be a sign of disordered development.

Elimination Disorders

Children who fail to achieve toilet training by the usual age (or developmental level, if they are mentally retarded) are diagnosed as having enuresis (poor control of urination) or encopresis (poor control of defecation). Both disorders occur more often in boys than in girls and seem to run in families. There also appear to be environmental influences; for example, the disorders are linked to child abuse. Behavior therapy is effective for enuresis and may also help encopresis. Sometimes, behavioral treatment is supplemented with cognitive therapy and antidepressants.

Oppositional Defiant Disorder and Conduct Disorder

Unruly, hard-to-manage, children may have an oppositional defiant disorder. They are the children who are frequently in trouble at school, and who may use temper tantrums to get their way. The behavior of such children can be modified by behavioral or cognitive-behavioral treatments. Conduct disorder is more serious and shares many of the features of antisocial personality disorder. Conduct disorders are relatively common and affect boys more often than girls. Childhood-onset disorders have worse outcomes than disorders that begin later. Although there is some evidence that conduct disorders are inherited, genetics is not the whole story. The environment also plays an etiological role. Parental neglect and exposure to antisocial models are particularly important.

Attention-Deficit/Hyperactivity Disorder

Children with attention-deficit/hyperactivity disorder (ADHD) are impulsive and distractible (mainly at school, but sometimes at home as well). Many are also hyperactive. ADHD is more common among boys than girls, and its incidence appears to be on the rise. Once a disorder only of children, ADHD is now being identified in adults as well. Many environmental factors have been blamed for ADHD at one time or another, but its cause remains unclear. Like that of most disorders, the etiology of ADHD probably involves an interaction between heredity and as-yet-unspecified environmental factors. Although many different drugs have been used to treat ADHD, stimulant drugs are the most common treatment. These drugs may improve the behavioral aspects of ADHD, but they do not have long-term beneficial effects on school performance (and they can have deleterious side effects). Cognitive-behavioral treatments can help many people with ADHD to focus their attention and change their behavior.

Tourette's and Other Tic Disorders

Tourette's disorder is characterized by sudden movements, strange utterances (swearing, barking), and multiple motor tics (sudden repetitive but irregular movements). The *DSM-IV* also identifies other tic disorders (chronic motor or vocal tic disorder, transient tic disorder) that share some of the symptoms of Tourette's disorder. Tic disorders affect boys more often than girls. The discovery that small doses of haloperidol, a dopamine-suppressing drug used to treat schizophrenia, suppress Tourette's symptoms in many people has led to the hypothesis that Tourette's patients may have an excess of the chemical dopamine. There is also evidence that the disorder is inherited. For those who need treatment in addition to drugs, behavior therapy and cognitive-behavior therapy have been used to help people relax and cope with the interpersonal and social problems caused by having a tic disorder.

Reactive Attachment Disorder

Children with a reactive attachment disorder fail to form strong emotional bonds with their parents (especially their mothers) by age 5 because of pathological care. There are two subtypes: children who fail to form attachments at all and those who form numerous superficial attachments. Once thought to be the rare result of extreme child abuse, the disorder is being diagnosed more frequently, especially among children adopted after the critical period for attachments to form (8–12 months). Through role playing, modeling, and other methods, children with this disorder may learn social-interaction skills. Because attachments are two-way processes, other family members will also need counseling or therapy to overcome the impediments to attachment formation.

Separation Anxiety Disorder and Selective Mutism

All young children are uneasy about separating from their mothers, but developmentally inappropriate separation anxiety can lead to a refusal to attend school and may presage adult anxiety disorders. Selective mutism is a rare disorder characterized by a lack of speech in some situations but not in others. Both disorders may also be associated with social phobia, avoidant personality disorder, and nightmares. In some cases, separation anxiety can be construed as a phobia and treated with cognitive restructuring and systematic desensitization. Self-modeling, in which children listen to specially constructed tapes of themselves talking to others, may be useful.

Pervasive Developmental Disorders

Pervasive developmental disorders are the most serious psychopathological conditions occurring in childhood. They are marked by poor interpersonal relationships, distorted thinking, defective perception, and inappropriate affect. There are four pervasive developmental disorders, all relatively rare. Autistic disorder and Asperger's are so similar that many clinicians look on Asperger's disorder as a milder form of autism. Both childhood disintegrative disorder and Rett's disorder involve a regression and loss of previously acquired skills. Rett's generally begins earlier and affects girls, whereas childhood disintegrative disorder affects mainly boys. The outcome for pervasive developmental disorders is variable. Some children never develop useful communication; others graduate from college and hold down responsible jobs. Even those in the latter group retain difficulties in interpersonal relations, however. In addition to poor attachments and communication problems, children with autism and Asperger's disorder also lack a "theory of mind." Although some children with pervasive developmental disorders have pockets of superior intellectual ability, this is rare. Most people with these disorders are mentally retarded. These disorders have been blamed on everything from smothering mothers to perceptual defects to viruses. The most likely etiology is the usual combination of genetic diathesis and an environmental trigger, such as a virus. Treatment focuses on teaching people with pervasive developmental disorders social and communication skills while also helping families to adjust. Planning for adulthood is a major challenge for all families.

Feeding and Eating Disorders

Anorexia nervosa and bulimia nervosa begin in adolescence or early adulthood. People with anorexia look emaciated but deny being ill, even when they are close to death. Most are convinced that they are overweight and need to diet even more. Those with anorexia of the restricting type lose weight by refraining from eating; the binge-eating/purging type have episodes of overeating followed by attempts to purge the food by vomiting or the use of laxatives. Binge eating is also the main symptom of bulimia, but people with bulimia do not lose significant amounts of weight. The *DSM-IV* appendix contains diagnostic criteria for a proposed binge-eating disorder characterized by uncontrolled eating but without purging or exercising. These people just eat, so they are obese. Pica is a strange eating disorder in which people eat inedible substances. Young children may also have eating disorders: rumination disorder is marked by regurgitation of food, whereas feeding disorder is manifested by inadequate eating. Anorexia and bulimia are most common among females, and their prevalence has increased markedly among women in their 20s and 30s over the second half of the 20th century. The prognosis for both disorders is poor. Every psychological paradigm has an explanation for eating disorders. Hormonal anomalies associated with anorexia and bulimia suggest physiological causes as well. Cognitive-behavior therapy aimed at helping people with eating disorders to change their distorted thinking may be helpful. Because adolescent females are at highest risk for developing eating disorders, many colleges have initiated primary prevention programs. These are similar to those designed to prevent substance abuse; they provide students with information about nutrition and health.

Key Terms

anorexia nervosa
Asperger's disorder
attachment
attention-deficit/hyper-
    activity disorder
autistic disorder
binge-eating disorder
bulimia nervosa
childhood disintegrative
    disorder
conduct disorder

critical period
developmental psycho-
    pathology
dyssomnias
elimination disorders
encopresis
enuresis
externalizing disorders
feeding disorder of infancy
    or early childhood
hyperactivity-impulsivity

inattention
internalizing disorders
nightmare disorder
oppositional defiant disorder
parasomnias
pica
reactive attachment disorder
    of infancy or early
    childhood
Rett's disorder
rumination disorder

selective mutism
self-modeling
separation anxiety disorder
sleep terror disorder
sleepwalking disorder
Tourette's disorder

Key Names

Hans Asperger
Bruno Bettelheim

Erik Erikson
Jean Itard

Leo Kanner
Jean Piaget

Andreas Rett
Georges Gilles de la Tourette

CHAPTER 13

CHAPTER OBJECTIVES

Sex is more revered, more vilified, more written about, more controversial, and, to many people, more significant than any other topic covered in this book. One chapter can hardly begin to cover the huge range of sexual interests and behaviors. The main focus of this chapter is the sexual disorders contained in the *DSM-IV*. At the same time, some related disorders of adult life (such as adjustment and sleep disorders) are touched on where relevant.

The main questions addressed in this chapter are

1. How do we decide when sexual behavior is disordered?
2. What are the various types of sexual disorders?
3. How can people with sexual disorders be helped?
4. Can sexual disorders be prevented?

Sexual and Related Problems of Adult Life

CONTENTS

Sex—it's a worldwide obsession. What to do, how to do it, and who to do it with are the central topics of movies, books, television shows, magazine articles, newspaper reports, popular music, Internet sites, and advertisements. Despite this avalanche of information, society's attitudes toward sex remain conflicted and confused. Should women who stray from their marriages be branded with a "scarlet letter," or should they be forgiven (like presidents)? Should people be encouraged to masturbate, or should the practice be condemned? Are some sex practices signs of mental illness? What is normal, anyway?

Because of its seemingly endless fascination, sex is the subject of a huge professional literature. This chapter focuses on only one aspect of this literature—the sexual and gender identity disorders described in the *DSM-IV*. The chapter is divided into three main sections. The first deals with the **paraphilias** (unusual sexual desires or acts), whereas the second section examines **sexual dysfunctions** (difficulties in performing sexual acts). The final section discusses **gender identity disorder** (discomfort with one's assigned sex role). Although the focus of the chapter is on sexual disorders, it is wrong to think about these problems as somehow separable from other aspects of a person's life. As you will see, an individual's sexual behavior is influenced by his or her genetic background, medical condition, personal history, use of substances, psychological state (especially the presence of anxiety or depression), and the prevailing cultural norms. To show how these factors come together to influence both normal and problematic sexual behavior, this chapter tells the story of four people: Peter Hall, Anne Lawrence, and Anne's two sons, Jared and Luke. Through a series of tragic circumstances, the lives of these four people crossed and were changed forever.

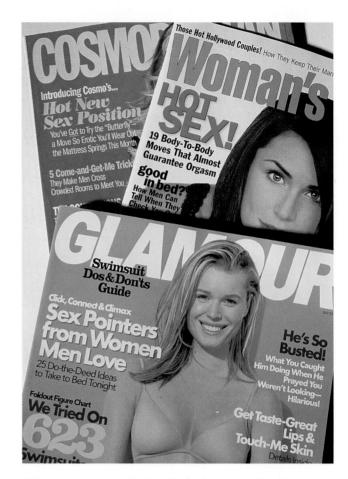

Although we are surrounded by talk about it, sex is still a controversial and confusing topic for many people.

THE PREDATOR

Peter Hall was born with a silver spoon in his mouth. His successful stockbroker father sent him to elite private schools, and his mother made sure that he received the best music lessons. Each summer, he went on trips to the cultural capitals of Europe. Now in his late 40s, Peter speaks five languages, drives a Jaguar sports car, and owns a yacht and three homes. He is a familiar figure at art galleries and chairs the museum board. Charming and urbane, Peter is especially well known for his charity work with underprivileged boys. Not only does he sponsor sports teams and camps, but he has also looked after wayward youths. He has provided them with emotional and financial support; some have even lived in one of his homes. So, imagine the shock to the community when Peter was arrested and charged with child sexual assault. Document 13.1 displays a newspaper account of the case against Hall.

DOCUMENT 13.1

Newspaper Story
Describing the Arrest
of Peter Hall

Chair of Museum Board Arrested for Child Sexual Assault

by Ron Nicks

Businessman Peter Hall, aged 48, was arrested by Metro Police and charged with seven counts of child sexual assault. Hall had been under investigation since police were approached by Mrs. Anne Lawrence, a divorced schoolteacher from Ross River. She claimed that Hall had sexually abused her sons, Jared, now aged 13, and Luke, aged 10, and that the abuse had gone on for a year.

"At first, I thought Peter was the best thing that ever happened to my boys. Their father abandoned us, and I had to raise them alone. They needed a father figure, and I thought Peter was it."

According to their mother, Jared and Luke met Hall last summer at the beach. They were admiring Hall's classic antique surfboard when he struck up a conversation with the boys. Later that afternoon, he invited Anne and her sons to his beachfront apartment for refreshments. In the apartment, the boys played with Hall's vast collection of video games and listened to his music CDs. They made plans to get together again the next day. After the summer, their relationship continued. On the weekends that Hall used the beachfront apartment, the boys were invited to join him. Often, their mother accompanied them.

"I went to his apartment many times," says Anne. "I always found Peter pleasant and entertaining. He was so refined and cultured. I thought we were friends. Jared and Luke adored Peter, and he treated them like the sons he never had. He introduced them to opera and classical music. I thought he was the ideal father."

Anne first began to suspect something was wrong when she found drugs (later identified as amphetamines) in Jared's drawer. She went to Hall for help. He offered to pay for counseling and to enroll Jared in a special program for substance-using teenagers. Because the program was located near his city home, Hall offered to have Jared live with him. What Hall neglected to tell Anne was that he was the source of Jared's amphetamines. Jared moved in with Hall, and Anne visited him on many weekends. Instead of improving with treatment, however, Jared seemed to get worse. According to Anne, he often seemed "dazed and strung out."

"One night I got a call from Peter telling me that Jared was 'very sick.' I hurried to Hall's home. I knew something was seriously wrong when I saw the police car parked outside. I ran inside. There was Jared, just lying there, unconscious from what turned out to be an overdose of sleeping pills. We got him to the hospital and had his stomach pumped. When he awoke, he told me that he had tried to kill himself to get away from Peter, who not only used him for sex but also made him have sex with Peter's friends."

Anne soon learned that Jared was not Hall's only victim; Luke had also been involved. The police investigation turned up five other boys who claimed that they, too, had been Hall's victims. Police inspector Philip Langton, who led the investigation, searched Hall's home after the arrest. "We found amphetamines and hundreds of photographs of naked boys, some as young as five years old. There were many computer games, toys, and videos—everything young boys might like. Hall's home computer was full of photos of boys, as well as contacts and connections to pedophile sites around the world."

Hall faces trial next March.

Hindus, like some Orthodox Jews, believe that women should not enter houses of worship while they are menstruating.

For most people, the idea of **pedophilia** (sexual activity with a prepubescent child) is simply incomprehensible. Yet it is precisely children's innocence and trust that makes them so attractive to pedophiles (Kincaid, 1998). Pedophiles, who seem to be exclusively male, generally focus on children below the age of 13. Most are satisfied to fantasize about sex with children or to collect child pornography. Others, like Peter Hall, act out their fantasies. The children involved may be their own or those of friends or relatives (McConaghy, 1998). Some pedophiles set out to meet children by becoming sports coaches, Big Brothers, or Scout leaders. A few prey on homeless street children. From a legal viewpoint, child sexual abuse is a crime that carries a deservedly severe punishment. From a clinical point of view, pedophilia is a psychological disorder. Specifically, it is one of the paraphilias—a group of unusual, harmful, or unacceptable sexual desires and acts.

PARAPHILIAS

What constitutes acceptable sexual behavior is largely a function of cultural mores. Activities considered normal in one time and place may be prohibited in another (Tannahill, 1989). For example, the Hebrews of biblical times forbade heterosexual intercourse while a woman was menstruating. Because menstruating women were considered unclean, they were required to undergo ritual cleansing in special baths and were refused entry to the Temple (a prohibition that still exists among Hindus today). The early Christians maintained many of the Hebrew prohibitions and added a few of their own. Premarital sex was out, and, even in marriage, sex was pro-

hibited on Sundays and other holy days. At best, sex was viewed as a necessary evil. The most devout people became nuns and priests and never had sex at all. During most of the medieval period, sex for any purpose other than procreation was condemned. Special care was required to protect men from seductive witches who sought to drain them of their "vital seed." The punishment for witches was death, sometimes by tying them to a stake and setting them afire.

During the reign of Britain's Queen Victoria, sex became a taboo topic. Sexual matters were not mentioned in polite society, and child-producing marital relations were considered the only "normal" sex acts. Queen Victoria refused to believe that there was such a thing as homosexual women. In the United States, people risked jail for revealing "deviant" desires (such as masturbation) to anyone, even their priest or doctor. Still, brothels catering to every kind of sexual whim thrived during the Victorian era. There seemed to be a hypocritical double standard in operation: Working-class prostitutes were despised, but their upper-class male clients did not lose their respectability. Perhaps not surprisingly, sexual repression did not make people lose interest in sex. As with any forbidden fruit, suppression actually made

In spite of the veneer of sexual repression in the Victorian era, people were very interested in sex, and sexology became a field of scientific study. Richard von Krafft-Ebing (1840–1902) published the first comprehensive nomenclature for sexual disorders in 1886.

One celebrated victim of the Victorians' ambivalence about sexual matters was the flamboyant Irish playwright Oscar Wilde. In 1895, the aristocratic father of his male lover engineered Wilde's arrest for homosexual practices. Wilde spent two years at hard labor and died three years later in 1900.

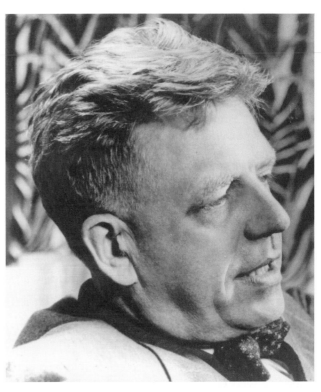

In the 1940s, the results of the surveys conducted by Alfred Kinsey (1894–1956) and his colleagues surprised the nation with evidence of more varied sexual practices than people had assumed.

people more, rather than less, interested in sex. It was no coincidence that Sigmund Freud, who made sex the central focus of his theory of human behavior, lived during the Victorian era.

Sex was also the focus of one of Freud's contemporaries, Richard von Krafft-Ebing (1840–1902). Krafft-Ebing was the first person to produce a comprehensive nomenclature for sexual disorders. His book, *Psychopathia Sexualis: A Medico-Forensic Study* (Krafft-Ebing, 1886), contained explicit descriptions of numerous sex acts. To preserve his reputation in those inhibited Victorian times, these passages were rendered in Latin. Only doctors and classical scholars could read them. Despite Krafft-Ebing's unshakeable belief that masturbation causes mental illness, some parts of his book were remarkably modern. For example, he differentiated *sexual dysfunctions* (an inability to maintain an erection, for example) from the *paraphilias*—a distinction identical to the one found in the *DSM-IV*. Krafft-Ebing was also aware of the debilitating effect of substance abuse and various medical conditions on sexual functioning. Krafft-Ebing sounded particularly modern when he argued that people with paraphilias are ill and need treat-

ment rather than punishment. Not surprisingly, Krafft-Ebing was in great demand as an expert witness for the defense in trials of people accused of sexual deviancy. Krafft-Ebing was also an active campaigner for homosexual law reform at a time when homosexuals were shunned and homosexual acts were punishable by imprisonment or banishment. Because of his social reform activities and extensive writings, Krafft-Ebing is widely acknowledged as both a liberalizing force in social attitudes and as founder of the field known today as **sexology** (the scientific study of human sexual behavior).

Despite Krafft-Ebing's work and the establishment of sexology as a scientific field (Horrocks & Campling, 1997), few scientists were willing to challenge the social taboos against researching, or even discussing, sexual behavior. A breakthrough occurred in the 1940s, when Alfred Kinsey (1894–1956) and his colleagues used surveys to paint a statistical portrait of the sexual behavior of 18,000 American men and women (Kinsey, Pomeroy, & Martin, 1948; Kinsey et al., 1953). Many of their findings were surprising, at least at the time. Practices that were considered rare and harmful (masturbation, for instance) were actually found to be quite common.

How to Be Smart About Sex

In the age of AIDS, sex is too serious a matter to be left to the spur of the moment. The consequences of sex can be quite serious unless you plan in advance. A lot of people are not taking precautions, however, because they are uncomfortable talking about sex. They find the subject embarrassing, and they fear that they may be rejected. Most people find it easier to have sex than to talk about it. Here are some things you can say to help make discussions easier.

First, introduce the topic of safer sex:

YOU: So, what do you think about this AIDS crisis? Do you think it's true what they have been writing about safer sex?

Second, reassure your partner:

YOU: I really enjoy being with you, but first we have to talk about safer sex.

If your partner objects to using protection, here are some replies:

PARTNER: I'm healthy.

YOU: I know, but I just don't want to worry about it and have it interfere with my enjoyment.

PARTNER: I can't believe you're so uptight.

YOU: I want you, but I don't want to die for it. I need to feel safe.

PARTNER: I thought you loved me.

YOU: By using protection, you can show me that you love me.

Homosexual experiences, once considered to be limited to people who were exclusively homosexual, were reported by people whose main sexual orientation was heterosexual. Kinsey found sexual behavior to be so diverse and variable that he concluded that practically any orientation is possible. Given the right early experiences and reinforcements, "most individuals might become conditioned in any direction, even into activities which they now consider quite unacceptable" (Kinsey et al., 1948, p. 678).

The sexual revolution of the 1960s, although exaggerated in its scope, did make people in Western countries more relaxed and accepting about sexual behavior. Even in polite society, sex came to be seen as more than just a way to produce children. It became accepted as a way to foster intimacy, solidify relationships, and give pleasure. Sexual experimentation came to be seen not as a sign of deviancy but as part of healthy development. For the first time in many American cities, sexually explicit literature and movies became readily available. By the 1990s, fear of sexually transmitted diseases, especially AIDS, had put an end to the wilder sexual experimentation that began in the 1960s. (Highlight 13.1 offers some tips for talking to a partner about sex.) Still, that turbulent decade has left a legacy. Today's society is less judgmental about sex and more willing to tolerate sexual experimentation in females as well as males. (Table 13.1 provides examples.) Undoubtedly, this more liberal attitude toward sex has allowed people who engage in "nonstandard" practices to feel less guilty about their behavior. In Chapter 1, we saw how homosexuality was transformed from a psychiatric disorder to a lifestyle. Masturbation, oral sex, and watching pornography are also no longer considered signs of psychological disorders. Still, the existence of a diagnostic category like the paraphilias suggests that there are some sex practices that we continue to find unacceptable. As you will see in the next section, these are mainly practices that cause suffering to the individual who engages in them or to other people.

Diagnosis

According to the *DSM-IV*, the paraphilias are characterized by intense sexual fantasies about, and urges to have (a) sex with nonhuman objects (bras or panties, for example), (b) sex that involves suffering on the part of oneself or one's partner, or (c) sex with children. The person need not act out these fantasies to receive the diagnosis, although many do. The *DSM-IV* paraphilias are listed in Table 13.2.

The main characteristics of the DSM-IV paraphilias are summarized in this section. To qualify for one of these diagnoses, a person must have fantasies and urges that last at least 6 months. During this period, people need not restrict themselves solely to paraphiliac fantasies or sex; they can engage in other types of sexual behavior as well. In most cases, however, paraphilias (more often, several paraphilias) become the person's dominant form of sexual expression. Like compulsions, paraphilias consume much of people's lives (Balyk, 1997; Kafka, 1997). Individuals may engage in their

TABLE 13.1 Sexual Experiences of University-Age Women

Ever performed (%)[a]	Average number of times in past month[b]	Activity
12.3	0.05	Anal intercourse
33.1	0.8	Caressing your partner's anal area
34.9	0.7	Masturbating alone
44.2	0.9	Intercourse: side by side
45.3	1.0	Having your anal area caressed
52.3	1.1	Intercourse: vaginal entry from rear
55.8	1.2	Intercourse: sitting position
63.9	1.8	Mutual petting of genitals to orgasm
67.4	1.7	Mutual oral stimulation of genitals
67.8	2.1	Intercourse: female "on top"
70.3	2.0	Oral stimulation of your partner's genitals
71.3	2.7	Intercourse: male "on top"
72.1	1.9	Having your genitals orally stimulated
79.7	2.8	Mutual undressing
81.3	3.2	Breast petting while in the nude
86.0	3.3	Stroking your partner's genitals
87.8	3.4	Having your genitals caressed
88.9	3.4	Your partner kissing your nude breasts
88.9	3.7	Erotic embrace while undressed
90.7	4.1	Kissing of sensitive (non-genital) areas of the body
91.1	4.0	Your partner lying on you while you are clothed
93.0	3.6	Breast petting while clothed
95.9	4.8	Deep kissing
98.8	5.6	Kissing on lips

[a]"Ever performed" is the percentage of women who experienced the activity at least once in their lives.

[b]For the past-month averages, women were asked to score each activity from 0 (did not occur) to 9 (twice or more per day).

Note: Adapted from Andersen & Cyranowski (1995).

DSM-IV TABLE 13.2 The *DSM-IV* Paraphilias

Exhibitionism	Pedophilia	Transvestic fetishism
Fetishism	Sexual masochism	Voyeurism
Frotteurism	Sexual sadism	Paraphilias not otherwise specified

paraphilia every day, sometimes several times each day. Some collect fetishistic objects (shoes, bras) or photographs depicting their preferred paraphiliac interest. Although some paraphiliacs are loners who keep their sexual behavior hidden, others are social enough to join interest groups of fellow paraphiliacs, who meet either in person or on the Internet. They may share paraphiliac objects or information, and, in some notorious cases of pedophilia, they may even share victims. Highlight 13.2 looks at the availability of sexually explicit material

on the Internet—and at its use by pornographers and pedophiles.

People with paraphilias are almost all male (McConaghy, 1998); it is rare for a female to meet the diagnostic criteria for any of the paraphilias other than masochism (where they are still the minority). Although the *DSM-IV* describes only a small number of paraphilias, it contains a "not otherwise specified" category that may include dozens, perhaps hundreds, more (Schewe, 1997). It seems that just about anything, from scuba

Surfing for Sex

At any moment in time, millions of people around the world are using search engines to surf the Internet for specific sites. What are they looking for? Most often, the answer is sex. It is the most frequently searched Internet topic. The second is erotica. Internet users search for both of these topics more often than they search for music (Elmer-Dewitt, 1995). There is, of course, nothing surprising about this. Our ancestors carved sexual pictures into the walls of caves. The ancient Greeks decorated pottery with sexual scenes and wrote sexual poems. The invention of still photography almost immediately produced sexually explicit photographs. As soon as movies were invented, they were used to film sexual activities. Next came VCRs. The Internet is just a new technology used for a very old purpose. For many people, it is an easier way to gain access to sexual material than was any previously available path. This is because of the relative

People in every society, including ancient Greece, have been interested in erotica. Its current popularity on the Internet should come as no surprise.

anonymity of the Net. People who might be too embarrassed to enter an adult sex shop or an erotic club find it easy to explore sexual material on the Internet without even leaving home.

In many cases, surfing the Internet for sex sites is harmless. Indeed, the Internet provides much useful information

about sexual behavior (Newman, 1997). But the Internet has a dark side as well. According to law enforcement officials, the Internet is also being used to procure children for illegal activities. Pornographers have used the Internet to provide pictures of children in sexual poses for pedophiles. These pictures, called "gifts," are actively traded by pedophiles living in many different countries. They also use the Internet to recruit young people to pose for such pictures and to engage in sex. Because of its anonymity, the Internet seems to remove inhibitions that might otherwise keep people from indulging their fantasies. The existence of pedophile sites on the Internet has caused many people to call for censorship and control. In a society that values free speech, however, control of antisocial activities must be balanced with protection of constitutional rights. Getting this balance correct is one of the major challenges facing legal authorities.

---

diving suits to toilet seats, can become imbued with erotic significance. Despite their diverse range, all paraphilias share a central characteristic—in every case, sexual behavior has been disconnected from a loving, consensual relationship with another adult.

Exhibitionism The *DSM-IV* defines **exhibitionism** as exposing one's genitals to a stranger, sometimes accompanied by masturbation (see Murphy, 1997, for a review). Affected individuals ("flashers") may be trying to shock the observer, and they often succeed. In some cases, exhibitionism may involve the fantasy that the stranger will find the display sexually arousing. The disorder is usually found among teenage and young adult males who grew up in sexually repressive homes and have little experience with women. Exhibitionism, indecent exposure, is the most common sexual offense.

Fetishism Using nonliving objects, such as shoes, bras, underpants, or leather clothing, in fantasy or directly to achieve sexual gratification is called **fetishism** (see Ma-

son, 1997, for a review). Some individuals have extensive fetish collections that they have purchased or, in some cases, stolen. They may masturbate while fondling the object, or they may ask their partners to don the object during sex. The fetishistic object is not just a stimulant (many men are attracted by women in high heels and sheer stockings); it is detached from the female and sexually stimulating on its own. For people with fetishism, sex is impossible without the fetish. Note that using objects specifically designed for sexual stimulation (vibrators, for example) is not considered a sign of fetishism. Fetishism begins in adolescence and tends to last a lifetime.

Frotteurism *Frottage* is French for "rub," and **frotteurism** involves touching or rubbing up against females, usually in crowded places (see Kreuger & Kaplan, 1997, for a review). Typically, the man gets behind a woman in a crowd and rubs his genitals against her buttocks or fondles her with his hands. This behavior may be accompanied by fantasies of a sexual relationship with the woman. Most men run away as soon as the woman re-acts. The behavior is most common in young men.

Pedophilia   Fantasizing about or engaging in sex with prepubescent children is termed **pedophilia.** According to the *DSM-IV*, pedophiles must be at least 5 years older than their victims. The law makes no such distinction. In most jurisdictions, sex with a minor aged 18 or less is always illegal. Most pedophiles prefer females, but some, like Peter Hall, prefer males, and others are aroused by both. Pedophiles may be sexually attracted only to children (exclusive type) or to both children and adults (nonexclusive type). Some pedophiles only fantasize about sex with children. Because they never act out their fantasies, they do not get into trouble with the law. Among pedophiles who do engage in sex with children, some fondle them or masturbate in front of them. Others engage in sexual intercourse with children, sometimes using force to achieve their ends. Pedophiles rationalize their behavior as "educating" the child or giving the child sexual pleasure, or they allege that the child seduced them. (This was Peter Hall's approach as illustrated in Document 13.2.) Pedophiles may limit their activities to their own children (*incest*) or to others they know, or they may prey on strangers. Some seek occupations (such as teaching) that bring them into contact with children. Pedophiles may physically threaten their victims to prevent disclosure. Pedophilia usually begins in adolescence and is highly resistant to punishment or treatment.

DOCUMENT 13.2

Excerpt From Transcript of Peter Hall's Trial in Superior Court for Sexual Assault

In the matter of: Peter Hall

Date: March 7, 1997

DISTRICT ATTORNEY: You have admitted to having sexual relations with many minor boys, including Jared Lawrence, yet you claim that you have not caused them any harm. Can you explain how both statements can be true?

PETER HALL: The boys loved me.

DISTRICT ATTORNEY: They loved you? Why?

PETER HALL: Because I loved them. These were not sordid one-night stands. I took care of these boys. I paid for their clothing and their games. I taught them about culture, about art, about life.

DISTRICT ATTORNEY: And about sex?

PETER HALL: Yes, that too. They learned to explore and enjoy their sexuality, and received pleasure in the process.

DISTRICT ATTORNEY: Were such young boys ready to explore their sexuality?

PETER HALL: You bet. Most of them came on to me first.

DISTRICT ATTORNEY: If they were so ready and derived such pleasure from their experiences, why did they need drugs?

PETER HALL: This was part of their education, and it enhanced their experiences.

DISTRICT ATTORNEY: As you say, you were involved with many boys. When they reached age 13 or so, you sent them away. Did you ever try to find out what happened to them?

PETER HALL: No, but I am sure they were all right. ■

Sexual Masochism   Sex involving real or imagined humiliation and suffering is described as **sexual masochism** (see Thornton & Mann, 1997, for a review). Females may fantasize about being held down and raped, for example. (Sexual masochism is the only paraphilia that seems to affect females, although they are still a minority.) Males may stick themselves with pins or give themselves electric shocks while masturbating. More dangerously, some may deprive themselves of oxygen by hanging from a noose or putting a plastic bag over their head (hyperoxyphilia). Such a practice has a high probability of being fatal (Uva, 1995). When partners are involved, masochistic acts include whipping, bondage, and being urinated on. Some couples carry out elaborate sex rituals involving fetishistic objects, such as

All sorts of leather and metal accessories are used by people who engage in sadistic-masochistic practices.

Rape Is Not Sex

Sexual penetration achieved against a person's will by menace or force or when the victim cannot give consent (because of mental retardation, illness, or intoxication) constitutes the crime known as rape. In some jurisdictions, oral or anal penetration is also considered rape when it takes place without consent. Rape is usually a crime committed by men against women, although homosexual rape also occurs (particularly in prisons). Rape should be differentiated from sex with a minor, which is sometimes called statutory rape. Sex with a minor is always a crime, even when both parties consent to the sex.

Because many rapes are not reported, it is difficult to know how often rape occurs, but we do know that it is fairly common. As we saw in Chapter 4, the effects of sexual assault are often devastating. In addition to any physical injury they suffer, rape victims may feel vul-

nerable, guilty, and depressed. The after-effects of rape may include a negative attitude toward sex, an anxiety disorder, substance abuse, or all three. In addition, victims whose cases come to trial must endure humiliating questioning from defense lawyers, who attempt to demonstrate that the victim somehow provoked the attack (Campbell, 1998). Considerable psychological and community support is expended each year helping rape victims to reestablish their lives (Campbell & Aherns, 1998).

Rape is not considered a paraphilia because it is not primarily a sexual act. Although rape involves sexual penetration, rapists may not have erections or reach orgasm during their attack. They seem to be motivated not by sex but by the need to dominate, degrade, and subjugate their victims (Brownmiller, 1993). This is why rapes often include sadistic acts. Victims have had their breasts

burned with cigarettes, their genitals mutilated, and, in extreme cases, they have been murdered.

A small number of rapes are committed by strangers, but most are committed by acquaintances (Parrot & Bechhofer, 1991). Often, the victim is intoxicated at the time. Because of its association with rape, the hypnotic drug Rohypnol (flunitrazepam) has been specifically targeted by legal authorities. According to federal law, courts may add up to 20 years to a convicted rapist's sentence if Rohypnol was used to facilitate the attack. This ban is seen as similar to gun control—target the drug and reduce the crime. In reality, it is like banning only one type of gun. There are many other tranquilizers and hypnotics that produce the same effect as Rohypnol. When abusers cannot find one, they substitute another (Calhoun et al., 1996).

---

leather-studded belts. Most of the time, physical damage is avoided, but, in some cases, masochists' desire to feel pain can lead to serious injury or even death.

Sexual Sadism   Fantasizing about or inflicting suffering or humiliation for sexual satisfaction is called **sexual sadism** (see Hucker, 1997b, for a review). The term *sadism* is derived from the name of the Marquis de Sade (1740–1814), who wrote about his need to inflict humiliation and pain on others. Sadistic behaviors include whipping, torturing, cutting, beating, pinching, and spanking. Some people with sexual sadism find masochistic partners; others impose their desires on unwilling partners. Sexual sadism inflicted on nonconsenting partners is a criminal offense. The severity of sadistic acts tends to increase over time and, when associated with antisocial personality disorder, may lead to rape or even murder (Firestone et al., 1998). Serial "lust murders," in which men rape, often mutilate, and then de-

liberately kill their female victims, may be an extreme form of sexual sadism. Note, however, that neither rape nor murder is a paraphilia. Both seem motivated as much by hate and aggression as by lust, as Highlight 13.3 makes clear in regard to rape.

Transvestic Fetishism   Cross-dressing for sexual pleasure by heterosexual males is called **transvestic fetishism** (Zucker & Blanchard, 1997). Most often, transvestic fetishists masturbate while wearing women's clothes. Individuals may begin by wearing one article of women's clothing, usually underwear, and stop there. Alternatively, they may progress to wearing an entire outfit and makeup. The behavior begins in childhood or adolescence and continues through adulthood and even through marriage. Cross-dressing to entertain an audience by homosexual males (*drag queens*) is not an example of transvestic fetishism. Some individuals find cross-dressing calming, even when no sex is involved. They

Cross-dressers, such as these members of the self-help group Crossroads, are transvestic festishists, not transexuals. They find emotional or sexual satisfaction in dressing like women, but their sexual orientation is usually heterosexual and they have no desire to be women.

may seek to live as women and may even have their sex surgically reassigned. In general, however, cross-dressing by males who believe they are really females is not a form of fetishism but a gender identity disorder (which is discussed later in this chapter).

Voyeurism   Sexual fulfillment and excitement gained by watching unsuspecting people disrobe or engage in sex is called **vouyeurism.** (Watching people who know they are being observed is not considered a paraphilia.) Usually, men masturbate while "peeping" or later as they recall what they have seen. In severe cases, this is the person's only form of sex. It begins in adolescence and tends to last a lifetime (see Kaplan & Kreuger, 1997, for a review).

Paraphilias Not Otherwise Specified   The *DSM-IV*'s category of paraphilias "not otherwise specified" encompasses a mixed collection of sexual behaviors and interests including making obscene phone calls, having sex with corpses or animals; deriving sexual pleasure from enemas; and *partialism,* which is an intense sexual attraction to a specific body part, most often breasts or buttocks.

It is difficult to know how frequently paraphilias occur because people with paraphilias rarely seek clinical assistance (McConaghy, 1998). The limited data that are available as to prevalence come mainly from surveys of people who have been convicted of sex crimes—which is hardly a representative sample of the general population. Convicted sex criminals are not even a representative sample of people with paraphilias because most paraphilias are not illegal. See Critical Thinking About Clinical Decisions 13.1 for a more detailed discussion about the relationship between sex crimes and the paraphilias.

Another reason why it is difficult to obtain accurate prevalence estimates is that paraphiliac behavior may be masked by other diagnoses. For example, some people only engage in paraphiliac behavior when intoxicated by alcohol or drugs while others display paraphiliac behavior only during psychotic episodes. These individuals will normally be diagnosed with substance intoxication or psychosis, respectively; their paraphiliac behavior may never be officially recorded. On the other hand, although it may be a difficult clinical judgment to make, people who deliberately use substances to help them act out their paraphiliac fantasies should probably be diagnosed as having a paraphilia because it is their primary disorder. (See the psychological assessment of Peter Hall in Document 13.3.)

DOCUMENT 13.3

Excerpts From Peter
Hall's Court–Ordered
Psychological
Evaluation

SUPERIOR COURT

Psychological Assessment

Date: March 3, 1997

Client: Peter Hall, 1232 Ocean View Road, Avalon; DOB: 3/17/1948

Tests Administered

Minnesota Multiphasic Personality Inventory (MMPI-2) 3/3/97

Wechsler Adult Intelligence Scale (WAIS-III) 3/3/97

Thematic Apperception Test (TAT) 3/3/97

Clinical interview

Psychologist: Dr. Stuart Berg

Referral: Judge L. Lyons, Superior Court

Reason for Referral: The client was referred by the Superior Court for a psychological assessment. He has been charged with indecent sexual assault and possession of illegal substances. The court has requested an evaluation of his psychological health and his competence to participate in his defense.

Behavioral Observations: Although the client was seen in the municipal jail, he seems to have been granted permission to wear his own clothing. He was dressed neatly, almost elegantly, and was wearing an expensive gold watch. At one point in our interview, he took a gold pen out of his pocket and tapped it quietly against the desk. His hair and nails were carefully groomed, and his shoes were buffed to a high shine.

    The client answered all questions carefully, was able to make eye contact, often smiled, and even made small jokes. He asked me questions about my educational background and mentioned how much he admired the university I attended. Overall, he gave the appearance of an educated person who has found himself caught in embarrassing circumstances and is determined to make the best of a difficult situation. The client was aware of the charges against him and claimed that the situation was "more complicated" than the police seemed to understand. He admitted to using drugs, especially amphetamines, but he said that they helped to heighten his sexual pleasure. He did not believe that he harmed the boys he had sex with, claiming instead that he never forced them and that they enjoyed and benefited from the experience.

Intellectual Assessment: The client's scores on the WAIS-III place him in the "above-average" range of intelligence. His verbal score was especially high, and there were no signs of deterioration or poor functioning in any area. . . .

Personality Assessment: The validity scales of the MMPI-2 were all in the average range, indicating that the profile could be safely interpreted. The main

Sex Crimes and Misdemeanors

In most states, it is illegal to have sexual relations with a person under 18. This crime is called *statutory rape* and is punishable by a prison sentence, even when both parties are willing participants. The purpose of statutory rape laws is to protect children, who may not be sufficiently mature to understand the consequences of their sexual behavior. Statutory rape is a sex crime, but it is not a psychological disorder. It does not appear in the *DSM-IV*, nor does date rape, acquaintance rape, or any other type of rape, even though they all are serious crimes. On the other hand, a man who feels guilty about dressing in women's clothing to obtain sexual fulfillment has a psychological disorder (transvestic fetishism), even though his behavior is perfectly legal and bothers no one except himself. Clearly, there is a disjunction between sex crimes and psychological disorders. Sex crimes need not be psychological disorders, and psychological disorders need not involve illegal behavior. Sounds pretty straightforward, does

it not? Unfortunately, the reality is far more complicated. Some paraphilias do involve crimes. For example, men who expose their genitals to female strangers are not only suffering from the paraphilia known as exhibitionism, they are also committing a misdemeanor (lewd behavior).

Sometimes, the distinctions between sex crimes and psychological disorders may appear quite odd. Consider pedophilia, for example. In most jurisdictions, an adult male over age 16 who engages in sexual behavior with a child, even just once, has committed the crime of child sexual assault. Does this person also have a psychological disorder? Probably not. The *DSM-IV* requires that pedophiliac behaviors occur over a period of at least 6 months before a diagnosis can be made. A one-time occurrence is not sufficient. Sometimes, continued sexual abuse may not be sufficient either. For example, the *DSM-IV* states that pedophilia can be diagnosed only when the "behaviors cause clinically signifi-

cant distress or impairment in social, occupational, or other important areas of functioning" (American Psychiatric Assn, 1994, p. 529). This seems to imply that sex with a child is not a sign of a psychological disorder when neither of the parties involved is significantly impaired. On the other hand, distressing *fantasies* about having sex with a child *are* sufficient for a diagnosis of pedophilia, even when no sex takes place and no child is harmed.

Some clinicians, and many legal experts, argue that the present diagnostic scheme is nonsensical. Most clinicians believe that children are *always* impaired by sexual abuse, even if such impairment does not appear significant at the time. The next *DSM* will almost certainly need to review its diagnostic criteria for the paraphilias to eliminate anomalies that allow fantasizers to be diagnosed as mentally disordered while those who act out the same fantasies may be considered normal.

features of the client's MMPI-2 are elevated Pd and Ma scale scores. This pattern is indicative of an ambitious person who eschews social norms and may have trouble delaying impulse gratification. This pattern of scores is found among people with antisocial personality disorder. . . .

The client's TAT responses tended to be short and guarded. However, on several occasions, his stories involved talented and brilliant older men mentoring younger boys (teaching them how to play a musical instrument, for example). In each case, the boy placed himself under the guidance of the adult, and, in each case, the boy was greatly helped by the relationship. . . . In one instance, the client described a mentor who was physically abused by a boy. This older man took this abuse gladly as a sign of the boy's emotional intimacy.

Overall, this client appears to view himself as smarter and more cultured than others. He sees himself as beyond the norms of society. . . . He tends to prefer interpersonal relationships in which he is the dominant party and has trouble delaying impulse gratification.

Diagnostic Considerations: Based on the history, interview, and test results, this client appears to meet the criteria for several *DSM-IV* diagnoses. He has engaged in pedophilia. He admits to using substances to heighten his sexual pleasure, but it is unclear whether this represents a disorder on its own. He does seem to have had a long-standing pattern of behavior that is characteristic of an antisocial personality disorder. His TAT suggests that he may have a tendency toward sexual masochism, as well. Despite his arrest, his global psychological functioning does not seem impaired, and there is nothing in either the intelligence test results nor the personality tests to indicate that the client is unable to participate in his defense.

Provisional Diagnosis

Axis I (clinical disorders): Pedophilia, substance abuse, sexual masochism

Axis II (personality disorders): Antisocial personality disorder

Axis III (general medical conditions): None

Axis IV (psychosocial and environmental problems): Arrest for child sexual assault and substance possession

Axis V (global assessment of functioning): 80+ (has minimal symptoms of distress, although his behavior may have caused distress to others)

Although we may not be able to estimate the incidence and prevalence of paraphilias with great precision, it is likely that they are fairly common. One need only look at the huge market for paraphiliac pornography (just check the Internet) to see that there must be many people with paraphiliac interests (American Psychiatric Assn, 1994).

Cultural Influences on Diagnosis   Even when other psychological disorders are ruled out, the line between the paraphilias and "normal" behavior remains blurry at best (Nakakuki, 1994). Some paraphilias appear to be little more than exaggerations of common sexual interests and behaviors. For example, many men are attracted to female breasts (just look at magazines and newspapers) but few take this interest to the extreme of partialism, in which sexual interest and pleasure are focused solely on breasts or some other part of the body. Although some paraphilias are exaggerations of everyday behavior, others are best described as violations of social norms, which vary from one culture to another. For example, a male who fondles the buttocks of a female stranger may qualify for the diagnosis of frotteurism in the United States, but may be considered just an amusing joker in Italy or Spain.

Sometimes, the distinction between what is normal and what is a paraphilia can seem quite artificial. For instance, masturbating while peeping through windows at unsuspecting couples is a sign of the paraphilia known as voyeurism, and it is illegal. On the other hand, masturbating while watching pornographic videos is not a sign of a psychological disorder, nor is it illegal (provided, of course, that it is done in private). To take another example, men who obtain sexual satisfaction by fondling women's underwear while masturbating may be diagnosed with the paraphilia known as fetishism. Curiously, this diagnosis does not apply to women who masturbate with penis-shaped vibrators. The *DSM-IV* defends this apparent contradiction by claiming that vibrators are designed for masturbation, whereas female underwear is not. By this definition, men who have sex with inflatable rubber dolls specifically designed for masturbation are normal, whereas those who use women's underwear have a psychological disorder. There may be a logical rule operating here, but it is not obvious.

In an attempt to make the distinction between paraphilias and normal behavior less arbitrary, the *DSM-IV* limits the diagnosis of paraphilia to people whose fantasies, urges, or behaviors cause significant distress or impairment to their social, occupational, or other important areas of functioning. In other words, if a paraphiliac interest does not bother the person or anyone else, then it does not signify a psychological disorder. As noted in Critical Thinking About Clinical Decisions 13.1, this distinction can produce absurd outcomes. Requiring that behavior produce significant distress before it is considered disordered means that men who happily have sex with uncomplaining children are normal, whereas those who are distressed by fantasies about sex with children are disordered.

Clearly, it is difficult to draw a firm line between sexually disordered and normal behavior. About the only thing we can say with conviction is that the paraphilias constitute a culturally unacceptable or personally distressing set of sexual fantasies, urges, and behaviors (some of which also involve criminal acts).

Etiology

How do people develop paraphilias? Probably, the same way that "normal" sexual behaviors develop—through a combination of biological instincts, cultural norms, and personal experiences. Because many people display more than one type of paraphilia, it is possible that there are general factors that dispose people to develop paraphilias. Some researchers have looked to physiology for these general factors; others, to social and psychological causes. As usual, the most likely cause of paraphiliac behavior is some combination of physiological and psychological variables.

Biological Causes Research on the biological causes of the paraphilias has concentrated on trying to find some physiological or anatomical difference between people with paraphilias and everyone else. Because sex drive is partly determined by hormone levels and because paraphilias affect mainly men, researchers have tried to demonstrate that men with paraphilias have higher levels of male sex hormones than people without paraphilias. Similarly, because brain damage can lead to odd sexual behavior in animals, scientists have tried to find evidence that people with paraphilias have brain damage. Although both lines of investigation have produced some confirmatory evidence (Collaer & Hines, 1995; Murphy, 1997), the data are far from conclusive. One problem is that hormone levels are not directly tied to paraphilias. Most men with high hormone levels do not meet the diagnostic criteria for a paraphilia. A second problem is that hormone levels are affected by various substances. Because people with paraphilias, especially

those convicted of sex crimes, may also use substances, it is not clear whether higher than normal hormone levels are the cause of paraphilias or the result of substance abuse (Langevin, 1992).

Because paraphilias are largely a male phenomenon and some types seem to run in families, researchers have suggested that they may be at least partly inherited. Again, there is some evidence supporting this view, although no specific hereditary mechanism for paraphilias has yet been uncovered (Langevin, 1993). Keep in mind that a trait does not have to be genetic to run in families. It is possible that members of each new generation are introduced to paraphiliac behavior by their forebears. Pedophilia, for example, may be the result of one generation molesting the next (Worling, 1995). In summary, it has not yet proved possible to identify a specific biological cause for any of the paraphilias. Progress is likely to remain slow because research volunteers are rare, and, consequently, sample sizes are small. The same problems apply to research on the potential social and psychological etiologies of the paraphilias.

Social and Psychological Causes Because it usually takes two people, sexual behavior is a social process. You must first locate a potential partner, ascertain whether your desire is reciprocated, and then initiate the behaviors that eventually lead to sex. In the paraphilias, one or more of these preliminaries has somehow gone awry—those with paraphilias have a kind of "courtship disorder" (Freund & Seto, 1998). For example, instead of reciprocal signaling and courtship, people with frotteurism simply fondle the object of their desire. Similarly, people with exhibitionism substitute their childish displays for more acceptable, and effective, means of seduction. In both cases, the paraphiliac behavior is unlikely to initiate an intimate interpersonal relationship. People with paraphilias appear to know this but feel unable to connect with others, except through paraphiliac behavior. Of course, they are doomed to fail. Women rarely fall in love with exhibitionists or strangers who grope them on trains. Yet men who engage in these behaviors continue to do so because their behavior is reinforced by the pleasure of orgasm.

How do paraphilias evolve? The answer probably depends on the specific paraphilia and the specific person (Laws & O'Donohue, 1997). There appear to be common factors that apply to practically all paraphilias, however, and these are just what you might expect (Furnham & Haraldsen, 1998). Specifically, people with paraphilias seem to have had childhood and adolescent experiences that limited their ability to be aroused by consensual sexual activity, increased their arousal by atypical stimuli, or restricted their ability to empathize with the victims of their paraphiliac behavior. For example, some people with paraphilias were led to consider themselves unattractive, a feeling that produced severe social anxiety. Instead of dating and courtship, they turned to less socially threatening forms of sexual fulfillment, such as the paraphilias. Some people with paraphilias come from environments that fostered repressive, guilt-producing attitudes toward sex. (Document 13.4 contains information on Peter Hall's background.) There is also evidence that some people with paraphilias were sexually abused as children (Worling, 1995). Their early experiences may have limited their ability to form intimate relationships later in life.

DOCUMENT 13.4

Excerpts From Court–Ordered Social Work Report on Peter Hall

Date: March 4, 1997

Social Worker: Li Cheong, MSW, psychiatric social worker

Referral: Judge Lyons requested this report on Peter Hall, who is charged with sexual assault and possession of illegal substances.

Sources: Court records, Anne Lawrence, Mrs. Maureen Hall, John O'Connor

Peter Hall is a successful businessperson. His bank estimates his net worth at $35 million. He was born into wealth. His family, stretching back at least 150 years, has owned a large food-processing company. His wit, sophistication, and money have brought him many friends among the rich and famous. Everyone from politicians to judges and artists attended his famous parties.

Like his two brothers, and all the male Halls before him, Peter was enrolled at age 10 in an elite private military academy. Until his graduation from college, his time at home was limited to school vacations. Although Peter's father had left home for another woman when Peter was only 8, Peter's mother, Maureen Hall, notes that Peter always seemed happy on his home visits. Things may have been different at school, however. Peter's classmate and lifetime friend John O'Connor reports that Peter was considered "girlish" by the other boys. He was bullied and teased, and on several occasions he was humiliated by having his head held in a toilet bowl.

Although Mrs. Hall claims to have been unaware of this bullying, she did note that Peter was never interested in girls. He did not date and seemed mainly to enjoy hanging around with younger boys. According to both Peter and his friend John, they were both actively homosexual by grade 10. Maureen claims to be unaware that Peter is homosexual, despite his never dating or getting married.

John and Peter lived together in Peter's expensive homes. According to the neighbors, there were usually young boys living there as well. These boys (the sons of Peter's foreign business associates) would bring their school friends to Peter's homes as well. John says that he and Peter would sometimes pick up "street kids" and boys on the beach. They would promise the boys money and allow them to use Peter's boat and video games in exchange for sex. According to Anne Lawrence, that is how Peter met her sons. . . . ∎

The psychological results of these early experiences—social anxiety, ignorance, guilt, fear (alone or in combination)—serve to misdirect sexual impulses away from intimate social relationships and toward other sexual outlets. Once this happens, practically anything can take on sexual connotations (Love, 1993). Articles of women's clothing, for example, can become fetishistic objects through classical conditioning. That is, they are conditioned stimuli whose presence during masturbation leads to their association with the conditioned response of orgasm (Rowan, 1988).

In addition to resulting from classical conditioning, paraphiliac learning can also take place through operant conditioning. For example, when they were children, people with transvestic fetishism may have been encouraged and rewarded for dressing as females. Over time, cross-dressing alone became a source of pleasure. Similarly, people who are too shy to make intimate contacts may have had their voyeuristic peeping reinforced by masturbation-induced orgasm. Modeling may also play a role in the development of paraphilias. Paraphiliac activity is common in pornography, and people without other sexual outlets may copy the behavior depicted in videos and magazines. Once tried, this behavior may be reinforced by masturbation and orgasm.

In contrast to behavioral theories about the etiology of paraphilias, psychodynamic explanations focus on the apparent symbolism of these disorders. For example, men who don women's clothing may be seeking a way out of their responsibilities (as fathers or providers). Similarly, people who seek physical punishment and humiliation during sex may be displaying guilt about their sexual urges, whereas those who find administering punishment sexually exciting may be overcoming feelings of inadequacy by seeking power over others.

Although they are difficult to prove, these psychodynamic hypotheses seem at least superficially plausible, and they do not exclude the possibility that paraphiliac behavior is learned. A complete explanation for paraphilias may need to include both conditioning and psychodynamic components. Because most people with paraphilias are men, biological factors will need to be incorporated as well. Finally, as already noted, substance use may provide the disinhibition that allows people with paraphilias to move beyond lonely masturbation to act out their fantasies. In other words, like most disorders, the paraphilias will almost certainly turn out to be the result of social, psychological, and biological factors.

Treatment and Prevention

Clinical psychologists have always considered the paraphilias difficult to treat (McConaghy, 1998). This is not surprising given that most people who undergo treatment are convicted sex offenders—men with the most severe, and most antisocial, paraphilias. People with mild paraphilias are rarely detected, let alone treated. Felons who participate in treatment are usually motivated by the promise of early release from jail, or they attend treatment after release as a parole requirement. Few are intrinsically motivated to change. Some, like Peter Hall, may not even admit that their behavior is disordered or harmful to others. Still, as you will see in this section, most of treatment research has been aimed at difficult-to-treat sex-criminal paraphiliacs, especially people with pedophilia (see Crolley et al., 1998, for example).

Even when clients are motivated to change, psychological treatments may not be up to the task (Furby, Weinrott, & Blackshaw, 1989). Psychodynamic therapy, based on insight and interpretation, has not been successful at "curing" paraphilias, nor has the most commonly applied form of behavior therapy—aversive conditioning. The idea behind aversive conditioning is to associate paraphiliac objects with negative stimuli, thereby transforming their sexually arousing properties into aversive ones (Maletzky, 1998). For example, to treat a person with a fetish for women's shoes, therapists pair a painful stimulus, such as an electric shock, with one of the fetishist's favorite shoes. Eventually, instead of sexual arousal, the sight of the shoe should elicit fear. Treating a pedophile is similar; an aversive stimulus is administered while the client looks at a photograph of a child (McConaghy, 1998).

Although aversive conditioning sounds as if it should work, its results have been disappointing. One problem is getting people motivated enough to complete a course of treatment (Jenkins-Hall, 1994). Because aversive conditioning is designed to be unpleasant (that is why it is called aversive), treatment dropouts are common. To make aversive conditioning more palatable, some therapists have used *covert sensitization*, in which aversive stimuli are presented, not directly (as in electric shock), but in the imagination (Dougher, 1993). For example, a client may be asked to imagine approaching a child and then, as the client becomes aroused, to conjure up an image of being caught in a sexual act with the child by disgusted relatives. Unfortunately, neither aversive conditioning nor covert sensitization, on their own, produces a significant reduction in paraphiliac behavior.

In an attempt to improve treatment outcomes, clinicians have devised cognitive-behavioral (multimodal) treatment programs (Marshall & Eccles, 1996). In addition to aversive conditioning, these treatments may include cognitive restructuring, desensitization (to overcome the anxiety produced by social and sexual situations), stress management, and skills training designed to help clients develop social relationships. To reorient clients' sexual attraction to more conventional stimuli, behavioral therapists may treat people with paraphilia by using *masturbatory reconditioning,* a technique which requires clients to supplement their paraphiliac masturbation fantasies with pictures or films of nude women (Laws & Marshall, 1991; P. Johnston, Hudson, & Marshall, 1992). The idea is that the clients will gradually reorient their fantasies and behavior away from paraphiliac objects and toward conventional sexual stimuli. To measure a change in orientation, researchers may use *phallometric testing,* which requires the man to wear a pressure-sensitive device called a plethysmograph on his penis. This device will reflect any sexual response that causes the penis to expand. In this way, researchers can determine whether they have been successful without having to rely on a person's verbal report (Lalumiere & Harris, 1998).

In cases of incest, family therapy may be employed to help family members come to grips with the perpetrator's behavior. *Relapse prevention* (see Chapter 6) may be used to help people recognize and avoid situations most likely to stimulate their paraphiliac behavior (McConaghy, 1998).

There is evidence that cognitive-behavioral treatment reduces the likelihood that paraphiliac behavior will be repeated (Marshall and Eccles, 1996; Marshall et al., 1996), but relapses still occur, especially among pedophiles with a long history of sex offenses and whose victims are boys rather than girls. Because of the relatively high likelihood of relapse, every so often there are

To detect whether the cause of male erectile disorder is physical or psychological, a man may be asked to wear a plethysmograph overnight to see whether he experiences erections while he is asleep.

calls for pedophiles (and others who commit sex offenses) to undergo calming brain operations or castration (Freund, 1980). Brain operations usually involve the destruction of parts of the hypothalamus, whereas castration requires the removal of the testes. Neither operation has been particularly successful (even castrated men may still engage in sex acts). As a consequence, these operations are rarely performed any more. Sex offenders are much more likely to be *chemically castrated* with drugs (Roesler & Witzum, 1998). For example, they may be given Depo-Provera (medroxyprogesterone), a birth control drug that reduces the level of the male sex hormone testosterone (Bradford, 1997). Lowering testosterone levels reduces sex drive and makes erections more difficult to achieve. In some cases, antidepressants, antipsychotics, and tranquilizers can have similar effects (Bourgeois & Klein, 1996). Because they may have to be taken for long periods, perhaps even a lifetime, drugs expose people to significant side effects, which may cause some people to drop out of treatment (Thibaut, Cordier, & Kuhn, 1996). Because the drugs simply lower sex drive while leaving sexual interests unchanged, clients are likely to return to their paraphiliac behaviors once these drugs are discontinued. For this reason, drugs should be supplemented with psychological treatment.

Because treatment is difficult and relapse a significant problem, many experts believe that prevention, especially of sex crimes, is the best way to use our scarce economic and health resources (Daro, 1994; Reppucci, Land, & Haugaard, 1998). Primary prevention efforts have so far been limited to censoring paraphiliac pornography. The idea is that pornographic materials may have two negative effects: (a) they may provoke naive viewers

into modeling unacceptable behaviors that, if reinforced through orgasm, may lead to the development of sexual disorders; and (b) they may stimulate people who already have antisocial sexual fantasies to act them out (Russell, 1998). In a society that values freedom of speech, a complete ban on pornography is impossible to achieve. About the best we can hope for is to keep pornography away from minors. Additionally, it is unclear whether pornography has as strong an effect on antisocial sexual behavior as many people believe (Howitt, 1995). For both of these reasons (legal rights to free speech and only modest research supporting pornography's pernicious effects), banning pornography has received less attention from psychological researchers than have various forms of secondary prevention.

One approach to secondary prevention uses school programs and public service announcements to warn children of potential dangers and to encourage them to report suspicious people or incidents (Reppucci et al., 1998; Rispens, Aldeman, & Goudena, 1997). A more extreme approach to secondary prevention is to keep sexual offenders locked away so that they cannot offend again. Several states have "sexual predator" laws that permit the legal authorities to conduct civil commitment proceedings for about-to-be-released prisoners deemed likely to repeat a sex offense (see the discussion on civil commitment in Chapter 9). The outcome of these proceedings can be indefinite involuntary incarceration in a mental hospital (Grudzinskas & Henry, 1997). Theoretically, people who have served their complete prison terms may remain in custody indefinitely. In practice, this rarely happens; most offenders are eventually released. To limit their opportunity to repeat their crimes and to allow members of the community to protect themselves and their children, many jurisdictions require police to register sex offenders and to inform community members when a registered sex offender moves into their neighborhood (Freeman-Longo, 1996). The original registration-notification law was enacted by the state of New Jersey in response to the brutal murder of Megan Kanka, a child kidnapped, raped, and murdered on her way home from school by a neighbor who turned out to be a twice-convicted sex offender. "Megan's Law" was quickly extended nationally. Using computer databases, police may soon be able to monitor convicted offenders anywhere in the United States.

The effectiveness of sexual predator laws in reducing sex crimes remains to be demonstrated (Berliner, 1996). In the meantime, these laws may have unintended consequences. For example, men who were convicted many years ago of consensual homosexual activity (behavior

Sleep Disorders

The parasomnias (night terrors, sleep-walking, nightmares) were discussed in Chapter 12. The *DSM-IV* also contains another set of sleep disorders known as the dyssomnias (see Vgontzas & Kales, 1999, for a review). The most common of these, **primary insomnia,** is difficulty in initiating or maintaining sleep or having sleep that is not perceived as restful. Most often it takes the form of either difficulty falling asleep or, as with Anne Lawrence, early awakening. (Early awakening is particularly common among people with depression.) People with insomnia become distressed by their poor sleep, and worry about getting a good night's sleep; the more worried they get, the less likely they are to sleep. Insomnia is more common as people get older. Often, insomnia starts with a stressful incident, as in Anne's case, but as the worry-

sleepless cycle takes over, it may become self-perpetuating. To meet the *DSM-IV* diagnostic criteria for primary insomnia, the problem must last at least 1 month and it must not simply be the result of another disorder or substance abuse.

In addition to primary insomnia, the *DSM-IV* includes several other dyssomnias. **Hypersomnia** is another name for excessive sleepiness. Sufferers may sleep 12 hours or more and still have difficulty awakening. **Narcolepsy** is marked by irresistible "sleep attacks" in which the person simply falls asleep in the middle of a meal, while working, or just about anywhere. This can happen several times a day and may be a sign of neurological illness. In **breathing-related sleep disorder,** breathing is made difficult during sleep by obstruction of the upper airways. This condition, which is associ-

ated with obesity, produces snoring, frequent awakenings, and, in severe cases, a brain-destroying lack of oxygen during sleep. The condition may respond to surgery, or mechanical devices may ensure unobstructed breathing during sleep. Finally, **circadian rhythm sleep disorder** is the *DSM-IV*'s name for a sleeping difficulty produced by changes in time or daily schedule. It is the most common symptom of jet lag, in which a person's sleep cycle becomes disrupted by changes in time zone.

Temporary sleep disorders may be assisted by medication, but long-term use of sedatives is likely to produce more harm than good. Fortunately, sleep disorders often respond to behavioral treatments designed to minimize anxiety about sleep.

which is no longer illegal in most jurisdictions) are being forced to register as sex offenders. Their neighbors are being notified, even though these men have never presented a threat to anyone (Riccardi & Leeds, 1997). In addition to the unanticipated outcomes, opponents of sexual predator laws decry their harshness to previous offenders. They say that it is unfair and cruel to turn former offenders who have paid their debt to society into social pariahs. Offenders are forced to suffer as social outcasts for the rest of their lives, even though they may never commit another crime. Rehabilitation, under such circumstances, may be difficult to achieve (who would want to give a job or live next door to a sex offender?).

The balancing argument given to justify such severe treatment is the even greater harm suffered by the victims of sex offenders, especially children. Victims of sex crimes may develop anxiety disorders (including post-traumatic stress disorder) and depression. Some may turn to substances for solace. Many will develop some type of sexual problem. Proponents argue that by preventing sex crimes, sexual predator laws (despite their stigmatizing brutality) produce more good than harm. The data are not yet available to settle this question. But there is no doubt that sex crimes can cause considerable

harm to the victims. Consider, for example, the cases of Jared and Luke Lawrence.

THE PREY

Peter Hall found it relatively easy to forge a relationship with Anne Lawrence and her sons. Anne was a divorced mother who welcomed a father figure in the life of her sons. Jared and Luke were overwhelmed by Hall's interest in them and awed by his houses, cars, boats, and huge collection of computer games and music. Anne told the police that she knew Hall was "homosexual," but what she did not say is that she found this comforting. Her attitudes toward heterosexual sex were ambivalent at best. After Jared's overdose, Anne entered psychological treatment. She was depressed and found it very difficult to get a good night's sleep. She would fall asleep but then wake up in the night and be unable to fall asleep again. This left her exhausted the next day. (Highlight 13.4 provides more information on sleep problems.) Anne Lawrence wanted help in dealing with her depression and blamed herself for what had happened to her son. During treatment, the focus turned to her sex life, which she described as full of problems both before and after she was divorced from her husband, Sean. Document 13.5 contains an excerpt from the transcript of one of Anne's psychotherapy sessions.

DOCUMENT 13.5

Excerpt From the Transcript of One of Anne Lawrence's Psychotherapy Sessions

THERAPIST: Can you tell me more about these sexual problems you refer to?

ANNE: It's a bit embarrassing.

THERAPIST: That's OK. Most people have trouble talking about sex.

ANNE: I know. It's so damn important to everyone. It certainly was to Sean. He left me and later moved in with someone much sexier than me. He said the reason was that I was so cold.

THERAPIST: Do you believe that you are not sexy?

ANNE: I used to go along with it, mostly to please Sean. But since the divorce, I have lost most of my interest in sex. I know people think about it and have fantasies, but I don't. To tell you the truth, I haven't had a sexual fantasy in years. One of the reasons I enjoyed spending time with Peter Hall was that I believed he was homosexual and therefore would not be interested in me sexually.

THERAPIST: Is there a reason for your lack of interest?

ANNE: Well, for one thing, I don't like undressing in front of anyone; I'm a little too fat. I was brought up to be modest. We never spoke about sex at home or at school; it was sort of "dirty." Another problem is that sex often hurts. You are supposed to get wet and swollen when you are excited; I rarely do.

THERAPIST: Was sex ever pleasurable for you?

ANNE: Sure, sometimes. But I have never had an orgasm during intercourse.

THERAPIST: Can you achieve an orgasm through masturbation?

ANNE: I don't know. I have never tried. ■

Sex also proved a problem for Jared. For many years after the overdose incident, he battled substance abuse, depression, and post-traumatic stress disorder. His school record was poor, and he seemed unable to get on with his life. As a young man, Jared gave a television interview as part of a documentary on the victims of pedophilia. He was asked about the lasting effects of Hall's victimization. A brief excerpt from this interview appears in Document 13.6.

DOCUMENT 13.6

Excerpt From Jared Lawrence's (age 18) Television Interview

INTERVIEWER: You described the balcony surrounding Peter Hall's beach apartment as "nightmare alley." What did you mean?

JARED: That's where they would have sex with us. Hall and his friends, they would pull down these blinds, for privacy. We would have to lie down on these lounge chairs with them, two boys to every adult. Then we would get started; it was a real orgy.

INTERVIEWER: It seems as if you are having trouble forgetting those times.

JARED: Yes. I have nightmares about it all the time.

INTERVIEWER: Have you ever had a girlfriend?

JARED: Yeah, but . . .

INTERVIEWER: But what?

JARED: They are hard to keep. I . . . usually shut off when they go emotional on me. . . . I get excited during, you know, when we are fooling around, but when it comes time for doing something . . .

INTERVIEWER: You cannot do anything?

JARED: No, I can't enter a woman. In fact, the whole idea makes me nauseous. ■

In different ways, and for different reasons, both Anne and Jared have developed what the *DSM-IV* calls sexual dysfunctions. Unlike the paraphilias, in which it is not performing the sex act that is the problem, but the target of the sex act, sexual dysfunctions actually interfere with performing sexual acts. As are most of the disorders described in this book, sexual dysfunctions are mainly exaggerations of common problems. At one time or another, practically everyone will have some problem performing a sex act. Fatigue, illness, stress, depression, and substance intoxication (alone or in combination) can make us either uninterested in sex or unable to perform sexually. When these everyday occurrences become persistent enough to disturb an individual or a relationship, the *DSM-IV* considers them to be dysfunctions.

SEXUAL DYSFUNCTIONS

As already noted, sexual dysfunctions make it difficult or impossible for people to have or enjoy sexual relations. They may be extremely distressing to those who have them, and, if they persist, sexual dysfunctions can

In the 1960s, William Masters and Virginia Johnson discovered new ways to record the physiological responses of people engaged in sexual behaviors.

lead to low self-esteem, anxiety about performance, and interpersonal problems. The *DSM-IV* categorizes sexual dysfunctions according to which aspect of sexual performance is affected. This categorization is based mainly on the work of Masters and Johnson, whose description of the phases of the human sexual response cycle is addressed next.

Human Sexual Response

Much of what we know today about the biological aspects of sexual behavior originated in the work of William H. Masters (1915–) and Virginia E. Johnson (1925–) in the 1960s (Masters & Johnson, 1967, 1970). They followed up Kinsey's sociological research with direct observations of people engaging in sexual behavior under controlled laboratory conditions. Although they were not the first to make such observations, Masters and Johnson developed important new ways to gather data. For example, to observe female physiological responses, they constructed a clear plastic artificial penis through which the vagina could be filmed during intercourse. Masters and Johnson had no difficulty finding volunteers. By the time they published their first book, they had filmed more than 700 volunteers and recorded data on more than 10,000 orgasms. Their work is not the last word, however. More recent investigations

have used increasingly sophisticated techniques, such as endoscopy and ultrasound imaging, to picture what really happens during sexual activity, especially during intercourse (Levin, 1998). These newer techniques have added much information to Masters and Johnson's original observations, although their main observations (described here) remain relatively unchallenged.

Masters and Johnson set out to describe how physical and psychological mechanisms work together to control sexual responsiveness. Before their observations, research attention was devoted primarily to understanding sexual genetics and anatomy. By the time Masters and Johnson began their work, these aspects of sexuality were already well understood (Figure 13.1). Males, who inherit an X chromosome from their mothers and a Y chromosome from their fathers, develop testes and a penis, whereas females, who inherit two X chromosomes, develop a uterus, ovaries, a vagina, and a particularly sensitive organ called the clitoris.

Sexual development is related to hormonal secretions. Surprisingly, both sexes produce male sex hormones (androgens) and female sex hormones (estrogens). It is the balance between hormones (androgens dominate in males, estrogens in females) that determines whether a child will display male or female sex characteristics. Sometimes, this balance is disturbed. Malfunctioning glands, for example, may result in a

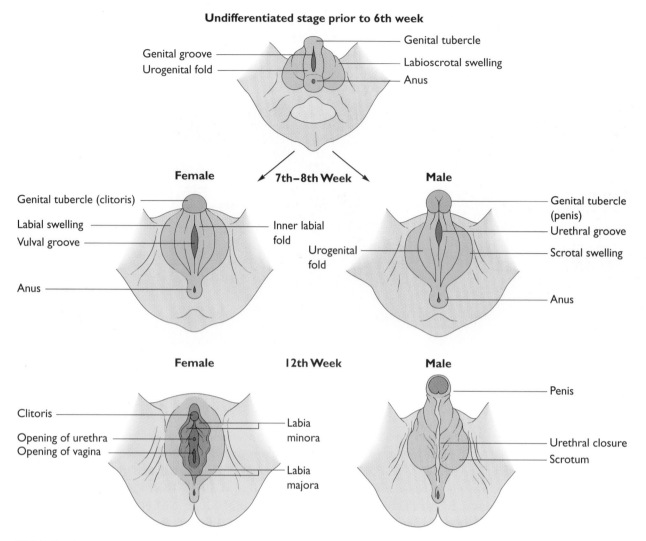

Undifferentiated stage prior to 6th week

Genital groove — Genital tubercle
Urogenital fold — Labioscrotal swelling
— Anus

Female — 7th–8th Week — **Male**

Genital tubercle (clitoris) — Genital tubercle (penis)
Labial swelling — Urethral groove
Vulval groove — Inner labial fold — Scrotal swelling
Urogenital fold
Anus — Anus

Female — 12th Week — **Male**

Clitoris — Penis
Opening of urethra — Labia minora
Opening of vagina — Urethral closure
— Labia majora — Scrotum

FIGURE 13.1 Embryonic-Fetal Differentiation of the External Reproductive Organs.
Female and male reproductive organs are formed from the same embryonic tissues. Genetic and hormonal instructions signal whether they will develop as male or female organs.

female fetus's being exposed to an excess of androgens. Even a brief exposure can produce dramatic effects. "Masculinized" females may grow up to be heavier, stronger, and more aggressive than their peers. They may also show more interest in sex. Surveys report that most males think about sex every day, often several times a day, whereas women think about sex a few times a week or less (Michael et al., 1995). Masculinized females may think about sex as often as males. "Feminized" male fetuses, who are exposed to an excess of estrogens, show the opposite pattern; they grow up with more feminine traits than their male peers. We shall have more to say about the development of sex role behavior and gender identity later in this chapter. For now, the important point to note is that, despite the physio-

logical and anatomical differences between the sexes, Masters and Johnson found that males and females follow a similar pattern of responses to sexual stimulation. Specifically, Masters and Johnson identified a sexual response cycle with several sequential phases (Figure 13.2). Although there is considerable individual variation in the duration of each phase, especially among females, the sequence of phases is typically the same for most people. The five phases of the sexual response cycle are described in Table 13.3.

In the course of their research, Masters and Johnson debunked many popular myths about sexual performance and satisfaction. For example, by taking careful measurements, they found that men with average-sized penises erroneously believed that their penises were

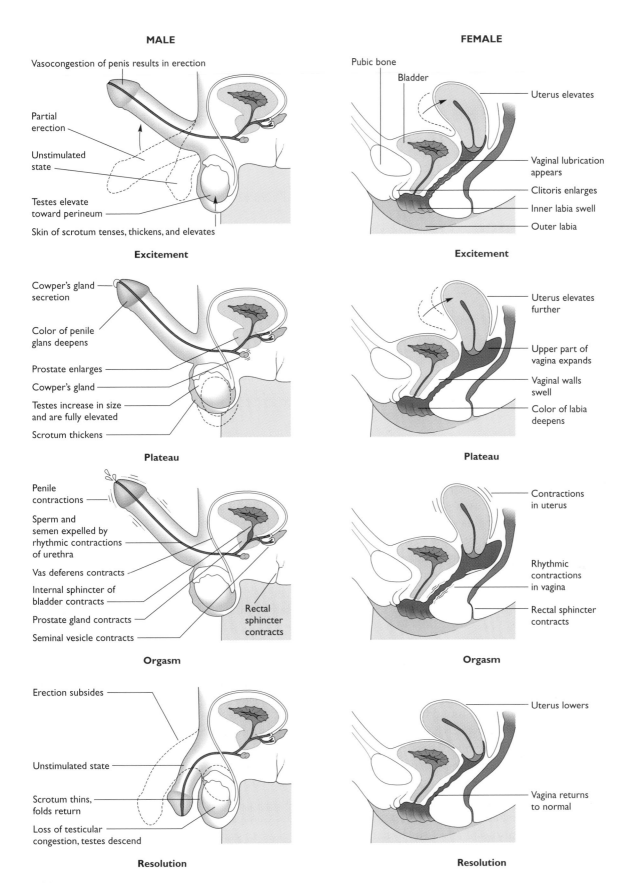

FIGURE 13.2 **Phases of the Sexual Response Cycle**

TABLE 13.3   Five Phases of the Sexual Response Cycle

1. *Desire.* A sexual cycle usually begins with desire, the motivation to engage in sexual activity. Desire can arise spontaneously or in response to a sexually arousing stimulus. In some cases, desire may not appear until sexual stimulation begins.

2. *Excitement.* The excitement phase begins with petting and foreplay, which causes sexual hormones to be secreted. Heart rate increases, and breathing becomes more rapid. The nipples become erect in women, and in many men as well. Some women develop a *sex flush,* a body rash that deepens in color with their degree of sexual arousal. Blood flows to the genitals, causing the penis and the clitoris to swell and become red. The lining of the vaginal walls becomes lubricated.

3. *Plateau.* The genitals continue to fill with blood, and the muscles become tense. The penis becomes erect, and the testes enlarge and are pulled up into the scrotum. The clitoris retracts under its hood and the tissues of the vagina swell. Psychologically, feelings of sexual excitement increase. This stage can last for from a few minutes to several hours.

4. *Orgasm.* Females experience strong genital sensations and warmth spreading in the pelvic area, followed by rhythmic muscle contractions causing the vaginal walls, uterus, and rectal sphincter muscle to contract and expand. Males first feel the ejaculate coming, followed by muscle contractions in the penis that propel semen through the urethra and out the urinary opening. For both sexes, a psychological sensation of orgasm (pleasurable release) accompanies these muscle contractions.

5. *Resolution.* The body gradually returns to its prior unstimulated condition. For men, there is a refractory period in which they are unable to have another orgasm no matter how much they are stimulated. This period varies from less than an hour for some men to many hours for others, depending on their age, fitness, and a host of other factors. Women may have multiple orgasms with no apparent refractory period, but the ability to have multiple orgasms varies considerably from one woman to the next.

---

smaller than average. Although there is considerable variability in the size of penises in their flaccid state, when erect, most organs are very close to the same size. In any event, they found that the vagina adjusts (getting smaller or larger) to accommodate any penis size. Masters and Johnson also exposed as false the Freudian distinction between clitoral and vaginal orgasms. Freud insisted that orgasms reached by masturbation are "immature" and that having vaginal orgasms (through intercourse) was evidence that a woman had progressed to the highest, "genital," stage of personality development. Contrary to Freud's assertions, Masters and Johnson showed that all female orgasms are caused by clitoral manipulation (direct in the case of masturbation and indirect during intercourse). They found that many psychologically healthy women never experience orgasm except by direct manual manipulation. Some women claim to be sexually fulfilled without experiencing orgasm at all, as Highlight 13.5 reports.

The *DSM-IV* categorizes sexual dysfunctions according to the phase of the sexual response cycle that they affect: Disorders of sexual desire affect the initial phase, disorders that affect sexual arousal arise in the excitement and plateau phases, and disorders that affect orgasm mainly affect the orgasmic phase. In addition, the *DSM-IV* contains sexual pain disorders, which affect

the specific mechanics of sexual intercourse. (The *DSM-IV* sexual dysfunctions are briefly summarized in Table 13.4.) Most of the literature on sexual dysfunctions deals with heterosexual couples. Similar sexual problems probably affect homosexual couples as well. However, because homosexual dysfunctions are not well documented, they are not discussed in detail in this chapter.

This chapter discusses each type of sexual dysfunction separately, but in practice they overlap and interact. For example, a person who cannot achieve an orgasm may lose the desire for sex. This individual may wind up with both an orgasmic disorder and a disorder of desire. Such multiple dysfunctions are the rule rather than the exception. Also keep in mind that sexual dysfunctions are highly charged emotionally. Anger, fear, resentment, shame, guilt, and humiliation are frequently associated with sexual dysfunctions. If the dysfunctions get out of hand, individuals may develop secondary disorders, particularly anxiety disorders and depression. These secondary disorders may be even more devastating to individuals and couples than are the sexual dysfunctions that trigger them.

Diagnosing a sexual dysfunction requires considerable clinical sensitivity. There is no objective way to decide where normal behavior ends and a sexual dysfunction begins. For example, the failure to reach orgasm is

Sex and the Big "O"

Is orgasm—the big "O"—the goal of sexual activity? Is it possible to have an intimate sexual relationship, and even be sexually satisfied, without having an orgasm? Some answers to these questions may be found in the results of the National Health and Social Life Survey, which questioned people about their sexual activities and satisfaction (Laumann et al., 1994; Laumann, Paik, & Rosen, 1999; Michael et al., 1995). In that survey, only 29% of females reported always having an orgasm with their partner during the preceding year. Yet 41% of women said that they were "extremely physically satisfied" by sex, and 39% reported "extreme emotional satisfaction." In other words, females did not need to have an orgasm to be physically and emotionally satisfied with sex. Tenderness, intimacy, and affection may be more important determinants of gratifi-

cation than having an orgasm.

The results for males were intriguing as well. Seventy-five percent claimed to always have had an orgasm while having sex with their partner during the preceding year. This is more than twice the percentage of females. On the other hand, 47% of males reported being extremely physically satisfied by sex, and 42% reported extreme emotional satisfaction. It seems that males are more likely to have orgasms than females, but their physical and emotional satisfaction with sex is not much different from the levels reported by females. In other words, for males as well as females, satisfaction is not directly tied to having an orgasm. Fulfillment, in a loving relationship, seems more a matter of expressing tender feelings than achieving an orgasm.

Despite these findings, many of the *DSM-IV* sexual dysfunctions involve ab-

sent, delayed, or too-rapid orgasms. Clearly, many people are troubled enough by their orgasmic performance to seek clinical assistance. What these survey results suggest is that their worries may be misplaced. People are able to have a satisfying sex life despite infrequent orgasms.

As an aside, when people were asked about their partners rather than themselves, 44% of men reported that their female partners always had an orgasm during sex. This figure is 14% higher than the one reported by females themselves. There are two possible explanations for this discrepancy: Men may not recognize the signs of orgasm in their partners, or their partners may have misled them into believing that they had had an orgasm in order to bolster their self-esteem.

---

not by itself a disorder. As we saw in Highlight 13.5, many women, and some men, report satisfying sex lives without having orgasms. Failure to have an orgasm becomes a problem only if it causes distress or interpersonal difficulty. The same is true of all of the sexual dysfunctions listed in the *DSM-IV*; they are problems only when the people involved decide they are. Because sexual behavior is affected by physiology and mood, the *DSM-IV* requires that other potential disorders (such as depression), substance abuse, and general medical conditions be ruled out before deciding that a person is suffering from a sexual dysfunction. Before making a diagnosis, the clinician must also assess whether a person's sexual performance is appropriate for his or her age (older people may require more stimulation than younger ones to become aroused or to reach orgasm). The clinician must also try to assess whether the person is getting adequate sexual stimulation. People with insensitive or inattentive partners may think they have a sexual dysfunction when they really have partners who don't know how to fulfill them (or don't care).

For each sexual dysfunction, the *DSM-IV* distinguishes between *lifelong* patterns that were present from

the person's first sexual activity and *acquired* ones that developed after a period of normal functioning. The latter are more likely to be the result of trauma or the secondary effect of some other disorder. The *DSM-IV* also distinguishes *generalized* problems, which occur in practically all sexual situations, from *situational* ones, in which the problems occur only with certain partners or in certain situations. The prognosis for situational problems is likely to be better than that for dysfunctions that occur in all sexual situations.

Sexual Desire Disorders

Desire is the complex set of feelings, cognitions, and fantasies that motivate people to engage in sex. Without desire, sex is little more than rubbing and friction. Women or men who, for whatever reason, lack desire for sex are said to have a sexual desire disorder. The *DSM-IV* describes two such disorders: hypoactive sexual desire disorder and sexual aversion disorder.

Anne Lawrence displays most of the characteristics of a lifelong generalized **hypoactive sexual desire disorder**—she has never had much interest in any type of

DSM-IV   TABLE 13.4   *DSM-IV* Sexual Dysfunctions

Disorders of desire

Hypoactive sexual desire disorder: Little desire for sexual activity and few sexual fantasies

Sexual aversion disorder: Fear and disgust at the thought of genital contact

Disorders of arousal

Female sexual arousal disorder: Inability to develop or maintain an adequate lubrication-swelling response long enough to complete sexual activity

Male erectile disorder: Inability to maintain an adequate erection long enough to complete sexual activity

Orgasmic disorders

Female orgasmic disorder: Delay in or absence of orgasm following normal sexual excitement

Male orgasmic disorder: Delay in or absence of orgasm following normal excitement

Premature ejaculation: Orgasm after a brief period of stimulation, before the person (or the partner) wishes it

Sexual pain disorder

Dyspareunia: Recurrent or persistent genital pain associated with intercourse (in males or females)

Vaginismus: Spasm of the vaginal muscles that interferes with penetration and intercourse

---

real or fantasy sex, and this lack of interest seems to have negatively affected her life. Specifically, her hypoactive sexual desire seems to have contributed to the breakdown of her marriage, and it may keep her from developing new relationships. Although hypoactive sexual desire disorder affects both men and women, it is more common in females. The disorder may appear at any time after puberty, but most often, it begins in adulthood after a period of psychosocial stress or physical illness. It also becomes more common with age.

Although it is possible for hypoactive sexual desire disorder to exist on its own, it rarely does. Disturbances in the other phases of the sexual response cycle—especially disturbances in sexual excitement or orgasm—frequently co-occur with hypoactive sexual desire disorder (Donahey & Carroll, 1993). In some cases, it is the inability to sustain sexual excitement or to reach orgasm that causes the person to lose interest in sex. Medical conditions, particularly those that cause pain during intercourse, various psychological disorders (depression and body dysmorphic disorder, to name two), and many drugs (including antidepressants) may also cause people to lose interest in sex. Anne's low desire may have several causes, including her sexually inhibited upbringing; self-consciousness about her appearance; and painful intercourse caused by dryness, which may be the result of a medical condition or an inability to sustain sexual excitement (see Document 13.5).

Hypoactive sexual desire disorder is one of the most common complaints of people who seek treatment for sexual problems, and it may be increasing in frequency (Rosen & Leiblum, 1995). Some people, such as Anne, lack desire for any type of sexual activity. In other cases, a person may lack desire for some sex acts (intercourse, for example) but may desire others (such as masturbation). As Anne did during her marriage, individuals with hypoactive sexual desire disorder may not initiate sexual activity but will go along if the partner insists.

Like practically all behaviors, sexual desire forms a continuum. People who fall at the low extreme have little desire for sex. The majority, who fall in the middle of the continuum, have an intermediate level of desire. Those who fall at the high extreme have a strong desire for frequent sex. (Figure 13.3 estimates how often people have sex.) Interestingly, the *DSM-IV* does not contain a "hyperactive sexual desire disorder." The authors of the *DSM-IV* may not believe that high levels of sexual desire can produce psychological problems. This is not the view of the general public, which seems to believe that sex addiction represents an important psychological problem. Highlight 13.6 looks at various definitions of the term.

If hypoactive sexual desire disorder can be characterized as an indifference toward sex, **sexual aversion disorder** is more like a severe phobia (Kaplan, 1995). Like Jared Lawrence, people who suffer from this disorder actively avoid genital contact with a partner; some may even avoid hugging or kissing. Many people with sexual aversion disorder say that they are afraid of sex; a few claim to loathe it. In extreme cases, people with sexual aversion disorder may have panic attacks when-

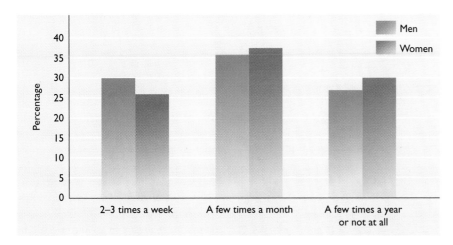

FIGURE 13.3 **How Often Do People Have Sex?** From: Laumann et al. (1994).

ever sex seems imminent. Like hypoactive sexual desire disorder, sexual aversion disorder is diagnosed only when it causes personal distress or interpersonal difficulty. People who can adjust (by giving up sex or finding accepting partners) do not receive the diagnosis. Like hypoactive sexual desire disorder, sexual aversion disorder may be the result of other sexual dysfunctions as well as various psychological and medical disorders. Most often, the condition can be traced back to a repressive sexual upbringing or to a sex-related trauma, such as sexual abuse. For example, because of his abuse by Peter Hall, Jared Lawrence seems to have learned to associate sex with fear and revulsion (see Document 13.6).

Sexual Arousal Disorders

Even when they desire to have sex, some people find it difficult to maintain the necessary level of arousal. That is, they have problems with the excitement phase of the sexual response cycle. The *DSM-IV* contains two sexual arousal disorders: female sexual arousal disorder and male erectile disorder.

Like Anne Lawrence, women with **female sexual arousal disorder** experience distress and personal difficulty because they do not produce the normal genital lubrication and swelling associated with sexual excitement (Morokoff, 1993). Dryness makes sex unpleasant, painful, and unfulfilling. Provided there is no clear medical reason for their failure to lubricate and it is not caused by a substance, the *DSM-IV* considers female sexual arousal disorder to have psychological origins. However, the *DSM-IV*'s concentration on genital lubrication may be misleading. Not all women who report dryness also report a lack of arousal or excitement.

Many women find that they can have satisfying sex by substituting artificial lubricants for natural ones. It seems that sexual arousal is a psychological state that is imperfectly measured by vaginal lubrication. Like the sexual desire disorders, arousal disorders can begin early in life or in adulthood and can affect all sexual situations or just some. Not surprisingly, arousal disorders are usually accompanied by orgasm disorders—it is not normally possible to have an orgasm if one is not sufficiently aroused.

The male equivalent of female sexual arousal disorder is **male erectile disorder,** which is defined as an inability to attain or sustain an erection until the completion of a sex act. Erectile disorder has replaced the older term *impotence,* which has false connotations (that the man is unable to have children or is an inadequate lover). Erectile disorder is the most common reason men visit clinics for help with a sexual dysfunction. It also accounts for hundreds of thousands of doctor visits each year (Laumann et al., 1999). After age 40, more than half of all men have some degree of erectile difficulty from time to time. In general, older men need more stimulation and take longer to achieve an erection than younger men. This is not a sign of a psychological disorder but of normal aging (Renshaw, 1996). Substances (antihypertension drugs, alcohol, tranquilizers), medical disorders (diabetes, spinal injury), and psychological disorders (such as depression) may affect a man's ability to attain or sustain an erection. However, the diagnosis of male erectile disorder is normally reserved for men whose dysfunction appears to have a large psychological component. For example, males who have erections while masturbating or during sleep are physically capable of having erections; thus their erectile dysfunction during

Addicted to Sex

Don Juan, the legendary profligate immortalized in poems, novels, and operas, was supposed to have made love to hundreds or even thousands of women before being dragged off to a fiery hell. Was he addicted to sex? Is such an addiction even possible? Many people seem to think so. **Sex addiction,** a term popularized by psychologist Patrick Carnes (1992), has become an industry, with its own books, treatments, and self-help organizations. At meetings around the world, members of Sexaholics Anonymous and Sex Addicts Anonymous proceed through 12-step therapy programs similar to the one used by Alcoholics Anonymous (see Chapter 6). The National Council on Sexual Addiction/Compulsivity publishes a professional journal (*Sexual Addiction and Compulsivity*) devoted to sexual addiction.

Although the term *sex addiction* may seem self-explanatory, descriptions of the behaviors that actually constitute sex addiction vary widely. According to the National Council on Sexual Addiction and Compulsion, sex addiction is reflected by multiple affairs, frequent masturbation, excessive use of prostitutes, or frequent paraphiliac behavior. About the only thing sex addicts share in common is a supposed inability to inhibit their sexual behavior, even in the face of ad-

The legendary figure Don Juan has become synonymous with sexual obsession. But is sexual addiction a real disorder equivalent to substance addiction?

verse consequences. Bill Clinton's apparent disregard for his reputation is cited by some as evidence that he might suffer from sex addiction.

It is fair to say that many lay people find it difficult to sympathize with a person addicted to sex. Instead of a serious psychological disorder, they consider sex addiction to be similar to chocolate addiction or shopping addiction or work-

aholism, a kind of overindulgence. Social critics view the concept of sex addiction as an attempt to medicalize, and thereby excuse, what would previously have been considered simply bad behavior or at best a lack of self-control (Kutchins & Kirk, 1997). Many professionals agree (Saulnier, 1996; also see Henkin & Carnes, 1998, for a debate by spokespersons for both sides). Unlike substance addiction, sex addiction does not involve physiological changes to the nervous system, chemical dependency, or a withdrawal syndrome. If it is a disorder at all, sex addiction is better described as a form of compulsive behavior than as an "addiction" similar to substance dependence. Perhaps this is why the *DSM-IV* does not recognize sex addiction as a distinct psychological disorder despite many attempts from advocates to have it included as an "official" diagnosis (Schneider, 1994). Instead of giving it a specific diagnosis, the *DSM-IV* considers compulsive sexual behavior a sign of some other disorder (Schneider & Irons, 1996) or the result of childhood sex abuse (Browning & Laumann, 1997). Why hypoactive sexual desire is considered a psychological disorder when hyperactive sexual desire is not remains one of the many curiosities of the *DSM-IV*.

sex is likely to have a psychological origin. They may feel guilty about sex or suffer from performance anxiety, for example. As in all sexual dysfunctions, male erectile disorder is diagnosed only when the dysfunction distresses the man or his partner.

Orgasmic Disorders

Some people have the desire for sex, enjoy foreplay, and become excited but have considerable difficulty achiev-

ing an orgasm. There may be physical reasons for this problem (medical conditions, substance intoxication) and psychological ones (such as performance anxiety). In some cases, both types of etiology are present simultaneously. An orgasmic disorder is diagnosed when psychological factors dominate. The *DSM-IV* describes three orgasmic disorders: female orgasmic disorder, male orgasmic disorder, and premature ejaculation.

Some women who have difficulty reaching orgasm lack interest in or are averse to sex in general. Once called *frigid,* such women are presumed to be uninterested in sex. On the other hand, there are women who are responsive to sexual stimuli as measured by self-report, vaginal lubrication, and genital swelling, but who nevertheless have great difficulty achieving an orgasm (Kaplan et al., 1996). The number of women who have difficulty reaching orgasm is large (Laumann et al., 1999). Ten to 15 percent of women never experience an orgasm at all. Another 10–15% experience them only rarely. Because most of these women, and their partners, are not distressed by their infrequent or nonexistent orgasms, they do not qualify for the diagnosis of **female orgasmic disorder.** Only those who are distressed or whose lack of orgasm causes interpersonal difficulty have an orgasmic disorder.

In the clinic, it is often difficult to determine whether a woman has an orgasmic disorder or whether she is just not getting the type or amount of stimulation she requires to achieve an orgasm. Women exhibit wide variability in the type and intensity of stimulation they require. Some women find intercourse sufficient stimulation to produce an orgasm, but many others do not. They are able to have an orgasm only when stimulated orally or manually. As already noted, despite Freud's claims to the contrary, their orgasms are physiologically identical to those achieved during intercourse. From a clinical viewpoint, a woman who fails to reach orgasm because she is not getting the stimulation she requires does not have an orgasmic disorder.

Male orgasmic disorder is the equivalent of female orgasmic disorder—it is a diagnosis applied to men who have trouble reaching orgasm despite being sexually excited. To qualify a man for the diagnosis, the difficulty achieving orgasm must be personally distressing or distressing to the man's partner. Moreover, the difficulty achieving orgasm must not be solely the result of a substance (alcohol, for example) or an illness (spinal cord injury). As in females, there is considerable variability among men in the focus, intensity, and duration of stimulation they require to reach orgasm. In the most common form of the disorder, men cannot reach orgasm during intercourse, but they can when given oral or manual stimulation. In some cases, males can reach orgasm only by masturbation. As already mentioned, as they age, men need a longer period of stimulation to achieve orgasm. As is the case for females, a man who is capable of orgasm but who is not receiving the stimulation he requires does not have an orgasmic disorder.

Premature ejaculation is the opposite of male orgasmic disorder—men with this disorder reach orgasm with minimal stimulation (see Rowland & Slob, 1997, for a review). For them, sex is over almost before it has begun. This reduces their satisfaction as well as the enjoyment of their partners. How quickly must a man reach orgasm for his ejaculation to be considered premature? There is no definitive answer. Some couples prolong intercourse for hours, whereas others are satisfied with a few minutes. In practice, ejaculation on insertion of the penis into the vagina or after a thrust or two is usually considered premature. Even then, a man is considered to have a disorder only if he is personally distressed by his premature ejaculation or if it disturbs his partner. Premature ejaculation is common among young, relatively inexperienced men, especially those whose sex lives have been dominated by situations where speed may be important (to avoid discovery, for instance).

Sexual Pain Disorders

The *DSM-IV* contains two disorders that are marked by pain in the genital area: dyspareunia and vaginismus. **Dyspareunia** refers to pain during sex (Butcher, 1999). It can affect both males and females and can vary from superficial to severe. In practically all cases, it causes distress to both the person with the pain and to his or her partner. Dyspareunia is diagnosed only when the pain is believed to have a strong psychological component. When the pain is solely the result of a medical or physiological condition (urinary tract infection, endometriosis, scar tissue, lack of lubrication) or a substance, the person does not have dyspareunia but "sexual dysfunction due to a general medical condition" or "substance-induced sexual dysfunction." In practice, it may be difficult to distinguish dyspareunia from the "somatization disorder" discussed in Chapter 7. Both involve pain with no clear physical explanation. Of course, in both cases, it is always possible that a physical cause exists but is being missed.

Vaginismus is the involuntary contraction of the perineal muscles surrounding the front part of the vagina whenever penetration of the vagina is attempted. The woman may have normal sexual desire and excitement and the ability to reach orgasm, but is unable to have intercourse. This can cause personal distress and disrupt relationships. The condition seems to be found most often in younger women who have negative attitudes toward sex and among victims of sexual abuse. Indeed, vaginismus has been construed as a conditioned fear response to sex, the result of abuse or an insensitive lover.

Epidemiology and Course

As we have seen, deciding whether a person has a sexual dysfunction takes considerable clinical skill. To make a diagnosis, the clinician must consider the person's age, health, substance use, and cultural background and must determine whether the person is receiving the stimulation necessary to build excitement and reach orgasm. In addition, the clinician must assess the degree of distress produced by the dysfunction in the individual and, where appropriate, the distress produced in the individual's partner. Because the diagnosis is so complex, surveys that ask people about their sexual problems are not likely to provide accurate data on the incidence or prevalence of sexual dysfunctions. Nevertheless, they can inform us about what people think about their sex lives.

One of the most carefully conducted surveys of the sex lives of Americans was analyzed by sociologist Edward Laumann and his colleagues (Laumann et al., 1994; Laumann et al., 1999; Michael et al., 1995). Their analyses, based on interviews with thousands of adults selected to reflect the American population, revealed that, at any given time, one third of men and 40% of women believe that they are suffering from some type of sexual dysfunction. Except for premature ejaculation, sexual dysfunctions are more commonly reported by women than by men. One third of women report that they lack interest in sex, and one quarter report being unable to experience orgasm over a period of months.

These numbers are large enough to suggest that many of us may confront a sexual dysfunction at some time in our lives. Whether we do depends on our age, race, gender, education, life circumstances, and physical condition. For instance, people who rate themselves as healthy have fewer sexual dysfunctions than those who consider themselves ill. Healthy or sick, married people report fewer sexual difficulties than single people. Whether they are divorced, widowed, or were never married, singles are more likely to have unsatisfying sex lives than married people. It seems that, despite what we see in the media, the singles sex scene is not as fulfilling as we may have been led to believe.

Analyses revealed important differences between men and women. Men report more sexual dysfunction as they get older, whereas women report more sexual problems when young (especially when they are also single). The reason for this difference is unclear. Perhaps young women have not yet learned what satisfies them sexually. The survey found that for both men and women, education is associated with greater sexual satisfaction.

Racial and ethnic differences, although small, were intriguing. African American women report lower sexual desire and pleasure than White women. White women, in turn, report more problems than Hispanic women. These racial and ethnic differences may reflect different cultural expectations.

Analyses found that patterns of sexual activity vary with age. Women are most sexually active in their 20s; their interest in sex declines markedly in their 50s. By age 60, 40% of women are no longer sexually active. Men maintain a fairly constant level of sexual activity until they reach their 60s, when they begin to slow down. Even in their 70s, however, men are more active than females 10 years younger. Of course, there are differences in sexual performance with age. Vaginal lubrication occurs more slowly, and men have more difficulty obtaining and sustaining erections. The subjective intensity of orgasms also seems to decrease with age. Nevertheless, with reasonable expectations, it is possible for couples to have satisfying sex lives well into old age.

Etiology

Each phase of the sexual response cycle depends on an intricate balance of social, psychological, and physiological forces. As shown in Figure 13.4, a disruption in any of these forces may result in a sexual dysfunction. It is worth keeping in mind, however, that the relationship between any single variable and a sexual dysfunction is never entirely predictable. Consider male sex hormones, for example. A certain level of testosterone is necessary to produce sexual desire, excitement, and orgasm. Testosterone levels decrease with age. This is one reason why older men have fewer sexual fantasies than younger men, whose testosterone levels are higher. The result may be hypoactive sexual desire, but not necessarily. Lower levels of testosterone may decrease an older male's spontaneous fantasies, but older men may make up for this by purposely seeking sexual stimulation from erotic films or extended foreplay. The result is that their interest in sex remains unchanged.

Social and cultural factors, especially parental attitudes, can have profound effects on sexual desire and arousal. People who grow up in cultures that repress sexuality may feel guilty about their sexual fantasies and urges. This guilt produces anxiety, which interferes with sexual enjoyment and performance. Women taught that sex is dirty and painful may develop vaginismus. Harmful or traumatic sexual experiences, such as those experienced by Jared Lawrence, can also result in sexual

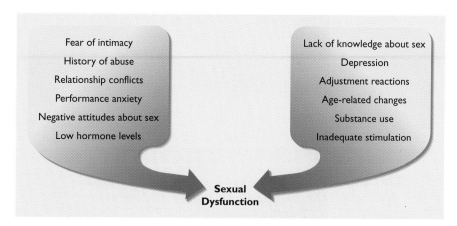

FIGURE 13.4 **Etiological Factors Contributing to Sexual Dysfunction**

DSM-IV TABLE 13.5 Diagnostic Criteria for Adjustment Disorder

A. The development of emotional or behavioral symptoms in response to an identifiable stresror(s) occurring within 3 months of the onset of the stressor(s).

B. These symptoms or behaviors are clinically significant as evidenced by either of the following:

   (1) marked distress that is in excess of what would be expected from exposure to the stressor

   (2) significant impairment in social or occupational (academic) functioning

C. The stress-related disturbance does not meet the criteria for another specific Axis I disorder (clinical disorder) and is not merely an exacerbation of a preexisting Axis I or Axis II disorder (Personality Disorder or Mental Retardation).

D. The symptoms do not represent Bereavement.

E. Once the stressor (or its consequences) has terminated, the symptoms do not persist for more than an additional 6 months.

Note: From American Psychiatric Association (1994, p. 626).

dysfunctions, but more often sexual dysfunctions arise from the problems of everyday life. Divorce, a death in the family, job loss, financial worries, relationship problems—practically anything that produces anxiety or depression can interfere with sexual functioning. If the sexual dysfunction is transitory and likely to disappear when the precipitating problem is resolved, the proper diagnosis is **adjustment disorder.** Adjustment disorders straddle the border between normality and pathology. They represent extreme but temporary reactions to everyday crises. Table 13.5 lists the main diagnostic criteria for adjustment disorder.

As already mentioned, medical conditions can adversely affect the sexual performance of both females and males. They can do this directly, by making performance physically impossible, or they can exert an indirect effect by making people too tired for sex. Sometimes, medical conditions and psychological factors

may interact. Take male erectile disorder as an example. Erectile disorder may result from poor circulation, which prevents blood from rushing to the genitals. This poor circulation could be caused by smoking, arteriosclerosis, and many other diseases including diabetes (Weinhardt & Carey, 1996). In some cases, damage to the spinal cord can destroy the reflexes necessary for an erection. Drugs such as alcohol, cannabis, tranquilizers, antihypertensives, antihistamines, and antidepressants can also cause erectile dysfunction. Once men begin having erectile problems, even occasionally, a vicious cycle may begin. The man begins to worry about his performance. His anxiety keeps him from becoming fully immersed in the sexual act. Instead, he takes on what Masters and Johnson call a *spectator role*—he watches his own reactions ("Am I developing an erection, or will I fail and be embarrassed?"). As his anxiety becomes worse, the chances of erectile failure increase.

This makes the man even more anxious, and the vicious cycle continues.

Treatment

Advice about sexual dysfunctions is not hard to find; in fact, it is difficult to avoid. Magazines, newspapers, television shows, and Internet sites are replete with advice about all areas of sexual functioning. Some of this advice is carefully researched and presented. For example, the Sexuality Information and Education Council of the United States disseminates information about sexuality through books, reports, and school curricula. On the other hand, much of what passes for sex information in popular media is superficial, poorly researched, and often just plain wrong. When sexual dysfunctions interfere with a couple's enjoyment of life, their safest course is to consult a professional who specializes in sexual problems.

Some dysfunctions require medical or physiological interventions. People whose sexual dysfunctions are caused by diseases such as diabetes may benefit from better treatment of their disease. People whose dysfunctions are the result of medications may benefit from having their medications reviewed and dosages adjusted. Getting people to stop using recreational drugs may also be helpful. In some cases, drug treatments may assist some people with sexual dysfunctions. Testosterone may help some men achieve and maintain erections (Rakic et al., 1997). Hormonal replacement therapy may help postmenopausal women maintain desire, reduce the pain of dyspareunia, and provide an adequate level of vaginal lubrication. (Vaginal lubricants may also help overcome dryness.) Although antidepressants may contribute to sexual dysfunction, they may also help men with premature ejaculation to last longer. Women with vaginismus may be helped by a program in which metal rods (dilators) of gradually larger diameter are inserted into the vagina until the woman can relax the vaginal muscles sufficiently to accommodate a penis.

To assist men with erectile disorders, a series of operations was developed in which pumps were implanted into the penis and inflated when the man wished to have intercourse (von Buehler & Herbert, 1998). These were soon supplanted by injectable drugs that produced erections (Riley & Riley, 1998). Neither of these methods was particularly practical or pleasant, so they were rarely used. With the release of sildenafil (Viagra), they have been rendered essentially obsolete. Sildenafil, which is successful at producing erections in most men with erectile disorder, has replaced practically

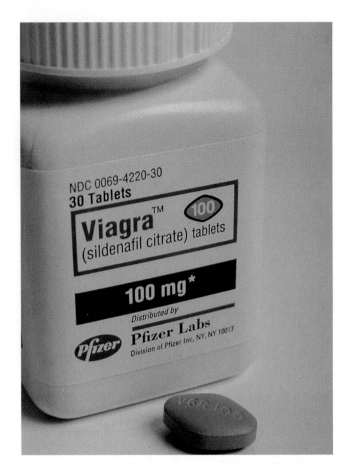

Sildenafil (Viagra), in the form of little blue pills, has virtually replaced all other methods of producing erections.

all other drugs and surgical procedures. It is taken about 1 hour before the man plans to have sex; its effects last for about 4 hours. Note that sildenafil does not produce an erection by itself; it is still necessary for the man to be sexually stimulated. Rather, the drug increases blood flow to the penis, thereby allowing the stimulated man to produce an erection. Sildenafil seems to be effective for erectile disorders caused by medical conditions as well as for disorders whose origins are mainly psychological (Rendell, Rajfer, & Wicker, 1999). The drug has become so popular that it is even being used by men who do not meet the diagnostic criteria for erectile disorder but who believe it will enhance their performance (Aldridge & Measham, 1999). Trials are also underway with women. Despite its popularity, sildenafil is not for everyone. Men with heart disease or circulatory disease who have not had sex for some time may find the strain of sildenafil-induced sex too much for their weak hearts. Anyone who takes medicine that contains nitrates (such as nitroglycerin used for circulatory disease) may find that sildenafil makes their blood pressure drop suddenly to a life-threatening level (Kloner & Jarow, 1999).

Although Viagra is clearly useful and popular, it is important to remember that the drug does not provide sex education, does not change attitudes, and does not treat any of the psychological disorders associated with erectile dysfunction, such as depression. Most important, it is not a cure (Segraves & Segraves, 1998). Take the drug away, and erectile dysfunction returns. Psychological treatments, on the other hand, are aimed at ameliorating sexual dysfunctions and preventing their return.

Until the middle of the 20th century, the psychological treatment approach to sexual disorders was the same as for other psychological disorders. That is, psychodynamic therapists saw these disorders as manifestations of underlying conflicts stemming from childhood experiences. Uncovering these unconscious conflicts, releasing the trapped emotions through catharsis, and "working though" their implications was the preferred mode of treatment. Unfortunately, this approach to treatment was not only expensive and time-consuming, it was also rarely effective. In the 1950s, behavioral psychologists attempted to devise more efficient and effective treatments for sexual dysfunctions. For example, systematic desensitization was used to help people overcome anxiety about sex. The behavioral approach to the treatment of sexual dysfunctions was given a major boost by Masters and Johnson, who followed up their research on the sexual response cycle with a set of brief, largely skill-based treatment techniques designed to be applied by couples working together. Their approach to treating sexual dysfunctions has been augmented and expanded over the years to form what is known today as **sex therapy** (Sarwer & Durlak, 1997). Modern sex therapy consists of a combination of treatment techniques that include sex education, communication skills training, cognitive-behavioral therapy, marital therapy, and, when necessary, insight-oriented therapy (O'Donohue, Dopke, & Swingen, 1997). In some cases, sex therapy also includes treatment for associated psychological disorders, such as substance abuse, anxiety, or depression.

Although people with psychological disorders need treatment that is tailored to their needs, there are some common factors that apply to most people with sexual dysfunction. First, treatment is almost always focused on couples, even when one partner has the identified problem. Second, educating couples about sex is crucial. Ignorance and misinformation about sex are important factors in almost every sexual dysfunction. (Highlight 13.7

debunks some common myths about sex.) Without such information, people often hold themselves to impossible standards. Women need to know that multiple orgasms during intercourse are very rare. Men need to know that everyone experiences erectile failure sometimes. Similarly, attitudes and maladaptive cognitions ("sex is dirty") need to be countered before progress can be made. A third common factor in practically all treatment programs is the need to overcome embarrassment and guilt about one's sexual needs and preferences. To accomplish this, individuals and couples in treatment may be asked to explore their bodies and to experiment with masturbation in order to identify what gives them pleasure. Once they discover their particular preferences, they must then learn to communicate these to their partners. For a fulfilling relationship, partners need to know what gives their lover pleasure, and what does not.

Masters and Johnson developed **sensate focus** as a way of helping couples learn about the sex practices that give them pleasure. Sensate focus requires that one partner actively stimulate the other, who focuses on the pleasurable feelings being induced. The couples then switch roles, so that each takes a turn giving and receiving stimulation. To conduct sensate focus, couples are encouraged to set aside time in quiet and relaxed settings. The active partner caresses the passive partner, giving pleasure but refraining from sexual intercourse. Treatment may begin by simply holding hands or giving one another back rubs. The idea is to concentrate on erotic sensations without the performance anxiety induced by the need to achieve orgasm. Without performance anxiety, couples are free to explore erotic pleasure in a nonthreatening atmosphere. As they learn more about what gives them pleasure and communicate this to one another, they gain confidence. Couples may also undergo cognitive restructuring to change mistaken attitudes and beliefs about sex. They learn that intercourse is not the only true form of sexual behavior, that masturbation is common and harmless, and that prolonged foreplay is not just for adolescents. Gradually, the couple proceeds to genital caresses and stimulation. They do not move on to intercourse until they can do so untroubled by performance anxiety. Masters and Johnson reported success rates of around 80% for their treatment. More recent studies have reported less-spectacular results, but sensate focus is still the treatment of choice for most couples (Sarwer & Durlak, 1997).

Specific techniques have been developed to deal with particular sexual dysfunctions. For example, the

Sex Myths

Although sexual dysfunctions and disorders have a multitude of interacting causes, ignorance about sex is almost always a contributor. Many of us are influenced by descriptions of sex in the media, which have contributed to unrealistic expectations and leave many people feeling inadequate. Some of the most common myths about sex are summarized here.

Sex equals erection, intercourse, and orgasm. This common myth is one of the main causes of sexual performance anxiety. When people convince themselves that sexual fulfillment depends on reaching a goal (orgasm), deviations from reaching the goal, even temporary ones, are likely to lead to anxiety. In reality, neither erections nor intercourse nor orgasms are necessary for pleasurable sex. Many couples report considerable satisfaction from kisses and caresses. Indeed, couples who learn to pleasure one another in circumstances where neither erections nor orgasms are required report more fulfilling sex lives than do those whose only goal is orgasm.

When it comes to sex, men must take the lead. This Victorian-era view can interfere with the sexual enjoyment of both men and women. It can also keep a man from ever learning what his partner desires. A better approach is for partners to communicate their needs and desires and to share responsibility for giving one another pleasure.

Men are always ready for sex. This is another anxiety-producing myth. Men who believe it become anxious whenever they fail to become immediately excited. In reality, men as well as women need to feel comfortable with their partner and with the situation in order to engage in pleasurable sex.

Women are not aroused by erotic films and books. This is totally untrue. Women find such materials stimulating—just have a look at the stories and pictures in magazines aimed at women.

Normal women achieve orgasm every time they have sex. Again, this may happen in the movies and in erotic literature, but it is not the case in real life. Individual differences allow some women to reach orgasm more easily than others. Even those women who reach orgasm easily do not have orgasms every time they have sex. Multiple orgasms are rarer still.

Menopause is the end of a woman's sex life. Although women who do not receive hormone replacement therapy may experience vaginal dryness, which can cause pain during intercourse, this is easily rectified by the application of vaginal lubrication. Many postmenopausal women report that not having to worry about pregnancy makes sex more pleasurable than when they were younger.

Sex should be spontaneous rather than planned. This may work in the movies, but in most people's busy lives, sex does not take place without planning.

start-stop technique for treating male erectile disorder begins with the partner's caressing the man until he gets an erection and then stopping. When the erection disappears, the partner repeats the caresses until the man is once again erect and then stops. When this start-stop cycle is repeated many times, the man gains confidence in his ability to achieve erections. He learns that his erections occur naturally in response to stimulation (provided that he does not focus on his performance). When the couple are ready to try intercourse, the *stuffing technique* can often assist. The female straddles the male, who is lying on his back, and stuffs his nonerect penis into her vagina. The male learns that he does not need an erection to accomplish entry or to give or receive pleasure. Again, this serves to give him self-confidence and take some of the pressure off performance.

The treatment of premature ejaculation may include a technique known as *pause and squeeze*. The male is stimulated until he signals that he feels orgasm coming. At that point, the partner stops stimulating the male and squeezes his penis—preventing orgasm. As this is repeated, ejaculation is gradually delayed. The couple then switches to vaginal stimulation in which brief periods of entry are followed by stopping until the male is able to engage in intercourse for a reasonable period of time without ejaculating.

These specific techniques work best when they are embedded in a multimodal treatment program that includes not just sex therapy but also education and cognitive restructuring (Wylie, 1997). Document 13.7 describes such a treatment program designed for Anne Lawrence and her new partner, Harry Cotes.

 UNIVERSITY HOSPITAL

University Health Service
Psychology Service

Assessment, Sexual History, and Conceptualization: Anne Lawrence is a 38-year-old divorced schoolteacher whose two boys were sexually abused by a family friend, who was later convicted of child molestation. Anne's first marriage ended in divorce, and she is currently in a "relationship" with Harry Cotes, a divorced lawyer, aged 40. Although they see each other often, they retain separate homes.

Anne grew up in a strict religious family and went to an all-girls religious school. She has no memory of sex ever being discussed in her home. She also received no sex education at school. She was overweight and self-conscious as a teenager and did not date. She had had only a few dates in college before she met Sean, her ex-husband. They dated for a year and married after graduation. According to Anne, they petted but never had intercourse until they were married. Anne cannot recall ever masturbating. Over time, however, she and Sean developed what Anne considered a mutually satisfying sex life. They engaged in some type of sexual behavior once a week, usually mutual fondling and intercourse. Anne reports being satisfied. This is why she was shocked when Sean told her that he found her "cold" and left her for one of her friends, a person Anne describes as "very sexy." They divorced, and Anne received custody of their two boys. Since then, Sean has largely stayed out of their lives.

Anne had no sex life for several years before meeting Harry, whose children attend the same school as hers. Their relationship initially centered around dinners and movies, but Harry has increasingly sought intimate relations. Anne says that she gets nervous whenever they get "physical." She can masturbate Harry, and with the aid of vaginal lubricant, she can have intercourse. However, these activities do not give her much pleasure. She rarely feels like having sex, and Harry's attempts to stimulate her have so far failed to induce much sexual excitement. She would like to have a "normal" sexual relationship, and so would Harry. This is why they came to treatment. A medical examination has revealed no physical impediment to Anne's sexual fulfillment. In addition, both partners are willing to participate in treatment and take mutual responsibility for overcoming their sexual problems.

Preliminary Diagnoses

Axis I (clinical disorders): Hypoactive sexual desire, female sexual arousal disorder, adjustment reaction (divorce)

Axes II (personality disorders) and III (general medical conditions): None

Axis IV (psychosocial and environmental problems): Divorce, victimization of children

Axis V (global assessment of functioning) GAF: 75

Treatment Plan

Education: Anne knows little about sexual anatomy and physiology. She also knows little about sex techniques. To increase her knowledge (and Harry's), the couple will be given instructional videotapes and books. In addition, several therapy sessions will be devoted to discussing these materials and to answering their questions.

Attitude change: Anne's restrictive upbringing, her abandonment, and the abuse of her sons have given her a negative attitude about sex. Not only is it dirty, she believes, but it leads husbands to abandon their families and causes people to perform evil deeds. Changing these attitudes by cognitive restructuring is an important aspect of treatment. The goal will be to show Anne that sex can be a way of showing love, trust, and commitment and that it can make relationships stronger and deeper. She will also be trained to use coping statements, such as "It is OK to enjoy sex."

Elimination of anxiety: The thought of sex makes Anne anxious. This inhibits her desire, her arousal, and her orgasms. Anne will be trained to use a "desire diary," in which she records the sexual feelings and thoughts she gets from books, films, or fantasies. The couple will also be encouraged to schedule time for themselves, away from their children, during which they can share pleasurable activities, both sexual and nonsexual. To help Anne overcome the revulsion she feels about the man who molested her children (a revulsion that may be coloring her view of sex in general), she will be encouraged to visit Peter Hall in prison, to express her feelings to him, and to reach some sort of closure. Sensate focus will be used to help desensitize Anne to the anxiety produced by sex. When there is no pressure on Anne to become aroused, she may be able to learn to enjoy caresses. Over successive weeks, the couple will become more intimate. The couple will also be taught to communicate their needs and to teach each other about what they like and dislike.

GENDER IDENTITY DISORDER

Luke Lawrence was only 9 years old when he first met Peter Hall. In his young life, he had already seen his father leave home for another woman, and then, while still in the fourth grade, he was forced to have sex with an older man and his friends. It was Peter Hall's habit to dress Luke in girl's clothing and to pretend that he was a little girl. This fantasy game seemed to excite Peter and his friends, but it left Luke conflicted and confused. He knew he was a boy, but he was being reinforced for dressing and acting like a girl. Sometimes he thought he would be better off as a girl, but he was a boy, wasn't he? As you can see in Document 13.8, Luke seems to have recovered, but not everyone is as lucky.

DOCUMENT 13.8

Excerpt From Luke's Interview (age 15) for a Television Documentary on Pedophilia

LUKE: Peter Hall made me wear girl's clothes and pretend to be a girl for him and his friends. He would give me presents, like dolls, if I would go along with the game. Sometimes, he would give me money, too. He would tell me how pretty I was and what a good girl I was. I began to associate being a girl with good things: feeling good, receiving gifts. I began to wish that I really was a girl so that I could always get that approval and those rewards. I practiced acting like a girl at home. When Peter went to jail, I still continued to think about being a girl, but as I began to mature, I thought about it less and less. Eventually, I stopped thinking about being a girl at all. I went to therapy for one year after Peter was arrested, and I learned how to like myself as I am. I also learned that what Peter did to me was not my fault. My therapist helped me make new friends. I have many now, both boys and girls. ■

Our sense of ourselves as male or female is known as our *gender identity*. Most of the time, gender identity is consistent with physical anatomy. Children with male genitals think and act as our culture expects males to act, and those with female genitalia think and act as culturally defined females. But this is not always the case. Consider, for example, the case of Billy Tipton, a transvestite jazz musician who married five wives and was

**DSM-IV TABLE 13.6   Main *DSM-IV* Diagnostic Criteria
for Gender Identity Disorder**

A. A strong and persistent cross-gender identification (not merely a desire for any perceived cultural advantages of being the opposite sex).

In children, the disturbance is manifested by four (or more) of the following:

(1) repeatedly stated desire to be, or insistence that he or she is, the other sex

(2) in boys, preference for cross-dressing or simulating female attire; in girls, insistence on wearing only stereotypical masculine clothing

(3) strong and persistent preferences for cross-sex roles in make-believe play or persistent fantasies of being the other sex

(4) intense desire to participate in the stereotypical games and pastimes of the other sex

(5) strong preference for playmates of the other sex

In adolescents and adults, the disturbance is manifested by symptoms such as a stated desire to be the other sex, frequent passing as the other sex, desire to live or be treated as the other sex, or the conviction that he or she has the typical feelings and reactions of the other sex.

B. Persistent discomfort with his or her sex or sense of inappropriateness in the gender role of that sex.

In children, the disturbance is manifested by any of the following: in boys, assertion that his penis or testes are disgusting or will disappear or assertion that it would be better not to have a penis, or aversion toward rough-and-tumble play and rejection of male stereotypical toys, games, and activities; in girls, rejection of urination in a sitting position, asserting that she has or will grow a penis, or assertion that she does not want to grow breasts or menstruate, or marked aversion toward normative feminine clothing.

In adolescents and adults, the disturbance is manifested by symptoms such as preoccupation with getting rid of primary and secondary sex characteristics (e.g., request for hormones, surgery, or other procedures to physically alter sexual characteristics to simulate the other sex) or belief that he or she was born the wrong sex.

C. The disturbance is not concurrent with a physical intersex condition.

D. The disturbance causes clinically significant distress or impairment in social, occupational, or other important areas of functioning.

Note: From American Psychiatric Association (1994, pp. 537–538).

found to be a biological woman only on death (Middlebrook, 1998). Born Dorothy in 1914, Tipton was raised at a time when jazz was a man's world. To have a career, a female musician had no choice but to pretend to be male. Tipton's impersonation must have been excellent because it fooled not only his fellow musicians but also his various wives. Exactly how Tipton managed sexually is something of a mystery, but her amazing life demonstrates that gender identity is a social and cultural construct that is only loosely related to the biological facts (McConaghy, 1997).

Description and Diagnosis

As Luke did, children may sometimes become confused about their gender identity. Some become convinced that their physical anatomy and their gender are in conflict. They may look like males, but emotionally they feel like females (or vice versa). According to the *DSM-IV*, such people may have a gender identity disorder. (Table 13.6 lists the main *DSM-IV* diagnostic criteria for this disorder.) The severity of gender identity disorder can range from feelings of dissatisfaction or unease (known as *gender dysphoria*) to wanting to change sex (known as *transsexualism*). People with gender identity disorder report that, even as children, they felt trapped in the wrong body (Rekers & Kilgus, 1998). Males say they were too "pretty" to be boys, whereas girls report feeling masculine (McDermid et al., 1998). Gender identity disorder—especially females who believe they are males—is rare.

Boys with a gender identity disorder may dress in female clothing and adopt behaviors associated with female sex roles. Some may even wish for their penises to disappear. Girls may act like boys. Such children may find themselves ostracized by their peers. Their

Changing the Sexual Orientation of Gay Men and Lesbians: An Ethical Quandary

In recent years, much progress has been made toward giving gay men and lesbians and their partners the same civil rights available to those who are heterosexual. Nevertheless, the hypocrisy of the military's "don't ask, don't tell" policy, which prohibits homosexuals from serving in the armed forces only if they admit to being homosexual, and the practice of humiliating people by publishing the names of gay men and lesbians who are passing as heterosexual (*outing*) show that we have a long way to

go before we can say that gay men and lesbians are truly accepted as equal members of society.

To escape prejudice, some gay men and lesbians may seek "treatment" to help them change their sexual orientation. Aversive conditioning and other behavioral techniques have been used for this purpose. Many clinicians believe that such treatment is misguided. It is not the homosexual individual who has a problem, but society. They argue that psychologists who attempt to change

someone's sexual orientation are simply legitimizing social prejudice. On the other side, some clinicians argue that it is unethical to ignore a client's wishes. If clients wish to change their sexual orientation, the clinician should not try to change their mind. To do so is to make the client subservient to the clinician's political views. Both sides feel strongly about their positions, and no professional consensus has yet been reached.

loneliness may lead to depression and other psychological disorders. At this relatively early stage, interventions designed to shelter children from teasing while re-

In the early part of the 20th century, only men played jazz, so Dorothy Tipton changed her identity and became Billy Tipton (center), and evidently no one—not even her five wives—knew that Billy was biologically a woman. Diane Middlebrook's biography of Tipton, Suits Me, *was published in 1998.*

inforcing culturally appropriate sex role behavior may keep the disorder from developing further (Soutter, 1996). Unfortunately, such treatment is not always available. Instead, children reach adolescence still confused about their gender identity. When sexual maturity occurs during adolescence, their biological sex becomes glaringly obvious. They can no longer pretend to be the opposite gender. To fit in, some learn to repress their feelings and play the sex role appropriate to their anatomy. A small number find this impossible; they endure adolescence and enter adulthood still wishing they were the opposite sex. Some decide to alter their sex through surgery.

Note that boys with gender identity disorder are not transvestic fetishists (they do not cross-dress to become sexually aroused) nor are they always homosexual (Menvielle, 1998). Homosexuals rarely wish to change their biological sex. Most are content being homosexual, although as discussed in Critical Thinking About Clinical Decisions 13.2, there are some exceptions.

Etiology and Treatment

The etiology of gender identity disorder is not clear (Zucker et al., 1992). As we have already seen, exposing a fetus to the hormones of the opposite sex can have masculinizing or feminizing effects on the brain. Animal research also suggests that fetal exposure to sex hormones may permanently affect gender identity while leaving sexual anatomy intact. Specifically, it appears

In the conservative 1950s, Christine Jorgenson's sex-change operation was publicized around the world because it was such an unusual event. These photographs show Jorgenson before and after the operation.

that brains may be "masculine" or "feminine" irrespective of whether the person has masculine or feminine genitalia. Consider, for example, the case of John, who became Joan in 1964 (Diamond & Sigmundson, 1997). Because of a surgical accident, John's penis was destroyed when he was 8 months old. He underwent surgery to give him female anatomy and was treated with female hormones. His case was famous at the time and was cited as evidence that sex roles are not fixed at birth but learned by social interaction. Yet, despite being treated as a girl, John continued to insist that he was a boy, and he reverted to being a male when he reached puberty. He eventually married and adopted children. It seemed that his identification as a male was set before birth and could not be changed by surgery or by being treated as a girl.

The notion that brains have a gender identity separate from the genitalia is also consistent with the observations made of people born with a condition known as *pseudohermaphroditism*. (A *hermaphrodite* is a person born with aspects of both female and male genitalia. Such birth accidents are rare and may be corrected by surgery.) A pseudohermaphrodite is a genetic male whose genitalia do not fully develop before birth. Pseudohermaphrodites are born looking like females and are usually raised as girls. They wear dresses and are encouraged to play female roles. When such children reach puberty, however, a sudden increase in the male sex hormone testosterone causes their genitalia to complete their development—that is, they develop a penis and testicles. Their voices become deeper, and they develop facial hair. It becomes clear that they are not females but males. What is important is that such children

also consider themselves men. They begin to act like men and play male roles. Although some have difficulty making the transition (Slijper et al., 1998), most do not. This suggests that gender identity is determined more by the "sex" of a person's brain than the appearance of a person's genitalia.

It has not been possible to demonstrate that all people with gender identity disorder have been exposed to opposite sex hormones during fetal development. Some may have developed their disorder for other reasons, such as the sexual trauma caused by abuse (see Document 13.8). In some cases, children who have the appearance of the opposite sex (pretty boys, tomboyish girls) may have been strongly reinforced for taking the opposite sex role (Fridell et al., 1996; McDermid et al., 1998). Eventually, they may have simply come to accept that they are the opposite sex. There are numerous other psychological hypotheses. For example, psychologists have suggested that children with gender identity disorder are the first-born or only children of parents who would have really preferred a child of the other sex. The evidence for this, and most other hypotheses, is equivocal at best (Zucker et al., 1998). At present, it is not possible to choose among these possibilities and, like that of most psychological disorders, the cause of gender identity disorder is most likely to be found in a combination of biological and psychological factors (Bradley & Zucker, 1997).

There are two ways to treat gender identity disorders: Change the person's sex role identity to match his or her anatomy, or change the anatomy to match the identity. The first option involves an immense psychological effort, which is not often successful. Hence, the option of changing anatomy has been taken up by thousands of people. Treatment usually begins by having the person live as the other sex for a trial period. During this period, the person is carefully monitored for other psychological disorders. Changing the sex of someone with a psychological disorder other than gender identity disorder is neither ethical nor sensible. People who are helped to overcome another psychological disorder may decide that they are perfectly happy with their existing sexual anatomy.

During the trial period, sex hormones are administered to produce many of the physical characteristics of the other sex. Specifically, men are given estrogen, which causes them to develop breasts and makes their body and facial hair disappear. Testosterone is given to females to deepen their voices, increase their muscle mass, and cause body and facial hair to develop. Some people stop at this point, content to live as if they were the other sex. Some go all the way and have sex-change surgery. Sex-change operations were first performed in the 1930s, but they did not become common until the 1950s, when George Jorgenson became Christine. Today, more than 1,000 sex-change operations take place every year in the United States. Males are made to look like females, and females are given artificial penises, which because they do not produce the normal male sexual response, may be augmented with pumps or other erection-imitating mechanical devices. Most people are satisfied with the results of their sex-change operations and go on to lead rewarding lives (Landen et al., 1998). A small number, particularly those with other psychological disorders, continue to have problems.

CHAPTER 13 IN PERSPECTIVE

Despite having more liberal attitudes than those of our parents, we remain conflicted and embarrassed about sex. Even modern couples find it difficult to discuss their sexual desires and needs; the result is much unnecessary suffering and unhappiness. There is also still considerable prejudice against those who are homosexual. Progress is being made, however. We know much more about sexual behavior than we did before, and our knowledge is being used to devise new treatments for those with sexual disorders and dysfunctions. As we enter the new millennium, there is increased hope that more people will be able to lead satisfying sexual lives. At the same time, we still have much to learn about aberrant sexual behaviors, especially pedophilia, which can devastate the lives of victim and perpetrator alike.

Key Ideas

Defining Abnormal Sexual Behavior
Acceptable sexual behavior is defined by cultural norms. Activities considered normal in one culture may be prohibited in another. Moreover, as our culture changes, so does our idea of normal sexual behavior. As noted in Chapter 1, homosexuality was once considered to be a sexual disorder but it no longer appears in the *DSM*.

Paraphilias
The paraphilias are characterized by unusual, disturbing, or harmful sexual fantasies and urges about sex with non-human objects, sex that involves suffering on the part of oneself or one's partner, or sex with children. The paraphilias listed in the *DSM-IV* include exhibitionism, fetishism, frotteurism, pedophilia, sexual masochism, sexual sadism, transvestic fetishism, voyeurism, and a large "other" category. Some paraphilias are exaggerations of everyday behavior; others involve serious crimes. Note, however, that not all apparently sexual crimes are paraphilias. For example, rape is excluded because it is more a crime of anger and aggression than one of sex. Although some paraphiliacs are loners who keep their sexual behavior hidden from others, many are social enough to join interest groups of fellow paraphiliacs, who meet either in person or on the Internet. Despite their diverse range, paraphilias share a common characteristic—in every case, sexual behavior has been disconnected from a loving, consensual relationship with another adult.

Etiology, Treatment, and Prevention of Paraphilias
Because paraphilias occur mainly in men, researchers have assumed that they must have some hereditary sex-linked cause. Unfortunately, no such etiology has been uncovered. On the other hand, there is evidence that people with paraphilias have childhood and adolescent experiences that may have distorted their sexual interests. Once people turn away from consensual sex, practically anything can take on sexual connotations through classical or operant conditioning. Some paraphilias may also symbolically represent unconscious sexual conflicts. Paraphilias have always been considered difficult to treat. Nevertheless, multimodal treatment programs that include education, skill training, and behavioral interventions have been able to help some people change their sexual behavior. Primary prevention efforts have so far been limited to censoring paraphiliac pornography. Secondary prevention has involved keeping potential sex criminals in custody and offender registration and in-

formation programs.

Sleep Disorders
In addition to the parasomnias discussed in Chapter 12, the *DSM-IV* contains a set of disorders known as the dyssomnias. These include primary insomnia (difficulty initiating or maintaining sleep), hypersomnia (excessive sleepiness), narcolepsy (sleep attacks), breathing-related sleep disorder (caused by obstruction of the upper airways), and circadian rhythm sleep disorder (produced by time changes). Primary insomnia often occurs in conjunction with other disorders.

Sexual Dysfunctions
Sexual dysfunctions are difficulties in sexual performance. Dysfunctions may affect any of the stages of human sexual response (desire, excitement, plateau, orgasm, resolution). Although they are described as separate disorders, the sexual dysfunctions often occur together. For example, a person who cannot achieve an orgasm may lose the desire for sex. Diagnosing sexual dysfunction requires clinical sensitivity. For example, a failure to reach orgasm is not by itself a disorder. The failure to have an orgasm becomes a problem only if it causes distress or interpersonal difficulty. Before making a diagnosis, the clinician must assess whether a person's sexual performance is appropriate for his or her age (older people may require more stimulation than younger ones to become aroused or to reach orgasm). The clinician must also try to assess whether the person is getting adequate sexual stimulation.

Types of Sexual Dysfunction
The *DSM-IV* includes two disorders of sexual desire: hypoactive sexual desire disorder and sexual aversion disorder. The first reflects a low level of sexual interest; the second, an active dislike of sex. Women with female sexual arousal disorder desire sex but do not seem to be able to become sufficiently aroused to have sex comfortably. Similarly, men with male erectile disorder desire sex but have difficulty sustaining an erection long enough to complete a sex act. Female or male orgasmic disorder is diagnosed when an individual has difficulty achieving orgasm, whereas premature ejaculation applies to men who reach orgasm too quickly. Finally, there are two sexual pain disorders: dyspareunia (pain during sexual intercourse) and vaginismus (involuntary contraction of the vaginal muscles, making penetration painful or impossible).

Causes and Treatment of Sexual Dysfunction
Sexual dysfunctions are common. They are influenced by medical conditions, substances, and psychological factors (especially performance anxiety). When they are temporary reactions to life circumstances such as divorce, they are better diagnosed as adjustment disorders. Some dysfunctions respond to medical or physiological interventions. However, many require multimodal sex therapy—a combination of treatment techniques that include sex education, communication skills training, cognitive-behavioral therapy, marital therapy, and insight-oriented therapy when necessary. In some cases, sex therapy also includes treatment for associated psychological disorders, such as substance abuse, anxiety, or depression.

Gender Identity Disorder
Our sense of ourselves as male or female is known as our gender identity. Most of the time, gender identity is consistent with physical anatomy, but some individuals become convinced that their physical anatomy and their gender are in conflict. They may look like males, but they feel like females (or vice versa). Males with gender identity disorder are not transvestic fetishists (they do not cross-dress to become sexually aroused) nor are they homosexual. Gender identity disorder may have hormonal origins, or it may be the result of early learning experiences. Treatment involves changing the person's sex role identity to match his or her anatomy or changing the anatomy to match the identity (usually through surgery).

Key Terms

adjustment disorder
breathing-related sleep
 disorder
circadian rhythm sleep
 disorder
dyspareunia
exhibitionism
female sexual arousal disorder
fetishism

frotteurism
gender identity disorder
hypersomnia
hypoactive sexual desire
 disorder
male erectile disorder
orgasmic disorder (female,
 male)
narcolepsy

paraphilia
pedophilia
premature ejaculation
primary insomnia
sensate focus
sex addiction
sex therapy
sexology
sexual aversion disorder

sexual dysfunction
sexual masochism
sexual sadism
transvestic fetishism
vaginismus

Key Names

Virginia E. Johnson
Alfred Kinsey

Richard von Krafft-Ebing
William H. Masters

Marquis de Sade

EPILOGUE

CHAPTER OBJECTIVES

The preceding 13 chapters summarize the field of abnormal psychology as it exists today. In this epilogue, we take a step back from the details of disorders, diagnoses, and scholarly debates to look at broader trends and more general issues. Abnormal psychology is currently in a state of flux; great progress has been made, but crucial questions remain unsettled. How much of our behavior (abnormal or normal) is the product of nature? How much are we influenced by nurture? Can we prevent mental disorders? What is the best way to deliver mental health services? In an era of managed care, is psychological treatment worth paying for? The answers to these questions will determine how abnormal psychology evolves over the 21st century.

The main questions addressed in this epilogue are

1. What is the current state of abnormal psychology?
2. As we enter the new millennium, what are the most important questions facing abnormal psychology?
3. How should abnormal psychology evolve to ensure that it meets its goals of understanding, treating, and preventing mental disorders?

Littleton, Colorado, and the Future of Abnormal Psychology

CONTENTS

In the *Journal of Mental Science*'s last edition for the year 1900, the editor lamented the "apparent inefficacy of medicine in the cure of insanity." He worried that, "though medical science has made great advances during the 19th century, our knowledge of the mental functions of the brain is still comparatively obscure" (quoted in Porter, 1997, p. 21). If brought back to life today, the author of these words could not help but be astonished at the progress that has been made in understanding mental disorders.

In the past 100 years, we have not only mapped the structural anatomy of the brain, but we also know a great deal about its functional anatomy. Modern imaging techniques have allowed us to observe how the various parts of the brain interact when we sleep, speak, feel emotions, and perform various cognitive tasks. At the molecular level, we understand how nerve impulses are propagated from one neuron to another, and we have identified the individual chemicals that make neural communication possible. And this is only the beginning. We now understand the genetic basis for many mental disorders. As a consequence, the symptoms of some disorders, such as PKU, are now preventable, and many others will soon be treatable by gene therapy.

Classical and instrumental conditioning (and the behavioral therapies derived from them); psychoanalytic, humanistic, family, and cognitive therapy; tranquilizers, antipsychotic drugs, antidepressant medications, and most of the psychological tests that clinicians use to assess behavior were developed in the past century. Scientists have refined the diagnostic and classification system for mental disorders so that the diagnostic process for mental disorders is just as reliable as that for general medical illnesses (S. Schwartz & Griffin, 1986; J. B. Williams et al., 1992). Moreover, the pace of new discoveries seems to be accelerating. In the final decade of the 20th century, nine new antidepressant medications and three new atypical antipsychotic drugs became available, and new drugs are on the horizon for obsessive-compulsive disorder and bipolar disorder. Psychological treatments have also become increasingly effective as they target some of the most crippling mental disorders, including depression and schizophrenia. For the first time in history, the majority of mental disorders are treatable. As you have seen in the preceding chapters, the lifelong suffering and social stigma that were once attached to most mental disorders have diminished considerably.

Abnormal psychology can be proud of its record of achievement. Yet, despite substantial scientific progress and increasingly sophisticated research methods (Sher & Trull, 1996), psychological disorders continue to exact an enormous toll on society. As we enter the 21st century, depression is the fourth leading cause of illness-related disability in the world (National Institute of Mental Health, 1998), and schizophrenia remains among the most debilitating of all disorders, medical or psychological. The preceding chapters have reviewed in some detail the current state of our knowledge of abnormal psychology. This epilogue examines broader trends and more general issues. The aim is to assess how far we have come and to make some predictions about how abnormal psychology will—and some judgments about how it *should*—develop over the 21st century. To provide a context for this discussion, the epilogue begins with a shocking reminder of the gaps that still exist in our knowledge of abnormal psychology.

DEATH ON A FINE SPRING DAY[1]

It was a sunny Tuesday in April; the temperature was 60° and there was a hint of summer in the air. The students of Littleton, Colorado's Columbine High School were getting ready for the end of their school year. It was lunchtime, and the cafeteria was full of teenagers discussing the prom, which had been held the previous weekend, and making plans for the upcoming summer. Members of the class of 1999 were looking forward to graduation in 3 weeks. About 50 students had skipped lunch to study for final exams in the library. Other students were working out in the gym or practicing in the music room. All in all, it was a normal school day—at least until the shooting started.

Students in the cafeteria heard the sounds first. They came from outside, in the parking lot—pop-pop-pop. Most students thought it was a prank, maybe someone lighting firecrackers. But they were wrong. The sounds were gunshots. Two young men in black trench coats were deliberately shooting students in the school parking lot. They shot a girl in the leg and a boy in the back. Within seconds, they shot another girl and another boy. One of the gunmen tossed a homemade pipe bomb into the parking lot. Then, walking slowly, almost casually, Dylan Klebold, 17, and Eric Harris, 18, two Columbine seniors, entered the cafeteria. They were armed with an assault rifle, sawed-off shotguns, and handguns. Once in the cafeteria, Harris opened his coat,

---

[1] The details of the events that took place in Littleton, Colorado, and the backgrounds of those involved were pieced together from a large variety of sources, including newspaper reports as well as school and court records.

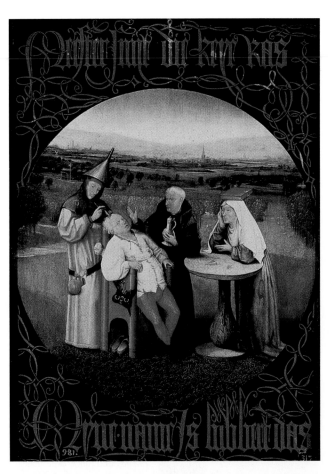

Our understanding and treatment of mental disorders has progressed since the 15th century. In The Extraction of the Stone of Madness (The Cure of Folly), *a satirical work painted in 1475–1480, Hieronymus Bosch depicts one of the common treatments of his day.*

revealing an assortment of homemade hand grenades. He tossed one into the cafeteria. The boys then began to shoot their schoolmates, laughing as they made their way through the cafeteria and into the school.

The 900 students in school that day ran for cover in classrooms, closets, bathrooms, under tables, anywhere. The gunmen were not fooled. As they moved through the school, they banged on locked doors, shouting, "We know you're in there." Some of those in hiding began to pray. Others called 911 on their cellular phones. Students and teachers who were near windows or exits escaped from the building and hid in the surrounding bushes. The armed sheriff's deputy who was permanently assigned to the school exchanged gunfire with the boys. Alerted by the 911 operator, backup officers began to arrive. They attended to those students and teachers who had managed to get out of the building. Meanwhile, inside the school, doors exploded in barrages of gunfire as Klebold and Harris made their way

from room to room. "All jocks stand up! We're going to kill every one of you," Harris is said to have yelled.

As time passed, the school parking lot began to overflow with police, bomb squads, fire fighters, SWAT teams, paramedics, worried parents, and, of course, hordes of media representatives. A little over an hour after the shooting started, the school grew silent. Although no one would know this for several more hours, Klebold and Harris had apparently turned their weapons on themselves. In the meantime, the world watched on television as students were removed from the school with their hands behind their heads and searched to be sure they were not also carrying guns or bombs. (The police thought that the killers might try to escape by pretending to be Columbine students—and, as it turned out, they were Columbine students.) Later, police found dozens of explosive devices in and around the school, including one huge bomb, fashioned from a 20-pound propane tank, hidden in the school's kitchen. Had it gone off, it would have totally destroyed the building. By the time the day was over, 30 people were being treated for their wounds (some were paralyzed), and 15 people were dead, including a teacher, 12 students, and the 2 shooters.

NORMAL KIDS

Eric Harris's father, Wayne, was an Air Force pilot, and, like all military families, the Harrises moved around a lot. As a youngster, Eric was fond of fishing and sports. He may have been a little shy, but otherwise he seemed a typical boy, and, to outsiders at least, the family appeared happy. Because the family had to relocate frequently, Eric's father encouraged him to participate in sports such as Little League as a way of making friends. Wayne Harris was often seen by neighbors shooting baskets with Eric and his older brother on a home basketball court. The Harris family moved to Littleton in 1993, when Wayne retired from the Air Force.

Dylan Klebold's father was a retired scientist who had turned to real estate and was financially successful. His mother worked at several careers, including a stint as a counselor in the local community college system. The Klebolds lived in a large house, drove expensive cars, and seemed relatively well off. As a youngster, Dylan Klebold was considered by neighbors and friends to be a "normal kid," quiet and a little shy, but easy to get along with.

Harris and Klebold quickly became good friends. They shared many interests, especially a love of com-

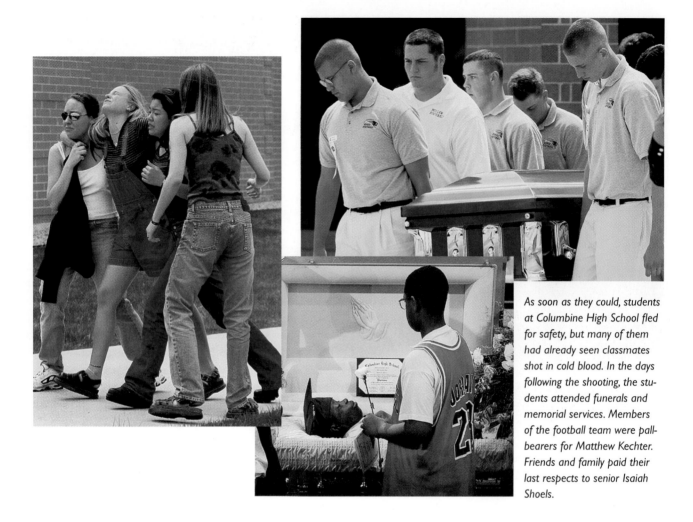

As soon as they could, students at Columbine High School fled for safety, but many of them had already seen classmates shot in cold blood. In the days following the shooting, the students attended funerals and memorial services. Members of the football team were pallbearers for Matthew Kechter. Friends and family paid their last respects to senior Isaiah Shoels.

puters. By the time they entered eighth grade, the two boys were immersed in computer games and would play them for hours. When they entered high school, the boys became increasingly isolated from other students. It is not clear why. Perhaps it was their shyness, or their "nerdy" interest in computers, or their lack of interest in sports, or their looks. Anyway, they seemed to be left out. They tried to join a school clique whose distinctive form of dress earned its members the name Trenchcoat Mafia. The members of this group wore long black coats to distinguish themselves from the expensively dressed "preps" and the sports-loving "jocks." However, even this "alternative" group was not anxious to have Klebold and Harris as members. The two boys wore long coats, but they never really made it past the periphery of this clique. As if to mark his separateness, Harris began to call himself "Reb." He also began to show a tendency toward melodrama. When he was 15, his homecoming date refused to go out with him again. In response, he staged a fake suicide complete with imitation blood splashed over his prostrate body. In the same girl's year-

book, Harris (who was studying German) wrote, "*Ich bin Gott*" ("I am God").

By the time Harris and Klebold reached their junior year of high school, they were no longer the clean-cut youths depicted in earlier photographs. Klebold had let his hair grow long and sported a scraggly beard. The two often spoke in German and decorated their clothing with Nazi insignia. Their appearance and behavior made them a target for bullying. Members of the school football team abused Klebold and Harris, called them names, and jostled them in the corridors.

It was also during their junior year that Harris and Klebold got into trouble with the law. They were convicted of breaking into a van and stealing electronic equipment. Because it was their first offense, they were enrolled in a special program designed to divert them from a criminal career. The program consisted of community service, individual counseling, and training in "anger management." According to the court counselor, the boys made excellent progress in the program. Indeed, they were not required to complete the program,

In their 1998 yearbook pictures, Dylan Klebold, left, and Eric Harris, right, look like typical suburban high school students, not young men who would go on a shooting rampage at their school a year later and kill themselves and 13 others.

and their criminal records were expunged. Just 3 months before the shootings, the court counselor described the boys as having bright futures. Harris was the subject of another police complaint a few months after the theft. He physically threatened a boy in his school and smashed the windshield of the student's car. The boy's father informed the police, but the police did not follow up the complaint nor inform those in charge of the diversion program. There were also reports that Harris had tried to enlist in the Marines but was rejected because he had been prescribed a psychoactive drug. Neither the police nor the court counselor seemed to know anything about this.

A year before the shootings, Harris began to keep a diary. It contained a detailed map of the school, notes of the ideal times to find large numbers of students in the cafeteria, and frequent references to Nazis and Adolf Hitler. In their senior year, Klebold and Harris made a video. They filmed student actors in long coats gunning down athletes in the school corridors. They submitted this film as a class project. Harris also created a Web site that contained, among other things, song lyrics about death and destruction.

On the Friday before the shootings, Harris and Klebold worked their regular jobs at a pizza restaurant. Sat-

urday night, Klebold attended the school prom. To the surprise of some, he brought a date. On Sunday, Klebold's BMW was parked outside the Harris home for most of the day. Neighbors heard noises coming from behind the Harrises' garage door; they sounded like breaking glass. Harris's parents were home at least part of the day. Tuesday, April 20, was the anniversary of Adolf Hitler's birthday. Klebold and Harris skipped school in the morning and showed up at lunchtime armed and ready to kill.

UNANSWERED QUESTIONS

In the days and weeks following the Columbine shootings, the public searched for an answer to the question "Why?" Newspapers, television, radio, and magazines were filled with facile "explanations" for the tragedy. The boys were part of a death-loving "Gothic" subculture or an alienated Trenchcoat Mafia (or both). They were driven to madness by violent video games or German techno-rock music (or both). They were corrupted by Internet chat groups. One writer suggested that the boys were alienated by having to attend a large school (Chenoweth, 1999). The need to find an explanation for

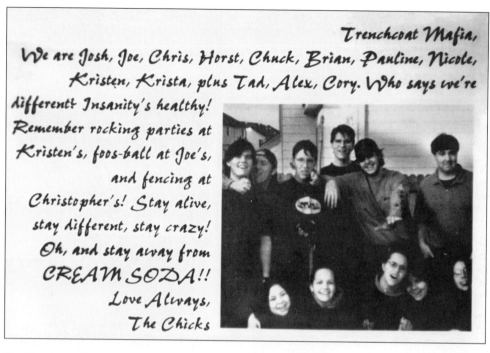

Trenchcoat Mafia,

We are Josh, Joe, Chris, Horst, Chuck, Brian, Pauline, Nicole, Kristen, Krista, plus Tad, Alex, Cory. Who says we're different? Insanity's healthy! Remember rocking parties at Kristen's, foos-ball at Joe's, and fencing at Christopher's! Stay alive, stay different, stay crazy! Oh, and stay away from CREAM SODA!! Love Always, The Chicks

The "Trenchcoat Mafia" (in a photo from the 1998 yearbook) prided themselves on being different, but their "insanity" took the form of parties and foos-ball, not videos and Web sites about death and destruction.

this tragedy was so strong, it did not seem to matter that many reported "facts" were incorrect. The boys were not Gothics, nor were they central figures in the Trenchcoat Mafia. Still, in an attempt to show that they were doing *something* to prevent violence, schools in several states banned black trench coats (Samuels & Benning, 1999).

Even those facts that were reported accurately present problems of interpretation. For example, the boys did attend a large school. Such schools may be alienating, but millions manage to graduate from them without becoming killers. Similarly, it is true that the boys played violent computer games. As noted in Chapter 10, exposure to violence is a risk factor for later violent behavior (Huesmann et al., 1997). In addition, there were seven school shootings in the preceding year that Harris and Klebold could have been copying (and more copycat shootings followed the incident at Littleton). To prevent future shootings, some people called for violent computer games and music with violent lyrics to be banned. Limiting freedom of speech may reduce the risk of violence, but not by much. Exposure to violence in the media, or even in real life, does not, by itself, turn a nonmurderer into a killer. Temperament and peer influences are more important determinants of violent behavior than is media violence (Adler & Denmark, 1995). There

may be more justification in calls to censor the Internet. After all, Harris and Klebold probably learned how to build their bombs from an Internet site. However, because censorship pits freedom of speech against (perhaps) greater public safety, it will be debated for some time.

Although they filled the media, debates about the adverse effects of large schools, violent games, long black coats, and antisocial Internet sites do not get to the heart of what most people really want to know—why did the boys want to kill their classmates and teachers, and could the killings have been prevented? As we discussed in Chapter 10, rare outbreaks of violence, such as the shootings at Littleton, are difficult to predict or to understand—they happen too infrequently. Yet the events that took place in Littleton have profound implications for the future of abnormal psychology, as the questions that follow highlight.

How Do We Ensure That the Scientific Findings of Abnormal Psychology Also Work in the Clinic?

Soon after the murders at Littleton, news reports surfaced that Eric Harris had been rejected by Marine Corps recruiters because he had been prescribed a psy-

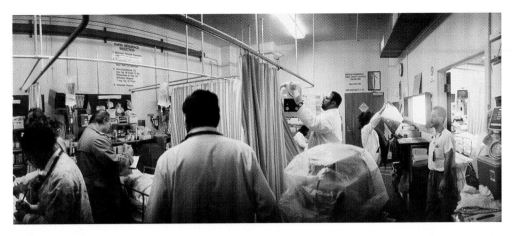

Limited by time and economics, clinicians, such as those in the trauma unit at Chicago's Cook County Hospital, are not always able to provide the treatment regimes that have proved efficacious in clinical trials.

choactive drug called Luvox (fluvoxamine). Fluvoxamine is a selective serotonin reuptake inhibitor (SSRI) approved by the U.S. Food and Drug Administration (FDA) for children up to age 17 for use in the treatment of obsessive-compulsive disorder. Because it is an SSRI like Prozac and Zoloft, doctors sometimes prescribe Luvox for depression as well, although there is no research showing its efficacy for childhood depression.

Prescribing a drug for a condition other than the one for which it is FDA approved is known as off-label use. Such prescriptions are not illegal; in fact, they are quite common (Vitiello & Jensen, 1997). Once a drug is approved for sale, doctors can prescribe it for any condition they deem appropriate, even one for which the drug's efficacy has never been tested. Similarly, psychologists are free to use therapeutic techniques such as cognitive therapy for any client they choose, even if cognitive therapy has never before been applied to the client's particular problem. In both cases, clinicians move away from the scientific "evidence base" that justifies a treatment to rely instead on their clinical judgment and intuition. The problem is that there are few ways to assess the outcomes of clinical judgment or intuition. Most psychotherapy (and drug) research is conducted in highly controlled clinical trials. In such trials, clients are carefully selected to be as similar to one another as possible. Great pains are taken to rule out extraneous factors. For example, trials of treatments for schizophrenia are usually conducted using people who are having their first episode of schizophrenia. They are preferred because they have not been "contaminated" by previous treatments. In trials, participants are randomly assigned to treatment and control conditions (and kept blind about

which group they are in). Clinicians who participate in such trials are carefully trained in the treatment protocol, and, where possible, they are also kept blind. Therapeutic regimes and processes are carefully specified so that all participants receive exactly the same treatment. By following these careful procedures, scientists can use statistical methods to measure a treatment's efficacy.

Unfortunately, even efficacious treatments may prove disappointing in the real world of the clinic. Not all clinicians are as carefully trained in applying a therapy as those who participate in a trial, and clients cannot be selected to meet certain criteria (such as having no previous episode of schizophrenia). Clinicians are confronted with people who are suffering, and they must try to help whomever they can. Sometimes, economics makes it difficult for clinicians to adhere to the same treatment regime used in a trial. For example, a trial may require 12 visits to a clinician, whereas a managed care organization may agree to pay for only 6. For these reasons, a treatment's effectiveness in the clinic is almost always lower than its efficacy in a clinical trial. (See Chapter 8 for more on the difference between efficacy and effectiveness.)

At present, psychologists have made few attempts to measure treatment effectiveness; most efforts go into measuring treatment efficacy. It is important to redress this imbalance because the effectiveness studies that have been done paint a pessimistic picture. Let us return to our example of schizophrenia. Up to 2 million people are treated for schizophrenia in the United States each year, and, at any given time, there are at least 100,000 in the hospital. Yet less than half of those in treatment are receiving the currently recommended doses of antipsychotic medications or the latest appropriate psychosocial treatments (Lehman, Steinwachs, and Survey Co-Investigators, 1998). In other words, a million people, and their families, are suffering more than they should because the latest research findings are not being applied in practice. This gap between research and practice is not unusual, nor is it confined to mental disorders. The same phenomenon occurs in many areas of medicine, such as cancer (Cronin et al., 1998). Clearly, we need to know why. Abnormal psychology needs to become much more concerned with how its findings are used in the clinic: Who is being treated, how are treatments being applied, and what are the outcomes? Collecting such data presents a great challenge. But without this information, the research findings of abnormal psychology will not be effectively transferred to the real world of the clinic.

Because effectiveness data on the outcomes of off-label prescriptions are not collected systematically and because privacy rights prevent us from knowing whether Eric Harris had either obsessive-compulsive disorder or depression (or some other disorder), we have no idea why he was prescribed fluvoxamine and whether the drug was of any help. We do know, however, that SSRIs may cause agitation and even manic episodes in some people. As you know from Chapter 8, manic behavior may include irritability and aggression. A student gunman named Kip Kinkel, who was involved in a school killing that took place before the one in Littleton, had taken an SSRI. For these reasons, some clinicians have claimed that school shooting rampages (including the one at Littleton) may be drug induced (Breggin, 1997). This seems a long shot. Although it is true that a small number of people may become agitated as a side effect of taking an SSRI, it is quite a stretch to argue that a drug prescribed for Eric Harris would induce him and Dylan Klebold to spend months making bombs, obtaining guns, and planning to murder their fellow students. Anyway, there is a fatal flaw in the theory. The local coroner did not find a trace of any psychoactive drug or alcohol in the bodies of either Eric Harris or Dylan Klebold.

Will the Biopsychosocial Model of Human Behavior Survive During the 21st Century?

Investigators found it difficult to believe that Eric Harris and Dylan Klebold could have accumulated such a huge arsenal of guns and bombs without their parents knowing anything about it. Police claimed that weapons and bombs were so easy to find in the Harris home that

Eric's parents must have known they were there. The police were so convinced that the Klebolds and the Harrises must have known of their sons' plans that they threatened to press charges against both sets of parents (although the nature of these charges was never specified). Clearly, in the minds of the police—and many others—the boys' parents should be held accountable for their sons' actions. Yet how much the parents knew is unclear. They denied any knowledge of the boys' plans and released press statements expressing profound love for their children. Friends and neighbors described both sets of parents as concerned and affectionate people who were shocked by the violent crimes committed by their children.

Earlier in this century, it would have been taken for granted by those working in the field of abnormal psychology that the parents were somehow to blame. Influenced by psychoanalysis and the radical behavioral view that all behavior is learned, psychologists would have sought explanations for the boys' behavior in their early childhood experiences. One fact that would surely have provoked professional interest is that, in counterpoint to his interest in Nazism, Dylan Klebold's mother is Jewish. Indeed, the Jewish Community Center in Columbus, Ohio, is named after his maternal grandfather, who was its major benefactor. Shortly before the shootings, at his family's Passover Seder, a traditional Jewish celebration, Dylan had participated by asking the customary four questions. Perhaps Klebold's act of violence was some sort of displaced anger at his mother. Alternatively, his interest in Nazism could have been a form of self-hate, perhaps the result of parental apathy or rejection.

In the past, a strong belief in nurture often led to the unfair blaming of parents for their children's disorders. Recall, for example, the "schizophrenogenic" mother who causes her child to develop schizophrenia (see Chapter 9) or the "refrigerator" mother who was supposed to be responsible for her child's autism (see Chapter 12). As we have seen in previous chapters, it is almost impossible to verify such hypotheses. Moreover, by the end of the 20th century, few psychologists even bothered to try. The prevailing views had changed; parental nurture had given way to nature and peer pressure as the major determiners of behavior.

One measure of the extent to which nature and peer influence have replaced nurture as an explanation for behavior is the huge sales of a book titled *The Nurture Assumption* by Judith Rich Harris (1998; see also Harris, 1995). According to Harris, whose book was something

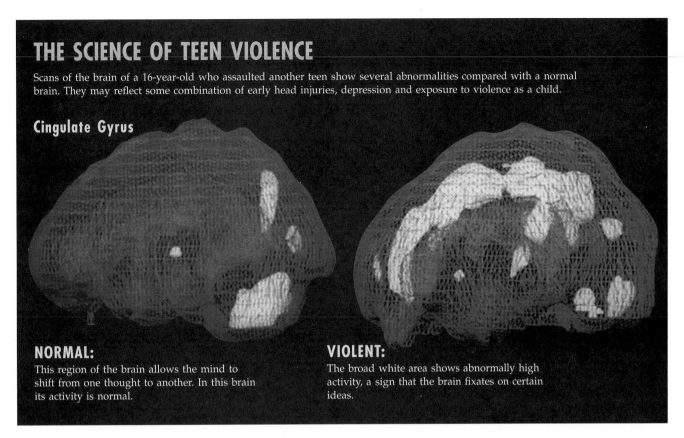

THE SCIENCE OF TEEN VIOLENCE

Scans of the brain of a 16-year-old who assaulted another teen show several abnormalities compared with a normal brain. They may reflect some combination of early head injuries, depression and exposure to violence as a child.

Cingulate Gyrus

NORMAL:
This region of the brain allows the mind to shift from one thought to another. In this brain its activity is normal.

VIOLENT:
The broad white area shows abnormally high activity, a sign that the brain fixates on certain ideas.

Biological and genetic explanations for violent behavior (such as this article in Newsweek *after the Littleton shootings) have become popular in recent years.*

of a publishing phenomenon, parents have only a minimal long-term effect on their child's personality. Indeed, their influence is so small that if children swapped parents, it would make little difference. Children, according to Harris, are influenced by their genes and their peers. Parents should not feel guilty about how their children turn out because they have little to do with it. In fact, children should feel guilty for causing their parents anguish and distress. For example, Harris notes that "difficult" children may cause parents to divorce.

Harris accumulated substantial evidence for her arguments. Twin and adoption studies have demonstrated the important role played by genetics in many disorders (as well as in personality, intelligence, and everyday behavior), but does this really mean that parenting makes no difference? Probably not. Parental abuse, neglect, and other early childhood experiences almost certainly affect later behavior. As we have seen in the preceding chapters, there is room for both nature and nurture in explaining most psychological disorders. Still, the present emphasis is clearly on biology. In 1999 alone, three books on youth violence were published

(Amen, 1999; Garbarino, 1999; Niehoff, 1999). Although each book admits that early experiences count, all three blame violence on biology—specifically, defects in various parts of the brain.

Why is this emphasis on nature so popular at this time in history? It could be a backlash. Those who emphasized the importance of nurture failed to deliver on many of their more ambitious promises. We still suffer from crime, poverty, mental retardation, and mental disorders. Habitual-criminal laws (which require those convicted of three felonies to be incarcerated for life with little or no attempt at rehabilitation), the growing popularity of psychoactive drugs (even for those who do not have mental disorders), and the increasingly widespread belief that genes are the dominant force in our behavior are all signs of a society that has become pessimistic about its ability to improve the human condition. If abnormal psychology is to have a future, it must confront this pessimism head-on. As you have seen in this book, research in abnormal psychology has deepened our understanding of human behavior and improved the quality of life for many people. These accomplishments were possible only because of the belief that human behavior can be modified by environmental forces. A major task for abnormal psychology is continuing to strengthen the biopsychosocial model of human behavior. By identifying the ways in which nature and nurture interact and proving to an increasingly skeptical public that nurture (especially early psychological interventions) can help to improve the quality of life of people with psychological disorders, abnormal psychology can retain its role as the unifying science of mental disorders.

To be fair to Harris, she does not argue that genes completely determine behavior. Her point is that peers are more significant than parents. Certainly, there is considerable evidence for the importance of peers. In the preceding chapters, we have seen how peer pressure contributes to substance abuse, eating disorders, and many other mental disorders. There is no doubt that youngsters, especially, are responsive to and imitate their peers. Rejection by peers can cause misery that even the most loving family may find difficult to overcome. In the aftermath of Littleton, teenagers from around the world posted messages to a special Internet site set up to allow them to express how they felt about the killings. Hundreds wrote about the anguish of being an "outcast." One cannot help but wonder whether the tragedy at Littleton would have taken place had Eric Harris and Dylan Klebold been accepted by their peers. Certainly, peer influences represent an important continuing research area for abnormal psychology.

How Do We Get Treatment and Prevention Services to Cooperate?

In the months leading up to the killings, Eric Harris and Dylan Klebold participated in a special diversion program administered by the county sheriff's department. To be eligible for this program, they signed contracts stating that they would not acquire firearms. They disregarded this promise and immediately began amassing guns and explosives. Yet, to the authorities, they seemed model members of the program. They appeared to understand the lessons of their anger-management classes. They paid fees on time, participated in counseling sessions, attended an ethics class, and fulfilled their community service obligations. The court officer who released them early from their diversion program believed that they had a bright future provided they worked hard and stayed motivated. No one involved in the program had any inkling that the boys were planning to blow up their school and kill their fellow students and teachers.

And these individuals were not the only ones who failed to notice anything awry. Eric Harris saw a physician and received a prescription for psychoactive medication. The boys attended a school that employed professional counselors. Klebold's mother was a counselor. Harris had been reported to the police for threatening violence. Yet no one predicted that the boys would explode in an orgy of killing. As we saw in Chapter 10, even when psychologists use specially designed assessment instruments, they are not very accurate at predicting rare violent events. Unaided clinical judgment (without assessment instruments) is even less effective. Clearly, there is still much for us to learn if we are to be able to predict and prevent violent behavior.

Yet, even with further research, we will still be unable to help people like Harris and Klebold unless we can foster better cooperation across service providers. In the case of Harris and Klebold, it seems as if there was little or no communication among these providers. The court counselors did not consult with the school, and neither seemed to have any communication with the physician who prescribed fluvoxamine (as already noted, fluvoxamine might not be the best drug to prescribe for someone with a tendency to violence).

Although it will always be difficult to predict rare violent events, it is possible that someone might have become alarmed had communication taken place among the various service providers. The police were informed that Eric Harris had threatened another student, but they did not communicate this information to those running the anger-management program (which Harris passed with flying colors). Teachers and school counselors knew that Eric and Dylan praised Hitler and had made a video that paralleled their later destructive orgy, but they did not communicate this information to the court counselors. (School officials may not even have known that the boys were in a diversion program.) Students were aware of Eric's hate-filled Web site, but they did not share this information with school counselors. Harris left weapons in plain sight in his home, and his neighbors heard the sounds of smashing glass, but this information somehow never got to those in authority who might have been able to intervene. Clearly, all these signs are easier to recognize in hindsight than in advance. Most teachers are not trained to note them, and others are too busy. The principal of Columbine High School told the press that he had never heard of the Trenchcoat Mafia until the killings. One of the great challenges for abnormal psychology in the new century will be to develop better communication networks among service providers.

Two generations check out the wares at a National Rifle Association gun show. Can abnormal psychology provide compelling evidence to social policy makers that restricting access to guns will reduce violence?

How Will Health Economics Affect Abnormal Psychology?

Although Eric Harris reportedly received psychiatric or psychological treatment, the nature of this treatment, and of the treated disorder, is not clear. Like Harris, millions of children and teenagers receive prescriptions for psychoactive drugs each year. The most common is Ritalin, which is usually prescribed for attention-deficit/hyperactivity disorder (see Chapter 12), and many prescriptions are written for antidepressants as well. Some of these prescriptions are written by psychiatrists and some by psychologists who have been given the right to prescribe psychoactive drugs in certain jurisdictions. However, the majority of the prescriptions are written by family physicians, often working for health maintenance organizations. In a desire to control costs, these organizations often prefer to treat behavior disorders with drugs rather than with psychological treatment because drugs are less expensive. The result is that, in many cases, a prescription is the only treatment the person receives. Without the close monitoring that is characteristic of a therapeutic relationship, there may be no one to know whether a person is harboring murderous or suicidal thoughts. Abnormal psychology must confront the realities of managed care by researching the patterns of care that people receive and by formulating treatment guidelines to help family

physicians improve the quality of the services they offer to people with mental disorders.

Will Abnormal Psychology Have a Role in Formulating Social Policy?

Whenever there is a particularly horrifying killing using guns, there are calls for greater gun control. America has notoriously lax gun laws and, as we saw in Chapter 10, one of the world's highest death rates from shootings. Following Littleton, many people, including the president of the United States, called on Congress to make it more difficult for people to obtain guns. Despite some long overdue reforms, America still has the least restrictive gun laws in the world. Many lawmakers hope that making access to guns more difficult will deter future killings. Clearly, Harris and Klebold could not have shot anyone had they not had guns. Still, it may be a long time before schools such as Columbine will be able to dispense with their security staffs and their sheriff's deputies.

The easy availability of guns is an important social problem. Abnormal psychology, if it is to have a practical effect on reducing violence, must help society to understand the cultural and psychological forces that glorify gun ownership. Why are guns so valued? Can we provide compelling evidence that restricting access to guns will reduce violence? If so, how can this evidence best be communicated? These questions constitute an important research agenda for abnormal psychology. Still, it was not simply access to guns that caused Harris and Klebold to kill their classmates and a teacher. Easy access to guns explains how they got the weapons; it does not explain why they used them. The roots of violence in early conduct disorders remain a crucial area for basic research.

THE WAY FORWARD

Abnormal psychology has a proud record of achievement, but there is still much work to be done. In the next 100 years, it is important for psychologists to focus on translating their discoveries into effective treatments for people who are treated not in research settings but in the messy world of the clinic, the schools, and the courts. It is not acceptable that half of all people with schizophrenia are receiving substandard treatment. A much better outcome is achievable, but it will require new research in areas that have not previously been studied. Generating knowledge in abnormal psychology is not an end in itself but should ultimately lead to better mental health for society. Progress in three interacting research domains—basic research, treatment research, and services research—will determine society's mental health well-being. Taken together, these domains represent a research agenda for the 21st century.

Basic Research

Much of the progress that has been made in understanding and helping people with mental disorders has come from basic research, which deals with the mechanisms of learning and habit formation, how social forces influence behavior, and the importance of biological factors such as genetics. This research has largely taken place within the context of the biopsychosocial model of human behavior. That is, everyone acknowledges that biological, psychological, and social factors interact to produce behavior (including mental disorders). However, few studies try to understand how the various factors interact—and, as we have seen, the field goes through fads during which one of the three factors is emphasized more than the others. Progress in the 21st century will come from clarifying how biology, psychology, and sociocultural studies can combine to help us understand mental disorders. This means more interdisciplinary research. Today, for example, some researchers

work on the genetics of depression, others on cognitions, others on pharmacology, and still others on seasonal changes in light. Real progress will come when these researchers begin working together. This can sometimes be physically difficult, but geographical boundaries can be overcome. The Internet is emerging as a primary source for organizing and manipulating information quickly and then making this information available worldwide. With this capacity for international collaboration, the challenge for abnormal psychology will be to present its research findings in a way that researchers from other disciplines can access on-line, evaluate, and contribute to in a collaborative manner.

Treatment Research

As already noted, treatment research must be broadened to measure effectiveness as well as efficacy, and researchers must also incorporate economic considerations into their research. In this era of managed care, it is no longer sufficient to know that a treatment has a positive effect in a clinical trial. What managed care providers want to know is whether the treatment is cost-effective in the clinic. That is, does the treatment produce a better outcome than less expensive alternatives? For example, would Eric Harris's life have had a different outcome if he had been treated with cognitive-behavioral therapy as opposed to drugs (which he may not have taken as prescribed)? Controlling costs without decreasing quality is a major challenge for everyone working in the field of abnormal psychology.

In the past, treatment research has focused on short-term outcomes, with follow-ups after a year or two at most. These studies are important for some disorders, but they are not always clinically meaningful. As are arthritis and diabetes, many mental disorders are lifelong and chronic. They require management strategies that may have to continue for years and that need to be aimed primarily at reducing relapses and teaching individuals how to live a high-quality life despite suffering the symptoms of a mental disorder. Psychological researchers must begin to take a lifelong management approach to certain disorders. To help clients, researchers will also have to evaluate new methods of treating people with chronic disorders.

It is also important for abnormal psychology to examine clinical practice and competencies. At present, data for determining whether a clinician is achieving good outcomes are not available. Researchers need to develop measures of the quality of mental health care. Once such measures have been devised, we can use

With advances in basic, treatment, and services research in the 21st century, abnormal psychology should be better able to recognize and treat people like Danielle Wood, Dylan Klebold, and Eric Harris and keep them from slipping through the cracks.

them to collect information on clinical practice and outcomes. Ultimately, these data can be used to develop clinical guidelines that represent "best practice." Clinicians who follow these guidelines will be basing their interventions on evidence, rather than intuition. There is already a shift away from clinical intuition and toward evidence-based clinical decision making (Frances et al., 1998). This trend will accelerate in the 21st century. As they are refined, treatment guidelines will be expanded to help clinicians decide which treatment to recommend next when the first one tried is unsuccessful. Off-label, or nonstandard, applications of treatments will still occur, but data on the outcomes of nonstandard treatments need to be collected so that they may be used to further refine clinical guidelines.

A perennial problem is the long time lag between clinical research and its practical application. Studies may take years to appear in published form and even longer to affect clinical practice. To get around this, scientists have formed data repositories in which the results of trials are collected. Some may later be published (and some are never published), but all are evaluated and used to help develop best-practice guidelines.

Services Research

It is important for clinicians to know more about how services are actually provided to clients. How, for example, did Eric Harris's doctor decide to prescribe fluvoxamine?

What was the content of the anger-management program in which Harris and Klebold participated? It is also vitally important that we find ways to foster better communication across service providers. At present, the treatment of mental disorders takes place in a complicated health system in which responsibility is divided among courts, managed care organizations, schools, jails, and private providers (medical and psychological). The lack of coordination among the various providers can have negative effects on treatment outcomes. As we saw in the case of Eric Harris and Dylan Klebold, health care providers, schools, social welfare providers, and juvenile justice counselors rarely talk to one another. In such a fragmented system, it is not surprising that some people fall through the cracks. Even the best treatments will not produce good outcomes if the systems for implementing the fail to work.

DANIELLE WOOD REVISITED

This book began with the story of Danielle Wood, a promising young woman who died while still in college. She probably took her own life, perhaps because of her early experiences, her temperament, her disappointments, or more likely because of all of these factors. It would be reassuring to think that 100 years from now, when we look back at the 21st century, such tragedies would be very rare events. With continued progress in basic research, we would know enough about how disorders develop to prevent many and to help alleviate others. With advances in basic research, we might understand how psychoactive and performance-enhancing drugs affected Danielle's judgment. We might also have better screening devices to ensure that her depression was noted and treated. We can hope that more effective treatments delivered in a high-quality environment and based on the latest evidence will be able to prevent those who feel despair from seeing no way out other than suicide. Perhaps we will finally have the integration among service providers that ensures coordinated care so that people like Danielle and Dylan Klebold and Eric Harris do not fall through the cracks of the system. As research progresses, we can be optimistic that the 21st century will continue to see great progress in alleviating the suffering of those with mental disorders and, in many cases, in preventing their occurrence in the first place. We know what needs to be done and, in most cases, how to do it. We must now get on with the job.

Glossary

ABAB experiment   An experimental design for determining the value of a specific treatment, with four phases: A—the psychologist collects baseline data on the frequency and intensity of the problem behaviors; B—treatment is introduced, and any changes in behavior are noted; A—treatment is discontinued while behavior continues to be monitored; B—treatment is reinstated and the problem behavior should again decrease if the treatment is effective.

acculturation   The process by which recent immigrants learn to adapt to their new culture; a process that almost always involves some degree of stress.

acculturative stress   Stress experienced by immigrants and members of minority cultures because of a conflict between assimilating into the majority culture and maintaining their ethnic or racial identity.

active phase of psychosis   The phase of schizophrenia in which periods of active symptoms alternate with periods of better functioning; patients are unaware that they are behaving strangely.

acute stress disorder   An anxiety disorder that is a short-term reaction to an emotional trauma.

adjustment disorder   Clinically significant emotional or behavioral symptoms (including anxiety, depression, and withdrawal) that develop in response to a crisis of everyday life, such as divorce, a death in the family, job loss, financial worries, or relationship problems.

adjustment disorder with depressive features   Feelings of sadness and self-doubt in reaction to a stressful life occurrence (loss of a job, for example) that dissipate within 6 months; a transient reaction to a stressful circumstance.

age adjustment (age standardization)   A statistical technique used to correct for differences in the age distribution of populations when comparing prevalence rates of a disorder in different countries.

agnosia   A failure to recognize familiar objects despite normal vision, touch, and hearing.

agoraphobia   An anxiety disorder characterized by fear of being alone away from help and protection; in extreme cases, a fear of leaving home.

alarm reaction   A reaction to fear (also called emergency reaction) in which the sympathetic nervous system and its associated glands increase the amount of sugar in the blood, speed up heart and respiration rates, reduce the blood supply to vessels near the skin, and increase the supply of proteins that cause blood clotting.

alcohol (ethanol)   A colorless, volatile liquid, C_2H_5OH; a psychoactive depressant derived mainly from fermented cereals or fruits.

amnestic disorders   Transient or chronic cognitive disorders characterized by loss of past memories or by an inability to learn new information; causes include traumatic brain injury,

stroke, exposure to highly toxic substances, brain disease, chronic substance abuse, and nutritional deficiencies.

anabolic steroids   Drugs derived from the hormone testosterone that help the body retain protein and thereby accelerate the growth of muscles, bones, and skin.

analogue experiment   An experiment whose variables are similar, or analogous, to the real-world variable the researcher wishes to study.

anhedonia   The inability to feel pleasure.

anorexia nervosa   An eating disorder that usually begins in adolescence or early adulthood and affects mainly females; involves extreme weight loss (at least 15% below the expected weight), intense fear of gaining weight, disturbance in the way one's body weight or shape is experienced, and amenorrhea.

antagonist   A chemical that reduces the potency of other chemicals.

antigens   Foreign cells, such as bacteria, that invade the body and provoke an immune response.

anti-psychiatrists   A group, whose best-known member was Thomas Szasz, that argued that if we accept that mental disorders are produced by environmental factors and personal failings, then mental disorders are not medical diseases but social dilemmas and are not the province of psychiatrists.

antisocial personality disorder   A personality disorder characterized by disregard for the rights of other people.

anxiety   A negative emotional state marked by foreboding and somatic signs of tension, such as a racing heart, sweating, and, often, difficulty breathing; similar to fear but with a less specific focus.

anxiety disorder   A psychological disorder defined by panic attacks that are frequent, that occur in combination with other symptoms, or that seriously affect a person's quality of life. According to *DSM-IV*, anxiety disorders include specific phobias, social phobia, obsessive-compulsive disorder, generalized anxiety disorder, panic disorder, agoraphobia, acute stress disorder, post-traumatic stress disorder, substance-induced anxiety disorder, and anxiety disorder produced by a general medical condition.

anxiety hierarchy   A series of gradually more frightening scenes; used in systematic desensitization.

aphasia   A language disorder usually associated with damage to the left cerebral hemisphere.

apraxia   An inability to carry out desired motor actions despite normal muscle control; for example, an inability to dress oneself.

Asperger's disorder   A pervasive developmental disorder that is similar to autistic disorder but without the serious language and communication problems.

attachment Strong emotional bond between two people, such as a child and mother or other primary caregiver.

attention-deficit/hyperactivity disorder (ADHD) A developmental disorder characterized by (1) persistent inattention that is maladaptive and inconsistent with developmental level or by (2) persistent hyperactivity and impulsivity that is maladaptive and inconsistent with developmental level or by (3) a combination of the two.

attribution An inference that we make about the causes of events, our own behavior, or the behavior of others.

autistic disorder A pervasive developmental disorder whose onset is before age 3 and that is characterized by poor social interactions, impaired communication, and odd motor behaviors.

avoidance learning Learning to respond to a signal in order to avoid exposure to an unpleasant stimulus.

avoidant personality disorder A Cluster C personality disorder characterized by extreme shyness and social discomfort; unlike people with schizoid personality disorder, people with this disorder would prefer to be sociable, but they avoid social contact for fear of embarrassment and criticism.

base rate The extent to which a particular trait or behavior exists in a population; also known as prevalence.

behavior modification Use of the principles of learning to help clients substitute desirable behaviors for undesirable ones. Also called behavior therapy.

behavioral assessment A heterogeneous set of techniques used by behavioral psychologists to describe the environmental conditions that elicit and maintain problem behaviors; a continuous process that tracks behavior throughout treatment and includes SORC analysis, behavioral interviewing, self-report measures, and direct observation of behavior.

behavioral contracting A treatment approach in which people are fined or rewarded depending on whether they keep to the terms of an agreement (a contract) they make to alter their behavior.

behavioral medicine A field of medicine that focuses on how psychological factors make people susceptible or resistant to illness, alter the course of an illness, determine compliance with medical treatment, and affect health-related behavior.

behaviorism The major alternative to psychoanalytic theory, this group of ideas was developed in the psychological laboratory rather than from clinical observations. John B. Watson coined the term, claiming that the focus of psychology should be objective evidence of behavior rather than thoughts or sensations.

belief A characteristic way of thinking about oneself and the world.

benzodiazepines Anxiolytic drugs that augment the inhibitory effect of gamma-aminobutyric acid (GABA), a neurotransmitter that inhibits neurons from firing. Examples are alprazolam, chlordiazepoxide, and diazepam.

binge-eating disorder An eating disorder proposed for inclusion in future *DSM* editions; it is characterized by uncontrolled eating, and the result is obesity.

biofeedback Using an instrument (such as a plethysmograph, an electromyograph, or a polygraph) to provide people with information about their physiological responses in order to help them change a behavior.

biopsychosocial A description of behavior used by modern clinical psychologists to indicate that biological, psychological, and social forces all interact to determine people's every action.

bipolar mood disorder A mood disorder characterized by a combination of depression with manic periods; termed manic depression by Kraepelin.

bipolar I disorder A bipolar mood disorder that mixes one or more manic or mixed episodes with one or more major depressive episodes.

bipolar II disorder A bipolar mood disorder characterized by recurrent major depressive episodes and at least one hypomanic episode.

body dysmorphic disorder An obsession with supposed defects in one's appearance, which can result in social isolation.

borderline personality disorder A Cluster B personality disorder characterized by instability in personal relationships, self-image, and affect, as well as noticeable impulsivity beginning in early adulthood.

breathing-related sleep disorder A dyssomnia in which breathing is difficult during sleep because of obstruction of the upper airways; associated with obesity, snoring, and frequent awakenings. In severe cases, it may result in a brain-destroying lack of oxygen during sleep.

brief psychotic disorder A disorder characterized by psychotic symptoms that last for less than 1 month.

Briquet's syndrome Now commonly known as somatization disorder, hysteria marked by multiple complaints; named for the French doctor Pierre Briquet (1796–1881).

bulimia nervosa An eating disorder that usually begins in adolescence or early adulthood and is characterized by recurrent episodes of binge eating followed by purging, fasting, or excessive exercise; self-evaluation is unduly influenced by body shape and weight.

caffeine A bitter white alkaloid, $C_8H_{10}N_4O_2$; a psychoactive stimulant found in coffee, tea, cocoa, and chocolate.

cannabis *Cannabis sativa,* a type of hemp plant that produces the psychoactive substances marijuana, hashish, and hash oil.

catatonic features Odd motor disturbances ranging from complete immobility to bizarre postures and movements; a diagnostic specifier for mood disorders.

catatonic subtype Schizophrenia whose main presenting feature is odd motor activity in which either stupor or excitement predominates: immobility, waxy flexibility, excessive motor activity, negativism, stereotyped movements, imitation of others, or odd movements.

categorical classification A classification system following Kraepelin that establishes diagnostic categories (by grouping symptoms to form syndromes, or disorders) and then assesses individuals to see how closely their symptoms match those of the category—i.e., whether they meet the "criteria" for the disorder. This approach emphasizes people's similarities and deemphasizes their uniqueness.

catharsis   The release of pent-up emotions.

childhood disintegrative disorder   A pervasive developmental disorder characterized by the deterioration, beginning between the ages of 2 and 10, of apparently normal development.

chlorpromazine   A neuroleptic drug that is one of the phenothiazines, which act by blocking certain dopamine receptors; brand name, Thorazine.

chorea   Brain syndromes characterized by involuntary, irregular, jerky movements; seen in a number of neurological diseases, including Huntington's disease.

circadian rhythm sleep disorder   A dyssomnia in which sleeping becomes difficult due to changes in time or daily schedule; an example is "jet lag."

circadian rhythms   Cyclic (24-hour) reflections of the body's biological clock.

classical conditioning   A type of learning in which a neutral stimulus is paired with a stimulus that elicits a physiological, behavioral, or emotional response; after repeated pairings, the neutral stimulus alone will produce the response. Also called Pavlovian conditioning.

clinical psychologist   A PhD or a PsyD who is a state-certified psychologist trained in the main areas of psychology with particular attention to mental disorders and research techniques. Clinical psychologists emphasize the causal and treatment roles of psychological factors.

cognitive (impairment) **disorders**   Disorders usually diagnosed among older people that are caused by temporary or permanent brain damage and attack the memories, personality traits, and cognitive skills that give each person a unique identity. The main cognitive disorders are dementia, delirium, and amnestic disorders.

cognitive triad   Negative attributions about the self, the world, and the future; believed by cognitive psychologists such as Beck to be one source of mood disorders.

collective unconscious   According to Carl Jung, the accumulated wisdom of a culture.

communication disorders   Difficulties with language, usually diagnosed in childhood. These disorders include expressive language disorder (poor vocabulary and verbal skills), mixed receptive-expressive language (difficulties in understanding and expression), phonological disorder (failure to use speech sounds appropriate for age and dialect), and stuttering.

comorbidity   The presence of two or more disorders.

compulsions   Ritualistic actions that a person feels driven to perform to ward off some calamity.

computerized tomography (CT)   An imaging technique that uses multiple beams of X rays to produce cross-sectional images and show outlines of structures in the body.

concordance rate   The proportion of identical twins or other family members who exhibit the same trait or disorder.

conditioned response (CR)   In classical conditioning, a learned response made to a previously neutral stimulus.

conditioned stimulus (CS)   In classical conditioning, the neutral stimulus that is paired with the stimulus eliciting a response (the unconditioned stimulus) and that eventually elicits the response by itself.

conduct disorder   A developmental disorder characterized by a repetitive and persistent pattern of behavior in which the basic rights of others or major age-appropriate societal norms or rules are violated; these behaviors include aggression against people and animals, destruction of property, deceitfulness or theft, and serious violations of rules.

consanguinity method   A research method that studies the relatives of a person with a disorder (a proband) to see if they also have the disorder, to examine whether the disorder is transmitted genetically.

control group   In an experiment, the group of subjects that does not receive the experimental treatment. The data from this group are compared with the data from the experimental group.

conversion disorder   Once known as hysteria, a somatoform disorder in which pseudoneurological symptoms (such as paralysis, blindness, deafness, seizures, odd tingling sensations, and anesthesias) affect sensory or motor functioning; does not include sexual symptoms.

conversion hysteria   According to Freudian theory, hysteria that is manifested by physical symptoms.

coping   Finding effective ways to adapt to the problems and difficulties presented by stress.

correlation   The degree and direction (positive or negative) of correspondence between two variables.

cost-effectiveness analysis   A tool used by health economists to determine which of several alternative health programs provides the greatest value for the money.

Creutzfeldt-Jakob disease   A spongiform encephalopathy whose symptoms are walking with a stiff gait, trouble maintaining balance, difficulty controlling voluntary movements, and diminished ability to plan ahead; as the disease progresses, memory defects, hallucinations, and delusions appear. The cause may be a virus transmitted by eating affected animals ("mad cow" disease) and a genetic diathesis to the virus.

criminal commitment   The commitment to a mental institution for assessment or treatment of people who are judged not responsible for their actions at the time of a crime and not capable of defending themselves in court.

criminology   A scientific field developed at the end of the 19th century to study the causes, prevention, and treatment of criminal behavior.

critical period   A limited period of development during which an organism is predisposed to acquiring certain behaviors. For example, young children find it easier to learn languages than do older children or adults.

cultural-familial retardation Retardation caused by a combination of environmental (cultural) and genetic (familial) factors.

cyclothymic disorder A bipolar mood disorder characterized by rapid cycling between hypomanic symptoms and symptoms of mild depression, which may be mixed with periods of normal moods.

defense mechanism An unconscious distortion of reality that provides relief from anxiety. Some of the principal defense mechanisms are repression, sublimation, projection, rationalization, reaction formation, and denial.

deinstitutionalization A movement begun in the 1960s to discharge mental patients and treat them in mental health centers and halfway houses in their home communities, where they could participate in daily life.

delirium A cognitive disorder characterized by cloudy consciousness accompanied by disorientation, memory deficits, perceptual disturbances (such as hallucinations), and language deficits. Causes include brain tumors, blows to the head, systemic diseases such as AIDS, and drug intoxication or withdrawal. Delirium can usually be differentiated from dementia by its rapid onset, short duration, alternating lucid intervals, the presence of hallucinations and delusions, and its minimal long-term effect on personality.

delirium tremens Delirium that occurs when alcohol is withdrawn from habitual drinkers.

delusion An idea that is either bizarre or false, but not both; an unsubstantiated belief.

delusional disorder A disorder characterized by at least 1 month of delusions that are false in character and having none of the other symptoms of schizophrenia.

dementia A cognitive disorder characterized by multiple cognitive deficits, including forgetfulness, disorientation, concrete thinking, and perseveration (repetitive speech or movements); the most common cognitive disorder. Dementia can usually be differentiated from delirium by its gradual onset, long duration, consistent severe cognitive impairment, absence of hallucinations and delusions, and permanent effect on personality.

dementia of the Alzheimer's type (DAT) A degenerative brain disorder that can occur in relatively young people ("pre-senile" dementia) and that is common among people with Down syndrome. Autopsies of the brains of people with DAT show neurofibrillary tangles, senile plaques, and arteriosclerosis; however, these abnormalities can also be found in older people who do not have DAT. Also called Alzheimer's disease.

dementia praecox Emil Kraepelin's term for a continuously deteriorating psychosis, whose symptoms begin early in life.

dependent personality disorder A Cluster C personality disorder characterized by a pervasive and excessive need to be taken care of that leads to submissive and clinging behavior and fear of separation.

dependent variable The variable observed by researchers for the effects of influence by the independent variable.

depersonalization disorder A disorder in which the sense of self becomes dissociated from the rest of the personality; often accompanied by derealization.

depressant A psychoactive chemical that lowers arousal and causes drowsiness; examples include alcohol, opioids (heroin), and sedatives and anxiolytics (tranquilizers).

depressive personality disorder A personality disorder being considered for possible inclusion in future editions of the *DSM*; the characteristic feature is a tendency toward negative cognitions and depressed behaviors that begins early in childhood. Similar to dysthymic disorder except that more emphasis is given to cognitions.

derealization The feeling that the world is not real or of living in a dream; often accompanies depersonalization disorder.

detoxification Removal of a psychoactive substance from the body.

developmental psychopathology The study of abnormal behavior in its developmental context; a specialized area of clinical psychology.

deviation IQ In intelligence tests, a measure of comparison of the performance of an individual with the performance of others of the same age.

dexamethasone suppression test (DST) A way to measure cortisol levels (abnormally high levels have been implicated in depression and other disorders); if the ingestion of dexamethasone does not suppress cortisol levels, then depression may be suspected, although high cortisol levels may be due to some other cause.

diagnostic specifier A feature associated with the diagnosis of a disorder.

dialectical behavior therapy A multimodal treatment strategy that combines group and individual therapy, supportive counseling, and behavioral contracting (usually an agreement not to harm oneself) with skill training aimed at improving and maintaining relationships.

diathesis-stress model of etiology A model of psychological breakdown that attributes it to a combination of vulnerability or predisposition (diathesis) and stress.

dimensional (approach to) **classification** Diagnosing a disorder by using a standard set of personality dimensions rather than the categories of *DSM-IV*.

disinhibition An inability to inhibit impulses, marked by sexual aggressiveness, social tactlessness, and impulsivity; often a sign of frontal lobe damage.

disorganized subtype Schizophrenia whose main presenting feature is incoherent speech accompanied by bizarre and sometimes childish behavior and flat or inappropriate affect.

dissociative amnesia Psychogenic memory loss.

dissociative disorders Disorders in which memories and sometimes identities become detached from one another in the absence of a brain disorder, resulting in the "disassociation" of the personality.

dissociative fugue   Retrograde amnesia (forgetting events that occurred before a traumatic event) coupled with leaving home and adopting a new identity.

dissociative identity disorder   Also known as multiple personality disorder, a disorder in which at least two separate identities come forward in turn to take charge of an individual's behavior.

double depression   Dysthymic disorder combined with occasional major depressive episodes.

double-blind experiment   An experiment in which neither the researchers nor the subjects know which subjects are receiving the experimental treatment and which are receiving the placebo; such an experiment avoids expectancy effects.

Down syndrome   A chromosomal defect (trisomy 21) causing intellectual and physical disabilities and characterized by distinctive physical features; originally named Down's syndrome (the term still used in Great Britain) for John Langdon Down, who first identified the syndrome.

DSM (Diagnostic and Statistical Manual)   A comprehensive list of mental disorders published by the American Psychiatric Association.

dyspareunia   A sexual dysfunction characterized by recurrent or persistent genital pain associated with intercourse; can affect males and females.

dyssomnias   Disturbances in the amount, quality, or timing of sleep.

dysthymic disorder   A chronic, relatively mild depressive disorder that lasts for at least 2 years.

effectiveness (of a treatment)   A real-world measure of treatment success; always lower than treatment efficacy.

efficacy (of a treatment)   A statistical measure of treatment success under ideal conditions; a treatment may produce statistically significant improvement (i.e., be efficacious) yet not necessarily be clinically effective.

ego   In psychoanalytic theory, the part of the adult personality that mediates between the id and the external world and allows the individual to satisfy important needs without violating the demands of civilized society.

Electra complex   In psychoanalytic theory, the forcing of females during the genital stage to repress their natural desire for their fathers and to identify with their mothers; analogous to Oedipal conflict, although its resolution is not as clear.

electroconvulsive therapy (ECT)   The use of electric shock to cure mental disorders; credited to Italian psychiatrist Ugo Cerletti.

elimination disorders   Failure to achieve toilet training by the usual age; enuresis (poor control of urination) and encopresis (poor control of defecation).

emergency reaction   An organism's physiological response to threat in which the sympathetic nervous system and hormones trigger deepened respiration, increased rate and strength of the heartbeat, release of red blood cells by the spleen, release of sugar by the liver, and increased blood flow to the brain; identified by Walter Cannon. Also known as alarm reaction.

emotion-focused coping   Managing feelings in order to reduce anxiety.

encopresis   Poor control of defecation after 4 years of age (or equivalent developmental level).

enuresis   Poor control of urination after 5 years of age (or equivalent developmental level).

eugenics   The study of hereditary improvement through selective breeding; literally, "the production of fine children."

euthanasia   The practice of killing hopelessly sick or injured individuals in a relatively painless way; mercy killing.

exhibitionism   A paraphilia characterized by the act of exposing one's genitals to a stranger, sometimes accompanied by masturbation; most common among adolescent and young adult males.

existential anxiety   According to existential theorists, the fear that arises from being solely responsible for giving meaning to one's life in an indifferent universe.

expectancies   Cognitions about what will happen in the future.

experimental group   In an experiment, a group of subjects to which something is done or some treatment is given. The data from this group are compared with the data from the control group.

expressed emotion   A psychological dimension describing the extent to which family members are hostile, critical, and overbearing; high levels of expressed emotion in relatives is closely related to relapse in people with schizophrenia.

externalizing disorders   Disorders characterized by "acting-out" behaviors that annoy or threaten others; difficult children are more at risk of developing these disorders than are easy or slow-to-warm-up children.

extroversion   An outgoing and sociable personality that, when extreme, can cause people to continuously seek stimulation.

factitious disorder   A disorder in which people pretend to be sick for no personal gain other than attention.

factor analysis   A statistical technique that uses correlations between variables to determine which dimensions (factors) go together.

false-positives   Incorrect positive test results. (Compare **true-positives**.)

fear survey   A self-report tool used to obtain quantitative information about fears. The person is asked to assign numeric values to fear-producing stimuli.

feeding disorder of infancy or early childhood   An eating disorder characterized by inadequate eating that is not due to a medical condition.

female orgasmic disorder   A sexual dysfunction characterized by delay in or absence of orgasm following normal sexual excitement.

female sexual arousal disorder   A sexual dysfunction characterized by inability to develop or maintain an adequate lubrication-swelling response long enough to complete sexual activity.

fetal alcohol syndrome Teratogenic damage to a fetus caused by the mother's heavy drinking during pregnancy; the pattern of defects includes retardation, hyperactivity, facial deformities, heart defects, and organ malfunctions.

fetishism A paraphilia characterized by using inanimate objects (such as shoes, bras, underpants, or leather clothing) in fantasy or directly in order to achieve sexual gratification.

fixation In psychoanalytic theory, the frustration of a child's achievement of pleasure during the oral stage, resulting in the individual's later craving satisfaction of oral needs.

flooding A technique in which fearful individuals are exposed to their most feared stimulus in order to become "flooded" with emotion. Because the fear is not reinforced, the exposure can cause the fear to extinguish.

fragile X syndrome A genetic defect (abnormal replication of the X chromosome) causing mental retardation; two times more common in females than in males; physical signs can include large ears and a long face.

free association A therapeutic technique developed by Sigmund Freud to help patients say what is on their mind rather than what they think the therapist wants to hear.

frotteurism A paraphilia that involves touching or rubbing up against females, usually in crowded places; may be accompanied by sexual fantasies.

functional disorder A behavioral disorder that has no physical basis; a term first applied by 19th-century researchers to "mental illnesses."

gender identity disorder Discomfort with one's assigned sex role; a strong and persistent identification with the other gender.

general adaptation syndrome (GAS) Stages of physical deterioration in response to long-term or frequently recurring threats; described by Hans Selye.

general paresis General paralysis of the insane; also, the psychological abnormalities caused by advanced syphilis.

generalized anxiety disorder An anxiety disorder characterized by free-floating anxiety in many situations without any objective threat.

genotype A person's genetic endowment.

gestalt therapy A humanistic treatment developed by Frederick Perls in which clients act out past experiences and dreams in an attempt to permit them to reexperience early conflicts and resolve them.

hallucinations Sensory experiences in the absence of external stimuli.

hallucinogen A psychoactive substance that produces distorted sensations and perceptions (hallucinations), such as THC and LSD.

hardiness A particular form of optimism that has been found to be negatively correlated with illness.

health maintenance organization (HMO) A corporation or other entity that provides health care for a fixed fee.

heritability The extent to which heredity contributes to a particular behavior disorder.

histrionic personality disorder A Cluster B personality disorder characterized by excessive emotionality and attention seeking in order to be the center of attention; once known as hysterical personality disorder.

hopelessness A construct that combines helplessness due to negative life experiences with negative expectancies.

Huntington's disease A form of chorea resulting from the progressive degeneration of the basal ganglia; symptoms also include memory impairment and personality changes; the cause is a single dominant gene.

hyperactivity-impulsivity Excessive restlessness and inability to wait one's turn; one of the symptoms of attention-deficit/hyperactivity disorder.

hypersomnia A dyssomnia characterized by excessive sleepiness.

hyperventilation Abnormally fast or deep respiration, which lowers the level of carbon dioxide in the blood, causing blood pressure to fall, the extremities to tingle, and, occasionally, fainting.

hypnosis An artificially induced state of relaxation or altered attention.

hypoactive sexual desire disorder A sexual dysfunction characterized by little desire for sexual activity and few sexual fantasies.

hypochondriasis A somatoform disorder characterized by the belief that one is ill despite a negative medical evaluation and physician reassurance to the contrary.

hypofrontality Diminished activity in the frontal lobes; found in schizophrenic subjects who are asked to perform abstract problem-solving tasks.

hypomanic episode An episode marked by an elated mood, little need for sleep, and intense periods of activity overlying a tendency to skip from one activity to another, an inability to complete plans, and a low tolerance for frustration; milder than a manic episode.

hypothyroidism A physical and mental condition marked by low levels of thyroxin, a hormone produced by the thyroid gland.

iatrogenic disorder An illness caused by treatment, such as an infection from surgery or an adverse reaction to a drug.

ICD (International Classification of Diseases) A comprehensive list of diseases, including mental disorders, published by the United Nations' World Health Organization (WHO).

id In psychoanalytic theory, the part of the adult personality ruled by the pleasure principle, which requires that biological needs, such as hunger, thirst, and sex, be immediately satisfied.

identification In psychoanalytic theory, the process by which children adopt their parents' standards of proper behavior and develop a superego.

identity crisis The challenge at Erik Erikson's fifth stage of personality development, which occurs between the ages of 12 and 20, to make important life choices about careers, goals, social commitments, and the type of person one wishes to become.

illusory correlation The incorrect belief that unrelated variables are correlated.

implosive therapy A technique in which fearful individuals are exposed to an image of their most feared stimulus rather than to the actual stimulus.

impulse-control disorders According to the *DSM-IV*, disorders characterized by "the failure to resist an impulse, drive, or temptation to perform an act that is harmful to the person or to others." Impulse-control disorders include intermittent explosive disorder, kleptomania, pyromania, pathological gambling, and trichotillomania.

inattention The inability to concentrate; one of the symptoms of attention-deficit/hyperactivity disorder.

incomplete penetrance Variations in the degree to which a genotype for a particular characteristic is expressed in the phenotype; also called variable expressivity.

independent variable An experimental variable manipulated by researchers.

inhalants Breathable, psychoactive chemical vapors produced by paint thinners, some glues, dry-cleaning fluid, aerosols, and gasoline.

insanity A legal term whose definition has varied with society's attitude toward crime and criminals. Usually, it means acting criminally because of a mental disorder and therefore not being responsible for one's actions and not capable of defending oneself in court. (See also **M'Naghten Rule** and **irresistible impulse rule**.)

intelligence quotient (IQ) A score, derived from an intelligence test, that represents a person's intellectual level relative to a reference group, such as people of the same age.

intermittent explosive disorder An impulse-control disorder characterized by aggressive, unprovoked outbursts in which a person assaults others or destroys property; found more often among men than women.

internalizing disorders Disorders, such as depression and anxiety, whose symptoms are directed inward.

interpersonal therapy (IPT) A form of psychodynamic therapy that aims to help clients examine the ways in which their present social behavior keeps them from forming satisfactory interpersonal relationships and to teach them skills to improve their ability to form supportive relationships.

interrater reliability The degree to which multiple observers agree in their classification of a behavior or set of behaviors.

irresistible impulse rule An insanity defense adopted by some American states; under this rule, a person who is unable to resist an impulse, as in a fit of passion, is considered temporarily insane and therefore not guilty of criminal behavior.

judgment heuristics A strategy used to simplify complex cognitive tasks by relying on rules of thumb.

kappa (κ) A statistical measure of interrater reliability.

kleptomania An impulse-control disorder characterized by the need to steal worthless objects in order to relieve tension.

learned helplessness Martin Seligman's theory of helplessness learned in response to tragedy and loss over which one believes one has no control; a characteristic of depressed people.

learning disorders The term used in *DSM-IV* for what have also been called learning disabilities and academic skills disorders. Learning disorders include difficulties in learning to read, write, and do mathematics; usually diagnosed in childhood.

libido In psychoanalytic theory, the psychological "energy" derived from the life instincts of survival, death, and aggression. The libido acts as "fuel" for the ego, the superego, and psychological functioning in general.

lifetime morbid risk The likelihood that a relative of someone with a particular disorder will suffer from that disorder during his or her lifetime.

limbic system The part of the brain associated with anxiety and other emotions.

lithium carbonate A naturally occurring substance that is effective in treating bipolar disorders.

living wills Advance directives stipulating when medical treatment should be discontinued.

localization of brain damage The process by which clinicians assess symptoms to deduce which area of the brain has sustained damage due to head injury, stroke, degenerative disease, cancer, or substance abuse.

locus of control One's belief about whether events are determined largely by external forces or by one's own actions.

lysergic acid diethylamide (LSD) A powerful hallucinogen derived from a fungus that grows on grain.

magnetic resonance imaging (MRI) An imaging technique that uses magnetic fields to attract protons in the body's hydrogen atoms and produce images of structures in the body. Functional MRI (fMRI) uses the magnetic signals produced by increased blood flow to active parts of the brain to map brain activity (or function).

mainstreaming Teaching children with mental retardation or learning disabilities in regular classes rather than segregating them into special ones.

major depressive disorder A serious unipolar mood disorder consisting of one or more major depressive episodes.

major depressive episode A serious depression (which may be characterized by anhedonia or agitation, changes in sleep patterns, changes in appetite, loss of interest in sex, and a wide variety of aches and pains) in response to a stressful circumstance.

male erectile disorder A sexual dysfunction characterized by inability to maintain an adequate erection long enough to complete sexual activity.

male orgasmic disorder A sexual dysfunction characterized by delay in or absence of orgasm following normal sexual excitement.

malingerer A person who pretends to be sick to avoid commitments or to gain some advantage.

managed care The attempt to control health care costs and maximize benefits by determining who will receive treatment and the type of treatment they will receive.

mania A mood disorder marked by extreme elation; one extreme of the mood spectrum.

manic episode An episode characterized by an overly elevated mood and sometimes by excessive irritability, grandiosity, and incoherence.

mediated learning Learning new behaviors due to the motivation (or mediation) of internal states, such as fear.

melancholia The early name for depression, believed to be derived from an excess of the bodily humor "black bile."

melancholic Lacking interest in previously enjoyable activities; a diagnostic specifier for mood disorders.

mental age The age level at which an individual is functioning intellectually.

mental retardation The failure of the intellectual abilities of an individual to develop at the same rate as those of his or her peers; usually diagnosed in childhood; can be inherited, acquired, or the result of genetic "accident." As defined in the *DSM-IV*, it is characterized by significantly below-average intellectual functioning, with an IQ of 70 or below, and concurrent deficits or impairments in adaptive functioning, both observed before the age of 18.

mental status examination A semistructured interview used mainly as a screening device to assess a person's current neurological and psychological status along several dimensions: memory, sensation, activity level, mood, and clarity of thought.

mentally ill chemical abusers (MICAs) People who suffer from substance dependence along with other psychological disorders; often young males who are poor, homeless, sickly, and likely to get into legal difficulties.

meta-analysis A set of techniques designed to find, appraise, and combine data across disparate studies.

milieu treatment Treatment of mental disorders in a mental hospital, where patients are sheltered from the everyday world, and doctors, nurses, and other staff create a joint culture in which patients interact socially and gain a sense of independence by participating in ward government. Today, this kind of long-term hospitalization has fallen out of favor, although it is still used to treat some people with schizophrenia.

mitral valve prolapse The protrusion of the mitral valve into the left atrium of the heart; produces symptoms similar to those seen in panic attacks, such as difficulty breathing, palpitations, and chest pain.

mixed episode The display of manic symptoms during a depressed mood.

M'Naghten Rule The strict insanity defense established in British law in the 19th century and adopted by many American states; under this rule, a person is deemed insane and not responsible for criminal behavior if he or she is suffering from a mental disorder and also unable to tell right from wrong.

modeling Learning by observation; a type of indirect conditioning.

monoamine oxidase (MAO) inhibitor A drug, such as reserpine or iproniazid, that regulates neurotransmitter reuptake and can be effective against depression; now largely replaced by less dangerous antidepressant drugs.

mood A period dominated by a specific emotion.

mood disorders Disorders characterized by persistent extremes of mood, ranging from depression to mania, that affect social and occupational functioning.

moral insanity A term used by British psychiatrists in the 19th century for an inherited illness that causes people to act in an antisocial fashion even when they appear to be normal.

moral treatment Treatment of mental disorders originated by Quaker philanthropist William Tuke in the late 18th century. The treatment involved kindness, comfort, calm, and inculcation of the Protestant work ethic coupled with manual work, organized recreation, establishment of healthy habits, and removal from the normal environment.

motor skills disorder Below-expected motor coordination skills marked by delays in walking and other motor skills, clumsiness, and poor handwriting that are not due to a medical condition; usually diagnosed in childhood.

multiaxial classification system A system, such as that used in the *DSM*, that bases a diagnosis on several axes, each of which represents a different type of information, such as the person's primary clinical diagnosis, any existing personality disorders, nonpsychiatric medical conditions, psychosocial or environmental problems, and a global assessment of psychological functioning.

multimodal treatment Treatment for substance dependence that combines several different methods, such as weaning people away from a substance, helping them manage their craving, and giving them skills to cope with social stress, anxiety, and other potential causes of substance abuse.

multiple-baseline experiment An experiment that measures several independent behaviors in the baseline phase to demonstrate a functional relationship between a treatment intervention and a behavior; useful in cases where it is undesirable to reverse a treatment effect, as in an ABAB experiment.

Munchausen syndrome A factitious disorder in which people go from hospital to hospital pretending to be ill in order to gain attention; in some cases, parents use their children as proxies for their own factitious disorder.

narcissistic personality disorder A Cluster B personality disorder characterized by a strong sense of superiority, grandiosity in fantasy or behavior, need for admiration, and lack of empathy beginning in early childhood; underlying these characteristics is a strong sense of self-doubt.

narcolepsy A dyssomnia characterized by irresistible "sleep attacks."

neurofibrillary tangles Disorganized tangles of neurofibrils, the narrow fibers within neurons that provide structural support and assist in transporting neurotransmitters and other chemicals. This brain abnormality is commonly found in the hippocampus and cerebral cortex of people with Alzheimer's disease.

neuroleptic drug A drug that acts on the nerves; an antipsychotic drug.

neuropsychological tests   Tests used to help clinicians make diagnoses and to assess the effects of treatment on people who have sustained head injuries, suffered strokes, developed degenerative diseases or cancer; who engage in substance abuse; or who have otherwise sustained organic brain damage.

neuroses   Distressing mental or behavioral symptoms that do not involve a break with reality. Freud originally characterized these as psychological disorders caused by anxiety, especially repressed sexual anxiety.

nicotine   A colorless, poisonous alkaloid, $C_{10}H_{14}N_2$, that is the primary psychoactive ingredient in tobacco and a stimulant so toxic that it is also used as a natural insecticide.

nightmare disorder   A developmental sleep disorder characterized by nightmares that are so frequent that they cause clinical distress or impair functioning.

normalization   The movement to deinstitutionalize people with mental retardation and to help them live as normal a life as possible at home and at school or in community-based facilities for adults.

nosology   A classification of diseases.

objective tests   Tests that are scored objectively (e.g., by counting) rather than interpreting responses, such as the Minnesota Multiphasic Personality Inventory (MMPI).

obsessions   Intrusive recurrent thoughts that seem irrational and uncontrollable to the individual experiencing them.

obsessive-compulsive disorder   An anxiety disorder characterized by intrusive recurrent thoughts (obsessions) or ritualistic actions (compulsions) or both.

obsessive-compulsive personality disorder   A Cluster C personality disorder characterized by a perfectionistic attitude toward daily life and a need to control one's routines and the behavior of other people; in females, sometimes found in conjunction with trichotillomania. A milder disorder than obsessive-compulsive disorder.

Oedipal conflict   In psychoanalytic theory, rivalry between son and father for mother's (wife's) love.

operant conditioning   A type of learning in which behaviors are reinforced or extinguished depending on their consequences; derived from the work of Edward L. Thorndike and B. F. Skinner. Also called instrumental conditioning.

opponent-process theory   The theory that any reaction to a stimulus is automatically followed by an opposite reaction (the opponent process) and that after repeated exposure to the stimulus, the opponent process becomes quicker and stronger. As applied to substance abuse, the initial reaction is the "high," and the opposite reaction is "crashing" and withdrawal symptoms.

oppositional defiant disorder   A developmental disorder characterized by a pattern of negativistic, hostile, and defiant behavior lasting at least 6 months.

pain disorder   A type of somatoform disorder in which the main physical complaint is pain.

panic attack   A period of intense fear or discomfort even though no objective threat is present.

panic disorder   An anxiety disorder characterized by fear of having panic attacks or being in places where panic attacks can occur.

paradigm   The conceptual framework within which a scientist works.

paradoxical intention   A therapeutic technique used in logotherapy (which was developed by Viktor Frankl) in which clients are directed to exaggerate their symptoms; they are not expected to carry out these instructions but rather to realize that they can control their symptoms rather than be controlled by them.

paranoid personality disorder   A Cluster A personality disorder whose defining feature is a pervasive distrust and suspiciousness of others; once viewed as a milder form of paranoid schizophrenia.

paranoid subtype   Schizophrenia whose main presenting feature is persecutory delusions or delusions of grandeur or both.

paraphilias   Sexual desires or acts that violate the norms of a culture. Paraphilias identified in the *DSM-IV* include exhibitionism, fetishism, frotteurism, pedophilia, sexual masochism, sexual sadism, transvestic fetishism, and voyeurism. Males are more likely than females to practice a paraphilia.

parasomnias   Abnormal behavioral or physiological events that occur during sleep, including nightmares, sleep terrors, and sleepwalking.

Parkinson's disease   A movement disorder characterized by tremors and jerky movements; caused by the destruction of dopamine-producing neurons.

passive-aggressive (or negativistic) personality disorder   A personality disorder being considered for possible inclusion in future editions of the *DSM;* the characteristic feature is negativistic attitudes and passive resistance to the demands of school and work by means of procrastination, "forgetfulness," stubbornness, and inefficiency.

pathological gambling   A common impulse-control disorder characterized by gambling despite personal loss and harm to one's family; whether this is really a disorder or simply irresponsible behavior has been the subject of controversy.

pedophilia   Fantasizing about or engaging in sexual activity with a prepubescent child; categorized as a paraphilia in *DSM-IV.*

performance anxiety   Fear of tests or speaking in front of other people ("stage fright"); in extreme cases, it can produce eating and sleeping disorders and make sufferers feel physically ill.

personality   According to the *DSM-IV,* a set of "enduring patterns of perceiving, relating to, and thinking about the environment and oneself, which are exhibited in a wide range of important social and personal contexts."

personality disorder   Maladaptive personality traits that negatively affect a person's life and that cause distress to self or others. According to the *DSM-IV,* personality disorders include paranoid personality, schizoid personality, schizotypal personality, antisocial personality, borderline personality,

histrionic personality, narcissistic personality, avoidant personality, dependent personality, and **obsessive-compulsive personality.**

personality traits Enduring aspects of personality.

phenothiazines Antipsychotic medications that can produce tremors and jerky movements and may reduce dopamine activity in the brain.

phenotype The way in which a genetic endowment is expressed physically.

phenylketonuria (PKU) An inherited metabolic defect causing difficulty in metabolizing the amino acid phenylalanine, an accumulation of which leads to severe mental retardation; can be controlled by eliminating phenylalanine from the diet.

physiognomy A pseudoscience, championed by Cesare Lombroso, based on the false idea that one's character can be determined by looking at the shape of one's facial features.

pica An eating disorder most often found among young children and pregnant women; it is characterized by persistent eating of nonnutritive substances, such as dirt, laundry starch, chalk, buttons, paper, cigarette butts, matches, sand, soap, and toothpaste.

Pick's disease Atrophy of the frontal and temporal lobes of the brain, which first appears after the age of 40; symptoms include the cognitive impairments usually associated with dementia as well as signs of frontal lobe damage, especially disinhibition.

placebo An inert substance used by the control group in an experiment testing the efficacy of another substance, such as a drug.

pleasure principle In psychoanalytic theory, the principle that rules the id and requires that biological needs, such as hunger, thirst, and sex, be immediately satisfied.

polygenic A disorder, such as schizophrenia, that is due to the interaction of two or more genes.

polygraph Commonly known as a *lie detector* (a term coined by William Marston, the creator of *Wonder Woman* comics), this device simultaneously measures respiration rate, heart rate, and several other forms of physiological activity.

polysubstance abuse The abuse of several substances.

positron emission tomography (PET) An imaging technique that shows the metabolic activity of radioactive glucose; used to provide images of brain function.

postpartum depression Depression whose onset occurs in the 4 weeks following childbirth; usually mild and brief, but intense episodes are possible and may be due to other pre-existing factors, including low self-esteem; a diagnostic specifier for a type of mood disorder.

post-traumatic stress disorder An anxiety disorder that is a long-term response to a traumatic incident, characterized by anxiety, emotional numbness, and the continual reliving of the traumatic event.

postvention Techniques aimed at helping relatives and friends of a suicide victim cope with their grief.

preconscious The part of mental functioning containing material that is not in immediate awareness but is available when needed, such as telephone numbers.

predictive validity The correlation of psychological tests with future behavior.

predictive value The ratio of true-positives to all positive results of a test.

premature ejaculation A sexual dysfunction characterized by orgasm after a brief period of stimulation.

premenstrual dysphoric disorder A depressed mood that seems to recur at the same time during each menstrual cycle; a disorder being considered for inclusion in the next *DSM*.

presentism The imposition of the standards of one civilization or generation on an earlier era.

prevalence The frequency of occurrence of a particular trait or behavior in a population; also known as base rate.

primary gain Keeping unacceptable conflicts at bay; a possible purpose of conversion disorders.

primary insomnia A dyssomnia characterized by difficulty in initiating or maintaining sleep or by having sleep that is not perceived as restful.

primary reinforcers Things that meet an organism's most basic needs, such as food, air, and water.

primary-process thinking Wish-fulfilling fantasies that provide a temporary solution to meeting biological needs, such as hunger, thirst, and sex.

proband A person with the disorder under investigation.

problem-focused coping Making a plan of action and dealing directly with a stressor.

prodromal phase of psychosis The first phase of schizophrenia, which precedes the disorder and is marked by a deterioration of functioning and negative symptoms, such as flattened affect or social withdrawal; patients may be aware that they are acting strangely.

prognosis A prediction about the course or outcome of a disorder.

projective personality tests Tests of personality traits based on the assumption that people project their unconscious drives, feelings, wishes, and conflicts onto the "screen" provided by ambiguous stimuli. The best-known test is the Rorschach inkblot test developed by Hermann Rorschach.

pseudodementia Symptoms of dementia (such as withdrawal from normal activities, loss of interest in everyday life, difficulty concentrating or sleeping, and confused, slow thought and speech) that are actually due to depression.

psychiatric nurse A nurse who has studied aspects of psychology and psychiatry and has experience working in psychiatric wards. These nurses, like psychiatrists, tend to view behavioral problems as analogous to medical illnesses.

psychiatrist An MD who has experience in the treatment of mental disorders and who is licensed by the state to practice medicine and certified by a professional board of psychiatry.

Psychiatrists conceptualize psychological problems as "illnesses" or "disorders."

psychoactive substance   A chemical that alters moods or behavior.

psychoanalyst   A mental health professional who is trained in the specific approach to treatment known as psychoanalysis, which is derived from the writings of Sigmund Freud. Psychoanalysis can be practiced by qualified psychiatrists, psychologists, and others. Psychoanalysts view behavioral problems as the result of unconscious conflicts arising from early childhood experiences.

psychological assessment   Psychologists' gathering of data about a client by tests, observations, interviews, and histories and their integrating and interpreting those data.

psychological autopsy   Interviews with a victim's friends and relatives to investigate whether the cause of death was suicide.

psychometrics   The science of psychological measurement.

psychoneuroimmunology   The study of the interactions among behavior, neurological and endocrine function, and the immune process.

psychopath   A person who has inherited the predilection to engage in criminal behavior; derived from Emil Kraepelin's term *constitutional psychopathic inferiority*.

psychopathology   The study of the origins, development, and symptoms of mental disorders.

psychophysiological disorders   Physical illnesses in whose etiology psychological factors play a significant role; also known as psychosomatic disorders.

psychoses   Disorders characterized by gross distortions of reality.

psychosomatic disorders   Physical illnesses in whose etiology psychological factors play a significant role; also known as psychophysiological disorders.

psychotherapy   Psychological treatment of maladaptive behavior.

psychotic features   Severe delusions or hallucinations; a diagnostic specifier for mood disorders.

pyromania   An impulse-control disorder characterized by the need to set fires in order to relieve tension and feel pleasure.

rapid eye movement (REM) sleep   The period of sleep when most dreams occur.

rapport   A warm and trusting relationship; the ideal for therapists and clients.

rational-emotive therapy   A type of therapy developed by Albert Ellis to expose and challenge irrational beliefs (or attributions) about oneself. It uses logical argument, modeling, and a variety of other techniques.

reactive attachment disorder of infancy or early childhood   According to *DSM-IV*, a developmental disorder caused by pathogenic care and characterized by a disturbance before the age of 5 in the ability to form attachments. In the inhibited subtype, children fail to develop strong attachments; in the disinhibited subtype, children form numerous superficial attachments but no strong primary attachment.

reactive measure   A response to self-monitoring (or to other experimental or assessment situations) that can affect behavior.

reliability   The extent to which a test yields consistent results.

repression   A defense mechanism used to keep traumatic and disturbing memories unconscious.

residual phase or **subtype**   Negative or mildly positive symptoms following the active phase of a schizophrenic episode; the third phase of schizophrenia.

response prevention   A behavioral treatment for obsessive-compulsive and somatoform disorders in which clients are exposed to anxiety-producing stimuli but prevented from performing their usual response. Because their anxiety is not reinforced by any harm coming to them, their anxiety can be extinguished.

Rett's disorder   A pervasive developmental disorder that involves the loss of previously acquired motor skills but is noted earlier than childhood disintegrative disorder; a physical characteristic is deceleration of head growth between ages 5 months and 48 months.

risk factors   Factors (such as genetic background, childhood experiences, drug abuse) that increase a person's chances of developing a particular disorder or contracting a particular disease.

rumination disorder   An eating disorder first noted in infancy or early childhood; it is characterized by regurgitation of food when the regurgitation is not due to a medical condition.

scaffolding   The use of assistive techniques and technologies to help children with mental retardation and learning disabilities perform at a higher level; examples for children with communication problems include sign language and computerized spell checkers, speech synthesizers, and talking calculators.

schizoaffective disorder   A disorder characterized by a combination of schizophrenic symptoms and mood disorder.

schizoid personality disorder   A Cluster A personality disorder whose defining features are the lack of social relationships and restricted emotional expression, which cause the individual distress, rather than delusion, obsession, or thought disorder; once described as "simple schizophrenia."

schizophrenia   The most common psychotic disorder; a split among cognitions within a single personality, characterized by a combination of hallucinations, delusions, disorganized speech, and odd motor movements. There are five subtypes: paranoid, disorganized, catatonic, undifferentiated, and residual.

schizophreniform disorder   A disorder with symptoms similar to schizophrenia but with a shorter duration.

schizotypal personality disorder   A Cluster A personality disorder whose defining feature is acute discomfort with and a reduced capacity for social relationships, accompanied by eccentric behaviors, peculiar thoughts, rambling speech, and odd appearance; similar to schizophreniform disorder.

seasonal affective disorder (SAD) A mood disorder characterized by seasonal depression, usually in winter, when there is less daylight.

secondary gain Symptoms reinforced or maintained because of the sympathy and attention they elicit.

secondary-process thinking In Freudian theory, the cognitive operation of the ego, which includes assessing new situations, anticipating future events, and working toward a goal.

selective mutism A developmental disorder characterized by consistent failure to speak in specific social situations despite speaking in other situations; does not apply to children (such as new immigrants) who are uncomfortable with the local language.

selective serotonin reuptake inhibitors (SSRIs) Antidepressant drugs (such as fluoxetine) that specifically block the reuptake of serotonin.

self-actualization The development of all aspects of the personality to their highest potential; a goal of Carl Jung's analytical psychology.

self-concept The sum total of a person's needs, plans, desires, values, perceptions, and memories.

self-modeling A therapeutic technique in which a patient's behavior in a comfortable situation is spliced into a similar but uncomfortable one by means of a video- or an audiotape; the patient thus becomes his or her own model, whose appropriate behavior is rewarded by the therapist.

self-monitoring Counting the number of times that one engages in a behavior and noting one's feelings or cognitions at the time; an important element of almost all behavioral assessment.

sensate focus A sex therapy technique that requires that partners take turns actively stimulating each other but refrain from sexual intercourse and focus instead on the pleasurable feelings being induced.

separation anxiety disorder Developmentally inappropriate and excessive anxiety about separation from home or from primary caregivers that negatively affects social and academic functioning.

sex addiction Inability to inhibit sexual behavior (reflected in multiple affairs, frequent masturbation, excessive use of prostitutes, or frequent paraphiliac behavior) even in the face of adverse consequences; not recognized by the *DSM-IV* as a distinct psychological disorder.

sex therapy Skill-based treatment techniques for sexual dysfunctions; developed by William Masters and Virginia Johnson.

sexology The scientific study of human sexual behavior.

sexual aversion disorder A sexual dysfunction characterized by fear and disgust at the thought of genital contact.

sexual dysfunctions Difficulties in performing sexual acts. These dysfunctions include disorders of desire and arousal, orgasmic disorders, and sexual pain disorders.

sexual masochism A paraphilia in which sexual activity involves real or imagined humiliation and suffering; the only paraphilia practiced by a significant number of females.

sexual sadism A paraphilia that involves fantasizing about or inflicting suffering or humiliation for sexual satisfaction.

shared psychotic disorder A disorder characterized by two or more people sharing a similar delusion; formerly known as *folie à deux.*

single photon emission computerized tomography (SPECT) An imaging technique that produces topographic maps of brain activity during cognition by monitoring blood flow from different areas of the brain.

single-subject experimental designs Experimental designs that measure behavior change in a single subject rather than in groups of subjects.

sleep terror disorder A developmental sleep disorder characterized by 15- to 30-minute episodes of terror and disorientation following a nightmare.

sleepwalking disorder A developmental sleep disorder characterized by unconsciously walking in one's sleep.

social phobia An anxiety disorder characterized by excessive fear of situations in which one may be evaluated by others; an exaggerated form of performance anxiety.

social stress theory The theory that poor people are exposed to more economic and social problems than are those who are better off; these problems produce extra stress, which, in turn, can be a causal factor in mental disorders.

social worker An MSW who is trained in social policy, sociology, interviewing, and counseling. A social worker's main goal is to integrate people into their communities. Social workers emphasize interpersonal causes of problem behavior.

sociopathic personality A person who engages in criminal behavior due to social factors such as discrimination, deprivation, and poor role models.

somatization disorder A psychological disorder characterized by a history of at least eight physical complaints spanning several bodily systems that cannot be attributed to a medical condition or substance abuse and are not consciously feigned.

somatoform disorders Disorders marked by physical symptoms, in the absence of obvious physical illness, that mimic those produced by physical disease.

SORC analysis Acronym summarizing the information that is essential for a behavioral analysis: the stimuli (S) that elicit the maladaptive behavior; organismic (O), or individual, characteristics that may affect the behavior; responses (R), the problem behaviors themselves; and the consequences (C), positive and negative, that follow the problem behavior.

special education A heterogeneous group of techniques (such as behavior modification, cognitive interventions, and drugs) used to help retarded and learning disabled children reach their goals.

specific phobia An anxiety disorder characterized by a fear of specific objects, organisms, or situations out of proportion to any objective threat.

specificity theory of psychosomatic illness   The theory that certain illnesses are related to specific personality types and that specific unconscious conflicts produce specific diseases; developed by Helen Flanders Dunbar and Franz Alexander.

St. Vitus' dance   A "dancing mania" recorded in medieval Europe and institutionalized in the 16th century as an annual event believed to protect dancers from illness. The term is used today to describe the odd muscle movements that accompany some forms of brain disorder, especially brain damage caused by high fevers.

standardization   The process by which tests are administered to a representative sample of the general population to develop norms that represent the distribution of scores in the population.

state-dependent learning   Learning that becomes associated with the conditions in which it occurred and that is best recalled when the individual is again in that state. For example, learning that takes place when a person is inebriated may be best recalled when the person drinks alcohol.

stimulant   A psychoactive chemical that increases alertness; examples include amphetamines, caffeine, cocaine, and nicotine.

stress   A general term for any stimulus or event that has (or is perceived to have) the potential to disrupt our equilibrium.

stress management   Various approaches to reducing stress. Direct approaches teach relaxation and other stress reduction skills; indirect reactions attempt to change cognitions and behaviors.

stressor   Anything that triggers stress, including physical threats, emotional experiences, unpleasant internal states, and the subjective feeling of being under pressure.

stroke   Interruption of the blood supply to a part of the brain, usually caused by a blood clot.

structured interview   An interview composed of questions that have been prepared in advance. Because of the uniformity of these interviews, they can be used before and after treatment to gauge the treatment's effectiveness.

subcortical dementia   Dementia characterized by psychomotor slowness and a memory defect; accompanies about one third of Parkinson's disease cases.

substance abuse disorder   Recurrent substance use that leads to significant impairment or distress.

substance dependence disorder   Chronic substance abuse that leads to a craving that profoundly shapes one's life. *Addiction* is an overused synonym.

substance intoxication disorder   A syndrome produced by exposure to a psychoactive substance; it may include mood lability, belligerence, cognitive impairment, and impaired social or occupational functioning.

substance-induced anxiety disorder   An anxiety disorder caused by using drugs or other substances.

substance-induced disorders   Intoxication, withdrawal syndromes, and sleep and anxiety disorders caused by the use of certain psychoactive substances.

substance-induced persisting dementia   Dementia caused by drugs or poisons that persists even after the substance is withdrawn.

substance use disorders   Substance abuse and substance dependence disorders, in contrast to substance-induced disorders.

suicidology   The scientific study of suicide.

superego   In psychoanalytic theory, the part of the adult personality that consists of an internalized moral code similar to a conscience.

supported employment   Adapting regular workplaces for the needs of mentally retarded and learning disabled workers rather than segregating them in sheltered workshops.

symptom-substitution hypothesis   According to psychoanalytic theory, if a symptom is treated without eliminating the underlying conflict, the conflict will simply manifest itself in the form of new symptoms.

syndrome   A group of symptoms that occur together, characterizing a specific condition or disorder.

systematic desensitization   A behavioral treatment for fears that gradually exposes people to feared situations at the same time that they are engaging in relaxation; developed by Joseph Wolpe.

tardive dyskinesia   An iatrogenic (medication-caused) movement disorder whose symptoms include facial grimaces, jerky movements, lip chewing, and other tics and odd movements; a side effect of long-term treatment of schizophrenia with neuroleptic drugs.

teratogenic agents   Drugs and other substances introduced during pregnancy that can produce fetal malformations.

test sensitivity   The probability of a true-positive result of a test.

test specificity   The probability of a true-negative result of a test.

THC   The abbreviation for delta-9-tetrahydrocannabinol, the psychoactive ingredient in marijuana; produces distorted sensations and perceptions, or hallucinations.

tic   A sudden and recurrent involuntary motor movement or vocalization.

tolerance   After repeated use, the need for increasing amounts of a psychoactive substance to achieve the desired effect.

Tourette's disorder   A tic disorder that begins in childhood and is characterized by multiple motor tics (sudden repetitive but irregular movements) and by strange utterances, which are exacerbated by stress; may be a genetically transmitted dominant trait caused by an excess of dopamine.

transference   The tendency for patients to transfer their habitual modes of interpersonal behavior to the therapist.

transitional stress   Stress due to the adjustments required by the transition from one developmental stage to another.

transvestic fetishism   A paraphilia practiced by heterosexual males who dress in women's clothing for sexual pleasure.

trichotillomania   An impulse-control disorder characterized by the pulling out of one's scalp, facial, or body hair; more common among women than men; a type of compulsion, but not the same as obsessive-compulsive disorder, and not associated with an obsession.

tricyclic antidepressants   One of several classes of antidepressant medications. An example is imipramine.

trisomy 21   A genetic defect (the triplication of the 21st chromosome) causing Down syndrome.

true-positives   Accurate test results (person who scores positive actually is positive). (Compare **false-positives.**)

two-process theory of avoidance learning   Avoidance learning that is based on both classical and instrumental conditioning.

Type A behavior   Unusually impatient, competitive, short-tempered behavior, some of the aspects of which may be risk factors.

unconditional positive regard   In Carl Rogers's client-centered therapy, the principle that individuals must be respected as people no matter how they behave.

unconditioned response (UCR)   In classical conditioning, the automatic (unlearned) response to the unconditioned stimulus.

unconditioned stimulus (UCS)   In classical conditioning, a stimulus that automatically (without any training) produces a specific unconditioned response.

unconscious   Mental functioning and materials (such as memories) that are out of immediate awareness.

undifferentiated somatoform disorder   A psychological disorder characterized by one or two physical complaints that cannot be attributed to a medical condition or to substance abuse and are not consciously feigned.

unipolar mood disorder   A mood disorder characterized by depressive episodes but not manic ones.

utilitarianism   A philosophy developed by the 18th-century philosopher Jeremy Bentham, who advocated social policies that led to "the greatest good for the greatest number."

utility   Subjective value of decision outcomes.

vaginismus   A sexual dysfunction characterized by involuntary contraction of the vaginal muscles that interferes with penetration and intercourse.

validity   The extent to which a test really measures what it is purported to measure.

variable expressivity   Variations in the degree to which a genotype for a particular characteristic is expressed in the phenotype; also called incomplete penetrance.

vascular dementia   Dementia cause by arteriosclerosis or a stroke (infarct or aneurysm cutting off the blood supply to a part of the brain).

voyeurism   A paraphilia in which sexual fulfillment and excitement are gained by watching unsuspecting people disrobe or engage in sex.

withdrawal syndrome   Physical reactions when withdrawing from a substance to which one has become addicted; irritability, restlessness, distractibility, and hunger in the case of nicotine withdrawal; tremor, sweating, nausea, and anxiety in the case of alcohol withdrawal.

References

Abadinsky, H. (1993). *Drug abuse: An introduction* (2nd ed.). Chicago: Nelson-Hall.

Abbey, S. E., & Garfinkel, P. E. (1991). Neurasthenia and chronic fatigue syndrome: The role of culture in the making of a diagnosis. *American Journal of Psychiatry, 148,* 1638–1646.

Abbott, R. D., Yin, Y., Reed, D. M., & Yano, K. (1986). Risk of stroke in male cigarette smokers. *New England Journal of Medicine, 315,* 717–720.

Abe, K., Oda, N., Ikenaga, K., & Yamada, T. (1993). Twin study on night terrors, fears and some physiological and behavioral characteristics in childhood. *Psychiatric Genetics, 3*(1), 39–43.

Abel, G. G., Rouleau, J., & Cunningham-Rathner, J. (1986). Sexually aggressive behavior. In W. J. Curran, A. L. McGarry, & S. Shah (Eds.), *Forensic psychiatry and psychology: Perspectives and standards for interdisciplinary practice* (pp. 289–314). Philadelphia: Davis.

Abel, J. L. (1993). Exposure with response prevention and serotonergic antidepressants in the treatment of obsessive-compulsive disorder: A review and implications for interdisciplinary treatment. *Behaviour Research and Therapy, 31,* 463–478.

Abrams, R., Swartz, C. M., & Vedak, C. (1991). Antidepressant effects of high-dose right unilateral electroconvulsive therapy. *Archives of General Psychiatry, 48*(8), 746–748.

Abwender, D. A., Trinidad, K. S., Jones, K. R., et al. (1998). Features resembling Tourette's syndrome in developmental stutterers. *Brain and Language, 62,* 455–464.

Accessibility to minors of cigarettes from vending machines—Broward County, Florida, 1996. (1996, Nov. 29). *Morbidity and Mortality Weekly Report (MMWR), 45*(47), 1036–1038 [Published erratum appears in *MMWR,* 1996, Dec. 6, *45*(48), 1060].

Achenbach, T. M. (1991). *Manual for the Child Behavior Checklist and 1991 profile.* Burlington, VT: University of Vermont, Dept. of Psychiatry.

Achenbach, T. M., & McConaughy, S. H. (1996). *Empirically based assessment of child and adolescent psychopathology: Practical applications* (2nd ed.). Newbury Park, CA: Sage.

Acklin, M. W. (1995). Integrative Rorschach interpretation. *Journal of Personality Assessment, 64*(2), 235–238.

Acklin, M. W., McDowell, C. J., II, & Orndoff, S. (1992). Statistical power and the

Rorschach: 1975–1991. *Journal of Personality Assessment, 59,* 366–379.

Adams, P. R., & Adams, G. R. (1984). Mount Saint Helens' ashfall: Evidence for a disaster stress reaction. *American Psychologist, 39,* 252–260.

Adams, S. G., Jr., Dammers, P. M., Saia, T. L., et al. (1994). Stress, depression, and anxiety predict average symptom severity and daily symptom fluctuation in systemic lupus erythematosus. *Journal of Behavioral Medicine, 17*(5), 459–477.

Adams, W., et al. (1993). Epidemiological evidence that maternal influenza contributes to the aetiology of schizophrenia: An analysis of Scottish, English, and Danish data. *British Journal of Psychiatry, 163,* 522–534.

Adelman, P. K., & Zajonc, R. B. (1989). Facial efference and the experience of emotion. *Annual Review of Psychology, 40,* 249–280.

Ader, R., & Cohen, N. (1975). Behaviorally conditioned immunosuppression. *Psychosomatic Medicine, 37,* 333–340.

Ader, R., & Cohen, N. (1993). Psychoneuroimmunology: Conditioning and stress. *Annual Review of Psychology, 44,* 53–85.

Adler, L. L., & Denmark, F. L. (Eds.). (1995). *Violence and the prevention of violence.* Westport, CT: Praeger.

Adler, N., Boyce, T., Chesney, M. A., et al. Socioeconomic status and health: The challenge of the gradient. *American Psychologist, 49,* 15–24.

Adler, T. (1990). Does the "new" MMPI beat the "classic"? *APA Monitor, 20,* 18–19.

Agarwal, D. P., & Goedde, H. W. (1991). The role of alcohol metabolizing enzymes in alcohol sensitivity, alcohol drinking habits, and incidence of alcoholism in Orientals. In T. N. Palmer (Ed.), *The molecular pathology of alcoholism: Molecular medicine* (pp. 211–237). Oxford, UK: Oxford University Press.

The age of Ritalin. (1998, Nov. 30). *Time,* p. 86.

Aiken, L. R. (1989). *Assessment of personality.* Boston: Allyn & Bacon.

Akbarian, S., Vinuela, A., Kim, J. J., et al. (1993). Distorted distribution of nicotinamide-adenine dinucleotide phosphate-diaphorase neurones in temporal lobe of schizophrenics implies anomalous cortical development. *Archives of General Psychiatry, 50*(3), 178–187.

Albano, A. M., & Barlow, D. H. (1996). Breaking the vicious cycle: Cognitive-behavioral group treatment for socially anxious youth. In E. D. Hibbs & P. S.

Jensen (Eds.), *Psychosocial treatments for child and adolescent disorders: Empirically based strategies for clinical practice* (pp. 43–62). Washington, DC: American Psychological Association.

Albano, A. M., Marten, P. A., Holt, C. S., et al. (1995). Cognitive-behavioral group treatment for social phobia in adolescents: A preliminary study. *Journal of Nervous and Mental Disease, 183*(10), 649–656.

Alden, L. E., Teschuk, M., & Tee, K. (1992). Public self-awareness and withdrawal from social interactions. *Cognitive Therapy and Research, 16,* 249–267.

Aldridge J., & Measham, F. (1999). Sildenafil (Viagra) is used as a recreational drug in England. *British Medical Journal, 318,* 669.

Alexander, P. J., Joseph, S., & Das, A. (1997). Limited utility of *ICD-10* and *DSM-IV* classification of dissociative and conversion disorders in India. *Acta Psychiatrica Scandinavica, 95*(3), 177–182.

Alford, B. A., & Beck, A. T. (1997). *The integrative power of cognitive therapy.* New York: Guilford Press.

Al-Issa, I. (1982). Does culture make a difference in psychopathology? In I. Al-Issa (Ed.), *Culture and psychopathology* (pp. 3–29). Baltimore: University Park Press.

Allen, I. V. (Ed.). (1993). *Spongiform encephalopathies.* Edinburgh, Scot.: Churchill Livingstone.

Allen, J. P., Moore C., Kuperminc, G., & Bell, K. (1998). Attachment and adolescent psychosocial functioning. *Child Development, 69,* 1406–1419.

Alleridge, P. (1985). Bedlam: Fact or fantasy? In W. F. Bynum, R. Porter, & M. Shepherd (Eds.), *The anatomy of madness: Vol. 2* (pp. 17–33). London: Tavistock.

Allgood-Merten, B., Lewinsohn, P. M., & Hops, H. (1990). Sex differences in adolescent depression. *Journal of Abnormal Psychology, 99,* 55–63.

Alloy, L. B., Kelley, K. A., Mineka, S., & Clements, C. M. (1990). Comorbidity, in anxiety and depressive disorders: A helplessness/hopelessness perspective. In J. D. Maser & C. R. Cloninger (Eds.), *Comorbidity in anxiety and mood disorders.* Washington, DC: American Psychiatric Press.

Alloy, L. B., Lipman, A. J., & Abramson, L. Y. (1992). Attributional style as a vulnerability factor for depression. *Cognitive Therapy and Research, 16,* 391–407.

Alpert, J. E., Uebelacker, L. A., McLean, N. E., et al. (1997). Social phobia, avoidant personality disorder and atypical depression: Co-occurrence and clinical implications. *Psychological Medicine, 27,* 627–633.

Altemus, M., Pigott, T., L'Heureux, F., et al. (1993). CSF somatostatin in obsessive-compulsive disorder. *American Journal of Psychiatry, 150*(3), 460–464.

Alterman, A. I., O'Brien, C. P., McLellan, A. T., et al. (1994). Effectiveness and costs of inpatient versus day hospital cocaine rehabilitation. *Journal of Nervous and Mental Disease, 182*(3), 157–163.

Altman, D. G., Foster, V., Rasenick-Douss, L., & Tye, J. B. (1989). Reducing the illegal sale of cigarettes to minors. *Journal of the American Medical Association, 261,* 80–83.

Altura, B. T., & Altura, B. M. (1981). Phencyclidine, lysergic acid diethylamide, and mescaline: Cerebral artery spasms and hallucinogenic activity. *Science, 212,* 1051–1052.

Amen, D. G. (1999). *Change your brain, change your life.* New York: Times Books.

American Association on Mental Retardation (AAMR). (1992). *Mental retardation: Definition, classification, and systems of support* (9th ed.). Washington, DC: Author.

American Medical Association Council on Scientific Affairs. (1990). The worldwide smoking epidemic: Tobacco, trade, use, and control. *Journal of the American Medical Association, 263,* 3312–3318.

American Psychiatric Association. (1952). *Diagnostic and statistical manual of mental disorders.* Washington, DC: Author.

American Psychiatric Association. (1968). *Diagnostic and statistical manual of mental disorders* (2nd ed.). Washington, DC: Author.

American Psychiatric Association. (1980). *Diagnostic and statistical manual of mental disorders* (3rd ed.). Washington, DC: Author.

American Psychiatric Association. (1987). *Diagnostic and statistical manual of mental disorders* (3rd ed., rev.). Washington, DC: Author.

American Psychiatric Association. (1991). *DSM-IV options book: Work in progress.* Washington, DC: Author.

American Psychiatric Association. (1994). *Diagnostic and statistical manual of mental disorders* (4th ed.). Washington, DC: Author.

American Psychological Association. (1986). *Guidelines for computer-based tests and interpretations.* Washington, DC: Author.

American Psychological Association. (1990). Ethical principles of psychologists. *American Psychologist, 45,* 390–395.

Amin, F., Siever, L. J., Silverman, J., et al. (1997). Plasma HVA in schizotypal personality disorder. In A. J. Friedhoff & F. Amin (Eds.), *Plasma homovanillic acid in schizophrenia: Implications for presynaptic*

dopamine dysfunction. Progress in psychiatry (pp. 133–149). Washington, DC: American Psychiatric Press.

Ammerman, R. T., & Hersen, M. (1992). *Assessment of family violence.* New York: Wiley.

Ammon, H. P. (1991). Biochemical mechanism of caffeine tolerance. *Archiv Der Pharmazie, 324*(5), 261–267.

Anastopoulos, A. D., Shelton, T. L., DuPaul, G. J., & Guevremont, D. C. (1993). Parent training for attention-deficit hyperactivity disorder: Its impact on parent functioning. *Journal of Abnormal Child Psychology, 21,* 581–596.

Andersen, A. E., Bowers, W., & Evans, K. (1997). Inpatient treatment of anorexia nervosa. In D. M. Garner & P. E. Garfinkel (Eds.), *Handbook of treatment for eating disorders* (2nd ed.) (pp. 327–353). New York: Guilford Press.

Andersen, A. E., & DiDomenico, L. (1992). Diet vs shape content of popular male and female magazines: A dose response relationship to the incidence of eating disorders? *International Journal of Eating Disorders, 11,* 283–287.

Andersen, B. L., & Cyranowski, J. M. (1995). Women's sexuality: Behaviors, responses, and individual differences. *Journal of Consulting and Clinical Psychology, 63,* 891–906.

Andersen, B. L., Kiecolt-Glaser, J. K., & Glaser, R. (1994). A biobehavioral model of cancer stress and disease course. *American Psychologist, 49*(5), 389–404.

Anderson, L. P. (1991). Acculturative stress: A theory of relevance to Black Americans. *Clinical Psychology Review, 11,* 685–702.

Anderson, R. M. (1994). *Practitioner's guide to clinical neuropsychology.* New York: Plenum.

Andreasen, N. C. (1984). *The broken brain.* New York: Harper & Row.

Andreasen, N. C. (1995). Posttraumatic stress disorder: Psychology, biology, and the Manichaean warfare between false dichotomies. *American Journal of Psychiatry, 152*(7), 963–965.

Andreasen, N. C. (1997). Linking mind and brain in the study of mental illnesses: A project for a scientific psychopathology. *Science, 275*(5306), 1586–1593.

Andreasen, N. C., & Carpenter, W. T., Jr. (1993). Diagnosis and classification of schizophrenia. *Schizophrenia Bulletin, 19,* 199–214.

Andreasen, N. C., Swayze, V. W., Flaum, M., et al. (1990). Ventricular enlargement in schizophrenia evaluated with computed tomographic scanning: Effects of gender, age, and stage of illness. *Archives of General Psychiatry, 47,* 1008–1015.

Anstey, K., & Brodaty, H. (1995). Antide-

pressants and the elderly: Double-blind trials 1987–1992. *International Journal of Geriatric Psychiatry, 10*(4), 265–279.

Antoni, M. H., Baggett, L., Ironson, G. I., et al. (1991). Cognitive-behavioral stress management intervention buffers distress responses and immunologic changes following notification of HIV-1 seropositivity. *Journal of Consulting and Clinical Psychology, 59*(6), 906–915.

Antony, M. M., Brown, T. A., Craske, M. G., et al. (1995). Accuracy of heartbeat perception in panic disorder, social phobia, and nonanxious subjects. *Journal of Anxiety Disorders, 9,* 355–371.

Apgar, V. (1953). A proposal for a new method of evaluation in the newborn infant. *Current Research in Anesthesia and Analgesia, 32,* 260.

Apter, A., Bleich, A., King, R. A., et al. (1993). Death without warning? A clinical postmortem study of suicide in 43 Israeli adolescent males. *Archives of General Psychiatry, 50,* 138–142.

Arana, G. W., Baldessarini, R. J., & Ornsteen, M. (1985). The dexamethasone suppression test for diagnosis and prognosis in psychiatry: Commentary and review. *Archives of General Psychiatry, 42,* 1193–1204.

Arendt, R. E., MacLean, W. E., Jr., & Baumeister, A. A. (1988). Critique of sensory integration therapy and its application in mental retardation. *American Journal on Mental Retardation, 92,* 401–411.

Aries, P. (1962). *Centuries of childhood: A social history of family life* (R. Baldick, Trans.). New York: Vintage Books.

Arieti, S. (1979). New views on the psychodynamics of phobias. *American Journal of Psychotherapy, 33,* 82–95.

Aronow, E., & Moreland, K. L. (1995). The Rorschach: Projective technique or psychometric test? *Journal of Personality Assessment, 64*(2), 213–228.

Aronow, E., Reznikoff, M., & Moreland, K. (1994). *The Rorschach technique: Perceptual basics, content interpretation, and applications.* Boston: Allyn & Bacon.

Asmundson, G. J. G., & Norton, G. R. (1993). Anxiety sensitivity and its relationship to spontaneous and cued panic attacks in college students. *Behaviour Research and Therapy, 31,* 199–201.

Assumpcao, F. B., Jr. (1998). Brief report: A case of chromosome 22 alteration associated with autistic syndrome. *Journal of Autism and Developmental Disorders, 28,* 253–256.

Attia, E., Haiman, C., Walsh, B. T., & Flater, S. R. (1998). Does fluoxetine augment the inpatient treatment of anorexia nervosa? *American Journal of Psychiatry, 155,* 548–551.

Attwood, T., & Wing, L. (1997). *Asperger's*

syndrome: A guide for parents and professionals. London: Jessica Kingsley.

Austin, L. S., Lydiard, R. B., Forey, M. D., & Zealberg, J. J. (1990). Panic and phobic disorders in patients with obsessive personality disorder. *Journal of Clinical Psychiatry, 51,* 456–458.

Australian Psychological Society Limited Board of Directors. (1994). *Guidelines relating to the reporting of recovered memories.* Sydney, NSW, Austral.: Author.

Ayuso-Gutierrez, J. L., Llorente, L. J., Ponce de Leon, C., & Ayuso-Mateos, J. L. (1993). HLA and panic disorder. *American Journal of Psychiatry, 150,* 838–839.

Azhar, M. Z., Varma, S. L., & Hakim, H. R. (1993). Phenomenological differences of hallucinations between schizophrenic patients in Penang and Kelantan. *Medical Journal of Malaysia, 48,* 146–152.

Bachman, J. G., Johnston, L. D., & O'Malley, P. M. (1993). *Monitoring the future: Questionnaire responses from the nation's high school seniors, 1992.* Ann Arbor, MI: Institute for Social Research.

Bach-y-Rita, P. (Ed.). (1987). *Recovery of function: Theoretical considerations for brain injury rehabilitation.* Lewiston, NY: Huber.

Backlar, P. (1998). Criminal behavior and mental disorder: Impediments to assigning moral responsibility. *Community Mental Health Journal, 34,* 3–12.

Baer, L., Jenike, M. A., Ricciardi, J. N., et al. (1990). Standardized assessment of personality disorders in obsessive-compulsive disorder. *Archives of General Psychiatry, 47,* 826–831.

Baer, L., Rauch, S. L., Ballantine, T., et al. (1995). Cingulotomy for intractable obsessive-compulsive disorder: Prospective long-term follow-up of 18 patients. *Archives of General Psychiatry, 52*(5), 384–392.

Bagley, C., & Tremblay, P. (1997). Suicidal behaviors in homosexual and bisexual males. *Crisis, 18,* 24–34.

Bakke, E. (1934). *The unemployed man.* New York: Dutton.

Bales, J. (1988, Dec.). *Vincennes. APA Monitor,* pp. 10–11.

Baltes, P. B. (1993). The ageing mind: Potential and limits. *Gerontologist, 33,* 580–594.

Balyk, E. D. (1997). Paraphilias as a subtype of obsessive-compulsive disorder: A hypothetical bio-social model. *Journal of Orthomolecular Medicine, 12,* 29–42.

Bandura, A. (1986). *Social foundations of thought and action: A social-cognitive theory.* Englewood Cliffs, NJ: Prentice-Hall.

Bandura, A., Adams, N. E., & Beyer, J. (1977). Cognitive processes mediating behavioral change. *Journal of Personality and Social Psychology, 35,* 125–139.

Bandura, A., O'Leary, A., Taylor, C. B., et al. (1987). Perceived self-efficacy and pain control: Opioid and nonopioid mecha-

nisms. *Journal of Personality and Social Psychology, 53,* 563–571.

Banks, S. M., & Kerns, R. D. (1996). Explaining high rates of depression in chronic pain: A diathesis-stress framework. *Psychological Bulletin, 119*(1), 95–110.

Barabasz, M., & Barabasz, A. (1996). Attention deficit disorder: Diagnosis, etiology and treatment. *Child Study Journal, 26,* 1–37.

Barahal, R. M., Waterman, J., & Martin, H. P. (1981). The social cognitive development of abused children. *Journal of Consulting and Clinical Psychology, 49,* 508–516.

Barber, M. E., Marzuk, P. M., Leon, A. C., et al. (1998). Aborted suicide attempts: A new classification of suicidal behavior. *American Journal of Psychiatry, 155,* 385–389.

Barcelo, F., & Gale, A. (1997). Electrophysiological measures of cognition in biological psychiatry: Some cautionary notes. *International Journal of Neuroscience, 92,* 219–240.

Barinaga, M. (1992). Pot, heroin unlock new areas for neuroscience. *Science, 258,* 1882–1884.

Barkley, R. A. (1990). Attention deficit disorders: History, definition, and diagnosis. In M. Lewis & S. M. Miller (Eds.), *Handbook of developmental psychopathology: Perspectives in developmental psychology* (pp. 65–75). New York: Plenum.

Barkley, R. A. (1996). Attention deficit/hyperactivity disorder. In E. J. Mash & R. A. Barkley (Eds.), *Child psychopathology* (pp. 63–112). New York: Guilford Press.

Barlow, D. H. (1988). *Anxiety and its disorders.* New York: Guilford Press.

Barlow, D. H., & Craske, M. G. (1994). *Mastery of your anxiety and panic* (MAP II). Albany, NY: Graywind.

Barlow, D. H., & Hersen, M. (1984). *Single case experimental designs.* New York: Pergamon.

Barlow, D. H., & Rapee, R. M. (1991). *Mastering stress: A lifestyle approach.* Dallas, TX: American Health Publishing.

Barlow, D. H., Rapee, R. M., & Brown, T. A. (1992). Behavioral treatment of generalized anxiety disorder. *Behavior Therapy, 23,* 551–570.

Baron, M. (1991). Genetics of manic depressive illness: Current status and evolving concepts. In P. R. McHugh & V. A. McKusick (Eds.), *Genes, brain, and behavior* (pp. 153–164). New York: Raven Press.

Baron, M., Risch, N., Hamburger, R., et al. (1987). Genetic linkage between X-chromosome markers and bipolar affective illness. *Nature, 326,* 289–292.

Baron-Cohen, S., (1995). *Mindblindness: An essay on autism and theory of mind.* Cambridge, MA: MIT Press.

Baron-Cohen, S. & Hammer, J. (1997). Parents of children with Asperger syndrome: What is the cognitive phenotype? *Journal of Cognitive Neuroscience, 9,* 548–554.

Baron-Cohen, S., Jolliffe, T., Mortimore, C., & Robertson, M. (1997). Another advanced test of theory of mind: Evidence from very high functioning adults with autism or Asperger syndrome. *Journal of Child Psychology and Psychiatry and Allied Disciplines, 38,* 813–822.

Barondes, S. H. (1993). *Molecules and mental illness.* New York: Scientific American Library.

Barr, C. E., Mednick, S. A., & Munk-Jorgensen, P. (1990). Exposure to influenza epidemics during gestation and adult schizophrenia: A 40-year study. *Archives of General Psychiatry, 47,* 869–874.

Barr, C. L., & Sandor, P. (1998). Current status of genetic studies of Gilles de la Tourette syndrome. *Canadian Journal of Psychiatry, 43,* 351–357.

Barrett, R. T. (1997). Making our own meanings: A critical review of media effects research in relation to the causation of aggression and social skills difficulties in children and anorexia nervosa in young women. *Journal of Psychiatric Mental Health Nursing, 4,* 179–183.

Barsky, A. J., Cleary, P. D., Sarnie, M. K., & Klerman, G. L. (1993). The course of transient hypochondriasis. *American Journal of Psychiatry, 150,* 484–488.

Barsky, A. J., Frank, C., Cleary, P., et al. (1991). The relation between hypochondriasis and age. *American Journal of Psychiatry, 148,* 923–928.

Barsky, A. J., Wyshak, G., & Klerman, G. L. (1992). Psychiatric comorbidity in *DSM-III-R* hypochondriasis. *Archives of General Psychiatry, 49,* 101–108.

Bartlett, D. L., & Steele, J. B. (1979). *Empire: The life, legend, and madness of Howard Hughes.* New York: Norton.

Bartlett, F. C. (1950). *Remembering.* Cambridge, UK: Cambridge University Press. (Original work published 1932)

Barton, M., & Volkmar, F. R. (1998). How commonly are known medical conditions associated with autism? *Journal of Autism and Developmental Disorders, 28,* 273–278.

Basedow, H. (1925). *The Australian aboriginal.* Adelaide, Austral.: F. W. Preece.

Basmajian, J. V. (1989). *Biofeedback: Principles and practice for clinicians.* Baltimore: Williams & Wilkins.

Bass, E., & Davis, L. (1988). *The courage to heal.* New York: Harper & Row.

Basso, M. R., Nasrallah, H. A., Olson, S. C., & Bornstein, R. A. (1997). Cognitive deficits distinguish patients with adolescent- and adult-onset schizophrenia. *Neuro-*

psychiatry, Neuropsychology, and Behavioral Neurology, 10(2), 107–112.

Bateson, G. (1959). Cultural problems posed by a study of the schizophrenic process. In A. Auerback (Ed.), *Schizophrenia: An integrated approach.* New York: Ronald Press.

Battaglia, M., Bernardeschi, L., Franchini, L., et al. (1995). A family study of schizotypal disorder. *Schizophrenia Bulletin, 21,* 33–45.

Battaglia, M., & Torgersen, S. (1996). Schizotypal disorder: At the crossroads of genetics and nosology. *Acta Psychiatrica Scandinavica, 94,* 303–310.

Baum, A., & Fleming, I. (1993). Implications of psychological research on stress and technological accidents. *American Psychologist, 48,* 665–672.

Bauman, M. L., Kemper, T. L., & Arin, D. M. (1995). Pervasive neuroanatomic abnormalities of the brain in three cases of Rett's syndrome. *Neurology, 45,* 1581–1586.

Baumeister, R. F., & Steinhilber, A. (1984). Paradoxical effects of supportive audiences on performance under pressure: The home field disadvantage in sports championships. *Journal of Personality and Social Psychology, 47,* 85–93.

Baumgarten, F. (1930). *Child prodigies: Psychological investigations.* Leipzig: Barth.

Baxter, L. R., Schwartz, J. M., Bergman, K. S., et al. (1992). Caudate glucose metabolic rate changes with both drug and behavior therapy for obsessive-compulsive disorder. *Archives of General Psychiatry, 49,* 681–689.

Baxter, L. R., Schwartz, J. M., Guze, B. H., et al. (1990). PET imaging in obsessive-compulsive disorder with and without depression. Symposium: Serotonin and its effects on human behavior (1989, Atlanta, GA). *Journal of Clinical Psychiatry, 51*(Suppl.), 61–69.

Bayer, R. (1981). *Homosexuality and American psychiatry.* New York: Basic Books.

Bayley, N. (1993). *Bayley Scales of Infant Development—2nd edition (BSID-II).* Lutz, FL: Psychological Assessment Resources.

Beardslee, W. R., Versage, E. M., & Gladstone, T. R. (1998). Children of affectively ill parents: A review of the past 10 years. *Journal of the American Academy of Child and Adolescent Psychiatry, 37,* 1134–1141.

Beats, B., Levy, R., & Forstl, H. (1991). Ventricular enlargement and caudate hyperdensity in elderly depressives. *Biological Psychiatry, 30*(5), 452–458.

Beauchemin, K. M., & Hays, P. (1997). Phototherapy is a useful adjunct in the treatment of depressed in-patients. *Acta Psychiatrica Scandinavica, 95*(5), 424–427.

Beauvais, P. (1996). Trends in drug use among American Indian students and dropouts, 1975–1994. *American Journal of Public Health, 86*(11), 1594–1598.

Bech, P. (1993). *Rating scales for psychopathology, health status, and quality of life.* New York: Springer-Verlag.

Beck, A. T. (1967). *Depression: Causes and treatment.* Philadelphia: University of Pennsylvania Press.

Beck, A. T. (1983). Cognitive therapy of depression: New perspectives. In P. J. Clayton & J. E. Barrett (Eds.), *Treatment of depression: Old controversies and new approaches.* New York: Raven Press.

Beck, A. T. (1991). Cognitive therapy: A 30-year perspective. *American Psychologist, 46,* 378–385.

Beck, A. T., & Clark, D. A. (1991). Anxiety and depression: An information processing perspective. In R. Schwarzer & R. A. Wicklund (Eds.), *Anxiety and self-focused attention* (pp. 41–54). London: Harwood Academic.

Beck, A. T., Emery, G., & Greenberg, R. L. (1985). *Anxiety disorders and phobias: A cognitive perspective.* New York: Basic Books.

Beck, A. T., Rush, A. J., Shaw, B. F., & Emery, G. (1979). *Cognitive therapy of depression.* New York: Guilford Press.

Beck, A. T., Steer, R., Kovacs, M., & Garrison, B. (1985). Hopelessness and eventual suicide: A 10-year prospective study of patients hospitalized with suicidal ideation. *American Journal of Psychiatry, 142,* 559–563.

Beck, A. T., & Steer, R. A. (1993). *Beck Depression Inventory* (rev. ed.). San Antonio, TX: Psychological Corporation.

Beck, S. J. (1961). *Rorschach's test.* New York: Grune & Stratton.

Becker, D. (1997). *Through the looking glass: Women and borderline personality disorder.* Boulder, CO: Westview Press.

Becker, R., Giacobini, E., & Barton, J. M. (Eds.). (1997). *Alzheimer's disease: From molecular biology to therapy.* Boston: Birkhauser.

Bekker, M. H. J. (1996). Agoraphobia and gender: A review. *Clinical Psychology Review, 16*(2), 129–146.

Belfer, P. L., & Glass, C. R. (1992). Agoraphobic anxiety and fear of fear: Test of a cognitive-attentional model. *Journal of Anxiety Disorders, 6,* 133–146.

Belitsky, C. A., Toner, B. B., Ali, A., et al. (1996). Sex-role attitudes and clinical appraisal in psychiatry residents. *Canadian Journal of Psychiatry, 41,* 503–508.

Bellack, A. S., & Hersen, M. (Eds.). (1988). *Behavioral assessment: A practical handbook.* New York: Pergamon.

Bellack, A. S., & Mueser, K. T. (1993). Psychosocial treatment for schizophrenia. *Schizophrenia Bulletin, 19,* 317–336.

Bellak, L. (1986). *The Thematic Apperception Test, the Children's Apperception Test, and the Senior Apperception Technique in clinical use* (4th ed.). Orlando: Academic Press.

Bellak, L. (1994). The schizophrenic syndrome and attention deficit disorder: Thesis, antithesis, and synthesis? *American Psychologist, 49*(1), 25–29.

Belsher, G., Wilkes, T. C. R., & Rush, A. J. (1995). An open multisite pilot study of cognitive therapy for depressed adolescents. *Journal of Psychotherapy Practice and Research, 4,* 52–66.

Benbow, C., & Lubinski, D. J. (Eds.). (1996). *Intellectual talent: Psychometric and social issues.* Baltimore: Johns Hopkins University Press.

Benca, R. M., Obermeyer, W. H., Thisted, R. A., & Gillin, J. C. (1992). Sleep and psychiatric disorders: A meta-analysis. *Archives of General Psychiatry, 49,* 651–668.

Bender, L. (1938). *A visual motor gestalt test and its clinical use.* New York: American Orthopsychiatric Association.

Bendetti, F., Sforzini, L., Colombo, C., et al. (1998). Low-dose clozapine in acute and continuation treatment of severe borderline personality disorder. *Journal of Clinical Psychiatry, 59,* 103–107.

Benedict, K. B., & Nacoste, D. B. (1990). Dementia and depression in the elderly: A framework for addressing difficulties in differential diagnosis. *Clinical Psychology Review, 10,* 513–537.

Benedict, R. (1934). *Patterns of culture.* Boston: Houghton Mifflin.

Bennett, P., Wallace, L., Carroll, D., & Smith, N. (1991). Treating type A behaviors and mild hypertension in middle-aged men. *Journal of Psychosomatic Research, 35,* 209–223.

Bennett, T. (1988). Use of the Halstead-Reitan Neuropsychological Test Battery in the assessment of head injury. *Cognitive Rehabilitation, 6,* 18–25.

Benowitz, N. (1990). Clinical pharmacology of caffeine. *Annual Review of Medicine, 41,* 277–288.

Bentall, R. P., & Pilgrim, D. (1993). Thomas Szasz, crazy talk and the myth of mental illness. *British Journal of Medical Psychology, 66,* 69–76.

Benton, M. K., & Schroeder, H. E. (1990). Social skills training with schizophrenics: A meta-analytic evaluation. *Journal of Consulting and Clinical Psychology, 58,* 741–747.

Berchick, R. J., & Wright, F. D. (1992). Guidelines for handling the suicidal patient: A cognitive perspective. In B. M. Bongar (Ed.), *Suicide: Guidelines for assessment, management, and treatment* (pp. 179–186). New York: Oxford University Press.

Berel, S., & Irving, L. M. (1998). Media and disturbed eating: An analysis of media influence and implications for prevention. *Journal of Primary Prevention, 18,* 415–430.

Berenbaum, H., & Oltmanns, T. F. (1992). Emotional experience and expression in schizophrenia and depression. *Journal of Abnormal Psychology, 101,* 37–44.

Berg, E. A. (1948). A simple objective test for measuring flexibility in thinking. *Journal of General Psychology, 39,* 15–22.

Bergman, A. J., Wolfson, M. A., & Walker, E. F. (1997). Neuromotor functioning and behavior problems in children at risk for psychopathology. *Journal of Abnormal Child Psychology, 25*(3), 229–237.

Bergner, M., Bobbit, R. A., Carter, W. B., & Gilson, B. S. (1981). The Sickness Impact Profile: Development and final revision of health status measure. *Medical Care, 19*(8), 787–805.

Berliner, L. (1996). Community notification of sex offenders: A new tool or a false promise? *Journal of Interpersonal Violence, 11,* 294–295.

Berman, A. L., & Jobes, D. A. (1991). *Adolescent suicide: Assessment and intervention.* Washington, DC: American Psychological Association.

Berman, I., Viegner, B., Merson, A., et al. (1997). Differential relationships between positive and negative symptoms and neuropsychological deficits in schizophrenia. *Schizophrenia Research, 25*(1), 1–10.

Berman, K. F., Torre, E. F., Daniel, D. G., & Weinberger, D. R. (1992). Regional cerebral blood flow in monozygotic twins discordant and concordant for schizophrenia. *Archives of General Psychiatry, 49,* 927–934.

Berman, M. E., Kavoussi, R. J., & Coccaro, E. F. (1997). Neurotransmitter correlates of human aggression. In D. M. Stoff, J. Breiling, & J. D. Maser (Eds.), *Handbook of antisocial behavior* (pp. 305–313). New York: Wiley.

Bermond, B., Fasotti, L., Nieuwenhuyse, B., & Schuerman, J. (1991). Spinal cord lesions, peripheral feedback and intensities of emotional feelings. *Cognition and Emotion, 5,* 201–220.

Bernard, L. C., Hutchison, S., Lavin, A., & Pennington, P. (1996). Ego-strength, hardiness, self-esteem, self-efficacy, optimism, and maladjustment: Health-related personality constructs and the "Big Five" model of personality. *Assessment, 3*(2), 115–131.

Bernard, P. G. (1994). *Closed-head injury: A clinical source book.* Charlottesville, VA: Michie Co.

Bernstein, D. P., Useda, D., & Siever, L. J. (1995). Paranoid personality disorder. In W. J. Livesley (Ed.), *The DSM-IV personality disorders. Diagnosis and treatment of mental disorders* (pp. 45–57). New York: Guilford Press.

Berrettini, W. H., Goldin, L. R., Gelernter, J., et al. (1990). X-chromosome markers and manic-depressive illness: Rejection of linkage to Xq28 in nine bipolar pedigrees. *Archives of General Psychiatry, 47*(4), 366–373.

Berrios, G. E. (1994). Development of contemporary views of dementia: Dementia and aging since the nineteenth century. In F. A. Huppert, C. Brayne, & D. W. O'Connor (Eds.), *Dementia and normal aging* (pp. 15–40). Cambridge, UK: Cambridge University Press.

Berry, J. W., & Fons, J. R. (1994). Acculturation and psychological adaptation: An overview. In A. Bouvy, F. J. R. van de Vijver, P. Boski, & P. G. Schmitz (Eds.), *Journeys into cross-cultural psychology* (pp. 129–141). Amsterdam: Swets & Zeitlinger.

Betancourt, H., & Lopez, S. R. (1993). The study of culture, ethnicity, and race in American psychology. *American Psychologist, 48*(6), 629–637.

Bettelheim, B. (1967). *The empty fortress.* New York: Free Press.

Bhagat, R. S., Allie, S. M., & Ford, D. L., Jr. (1995). Coping with stressful life events: An empirical analysis. In R. Crandall & P. L. Perrewe (Eds.), *Occupational stress: A handbook* (pp. 93–112). Philadelphia: Taylor & Francis.

Biggins, C. A., Boyd, J. L., Harrop, F. M., et al. (1992). A controlled longitudinal study of dementia in Parkinson's disease. *Journal of Neurology, Neurosurgery, and Psychiatry, 55,* 566–571.

Bigler, E. D. (1997). Neuroimaging in normal aging and dementia. In P. D. Nussbaum (Ed.), *Handbook of neuropsychology and aging: Critical issues in neuropsychology* (pp. 409–421). New York: Plenum.

Binzer, M., Andersen, P. M., & Kullgren, G. (1997). Clinical characteristics of patients with motor disability due to conversion disorder: A prospective control group study. *Journal of Neurology, Neurosurgery and Psychiatry, 63*(1), 83–88.

Birnbaum, M. H. (1992). Predicting health from stress: Response to Crandall. *Psychological Science, 3*(5), 319–320.

Birren, J. E., & Fisher, L. M. (1995). Age and speed of behavior: Possible consequences for psychological functioning. *Annual Review of Psychology, 46,* 329–353.

Black, B., & Uhde, T. W. (1992). Elective mutism as a variant of social phobia. *Journal of the American Academy of Child and Adolescent Psychiatry, 31,* 1090–1094.

Black, D. W. (1998). Recognition and treatment of obsessive-compulsive spectrum disorders. In R. P. Swinson & M. M. Antony (Eds.), *Obsessive-compulsive disorder: Theory, research, and treatment* (pp. 426–457). New York: Guilford Press.

Black, D. W., Noyes, R., Goldstein, R., & Blum, N. (1992). A family study of obsessive-compulsive disorder. *Archives of General Psychology, 49,* 362–368.

Black, D. W., Noyes, R., Pfohl, B., et al. (1993). Personality disorder in obsessive-compulsive volunteers, well comparison subjects, and their first degree relatives. *American Journal of Psychiatry, 150,* 1226–1232.

Black, S. T., & Lester, D. (1995). Distinguishing suicide notes from completed and attempted suicides. *Perceptual and Motor Skills, 81*(3, Pt. 1), 802.

Blanchard, E. B. (1992). Psychological treatment of benign headache disorders. *Journal of Consulting and Clinical Psychology, 60,* 537–551.

Blanchard, E. B. (1994). Behavioral medicine and health psychology. In A. E. Bergin & S. L. Garfield (Eds.), *Handbook of psycho-therapy and behavior change* (4th ed.) (pp. 701–733). New York: Wiley.

Blatt, S. J., & Zuroff, D. (1992). Interpersonal readiness and self-definition: Two prototypes for depression. *Clinical Psychological Review, 12,* 527–562.

Blazer, D. G., Hughes, D., George, L. K., et al. (1991). Generalized anxiety disorder. In L. N. Robins & D. A. Gegier (Eds.), *Psychiatric disorders in America* (pp. 180–203). New York: Free Press.

Bleuler, E. (1952). *Dementia praecox or the group of schizophrenias.* New York: International Universities Press. (Original work published 1911)

Bliss, E. L. (1986). *Multiple personality, allied disorders and hypnosis.* Oxford: Oxford University Press.

Bliss, E. L., Larson, E. M., & Nakashima, S. R. (1983). Auditory hallucinations and schizophrenia. *Journal of Nervous and Mental Disease, 171,* 30–33.

Block, M. A., (1997). *No more Ritalin: Treating ADHD without drugs.* New York: Kensington.

Blum, K., & Noble, E. (1993). Alcoholism and the D_2 dopamine receptor gene. *Journal of the American Medical Association, 273*(13), 1547–1548.

Blum, K., Noble, E. P., Sparkes, R. S., et al. (Eds.). (1997). *Handbook of psychiatric genetics.* Boca Raton, FL: CRC Press.

Blum, K., Sheridan, P. J., Wood, R. C., et al. (1996). The D_2 dopamine receptor gene as a determinant of reward deficiency syndrome. *Journal of the Royal Society of Medicine, 89*(7), 396–400.

Blum, N. J., Kell, R. S., Starr, H. L., et al. (1998). Case study: Audio feedforward treatment of selective mutism. *Journal of the American Academy of Child and Adolescent Psychiatry, 37,* 40–43.

Bock, G., & Marsh, J. (Eds.). (1990). *The biology of nicotine dependence.* New York: Wiley.

Boffeli, T. J., & Guze, S. B. (1992). The simulation of neurological disease. *Psychiatric Clinics of North America, 15,* 301–310.

Bogolub, E. B. (1995). *Helping families through divorce: An eclectic approach.* New York: Springer-Verlag.

Bohman, M. (1996). Predisposition to criminality: Swedish adoption studies in retrospect. *Ciba Foundation Symposium, 194,* 99–109.

Bokey, K. (1993). Conversion disorder revisited: Severe parasomnia discovered. *Australian and New Zealand Journal of Psychiatry, 27,* 694–698.

Bolger, J. P., Carpenter, B. C., & Strauss, M. E. (1994). Behavior and affect in Alzheimer's disease. *Clinics in Geriatric Medicine, 10,* 315–337.

Bolger, N., & Eckenrode, J. (1991). Social relationships, personality, and anxiety during a major stressful event. *Journal of Personality and Social Psychology, 61,* 440–449.

Bolte, E. R. (1998). Autism and *Clostridium tetani. Medical Hypotheses, 51,* 133–144.

Bone, S., & Oldham, J. M. (1994). Paranoia: Historical considerations. In J. M. Oldham & S. Bone (Eds.), *Paranoia: New psychoanalytic perspectives* (pp. 3–15). Madison, CT: International Universities Press.

Bongar, B. M. (1991). *The suicidal patient: Clinical and legal standards of care.* Washington, DC: American Psychological Association.

Boon, S., & Draijer, N. (1993). Multiple personality disorder in the Netherlands: A clinical investigation of 71 patients. *American Journal of Psychiatry, 150,* 489–494.

Booth, P. G., & Murphy, D. (1997). Measuring outcomes in the treatment of alcohol dependency. *Journal of Psychiatric and Mental Health Nursing, 4*(1), 17–22.

Borden, J. W., Lowenbraun, P. B., Wolff, P. L., & Jones, A. (1993). Self-focused attention in panic disorder. *Cognitive Therapy and Research, 17,* 413–425.

Bordens, K. S., & Abbott, B. B. (1999). *Research design and methods: A process approach* (4th ed.). Mountain View, CA: Mayfield.

Boring, E. G. (1950). *A history of experimental psychology* (2nd ed.). New York: Appleton-Century-Crofts.

Boris, N. W., & Zeanah, C. H. (1998). Clinical disturbances of attachment in infancy and early childhood. *Current Opinions in Pediatrics, 10,* 365–368.

Boris, N. W., Zeanah, C. H., Larrieu, J. A., et al. (1998). Attachment disorders in infancy and early childhood: A prelimi-nary investigation of diagnostic criteria. *American Journal of Psychiatry, 155,* 295–297.

Borison, R. L. (1995). Clinical efficacy of serotonin-dopamine antagonists relative to classic neuroleptics. *Journal of Clinical Psychopharmacology, 15* (1, Suppl. 1), 24S–29S.

Borkovec, T. D., & Inz, J. (1990). The nature of worry in generalized anxiety disorder: A predominance of thought activity. *Behaviour Research and Therapy, 28,* 153–158.

Bornstein, R. F. (1993). *The dependent personality.* New York: Guilford Press.

Bornstein, R. F. (1997a). Dependent personality disorder in the *DSM-IV* and beyond. *Clinical Psychology Science and Practice, 4,* 175–187.

Bornstein, R. F. (1997b). Pharmacological treatments for borderline personality disorder: A critical review of the empirical literature. In S. Fisher & R. P. Greenberg (Eds.), *From placebo to panacea: Putting psychiatric drugs to the test* (pp. 281–304). New York: Wiley.

Borum, R. (1996). Improving the clinical practice of violence risk assessment. *American Psychologist, 51,* 945–956.

Børup, C., Kaiser, A., & Jensen, E. (1992). Long-term Antabuse treatment: Tolerance and reward deficiency syndrome and reasons for withdrawal. *Acta Psychiatrica Scandinavica, 86*(Suppl. 369), 47–49.

Boscarino, J. A. (1995). Post-traumatic stress and associated disorders among Vietnam veterans: The significance of combat exposure and social support. *Journal of Traumatic Stress, 8*(2), 317–336.

Boscarino, J. A. (1996). Posttraumatic stress disorder, exposure to combat, and lower plasma cortisol among Vietnam veterans: Findings and clinical implications. *Journal of Consulting and Clinical Psychology, 64*(1), 191–201.

Boswell, J. (1933). *The life of Dr. Johnson.* London: J. M. Dent & Sons.

Bouchard, T. J., Jr. (1996). Behavioural genetic studies of intelligence: Yesterday and today. The long journey from plausibility to proof. (The Galton Lecture.) *Journal of Biosocial Science, 28,* 527–555.

Bouchard, T. J., Jr., & Propping, P. (Eds.). (1993). *Twins as a tool of behavioral genetics.* Chichester, UK: Wiley.

Boulton, A. A., Baker, G. B., & Hiscock, M. (1990). *Neuropsychology.* Clifton, NJ: Humana Press.

Bourgeois, J. A., & Klein, M. (1996). Risperidone and fluoxetine in the treatment of pedophilia with comorbid dysthymia. *Journal of Clinical Psychopharmacology, 16,* 257–258.

Bourgeois, M. S. (1992). Evaluating memory wallets in conversations with persons with dementia. *Journal of Speech and Hearing Research, 35,* 1344–1357.

Bourne, E. J. (1990). *The anxiety and phobia workbook.* Oakland, CA: New Harbinger.

Bourne, P. G. (1970). *Men, stress, and Vietnam.* Boston: Little, Brown.

Boutelle, K. N. (1998). The use of exposure with response prevention in a male anorexic. *Journal of Behavior Therapy and Experimental Psychiatry, 129,* 79–84.

Bower, G. H. (1981). Mood and memory. *American Psychologist, 15,* 60–69.

Bowers, L. B. (1990). Traumas precipitating female delinquency: Implications for assessment, practice and policy. *Child and Adolescent Social Work Journal, 7,* 389–402.

Bowlby, J. (1951). *Maternal care and maternal health.* Geneva: World Health Organization.

Boyd, J., & Crump, R. (1991). Westphal's agoraphobia. *Journal of Anxiety Disorders, 5,* 77–86.

Boyle, M. (1991). *Schizophrenia: A scientific delusion?* New York: Routledge.

Bracha, H. S., Torrey, E. F., Gottesman, I. I., et al. (1992). Second-trimester markers of fetal size in schizophrenia: A study of monozygotic twins. *American Journal of Psychiatry, 149,* 1355–1361.

Bradford, J. (1997). Medical interventions in sexual deviance. In D. R. Laws & W. T. O'Donohue (Eds.), *Sexual deviance: Theory, assessment, and treatment* (pp. 449–464). New York: Guilford Press.

Bradley, C. (1994). Contributions of psychology to diabetes management. *British Journal of Clinical Psychology, 33*(Pt. 1), 11–21.

Bradley, C. (1995). Health beliefs and knowledge of patients and doctors in clinical practice and research. *Patient Education and Counseling, 26*(1–3), 99–106.

Bradley, S. J., & Zucker, K. J. (1997). Gender identity disorder: A review of the past 10 years. *Journal of the American Academy of Child and Adolescent Psychiatry, 36,* 872–880.

Brady, E. U., & Kendall, P. C. (1992). Comorbidity of anxiety and depression in children and adolescents. *Psychological Bulletin, 111,* 244–255.

Brain, P. F., & Susman, E. J. (1997). Hormonal aspects of aggression and violence. In D. M. Stoff, J. Breiling, & J. D. Maser (Eds.), *Handbook of antisocial behavior* (pp. 314–323). New York: Wiley.

Brand, N., Verspui, L., & Oving, A. (1997). Induced mood and selective attention. *Perceptual and Motor Skills, 84,* 455–463.

Brannon, L., & Feist, J. (1992). *Health psychology* (2nd ed.). Belmont, CA: Wadsworth.

Brannon, L., & Feist, J. (1997). *Health psychology: An introduction to behavior and health* (3rd ed.). Pacific Grove, CA: Brooks/Cole.

Braswell, L., & Bloomquist, M. L. (1991). *Cognitive behavioral therapy with ADHD children: Child, family, and school interventions.* New York: Guilford Press.

Brawman-Mintzer, O., & Lydiard, R. B. (1996). Generalized anxiety disorder: Issues in epidemiology. *Journal of Clinical Psychiatry, 7,* 3–8.

Brayne, C. (1993). Research and Alzheimer's disease: An epidemiological perspective. *Psychological Medicine, 23,* 287–296.

Brazier, D. K., & Venning, H. E. (1997). Conversion disorders in adolescents: A practical approach to rehabilitation. *British Journal of Rheumatology, 36*(5), 594–598.

Brecher, E. M. (1972). *Licit and illicit drugs.* Boston: Little, Brown.

Breen, M. J. (1989). Cognitive and behavioral differences in ADHD boys and girls. *Journal of Child Psychology and Psychiatry and Allied Disciplines, 30,* 711–716.

Breggin, P. R. (1997). *Brain-disabling treatments in psychiatry.* New York: Springer-Verlag.

Breier, A. (1993). Paranoid disorder: Clinical features and treatment. In D. L. Dunner (Ed.), *Current psychiatric therapy* (pp. 154–159). Philadelphia: Saunders.

Breier, A. (1995). Serotonin, schizophrenia, and antipsychotic drug action. *Schizophrenia Research, 14,* 187–202.

Breier, A., Schreiber, J. L., Dyer, J., & Pickar, D. (1991). National Institute of Mental Health longitudinal study of chronic schizophrenia: Prognosis and predictors of outcome. *Archives of General Psychiatry, 48,* 239–246.

Bremer, J., & Herzog, D. (1997). Are insurance agencies making treatment decisions? *Journal of the American Academy of Child and Adolescent Psychiatry, 36,* 1488–1489.

Bremner, J. D., Krystal, J. H., Charney, D. S., & Southwick, S. M. (1996). Neural mechanisms in dissociative amnesia for childhood abuse: Relevance to the current controversy surrounding the "false memory syndrome." *American Journal of Psychiatry, 153*(7, Suppl.), 71–82.

Bremner, J. D., Krystal, J. H., Southwick, S. M., & Charney, D. S. (1995). Functional neuroanatomical correlates of the effects of stress on memory. Special Issue: Research on traumatic memory. *Journal of Traumatic Stress, 8*(4), 527–553.

Bremner, J. D., Southwick, S. M., David, R., & Yehuda, R. (1993). Childhood physical abuse and combat-related posttraumatic stress disorder in Vietnam veterans. *American Journal of Psychiatry, 150,* 235–239.

Brennan, P. A., & Mednick, S. (1997). Medical histories of antisocial individuals.

In D. M. Stoff, J. Breiling, & J. D. Maser (Eds.), *Handbook of antisocial behavior* (pp. 269–279). New York: Wiley.

Brenner, D. E., Kukull, W. A., van Belle, G., et al. (1993). Relationship between cigarette smoking and Alzheimer's disease in a population-based case-control study. *Neurology, 43,* 293–300.

Brenner, H. D., Hodel, B., Roder, V., & Corrigan, P. (1992). Treatment of cognitive dysfunctions and behavioral deficits in schizophrenia. *Schizophrenia Bulletin, 18,* 21–26.

Brenner, M. H. (1973). *Mental illness and the economy.* Cambridge, MA: Harvard University Press.

Brent, D. A., Perper, J. A., Goldstein, C. E., et al. (1988). Risk factors for adolescent suicide: A comparison of adolescent suicide victims with suicidal inpatients. *Archives of General Psychiatry, 45,* 581–588.

Breslau, N., Davis, G. C., Andreski, P., & Peterson, E. (1991). Traumatic events and posttraumatic stress disorder in an urban population of young adults. *Archives of General Psychiatry, 48,* 216–222.

Breslau, N., Kilbey, M. M., & Andreski, P. (1993). Nicotine dependence and major depression: New evidence from a prospective investigation. *Archives of General Psychiatry, 50,* 31–35.

Breuer, J., & Freud, S. (1956). *Studies on hy-steria.* In J. Strachey & A. Strachey (Ed. and Trans.), *International psychoanalytical library* (no. 50). London: Hogarth Press. (Original work published 1895)

Brewin, C. R., Andrews, B., & Gotlib, I. H. (1993). Psychopathology and early experience: A reappraisal of retrospective reports. *Psychological Bulletin, 113,* 82–98.

Briquet, P. (1859). *Traité clinique et thérapeutique de l'hystérie* [Symptoms and treatment of hysteria]. Paris: J-b Bailliere et fils.

Broadbent, D. E. (1973). *In defence of empirical psychology.* London: Metheun.

Broadbent, D. E., Baddeley, A., & Reason, J. T. (Eds.). (1990). *Human factors in hazardous situations.* Oxford: Clarendon Press.

Broca, P. (1861). Perte de la parole. Ramollissement chronique et destruction partielle du lobe anterieur gauche de cervau. *Bulletin de la Société d'Anthropologie, 2,* 235–238.

Brody, L. E., & Mills, C. J. (1997). Gifted children with learning disabilities: A review of the issues. *Journal of Learning Disabilities, 30,* 282–296.

Brody, N., & Crowley, M. J. (1995). Environmental (and genetic) influences on personality and intelligence. In D. H. Saklofske & M. Zeidner (Eds.), *International handbook of personality and intelli-*

gence: Perspectives on individual differences (pp. 59–80). New York: Plenum.

Broman, S. H., Nichols, P. L., & Kennedy, W. (1975). *Preschool IQ: Prenatal and early development correlates.* Hillsdale, NJ: Erlbaum.

Brown, D. R., Eaton, W. W., & Sussman, L. (1990). Racial differences in prevalence of phobic disorders. *Journal of Nervous and Mental Disease, 178,* 434–441.

Brown, F. W., Golding, J. M., & Smith, G. R. (1990). Psychiatric comorbidity in primary somatization disorder. *Psychosomatic Medicine, 52,* 445–451.

Brown, G. W., & Harris, T. O. (1989). Depression. In G. W. Brown & T. O. Harris (Eds.), *Life events and illness* (pp. 49–93). New York: Guilford Press.

Brown, G. W., & Harris, T. O. (1993). Aetiology of anxiety and depressive disorders in an inner-city population: I. Early adversity. *Psychological Medicine, 23*(1), 143–154.

Brown, J. (1992). *The definition of a profession: The authority of metaphor in the history of intelligence testing, 1890–1930.* Princeton, NJ: Princeton University Press.

Brown, J. K., & Kerns, B. (Eds.). (1985). *In her prime.* South Hadley, MA: Bergin & Garvey.

Brown, J. L., & Pollitt, E. (1996). Malnutrition, poverty and intellectual development. *Scientific American, 274,* 38–43.

Brown, T. A., & Barlow, D. H. (1992). Comorbidity among anxiety disorders: Implications for treatment and *DSM-IV.* *Journal of Consulting and Clinical Psychology, 60,* 835–844.

Brown, T. A., Barlow, D. H., & Liebowitz, M. R. (1994). The empirical basis of generalized anxiety disorder. *American Journal of Psychiatry, 151*(9), 1272–1280.

Brown, T. A., O'Leary, T. A., & Barlow, D. H. (1993). Generalized anxiety disorder. In D. H. Barlow (Ed.), *Clinical handbook of psychological disorders: A step-by-step treatment manual* (2nd ed.) (pp. 137–188). New York: Guilford Press.

Brownell, K. D., & Stunkard, A. J. (1982). The double-blind in danger: Untoward consequences of informed consent. *American Journal of Psychiatry, 139*(11), 1487–1489.

Browning, C. R., & Laumann, E. O. (1997). Sexual contact between children and adults: A life perspective. *American Psychological Review, 62,* 540–560.

Brownlee-Duffeck, M., Peterson, L., Simonds, J. F., et al. (1987). The role of health beliefs in the regimen adherence and metabolic control of adolescents and adults with diabetes mellitus. *Journal of Consulting and Clinical Psychology, 55*(2), 139–144.

Brownmiller, S. (1993). *Against our will: Men, women and rape.* New York: Fawcett.

Bruch, H. (1978). *The golden cage: The enigma of anorexia nervosa.* Cambridge, MA: Harvard University Press.

Brunia, C. H. M., Mulder, G., & Verbaten, M. N. (1991). *Event-related brain research.* Amsterdam: Elsevier.

Bryant, R. A., & McConkey, R. M. (1989). Visual conversion disorder: A case analysis of the influence of visual information. *Journal of Abnormal Psychology, 98,* 326–329.

Buchsbaum, M. S., Yang, S., Hazlett, E., et al. (1997). Ventricular volume and asymmetry in schizotypal personality disorder and schizophrenia assessed with magnetic resonance imaging. *Schizophrenia Research, 27,* 45–53.

Buchwald, A. M., & Rudick-Davis, D. (1993). The symptoms of major depression. *Journal of Abnormal Psychology, 102*(2), 197–205.

Buck, J. (1981). *The House-tree-person technique: A revised manual.* Los Angeles: Western Psychological Services.

Buist, A., & Barnett, B. (1995). Childhood sexual abuse: A risk factor for depression? *Australian and New Zealand Journal of Psychiatry, 29,* 604–608.

Burchfiel, C. M., Marcus, E. B., Curb, J. D., et al. (1995). Effects of smoking and smoking cessation on longitudinal decline in pulmonary function. *American Journal of Respiratory and Critical Care Medicine, 151*(6), 1778–1785.

Burchfield, S. R. (1985). *Stress: Psychological and physiological interactions.* Washington, DC: Hemisphere.

Burge, D., & Hammen, C. (1991). Maternal communication: Predictors of outcome at follow-up in a sample of children at high and low risk for depression. *Journal of Abnormal Psychology, 100,* 174–180.

Burke, K. C., Burke, J. D., Regier, D. A., & Rae, D. S. (1990). Age at onset of selected mental disorders in five community populations. *Archives of General Psychiatry, 47,* 511–518.

Burnam, M. A. (1996, Fall). Measuring outcomes of care for substance use and mental disorders. *New Directions in Mental Health Services, 71,* 3–17.

Burns, D. D., Sayers, S. L., & Moras, K. (1994). Intimate relationships and depression: Is there a causal connection? *Journal of Consulting and Clinical Psychology, 62*(5), 1033–1043.

Burt, C. (1935). *The subnormal mind.* New York: Oxford University Press.

Burt, D. B., Zembar, M. J., & Niederehe, G. (1995). Depression and memory impairment: A meta-analysis of the association, its pattern, and specificity. *Psychological Bulletin, 117,* 285–305.

Burton, R. (1977). *Anatomy of melancholy: What it is, with all the kinds, causes, symptomes, prognostickes and severall cures of it*

(Reprint of the 1932 ed. published by J. M. Dent, London and Dutton, New York). New York: Vintage Books. (Original work published 1621)

Bushman, B. J. (1993). Human aggression while under the influence of alcohol and other drugs: An integrative research review. *Psychological Science, 2,* 148–152.

Buss, A. H. (1986). A theory of shyness. In W. H. Jones, J. M. Cheek, & S. R. Briggs (Eds.), *Shyness: Perspectives on research and treatment* (pp. 39–46). New York: Plenum.

Butcher, J. (1999). ABC of sexual health. Female sexual problems. II: Sexual pain and sexual fears. *British Medical Journal, 318,* 110–112.

Butcher, J. N. (Ed.). (1987). *Computerized psychological assessment: A practitioner's guide.* New York: Basic Books.

Butcher, J. N., Dahlstrom, W. G., Graham, J. R., et al. (1989a). *Manual for the restandardized Minnesota Multiphasic Personality Inventory, MMPI-2: An administrative and interpretive guide.* Minneapolis: University of Minnesota Press.

Butcher, J. N., Dahlstrom, W. G., Graham, J. R., et al. (1989b). *Minnesota Multiphasic Personality Inventory–2: Manual for administration and scoring.* Minneapolis: University of Minnesota Press.

Butcher, J. N., & Williams, C. L. (1992). *Essentials of MMPI-2 and MMPI-A interpretation.* Minneapolis: University of Minnesota Press.

Butcher, J. N., Williams, C. L., Graham, J. R., et al. (1992). *MMPI-A: Manual for administration, scoring and interpretation.* Minneapolis: University of Minnesota Press.

Butler, G., Fennel, M., Robson, P., & Gilder, M. (1991). A comparison of behavior therapy and cognitive therapy in the treatment of generalized anxiety disorder. *Journal of Consulting and Clinical Psychology, 59,* 167–175.

Butters, N., Delis, D. C., & Lucas, J. A. (1995). Clinical assessment of memory disorders in amnesia and dementia. *Annual Review of Psychology, 46,* 493–523.

Buysse, D. J., Morin, C. M., & Reynolds, C. F., III. (1995). Sleep disorders. In G. O. Gabbard (Ed.), *Treatments of psychiatric disorders, Vol. 2* (2nd ed.) (pp. 2395–2453). Washington, DC: American Psychiatric Press.

Byrne, A. (1996). Harm minimization approaches to drug misuse: Current challenges in evaluation. *Substance Use and Misuse, 31*(14), 2017–2028.

Bystritsky, A., & Waikar, S. V. (1994). Inert placebo versus active medication: Patient blindability in clinical pharmacological trials. *Journal of Nervous and Mental Disease, 182,* 475–485.

Cacioppo, J. T. (1994). Social neuroscience:

Autonomic, neuroendocrine, and immune response to stress. *Psychophysiology, 31,* 113–128.

Cadoret, R. J., O'Gorman, T., Troughton, E., & Heywood, E. (1987). An adoption study of genetic and environmental factors in drug abuse. *Archives of General Psychiatry, 43,* 1131–1136.

Cairns, E., McWhirter, L., Barry, R., & Duffy, U. (1991). The development of psychological well-being in late adolescence. *Journal of Child Psychology and Psychiatry and Allied Disciplines, 32,* 635–643.

Caldwell, C., & Gottesman, I. I. (1992). Schizophrenia—A high-risk factor for suicide: Clues to risk reduction. *Suicide and Life-Threatening Behavior, 2,* 479–493.

Caldwell, S., & White, K. (1991). Co-creating a self-help recovery movement: Serving persons with dual disorders of mental illness and substance abuse. *Psychosocial Rehabilitation Journal, 15*(2), 91–95.

Calhoun, K. S., & Resick, P. A. (1993). Posttraumatic stress disorder. In D. H. Barlow (Ed.), *Clinical handbook of psychological disorders: A step-by-step treatment manual* (2nd ed.) (pp. 48–98). New York: Guilford Press.

Calhoun, S. R., Wesson, D. R., Galloway, G. P., et al. (1996). Abuse of flunitrazepam (Rohypnol) and other benzodiazepines in Austin and South Texas. *Journal of Psychoactive Drugs, 28,* 183–189.

Callahan, C. M., & Rivara, F. P. (1992). Urban high school youth and handguns: A school-based survey. *Journal of the American Medical Association, 267,* 3038–3042.

Callner, D. A. (1975). Behavioral treatment approaches to drug abuse: A critical review of the research. *Psychological Bulletin, 82*(2), 143–164.

Camp, B. W., Broman, S. H., Nichols, P. L., & Leff, M. (1998). Maternal and neonatal risk factors for mental retardation: Defining the "at-risk" child. *Early Human Development, 50,* 159–173.

Campbell, E. (1996). Should drugs be decriminalized? [Editorial]. *Alabama Medicine, 65*(8–10), 16.

Campbell, R. (1998). The community response to a rape victim's experiences with the legal, medical, and mental health systems. *American Journal of Community Psychology, 26,* 355–379.

Campbell, R., & Aherns, C. E. (1998). Innovative community services for rape victims: An application of multiple case study methodology. *American Journal of Community Psychology, 26,* 537–571.

Canada court denies woman right to an assisted suicide. (1993, March 9). *New York Times,* p. A, 8:1.

Cannon, T. D., Mednick, S. A., & Parnas, J. (1990). Antecedents of predominantly negative and predominantly positive-symptom schizophrenia in a high-risk population. *Archives of General Psychiatry, 50,* 551–564.

Cannon, W. B. (1939). *The wisdom of the body.* New York: Norton.

Cantwell, D. P. (1996). Attention deficit disorder: A review of the past 10 years. *Journal of the American Academy of Child and Adolescent Psychiatry, 35,* 978–987.

Cao, Q., Martinez, M., Zhang, J., et al. (1997). Suggestive evidence for a schizophrenia susceptibility locus on chromosome 6q and a confirmation in an independent series of pedigrees. *Genomics, 43*(1), 1–8.

Caplan, L. J., & Lipman, P. D. (1995). Age and gender differences in the effectiveness of map-like learning aids in memory for routes. *Journals of Gerontology, Series B: Psychological Sciences & Social Sciences, 50B*(3), P126–P133.

Caporael, L. (1976). Ergotism: The satan loosed in Salem. *Science, 192,* 21–26.

Caputo, R. A. (1993). Volatile substance misuse in children and youth: A consideration of theories [Review]. *International Journal of the Addictions, 28*(10), 1015–1032.

Cardena, E., & Spiegel, D. (1993). Dissociative reactions to the San Francisco Bay Area earthquake of 1989. *American Journal of Psychiatry, 150,* 474–478.

Carey, G., & Goldman, D. (1997). The genetics of antisocial behavior. In D. M. Stoff, J. Breiling, & J. D. Maser (Eds.), *Handbook of antisocial behavior* (pp. 243–254). New York: Wiley.

Carlson, C. L., & Lahey, B. B. (1988). Conduct and attention disorders. In J. C. Witt, S. Elliott, & F. M. Gresham (Eds.), *Handbook of behavior therapy in education* (pp. 653–677). New York: Plenum.

Carlson, K. J., Eisenstat, S. A., & Ziporyn, T. (1996). *The Harvard guide to women's health.* Cambridge, MA: Harvard University Press.

Carlsson, A., Hansson, L. O., Waters, N., & Carlsson, M. L. (1997). Neurotransmitter aberrations in schizophrenia: New perspectives and therapeutic implications. *Life Sciences, 61*(2), 75–94.

Carmelli, D., Swan, G. E., Robinette, D., & Fabsitz, R. (1992). Genetic influences on smoking—A study of male twins. *New England Journal of Medicine, 327,* 829–833.

Carnes, P. J. (1992). *Don't call it love: Recovery from sexual addiction.* New York: Bantam Books.

Carpenter, W. T. (1994). The deficit syndrome. *American Journal of Psychiatry, 151,* 327–329.

Carpenter, W. T., & Strauss, J. S. (1991). The prediction of outcome in schizophrenia. IV: Eleven-year follow-up of the Washington IPSS cohort. *Journal of Nervous and Mental Disease, 179,* 517–525.

Carratala, F., Galan, F., Moya, M., et al. (1998). A patient with autistic disorder and a 20/22 chromosomal translocation. *Developmental Medicine and Child Neurology, 40,* 492–495.

Carroll, D., Smith, G. D., & Bennett, P. (1994). Health and socioeconomic status. *Psychologist, 7,* 122–125.

Carroll, K. M., & Schottenfeld, R. (1997). Nonpharmacologic approaches to substance abuse treatment. *Medical Clinics of North America, 81*(4), 927–944.

Carroll, L., Hoenigmann-Stovall, N., King, A., et al. (1998). Interpersonal consequences of narcissistic and borderline personality disorders. *Journal of Social and Clinical Psychology, 17,* 38–49.

Carson, R. C. (1989). Personality. *Annual Review of Psychology, 40,* 227–248.

Carson, R. C., & Butcher, J. N. (1992). *Abnormal psychology and modern life* (9th ed.). New York: HarperCollins.

Carson, R. C., & Sanislow, C. A. (1993). The schizophrenias. In P. B. Sutker & H. E. Adams (Eds.), *Comprehensive handbook of psychopathology* (pp. 295–333). New York: Plenum.

Cash, T. F., & Deagle, E. A., III. (1997). The nature and extent of body image disturbances in anorexia nervosa and bulimia nervosa: A meta analysis. *International Journal of Eating Disorders, 22,* 107–112.

Cassileth, B. R., Lusk, E. J., Miller, D. S., et al. (1985). Psychological correlates of survival in advanced malignant disease? *New England Journal of Medicine, 312,* 1551–1555.

Castillo, C. S., Starkstein, S. E., Fedoroff, J. P., & Price, T. R. (1993). Generalized anxiety disorder after stroke. *Journal of Nervous and Mental Disease, 181,* 100–106.

Catalano, R. A. (Ed.). (1998). *When autism strikes: Families cope with childhood disintegrative disorder.* New York: Plenum.

Cattell, R. B., Eber, H. W., & Tatsuoka, M. M. (1970). *Handbook for the Sixteen Personality Factor Questionnaire.* Champaign, IL: Institute for Personality and Ability Testing.

Cautela, J. (1996). A behaviour therapy approach to pervasive anxiety. *Behaviour Research and Therapy, 4,* 99–109.

Centers for Disease Control. (1991). Attempted suicide among high school students: United States (1990). *Morbidity and Mortality Weekly Report, 40,* 633–635.

Centers for Disease Control. (1997). *Morbidity and Mortality Weekly Report, 46,* 448–451.

Cerezo, M. A., & Pons-Salvador, G. (1998). Modifying the family process in two cases of physical child abuse and secondary functional encopresis. *Child Maltreatment: Journal of the American Professional Society on the Abuse of Children, 3,* 171–185.

Cernovsky, Z. Z., Landmark, J. A., & O'Reilly, R. L. (1997). Symptom patterns in schizophrenia for men and women. *Psychological Reports, 80*(3, Pt. 2), 1267–1271.

Chandrassekaran, R., Goswami, U., & Sivakumar, V. (1994). Hysterical neurosis: A follow-up study. *Acta Psychiatrica Scandinavica, 89,* 78–80.

Chapman, L. J., & Chapman, J. P. (1969). Illusory correlation as an obstacle to the use of valid diagnostic signs. *Journal of Abnormal Psychology, 74,* 271–287.

Chappel, J. N. (1993). Long-term recovery from alcoholism. *Psychiatric Clinics of North America, 16,* 177–187.

Chappell, P. B., Scahill, L. D., & Leckman, J. F. (1997). Future therapies of Tourette syndrome. *Neurologic Clinics, 15,* 429–450.

Charlton, B. G. (1990). A critique of biological psychiatry. *Psychological Medicine, 20,* 3–6.

Chase, M. (1993, May 28). Psychiatrists declare severe PMS a depressive disorder. *Wall Street Journal,* pp. B1, B6.

Chassin, L., Pillow, D. R., Curran, P. J., et al. (1993). Relation of parental alcoholism to early adolescent substance abuse: A test of three mediating mechanisms. *Journal of Abnormal Psychology, 102,* 3–19.

Chen, Y. W., & Dilsaver, S. C. (1995). Comorbidity for obsessive-compulsive disorder in bipolar and unipolar disorders. *Psychiatry Research, 59*(1–2), 57–64.

Chenoweth, K. (1999, May 13). Assembly lines for alienated teens. *Washington Post,* p. A3.

Chesebro, B. W. (Ed.). (1991). *Transmissible spongiform encephalopathies: Scrapie, BSE and related human disorders.* Berlin: Springer-Verlag.

Chess, S., & Alexander, T. (1995). *Temperament in clinical practice.* New York: Guilford Press.

Chess, S., & Alexander, T. (1999). *Goodness of fit: Clinical applications from infancy through adult life.* Pacific Grove, CA: Brooks/Cole.

Chin, A. E., Hedberg, K., Higginson, G. K., & Fleming, D. W. (1999). Legalized physician-assisted suicide in Oregon—The first year's experience. *New England Journal of Medicine, 340,* 577–583.

Chisholm, K., Carter, M. C., Ames, E. W., & Morison, S. J. (1995). Attachment security and indiscriminately friendly behavior in children adopted from Romanian orphanages. *Development and Psychopathology, 7,* 283–294.

Chomsky, N. (1973). *For reasons of state.* New York: Pantheon Books.

Chomsky, N. (1980). *Rules and representations.* Oxford: Blackwell.

Chor, P. N., Mercier, M. A., & Halper, I. S. (1988). Use of cognitive therapy for treatment of a patient suffering from a bipolar affective disorder. *Journal of Cognitive Psychotherapy, 2,* 51–58.

Christen, A. G. (1996). Smokeless tobacco usage: A growing and menacing addiction among Hoosier children and young adults. *Indiana Medicine, 89*(2), 176–180.

Christensen, L., Bourgeois, A., & Cockroft, R. (1993). Electroencephalographic concomitants of a caffeine-induced panic reaction. *Journal of Nervous and Mental Disease, 181,* 327–330.

Christensen-Szalanski, J. J. J., Beck, D. E., Christensen-Szalanski, C. M., & Koepsell, T. D. (1983). The effect of journal coverage on physician's perception of risk. *Journal of Applied Psychology, 68,* 278–284.

Christenson, G. A., Ristvedt, S. L., & Mackenzie, T. B. (1993). Identification of trichotillomania cue profiles. *Behaviour Research and Therapy, 31,* 315–320.

Christianson, S-A. (1992). Emotional stress and eyewitness memory: A critical review. *Psychological Bulletin, 112*(2), 284–309.

Chung, R., & Okazaki, S. (1991). Counseling Americans of Southeast Asian descent: The impact of the refugee experience. In C. C. Lee & B. L. Richardson (Eds.), *Multicultural issues in counseling: New approaches to diversity* (pp. 107–126). Alexandria, VA: American Association for Counseling and Development.

Chung, R. C., & Singer, M. K. (1995). Interpretation of symptom presentation and distress: A Southeast Asian refugee example. *Journal of Nervous and Mental Disease, 183*(10), 639–648.

Ciminero, A. R., Calhoun, K. S., & Adams, H. E. (Eds.). (1986). *Handbook of behavioral assessment.* New York: Wiley.

Citrome, L., & Volavka, J. (1997). Psychopharmacology of violence. Part I: Assessment and acute treatment. *Psychiatric Annals, 27,* 691–695.

Clare, A. (1989). National variations in medical practice. *British Medical Journal, 298,* 1334.

Clarizio, H. F. (1997). Conduct disorder: Developmental considerations. *Psychology in the Schools, 34,* 253–265.

Clark, D., & Salkovskis, P. M. (1990). *Cognitive model of panic: A comparative outcome study.* Paper presented at the International Conference on Panic Disorders, Gothenberg, Sweden.

Clark, D. A., & Purdon, C. L. (1995). The assessment of unwanted intrusive thoughts: A review and critique of the literature. *Behaviour Research and Therapy, 33*(8), 967–976.

Clark, D. C., & Fawcett, J. (1992). Review of empirical risk factors for the evaluation of the suicidal patient. In B. M. Bongar (Ed.), *Suicide: Guidelines for assessment,* *management, and treatment.* New York: Oxford University Press.

Clark, D. C., & Horton-Deutsch, S. L. (1992). Assessment in absentia: The value of the psychological autopsy method for studying antecedents of suicide and predicting future suicide. In R. W. Maris, A. L. Berman, J. R. Maltsberger, & R. I. Yufit (Eds.), *Assessment and prediction of suicide* (pp. 145–182). New York: Guilford Press.

Clark, D. M., & Beck, A. T. (1988). Cognitive approaches. In C. G. Last & M. Hersen (Eds.), *Handbook of anxiety disorders* (pp. 362–385). New York: Pergamon.

Clark, L. A., & Watson, D. (1991). A tripartite model of anxiety and depression: Psychometric evidence and taxometric implications. *Journal of Abnormal Psychology, 100*(3), 316–336.

Clark, L. A., Watson, D., & Mineka, S. (1994). Temperament, personality, and the mood and anxiety disorders. *Journal of Abnormal Psychology, 103,* 103–116.

Clarke, V. A., Frankish, C. J., & Green, L. W. (1997). Understanding suicide among indigenous adolescents: A review using the PRECEDE model. *Injury Prevention, 3*(2), 126–134.

Cleckley, H. (1976). *The mask of sanity.* St. Louis: Mosby.

Cline, T., & Baldwin, S. (1994). *Selective mutism in children.* London: Whurr.

Cloninger, C. A. (1987). Neurogenetic adaptive mechanisms in alcoholism. *Science, 236,* 410–416.

Cloninger, C. R., Bayon, C., & Przybeck, T. R. (1997). Epidemiology and Axis I comorbidity of antisocial personality. In D. M. Stoff, J. Breiling, & J. D. Maser (Eds.), *Handbook of antisocial behavior* (pp. 12–21). New York: Wiley.

Cloninger, C. R., Martin, R. L., Guze, S. P., & Clayton, P. J. (1986). A prospective follow-up and family study of somatization in men and women. *American Journal of Psychiatry, 143*(7), 873–878.

Cloninger, C. R., Sigvardsson, S., von Knorring, A-L, & Bohman, M. (1984). An adoption study of somatoform disorders. II: Identification of two discrete somatoform disorders. *Archives of General Psychiatry, 41,* 863–871.

Clum, A., & Knowles, S. L. (1991). Why do some people with panic disorder become avoidant? A review. *Clinical Psychology Review, 11,* 295–314.

Coates, T. J. (1990). Strategies for modifying sexual behavior for primary and secondary prevention of HIV disease. *Journal of Consulting and Clinical Psychology, 58*(1), 57–69.

Coatsworth, J. D., Szapocznik, J., Kurtines, W., & Santisteban, D. A. (1997). Culturally competent psychosocial interventions with antisocial problem behavior in Hispanic youths. In D. M. Stoff, J. Breiling, & J. D. Maser (Eds.), *Handbook of antisocial behavior* (pp. 395–404). New York: Wiley.

Cobb, N. J. (1998). *Adolescence: Continuity, change, and diversity* (3rd ed.). Mountain View, CA: Mayfield.

Coe, C. L., Rosenberg, L. T., Fischer, M., & Levine, S. (1987). Psychological factors capable of preventing the inhibition of antibody responses in separated infant monkeys. *Child Development, 58,* 1420–1430.

Cohen, D. R., & Henderson, J. B. (1988). *Health, prevention and economics.* Oxford: Oxford University Press.

Cohen, J. (1960). A coefficient of agreement for nominal scales. *Educational and Psychological Measurement, 20,* 37–46.

Cohen, J. (1968). Weighted kappa: Nominal scale agreement with provision for scaled disagreement or partial credit. *Psychological Bulletin, 70,* 213–220.

Cohen, R. J., Swerdlik, M. E., & Phillips, S. M. (1996). *Psychological testing and assessment: An introduction to tests and measurement* (3rd ed.). Mountain View, CA: Mayfield.

Cohen, R. J., Swerdlik, M. E., & Smith, D. K. (1992). *Psychological testing and assessment: An Introduction to tests and measurements* (2nd ed.). Mountain View, CA: Mayfield.

Cohen, S., Tyrell, D. A., & Smith, A. P. (1993). Negative life events, perceived stress, negative affect, and susceptibility to the common cold. *Journal of Personality and Social Psychology, 64*(1), 131–140.

Cohen, S., & Williamson, G. M. (1991). Stress and infectious disease in humans. *Psychological Bulletin, 109,* 5–24.

Coleman, E. A., Honeycutt, G., Ogden, B., et al. (1997). Assessing substance abuse among health care students and the efficacy of educational interventions. *Journal of Professional Nursing, 13*(1), 28–37.

Collaer, M. L., & Hines, M. (1995). Human behavioral sex differences: A role for gonadal hormones during early development? *Psychological Bulletin, 8,* 55–107.

Collins, F. S. (1995). Ahead of schedule and under budget: The Genome Project passes its fifth birthday. *Proceedings of the National Academy of Sciences of the United States of America, 92*(24), 10821–10823.

Combs, G., Jr., & Ludwig, A. M. (1982). Dissociative disorders. In J. H. Greist, J. W. Jefferson, & R. L. Spitzer (Eds.), *Treatment of mental disorders.* New York: Oxford University Press.

Comer, R. J. (1992). *Abnormal psychology.* New York: Freeman.

Compton, W. M., Helzer, J. E., Hwu, H., et al. (1991). New methods in cross-cultural psychiatry: Psychiatric illness in Taiwan and the United States.

American Journal of Psychiatry, 148(12), 1697–1704.

Comstock, B. S. (1992). Decision to hospitalize and alternatives to hospitalization. In B. M. Bongar (Ed.), *Suicide: Guidelines for assessment, management and treatment* (pp. 204–217). New York: Oxford University Press.

Condon, J. T., & Corkindale, C. (1997). The correlates of antenatal attachment in pregnant women. *British Journal of Medical Psychology, 70,* 359–372.

Conrad, M., & Hammen, C. L. (1993). Protective and resilience factors in high and low risk children: A comparison of unipolar, bipolar, medically ill, and normal mothers. *Development and Psychopathology, 5,* 593–607.

Constans, J. I., Foa, E. B., Franklin, M. E., & Matthews, A. (1995). Memory for actual and imagined events in OC checkers. *Behaviour Research and Therapy, 33*(6), 665–672.

Cook, C. C. H., & Gurling, H. M. D. (1991). Genetic factors in alcoholism. In T. N. Palmer (Ed.), *The molecular pathology of alcoholism* (pp. 182–210). New York: Oxford University Press.

Cook, J. A. L. (1997). Play therapy for selective mutism. In H. G. Kaduson, D. M. Cangelosi, & C. E. Schaefer (Eds.), *The playing cure: Individualized play therapy for specific childhood problems* (pp. 83–115). Child Therapy series. Northvale, NJ: Jason Aronson.

Cook, M., & Mineka, S. (1991). Selective associations in the origins of phobic fears and their implications for behavior therapy. In P. R. Martin (Ed.), *Handbook of behavior therapy and psychological science: An integrative approach* (pp. 413–434). Oxford: Pergamon.

Coons, P. (1991). Iatrogenesis and malingering of multiple personality disorder in the forensic evaluation of homicide defendants. *Psychiatric Clinics of North America, 14,* 757–768.

Coons, P. M. (1986). Treatment progress in 20 patients with multiple personality disorder. *Journal of Nervous and Mental Disease, 174,* 715–721.

Coons, P. M., Bowman, E. S., & Milstein, V. (1988). Multiple personality disorder: A clinical investigation of 50 cases. *Journal of Nervous and Mental Disease, 176,* 519–527.

Coons, P. M., & Bradley, K. (1985). Group psychotherapy with multiple personality patients. *Journal of Nervous and Mental Disease, 173,* 515–521.

Cooper, J. E., et al. (1972). *Psychiatric diagnosis in New York and London* (Maudsley Monograph No. 20). London: Oxford University Press.

Cooper, M. (1997). Cognitive theory in anorexia nervosa and bulimia nervosa:

A review. *Behavioural and Cognitive Psychotherapy, 25,* 113–145.

Cooper, M. L., Russell, M., Skinner, J. B., et al. (1992). Stress and alcohol use: Moderating effects of gender, coping, and alcohol expectancies. *Journal of Abnormal Psychology, 101,* 139–152.

Cooper, P., & Ideus, K. (1995). Is attention deficit hyperactivity disorder a Trojan horse? *Support for Learning, 10,* 29–34.

Cooper, P. L., Ford, D. E., Mead, L. A., et al. (1997). Exercise and depression in midlife. *American Journal of Public Health, 87,* 670–673.

Cooter, R. (1984). *The cultural meaning of popular science: Phrenology and the organization of consent in nineteenth century Britain.* Cambridge, UK: Cambridge University Press.

Copeland, J., & Hall, W. (1992). A comparison of women seeking drug and alcohol treatment in a specialist women's and two traditional mixed-sex treatment services. *British Journal of Addiction, 87*(9), 1293–1302.

Copestake, P. (1993). Aluminium and Alzheimer's: An update. *Food and Chemical Toxicology, 31,* 670–683.

Corcoran, M. A., & Gitlin, L. N. (1992). Dementia management: An occupational therapy home-based intervention for caregivers. *American Journal of Occupational Therapy, 46,* 801–808.

Corder, E. H., Saunders, A. M., Strittmatter, W. J., et al. (1993). Gene dose of apolipoprotein E Type 4 allele and the risk of Alzheimer's disease in late onset families. *Science, 261,* 921–923.

Cornblatt, B. A., Lenzenweger, M. F., Dworkin, R. H., & Erlenmeyer-Kimling, L. (1992). Childhood attentional dysfunctions predict social deficits in unaffected adults at risk for schizophrenia. *British Journal of Psychiatry, 16* (Suppl. 18), 59–64.

Corrigan, P. W. (1995). Wanted: Champions of psychiatric rehabilitation. *American Psychologist, 50,* 514–521.

Coryell, W., Endicott, J., & Keller, M. (1992). Major depression in a nonclinical sample: Demographic and clinical risk factors for first onset. *Archives of General Psychiatry, 49,* 117–125.

Coryell, W., Scheftner, W., Keller, M., et al. (1993). The enduring psychosocial consequences of mania and depression. *American Journal of Psychiatry, 150,* 720–727.

Coryell, W., & Winokur, G. (1992). Course and outcome. In E. S. Paykel (Ed.), *Handbook of affective disorders* (2nd ed.) (pp. 89–110). New York: Guilford Press.

Coryell, W., Winokur, G., Shea, T., et al. (1994). The long-term stability of depressive subtypes. *American Journal of Psychiatry, 151,* 199–204.

Cote, J. E. (1994). *Adolescent storm and stress: An evaluation of the Mead-Freeman controversy.* Hillsdale, NJ: Erlbaum.

Cotrufo, P., Barretta, V., & Monteleone, P. (1997). An epidemiological study on eating disorders in two high schools in Naples. *European Psychiatry, 12,* 342–344.

Cotterill, J. A. (1996). Body dysmorphic disorder. *Dermatology Clinics, 14*(3), 457–463.

Cowart, V. S. (1989). If youngsters overdose with anabolic steroids, what's the cost anatomically and otherwise? *Journal of the American Medical Association, 261,* 1856–1857.

Cowen, E. L., Work, W. C., & Wyman, P. A. (1997). The Rochester Child Resilience Project (RCRP): Facts found, lessons learned, future directions divined. In S. S. Luthar & J. A. Burack (Eds.), *Developmental psychopathology: Perspectives on adjustment, risk, and disorder* (pp. 527–547). New York: Cambridge University Press.

Coyne, J. C., & Downey, G. (1991). Social factors and psychopathology: Stress, social support, and coping processes. *Annual Review of Psychology, 42,* 401–425.

Craig, T. J., Bromet, E. J., Jandorf, L., et al. (1997). Diagnosis, treatment, and six-month outcome status in first-admission psychosis. *Annals of Clinical Psychiatry, 9*(2), 89–97.

Craig, T. J., Siegel, C., Hopper, K., et al. (1997). Outcome in schizophrenia and related disorders compared between developing and developed countries: A recursive partitioning re-analysis of the WHO DOSMD data. *British Journal of Psychiatry, 170,* 229–233.

Crandall, C. S., Preisler, J. J., & Aussprung, J. (1992). Measuring life event stress in the lives of college students: The Undergraduate Stress Questionnaire (USQ). *Journal of Behavioral Medicine, 15,* 627–662.

Craske, M. G., & Barlow, D. H. (1991). Contributions of cognitive psychology to assessment and treatment of anxiety. In P. R. Martin (Ed.), *Handbook of behavior therapy and psychological science: An integrative approach* (pp. 151–168). Oxford: Pergamon.

Craske, M. G., & Barlow, D. H. (1993). Panic disorder and agoraphobia. In D. H. Barlow (Ed.), *Clinical handbook of psychological disorders: A step-by-step treatment manual.* (2nd ed.) (pp. 1–47). New York: Guilford Press.

Craske, M. G., Brown, T. A., & Barlow, D. H. (1991). Behavioral treatment of panic disorder: A two-year follow-up. *Behavior Therapy, 22,* 289–304.

Craske, M. G., Rapee, R. M., & Barlow, D. H. (1992). Cognitive-behavioral treatment of panic disorder, agoraphobia, and generalized anxiety disorder. In

S. M. Turner, K. S. Calhoun, & H. E. Adams (Eds.), *Handbook of clinical behavior therapy* (2nd ed.) (pp. 39–65). New York: Wiley.

Crawford, J. R., Parker, D. M., & McKinlay, W. W. (Eds.). (1992). *A handbook of neuropsychological assessment.* Hillsdale, NJ: Erlbaum.

Critchley, M., & Critchley, E. A. (1978). *Dyslexia defined.* Springfield, IL: Thomas.

Crolley, J., Roys, D., Thyer, B. A., et al. (1998). Evaluating outpatient behavior therapy of sex offenders: A pretest-posttest study. *Behavior Modification, 22,* 485–501.

Cromwell, R. L. (1993). A summary view of schizophrenia. In R. L. Cromwell & C. R. Snyder (Eds.), *Schizophrenia: Origins, processes, treatment, and outcome* (pp. 335–349). New York: Oxford University Press.

Cromwell, R. L., & Snyder, C. R. (Eds.). (1993). *Schizophrenia: Origins, processes, treatment, and outcome.* New York: Oxford University Press.

Cronin, K. A., Weed, D. L., Connor, R. J., et al. (1998). Case-control studies of cancer screening: Theory and practice. *Journal of the National Cancer Institute, 90,* 498–504.

Cross-National Collaborative Study Group. (1992). The changing rate of major depression: Cross-national comparisons. *Journal of the American Medical Association, 268,* 3098–3105.

Crow, T. J. (1997). Schizophrenia as failure of hemispheric dominance for language. *Trends in Neuroscience, 20*(8), 339–343.

Crow, T. J., & Done, D. J. (1992). Prenatal exposure to influenza does not cause schizophrenia. *British Journal of Psychiatry, 161,* 390–393.

Crowe, R. R., Noyes, R., Pauls, D. L., & Slymen, D. J. (1983). A family study of panic disorder. *Archives of General Psychiatry, 40,* 1065–1069.

Crusio, W. E. (1996). The neurobehavioral genetics of aggression. *Behavior Genetics, 26,* 459–461.

Cummings, J. L. (1990). *Subcortical dementia.* New York: Oxford University Press.

Cummings, J. L. (1992). Neuropsychiatric aspects of Alzheimer's disease and other dementing illnesses. In S. C. Yudofsky & R. E. Hales (Eds.), *Textbook of neuropsychiatry* (2nd ed.) (pp. 605–620). Washington, DC: American Psychiatric Press.

Cutter, M. A. G., & Shelp, E. E. (Eds.). (1991). *Competency: A study of informal competency determinations in primary care.* Boston: Kluwer Academic.

Cutting, J. C. (1994). Evidence for right hemisphere damage in schizophrenia. In A. S. David & J. C. Cutting (Eds.), *The neuropsychology of schizophrenia* (pp. 231–244). Hillsdale, NJ: Erlbaum.

Dackis, C. A., & Gold, M. S. (1991). Inpa-tient treatment of drug and alcohol addiction. In N. S. Miller (Ed.), *Comprehensive handbook of drug and alcohol addiction* (pp. 1233–1244). New York: Dekker.

Dadds, M. R. (1997). Conduct disorder. In R. T. Ammerman & M. Hersen (Eds.), *Handbook of prevention and treatment with children and adolescents: Intervention in the real world context* (pp. 521–550). New York: Wiley.

Dager, S. R., Kenny, M. A., Artru, A. A., et al. (1993). Effects of sodium lactate infusion on cisternal lactate and carbon dioxide levels. *American Journal of Psychiatry, 150*(10), 1568.

Dahl, A. A. (1996). The relationship between social phobia and avoidant personality disorder: Workshop report 3. *International Clinical Psychopharmacology, 11* (Suppl. 3), 109–112.

Dahlstrom, W. G. (1985). The development of psychological testing. In G. A. Kimble & K. Schlesinger (Eds.), *Topics in the history of psychology, Vol. 2* (pp. 63–114). Hillsdale, NJ: Erlbaum.

Dahlstrom, W. G., Welsh, G. S., & Dahlstrom, L. (1972). *An MMPI handbook, Vol. 1: Clinical interpretation* (rev. ed.). Minneapolis: University of Minnesota Press.

Dalgleish, T., Joseph, S., Thrasher, S., & Tranah, T. (1996). Crisis support following the *Herald of Free-Enterprise* disaster: A longitudinal perspective. *Journal of Traumatic Stress, 9,* 833–845.

Dalgleish, T., Rosen, K., & Marks, M. (1996). Rhythm and blues: The theory and treatment of seasonal affective disorder. *British Journal of Clinical Psychology, 35*(Pt. 2), 163–182.

Dally, P. J. (1969). *Anorexia nervosa.* New York: Grune & Stratton.

Daly, J. A., & Buss, A. H. (1984). The transitory causes of audience anxiety. In J. A. Daly & J. C. McCroskey (Eds.), *Avoiding communication: Shyness, reticence, and communication apprehension* (pp. 67–78). Beverly Hills, CA: Sage.

Daniel, E. L. (1988). Development of a campus food service nutrition education program. *Journal of College Student Development, 29,* 276–278.

Dar, R., Serlin, R. C., & Omer, H. (1994). Misuse of statistical tests in three decades of psychotherapy research. *Journal of Consulting and Clinical Psychology, 62,* 75–82.

Daro, D. A. (1994). Prevention of child sexual abuse. *Future of Children, 4,* 198–223.

Darves-Bornoz, J. M., Degiovanni, A., & Gaillard, P. (1995). Why is dissociative disorder infrequent in France? *American Journal of Psychiatry, 152*(10), 1530–1531.

Darwin, C. R. (1872). *The expression of emotions in man and animals.* London: John Murray.

Dasen, P. R., Berry, J. W., & Sartorius, N. (Eds.). (1988). *Health and cross-cultural psychology: Toward applications.* Beverly Hills, CA: Sage.

Dauphinais, P., & King, J. (1992). Psychological assessment with American Indian children. *Applied and Preventative Psychology, 1,* 97–110.

Davey, G. C. L. (1992). Classical conditioning and the acquisition of human fears and phobias: A review and synthesis of the literature. *Advances in Behaviour Research and Therapy, 14*(1), 29–66.

Davey, G. C. L. (1994). Self-reported fears to common indigenous animals in an adult UK population: The role of disgust sensitivity. *British Journal of Psychology, 85* (Pt. 4), 541–554.

Davey, G. C. L. (1995). Preparedness and phobias: Specific evolved associations or a generalized expectancy bias? *Behavioral and Brain Sciences, 18*(2), 289–325.

Davey, G. C. L., Burgess, I., & Rashes, R. (1995). Coping strategies and phobias: The relationship between fears, phobias and methods of coping with stressors. *British Journal of Clinical Psychology, 34*(3), 423–434.

David, A. S., & Cutting, J. C. (Eds.). (1994). *The neuropsychology of schizophrenia.* Hillsdale, NJ: Erlbaum.

David, E. G. (1998). *Autism and the family: Problems, prospects, and coping with the disorder.* Springfield, IL: Thomas.

Davidson, J. R., Hughes, D., Blazer, D. G., & George, L. K. (1991). Posttraumatic stress disorder in the community: An epidemiological study. *Psychological Medicine, 21,* 713–721.

Davidson, J. R., Kundler, H., Smith, R., et al. (1990). Treatment of posttraumatic stress disorder with amitriptyline and placebo. *Archives of General Psychiatry, 47,* 259–268.

Davidson, L., & McGlashan, T. H. (1997). The varied outcomes of schizophrenia. *Canadian Journal of Psychiatry, 42*(1), 34–43.

Davidson, R. J. (1992). Emotion and affective style: Hemispheric substrates. *Psychological Science, 3,* 39–43.

Davis, J. O., & Phelps, J. A. (1995). Twins with schizophrenia: Genes or germs? *Schizophrenia Bulletin, 21,* 13–18.

Davison, G. C., & Neale, J. M. (1990). *Abnormal psychology* (5th ed.). New York: Wiley.

Dawber, T. R. (1980). *The Framingham study: The epidemiology of atherosclerotic disease.* Cambridge, MA: Harvard University Press.

Dawes, R. M. (1988). *Rational choice in an uncertain world.* New York: Harcourt Brace Jovanovich.

Dawes, R. M., & Corrigan, B. (1974). Linear models in decision making. *Psychological Bulletin, 81,* 95–106.

Dawes, R. M., Faust, D., & Meehl, P. E. (1989). Clinical versus actuarial judgment. *Science, 243*, 1668–1674.

Dawson, G., Meltzoff, A. N., Osterling, J., & Rinaldi, J. (1998). Neuropsychological tests: Neuropsychological correlates of early symptoms of autism. *Child Development, 69*, 1276–1285.

Deakin, F. W., Simpson, M. D., Slater, P., & Hellewell, J. S. (1997). Familial and developmental abnormalities of front lobe function and neurochemistry in schizophrenia. *Journal of Psychopharmacology, 11*(2), 133–142.

de Almeida-Filho, N., Santana, U. S., Pinto, I. M., & de Carvalho-Neto, J. A. (1991). Is there an epidemic of drug misuse in Brazil? A review of the epidemiological evidence (1977–1988). *International Journal of the Addictions, 26*, 355–369.

Dean, C., & Surtees, P. B. (1989). Do psychological factors predict breast cancer? *Journal of Psychosomatic Research, 33*, 561–569.

de Beurs, E., van Balkom, A. J., Lange, A., et al. (1995). Treatment of panic disorder with agoraphobia: Comparison of fluvoxamine, placebo, and psychological panic management combined with exposure and of exposure in vivo alone. *American Journal of Psychiatry, 152*(5), 683–691.

Decker, T. W., Cline-Elsen, J., & Gallagher, M. (1992). Relaxation therapy as an adjunct in radiation oncology. *Journal of Clinical Psychology, 48*, 388–393.

Deister, A., & Marneros, A. (1993). Predicting the long-term outcome of affective disorders. *Acta Psychiatrica Scandinavica, 88*(3), 174–177.

Delameter, A. M., Bubb, J., Kurtz, S. M., et al. (1987). Stress and coping in relation to adolescents with Type 1 diabetes mellitus. *Journal of Pediatric Psychology, 13*, 69–86.

DeLisi, L. E., Sakuma, M., Tew, W., et al. (1997). Schizophrenia as a chronic active brain process: A study of progressive brain structural change subsequent to the onset of schizophrenia. *Psychiatry Research, 74*(3), 129–140.

Delong, R. (1995). Medical and pharmacological treatment of learning disabilities. *Journal of Child Neurology, 10* (Suppl. 1), S92–S95.

Dembroski, T. M., & MacDougall, J. M. (1983). Behavioral and psychophysiological perspectives on coronary-prone behavior. In T. M. Dembroski, T. H. Schmidt, & G. Blumchen (Eds.), *Biobehavioral bases of coronary heart disease.* New York: Karger.

Demopulos, C., Fava, M., McLean, N. E., et al. (1996). Hypochondriacal concerns in depressed outpatients. *Psychosomatic Medicine, 58*, 314–320.

Depue, R. A., & Iacono, W. G. (1989). Neurobehavioral aspects of affective disorders. *Annual Review of Psychology, 40*, 457–492.

Depue, R. A., Slater, J. F., Wolfstetter-Kausch, H., et al. (1981). A behavioral paradigm for identifying persons at risk for bipolar depressive disorder: A conceptual framework and five validation studies. *Journal of Abnormal Psychology, 90*(5), 381–437.

Derry, S. J. (1988). Putting learning strategies to work. *Educational Leadership, 46*, 4–10.

Devlin, M. J. (1998). Eating disorders: Progress and problems. *Science, 280*, 1387–1390.

Dew, M. A., Bromet, E. J., Brent, D., & Greenhouse, J. (1987). A quantitative review of the effectiveness of suicide prevention centers. *Journal of Consulting and Clinical Psychology, 55*, 239–244.

de Wilde, E. J., Kienhurst, C. W. M., Diekstra, R. F. W., & Wolters, W. H. G. (1993). The specificity of psychological characteristics of adolescent suicide attempters. *Journal of the American Academy of Child and Adolescent Psychiatry, 32*, 51–59.

Dhondt, J. L., Farriaux, J. P., Sailly, J. C., & Lebrun, T. (1991). Economic evaluation of cost-benefit ratio of neonatal screening procedure for phenylketonuria and hypothyroidism. *Journal of Inherited Metabolic Disease, 14*(4), 633–639.

Diamond, M., & Sigmundson, H. K. (1997). Sex reassignment at birth: Long-term review and clinical implications. *Archives of Pediatric and Adolescent Medicine, 151*, 298–304.

Diamond, S. (1980). Wundt before Leipzig. In R. W. Reiber (Ed.), *Wilhelm Wundt and the making of scientific psychology* (pp. 3–70). New York: Plenum.

Dick, C. L., Bland, R. C., & Newman, S. C. (1994). Epidemiology of psychiatric disorders in Edmonton: Panic disorder. *Acta Psychiatrica Scandinavica, Supplementum, 376*, 45–53.

Di Nardo, P. A., Brown, T. A., & Barlow, D. H. (1994). *Anxiety disorders interview schedule for DSM-IV (ADIS-IV).* Albany, NY: Graywind.

Di Nardo, P. A., Moras, K., Barlow, D. H., & Rapee, R. M. (1993). Reliability of *DSM-III-R* anxiety disorder categories: Using the Anxiety Disorders Interview Schedule–Revised (ADIS-R). *Archives of General Psychiatry, 50*, 251–256.

Dinwiddie, S. H. (1994). Abuse of inhalants: A review. *Addiction, 89*(8), 925–939.

Dinwiddie, S. H. (1996). Genetics, antisocial personality, and criminal responsibility. *Bulletin of the American Academy of Psychiatry and Law, 24*, 95–108.

Dinwiddie, S. H., & Reich, T. (1993). Attribution of antisocial symptoms in coexis-

tent antisocial personality disorder and substance abuse. *Comprehensive Psychiatry, 34*, 235–242.

Dobson, D. J., McDougall, G., Busheikin, J., & Aldous, J. (1995). Effects of social skills training and social milieu treatment on symptoms of schizophrenia. *Psychiatric Services, 46*(4), 376–380.

Dobson, K. (Ed.). (1988). *Handbook of cognitive behavioral therapies.* New York: Guilford Press.

Doctor, R. M., & Kahn, A. P. (1989). *The encyclopedia of phobias, fears, and anxieties.* New York: Facts on File.

Dodd, S. L., Herb, R. A., & Powers, S. K. (1993). Caffeine and endurance performance: An update. *Sports Medicine, 15*, 14–23.

Dodge, K. A. (1993). Social-cognitive mechanisms in the development of conduct disorder and depression. *Annual Review of Psychology, 44*, 559–584.

Dohr, K. B., Rush, A. J., & Bernstein, I. H. (1989). Cognitive biases and depression. *Journal of Abnormal Psychology, 98*(3), 263–267.

Dohrenwend, B. S., Krasnoff, L., Askenasy, A. R., & Dohrenwend, B. P. (1982). Exemplification of a method for scaling life events: The PERI Life Events Scale. *Journal of Health and Social Behavior, 19*, 205–229.

Doll, E. A. (1965). *Vineland Social Maturity Scale: Manual of directions* (rev. ed.). Minneapolis: Educational Test Bureau.

Dollard, J., & Miller, N. E. (1950). *Personality and psychotherapy.* New York: McGraw-Hill.

Donahey, K. M., & Carroll, R. A. (1993). Gender differences in factors associated with hypoactive sexual desire. *Journal of Sex and Marital Therapy, 19*, 25–40.

Doogan, S., & Thomas, G. V. (1992). Origins of fear of dogs in adults and children: The role of conditioning processes and prior familiarity with dogs. *Behaviour Research and Therapy, 30*(4), 387–394.

Dougher, M. J. (1993). Covert sensitization in the treatment of deviant sexual arousal. In J. R. Cautela, A. J. Kearney, et al. (Eds.), *Covert conditioning casebook* (pp. 199–207). Pacific Grove, CA: Brooks/Cole.

Douglass, H. M., Moffitt, T. E., Dar, R., et al. (1995). Obsessive-compulsive disorder in a birth cohort of 18-year-olds: Prevalence and predictors. *Journal of the American Academy of Child and Adolescent Psychiatry, 34*(11), 1424–1431.

Dreger, R. M. (1982). The classification of children and their emotional problems: An overview—II. *Clinical Psychology Review, 2*, 261–271.

Drinnan, M. J., & Marmor, M. F. (1991). Functional visual loss in Cambodian refugees: A study of cultural factors in ophthalmology. *European Journal of Ophthalmology, 1,* 115–118.

Droogan, J., & Bannigan, K. A. (1997). Review of psychosocial family interventions for schizophrenia. *Nursing Times, 93*(26), 46–47.

Dryfoos, J. G. (1990). *Adolescents at risk: Prevalence and prevention.* New York: Oxford University Press.

Dubois, P. H. (1970). *The history of psychological testing.* Boston: Allyn & Bacon.

Duckett, S. (1991). The normal aging human brain. In S. Duckett (Ed.), *The pathology of the aging human nervous system* (pp. 1–9). Philadelphia: Lea & Febiger.

Duclos, P., & Ward, B. J. (1998). Measles vaccines: A review of adverse events. *Drug Safety, 19,* 435–454.

Duggan, C. F., Lee, A. S., & Murray, R. M. (1991). Do different subtypes of hospitalized depressives have different long-term outcomes? *Archives of General Psychiatry, 48,* 308–312.

Dujovne, V. F., Barnard, M. U., & Rapoff, M. A. (1995). Pharmacological and cognitive behavioral approaches in the treatment of childhood depression: A review and critique. *Clinical Psychology Review, 15*(7), 589–611.

Duke University School of Medicine. (1999). Basic neurobiology, Slide 18. Available: http://www.neuro.duke.edu/COURSES/202/99/medschool99chapter6/sld018.htm; last visited 3/15/99.

Dummit, E. S., III, Klein, R. G., Tancer, N. K., et al. (1997). Systematic assessment of 50 children with selective mutism. *Journal of the American Academy of Child and Adolescent Psychiatry, 36,* 653–660.

Dunlap, K. (1932). *Habits: Their making and unmaking.* New York: Liveright.

Dunn, G. E., Paolo, A. M., Ryan, J. J., & Van Fleet, J. N. (1994). Belief in the existence of multiple personality disorder among psychologists and psychiatrists. *Journal of Clinical Psychology, 50,* 454–457.

Durkheim, É. (1951). *Suicide.* (J. A. Spaulding & G. Simpson, Trans.). Glencoe, IL: Free Press. (Original work published 1897)

Dusenbury, L., Falco, M., & Lake, A. (1997). A review of the evaluation of 47 drug abuse prevention curricula available nationally. *Journal of School Health, 67*(4), 127–132.

Dykman, B. M., Horowitz, L. M., Abramson, L. Y., & Usher, M. (1991). Schematic and situational determinants of depressed and nondepressed students' interpretation of feedback. *Journal of Abnormal Psychology, 100,* 45–55.

Eagles, J. M. (1991). The relationship between schizophrenia and immigration: Are there alternatives to psychosocial models? *British Journal of Psychiatry, 159,* 783–789.

Eagles, J. M., Gibson, I., Bremner, M. H., et al. (1990). Obstetric complications in *DSM-III* schizophrenics and their siblings. *Lancet, 335,* 1139–1141.

Eagly, A. H. (1995). The science and politics of comparing men and women. *American Psychologist, 50,* 145–158.

Eaton, W. W. (1985). Epidemiology of schizophrenia. *Epidemiological Reviews, 7,* 105–126.

Eaton, W. W. (1991). Update on the epidemiology of schizophrenia. *Epidemiological Reviews, 13,* 320–328.

Eaton, W. W., Mortensen, P. B., Herrman, H., et al. (1992). Long-term course of hospitalization for schizophrenia: Part I. Risk for rehospitalization. *Schizophrenia Bulletin, 18,* 217–228.

Eaves, L., Silberg, J., Hewitt, J. K., et al. (1993). Genes, personality, and psychopathology: A latent class analysis of liability to symptoms of attention deficit hyperactivity disorder in twins. In R. Plomin & G. E. McClearn (Eds.), *Nature, nurture and psychology* (pp. 285–303). Washington, DC: American Psychological Association.

Eaves, L. J., Silberg, J., Maes, H. H., et al. (1997). Genetics and developmental psychopathology 2: The main effects of genes and environment on behavioral problems in the Virginia Twin Study of Adolescent Behavioral Development. *Journal of Child Psychology and Psychiatry, 38,* 965–980.

Ebmeier, K. P., Lawrie, S. M., Blackwood, D. H., et al. (1995). Hypofrontality revisited: A high resolution single photon emission computed tomography study in schizophrenia. *Journal of Neurology, Neurosurgery and Psychiatry, 58,* 452–456.

Eccles, J. S., Midgley, C., Wigfield, A., et al. (1993). The impact of stage-environment fit on young adolescents' experiences in schools and families. *American Psychologist, 48,* 90–101.

Edelmann, R. J. (1992). *Anxiety: Theory, research, and intervention in clinical and health psychology.* Chichester, UK: Wiley.

Edelson, S. M., Rimland, B., Berger, C. L., & Billings, D. (1998). Evaluation of a mechanical hand-support for facilitated communication. *Journal of Autism and Developmental Disorders, 28,* 153–157.

Edgerton, R. B., & Cohen, A. (1994). Culture and schizophrenia: The DOSMD challenge. *British Journal of Psychiatry, 164,* 222–231.

Edman, G., Asberg, M., Levander, S., & Schalling, D. (1986). Skin conductance habituation and cerebrospinal fluid 5-hydroxinoleactic acid in suicidal patients. *Archives of General Psychiatry, 43,* 586–592.

Edwards, A. J. (1994). *When memory fails: Helping the Alzheimer's and dementia patient.* New York: Plenum.

Edwards, A. L. (1959). *Edwards Personal Preference Schedule.* New York: Psychological Corporation.

Edwards, G., & Peters, T. J. (Eds.). (1994). *Alcohol and alcohol problems.* Edinburgh, Scot.: Churchill Livingstone.

Edwards, J. R., Cooper, C., Pearl, S. G., et al. (1990). The relationship between psychosocial factors and breast cancer: Some unexpected results. *Behavioral Medicine, 5,* 14–19.

Egeland, J. A., Gerhard, D. S., Pauls, D. L., et al. (1987). Bipolar affective disorders linked to DNA markers on chromosome 11. *Nature, 325*(6107), 783–787.

Egeland, J. A., & Hostetter, A. M. (1983). Amish study I: Affective disorders among the Amish. *American Journal of Psychiatry, 140,* 56–61.

Ehlers, A., & Breuer, P. (1992). Increased cardiac awareness in panic disorder. *Journal of Abnormal Psychology, 101,* 371–382.

Ehlers, A., Margraf, J., Roth, W. T., et al. (1988). Anxiety induced by false heart-rate feedback in patients' panic disorder. *Behaviour Research and Therapy, 26,* 1–11.

Eifert, G. H. (1992). General and specific fears in referred and self-referred adult patients with extreme dental anxiety. *Behaviour Research and Therapy, 30,* 329–345.

Einhorn, H. J. (1988). Diagnosis and causality in clinical and statistical prediction. In D. C. Turk & P. Salovey (Eds.), *Reasoning, inference and judgment in clinical psychology* (pp. 51–70). New York: Free Press.

Eisler, I., Dare, C., Russell, G. F. M., et al. (1997). Family and individual therapy in anorexia nervosa: A 5-year follow-up. *Archives of General Psychiatry, 54,* 1025–1030.

Ekman, P. (Ed.). (1982). *Emotion in the human face.* Cambridge, UK: Cambridge University Press.

Ekman, P., & Davidson, R. J. (1993). Voluntary smiling changes regional brain activity. *Psychological Science, 4,* 342–345.

Ekselius, L., Eriksson, M., von Knorring, L., & Linder, J. (1997). Comorbidity of personality disorders and major depression in patients with somatoform pain disorders or medical illnesses with long-standing work disability. *Scandinavian Journal of Rehabilitation Medicine, 29*(2), 91–96.

Elkin, I., Parloff, M. B., Hadley, S. W., & Autry, J. H. (1985). NIMH treatment of depression collaborative research program. *Archives of General Psychiatry, 42,* 305–316.

Ellard, J. (1989). *Some rules for killing people: Essays on madness, murder and the mind.* North Ryde, NSW, Austral.: Angus & Robertson.

Ellason, J. W., & Ross, C. A. (1997). Two-year

follow-up of inpatients with dissociative identity disorder. *American Journal of Psychiatry, 154*(6), 832–839.

Ellenberger, H. (1954). The life and work of Hermann Rorschach (1884–1922). *Bulletin of the Menninger Clinic, 18*, 173–219.

Elliott, C. (1991). The rules of insanity. Commentary on psychopathic disorder: A category mistake? *Journal of Medical Ethics, 17*, 89–90.

Elliot, D., & Goldberg, L. (1996). Intervention and prevention of steroid use in adolescents. *American Journal of Sports Medicine, 24*(6 Suppl.), S46–S47.

Ellis, A. (1962). *Reason and emotion in psychotherapy.* New York: Lyle Stewart.

Ellis, A., & Dryden, W. (1997). *The practice of rational emotive behavior therapy* (2nd ed.). New York: Springer-Verlag.

Ellis, H. D., & de Pauw, K. W. (1994). The cognitive neuropsychiatric origins of the Capgras delusion. In A. S. David & J. C. Cutting (Eds.), *The neuropsychology of schizophrenia* (pp. 317–335). Hillsdale, NJ: Erlbaum.

Ellison, G. D., & Bresler, D. E. (1974). Tests of emotional behavior in rats following depletion of norepinephrine, of serotonin, or of both. *Psychopharmacology, 34*, 275–280.

Elmer-Dewitt, P. (1995, July 3). On a screen near you. *Time*, p. 38.

Emanuels, Z. L., & Emmelkamp, P. M. (1997). Spouse-aided therapy with depression. *Behavior Modification, 21*, 62–77.

Emerson, E., & Hatton, C. (1996). Deinstitutionalisation in the UK and Ireland: Outcomes for service users. *Australia and New Zealand Journal of Developmental Disabilities, 21*, 17–37.

Emery, R. E., & Coiro, M. J. (1998). Some costs of coping: Stress and distress among children from divorced families. In D. Cicchetti & S. L. Toth (Eds.), *Rochester Symposium on Developmental Psychopathology, Vol. 8: Developmental perspectives on trauma: Theory, research, and intervention* (pp. 435–462). Rochester, NY: University of Rochester Press.

Emmelkamp, P. M. (1994). Behavior therapy with adults. In A. E. Bergin & S. L. Garfield (Eds.), *Handbook of psychotherapy and behavior change* (4th ed.). New York: Wiley.

Emrick, C. D., Tonigan, J. S., Montgomery, H., & Little, L. (1993). Alcoholics Anonymous: What is currently known? In B. S. McCrady & W. R. Miller (Eds.), *Research on Alcoholics Anonymous: Opportunities and alternatives* (pp. 41–76). New Brunswick, NJ: Rutgers Center of Alcohol Studies.

Epstein, L. H. (1992). Role of behavior theory in behavioral medicine. *Journal of Consulting and Clinical Psychology, 60*, 493–498.

Erdberg, P. (1985). The Rorschach. In C. S. Newmark (Ed.), *Major psychological assessment instruments* (pp. 65–88). Boston: Allyn & Bacon.

Erikson, E. H. (1967). *Identity and the life cycle: Selected papers.* New York: International Universities Press.

Eriksson, N. G., & Lundin, T. (1996). Early traumatic stress reactions among Swedish survivors of the m/s *Estonia* disaster. *British Journal of Psychiatry, 169*(6), 713–716.

Erlenmeyer-Kimling, L., & Cornblatt, B. A. (1992). A summary of attentional findings in the New York High-Risk Project. *Journal of Psychiatric Research, 26*, 405–426.

Ernst, C., & Angst, J. (1992). The Zurich Study. XII. Sex differences in depression: Evidence from longitudinal epidemiological data. *European Archives of Psychiatry and Clinical Neuroscience, 241*(4), 222–230.

Eron, L. D. (1997). The development of antisocial behavior from a learning perspective. In D. M. Stoff, J. Breiling, & J. D. Maser (Eds.), *Handbook of antisocial behavior* (pp. 140–147). New York: Wiley.

Ervin, R. A., Bankert, C. L., & DuPaul, G. J. (1996). Treatment of attention-deficit/hyperactivity disorder. In M. A. Reinecke & F. M. Dattilio (Eds.), *Cognitive therapy with children and adolescents: A casebook for clinical practice* (pp. 38–61). New York: Guilford Press.

Escobar, J. I. (1996). Overview of somatization: Diagnosis, epidemiology, and management. *Psychopharmacology Bulletin, 32*(4), 589–596.

Escobar, J. I., Burnam, M. A., Karno, M., et al. (1987). Somatization in the community. *Archives of General Psychiatry, 44*, 713–720.

Espeland, K. E. (1997). Inhalants: The instant, but deadly high. *Pediatric Nursing, 23*(1), 82–86.

Esquirol, J. E. D. (1832). *Alienation mentale.* Paris: Librairie Medicale de Crochard.

Estimates of retailers willing to sell tobacco to minors—California, August–September 1995 and June–July 1996. (1996, Dec. 20). *Morbidity and Mortality Weekly Report (MMWR), 45*(50), 1095–1099.

Evans, D. L., Folds, J. D., Pettito, J. M., & Golden, R. N. (1992). Circulating natural killer cell phenotypes in men and women with major depression: Relation to cytotoxic activity and severity of depression. *Archives of General Psychology, 49*, 388–395.

Evans, J. St. B. T. (1989). Some causes of bias in expert opinion. *Psychologist, 2*, 112–113.

Evans, M. D., Hollon, S. D., Derubeis, R. J., et al. (1992). Differential relapse following cognitive therapy and pharmacotherapy for depression. *Archives of General Psychiatry, 49*, 802–808.

Evans, R. I., Smith, C. K., & Raines, B. E. (1984). Deterring cigarette smoking in adolescents: A psychosocial-behavioral analysis of an intervention strategy. In A. Baum, S. E. Taylor, & J. E. Singer (Eds.), *Handbook of psychology and health, Vol. 4: Social psychological aspects of health* (pp. 301–318). Hillsdale, NJ: Erlbaum.

Ewing, S. E., Falk, W. E., & Otto, M. W. (1996). The recalcitrant patient: Treating disorders of personality. In M. H. Pollack & M. W. Otto (Eds.), *Challenges in clinical practice: Pharmacologic and psychosocial strategies* (pp. 355–379). New York: Guilford Press.

Exner, J. E. (1990). *A Rorschach workbook for the comprehensive system* (2nd ed.). Asheville, NC: Rorschach Workshops.

Exner, J. E., Jr. (1986). *The Rorschach: A comprehensive system* (2nd ed.). New York: Wiley.

Eysenck, H. J. (1991). *Smoking, personality, and stress: Psychosocial factors in the prevention of cancer and coronary heart disease.* New York: Springer-Verlag.

Eysenck, H. J., & Eysenck, S. B. G. (1975). *Manual of the Eysenck Personality Questionnaire.* San Diego: Educational and Industrial Testing Service.

Eysenck, M. W. (1992). *Anxiety: The cognitive perspective.* Hove, UK: Erlbaum.

Ezzy, D. (1993). Unemployment and mental health: A critical review. *Social Science and Medicine, 37*, 41–52.

Fackelmann, K. A. (1993). Marijuana and the brain: Scientists discover the brain's own THC. *Science, 143*, 88–94.

Falloon, I. R. H., Brooker, C., & Graham-Hole, V. (1992). Psychosocial interventions for schizophrenia. *Archives of General Psychiatry, 42*, 887–896.

Falsetti, S. A., Resnick, H. S., Dansky, B. S., et al. (1995). Relationship of stress to panic disorder: Cause or effect? In C. M. Mazure (Ed.), *Does stress cause psychiatric illness?* Washington, DC: American Psychiatric Association.

Faraone, S. V., Biederman, J., & Mick, E. (1997). Symptom reports by adults with attention deficit hyperactivity disorder: Are they influenced by attention deficit hyperactivity disorder in their children? *Journal of Nervous and Mental Disease, 185*, 583–584.

Faraone, S. V., Kremen, W. S., & Tsuang, M. T. (1990). Genetic transmission of major affective disorders: Quantitative models and linkage analysis. *Psychological Bulletin, 108*, 109–127.

Faravelli, C., Pallanti, S., Biondi, F., & Paterniti, S. (1992). Onset of panic disorder. *American Journal of Psychiatry, 149*(6), 827–828.

Faravelli, C., Salvatori, S., Galassi, F., et al.

(1997). Epidemiology of somatoform disorders: A community survey in Florence. *Social Psychiatry and Psychiatric Epidemiology, 32*(1), 24–29.

Faris, R. E. L., & Dunham, H. W. (1939). *Mental disorders in urban areas: An ecological study of schizophrenia and other psychoses.* Chicago: University of Chicago Press.

Farlow, M., Ghetti, B., Benson, M. D., et al. (1992). Low cerebrospinal-fluid concentrations of soluble amyloid β-protein precursor in hereditary Alzheimer's disease. *Lancet, 340,* 453–454.

Farmer, A. E., & Blewitt, A. (1993). Drug treatment of resistant schizophrenia: Limitations and recommendations. *Drugs, 45*(3), 374–383.

Farmer, R., & Nelson-Gray, R. O. (1990). Personality disorders and depression: Hypothetical relations, empirical findings, and methodological considerations. *Clinical Psychology Review, 10,* 453–476.

Faron, L. C. (1968). *The Mapuche Indians of Chile.* New York: Holt Rinehart Winston.

Farrell, J. M., & Shaw, I. A. (1994). Emotional awareness training: A prerequisite to effective cognitive-behavioral treatment of borderline personality disorder. *Cognitive and Behavioral Practice, 1,* 71–91.

Fava, M., Alpert, J. E., Borus, J. S., et al. (1996). Patterns of personality disorder comorbidity in early-onset versus late-onset major depression. *American Journal of Psychiatry, 153,* 1308–1312.

Fava, M., Rosenbaum, J. F., Pava, J. A., et al. (1993). Anger attacks in unipolar depression. Part 1: Clinical correlates and response to fluoxetine treatment. *American Journal of Psychiatry, 150*(8), 1158–1163.

Favaro, A., & Santonastaso, P. (1997). Suicidality in eating disorders: Clinical and psychological correlates. *Acta Psychiatrica Scandinavica, 95,* 508–514.

Fawzy, F. I., Fawzy, N. W., Hyun, C. S., et al. (1993). Malignant melanoma: Effects of an early structured psychiatric intervention, coping, and affective state on recurrence and survival 6 years later. *Archives of General Psychiatry, 50,* 681–689.

Feather, N. (1990). *The psychological impact of unemployment.* New York: Springer-Verlag.

Feehan, C. J. (1995). Enuresis secondary to sexual assault. *Journal of the American Academy of Child and Adolescent Psychiatry, 34,* 1404.

Fenichel, O. (1946). *The psychoanalytic theory of neuroses.* London: Routledge & Kegan Paul.

Fennig, S., Bromet, E. J., Karant, M. T., et al. (1996). Mood-congruent versus mood-incongruent psychotic symptoms in first-admission patients with affective disorder. *Journal of Affective Disorders, 37*(1), 23–29.

Fernandez, E., & Sheffield, J. (1995). Psychosocial stressors predicting headache occurrence: The major role of minor hassles. *Headache Quarterly, 6*(3), 215–220.

Ferster, C. B. (1961). Positive reinforcement and behavioral deficits of autistic children. *Child Development 32,* 437–456.

Fichtner, C. G., Hanrahan, P., & Luchins, D. J. (1998). Pharmacoeconomic studies of atypical antipsychotics: Review and perspective. *Psychiatric Annals, 28,* 381–396.

Fielding, J. E. (1985). Smoking: Health effects and control. *New England Journal of Medicine, 313,* 491–498.

Figueroa, E. F., Silk, K. R., Huth, A., & Lohr, N. E. (1997). History of childhood sexual abuse and general psychopathology. *Comprehensive Psychiatry, 38*(1), 23–30.

Filley, C. M. (1995). Neuropsychiatric features of Lewy body disease. *Brain and Cognition, 28,* 229–239.

Fils-Aime, M. L. (1993). Sedative-hypnotic abuse. In D. L. Dunner (Ed.), *Current psychiatric therapy* (pp. 124–131). Philadelphia: Saunders.

Fink, P. (1992). The use of hospitalizations by persistent somatizing patients. *Psychological Medicine, 22,* 173–180.

Finney, J. W., & Moos, R. H. (1991). The long-term course of treated alcoholism. I: Mortality, relapse and remission rates and comparisons with community controls. *Journal of Studies on Alcohol, 52,* 44–54.

Firestone, P., Bradford, J. M., Greenberg, D. M., et al. (1998). Homicidal and nonhomicidal child molesters: Psychological, phallometric, and criminal features. *Sexual Abuse: Journal of Research and Treatment, 10,* 305–323.

First, M. B., Donovan, S., & Frances, A. (1996). Nosology of chronic mood disorders. *Psychiatric Clinics of North America, 19*(1), 29–39.

Fisch, H. U., Hammond, K. R., Joyce, C. R. B., & O'Reilly, M. (1981). An experimental study of the clinical judgement of general physicians in evaluating and prescribing for depression. *British Journal of Psychiatry, 138,* 100–109.

Fischer, C., Hatzidimitriou, G., Wlos, J., et al. (1995). Reorganization of ascending 5-HT axon projections in animals previously exposed to recreational drug (+/−) 3,4-methylenedioxymethamphetamine (MDMA, "ecstasy"). *Journal of Neuroscience, 15*(8), 5476–5485.

Fischer, D. G., & Elnitsky, S. (1990). A factor analytic study of two scales measuring dissociation. *American Journal of Clinical Hypnosis, 31,* 201–207.

Fischer, P. J., & Breakey, W. R. (1991). The epidemiology of alcohol, drug, and mental disorders among homeless persons. *American Psychologist, 46,* 1115–1128.

Fischer, P. M., Richards, J. W., Jr., Berman, E. J., & Krugman, D. M. (1989). Recall and eye tracking study of adolescents viewing tobacco advertisements. *Journal of the American Medical Association, 261,* 84–89.

Fischhoff, B. (1982). For those condemned to study the past: Heuristics and biases in hindsight. In D. Kahneman, P. Slovic, & A. Tversky (Eds.), *Judgment under uncertainty: Heuristics and biases* (pp. 335–354). Cambridge, UK: Cambridge University Press.

Fishbain, D. A. (1996). Where have two *DSM* revisions taken us for the diagnosis of pain disorder in chronic pain patients? *American Journal of Psychiatry, 153*(1), 137–138.

Fishbain, D. A., & Goldberg, M. (1991). The misdiagnosis of conversion disorder in a psychiatric emergency service. *General Hospital Psychiatry, 13,* 177–181.

Fisher, B. C., & Beckley, R. A. (1998). *Attention deficit disorder: Practical coping methods.* Boca Raton, FL: CRC Press.

Fisher, D. G., Lankford, B. A., & Galea, R. P. (1996). Therapeutic community retention among Alaska natives: Akeela House. *Journal of Substance Abuse Treatment, 13*(3), 265–271.

Fisher, K. K., Glasgow, R. E., & Terborg, J. R. (1990). Worksite smoking cessation: A meta-analysis of controlled studies. *Journal of Occupational Medicine, 32,* 429–439.

Fiske, S. T. (1992). Thinking is for doing: Portraits of social cognition from daguerreotype to laserphoto. *Journal of Personality and Social Psychology, 63,* 877–889.

Fitts, S. N., Gibson, P., Redding, C. A., & Deiter, P. J. (1989). Body dysmorphic disorder: Implications of its validity as a *DSM-III-R* clinical syndrome. *Psychological Reports, 64,* 655–658.

FitzGerald, M. L., Braudaway, C. A., Leeks, D., et al. (1993). Debriefing: A therapeutic intervention. *Military Medicine, 158*(8), 542–545.

Flach, F. (1990). The resilience hypothesis and posttraumatic stress disorder. In M. E. Wolf & A. D. Mosnaim (Eds.), *Posttraumatic stress disorder: Etiology, phenomenology, and treatment* (pp. 37–45). Washington, DC: American Psychiatric Press.

Flakierska-Praquin, N., Lindstroem, M., & Gillberg, C. (1997). School phobia with separation anxiety disorder: A comparative 20- to 29-year follow-up study of 35 school refusers. *Comprehensive Psychiatry, 38,* 17–22.

Fleischhacker, W. W., & Hummer, M. (1997). Drug treatment of schizophrenia in the 1990s: Achievements and future possibilities in optimising outcomes. *Drugs, 53*(6), 915–929.

Flett, G. L., Vredenburg, K., & Krames, L. (1997). The continuity of depression in clinical and nonclinical samples. *Psychological Bulletin, 121,* 395–416.

Flint, A. J. (1994). Epidemiology and comorbidity of anxiety disorders in the elderly. *American Journal of Psychiatry, 151*(5), 640–649.

Flint, A. J. (1997). Epidemiology and comorbidity of anxiety disorders in later life: Implications for treatment. *Clinical Neuroscience, 4*(1), 31–36.

Flynn, J. R. (1984). The mean IQ of Americans: Massive gains 1932 to 1978. *Psychological Bulletin, 95,* 29–51.

Flynn, J. R. (1987). Massive IQ gains in 14 nations: What IQ tests really measure. *Psychological Bulletin, 101,* 171–191.

Foa, E., Rothbaum, B. O., Riggs, D. S., & Murdock, T. B. (1991). Treatment of posttraumatic stress disorder in rape victims: A comparison between cognitive behavioral procedures and counseling. *Journal of Consulting and Clinical Psychology, 59,* 715–723.

Foa, E. B., Hearst-Ikeda, D., & Perry, K. J. (1995). Evaluation of a brief cognitive-behavioral program for the prevention of PTSD in recent assault victims. *Journal of Consulting and Clinical Psychology, 63* (6), 948–955.

Fokias, D., & Tyler, P. (1995). Social support and agoraphobia: A review. *Clinical Psychology Review, 15*(4), 347–366.

Foley, H. A., Carlton, C. O., & Howell R. J. (1996). The relationship of attention deficit hyperactivity disorder and conduct disorder to juvenile delinquency: Legal implications. *Bulletin of the American Academy of Psychiatry and Law, 24,* 333–345.

Folkman, S., & Lazarus, R. S. (1990). Coping and emotion. In N. Stein & B. Leventhal (Eds.), *Psychological and biological approaches to emotion* (pp. 313–332). Hillsdale, NJ: Erlbaum.

Folks, D. G., Ford, C. V., & Regan, W. M. (1984). Conversion symptoms in a general hospital. *Psychosomatics, 25,* 285–295.

Folnegovic, Z., & Folnegovic-Smalc, V. (1992). Schizophrenia in Croatia: Interregional differences in prevalence and a comment on constant incidence. *Journal of Epidemiology and Community Health, 46*(3), 248–255.

Folstein, S. E., Bisson, E., Santangelo, S. L., & Piven, J. (1998). Finding specific genes that cause autism: A combination of approaches will be needed to maximize power. *Journal of Autism and Developmental Disorders, 28,* 439–445.

Folstein, S. E., & Folstein, M. F. (1998). Genetic counseling in Alzheimer's disease and Huntington's disease: Principles and practice. In M. F. Folstein (Ed.), *Neurobiology of primary dementia* (pp. 329–364). Washington, DC: American Psychiatric Press.

Fones, C. (1996). Posttraumatic stress disorder occurring after painful childbirth. *Journal of Nervous and Mental Disease, 184*(3), 195–196.

Fontaine, K. R., & Jones, L. C. (1997). Self-esteem, optimism and postpartum depression. *Journal of Clinical Psychology, 53,* 59–63.

Ford, C., & Neale, J. M. (1985). Effects of a helplessness induction on judgements of control. *Journal of Personality and Social Psychology, 49,* 1330–1336.

Ford, C. V., & Folks, D. G. (1985). Conversion disorders: An overview. *Psychosomatics, 26,* 371–383.

Ford, M. R., & Widiger, T. A. (1989). Sex bias in the diagnosis of histrionic and antisocial personality disorders. *Journal of Consulting and Clinical Psychology, 57,* 301–305.

Foreman, D. M., & Thambirajah, M. S. (1996). Conduct disorder, enuresis and specific developmental delays in two types of encopresis: A case note study of 63 boys. *European Child and Adolescent Psychiatry, 15,* 33–37.

Forrest, A. R. (1997). Ethical aspects of workplace urine screening for drug abuse. *Journal of Medical Ethics, 23*(1), 12–17.

Fossey, L., Papiernik, E., & Bydlowski, M. (1997). Postpartum blues: A clinical syndrome and predictor of postnatal depression. *Journal of Psychosomatic Obstetrics and Gynecology, 18,* 17–21.

Foucault, M. (1967). *Madness and civilization.* London: Tavistock.

Frances, A. J., Kahn, D. A., Carpenter, D., et al. (1998). The expert consensus guidelines for treating depression in bipolar disorder. *Journal of Clinical Psychiatry, 59* (Suppl. 4), 73–79.

Francis, M. E., & Pennebaker, J. W. (1992). Putting stress into words: The impact of writing on physiological, absentee, and self-reported emotional well-being measures. *American Journal of Health Promotion, 6*(4), 280–287.

Frank, E., Kupfer, D. J., Perel, J. M., et al. (1990). Three-year outcomes for maintenance therapies in recurrent depression. *Archives of General Psychiatry, 47*(12), 1093–1099.

Frank, G. (1990). Research on the clinical usefulness of the Rorschach. I: The diagnosis of schizophrenia. *Perceptual and Motor Skills, 71,* 573–578.

Frank, L. G. (1939). Projective methods for the study of personality. *Journal of Psychology, 8,* 389–413.

Frankel, F. H. (1994). The concept of flashbacks in historical perspective. *International Journal of Clinical and Experimental Hypnosis, 42*(4), 321–336.

Frankl, V. E. (1973). *The doctor and the soul: From psychotherapy to logotherapy.* New York: Knopf.

Frankl, V. E. (1978). *The unheard cry for meaning: Psychotherapy and humanism.* London: Hodder & Stoughton.

Frazier, P. A. (1991). Self-blame as a mediator of postrape depressive symptoms. *Journal of Social and Clinical Psychology, 10*(1), 47–57.

Freedman, A. M. (1995). The biopsychosocial paradigm and the future of psychiatry. *Comprehensive Psychiatry, 36*(6), 397–406.

Freedman, R., Waldo, M., Bickford-Wimer, P., & Nagamoto, H. (1991). Elementary neuronal dysfunctions in schizophrenia. *Schizophrenia Research, 4*(2), 233–243.

Freeman, C. (1998). Drug treatment for bulimia nervosa. *Neuropsychobiology, 37,* 72–79.

Freeman, D. (1983). *Margaret Mead and Samoa: The making and unmaking of an anthropological myth.* Canberra: Australian National University Press.

Freeman, R. D. (1997). Attention deficit hyperactivity disorder in the presence of Tourette syndrome. *Neurologic Clinics, 15,* 411–420.

Freeman-Longo, R. E. (1996). Feel good legislation: Prevention or calamity. *Child Abuse and Neglect, 120,* 95–101.

Freiberg, P. (1991). Suicide in family, friends is familiar to many teens. *APA Monitor, 22,* 36–37.

Fremon, C. (1991, Jan. 27). Love and death. *Los Angeles Times Magazine,* pp. 17–35.

Fremouw, W. J., Perczel, W. J., & Ellis, T. E. (1990). *Suicide risk: Assessment and response guidelines.* Elmsford, NY: Pergamon.

Freud, S. (1959b). Mourning and melancholia. In E. Jones (Ed.), (A. Strachey & J. Strachey, Trans.), *Sigmund Freud: Collected papers, Vol. 4* (pp. 152–170). New York: Basic Books. (Original work published 1917)

Freud, S. (1938). Psychopathology of everyday life. In A. A. Brill (Ed. and Trans.), *The basic writings of Sigmund Freud.* New York: Modern Library. (Original work published 1904)

Freud, S. (1959a). Analysis of a phobia in a five-year-old boy. In E. Jones (Ed.), (A. Strachey & J. Strachey, Trans.), *Sigmund Freud: Collected papers, Vol. 3* (pp. 149–289). New York: Basic Books. (Original work published 1909)

Freud, S. (1959c). Notes upon a case of obsessional neurosis. In E. Jones (Ed.), (A. Strachey & J. Strachey, Trans.), *Sigmund Freud: Collected papers, Vol. 3* (pp. 296–373). New York: Basic Books. (Original work published 1909)

Freud, S. (1960). *A general introduction to psychoanalysis* (rev. ed.) (J. Riviere, Trans.). New York: Washington Square Press. (Original work published 1917)

Freund, K. (1980). Therapeutic sex drive reduction. *Acta Psychiatrica Scandinavica, 287,* 5–38.

Freund, K., & Seto, M. C. (1998). Preferential rape in the theory of courtship disorder. *Archives of Sexual Behavior, 27,* 433–443.

Freund, K. M., Belanger, A. J., D'Agostino, R. B., & Kannel, W. B. (1993). The health risks of smoking. The Framingham study: 34 years of follow-up. *Annals of Epidemiology, 3*(4), 417–424.

Fridell, S. R., Zucker, K. J., Bradley, S. J., et al. (1996). Physical attractiveness of girls with gender identity disorder. *Archives of Sexual Behavior, 25,* 17–31.

Friedman, A. F., Webb, J. T., & Lewak, R. (1990). *Psychological assessment with the MMPI.* Hillsdale, NJ: Erlbaum.

Friedman, H. S., & Booth-Kewley, S. (1987). The "disease-prone personality": A meta analytic view of the construct. *American Psychologist, 42,* 539–555.

Friedman, M., & Ulmer, D. (1984). *Treating Type A behavior and your heart.* New York: Fawcett Crest.

Friedman, R. C., & Rogers, K. B. (Eds.). (1998). *Talent in context: Historical and social perspectives on giftedness.* Washington, DC: American Psychological Association.

Friedman, S., Jones, J. C., Chernen, L., & Barlow, D. H. (1992). Suicidal ideation and suicide attempts among patients with panic disorder: A survey of two outpatient clinics. *American Journal of Psychiatry, 149*(5), 680–685.

Friedman, S. L., & Sigman, M. D. (Eds.). (1992). *The psychological development of low-birthweight children.* Norwood, NJ: Ablex.

Friedrich, G., & Goss, B. (1983). Systematic desensitization. In J. A. Daly & J. C. McCroskey (Eds.), *Avoiding communication: Shyness, reticence, and communication apprehension* (pp. 173–188). Beverly Hills, CA: Sage.

Friman, P. C., & Jones, K. M. (1998). Elimination disorders in children. In T. S. Watson & F. M. Gresham (Eds.), *Handbook of child behavior therapy: Issues in clinical child psychology* (pp. 239–260). New York: Plenum.

Frischauf, E. (1997). Drug therapy in autism. *Journal of the American Academy of Child and Adolescent Psychiatry, 36,* 577.

Frischholz, E. J., Braun, B. G., Lipman, L. S., & Sachs, R. (1992). Suggested posthypnotic amnesia in psychiatric patients and normals. *American Journal of Clinical Hypnosis, 35,* 29–39.

Frith, U. (1989). *Autism: Explaining the enigma.* Cambridge, MA: Blackwell.

Fromm-Reichmann, F. (1948). Notes on the development of treatment of schizophrenics by psychoanalytic psychotherapy. *Psychiatry, 11,* 263–273.

Frost, J. J., & Wagner, H. N., Jr. (Eds.). (1990). Quantitative imaging: *Neuroreceptors, neurotransmitters, and enzymes.* New York: Raven Press.

Frueh, B. C., Turner, S. M., & Beidel, D. C. (1995). Exposure therapy for combat-related PTSD: A critical review. *Clinical Psychology Review, 15*(8), 799–817.

Fry, R. P., Crisp, A. H., & Beard, R. W. (1997). Sociopsychological factors in chronic pelvic pain: A review. *Journal of Psychosomatic Research, 42*(1), 1–15.

Fryers, T. (1993). Epidemiological thinking in mental retardation: Issues in taxonomy and population frequency. In N. W. Bray (Ed.), *International Review of Research in Mental Retardation, Vol. 19.* Novato, CA: Academic Therapy Publications.

Fukuda, K., Straus, S. E., Hickie, I., et al. (1994). The chronic fatigue syndrome: A comprehensive approach to its definition and study. International Chronic Fatigue Syndrome Study Group. *Annals of Internal Medicine, 121*(12), 953–959.

Fulford, K. W. M. (1989). *Moral theory and medical practice.* Cambridge, UK: Cambridge University Press.

Fulton, M., & Winokur, G. (1993). A comparative study of paranoid and schizoid personality disorders. *American Journal of Psychiatry, 150,* 1363–1367.

Furby, L., Weinrott, M. R., & Blackshaw, L. (1989). Sex offender recidivism: A review. *Psychological Bulletin, 105,* 3–30.

Furnham, A., & Haraldsen, E. (1998). Lay theories of etiology and "cure" for four types of paraphilia: Fetishism; pedophilia; sexual sadism; and voyeurism. *Journal of Clinical Psychology, 54,* 689–700.

Fyer, A. J., Mannuzza, S., Chapman, T. F., et al. (1993). A direct interview family study of social phobia. *Archives of General Psychiatry, 50,* 286–293.

Gabbard, G. O. (1990). *Psychodynamic psychiatry in clinical practice.* Washington, DC: American Psychiatric Press.

Gabbard, G. O., Horwitz, L., Allen, J. G., et al. (1994). Transference interpretation in the psychotherapy of borderline patients: A high-risk, high-gain phenomenon. *Harvard Review of Psychiatry, 2,* 59–69.

Gabbay, F. H. (1992). Behavior: Genetic strategies in the study of emotion. *Psychological Science, 3,* 50–55.

Gabel, S., Stadler, J., Bjorn, J., et al. (1994). Sensation seeking in psychiatrically disturbed youth: Relationship to biochemical parameters in behavior problems. *Journal of the American Academy of Child and Adolescent Psychiatry, 33,* 123–129.

Gaines, R. (1995). The treatment of children. In M. Lionells, J. Fiscalini, C. H. Mann, & D. B. Stern (Eds.), *Handbook of interpersonal psychoanalysis* (pp. 751–769). Hillsdale, NJ: Analytic Press.

Gajdusek, D. V. (1977). Unconventional viruses and the origin and disappearance of kuru. *Science, 197,* 943–960.

Galanter, M. (1993). Network therapy for addiction: A model for office practice. *American Journal of Psychiatry, 150*(1), 28–35.

Gale, A. (Ed.). (1988). *The polygraph test: Lies, truth and science.* London: Sage.

Gambini, O., Campana, A., Macciardi, F., & Scarone, S. (1997). A preliminary report of a strong genetic component for thought disorder in normals: A twin study. *Neuropsychobiology, 36*(1), 13–18.

Garbarino, J. (1999). *Lost boys: Why our sons turn violent and how we can save them.* New York: Free Press.

Garber, S. W., Spizman, R. F., & Garber, M. D. (1997). *Beyond Ritalin: Facts about medication and other strategies for helping children, adolescents, and adults with attention deficit disorders.* New York: HarperCollins.

Garcia, J., & Rusiniak, K. W. (1980). What the nose learns from the mouth. In D. Muller-Schwarze & R. M. Silverstein (Eds.), *Chemical signals: Vertebrates and aquatic invertebrates* (pp. 141–156). New York: Plenum.

Gard, A., Gilman, L., & Gorman, J. (1993). *Speech and language developmental chart* (2nd ed.). Austin, TX: Pro-Ed.

Gardner, W., Lidz, C. W., Mulvey, E. P., et al. (1996). A comparison of actuarial methods for identifying repetitively violent patients. *Law and Human Behavior, 20,* 35–48.

Garfinkel, P. E., & Garner, D. M. (1982). *Anorexia nervosa: A multidimensional perspective.* New York: Brunner/Mazel.

Garfinkel, P. E., & Walsh, B. T. (1997). Drug therapies. In D. M. Garner & P. E. Garfinkel (Eds.), *Handbook of treatment for eating disorders* (2nd ed.) (pp. 372–380). New York: Guilford Press.

Garland, A. F., & Zigler, E. (1993). Adolescent suicide prevention: Current research and social policy implications. *American Psychologist, 48*(2), 169–182.

Garner, D. M., & Garfinkel, P. E. (1980). Sociocultural factors in anorexia nervosa. *Lancet, 2,* 674.

Garner, D. M., Vitousek, K. M., & Pike, K. M. (1997). Cognitive-behavioral therapy for anorexia nervosa. In D. M. Garner & P. E. Garfinkel (Eds.), *Handbook of treatment for eating disorders* (2nd ed.) (pp. 94–144). New York: Guilford Press.

Garry, M., Loftus, E. F., & Brown, S. W. (1994). Memory: A river runs through it. Special Issue: The recovered memory/

false memory debate. *Consciousness and Cognition: An International Journal, 3*(3–4), 438–451.

Garver, D. L. (1997). The etiologic heterogeneity of schizophrenia. *Harvard Review of Psychiatry, 4*(6), 317–327.

Gatz, M., & Smyer, M. A. (1992). The mental health system and older adults in the 1990s. *American Psychologist, 47,* 741–751.

Gaub, M., & Carlson, C. L. (1997). Gender differences in ADHD: A meta analysis and critical review. *Journal of the American Academy of Child and Adolescent Psychiatry, 36,* 1036–1045.

Gauthier, J., Côté, G., & French, D. (1994). The role of home practice in the thermal biofeedback treatment of migraine headache. *Journal of Consulting and Clinical Psychology, 62*(1), 180–184.

Gawin, F. H., & Kleber, H. D. (1992). Evolving conceptualizations of cocaine dependence. In T. R. Rosen & H. D. Kleber (Eds.), *Clinician's guide to cocaine addiction: Theory, research, and treatment* (pp. 33–52). New York: Guilford Press.

Geen, R. (1997). Psychophysiological approaches to personality. In R. Hogan, J. A. Johnson, & S. R. Briggs (Eds.), *Handbook of personality psychology* (pp. 387–414). San Diego: Academic Press.

Geldmacher, D. S., & Whitehouse, P. J., Jr. (1997). Differential diagnosis of Alzheimer's disease. *Neurology, 48* (5, Suppl. 6), S2–S9.

Gelenberg, A. J., Bassuk, E. L., & Schoonover, S. C. (1991). *The practitioner's guide to psychoactive drugs* (3rd ed.). New York: Plenum.

Gelman, D., & Katel, P. (1993, April 5). The trauma after the storm. *Newsweek.*

George, L. K., Landoman, R., Blazer, D. G., & Anthony, J. C. (1991). Cognitive impairment. In L. N. Robins & D. A. Regier (Eds.), *Psychiatric disorders in America* (pp. 291–327). New York: Free Press.

George, M. S., & Ballenger, J. C. (1992). The neuroanatomy of panic disorder: The emerging role of the right parahippocampal region. *Journal of Anxiety Disorder, 6,* 181–188.

George, M. S., Trimble, M. R., Ring, H. A., et al. (1993). Obsessions in obsessive-compulsive disorder with and without Gilles de la Tourette's syndrome. *American Journal of Psychiatry, 150,* 93–97.

Gerin, W., Pieper, C., Levy, R., & Pickering, T. G. (1992). Social support in social interaction: A moderator of cardiovascular activity. *Psychosomatic Medicine, 54,* 324–336.

Gershon, E. O., & Rieder, R. O. (1992, Sept.). Major disorders of mind and brain. *Scientific American,* p. 131.

Gershon, E. S., Hamovit, J. H., Guroff, J. J., & Nurnberger, J. I. (1987). Birth-cohort changes in manic and depressive disorders in relatives of bipolar and schizoaffective patients. *Archives of General Psychiatry, 44,* 314–319.

Gersten, S. P. (1993). Tardive dyskinesia-like syndromes with clomipramine. *American Journal of Psychiatry, 150,* 165–166.

Gerstley, L. J., Alterman, A. I., McLellan, A. T., & Woody, G. E. (1990). Antisocial personality disorder in patients with substance abuse disorders: A problematic diagnosis? *American Journal of Psychiatry, 147,* 173–178.

Getka, E. J., & Glass, C. R. (1992). Behavioral and cognitive-behavioral approaches to the reduction of dental anxiety. *Behavior Therapy, 23,* 433–448.

Geyer, S. (1993). Life events, chronic difficulties and vulnerability factors preceding breast cancer. *Social Science and Medicine, 37,* 1545–1555.

Gfroerer, J. C., Greenblatt, J. C., & Wright, D. A. (1997). Substance use in the U.S. college-age population: Differences according to educational status and living arrangement. *American Journal of Public Health, 87*(1), 62–65.

Ghosch, A., Marks, I. M., & Carr, A. C. (1988). Therapist contact and outcome of self-exposure treatment for phobias. *British Journal of Psychiatry, 152,* 234–238.

Gibbons, F. X., McGovern, P. G., & Lando, H. A. (1991). Relapse and risk perception among members of a smoking cessation clinic. *Health Psychology, 210,* 42–45.

Gil, K., Williams, D., Keefe, F., & Beckham, J. (1990). The relationship of negative thoughts to pain and psychological distress. *Behavior Therapy, 21,* 349–362.

Gilberstadt, H., & Duker, J. (1965). *A handbook for clinical and actuarial MMPI interpretation.* Philadelphia: Saunders.

Gillberg, C. (1997). Physical investigations in mental retardation. *Journal of Child Psychology, Psychiatry, and Allied Disciplines, 38,* 889–897.

Gillberg, C. (1998). Chromosomal disorders and autism. *Journal of Autism and Developmental Disorders, 28,* 415–425.

Gillberg, C., Melander, H., von-Knorring, A. L., et al. (1997). Long term stimulant treatment of children with attention deficit hyperactivity disorder symptoms: A randomized, double blind, placebo controlled trial. *Archives of General Psychiatry, 54,* 857–864.

Gillberg, I. A., Hellgren, L., & Gillberg, C. (1993). Psychotic disorders diagnosed in adolescence: Outcome at age 30 years. *Journal of Child Psychology and Psychiatry and Allied Disciplines, 34*(7), 1173–1185.

Ginsberg, H. P. (1997). Mathematics learning disabilities: A view from developmental psychology. *Journal of Learning Disabilities, 30,* 20–33.

Giordano, P. C., & Cernkovich, S. A. (1997). Gender and antisocial behavior. In D. M. Stoff, J. Breiling, & J. D. Maser (Eds.), *Handbook of antisocial behavior* (pp. 496–510). New York: Wiley.

Gitlin, M. J. (1990). *The psychotherapist's guide to psychopharmacology.* New York: Free Press.

Gitlin, M. J. (1993). Pharmacotherapy of personality disorders: Conceptual framework and clinical strategies. *Journal of Clinical Pharmacology, 13,* 343–353.

Glass, A. G., & Hoover, R. N. (1989). The emerging epidemic of melanoma and squamous cell skin cancer. *Journal of the American Medical Association, 262,* 2097–2100.

Glass, C. R., & Shea, C. A. (1986). Cognitive therapy for shyness and social anxiety. In W. H. Jones, J. M. Cheek, & S. R. Briggs (Eds.), *Shyness: Perspectives on research and treatment* (pp. 315–328). New York: Plenum.

Glavin, D. K., Franklin, J., & Francis, R. J. (1990). Substance abuse and suicidal behavior. In S. Blumenthal & D. Kupfer (Eds.), *Suicide over the life cycle: Risk factors, assessment, and treatment of suicidal patients* (pp. 177–204). Washington, DC: American Psychiatric Press.

Gleitman, H. (1981). *Psychology.* New York: Norton.

Goble, F. G. (1970). *The third force: The psychology of Abraham Maslow.* New York: Washington Square Press.

Goeders, N. E., & Guerin, G. F. (1994). Noncontingent electric footshock facilitates the acquisition of intravenous cocaine self-administration in rats. *Psychopharmacology, 114,* 63–70.

Goffman, E. (1961). *Asylums: Essays on the social situation of mental patients and other inmates.* Garden City, NY: Doubleday.

Gold, P. W., Goodwin, F. K., & Chrousos, G. P. (1988). Clinical and biochemical manifestations of depression: Relation to the neurobiology of stress. *New England Journal of Medicine, 319,* 348–353.

Goldberg, L. (1993). The structure of phenotypic personality traits. *American Psychologist, 48,* 26–34.

Goldberg, R. J. (1995). Diagnostic dilemmas presented by patients with anxiety and depression. *American Journal of Medicine, 98*(3), 278–284.

Goldblatt, M., Silverman, M. M., & Schatzberg, A. F. (1998). Psychopharmacological treatment of suicidal inpatients. In B. Bongar & A. L. Berman (Eds.), *Risk management with suicidal patients* (pp. 110–129). New York: Guilford Press.

Golden, C. J. (1989). The Luria-Nebraska Neuropsychological Battery. In C. S. Newmark (Ed.), *Major psychological assessment instruments, Vol. 2* (pp. 165–188). Boston: Allyn & Bacon.

Golding, J. M., Smith, G. R., & Kashner, T. M. (1991). Does somatization disorder occur in men? *Archives of General Psychiatry, 48*, 231–235.

Goldman, H. H. (1988). Psychiatric epidemiology and mental health services research. In H. H. Goldman (Ed.), *Review of general psychiatry* (pp. 143–156). Norwalk, CT: Appleton & Lange.

Goldman, L. S., Genel, M., Bezman, R. J., & Slanetz, P. J. (1998). Diagnosis and treatment of attention-deficit/hyperactivity disorder in children and adolescents. *Journal of the American Medical Association, 279*, 1100–1107.

Goldstein, A. (1994). *Addiction: From biology to drug policy.* New York: Freeman.

Goldstein, A. J., & Chambless, D. L. (1978). A reanalysis of agoraphobic behavior. *Behavior Therapy, 9*, 47–59.

Goldstein, A. P., Reagles, K. W., & Amann, L. L. (1990). *Refusal skills: Preventing drug use in adolescents.* Champaign, IL: Research Press.

Goldstein, M. J. (1988). Gender differences in the course of schizophrenia. *American Journal of Psychiatry, 145*, 684–689.

Goldstein, R. B., Black, D. W., Nasrallah, A., & Winokur, G. (1991). The prediction of suicide: Sensitivity, specificity, and predictive value of a multivariate model applied to suicide among 1,906 patients with affective disorders. *Archives of General Psychiatry, 48*, 418–422.

Goldstein, S., & Goldstein, M. (1998). *Managing attention deficit hyperactivity disorder in children: A guide for practitioners* (2nd ed.). New York: Wiley.

Goldston, D. B., Kovacs, M., Ho, V. Y., et al. (1994). Suicidal ideation and suicide attempts among youth with insulin-dependent diabetes mellitus. *Journal of the American Academy of Child and Adolescent Psychiatry, 33*, 240–246.

Gomberg, E. L. (1988). Alcoholic women in treatment: The question of stigma and age. *Alcohol and Alcoholism, 23*, 507–514.

Gooch, J. L., Wolcott, R., & Speed, J. (1997). Behavioral management of conversion disorder in children. *Archives of Physical Medicine and Rehabilitation, 78*(3), 264–268.

Goodman, A. B. (1994). Medical conditions in Ashkenazi schizophrenic pedigrees. *Schizophrenia Bulletin, 20*, 507–517.

Goodwin, D. W., & Guze, S. B. (1984). *Psychiatric diagnosis* (3rd ed.). New York: Oxford University Press.

Goodwin, F. K., & Jamison, K. R. (Eds.). (1990). *Manic depressive illness.* New York: Oxford University Press.

Gordis, E. (1991). *Alcohol research: Promise for the decade.* Rockville, MD: National Institute of Alcohol Abuse and Alcoholism.

Gordon, C. T., State, R. C., Nelson, J. E., & Hamburger, S. D. (1993). A 2- to 7-year follow-up study of 54 obsessive-compulsive children and adolescents. *Archives of General Psychiatry, 50*, 429–439.

Gordon, W. A., & Hibbard, M. R. (1997). Poststroke depression: An examination of the literature. *Archives of Physical Medicine and Rehabilitation, 78*, 658–663.

Gorenstein, E. E. (1992). *The science of mental illness.* San Diego: Academic Press.

Gorman, D. M. (1993). A review of studies comparing checklist and interview methods of data collection in life event research. *Behavioral Medicine, 19*(2), 66–73.

Gorman, J. M., Papp, L., & Klein, D. F. (1990). Biological models of panic disorder. In G. D. Burrows, M. Roth, & R. Noyes, Jr. (Eds.), *Handbook of anxiety, Vol. 3* (pp. 59–77). Amsterdam: Elsevier.

Gorwood, P., Ades, J., & Parmentier, G. (1998). Anorexia nervosa in one monozygotic twin. *American Journal of Psychiatry, 155*, 708.

Gotlib, I. H. (1992). Interpersonal and cognitive aspects of depression. *Current Directions in Psychological Science, 1*, 149–154.

Gotlib, I. H., & Hammen, C. (1992). *Psychological aspects of depression: Toward a cognitive-interpersonal integration.* New York: Wiley.

Gottesman, I., & Shields, J. (1972). *Schizophrenia and genetics: A twin study vantage point.* New York: Academic Press.

Gottesman, I. I. (1991). *Schizophrenia genesis: The origins of madness.* New York: Freeman.

Gottesman, I. I., & Bertelsen, A. (1989). Dual mating studies in psychiatry: Offspring of inpatients with examples from reactive (psychogenic) psychoses. *International Review of Psychiatry, 1*, 287–295.

Gottleib, A. M., Killen, J. D., Marlatt, G. A., & Taylor, C. B. (1987). Psychological and pharmacological influences in cigarette smoking withdrawal: Effects of nicotine gum and expectancy on smoking withdrawal symptoms and relapse. *Journal of Consulting and Clinical Psychology, 55*, 606–608.

Gottschalk, L. A., Rebello, T., Buchsbaum, M. S., et al. (1991). Abnormalities in hair trace elements as indicators of aberrant behavior. *Comprehensive Psychiatry, 32*, 229–237.

Gould, M., Wallenstein, S., Kleinman, M., et al. (1990). Suicide clusters: An examination of age-specific effects. *American Journal of Public Health, 80*, 211–214.

Gould, M. S., Bird, H., & Jaramillo, B. S. (1993). Correspondence between statistically derived behavior problem syndromes and child psychiatric diagnoses in a community sample. *Journal of Abnormal Child Psychology, 21*, 287–313.

Gould, S. J. (1996). *The mismeasure of man.* New York: Norton.

Gowers, S. G., Jones, J. C., Kiana, S., et al. (1995). Family functioning: A correlate of diabetic control? *Journal of Child Psychology and Psychiatry and Allied Disciplines, 36*(6), 993–1001.

Goyette, C. H., Conners, C. K., & Ulrich, R. F. (1978). Normative data on revised Conners parent and teacher rating scales. *Journal of Abnormal Psychology, 6*, 221–236.

Grabowski, J., & VandenBos, G. R. (1992). *Pharmacology: Basic mechanisms and applied interventions.* Washington, DC: American Psychological Association.

Graham, J. R. (1987). *The MMPI: A practical guide.* New York: Oxford University Press.

Grandin, T., & Sacks, O. (1996). *Thinking in pictures and other reports from my life with autism.* New York: Vintage Books.

Grandin, T., & Scariano, M. M. (1996). *Emergence: Labeled autistic.* New York: Warner Books.

Granholm, E., Morris, S. K., Sarkin, A. J., et al. (1997). Pupillary responses index overload of working memory resources in schizophrenia. *Journal of Abnormal Psychology, 106*(3), 458–467.

Grant, S., London, E. D., Newlin, D. B., et al. (1996). Activation of memory circuits during cue-elicited cocaine craving. *Proceedings of the National Academy of Sciences of the United States of America, 93*(21), 12040–12045.

Gray, J. A. (1987). *The psychology of fear and stress.* Cambridge, UK: Cambridge University Press.

Gray, J. A. (1991). Fear, panic, and anxiety: What's in a name? *Psychological Inquiry, 2*(1), 72–96.

Green, A. (1978). Self-destructive behavior in battered children. *American Journal of Psychiatry, 135*, 579–582.

Greenberg, R. P., Bornstein, R. F., Greenberg, M. D., & Fisher, S. (1992). A meta-analysis of antidepressant outcome under "blinder" conditions. *Journal of Consulting and Clinical Psychology, 60*, 664–669.

Greenberg, R. P., Bornstein, R. F., Zborowski, M. J., et al. (1994). A meta-analysis of fluoxetine outcome in the treatment of depression. *Journal of Nervous and Mental Disease, 182*(10), 547–551.

Greenhill, L. L. (1998). Attention deficit/hyperactivity disorder. In B. T. Walsh (Ed.), *Child psychopharmacology* (pp. 29–64). Review of Psychiatry series. Washington, DC: American Psychiatric Press.

Gregory, R. J. (1992). *Psychological testing.* Boston: Allyn & Bacon.

Greist, J. H. (1994). Behavior therapy for obsessive-compulsive disorder. *Journal of Clinical Psychiatry, 55*(Suppl.), 60–68.

Gresham, F. M., & MacMillan, D. L. (1998).

Early intervention project: Can its claims be substantiated and its effects replicated? *Journal of Autism and Developmental Disorders, 28,* 5–13.

Grinspoon, L., & Bakalar, J. B. (1993). *Marihuana, the forbidden medicine.* New Haven, CT: Yale University Press.

Grob, G. N. (1991). The origins of *DSM-I:* A study in appearance and reality. *American Journal of Psychiatry, 148,* 421–431.

Gross, T. V., Manor, O., & Shalev, R. S. (1996). Developmental dyscalculia: Prevalence and demographic features. *Developmental Medicine and Child Neurology, 38,* 25–33.

Groth-Marnat, G. (1990). *Handbook of psychological assessment* (2nd ed.). New York: Wiley.

Group for the Advancement of Psychiatry. (1989). *Suicide and ethnicity in the United States.* New York: Brunner/Mazel.

Grove, W. M., Clementz, B. A., Iacono, W. G., & Katsansis, J. (1992). Smooth pursuit ocular motor dysfunction in schizophrenia: Evidence for a major gene. *American Journal of Psychiatry, 149,* 1362–1368.

Grove, W. M., Lebow, B. S., Clementz, B. A., et al. (1991). Familial prevalence and co-aggregation of schizotype indicators: A multitrait family study. *Journal of Abnormal Psychology, 100*(2), 115–121.

Grubb, A. (1994). *Decision-making and problems of incompetence.* New York: Wiley.

Grudzinskas, A. J., Jr., & Henry, M. G. (1997). Kansas v. Hendricks. *Journal of the American Academy of Psychiatry and Law, 25,* 607–612.

Gruen, R. J., Folkman, S., & Lazarus, R. S. (1988). Centrality and individual differences in the meaning of daily hassles. *Journal of Personality and Social Psychology, 56,* 743–762.

Grych, J. H., & Fincham, F. D. (1997). Children's adaptation to divorce: From description to explanation. In S. A. Wolchik & I. N. Sandler (Eds.), *Handbook of children's coping: Linking theory and intervention* (pp. 159–193). Issues in Clinical Child Psychology. New York: Plenum.

Guillemin, J. (1992). Planning to die. *Society, 29,* 29–33.

Gull, W. W. (1874). Anorexia nervosa. *Transactions of the Clinical Society of London, 7,* 22–27.

Gunatilake, S. B., De-Silva, H. J., & Ranasinghe, G. (1997). Twenty-seven venous cutdowns to treat pseudostatus epilepticus. *Seizure, 6*(1), 71–72.

Gunderson, J. G., Berkowitz, C., & Ruiz-Sancho, A. (1997). Families of borderline patients: A psychoeducational approach. *Bulletin of the Menninger Clinic, 61,* 446–457.

Gunderson, J. G., Ronningstam, E., & Smith, L. E. (1995). Narcissistic personal-

ity disorder. In W. J. Livesley (Ed.), *The DSM-IV personality disorders: Diagnosis and treatment of mental disorders* (pp. 201–212). New York: Guilford Press.

Gunderson, J. G., Zanarini, M. C., & Kisiel, C. L. (1995). Borderline personality disorder. In W. J. Livesley (Ed.), *The DSM-IV personality disorders: Diagnosis and treatment of mental disorders* (pp. 141–157). New York: Guilford Press.

Gur, R. E., & Pearlson, G. D. (1993). Neuroimaging in schizophrenia research. *Schizophrenia Bulletin, 19*(2), 337–353.

Gureje, O., Simon, G. E., Ustun, T. B., & Goldberg, D. P. (1997). Somatization in cross-cultural perspective: A World Health Organization study in primary care. *American Journal of Psychiatry, 154*(7), 989–995.

Gusella, J., MacDonald, M., Ambrose, C., & Duyao, M. (1993). Molecular genetics of Huntington's disease. *Archives of Neurology, 50,* 1157–1163.

Gustafsson, P. A. (1987). *Family interaction and family therapy in childhood psychosomatic disease.* Unpublished doctoral dissertation, Linkping University, Sweden.

Guze, S. B. (1993). Genetics of Briquet's syndrome and somatization disorder: A review of family, adoption, and twin studies. *Annals of Clinical Psychiatry, 5*(4), 225–230.

Guze, S. B., Cloninger, C. R., Martin, R. L., & Clayton, P. (1986). A follow-up and family study of Briquet's syndrome. *British Journal of Psychiatry, 149,* 17–23.

Haaga, D. A., & Davison, G. C. (1989). Outcome studies of rational-emotive therapy. In M. Bernard & R. DeGiuseppe (Eds.), *Inside rational-emotive therapy.* New York: Academic Press.

Haaga, D.A., Dyck, M. J., & Ernst, D. (1991). Empirical status of cognitive theory of depression. *Psychological Bulletin, 110,* 215–236.

Hadwin, J., Baron-Cohen, S., Howlin, P., & Hill, K. (1997). Does teaching theory of mind have an effect on the ability to develop conversation in children with autism? *Journal of Autism and Developmental Disorders, 27,* 519–537.

Haenen, M. A., Schmidt, A. J., Kroeze, S., & van-den-Hout, M. A. (1996). Hypochondriasis and symptom reporting—The effect of attention versus distraction. *Psychotherapy and Psychosomatics, 65*(1), 43–48.

Häfner, H., Behrens, S., de Vry, J., & Gattaz, W. F. (1991). Oestradiol enhances the vulnerability threshold for schizophrenia in women by an early effect on dopaminergic neurotransmission: Evidence from an epidemiological study and from animal experiments. *European Archives of Psychiatry and Clinical Neuroscience, 241*(1), 65–68.

Häfner, H., & Gattaz, W. F. (1991). Is schizophrenia disappearing? *European Archives of Psychiatry and Clinical Neuroscience, 240,* 374–376.

Hagerman, R. J. (1996). Fragile X syndrome. *Child and Adolescent Psychiatric Clinics of North America, 5,* 895–911.

Haggerty, J. J., Jr., & Prange, A. J., Jr. (1995). Borderline hypothyroidism and depression. *Annual Review of Medicine, 46,* 37–46.

Hagnell, O., Franck, A., Grasbeck, A., et al. (1992). Vascular dementia in the Lund study. I: A prospective, epidemiological study of incidence and risk from 1957–1972. *Neuropsychobiology, 26,* 43–49.

Halford, W. K., & Hayes, R. (1991). Psychological rehabilitation of chronic schizophrenic patients: Recent findings on social skills training and family psychoeducation. *Clinical Psychology Review, 11,* 23–44.

Hall, P., & Brockington, I. F. (1991). *The closure of mental hospitals.* London: Gaskell.

Hallfors, D. D., & Saxe, L. (1993). The dependence potential of short half-life benzodiazepines: A meta-analysis. *American Journal of Public Health, 83*(9), 1300–1304.

Hamburger, M. E., Lilienfeld, S. O., & Hogben, M. (1996). Psychopathy, gender, and gender roles: Implications for antisocial and histrionic personality disorders. *Journal of Personality Disorders, 10,* 41–55.

Hamilton, N. (1991). Intake and diagnosis of drug dependent women. In *National Conference on Drug Abuse Research and Practice conference highlights.* Rockville, MD: National Institute on Drug Abuse.

Hamling, J. E., Harris, G. T., & Rice, M. E. (1997). Risk appraisal and management of violent behavior. *Psychiatric Services, 48,* 1168–1176.

Hammen, C. (1991a). *Depression runs in families: The social context of risk and resilience in children of depressed mothers.* New York: Springer-Verlag.

Hammen, C. (1991b). The generation of stress in the course of unipolar depression. *Journal of Abnormal Psychology, 100,* 555–561.

Hammen, C., Burge, D., Burney, E., & Adrian, C. (1990). Longitudinal study of diagnoses in children of women with unipolar and bipolar affective disorder. *Archives of General Psychiatry, 47*(12), 1112–1117.

Hammen, C., Ellicott, A., & Gitlin, M. (1992). Stressors and sociotropy/autonomy: A longitudinal study of their relationship to the course of bipolar disorder. *Cognitive Therapy and Research, 16,* 409–418.

Handwerk, M. L., & Marshall, R. M. (1998). Behavioral and emotional problems of students with learning disabilities, serious emotional disturbance, or both conditions. *Journal of Learning Disabilities, 30*, 635–642.

Hansell, S. (1997). Treatment of comorbid schizophrenia and substance abuse disorders. *New Directions in Mental Health Services, Spring*(73), 65–73.

Harangozo, J., Magyar, I., & Faludy, G. (1991). Use of benzodiazepines in psychiatry. *Therapia Hungarica, 39*(3), 103–111.

Hardie, D. G. (1991). *Biochemical messengers: Hormones, neurotransmitters, and growth factors.* London: Chapman & Hall.

Harding, C. M., Zubin, J., & Strauss, J. S. (1992). Chronicity in schizophrenia: Revisited. *British Journal of Psychiatry, 161*(Suppl. 18), 27–37.

Hare, E. H. (1988). Schizophrenia as a recent disease. *British Journal of Psychiatry, 153,* 521–531.

Hare, R. D. (1996). Psychopathy: A clinical construct whose time has come. *Criminal Justice and Behavior, 23*, 25–54.

Hare, R. D., Hart, S. D., & Harpur, T. J. (1991). Psychopathy and the *DSM-IV* criteria for antisocial personality disorder. *Journal of Abnormal Psychology, 100*, 391–398.

Harlow, H., & Suomi, S. J. (1976). Production of depressive behaviors in young monkeys. *Journal of Autism and Childhood Schizophrenia, 1*, 246–255.

Harlow, K. C., & Swint, J. M. (1989). Patterns and economic effects of drug overdose mortality in Texas: 1980–1986. *Journal of Drug Education, 19*, 165–182.

Harmon, R. J., Bender, B. G., Linden, M. G., & Robinson, A. (1998). Transition from adolescence to early adulthood: Adaptation and psychiatric status of women with 47, XXX. *Journal of the American Academy of Child and Adolescent Psychiatry, 37*, 286–291.

Harper, P. S. (1991). *Huntington's disease.* London: Saunders.

Harper, P. S. (1993). *Practical genetic counseling* (4th ed.). Boston: Butterworth-Heinemann.

Harpur, T. J., & Hare, R. D. (1994). Assessment of psychopathy as a function of age. *Journal of Abnormal Psychology, 103*, 604–609.

Harran, S. M., & Ziegler, D. J. (1991). Cognitive appraisal of daily hassles in college students displaying high or low irrational beliefs. *Journal of Rational Emotive and Cognitive Behavior Therapy, 9*, 265–271.

Harrington, R. C., Fudge, H., Rutter, M., et al. (1990). Adult outcomes of childhood and adolescent depression. I: Psychiatric status. *Archives of General Psychiatry, 47*, 465–473.

Harris, B. (1979). What ever happened to Little Albert? *American Psychologist, 34*, 151–160.

Harris, G. T., Rice, M. E., & Quinsey, V. L. (1993). Violent recidivism of mentally disordered offenders. *Criminal Justice and Behavior, 20*, 315–335.

Harris, J. R. (1995). Where is the child's environment? A group socialization theory of development. *Psychological Review, 102*, 458–489.

Harris, J. R. (1998). *The nurture assumption.* New York: Free Press.

Harris, L., and Associates. (1994). *The N.O.D. / Harris survey on employment of people with disabilities.* New York: Author.

Harris, M. B., Deary, I. J., & Wilson, J. A. (1996). Life events and difficulties in relation to the onset of globus pharyngis. *Journal of Psychosomatic Research, 40*(6), 603–615.

Harrison, P. A., Fulkerson, J. A., & Beebe, T. J. (1997). Multiple substance use among adolescent physical and sexual abuse victims. *Child Abuse and Neglect, 21*(6), 529–539.

Harrow, M., Goldberg, J. F., Grossman, L. S., & Meltzer, H. Y. (1990). Outcome in manic disorders: A naturalistic follow-up study. *Archives of General Psychiatry, 47*, 665–671.

Hart, S. D., & Hare, R. D. (1997). Psychopathy: Assessment and association with criminal conduct. In D. M. Stoff, J. Breiling, & J. D. Maser (Eds.), *Handbook of antisocial behavior* (pp. 22–35). New York: Wiley.

Hartlage, S., Alloy, L. B., Vazquez, C., & Dykman, B. (1993). Automatic and effortful processing in depression. *Psychological Bulletin, 113*, 247–278.

Hartlage, S., Arduino, K., & Alloy, L. B. (1998). Depressive personality characteristics: State dependent concomitants of depressive disorder and traits independent of current depression. *Journal of Abnormal Psychology, 107*, 349–354.

Hartwell, C. E. (1996). The schizophrenogenic mother concept in American psychiatry. *Psychiatry Interpersonal and Biological Processes, 59*(3), 274–297.

Harver, A. (1994). Effects of feedback on the ability of asthmatics to detect increases in the flow resistance component of breathing. *Health Psychology, 13*, 52–62.

Harvey, A. G., & Rapee, R. M. (1995). Cognitive-behavior therapy for generalized anxiety disorder. *Psychiatric Clinics of North America, 18*(4), 859–870.

Harvey, W. (1847). *The works of William Harvey.* London: Sydneham Society. (Original work published 1649)

Hasan, M. K., & Mooney, D. (1994). Alzheimer's disease: A new hope. *West Virginia Medical Journal, 90*(10), 418–419.

Hashimoto, T., Kawano, N., Fukuda, K., et al. (1998). Proton magnetic resonance spectroscopy of the brain in three cases

of Rett syndrome: Comparison with autism and normal controls. *Acta Neurologica Scandinavica, 98*, 8–14.

Haslam, N., & Beck, A. T. (1994). Subtyping major depression: A taxometric analysis. *Journal of Abnormal Psychology, 103*, 686–692.

Hatch, J. P., Fisher, J. G., & Rugh, J. D. (Eds.). (1987). *Biofeedback: Studies in clinical efficacy.* New York: Plenum.

Hathaway, S. R., & McKinley, J. C. (1943). *The Minnesota Multiphasic Personality Inventory* (rev. ed.). Minneapolis: University of Minnesota Press.

Hathaway, S. R., McKinley, J. C., & Butcher, J. N. (1990). *Minnesota Multiphasic Personality Inventory–2.* (2nd ed.). Minneapolis: University of Minnesota Press.

Haug, M., Brain, P. F., & Aron, C. (1991). *Heterotypical behaviour in man and animals.* London: Chapman & Hall.

Hawton, K. (1989). Controlled studies of psychosocial intervention following attempted suicide. In S. D. Platt & N. Kreitman (Eds.), *Current research on suicide and parasuicide.* Edinburgh, Scot.: Edinburgh University Press.

Hawton, K., Kimkin, S., Fagg, J., et al. (1995). Suicide in Oxford University students, 1976–1990. *British Journal of Psychiatry, 166*, 44–50.

Hayden, M. F. (1997). Class-action civil rights litigation for institutionalized persons with mental retardation and other developmental disabilities: A review. *Mental and Physical Disability Law Reporter, 21*, 411–423.

Hayden, T. L. (1980). Classification of elective mutism. *Journal of the American Academy of Child Psychiatry, 19*, 118–133.

Haynes, S.G., Feinleib, M., & Eaker, E. D. (1983). Type A behavior and the ten-year incidence of coronary heart disease in the Framingham heart study. In R. H. Rosenman (Ed.), *Psychosomatic risk factors and coronary heart disease: Indications for specific preventive therapy: A colloquium held during the International Symposium on Psychophysiological Risk Factors of Cardiovascular Diseases* (pp. 80–92). Bern, Stuttgart: Huber.

Hays, L. R., Cheever, T., & Patel, P. (1996). Medical student suicide 1989–1994. *American Journal of Psychiatry, 153*, 553–555.

Hays, R. B., Turner, H., & Coates, T. J. (1992). Social support, AIDS-related symptoms, and depression among gay men. *Journal of Consulting and Clinical Psychology, 60*, 463–469.

Haywood, T. W., Kravitz, H. M., Grossman, L. S., et al. (1995). Predicting the "revolving door" phenomenon among patients with schizophrenic, schizoaffective, and affective disorders. *American Journal of Psychiatry, 152*(6), 856–861.

Hazell, P. (1993). Adolescent suicide clusters: Evidence, mechanisms and prevention. *Australian and New Zealand Journal of Psychiatry, 27,* 653–665.

Healy, A. F., & Bourne, L. E., Jr. (Eds.). (1995). *Learning and memory of knowledge and skills: Durability and specificity.* Thousand Oaks, CA.: Sage.

Hebb, D. O. (1946). On the nature of fear. *Psychological Review, 53,* 259–276.

Hebebrand, J., Klug, B., Fimmers, R., & Seuchter, S. A. (1997). Rates for tic disorders and obsessive-compulsive symptomatology in families of children and adolescents with Gilles de la Tourette syndrome. *Journal of Psychiatric Research, 31,* 519–530.

Heehs, P. (1997). Genius, mysticism, and madness. *Psychohistory Review, 26,* 45–75.

Hegarty, J. D., Baldessarini, R. J., Tohen, M., et al. (1994). One hundred years of schizophrenia: A meta-analysis of the outcome literature. *American Journal of Psychiatry, 151*(10), 1409–1416.

Heikkinen, M., Aro, H. M., & Lonnqvist, J. K. (1993). Life events and social support in suicide. *Suicide and Life-Threatening Behavior, 23*(4), 343–358.

Heila, H., Isometsa, E. T., Henriksson, M. M., et al. (1997). Suicide and schizophrenia: A nationwide psychological autopsy study on age- and sex-specific clinical characteristics of 92 suicide victims with schizophrenia. *American Journal of Psychiatry, 154*(9), 1235–1242.

Heilbronner, R. L. (1980). *The worldly philosophers.* New York: Touchstone.

Heilbrun, A. B., Jr. (1993). Hallucinations. In C. G. Costello (Ed.), *Symptoms of schizophrenia* (pp. 56–91). New York: Wiley.

Heimberg, R. G., & Barlow, D. H. (1991). New developments in cognitive-behavioral therapy for social phobia. 11th National Conference on Anxiety Disorders: Social phobia: Advances in understanding and treatment. *Journal of Clinical Psychiatry, 52*(Suppl.), 21–30.

Heimberg, R. G., Dodge, C. S., Hope, D. A., & Kennedy, C. R. (1990). Cognitive behavioral group treatment for social phobia: Comparison with a credible placebo control. *Cognitive Therapy and Research, 14,* 1–23.

Heimberg, R. G., Holt, C. S., Schneier, F. R., et al. (1993). The issue of subtypes in the diagnosis of social phobia. *Journal of Anxiety Disorders, 7*(3), 249–269.

Heimberg, R. G., Hope, D. A., Dodge, C. S., & Becker, R. E. (1990). DSM-III-R subtypes of social phobia: Comparison of generalized social phobics and public speaking phobics. *Journal of Nervous and Mental Disease, 178,* 172–179.

Heimberg, R. G., & Juster, H. R. (1994). Treatment of social phobia in cognitive-

behavioral groups. *Journal of Clinical Psychiatry, 55*(6, Suppl.), 38–46.

Heineman, E. F., Zahm, S. H., McLaughlin, J. K., & Vaught, J. B. (1994). Increased risk of colorectal cancer among smokers: Results of a 26-year follow-up of U.S. veterans and a review. *International Journal of Cancer, 59*(6), 728–738.

Heinrichs, R. W. (1993). Schizophrenia and the brain. *American Psychologist, 48,* 221–223.

Heishman, S. J., & Henningfield, J. E. (1992). Stimulus functions of caffeine in humans: Relation to dependence potential. *Neuroscience and Behavioral Reviews, 16,* 273–287.

Hellstrom, K., Fellenius, J., & Öst, L. (1996). One versus five sessions of applied tension in the treatment of blood phobia. *Behaviour Research and Therapy, 34*(2), 101–112.

Helzer, J. E., Bucholz, K., & Robins, L. N. (1992). Five communities in the United States: Results of the epidemiologic catchment area survey. In J. E. Helzer & G. J. Canino (Eds.), *Alcoholism in North America, Europe, and Asia: A coordinated analysis of population data from ten regions* (pp. 71–95). New York: Oxford University Press.

Helzer, J. E., & Canino, G. (1992). Comparative analyses of alcoholism in 10 cultural regions. In J. Helzer & G. Canino (Eds.), *Alcoholism in North America, Europe, and Asia: A coordinated analysis of population data from ten regions* (pp. 131–155). New York: Oxford University Press.

Henderson, A. S. (1994). *Dementia: Epidemiology of mental disorders and psychosocial problems.* Geneva: World Health Organization.

Henggeler, S. W., Schoenwald, S. K., Borduin, C. M., et al. (1998). *Multisystemic treatment of antisocial behavior in children and adolescents. Treatment manuals for practitioners.* New York: Guilford Press.

Henkin, W. A., & Carnes, P. J. (1998). Is sex addiction a myth? In S. Nolen-Hoeksema (Ed.), *Clashing views on abnormal psychology: A taking sides custom reader* (pp. 196–215). Guilford, CT: Dushkin/McGraw-Hill.

Henriksson, M. M., Isometsa, E. T., Kuoppasalmi, K. I., et al. (1996). Panic disorder in completed suicide. *Journal of Clinical Psychiatry, 57*(7), 275–281.

Henry, B., & Moffitt, T. E. (1997). Neuropsychological and neuroimaging studies of juvenile delinquency and adult criminal behavior. In D. M. Stoff, J. Breiling, & J. D. Maser (Eds.), *Handbook of antisocial behavior* (pp. 280–288). New York: Wiley.

Herlihy, B. (1993). Mandy: Out in the world. In L. B. Golden & M. L. Norwood (Eds.), *Case studies in child counseling* (pp. 63–73). New York: Merrill/Macmillan.

Hermann, D. H. J. (1990). Autonomy, self-determination, the right of involuntarily committed persons to refuse treatment, and the use of substituted judgments in medication decisions involving incompetent persons. *International Journal of Law and Psychiatry, 13,* 361–385.

Hernandez, D., & Fisher, E. M. C. (1996). Down syndrome genetics: Unravelling a multifactorial disorder. *Human Molecular Genetics, 5,* 1411–1416.

Herning, R. I., Jones, R. T., Bachman, J., & Mines, A. H. (1981). Puff volume increases when low nicotine cigarettes are smoked. *British Medical Journal, 283,* 187–189.

Herrnstein, R. J., & Murray, C. A. (1994). *The bell curve: Intelligence and class structure in American life.* New York: Free Press.

Hersen, M., & Bellack, A. S. (Eds.). (1988). *Dictionary of behavioral assessment techniques.* New York: Pergamon.

Hersen, M., Bellack, A. S., Himmelhoch, J. M., & Thase, M. E. (1984). Effects of social skill training, amitriptyline, and psychotherapy in unipolar depressed women. *Behavior Therapy, 15,* 21–40.

Hersen, M., Kazdin, A. E., & Bellack, A. S. (1983). *The clinical psychology handbook.* New York: Pergamon.

Heston, L. L. (1966). Psychiatric disorders in foster home reared children of schizophrenic mothers. *British Journal of Psychiatry, 112,* 819–825.

Heston, L. L., & White, J. A. (1991). *The vanishing mind: A practical guide to Alzheimer's disease and other dementias.* New York: Freeman.

Higgins, S. T., Budney, A. J., Bickel, W. K., et al. (1993). Achieving cocaine abstinence with a behavioral approach. *American Journal of Psychiatry, 150,* 763–769.

Higuchi, S., Suzuki, K., Yamada, K., et al. (1993). Alcoholics with eating disorders: Prevalence and clinical course: A study from Japan. *British Journal of Psychiatry, 162,* 403–406.

Hilgard, E. R. (1994). Neodissociation theory. In S. J. Lynn & J. W. Rhue (Eds.), *Dissociation: Clinical and theoretical perspectives* (pp. 32–51). New York: Guilford Press.

Hilgard, E. R., & Bower, G. H. (1975). *Theories of learning.* Englewood Cliffs, NJ: Prentice-Hall.

Hill, K. K., & Maloney, M. J. (1997). Treating anorexia nervosa patients in the era of managed care. *Journal of the American Academy of Child and Adolescent Psychiatry, 36,* 1632–1633.

Hill, R. D., Rigdon, M., & Johnson, S. (1993). Behavioral smoking cessation treatment for older chronic smokers. *Behavior Therapy, 24,* 321–329.

Hinde, R. A. (1954). Factors governing the changes in strength of a partially inborn response, as shown by the mobbing behavior of the chaffinch (*Fringilla coelebs*). II: The waning of the response. *Proceedings of the Royal Society, Series–B, 142,* 331–358.

Hindmarch, I. (1990). Cognitive impairment with anti-anxiety agents: A solvable problem? In D. Wheatley (Ed.), *The anxiolytic jungle: Where, next?* (pp. 49–61). Chichester, UK: Wiley.

Hinshaw, S. P., & Zupan, B. A. (1997). Assessment of antisocial behavior in children and adolescents. In D. M. Stoff, J. Breiling, & J. D. Maser (Eds.), *Handbook of antisocial behavior* (pp. 36–50). New York: Wiley.

Hinshelwood, J. (1917). *Congenital word blindness.* London: Lewis.

Hiroto, D. S., & Seligman, M. E. P. (1975). Generality of learned helplessness in man. *Journal of Personality and Social Psychology, 31,* 311–327.

Hirschfeld, R. M. A. (1994). Major depression, dysthymia and depressive personality disorder. *British Journal of Psychiatry, 165*(Suppl. 26), 23–30.

Hirschfeld, R. M. A. (1995). "Depressive personality disorder." Reply. *Journal of Clinical Psychiatry, 56,* 266.

Hirschfeld, R. M. A. (1997). Pharmacotherapy of borderline personality disorder. *Journal of Clinical Psychiatry, 58*(Suppl. 14), 48–52.

Hirschfeld, R. M. A., Keller, M. B., Panico, S., et al. (1997). The National Depressive and Manic-Depressive Association consensus statement on the undertreatment of depression. *Journal of the American Medical Association, 277,* 333–340.

Hirschfeld, R. M. A., Shea, M. T., & Weise, R. (1995). Dependent personality disorder. In W. J. Livesley (Ed.), *The DSM-IV personality disorders: Diagnosis and treatment of mental disorders* (pp. 239–256). New York: Guilford Press.

Hitchcock, P. B., & Mathews, A. (1992). Interpretation of bodily symptoms in hypochondriasis. *Behaviour Research and Therapy, 30,* 223–234.

Ho, B. C., Andreasen, N., & Flaum, M. (1997). Dependence on public financial support early in the course of schizophrenia. *Psychiatric Services, 48*(7), 948–950.

Hobbes, T. (1973). *Leviathan.* New York: Dutton. (Original work published 1670)

Hobfoll, S. E., Spielberger, C. D., Breznitz, S., et al. (1991). War-related stress: Addressing the stress of war and other traumatic events. *American Psychologist, 46,* 848–855.

Hobson, H. J. (1994). *The chemistry of conscious states: How the brain changes the mind.* Boston: Little, Brown.

Hockey, R. (1983). *Stress and fatigue in human performance.* New York: Wiley.

Hoek, H. W., Susser, E., Buck, K. A., & Lumey, L. H. (1996). Schizoid personality disorder after prenatal exposure to famine. *American Journal of Psychiatry, 153,* 1637–1639.

Hoek, H. W., van Harten, P. N., van Hoeken, D., & Susser, E. (1998). Lack of relation between culture and anorexia nervosa: Results of an incidence study on Curacao. *New England Journal of Medicine, 338,* 1231–1232.

Hoffman, L. (1994). *Eating disorders.* Rockville, MD: National Institutes of Health.

Hoffman, R. E., & Rapaport, J. (1994). A psycholinguistic study of auditory/verbal hallucinations: Preliminary findings. In A. S. David & J. C. Cutting (Eds.), *The neuropsychology of schizophrenia* (pp. 255–267). Hillsdale, NJ: Erlbaum.

Hofmann, S. G., Ehlers, A., & Roth, W. T. (1995). Conditioning theory: A model for the etiology of public speaking anxiety? *Behaviour Research and Therapy, 33*(5), 567–571.

Hofmann, S. G., Newman, M. G., Becker, E., et al. (1995). Social phobia with and without avoidant personality disorder: Preliminary behavior therapy outcome findings. *Journal of Anxiety Disorders, 9,* 427–438.

Hogan, R. A. (1968). The implosive technique. *Behaviour Research and Therapy, 6,* 423–431.

Hogan, R. A., & Kirchner, J. H. (1968). Implosive, eclectic verbal and bibliotherapy in the treatment of fears of snakes. *Behaviour Research and Therapy, 6*(2), 167–171.

Hogarty, G. E. (1993). Prevention of relapse in chronic schizophrenic patients. *Journal of Clinical Psychiatry, 54*(Suppl.), 18–23.

Hoge, S. K., Appelbaum, P. S., Lawler, T., et al. (1991). A prospective, multicenter study of patients' refusal of antipsychotic medication. *Archives of General Psychiatry, 47,* 949–956.

Holahan, C. J., & Moos, R. H. (1991). Life stressors, personal and social resources, and depression: A 4-year structure model. *Journal of Abnormal Psychology, 100,* 31–38.

Holbrook, M. I. (1997). Anger management training in prison inmates. *Psychological Reports, 81,* 623–626.

Holden, C. (1980). A new visibility for gifted children. *Science, 210,* 879–882.

Holding, D. (1983). Fatigue. In G. R. J. Hockey (Ed.), *Stress and fatigue in human performance.* New York: Wiley.

Hollander, E., DeCaria, C. M., Nitescu, A., et al. (1992). Serotonergic function in obsessive-compulsive disorder: Behavior and neuroendocrine responses to oral m-chlorophenylpiperazine and fenfluramine in patients and healthy volunteers. *Archives of General Psychiatry, 49* (1), 21–28.

Hollander, E., Simeon, D., Gross, S., et al. (1997). Feeling unreal: 30 cases of *DSM-III-R* depersonalization disorder. *American Journal of Psychiatry, 154*(8), 1107–1113.

Hollandsworth, J. G., Jr. (1990). *The physiology of psychological disorders: Schizophrenia, depression, anxiety and substance abuse.* New York: Plenum.

Hollifield, M., Katon, W., Spain, D., & Pule, L. (1990). Anxiety and depression in a village in Lesotho, Africa: A comparison with the United States. *British Journal of Psychiatry, 156,* 343–350.

Hollingshead, A. B., & Redlich, F. C. (1958). *Social class and mental illness: A community study.* New York: Wiley.

Hollon, S. D. (1996). The efficacy and effectiveness of psychotherapy relative to medications. *American Psychologist, 51*(10), 1025–1030.

Hollon, S. D., DeRubeis, R. J., Evans, M. D., et al. (1992). Cognitive therapy and pharmacotherapy for depression: Singly and in combination. *Archives of General Psychiatry, 49,* 774–781.

Hollon, S. D., Shelton, R. C., & Davis, D. D. (1993). Cognitive therapy and pharmacotherapy for depression. *Journal of Consulting and Clinical Psychology, 61,* 270–275.

Hollon, S. D., Shelton, R. C., & Loosen, P. T. (1991). Cognitive therapy and pharmacotherapy for depression. *Journal of Consulting and Clinical Psychology, 59,* 88–99.

Hollweg, M. (1998). Modification of criminal law and its impact on psychiatric expert opinions. *International Journal of Law and Psychiatry, 21,* 109–116.

Holmes, A., & Nadelson, C. C. (1999). *Psychological effects of cocaine and crack.* Encyclopedia of Psychological Disorders. Broomall, PA: Chelsea House.

Holmes, C. A. (1991). Psychopathic disorder: A category mistake? *Journal of Medical Ethics, 17,* 77–85.

Holmes, T. H., & Rahe, R. H. (1967). The Social Readjustment Rating Scale. *Journal of Psychosomatic Research, 11,* 213–218.

Holsboer, F. (1992). The hypothalamic-pituitary-adrenocortical system. In E. S. Paykel (Ed.), *Handbook of affective disorders* (2nd ed.). New York: Guilford Press.

Holtzman, W. H. (1961). *Guide to administration and scoring: Holtzman Inkblot Technique.* New York: Psychological Corporation.

Honig, H., & Praag, M. (1997). *Neurobiological, psychopathological, and therapeutic advances.* New York: Wiley.

Hooker, E. (1957). The adjustment of the male overt homosexual. *Journal of Projective Techniques, 21,* 18–31.

Hooker, E. (1993). Reflections of a 40-year exploration: A scientific view of homosexuality. *American Psychologist, 48,* 450–453.

Hooley, J. M., & Teasdale, J. D. (1989). Predictors of relapse in unipolar depressives: Expressed emotion, marital distress, and perceived criticism. *Journal of Abnormal Psychology, 98,* 229–235.

Hooper, S. R., & Bundy, M. B. (1998). Learning characteristics of individuals with Asperger syndrome. In E. Schopler & G. Mesibov (Eds.), *Asperger syndrome or high-functioning autism? Current issues in autism* (pp. 317–342). New York: Plenum.

Hooten, W. M., & Pearlson, G. (1996). Delirium caused by tacrine and ibuprofen interaction. *American Journal of Psychiatry, 153,* 842.

Hope, D. (1998, Aug. 12). Dead time stories. *Australian,* p. 9.

Hope, D. A., & Heimberg, R. G. (1993). Social phobia and social anxiety. In D. H. Barlow (Ed.), *Clinical handbook of psychological disorders: A step-by-step treatment manual* (2nd ed.) (pp. 99–136). New York: Guilford Press.

Horn, M. (1993, Nov.). Memories lost and found. *U.S. News & World Report,* pp. 52–63.

Hornabacher, M. (1998). *Wasted: A memoir of anorexia and bulimia.* New York: HarperCollins.

Horney, K. (1937). *The neurotic personality of our time.* London: Routledge & Kegan Paul.

Horowitz, M. J. (1997). Psychotherapy of histrionic personality disorder. *Journal of Psychotherapy Practice and Research, 6,* 93–107.

Horrocks, R., & Campling, J. (1997). *An introduction to the study of sexuality.* New York: St. Martin's Press.

Horwath, E., Johnson, J., & Horning, C. D. (1993). Epidemiology of panic disorder in African-Americans. *American Journal of Psychiatry, 150,* 465–469.

Horwath, E., Lish, J. D., Johnson, J., et al. (1993). Agoraphobia without panic: Clinical reappraisal of an epidemiologic finding. *American Journal of Psychiatry, 150*(10), 1496–1501.

Horwitz, L., Gabbard, G. O., Allen, J. G., et al. (1996). *Borderline personality disorder: Tailoring the psychotherapy to the patient.* Washington, DC: American Psychiatric Press.

Hotelling, K. A. (1988). A model for addressing the problem of bulimia on college campuses. *Journal of College Student Psychotherapy, 3,* 241–255.

Hovanitz, C. A., & Wander, M. R. (1990). Tension headache: Disregulation at some levels of stress. *Journal of Behavioral Medicine, 13,* 539–560.

Howard, K., & Rockwood, K. (1995). Quality of life in Alzheimer's disease. *Dementia, 6,* 113–116.

Howard, K. I., Moras, K., Brill, P. L., et al. (1996). Evaluation of psychotherapy: Efficacy, effectiveness, and patient progress. *American Psychologist, 51*(10), 1059–1064.

Howard, R., Castle, D., Wessely, S., & Murray, R. (1993). A comparative study of 470 cases of early-onset and late-onset schizophrenia. *British Journal of Psychiatry, 163,* 352–357.

Howitt, D. (1995). Pornography and the paedophile: Is it criminogenic? *British Journal of Medical Psychology, 68*(Pt. 1), 15–27.

Howlin, P. (1997). *Autism: Preparing for adulthood.* London: Routledge.

Howlin, P. (1998). Psychological and educational treatments for autism. *Journal of Child Psychology and Psychiatry and Allied Disciplines, 39,* 307–322.

Howlin, P., & Barron-Cohen, S. (1998). *Teaching children with autism to mind read: A practical guide for teachers and parents.* New York: Wiley.

Hoyer, G., & Lund, E. (1993). Suicide among women related to number of children in marriage. *Archives of General Psychiatry, 50,* 134–137.

Hoyle, S. G. (1995). Long-term treatment of emotionally disturbed adoptees and their families. *Clinical Social Work Journal, 23,* 429–440.

Hser, Y., Anglin, M. D., & Powers, K. (1993). A 24-year follow-up of California narcotics addicts. *Archives of General Psychiatry, 50,* 577–584.

Hsu, L. K., & Folstein, M. F. (1997). Somatoform disorders in Caucasian and Chinese Americans. *Journal of Nervous and Mental Disease, 185*(6), 382–387.

Hucker, S. J. (1997a). Impulsivity in *DSM-IV* impulse-control disorders. In D. Webster & M. A. Jackson (Eds.), *Impulsivity: Theory, assessment, and treatment* (pp. 195–211). New York: Guilford Press.

Hucker, S. J. (1997b). Sexual sadism: Psychopathology and theory. In D. R. Laws & W. T. O'Donohue (Eds.), *Sexual deviance: Theory, assessment, and treatment* (pp. 194–209). New York: Guilford Press.

Huebner, R. A., & Emery, L. J. (1998). Social psychological analysis of facilitated communication: Implications for education. *Mental Retardation, 36,* 259–268.

Huesmann, L. R., Moise, J. F., & Podolski, C. L. (1997). The effects of media violence on the development of antisocial behavior. In D. M. Stoff, J. Breiling, & J. D. Maser (Eds.), *Handbook of antisocial behavior* (pp. 181–193). New York: Wiley.

Hughes, D., Morris, S., & McGuire, A. (1997). The cost of depression in the elderly: Effects of drug therapy. *Drugs and Aging, 10,* 59–68.

Hughes, J. R. (1993). Pharmacotherapy for smoking cessation: Unvalidated assumptions, anomalies, and suggestions for future research. *Journal of Consulting and Clinical Psychology, 61,* 751–760.

Hughes, J. R., Gust, S. W., Skoog, K., et al. (1991). Symptoms of tobacco withdrawal: A replication and extension. *Archives of General Psychiatry, 48,* 52–61.

Humphry, D. (1991). *Final exit: The practicalities of self-deliverance and assisted suicide for the dying.* Eugene, OR: Hemlock Society.

Hunt, C., & Andrews, G. (1995). Comorbidity in the anxiety disorders: The use of a life-chart approach. *Journal of Psychiatric Research, 29*(6), 467–480.

Hunter, R., & MacAlpine, I. (1963). *Three hundred years of psychiatry.* Oxford: Oxford University Press.

Huntington, D. D., & Bender, W. N. (1993). Adolescents with learning disabilities at risk? Emotional well-being, depression, suicide. *Journal of Learning Disabilities, 26,* 159–166.

Huon, G. F., Braganza, C., Brown, L. B., et al. (1998). Reflections on prevention in dieting induced disorders. *International Journal of Eating Disorders, 23,* 455–458.

Huppert, F. A., Brayne, C., & O'Connor, D. W. (Eds.). (1994). *Dementia and normal aging.* Cambridge, UK: Cambridge University Press.

Hurt, C. (1998, March 7). Ritalin: The calm and the controversy. *Gannett News Service Bulletin.*

Husten, C. G., Chrisman, J. H., & Reddy, M. N. (1996). Trends and effects of cigarette smoking among girls and women in the United States, 1965–1993. *Journal of the American Medical Women's Association, 51*(1–2), 11–18.

Iacono, W. G., & Beiser, M. (1992). Where are the women in first-episode studies of schizophrenia? *Schizophrenia Bulletin, 18,* 471–480.

Iacono, W. G., & Clementz, B. A. (1993). A strategy for elucidating genetic influences on complex psychopathological syndromes (with special reference to ocular motor functioning and schizophrenia). In L. J. Chapman, J. P. Chapman, & D. Fowles (Eds.), *Progress in experimental personality and psychopathology research* (pp. 11–65). New York: Springer-Verlag.

Iacono, W. G., & Grove, W. M. (1991). Schizophrenia reviewed: Toward an integrative genetic model. *Psychological Science, 4,* 273–276.

Ingham, R., & Bennett, P. (1990). Health psychology in community settings: Models and methods. In P. Bennett, J. Weinman, & P. Spurgeon (Eds.), *Current developments in health psychology.* London: Harwood Academic.

Insel, P. M., & Roth, W. T. (2000). *Core concepts in health—2000 update* (8th ed.) (p. 254). Mountain View, CA: Mayfield.

International Society for the Study of Dissociation (ISSD). (1997). *Guidelines for treating dissociative identity disorder.* Glenview, IL: Author.

Ishii, T., Allsop, D., & Selkoe, D. J. (1991). *Frontiers of Alzheimer research: Proceedings of the 5th International Symposium of the Psychiatric Research Institute of Tokyo (PRIT).* New York: Excerpta Medica.

Islam, S., Durkin, M. S., & Zaman, S. S. (1993). Socioeconomic status and the prevalence of mental retardation in Bangladesh. *Mental Retardation, 31,* 412–417.

Ito, T. A., Miller, N., & Pollock, V. E. (1996). Alcohol and aggression: A meta-analysis on the moderating effects of inhibitory cues, triggering events, and self-focused attention. *Psychological Bulletin, 120,* 60–82.

Iwamoto, S., & Yoshida, K. (1997). School refusal in Japan: The recent dramatic increase in incidence is a cause for concern. *Social Behavior and Personality, 25,* 315–319.

Jablensky, A., & Cole, S. W. (1997). Is the earlier age at onset of schizophrenia in males a confounded finding? Results from a cross-cultural investigation. *British Journal of Psychiatry, 170,* 234–240.

Jablensky, A., & Sartorius, N. (1975). Culture and schizophrenia. *Psychological Medicine, 5,* 113–124.

Jablensky, A., Sartorius, N., Ernberg, G., et al. (1992). Schizophrenia: Manifestations, incidence and course in different cultures. A World Health Organization ten-country study. *Psychological Medicine Monographs Supplement, 20,* 1–97 [published erratum appears in *Psychological Medicine Monographs Supplement 22*(4), following 1092].

Jackson, D. N. (1989). *Personality Research Form manual* (3rd ed.). Port Huron, MI: Sigma Assessment Systems.

Jackson, H., Hess, P. M., & van-Dalen, A. (1995). Preadolescent suicide: How to ask and how to respond. *Families in Society, 76*(5), 267–279.

Jackson, J. L., Calhoun, K., Amick, A. E., et al. (1990). Young adult women who experienced childhood intrafamilial sexual abuse: Subsequent adjustment. *Archives of Sexual Behavior, 19,* 211–221.

Jackson, T. (1999). Differences in psychosocial experiences of employed, unemployed, and student samples of young adults. *Journal of Psychology, 133,* 49–60.

Jacob, R. G., Furman, J. M., Durrant, J. D., & Turner, S. M. (1996). Panic, agoraphobia, and vestibular dysfunction. *American Journal of Psychiatry, 153*(4), 503–512.

Jacobs, G. A., Quevillon, R. P., & Stricherz,

M. (1990). Lessons from the aftermath of Flight 232: Practical considerations for the mental health profession's response to air disasters. *American Psychologist, 45,* 1329–1335.

Jacobs, S. (1993). *Pathologic grief: Maladaption to loss.* Washington, DC: American Psychiatric Press.

Jacobson, E. (1938). *Progressive relaxation.* Chicago: University of Chicago Press.

Jacobson, N. S., & Christensen, A. (1996). Studying the effectiveness of psychotherapy: How well can clinical trials do the job? *American Psychologist, 51*(10), 1031–1039.

Jaffe, J. H. (1991). Opiates. In I. B. Glass (Ed.), *The international handbook of addiction behaviour* (pp. 64–68). London: Tavistock/Routledge.

James, F. E. (1991). Saint Vitus' dance [Letter]. *Journal of the Royal Society of Medicine, 84*(1), 60.

James, W. (1892). *Psychology.* London: Macmillan.

Jamison, S. (1997). *Assisted suicide: A compassionate and responsible guide for helping professionals.* San Francisco: Jossey-Bass.

Janca, A., Isaac, M., Bennett, L. A., & Tacchini, G. (1995). Somatoform disorders in different cultures—A mail questionnaire survey. *Social Psychiatry and Psychiatric Epidemiology, 30*(1), 44–48.

Jancar, J., & Jancar, P. J. (1996). Longevity in Down syndrome: A twelve year survey (1984–1995). *Italian Journal of Intellective Impairment, 9,* 27–30.

Jansen, M. A. (1996). Prevention research for alcohol and other drugs: A look ahead to what is needed. *Substance Use and Misuse, 31*(9), 1217–1222.

Jason, L., Billows, W., Schnopp-Wyatt, D., & King, C. (1996). Reducing the illegal sales of cigarettes to minors: Analysis of alternative enforcement schedules. *Journal of Applied Behavior Analysis, 29*(3), 333–344.

Jawed, S. Y. (1991). A survey of psychologically ill Asian children. *British Journal of Psychiatry, 158,* 268–270.

Jehu, D. (1992). Adult survivors of sexual abuse. In R. T. Ammerman & M. Hersen (Eds.), *Assessment of family violence* (pp. 348–370). New York: Wiley.

Jellinek, E. M. (1946). Phases in the drinking histories of alcoholics. *Quarterly Journal of Studies in Alcohol, 7,* 1–88.

Jenaway, A., & Swinton, M. (1993). Triplets where monozygotic siblings are concordant for arson. *Medicine, Science, and the Law, 33,* 351–353.

Jenike, M. A. (1986). Theories of etiology. In M. A. Jenike, L. Baer, & W. E. Minichiello (Eds.), *Obsessive-compulsive disorders.* Littleton, MA: PSG Publishing.

Jenike, M. A. (1990). Psychotherapy. In A. S.

Bellack & M. Hersen (Eds.), *Handbook of comparative treatments for adult disorders* (pp. 245–255). New York: Wiley.

Jenike, M. A., Baer, L., Ballantine, T., et al. (1991). Cingulotomy for refractory obsessive-compulsive disorder: A long-term follow-up of 33 patients. *Archives of General Psychiatry, 48*(6), 548–555.

Jenkins, A. J., Keenan, R. M., Henningfield, J. E., & Cone, E. J. (1994). Pharmacokinetics and pharmacodynamics of smoked heroin. *Journal of Analytical Toxicology, 18,* 317–330.

Jenkins, C. D., Zyzanski, S. J., & Rosenman, R. H. (1979). *Jenkins Activity Survey.* New York: Psychological Corporation.

Jenkins-Hall, K. (1994). Outpatient treatment of child molesters: Motivational factors and outcome. *Journal of Offender Rehabilitation, 21,* 139–150.

Jensen, E. J., Schmidt, E., Pedersen, B., & Dahl, R. (1991). Effect on smoking cessation of silver acetate, nicotine and ordinary chewing gum. *Psychopharmacology, 104,* 470–474.

Jensen, G. B., & Pakkenberg, B. (1993). Do alcoholics drink their neurons away? *Lancet, 342,* 1201–1204.

Jensen, M. P., Turner, J. A., Romano, J. M., & Karoly, P. (1991). Coping with chronic pain: A critical review of the literature. *Pain, 47,* 249–283.

Jerome, J. K. (1964). *Three men in a boat.* Harmondsworth, UK: Penguin. (Original work published 1889)

Jerusalem, M. (1990). Temporal patterns of stress appraisals for high- and low-anxious subjects. *Anxiety Research, 3,* 113–129.

Jeste, D. V., & Caligiuri, M. P. (1993). Tardive dyskinesia. *Schizophrenia Bulletin, 19,* 303–316.

Jiang, W., Babyak, M., Krantz, D. S., et al. (1996). Mental stress–induced myocardial ischemia and cardiac events. *Journal of the American Medical Association, 275* (21), 1651–1656.

Jilek, W. G. (1995). Emil Kraepelin and comparative sociocultural psychiatry. *European Archives of Psychiatry and Clinical Neuroscience, 245,* 231–238.

Johnson, B. D., Natarajan, M., Dunlap, E., et al. (1994). Crack abusers and noncrack abusers: Profiles of drug use, drug sales and nondrug criminality. *Journal of Drug Issues, 24,* 117–141.

Johnson, J., Weissman, M. M., & Klerman, G. L. (1990). Panic disorder, comorbidity and suicide attempts. *Archives of General Psychiatry, 47,* 805–808.

Johnson, K. A., Jones, K., Holman, B. L., et al. (1998). Preclinical prediction of Alzheimer's disease using SPECT. *Neurology, 50,* 1563–1571.

Johnson, S. K., DeLuca, J., & Natelson, B. H. (1996). Assessing somatization disorder in the chronic fatigue syndrome. *Psychosomatic Medicine, 58*, 50–57.

Johnson, T. P., Freels, S. A., Parsons, J. A., & Vangeest, J. B. (1997). Substance abuse and homelessness: Social selection or social adaptation? *Addiction, 92*(4), 437–445.

Johnston, L. D., O'Malley, P. M., & Bachman, J. G. (1995). *National survey results on drug use from the Monitoring the Future Study, 1975–1994. Volume I: Secondary school students.* (NIH Pub. No. 95-4026). *Volume II: College students and young adults.* (1996). (NIH Pub. No. 96-4027). Rockville, MD: National Institute on Drug Abuse.

Johnston, L. D., O'Malley, P. M., & Bachman, J. G. (1996). *National survey results on drug use from the Monitoring the Future Study, 1975–1995. Volume I: Secondary school students.* (NIH Pub. No. 97-4139). Rockville, MD: National Institute on Drug Abuse.

Johnston, P., Hudson, S. M., & Marshall, W. L. (1992). The effects of masturbatory reconditioning with nonfamilial child molesters. *Behavior Research and Therapy, 30*, 559–561.

Joiner, T. E., Alfano, M. S., & Metalsky, G. I. (1992). When depression breeds contempt: Reassurance seeking, self-esteem, and rejection of depressed college students by their roommates. *Journal of Abnormal Psychology, 101*, 165–173.

Jolly, J. B., Dyck, M. J., Kramer, T. A., & Wherry, J. N. (1996). The relations between sociotropy and autonomy, positive and negative affect and two proposed depression subtypes. *British Journal of Clinical Psychology, 35*(1), 91–101.

Jones, E. E. (1993). Introduction to special section: Single-case research in psychotherapy. *Journal of Consulting and Clinical Psychology, 61*, 371–372.

Jones, G. (1995). More than just a game: Research developments and issues in competitive anxiety in sport. *British Journal of Psychology, 86*(Pt. 4), 449–478.

Jones, I. H., & Horne, D. J. de L. (1973). Psychiatric disorders among Aborigines of the Australian western desert: Further data and discussion. *Social Science and Medicine, 7*, 219–228.

Jones, J. B., & Barklage, N. E. (1990). Conversion disorder: Camouflage for brain lesions in two cases. *Archives of Internal Medicine, 150*, 1343–1345.

Jones, M. C. (1924a). The elimination of children's fears. *Journal of Experimental Psychology, 7*, 382–390.

Jones, M. C. (1924b). A laboratory study of fear: The case of Peter. *Journal of Genetic Psychology, 31*, 308–315.

Jones, P. B., Bebbington, P., Foerster, A., et al. (1993). Premorbid social underachievement in schizophrenia: Results from the Camberwell Collaborative

Study. *British Journal of Psychiatry, 162*, 65–71.

Jones, W. H., Cheek, J. M., & Briggs, S. R. (Eds.). (1986). *Shyness: Perspectives on research and treatment.* New York: Plenum.

Jones-Brando, L. V., Buthod, J. L., Holland, L. E., et al. (1997). Metabolites of the antipsychotic agent clozapine inhibit the replication of human immunodeficiency virus type 1. *Schizophrenia Research, 25*(1), 63–70.

Jorgensen, R. S., Johnson, B. T., Kolodziej, M. E., & Schreer, G. F. (1996). Elevated blood pressure and personality: A meta-analytic review. *Psychological Bulletin, 120*(2), 293–320.

Joseph, S. (1997). *Personality disorders: New symptom-focused drug therapy.* New York: Haworth Medical Press.

Jozsvai, E., Richards, B., & Leach, L. (1996). Behavior management of a patient with Creutzfeldt-Jacob disease. *Clinical Gerontologist, 16*, 11–17.

Julkunen, J., Idanpaan-Heikkila, U., & Saarinen, T. (1993). Components of type A behavior and the first-year prognosis of myocardial infarction. *Journal of Psychosomatic Research, 37*, 11–18.

Jung, C. G. (1910). The association method. *American Journal of Psychology, 21*, 219–269.

Juster, H. R., Heimberg, R. G., & Holt, C. S. (1996). Social phobia: Diagnostic issues and review of cognitive behavioral treatment strategies. *Progress in Behavior Modification, 30*, 74–98.

Justice, B. (1994). Critical life events and the onset of illness. *Comprehensive Therapy, 20*(4), 232–238.

Kafka, M. O. (1997). Hypersexual desire in males: An operational definition and clinical implications for males with paraphilias and paraphilia-related disorders. *Archives of Sexual Behavior, 26*, 505–526.

Kagan, J., & Snidman, N. (1991). Infant predictors of inhibited and uninhibited profiles. *Psychological Science, 2*, 40–44.

Kagitçibasi, Ç., & Berry, J. W. (1989). Cross-cultural psychology: Current research and trends. *Annual Review of Psychology, 40*, 493–531.

Kahneman, D., Slovic, P., & Tversky, A. (Eds.). (1982). *Judgement under uncertainty: Heuristics and biases.* Cambridge, UK: Cambridge University Press.

Kalin, N. H. (1993, May). The neurobiology of fear. *Scientific American*, pp. 94–101.

Kallman, F. J. (1938). *The genetics of schizophrenia.* New York: Augustin.

Kalus, O., Bernstein, D. P., & Siever, L. J. (1995). Schizoid personality disorder. In W. J. Livesley (Ed.), *The DSM-IV personality disorders: Diagnosis and treatment of mental disorders* (pp. 58–70). New York: Guilford Press.

Kandel, D. B., & Logan, J. A. (1984). Patterns of drug use from adolescence to young adulthood. 1: Periods of risk for initiation, continued use, and discontinuation. *American Journal of Public Health, 74*, 660–666.

Kane, J. M. (1997). What can we achieve by implementing a compliance-improvement program? *International Clinical Psychopharmacology, 12*(Suppl. 1), S43–S46.

Kane, J. M., & Marder, S. R. (1993). Psychopharmacologic treatment of schizophrenia. *Schizophrenia Bulletin, 19*, 287–302.

Kanner, A. D., Coyne, J. C., Schaefer, C., & Lazarus, R. S. (1981). Comparison of two modes of stress measurement: Daily hassles and uplifts versus major life events. *Journal of Behavioral Medicine, 4*, 1–39.

Kanner, L. (1943). Autistic disturbances of affective contact. *Nervous Child, 2*, 217–250.

Kaplan, H. B. (1996). Perspectives on psychosocial stress. In H. B. Kaplan (Ed.), *Psychosocial stress: Perspectives on structure, theory, life-course, and methods* (pp. 3–24). San Diego: Academic Press.

Kaplan, H. S. (1995). Sexual aversion disorder: The case of the phobic virgin, or an abused child grows up. In R. C. Rosen & S. R. Leiblum (Eds.), *Case studies in sex therapy* (pp. 65–80). New York: Guilford Press.

Kaplan, H. S., Schiavi, R. C., Rosenbaum, M. B., et al. (1996). Sexual and gender identity disorders. In G. O. Gabbard & S. D. Atkinson (Eds.), *Synopsis of treatments of psychiatric disorders* (2nd ed.) (pp. 771–872). Washington, DC: American Psychiatric Press.

Kaplan, M. (1983). A woman's view of the *DSM-III. American Psychologist, 38*, 786–792.

Kaplan, M. S., & Kreuger, R. B. (1997). Voyeurism: Psychopathology and theory. In D. R. Laws & W. T. O'Donohue (Eds.), *Sexual deviance: Theory, assessment, and treatment* (pp. 297–310). New York: Guilford Press.

Kaprio, J., Koskenvuy, M., & Rita, H. (1987). Mortality after bereavement: A prospective study of 95,647 widowed persons. *American Journal of Public Health, 7*, 283–287.

Karayiorgou, M., & Gogos, J. A. (1997). Dissecting the genetic complexity of schizophrenia. *Molecular Psychiatry, 2*(3), 211–223.

Karno, M., Golding, J. M., Sorenson, S. B., & Burnam, M. A. (1988). The epidemiology of obsessive-compulsive disorder in 5 U.S. communities. *Archives of General Psychiatry, 45*, 1094–1099.

Karno, M., Hough, R. L., Burnam, M. A., et al. (1987). Lifetime prevalence of specific psychiatric disorders among Mexican

Americans and non-Hispanic Whites in Los Angeles. *Archives of General Psychiatry, 44,* 695–701.

Karon, B. P. (1978). Projective tests are valid. *American Psychologist, 33*(8), 764–765.

Kasper, S., Wehr, T. A., Bartko, J. J., et al. (1989). Epidemiological findings of seasonal changes in mood and behavior: A telephone survey of Montgomery County, Maryland. *Archives of General Psychiatry, 46,* 823–833.

Katerndahl, D. A. (1992). Natural history of phobic anxiety. *Family Practice Research Journal, 12*(4), 401–409.

Katerndahl, D. A. (1993). Panic and prolapse: Meta-analysis. *Journal of Nervous and Mental Disease, 181,* 539–544.

Katerndahl, D. A., & Realini, J. P. (1993). Lifetime prevalence of panic states. *American Journal of Psychiatry, 150,* 246–249.

Kates, W. R., Mostofsky, S. H., Zimmerman, A. W., et al. (1998). Neuroanatomical and neurocognitive differences in a pair of monozygous twins discordant for strictly defined autism. *Annals of Neurology, 43,* 782–791.

Katsanis, J., & Iacono, W. G. (1991). Clinical neuropsychological and brain structural correlates of smooth-pursuit eye tracking performance in chronic schizophrenia. *Journal of Abnormal Psychology, 100,* 526–534.

Katsanis, J., Kortenkamp, S., Iacono, W. G., & Grove, W. M. (1997). Antisaccade performance in patients with schizophrenia and affective disorder. *Journal of Abnormal Psychology, 106*(3), 468–472.

Katusic, S. K., Colligan, R. C., Beard, C. M., et al. (1996). Mental retardation in a birth cohort, 1976–1980, Rochester, Minnesota. *American Journal on Mental Retardation, 100,* 335–344.

Katz, I. R. (1993). Delirium. In D. L. Dunner (Ed.), *Current psychiatric therapy* (pp. 65–73). Philadelphia: Saunders.

Katz, R., & McGuffin, P. (1993). The genetics of affective disorders. In L. J. Chapman, L. P. Chapman, & D. Fowles (Eds.), *Progress in experimental personality and psychopathology research.* New York: Springer-Verlag.

Katz, S. (1994). Twenty years later: A follow-up study of graduates of two sheltered workshop programmes in Israel. *British Journal of Developmental Disabilities, 40,* 4–14.

Katz, S., Kravetz, S., & Marks, Y. (1997). Parents' and doctors' attitudes toward facial plastic surgery for persons with Down syndrome. *Journal of Intellectual and Developmental Disability, 22,* 265–273.

Kaufman, A. S. (1990). *Assessing adolescent and adult intelligence.* Boston: Allyn & Bacon.

Kavanagh, D. J. (1992). Recent develop-

ments in expressed emotion and schizophrenia. *British Journal of Psychiatry, 160,* 601–620.

Kavoussi, R., Armstead, P., & Coccaro, E. (1997). The neurobiology of impulsive aggression. *Psychiatric Clinics of North America, 20,* 453–472.

Kazdin, A. K. (1978). *A history of behavior modification.* Baltimore: University Park Press.

Keane, T. M., Caddell, J. M., & Taylor, K. L. (1988). Mississippi Scale for Combat-Related Posttraumatic Stress Disorder: Three studies in reliability and validity. *Journal of Consulting and Clinical Psychology, 56*(1), 85–90.

Keane, T. M., Gerardi, R. J., Quinn, S. J., & Litz, B. T. (1992). Behavioral treatment of posttraumatic stress disorder. In S. M. Turner, K. S. Calhoun, & H. E. Adams (Eds.), *Handbook of clinical behavior therapy* (2nd ed.) (pp. 87–89). New York: Wiley.

Keefe, R. S. E., Silverman, J. M., Mohs, R. C., et al. (1997). Eye tracking, attention, and schizotypal symptoms in nonpsychotic relatives of patients with schizophrenia. *Archives of General Psychiatry, 54,* 169–176.

Keith, S. J., Regier, D. A., & Rae, D. S. (1991). Schizophrenic disorders. In L. N. Robins & D. A. Regier (Eds.), *Psychotic disorders in America: The epidemiologic catchment area study.* New York: Free Press.

Keller, M. B. (1988). Diagnostic issues and clinical course of unipolar illness. In A. J. Frances & R. E. Hales (Eds.), *Review of psychiatry.* Washington, DC: American Psychiatric Press.

Keller, M. B., Baker, L. A., & Russell, C. W. (1993). Classification and treatment of dysthymia. In D. L. Dunner (Ed.), *Current psychiatric therapy.* Philadelphia: Saunders.

Kelley, G. A. (1955). *The psychology of personal constructs.* New York: Norton.

Kelley, S. J. (1986). Learned helplessness in the sexually abused child. *Issues in Comprehensive Pediatric Nursing, 9*(3), 193–207.

Kellner, R. (1985). Functional somatic symptoms and hypochondriasis. *Archives of General Psychiatry, 42,* 821–833.

Kellner, R., Hernandez, J., & Pathak, D. (1992). Hypochondriacal fears and beliefs, anxiety and somatization. *British Journal of Psychiatry, 160,* 525–532.

Kelly, J. A., Murphy, D. A., Sikkema, K. L., & Kalichman, S. C. (1993). Psychological interventions to prevent HIV infection are urgently needed. *American Psychologist, 48,* 1023–1034.

Kelly, J. B. (1998). Marital conflict, divorce and children's adjustment. *Child and Adolescent Psychiatric Clinics of North America, 7,* 259–271.

Kelly, W. L. (1991). *Psychology of the unconscious: Mesmer, Janet, Freud, Jung, and cur-*

rent issues. Buffalo, NY: Prometheus Books.

Kelsoe, J. R., Ginns, E. I., Egeland, J. A., et al. (1989). Re-evaluation of the linkage relationship between chromosome 11p loci and the gene for bipolar affective disorder in the Old Order Amish. *Nature, 342*(6247), 238–243.

Keltner, N. L. (1995). Risperidone: The search for a better antipsychotic. *Perspectives in Psychiatric Care, 31*(1), 30–33.

Kemeny, M. E., Weiner, H., Taylor, S. E., et al. (1994). Repeated bereavement, depressed mood, and immune parameters in HIV seropositive and symptomatic gay men. *Health Psychology, 13,* 14–24.

Kemper, T. L., & Bauman, M. (1998). Neuropathology of infantile autism. *Journal of Neuropathology and Experimental Neurology, 57,* 645–652.

Kendell, R. E., Cooper, J. E., & Gourley, A. J. (1971). Diagnostic criteria of American and British psychiatrists. *Archives of General Psychiatry, 25,* 123–130.

Kendell, R. E., & Kemp, I. W. (1989). Maternal influence in the etiology of schizophrenia. *Archives of General Psychiatry, 46,* 878–882.

Kendler, K. S., & Diehl, S. R. (1993). The genetics of schizophrenia: A current, genetic-epidemiologic perspective. *Schizophrenia Bulletin, 19,* 261–285.

Kendler, K. S., Heath, A. C., Neale, M. C., et al. (1992). A population-based twin study of alcoholism in women. *Journal of the American Medical Association, 268,* 1877–1882.

Kendler, K. S., Neale, M. C., Kessler, R. C., et al. (1992). The genetic epidemiology of phobias in women. *Archives of General Psychiatry, 49,* 273–281.

Kendler, K. S., & Walsh, D. (1995). Schizotypal personality disorder in parents and the risk for schizophrenia in siblings. *Schizophrenia Bulletin, 21,* 47–52.

Kendler, K. S., Walters, E. E., Truett, K. R., et al. (1994). Sources of individual differences in depressive symptoms: Analysis of two samples of twins and their families. *American Journal of Psychiatry, 151* (11), 1605–1614.

Kent, D. A., Tomasson, K., & Coryell, W. (1995). Course and outcome of conversion and somatization disorders: A four-year follow-up. *Psychosomatics, 36*(2), 138–144.

Kern, R. S., Green, M. F., & Goldstein, M. J. (1995). Modification of performance on the span of apprehension, a putative marker of vulnerability to schizophrenia. *Journal of Abnormal Psychology, 104,* 385–389.

Kern, R. S, Kuehnel, T. G., Teuber, J., & Hayden, J. L. (1997). Multimodal cognitive-behavior therapy for borderline personality disorder with self-injurious behavior. *Psychiatric Services, 48,* 1131–1133.

Kernberg, P. F., Hajal, F., & Normandin, L. (1998). A retrospective record review study of descriptive characteristics. In E. F. Ronningstam (Ed.), *Disorders of narcissism: Diagnostic, clinical, and empirical implications* (pp. 437–456). Washington, DC: American Psychiatric Press.

Kertesz, A. (1996). Pick complex and Pick's disease: The nosology of frontal lobe dementia, primary progressive aphasia, and corticobasal ganglionic degeneration. *European Journal of Neurology, 3,* 280–282.

Kessler, D. A., Barnett, P. S., Witt, A., et al. (1997). The legal and scientific basis for FDA's assertion of jurisdiction over cigarettes and smokeless tobacco. *Journal of the American Medical Association, 277*(5), 405–409.

Kessler, R. C., McGonagle, K. A., Zhao, S., et al. (1994). Lifetime and 12-month prevalence of *DSM-III-R* psychiatric disorders in the United States. *Archives of General Psychiatry, 51,* 8–19.

Kessler, R. C., Sonnega, A., Bromet, E., et al. (1995). Posttraumatic stress disorder in the National Comorbidity Survey. *Archives of General Psychiatry, 52*(12), 1048–1060.

Kevorkian, J. (1988). The last fearsome taboo: Medical aspects of planned death. *Medicine and Law, 7*(1), 1–14.

Keyes, D. (1981). *The minds of Billy Milligan.* New York: Random House.

Kiecolt-Glaser, J. K., & Glaser, R. (1992). Psychoneuroimmunology: Can psychological interventions modulate immunity? *Journal of Consulting and Clinical Psychology, 60,* 569–575.

Kihlstrom, J. F., Barnhardt, T. M., & Tataryn, D. J. (1992). The psychological unconscious: Found, lost, and regained. *American Psychologist, 47,* 788–791.

Kihlstrom, J. F., Glisky, M. L., & Angiulo, M. J. (1994). Dissociative tendencies and dissociative disorders. *Journal of Abnormal Psychology, 103,* 117–124.

Kihlstrom, J. F., Tataryn, D. J., & Hoyt, I. P. (1993). Dissociative disorders. In P. B. Sutker and H. E. Adams (Eds.), *Comprehensive handbook of psychopathology* (2nd ed.). New York: Plenum.

Kincaid, J. R. (1998). *Erotic innocence: The culture of child molesting.* Durham, NC: Duke University Press.

King, N. J., Gullione, E., Tonge, B. J., & Ollendick, T. H. (1993). Self-reports of panic attacks and manifest anxiety in adolescents. *Behaviour Research and Therapy, 31,* 111–116.

King, N. J., & Tonge, B. J. (1992). Treatment of childhood anxiety disorders using behaviour therapy and pharmacotherapy. *Australian and New Zealand Journal of Psychiatry, 26*(4), 644–651.

Kingdon, D. G., & Turkington, D. (1991). The use of cognitive behavior therapy with a normalizing rationale in schizophrenia. *Journal of Nervous and Mental Disease, 179,* 207–211.

Kinsella, J. E., Frankel, E., German, B., & Kanner, J. (1993). Possible mechanisms for the protective role of antioxidants in wine and plant foods. *Food Technology, 47,* 85–89.

Kinsey, A. C., Pomeroy, W. B., & Martin, C. E. (1948). *Sexual behavior in the human male.* Philadelphia: Saunders.

Kinsey, A. C., Pomeroy, W. B., Martin, C. E., & Gebhard, P. H. (1953). *Sexual behavior in the human female.* Philadelphia: Saunders.

Kinzie, J. D., Leung, P. K., Boehnlein, J., & Matsunaga, D. (1992). Psychiatric epidemiology of an Indian village: A 19-year replication study. *Journal of Nervous and Mental Disease, 180,* 33–39.

Kinzl, J. F., Traweger, C. H., & Biebl, W. (1995). Family background and sexual abuse associated with somatization. *Psychotherapy and Psychosomatics, 64*(2), 82–87.

Kiple, K. F. (1993). *The Cambridge world history of human disease.* Cambridge, UK: Cambridge University Press.

Kirk, S. A., & Kutchins, H. (1992). *The selling of DSM: The rhetoric of science in psychiatry.* New York: Aldine.

Kirkby, K., Daniels, B., Jones, I., & McInnes, M. A. (1997). Survey of social outcome in schizophrenia in Tasmania. *Australia and New Zealand Journal of Psychiatry, 31*(3), 405–410.

Kirkby, K. C., Menzies, R. G., Daniels, B. A., & Smith, K. L. (1995). Aetiology of spider phobia: Classificatory differences between two origins instruments. *Behaviour Research and Therapy, 33*(8), 955–958.

Kirmayer, L. J., Robbins, J. M., & Paris, J. (1994). Somatoform disorders: Personality and social matrix of distress. *Journal of Abnormal Psychology, 103,* 125–136.

Kirov, G., & Murray, R. (1997). The molecular genetics of schizophrenia: Progress so far. *Molecular Medicine Today, 3*(3), 124–130.

Kirsner, J. B., & Shorter, R. G. (1980). *Inflammatory bowel disease* (2nd ed.). Philadelphia: Lea & Febiger.

Kissane, D. W., McKenzie, D. P., & Bloch, S. (1997). Family coping and bereavement outcome. *Palliative Medicine, 11,* 191–201.

Kitamura, T., Shima, S., Sugawara, M., et al. (1996). Clinical and psychosocial correlates of antenatal depression: A review. *Psychotherapy and Psychosomatics, 65,* 117–123.

Klein, D. F. (1964). Delineation of two drug-responsive anxiety syndromes. *Psychopharmacologia, 5,* 397–408.

Klein, D. N., Kocsis, J. H., McCullough, J. P., et al. (1996). Symptomatology in dysthymic and major depressive disorder. *Psychiatric Clinics of North America, 19*(1), 41–53.

Klein, D. N., & Shih, J. H. (1998). Depressive personality: Associations with *DSM-III-R* mood and personality disorders and negative and positive affectivity, 30-month stability, and prediction of course of Axis I depressive disorders. *Journal of Abnormal Psychology, 107,* 319–327.

Klein, D. N., Taylor, E. B., Dickstein, S., & Harding, K. (1988). The early-late onset distinction in *DSM-III-R* dysthymia. *Journal of Affective Disorders, 14*(1), 25–33.

Klein, R. G. (1995). Is panic disorder associated with separation anxiety disorder? *Clinical Neuropharmacology, 18*(Suppl. 2), S7–S14.

Kleinknecht, R. A. (1986). *The anxious self.* New York: Human Services Press.

Kleinknecht, R. A. (1994). Acquisition of blood, injury, and needle fears and phobias. *Behaviour Research and Therapy, 32*(8), 817–823.

Kleinman, A. (1986). *Social origins of distress and disease: Depression neurasthenia and pain in modern China.* New Haven, CT: Yale University Press.

Kleinman, A. (1991, April). *Culture and DSM-IV: Recommendations for the introduction and for the overall structure.* Paper presented at the Conference on Culture and *DSM-IV,* Pittsburgh, PA.

Kleinman, A., & Good, B. (1985). *Culture and depression: Studies in the anthropology and cross-cultural psychiatry of affect and disorder.* Berkeley: University of California Press.

Klerman, G. L. (1982). Practical issues in the treatment of depression and mania. In E. S. Paykel (Ed.), *Handbook of affective disorders.* New York: Guilford Press.

Klerman, G. L. (1988). Depression and related disorders of mood (affective disorders). In A. M. Nicholi, Jr. (Ed.), *The new Harvard guide to psychiatry.* Cambridge, MA: Harvard University Press.

Kline, N. S. (1954). Use of *Rauwolfia serpentia* in neuropsychiatric conditions. *Annals of the New York Academy of Science, 54,* 107–132.

Klingner, J. K., Vaughn, S., Schumm, J. S., et al. (1998). Inclusion or pull-out: Which do students prefer? *Journal of Learning Disabilities, 31,* 148–158.

Kloner, R. A., & Jarow, J. P. (1999). Erectile dysfunction and sildenafil citrate and cardiologists. *American Journal of Cardiology, 83,* 576–552.

Klonoff, E. A., & Landrine, H. (1997). *Preventing misdiagnosis of women: A guide to physical disorders that have psychiatric symptoms.* Thousand Oaks, CA: Sage.

Klosko, J. S., Barlow, D. H., Tassinari, R. B., & Cerny, J. A. (1990). Comparison of alprazolam and cognitive behavior therapy in the treatment of panic disorder: A preliminary report. In I. Hand & H. U. Wittichen (Eds.), *Treatment of panic and phobias: Models of application and factors affecting outcome.* Berlin: Springer-Verlag.

Kluft, R. P. (1984). An introduction to multiple personality disorder. *Psychiatric Annals, 7,* 19–24.

Kluft, R. P. (1985). The treatment of multiple personality disorder: Current concepts. In F. Flach (Ed.), *Directions in psychiatry.* New York: Hatherleigh.

Kluft, R. P. (1987). First-rank symptoms as a diagnostic clue to multiple personality disorder. *American Journal of Psychiatry, 144,* 293–298.

Kluft, R. P. (1988). The dissociative disorders. In J. A. Talbott, R. E. Hales, & S. C. Yudofsky (Eds.), *The American Psychiatric Press textbook of psychiatry.* Washington, DC: American Psychiatric Press.

Kluft, R. P. (1991). Multiple personality disorder. In A. Tasman & S. M. Goldfinger (Eds.), *American Psychiatric press review of psychiatry, Vol. 10.* Washington, DC: American Psychiatric Press.

Kluft, R. P. (Ed.). (1985). *Childhood antecedents of multiple personality.* Washington, DC: American Psychiatric Press.

Knable, M. B., & Weinberger, D. R. (1997). Dopamine, the prefrontal cortex and schizophrenia. *Journal of Psychopharmacology, 11*(2), 123–131.

Knight, R. G., Williams, S., McGee, R., et al. (1997). Psychometric properties of the Centre for Epidemiologic Studies in Depression Scale (CES-D) in a sample of women in middle life. *Behaviour Research and Therapy, 35,* 373–380.

Knoppers, B. M., & Chadwick, R. (1994). The Human Genome Project: Under an international ethical microscope. *Science, 265*(5181), 2035–2036.

Kobasa, S. C., Hilker, R. J., & Maddi, S. R. (1979). Psychological hardiness. *Journal of Occupational Medicine, 21,* 595–598.

Koegel, R. L., Schreibman, L., O'Neill, R. E., & Burke, J. C. (1983). The personality and family interaction characteristics of parents of autistic children. *Journal of Consulting and Clinical Psychology, 51,* 683–692.

Koerner, K., & Linehan, M. M. (1997). Case formulation in dialectical behavior therapy for borderline personality disorder. In T. D. Eells (Ed.), *Handbook of psychotherapy case formulation* (pp. 340–367). New York: Guilford Press.

Kohlenberg, R. J. (1973). Behavioristic approach to multiple personality. *Behavior Therapy, 4,* 137–140.

Kohlenberg, R. J., & Tsai, M. (1991). *Functional analytic psychotherapy.* New York: Plenum.

Kohn, P. M., & Macdonald, J. E. (1992). The survey of recent life experiences: A decontaminated Hassles Scale for adults. *Journal of Behavioral Medicine, 15,* 221–236.

Koller, W. C., & Paulson, G. (Eds.). (1995). *Therapy of Parkinson's disease.* New York: Dekker.

Kopp, S., & Gillberg, C. (1997). Selective mutism: A population based study. A research note. *Journal of Child Psychology and Psychiatry, 38,* 257–262.

Koppitz, E. M. (1975). *The Bender-Gestalt Test for young children.* New York: Grune & Stratton.

Korenberg, J. R., Chen, X. N., Schipper, R., et al. (1994). Down syndrome phenotypes: The consequences of chromosomal imbalance. *Proceedings of the National Academy of Sciences, 91,* 4997–5001.

Korenman, S. G., & Barchas, J. D. (1993). *Biological basis of substance abuse.* New York: Oxford University Press.

Koss, M. P. (1993). Rape: Scope, impact, interventions, and public policy responses. *American Psychologist, 48,* 1062–1069.

Koszewski, W. M., Newell, G. K., & Higgins, J. J. (1990). Effect of a nutrition education program on the eating attitudes and behaviors of college women. *Journal of College Student Development, 31,* 203–210.

Kovacs, M., & Feinberg, T. (1982). Coping with juvenile onset diabetes mellitus. In A. Baum & J. Singer (Eds.), *Handbook of psychology and health, Vol. 2* (pp. 165–212). Hillsdale, NJ: Erlbaum.

Kovacs, M., Kass, R., Schnell, T., et al. (1989). Family functioning and metabolic control in school-aged children with IDDM. *Diabetes Care, 12,* 409–414.

Kowall, N. W., Beal, M. F., Busciglio, J., et al. (1991). An in vivo model for the neurodegenerative effects of β-amyloid and protection by substance P. *Proceedings of the National Academy of Sciences, 88,* 7247–7251.

Kozielecki, J. (1981). *Psychological decision theory.* London: Reidel.

Kraepelin, E. (1919). Signs of mental disorder. *Alienist and Neurologist, 40,* 85 [cited in Bleuler, 1952].

Krafft-Ebing, R. von. (1886). *Psychopathia sexualis: A medico-forensic study* (H. E. Wedeck, Trans.). New York: G. Putnam & Sons.

Kratochwill, T. R., & Sheridan, S. M. (1990). Advances in behavioral assessment. In T. B. Gutkin & C. R. Reynolds (Eds.), *The handbook of school psychology* (2nd ed.) (pp. 328–364). New York: Wiley.

Kreuger, R. B., & Kaplan, M. S. (1997). Frotteurism: Assessment and treatment. In D. R. Laws & W. T. O'Donohue (Eds.), *Sexual deviance: Theory, assessment, and treatment* (pp. 131–151). New York: Guilford Press.

Krull, F., & Schifferdecker, M. (1990). Inpatient treatment of conversion disorder: A clinical investigation of outcome. *Psychotherapy and Psychosomatics, 53,* 164–165.

Krystal, J. H., Kosten, T. R., Southwick, S., et al. (1989). Neurobiological aspects of PTSD: Review of clinical and preclinical studies. *Behavior Therapy, 20,* 177–198.

Krystal, J. H., Woods, S. W., Hill, C. L., & Charney, D. S. (1991). Characteristics of panic attack subtypes: Assessment of spontaneous panic, situational panic, sleep panic, and limited symptom attacks. *Comprehensive Psychiatry, 32*(6), 474–480.

Kubicek, L. F. (1980). Organization in two mother-infant interactions involving a normal infant and his fraternal brother who was later diagnosed as autistic. In T. M. Field, S. Golaber, D. Stern, & A. M. Sostek (Eds.), *High-risk infants and children: Adult and peer interactions.* New York: Academic Press.

Kuch, K., & Cox, B. J. (1992). Symptoms of PTSD in 124 survivors of the Holocaust. *American Journal of Psychiatry, 149,* 337–340.

Kuhn, T. S. (1962). *The structure of scientific revolutions.* Chicago: University of Chicago Press.

Kuipers, L. (1992). Expressed emotion research in Europe. *British Journal of Clinical Psychology, 31,* 429–443.

Kulhara, P. (1994). Outcome of schizophrenia: Some transcultural observations with particular reference to developing countries. *European Archives of Psychiatry and Clinical Neuroscience, 244,* 227–235.

Kumar, R. C. (1997). "Anybody's child": Severe disorders of mother to infant bonding. *British Journal of Psychiatry, 171,* 175–178.

Kumpulainen, K., Raesaenen, E., Raaska, H., & Somppi, V. (1998). Selective mutism among second-graders in elementary school. *European Child and Adolescent Psychiatry, 7,* 24–29.

Kunce, L., & Mesibov, G. B. (1998). Educational approaches to high-functioning autism and Asperger syndrome. In E. Schopler & G. B. Mesibov (Eds.), *Asperger syndrome or high-functioning autism? Current issues in autism* (pp. 227–261). New York: Plenum.

Kunugi , H., Nanko, S., Takei, N., et al. (1995). Schizophrenia following in-utero exposure to the 1957 influenza epidemic in Japan. *American Journal of Psychiatry, 152,* 450–452.

Kupfer, D. J., Frank, E., Perel, J. M., et al. (1992). Five-year outcome for maintenance therapies in recurrent depression.

Archives of General Psychiatry, 49, 769–773.

Kupfer, D. J., Monk, T. H., & Barchas, J. D. (1988). *Biological rhythms and mental disorders.* New York: Guilford Press.

Kupfersmid, J. (1992). The "defense" of Sigmund Freud. *Psychotherapy, 29,* 297–309.

Kurtz, L. (1995). Coping processes and behavioral outcomes in children of divorce. *Canadian Journal of School Psychology, 11* (1), 52–64.

Kushner, M. B., Sher, K. J., & Beitman, B. D. (1990). The relation between alcohol problems and the anxiety disorders. *American Journal of Psychiatry, 147,* 685–695.

Kushner, M. G., Thomas, A. M., Bartels, K. M., & Beitman, B. D. (1992). Panic disorder history in the families of patients with angiographically normal coronary arteries. *American Journal of Psychiatry, 149,* 1563–1567.

Kutcher, S., Kachur, E., Marton, P., et al. (1992). Substance abuse among adolescents with chronic mental illnesses: A pilot study of descriptive and differentiating features. *Canadian Journal of Psychiatry, 37*(6), 428–431.

Kutchins, H., & Kirk, S. A. (1997). *Making us crazy.* DSM: *The psychiatric bible and the creation of mental disorders.* New York: Free Press.

Labbate, L. A., & Snow, M. P. (1992). Posttraumatic stress symptoms among soldiers exposed to combat in the Persian Gulf. *Hospital and Community Psychiatry, 43*(8), 831–833.

Lackner, J. M., Carosella, A., & Feuerstein, M. (1996). Pain expectancies, pain, and functional self-efficacy expectancies as determinants of disability in patients with chronic low back disorders. *Journal of Consulting and Clinical Psychology, 64*(1), 221–224.

Lacks, P. (1984). *Bender-Gestalt screening for brain function.* New York: Wiley.

La Fond, J. Q., & Durham, M. L. (1992). *Back to the asylum: The future of mental health law and policy in the United States.* New York: Oxford University Press.

LaFrance, A. B. (1995). Mental commitments: The judicial function: A case perspective. *Journal of Psychiatry and Law, 23*(1), 3–153.

Lahey, B. B., & Loeber, R. (1997). Attention deficit/hyperactivity disorder, oppositional defiant disorder, conduct disorder, and adult antisocial behavior: A life span perspective. In D. M. Stoff, J. Breiling, & J. D. Maser (Eds.), *Handbook of antisocial behavior* (pp. 51–59). New York: Wiley.

Lahey, B. B., Pelham, W. E., Stein, M. A., et al., (1998). Validity of *DSM-IV* attention-deficit/hyperactivity disorder for younger children. *Journal of the Ameri-*

can Academy of Child and Adolescent Psychiatry, 37, 695–702.

Lahey, B. B., Piacentini, J. C., McBurnett, K., et al. (1988). Psychopathology in the parents of children with conduct disorder and hyperactivity. *Journal of the American Academy of Child and Adolescent Psychiatry, 27,* 163–170.

Lalumiere, M. L., & Harris, G. T. (1998). Common questions regarding the use of phallometric testing with sexual offenders. *Sexual Abuse: Journal of Research and Treatment, 10,* 227–237.

Lamb, H. R., & Grant, R. W. (1982). The mentally ill in an urban county jail. *Archives of General Psychiatry, 39,* 17–22.

Lamb, M. E., Sternberg, K. J., & Thompson, R. A. (1997). The effects of divorce custody arrangements on children's behavior, development, and adjustment. *Family and Conciliation Courts Review, 35,* 393–404.

Landen, M., Walinder, J., Hambert, G., et al. (1998). Factors predictive of regret in sex reassignment. *Acta Psychiatrica Scandinavica, 97,* 284–289.

Langer, L. M., & Tubman, J. G. (1997). Risky sexual behavior among substance-abusing adolescents: Psychosocial and contextual factors. *American Journal of Orthopsychiatry, 67*(2), 315–322.

Langevin, R. A. (1992). Biological factors contributing to paraphilic behavior. *Psychiatric Annals, 22,* 309–314.

Langevin, R. A. (1993). A comparison of neuroendocrine and genetic factors in homosexuality and in pedophilia. *Annals of Sex Research, 6,* 67–76.

Lanyon, R. I. (1987). The validity of computer-based personality assessment products: Recommendations for the future. *Computers in Human Behavior, 3,* 225–238.

Larkin, A. S., & Gurry, S. (1998). Brief report: Progress reported in three children with autism using daily life therapy. *Journal of Autism and Developmental Disorders, 28,* 339–342.

Larsen, F. W., & Mouridsen, S. E. (1997). The outcome in children with childhood autism and Asperger syndrome originally diagnosed as psychotic: A 30-year follow-up study of subjects hospitalized as children. *European Child and Adolescent Psychiatry, 6,* 181–190.

Last, C. G., Hersen, M., Kazdin, A., et al. (1991). Anxiety disorders in children and their families. *Archives of General Psychiatry, 48,* 923–924.

Laumann, E. O., Michael, R. T., & Gagnon, J. H. (1994). *The social organization of sexuality: Sexual practices in the United States.* Chicago: University of Chicago Press.

Laumann, E. O., Paik, A., & Rosen, R. C. (1999). Sexual dysfunction in the United States: Prevalence and predictors. *Jour-*

nal of the American Medical Association, 281, 537–544.

Laws, D. R., & Marshall, W. L. (1991). Masturbatory reconditioning with sexual deviates: An evaluative review. *Advances in Behaviour Research and Therapy, 13,* 13–25.

Laws, D. R., & O'Donohue, W. T. (Eds.). (1997). *Sexual deviance: Theory, assessment, and treatment.* New York: Guilford Press.

Lazar, S. G., & Gabbard, G. O. (1997). The cost-effectiveness of psychotherapy. *Journal of Psychotherapy Practice and Research, 6,* 307–314.

Lazarus, A. A. (1989). Mulitmodal therapy. In R. J. Corsini, & D. Wedding (Eds.), *Current psychotherapies* (pp. 503–544). Itasca, IL: Peacock.

Lazarus, R. S. (1993). From psychological stress to the emotions: A history of changing outlooks. *Annual Review of Psychology, 44,* 1–21.

Lear, D. (1995). Sexual communication in the age of AIDS: The construction of risk and trust among young adults. *Social Science and Medicine, 41*(9), 1311–1323.

Leavitt, F. (1997). False attribution of suggestibility to explain recovered memory of childhood sexual abuse following extended amnesia. *Child Abuse and Neglect, 21*(3), 265–272.

Lee, A., & Hobson, R. P. (1998). On developing self-concepts: A controlled study of children and adolescents with autism. *Journal of Child Psychology and Psychiatry, 39,* 1131–1144.

Lee, M. I., & Miltenberger, R. G. (1996). School refusal behavior: Classification, assessment, and treatment issues. *Education and Treatment of Children, 19,* 474–486.

Lee, S. H., Rao, K. C. V. G., & Zimmerman, R. A. (Eds.). (1992). *Cranial MRI and CT* (2nd ed.). New York: McGraw-Hill.

Lee, T. F. (1991). *The Human Genome Project: Cracking the genetic code of life.* New York: Plenum.

Leenaars, A. A. (1988). *Suicide notes: Predictive clues and patterns.* New York: Human Sciences Press.

Leenaars, A. A. (1992). Suicide notes, communication, and ideation. In R. W. Maris, A. L. Berman, J. T. Maltsberger, & R. I. Yufit (Eds.), *Assessment and prediction of suicide.* New York: Guilford Press.

Leenaars, A. A. (1996). Suicide notes at symbolic ages. *Psychological Reports, 78*(3, Pt. 1), 1034.

Leenaars, A. A. (Ed.). (1993). *Suicidology: Essays in honour of Edwin S. Shneidman.* Northvale, NJ: Aronson.

Lefcourt, H. M. (1992). Durability and impact of the locus of control concept. *Psychological Bulletin, 112,* 411–414.

Leff, J. (1992). Transcultural aspects. In E. S. Paykel (Ed.), *Handbook of affective disor-*

ders (2nd ed.) (pp. 539–550). New York: Guilford Press.

Lefley, H. P. (1992). Expressed emotion: Conceptual, clinical and social policy issues. *Hospital and Community Psychiatry, 43*, 591–598.

Lehman, A. F., Steinwachs, D. M., & Survey Co-Investigators. (1998). Patterns of usual care for schizophrenia: Initial results from the Schizophrenia Patient Outcomes Research Team (PORT) Client Survey. *Schizophrenia Bulletin, 24*, 11–20.

Lehrer, P. M., & Woolfolk, R. L. (1993). *Principles and practice of stress management* (2nd ed.). New York: Guilford Press.

Leibenluft, E., Fiero, P. L., & Rubinow, D. R. (1994). Effects of the menstrual cycle on dependent variables in mood disorder research. *Archives of General Psychiatry, 51*, 761–781.

Leibenluft, E., & Wehr, T. (1992). Is sleep deprivation useful in the treatment of depression? *American Journal of Psychiatry, 149*, 159–168.

Leigh, P. N., & Swash, M. (1995). *Motor neuron disease: Biology and management.* New York: Springer-Verlag.

Leitenberg, H. (Ed.). (1990). *Handbook of social and evaluation anxiety.* New York: Plenum.

Lejoyeus, M., & Ades, J. (1997). Antidepressant medication: A review of the literature. *Journal of Clinical Psychiatry, 58* (Suppl. 7), 11–15.

Lenane, M. C., Swedo, S. E., Leonard, H., et al. (1990). Psychiatric disorders in first degree relatives of children and adolescents with obsessive-compulsive disorder. *Journal of the American Academy of Child and Adolescent Psychiatry, 29*(3), 407–412.

Lendon, C. L., Ashall, F., & Goate, A. M. (1997). Exploring the etiology of Alzheimer disease using molecular genetics. *Journal of the American Medical Association, 277*, 825–831.

Lenihan, G., & Kirk, W. G. (1990). Using paraprofessionals in the treatment of eating disorders. *Journal of Counseling and Development, 68*, 332–335.

Lenneberg, E. H. (1967). *Biological foundations of language.* New York: Wiley.

Lennox, N. G., & Kerr, M. P. (1997). Primary health care and people with intellectual disability: The evidence base. *Journal of Intellectual Disability Research, 41*, 365–372.

Leonard, B. E., & Song, C. (1996). Stress and the immune system in the etiology of anxiety and depression. *Pharmacology, Biochemistry and Behavior, 54*(1), 299–303.

Lesage, A., & Lamoontagne, Y. (1985). Paradoxical intention and exposure in vivo in the treatment of psychogenic nausea: Report of two cases. *Behavioral Psychotherapy, 13*, 69–75.

Lesch, K. P., Hoh, A., Disselkamp-Tietze, J., et al. (1991). 5-Hydroxytryptamine 1A receptor responsivity in obsessive-compulsive disorder: Comparison of patients and controls. *Archives of General Psychiatry, 48*(6), 540–547.

Lester, D. (1986). Genetics, twin studies, and suicide. *Suicide and Life Threatening Behavior, 16*, 274–285.

Leung, A. K., & Robson, W. L. (1993). Nightmares. *Journal of the American Medical Association, 85*, 233–235.

Levenson, R. W. (1992). Autonomic nervous system differences among emotions. *Psychological Science, 3*, 23–27.

Levin, M. R., Ashmore, C. S., Kendall, P. C., et al. (1996). Treatment of separation anxiety disorder. In M. A. Reinecke & F. Dattilo (Eds.), *Cognitive therapy with children and adolescents: A casebook for clinical practice* (pp. 153–174). New York: Guilford Press.

Levin, R. J. (1998). Sex and the human female reproductive tract—what really happens during and after coitus. *Journal of Impotence Research* (Suppl. 1), S14–S21.

Levinson, D. F., & Simpson, G. M. (1992). Blacks, schizophrenia, and neuroleptic treatment: In reply. *Archives of General Psychiatry, 49*, 165.

Levitt, A. J., Joffe, R. T., Moul, D. E., et al. (1993). Side effects of light therapy in seasonal affective disorder. *American Journal of Psychiatry, 150*, 650–652.

Levitt, A. J., Wesson, V. A., Joffe, R. T., et al. (1996). A controlled comparison of light box and head-mounted units in the treatment of seasonal depression. *Journal of Clinical Psychiatry, 57*(3), 105–110.

Levy, D. L., Holzman, P. S., Matthysse, S., & Mendell, N. R. (1993). Eye tracking dysfunction and schizophrenia: A critical perspective. *Schizophrenia Bulletin, 19*, 461–537.

Levy, T. M., & Orlans, M. (1998). *Attachment, trauma, and healing: Understanding and treating attachment disorder in children and families.* Washington, DC: Child Welfare League of America.

Lewander, T. (1992). Differential development of therapeutic drugs for psychosis. *Clinical Neuropharmacology, 15*(Suppl. 1), 654–655.

Lewine, R. R. J. (1991). Ontogenetic implications of sex differences in schizophrenia. In E. F. Walker (Ed.), *The behavioral management of anxiety, depression, and pain.* New York: Brunner/Mazel.

Lewinsohn, P. M. (1974). A behavioral approach to depression. In R. J. Friedman & M. M. Katz (Eds.), *The psychology of depression: Contemporary theory and research.* Washington, DC: Winston-Wiley.

Lewinsohn, P. M., Clarke, G. N., Hops, H., & Andrews, J. (1990). Cognitive behavioral treatment for depressed adolescents. *Behavior Therapy, 21*, 385–401.

Lewinsohn, P. M., Hops, H., Roberts, R. E., et al. (1993). Adolescent psychopathology: Prevalence and incidence of depression and other *DSM-III-R* disorders in high school students. *Journal of Abnormal Psychology, 102*, 133–144.

Lewinsohn, P. M., Mischel, W., Chaplin, W., & Barton, R. (1980). Social competence and depression: The role of illusory self-perceptions. *Journal of Abnormal Psychology, 89*, 203–212.

Lewinsohn, P. M., Rohde, P., & Seeley, J. R. (1993). Psychosocial characteristics of adolescents with a history of suicide attempt. *Journal of the American Academy of Child and Adolescent Psychiatry, 32*, 60–68.

Lewinsohn, P. M., Rohde, P., Seeley, J. R., & Fischer, S. A. (1993). Age-cohort changes in the lifetime occurrence of depression and other mental disorders. *Journal of Abnormal Psychology, 102*(1), 110–120.

Lewinsohn, P. M., Zeiss, A. M., & Duncan, E. M. (1989). Probability of relapse after recovery from an episode of depression. *Journal of Abnormal Psychology, 98*, 107–116.

Lewis, C. E. (1991). Neurochemical mechanisms of chronic antisocial behavior (psychopathy): A literature review. *Journal of Nervous and Mental Disease, 179*, 720–727.

Lewis, G., Davis, A., Andreasson, S., & Allebeck, P. (1992). Schizophrenia and city life. *Lancet, 340*, 137–140.

Lewis, M. S. (1992). Age incidence and schizophrenia. Part 1: The season of birth controversy. *Schizophrenia Bulletin, 15*, 59–73.

Lewy, A. J. (1993). Seasonal mood disorders. In D. L. Dunner (Ed.), *Current psychiatric therapy* (pp. 220–225). Philadelphia: Saunders.

Lezak, M. D. (1983). *Neuropsychological assessment* (2nd ed.). New York: Oxford University Press.

Lezak, M. D. (1995). *Neuropsychological assessment* (3rd ed.). New York: Oxford University Press.

Liberman, R. P., & Green, M. F. (1992). Whither cognitive-behavioral therapy for schizophrenia? *Schizophrenia Bulletin, 18*, 27–36.

Lichtenstein, E., & Glasgow, R. E. (1992). Smoking cessation: What have we learned over the past decade? *Journal of Consulting and Clinical Psychology, 60*, 518–527.

Lidz, C. W., Mulvey, E. P., & Gardner, W. (1993). The accuracy of predictions of violence to others. *Journal of the American Medical Association, 269*, 1007–1011.

Lieberman, J. A., Mailman, R. B., Duncan, G., et al. (1998). Serotonergic basis of antipsychotic drug effects in schizophrenia. *Biological Psychiatry, 44*, 1099–1117.

Lifton, R. J. (1976). Advocacy and corruption in the healing profession. In N. L. Goldman & D. R. Segal (Eds.), *The social psychology of military service.* Beverly Hills, CA: Sage.

Lilienfeld, A., & Graham, S. (1958). Validity of determining circumcision status by questionnaire as related to epidemiological studies of cancer of the cervix. *Journal of the National Cancer Institute, 21,* 713–770.

Lilienfeld, S. O. (1992). The association between antisocial personality and somatization disorders: A review and integration of theoretical models. *Clinical Psychology Review, 12,* 641–662.

Lin, K., Poland, R. E., Nuccio, I., et al. (1989). A longitudinal assessment of haloperidol doses and serum concentrations in Asian and Caucasian schizophrenic patients. *American Journal of Psychiatry, 146,* 1307–1311.

Lincoln, A., Courchesne, E., Allen, M., et al. (1998). Neurobiology of Asperger syndrome: Seven case studies and quantitative magnetic resonance imaging findings. In E. Schopler & G. B. Mesibov (Eds.), *Asperger syndrome or high-functioning autism? Current issues in autism* (pp. 145–163). New York: Plenum.

Lindenmayer, J. P. (1993). Recent advances in pharmacotherapy of schizophrenia. *Psychiatric Annals, 23,* 201–208.

Lindesay, J. (1991). Phobic disorders in the elderly. *British Journal of Psychiatry, 159,* 531–541.

Lindesay, J., Macdonald, A., & Starke, I. (1990). *Delirium in the elderly.* New York: Oxford University Press.

Lindsay, D. S., & Read, J. D. (1994). Psychotherapy and memories of childhood sexual abuse: A cognitive perspective. *Journal of Applied Cognitive Psychology, 8,* 281–338.

Lipman, A. J., & Kendall, P. C. (1992). Drugs and psychotherapy: Comparison, contrasts, and conclusions. *Applied and Preventive Psychology, 1,* 141–148.

Lipowski, Z. J. (1990). *Delirium: Acute confusional states.* New York: Oxford University Press.

Lively, S., Friedrich, R. M., & Buckwalter, K. C. (1995). Sibling perception of schizophrenia: Impact on relationships, roles, and health. *Issues in Mental Health Nursing, 16,* 225–238.

Livesley, W. J., Schroeder, M. L., Jackson, D. N., & Jang, K. L. (1994). Categorical distinctions in the study of personality disorder: Implications for classification. *Journal of Abnormal Psychology, 103,* 6–17.

Livesley, W. J., & West, M. (1986). The *DSM-III* distinction between schizoid and avoidant personality disorders. *Canadian Journal of Psychiatry, 31,* 59–62.

Livingston, K. (1997). Ritalin: Miracle drug or cop out? *Public Interest, 127,* 04.

Lo, S. K., Blaze-Temple, D., Binns, C. W., & Ovenden, C. (1993). Adolescent cigarette consumption: The influence of attitudes and peer drug use. *International Journal of the Addictions, 28*(14), 1515–1530.

Loeber, R. (1991). Antisocial behavior: More enduring than changeable? *Journal of the American Academy of Child and Adolescent Psychiatry, 30,* 393–397.

Loeber, R., & Hay, D. (1997). Key issues in the development of aggression and violence from childhood to early adulthood. *Annual Review of Psychology, 48,* 371–410.

Loewenstein, R. J. (1991). Psychogenic amnesia and psychogenic fugue: A comprehensive review. In A. Tasman & S. M. Goldfinger (Eds.), *American Psychiatric Press review of psychiatry, Vol. 10.* Washington, DC: American Psychiatric Association.

Loftus, E. (1979). *Eyewitness testimony.* Cambridge, MA: Harvard University Press.

Loftus, E. (1993). The reality of repressed memories. *American Psychologist, 48,* 518–537.

Loftus, E. F., & Rosenwald, L. A. (1995). Recovered memories: Unearthing the past in court. *Journal of Psychiatry and Law, 23*(3), 349–361.

Logan, A. C., & Goetsch, V. L. (1993). Attention to external threat cues in anxiety states. *Clinical Psychology Review, 13,* 541–559.

Lohiya, G. S., Crinella, F. M., Figueroa, L. T., et al. (1996). Lead exposure of people with developmental disabilities: Success of control measures. *Mental Retardation, 34,* 215–219.

Lopez, S., & Hernandez, P. (1986). How culture is considered in evaluations of psychopathology. *Journal of Nervous and Mental Disease, 176,* 598–606.

Lopez, S., & Nunez, J. A. (1987). Cultural factors considered in selected diagnostic criteria and interview schedules. *Journal of Abnormal Psychology, 96,* 270–272.

Love, B. (1993). *The encyclopedia of unusual sex practices.* Emory, CA: Barricade Books.

Loza, W., & Dhaliwal, G. K. (1997). Psychometric evaluation of the Risk Appraisal Guide (RAG): A tool for assessing violent recidivism. *Journal of Interpersonal Violence, 12,* 779–793.

Lubin, B., Larsen, R. M., & Matarazzo, J. D. (1984). Patterns of psychological test usage in the United States: 1935–1982. *American Psychologist, 39,* 451–455.

Lukas, C., & Seiden, H. M. (1990). *Silent grief: Living in the wake of suicide.* New York: Bantam Books.

Lukas, S. E. (1985). *Amphetamines: Danger in the fast lane.* New York: Chelsea House.

Lukas, S. E., Sholar, M., Lundahl, K. H., et al. (1996). Sex differences in plasma cocaine levels and subjective effects after acute cocaine administration in human volunteers. *Psychopharmacology, 125,* 346–354.

Luntz, B. K., & Widom, C. S. (1994). Antisocial personality disorder in abused and neglected children grown up. *American Journal of Psychiatry, 151,* 670–674.

Lussier, R. G., Steiner, J., Grey, A., & Hansen, C. (1997). Prevalence of dissociative disorders in an acute care day hospital population. *Psychiatric Services, 48*(2), 244–246.

Lykken, D. T. (1957). A study of anxiety in the sociopathic personality. *Journal of Abnormal and Social Psychology, 55,* 6–10.

Lykken, D. T. (1981). *A tremor in the blood: Uses and abuses of the lie detector.* New York: McGraw-Hill.

Lykken, D. T. (1982, Sept.). Fearlessness: Its carefree charm and deadly risks. *Psychology Today,* pp. 20–28.

Lyness, S. A. (1993). Predictors of differences between type A and B individuals in heart rate and blood pressure reactivity. *Psychological Bulletin, 114,* 266–295.

MacAvoy, M. G., & Bruce, C. J. (1995). Comparison of the smooth eye tracking disorder of schizophrenics with that of nonhuman primates with specific brain lesions. *International Journal of Neuroscience, 80,* 117–151.

Mace, C. J., & Trimble, M. R. (1996). Ten-year prognosis of conversion disorder. *British Journal of Psychiatry, 169*(3), 282–288.

Machover, K. (1949). *Personality projection in the drawing of the human face.* Springfield, IL: Thomas.

Mackintosh, N. J. (Ed.). (1995). *Cyril Burt: Fraud or framed?* Oxford: Oxford University Press.

MacLeod, C., & Matthews, A. M. (1991). Cognitive-experimental approaches to the emotional disorders. In P. R. Martin (Ed.), *Handbook of behavior therapy and psychological science: An integrative approach* (pp. 116–150). Elmsford, NY: Pergamon.

MacMillan, D., & Reschly, D. J. (1998). Overrepresentation of minority students: The case for greater specificity or reconsideration of the variables examined. *Journal of Special Education, 32,* 15–24.

Maes, S., Leventhal, H., & de Ridder, D. T. D. (1996). Coping with chronic diseases. In M. Zeidner & N. S. Endler (Eds.), *Handbook of coping: Theory, research, applications* (pp. 221–251). New York: Wiley.

Magee, W. J., Eaton, W. W., Wittchen, H., et al. (1996). Agoraphobia, simple phobia, and social phobia in the National Comorbidity Survey. *Archives of General Psychiatry, 53*(2), 159–168.

Magura, S., & Kang, S. Y. (1996). Validity of self-reported drug use in high-risk populations: A meta-analytical review. *Substance Use and Misuse, 31*(9), 1131–1153.

Mahendra, B. (1988). *Dementia: A survey of the syndrome of dementia* (2nd ed.). Boston: MTP Press.

Maher, B. A., & Maher, W. B. (1985). Psychopathology. II: From the eighteenth century to modern times. In G. A. Kimble & K. Schlesinger (Eds.), *Topics in the history of psychology, Vol. 2* (pp. 295–330). Hillsdale, NJ: Erlbaum.

Maher, B. A., & Spitzer, M. (1993). Delusions. In C. G. Costello (Ed.), *Symptoms of schizophrenia* (pp. 92–120). New York: Wiley.

Maher, W. B., & Maher, B. A. (1982). The ship of fools: Stultifera navis or ignis fatuus? *American Psychologist, 37*, 756–761.

Maher, W. B., & Maher, B. A. (1985). Psychopathology. I: From ancient times to the eighteenth century. In G. A. Kimble & K. Schlesinger (Eds.), *Topics in the history of psychology, Vol. 2* (pp. 251–294). Hillsdale, NJ: Erlbaum.

Mahler, M. (1979). On the first three subphases of the separation-individuation process. In *Selected papers of Margaret Mahler, Vol. 2*. New York: Jason Aronson.

Mahoney, W. J., Szatmari, P., MacLean, J. E., et al. (1998). Reliability and accuracy of differentiating pervasive developmental disorder subtypes. *Journal of the American Academy of Child and Adolescent Psychiatry, 37*, 278–285.

Maier, S. F., Watkins, L. R., & Fleshner, M. (1994). Psychoneuroimmunology: The interface between behavior, brain, and immunity. *American Psychologist, 49*, 1004–1017.

Maier, W., Lichtermann, D., Minges, J., & Heun, R. (1994). Personality disorders among the relatives of schizophrenia patients. *Schizophrenia Bulletin, 20*, 481–493.

Mail, G., & Johnson, S. (1993). Boozing, sniffing, and toking: An overview of the past, present and future of substance abuse by American Indians [Editorial]. *American Indian and Alaska Native Mental Health Research 1993, 5*(2), 1–33.

Maisto, S. A., Galizio, M., & Connors, G. J. (1991). *Drug use and misuse*. Fort Worth, TX: Holt, Rinehart & Winston.

Makintosh, N. J. (1983). *Conditioning and associative learning*. Oxford: Clarendon Press.

Maklin, R. (1987). *Mortal choices: Bioethics in today's world*. New York: Pantheon.

Malaspina, D., Quitkina, H. M., & Kaufman, C. A. (1994). Epidemiology and genetics of neuropsychiatric disorders. In S. C. Yudofsky & R. E. Hales (Eds.), *Synopsis of neuropsychiatry* (pp. 157–186).

Washington, DC: American Psychiatric Press.

Maletzky, B. M. (1998). The paraphilias: Research and treatment. In P. E. Nathan & J. M. Gorman (Eds.), *A guide to treatments that work* (pp. 472–500). New York: Oxford University Press.

Malinowski, B. K. (1927). *Sex and repression in savage society*. London: Routledge & Kegan Paul.

Mandalos, G. E., & Szarek, B. L. (1990). Dose-related paranoid reaction associated with fluoxetine. *Journal of Nervous and Mental Disease, 178*, 57–58.

Mandler, G., & Sarason, S. B. (1952). A study of anxiety and learning. *Journal of Abnormal and Social Psychology, 47*, 166–173.

Manicavasagar, V., Silove, D., & Hadzi-Pavlovic, D. (1998). Subpopulations of early separation anxiety: Relevance to risk of adult anxiety disorders. *Journal of Affective Disorders, 48*, 181–190.

Manley, A. (1992). Comorbidity of mental and addictive disorders. *Journal of Health Care for the Poor and Underserved, 3*(1), 60–72.

Mann, J. J., McBride, P. A., Brown, R. P., et al. (1992). Relationship between central and peripheral serotonin indexes in depressed and suicidal psychiatric inpatients. *Archives of General Psychiatry, 49*, 442–446.

Manuzza, S., Klein, R. G., Bessler, A., et al. (1993). Adult outcome of hyperactive boys. *Archives of General Psychiatry, 50*, 565–576.

Mapou, R. L., & Spector, J. (Eds.). (1995). *Clinical neuropsychological assessment: A cognitive approach*. New York: Plenum.

Marcuccilli, C. J., & Miller, R. J. (1994). ANS stress response: Too hot to handle. *Trends in Neuroscience, 17*, 135–138.

Marcus, J., Hans, S. L., Nagler, S., et al. (1987). Review of the NIMH Israeli kibbutz-city study and the Jerusalem infant development study. *Schizophrenia Bulletin, 13*, 425–437.

Marengo, J. T., & Harrow, M. (1993). Thought disorder. In C. G. Costello (Ed.), *Symptoms of schizophrenia* (pp. 27–55). New York: Wiley.

Margolin, D. I. (1992). *Cognitive neuropsychology in clinical practice*. New York: Oxford University Press.

Margolin, R. (1991). Neuroimaging. In J. Sadavoy, L. W. Lazarus, & L. F. Jarvik (Eds.), *Comprehensive review of geriatric psychiatry* (pp. 245–271). Washington, DC: American Psychiatric Press.

Margraf, J., Barlow, D. H., Clark, D. M., & Telch, M. J. (1993). Psychological treatment of panic: Work in progress on outcome, active ingredients, and follow-up. *Behaviour Research and Therapy, 31*, 1–8.

Margraf, J., & Ehlers, A. (1990). Biological models of panic disorder and agoraphobia: Theory and evidence. In G. D. Burrows, M. Roth, & R. Noyes, Jr. (Eds.), *Handbook of anxiety, Vol. 3: The neurobiology of anxiety* (pp. 79–139). Amsterdam: Elsevier.

Maris, R., Berman, A. L., Maltsberger, J. T., & Yuflt, R. I. (Eds.). (1992). *Assessment and prediction of suicide*. New York: Guilford Press.

Maris, R. W. (1992). How are suicides different? In R. Maris, A. L. Berman, J. T. Maltsberger, & R. I. Yuflt (Eds.), *Assessment and prediction of suicide*. New York: Guilford Press.

Marks, I. M. (1987). *Fears, phobias and rituals: Panic, anxiety and their disorders*. New York: Oxford University Press.

Marks, I. M. (1994). Behavior therapy as an aid to self-care. *Current Directions in Psychological Science, 3*, 19–22.

Markson, L. J., Kern, D. C., Annas, G. J., & Glantz, L. H. (1994). Physician assessment of patient competence. *Journal of the American Geriatrics Society, 42*, 1074–1080.

Maron, D. J., & Fortmann, S. P. (1987). Nicotine yield and measures of cigarette smoke exposure in a large population: Are lower-yield cigarettes safer? *American Journal of Public Health, 77*, 546–549.

Marquis, J. N. (1991). A report on seventy-eight cases treated by eye movement desensitization. *Journal of Behavior Therapy and Experimental Psychiatry, 22*, 187–192.

Marriage, K. J., Miles, T., Stokes, D., & Davey, M. (1993). Clinical and research implications of the co-occurrence of Asperger's and Tourette syndromes. *Australian and New Zealand Journal of Psychiatry, 27*, 666–672.

Marshall, E., & Pennisi, E. (1996). NIH launches the final push to sequence the genome. *Science, 272*(5259), 188–189.

Marshall, W. L., Bryce, P., Hudson, S. M., et al. (1996). The enhancement of intimacy and the reduction of loneliness among child molesters. *Journal of Family Violence, 11*, 219–235.

Marshall, W. L., & Eccles, A. (1996). Cognitive-behavioral treatment of sex offenders. In V. B. Van Hasselt & M. Hersen (Eds.), *Sourcebook of psychological treatment manuals for adult disorders* (pp. 295–332). New York: Plenum.

Martin, G., & Pear, J. (1992). *Behavior modification: What it is and how to do it*. Englewood Cliffs, NJ: Prentice-Hall.

Martin, P. R. (1993). *Psychological management of chronic headaches*. New York: Guilford Press.

Martin, P. R., Adinoff, B., Lane, E., et al. (1995). Fluvoxamine treatment of alcoholic amnestic disorder. *European Neuropsychopharmacology, 5*, 27–33.

Martin, P. R., Marie, G. V., & Nathan, P. R. (1992). Psychophysiological mechanisms of chronic headaches: Investigation using pain induction and pain reduction procedures. *Journal of Psychosomatic Research, 36,* 137–148.

Martin, R. (1997). Narcan therapy [Letter]. *Southern Journal of Medicine, 90*(1), 95–96.

Martin, R. A., Velicer, W. F., & Fava, J. L. (1996). Latent transition analysis to the stages of change for smoking cessation. *Addictive Behaviors, 21*(1), 67–80.

Martinez-Taboas, A. (1996). Repressed memories: Some clinical data contributing toward its elucidation. *American Journal of Psychotherapy, 50*(2), 217–230.

Martini, F. (1989). *Fundamentals of anatomy and physiology* (4th ed.). New York: Prentice-Hall.

Marttunen, M. J., Aro, H. M., Henriksson, M. M., & Loennqvist, J. K. (1991). Mental disorders in adolescent suicide: *DSM-III-R* Axes I and II diagnoses in suicides among 13- to 19-year-olds in Finland. *Archives of General Psychiatry, 48,* 834–839.

Marzuk, P. M., Tardiff, K., Leon, A. C., et al. (1992). Prevalence of cocaine use among residents of New York City who committed suicide during a one-year period. *American Journal of Psychiatry, 149*(3), 371–375.

Mash, E. J., & Terdal, L. G. (Eds.). (1981). *Behavioral assessment of childhood disorders.* New York: Guilford Press.

Maslow, A. (1970). *Motivation and personality* (2nd ed.). New York: Harper & Row.

Mason, A., Banerjee, S., Eapen, V., et al. (1998). The prevalence of Tourette syndrome in a mainstream school population. *Developmental Medicine and Child Neurology, 40,* 292–296.

Mason, F. L. (1997). Fetishism: Psychopathology and theory. In D. R. Laws & W. T. O'Donohue (Eds.), *Sexual deviance: Theory, assessment, and treatment* (pp. 75–91). New York: Guilford Press.

Mason, P., Harrison, G., Croudace, T., et al. (1997). The predictive validity of a diagnosis of schizophrenia. A report from the International Study of Schizophrenia (ISoS) coordinated by the World Health Organization and the Department of Psychiatry, University of Nottingham. *British Journal of Psychiatry, 170*(4), 321–327.

Masson, J. M. (1992). *The assault on the truth: Freud's suppression of the seduction theory.* New York: Penguin Books.

Masters, J. S., & Masters, A. L. (1997). Freeman, militias, Christian patriots: Dangerous menace, or ridiculous mouse? *Journal of Psychohistory, 25,* 81–95.

Masters, W. H., & Johnson, V. E. (1967). *Human sexual response.* Boston: Little, Brown.

Masters, W. H., & Johnson, V. E. (1970). *Human sexual inadequacy.* Boston: Little, Brown.

Masuda, M., & Holmes, T. H. (1967). The Social Readjustment Scale: A cross-cultural study of Japanese and Americans. *Journal of Psychosomatic Research, 11,* 227–237.

Matarazzo, J. D. (1983). The reliability of psychiatric and psychological diagnosis. *Clinical Psychology Review, 3,* 103–145.

Matarazzo, J. D. (1986). Computerized clinical psychological test interpretations: Unvalidated plus all mean and no sigma. *American Psychologist, 41,* 14–24.

Matchett, G., & Davey, G. C. L. (1991). A test of a disease-avoidance model of animal phobias. *Behaviour Research and Therapy, 29,* 91–94.

Mathew, R. J., Wilson, W. H., Humphreys, D., & Lowe, J. V. (1993). Depersonalization after marijuana smoking. *Biological Psychiatry, 33,* 431–441.

Mathews, A., & MacLeod, C. (1994). Cognitive approaches to emotion and emotional disorders. *Annual Review of Psychology, 45,* 25–50.

Matsuoka, N., & Satoh, M. (1998). FK960, a novel potential anti-dementia drug, augments long-term potentiation in mossy fiver-CA3 pathway of guinea pig hippocampal slices. *Brain Research, 794,* 248–254.

Maughn, B., & McCarthy, G. (1997). Childhood adversities and psychosocial disorders. *British Medical Bulletin, 53,* 156–169.

Maurer, K., Riederer, P., & Beckmann, H. (Eds.). (1990). *Alzheimer's disease: Epidemiology, neuropathology, neurochemistry and clinics.* New York: Springer-Verlag.

Mavissakalian, M. (1993). Combined behavioral therapy and pharmacotherapy of agoraphobia. *Journal of Psychiatric Research, 1,* 179–191.

Max, W. (1993). The economic impact of Alzheimer's disease. *Neurology, 43*(8, Suppl. 4), S6–S10.

May, B. (1991). Diabetes. In M. Pitts & K. Phillips (Eds.), *The psychology of health and illness: An introduction.* London: Routledge.

May, R., Angel, E., & Ellenberger, H. F. (1958). *Existence: A new dimension in psychiatry and psychology.* New York: Basic Books.

Mays, V. M., & Cochran, S. D. (1988). Issues in the perception of AIDS risk and risk reduction activities by Black and Hispanic/Latino women. *American Psychologist, 43*(11), 949–957.

Mazumdar, P. M. H. (1992). *Eugenics, human genetics and human failings: The Eugenics Society, its sources and its critics in Britain.* London: Routledge.

McAllister, L. W. (1986). *A practical guide to CPI interpretation.* Palo Alto, CA: Consulting Psychologists Press.

McBride, H. E. A., & Siegel, L. S. (1997). Learning disabilities and adolescent suicide. *Journal of Learning Disabilities, 30,* 652–659.

McCauley, J., Kern, D. E., & Kolodner, K. (1997). Clinical characteristics of women with a history of child abuse: Unhealed wounds. *Journal of the American Medical Association, 277,* 1362–1368.

McClannahan, L. E., & Krautz, P. J. (1999). *Activity schedules for children with autism: A guide for parents and professionals.* Topics in Autism series. Bethesda, MD: Woodbine House.

McClure, E., Rogeness, G. A., & Thompson, N. M. (1997). Characteristics of adolescent girls with depressive symptoms in a so-called normal sample. *Journal of Affective Disorders, 42,* 187–197.

McConaghy, N. (1997). Sexual and gender identity disorders. In S. Turner & M. Hersen (Eds.), *Adult psychopathology and diagnosis* (3rd ed.) (pp. 409–464). New York: Wiley.

McConaghy, N. (1998). Pedophilia: A review of the evidence. *Australian and New Zealand Journal of Psychiatry, 32,* 252–265.

McCreadie, R. G. (1997). The Nithsdale schizophrenia surveys. 16: Breast-feeding and schizophrenia: Preliminary results and hypotheses. *British Journal of Psychiatry, 170,* 334–337.

McCreery, J. M., & Walker, R. D. (1993). Alcohol problems. In D. L. Dunner (Ed.), *Current psychiatric therapy* (pp. 92–98). Philadelphia: Saunders.

McCroskey, J. C. (1983). Self-report measurement. In J. Daly & J. C. McCroskey (Eds.), *Avoiding communication: Shyness, reticence, and communication apprehension* (pp. 81–94). Beverly Hills, CA: Sage.

McCullough, L. (1993). An anxiety-reduction modification of short-term dynamic psychotherapy (STDP): A theoretical "melting pot" of treatment techniques. In J. R. Gold (Ed.), *Comprehensive handbook of psychotherapy integration* (pp. 139–149). New York: Plenum.

McCurdy, H. G. (1941). A note on the dissociation of a personality. *Character and Personality, 10,* 33–41.

McDaniel, J. S., Desoutter, L., Firestone, S., & McDonnell, K. (1992). Factitious disorder resulting in bilateral mastectomies. *General Hospital Psychiatry, 14,* 353–356.

McDermid, S. A., Zucker, K. J., Bradley, S., et al. (1998). Effects of physical appearance on masculine trait ratings of boys and girls with gender identity disorder. *Archives of Sexual Behavior, 27,* 253–267.

McDermott, S. W., & Altekruse, J. M. (1994). Dynamic model for preventing mental retardation in the population: The importance of poverty and deprivation. *Research in Developmental Disabilities, 15,* 49–65.

McDougall, W. (1926). *Outline of abnormal psychology*. New York: Scribner.

McDowell, J. E., & Clementz, B. A. (1997). The effect of fixation condition manipulations on antisaccade performance in schizophrenia: Studies of diagnostic specificity. *Experimental Brain Research, 115*(2), 333–344.

McElroy, S. L., Keck, P. E., Pope, H. G., et al. (1992). Clinical and research implications of the diagnosis of dysphoric or mixed mania or hypomania. *American Journal of Psychiatry, 149*(12), 1633–1644.

McElroy, S. L., Pope, H. G., Jr., Keck, P. E., Jr., et al. (1996). Are impulse-control disorders related to bipolar disorder? *Comprehensive-Psychiatry, 37*, 229–240.

McFall, M., Mackay, P., & Donovan, D. (1992). Combat-related posttraumatic stress disorder and severity of substance abuse in Vietnam veterans. *Journal of Studies on Alcohol, 53*(4), 357–363.

McGee, R., Williams, S., & Elwood, M. (1994). Depression and the development of cancer: A meta-analysis. *Social Science and Medicine, 38*(1), 187–192.

McGlashan, T. H., & Fenton, W. S. (1991). Classical subtypes for schizophrenia: Literature review for *DSM-IV. Schizophrenia Bulletin, 17*, 609–623.

McGue, M. (1992). When assessing twin concordance, use the probandwise not the pairwise rate. *Schizophrenia Bulletin, 18*, 171–176.

McGuffin, P., Katz, R., & Rutherford, J. (1991). Nature, nurture, and depression: A twin study. *Psychological Medicine, 21*, 329–335.

McGuffin, P., Owen, M. J., O'Donovan, M. C., et al. (1994). *Seminars in psychiatric genetics*. London: Gaskell.

McGuire, P. K., Shah, G. M. S., & Murray, R. M. (1993). Increased blood flow in Broca's area during auditory hallucinations in schizophrenia. *Lancet, 342*, 703–706.

McIntosh, J. L. (1991). Epidemiology of suicide in the U.S. In A. A. Leenaars (Ed.), *Life span perspectives of suicide* (pp. 55–70). New York: Plenum.

McIntosh, J. L. (1992). Suicide of the elderly. In B. Bongar (Ed.), *Suicide: Guidelines for assessment, management, and treatment*. New York: Oxford University Press.

McKay, D., & Neziroglu, F. (1996). Social skills training in a case of obsessive-compulsive disorder with schizotypal personality disorder. *Journal of Behavior Therapy and Experimental Psychiatry, 27*, 189–194.

McKay, D., Todaro, J., Neziroglu, F., et al. (1997). Body dysmorphic disorder: A preliminary evaluation of treatment and maintenance using exposure with response prevention. *Behaviour Research and Therapy, 35*(1), 67–70.

McKay, I. (1991). Psychopathic disorder: A category mistake? A legal response to Colin Holmes. *Journal of Medical Ethics, 17*, 86–88.

McKim, W. A. (1991). *Drugs and behavior: An introduction to behavioral pharmacology* (2nd ed.). Englewood Cliffs, NJ: Prentice-Hall.

McKinnon, W., Weisse, C. S., Reynolds, C. P., et al. (1989). Chronic stress, leukocyte subpopulations, and humoral response to latent viruses. *Health Psychology, 8*(4), 389–402.

McKnight, D. L., Nelson-Gray, R. O., & Barnhill, J. (1992). Dexamethasone suppression test and response to cognitive therapy and antidepressant medication. *Behavior Therapy, 23*, 99–111.

McLellan, A. T. (1992). Measurement issues in the evaluation of experimental treatment interventions. *NIDA Research Monograph, 117*, 18–30.

McLaren, N. (1998). A critical review of the biopsychosocial model. *Australian and New Zealand Journal of Psychiatry, 32*, 86–92.

McLeod, D. M., Eveland, W. P., & Nathanson, A. I. (1997). Support for censorship of violent and misogynic rap lyrics: An analysis of the third-person effect. *Communication Research, 24*, 153–174.

McLeod, J. D., Kessler, R. C., & Landis, K. R. (1992). Speed of recovery from major depressive episodes in a community sample of married men and women. *Journal of Abnormal Psychology, 101*(2), 277–286.

McLin, W. M. (1992). Introduction to issues in psychology and epilepsy. *American Psychologist, 47*, 1124–1125.

McMahon, R. J. (1984). Behavioral checklists and rating scales. In T. Ollendick & M. Hersen (Eds.), *Child behavioral assessment* (pp. 80–105). New York: Pergamon.

McNally, S. E., & Goldberg, J. O. (1997). Natural cognitive coping strategies in schizophrenia. *British Journal of Medical Psychology, 70*(Pt. 2), 159–167.

McNeill, P. M. (1993). *The ethics and politics of human experimentation*. Cambridge, UK: Cambridge University Press.

McNulty, P. A. F. (1997a). Prevalence and contributing factors of eating disorder behaviors in active duty navy men. *Military Medicine, 162*, 753–758.

McNulty, P. A. F. (1997b). Prevalence and contributing factors of eating disorder behaviors in a population of female navy nurses. *Military Medicine, 162*, 703–706.

McPherson, S. (1996). Neuropsychological aspects of vascular dementia. *Brain and Cognition, 31*, 269–282.

McQuiston, J. T. (1993, Feb. 23). Suffolk mother's illness imperils son, judge rules. *New York Times*, pp. B1, B2.

McReynolds, P. (1989). Diagnosis and clinical assessment: Current status and major issues. *Annual Review of Psychology, 40*, 83–108.

Mead, M. (1949). *Coming of age in Samoa: A psychological study of primitive youth for western civilization*. New York: New American Library.

Meador-Woodruff, J. H. (1999). Meador-Woodruff Laboratory, Mental Health Research Institute, Department of Psychiatry, University of Michigan Medical Center. Available: http://www-personal.umich.edu/~jimmw/ [Last visited 3/15/99].

Mednick, S. A., Machon, R. A., Huttunen, M. O., & Bonett, D. (1988). Adult schizophrenia following prenatal exposure to an influenza epidemic. *Archives of General Psychiatry, 45*, 189–192.

Mednick, S. A., & Schulsinger, F. (1968). Some premorbid characteristics related to breakdown in children with schizophrenic mothers. *Journal of Psychiatric Research, 6*(Suppl. 1), 354–362.

Meehan, P. J., Lamb, J. A., Saltzman, L. E., & O'Corroll, P. W. (1992). Attempted suicide among young adults: Progress toward a meaningful estimate of prevalence. *American Journal of Psychiatry, 149*, 41–44.

Meehl, P. E. (1954). *Clinical versus statistical prediction: A theoretical analysis and review of the evidence*. Minneapolis: University of Minnesota Press.

Meehl, P. E. (1990). Toward an integrated theory of schizotaxia, schizotypy, and schizophrenia. *Journal of Personality Disorders, 4*(1), 1–99.

Mehl, A. L., Coble, L., & Johnson, S. (1990). Munchausen syndrome by proxy: A family affair. *Child Abuse and Neglect, 14*, 577–585.

Meichenbaum, D. (1977). *Cognitive-behavior modification: An integrative approach*. New York: Plenum.

Meichenbaum, D. (1985). *Stress inoculation training*. New York: Pergamon.

Meissner, W. W., Stone, M. H., Meloy, J. R., et al. (1996). Personality disorders. In G. O. Gabbard & S. D. Atkinson (Eds.), *Synopsis of treatments of psychiatric disorders* (2nd ed.) (pp. 947–1010). Washington, DC: American Psychiatric Press.

Meketon, M. J. (1983). Indian mental health: An orientation. *American Journal of Orthopsychiatry, 53*, 110–115.

Mellon, M. W., & Stern, H. P. (1998). Elimination disorders. In R. T. Ammerman & J. V. Campo (Eds.), *Handbook of pediatric psychology and psychiatry, Vol. 1: Psychological and psychiatric issues in the pediatric setting* (pp. 182–198). Boston: Allyn & Bacon.

Meltzer, H. Y. (1992). The role of dopamine in schizophrenia. In J. Lindenmayer & S. R. Kay (Eds.), *New biological vistas on schizophrenia*. New York: Brunner/Mazel.

Meltzer, H. Y. (1993). Serotonin-dopamine interactions and atypical antipsychotic drugs. *Psychiatric Annals, 23*, 193–200.

Meltzer, L. J. (Ed.). (1993). *Strategy assessment and instruction for students with learning disabilities: From theory to practice.* Austin, TX: Pro-Ed.

Melzack, R., & Wall, P. D. (1982). *The challenge of pain.* New York: Basic Books.

Mendez, M. F., Selwood, A., Mastri, A. R., & Frey, W. H. (1993). Pick's disease versus Alzheimer's: A comparison of clinical characteristics. *Neurology, 43*, 289–292.

Menezes, P. R., Rodrigues, L. C., & Mann, A. H. (1997). Predictors of clinical and social outcomes after hospitalization in schizophrenia. *European Archives of Psychiatry and Clinical Neuroscience, 247*(3), 137–145.

Menninger, W. W. (1994). Psychotherapy and integrated treatment of social phobia and comorbid conditions. *Bulletin of the Menninger Clinic, 58*(2, Suppl. A), A84–A90.

Mental health: Does therapy help? (1995, Nov.). *Consumer Reports,* pp. 734–739.

Menvielle, E. J. (1998). Gender identity disorder. *Journal of the American Academy of Child and Adolescent Psychiatry, 37,* 243–244.

Menzies, R. G., & Clarke, C. J. (1993). A comparison of in vivo and vicarious exposure in the treatment of childhood water phobia. *Behaviour Research and Therapy, 31,* 9–15.

Menzies, R. G., & Clarke, J. C. (1995). The etiology of acrophobia and its relationship to severity and individual response patterns. *Behaviour Research and Therapy, 33*(7), 795–803.

Merckelbach, H., Arntz, A., Arrindell, W. A., & de Jong, P. J. (1992). Pathways to spider phobia. *Behaviour Research and Therapy, 30,* 543–546.

Merckelbach, H., de Jong, P. J., Muris, P., & van den Hout, M. A. (1996). The etiology of specific phobias: A review. *Clinical Psychology Review, 16*(4), 337–361.

Merckelbach, H., de Ruiter, C., van den Hout, M. A., & Hoekstra, R. (1989). Conditioning experiences and phobias. *Behaviour Research and Therapy, 27,* 657–662.

Merskey, H. (1992). The manufacture of personalities: The production of multiple personality disorder. *British Journal of Psychiatry, 160,* 327–340.

Merskey, H. (1995). Multiple personality disorder and false memory syndrome. *British Journal of Psychiatry, 166*(3), 281–283.

Merson, S., Tyrer, P., Duke, P. J., & Henderson, F. (1994). Interrater reliability of *ICD-10* guidelines for the diagnosis of personality disorders: Clinicians still have difficulty agreeing on personality disorder diagnoses. *Journal of Personality Disorders, 8,* 89–95.

Metalsky, G. I., Joiner, T. E., Hardin, T. S., & Abramson, L. Y. (1993). Depressive reactions to failure in a naturalistic setting: A test of the hopelessness and self-esteem theories of depression. *Journal of Abnormal Psychology, 102,* 101–109.

Mezzich, J. E., Dow, J. T., Ganguli, R., et al. (1994). Computerized initial and discharge evaluations. In J. E. Mezzich, M. R. Jorge, & I. M. Salloum (Eds.), *Psychiatric epidemiology: Assessment concepts and methods* (pp. 281–315). Baltimore: Johns Hopkins University Press.

Mialet, J. P., Pope, H. G., & Yurgelun, T. D. (1996). Impaired attention in depressive states: A non-specific deficit? *Psychological Medicine, 26,* 1009–1020.

Michael, R. T., Gagnon, J. H., Laumann, E. O., et al. (1995). *Sex in America: A definitive survey.* New York: Warner Books.

Michelson, L. K., & Marchione, K. (1991). Behavioral, cognitive, and pharmacological treatments of panic disorder with agoraphobia: Critique and synthesis. *Journal of Consulting and Clinical Psychology, 59,* 100–114.

Miczek, K. A., Hubbard, N., & Cantuti-Castelvetri, I. (1995). Increased cocaine self-administration after social stress. *Neuroscience Abstracts, 21,* 1954 (Abstract No. 766.9).

Middlebrook, D. W. (1998). *Suits me: The double life of Billy Tipton.* Boston: Houghton Mifflin.

Miklowitz, D. J., Celligan, D. I., Gitlin, M. J., et al. (1991). Communication deviance in the families of schizophrenic and manic patients. *Journal of Abnormal Psychology, 100,* 163–173.

Miklowitz, D. J., & Goldstein, M. J. (1990). Behavioral family treatment for patients with bipolar affective disorder. *Behavior Modification, 14,* 457–489.

Miklowitz, D. J., & Goldstein, M. J. (1993). Mapping the intrafamilial environment of the schizophrenic patient. In R. L. Cromwell & C. R. Snyder (Eds.), *Schizophrenia: Origins, processes, treatment, and outcome* (pp. 313–332). New York: Oxford University Press.

Milgrom, P., Vignesha, H., & Weinstein, P. (1992). Adolescent dental fear and control: Prevalence and theoretical implications. *Behaviour Research and Therapy, 30,* 367–373.

Miller, B. A., Downs, W. R., & Testa, M. (1993). Interrelationships between victimization experiences and women's alcohol use. *Journal of Studies on Alcohol* (Suppl. 11), 109–117.

Miller, H. L., Coombs, D. W., Leeper, J. D., & Bartan, S. N. (1984). An analysis of the effects of suicide prevention facilities on suicide rates in the United States. *American Journal of Public Health, 74,* 340–343.

Miller, J. R. (1994). Fear of success: Psychodynamic implications. *Journal of the American Academy of Psychoanalysis, 22*(1), 129–136.

Miller, L. (1997). Freud and consciousness: The first one hundred years of neuropsychodynamics in theory and clinical practice. *Seminars in Neurology, 17*(2), 171–177.

Miller, M. A., & Rahe, R. H. (1997). Life changes scaling for the 1990s. *Journal of Psychosomatic Research, 43*(3), 279–292.

Miller, N. E. (1948). Studies of fear as an acquirable drive. I: Fear as motivation and fear reduction as reinforcement in the learning of new responses. *Journal of Experimental Psychology, 38,* 89–101.

Miller, N. E. (1974). Applications of learning and biofeedback to psychiatry and medicine. In A. M. Friedman, H. I. Kaplan, & B. Sadock (Eds.), *Comprehensive textbook of psychiatry* (2nd ed.). Baltimore: Williams & Wilkins.

Miller, N. S., Gold, M. S., & Pottash, A. C. (1989). A 12-step treatment approach for marijuana (cannabis) dependence. *Journal of Substance Abuse Treatment, 6,* 241–250.

Miller, P. M., Smith, G. T., & Goldman, M. S. (1990). Emergence of alcohol expectancies in childhood: A possible critical period. *Journal of Studies on Alcohol, 51,* 343–349.

Miller, S. D., & Triggiano, P. J. (1992). The psychophysiological investigation of multiple personality disorder. *American Journal of Clinical Hypnosis, 35,* 47–61.

Miller, S. M., Shoda, Y., & Hurley, K. (1996). Applying cognitive-social theory to health-protective behavior: Breast self-examination in cancer screening. *Psychological Bulletin, 119*(1), 70–94.

Miller, W. R., Leckman, A. L., Delaney, H. D., & Tinchom, M. (1992). Long-term follow-up of behavioral self-control training. *Journal of Studies on Alcohol, 51,* 108–115.

Millon, T., & Radovanov, J. (1995). Controversial passive-aggressive (negativistic) personality disorder. In W. J. Livesley (Ed.), *The DSM-IV personality disorders: Diagnosis and treatment of mental disorders* (pp. 312–325). New York: Guilford Press.

Mineka, S. (1979). The role of fear in theories of avoidance learning, flooding and extinction. *Psychological Bulletin, 86,* 985–1010.

Mineka, S. (1985). The frightful complexity of the origins of fears. In F. R. Brush & J. B. Overmier (Eds.), *Affect, conditioning, and cognition: Essays on the determinants of behavior.* Hillsdale, NJ: Erlbaum.

Mineka, S. (1992). Evolutionary memories, emotional processing, and the emotional disorders. In D. Medin (Ed.), *The psychology of learning and motivation, Vol. 28.* New York: Academic Press.

Mineka, S., & Sutton, S. K. (1992). Cognitive biases and the emotional disorders. *Psychological Science, 3*(1), 65–69.

Mineka, S., & Zinbarg, R. (1991). Animal models of psychopathology. In C. E. Walker (Ed.), *Clinical psychology: Historical and research foundations. Applied clinical psychology* (pp. 51–86). New York: Plenum.

Minnis, H., Ramsay, R., & Campbell, L. (1996). Reactive attachment disorder: Usefulness of a new clinical category. *Journal of Nervous and Mental Disease, 184,* 440.

Mintz, J., Mintz, L. I., Aruda, M. J., & Hwang, S. S. (1992). Treatments of depression and the functional capacity to work. *Archives of General Psychiatry, 49,* 761–768.

Minuchin, S., Rosman, B. L., & Baker, L. (1978). *Psychosomatic families.* Cambridge, MA: Harvard University Press.

Mischel, W. (1968). *Personality and assessment.* New York: Wiley.

Mischel, W. (1973). Toward a cognitive social learning reconceptualization of personality. *Psychological Review, 80*(4), 252–283.

Mischel, W. (1997). Consistency and specificity in behavior. In D. C. Funder & D. J. Ozer (Eds.), *Pieces of the personality puzzle: Readings in theory and research.* New York: Norton.

Modestin, J. (1992). Multiple personality disorder in Switzerland. *American Journal of Psychiatry, 149,* 88–92.

Modestin, J., Ammann, R., & Wurmle, O. (1995). Season of birth: Comparison of patients with schizophrenia, affective disorders and alcoholism. *Acta Psychiatrica Scandinavica, 91*(2), 140–143.

Modestin, J., Berger, A., & Ammann, R. (1996). Mental disorder and criminality: Male alcoholism. *Journal of Nervous and Mental Disease, 184*(7), 393–402.

Modestin, J., Hug, A., & Ammann, R. (1997). Criminal behavior in males with affective disorders. *Journal of Affective Disorders, 42,* 29–38.

Moffitt, T. E. (1993). Adolescence-limited and life-course-persistent antisocial behavior: A developmental taxonomy. *Psychological Review, 100,* 674–701.

Mogil, J. S., Sternberg, W. F., Kest, B., et al. (1993). Sex differences in the antagonism of swim stress-induced analgesia: Effects of gonadectomy and estrogen replacement. *Pain, 53,* 17–25.

Molloy, D. W., Alemayehu, E., & Roberts, R. (1991). Reliability of a standardized Mini-Mental State examination compared with the traditional Mini-Mental State examination. *American Journal of Psychiatry, 148,* 102–105.

Monahan, J. (1981). *The clinical prediction of violent behavior.* Washington, DC: U.S. Government Printing House.

Monahan, J. (1992). Mental disorder and violent behavior: Perceptions and evidence. *American Psychologist, 47,* 511–521.

Monahan, J., & Steadman, H. J. (1996). Violent storms and violent people: How meteorology can inform risk communication in mental health law. *American Psychologist, 51,* 931–938.

Monking, H. S., Hornung, W. P., Stricker, K., & Buchkremer, G. (1997). Expressed-emotion development and course of schizophrenic illness: Considerations based on results of a CFI replication. *European Archives of Psychiatry and Clinical Neuroscience, 247*(1), 31–34.

Monroe, S. M., Roberts, J. E., Kupfer, D. J., & Frank, E. (1996). Life stress and treatment course of recurrent depression. II: Postrecovery associations with attrition, symptom course, and recurrence over 3 years. *Journal of Abnormal Psychology, 105*(3), 313–328.

Monroe, S. M., & Simons, A. D. (1991). Diathesis-stress theories in the context of life stress research: Implications of the depressive disorders. *Psychological Bulletin, 110,* 406–425.

Monroe, S. M., Thase, M. E., & Simons, A. D. (1992). Social factors and the psychobiology of depression: Relations between life stress and rapid eye movement sleep latency. *Journal of Abnormal Psychology, 101,* 528–537.

Montgomery, H. A., Miller, W. R., & Tonigan, J. S. (1993). Differences among AA groups: Implications for research. *Journal of Studies on Alcohol, 54,* 502–504.

Montgomery, S. A., & Corn, T. (1994). *The psychopharmacology of depression.* New York: Oxford University Press.

Moore, D. R., & Arthur, J. L. (1983). Juvenile delinquency. In T. Ollendick & M. Hersen (Eds.), *Handbook of child psychopathology.* New York: Plenum.

Moore, N. A., Leander, J. D., Benvenga, M. J., et al. (1997). Behavioral pharmacology of olanzapine: A novel antipsychotic drug. *Journal of Clinical Psychiatry, 58*(Suppl. 10), 37–44.

Morano, C. D., Cisler, R. A., & Lemerond, J. (1993). Risk factors for adolescent suicidal behavior: Loss, insufficient familial support, and hopelessness. *Adolescence, 28*(112), 851–865.

Moreau, D., & Weissman, M. M. (1992). Panic disorder in children and adolescents: A review. *American Journal of Psychiatry, 149,* 1306–1314.

Moreland, K. L., Reznikoff, M., & Aronow, E. (1995). Integrating Rorschach interpretation by carefully placing more of your eggs in the content basket. *Journal of Personality Assessment, 64*(2), 239–242.

Morgan, H. (Ed.). (1996). *Adults with autism: A guide to theory and practice.* Cambridge, UK: Cambridge University Press.

Morgenstern, H., & Glazer, W. M. (1993). Identifying risk factors for tardive dyskinesia among long-term outpatients maintained with neuroleptic medications: Results of the Yale tardive dyskinesia study. *Archives of General Psychiatry, 50,* 723–733.

Morgenstern, J., Langenbucher, J., Labouvie, E., & Miller, K. J. (1997). The comorbidity of alcoholism and personality disorders in a clinical population: Prevalence and relation to alcohol typology variables. *Journal of Abnormal Psychology, 106,* 74–84.

Morison, S. J., Ames, E. W., & Chisholm, K. (1995). The development of children adopted from Romanian orphanages. *Merrill Palmer Quarterly, 41,* 411–430.

Morokoff, P. J. (1993). Female sexual arousal disorder. In W. O'Donohue & J. H. Geer (Eds.), *Handbook of sexual dysfunctions: Assessment and treatment* (pp. 157–199). Boston: Allyn & Bacon.

Morota, N., Deletis, V., Kiprovski, K., et al. (1994). The use of motor-evoked potentials in the diagnosis of psychogenic quadriparesis: A case study. *Pediatric Neurosurgery, 20,* 203–206.

Morris, M. J., & Harper, P. S. (1991). Prediction and prevention in Huntington's disease. In P. McGuffin & R. Murray (Eds.), *The new genetics and mental illness* (pp. 281–298). Oxford: Butterworth-Heinemann.

Morris, R., & Morris, D. (1965). *Men and snakes.* New York: McGraw-Hill.

Morse, J. M., & Johnson, J. L. (Eds.). (1991). *The illness experience: Dimensions of suffering.* Newbury Park, CA: Sage.

Morse, T. E., Schuster, J. W., & Sandknop, P. A. (1996). Grocery shopping skills for persons with moderate to profound intellectual disabilities: A review of the literature. *Education and Treatment of Children, 19,* 487–517.

Moss, E., Rousseau, D., Parent, S., et al. (1998). Correlates of attachment at school age: Maternal reported stress, mother-child interaction, and behavior problems. *Journal of Child Development, 69,* 1390–1405.

Mowrer, O. H. (1939). A stimulus-response analysis of anxiety and its role as a reinforcing agent. *Psychological Review, 46,* 553–565.

Mowrer, O. H., & Mowrer, W. M. (1938). Enuresis, a method for its study and treatment. *American Journal of Orthopsychiatry, 8,* 426–459.

Mowrer, O. H., & Viek, P. (1948). An experimental analog of fear from a sense of helplessness. *Journal of Abnormal and Social Psychology, 43*, 193–200.

Mudford, O. C. (1995). Review of the gentle teaching data. *American Journal on Mental Retardation, 99*, 345–355.

Mueser, K. T., Bellack, A. S., Morrison, R. L., & Wade, J. H. (1990). Gender, social competence, and symptomatology in schizophrenia: A longitudinal analysis. *Journal of Abnormal Psychology, 99*(2), 138–147.

Muhlin, G. L. (1979). Mental hospitalization of the foreign-born and the role of cultural isolation. *International Journal of Social Psychiatry, 25*(4), 258–266.

Mulac, A., & Wiemann, J. M. (1983). Observer-perceived communicator anxiety. In J. A. Daly & J. C. McCroskey (Eds.), *Avoiding communication: Shyness, reticence, and communication apprehension* (pp. 107–121). Beverly Hills, CA: Sage.

Mullins, L. L., Olson, R. A., & Chaney, J. M. (1992). A social learning/family systems approach to the treatment of somatoform disorders in children and adolescents. *Family Systems Medicine, 10*(2), 201–212.

Munoz, R. F. (1993). The prevention of depression: Current research and practice. *Applied and Preventive Psychology, 2*, 21–33.

Murphy, C. C., Yeargin-Allsopp, M., Decoufle, P., & Drews, C. D. (1995). The administrative prevalence of mental retardation in 10-year-old children in metropolitan Atlanta, 1985 through 1987. *American Journal of Public Health, 85*, 319–323.

Murphy, D. L., Pigott, T. A., & Insel, T. R. (1990). Obsessive-compulsive disorder and anxiety. In G. D. Burrows, M. Roth, & R. Noyes, Jr. (Eds.), *Handbook of Anxiety, Vol. 3: The neurobiology of anxiety* (pp. 269–287). Amsterdam: Elsevier.

Murphy, E. (1991). *After the asylums*. London: Faber & Faber.

Murphy, G. E., Wetzel, R. D., Robins, E., & McEvoy, L. (1992). Multiple risk factors predict suicide in alcoholism. *Archives of General Psychiatry, 49*, 459–463.

Murphy, W. D. (1997). Exhibitionism: Psychopathology and theory. In D. R. Laws & W. T. O'Donohue (Eds.), *Sexual deviance: Theory, assessment, and treatment* (pp. 22–39). New York: Guilford Press.

Murray, H. A. (1943). *Thematic Apperception Test manual*. Cambridge, MA: Harvard University Press.

Murray, J. B. (1997). Psychophysiological aspects of Tourette's syndrome. *Journal of Psychology, 141*, 615–626.

Murray, T. J. (1982). Dr. Samuel Johnson's abnormal movements. In A. J. Friedhoff & T. N. Chase (Eds.), *Gilles de la Tourette syndrome*. New York: Raven Press.

Murrell, J., Farolow, M., Ghetti, B., & Benson, M. D. (1991). A mutation in the amyloid precursor protein associated with Alzheimer's disease. *Science, 254*, 97–99.

Muscat, J. E., Stellman, S. D., Hoffmann, D., & Wynder, E. L. (1997). Smoking and pancreatic cancer in men and women. *Cancer Epidemiology, Biomarkers and Prevention, 6*(1), 15–19.

Musser, W. S., & Akil, M. (1996). Clozapine as a treatment for Parkinson's disease: A review. *Journal of Neuropsychiatry and Clinical Neurosciences, 8*, 1–9.

Musto, D. F. (1992). America's first cocaine epidemic: What did we learn? In T. R. Kosten & H. D. Kleber (Eds.), *Clinician's guide to cocaine addiction: Theory, research, and treatment* (pp. 3–15). New York: Guilford Press.

Myers, I. B., & McCaulley, M. H. (1985). *A guide to the development and use of the Myers-Briggs type indicator*. Palo Alto, CA: Consulting Psychologists Press.

Myers, J. K., Weissman, M. M., Tischler, G. L., et al. (1984). Six-month prevalence of psychiatric disorders in three communities, 1980–1982. *Archives of General Psychiatry, 41*, 959–967.

Myers, M. G., Stewart, D. G., & Brown, S. A. (1998). Progression from conduct disorder to antisocial personality disorder following treatment for adolescent substance abuse. *American Journal of Psychiatry, 155*, 479–485.

Myers, W. A. (1992). Body dysmorphic disorder. *American Journal of Psychiatry, 149*, 718.

Myhr, G. (1998). Autism and other pervasive developmental disorders: Exploring the dimensional view. *Canadian Journal of Psychiatry, 43*, 589–595.

Nagatsu, T., Narabayashi, H., & Yoshida, M. (Eds.). (1991). *Parkinson's disease: From clinical aspects to molecular basis*. New York: Springer-Verlag.

Nageotte, C., Sullivan, G., Duan, N., & Camp, P. L. (1997). Medication compliance among the seriously mentally ill in a public mental health system. *Social Psychiatry and Psychiatric Epidemiology, 32*(2), 49–56.

Naglieri, J. A., & Reardon, S. M. (1993). Traditional IQ is irrelevant to learning disabilities—intelligence is not. *Journal of Learning Disabilities, 26*, 127–133.

Nair, T. R., Christensen, J. D., Kingsbury, S. J., et al. (1997). Progression of cerebroventricular enlargement and the subtyping of schizophrenia. *Psychiatry Research, 74*(3), 141–150.

Nakakuki, M. (1994). Normal and developmental aspects of masochism: Transcultural and clinical implications. *Psychiatry, 57*, 244–245.

Nasar, S. (1998). *A beautiful mind*. New York: Simon & Schuster.

Nass, R. D. (1993). Sex differences in learning abilities and disabilities. *Annals of Dyslexia, 43*, 61–77.

Nathan, P. E. (1993). Alcoholism: Psychopathology, etiology, and treatment. In P. B. Sutker & H. E. Adams (Eds.), *Comprehensive handbook of psychopathology* (pp. 451–476). New York: Plenum.

National Center for Health Statistics. (1992). Advance report of final mortality statistics, 1989. *NCHS Monthly Vital Statistics Report, 40*.

National Institute of Mental Health (NIMH), National Advisory Mental Health Council Workgroup on Mental Disorders. (1998). *Priorities for prevention research at NIMH*. (NIH Publication No. 98-4321). Rockville, MD: Author.

National Insitute of Mental Health (NIMH), Research Task Force. (1975). *Research in the service of mental health*. Rockville, MD: Author.

National Institute on Alcohol Abuse and Alcoholism. (1992, Jan.). *Alcohol Alert #15: Alcohol and AIDS*. Rockville, MD: Author.

National Institute on Drug Abuse (1996a). Cross-cultural comparison of substance abuse: Results from the 12-site WHO study on reliability and validity. *NIDA Research Monograph, 162*, 79–81.

National Institute on Drug Abuse (1996b). Inhalant abuse: Our least understood drug problem. *NIDA Research Monograph, 162*, 57–59.

Neal, A. M., & Turner, S. M. (1991). Anxiety disorders research with African Americans: Current status. *Psychological Bulletin, 109*(3), 400–410.

Needleman, H. L. (1992). *Human lead exposure*. Boca Raton, FL: CRC Press.

Neisser, U., & Harsch, N. (1992). Phantom flashbulbs: False recollections of hearing news about *Challenger*. In E. Winograd & U. Neisser (Eds.), *Affect and accuracy in recall: Studies of "flashbulb" memories* (pp. 9–31). New York: Cambridge University Press.

Nelkin, D. (1995, Oct. 5). Hunting a link between crime and genes. *Star Tribune*, p. 23A.

Nemeroff, C. B. (1998, June). The neurobiology of depression. *Scientific American*. Available: http://www.sciam.com/1998/0698issue/0698nemeroffbox3.html.

Ness, D. E., & Pfeffer, C. R. (1990). Sequelae of bereavement resulting from suicide. *American Journal of Psychiatry, 147*, 279–285.

Neumaerker, K. J., Bettle, N., Bettle, O., et al. (1998). The Eating Attitudes Test: Comparative analysis of female and male students at the Public Ballet School of Berlin. *European Child and Adolescent Psychiatry, 7*, 19–23.

Neuman, R. J., Geller, B., Rice, J. P., & Todd,

R. D. (1997). Increased prevalence and earlier onset of mood disorders among relatives of prepubertal versus adult probands. *Journal of the American Academy of Child Psychiatry, 36,* 466–473.

Newman, B. (1997). The use of online services to encourage exploration of ego-dystonic sexual interests. *Journal of Sex Education and Therapy, 22,* 45–48.

Newman, C. (1998). Cognitive therapy for borderline personality disorder. In L. VandeCreek & S. Knapp (Eds.), *Innovations in clinical practice: A source book. Vol. 16* (pp. 17–38). Sarasota, FL: Professional Resources Press.

Newman, M. G., Hofmann, S. G., Trabert, W., et al. (1994). Does behavioral treatment of social phobia lead to cognitive changes? *Behavior Therapy, 25*(3), 503–517.

Nezu, A. M., Nezu, C. M., & Perri, M. G. (1989). *Problem-solving therapy for depression.* New York: Wiley.

Nichols-Hoppe, K. T., & Beach, L. R. (1990). The effects of test anxiety and task variables on predecisional information search. *Journal of Research in Personality, 24,* 163–172.

Nicholson, S. D., & Roberts, G. A. (1994). Patients who (need to) tell stories. *British Journal of Hospital Medicine, 51,* 546–549.

NIDA. *See* National Institute on Drug Abuse.

Niehoff, D. (1999). *The biology of violence.* New York: Free Press.

Nielsen, S., Moller-Madsen, S., Isager, T., et al. (1998). Standardized mortality in eating disorders: A quantitative summary of previously published and new evidence. *Journal of Psychosomatic Research, 44,* 413–434.

Nigg, J. Y., & Goldsmith, H. H. (1994). Genetics of personality disorders: Perspectives from personality and psychopathology research. *Psychological Bulletin, 115,* 346–380.

NIMH/NIH Consensus Development Conference Statement. (1985). Mood disorders: Pharmacologic prevention of recurrences. *American Journal of Psychiatry, 142,* 469–476.

Nolen-Hoeksema, S. (1991). Responses to depression and their effects on the duration of depressive episodes. *Journal of Abnormal Psychology, 100,* 569–582.

Nolen-Hoeksema, S., Girgus, J. S., & Seligman, M. E. (1992). Predictors and consequences of childhood depressive symptoms: A 5-year longitudinal study. *Journal of Abnormal Psychology, 101,* 405–422.

Noll, R. B., Zucker, R. A., & Greenberg, G. S. (1990). Identification of alcohol by smell among preschoolers: Evidence for early socialization about drugs occurring in the home. *Child Development, 61,* 1520–1527.

Norbeck, J. S. (1984). The Norbeck Social Support Questionnaire. *Birth Defects: Original Article Series, 20*(5), 45–57.

Norman, M. G., & Malla, A. K. (1993). Stressful life events and schizophrenia. I: A review of the research. *British Journal of Psychiatry, 162,* 161–166.

Norris, J. W., & Hachinski, V. C. (Eds.). (1991). *Prevention of stroke.* New York: Springer-Verlag.

North, C. S., & Ryall, J. E. (1997). Psychiatric illness in female physicians: Are high rates of depression an occupational hazard? *Postgraduate Medicine, 101,* 233–236, 239–240, 242.

Noshirvani, H. F., Kasvikis, Y., Marks, I. M., et al. (1991). Gender-divergent aetiological factors in obsessive-compulsive disorder. *British Journal of Psychiatry, 158,* 260–263.

Novins, D. K., Beals, J., Shore, J. H., & Manson, S. M. (1996). Substance abuse treatment of American Indian adolescents: Comorbid symptomatology, gender differences, and treatment patterns. *Journal of the American Academy of Child and Adolescent Psychiatry, 35*(12), 1593–1601.

Noyes, R., Holt, C. S., Happel, R. L., et al. (1997). A family study of hypochondriasis. *Journal of Nervous and Mental Disease, 185*(4), 223–232.

Noyes, R., Woodman, C., Garvey, M. J., et al. (1992). Generalized anxiety vs. panic disorder: Distinguishing characteristics and patterns of comorbidity. *Journal of Nervous and Mental Disease, 180,* 369–379.

Nuechterlein, K. H. (1991). Vigilance in schizophrenia and related disorders. In S. R. Steinhauer, J. H. Gruzelier, & J. Zubin (Eds.), *Handbook of schizophrenia: Neuropsychology, psychophysiology and information processing, Vol. 5* (pp. 397–433). Amsterdam: Elsevier.

Nuechterlein, K. H., Buchsbaum, M. S., & Dawson, M. E. (1994). Neuropsychological vulnerability to schizophrenia. In A. S. David & J. C. Cutting (Eds.), *The neuropsychology of schizophrenia* (pp. 53–78). Hillsdale, NJ: Erlbaum.

Nunn, K. P. (1996). Personal hopefulness: A conceptual review of the relevance of the perceived future to psychiatry. *British Journal of Medical Psychology, 69*(3), 227–245.

Nutt, D., & Lawson, C. (1992). Panic attacks: A neurochemical overview of models and mechanisms. *British Journal of Psychiatry, 160,* 165–178.

Oatley, K., & Jenkins, J. M. (1992). Human emotions: Function and dysfunction. *Annual Review of Psychology, 43,* 55–85.

Ochitil, H. (1982). Conversion disorder. In J. H. Greist, J. W. Jefferson, & R. L. Spitzer (Eds.), *Treatment of mental disorders.* New York: Oxford University Press.

O'Connor, D. (1983). *Glue sniffing and volatile substance abuse: Case studies of children and young adults.* Brookfield, VT: Gower.

O'Connor, D. W., Pollitt, P. A., Roth, M., et al. (1990). Memory complaints and impairment in normal, depressed, and demented elderly persons identified in a community survey. *Archives of General Psychiatry, 47,* 224–227.

O'Connor, K., & Stravynski, A. (1982). Evaluation of smoking typology by use of a specific behavioral substitution method of self-control. *Behavior Research and Therapy, 20,* 279–288.

O'Connor, T. G., Deater-Deckard, K., Fulker, D., et al. (1998). Genotype-environment correlations in late childhood and early adolescence: Antisocial behavioral problems and coercive parenting. *Developmental Psychology, 34,* 970–981.

O'Donnell, I., Farmer, R., & Catalan, J. (1993). Suicide notes. *British Journal of Psychiatry, 163,* 45–48.

O'Donohue, W., Dopke, C. A., & Swingen, D. N. (1997). Psychotherapy for female sexual dysfunction: A review. *Clinical Psychology Review, 17,* 537–566.

OECD. *See* Organization for Economic Cooperation and Development.

Offord, D. R., Boyle, M. H., & Racine, Y. A. (1991). The epidemiology of antisocial behavior in childhood and adolescence. In D. J. Pepler & K. H. Rubin (Eds.), *The development and treatment of childhood aggression* (pp. 31–54). Hillsdale, NJ: Erlbaum.

O'Grady, J. C. (1990). The prevalence and diagnostic significance of Schneiderian first-rank symptoms in a random sample of acute psychiatric in-patients. *British Journal of Psychiatry, 156,* 496–500.

Ohman, A. (1979). Fear relevance, autonomic conditioning and phobias: A laboratory model. In P. O. Sjoden, S. Bates, & W. S. Dockens III (Eds.), *Trends in behavior therapy* (pp. 107–133). New York: Academic Press.

Ohman, A., & Soares, J. J. F. (1993). On the autonomic nature of phobic fear: Conditioned electrodermal responses to masked fear-relevant stimuli. *Journal of Abnormal Psychology, 102,* 121–132.

Okagaki, L., & Frensch, P. A. (1998). Parenting and children's school achievement: A multiethnic perspective. *American Educational Research Journal, 35,* 123–144.

Okasha, A., Saad, A., Khalikl, A. H., et al. (1994). Phenomenology of obsessive-compulsive disorder: A transcultural study. *Comprehensive Psychiatry, 35,* 191–197.

Okazaki, S. (1997). Sources of ethnic differences between Asian Americans and White American college students on measures of depression and social anxiety. *Journal of Abnormal Psychology, 106*, 52–60.

Okun, B. F. (1982). *Effective helping: Interviewing and counseling techniques.* Monterey, CA: Brooks/Cole.

Oldham, J. M., & Bone, S. (Eds.). (1994). *Paranoia: New psychoanalytic perspectives.* Madison, CT: International Universities Press.

Oldham, J. M., Skodol, A. E., Kellman, H. D., et al. (1995). Comorbidity of axis I and axis II disorders. *American Journal of Psychiatry, 152*(4), 571–578.

Olds, J. (1956). Pleasure centers in the brain. *Scientific American, 195*, 105–116.

Oldstone, M. B. A., & Vitkovic, L. (Eds.). (1995). *Pathogenesis of HIV infection of the brain: Impact on function and behavior.* Berlin: Springer-Verlag.

O'Leary, A. (1990). Stress, emotion, and human immune function. *Psychological Bulletin, 108*, 363–382.

O'Leary, K. D. (1980). Pills or skills for hyperactive children? *Journal of Applied Behavior Analysis, 13*, 191–204.

Ollendick, T. H., & King, N. J. (1991). Origins of childhood fears: An evaluation of Rachman's theory of fear acquisition. *Behaviour Research and Therapy, 29*, 117–123.

O'Malley, S. S., Jaffe, A. J., Chang, G., et al. (1996). Six-month follow-up of naltrexone and psychotherapy for alcohol dependence. *Archives of General Psychiatry, 53*(3), 217–224.

Ondersma, S. J., & Walker, C. (1998). Elimination disorders. In T. H. Ollendick & M. Hersen (Eds.), *Handbook of child psychopathology* (3rd ed.) (pp. 355–378). New York: Plenum.

O'Neil, H. F., Jr., & Spielberger, C. D. (1979). *Cognitive and affective learning strategies.* New York: Academic Press.

Ono, Y., Yoshimura, K., Sueoka, R., et al. (1996). Avoidant personality disorder and taijin kyoufu: Sociocultural implications of the WHO/ADAMHA International Study of Personality Disorders in Japan. *Acta Psychiatrica Scandinavica, 93*, 172–176.

Onstad, S., Skre, I., Torgersen, S., & Kringlin, E. (1991). Twin concordance for DSM-III-R schizophrenia. *Acta Psychiatrica Scandinavica, 83*, 395–401.

Organization for Economic Cooperation and Development. (1992). *U.S. health at the cross-roads.* Paris: Author.

Orne, M. T., Dinges, D. F., & Orne, E. C. (1984). On the differential diagnosis of multiple personality in a forensic case. *International Journal of Clinical and Experimental Hypnosis, 32*, 118–169.

Oscar-Berman, M., & Evert, D. L. (1997). Alcoholic Korsakoff's syndrome. In P. D. Nussbaum (Ed.), *Handbook of neuropsychology and aging: Critical issues in neuropsychology* (pp. 201–215). New York: Plenum.

O'Shea, R. M., Corah, N. L., & Ayer, W. A. (1984). Sources of dentists' stress. *Journal of the American Dental Association, 109*, 48–51.

Oskamp, S. (1965). Overconfidence in case-study judgments. *Journal of Consulting Psychology, 29*, 261–265.

Öst, L. G. (1991). Acquisition of blood and injection phobia and anxiety response patterns in clinical patients. *Behavior Research and Therapy, 29*, 323–332.

Öst, L. G., Sterner, U., & Fellenius, J. (1989). Applied tension, applied relaxation, and the combination in the treatment of blood phobia. *Behavior Research and Therapy, 27*, 109–121.

Ostrow, D. G. (Ed.). (1990). *Behavioral aspects of AIDS.* New York: Plenum.

Otto, M. W., Pollack, M. H., Sachs, G. S., et al. (1993). Discontinuation of benzodiazepine treatment: Efficacy of cognitive-behavioral therapy for patients with panic disorder. *American Journal of Psychiatry, 150*(10), 1485–1490.

Overholser, J. C., Spirito, A., & Adams, D. (1999). Suicide attempts and completion during adolescence: A biopsychosocial perspective. In A. J. Goreczny & M. Hersen (Eds.). *Handbook of pediatric and adolescent health psychology* (pp. 413–428). Boston: Allyn & Bacon.

Overmier, J. B., & LoLordo, V. M. (1998). Learned helplessness. In W. T. O'Donohue (Ed.), *Learning and behavior therapy* (pp. 352–373). Boston: Allyn & Bacon.

Owens, S. M. (1997). Criminal responsibility and multiple personality defendants. *Mental and Physical Disability Law Reporter, 21*(1), 133–143.

Oyama, O., & Andrasik, F. (1992). Behavioral strategies in the prevention of disease. In S. M. Turner, K. S. Calhoun, & H. E. Adams (Eds.), *Handbook of clinical behavior therapy* (2nd ed.) (pp. 397–413). New York: Wiley.

Padgett, D. K. (Ed.). (1995). *Handbook on ethnicity, aging, and mental health.* Westport, CT: Greenwood Press.

Paffenbarger, R. S., Hyde, R. T., Wing, A. L., & Hsieh, C. C. (1986). Physical activity, all-cause mortality, and longevity of college alumni. *New England Journal of Medicine, 314*, 605–613.

Page, G. G., Ben-Eliyahu, S., Yirmiya, R., & Liebeskind, J. C. (1993). Morphine attenuates surgery-induced enhancement of metastatic colonization in rats. *Pain, 54*(1), 21–28.

Painter, K. (1992, March 25). Drunken-driving casualties aren't the only victims of alcohol abuse. *USA Today*, p. 5D.

Palermo, G. B., Liska, F. J., Palermo, M. T., & dal-Forno, G. (1992). "On the predictability of violent behavior: Considerations and guidelines": Response. *Journal of Forensic Sciences, 37*, 950–955.

Palinkas, L. A., Petterson, J. S., Russell, J., & Downs, M. A. (1993). Community patterns of psychiatric disorders after the Exxon *Valdez* oil spill. *American Journal of Psychiatry, 150*, 1517–1523.

Palmer, B. W., Heaton, R. K., Paulsen, J. S., et al. (1997). Is it possible to be schizophrenic yet neuropsychologically normal? *Neuropsychology, 11*(3), 437–446.

Pamuk, E., Makuc, D., Heck, K., et al. (1998). Death rates for suicide, according to sex, detailed race, Hispanic origin, and age: United States, selected years 1950–96. *Socioeconomic status and health chartbook*, Table 48. In *Health, United States, 1998.* Hyattsville, MD: National Center for Health Statistics.

Panchen, A. L. (1992). *Classification, evolution, and the nature of biology.* Cambridge, UK: Cambridge University Press.

Panksepp, J. (1990). The psychoneurology of fear: Evolutionary perspectives and the role of animal models in understanding human anxiety. In G. D. Burrows, M. Roth, & R. Noyes, Jr. (Eds.), *The neurobiology of anxiety, Vol. 3* (pp. 3–58). Amsterdam: Elsevier.

Papp, L. A., Coplan, J., & Gorman, J. M. (1992). Neurobiology of anxiety. In A. Tasman & M. B. Riba (Eds.), *Review of psychiatry, Vol. 11.* Washington, DC: American Psychiatric Press.

Papp, L. A., Klein, D. F., & Gorman, J. M. (1993). Carbon dioxide hypersensitivity, hyperventilation, and panic disorder. *American Journal of Psychiatry, 150*, 1149–1157.

Papp, L. A., Klein, D. F., Martinez, J., et al. (1993). Diagnostic and substance specificity of carbon-dioxide-induced panic. *American Journal of Psychiatry, 150*, 250–257.

Paradis, C. M., Freidman, S., Hatch, M., & Lazar, R. M. (1992). Obsessive-compulsive disorder onset after removal of brain tumor. *Journal of Nervous and Mental Disease, 180*(8), 535–536.

Paris, J. (1996). Cultural factors in the emergence of borderline pathology. *Psychiatry: Interpersonal and Biological Processes, 59*, 185–192.

Paris, J. (1997). Antisocial and borderline personality disorders: Two separate diagnoses or two aspects of the same psychopathology? *Comprehensive Psychiatry, 38*, 237–242.

Paris, J. (1998). Does childhood trauma cause personality disorders in adults? *Canadian Journal of Psychiatry, 143*, 148–153.

Parker, J. D., Taylor, G. J., Bagby, R. M., & Acklin, M. W. (1993). Alexithymia in panic disorder and simple phobia: A comparative study. *American Journal of Psychiatry, 150*(7), 1105–1107.

Parker, P. E. (1993). A case report of Munchausen syndrome with mixed psychological features. *Psychosomatics, 34*(4), 360–364.

Parkin, A. J. (1993). *Neuropsychology of the amnesic syndrome.* Hove, UK: Erlbaum.

Parnas, J., Cannon, T. D., Jacobsen, B., et al. (1993). Lifetime *DSM-III-R* diagnostic outcomes in the offspring of schizophrenic mothers: Results from the Copenhagen high-risk study. *Archives of General Psychiatry, 50*, 707–714.

Parrot, A., & Bechhofer, L. (1991). *Acquaintance rape: The hidden crime.* New York: Wiley.

Parrott, A. (1991). Social drugs: Their effects upon health. In M. Pitts & K. Phillips (Eds.), *The psychology of health: An introduction* (pp. 199–213). London: Routledge.

Parry, B. L. (1997). Psychobiology of premenstrual dysphoric disorder. *Seminar in Reproductive Endocrinology, 15*, 55–68.

Pasamanick, B. (1959). *Epidemiology of mental disorder: A symposium to commemorate the centennial of the birth of Emil Kraepelin.* Washington, DC: American Association for the Advancement of Science.

Pasquier, F., & Petit, H. (1997). Frontotemporal dementia: Its rediscovery. *European Neurology, 38*, 1–6.

Patrick, C. J., Cuthbert, B. N., & Lang, P. J. (1994). Emotion in the criminal psychopath: Fear image processing. *Journal of Abnormal Psychology, 103*, 523–534.

Patten, C. A., Gillin, J. C., Farkas, A. J., et al. (1997). Depressive symptoms in California adolescents: Family structure and parental support. *Journal of Adolescent Health, 20*, 271–278.

Patten, S. B., & Love, E. J. (1994). Drug-induced depression. Incidence, avoidance and management. *Drug Safety, 10*(3), 203–219.

Patten, S. B., & Love, E. J. (1997). Drug-induced depression. *Psychotherapy and Psychosomatics, 66*, 63–73.

Patterson, D. (1995). The integrated map of human chromosome 21. In C. Epstein, D. Patterson, & L. Nadel (Eds.), *Etiology and pathogenesis of Down syndrome* (pp. 43–55). New York: Wiley.

Paul, G. L., & Lentz, R. J. (1977). Psychosocial treatment of chronic mental patients: Milieu versus social learning programs. *Psychological Medicine, 20*, 383–394.

Pauli, P., Marquardt, C., Hartl, L., et al. (1991). Anxiety induced by cardiac perceptions in patients with panic attacks: A field study. *Behaviour Research and Therapy, 29*, 137–145.

Pauls, D. L., Leckman, J. F., & Cohen, D. F. (1993). Familial relationship between Gilles de la Tourette's syndrome, attention disorder, learning disabilities, speech disorders, and stuttering. *Journal of the American Academy of Child and Adolescent Psychiatry, 32*, 1044–1050.

Paurohit, N., Dowd, E. T., & Cottingham, H. F. (1982). The role of verbal and nonverbal cues in the formation of first impressions of Black and White counselors. *Journal of Counseling Psychology, 4*, 371–378.

Pawliuk, N., Grizenko, N., Chan-Yip, A., et al. (1996). Acculturation style and psychological functioning in children of immigrants. *American Journal of Orthopsychiatry, 66*(1), 111–121.

Pawluck, D. E., & Gorey, K. M. (1998). Secular trends in the incidence of anorexia nervosa: Integrative review of population-based studies. *International Journal of Eating Disorders, 23*, 347–352.

Paykel, E. S. (1995). Psychotherapy, medication combinations, and compliance. *Journal of Clinical Psychiatry, 56*(Suppl. 1), 24–30.

Paykel, E. S. (Ed.). (1982). *Handbook of affective disorders.* New York: Guilford Press.

Paykel, E. S., Brayne, C., Huppert, F. A., et al. (1994). Incidence of dementia in a population older than 75 years in the United Kingdom. *Archives of General Psychiatry, 51*, 325–332.

Paykel, E. S., & Cooper, Z. (1982). Life events and social stress. In E. S. Paykel (Ed.), *Handbook of affective disorders.* New York: Guilford Press.

Payne, R. L. (1992). First person account: My schizophrenia. *Schizophrenia Bulletin, 18*, 725–728.

Payton, S. (1992). The concept of the person in the *parens patriae* jurisdiction over previously competent persons. *Journal of Medicine and Philosophy, 17*, 605–645.

Pearlson, G. D., Harris, G. J., Powers, R. E., et al. (1992). Quantitative changes in mesial temporal volume, regional cerebral blood flow, and cognition in Alzheimer's disease. *Archives of General Psychiatry, 49*, 402–408.

Pedersen, N. L., & Gatz, M. (1991). Twin studies as a tool for bridging the gap between genetics and epidemiology of dementia: The study of dementia in Swedish twins [Abstract]. *Gerontologist, 31*, 333.

Peet, M., & Peters, S. (1995). Drug-induced mania. *Drug Safety, 12*(2), 146–153.

Pelka, F. (1997). Unequal justice: Preserving the rights of the mentally retarded in the criminal justice system. *Humanist, 57*, 28–33.

Pendery, M. L., Maltzman, I. M., & West, L. J. (1982). Controlled drinking by alcoholics? New findings and a reevaluation of a major affirmative study. *Science, 217*, 169–175.

Pennebaker, J. W. (1993). Putting stress into words: Health, linguistic, and therapeutic implications. *Behaviour Research and Therapy, 31*, 539–548.

Pennington, B. F., Rogers, S. J., Bennetto, L., et al. (1997). Validity tests of the executive dysfunction hypothesis of autism. In J. Russell (Ed.), *Autism as an executive disorder* (pp. 143–178). New York: Oxford University Press.

Peralta, V., Cuesta, M. J., & de Leon, J. (1995). Positive and negative symptoms/syndromes in schizophrenia: Reliability and validity of different diagnostic systems. *Psychological Medicine, 25*(1), 43–50.

Perkins, D. V. (1982). The assessment of stress using life event scales. In L. Goldberger & S. Brexnitz (Eds.), *Handbook of stress: Theoretical and clinical aspects.* New York: Free Press.

Perls, F. C., Hefferline, R. F., & Goodman, P. (1973). *Gestalt therapy: Excitement and growth in the human personality.* Harmondsworth, UK: Penguin.

Perry, S. V., Fishman, B., Jacobsberg, L., & Frances, A. (1992). Relationship over 1 year between lymphocyte subsets and psychosocial variables among adults with infection by human immunodeficiency virus. *Archives of General Psychiatry, 49*, 396–401.

Persons, J. B. (1995). Are all psychotherapies cognitive? Special issue: Psychotherapy integration and cognitive psychotherapy. *Journal of Cognitive Psychotherapy: An International Quarterly, 9*(3), 185–194.

Peselow, E. D., Robins, C. J., Sanfilipo, M. P., et al. (1992). Sociotropy and autonomy: Relationship to antidepressant drug treatment response and endogenous-nonendogenous dichotomy. *Journal of Abnormal Psychology, 101*, 479–486.

Peterson, B. S., & Cohen, D. J. (1998). The treatment of Tourette's syndrome: Multimodal, developmental intervention. *Journal of Clinical Psychiatry, 59* (Suppl. 1), 62–72.

Peterson, C., Maier, S. F., & Seligman, M. E. P. (1993). *Learned helplessness: A theory for the age of personal control.* New York: Oxford University Press.

Peterson, L., & Roberts, M. C. (1992). Complacency, misdirection, and effective prevention of children's injuries. *American Psychologist, 47*(8), 1040–1044.

Peterson, L. G., & O'Shanick, G. J. (Eds.). (1986). *Psychiatric aspects of trauma.* London: Karger.

Petty, R. G. (1998). Management of chronic psychotic ambulatory outpatients. *Journal of Clinical Psychiatry, 59*(Suppl. 19), 30–35.

Peyrot, M., & Rubin, R. R. (1997). Levels and risks of depression and anxiety symptomatology among diabetic adults. *Diabetes Care, 20,* 585–590.

Pfeffer, C. R. (1990). Manifestation of risk factors. In G. MacLean (Ed.), *Suicide in children and adolescents.* Toronto: Hogrefe & Huber.

Pfeffer, C. R., Klerman, G. L., Hurt, S. W., et al. (1993). Suicidal children grow up: Rates and psychosocial risk factors for suicide attempts during follow-up. *Journal of the American Academy of Child and Adolescent Psychiatry, 32,* 106–113.

Pfohl, B., & Blum, N. (1995). Obsessive-compulsive personality disorder. In W. J. Livesley (Ed.), *The DSM-IV personality disorders: Diagnosis and treatment of mental disorders* (pp. 261–276). New York: Guilford Press.

Phelps, L. (Ed.). (1998). *Health-related disorders in children and adolescents: A guidebook for understanding and educating.* Washington, DC: American Psychological Association.

Phelps, L., & Grabowski, J. (1992). Fetal alcohol syndrome: Diagnostic features and psychoeducational risk factors. *School Psychology Quarterly, 7,* 112–128.

Phillips, K. A. (1991). Body dysmorphic disorder: The distress of imagined ugliness. *American Journal of Psychiatry, 148,* 1138–1149.

Phillips, K. A. (1996). Pharmacologic treatment of body dysmorphic disorder. *Psychopharmacology Bulletin, 32*(4), 597–605.

Phillips, K. A., & Gunderson, J. G. (1996). Personality disorders. In R. E. Hales & S. C. Yudofsky (Eds.), *The American Psychiatric Press synopsis of psychiatry* (pp. 653–680). Washington, DC: American Psychiatric Press.

Phillips, K. A., Hirschfeld, R. M. A., Shea, M. T., & Gunderson, J. G. (1995). Depressive personality disorder. In W. J. Livesley (Ed.), *The DSM-IV personality disorders: Diagnosis and treatment of mental disorders* (pp. 287–302). New York: Guilford Press.

Phillips, K. A., McElroy, S. L., Keck, P. E., et al. (1993). Body dysmorphic disorder: 30 cases of imagined ugliness. *American Journal of Psychiatry, 150,* 302–308.

Piaget, J., Gruber, H. E., & Voneche, J. J. (1995). *The essential Piaget.* New York: Jason Aronson.

Piccinelli, M., & Simon, G. (1997). Gender and cross-cultural differences in somatic symptoms associated with emotional distress: An international study in primary care. *Psychological Medicine, 27*(2), 433–444.

Pierce, J. P., Fiore, M. C., Novotny, T. E., et al. (1989). Trends in cigarette smoking in the United States: Projections to the year 2000. *Journal of the American Medical Association, 261,* 61–65.

Pierce, K. A., and Kirkpatrick, D. R. (1992). Do men lie on fear surveys? *Behaviour Research and Therapy, 30,* 415–418.

Pigott, T. A., Pato, M. T., Bernstein, S. E., et al. (1990). Controlled comparisons of clomipramine and fluoxetine in the treatment of obsessive-compulsive disorder: Behavioral and biological results. *Archives of General Psychiatry, 47*(10), 926–932.

Pike, K. M. (1998). Long-term course of anorexia nervosa: Response, relapse, remission, and recovery. *Clinical Psychology Review, 18,* 447–475.

Pilkonis, P. A., & Klein, K. R. (1997). Commentary on the assessment and diagnosis of antisocial behavior and personality. In D. M. Stoff, J. Breiling, & J. D. Maser (Eds.), *Handbook of antisocial behavior* (pp. 109–112). New York: Wiley.

Pine, D. S., & Grun, J. (1998). Anxiety disorders. In B. T. Walsh (Ed.), *Child psychopharmacology* (pp. 115–148). Review of Psychiatry series. Washington, DC: American Psychiatric Press.

Pinel, P. (1962). *A treatise on insanity.* New York: Hafner. (Original work published 1801)

Piotrowski, C., & Keller, J. W. (1989). Psychological testing in outpatient mental health facilities: A national study. *Professional Psychology: Research and Practice, 20,* 423–425.

Piotrowski, C., & Keller, J. W. (1991). Psychological testing in outpatient mental health facilities: Survey of APA Division 38 clinicians. *Professional Psychology: Research and Practice, 21,* 99–106.

Piper, A., Jr. (1994). Multiple personality disorder. *British Journal of Psychiatry, 164,* 600–612.

Pisani, V. C., Fawcett, J., Clark, D. C., & McGuire, M. (1993). The relative contributions of medication adherence and AA meeting attendance to abstinent outcome for chronic alcoholics. *Journal of Studies on Alcohol, 54,* 115–119.

Pitman, R. K., Orr, S. P., Forgue, D. F., et al. (1990). Psychophysiologic responses to combat imagery of Vietnam veterans with posttraumatic stress disorder vs other anxiety disorders. *Journal of Abnormal Psychology, 99*(1), 49–54.

Piven, J., & O'Leary, D. (1997). Neuroimaging in autism. *Child and Adolescent Psychiatric Clinics of North America, 6,* 305–323.

Planet Press. (1985). *California Adaptive Behavior Scale.* Newport Beach, CA: Author.

Plassmann, R. (Ed.). (1994). Factitious disease. Special issue. *Psychotherapy and Psychosomatics, 62*(1–2), 1–139.

Pliszka, S. R., McCracken, J. T., & Maas, J. W. (1996). Catecholamines in attention deficit hyperactivity disorder: Current perspectives. *Journal of the American Academy of Child and Adolescent Psychiatry, 35,* 264–272.

Plomin, R., Defries, J. C., McClearn, G. E., & Rutter, M. (1997). *Behavioral genetics* (3rd ed.). New York: Freeman.

Plomin, R., & Rende, R. (1991). Human behavioral genetics. *Annual Review of Psychology, 42,* 161–190.

Plotnikoff, N., Murgo, A., Faith, R., & Wybran, J. (Eds.). (1991). *Stress and immunity.* Boca Raton, FL: CRC Press.

Plutchik, R., & Van Praag, H. M. (1997). Suicide, impulsivity and antisocial behavior. In D. M. Stoff, J. Breiling, & J. D. Maser (Eds.), *Handbook of antisocial behavior* (pp. 101–108). New York: Wiley.

Pober, B. R., & Dykens, E. M. (1996). Williams syndrome: An overview of medical, cognitive, and behavioral features. *Child and Adolescent Psychiatric Clinics of North America, 5,* 929–943.

Pokorny, A. D. (1993). Suicide prediction revisited. *Suicide and Life-Threatening Behavior, 23*(1), 1–10.

Polcin, D. (1992). Issues in the treatment of dual-diagnosis clients who have mental illness. *Professional Psychology: Research and Practice, 23*(1), 30–37.

Poling, A., Gadow, K. D., & Cleary, J. (1991). *Drug therapy for behavior disorders.* New York: Pergamon.

Pollack, M. H., Kradin, R., Otto, M. W., et al. (1996). Prevalence of panic in patients referred for pulmonary function testing at a major medical center. *American Journal of Psychiatry, 153*(1), 110–113.

Pomerlau, O. F., & Pomerlau, C. S. (1990). Behavioral studies in humans: Anxiety, stress, and smoking. In G. Bock & J. Marsh (Eds.), *The biology of nicotine dependence* (pp. 225–234). New York: Wiley.

Poon, L. W., & Siegler, I. C. (1991). Psychological aspects of normal aging. In J. Sadavoy, L. W. Lazarus, & L. F. Jarvik (Eds.), *Comprehensive review of geriatric psychiatry* (pp. 117–145). Washington, DC: American Psychiatric Press.

Popenoe, D. (1996). *Life without father.* New York: Free Press.

Popper, C. W. (1997). Antidepressants in the treatment of attention deficit/hyperactivity disorder. *Journal of Clinical Psychiatry, 58*(Suppl. 14), 14–29.

Popper, C. W., & Steingard, R. J. (1996). Disorders usually first diagnosed in infancy, childhood or adolescence. In R. E. Hales & S. C. Yudofsky (Eds.), *The American Psychiatric Press synopsis of psychiatry* (pp. 681–774). Washington, DC: American Psychiatric Press.

Portegies, P., & Rosenberg, N. R. (1998). AIDS dementia complex: Diagnosis and drug treatment options. *CNS-Drugs, 9,* 31–40.

Porter, R. (1997, Oct. 10). Lunatic ideas and the truth about asylums. *The* [London] *Times Higher Education Supplement,* p. 21.

Post, J. M. (1997). Narcissism and the quest for political power. In C. S. Ellman & J. Reppen (Eds.), *Omnipotent fantasies and the vulnerable self: The library of clinical psychoanalysis* (pp. 195–232). Northvale, NJ: Jason Aronson.

Post, R. M. (1992). Transduction of psychosocial stress into the neurobiology of recurrent affective disorder. *American Journal of Psychiatry, 149*(8), 999–1010.

Potter, L. B., & Mercy, J. A. (1997). Public health perspective on interpersonal violence among youths in the United States. In D. M. Stoff, J. Breiling, & J. D. Maser (Eds.), *Handbook of antisocial behavior* (pp. 3–11). New York: Wiley.

Potter, W. Z., & Manji, H. K. (1993). Are monoamine metabolites in cerebral spinal fluid worth measuring? *Archives of General Psychiatry, 50,* 653–656.

Potts, M. K. (1994). Long-term effects of trauma: Post-traumatic stress among civilian internees of the Japanese during World War II. *Journal of Clinical Psychology, 50*(5), 681–698.

Powell, E. C., Sheehan, K. M., & Christoffel, K. K. (1996). Firearm violence among youth: Public health strategies for prevention. *Annals of Emergency Medicine, 28*(2), 204–212.

Powell, G., & Clibbens, J. (1994). Actions speak louder than words: Signing and speech intelligibility in adults with Down's syndrome. *Down Syndrome Research and Practice, 2,* 127–129.

Presley, C. A., & Meilman, P. W. (1992). *Alcohol and drugs on American college campuses: A report to college presidents.* Carbondale, IL: Southern Illinois University Press.

Pribor, E. F., Yutzy, S. H., Dean, J. T., & Wetzel, R. D. (1993). Briquet's syndrome, dissociation and abuse. *American Journal of Psychiatry, 150*(10), 1507–1511.

Price, T. R. P., Goetz, K. L., & Lovell, M. R. (1992). Neuropsychiatric aspects of brain tumors. In S. C. Yudofsky & R. E. Hales (Eds.), *The American Psychiatric Press textbook of neuropsychiatry* (pp. 473–497). Washington, DC: American Psychiatric Press.

Price, V. A. (1988). Research and clinical issues in treating type A behavior. In B. K. Houston & C. R. Snyder (Eds.), *Type A behavior pattern: Research, theory, and intervention.* New York: Wiley.

Prichard, J. C. (1835). *Treatise on insanity and other disorders affecting the mind.* Philadelphia: Hasell, Barrington & Haswell.

Prien, R. F., & Potter, W. Z. (1993). Maintenance treatment for mood disorders. In D. L. Dunner (Ed.), *Current psychiatric therapy* (pp. 255–260). Philadelphia: Saunders.

Prince, M. (1908). *The dissociation of a personality.* London: Longmans Green.

Prinz, R. J., & Connell, C. M. (1997). Conduct disorders and antisocial behavior. In R. T. Ammerman & M. Hersen (Eds.), *Handbook of prevention and treatment with children and adolescents: Intervention in the real world context* (pp. 238–258). New York: Wiley.

Prior, M., Eisenmajer, R., Leekam, S., et al. (1998). Are there subgroups within the autistic spectrum? A cluster analysis of a group of children with autistic spectrum disorders. *Journal of Child Psychology and Psychiatry, 39,* 893–902.

Pritchard, C. (1992). Is there a link between suicide in young men and unemployment? A comparison of the UK with other European Community countries. *British Journal of Psychiatry, 160,* 750–756.

Pritchard, C. W., & Teo, P. Y. (1994). Preterm birth, low birthweight and the stressfulness of the household role for pregnant women. *Social Science and Medicine, 38* (1), 89–96.

Probst, M., Vandereycken, W., Van Coppenolle, H., et al. (1995). The Body Attitude Test for patients with an eating disorder: Psychometric characteristics of a new questionnaire. *Eating Disorders: The Journal of Treatment and Prevention, 3,* 133–144.

Probst, M., Vandereycken, W., Van Coppenolle, H., & Pieters, G. (1998). Body size estimation in anorexia nervosa patients: The significance of overestimation. *Journal of Psychosomatic Research, 44,* 451–456.

Prochaska, J. O. (1996). A stage paradigm for integrating clinical and public health approaches to smoking cessation. *Addictive Behaviors, 21*(6), 721–732.

Pu, T., Mohamed, E., Imam, K., & El-Roey, A. M. (1986). One hundred cases of hysteria in eastern Lybia. *British Journal of Psychiatry, 148,* 606–609.

Puente, A. E., & Salazar, G. D. (1998). Assessment of minority and culturally diverse children. In A. Prifitera & D. H. Saklofske (Eds.), *WISC-III clinical use and interpretation: Scientist-practitioner perspectives* (pp. 227–248). San Diego: Academic Press.

Pueschel, S. M., & Sustrova, M. (1997). *Adolescents with Down syndrome: Toward a more fulfilling life.* Baltimore: Brookes.

Purcell, T. B. (1991). The somatic patient. *Emergency Medicine Clinics of North America, 9,* 137–159.

Purdon, C., & Clark, D. A. (1993). Obsessive-intrusive thoughts in nonclinical subjects. I: Content and relations with depressive, anxious, and obsessional symptoms. *Behaviour Research and Therapy, 31,* 713–720.

Putnam, F. W. (1989). *Diagnosis and treatment of multiple personality disorder.* New York: Guilford Press.

Putnam, F. W. (1991). Dissociative phenomena. In A. Tasman & S. M. Goldfinger (Eds.), *American Psychiatric Press review of psychiatry, Vol. 10.* Washington, DC: American Psychiatric Press.

Putnam, F. W. (1992). Altered states: Peeling away the layers of a multiple personality. *Sciences, 32*(6), 30–36.

Putnam, F. W., Guroff, J. J., Silberman, E. K., et al. (1986). The clinical phenomenology of multiple personality disorder: Review of 100 recent cases. *Journal of Clinical Psychiatry, 57,* 285–293.

Putnam, F. W., & Loewenstein, R. J. (1993). Treatment of multiple personality disorder: A survey of current practices. *American Journal of Psychiatry, 150,* 1048–1052.

Putnam, F. W., Zahn, T. P., & Post, R. M. (1990). Differential autonomic nervous system activity in multiple personality disorder. *Psychiatric Research, 31,* 251–260.

Quadrel, M. J., Fischhoff, B., & Davis, W. (1993). Adolescent (in)vulnerability. *American Psychologist, 48,* 102–116.

Quick, J. C., Murphy, L. R., & Hurrell, J. J., Jr. (Eds.). (1992). *Stress and well-being at work: Assessments and interventions for occupational mental health.* Washington, DC: American Psychological Association.

Quill, T., Cassel, C. K., & Meier, D. E. (1992). Care of the hopelessly ill. *New England Journal of Medicine, 19,* 1380–1384.

Quinsey, V. L., Harris, G. T., Rice, M. E., & Cormier, C. A. (1998). *Violent offenders: Appraising and managing risk.* Washington, DC: American Psychological Association.

Quon, D., Wang, Y., Catalano, R., et al. (1991). Formation of β-amyloid protein deposits in strains of transgenic mice. *Nature, 352,* 239–241.

Rabinowitz, J., Mark, M., Popper, M., et al. (1995). Predicting revolving-door patients in a 9-year national sample. *Social Psychiatry and Psychiatric Epidemiology, 30*(2), 65–72.

Rabkin, J. G., Williams, J. B., Remien, R. H., et al. (1991). Depression, distress, lymphocyte subsets, and human immunodeficiency virus symptoms on two occasions in HIV-positive homosexual men. *Archives of General Psychiatry, 48*(2), 111–119.

Rachman, S. (1991). Neo-conditioning and the classical theory of fear acquisition. *Clinical Psychology Review, 121*, 155–173.

Rachman, S. J., & Hodgson, R. (1980). *Obsessions and compulsions*. Englewood Cliffs, NJ: Prentice-Hall.

Radley, A. (Ed.). (1993). *Worlds of illness. Biographical and cultural perspectives on health and disease*. London: Routledge.

Ragland, D. R., & Brand, R. J. (1988a). Coronary heart disease mortality in the Western Collaborative Group Study: Follow-up experience of 22 years. *American Journal of Epidemiology, 127*, 462–475.

Ragland, D. R., & Brand, R. J. (1988b). Type A behavior and mortality from coronary heart disease. *New England Journal of Medicine, 318*, 65–69.

Raine, A. (1997). Antisocial behavior and psychophysiology: A biosocial perspective and a prefrontal dysfunction hypothesis. In D. M. Stoff, J. Breiling, & J. D. Maser (Eds.), *Handbook of antisocial behavior* (pp. 289–304). New York: Wiley.

Raine, A., Benishay, D., Lencz, T., & Scarpa, A. (1997). Abnormal orienting in schizotypal personality disorder. *Schizophrenia Bulletin, 23*, 75–82.

Raja, M., Azzoni, A., & Giammarco, V. (1998). Diabetes insipidus and polydipsia in a patient with Asperger's disorder and an empty sella: A case report. *Journal of Autism and Developmental Disorders, 28*, 235–239.

Rakic, Z., Starcevic, V., Starcevic, V. P., et al. (1997). Testosterone treatment in men with erectile disorder and low levels of testosterone in serum. *Archives of Sexual Behavior, 26*, 495–504.

Rao, S. M., Huber, S. J., & Bornstein, R. A. (1992). Emotional changes with multiple sclerosis and Parkinson's disease. *Journal of Consulting and Clinical Psychology, 60*, 369–378.

Rapaport, D., Gill, M. M., & Scoffer, R. (1968). *Diagnostic psychological testing* (rev. ed.). New York: International Universities Press.

Rapaport, M. H., Paniccia, G., & Judd, L. L. (1995). A review of social phobia. *Psychopharmacology Bulletin, 31*(1), 125–129.

Rapee, R. M. (1991a). The conceptual overlap between cognition and conditioning in clinical psychology. *Clinical Psychology Review, 11*, 193–203.

Rapee, R. M. (1991b). Generalized anxiety disorder: A review of clinical features and theoretical concepts. *Clinical Psychology Review, 11*, 419–440.

Rapee, R. M. (1993). Psychological factors in panic disorder. *Advances in Behaviour Research and Therapy, 15*(1), 85–102.

Rapee, R. M., Mattick, R., & Murrell, E. (1986). Cognitive mediation in the affective component of spontaneous panic attacks. *Journal of Behavior Therapy and Experimental Psychiatry, 17*, 245–253.

Rapee, R. M., Sanderson, W. C., McCauley, P. A., & Di Nardo, P. A. (1992). Differences between panic disorder and other *DSM-III-R* anxiety disorders. *Behaviour Research and Therapy, 30*, 45–52.

Raphael, K. G., Cloitre, M., & Dohrenwend, B. P. (1991). Problems of recall and misclassification with checklist methods of measuring stressful life events. *Health Psychology, 8*, 747–752.

Rapin, I., & Katzman, R. (1998). Neurobiology of autism. *Annals of Neurology, 43*, 7–14.

Rapoport, J. L., Buchsbaum, M. S., Zahne, T. P., et al. (1978). Dextroamphetamine: Cognitive and behavioral effects in normal prepubertal boys. *Science, 199*, 560–563.

Raskind, M. H., & Higgins, E. L. (1998). Assistive technology for postsecondary students with learning disabilities: An overview. *Journal of Learning Disabilities, 31*, 27–40.

Raspe, R. E. (1969). *Baron Munchausen's narrative of his marvelous travels and campaigns in Russia*. New York: Pantheon Books. (Original work published 1784)

Rathus, S. A., & Nevid, J. S. (1992). *Adjustment and growth: The challenges of life* (5th ed.). Ft. Worth, TX: Harcourt Brace Jovanovich.

Raver, C. C., & Zigler, E. F. (1997). Focus section: New perspectives on Head Start. Social competence, an untapped dimension in evaluating Head Start's success. *Early Childhood Research Quarterly, 12*, 363–385.

Ray, J. J. (1991). If "A-B" does not predict heart disease, why bother with it? A comment on Ivancevich & Matteson. *British Journal of Medical Psychology, 64*(1), 85–90.

Ray, O., & Ksir, C. (1993). *Drugs, society, and human behavior*. St. Louis: Mosby.

Ray, W. A., Gurwitz, J., Decker, M. D., & Kennedy, D. L. (1992). Medications and the safety of the older driver: Is there a basis for concern? Special Issue: Safety and mobility of elderly drivers: II. *Human Factors, 34*(1), 33–47.

Raz, S., & Raz, N. (1990). Structural brain abnormalities in the major psychoses: A quantitative review of evidence from computerized imaging. *Psychological Bulletin, 108*, 93–98.

Read, S. L., Miller, B. L., Mena, I., et al. (1995). SPECT in dementia: Clinical and pathological correlation. *Journal of the American Geriatrics Society, 43*, 1243–1247.

Reardon, W., Hughes, H. E., Green, S. H., et al. (1992). Anal abnormalities in childhood myotonic dystrophy—A possible source of confusion in child sexual abuse. *Archives of Disease in Childhood, 67*(4), 527–528.

Regier, D. A., Farmer, M. E., Raye, D. S., et al. (1990). Comorbidity of mental disorders with drug and alcohol abuse: Results from the epidemiologic catchment area (ECA) study. *Journal of the American Medical Association, 264*, 2511–2518.

Regier, D. A., Narrow, W. E., Rae, D. S., et al. (1993). The de facto U.S. mental and addictive disorders service system: Epidemiologic catchment area prospective 1-year prevalence rates of disorders and services. *Archives of General Psychiatry, 50*(2), 85–94.

Register, A. C., Beckham, J. C., May, J. G., & Gustafson, D. J. (1991). Stress inoculation bibliotherapy in the treatment of test anxiety. *Journal of Counseling Psychology, 38*, 115–119.

Reich, J. (1996). The morbidity of *DSM-III-R* dependent personality disorder. *Journal of Nervous and Mental Disease, 184*, 22–26.

Reicher, A., Maurer, K., Loffler, W., & Fatkenheuer, B. (1991). Gender differences in age at onset and course of schizophrenic disorder. In H. Hafner & W. F. Gattaz (Eds.), *Search for the causes of schizophrenia, Vol. 2* (pp. 14–33). Berlin: Springer-Verlag.

Reid, D. K. (1998). Scaffolding: A broader view. *Journal of Learning Disabilities, 31*, 386–396.

Reid, D. K., Hresko, W. P., & Swanson, H. L. (1996). *Cognitive approaches to learning disabilities* (3rd ed.). Austin, TX: Pro-Ed.

Reid, J. B., & Eddy, J. M. (1997). The prevention of antisocial behavior: Some considerations in the search for effective interventions. In D. M. Stoff, J. Breiling, & J. D. Maser (Eds.), *Handbook of antisocial behavior* (pp. 343–356). New York: Wiley.

Rein, W., & Turjanski, S. (1997). Clinical update on amisulpride in deficit schizophrenia. *International Clinical Psychopharmacology, 12*(Suppl. 2), S19–S27.

Reitan, R. M., & Wolfson, D. (1985). *The Halstead-Reitan Neuropsychological Test Battery: Theory and clinical interpretation*. Tucson, AZ: Neuropsychology Press.

Rekers, G. A., & Kilgus, M. D. (1998). Diagnosis and treatment of gender identity disorders in children and adolescents. In L. VandeCreek & S. Knapp (Eds.), *Innovations in clinical practice: A sourcebook, Vol. 16* (pp. 127–141). Sarasota, FL: Professional Resources Press.

Remington, P. L., Forman, M. R., Gentry, E. M., et al. (1985). Current smoking trends in the United States: The 1981–1983 Behavioral Risk Factor surveys. *Journal of the American Medical Association, 253*, 2975–2978.

Rendell, M. S., Rajfer, J., Wicker, P. A., et al. (1999). Sildenafil for treatment of erectile dysfunction in men with diabetes: A randomized controlled trial. *Journal of the American Medical Association, 281,* 421–426.

Renshaw, D. C. (1996). Sexuality and ageing. In J. Sadavoy & L. Lazarus (Eds.), *Comprehensive review of geriatric psychiatry II* (2nd ed.) (pp. 713–729). Washington, DC: American Psychiatric Press.

Reppucci, N. D., Land, D., & Haugaard, J. J. (1998). Child sexual abuse prevention programs that target young children. In P. K. Trickett & C. J. Schellenbach (Eds.), *Violence against children in the family and the community* (pp. 317–337). Washington, DC: American Psychological Association.

Reubart, D. (1985). *Anxiety and musical performance: On playing the piano from memory.* New York: Da Capo Press.

Rey, J. M., & Walter, G. (1997). Half a century of ECT use in young people. *American Journal of Psychiatry, 154,* 595–602.

Reynolds, C. R. (1994). *Cognitive assessment: A multidisciplinary perspective.* New York: Plenum.

Reynolds, C. R. (1995). Test bias and the assessment of intelligence and personality. In D. H. Saklofske & D. Zeidner (Eds.), *International handbook of personality and intelligence: Perspectives on individual differences* (pp. 545–573). New York: Plenum.

Reznek, L. (1998). *Evil or ill? Justifying the insanity defence.* London: Routledge.

Ribas, D. (1998). Autism as the defusion of drives. *International Journal of Psycho-Analysis, 79,* 529–538.

Riccardi, N., & Leeds, J. (1997, Feb. 24). Megan's law calling up old, minor offenses. *Los Angeles Times,* pp. A1, A16.

Rich, C. L., Young, J. G., Fowler, R. C., et al. (1990). Guns and suicide: Possible effects of some specific legislation. *American Journal of Psychiatry, 147,* 342–346.

Richters, M. M., & Volkmar, F. R. (1994). Reactive attachment disorder of infancy or early childhood. *Journal of the American Academy of Child and Adolescent Psychiatry, 33,* 328–332.

Rickels, K., Schweizer, E., Case, W. G., & Greenblatt, D. J. (1990). Long-term therapeutic use of benzodiazepines. I: Effects of abrupt discontinuation. *Archives of General Psychiatry, 47,* 899–907.

Riding, A. (1992, Nov. 17). New catechism for Catholics defines sins of the modern world. *New York Times,* p. A14.

Riemann, D., Hohagen, F., Konig, A., et al. (1996). Advanced vs. normal sleep timing: Effects on depressed mood after response to sleep deprivation in patients with a major depressive disorder. *Journal of Affective Disorders, 37*(2–3), 121–128.

Riggs, D. S., & Foa, E. B. (1993). Obsessive-compulsive disorder. In D. H. Barlow (Ed.), *Clinical handbook of psychological disorders: A step-by-step treatment manual* (2nd ed.) (pp. 189–239). New York: Guilford Press.

Riley, A. J., & Riley, E. J. (1998). Psychological and behavioral aspects of intercavernosal injection therapy for erectile disorder. *Sexual and Marital Therapy, 13,* 273–284.

Rimm, S. (1986). *Underachievement syndrome: Causes and cures.* Watertown, WI: Apple.

Rispens, J., Aldeman, A., & Goudena, P. P. (1997). Prevention of child sexual abuse victimization: A meta analysis of school programs. *Child Abuse and Neglect, 21,* 975–987.

Ritchie, E. C. (1992). Treatment of gas mask phobia. *Military Medicine, 157*(2), 104–106.

Rivara, F. P., Mueller, B. A., Somes G., et al. (1997). Alcohol and illicit drug abuse and the risk of violent death in the home. *Journal of the American Medical Association, 278*(7), 569–575.

Rivera-Tovar, A. D., Pilkonis, P., & Frank, E. (1992). Symptom patterns in the late luteal-phase dysphoric disorder. *Journal of Psychopathology and Behavioral Assessment, 14,* 189–199.

Robbins, W. (1986, Feb. 11). 3rd suicide stuns students in Omaha. *New York Times,* p. A14.

Roberts, G. A. (1991). Delusional belief and meaning in life: A preferred reality? *British Journal of Psychiatry, 159,* 20–29.

Robin, A. L., Gilroy, M., & Dennis, A. B. (1998). Treatment of eating disorders in children and adolescents. *Clinical Psychology Review, 18,* 421–446.

Robins, C. J. (1990). Congruence of personality and life events in depression. *Journal of Abnormal Psychology, 99*(4), 393–397.

Robins, C. J., & Luten, A. G. (1991). Sociotropy and autonomy: Differential patterns of clinical presentation in unipolar depression. *Journal of Abnormal Psychology, 100,* 74–77.

Robins, L. N. (1966). *Deviant children grow up: A sociological and psychiatric study of sociopathic personality.* Baltimore: Williams & Wilkins.

Robins, L. N., Helzer, J. E., Weissman, M. M., et al. (1984). Lifetime prevalence of specific psychiatric disorders in three sites. *Archives of General Psychiatry, 41,* 949–958.

Robinson, L. A., Berman, J. S., & Neimeyer, R. A. (1990). Psychotherapy for the treatment of depression: A comprehensive review of controlled outcome research. *Psychological Bulletin, 108,* 30–49.

Robinson, P., Katon, W., Von-Korff, M., et al. (1997). The education of depressed primary care patients: What do patients think of interactive booklets and a video? *Journal of Family Practice, 44,* 562–571.

Robinson, S., & Birchwood, M. (1991). The relationship between catastrophic cognitions and the components of panic disorder. *Journal of Cognitive Psychotherapy: An International Quarterly, 5,* 175–186.

Rochefort, D. A. (1993). *From poorhouses to homelessness.* Westport, CT: Auburn House.

Rodin, G., & Izenberg, S. (1997). Treating the narcissistic personality disorder. In M. Rosenbluth & I. D. Yalom (Eds.), *Treating difficult personality disorders: The Jossey-Bass library of current clinical technique* (pp. 107–122). San Francisco: Jossey-Bass.

Rodin, J. (1986). Aging and health: Effects of the sense of control. *Science, 233,* 1271–1276.

Rodin, J., & Salovey, P. (1989). Health psychology. *Annual Review of Psychology, 40,* 533–579.

Roebuck, K. (1997, Aug. 11). Defense rejected in adopted boy's death. *U.S. News & World Report,* p. 123.

Roeleveld, N., Zielhuis, G. A., & Gabreels, F. (1997). The prevalence of mental retardation: A critical review of the recent literature. *Developmental Medicine and Child Neurology, 39,* 125–132.

Roesler, A., & Witzum, E. (1998). Treatment of men with paraphilia with a long-acting analogue of gonadotropin-releasing hormone. *New England Journal of Medicine, 338,* 416–422.

Rogers, C. R. (1951). *Client-centered therapy: Its current practice, implications and theory.* London: Constable.

Rogers, C. R. (1967). *On becoming a person: A therapist's view of psychotherapy.* London: Constable.

Rogers, C. R., & Dymond, R. F. (Eds.). (1954). *Psychotherapy and personality change: Coordinated research studies in the client centered approach.* Chicago: University of Chicago Press.

Rogers, J. R. (1990). Female suicide: The trend toward increased lethality in method of choice and its implications. *Journal of Counseling and Development, 69,* 37–41.

Rogers, J. R. (1992). Suicide and alcohol: Conceptualizing the relationship from a cognitive-social paradigm. *Journal of Counseling and Development, 70*(4), 540–543.

Rogers, M. P., Weinshenker, N. J., Warshaw, M. G., et al. (1996). Prevalence of somatoform disorders in a large sample of patients with anxiety disorders. *Psychosomatics, 37*(1), 17–22.

Rogers, N. B., Hawkins, B. A., & Eklund, S. J. (1998). The nature of leisure in the lives of older adults with intellectual disability. *Journal of Intellectual Disability Research, 42,* 122–130.

Rogers, R., Johansen, J., Chang, J. J., & Salekin, R. T. (1997). Predictors of adolescent psychopathy: Oppositional and conduct-disordered symptoms. *Journal of the American Academy of Psychiatry and the Law, 25,* 261–271.

Rohde, P., Lewinsohn, P. M., & Seeley, J. R. (1990). Are people changed by the experience of having an episode of depression? A further test of the scar hypothesis. *Journal of Abnormal Psychology, 99,* 264–271.

Roitman, S. E. L., Cornblatt, B. A., Bergman, A., et al. (1997). Attentional functioning in schizotypal personality disorder. *American Journal of Psychiatry, 154,* 655–660.

Roitt, I. M. (1994). *Essential immunology* (8th ed.). Oxford: Blackwell Scientific.

Roizen, N. J. (1997). Down syndrome. In M. L. Batshaw (Ed.), *Children with disabilities* (4th ed.) (pp. 361–376). Baltimore: Brookes.

Romieu, I., Carreon, T., Lopez, L., et al. (1995). Environmental urban lead exposure and blood lead levels in children of Mexico City. *Environmental Health Perspectives, 103*(11), 1036–1040.

Ronningstam, E. F. (1998). Narcissistic personality disorder and pathological narcissism: Long-term stability and presence in Axis I disorders. In E. F. Ronningstam (Ed.), *Disorders of narcissism: Diagnostic, clinical, and empirical implications* (pp. 375–413). Washington, DC: American Psychiatric Press.

Room, R. (1996). Gender roles and interactions in drinking and drug use. *Journal of Substance Abuse, 8*(2), 227–239.

Rorschach, H. (1921). *Psychodiagnostics.* (P. Lemkau & B. Kroneberg, Trans.). New York: Grune & Stratton.

Rosal, M. C., Ockene, J. K., Barrett, S. V., et al. (1997). A longitudinal study of students' depression at one medical school. *Academic Medicine, 72,* 542–546.

Rose, R. J. (1995). Genes and human behavior. *Annual Review of Psychology, 46,* 625–654.

Rosen, G. (1969). *Madness in society.* Chicago: University of Chicago Press.

Rosen, J. C., & Ramirez, E. (1998). A comparison of eating disorders and body dysmorphic disorder on body image and psychological adjustment. *Journal of Psychosomatic Research, 44,* 441–449.

Rosen, K. V., & Tallis, F. (1995). Investigation into the relationship between personality traits and OCD. *Behaviour Research and Therapy, 33*(4), 445–450.

Rosen, L. N., Targum, S. D., Terman, M., et al. (1990). Prevalence of seasonal affective disorder at four latitudes. *Psychiatry Research, 31,* 131–144.

Rosen, R. C., & Leiblum, S. R. (1995). Hypoactive sexual desire. *Psychiatric Clinics of North America, 18,* 107–121.

Rosenbaum, J. F., & Zajecka, J. (1997). Clinical management of antidepressant discontinuation. *Journal of Clinical Psychiatry, 58*(Suppl. 7), 37–40.

Rosenbaum, M. (1980). The role of the term *schizophrenia* in the decline of the diagnosis of multiple personality. *Archives of General Psychiatry, 37,* 1383–1385.

Rosenbaum, M. (1990). The role of depression in couples involved in murder-suicide and homicide. *American Journal of Psychiatry, 147,* 1036–1039.

Rosenberg, H. (1993). Prediction of controlled drinking by alcoholics and problem drinkers. *Psychological Bulletin, 113,* 129–139.

Rosenberger, P. B., Wheeldeen, J. A., & Kalotkin, M. (1976). The effect of haloperidol on stuttering. *American Journal of Psychiatry, 133,* 331–334.

Rosenbluth, M., & Yalom, I. D. (Eds.). (1997). *Treating difficult personality disorders.* San Francisco: Jossey-Bass.

Rosenhan, D. L. (1973). On being sane in insane places. *Science, 179,* 250–258.

Rosenheck, R., Cramer, J., Xu, W., et al. (1997). A comparison of clozapine and haloperidol in hospitalized patients with refractory schizophrenia. Department of Veterans Affairs Cooperative Study Group on Clozapine in Refractory Schizophrenia. *New England Journal of Medicine, 337*(12), 809–815.

Rosenman, R. H. (1986). Current and past history of type A behavior pattern. In T. H. Schmidt, T. M. Dembroski, & C. Blumchen (Eds.), *Biological and psychological factors in cardiovascular disease* (pp. 15–40). New York: Springer-Verlag.

Rosenman, R. H., Brand, R. J., Jenkins, C. D., et al. (1975). Coronary heart disease in the Western Collaborative Group study: Final follow-up of 8 1/2 years. *Journal of the American Medical Association, 233,* 872–877.

Rosenthal, D. (1963). *The Genain quadruplets: A case study and theoretical analysis of heredity and environment in schizophrenia.* New York: Basic Books.

Rosenthal, N. E., & Blehar, M. C. (Eds.). (1989). *Seasonal affective disorders and psychotherapy.* New York: Guilford Press.

Rosenthal, R., & Jacobson, L. (1968). *Pygmalion in the classroom.* New York: Holt, Rinehart & Winston.

Ross, C. A. (1989). *Multiple personality disorder: Diagnosis, clinical features and treatment.* New York: Wiley.

Ross, C. A. (1991). Epidemiology of multiple personality disorder and dissociation. *Psychiatric Clinics of America, 14,* 503–517.

Ross, C. A., Anderson, G., Fleischer, W. P., & Norton, G. R. (1991). The frequency of multiple personality disorder among psychiatric inpatients. *American Journal of Psychiatry, 148,* 1717–1720.

Ross, C. A., Miller, S. D., Reagor, P., et al. (1990). Structured interview data on 102 cases of multiple personality from four centers. *American Journal of Psychiatry, 147*(5), 596–601.

Ross, C. A., & Norton, G. R. (1989). Differences between men and women with multiple personality disorder. *Hospital and Community Psychiatry, 40,* 186–188.

Ross, C. A., Norton, G. R., & Wozney, K. (1989). Multiple personality disorder: An analysis of 236 cases. *Canadian Journal of Psychiatry, 304,* 413–418.

Ross, E. B. (1997). *A ray of hope for those left behind.* New York: Plenum.

Ross, K., & Handy, J. A. (1997). Family perceptions of anorexia nervosa: A qualitative study of two families' histories. In G. M. Habermann (Ed.), *Looking back and moving forward: 50 years of New Zealand psychology* (pp. 232–239). Wellington, NZ: New Zealand Psychological Society.

Rost, K. M., Atkins, R. N., Brown, F. W., & Smith, G. R. (1992). The comorbidity of *DSM-III-R* personality disorders in somatization disorder. *General Hospital Psychiatry, 14,* 322–326.

Rotter, J. B., & Rafferty, J. E. (1950). *Manual for the Rotter Incomplete Sentences Blank: College form.* New York: Psychological Corporation.

Rounsaville, B., Kranzler, H. R., Ball, S., et al. (1998). Personality disorders in substance abusers: Relation to substance use. *Journal of Nervous and Mental Disease, 186,* 87–95.

Rowan, E. L. (1988). Pedophilia. *Journal of Social Work and Human Sexuality, 7,* 91–100.

Rowland, D. L., & Slob, A. K. (1997). Premature ejaculation: Psychophysiological considerations in theory, research, and treatment. *Annual Review of Sex Research, 8,* 224–253.

Roy, A., & Draper, R. (1995). Suicide among psychiatric hospital in-patients. *Psychological Medicine, 25*(1), 199–202.

Roy, A., Karoum, F., & Pollack, S. (1992). Marked reduction in indexes of dopamine metabolism among patients with depression who attempted suicide. *Archives of General Psychiatry, 49,* 447–450.

Roy, A., Rylander, G., & Sarchiapone, M. (1997). Genetics of suicide: Family studies and molecular genetics. In D. M. Stoff & J. J. Mann (Eds.), *The neurobiology of suicide: From the bench to the clinic. An-*

nals of the New York Academy of Sciences, 836, 135–157. New York: New York Academy of Sciences.

Roy, A., Segal, N. L., Centerwall, B. S., & Robinette, D. (1991). Suicide in twins. Archives of General Psychiatry, 48, 29–32.

Roy, A., Segal, N. L., & Sarchiapone, M. (1995). Attempted suicide among living co-twins of twin suicide victims. American Journal of Psychiatry, 152(7), 1075–1076.

Rubin, R. R., & Peyrot, M. (1992). Psychosocial problems and interventions in diabetes: A review of the literature. Diabetes Care, 15(11), 1640–1657.

Rudolph, K. D., Hammen, C., & Burge, D. (1997). A cognitive-interpersonal approach to depressive symptoms in preadolescent children. Journal of Abnormal Child Psychology, 25, 33–45.

Rund, B. R., Oie, M., & Sundet, K. (1996). Backward-masking deficit in adolescents with schizophrenic disorders or attention deficit hyperactivity disorder. American Journal of Psychiatry, 153(9), 1154–1157.

Rush, A. J. (1993). Mood disorders in DSM-IV. In D. L. Dunner (Ed.), Current psychiatric therapy (pp. 189–195). Philadelphia: Saunders.

Rush, A. J., Beck, A. T., Kovacs, M., & Hollon, S. D. (1977). Comparative efficacy of cognitive therapy and pharmacotherapy in the treatment of depressed outpatients. Cognitive Therapy and Research, 1, 17–38.

Rush, A. J., & Weissenburger, J. E. (1994). Melancholic symptom features and DSM-IV. American Journal of Psychiatry, 151(4), 489–498.

Russell, D. E. H. (1998). Dangerous relationships: Pornography, misogyny, and rape. Thousand Oaks, CA: Sage.

Russell, J. (Ed.). (1998). Autism as an executive disorder. Oxford: Oxford University Press.

Rutter, D., Quine, L., & Chesham, D. J. (1993). Social psychological approaches to health. New York: Harvester.

Rutter, M. (1996). Introduction: Concepts of antisocial behavior, of cause, and of genetic influences. Ciba Foundation Symposium, 194, 1–15.

Ryan, C., & Morrow, L. (1986). Self-esteem in diabetic adolescents: Relationship between age at onset and gender. Journal of Consulting and Clinical Psychology, 54, 730–731.

Ryan, J. J., & Lewis, C. V. (1988). Comparison of normal controls and recently detoxified alcoholics on the Wechsler Memory Scale–Revised. Clinical Neuropsychologist, 2, 173–180.

Ryan, W. D. (1992). The pharmacologic treatment of child and adolescent depression. Psychiatric Clinics of North America 15, 29–40.

Ryland, D. H., & Kruesi, M. J. P. (1992). Suicide among adolescents. International Review of Psychiatry, 4, 117–129.

Sable, P. (1997). Attachment, detachment and borderline personality disorder. Psychotherapy, 34, 171–181.

Saccomani, L., Savoini, M., Cirrincione, M., et al. (1998). Long-term outcome of children and adolescents with anorexia nervosa: Study of comorbidity. Journal of Psychosomatic Research, 44, 565–571.

Sachdev, P., & Hay, P. (1995). Does neurosurgery for obsessive-compulsive disorder produce personality change? Journal of Nervous and Mental Disease, 183(6), 408–413.

Sacks, O. W. (1998). The man who mistook his wife for a hat: And other clinical tales. New York: Touchstone Books.

Sadovnick, A. D., Remick, R. A., Lam, R., et al. (1994). Mood Disorder Service genetic database: Morbidity risks for mood disorders in 3,942 first-degree relatives of 671 index cases with single depression, recurrent depression, bipolar I, or bipolar II. American Journal of Medical Genetics, 54(2), 132–140.

Sadowski, C., & Kelley, M. L. (1994). Social problem solving in suicidal adolescents. Journal of Consulting and Clinical Psychology, 61, 121–127.

Safer, D. J., Zito, J. M., & Fine, E. M. (1996). Increased methylphenidate usage for attention deficit disorder in the 1990s. Pediatrics, 98, 1084–1088.

Salama, A. A. (1988). The antisocial personality (the sociopathic personality). Psychiatric Journal of the University of Ottawa, 13, 149–153.

Sales, G. N. (1993). The health care proxy for mental illness: Can it work and should we want it to? Bulletin of the American Academy of Psychiatry and the Law, 21(2), 161–179.

Salkovskis, P. M., & Warwick, H. M. C. (1988). Morbid preoccupations, health anxiety, and reassurance: A cognitive behavioral approach to hypochondriasis. Behaviour Research and Therapy, 24, 597–602.

Salmon, E., Degueldre C., Franco, G., et al. (1996). Frontal lobe dementia presenting as personality disorder. Acta Neurologica Belgica, 96, 130–134.

Salmon, P., & Calderbank, S. (1996). The relationship of childhood physical and sexual abuse to adult illness and behavior. Journal of Psychosomatic Research, 40(3), 329–336.

Salzman, C., Wolfson, A. N., Schatzberg, A., et al. (1995). Effect of fluoxetine on anger in symptomatic volunteers with border-line personality disorder. Journal of Clinical Psychopharmacology, 15, 23–29.

SAMHSA. See Substance Abuse and Mental Health Services Administration.

Samuels, C. A., & Benning, V. (1999, May 14). Prince William County proposes ban on coats in class. Washington Post, p. B6.

Sanders, B., & Giolas, M. H. (1991). Dissociation and childhood trauma in psychologically disturbed adolescents. American Journal of Psychiatry, 148, 50–54.

Sanderson, W. C., Rapee, R. M., & Barlow, D. H. (1989). The influence of an illusion of control on panic attacks induced via inhalation of 5.5% carbon dioxide–enriched air. Archives of General Psychiatry, 46, 157–162.

Sapir, E. (1929). The status of linguistics as a science. Language, 5, 207–214.

Sapolsky, R. (1992). Stress, the aging brain, and the mechanisms of neuron death. Cambridge, MA: MIT Press.

Sapolsky, R. (1998). Why zebras don't get ulcers: An updated guide to stress, stress-related diseases and coping. New York: Freeman.

Sarasalo, E., Bergman, B., & Toth, J. (1996). Personality traits and psychiatric and somatic morbidity among kleptomaniacs. Acta Psychiatrica Scandinavica, 94, 358–364.

Sarason, I. G. (1984). Stress, anxiety, and cognitive interference: Reactions to tests. Journal of Personality and Social Psychology, 46, 929–938.

Sarason, I. G. (1991). Anxiety, self-preoccupation and attention. In R. Schwarzer & R. A. Wicklund (Eds.), Anxiety and self-focused attention (pp. 9–14). London: Harwood Academic.

Sarason, I. G. (Ed.). (1980). Test anxiety: Theory, research and applications. Hillsdale, NJ: Erlbaum.

Sarason, S. B. (1949). Psychological problems in mental deficiency. New York: Harper.

Sarbin, T. R., & Mancuso, J. C. (1980). Schizophrenia: Medical diagnosis or moral verdict? Elmsford, NY: Pergamon.

Sarton, G. A. L. (1954). Galen of Pergamon. Lawrence: University of Kansas Press.

Sartorius, N. (1997). Fighting schizophrenia and its stigma: A new World Psychiatric Association educational programme [Editorial]. British Journal of Psychiatry, 170, 297.

Sartorius, N., Davidian, H., Ernberg, G., et al. (1983). Depressive disorders in different cultures: Report on the WHO collaborative study on standardized assessment of depressive disorders. Geneva: World Health Organization.

Sartorius, N., Jablensky, A., Korten, A., et al. (1986). Early manifestations and first-contact incidence of schizophrenia in different cultures: A preliminary report on the initial evaluation phase of the WHO Collaborative Study on Determinants of Outcome of Severe Mental Disorders. *Psychological Medicine, 16*, 909–928.

Sarwer, D. B., & Durlak, J. A. (1997). A field trial of the effectiveness of behavioral treatment for sexual dysfunctions. *Journal of Sex and Marital Therapy, 23*, 87–97.

Sattler, J. M. (1992). *Assessment of children* (3rd ed.). San Diego: Author.

Saulnier, C. F. (1996). Sex addiction: A problematic concept. *Journal of Applied Social Sciences, 20*, 159–168.

Savage, C. R. (1997). Neuropsychology of subcortical dementias. *Psychiatric Clinics of North America, 20*, 911–931.

Saxe, L., Dougherty, D., & Cross, T. (1985). The validity of polygraph testing: Scientific analysis and public controversy. *American Psychologist, 40*, 355–366.

Sayette, M. A. (1993). An appraisal-disruption model of alcohol's effects on stress responses in social drinkers. *Psychological Bulletin, 114*(3), 459–476.

Schachter, S. (1980). Urinary pH and the psychology of nicotine addiction. In P. O. Davidson & S. M. Davidson (Eds.), *Behavioral medicine: Changing health lifestyles* (pp. 70–93). New York: Brunner/Mazel.

Schacter, S., & Singer, J. E. (1962). Cognitive, social, and physiological determinants of emotional state. *Psychological Review, 69*, 379–399.

Schaffer, H. R., & Emerson, P. (1964). The development of social attachments in infancy. *Monographs of the Society for Research in Child Development, 29* (3, whole no. 94).

Scheff, T. J. (1966). *Being mentally ill: A sociological theory.* London: Weidenfield & Nicolson.

Scheff, T. J. (Ed.). (1975). *Labelling madness.* Englewood Cliffs, NJ: Prentice-Hall.

Scheflin, A. W., & Brown, D. (1996). Repressed memory or dissociative amnesia: What science says. *Journal of Psychiatry and Law, 24*(2), 143–188.

Scheltens, P., & van Gool, W. A. (1997). Emerging treatments in dementia. *European Neurology, 38*, 184–189.

Schewe, P. A. (1997). Paraphilia not otherwise specified: Assessment and treatment. In D. R. Laws & W. T. O'Donohue (Eds.), *Sexual deviance: Theory, assessment, and treatment* (pp. 424–433). New York: Guilford Press.

Schickedanz, J. A., Schickedanz, D. I, Forsyth, P. D., & G. A. Forsyth (1993). *Understanding children and adolescents* (3rd ed.). Needham Heights, MA: Allyn and Bacon.

Schildkraut, J. J. (1965). The catecholamine hypothesis of affective disorders: A re-

view of supporting evidence. *American Journal of Psychiatry, 122*, 509–522.

Schildkraut, J. J., Hirshfeld, A. J., & Murphy, J. M. (1994). Mind and mood in modern art. II: Depressive disorders, spirituality, and early deaths in the abstract expressionist artists of the New York School. *American Journal of Psychiatry, 151*, 482–488.

Schlager, D. S. (1994). Early-morning administration of short-acting β blockers for treatment of winter depression. 5th Annual Meeting on Light Treatment and Biological Rhythms (1993, San Diego, CA). *American Journal of Psychiatry, 151* (9), 1383–1385.

Schleifer, S. J., Keller, S. E., Bartlett, J. A., et al. (1996). Immunity in young adults with major depressive disorder. *American Journal of Psychiatry, 153*(4), 477–482.

Schlosser, S., Black, D. W., Blum, N., & Goldstein, R. B. (1994). The demography, phenomenology, and family history of 22 persons with compulsive hair pulling. *Annals of Clinical Psychiatry, 6*, 147–152.

Schmidt, L. R., Schwenkmezger, P., & Dlugosch, G. E. (1990). The scope of health psychology. In L .R. Schmidt, P. Schwenkmezger, J. Weinman, & S. Maes (Eds.), *Theoretical and applied aspects of health psychology* (pp. 3–28). London: Harwood Academic.

Schmidt, U., Tiller, J., Blanchard, M., et al. (1997). Is there a specific trauma precipitating anorexia nervosa? *Psychological Medicine, 27*, 523–530.

Schmoll, H. J., Tewes, U., & Plotnikoff, N. P. (Eds.). (1992). *Psychoneuroimmunology.* Lewiston, NY: Hogrefe & Huber.

Schneider, J. P. (1994). Sex addiction: Controversy within mainstream addiction medicine, diagnosis based on the *DSM-III-R*, and physician case histories. *Sexual Addiction and Compulsivity, 1*, 19–44.

Schneider, J. P., & Irons, R. (1996). Differential diagnosis of addictive sexual disorders using the *DSM-IV. Sexual Addiction and Compulsivity, 3*, 7–21.

Schneider, K. (1959). *Clinical psychopathology.* New York: Grune & Stratton.

Schneier, F. R., Johnson, J., Hornig, C. D., et al. (1992). Social phobia: Comorbidity and morbidity in an epidemiologic sample. *Archives of General Psychiatry, 49*, 282–288.

Schooler, N. R. (1993). Antipsychotic medications and schizophrenia: Effects in acute and maintenance treatment of the illness. In R. L. Cromwell & C. R. Snyder (Eds.), *Schizophrenia: Origins, processes, treatment, and outcome* (pp. 284–295). New York: Oxford University Press.

Schooling, A., & Emmelkamp, P. M. (1993). Cognitive and behavioural treatments of fear of blushing, sweating and trem-

bling. *Behaviour Research and Therapy, 31*, 155–170.

Schopler, E., Mesibov, G. B., & Kunce, L. J. (Eds.). (1998). *Asperger syndrome or high-functioning autism?* New York: Plenum.

Schorling, J. B., & Buchsbaum, D. (1997). Screening for alcohol abuse. *Medical Clinics of North America, 81*(4), 845–865.

Schreiber, F. R. (1975). *Sybil.* Ringwood, Victoria, Australia: Penguin Books.

Schreiber, H., Stolz-Born, G., Born, J., et al. (1997). Visually-guided saccadic eye movements in adolescents at genetic risk for schizophrenia. *Schizophrenia Research, 25*(2), 97–109.

Schroeder, S. R. (Ed.). (1987). *Toxic substances and mental retardation: Neurobehavioral toxicology and teratology.* Washington, DC: American Association on Mental Deficiency.

Schuckit, M. A. (1996). Recent developments in the pharmacotherapy of alcohol dependence. *Journal of Consulting and Clinical Psychology, 64*(4), 669–676.

Schuckit, M. A., & Smith, T. L. (1996). An 8-year follow-up of 450 sons of alcoholic and control subjects. *Archives of General Psychiatry, 53*(3), 202–210.

Schuckit, M. A., Smith, T. L., Anthenelli, R., & Irwin, M. (1993). Clinical course of alcoholism in 636 male inpatients. *American Journal of Psychiatry, 150*(5), 786–792.

Schulman, P., Keith, D., & Seligman, M. E. P. (1993). Is optimism heritable? A study of twins. *Behaviour Research and Therapy, 31*, 569–574.

Schupf, N., Kapell, D., Nightingale, B., et al. (1998). Earlier onset of Alzheimer's disease in men with Down syndrome. *Neurology, 50*, 991–995.

Schutz, C. G., Chilcoat, H. D., & Anthony, J. C. (1994). The association between sniffing inhalants and injecting drugs. *Comprehensive Psychiatry, 35*(2), 99–105.

Schwab, S. G., Eckstein, G. N., Hallmayer, J., et al. (1997). Evidence suggestive of a locus on chromosome 5q31 contributing to susceptibility for schizophrenia in German and Israeli families by multipoint affected sib-pair linkage analysis. *Molecular Psychiatry, 2*(2), 156–160.

Schwartz, J. L. (1987). *Review and evaluation of smoking cessation methods, the United States and Canada, 1978–1985* (NIH Publication No. 87–2940). Washington, DC: U.S. Government Printing Office.

Schwartz, J. M., Stoessel, P. W., Baxter, L. R., et al. (1996). Systematic changes in cerebral glucose metabolic rate after successful behavior modification treatment of obsessive-compulsive disorder. *Archives of General Psychiatry, 53*(2), 109–113.

Schwartz, S. (1981). Language disabilities in infantile autism: A brief review and comment. *Applied Psycholinguistics, 7*, 25–31.

Schwartz, S. (1982). Is there a schizophrenic language? *Behavioral and Brain Sciences, 5*(4), 579–626.

Schwartz, S. (1986). *Classic studies in psychology.* Mountain View, CA: Mayfield.

Schwartz, S. (1991). Clinical decision making. In P. R. Martin (Ed.), *Handbook of behavior therapy and psychological sciences: An integrative approach* (pp. 196–215). New York: Pergamon.

Schwartz, S. (1993). *Classic studies in abnormal psychology.* Mountain View, CA: Mayfield.

Schwartz, S. (1994). Applications of heuristics and biases in the judgement of physicians. In L. Heath, et al. (Eds.), *Applications of heuristics and biases to social issues.* New York: Plenum.

Schwartz, S., & Griffin, T. (1986). *Medical thinking: The psychology of medical judgment and decision making.* New York: Springer-Verlag.

Schwartz, S., Griffin, T., & Fox, J. (1989). Clinical expert systems versus linear models: Do we really have to choose? *Behavioral Science, 34,* 305–311.

Schwartz, S., & Johnson, J. H. (1985). *Psychopathology of childhood* (2nd ed.). Elmsford, NY: Pergamon.

Schwartz, S., Richardson, J., & Glasziou, P. P. (1993). Quality-adjusted life years: Origins, measurements, applications, objections. *Australian Journal of Public Health, 17*(3), 272–278.

Schwarz, J. R. (1981). *The Hillside strangler: A murderer's mind.* New York: New American Library.

Schwarz, K., Harding, R., Harrington, D., & Farr, B. (1993). Hospital management of a patient with intractable factitious disorder. *Psychosomatics, 34,* 265–267.

Schwarzer, R., & Wicklund, R. A. (Eds.). (1991). *Anxiety and self-focused attention.* London: Harwood Academic.

Schweizer, E., Patterson, W., Rickels, K., & Rosenthal, M. (1993). Double-blind placebo-controlled study of a once-a-day, sustained-release preparation of alprazolam for the treatment of panic disorder. *American Journal of Psychiatry, 150,* 1210–1215.

Schweizer, E., Rickels, K., Case, G., & Greenblatt, D. J. (1990). Long-term therapeutic use of benzodiazepines: Effects of gradual taper. *Archives of General Psychiatry, 47*(10), 908–915.

Scott, D. M., Wagner, J. C., & Barlow, T. W. (1996). Anabolic steroid use among adolescents in Nebraska schools. *American Journal of Health-System Pharmacy, 53*(17), 2068–2072.

Scott, M. L., Golden, C. J., Ruedrich, S. L., & Bishop, R. J. (1983). Ventricular enlargement in major depression. *Psychiatry Research, 8*(2), 91–93.

Scull, A. (1979). *Museums of madness: The social organization of insanity in nineteenth century England.* London: Allen Lane.

Scull, A. (1989). *Social order/mental disorder: Anglo-American psychiatry in historical perspective.* Berkeley: University of California Press.

Seal, B. C., & Bonvillian, J. D. (1997). Sign language and motor functioning in students with autistic disorder. *Journal of Autism and Developmental Disorders, 27,* 437–466.

Sechenov, I. M. (1863). Reflexes of the brain. In I. V. Sechenov (Ed.), *Selected works* (pp. 263–336). Moscow: Moscow State Publishing House for Biological and Medical Literature.

Segal, Z. V., Shaw, B. F., Vella, D. D., & Katz, R. (1992). Cognitive and life stress predictors of relapse in remitted unipolar depressed patients: Test of the congruency hypothesis. *Journal of Abnormal Psychology, 101,* 26–37.

Segraves, R. T., & Segraves, K. B. (1998). Pharmacotherapy for sexual disorders: Advantages and pitfalls. *Sexual and Marital Therapy, 13,* 295–309.

Seifert, C. D. (1990). *Theories of autism.* Lanham, MD: University Press of America.

Seligman, M. E. P. (1975). *Helplessness: On depression, development and death.* San Francisco: W. H. Freeman.

Seligman, M. E. P. (1995). The effectiveness of psychotherapy: The *Consumer Reports* study. *American Psychologist, 50*(12), 965–974.

Selikowitz, M. (1997). *Down syndrome: The facts* (2nd ed.). Oxford: Oxford University Press.

Selling, L. S. (1940). *Men against madness.* New York: Greenberg.

Selye, H. (1950). *The physiology and pathology of exposure to stress: A treatise on the concept of the general adaptation syndrome and the diseases of adaptation.* Montreal: Acta.

Selye, H. (1976). *Stress in health and disease.* Woburn, MA: Butterworth.

Shaffer, J. W., Graves, P. L., Swank, R. T., & Pearson, T. A. (1987). Clustering of personality traits in youth and the subsequent development of cancer among physicians. *Journal of Behavioral Medicine, 10,* 441–447.

Shafran, R., Booth, R., & Rachman, S. (1993). The reduction of claustrophobia. II: Cognitive analysis. *Behaviour Research and Therapy, 31,* 75–85.

Shahidi, S., & Salmon, P. (1992). Contingent and noncontingent biofeedback training for type A and B healthy adults: Can type A's relax by competing? *Journal of Psychosomatic Research, 36,* 477–483.

Shajahan, P. M., O'Carroll, R. E., Glabus, M. F., et al. (1997). Correlation of auditory 'oddball' P300 with verbal memory deficits in schizophrenia. *Psychological Medicine, 27*(3), 579–586.

Shalev, A. Y., Orr, S. P., Peri, T., et al. (1992). Physiologic responses to loud tones in Israeli patients with posttraumatic stress disorder. *Archives of General Psychiatry, 49*(11), 870–875.

Shantz, C. U., & Hartup, W. W. (Eds.). (1992). *Conflict in child and adolescent development.* Cambridge, UK: Cambridge University Press.

Shao, W. A., Williams, J. W., Jr., Lee, S., et al. (1997). Knowledge and attitudes about depression among non-generalists and generalists. *Journal of Family Practice, 44,* 161–168.

Shapiro, A. K., Shapiro, E. S., Bruun, R. D., & Sweet, R. D. (Eds.). (1978). *Gilles de la Tourette syndrome.* New York: Raven Press.

Shapiro, A. K., Shapiro, E. S., Young, J. G., & Feinberg, T. E. (1998). *Gilles de la Tourette syndrome* (2nd ed.). New York: Lippincott-Raven.

Shapiro, J. P. (1991). Interviewing people about psychological issues associated with sexual abuse. *Psychotherapy, 28,* 55–65.

Shapiro, L., Rosenberg, D., Lauerman, J. F., & Sparkman, R. (1993, April 19). Rush to judgment. *Newsweek,* pp. 54–60.

Sharif, Z., Gewirtz, G., & Iqbal, N. (1993). Brain imaging in schizophrenia: A review. *Psychiatric Annals, 23,* 123–134.

Sharma, S., & Sud, A. (1990). Examination stress and test anxiety: A cross-cultural perspective. *Psychology and Developing Societies, 2,* 183–201.

Shaw, D. S., & Winslow, E. B. (1997). Precursors and correlates of antisocial behavior from infancy to preschool. In D. M. Stoff, J. Breiling, & J. D. Maser (Eds.), *Handbook of antisocial behavior* (pp. 148–158). New York: Wiley.

Shaw, W., Rimland, B., Semon, B., & Lewis, L. (1998). *Biological treatments for autism and PDD.* Toronto: Sunflower.

Shear, M., Cooper, A. M., Klerman, G. L., et al. (1993). A psychodynamic model of panic disorder. *American Journal of Psychiatry, 150,* 859–866.

Sheehan, P. W., Grigg, L., & McCann, T. (1984). Memory following exposure to false information in hypnosis. *Journal of Abnormal Psychology, 93,* 259–265.

Sheikh, J. I. (1992). Anxiety and its disorders in old age. In J. E. Birren, K. Sloan, & G. D. Cohen (Eds.), *Handbook of mental health and aging* (pp. 410–432). New York: Academic Press.

Shenton, M. E., Kikinis, R., Jolesz, F. A., et al. (1992). Abnormalities of the left temporal lobe and thought disorder in schizophrenia: A quantitative magnetic resonance imaging study. *New England Journal of Medicine, 327,* 604–612.

Sher, K. J., & Trull, T. J. (1996). Methodological issues in psychopathology research. *Annual Review of Psychology, 47,* 371–400.

Sherbourne, C. D., Jackson, C. A., Meredith, L. S., et al. (1996). Prevalence of comorbid anxiety disorders in primary care outpatients. *Archives of Family Medicine, 5*(1), 27–34.

Sherman, D. K., McGue, M. K., & Iacono, W. G. (1997). Twin concordance for attention deficit hyperactivity disorder: A comparison of teachers' and mothers' reports. *American Journal of Psychiatry, 154,* 532–535.

Sherman, Y. (1995). Depressive personality disorder. *Journal of Clinical Psychiatry, 56,* 266.

Shillitoe, R., & Christie, M. (1990). Psychological approaches to the management of chronic illness: The example of diabetes mellitus. In P. Bennett, J. Weinman, & P. Spurgeon (Eds.), *Current developments in health psychology* (pp. 177–208). New York: Harwood Academic.

Shneidman, E. S. (1992). What do suicides have in common? Summary of the psychological approach. In B. Bongar (Ed.), *Suicide: Guidelines for assessment, management, and treatment.* New York: Oxford University Press.

Shneidman, E. S. (1993). Suicide as psychache. *Journal of Nervous and Mental Disease, 181,* 147–149.

Shneidman, E. S. (1998). Further reflections on suicide and psychache. *Suicide and Life-Threatening Behavior, 28*(3), 245–250.

Shneidman, E. S., Farberow, N. L., & Litman, R. E. (1970). *The psychology of suicide.* New York: Jason Aronson.

Showalter, E. (1985). *The female malady.* New York: Pantheon Books.

Shuster, B. (1998, Aug. 23). Living in fear. *Los Angeles Times,* p. A1.

Shweder, R. A., & Sullivan, M. A. (1993). Cultural psychology: Who needs it? *Annual Review of Psychology, 44,* 497–523.

Siegman, A. W., & Smith, T. W. (Eds.). (1993). *Anger, hostility and the heart.* Hillsdale, NJ: Erlbaum.

Siever, L. J. (1995). Brain structure/function and the dopamine system in schizotypal personality disorder. In A. Raine & T. Lencz (Eds.), *Schizotypal personality* (pp. 272–286). New York: Cambridge University Press.

Sigerist, H. E. (1943). *Civilization and disease.* Ithaca, NY: Cornell University Press.

Sigvardsson, S., Bohman, M., & Cloninger, C. R. (1996). Replication of the Stockholm adoption study of alcoholism: Confirmatory cross-fostering analysis. *Archives of General Psychiatry, 53*(8), 681–687.

Silverman, K., Evans, S. M., Strain, E. C., & Griffiths, R. R. (1992). Withdrawal syndrome after the double-blind cessation of caffeine consumption. *New England Journal of Medicine, 327,* 1109–1114.

Silverman, K., Higgins, S. T., Brooner, R. K., & Montoya, I. D. (1996). Sustained cocaine abstinence in methadone maintenance patients through voucher-based reinforcement therapy. *Archives of General Psychiatry, 53*(5), 409–415.

Simon, B. (1978). *Mind and madness in ancient Greece.* Ithaca, NY: Cornell University Press.

Simon, H. A. (1957). *Models of man: Social and rational.* New York: Wiley.

Simonoff, E. (1998). Genetic counseling in autism and pervasive developmental disorders. *Journal of Autism and Developmental Disorders, 28,* 447–456.

Simonoff, E., Bolton, P., & Rutter, M. (1996). Mental retardation: Genetic findings, clinical implications and research agenda. *Journal of Child Psychology and Psychiatry, 37*(3), 259–280.

Simonoff, E., Bolton, P., & Rutter, M. (1998). Genetic perspectives on mental retardation. In J. A. Burack & R. M. Hodapp (Eds.), *Handbook of mental retardation and development* (pp. 41–79). New York: Cambridge University Press.

Simons, D., Goode, S., & Fombonne, E. (1997). Elective mutism and chromosome 18 abnormality. *European Child and Adolescent Psychiatry, 6,* 112–114.

Simons, R. C., & Hughes, C. C. (Eds.). (1985). *The culture-bound syndromes.* Boston: Reidel.

Simpson, R. L., & Myles, B. I. (Eds.). (1998). *Educating children with autism: Strategies for effective practice.* Austin, TX: Pro-Ed.

Sisson, J. C., Schoomaker, E. B., & Ross, J. C. (1976). Clinical decision analysis: The hazard of using additional data. *Journal of the American Medical Association, 236,* 1259–1263.

Sizemore, C. (1989). *A mind of my own.* New York: Morrow.

Skinner, B. F. (1948). "Superstition" in the pigeon. *Journal of Experimental Psychology, 38,* 168–172.

Skinner, B. F. (1971). *Beyond freedom and dignity.* New York: Knopf.

Skinner, B. F. (1976). *Walden Two.* New York: Macmillan.

Skodol, A. E., Gallaher, P. E., & Oldham, J. M. (1996). Excessive dependency and depression: Is the relationship specific? *Journal of Nervous and Mental Disease, 184,* 165–171.

Skodol, A. E., Oldham, J. M., Hyler, S. E., et al. (1995). Patterns of anxiety and personality disorder comorbidity. *Journal of Psychiatric Research, 29*(5), 361–374.

Skoog, I. (1994). Risk factors for vascular dementia: A review. *Dementia, 5,* 137–144.

Skoog, I., Nilsson, L., Palmer, B., et al. (1993). A population-based study of dementia in 85-year-olds: A reply. *New England Journal of Medicine, 328,* 153–158.

Skowron, E. A., & Friedlander, M. L. (1994). Psychological separation, self-control, and weight preoccupation among elite women athletes. *Journal of Counseling and Development, 72,* 310–315.

Slater, E., & Glithero, E. (1965). A follow-up of patients diagnosed as suffering from hysteria. *Journal of Psychosomatic Research, 9,* 9–13.

Slijper, F. M. E., Drop, S. L. S., Molenaar, J. S., et al. (1998). Long-term psychological evaluation of intersex children. *Archives of Sexual Behavior, 27,* 125–144.

Sloan, J. H., Rivara, F. P., Reay, D. T., et al. (1990). Firearm regulations and rates of suicide: A comparison of two metropolitan areas. *New England Journal of Medicine, 322,* 369–373.

Sloan, P., Arsenault, L., Hilsenroth, M., & Harvill, L. (1995). Use of the Mississippi Scale for Combat-Related PTSD in detecting war-related, non-combat stress symptomatology. *Journal of Clinical Psychology, 51*(6), 799–801.

Sloboda, J. A. (1990). Combating examination stress among university students: Action research in an institutional context. *British Journal of Guidance and Counselling, 18,* 124–136.

Small, J. C., Klapper, M. H., Milstein, V., et al. (1991). Carbamazine compared with lithium in the treatment of mania. *Archives of General Psychiatry, 48,* 915–921.

Smeets, M. A. M., Smit, F., Panhuysen, G. E. M., & Ingleby, J. D. (1998). Body perception index: Benefits, pitfalls, ideas. *Journal of Psychosomatic Research, 44,* 457–464.

Smith, B., & Surgan, B. (1996). Model mental health program serves war-weary Sarajevo. *Psychology International, 7*(4), 1–4.

Smith, D. B. (Ed.). (1990). *Epilepsy: Current approaches to diagnosis and treatment.* New York: Raven Press.

Smith, D. M., & Atkinson, R. M. (1997). Alcoholism and dementia. In A. M. Gurnack (Ed.), *Older adults' misuse of alcohol, medicines, and other drugs: Research and practice issues* (pp. 132–157). New York: Springer-Verlag.

Smith, E., North, C., & Spitznagel, E. (1993). Alcohol, drugs, and psychiatric comorbidity among homeless women: An epidemiologic study. *Journal of Clinical Psychiatry, 54*(3), 82–87.

Smith, K. L., Michael, W. B., & Hocevar, D. (1990). Performance on creativity measures with examination instructions intended to induce high or low levels of test anxiety. *Creativity Research Journal, 3,* 265–280.

Smith, N. M., Floyd, M. R., Scogin, F., et al.

(1997). Three-year follow-up of bibliotherapy for depression. *Journal of Consulting and Clinical Psychology, 65,* 324–327.

Smith, R. E., Smoll, F. L., & Barnett, N. P. (1995). Reduction of children's sport performance anxiety through social support and stress-reduction training for coaches. *Journal of Applied Developmental Psychology, 16*(1), 125–142.

Smith, R. E., & Winokur, G. (1991). Mood disorders (bipolar). In M. Hersen & D. M. Turner (Eds.), *Adult psychopathology and diagnosis.* New York: Wiley.

Smith, T., Klevstrand, M., & Lovaas, O. I. (1995). Behavioral treatment of Rett's disorder: Ineffectiveness in three cases. *American Journal on Mental Retardation, 100,* 317–322.

Smith, T., Snyder, C. R., & Perkins, S. C. (1983). Self-serving function of hypochondriacal complaints: Physical symptoms as self-handicapping strategies. *Journal of Personality and Social Psychology, 44,* 787–797.

Snaith, P. (1992). Body image disorders. *Psychotherapy and Psychosomatics, 58,* 119–124.

Snyder, S. (1991). Drugs, neurotransmitters and the brain. In P. Corsi (Ed.), *The enchanted loom: Chapters in the history of neuroscience* (pp. 299–314). New York: Oxford University Press.

Snyderman, M., & Rothman, S. (1988). *The IQ controversy: The media and public policy.* New Brunswick, NJ: Transaction Books.

Sobell, M. B., & Sobell, L. C. (1976). Second-year treatment outcome of alcoholics treated by individualized behaviour therapy: Results. *Behaviour Research and Therapy, 14*(3), 195–215.

Sobell, M. B., & Sobell, L. C. (1993). *Problem drinkers: Guided self-change treatment.* New York: Guilford Press.

Society for Neuroscience. (1998, Oct.). Brain briefings: Nicotine and the brain. Available: http://www.sfn.org/briefings/nicotine.html [Last visited 2/19/99].

Sokol, M. S., & Pfeffer, C. R. (1992). Suicidal behavior of children. In B. Bongar (Ed.), *Suicide: Guidelines for assessment, management, and treatment.* New York: Oxford University Press.

Solomon, R. L. (1980). The opponent-process theory of acquired motivation: The costs of pleasure and the benefits of pain. *American Psychologist, 35,* 691–712.

Solomon, Z., Laor, N., Weiler, D., & Muller, U. F. (1993). The psychological impact of the Gulf War: A study in acute stress in Israeli evacuees. *Archives of General Psychiatry, 50,* 320–321.

Solomon, Z., Mikulincev, M., & Flum, H. (1988). Negative life events, coping response, and combat-related psychopathology: A prospective study. *Journal of Abnormal Psychology, 97,* 302–307.

Solyom, C., & Solyom, L. (1990). A treatment program for functional paraplegia/Munchausen's syndrome. *Journal of Behavior Therapy and Experimental Psychiatry, 21,* 225–230.

Sorenson, S. B., & Rutter, C. M. (1991). Transgenerational patterns of suicide attempt. *Journal of Consulting and Clinical Psychology, 59,* 861–866.

Soutter, A. (1996). A longitudinal study of three cases of gender identity disorder of childhood successfully resolved in the school setting. *School Psychology International, 17,* 49–57.

Spanos, N. P. (1986). Hypnosis, nonvolitional responding, and multiple personality. In B. Maher & W. Maher (Eds.), *Progress in experimental personality research* (pp. 1–62). New York: Academic Press.

Spanos, N. P. (1994). Multiple identity enactments and multiple personality disorder: A sociocognitive perspective. *Psychological Bulletin, 116,* 143–165.

Spanos, N. P., Weekes, J. R., & Bertrand, L. D. (1985). Multiple personality: A social psychological perspective. *Journal of Abnormal Psychology, 94,* 362–376.

Spiegel, D. (1997). Trauma, dissociation, and memory. *Annals of the New York Academy of Sciences, 821,* 225–237.

Spiegel, D., Bloom, J. R., Kramer, H. C., & Gotheil, E. (1989). Effect of psychosocial treatment on survival of patients with metastatic breast cancer. *Lancet, 14,* 888–891.

Spiegel, R., & Irwin, P. (1996). Designing dementia treatment studies: Diagnosis, efficacy criteria and duration. *European Psychiatry, 11,* 149–154.

Spielberger, C. D. (1980). *Test anxiety manual.* Palo Alto, CA: Consulting Psychologists Press.

Spielberger, C. D. (1983). *State-Trait Anxiety Inventory: A comprehensive bibliography.* Palo Alto, CA: Consulting Psychologists Press.

Spielberger, C. D. (1984). *State-Trait Anxiety Inventory (STAI).* Palo Alto, CA: Consulting Psychologists Press.

Spiess, K., Sachs, G., Moser, G., et al. (1994). Psychological moderator variables and metabolic control in recent-onset Type 1 diabetic patients—A two-year longitudinal study. *Journal of Psychosomatic Research, 38*(3), 249–258.

Spirito, A., Overholser, J., & Hart, K. (1991). Cognitive characteristics of adolescent suicide attempters. *Journal of the American Academy of Child and Adolescent Psychiatry, 30,* 604–608.

Spitz, H. H. (1997). *Nonconscious movements: From mystical messages to facilitated communication.* Mahwah, NJ: Erlbaum.

Spitz, R. (1945). Hospitalism: An inquiry into the genesis of psychiatric conditions in early childhood. *Psychoanalytic Study of the Child, 1,* 53–74.

Spitz, R. (1946). Hospitalism: A follow-up report. *Psychoanalytic Study of the Child, 2,* 113–117.

Spitzer, R. L., Williams, J. B. W., Gibbon, M., & First, M. B. (1992). The structured clinical interview for *DSM-III-R* (SCID). *Archives of General Psychiatry, 49,* 624–629.

Spitzer, R. L., Williams, J. B. W., & Skodol, A. E. (1983). *International perspectives on DSM-III.* Washington, DC: American Psychiatric Press.

Sponheim, E., & Skjeldal, O. (1998). Autism and related disorders: Epidemiological findings in a Norwegian study using *ICD-10* diagnostic criteria. *Journal of Autism and Developmental Disorders, 28,* 217–227.

Spoont, M. R. (1992). Modulatory role of serotonin in neural information processing: Implications for human psychopathology. *Psychological Bulletin, 112,* 330–350.

Spores, J. C. (1988). *Running amok: An historical inquiry.* Athens: Ohio University Center for International Studies.

Sprauve, M. E., Lindsay, M. K., Herbert, S., & Graves, W. (1997). Adverse perinatal outcome in parturients who use crack cocaine. *Obstetrics and Gynecology, 89*(5, Pt. 1), 674–678.

Sprenger, J., & Krämer, H. (1948). *Malleus maleficarum.* (M. Summers, Trans.). London: Pushkin Press. (Original work published 1486)

Squire, L. R., & Butters, N. (Eds.). (1992). *Neuropsychology of memory.* New York: Guilford Press.

Staats, A. W., & Heiby, E. M. (1985). Paradigmatic behaviorism's theory of depression: Unified, explanatory, and heuristic. In S. Reiss & R. R. Bootzin (Eds.), *Theoretical issues in behavioral therapy* (pp. 279–330). Orlando, FL: Academic Press.

Staley, D., Wand, R., & Shady, G. (1997). Tourette disorder: A cross-cultural review. *Comprehensive Psychiatry, 38,* 6–16.

Stallings, M. C., Cherny, S. S., Young, S. E., et al. (1997). The familial aggregation of depressive symptoms, antisocial behavior, and alcohol abuse. *American Journal of Medical Genetics, 74,* 183–191.

Steadman, H., Monahan, J., Applebaum, P., et al. (1994). Designing a new generation of risk assessment research. In J. Monahan & H. Steadman (Eds.), *Violence and mental disorder: Developments in risk assessment* (pp. 297–318). Chicago: University of Chicago Press.

Steele, C. M., & Josephs, R. A. (1990). Alcohol myopia: Its prized and dangerous effects. *American Psychologist, 45*(8), 921–933.

Steen, R. G. (1996). *DNA and destiny: Nature and nurture in human behavior.* New York: Plenum.

Stein, D. J., & Hollander, E. (1997). The spectrum of obsessive-compulsive-related disorders. In D. J. Stein & M. H. Stone (Eds.), *Essential papers on obsessive-compulsive disorder.* Essential papers in psychoanalysis (pp. 373–399). New York: New York University Press.

Stein, D. J., Hollander, E., Cohen, L., et al. (1993). Neuropsychiatric impairment in impulsive personality disorders. *Psychiatry Research, 48,* 257–266.

Stein, M., Miller, A. H., & Trestman, R. L. (1991). Depression, the immune system, and health and illness. *Archives of General Psychiatry, 48,* 171–177.

Stein, M. B., Walker, J. R., & Forde, D. R. (1996). Public speaking fears in a community sample: Prevalence, impact on functioning, and diagnostic classification. *Archives of General Psychiatry, 53*(2), 169–174.

Stein, M. D., & Cyr, M. G. (1997). Women and substance abuse. *Medical Clinics of North America, 81*(4), 979–998.

Stein, S. (1987). Computer-assisted diagnosis for children and adolescents. In J. N. Butcher (Ed.), *Computerized psychological assessment: A practitioner's guide* (pp. 145–158). New York: Basic Books.

Steinberg, M., & Hall, P. (1997). The SCID-D diagnostic interview and treatment planning in dissociative disorders. *Bulletin of the Menninger Clinic, 61*(1), 108–120.

Steinberg, M. D., & Youngner, S. J. (Eds.). (1998). *End-of-life decisions: A psychosocial perspective.* Washington, DC: American Psychiatric Press.

Steinbrook, R. (1992). The polygraph test: A flawed diagnostic method. *New England Journal of Medicine, 327*(2), 122–123.

Steinfels, P. (1993, Feb. 14). Help for the helping hands in death. *New York Times, iv:* 1:1.

Steinhausen, H. C., & Adamek, R. (1997). The family history of children with elective mutism: A research report. *European Journal of Child and Adolescent Psychiatry, 6,* 107–111.

Stephenson, W. (1953). *The study of behavior: Q technique and its methodology.* Chicago: University of Chicago Press.

Stephney, R. (1980). Smoking behavior: A psychology of the cigarette habit. *British Journal of Diseases of the Chest 74*(4), 325–344.

Steptoe, A. (1991). Invited review: The links between stress and illness. *Journal of Psychosomatic Research, 35,* 633–644.

Steptoe, A., & Fidler, H. (1987). Stage fright in orchestral musicians: A study of cog-

nitive and behavioural strategies in performance anxiety. *British Journal of Psychology, 78,* 241–249.

Stern, Y., Gurland, B., Tatemichi, T. K., et al. (1994). Influence of education and occupation on the incidence of Alzheimer's disease. *Journal of the American Medical Association, 271,* 1004–1010.

Sternberg, R. J., & Davidson, J. E. (Eds.). (1986). *Conceptions of giftedness.* New York: Cambridge University Press.

Stevenson, E. K., Hudgens, R. W., Held, C. P., et al. (1972). Suicidal communication by adolescents: Study of two matched groups of 60 teenagers. *Diseases of the Nervous System, 33,* 112–122.

Stevenson, J., & Meares, R. (1992). An outcome study of psychotherapy for patients with borderline personality disorder. *American Journal of Psychiatry, 149,* 358–362.

Stevenson, R. E., Massey, P. S., Schroer, R. J., et al. (1996). Preventable fraction of mental retardation: Analysis based on individuals with severe mental retardation. *Mental Retardation, 34,* 182–188.

Stevenson, R. L. (1896). *The strange case of Doctor Jekyll and Mr. Hyde.* London: Longmans Green.

Stober, G., Franzek, E., & Beckmann, H. (1997). Maternal infectious illness and schizophrenia. *American Journal of Psychiatry, 154*(2), 292–293.

Stoff, D. M., Breiling, J., & Maser, J. D. (Eds.). (1997). *Handbook of antisocial behavior.* New York: Wiley.

Stokes, P. (1993). Fluoxetine: A five-year review. *Clinical Therapeutics, 15,* 216–243.

Stone, M. (1985). Shellshock and psychologists. In W. F. Bynum, R. Porter, & M. Shepherd (Eds.), *The anatomy of madness, Vol. 2* (pp. 242–247). London: Tavistock.

Stone, M. H. (1993). *Abnormalities of personality: Within and beyond the realm of treatment.* New York: Norton.

St. Onge, S. (1995). Systematic desensitization. In M. Ballou (Ed.), *Psychological interventions: A guide to strategies* (pp. 95–115). Westport, CT: Praeger/Greenwood.

Stopa, L., & Clark, D. M. (1993). Cognitive processes in social phobia. *Behaviour Research and Therapy, 31*(3), 255–267.

Straub, R. E., MacLean, C. J., O'Neill, F. A., et al. (1997). Support for a possible schizophrenia vulnerability locus in region 5q22-31 in Irish families. *Molecular Psychiatry, 2*(2), 148–155.

Straube, E. R. (1993). The heterogeneous prognosis of schizophrenia: Possible determinants of the short-term and 5-year outcomes. In R. L. Cromwell & C. R. Snyder (Eds.), *Schizophrenia: Origins, processes, treatment, and outcome* (pp. 258–327). New York: Oxford University Press.

Straus, M. A., & Donnelly, D. A. (1994).

Beating the devil out of them: Corporal punishment in American families. New York: Lexington Books/Macmillan.

Strauss, A. A., & Kephart, N. C. (1955). *Psychopathology and education of the brain-injured child, Vol. 2.* New York: Grune & Stratton.

Stravynski, A. (1995). Social sensitivity: A shared feature of all phobias. *British Journal of Clinical Psychology, 34*(3), 343–351.

Stravynski, A., Belisle, M., Marcouiller, M., et al. (1994). The treatment of avoidant personality disorder by social skills training in the clinic or in real-life settings. *Canadian Journal of Psychiatry 39,* 377–383.

Stray-Gundersen, K. (Ed.). (1995). *Babies with Down syndrome: A new parents' guide* (2nd ed.). Bethesda, MD: Woodbine House.

Strehlow, K. S. (1985). *The operation of fear in traditional Aboriginal society in Central Australia.* Prospect, S. Austral.: Strehlow Foundation.

Strelau, J. (1998). *Temperament: A psychological perspective.* New York: Plenum.

Streuning, J. P., & Gray, G. C. (1990). An epidemic of respiratory complaints exacerbated by psychogenic illness in a military recruit population. *American Journal of Epidemiology, 152,* 1120–1129.

Strickland, B. R. (1992). Women and depression. *Current Directions in Psychological Science, 1,* 132–135.

Stritzke, W. G. K., Lang, A. R., & Patrick, C. J. (1996). Beyond stress and arousal: A reconceptualization of alcohol-emotion relations with reference to psychophysiological methods. *Psychological Bulletin, 120*(3), 376–395.

Strober, M., Freeman, R., & Morrell, W. (1997). The long-term course of severe anorexia nervosa in adolescents: Survival analysis of recovery, relapse, and outcome predictors over 10–15 years in a prospective study. *International Journal of Eating Disorders, 22,* 339–360.

Strother, C. R. (1973). Minimal cerebral dysfunction: An historical overview. *Annals of the New York Academy of Sciences, 205,* 6–17.

Strub, R. L., & Black, F. W. (1985). *The mental status examination in neurology.* Philadelphia: Davis.

Stuss, D. T., Gow, C. A., & Hetherington, C. R. (1992). "No longer Gage": Frontal lobe dysfunction and emotional changes. *Journal of Consulting and Clinical Psychology, 60*(3), 349–359.

Substance Abuse and Mental Health Services Administration (SAMHSA). (1994). *1993 preliminary estimates from the Drug Abuse Warning Network: 1993 preliminary estimates of drug-related emergency department episodes.* (Advance Report No. 8, Dec. 1994). Rockville, MD: U.S. Department of Health and Human Services, Public Health Service.

Substance Abuse and Mental Health Services Administration (SAMHSA), Office of Applied Studies. (1995). *National household survey on drug abuse: Main findings 1992*. (Publication No. SMA 94-3012). Rockville, MD: U.S. Department of Health and Human Services, Public Health Service.

Sud, A. (1990). A comparative study of test anxiety across Indian and Italian cultures. *Psychological Studies, 35*, 69–75.

Sue, D., Sue, D., & Sue, S. (1994). *Understanding abnormal behavior* (4th ed.). Boston: Houghton Mifflin.

Sue, D. W., & Sue, D. (1990). *Counseling the culturally different: Theory and practice* (2nd ed.). New York: Wiley.

Sullivan, G., Young, A. S., & Morgenstern, H. (1997). Behaviors as risk factors for rehospitalization: Implications for predicting and preventing admissions among the seriously mentally ill. *Social Psychiatry and Psychiatric Epidemiology, 32*(4), 185–190.

Sullivan, J. T., & Sellers, E. M. (1992). Detoxification for triazolam physical dependence. *Journal of Clinical Psychopharmacology, 12*(2), 124–127.

Sullivan, P. F., Bulik, C. M., Fear, J. L., & Pickering, A. (1998). Outcome of anorexia nervosa: A case control study. *American Journal of Psychiatry, 155*, 939–946.

Summerfield, D., & Hume, F. (1993). War and posttraumatic stress disorder: The question of social context. *Journal of Nervous and Mental Disease, 181*, 522.

Summerville, M. B., Abbate, M. F., Siegel, A. M., et al. (1992). Psychopathology in urban female minority adolescents with suicide attempts. *Journal of the American Academy of Child and Adolescent Psychiatry, 31*, 663–668.

Sunaert, S., Dymarkowski, S., Van-Oostende, S., et al. (1998). Functional magnetic resonance imaging (fMRI) visualises the brain at work. *Acta Neurologica Belgica, 98*, 8–16.

Sung, H., Hawkins, B. A., Eklund, S. J., et al. (1997). Depression and dementia in ageing adults with Down syndrome: A case study approach. *Mental Retardation, 35*, 27–38.

Suomi, S. J. (1991). Primate separation models of affective disorders. In J. Madden, IV (Ed.), *Neurobiology of learning, emotion and affect*. New York: Raven Press.

Suppes, T., Baldessarini, R. J., Faedda, G. L., & Tohen, M. (1991). Risk of recurrence following discontinuation of lithium treatment in bipolar disorder. *Archives of General Psychiatry, 48*, 1082–1088.

The Surgeon General's 1990 report on the health benefits of smoking cessation. (1990, Oct. 5).

Executive summary (pp. 2–10). *MMWR Recommendations and Reports* (RR-12). Washington, DC: U.S. Government Printing Office.

Sussman, S. (1996). Development of a school-based drug abuse prevention curriculum for high-risk youths. *Journal of Psychoactive Drugs, 28*(2), 169–182.

Sutcliffe, J. P., & Jones, J. (1962). Personal identity, multiple personality, and hypnosis. *International Journal of Clinical and Experimental Hypnosis, 10*, 231–269.

Sutker, P. B. (1994). Psychopathy: Traditional and clinical antisocial concepts. *Progress in Personality and Psychopathology Research*, 73–120.

Sutker, P. B., Allain, A. N., & Winstead, D. K. (1993). Psychopathology and psychiatric diagnoses of World War II Pacific theater prisoner of war survivors and combat veterans. *American Journal of Psychiatry, 150*, 240–245.

Sutker, P. B., Davis, J. M., Uddo, M., & Ditta, S. R. (1995). Assessment of psychological distress in Persian Gulf troops: Ethnicity and gender comparisons. *Journal of Personality Assessment, 64*(3), 415–427.

Sutker, P. B., Uddo, M., Brailey, K., et al. (1994). Psychological symptoms and psychiatric diagnoses in Operation Desert Storm troops serving graves registration duty. *Journal of Traumatic Stress, 7*(2), 159–171.

Swan, N. (1999). Drug abuse cost to society set at $97.7 billion, continuing steady increase since 1975. *NIDA Notes, 13*, 4 (whole number). Washington, DC.

Swanson, M. C., Bland, R. C., & Newman, S. C. (1994). Epidemiology of psychiatric disorders in Edmonton: Antisocial personality disorders. *Acta Psychiatrica Scandinavica, 376*(Suppl.), 63–70.

Swartz, L. (1985). Anorexia nervosa as a culture-bound syndrome. *Social Science and Medicine, 20*, 725–730.

Swedo, S. E., Leonard, H. L., Schapiro, M. B., et al. (1993). Sydenham's chorea: Physical and psychological symptoms of St. Vitus dance. *Pediatrics, 91*(4), 706–713.

Swendsen, J. D. (1997). Anxiety, depression, and their comorbidity: An experience sampling test of the helplessness-hopelessness theory. *Cognitive Therapy and Research, 21*(1) 97–114.

Swinson, R. P., & Cox, B. J. (1993). Diagnostic validity in genetics research on generalized anxiety disorder. *Archives of General Psychiatry, 50*, 916.

Swinson, R. P., Soulios, C., Cox, B. J., & Kuch, K. (1992). Brief treatment of emergency room patients with panic attacks. *American Journal of Psychiatry, 149*, 944–946.

Sykora, C., Grilo, C. M., Wilfley, D. E., & Brownell, K. D. (1993). Eating, weight,

and dieting disturbances in male and female lightweight and heavyweight rowers. *International Journal of Eating Disorders, 14*, 203–211.

Szasz, T. (1986). The case against suicide prevention. *American Psychologist, 41*, 806–812.

Szasz, T. S. (1961). *The myth of mental illness: Foundations of a theory of personal conduct*. New York: Obeyer-Harper.

Szasz, T. S. (1971). *The manufacture of madness*. London: Routledge & Kegan Paul.

Szatmari, P. (1998). Differential diagnosis of Asperger disorder. In E. Schopler & G. B. Mesibov (Eds.), *Asperger syndrome or high-functioning autism? Current issues in autism* (pp. 61–76). New York: Plenum.

Szymanski, L. S., & Stark, J. (1996). Mental retardation: Past, present and future. *Child and Adolescent Psychiatry Clinics of North America, 5*, 769–780.

Tagamets, M. A., & Horwitz, B. (1998). Integrating electrophysiological and anatomical experimental data to create a large-scale model that simulates a delayed match-to-sample human brain imaging study. *Cerebral Cortex, 8*, 310–320.

Talcott, G. W., Fiedler, E. R., Pascale, R. W., et al. (1995). Is weight gain after smoking cessation inevitable? *Journal of Consulting and Clinical Psychology, 63*(2), 313–316.

Tancer, N. K. (1992). Elective mutism: A review of the literature. In B. B. Lahey & A. E. Kazdin (Eds.), *Advances in clinical child psychology, Vol. 14* (pp. 265–288). New York: Plenum.

Tannahill, R. (1989). *Sex in history*. London: Cardinal.

Tanner, C. M., & Goldman, S. M. (1997). Epidemiology of Tourette syndrome. *Neurologic Clinics, 15*, 395–402.

Tapper, A. (1996). State of the family: Recent research in Australia. In B. Maley, B. Berger, P. Morgan, et al. (Eds.), *Home repairs: Building stronger families to resist social decay* (pp. 49–66). Sydney: Centre for Independent Studies.

Taylor, S. (1991). *Health psychology* (2nd ed.). New York: McGraw-Hill.

Taylor, S., & Hyler, S. E. (1993). Update on factitious disorders. *International Journal of Psychiatry in Medicine, 23*, 81–94.

Taylor, S., & Koch, W. J. (1995). Anxiety disorders due to motor vehicle accidents: Nature and treatment. *Clinical Psychology Review, 15*(8), 721–738.

Taylor, S., Koch, W. J., & McNally, R. J. (1992). How does anxiety sensitivity vary across the anxiety disorders? *Journal of Anxiety Disorders, 6*(3), 249–259.

Taylor, S. E., & Aspinwall, L. G. (1996). Mediating and moderating processes in psychosocial stress: Appraisal, coping, resistance, and vulnerability. In H. B.

Kaplan (Ed.), *Psychosocial stress: Perspectives on structure, theory, life-course, and methods* (pp. 71–110). San Diego: Academic Press.

Taylor, S. E., Lichtman, R. R., Wood, J. V., et al. (1984). Breast self-examination among diagnosed breast cancer patients. *Cancer, 54,* 2528–2532.

Taylor, W. S., & Martin, M. F. (1944). Multiple personality. *Journal of Abnormal and Social Psychology, 39,* 281–300.

Teplin, L. A. (1990). The prevalence of severe mental disorder among male urban jail detainees: Comparison with the epidemiologic catchment area program. *American Journal of Public Health, 80,* 663–669.

Teri, L., & Wagner, A. (1992). Alzheimer's disease and depression. *Journal of Consulting and Clinical Psychology, 60,* 379–391.

Tesser, A. (1993). The importance of heritability in psychological research: The case of attitudes. *Psychological Review, 100,* 129–142.

Thara, R., Padmavati, R., & Nagaswami, V. (1993). Schizophrenia in India: Epidemiology, phenomenology, course and outcome. *International Review of Psychiatry, 5*(2–3), 157–163.

Thibaut, F., Cordier, B., & Kuhn, M. (1996). Gonadotrophin hormone releasing hormone agonist in cases of severe paraphilia: A lifetime treatment? *Psychoneuroendocrinology, 21,* 411–419.

Thigpen, C., & Cleckley, H. (1957). *The three faces of Eve.* New York: McGraw-Hill.

Thomas, A. M., & LoPiccolo, J. (1994). Sexual functioning in persons with diabetes: Issues in research, treatment and education. *Clinical Psychology Review, 14,* 61–86.

Thomas, L. (1979). Medical lessons from history. In L. Thomas (Ed.), *The Medusa and the snail* (pp. 131–144). New York: Viking.

Thomason, B. T., Brantley, P. J., Jones, G. N., & Herbert, T. (1992). The relationship between stress and disease activity in rheumatoid arthritis. *Journal of Behavioral Medicine, 15,* 215–220.

Thompson, E. L. (1978). Smoking education programs, 1960–1976. *American Journal of Public Health, 68,* 250–257.

Thompson, J. W., Belcher, J. R., DeForge, B. R., et al. (1995). Trends in the inpatient care of persons with schizophrenia. *Schizophrenia Bulletin, 21,* 75–85.

Thoreson, C. E., & Powell, L. H. (1992). Type A behavior pattern: New perspectives on theory, assessment, and intervention. *Journal of Consulting and Clinical Psychology, 60,* 595–604.

Thorndike, R. L., Hagen, E. P., & Sattler, J. (1986). *The Stanford-Binet Intelligence Scale: Guide for administering and scoring* (4th ed.). Chicago: Riverside.

Thornton, C., & Russell, J. (1997). Obsessive-compulsive comorbidity in the dieting disorders. *International Journal of Eating Disorders, 121,* 83–87.

Thornton, D., & Mann, R. (1997). Sexual masochism: Assessment and treatment. In D. R. Laws & W. T. O'Donohue (Eds.), *Sexual deviance: Theory, assessment, and treatment* (pp. 240–252). New York: Guilford Press.

Tienari, P. (1991). Interaction between genetic vulnerability and family environment: The Finnish Adoptive Family Study of schizophrenia. *Acta Psychiatrica Scandinavica, 84,* 460–465.

Tienari, P., Sorri, A., Lahti, I., et al. (1987). Genetic and psychosocial factors in schizophrenia: The Finnish Adoptive Family Study. *Schizophrenia Bulletin, 13,* 477–484.

Tischler, G. L. (Ed.). (1987). *Diagnosis and classification in psychiatry: A critical appraisal.* Cambridge, UK: Cambridge University Press.

Tollefson, G. D. (1993). Major depression. In D. L. Dunner (Ed.), *Current psychiatric therapy.* Philadelphia: Saunders.

Tomasson, K., Kent, D., & Coryell, W. (1991). Somatization and conversion disorders: Comorbidity and demographics at presentation. *Acta Psychiatrica Scandinavica, 84*(3), 288–293.

Tompson, M. C., Asarnow, J. R., Hamilton, E. B., et al. (1997). Children with schizophrenia-spectrum disorders: Thought disorder and communication problems in a family interactional context. *Journal of Child Psychology and Psychiatry and Allied Disciplines, 38*(4), 421–429.

Tonkin, R. S. (1997). Evaluation of a summer camp for adolescents with eating disorders. *Journal of Adolescent Health, 20,* 412–413.

Torgersen, S. (1986). Genetics of somatoform disorder. *Archives of General Psychiatry, 43,* 502–505.

Torgersen, S. (1990). Genetics of anxiety and its clinical implications. In G. Burrows, M. Roth, & R. Noyes (Eds.), *Handbook of anxiety, Vol. 3: The neurobiology of anxiety* (pp. 381–407). Amsterdam: Elsevier.

Torrey, E. F. (1980). *Schizophrenia and civilization.* New York: Jason Aronson.

Torrey, E. F. (1988). *Nowhere to go: The tragic odyssey of the homeless mentally ill.* New York: Harper & Row.

Torrey, E. F. (1992). Are we overestimating the genetic contribution to schizophrenia? *Schizophrenia Bulletin, 18,* 159–170.

Torrey, E. F., Bowler, A. E., Taylor, E. H., & Gottesman, I. I. (1994). *Schizophrenia and manic-depressive disorder: The biological roots of the mental illness as revealed by the landmark study of identical twins.* New York: Basic Books.

Torrey, E. F., Stieber, J., Ezekiel, J., et al. (1992). *Criminalizing the seriously mentally ill.* Washington, DC: Public Citizens Health Research Group and National Alliance for the Mentally Ill.

Touyz, S. W., & Beumont, P. J. V. (1997). Behavioral treatment to promote weight gain in anorexia nervosa. In D. M. Garner & P. E. Garfinkel (Eds.), *Handbook of treatment for eating disorders* (2nd ed.) (pp. 361–371). New York: Guilford Press.

Trent, J. W. (1995). *Inventing the feeble mind: A history of mental retardation in the United States.* Berkeley: University of California Press.

Trèves, T. A. (1991). Epidemiology of Alzheimer's disease. *Psychiatric Clinics of North America, 14,* 251–265.

Trimpey, M., & Davidson, S. (1994). Chaos, perfectionism, and sabotage: Personality disorders in the workplace. *Issues in Mental Health Nursing, 15,* 27–36.

True, W. R., Rice, J., Eisen, S. A., & Heath, A. C. (1993). A twin study of genetic and environmental contributions to liability for posttraumatic stress symptoms. *Archives of General Psychiatry, 50,* 257–264.

Tryon, G. S. (1980). The measurement and treatment of test anxiety. *Review of Educational Research, 50,* 343–372.

Trzepacz, P. T., & Baker, R. W. (1993). *The psychiatric mental status examination.* New York: Oxford University Press.

Tsevat, J. (1992). Impact and cost-effectiveness of smoking interventions. *American Journal of Medicine, 93*(1A), 43S–47S.

Tsuang, D., & Coryell, W. (1993). An 8-year follow-up of patients with *DSM-III-R* psychotic depression, schizoaffective disorder, and schizophrenia. *American Journal of Psychiatry, 150,* 1182–1188.

Tsuang, M. T., & Faraone, S. V. (1996). The inheritance of mood disorders. In L. L. Hall (Ed.), *Genetics and mental illness: Evolving issues for research and society* (pp. 79–109). New York: Plenum.

Tsuda, A., Ida, Y., Satoh, H., et al. (1989). Stressor predictability and rat brain noradrenaline metabolism. *Pharmacology, Biochemistry and Behavior, 32*(2), 569–572.

Tuan, Y. F. (1980). *Landscapes of fear.* Oxford: Basil Blackwell.

Tucker, W. H. (1997). Re-reconsidering Burt: Beyond a reasonable doubt. *Journal of the History of the Behavioral Sciences, 33,* 145–162.

Tulving, E. (1993). What is episodic memory? *Current Directions in Psychological Science, 2*(3), 67–70.

Tune, L., & Ross, C. (1994). Delirium. In C. E. Coffey & J. L. Cummings (Eds.), *The American Psychiatric Press textbook of geriatric neuropsychiatry* (pp. 351–365). Washington, DC: American Psychiatric Press.

Tupper, E. D., & Cicernone, K. D. (1991). *The neuropsychology of everyday life: Issues in development and rehabilitation.* Boston: Kluwer.

Turk, D. C., & Salovey, P. (1988). *Reasoning, inference, and judgment in clinical psychology.* New York: Free Press.

Turkheimer, E., & Parry, C. D. H. (1992). Why the gap? *American Psychologist, 47,* 646–655.

Turner, S. (1996). Progress in social independent functioning of young people with Down's syndrome. *Journal of Intellectual Disability Research, 40,* 39–48.

Turner, S. M., Beidel, D. C., Borden, J. W., et al. (1991). Social phobia: Axis I and II correlates. *Journal of Abnormal Psychology, 100*(1), 102–106.

Turner, S. M., Beidel, D. C., & Cooley-Quille, M. R. (1995). Two-year follow-up of social phobias treated with social effectiveness therapy. *Behaviour Research and Therapy, 33*(5), 553–555.

Turner, S. M., Beidel, D. C., Long, P. J., & Greenhouse, J. (1992). Reduction of fear in social phobics: An examination of extinction patterns. *Behavior Therapy, 23,* 389–403.

Turner, S. M., Beidel, D. C., & Townsley, R. M. (1992). Behavioral treatment for social phobia. In S. M. Turner, K. S. Calhoun, & H. E. Adams (Eds.), *Handbook of clinical behavior therapy* (2nd ed.) (pp. 13–37). New York: Wiley.

Turner, W. M., & Tsuang, M. Y. (1990). Impact of substance abuse on the course and outcome of schizophrenia. *Schizophrenia Bulletin, 16,* 76–87.

Twachtman-Cullen, D. T. (1998). *A passion to believe: Autism and the facilitated communication phenomenon.* Essays in Developmental Science. New York: Westview (distributed by HarperCollins).

Tyrer, P. (1994). What are the borders of borderline personality disorder? *Acta Psychiatrica Scandinavica, 89*(Suppl.), 38–44.

Ullmann, L. P., & Krasner, L. (1975). *A psychological approach to abnormal behavior* (2nd ed.). Englewood Cliffs, NJ: Prentice-Hall.

Unger, D. D., Parent, W., Gibson, K., et al. (1998). An analysis of the activities of employment specialists in a natural support approach to supported employment. *Focus on Autism and Other Developmental Disabilities, 13,* 27–38.

Unnewehr, S., Schneider, S., Florin, I., & Margraf, J. (1998). Psychopathology in children of patients with panic disorder or animal phobia. *Psychopathology, 31,* 69–84.

Unutzer, J., Patrick, D. L., Simon, G., et al. (1997). Depressive symptoms and the cost of health services in HMO patients aged 65 years and older: A 4-year prospective study. *Journal of the American Medical Association, 277,* 1618–1623.

U.S. Department of Health and Human Services. (1988). *The health consequences of smoking. Nicotine addiction: A report of the Surgeon General.* (DHHS Publication No. 88-8406). Washington, DC: U.S. Government Printing Office.

U.S. Department of Health and Human Services. (1990). *The health benefits of smoking cessation: A report of the Surgeon General* (DHHS Publication No. CDC 90-8416). Washington, DC: U.S. Government Printing Office.

Uva, J. L. (1995). Review: Autoerotic asphyxiation in the United States. *Journal of Forensic Sciences, 40,* 574–581.

Vaillant, G. E. (1992). Is there a natural history of addiction? In C. P. O'Brien & J. H. Jaffe (Eds.), *Addictive states* (pp. 41–58). New York: Raven Press.

Valentine, C. W. (1930). The innate bases of fear. *Journal of Genetic Psychology, 37,* 394–414.

van-Bemmel, A. L. (1997). The link between sleep and depression: The effects of antidepressants on EEG sleep. *Journal of Psychosomatic Research, 42*(6), 555–564.

Vandereycken, W., & Van Deth, R. (1994). *From fasting saints to anorexic girls: The history of self-starvation.* New York: New York University Press.

van der Feltz-Cornelis, C. M., & van Dyck, R. (1997).The notion of somatization: An artefact of the conceptualization of body and mind. *Psychotherapy and Psychosomatics, 66*(3), 117–127.

Vanderlinden, J., van Dyck, R., Vandereycken, W., et al. (1993). The Dissociation Questionnaire (DIS-Q): Development and characteristics of a new self-report questionnaire. *Clinical Psychology and Psychotherapy, 1,* 21–27.

van Gorp, W. G., & Buckingham, S. L. (Eds.). (1998). *Practitioner's guide to the neuropsychiatry of HIV/AIDS.* New York: Guilford Press.

Van Ierssel, A. J., Mieremet-Ooms, M. A., Van der Zon, J. M., et al. (1997). Suppression of intestinal mucosal natural killer cells by corticosteroids. *Alimentary Pharmacological Therapy, 11,* 347–353.

Van-Reekum, R. (1993). Acquired and developmental brain dysfunction in borderline personality disorder. *Canadian Journal of Psychiatry, 38*(Suppl. 1), 4–10.

Van Rood, Y. R., Bogaards, M. M., Goulmy, E., & Van Houwelingen, H. C. (1993). The effects of stress and relaxation on the in vitro immune response in man: A meta-analytic study. *Journal of Behavioral Medicine, 16,* 163–181.

Van-Sweden, B., Van-Erp, M. G., & Mesotten, F. (1997). Auditory information processing in schizophrenia. *Neuropsychobiology, 35*(4), 191–196.

Vasterling, J., Jenkins, R. A., Tope, D. M., &

Burish, T. G. (1993). Cognitive distraction and relaxation training for the control of side effects due to cancer chemotherapy. *Journal of Behavioral Medicine, 16,* 65–80.

Veale, D., Boocock, A., Gournay, K., et al. (1996). Body dysmorphic disorder: A survey of fifty cases. *British Journal of Psychiatry, 169*(2), 196–201.

Veale, D., Gournay, K., Dryden, W., et al. (1996). Body dysmorphic disorder: A cognitive behavioural model and pilot randomised controlled trial. *Behaviour Research and Therapy, 34*(9), 717–729.

Vega, W., & Rumbaut, R. G. (1991). Ethnic minorities and mental health. *Annual Review of Sociology, 17,* 351–383.

Velligan, D. I., Mahurin, R. K., Diamond, P. L., et al. (1997). The functional significance of symptomatology and cognitive function in schizophrenia. *Schizophrenia Research, 25*(1), 21–31.

Velligan, D. I., Mahurin, R. K., Eckert, S. L., et al. (1997). Relationship between specific types of communication deviance and attentional performance in patients with schizophrenia. *Psychiatry Research, 70*(1), 9–20.

Ventura, J., Nuechterlein, K. H., Lukoff, D., & Hardesty, J. P. (1989). A prospective study of stressful life events and schizophrenia relapse. *Journal of Abnormal Psychology, 98,* 407–411.

Verberg, E. M., Abwender, D. A., Ewell, K. K., et al. (1992). Social anxiety and peer relationships in early adolescence: A prospective analysis. *Journal of Clinical Child Psychology, 21,* 189–196.

Verdoux, H., Geddes, J. R., Takei, N., et al. (1997). Obstetric complications and age at onset in schizophrenia: An international collaborative meta-analysis of individual patient data. *American Journal of Psychiatry, 154*(9), 1220–1227.

Vetter, P., & Köller, O. (1993). Stability of diagnosis in various psychiatric disorders: A study of long-term course. *Psychopathology, 26,* 173–180.

Vgontzas, A. N., & Kales, A. (1999). Sleep and its disorders. *Annual Review of Medicine, 50,* 387–400.

Vialle, W. (1994). "Termanal" science? The work of Lewis Terman revisited. *Roeper Review, 17,* 32–38.

Victor, M. (1971). *The Wernicke-Korsakoff syndrome: A clinical and pathological study of 245 patients, 82 with post-mortem examinations.* Philadelphia: Davis.

Viederman, M. (1986). Somatoform and factitious disorders. In A. M. Cooper, A. J. Frances, & M. H. Sacks (Eds.), *The personality disorders and neuroses.* Philadelphia: Lippincott.

Violanti, J. M. (1996). The impact of cohesive groups in the trauma recovery context: Police spouse survivors and duty-related death. *Journal of Traumatic Stress, 9*(2), 379–386.

Visser, F. E., Aldenkamp, A. P., van-Huffelen, A. C., & Kuilman, M. (1997). Prospective study of the prevalence of Alzheimer-type dementia in institutionalized individuals with Down syndrome. *American Journal on Mental Retardation, 101,* 400–412.

Visser, S., & Bouman, T. K. (1992). Cognitive behavioural approaches to the treatment of hypochondriasis: Six single-case crossover studies. *Behaviour Research and Therapy, 30,* 301–306.

Vitelli, R. (1997). Comparison of early and late start models of delinquency in adult offenders. *International Journal of Offender Therapy and Comparative Criminology, 41,* 351–357.

Vitiello, B., & Jensen, P. (1997). Medication development and testing in children and adolescents. *Archives of General Psychiatry, 54,* 871–876.

Vogel, W. H., & Bower, D. B. (1991). Stress, immunity, and cancer. In N. Plotnikoff, A. Murgo, R. Faith, & J. Wybran (Eds.), *Stress and immunity* (pp. 493–508). Boca Raton, FL: CRC Press.

Voglmaier, M. M., Seidman, L. J., Salisbury, D., & McCarley, R. W. (1997). Neuropsychological dysfunction in schizotypal personality disorder: A profile analysis. *Biological Psychiatry, 41,* 530–540.

Volkmar, F. R. (1996). The disintegrative disorders: Childhood disintegrative disorder and Rett's disorder. In F. R. Volkmar (Ed.), *Psychoses and pervasive developmental disorders in childhood and adolescence* (pp. 223–248). Washington, DC: American Psychiatric Press.

Volkmar, F. R. (Ed.). (1998). *Autism and pervasive developmental disorders.* Cambridge, UK: Cambridge University Press.

Volkmar, F. R., Klin, A., & Pauls, D. (1998). Nosological and genetic aspects of Asperger syndrome. *Journal of Autism and Developmental Disorders, 28,* 457–463.

Volterra, V., Capirci, O., Pezzini, G., et al. (1996). Linguistic abilities in Italian children with Williams syndrome. *Cortex, 32,* 663–677.

von Buehler, J. M., & Herbert, P. (1998). Vacuum and constriction devices for erectile disorder: An integrative view. *Sexual and Marital Therapy, 13,* 257–272.

Von Korff, M., Ormel, J., Katon, W., & Lin, E. H. B. (1992). Disability and depression among utilizers of health care. *Archives of General Psychiatry, 49,* 91–100.

Vredenburg, K., Flett, G. L., & Krames, L. (1993). Analogue versus clinical depression: A critical reappraisal. *Psychological Bulletin, 113,* 327–344.

Vygotsky, L. S. (1986). *Thought and language.* Cambridge, MA: MIT Press.

Waddington, J. L., & Youssef, H. A. (1994). Evidence for a gender-specific decline in the rate of schizophrenia in rural Ireland over a 50-year period. *British Journal of Psychiatry, 164,* 171–176.

Wade, S. L., Monroe, S. M., & Michelson, L. K. (1993). Chronic life stress and treatment outcome in agoraphobia with panic attacks. *American Journal of Psychiatry, 150,* 1491–1495.

Waikar, S. V., & Craske, M. G. (1997). Cognitive correlates of anxious and depressive symptomatology: An examination of the hopelessness/helplessness model. *Journal of Anxiety Disorders, 11,* 1–16.

Wakefield, H., & Underwager, R. (1992). Recovered memories of alleged sexual abuse: Lawsuits against parents. *Behavioral Sciences and the Law, 10,* 483–507.

Waldie, K., & Spreen, O. (1993). The relationship between learning disabilities and persisting delinquency. *Journal of Learning Disabilities, 26,* 417–423.

Waldinger, R. J., & Frank, A. F. (1989). Clinicians' experiences in combining medication and psychotherapy in the treatment of borderline patients. *Hospital and Community Psychiatry, 40,* 712–718.

Waldo, M., & Harman, M. J. (1998). Borderline personality disorder and relationship enhancement marital therapy. In J. Carlson & L. Sperry (Eds.), *The disordered couple* (pp. 285–297). Bristol, PA: Brunner/Mazel.

Waldrow, I. (1991). Effects of labor force participation on sex differences in mortality and morbidity. In M. Frankenhauser, A. Lundberg, & M. Chesney (Eds.), *Women, work, and health: Stress and opportunities.* New York: Plenum.

Walker, E., Davis, D., & Baum, K. (1993). Social withdrawal. In C. G. Costello (Ed.), *Symptoms of schizophrenia* (pp. 227–260). New York: Wiley.

Walker, E. F., Grimes, K. E., Davis, D. M., & Smith, A. J. (1993). Childhood precursors of schizophrenia: Facial expressions of emotion. *American Journal of Psychiatry, 150,* 1654–1660.

Walker, E. F., & Lewine, R. J. (1990). Prediction of adult-onset schizophrenia from childhood home movies of patients. *American Journal of Psychiatry, 147,* 1052–1056.

Walker, M., Moreau, D., & Weissman, M. M. (1990). Parents' awareness of children's suicide attempts. *American Journal of Psychiatry, 147,* 1364–1366.

Wall, P. D., Melzack, R., & Bonica, J. (Eds.). (1994). *Textbook of pain* (3rd ed.). Edinburgh, Scot.: Churchill Livingstone.

Wallace, J., & O'Hara, M. W. (1992). Increases in depressive symptomatology in the rural elderly: Results from a cross-sectional and longitudinal study. *Journal of Abnormal Psychology, 101*(3), 398–404.

Walsh, B. T., & Devlin, M. J. (1998). Eating disorders: Progress and problems. *Science, 280,* 1387–1390.

Walsh, B. T., & Kahn, C. B. (1997). Diagnostic criteria for eating disorders: Current concerns and future directions. *Psychopharmacology Bulletin, 33,* 369–372.

Walsh, K. (1987). *Neuropsychology: A clinical approach.* Edinburgh, Scot.: Churchill Livingstone.

Walter, G., & Rey, J. M. (1997). An epidemiological study of the use of ECT in adolescents. *Journal of the American Academy of Child Psychiatry, 36,* 809–815.

Walther, V. N. (1997). Postpartum depression: A review for perinatal social workers. *Social Work in Health Care, 24*(3–4), 99–111.

Waltrip, R. W., II, Buchanan, R. W., Summerfelt, A., et al. (1995). Borna disease virus and schizophrenia. *Psychiatry Research, 56*(1), 33–44.

Wang, S. (1997). Traumatic stress and attachment. *Acta Physiologica Scandinavica, 640,* 164–169.

Warneke, L. B. (1991). Benzodiazepines: Abuses and new use. *Canadian Journal of Psychiatry, 36,* 194–205.

Warner, E. A., Kosten, T. R., & O'Connor, P. G. (1997). Pharmacotherapy for opioid and cocaine abuse. *Medical Clinics of North America, 81*(4), 909–925.

Warner, J. (1992). Before there was 'alcoholism': Lessons from the medieval experience with alcohol. *Contemporary Drug Problems, Fall,* 409–429.

Warner, R., & de Girolamo, G. (1995). *Schizophrenia.* Geneva: World Health Organization.

Warner, R., de Girolamo, G., & Warburton, D. (1989). Is nicotine use an addiction? *Psychologist, 4,* 166–170.

Warren, R., & Zgourides, G. D. (1991). *Anxiety disorders: A rational-emotive perspective.* New York: Pergamon.

Warshaw, M. G., Fierman, E., Pratt, L., et al. (1993). Quality of life and dissociation in anxiety disorder patients with histories of trauma or PTSD. *American Journal of Psychiatry, 150*(10), 1512–1516.

Warwick, H. M., Clark, D. M., Cobb, A. M., & Salkovskis, P. M. (1996). A controlled trial of cognitive-behavioural treatment of hypochondriasis. *British Journal of Psychiatry, 169*(2), 189–195.

Warwick, H. M. C., & Marks, I. M. (1988). Behavioural treatment of illness phobia and hypochondriasis: A pilot study of 17 cases. *British Journal of Psychiatry, 152,* 239–241.

Watson, G. C., & Buranen, C. (1979). The frequency and identification of false positive conversion reactions. *Journal of Nervous and Mental Disease, 167,* 243–247.

Watson, J. B. (1913). Psychology as the behaviorist views it. *Psychology Review, 20,* 158–177.

Watson, J. B. (1930). *Behaviorism* (rev. ed.). New York: Norton.

Watson, J. B., & Rayner, R. (1920). Conditioned emotional reactions. *Journal of Experimental Psychology, 3*, 1–14.

Watt, N. F., & Saiz, C. (1991). Longitudinal studies of premorbid development of adult schizophrenics. In E. F. Walker (Ed.), *Schizophrenia: A life-course in developmental perspective*. San Diego: Academic Press.

Weakley, M. M., Petti, T. A., & Karwisch, G. (1997). Case study: Chewing gum treatment of rumination in an adolescent with an eating disorder. *Journal of the American Academy of Child and Adolescent Psychiatry, 36*, 1124–1127.

Webb, J. T., McNamara, K. M., & Rodgers, D. A. (1981). *Configural interpretations of the MMPI and CPI* (rev. ed.). Columbus: Ohio Psychology Publishing.

Wechsler, D. (1981). *Manual for the Wechsler Adult Intelligence Scale–Revised*. San Antonio, TX: Psychological Corporation.

Wechsler, D. (1987). *Wechsler Memory Scale–Revised manual*. New York: Psychological Corporation.

Wechsler, D. (1989). *Manual for the Wechsler Preschool and Primary Scale of Intelligence–Revised*. San Antonio, TX: Psychological Corporation.

Wechsler, D. (1991). *Wechsler Intelligence Scale for Children* (3rd ed.). San Antonio, TX: Psychological Corporation.

Wechsler, D. (1997). *Wechsler Adult Intelligence Scale* (3rd ed.). San Antonio, TX: Psychological Corporation.

Weckowicz, T., & Liebel-Weckowicz, H. P. (1990). *A history of great ideas in abnormal psychology*. Amsterdam: North Holland.

Weddington, W. W. (1992). Use of pharmacologic agents in the treatment of addiction. *Psychiatric Annals, 22*, 425–429.

Wehman, P. H., Revell, W. G., Kregel, J., et al. (1991). Supported employment: An alternative model for vocational rehabilitation of persons with severe neurologic, psychiatric, or physical disability. *Archives of Physical and Medical Rehabilitation, 72*, 101–105.

Wehr, T. A. (1989). Seasonal affective disorder: A historical review. In N. E. Rosenthal & M. C. Blehar (Eds.), *Seasonal affective disorders and phototherapy*. New York: Guilford Press.

Wehr, T. A. & Rosenthal, N. E. (1989). Seasonality and affective illness. *American Journal of Psychiatry, 146*(7), 829–839.

Weiner, B. (1993). On sin versus sickness: A theory of perceived responsibility and social motivation. *American Psychologist, 48*(9), 957–965.

Weiner, B. A., & Wettstein, R. M. (1993). *Legal issues in mental health care*. New York: Plenum.

Weiner, M. F. (1996). Diagnosis of dementia. In M. F. Weiner (Ed.), *The dementias: Diagnosis, management, and research* (2nd ed.) (pp. 1–41). Washington, DC: American Psychiatric Press.

Weiner, R. D., & Coffey, C. E. (1988). Indications for the use of electroconvulsive therapy. In A. J. Frances & R. E. Hales (Eds.), *Review of psychiatry*. Washington, DC: American Psychiatric Press.

Weinhardt, L. S., & Carey, M. P. (1996). Prevalence of erectile disorder among men with diabetes mellitus: Comprehensive review, methodological critique, and suggestions for future research. *Journal of Sex Research, 33*, 205–214.

Weishaar, M. E., & Beck, A. T. (1992). Hopelessness and suicide. *International Review of Psychiatry, 4*, 177–184.

Weisman, A. G. (1997). Understanding cross-cultural prognostic variability for schizophrenia. *Cultural Diversity and Mental Health, 3*, 23–35.

Weiss, C. R., & Orysh, L. K. (1994). Group counseling for eating disorders: A two-phase treatment program. *Journal of College Student Development, 35*, 487–488.

Weiss, J. M. (1977). Psychological and behavioral influences on gastrointestinal lesions in animal models. In J. D. Maser & M. E. P. Seligman (Eds.), *Psychopathology: Experimental models* (pp. 232–269). San Francisco: W. H. Freeman.

Weissberg, M. (1993). Multiple personality disorder and iatrogenesis: The cautionary tale of Ann O. *International Journal of Clinical and Experimental Hypnosis, 41*, 15–34.

Weissman, M. M. (1993). Family genetic studies of panic disorder. Conference on Panic and Anxiety: A decade of progress (1990, Geneva, Switzerland). *Journal of Psychiatric Research, 27*(Suppl. 1), 69–78.

Weissman, M. M., Bland, R. C., Canino, G. J., et al. (1994). The cross national epidemiology of obsessive compulsive disorder: The Cross National Collaborative Group. *Journal of Clinical Psychiatry, 55*(3, Suppl.), 5–10.

Weissman, M. M., Bruce, M. L., Leaf, P. J., et al. (1991). Affective disorders. In L. N. Robins & D. A. Reiger (Eds.), *Psychiatric disorders of America: The epidemiologic catchment area study* (pp. 53–80). New York: Free Press.

Weissman, M. M., Leaf, P., Tischler, G., et al. (1988). Affective disorder in five United States communities. *Psychological Medicine, 18*, 141–153.

Welford, A. T. (1968). *Fundamentals of skill*. London: Methuen.

Wells, K. B., Burnam, A., Rogers, W., et al. (1992). The course of depression in adult outpatients: Results from the medical outcomes study. *Archives of General Psychiatry, 49*, 788–794.

Wells, K. B., Stewart, A., Hays, R. D., et al. (1989). The functioning and well-being of depressed patients: Results from the medical outcomes study. *Journal of the American Medical Association, 262*, 914–919.

Wender, P. (1997). Attention deficit hyperactivity disorder in adults: A wide view of a widespread condition. *Psychiatric Annals, 27*, 556–562.

Wender, P. H. (1995). *Attention-deficit hyperactivity disorder in adults*. New York: Oxford University Press.

Wender, P. H., et al. (1974). Cross-fostering: A research strategy for clarifying the role of genetic and experiential factors in the etiology of schizophrenia. *Archives of General Psychiatry, 30*, 121–128.

Wender, P. H., Kety, S. S., Rosenthal, D., et al. (1986). Psychiatric disorders in the biological and adoptive families of adopted individuals with affective disorder. *Archives of General Psychiatry, 43*, 923–929.

Wernicke, C. (1874). *Der aphasische symptomen-komplex*. Breslau: Cohn & Weigart.

Werry, J. S., Methven, R. R. J., Fitzpatrick, J., & Dixon, H. (1983). The inter-rater reliability of the *DSM-III* in children. *Journal of Abnormal Child Psychology, 11*, 341–354.

Wertlieb, D. L., Jacobson, A., & Hauser, S. T. (1990). The child with diabetes. In P. T. Costa & G. R. VandenBos (Eds.), *Psychosocial aspects of serious illness: Chronic conditions, fatal diseases and clinical care* (pp. 65–101). Washington, DC: American Psychological Association.

Wertman, B. G., Sostrin, S. V., Pavlova, Z., & Lundberg, G. D. (1980). Why do physicians order laboratory tests? A study of laboratory test request and use patterns. *Journal of the American Medical Association, 243*, 2080–2082.

Westling, B. E., & Öst, L. G. (1995). Cognitive bias in panic disorder patients and changes after cognitive-behavioural treatments. *Behaviour Research and Therapy, 33*(5), 585–588.

Weston, S. C., & Siever, L. J. (1993). Biologic correlates of personality disorders. *Journal of Personality Disorders* (Suppl. 1), 129–148.

What caffeine can do for you—and to you. (1997, Sept.). *Consumer Reports on Health.*

Wheatley, D. (1990). The stress profile. *British Journal of Psychiatry, 156*, 685–688.

Wheeler, M. (1998). *Toilet training for individuals with autism and related disorders*. Arlington, TX: Future Horizons.

Wheelis, J., & Gunderson, J. G. (1998). A little cream and sugar: Psychotherapy with a borderline patient. *American Journal of Psychiatry, 155*, 114–122.

Whiffen, V. E. (1992). Is postpartum depression a distinct diagnosis? *Clinical Psychology Review, 12*, 485–508.

White, J., Davison, G. C., Haaga, D. A. F., & White, K. (1992). Articulated thoughts and cognitive distortion in depressed and nondepressed psychiatric patients. *Journal of Nervous and Mental Disease, 180,* 77–81.

White, K., & Cole, J. O. (1990). Pharmacotherapy. In A. S. Bellack & M. Hersen (Eds.), *Handbook of comparative treatments for adult disorders* (pp. 266–284). New York: Wiley.

Whitehouse, P. J., Friedland, R. P., & Strauss, M. E. (1992). Neuropsychiatric aspects of degenerative dementias associated with motor dysfunction. In S. C. Yudofsky & R. E. Hales (Eds.), *The American Psychiatric Press textbook of neuropsychiatry* (pp. 453–468). Washington, DC: American Psychiatric Press.

Whitney, L., Ruiz, P., & Langenbach, M. (1994). Detaining psychiatric patients. In T. Sensky, C. Katona, & S. Montgomery (Eds.), *Psychiatry in Europe* (pp. 137–142). London: Gaskell.

WHO. *See* World Health Organization.

Whybrow, P. C. (1994). Of the muse and moods mundane. *American Journal of Psychiatry, 151,* 477–479.

Whybrow, P. C., Akiskal, H. S., & McKinney, W. T., Jr. (1994). *Mood disorders: Towards a new psychobiology.* New York: Plenum.

Widiger, T. A. (1991). Personality disorder dimensional models proposed for the *DSM-IV. Journal of Personality Disorders, 5,* 386–398.

Widiger, T. A., & Corbitt, E. M. (1997). Comorbidity of antisocial personality disorder with other personality disorders. In D. M. Stoff, J. Breiling, & J. D. Maser (Eds.), *Handbook of antisocial behavior* (pp. 75–82). New York: Wiley.

Widiger, T. A., & Rogers, J. H. (1989). Prevalence and comorbidity of personality disorders. *Psychiatry Annual, 19,* 132–136.

Widiger, T. A., & Trull, T. J. (1991). Diagnosis and clinical assessment. *Annual Review of Psychology, 42,* 109–133.

Wiens, A. N. (1983). The assessment interview. In I. D. Weiner (Ed.), *Clinical methods in psychology* (2nd ed.) (pp. 3–57). New York: Wiley.

Wilkinson, J. G. (1975). Techniques of ancient skull surgery. *Natural History, 84,* 94–101.

Williams, J. B., Gibbon, M., First, M. B., et al. (1997). The Structured Clinical Interview for *DSM-III-R* (SCIUD). II: Multisite test-retest reliability. *Archives of General Psychiatry, 49,* 630–636.

Williams, J. E., & Best, D. L. (1988). *Sex and psyche: Gender roles and self-concept viewed cross-culturally.* Newbury Park, CA: Sage.

Williams, K. C. (1996). Piagetian principles: Simple and effective application. *Journal of Intellectual Disability Research, 40,* 110–119.

Williams, P. G., Wiebe, D. J., & Smith, T. W. (1992). Coping processes as mediators of the relationship between hardiness and health. *Journal of Behavioral Medicine, 15,* 237–255.

Williams, R. (1989). *The trusting heart: Great news about type A behavior.* New York: Time Books.

Williams, R. C. (1991). *Molecular biology in clinical medicine.* New York: Elsevier.

Williamson, D. A., Duchmann, E. G., Barker, S. E., & Bruno, R. M. (1998). Anorexia nervosa. In V. B. Van Hasselt & M. Hersen (Eds.), *Handbook of psychological treatment protocols for children and adolescents* (pp. 413–434). Mahwah, NJ: Erlbaum.

Willis, C. G. (1987). Myers-Briggs type indicator. In D. J. Keyser & R. C. Sweetland (Eds.), *Test critiques compendium* (pp. 327–336). Kansas City, MO: Test Corporation of America.

Willis, E., & Strasburger, V. C. (1998). Media violence. *Pediatric Clinics of North America, 45,* 319–331.

Wilsnack, S. C., Vogeltanz, N. D., Klassen, A. D., & Harris, T. R. (1997). Childhood sexual abuse and women's substance abuse: National survey findings. *Journal of Studies on Alcohol, 58*(3), 264–271.

Wilson, D. K., Wallston, K. A., King, J. E., et al. (1993). Validation of smoking abstinence in newly diagnosed cardiovascular patients. *Addictive Behaviors, 18*(4), 421–429.

Wilson, F. R., Omeltschenko, L., & Yager, G. G. (1991). Coping with test stress: Microcomputer software for treatment of test anxiety. *Journal of Behavior Therapy and Experimental Psychiatry, 22,* 131–139.

Wilson, G. T., & Fairburn, C. G. (1998). Treatments for eating disorders. In P. E. Nathan & J. M. Gorman (Eds.), *A guide to treatments that work* (pp. 501–530). New York: Oxford University Press.

Wilson, J. P., & Raphael, B. (Eds.). (1993). *International handbook of traumatic stress syndromes.* New York: Plenum.

Wilson, M. (1993). *DSM-III* and the transformation of American psychiatry: A history. *American Journal of Psychiatry, 150,* 399–410.

Wilson, S. A., Becker, L. A., & Tinker, R. H. (1995). Eye movement desensitization and reprocessing (EMDR) treatment for psychologically traumatized individuals. *Journal of Consulting and Clinical Psychology, 63*(6), 928–937.

Wing, L. (1998). The history of Asperger syndrome. In E. Schopler, G. B. Mesibov, & L. J. Kunce (Eds.), *Asperger syndrome or high-functioning autism? Current issues in autism* (pp. 11–28). New York: Plenum.

Winker, M. A. (1994). Tacrine for Alzheimer's disease: Which patient, which dose? *Journal of the American Medical Association, 271,* 1023–1024.

Winokur, G., Coryell, W., Endicott, J., & Akiskal, H. (1993). Further distinctions between manic-depressive illness (bipolar disorder) and primary depressive illness (unipolar depression). *American Journal of Psychiatry, 150,* 1176–1181.

Wirt, R. D., Lachar, D., Klinedinst, J. K., & Seat, P. D. (1977). *Multidimensional evaluation of child personality: Manual for the Personality Inventory for Children.* Los Angeles: Western Psychological Services.

Wise, M. G., & Brandt, G. T. (1992). Delirium. In S. C. Yudofsky & R. E. Hales (Eds.), *The American Psychiatric Press textbook of neuropsychiatry* (pp. 291–310). Washington, DC: American Psychiatric Press.

Wiseman, M. A., Gray, J. J., Mosimann, J. E., & Ahrens, A. H. (1992). Cultural expectations of thinness in women: An update. *International Journal of Eating Disorders, 11,* 85–89.

Wisner, K. L., & Stowe, Z. N. (1997). Psychobiology of postpartum mood disorders. *Seminars in Reproductive and Renal Endocrinology, 15,* 77–89.

Wittchen, H. U., Kessler, R. C., Zhao, S., & Abelson, J. (1995). Reliability and clinical validity of UM-CIDI *DSM-III-R* generalized anxiety disorder. *Journal of Psychiatric Research, 29*(2), 95–110.

Wittchen, H. U., Reed, V., & Kessler, R. C. (1998). The relationship of agoraphobia and panic in a community sample of adolescents and young adults. *Archives of General Psychiatry, 55,* 1017–1024.

Wolitzky, D. L. (1995). The theory and practice of traditional psychoanalytic psychotherapy. In A. S. Gurman & S. B. Messer (Eds.), *Essential psychotherapies: Theory and practice* (pp. 12–54). New York: Guilford Press.

Wolitzky, D. L., & Eagle, M. N. (1990). Psychotherapy. In A. S. Bellack & M. Hersen (Eds.), *Handbook of comparative treatments for adult disorders* (pp. 123–143). New York: Wiley.

Wolkoff, D. A. (1997). Methamphetamine abuse: An overview for health care professionals. *Hawaii Medical Journal, 56*(2), 34–36, 44.

Wolpe, J. (1958). *Psychotherapy by reciprocal inhibition.* Stanford, CA: Stanford University Press.

Wolpe, J. (1969). Basic principles and practices of behavior therapy of neuroses. *American Journal of Psychiatry, 125,* 1242–1247.

Wolpe, J. (1981). *Our useless fears.* Boston: Houghton Mifflin.

Wolpe, J. (1982). *The practice of behavior therapy* (3rd ed.). Elmsford, NY: Pergamon.

Wood, A., Tollefson, G. D., & Birkett, M. (1993). Pharmacotherapy of obsessive compulsive disorder—Experience with fluoxetine. *International Clinical Psychopharmacology, 8*(4), 301–306.

Wood, R. L. (Ed.). (1990). *Neurobehavioural sequelae of traumatic brain injury.* London: Taylor & Francis.

Woody, R. H., & Woody, J. D. (Eds.). (1972). *Clinical assessment in counseling and psychotherapy.* New York: Appleton-Century-Crofts.

Woolf, C. M. (1997). Does the genotype for schizophrenia often remain unexpressed because of canalization and stochastic events during development? *Psychological Medicine, 27*(3), 659–668.

Woolf, L., & Jackson, B. (1996). 'Coffee and condoms': The implementation of a sexual health programme in acute psychiatry in an inner city area. *Journal of Advanced Nursing, 23*(2), 299–304.

Working Group on the Investigation of Memories of Childhood Abuse. (1996). *Final report.* Washington, DC: American Psychological Association.

World Health Organization. (1992). *The ICD-10 classification of mental and behavioural disorders: Clinical descriptions and diagnostic guidelines.* Geneva: Author.

World Health Organization. (1993). *The ICD-10 classification of mental and behavioural disorders: Diagnostic criteria for research.* Geneva: Author.

Worling, J. R. (1995). Sexual abuse histories of adolescent male sex offenders: Differences on the basis of the age and gender of their victims. *Journal of Abnormal Psychology, 104*, 610–613.

Wormser, G. P. (Ed.). (1992). *AIDS and other manifestations of HIV infection.* New York: Raven Press.

Wren, F. J., & Tarbell, S. E. (1998). Feeding and growth disorders. In R. T. Ammerman & J. V. Campo (Eds.), *Handbook of pediatric psychology and psychiatry, Vol. 2: Disease, injury, and illness* (pp. 133–165). Boston: Allyn & Bacon.

Wright, H. H., Holmes, G. R., Cuccaro, M. L., et al. (1994). A guided bibliography of the selective mutism (elective mutism) literature. *Psychological Reports, 74*(3, Pt. 1), 995–1007.

Wright, S. J. (1990). Health status measurement: Review and prospects. In P. Bennett, J. Weinman, & P. Spurgeon (Eds.), *Current developments in health psychology* (pp. 93–104). London: Harwood Academic.

Wu, J. C., & Bunney, W. E. (1990). The biological basis of an antidepressant response to sleep deprivation and relapse: Review and hypothesis. *American Journal of Psychiatry, 147*, 14–21.

Wu, J. M. (1990). Summary and concluding remarks. In J. M. Wu (Ed.), *Proceedings of the International Symposium at McGill University* (pp. 367–375). Lexington, MA: Heath.

Wyatt, T. A. (1996). Betel nut chewing and selected psychophysiological variables. *Psychological Reports, 79*(2), 451–463.

Wyler, A. R., Masuda, M., & Holmes, T. H. (1971). Magnitude of the life events and seriousness of illness. *Journal of Psychosomatic Medicine, 33*, 115–122.

Wylie, K. R. (1997). Treatment outcome of brief couple therapy in psychogenic male erectile disorder. *Archives of Sexual Behavior, 26*, 527–545.

Wynne, L. C., & Singer, M. T. (1963). Thought disorder and family relations of schizophrenics. II: A classification of forms of thinking. *Archives of General Psychiatry, 9*, 199–206.

Yaeger, C. A., & Lewis, D. O. (1997). False memories of cult abuse. *American Journal of Psychiatry, 154*(3), 435.

Yalom, I. D. (1980). *Existential psychotherapy.* New York: Basic Books.

Yamamoto, J., Silva, J. A., Sasao, T., et al. (1993). Alcoholism in Peru. *American Journal of Psychiatry, 150*, 1059–1062.

Yang, B., Stack, S., & Lester, D. (1992). Suicide and unemployment: Predicting the smoothed trend and yearly fluctuations. *Journal of Socio-Economics, 21*, 39–41.

Yap, P. M. (1951). Mental diseases peculiar to certain cultures: A survey of comparative psychiatry. *Journal of Mental Science, 97*, 313–327.

Yapko, M. D. (1994). *Suggestions of abuse: True and false memories of childhood sexual trauma.* New York: Simon & Schuster.

Yarbrough, D. W., & Schaffer, J. L. (1990). A comparison of school-related anxiety experienced by nontraditional versus traditional students. *College Student Journal, 24*, 81–90.

Yates, A. J. (1970). *Behavior therapy.* New York: Wiley.

Yehuda, R., Kahana, B., Binder-Brynes, K., et al. (1995). Low urinary cortisol excretion in Holocaust survivors with posttraumatic stress disorder. *American Journal of Psychiatry, 152*(7), 982–986.

Yesalis, C. E., & Bahrke, M. S. (1995). Anabolic-androgenic steroids: Current issues. *Sports Medicine, 19*(5), 326–340.

Yi, D. (1991). Alcohol. In N. S. Miller (Ed.), *Comprehensive handbook of drug and alcohol addiction.* New York: Marcel Dekker.

Yirmiya, N., Erel, O., Shaked, M., & Solomonica, L. D. (1998). Meta-analyses comparing theory of mind abilities of individuals with autism, individuals with mental retardation, and normally developing individuals. *Psychological Bulletin, 124*, 283–307.

Yodofsky, S. C., & Hales, R. E. (Eds.). (1995). Delerium, dementia, and amnestic and other disorders. In G. O. Gabbard (Ed.), *Treatments of psychiatric disorders* (2nd ed.) (pp. 413–531). Washington, DC: American Psychiatric Press.

Yoshino, A., & Kato, M. (1996). Prediction of 3-year outcome of treated alcoholics by an empirically derived multivariate typology. *American Journal of Psychiatry, 153*(6), 829–830.

Young, C. R., Longhurst, J. G., Bowers, M. B., Jr., & Mazure, C. M. (1997). The expanding indications for clozapine. *Experimental and Clinical Psychopharmacology, 5*(3), 216–234.

Yudofsky, S., Silver, J., & Hales, R. (1993). Cocaine and aggressive behavior: Neurobiological and clinical perspectives. *Bulletin of the Menninger Clinic, 57*(2), 218–226.

Yue, X. (1994). A comparative study of test anxiety among Chinese and American high school students. *Bulletin of the Hong Kong Psychological Society*, No. 32–33, 47–59.

Yuille, J. C. (Ed.). (1989). *Credibility assessment.* Boston: Kluwer.

Zakowski, S., Hall, M. H., & Baum, A. (1992). Stress, stress management, and the immune system. *Applied and Preventive Psychology, 1*, 1–13.

Zanarini, M. C. (Ed.). (1997). *Role of sexual abuse in the etiology of borderline personality disorder.* Washington, DC: American Psychiatric Press.

Zanarini, M. C., & Gunderson, J. G. (1997). Differential diagnosis of antisocial and borderline personality disorder. In D. M. Stoff, J. Breiling, & J. D. Maser (Eds.), *Handbook of antisocial behavior* (pp. 83–91). New York: Wiley.

Zarate, R., & Agras, W. S. (1994). Psychosocial treatment of phobia and panic disorders. *Psychiatry, 57*(2), 133–141.

Zauszniewski, J. A. (1997). Teaching resourcefulness skills to older adults. *Journal of Gerontological Nursing, 23*, 14–20.

Zeanah, C. H., Jr. (Ed.). (1993). *Handbook of infant mental health.* New York: Guilford Press.

Zenderland, L. (1998). *Measuring minds: Henry Herbert Goddard and the origins of American intelligence testing.* Cambridge Studies in the History of Psychology. Cambridge, UK: Cambridge University Press.

Zetlin, A. G., & Morrison, G. M. (1998). Adaptation through the life span. In J. Burack & R. M. Hodapp (Eds.), *Handbook of mental retardation and development* (pp. 481–503). New York: Cambridge University Press.

Zheng, D., Macera, C. A., Croft, J. B., et al. (1997). Major depression and all-cause mortality among White adults in the

United States. *Annals of Epidemiology, 7,* 213–218.

Ziegler, D. K., & Schlemmer, R. B. (1994). Familial psychogenic blindness and headache: A case study. *Journal of Clinical Psychiatry, 55,* 114–117.

Zigler, E. (1967). Familial mental retardation: A continuing dilemma. *Science, 155,* 292–298.

Zigler, E. (1995). Can we "cure" mild mental retardation among individuals in the lower socioeconomic stratum? *American Journal of Public Health, 85,* 302–304.

Zilboorg, G., & Henry, G. (1941). *A history of medical psychology.* New York: Norton.

Zimbardo, P. G. (1977). *Shyness: What it is, what to do about it.* Reading, MA: Addison-Wesley.

Zinbarg, R. E., Barlow, D. H., Brown, T. A., & Hertz, R. M. (1992). Cognitive-behavioral approaches to the nature and treatment of anxiety disorders. *Annual Review of Psychology, 43,* 235–268.

Zinbarg, R. E., Barlow, D. H., Liebowitz, M., et al. (1994). The *DSM-IV* field trial for mixed anxiety-depression. *American Journal of Psychiatry, 151,* 1153–1162.

Zlotnick, C. (1997). Posttraumatic stress disorder (PTSD), PTSD comorbidity, and childhood abuse among incarcerated women. *Journal of Nervous and Mental Disease, 185,* 761–763.

Zoccolillo, M. (1993). Gender and the development of conduct disorder. *Development and Psychopathology, 5,* 65–78.

Zoccolillo, M., Tremblay, R., & Vitaro, F. (1996). *DSM-III-R* and *DSM-III* criteria for conduct disorder in preadolescent girls: Specific but insensitive. *Journal of the American Academy of Child and Adolescent Psychiatry, 35,* 461–470.

Zucker, K. J., & Blanchard, R. (1997). Transvestic fetishism: Psychopathology and theory. In D. R. Laws & W. T. O'Donohue (Eds.), *Sexual deviance: Theory, assessment, and treatment* (pp. 253–279). New York: Guilford Press.

Zucker, K. J., Bradley, S. J., Sullivan, C. B., et al. (1992). Gender identity disorder in children. *Annual Review of Sex Research, 3,* 73–120.

Zucker, K. J., Lightbody, S., Pecore, K., et al. (1998). Birth order in girls with gender identity disorder. *European Child and Adolescent Psychiatry, 7,* 30–35.

Zuger, A. (1993, July). The Baron strikes again. *Discover,* pp. 28–30.

Credits

Text and Illustration

Diagnostic Criteria reprinted with permission from the *Diagnostic and Statistical Manual of Mental Disorders, Fourth Edition.* Copyright © 1994 American Psychiatric Association. **Chapter 1** Fig. 1.1, from J. A. Schickedanz, D. I. Schickedanz, P. D. Forsyth and G. A. Forsyth, *Understanding Children and Adolescents, Third Edition.* Copyright © 1998 by Allyn & Bacon. Reprinted by permission. **Chapter 2** Fig. 2.5, from S. Schwartz and J. H. Johnson, *Psychopathology of Childhood,* (2nd ed.), Copyright © 1992 Allyn and Bacon. Reprinted with permission from the publisher. **Chapter 3** Table 3.1, copyright © 1986 by The Riverside Publishing Co. Reproduced from Stanford-Binet Intelligence Scale, Fourth Edition, by Robert L. Thorndike, Elizabeth P. Hagen, and Jerome M. Sattler, with permission from the publisher. Document 3.8 and Table 3.2, Basic Profile for the Minnesota Multiphasic Personality Inventory-2 (MMPI-2). Copyright © 1942, 1943, renewed 1970, 1989 The Regents of the University of Minnesota. All rights reserved. Reproduced by permission of the publisher. MMPI-2 and Minnesota Multiphasic Personality Inventory-2 are trademarks owned by the University of Minnesota. Fig. 3.4, reprinted with permission from "A Visual Motor Gestalt Test and Its Clinical Use," *American Orthopsychiatric Association Research Monographs,* No. 3. Copyright © 1938 by Lauretta Bender, MD and American Orthopsychiatric Association. All rights reserved. Bender ® is a trademark registered in the U.S. Patent and Trademark Office. Fig. 3.5, adapted from Kenneth S. Bordens and Bruce B. Abbott, *Research Design and Methods: A Process Approach, Fourth Edition,* Mayfield, 1999, Fig. 10-5, p. 288. With permission from the publisher. **Chapter 4** Fig. 4.8, from Martin E. P. Seligman and Jack D. Maser, *Psychopathology: Experimental Models,* W. H. Freeman, 1977. Reprinted with permission from the authors. **Chapter 5** Fig. 5.5, from Frederic H. Martini, *Fundamentals of Anatomy and Physiology, Fourth Edition.* Copyright © 1989 Prentice-Hall, Inc. Adapted by permission of Prentice-Hall, Inc., Upper Saddle River, NJ. Table 5.1, reprinted from Miller and Rahe, "Life Changes Scaling for the 1990s," *Journal of Psychosomatic Research,* Vol. 43, 1997. Copyright © 1997 Elsevier Science. With permission from Elsevier Science. Table 5.2, from A. D. Kanner, J. C. Coyne, C. Schaefer, R. S. Lazarus, "Comparison of Two Models of Stress Measurement: Daily Hassles and Uplifts Versus Major Life Events," *Journal of Behavioral Medicine,* 4, 1981, pp. 1–39. Reprinted with permission from Plenum Publishing Corporation. **Chapter 6** Fig. 6.5, from R. Stephney, "Smoking Behavior: A Psychology of the Cigarette Habit," *British Journal of Diseases of the Chest,* 1980, Vol. 74, No. 4, pp. 325–344. (Currently being published as *Respiratory Medicine.*) Adapted with permission from W. B. Saunders Co. Ltd. Table 6.9, from A. P. Goldstein, K. W. Reagles, and L. L. Amann, *Refusal Skills: Preventing Drug Use in Adolescence,* Champaign, IL: Research Press, 1990. Copyright © 1990 by A. P. Goldstein, K. W. Reagles, L. L. Amann. Reprinted by permission. **Chapter 7** Fig. 7.1, part b copyright © 1989 Novartis. Reprinted with permission from the *Atlas of Human Anatomy,* illustrated by Frank H. Netter, MD. All rights reserved. **Chapter 8** Doc. 8.4 From A.T. Beck and R.A. Steer, Beck Depression Inventory, rev. ed. Copyright © 1993 The Psychological Corporation. Reproduced by permission. All rights reserved. Fig. 8.2, from Elliot S. Gershon and O. Rieder, "Major Disorders of Mind and Brain," *Scientific American,* September 1992, p. 131, illustration by Johnny Johnson. Copyright © 1992 by Scientific American, Inc. All rights reserved. **Chapter 9** Fig. 9.3, R. E. L. Faris and H. W. Dunham, *Mental Disorders in Urban Areas,* University of Chicago Press, 1939. Fig. 9.4, courtesy of James H. Meador-Woodruff, MD, University of Michigan Medical Center. **Chapter 11** Document 11.4, adapted from *California Adaptive Behavior Scale.* Copyright © 1995 Planet Press Enterprises. Adapted with permission from the publisher. Fig. 11.3, from S. H. Broman, P. L. Nichols, W. A. Kennedy, *Preschool IQ: Prenatal and Early Developmental Correlates,* Lawrence Erlbaum Associates, Inc., 1975. Reprinted with permission from the publisher. **Chapter 12** Fig. 12.2, adapted from U. Frith, *Autism: Explaining the Enigma,* Blackwell, 1989. Illustration copyright © 1989 Axel Scheffler. **Chapter 13** Table 13.1, from B. L. Andersen and J. M. Cyranowski, "Women's Sexuality: Behaviors, Responses, and Individual Differences," *Journal of Consulting and Clinical Psychology,* 1995, 63, 891–906. Copyright © 1995 by the American Psychological Association. Adapted with permission.

Photographic

p. xxiv, © Murdoch University Media Services, courtesy of the author. **Chapter 1** p. 11, © Bill Aron/PhotoEdit; p. 14, © The Granger Collection, New York; p. 15, © The Granger Collection, New York; p. 17, © Scala/Art Resource, NY; p. 19, © A. Ramey/PhotoEdit; p. 20, © Rick Romagosa/San Francisco Examiner/SABA; p. 22, © AP/Wide World Photos; p. 24, © The Granger Collection, New York; p. 25, © John Chiasson/Liaison Agency, Inc.; p. 26, © Leonard Freed/Magnum Photos, Inc.; p. 27, © The Granger Collection, New York; p. 30, © The Granger Collection, New York; p. 33, © Custom Medical Stock Photo, All Rights Reserved; p. 34, © David K. Crow/PhotoEdit; p. 37, © Amy E. Powers/Liaison Agency, Inc. **Chapter 2** p. 46L, © Popperfoto/Archive Photos; p. 46R, © Express Newspapers/Archive Photos; p. 47, courtesy National Institute of Mental Health; p. 51, © AKG London; p. 56, reproduced from the Collections of the Library of Congress; p. 60, © The Granger Collection, New York; p. 61L, © The Granger Collection, New York; p. 61R, © AP/Wide World Photos; p. 65, Archives of the History of American Psychology, The University of Akron; p. 66, © The Granger Collection, New York; p. 68, courtesy Professor Benjamin Harris, University of Wisconsin, Parkside; p. 71, © Tony Freeman/PhotoEdit; p. 76, © Bruce Hoertel/Liaison Agency, Inc.; p. 79, courtesy Albert Ellis; p. 81, Archives of the History of American Psychology, The University of Akron; p. 84, © Cindy Reiman/Impact Visuals; p. 86L, © Mansell Collection/Time, Inc.; p. 86R, © Michael Newman/PhotoEdit; p. 87, © A. Ramey/PhotoEdit; p. 88, © The Granger Collection, New York; p. 89, © R. Crandall/The Image Works. **Chapter 3** p. 97, Everett Collection; p. 100TL, © Corbis-Bettmann; pp. 100TR, 100B, Archives of the History of American Psychology, The University of Akron; p. 101, courtesy Archives of the History of American Psychology Literature Collection; p. 104, © Bill Aron/PhotoEdit; p. 106, reprinted by permission of the publishers from Henry A. Murray, Thematic Apperception Test, Cambridge, MA, Harvard University Press, © 1943 by the President and Fellows of Harvard College, © 1971 by Henry A. Murray; p. 115, © Jeff Greenberg/PhotoEdit; p. 117, © Reuters/Eric Miller/Archive Photos; p. 118, © The Granger Collection, New York; pp. 122L, 122R, © Joel Gordon; p. 126, © Tasso Taraboulsi/SABA. **Chapter 4** p. 136, © D. Hudson/Sygma; p. 145, Everett Collection; p. 147, © Elizabeth Crews/The Image Works; p. 149, © N. Rowan/The Image Works; p. 155, © Michael Schwarz/The Image Works; p. 158, © Ulrike Welsch/PhotoEdit; p. 164, Photofest; p. 170, courtesy National Institute of Mental Health; p. 171, collection of the Whitney Museum of

Name Index

Abadinsky, H., 246
Abbey, S. E., 198
Abbott, B. B., 116
Abbott, R. D., 242
Abe, K., 148
Abel, G. G., 116
Abel, J. L., 170
Abrams, R., 348
Abramson, L. Y., 343
Abwender, D. A., 521
Achenbach, T. M., 509, 512
Acklin, M. W., 107
Adams, D., 18
Adams, G. R., 206
Adams, H. E., 114
Adams, N. E., 79–80
Adams, P. R., 206
Adams, S. G., Jr., 207
Adams, W., 396
Ader, R., 213, 214
Ades, J., 346, 545
Adler, A., 61, 62, 93
Adler, L. L., 437, 600
Adler, N., 207
Adler, T., 108
Agarwal, D. P., 256
Agras, W. S., 154
Aherns, C. E., 562
Aiken, L. R., 106
Akbarian, S., 396
Akil, M., 492
Albano, A. M., 155, 156
Aldeman, A., 570
Alden, L. E., 151
Aldridge, J., 584
Alemayehu, E., 98
Alexander, F., 200–201, 229
Alexander, P. J., 294, 297
Alexander, T., 509
Alfano, M. S., 344
Alford, B. A., 77
Ali, M., 491
Al-Issa, I., 21, 28, 91
Allain, A. N., 136
Allen, I. V., 493
Allen, J. P., 522
Alleridge, P., 403
Allgood-Merten, B., 328
Allie, S. M., 217
Alloy, L. B., 343, 344, 455
Allsop, D., 495
Alpert, J. E., 422, 452, 453
Altekruse, J. M., 482
Altemus, M., 169
Alterman, A. I., 261
Altura, B. M., 249
Altura, B. T., 249
Alzheimer, A., 494, 503
Amen, D. G., 603
American Association on Mental Retardation (AAMR), 464, 469

American Medical Association Council on Scientific Affairs, 241
American Psychiatric Association, 8, 26, 50, 118–119, 121, 124, 125, 139, 145, 152, 153, 154, 162, 167, 168, 172, 180, 233, 249, 250, 257, 258, 259, 260, 285, 287, 289, 296, 299, 301, 302, 304, 306, 308, 324, 325, 327, 328, 330, 376, 416, 418, 419, 425, 431, 442, 443, 446, 448, 449, 451, 452, 453, 454, 465, 487, 497, 510, 512, 14, 516, 517, 520, 524, 527, 530, 531, 534, 535, 541, 543, 565, 566, 583, 589
American Psychological Association (APA), 35–36, 53, 111
Ames, E. W., 525
Amin, F., 447
Ammann, R., 248, 296, 328
Ammerman, R. T., 18
Ammon, H. P., 239
Anastopoulos, A. D., 519
Andersen, A. E., 545, 547
Andersen, B. L., 559
Andersen, P. M., 297
Anderson, B. L., 220
Anderson, L. P., 206
Andrasik, F., 195
Andreasen, N. C., 49, 121, 181, 370, 375, 399, 401
Andreski, P., 244
Andrews, B., 311
Andrews, G., 165
Angel, E., 81
Angiulo, M. J., 291
Anglin, M. D., 246
Angst, J., 328
Anstey, K., 346
Anthony, J. C., 268
Antoni, M. H., 214
Antony, M. M., 175
Apter, A., 360
Arduino, K., 455
Arendt, R. E., 480
Aries, P., 508
Arieti, S., 156
Arin, D. M., 537
Aristotle, 15, 198
Armstead, P., 434
Arana, G. W., 338
Aro, H. M., 18
Aron, C., 15
Aronow, E., 107
Arthur, J. L., 515
Ashall, F., 484
Asmundson, G. J. G., 139
Asperger, H., 531, 551
Aspinwall, L. G., 216
Assumpcao, F. B., Jr., 537
Atkinson, R. M., 491
Attia, E., 547
Attwood, T., 534
Aussprung, J., 207

Australian Psychological Society, 311
Avicenna (Ibn Senna), 322
Ayuso-Gutierrez, J. L., 173
Azhar, M. Z., 277
Azzoni, A., 537

Bachman, J. G., 232
Backlar, P., 433
Baddeley, A., 214
Baer, L., 170
Bagley, C., 356
Bahrke, M. S., 10, 14
Bakalar, J. B., 248, 252, 253
Baker, G. B., 111
Baker, L., 544
Baker, L. A., 332
Baker, R. W., 98
Bakke, E., 87
Baldessarini, R. J., 338
Baldwin, S., 527
Bales, J., 215
Ballenger, J. C., 173
Balyk, E. D., 558
Bandura, A., 70, 79–80, 103, 150, 212
Bankert, C. L., 519
Banks, S. M., 210
Bannigan, K. A., 409
Barabasz, A., 518
Barabasz, M., 518
Barahal, R. M., 18
Barber, M. E., 448
Barcelo, F., 489
Barchas, J. D., 254, 338
Barinaga, M., 246
Barklage, N. E., 296
Barkley, R. A., 516, 518
Barlow, D. H., 116, 142, 152, 156, 158, 162, 164, 172, 174, 175, 176, 223
Barlow, T. W., 240
Barnard, M. U., 75
Barnett, B., 359
Barnett, N. P., 155
Barnhardt, T. M., 295
Barnhill, J., 338
Baron, M., 335
Baron-Cohen, S., 533, 537, 539
Barondes, S. H., 140, 146
Barr, C. E., 396
Barr, C. L., 520
Barrett, R. T., 436
Barretta, V., 543
Barsky, A. J., 303, 304
Bartlett, D. L., 165
Bartlett, F. C., 310, 315
Barton, J. M., 498
Barton, M., 537
Basedow, H., 146
Basmajian, J. V., 73
Bass, E., 311
Basso, M. R., 387
Bassuk, E. L., 159

Subject Index